ENCYCLOPEDIA of WORLD RELIGIONS CULTS & the OCCULT

Compiled by

Mark Water

Advancing the Ministries of the Gospel

AMG *Publishers*

God's Word to you is our highest calling.

Encyclopedia of World Religions, Cults, and the Occult

AMG Publishers
6815 Shallowford Road
Chattanooga, Tennessee 37421

Copyright © 2006 John Hunt Publishing Ltd
Text © 2006 Mark Water
Typography: BookDesign™, London, UK

ISBN 0-89957-460-2

Printed in the United States of America
11 10 09 08 07 06 –MV– 6 5 4 3 2 1

CONTENTS

PART ONE

WORLD RELIGIONS

Introduction

Christianity

Islam

Hinduism

Buddhism

Sikhism

Taoism

Judaism

Jainism

Confucianism

Bahai

Shintoism

Zoroastrianism

Atheism, agnosticism, and non-
religious worldviews

PART TWO

CULTS

Introduction

Four traditional "Christian" cults

Mormonism

Jehovah's Witnesses

Christian Science

Christadelphianism

Other cults

Apocalyptic cults

Hare Krishna

New Age Movement

Scientology

Swedenborgianism

The Family/Children of God

Theosophy

Transcendental Meditation

Unification Church (Moonies)

Unity School of Christianity

The Way International

PART THREE

OTHER TRAILS

Freemasonry

Seventh-Day Adventists

Worldwide Church of God

PART FOUR

THE OCCULT

Introduction

Divination

Magic, Magick

Spiritism and spiritualism

CONTENTS IN DETAIL

PART ONE, WORLD RELIGIONS

Introduction   4

Christianity

Section One: General

1   An overview   11
2   Christianity's founder   12
3   Christianity's holy book   20
4   Facts and figures   23
5   Christian practices   24
6   Christian beliefs   38
7   Worship   39
8   Groupings within Christianity   40
9   Comparison of Christianity with world religions   64
10   Glossary   65

Section Two: Roman Catholicism

1   Introduction   75
2   Encyclicals   76
    Ad Caeli Reginam
3   Doctrines   86
    The pope
    Final authority: the Bible or tradition?
    Mary
    Purgatory
    Justification
    Transubstantiation
    The Mass
4   Glossary   91
5   Quotations   94

Islam

1   An overview   99
2   Islam's founder   100
3   Islam's holy book   103
4   Facts and figures   114

5	Islamic practices	115
6	Islamic beliefs	117
7	Islamic worship	121
8	Groupings within Islam	122
9	Comparison with Christianity	124
10	Glossary	126

Hinduism

1	An overview	133
2	Founder of Hinduism	134
3	Holy books	135
4	Facts and figures	189
5	Practices	190
6	Beliefs	191
7	Worship	196
8	Groupings within Hinduism	197
9	Swamiji: Yoga in Daily Life	198
10	Quotations about Hinduism	199
11	Comparison with Christianity	205
12	Glossary	207

Buddhism

1	An overview	213
2	Buddhism's founder	214
3	Buddhism's holy book	218
4	Facts and figures	242
5	Buddhist practices	243
6	Buddhist beliefs	244
7	Worship	247
8	Groupings within Buddhism	249
9	In praise of Buddhism	253
10	Comparison with Christianity	256
11	Glossary	257

Sikhism

1	An overview	263
2	Founders of Sikhism	264
3	Sikh's holy book	267
4	Facts and figures	275
5	Sikh practices	276
6	Sikh beliefs	279
7	Sikh worship	280
8	Sikh groups	283
9	Comparison with Hinduism and Christianity	283
10	Glossary	284

Taoism

1	An overview	289
2	Taoism's founders	290
3	Taoist holy book	291
4	Facts and figures	316
5	Taoist practices	317
6	Taoist beliefs	318
7	Worship	319
8	Comparison with Christianity	321
9	Glossary	322

Judaism

1	An overview	327
2	Judaism's founders	328
3	Jewish holy book	328
4	Facts and figures	332
5	Jewish practices	332
6	Jewish beliefs	335
7	Worship	351
8	Groupings within Judaism	357
9	Famous Jews	358
10	Comparison with Christianity	359
11	Glossary	360

Jainism

1	An overview	367
2	Founder of Jainism	368
3	Jainist holy books	369
4	Facts and figures	375
5	Jainist practices	376
6	Jainist beliefs	378
7	Jainist worship	383
8	Jainist groupings	385
9	Famous Jainists	385
10	Quotations about Jainism	385
11	Glossary	387

Confucianism

1	An overview	391
2	Founder of Confucianism	392
3	Confucian holy books	393
4	Facts and figures	403
5	Confucian practices	404
6	Confucian beliefs	405
7	Worship	407
8	Famous Confucianists	407
9	Glossary	408

Bahai
   1   An overview   411
   2   Bahai's founder   412
   3   Bahai's holy books   414
   4   Facts and figures   420
   5   Bahai practices   420
   6   Bahai beliefs   421
   7   Bahai worship   430
   8   Comparison of Bahai faith with Christianity   431
   9   Glossary   432

Shintoism
   1   An overview   439
   2   Shinto's founder   440
   3   Shinto holy books   440
   4   Facts and figures   449
   5   Shinto practices   449
   6   Shinto beliefs   451
   7   Shinto Worship   452
   8   Groupings within Shintoism   455
   9   Glossary   456

Zoroastorianism
   1   An overview   461
   2   Zoroastrian's founder   462
   3   Zoroastrian holy book   463
   4   Facts and figures   467
   5   Zoroastrian practices   467
   6   Zoroastrian beliefs   469
   7   Worship   472
   8   Groupings within Zoroastrianism   472
   9   Glossary   473

Atheism, agnosticism, and non-religious worldviews
   1   Non-religious worldviews   477
   2   Famous agnostics   480
   3   Sound-bites against religion and Christianity   481
   4   Arguments for the existence of God   483
   5   Answering atheists   484

PART TWO, CULTS

Introduction   **487**
Four traditional "Christian" cults
   Mormonism
   Jehovah's Witnesses
   Christian Science
   Christadelphianism

Mormonism
1 An overview 491
2 Mormon's founder 492
3 Mormon holy books 505
4 Facts and figures 517
5 Mormon practices 518
6 Mormon beliefs 520
7 Worship 524

Jehovah's Witnesses
1 An overview 529
2 Founder 529
3 Jehovah's Witnesses' holy book 530
4 Facts and figures 532
5 Jehovah's Witnesses' practices 533
6 Jehovah's Witnesses' beliefs 536
7 Worship 539
8 Glossary 539

Christian Science
1 An overview 543
2 Founder 543
3 Christian Science's holy book 547
4 Facts and figures 549
5 Christian Science practices 549
6 Christian Science beliefs 550
7 Worship 556

Christadelphians
1 An overview 559
2 Founder 559
3 Christadelphian holy book 560
4 Facts and figures 564
5 Christadelphian practices 565
6 Christadelphian beliefs 565
7 Worship 568

Other cults
Apocalyptic cults
Hare Krishna
New Age Movement
Scientology
Swedenborgianism
The Family/Children of God
Theosophy

Transcendental Meditation
Unification Church (Moonies)
Unity School of Christianity
The Way International

Apocalyptic cults
1 An overview   571
2 The Apocalyptic cults   572
   Aum Shinri Kyo
   The Family
   Branch Davidians
   Heaven's Gate
   Jeffrey Lundgren
   Movement for the Restoration of the Ten Commandments of God (Uganda)
   The People's Temple
   Solar Temple

Hare Krishna
1 An overview   579
2 Founder   580
3 Hare Krishna's holy book   580
4 Facts and figures   580
5 Hare Krishna practices   581
6 Hare Krishna beliefs   583
7 Worship   586
8 Quotations   587

New Age Movement
1 An overview   591
2 Founder   592
3 New Age's holy book   593
4 Facts and figures   593
5 New Age practices   594
6 New Age beliefs   594
7 Worship   596
8 Links to the NAM   596
9 Quotations   597
10 Glossary   598

Scientology
1 An overview   603
2 Founder   604
3 Scientology's holy book   607
4 Facts and figures   607
5 Scientology practices   608
6 Scientology beliefs   609
7 Scientology groupings   612
8 Worship   612
9 Quotations   613

Swedenborgianism

1	An overview	617
2	Founder	618
3	Swedenborgianism's holy book	619
4	Facts and figures	620
5	Swedenborgianism's practices	620
6	Swedenborgianism's beliefs	620
7	Worship and structure of Church	621
8	Famous Swedenborg fellow-travelers	623
9	Quotations	624

The Family/Children of God

1	An overview	627
2	Founder	628
3	Children of God's holy book	629
4	Facts and figures	630
5	Children of God practices	630
6	Children of God beliefs	633

Theosophy

1	An overview	637
2	Founder	638
3	Theosophy's holy book	639
4	Facts and figures	639
5	Theosophy practices	640
6	Theosophy beliefs	640
7	Worship	646
8	Quotations	647

Transcendental Meditation

1	An overview	651
2	Founder	652
3	Transcendental Meditation's holy book	652
4	Facts and figures	652
5	Transcendental Meditation's practices	653
6	Transcendental Meditation's beliefs	654
7	The Bible and meditation	654
8	Christian evaluation	655

Unification Church (Moonies)

1	An overview	659
2	Founder	660
3	Unification Church's holy book	660
4	Facts and figures	661
5	Unification Church's practices	662
6	Unification Church's beliefs	663
7	Worship	676

Unity School of Christianity
1   An overview   679
2   Founder   679
3   Unity School of Christianity's holy book   680
4   Facts and figures   680
5   Unity School of Christianity practices   681
6   Unity School of Christianity beliefs   681
7   Christian evaluation   682

The Way International
1   An overview   685
2   Founder   686
3   The Way International's holy book   687
4   Facts and figures   687
5   The Way International's practices   688
6   The Way International's beliefs   688
7   Worship   689

PART THREE, OTHER TRAILS

Introduction   692

Freemasonry
1   An overview   695
2   Founder   696
3   Freemasonry's holy book   697
4   Facts and figures   700
5   Freemasonry practices   701
6   Freemasonry beliefs   702
7   Worship   703
8   Quotations   704

Seventh-day Adventists
1   An overview   709
2   Founder   709
3   Seventh-day Adventists' holy book   710
4   Facts and figures   711
5   Seventh-day Adventist practices   714
6   Seventh-day Adventist beliefs   715
7   Seventh-day Adventist groups   725
8   Quotations   725

Worldwide Church of God
1   An overview   727
2   Founder   727
3   Worldwide Church of God's holy book   729
4   Facts and figures   730
5   Worldwide Church of God practices   730

6   Worldwide Church of God beliefs   732
7   Splits from the Worldwide Church of God   733
8   Quotations   734

Part Four, The Occult

Introduction   739

1 Divination   743
   Introduction
   A   Astrology   744
     (i)   The Zodiac
       a. Two poems
       b. The twelve signs of the Zodiac
     (ii)   Fortune-tellers
     (iii) Horoscopes
   B   Tarot cards   750
     (i)   Cartomancy
   C   Crystal ball, mirrors, and psychometry   752
   D   Palm reading, phrenology   752
   E   Rod and pendulum   753
   F   Tea leaf reading   753
   G   Dice and dominoes   754
   H   *I Ching*   754
   I   Snail shells and coconuts   754
   J   Tables of fate and the wheel of fortune   754
   K   Telepathy, clairvoyance   755
   L   Dreams   755
   M   Numerology   755
   N   Selenomancia   755

2 Magic, Magick   756
   Introduction   756
   A   White magic, black magic   756
     (i)   Introduction
     (ii)   Biblical assessment
     (iii) Acupuncture
     (iv)   Typical rite of magic
   B   Witchcraft   759
     (i)   Introduction
     (ii)   Witchcraft assessed
     (iii) Types of witchcraft
     (iv)   Witch doctors
     (v)   Membership and history
     (vi)   What it is
     (vii) Covens
     (viii) Women

       (ix)   Gods

       (x)   Esbat and Sabbat

       (xi)   The rite

   C   Wicca   762

       Introduction

       History and background of Wicca

       Wicca beliefs and practices

       Mother Goddess, Horned God

       Maiden, Mother, and Crone

       Mother Goddess' names

       Horned God

       Horned God's names

       A Wicca view of god

       The Wiccan Rede

       The Law of the Three

       Relativism and moral relativity

       Wicca practices

   D   The Church of Satan   768

       What it is

       Founder

       Revered texts

       The Satanic Bible

       Nine Satanic Statements

       Satanic sins

       Black mass

3 Spiritism and spiritualism   770

       Introduction   770

       History of spiritism   770

       Extent of spiritism and spiritualism   770

       Spiritism and Christianity   771

       The creed of Spiritualism   771

       Séances   771

       Critical view of séances

       Séances in churches

       The spirit world   772

       Poltergeists

       Ouija boards

Glossary   773

PART ONE

WORLD RELIGIONS

CONTENTS

Introduction
Christianity
Islam
Hinduism
Buddhism
Sikhism
Taoism
Judaism
Jainism
Confucianism
Bahai
Shinto
Zoroastrianism
Atheism, agnosticism, and non-religious worldviews

INTRODUCTION

The most frequent way of listing world religions is according to what has become known as "The Classical World Religions' List." This list contains the following world religions (in alphabetical order):

- Bahai
- Buddhism
- Christianity
- Confucianism
- Hinduism
- Islam
- Jainism
- Judaism
- Shinto
- Sikhism
- Taoism
- Zoroastrianism

The Encyclopedia of World Religions, Cults, and the Occult follows the classical list of the twelve world religions, and looks at them in the order of their approximate size, starting with the world's largest, in terms of numbers of adherents, Christianity.

FACTUAL INFORMATION

The Encyclopedia of World Religions, Cults, and the Occult attempts to show each world religion from the viewpoint of the religion itself. It does not set out to discredit any worldview or religious belief. For this reason, extensive quotations from the sacred scriptures of different world religions are included. Reading them is one of the quickest ways of gaining an understanding about each world religion. Often their influence, even in the West, is far more significant than their number of "official" adherents might suggest. Extracts from, or, in some cases, the entire contents of, the following are included:

- Bahai's The *Kitab-i-Aqbas*
- Buddhism's *Dhammapada*
- Confucius' *Analects*
- Hindu's The *Bhagavad Gita*
- Islam's Qur'an
- Jainist's *Agamas*
- Shinto's *Kojiki*
- Sikh's *Guru Granth Sahib*
- Taoist's *Tao-te-ching*, and
- Zoroastrianism's *Avesta*,

CHRISTIANITY

One of the main objectives of *The Encyclopedia of World Religions, Cults, and the Occult* is to compare each world religion with Christianity. It is written primarily for Christians, to help them to have a better understanding of their religion, and to see it in relation to other faiths. So one of the features of this encyclopedia is that there is often a section in a religion that holds up some of the

major beliefs of that religion against the
yardstick of biblical teaching.

ORGANIZATION

The entries focus on major beliefs so that
comparisons can be made. Throughout the
Encyclopedia a broad range of Christian belief
and practice is covered, but examples are
selected primarily from the best of the
evangelical tradition down the ages, as being
closest to the Bible, rather than from different
Church traditions.

IS CHRISTIANITY UNIQUE?

One of the driving forces in Islam, in contrast
to some religions, is that all people in the
world should become Muslim. Is it right for
Christians likewise to aim at global
evangelization? Only if Christianity is unique
and if it is true. And this is the claim made by
most Christian commentators, on the basis of
their understanding of the Gospels:

> This is the unique element in the gospel,
> which tells us that what we could never
> do, God has done. We cannot climb up to
> heaven to discover God, but God has
> come down to earth, in the person of his
> Son, to reveal himself to us in the only
> way we could really understand: in terms
> of a human life.
> *J. N. D. Anderson*

The distinction between Christianity and
all other systems of religion consists
largely in this, that in these others, men
are found seeking after God, while
Christianity is God seeking after men.
Thomas Arnold, Literature and Dogma

I have read in Plato and Cicero sayings
that are very wise and beautiful; but I
never read in either of them: "Come unto
me all ye that labor and are heavy laden
and I will give thee rest."
Augustine of Hippo

There are many religions in the world,
but only one Christianity, for only
Christianity has a God who gave himself
for mankind. World religions attempt to

reach up to God; Christianity is God
reaching down to man.
Billy Graham

Do we have a right to defy the whole
world, to boast that only our cause is
right? We must conclude: I know that my
cause is right, though the whole world
may say otherwise. Do not think: I shall
stay with the majority, for the fact that the
greater part of mankind is in darkness is
nothing new.
Martin Luther

Christianity is different from all other
religions. They are the story of man's
search for God. The Gospel is the story of
God's search for man.
Dewi Morgan

Christianity is God reaching down to
humanity. Other religions are a matter of
men and women seeking and struggling
toward God.
Luis Palau

Only the Judeo-Christian tradition
contains worship of an infinite personal
being.
Francis Schaeffer

The Christian religion is distinctive in
that it claims that God can be known as a
personal God only in his self-revelation in
the Scriptures.
Francis Schaeffer

In religion outside of Christianity man
cannot normally reach to an experience of
God except in a vague and often nameless
way.
Edward Schillebeeckx

Christianity is a religion of salvation, and
there is nothing in the non-Christian
religions to compare with this message of
a God who loved, and came after, and
died for, a world of lost sinners.
John Stott

Our claim to uniqueness is not of a
system or church but Jesus Christ alone.

The uniqueness of Jesus Christ and his finality, that we alone defend.

John R. W. Stott

Every religion except one puts upon you doing something in order to recommend yourself to God. It is only the religion of Christ which was not sold out to us on certain conditions to be fulfilled by ourselves.

Augustus Toplady

WITNESSING TO OTHER FAITHS

It is the hope of the editor that as a result of reading through the sections on the different world faiths, the reader will be better enabled to see the most effective way to witness to a member of a particular non-Christian faith.

For example, when speaking with Jews, it is helpful to use words that emphasize the links that the Christian faith has with Judaism. Thus, instead of always using the title "Christ," which is derived from the Greek word for "the Anointed One," it may be helpful to refer to Jesus as God's "Messiah," a word based on the Hebrew. In the same way, communication is aided if Christians refer, not to "the Old Testament," but rather to "the Hebrew Scriptures."

STATISTICS

Of the people in the world who adhere to a major world religion, half are either Christians or Muslims.

Over 75% of the world's population are members of seven major world religions: Hinduism, Judaism, Buddhism, Confucianism, Taoism, Christianity, and Islam.

It is, however, difficult to be exact about numbers. Many of the accepted figures are based on out-of-date census forms. It is also far from easy to say with absolute confidence that there are, for example, one billion Hindus in the world. Does that include "lapsed" Hindus? Does that include "practicing" Hindus, or Hindus who are children? Does it include members of Hindu families, or "practicing" Hindus who have severe doubts about their faith? And this of course, applies equally to Christians.

So the facts and figures in *The Encyclopedia of World Religions, Cults, and the Occult* should be taken as estimates that have been made in good faith, on the best available data.

ISLAM V. CHRISTIANITY

There is one trend concerning the different world religions about which most commentators are agreed. At present, numerically, the largest world religion is Christianity (assuming that Protestants and non-Protestants are included under the broad heading of "Christian"). It is also generally agreed that the second largest world religion is Islam. Islam is growing at a significantly faster rate each year than Christianity. Indeed, it is the fastest growing major religion in the world today. From a population base of 200 million in 1900, Islam grew more than fivefold during the twentieth century.

The change in Muslim/Roman Catholic demographics over the past thirty years is striking. In 1970 there were 554 million Muslims in the world, and 666 million Roman Catholics. But it has been estimated that if the present rates of growth of Islam and Christianity remain constant, by about 2015 Islam will have replaced Christianity as the world's largest religion.

WHO LIVES WHERE?

For Christians, especially for Christians who put the importance of following biblical principles above allegiance to a Christian denomination, the following table makes sobering reading, for out of the top twenty most populated countries in the world, only three claim that the most popular religion is Protestant Christianity.

Rank by population	Country	Most popular religion
1	China	Taoist
2	India	Hindu (also has 200 million Muslims)
3	United States	Christianity (mostly Protestant)

4	Indonesia	Muslim
5	Brazil	Christianity (mostly Roman Catholic)
6	Russia	Christianity (Russian Orthodox)
7	Pakistan	Islam
8	Bangladesh	Islam
9	Japan	Shinto and Buddhism
10	Nigeria	Islam
11	Mexico	Christianity (Roman Catholic)
12	Germany	Christianity (Protestant)
13	Philippines	Christianity (Roman Catholic)
14	Vietnam	Buddhist
15	Egypt	Islam
16	Turkey	Islam
17	Iran	Islam
18	Ethiopia	Islam
19	Thailand	Buddhism
20	United Kingdom	Christianity (Protestant)

PROTESTANTS AND ROMAN CATHOLICS

The entry on Christianity ends with an appraisal of Roman Catholicism from a critical Protestant viewpoint. While some Protestants are happy about having dialogue with Roman Catholics, others are still upset that Billy Graham ever shared a speaking platform with any Roman Catholic.

CHRISTIAN MISSION

Christians usually emphasize the numerical strength of Christianity, for while there were under 660 million Christians in the world in 1900, there were 2 billion in the year 2000. But these figures are less impressive when looked at in the light of the increase in world population and the advances made by many other world religions. For example, in 1900, 34.5% of the world's population were Christians, but in 2002 that number had decreased to only 33.1%.

Christianity is also under attack from atheistic philosophy. For this reason, *The Encyclopedia of World Religions, Cults, and the Occult* has a concluding chapter on atheism, agnosticism, and non-religious worldviews.

PAUL AND OTHER FAITHS

Christians can take their cue from the apostle Paul. He lived in a world of non-Christian beliefs. He did not cut himself off from them. In his sermon at Athens, he even quoted secular poetry. His attitude towards non-Christians and their beliefs and the ways he applied the gospel to them remain guidelines for any who seek to follow the last words of Jesus in Matthew's Gospel: "Therefore go and make disciples of all nations, baptizing them in the name of the Father and of the Son and of the Holy Spirit, and teaching them to obey everything I have commanded you. And surely I am with you always, to the very end of the age" (Matthew 28:19-20).

PAUL IN ATHENS

While Paul was waiting for them in Athens, he was greatly distressed to see that the city was full of idols. So he reasoned in the synagogue with the Jews and the God-fearing Greeks, as well as in the marketplace day by day with those who happened to be there. A group of Epicurean and Stoic philosophers began to dispute with him. Some of them asked, "What is this babbler trying to say?" Others remarked, "He seems to be advocating foreign gods." They said this because Paul was preaching the good news about Jesus and the resurrection. Then they took him and brought him to a meeting of the Areopagus, where they said to him, "May we know what this new teaching is that you are presenting? You are bringing some strange ideas to our ears, and we want to know what they mean." (All the Athenians and the foreigners who lived there spent their time doing nothing but talking about and listening to the latest ideas.)

Paul then stood up in the meeting of the Areopagus and said: "Men of Athens! I see that in every way you are very religious. For as I walked around and looked carefully at your objects of worship, I even found an altar with this inscription: TO AN UNKNOWN GOD. Now what you worship as something unknown I am going to proclaim to you.

"The God who made the world and everything in it is the Lord of heaven and earth and does not live in temples built by hands. And he is not served by human hands, as if he needed anything, because he himself gives all men life and breath and everything else. From one man he made every nation of men, that they should inhabit the whole earth; and he determined the times set for them and the exact places where they should live. God did this so that men would seek him and perhaps reach out for him and find him, though he is not far from each one of us. 'For in him we live and move and have our being.' As some of your own poets have said, 'We are his offspring.'

"Therefore since we are God's offspring, we should not think that the divine being is like gold or silver or stone-an image made by man's design and skill. In the past God overlooked such ignorance, but now he commands all people everywhere to repent. For he has set a day when he will judge the world with justice by the man he has appointed. He has given proof of this to all men by raising him from the dead."

When they heard about the resurrection of the dead, some of them sneered, but others said, "We want to hear you again on this subject." At that, Paul left the Council. A few men became followers of Paul and believed. Among them was Dionysius, a member of the Areopagus, also a woman named Damaris, and a number of others.

Acts 17:16-34

Today we again live in a world where people seek many unknown and strange gods. My prayer is that Part One of *The Encyclopedia of World Religions, Cults, and the Occult* may help you in your belief and witness.

CHRISTIANITY:
SECTION ONE: GENERAL

CONTENTS

1	An overview	11
2	Christianity's founder	12
3	Christianity's holy book	20
4	Facts and figures	23
5	Christian practices	24
6	Christian beliefs	38
7	Worship	39
8	Groupings within Christianity	40
9	Comparison of Christianity with world religions	64
10	Glossary	65

1 AN OVERVIEW

DEFINITION

The Christian religion is based on the teachings of Jesus and on the belief that he is the incarnate Son of God. Christians are disciples of Jesus Christ.

Factfile
- Date of origin: c. AD 30
- Founder: Jesus Christ
- Holy book: Bible
- Number of adherents: more than 2.2 billion

SUMMARY

The Christian religion teaches me two points–that there is a God whom men can know, and that their nature is so corrupt that they are unworthy of him.

Blaise Pascal

We are told that Christ was killed for us, that his death has washed out our sins, and that by dying he disabled death itself. That is the formula. That is Christianity. That is what has to be believed.

C. S. Lewis

SUMMARY OF PRACTICES

Christianity is not primarily a theological system, an ethical system, a ritual system, a social system or an ecclesiastical system – it is a person: it's Jesus Christ, and to be a Christian is to know him and to follow him and believe in him.

John R. W. Stott

There are no formal practices in Christianity of the kind that are found in, say, Islam. But over the centuries a number have emerged as essential planks of the faith, with different traditions within Christianity giving differing weights to each. Such essentials include spending time with God in prayer and worship, spending time with fellow-Christians in Christian fellowship, being baptized and attending the Lord's Supper, and living a Christian life in line with the teaching of Jesus.

SUMMARY OF BELIEFS

Christians believe in:
The Trinity
God
Jesus
The Holy Spirit

THE TRINITY

The vast majority of Christian Churches take belief in the Trinity as their defining feature. Christianity affirms that there is only one God who exists as three distinct persons. Although the word "Trinity" never appears in the Bible, the concept of God as God the Father, and God the Son, and God the Holy Spirit is deduced from a number of biblical passages where the three "persons" of the Trinity are mentioned together. (See Matthew 3:16,17; 28:19; Luke 1:35; John 14:26; 15:26; 2 Corinthians 13:14.)

BELIEF IN GOD
God is the almighty creator and sustainer of the universe. (Genesis 1).
God is both perfectly loving, and perfectly just. (Jeremiah 31:3; Romans 2:2; 5:8).
God is all-powerful, all-seeing, all-knowing. (1 Samuel 2:3; Psalm 65:6).

BELIEF IN JESUS
Jesus was God in human form.
Jesus lived on earth and taught and performed miracles.
He was crucified dying as a sacrifice for our sins.
He conquered death and rose again to life through his resurrection.
He ascended into heaven and acts as the link between God and humankind.

(See following section "Christianity's founder" for relevant Bible references.)

BELIEF IN THE HOLY SPIRIT
Like the Father and the Son, the Holy Spirit acts as only a person can: he hears, convinces, speaks, testifies, shows, leads, guides, teaches, prompts speech, commands, forbids, desires, helps, and prays with groans. (See John 14:26; 16:7-15; 15:26; Acts 2:4; 8:29; 13:2; 16:6-7; 21:11; Romans 8:14, 16; 26-27; Galatians 4 :6; 5:17-18; Hebrews 3:7; 10:15; 1 Peter 1:11; Revelation 2:7.)

Jesus stated that the Holy Spirit mediates knowledge of, and union with Jesus himself, even though he has now ascended and has been glorified.

2 CHRISTIANITY'S FOUNDER

A	Facts about Jesus
B	Jesus' claims
C	Jesus made statements only God would make
D	Christ and the attributes of deity
E	The deity's prerogatives
F	Scriptural declarations that Christ is God
G	Names and titles of God are attributed to Christ
H	First-century testimonies
I	The early Church's testimony to the deity of Christ

A FACTS ABOUT JESUS
Christians are convinced that Jesus was an historical figure who lived over two thousand years ago in the land of Israel. He taught large groups of people about God, performed many miracles and was crucified on a cross.

The Bible teaches the following facts about Jesus:

• MIRACULOUS CONCEPTION
Jesus was conceived in a miraculous way. Joseph was only Jesus' foster father, for Jesus' true Father was God himself. Mary became pregnant with Jesus while she was still a virgin.

• GOD-APPOINTED
Jesus was sent, and anointed by God himself for a unique mission, which included being a teacher and performing scores of miracles.

• JESUS AND HIS DEATH
Jesus' death was a voluntary, substitutionary act of love, which now enables people to have their sins forgiven and to enjoy spiritual life with God

himself. "For God so loved the world, that he gave his only begotten Son, that whosoever believeth in him should not perish, but have everlasting life" (John 3:16).

Jesus died on the cross to pay the penalty for our sins (1 John 2:2, Romans 3:25).

- THE DEITY OF JESUS
  Jesus was God in the flesh (John 1:1, 14). Many religious leaders of his own day wanted Jesus killed because they said he committed blasphemy by claiming to be God. (See John 5:18; 10:29-33; Luke 22:66-71.)

- SINLESS PERFECTION
  Jesus lived a perfect, sinless life (2 Corinthians 5:21; 1 Peter 2:22; 1 John 3:5).

- JESUS' RESURRECTION
  Jesus rose again from the dead (1 Corinthians 15:3-5; Acts 1:1-3).

B JESUS' CLAIMS
Jesus made the following claims about himself.

HEAVEN
"No one has ever gone into heaven except the one who came from heaven—the Son of Man" (John 3:13).

THE BREAD OF LIFE
"For the bread of God is he who comes down from heaven and gives life to the world. . . . I am the bread of life. He who comes to me will never go hungry, and he who believes in me will never be thirsty" (John 6:33, 35).

TEACHING IS FROM GOD
"My teaching is not my own. It comes from him who sent me. If anyone chooses to do God's will, he will find out whether my teaching comes from God or whether I speak on my own" (John 7:16-17).

LIGHT
"I am the light of the world. Whoever follows me will never walk in darkness, but will have the light of life" (John 8:12).

FROM HEAVEN
"You are from below; I am from above. You are of this world; I am not of this world"(John 8:23).

FROM ETERNITY
"I tell you the truth," Jesus answered, "before Abraham was born, I am!" (John 8:58).

UNITED WITH GOD THE FATHER
"I and the Father are one" (John 10:30). "All that belongs to the Father is mine" (John 16:15).

RESURRECTION
"I am the resurrection and the life. He who believes in me will live, even though he dies" (John 11:25).

SENT BY GOD
"When a man believes in me, he does not believe in me only, but in the one who sent me. When he looks at me, he sees the one who sent me" (John 12:44-45).

TEACHER AND LORD
"You call me 'Teacher' and 'Lord,' and rightly so, for that is what I am" (John 13:13).

RETURN PROMISED
"And if I go and prepare a place for you, I will come back and take you to be with me that you also may be where I am" (John 14:3).

GOD
"Anyone who has seen me has seen the Father" (John 14:9).

VICTORIOUS
"I have overcome the world" (John 16:33).

C JESUS MADE STATEMENTS ONLY GOD WOULD MAKE
"Then Jesus came to them and said, 'All authority in heaven and on earth has been given to me'" (Matthew 28:18).

"Whoever believes in the Son has eternal life, but whoever rejects the Son will not see life, for God's wrath remains on him" (John 3:36).

"I tell you the truth, whoever hears my word and believes him who sent me has eternal life and will not be condemned; he has crossed over from death to life" (John 5:24; see John 10:27, 28; 11:25).

"For I have come down from heaven not to do my will but to do the will of him who sent me" (John 6:38).

"While I am in the world, I am the light of the world" (John 9:5).

"When he looks at me, he sees the one who sent me" (John 12:45; see John 14:7-11; 17:5).

"There is a judge for the one who rejects me and does not accept my words; that very word which I spoke will condemn him at the last day" (John 12:48).

"Jesus answered, 'I am the way and the truth and the life. No one comes to the Father except through me'" (John 14:6).

"I am the vine; you are the branches. If a man remains in me and I in him, he will bear much fruit; apart from me you can do nothing" (John 15:5).

"I have told you these things, so that in me you may have peace. In this world you will have trouble. But take heart! I have overcome the world" (John 16:33).

"And now, Father, glorify me in your presence with the glory I had with you before the world began" (John 17:5).

No mere human being could genuinely make the following claims. They reveal the unique relationship between God and Christ.

"He who receives me, receives the One who sent me" (Matthew 10:40).

"No one knows the Father except the Son" (Matthew 11:27).

"My Father is working until now and I am working" (John 5:17).

"Whatever the Father does, these things the Son also does in like manner" (John 5:19).

"He who does not honor the Son does not honor the Father" (John 5:23).
"If you knew me, you know my Father also" (John 8:19).

"When he looks at me, he see the one who sent me" (John 12:45).

"Trust in God; trust also in me" (John 14:1).

"He who hates me hates my Father as well" (John 15:23).

> If Christ is not God, He is a deceiver or is self-deceived, and in either case, Christ, if not God, is not good.
> *Dr. H. Strong*

D CHRIST AND THE ATTRIBUTES OF DEITY
The following Bible verses show that Jesus Christ is said to have possessed the attributes of God.

ETERNITY
In the beginning, Christ always was: John 1:1, 2, 14, 15.
Jesus had glory with God before the world was created: John 17:5.

OMNIPRESENCE
He is with us always: Matthew 28:20.
He is in every believer: John 14:20-23.
He fills all: Ephesians 1:23; 4:20.

OMNISCIENCE
He knows people's thoughts: Mark 2:8; Luke 6:8; 11:17.
He knew how he would die: Matthew 16:21; John 12:33.
He knew the Father: Matthew 11:27 (only God can know himself [1 Corinthians 2:11, 16]).
He knew who would betray him: John 6:64, 70-71.

He knew the future: John 2:19-22; John 18:4; John 13:19; Matthew 24:35.
He knew all men: John 2:24, 25.

OMNIPOTENCE AND SOVEREIGNTY
He is the Almighty: Revelation 1:8.
He does whatever the Father does: John 5:19.
He upholds all things: Colossians 1:17; Hebrews 1:3.
All authority, including over all humankind, is given to him: Matthew 28:18; John 17:2, 3.
He is the head over all rule and authority: Colossians 2:10.
He has power to subject all things unto himself: Philippians 3:21.
He will reign until he has put all enemies under his feet: 1 Corinthians 15:25.
He exerts control over his own life and death: John 10:18.
He is the ruler of the kings of the earth: Revelation 1:5.
He has power over nature: Luke. 8:25.
He is Lord of all: Revelations 19:16; 1 Peter 3:22, Colossians 1:18; Acts 10:36.

IMMUTABILITY
He is always and forever the same: Hebrews 13:8; compare Hebrews 1:12, 8, 10.
His words will never pass away: Matthew 24:35.

HOLY
He is holy: Revelation 3:7.
He knew no sin: 2 Corinthians 5:21.
He is without sin: Hebrews 4:15.
He is holy, innocent, undefiled, and separated from sinners: Hebrews 7:26.
He is unblemished and spotless: 1 Peter 1:19.
He committed no sin: John 8:46; 1 John 3:5; 1 Peter 2:22.

TRUTH
He is full of grace and truth: John 1:14.
The truth is in Jesus: Ephesians 4:21.
He is the truth: John 14:6.

CONCLUSION
If the major attributes of deity are attributed to Jesus Christ, it is correct to conclude that he is God.

E THE DEITY'S PREROGATIVES
The following prerogatives, which belong exclusively to the deity, are also attributed to Jesus Christ
Raising the dead while on earth (Matthew 9:25, the Synagogue official's daughter; Luke 7:12-16, the widow's son; John 11:44, Lazarus; John 2:19-22, himself).

Doing the works of God (John 10:37-39).

Giving eternal life (John 17:2; John 10:28).

Worshiped by angels (Psalm 148:2): God – Hebrews 1:6; Jesus – Luke 4:8.

Addressed in prayer (Acts 7:59).

Providence and eternal dominion (Luke 10:22; John 3:35; 17:2; Ephesians 1:2; Colossians 1:17; Hebrews 1:3; Revelation 1:5).

Power to transform the bodies of all believers (Philippians 3:21).

Raising the dead for judgment (John 5:24-29; Acts 10:42; Acts 17:31).

Worshiped by people. Only God is worthy of worship (Psalm 95:6). Neither people (Acts 10:25-6), nor angels (Revelation 19:10) are to receive worship, but God alone (Luke 4:8). Jesus received worship from:

- the man born blind (John 9:38)
- the disciples (Matthew 14:33; 28:17)
- the wise men (Matthew 2:2, 11)
- the young ruler (Matthew 9:18)
- women (Matthew 28:9)
- the disciples (Matthew 28:17)
- the demons (Mark 3:11; 5:6)
- everyone (Philippians 2:10, 11)
- the four elders (Revelation 5:14).

Forgiving sin (Matthew 1:21; Mark 2:7).

Sending the Holy Spirit (a creature cannot send God; John 16:7; cf. 14:26).

The baptismal formula shows Christ clearly asserting his deity (Matthew 28:19).

A comment from the great Puritan preacher B. B. Warfield on this key verse is helpful here.

> The precise form of the formula must be carefully observed. It does not read: "In the names" (plural)—as if there were three beings enumerated, each with its distinguishing name. Nor yet: "In the name of the Father, Son and Holy Spirit," as if there were one person, going by a threefold name. It reads: "In the name (singular) of the Father and of the (article repeated) Son, and of the (article repeated) Holy Spirit," carefully distinguishing three persons, though uniting them all under one name. The name of God was to the Jews Jehovah, and to name the name of Jehovah upon them was to make them His. What Jesus did in this great injunction was to command His followers to name the name of God upon their converts, and to announce the name of God which is to be named on their converts in the threefold enumeration of "the Father" and "the Son" and "the Holy Spirit." As it is unquestionable that He here intended Himself by "the Son," He here places Himself by the side of the Father and Spirit, as together with them constituting the one God. It is, of course, the Trinity which he is describing and that is as much as to say that He announces Himself as one of the persons of the Trinity.
>
> *B. B. Warfield*

F SCRIPTURAL DECLARATIONS THAT CHRIST IS GOD

The Bible has plenty of teaching about Christ's deity.

Isaiah 9:6: "For to us a child is born . . . and he will be called Mighty God."

Matthew 1:23: "'. . . and they will call him Immanuel'—which means, 'God with us.'" (See also Isaiah 7:14.)

John 1:1, 14: "The Word was God. . . . The Word became flesh and made his dwelling among us."

John 1:18: "No one has ever seen God, but God the One and Only, who is at the Father's side has made him known."

John 20:28: Thomas said to him [Jesus] "My Lord and my God!"

Acts 20:28: "Be shepherds of the church of God, which he bought with his own blood."

Romans 9:5: "Christ, who is God over all, forever praised!"

1 Corinthians 1:24: "Christ the power of God and the wisdom of God."

2 Corinthians 4:4: "Christ, who is the image of God."

Philippians 2:6, "being in very nature God."

Colossians 1:15-17: "He is the image of the invisible God . . . and in him all things hold together."

Colossians 2:9: "In Christ all the fullness of the Deity lives in bodily form."

Titus 2:13: "Our great God and Savior, Jesus Christ."

Hebrews 1:3: "The Son is the radiance of God's glory and the exact representation of his being, sustaining all things by his powerful word."

Hebrews 1:8: "But about the Son he says, 'Your throne, O God, will last for ever and ever.'"

2 Peter 1:1: "Our God and Savior Jesus Christ."

1 John 5:20: ". . . Jesus Christ. He is the true God and eternal life."

PEOPLE IN THE BIBLE WHO TESTIFIED TO CHRIST'S DEITY

The High Priest: "You have heard the blasphemy" (Mark 14:61-64).

Peter: "The Son of the living God" (Matthew 16:16; to a Jew, this made him God's equal, see John 5:18).

John: "Making himself [Jesus] equal with God" (John 5:18).

The Jews: "You, a mere man, claim to be God" (John 10:33).

Thomas: "My Lord and my God!" (John 20:28).

G NAMES AND TITLES OF GOD ARE ATTRIBUTED TO CHRIST

This can be demonstrated by comparing the descriptions of God in the Old Testament which are also used of Jesus Christ in the New Testament.

1. The first and the last: Isaiah 41:4; 44, 6; 48:12 / Revelation 2:8; 22:13

2. I AM: Exodus 3:14 / John 8:58; John 13:19

3. Author of eternal words: Isaiah. 40:8; Psalm 119:89 / Matthew 24:35; John 6:68

4. Light: Psalm 27:1 / John 1:4-9; 8:12; 1 John 1:5

5. Rock: Deuteronomy 32:31; Psalm 18:2; Isaiah 8:14; Psalm 92:15 / 1 Peter 2:6-8; 1 Corinthians 10:4

6. Bridegroom: Isaiah 62:5; Hosea 2:16 / Mark 2:19; Revelation 21:2

7. Shepherd: Psalm 23:1 / John 10:11; Hebrews 13:20

8. Forgiver of sins: Jeremiah 31:34 / Mark 2:5-7; Acts 5:31

9. Redeemer: Hosea 13:14; Psalm 130:7 / Titus 2:13, 14; Revelation 5:9

10. Savior: Isaiah 43:3; Hosea 13:4 / 2 Peter 1:1, 11; Titus 2:10-13; Acts 4:12 (compare Titus 1:3)

11. The Lord of Glory: Isaiah 42:8 / John 17:1-5; 1 Corinthians 2:8

12. Judge: Joel 3:12 / Matthew 25:31-46

13. The second coming God: Zechariah 14:5 / Matthew 16:27; 24:29-31

14. The first coming God: Isaiah 40:3 / Matthew 3:3

15. King of glory: Psalm 24:7, 10 / 1 Corinthians 2:8; John 17:5

16. Jehovah our righteousness: Jeremiah 23:5, 6 / 1 Corinthians 1:30

17. Jehovah the first and last: Isaiah 44:6; 48:12-16 / Revelation 1:8, 17; 22:13

18. Jehovah above all: Psalm 97:9 / John 3:31

19. Jehovah's fellow and equal: Zechariah 13:7 / Philippians 2:6

20. The Lord Almighty: Isaiah 6:1-3; 8:13-14 / John 12:41; 1 Peter 2:8

21. Jehovah: Psalm 110:1 / Matthew 22:42-45

22. Jehovah the shepherd: Isaiah 40:11 / Hebrews 13:20

23. Jehovah, for whose glory all things were created: Proverbs 16:4 / Colossians 1:16

24. Jehovah the messenger of the covenant: Malachi 3:1 / Luke 7:27

25. Invoked as Jehovah: Joel 2:32; Isaiah 45:22 / 1 Corinthians 1:2

26. The eternal God and creator: Psalm 102:24-27 / Hebrews 1:8, 10-12

27. The great God and Savior: Isaiah 43:11-12 / Titus 1:3-4; 2:10, 13; 3:4-6

28. God the judge: Ecclesiastes 12:14 / 1 Corinthians 4:5; 2 Corinthians 5:10; 2 Timothy 4:1

29. Emmanuel: Isaiah 7:14 / Matthew 1:23

30. The Holy One: 1 Samuel 2:2 / Acts 3:14

31. Lord of the Sabbath: Genesis 2:3 / Matthew 12:8

32. Lord of all: 1 Chronicles 29:11-12 / Acts 10:36; Romans 10:11-13

33. Creator of all things: Isaiah 40:28; Psalm 148:1-5 / John 1:3; Colossians 1:16

34. Supporter, preserver of all things: Nehemiah 9:6 / Colossians 1:17

35. Stumbling rock of offense: Isaiah 8:13-14 / Romans 9:32-33; 1 Peter 2:8; Acts 4:11

36. All will confess that he is Lord: Isaiah 45:23 (Jehovah) / Philippians 2:11 (Jesus)

37. The judge of all men: Psalm 98:9 / Acts 17:31

38. Raiser of the dead: 1 Samuel 2:6; Psalm 119 (11 times) / John 11:25; 5:21; Luke 7:12-16

39. Co-sender of the Holy Spirit: John 14:16 (the Father sends) / (Jesus sends) John 15:26

40. Led captivity captive: Psalm 68:18 / Ephesians 4:7, 8

41. Seen by Isaiah: Isaiah 6:1 / John 12:41

42. Judge of the nations: Joel 3:12 / Matthew 25:31-41

43. Salvation by calling on the name of the Lord: Joel 2:32 / Romans 10:13

H FIRST-CENTURY TESTIMONIES

This is the disciple who testifies to these things [about Jesus] and who wrote them down. We know that his testimony is true.

John the apostle, John 21:24

I myself have carefully investigated everything from the beginning . . . so that you may know the certainty of the things you have been taught.

Dr. Luke, Luke 1:3, 4

After his [Jesus'] suffering, he showed himself to these men [apostles] and gave many convincing proofs that he was alive. He appeared to them over a period of forty days and spoke about the kingdom of God.

Dr. Luke, Acts 1:3

But I have had God's help to this very day, and so I stand here and testify to small and great alike. I am saying nothing beyond what the prophets and Moses said would happen. . . . What I am saying is true and reasonable. The king is familiar with these things, and I can speak freely to him. I am convinced that none of this has escaped his notice, because it was not done in a corner.

The apostle Paul, Acts 26:22, 25b-26

We did not follow cleverly invented stories when we told you about the power and coming of our Lord Jesus Christ, but we were eyewitnesses of his majesty.

The apostle Peter, 2 Peter 1:16

I THE EARLY CHURCH'S TESTIMONY TO THE DEITY OF CHRIST

IGNATIUS OF ANTIOCH (30-107)

In his letters to the Ephesians, to the Romans, to the Magnesians and in other letters, Ignatius wrote: "Jesus Christ our God;" "who is God and man;" "received knowledge of God, that is, Jesus Christ;" "for our God, Jesus the Christ;" "for God was manifest as man;" "Christ, who was from eternity with the Father;" "from God, from Jesus Christ;" "from Jesus Christ, our God;" "Our God, Jesus Christ;" "suffer me to follow the example of the passion of my God;" "Jesus Christ the God;" and, "Our God Jesus Christ."

JUSTIN MARTYR (100-165)

Justin Martyr wrote of Jesus, "who . . . being the first-begotten Word of God, is even God." In his *Dialogue with Trypho*, he stated that, "God was born from a virgin" and that Jesus was "worthy of worship" and of being "called Lord and God."

TATIAN (110-172)

This early apologist wrote, "We do not act as fools, O Greeks, nor utter idle tales when we announce that God was born in the form of man."

IRENAEUS OF LYONS AND ROME (120-202)

Irenaeus wrote that Jesus was "perfect God and perfect man;" "not a mere man . . . but was very God;" and that "He is in himself in his own right . . .God, and Lord, and King eternal" and spoke of "Christ Jesus, our Lord, and God, and Savior and King."

TERTULLIAN OF CARTHAGE (C.150-212)

Tertullian said of Jesus, "Christ is also God" because "that which has come forth from God [in the virgin birth] is at once God and the Son of God, and the two are one . . . in His birth, God and man united." Jesus is "both Man and God, the Son of Man and the Son of God."

He wrote of Jesus that, "He is God and man . . . We have here a dual condition - not fused but united - in one person, Jesus as God and man."

HIPPOLYTUS (170-235)

He said, "[It is] the Father who is above all, the Son who is through all, and the Holy Spirit who is in all. And we cannot otherwise think of one God, but by believing in truth in Father and Son and Holy Spirit. . . . For it is through this Trinity that the Father is glorified . . . The whole Scriptures, then, proclaim this truth." And, "the Logos is God, being the substance of God."

GREGORY THAUMATURGUS OF NEO-CAESAREA (205-270)

"All [the persons] are one nature, one essence, one will, and are called the Holy Trinity; and these also are names subsistent, one nature in three persons, and one genus [kind]." Gregory Thaumaturgus referred to Jesus as "God of God" and "God the Son."

ORIGEN OF ALEXANDRIA (C. 185-C. 254)

Origen stated that Christ was "God and man." In AD 254 he wrote, "Jesus Christ . . . while he was God, and though made man, remained God as he was before."

ATHANASIUS (293-373)

Athanasius wrote of Jesus, "He always was and is God and Son," and "He who is eternally God . . . also became man for our sake."

LUCIAN OF ANTIOCH (C. 300)

"We believe in . . . one Lord Jesus Christ, his Son, the only-begotten God . . . God of God."

CYRIL OF JERUSALEM (C. 350)

Cyril wrote: "We believe in . . . One Lord Jesus Christ, the only begotten Son of God . . . very God, by whom all things were made."

EPIPHANIUS OF CONSTANTIA (C. 374)

"We believe . . . in one Lord Jesus Christ . . . of the substance of the Father, Light of Light, very God of very God."

AUGUSTINE OF HIPPO (354-430)

Augustine declared that Christians, "believe that Father, Son, and Holy Spirit are one God, maker and ruler of the whole creation: that Father is not Son, nor Holy Spirit Father or Son; but a Trinity of mutually related Persons, and a unity of equal essence," and that therefore, "the Father is God, the Son is God, and the Holy Spirit God; and all together are one God."

3 CHRISTIANITY'S HOLY BOOK

INTRODUCTION

Christianity finds all its doctrines stated in the Bible, and Christianity denies no part, nor attempts to add anything to the word of God.

Billy Graham

The Bible was written over a period of 1,500 years, by over forty authors, from three different continents—Asia, Africa and Europe.

The authors of the Bible were a varied collection of people, including:

- an Egyptian prince
- a housewife
- a priest
- scribes
- a farmer
- prophets

- a military general
- fishermen
- kings
- shepherds
- a herdsman
- a politician
- a doctor
- a tax collector
- a rabbinical scholar
- a half-brother of Jesus

A UNIQUE BOOK

The Bible claims to be "the word of God" (Proverbs 30:5; Matthew 15:6) and in this sense Christians believe that it is unique among "holy books." It reveals the character of God and records the interaction of God in history with individual people and nations. It shows the meaning of life and human beings' responsibility to their creator.

A LIBRARY
The Bible is a collection of books. It has been called, "the book of books."

BEST SELLER
The Bible is the world's all-time best seller.

TWO MAJOR SECTIONS
The Bible is divided into two sections: the Old Testament and the New Testament.
OLD TESTAMENT BIBLE BOOKS
Genesis
Exodus
Leviticus
Numbers
Deuteronomy
Joshua
Judges
Ruth
1 & 2 Samuel
1 & 2 Kings
1 & 2 Chronicles
Ezra
Nehemiah
Esther
Job
Psalms
Proverbs
Ecclesiastes
Song of Solomon
Isaiah
Jeremiah
Lamentations
Ezekiel
Daniel
Hosea
Joel
Amos
Obadiah
Jonah
Micah
Nahum
Habakkuk
Zephaniah

Haggai
Zechariah
Malachi

NEW TESTAMENT BIBLE BOOKS
Matthew
Mark
Luke
John
Acts
Romans
1 Corinthians
2 Corinthians
Galatians
Ephesians
Philippians
Colossians
1 & 2 Thessalonians
1 Timothy
2 Timothy
Titus
Philemon
Hebrews
James
1 & 2 Peter
1, 2, & 3 John
Jude
Revelation

THE OLD TESTAMENT
The King James Version of the Old Testament has:
39 books
929 chapters
23,214 verses
593,493 words
Longest book: Psalms
Shortest book: Obadiah (third shortest book in the Bible)

THE NEW TESTAMENT
The King James Version of the New Testament has:
27 books
260 chapters
7,959 verses
181,253 words
Longest book: Acts
Shortest book in the Bible: 3 John (with the fewest number of words. 2 John has more words, but one fewer verses.)

5 history books (Acts and the Gospels: Matthew, Mark, Luke, John)
21 letters (epistles)
1 book of prophecy (Revelation)

THE NINE SUB-SECTIONS OF THE BIBLE.

The Bible's books are arranged by *type*, rather than in chronological order.

(I) BOOKS OF MOSES AND THE LAW
Genesis
Exodus
Leviticus
Numbers
Deuteronomy

(II) HISTORY BOOKS (ABOUT GOD'S CHOSEN PEOPLE, ISRAEL)
Joshua
Judges
Ruth
1 & 2 Samuel
1 & 2 Kings
1 & 2 Chronicles
Ezra
Nehemiah
Esther

(III) WISDOM BOOKS
Job
Psalms
Proverbs
Ecclesiastes
Song of Solomon

(IV) PROPHETS' BOOKS
Isaiah
Jeremiah
Lamentations
Ezekiel
Daniel
Hosea
Joel
Amos
Obadiah
Jonah
Micah

Nahum
Habakkuk
Zephaniah
Haggai
Zechariah
Malachi

(V) GOSPELS (JESUS' LIFE AND THE WAY OF SALVATION)
Matthew
Mark
Luke
John

(VI) HISTORY OF THE EARLY CHURCH
Acts

(VII) PAUL'S LETTERS
Romans
1 Corinthians
2 Corinthians
Galatians
Ephesians
Philippians
Colossians
1Thessalonians
2 Thessalonians
1 Timothy
2 Timothy
Titus
Philemon

(VIII) OTHER NEW TESTAMENT LETTERS
Hebrews
James
1 Peter
2 Peter
1 John
2 John
3 John
Jude

(IX) APOCALYPSE
Revelation

4 FACTS AND FIGURES

INTRODUCTION

Christianity is the world's biggest religion, with more than 2,200 million followers worldwide.

THROUGHOUT THE WORLD
MAJOR TRADITIONAL BRANCHES OF CHRISTIANITY

Roman Catholic	1,100,000,000
Protestant	500,000,000
Other Christians	300,000,000
Orthodox	250,000,000
Anglicans and Episcopalians	77,000,000

MAJOR DENOMINATIONAL GROUPINGS OF CHRISTIANS

Roman Catholic	1,100,000,000
Orthodox/Eastern Christian	250,000,000
Pentecostal	150,000,000
Reformed/Presbyterian/Congregational	80,000,000
Anglican/Episcopalian	77,000,000
Baptist	75,000,000
Methodist	70,000,000
Lutheran	65,000,000
Brethren	1,500,000
Mennonite	1,250,000
Friends (Quakers)	300,000

PROTESTANTS

Conservative Protestant	200,000,000
Liberal Protestant	150,000,000

LARGEST NATIONAL CHRISTIAN POPULATIONS

Rank	Nation	Number	Percentage of population
1	USA	250,000,000	85%
2	Brazil	150,000,000	93%
3	Mexico	90,000,000	99%
4	Russia	80,000,000	60%
5	China	75,000,000	6%
6	Germany	70,000,000	80%
7	Philippines	65,000,000	92%
8	United Kingdom	50,000,000	85%
9	Italy	50,000,000	89%
10	France	45,000,000	97%
11	Nigeria	40,000,000	46%

IN THE USA
The top ten (all-inclusive) Christian states by percentage of population

Rank	State	Percentage of population
1	Utah	80%
2	North Dakota	76%
3	Rhode Island	75%
4	Alabama	71%
5	Louisiana	70%
6	Mississippi	69%
7	South Dakota	68%
8	Oklahoma	67%
9	Minnesota	64%
10	Wisconsin	62%

The top ten (all-inclusive) Christian states by number of adherents

Rank	State	Number of adherents
1	Wisconsin	3,125,000
2	Louisiana	3,100,000
3	Alabama	2,900,000
4	Minnesota	2,800,000
5	Oklahoma	2,200,000
6	Mississippi	1,00,000
7	Utah	1,400,000
8	Rhode Island	800,000
9	North Dakota	500,000
10	South Dakota	490,000

5 CHRISTIAN PRACTICES

INTRODUCTION

A   Roman Catholics and the seven sacraments
B   *The Abstract of Principles*
C   Christian mission
    (i) History of Christian missions
    (ii) Timeline of the spread of the Christian gospel

Christians set out to live their lives in accordance with the teachings in the New Testament. They belong to a local Christian fellowship, participating in a number of Christian sacraments, and usually attend a worship service on Sundays.

There is a great deal of common ground between Roman Catholics and Protestants, but there are major differences in teaching about worship and the Christian sacraments. The following seven extracts from *The Catholic Encyclopedia,* 1908, give a fair overview of Roman Catholic teaching on the sacraments. By way of contrast, *The Abstract of Principles* represent the beliefs of many Protestant evangelicals.

From the first recorded Christian sermon on the day of Pentecost Christianity has been an evangelizing and missionary religion. The section on Christian mission summarizes two thousand years of this vital aspect of Christianity.

A ROMAN CATHOLICS AND THE SEVEN SACRAMENTS

(See also Section Two: Roman Catholism, on pages 73-95)

(I) BAPTISM

One of the seven sacraments of the Christian Church; frequently called the "first sacrament," the "door of the sacraments," and the "door of the Church."

> The Roman Catechism (Ad parochos, De bapt., 2, 2, 5) defines baptism thus: Baptism is the sacrament of regeneration by water in the word (*per aquam in verbo*). St. Thomas Aquinas (III:66:1) gives this definition: "Baptism is the external ablution of the body, performed with the prescribed form of words." Later theologians generally distinguish formally between the physical and the metaphysical defining of this sacrament. By the former they understand the formula expressing the action of ablution and the utterance of the invocation of the Trinity; by the latter, the definition: "Sacrament of regeneration" or that

institution of Christ by which we are reborn to spiritual life. The term "regeneration" distinguishes baptism from every other sacrament, for although penance revivifies men spiritually, yet this is rather a resuscitation, a bringing back from the dead, than a rebirth. Penance does not make us Christians; on the contrary, it presupposes that we have already been born of water and the Holy Ghost to the life of grace, while baptism on the other hand was instituted to confer upon men the very beginnings of the spiritual life, to transfer them from the state of enemies of God to the state of adoption, as sons of God. The definition of the Roman Catechism combines the physical and metaphysical definitions of baptism. "The sacrament of regeneration" is the metaphysical essence of the sacrament, while the physical essence is expressed by the second part of the definition, i.e. the washing with water (matter), accompanied by the invocation of the Holy Trinity (form). Baptism is, therefore, the sacrament by which we are born again of water and the Holy Ghost, that is, by which we receive in a new and spiritual life, the dignity of adoption as sons of God and heirs of God's kingdom.

William H. W. Fanning, The Catholic Encyclopedia, *1908*

(II) CONFIRMATION

A sacrament in which the Holy Ghost is given to those already baptized in order to make them strong and perfect Christians and soldiers of Jesus Christ.

T. B. Scannell, The Catholic Encyclopedia, *1908*

(III) EUCHARIST

(Greek, *eucharistia*, "thanksgiving")

The name given to the Blessed Sacrament of the Altar in its twofold aspect of sacrament and Sacrifice of Mass, and in which Jesus Christ is truly present under the bread and wine. Other titles are used, such as "Lord's Supper" (Coena Domini), "Table of the Lord" (Mensa Domini), the "Lord's Body" (Corpus Domini), and the "Holy of Holies" (Sanctissimum), to which may be added the following expressions, and somewhat altered from their primitive meaning: "Agape" (Love-Feast), "Eulogia" (Blessing), "Breaking of Bread", "Synaxis" (Assembly), etc.; but the ancient title "Eucharistia" appearing in writers as early as Ignatius, Justin, and Irenæus, has taken precedence in the technical terminology of the Church and her theologians. The expression "Blessed Sacrament of the Altar", introduced by Augustine, is at the present day almost entirely restricted to catechetical and popular treatises. This extensive nomenclature, describing the great mystery from such different points of view, is in itself sufficient proof of the central position the Eucharist has occupied from the earliest ages, both in the Divine worship and services of the Church and in the life of faith and devotion which animates her members. The Church honors the Eucharist as one

of her most exalted mysteries, since for sublimity and incomprehensibility it yields in nothing to the allied mysteries of the Trinity and Incarnation. These three mysteries constitute a wonderful triad, which causes the essential characteristic of Christianity, as a religion of mysteries far transcending the capabilities of reason, to shine forth in all its brilliance and splendor, and elevates Catholicism, the most faithful guardian and keeper of our Christian heritage, far above all pagan and non-Christian religions.

J. Pohle, The Catholic Encyclopedia, *1908*

(IV) EXTREME UNCTION

A sacrament of the New Law instituted by Christ to give spiritual aid and comfort and perfect spiritual health, including, if need be, the remission of sins, and also, conditionally, to restore bodily health, to Christians who are seriously ill; it consists essentially in the unction by a priest of the body of the sick person, accompanied by a suitable form of words.

P. J. Toner, The Catholic Encyclopedia, *1908*

(V) SACRAMENT OF MARRIAGE

That Christian marriage (i.e. marriage between baptized persons) is really a sacrament of the New Law in the strict sense of the word is for all Catholics an indubitable truth. According to the Council of Trent this dogma has always been taught by the Church, and is thus defined in canon i, Sess. XXIV: "If any one shall say that matrimony is not truly and properly one of the Seven Sacraments of the Evangelical Law, instituted by Christ our Lord, but was invented in the Church by men, and does not confer grace, let him be anathema." The occasion of this solemn declaration was the denial by the so-called Reformers of the sacramental character of marriage. Calvin in his "Institutions", IV, xix, 34, says: "Lastly, there is matrimony, which all admit was instituted by God, though no one before the time of Gregory regarded it as a sacrament. What man in his sober senses could so regard it? God's ordinance is good and holy; so also are agriculture, architecture, shoemaking, hair-cutting legitimate ordinances of God, but they are not sacraments". And Luther speaks in terms equally vigorous. In his German work, published at Wittenberg in 1530 under the title "Von den Ehesachen", he writes (p. 1): "No one indeed can deny that marriage is an external worldly thing, like clothes and food, house and home, subject to worldly authority, as shown by so many imperial laws governing it." In an earlier work (the original edition of "De captivitate Babylonica") he writes: "Not only is the sacramental character of matrimony without foundation in Scripture; but the very traditions, which claim such sacredness for it, are a mere jest"; and two pages further on: "Marriage may therefore be a figure of Christ and the Church; it is, however, no Divinely instituted sacrament, but the invention of men in the Church, arising from ignorance of the subject." The Fathers of the Council of Trent evidently had the latter passage in mind.

But the decision of Trent was not the first given by the Church. The Council of Florence, in the Decree for the Armenians, had already declared: "The seventh sacrament is matrimony, which is a figure of the union of Christ, and the Church, according to the words of the Apostle: This is a great sacrament, but I speak in Christ and in the Church.'" And Innocent IV, in the profession of faith prescribed for the Waldensians (December 18, 1208), includes matrimony among the sacraments (Denziger-Bannwart, "Enchiridion", n. 424). The acceptance of the sacraments administered in the Church had been prescribed in general in the following words: "And we by no means reject the sacraments which are administered in it (the Roman Catholic Church), with the co-operation of the inestimable and invisible power of the Holy Ghost, even though they be administered by a sinful priest, provided the Church recognizes

him", the formula then takes up each sacrament in particular, touching especially on those points which the Waldensians had denied: "Therefore we approve of baptism of children . . . confirmation administered by the bishop . . . the sacrifice of the Eucharist . . . . We believe that pardon is granted by God to penitent sinners . . . we hold in honor the anointing of the sick with consecrated oil . . . we do not deny that carnal marriages are to be contracted, according to the words of the Apostle." It is, therefore, historically certain that from the beginning of the thirteenth century the sacramental character of marriage was universally known and recognized as a dogma.

A. Lehmkuhl, The Catholic Encyclopedia, *1908*

(VI) HOLY ORDERS

Order is the appropriate disposition of things equal and unequal, by giving each its proper place (St. Aug., "De civ. Dei," XIX, xiii). Order primarily means a relation. It is used to designate that on which the relation is founded and thus generally means rank (St. Thom., "Suppl.", Q. xxxiv, a.2, ad 4um). In this sense it was applied to clergy and laity (St. Jer., "In Isaiam", XIX, 18; St. Greg. the Great, "Moral.", XXXII, xx). The meaning was restricted later to the hierarchy as a whole or to the various ranks of the clergy. Tertullian and some early writers had already used the word in that sense, but generally with a qualifying adjective (Tertullian, "De exhort. cast.", vii, ordo sacerdotalis, ordo ecclesiasticus; St. Greg. of Tours, "Vit. patr.", X, i, ordo clericorum). Order is used to signify not only the particular rank or general status of the clergy, but also the outward action by which they are raised to that status, and thus stands for ordination. It also indicates what differentiates laity from clergy or the various ranks of the clergy, and thus means spiritual power. The Sacrament of Order is the sacrament by which grace and spiritual power for the discharge of ecclesiastical offices are conferred.

Christ founded His Church as a supernatural society, the Kingdom of God. In this society there must be the power of ruling; and also the principles by which the members are to attain their supernatural end, viz., supernatural truth, which is held by faith, and supernatural grace by which man is formally elevated to the supernatural order. Thus, besides the power of jurisdiction, the Church has the power of teaching (magisterium) and the power of conferring grace (power of order). This power of order was committed by our Lord to His Apostles, who were to continue His work and to be His earthly representatives. The Apostles received their power from Christ: "as the Father hath sent me, I also send you" (John, xx, 21). Christ possessed fullness of power in virtue of His priesthood - of His office as Redeemer and Mediator. He merited the grace which freed man from the bondage of sin, which grace is applied to man mediately by the Sacrifice of the Eucharist and immediately by the sacraments. He gave His Apostles the power to offer the Sacrifice (Luke, xxii, 19), and dispense the sacraments (Matt., xxviii, 18; John, xx, 22, 23); thus making them priests. It is true that every Christian receives sanctifying grace which confers on him a priesthood. Even as Israel under the Old dispensation was to God "a priestly kingdom" (Exod., xix, 4-6), thus under the New, all Christians are "a kingly priesthood" (I Pet., ii, 9); but now as then the special and sacramental priesthood strengthens and perfects the universal priesthood (cf. II Cor., iii, 3, 6; Rom., xv, 16).

H. Ahaus, The Catholic Encyclopedia, *1908*

(VII) THE SACRAMENT OF PENANCE

Penance is a sacrament of the New Law instituted by Christ in which forgiveness of sins committed after baptism is granted through the priest's absolution to those who with true sorrow confess their sins and promise to satisfy for the same. It is called a "sacrament" not simply a function or ceremony, because it is an outward sign instituted by Christ to impart grace to the soul. As an outward sign it comprises the actions of the penitent in presenting himself to the priest and accusing himself of his sins, and the actions of the priest in pronouncing absolution and imposing satisfaction. This whole procedure is usually called, from one of its parts, "confession", and it is said to take place in the "tribunal of penance", because it is a judicial process in which the penitent is at once the accuser, the person accused, and the witness, while the priest pronounces judgment and sentence. The grace conferred is deliverance from the guilt of sin and, in the case of mortal sin, from its eternal punishment; hence also reconciliation with God, justification. Finally, the confession is made not in the secrecy of the penitent's heart nor to a layman as friend and advocate, nor to a representative of human authority, but to a duly ordained priest with requisite jurisdiction and with the "power of the keys", i.e., the power to forgive sins which Christ granted to His Church. *Edward J. Hanna,* The Catholic Encyclopedia, *1908*

B THE ABSTRACT OF PRINCIPLES

Most Protestants hold that there are only two Christian sacraments: baptism and the Lord's Supper.

The Abstract of Principles (1858) remains a clear and succinct statement of beliefs commonly held by Southern Baptists. It stipulates the following about the Church, baptism, and the Lord's Supper.

THE CHURCH

The Lord Jesus is the head of the church which is composed of all his true disciples, and in him is invested supremely all power for its government. According to his commandment, Christians are to associate themselves into particular societies or churches; and to each of these churches he hath given needful authority for administering that order, disciple and worship which he hath appointed. The regular officers of a church are bishop or elders, and deacons.

See Matthew16:15-19; Acts 2:41-42, 47;
Ephesians 1:22-23; Colossians 1:18; 1
Timothy 3:1-15; 1 Peter 3:1-4.

BAPTISM

Baptism is an ordinance of the Lord Jesus,
obligatory upon every believer, wherein
he is immersed in water in the name of
the Father, and of the Son, and of the
Holy Spirit, as a sign of his fellowship
with the death and resurrection of Christ,
of remission of sins, and of his giving
himself up to God, to live and walk in
newness of life. It is prerequisite to church
fellowship, and to participation in the
Lord's Supper.
See Matthew 28:19-20; Mark1:9-11;
Romans 6:3-5.

THE LORD'S SUPPER

The Lord's Supper is an ordinance of Jesus
Christ, to be administered with the
elements of bread and wine, and to be
observed by his churches till the end of
the world. It is in no sense a sacrifice, but
is designed to commemorate his death, to
confirm the faith and other graces of
Christians, and to be a bond, pledge and
renewal of their communion with him,
and of their church fellowship.
See Matthew 26:26-30; Mark 14:22-26;
1Corinthians 11:23-29.

C CHRISTIAN MISSION

Mission is seen to be God's will as it is plainly
stated throughout the Bible, including the
Old Testament. Since the Lausanne Congress
of 1974, a widely-accepted definition of
Christian mission has been "to form a viable
indigenous church-planting movement." This
definition is motivated by theological analysis
of the acts required to enhance God's
reputation (usually translated as "glory" or
"honor"), and summarizes the acts of Jesus'
ministry, which is taken as a model for
all ministries.

- The movement must "plant" (start)
  churches because the process of forming
  godly disciples is necessarily social.

- "Church" should be understood in the
  widest sense as an organization of
  believers. It is not a building. Many
  churches start by meeting in houses.
  Discipling is required to grow the number
  of believers to the largest extent, and
  maximize their quality and therefore the
  acceptability of their worship to God and
  their outreach.

- "Viable" means that the movement is self-
  governing, self-supporting and self-
  propagating. This is the famous "three-
  self" formula put forward by Henry Venn
  of the London Church Missionary
  Society in the century.

- "Indigenous" means that people who are
  native to a culture have all the needed
  abilities and accept all the required duties.
  Only such people can adapt the gospel to
  their culture, maximizing both natural,
  high-quality worship and the number of
  people that can be reached in that culture.

- It must be a "movement," because special
  organization is required for the task of
  planting churches. This movement
  naturally forms cross-cultural missions
  when people who understand and accept
  church-planting duties go to others
  outside their culture, as Christ
  commanded in the great commission
  (Matthew 28:18-20). Thus the cycle
  is repeated.

(I) HISTORY OF CHRISTIAN MISSIONS
According to the documents of the Lausanne
Committee for World Evangelization, the
biblical authority for missions begins in
Genesis 12:1-3 where Abraham is blessed so
that through him and his descendants all the
"peoples" of the world may be blessed. Others
point to God's wish, often expressed in the
Bible, that all peoples of the earth should
worship him. Christian missions go,
therefore, where worship is not, in order to
bring worship to God.
In this view, the mission of the Israelites
was that of being a people placed in the midst
of the other nations so that they could

proclaim the creator God who had blessed them. This view is confirmed in many OT scriptures, (for example, Exodus 19:4-6; Psalm 67) as well as in the structure of the Temple (its outer court was "the court of the Gentiles").

Several teachers, including John R. W. Stott, believe that a prominent prophecy in the Old Testament often unfolds continually and is manifested in three situations: the immediate historical situation following the prophecy; a church-based intermediate situation; and an eschatological, end-of-time situation (Genesis 12:1-3 is a good example).

The first, and most famous, missionary was St. Paul. He contextualized the gospel for the Greek and Roman cultures, permitting it to leave its Jewish context. This cultural fluidity was then, as it is now, a source of friction between Paul and some members of the sending church. In such a contextualization, the object is to take the essential seed of the gospel, and plant it in the soil of the foreign culture so that every practice not essential to the gospel is indigenous. This permits the indigenous church to grow more rapidly by reducing cultural barriers that hinder acceptance of the gospel.

In the early Christian era, most missions were by monks. Monasteries followed disciplines and supported missions, libraries and practical research, all of which were perceived as works to reduce human misery and suffering, thus enhancing the reputation of God. Nestorian communities, for example, evangelized large areas of North Africa before the time of Muhammad and Cistercians evangelized much of northern Europe, as well as developing most of European agriculture's classic techniques. Later, Jesuits were sent to China.

For nearly a hundred years after the Reformation, the Protestant Churches were preoccupied with their struggle with the Roman Catholic Church, and were not missionary-sending Churches. But in the centuries that followed, the Protestant Churches sent increasing numbers of missionaries to previously unreached people.

In North America, missionaries to the native Americans included Jonathan Edwards, the well-known preacher of the Great Awakening, who in his later years retired from the very public life of his early career to go as a missionary to the Housatonic Native Americans. He became a staunch advocate for them against cultural imperialism.

In areas where European culture has been established in the midst of indigenous peoples, the cultural distance between Christians of differing cultures has been difficult to overcome. One early solution was the creation of segregated "praying towns" of Christian natives. This pattern of grudging acceptance of converts was later repeated in Hawaii by missionaries from that same New England.

In Spanish colonization of the Americas, the Catholic missionaries learned the languages of the Amerindians and devised writing systems for them. Then they preached to them in those languages (Quechua, Guarani, Nahuatl), instead of Spanish, to keep Indians away from "sinful" whites. An extreme case was the Guarani Reductions, a theocratic semi-independent region established by the Jesuits.

Around 1780, an indigent Baptist cobbler named William Carey began reading about James Cook's Polynesian journeys. His interest grew to a furious sort of "backwards homesickness," inspiring him to obtain Baptist orders, and eventually write his famous 1792 pamphlet, *An Enquiry into the Obligation of Christians to use Means for the Conversion of Heathen.* Far from being a dry book of theology, Carey's work used the best available geographic and ethnographic data to map and count the number of people who had never heard the gospel. It formed a movement that has grown with increasing speed from Carey's day to ours.

Not long after the publication of Carey's pamphlet, he and his friends formed the first missionary society, enabling him to go as a missionary to India. In India, Carey is well-known, having translated and printed numerous books, scientific as well as religious. He translated not just from English to Bengali and Sanskrit, but also translated the *Vedas* into

English, producing the first authoritative English versions. He started the first Bengali newspaper, formed horticultural societies and universities to teach farming and useful arts, and successfully fought the ancient evils of infant exposure and wife-burning (Suttee).

Carey's example was followed by a number of missions to seaside and port cities, the China Overseas Missionaries and Moravian Church being two of the more famous.

The next great wave of missions, starting about 1850, was to inland areas. Leading the way was Hudson Taylor with his China Inland Mission. Taylor was a thorough-going nativist, offending the missionaries of his era by wearing Chinese clothing and speaking Chinese at home. His mission was one of the few that actually began to persuade Chinese to follow Christ. His books, speaking, and example led to the formation of numerous inland missions, and the Student Volunteer Movement (SVM), which from 1850 to about 1950 sent nearly 10,000 missionaries to inland areas, often at great personal sacrifice. Many early SVM missionaries to areas with endemic tropical diseases left with their belongings packed in a coffin, aware that 80% of them would die within two years.

The next wave of missions was started by two missionaries, Cameron Townsend and Donald McGavran, around 1935. These men realized that although earlier missionaries had reached geographic areas, there were numerous ethnographic groups that were isolated by language or class from the groups the missionaries had reached. Cameron formed Wycliffe Bible Translators to translate the Bible into native languages. McGavran concentrated on finding bridges to cross the class and cultural barriers in places like India, which has upwards of 4,600 peoples, separated by a combination of language, culture and caste.

In the past, Christian missionaries sometimes worked hand-in-hand with colonialism, as during the European colonization of the Americas, Africa, and Asia. Sometimes, they have damaged those cultures and led natives to acculturation. On the other hand, missionaries have sometimes helped to save cultures from destruction by economic and political forces.

Most modern missionaries and missionary societies have repudiated cultural imperialism, and focus on spreading the gospel and translating the Bible. Sometimes, missionaries have been vital in preserving and documenting the culture of the peoples among whom they live.

Often missionaries provide welfare and health services. Thousands of schools, orphanages, and hospitals have been established by missions.

One of the quietest, yet most far-reaching, services provided by missionaries started with the "Each one, teach one" literacy program begun by Dr. Frank Laubach in the Philippines in 1935. The program has since spread around the world and has brought literacy to the least enabled members of many societies.

The word "mission" was historically often applied to the building - the "mission station" - in which the missionary lived or worked. In some colonies, these mission stations became a focus of settlement of displaced or formerly nomadic people. Particularly in rural Australia, missions became localities or ghettoes on the edges of towns, home to many Aborigines. When used in this context in a racist way, the word may be seen as derogatory.

Most modern missionaries avoid creating mission stations, and live in a totally native milieu, with a native family if possible, to speed language acquisition and to maintain a relevant connection between the work of the missionary and the people among whom the mission is established.

As Christianity has spread to other peoples, it has simultaneously declined in most of the sending nations. This generation witnesses the mission nations returning missionaries to the sending nations. However, at the same time, their deeds have greatly contributed to the extinction, or decline of indigenous religions, customs and culture. One good example is the tribes in north-east India.

As a matter of strategy, evangelical Christians in Europe and North America now focus on what they call the "10/40 window," a band of countries between 10 and 40 degrees north latitude and reaching from western Africa through Asia. It's an area that includes 35% of the world's landmass, 90% of the world's poorest peoples and 95% of those who have yet to hear anything about Christianity.

(II) TIMELINE OF THE SPREAD OF THE CHRISTIAN GOSPEL

c. 29   Pentecost and birth of the Christian Church

c. 34   Stephen stoned, Christians scattered by persecution; Philip, a deacon, baptizes a convert, an Ethiopian pilgrim

c. 39   Peter preaches to the Gentiles

c. 48   Paul (formerly known as Saul of Tarsus) begins his first missionary journey to modern-day Turkey

c. 51   Paul begins his second missionary journey, a trip that will take him through Turkey and on into modern-day Greece

c. 52   The apostle Thomas arrives in India and founds church that subsequently becomes Indian Orthodox Church (and its various descendants)

c. 54   Paul begins his third missionary journey

c. 60   Paul journeys to Rome

c. 180   Pantaenus preaches in India

c. 300   Ulfilas goes to the Goths in present-day Romania

328   Frumentius takes the gospel to Ethiopia

386   Augustine of Hippo converted

410   The New Testament appears in Armenian language

432   Patrick goes to Ireland as a missionary

496   Conversion of Clovis I, king of Franks in Gaul, along with 3,000 warriors

c. 528   Benedict destroys pagan temple at Monte Cassino (Italy) and builds monastery

c. 563   Columba sails from Ireland to Scotland

596   Gregory the Great sends Augustine to (what is now) England

631   Conversion of the East Angles

635   First Christian missionaries (Nestorian monks from Asia Minor and Persia) arrive in China; Aidan launches crusade into heart of Northumbria (England)

637   Lombards become Christian

692   Willibrord and eleven companions cross the North Sea to become missionaries to the Frisians (in modern Holland)

697   Muslims overrun Carthage, capital of North Africa

722   Boniface goes to Germanic tribes

823   Ansgar goes to Sweden

830   Scotch-born Erluph, bishop of Werden, is evangelizing in (what is now) Germany when he is killed by the Vandals

869   Cyril and Methodius go to the Slavs

864   Conversion of Prince Boris of Bulgaria

1000   Leif the Lucky evangelizes Greenland

1219   Francis of Assisi presents the gospel to the Sultan of Egypt

1266   The Khan sends Marco Polo's father and uncle, Niccolo and Maffeo Polo, back to Europe with a request to the pope to send 100 missionaries (only two responded and they turned back before reaching Mongolia)

1276   Ramon Lull opens training center to send missionaries to North Africa

1289   Franciscan friars begin mission work in China

1294   Franciscan John of Monte Corvino goes to China

1329   Nicea falls to Muslim Ottoman Turks

1368   Collapse of the Franciscan mission in China as Ming Dynasty abolishes Christianity

1382   Bible translated into English from Latin

1453   Constantinople falls to the Muslim Ottoman Turks who make it their capital

1500   Franciscans enter Brazil with Cabral

1510   Dominicans begin work in Haiti

1526   Franciscans enter Florida

1537   Pope Paul III orders that the Indians of the New World be brought to

1542 Christ "by the preaching of the divine word, and with the example of the good life."

1542 Francis Xavier, having two years previously launched the missionary work of the Society of Jesus, goes to the Portuguese colony of Goa in South India; Franciscans reach what is now New Mexico

1555 John Calvin sends Huguenots to Brazil

1564 Legaspi begins Augustinian work in Philippine Islands

1577 Dominicans enter Mozambique and penetrate inland, burning Muslim mosques as they go

1582 Jesuits begin mission work in China, introduce Western science, mathematics, and astronomy

1597 Twenty-six Japanese Christians are crucified for their faith by General Toyotomi Hideyoshi in Nagasaki, Japan. By 1640, thousands of Japanese Christians have been martyred

1601 Matteo Ricci goes to China

1605 Roberto de Nobili goes to India

1612 Jesuits found a mission for the Abenakis in Maine

1614 Anti-Christian edicts issued in Japan

1622 Pope Gregory VI founds the Sacred Congregation for the Propagation of the Faith

1628 College of Propaganda established in Rome to train "native clergy" from all over the world

1644 John Eliot begins ministry to Algonquin Indians in North America

1649 Society for the Propagation of the Gospel in New England formed to reach the Indians of New England

1651 Count Truchsess, prominent Lutheran layman, asked the theological faculty of Wittenberg why Lutherans were not sending out missionaries in obedience to the Great Commission

1658 Paris Foreign Missions Society established by Jesuit Alexandre de Rhodes

1661 George Fox, founder of the Society of Friends (Quakers) sends three missionaries to China (although they arrived at their destination)

1664 Justinian Von Welz goes to Dutch Guinea (now called Surinam)

1670 Jesuits establish missions on the Orinoco River in Venezuela

1698 Society for Promoting Christian Knowledge organized by Anglicans

1701 Society for the Propagation of the Gospel in Foreign Parts

1705 Danish-Halle mission to India begins with Bartholomaus Ziegenbalg and Heinrich Plutschau

1719 Isaac Watts writes missionary hymn "Jesus Shall Reign Where'er the Sun"

1722 Hans Egede goes to Greenland

1723 Robert Millar publishes *A History of the Propagation of Christianity and the Overthrow of Paganism*

1732 Moravians launch missionary outreach in Caribbean

1733 Moravians go to Greenland

1735 John Wesley goes to Indians in Georgia as missionary with the Society for the Propagation of the Gospel

1736 Anti-Christian edicts in China

1743 David Brainerd starts ministry to North American Indians

1746 From Boston, a call is issued to the Christians of the New World to enter into a seven-year "Concert of Prayer" for missionary work

1747 Jonathan Edwards appeals for prayer for world missions

1750 Jonathan Edwards, preacher of the First Great Awakening, having been banished from his church at Northampton, Massachusetts, goes as a missionary to the nearby Housatonic Indians

1750 Christian Frederic Schwartz goes to India with Danish-Halle Mission

1769 Father Junípero Serra founds Mission San Diego de Alcala, first of the twenty-one California missions

1776 The first baptism of an Eskimo by a Lutheran pastor takes place in Labrador

1782	Freed slave George Lisle goes to Jamaica as missionary
1786	John Marrant, a free black from New York City, preaches to "a great number of Indians and white people" at Green's Harbor, Newfoundland. Marrant's cross-cultural ministry led him to take the Christian gospel to the Cherokee, Creek, Catawar, and Housaw Indians
1792	William Carey writes *Enquiry into the Obligations of Christians to use means for the conversion of the heathen* and forms the Baptist Missionary Society to support him in establishing missionary work in India
1795	The London Missionary Society is formed
1797	London Missionary Society enters Tahiti
1799	The Church Missionary Society (Church of England) is formed; John Vanderkemp, Dutch physician, goes to Cape Colony, Africa; Religious Tract Society organized
1804	British and Foreign Bible Society formed; Church Missionary Society enters Sierra Leone
1806	Haystack prayer meeting at Williams College; Henry Martyn lands in Calcutta
1807	First Protestant missionary to China, Robert Morrison, begins work in Canton
1809	National Bible Society of Scotland organized
1810	The American Board of Commissioners for Foreign Missions is formed
1811	English Wesleyans enter Sierra Leone
1812	First American foreign missionary, Adoniram Judson, arrives in Serampore and soon goes to Burma
1813	The Methodists form the Wesleyan Missionary Society
1814	First recorded baptism of a Chinese convert, Cai Gao; American Baptist Foreign Mission Society formed; Netherlands Bible Society founded
1815	American Board of Commissioners open work on Ceylon; Basel Missionary Society organized
1816	Robert Moffat arrives in Africa; American Bible Society founded
1817	James Thompson begins distributing Bibles throughout Latin America
1819	John Scudder, the missionary physician, joins the Ceylon Mission; Wesleyan Methodists start work in Madras, India; Reginald Heber writes words to missionary classic "From Greenland's Icy Mountains"
820	Hiram Bingham goes to Hawaii (Sandwich Islands)
1821	African-American Lott Carey, a Baptist missionary, sails with twenty-eight colleagues from Norfolk, VA to Sierra Leone
1822	Paris Evangelical Missionary Society established
1823	Scottish Missionary Society workers arrive in Bombay, India
1825	George Boardman goes to Burma
1826	American Bible Society sends first shipment of Bibles to Mexico
1828	Basel Mission begins work at Christiansborg, Accra (Africa); Karl F. A. Gutzlaff of the Netherlands Missionary Society lands in Bangkok, Thailand; Rhenish Missionary Association formed
1830	Alexander Duff arrives in Calcutta; baptism of Taufa'ahau Tupou, king of Tonga, by a Western missionary
1831	American Congregational missionaries arrive in Thailand, withdrawing in 1849 without a single convert
1833	Baptist work in Thailand begins with John Taylor Jones; American Methodist missionary Melville Box arrives in Liberia
1834	American Presbyterian Mission opens work in India in the Punjab
1835	Rhenish Missionary Society begins work among the Dayaks on Borneo (Indonesia)
1836	Plymouth Brethren begin work in Madras, India; George Müller begins his work with orphans in Bristol, England
1839	Entire Bible in Tahiti published

1840   David Livingstone is in present-day Malawi (Africa) with the London Missionary Society; American Presbyterians enter Thailand and labor for eighteen years before seeing their first Thai convert

1844   Swiss Johann Krapf begins work on Zanzibar

1852   Zenana (women) and Medical Missionary Fellowship formed in England to send out single women missionaries

1854   London Missionary Conference; New York Missionary Conference

1856   Presbyterians start work in Colombia with the arrival of Henry Pratt

1857   Bible translated into Tswana language

1858   John G. Paton begins work in New Hebrides; Elizabeth Freeman martyred in India; Basel Evangelical Missionary Society begins work in western Sumatra (Indonesia)

1859   Protestant missionaries arrive in Japan

1860   United Lutheran Church begins work in Liberia; Liverpool Missionary Conference; Cyrus Hamlin establishes Robert College in Constantinople

1861   Sarah Doremus founds the Women's Union Missionary Society; Episcopal Church opens work in Haiti; Rhenish Mission goes to Indonesia under Ludwig Nommensen

1862   Paris Evangelical Missionary Society opens work in Senegal

1864   Baptists enter Argentina

1865   The China Inland Mission is founded by James Hudson Taylor; James Laidlaw Maxwell plants first viable church in Formosa (Taiwan)

1867   Methodists start work in Argentina; Scripture Union established

1868   Robert Bruce goes to Iran

1870   Clara Swain, the very first female missionary medical doctor, arrives at Bareilly, India

1871   Henry Stanley finds David Livingstone in central Africa; George Leslie Mackay plants church in northern Formosa

1872   First All-India Missionary Conference with 136 participants

1873   Regions Beyond Missionary Union founded in London in connection with the East London Training Institute for Home and Foreign Missions

1876   Mary Slessor goes to the Calabar region of Nigeria

1877   James Chalmers goes to New Guinea

1881   Methodist work in Lahore, Pakistan, starts in the wake of revivals under Bishop William Taylor; North Africa Mission (now Arab World Ministries) founded on work of Edward Glenny in Algeria

1882   A. B. Simpson founds missionary training school in Nyack, New York

1883   Salvation Army enters West Pakistan

1885   Horace Underwood, Presbyterian missionary, and Henry Appenzellar, Methodist missionary, arrive in Korea; Scottish Ion Keith-Falconer goes to Aden on the Arabian peninsula; "Cambridge Seven" (C. T. Studd, M. Beauchamp, W. W. Cassels, D. E. Hoste, S. P. Smith, A. T. Polhill-Turner, C. H. Polhill-Turner) go to China as missionaries

1886   Student Volunteer Movement launched as 100 university and seminar students at Moody's conference grounds at Mount Hermon, Massachusetts, sign the Princeton Pledge: "I purpose, God willing, to become a foreign missionary."

1887   A. B. Simpson founds the Christian & Missionary Alliance

1888   Jonathan Goforth sails to China; Student Volunteer Movement for Foreign Missions officially organized with John R. Mott as chairman and Robert Wilder as traveling secretary. The movement's motto, coined by Wilder, was: "The evangelization of the world in this generation;" Scripture Gift Mission founded

1889   Samuel Moffett sails from US for Korea, establishes Presbyterian Mission there

1890 Central American Mission founded by C. I. Scofield, editor of the Scofield Reference Bible; The Scandinavian Alliance (now The Evangelical Alliance Mission) founded; Methodist Charles Gabriel writes missionary song "Send the Light"

1891 Samuel Zwemer goes to Arabia

1892 Redcliffe Missionary Training College founded in Chiswick (London)

1893 Eleanor Chestnut goes to India as Presbyterian medical missionary; Sudan Interior Mission founded

1895 Africa Inland Mission formed by Peter Cameron Scott

1897 Presbyterian Church, USA begins work in Venezuela

1899 James Rodgers arrives in Philippines with the Presbyterian Mission; Central American Mission enters Guatemala

1900 American Friends open work in Cuba; Ecumenical Missionary Conference in Carnegie Hall, New York (162 mission boards represented); 189 missionaries and their children killed in Boxer rebellion in China

1901 John Diaz goes to Cape Verde Islands; Maude Cary sails for Morocco; Disciples of Christ open work in northern Luzon (Philippines); Oriental Missionary Society founded by Charles Cowman (his wife is the compiler of the popular devotional book *Streams in the Desert*)

1902 Swiss members of Christian Missions in Many Lands enter Laos; California Yearly Meeting of Friends opens work in Guatemala

1903 Church of the Nazarene enters Mexico

1906 The Azusa Street Revivals

1906 The Evangelical Alliance Mission (TEAM) opens work in Venezuela with T. J. Bach and John Christiansen

1907 Harmon Schmelzenbach sails for Africa; Presbyterians and Methodists open Union Theological Seminary in Manila, Philippines; Bolivian Indian Mission founded by George Allen

1908 Gospel Missionary Union opens work in Colombia with Charles Chapman and John Funk

1910 C. T. Studd establishes Heart of Africa Mission (now called Worldwide Evangelization Crusade); Edinburgh (Scotland) Missionary Conference

1911 Christian & Missionary Alliance enters Vietnam

1912 Conference of British Missionary Societies formed

1917 Interdenominational Foreign Mission Association (IFMA) founded

1920 Church of the Nazarene enters Syria

1921 Founding of International Missionary Council (IMC); Norwegian Mission Council formed

1924 Bible Churchman's Missionary Society opens work in Upper Burma; Baptist Mid-Missions begins work in Venezuela

1927 Near East Christian Council established

1928 Cuba Bible Institute (West Indies Mission) opens; Jerusalem Conference of IMC

1929 Christian & Missionary Alliance enters East Borneo (Indonesia)

1930 Christian & Missionary Alliance starts work among Baouli tribe in the Côte d'Ivoire

1931 HCJB radio station started in Quito, Ecuador, by Clarence Jones; Baptist Mid-Missions enters Liberia

1932 Assemblies of God open work in Colombia; Laymen's Missionary Inquiry

1933 Gladys Aylward (subject of movie "The Inn of the Sixth Happiness") arrives in China

1934 William Cameron Townsend begins the Summer Institute of Linguistics

1935 Dr. Frank C. Laubach, American missionary to the Philippines, perfects the "Each one teach one" literacy program, which was used worldwide to teach 60 million people to read in their own language

1938 West Indies Mission enters Dominican Republic; Church Society forced out of Egypt; Madras World Missionary Conference held; Dr. Orpha Speicher oversees construction of Reynolds Memorial Hospital in central India

1940 Marianna Slocum begins translation work in Mexico

1941 Joy Ridderhof founds Gospel Recordings

1942 William Cameron Townsend founds Wycliffe Bible Translators; New Tribes mission founded

1943 World Gospel Mission (National Holiness Missionary Society) enters Honduras; five missionaries with New Tribes Mission martyred

1945 Missionary Aviation Fellowship formed; Far East Broadcasting Company (FEBC) founded; Evangelical Foreign Missions Association formed by denominational mission boards

1946 First Inter-Varsity missionary convention (now called "Urbana"); United Bible Societies formed; Missionary Aviation Fellowship purchases its first aircraft, a 1933 four-place Waco biplane

1947 Conservative Baptist Foreign Mission Society begins work among the Senufo people tribe in the Côte d'Ivoire

1948 Alfredo del Rosso merges his Italian Holiness Mission with the Church of the Nazarene, thus opening Nazarene work on the European continent; Don Owens goes to Korea

1949 Southern Baptist Mission opens work in Venezuela

1950 Paul Orjala arrives in Haiti; radio station 4VEH, owned by Oriental Missionary Society, starts broadcasting from near Cap Haitien, Haiti

1951 World Evangelical Fellowship organized; Bill and Vonette Bright create Campus Crusade for Christ at UCLA

1952 Church of the Nazarene enters New Zealand

1954 Mennonite Board of Missions and Charities opens work in Cuba

1955 Donald McGavran publishes *Bridges of God*; Dutch missionary "Brother Andrew" makes first of many Bible smuggling trips into Communist Eastern Europe

1956 Edward McCully, Peter Fleming, Jim Elliot, Roger Youderian and Nate Saint die in Ecuador at the hands of Auca Indians on the Curaray River; Assemblies of God open work in Senegal

1958 Rochunga Pudaite completes translation of Bible into Hmar language (India)

1959 Radio Lumiere founded in Haiti by West Indies Mission (now World Team)

c. 1960 Kenneth Strachan starts Evangelism-in-Depth in Central America

1962 Don Richardson goes to Sawi tribe in Papua New Guinea

1963 Theological Education by Extension movement launched in Guatemala by Ralph Winter and James Emery

1964 In separate incidents rebels in the Congo kill missionaries Paul Carlson and Irene Ferrel as well as brutalizing missionary doctor Helen Roseveare; Carlson is featured on December 4 TIME magazine cover

1966 Red Guards destroy churches in China; Berlin Congress on Evangelism; Missionaries expelled from Burma; *God's Smuggler* published

1970 Frankfurt Declaration on Mission

1971 Gustavo Gutierrez publishes *A Theology of Liberation*

1973 Church of the Nazarene enters Indonesia and Portugal; first All-Asia Mission Consultation convenes in Seoul, Korea, with twenty-five delegates from fourteen countries; founding of American Society of Missiology

1974 Ralph Winter talks about "hidden" or unreached peoples at Lausanne Congress of World Evangelism

1975 Nazarene missionaries Armand Doll and Hugh Friberg imprisoned in Mozambique

1976 US Center for World Mission founded; 1600 Chinese assemble in Hong Kong for the Chinese Congress on World Evangelization; Islamic World Congress calls for withdrawal of missionaries; Peace Child appears in *Reader's Digest*

1977 Evangelical Fellowship of India sponsors the All-India Congress on Mission and Evangelization

1979 Production of JESUS film commissioned by Bill Bright of Campus Crusade for Christ; Mother Teresa awarded Nobel Peace Prize; PIONEERS is founded, the first missionary agency with a sole focus on the "unreached people groups" paradigm

1980 Philippine Congress on Discipling a Whole Nation; LCWE Conference in Pattaya

1981 Colombian terrorists kidnap and kill Wycliffe Bible Translator Chet Bitterman

1982 Third World Theologians Consultation in Seoul; story on "The New Missionary" makes December 27 cover of *TIME* magazine; Andes Evangelical Mission (formerly Bolivian Indian Mission) merges into SIM (formerly Sudan Interior Mission)

1984 STEM (Short Term Evangelical Mission teams) ministries founded by Roger Petersen

1986 Entire Bible published in Haitian Creole

1987 Second International Conference on Missionary Kids (MKs) held in Quito, Ecuador

1988 Wycliffe Bible Translators complete their 300th New Testament translation (Cotabato Manobo language of the Philippines)

1989 Adventures In Missions (AIM) founded by Seth Barnes

1994 Church of the Nazarene enters Bulgaria

1994 Saint Liibaan of Somalia (Liibaan Ibraahim Hassan) was martyred by Islamic militants in the Somali capital of Mogadishu

1995 Nazarene missionary Don Cox abducted in Quito, Ecuador

1999 Radical Hindus murder veteran Australian missionary Graham Stewart Stains and his two sons as they are sleeping in a car in eastern India

2000 Unidentified militants detonated two bombs in a Christian church in Dushanbe, Tajikistan, killing seven persons and injuring seventy others. The church was founded by a Korean-born US citizen, and most of those killed and wounded were Korean

2001 Six masked gunmen shot up a church in Bahawalpur, Pakistan, killing fifteen Pakistani Christians

2002 Militants threw grenades into the Protestant International Church in Islamabad, Pakistan, during a church service. Five persons were killed and forty-six were wounded

6 CHRISTIAN BELIEFS

A Creeds
B The Apostles' Creed
C The Nicene Creed

A CREEDS

Since New Testament days, summaries of the Christian faith have been formulated into creeds.

B THE APOSTLES' CREED

The Apostles' Creed, also known as the "Old Roman Creed," is the earliest known Christian creed, dating back to some time in the second, or even first, century AD. Though not written by the apostles, it is thought to reflect their teaching.

> I believe in God the Father, Almighty, Maker of heaven and earth:
> And in Jesus Christ, his only begotten Son, our Lord:
> Who was conceived by the Holy Ghost, born of the Virgin Mary:
> Suffered under Pontius Pilate; was crucified, dead and buried: He descended into hell:
> The third day he rose again from the dead:
> He ascended into heaven, and sits at the right hand of God the Father Almighty:
> From thence he shall come to judge the quick and the dead:
> I believe in the Holy Ghost:
> I believe in the holy catholic church: the communion of saints:
> The forgiveness of sins:
> The resurrection of the body:
> And the life everlasting. Amen.

C THE NICENE CREED

Commonly known as the Nicene Creed, this creed is actually the Creed of Constantinople (AD 381), written about sixty years after the Council of Nicea and the "original" Nicene Creed (AD 325). The original form did not include any description of the person and work of the Holy Spirit, and added a pronouncement of anathema on anyone who did not believe in the full deity of Jesus as described in the creed.

> I believe in one God, the Father Almighty, Maker of heaven and earth, and of all things visible and invisible.
> And in one Lord Jesus Christ, the only-begotten Son of God, begotten of the Father before all worlds; God of God, Light of Light, very God of very God; begotten, not made, being of one substance with the Father, by whom all things were made.
> Who, for us men for our salvation, came down from heaven, and was incarnate by the Holy Spirit of the virgin Mary, and was made man; and was crucified also for us under Pontius Pilate; He suffered and was buried; and the third day He rose again, according to the Scriptures; and ascended into heaven, and sits on the right hand of the Father; and He shall come again, with glory, to judge the quick and the dead; whose kingdom shall have no end.
> And I believe in the Holy Ghost, the Lord and Giver of Life; who proceeds from the Father and the Son; who with the Father and the Son together is worshiped and glorified; who spoke by the prophets.
> And I believe one holy catholic and apostolic Church. I acknowledge one baptism for the remission of sins; and I look for the resurrection of the dead, and the life of the world to come. Amen.

7 WORSHIP

BASIC PRINCIPLES

The following Bible verses, taken from a paraphrase by J. B. Phillips, summarize some of the important principles Christians follow in their approach to worshiping God.

HOW MANY PEOPLE ARE NEEDED TO BECOME A "CHURCH" IN WORSHIP?

"I tell you once more that if two of you on earth agree in asking for anything it will be granted to you by my Heavenly Father. For wherever two or three people come together in my name, I am there, right among you!" Matthew 18:19-20

RELIGIOUS PRACTICES

"One man thinks some days of more importance than others. Another man considers them all alike. Let every one be definite in his own convictions. If a man specially observes one particular day, he does to "to God". The man who eats, eats "to God", for he thanks God for the food. The man who fasts also does it "to God", for he thanks God for the benefits of fasting." Romans 14:5-6

WHEN YOU MEET TO WORSHIP

". . . whenever you meet (in worship) be ready to contribute a psalm, a piece of teaching, a spiritual truth, or a "tongue" with an interpreter.

Everything should be done to make your church strong in the faith." 1 Corinthians 14:26b

PREACHING, TONGUES AND ORDERLINESS

". . . set your heart on preaching the word of God, while not forbidding the use of "tongues". Let everything be done decently and in order." 1 Corinthians 14:39-40

WORSHIP IN EVERYDAY LIFE

"Express your joy in singing among yourselves psalms and hymns and spiritual songs, making music in your hearts for the ears of God! Thank God at all times for everything, in the name of our Lord Jesus Christ." Ephesians 5:19-20a

"Teach and help one another along the right road with your psalms and hymns and Christian songs, singing God's praises with joyful hearts." Colossians 3:16b

PAUL'S TEACHING ON WORSHIP

"Here then is my charge: First, supplications, prayers, intercessions and thanksgivings should be made on behalf of all men: for kings and rulers in positions of responsibility, so that our common life may be lived in peace and quiet, with a proper sense of God and of our responsibility to him for what we do with our lives. . . . I want the men to pray in all the churches with sincerity, without resentment or doubt in their minds." 1 Timothy 2:1-2, 8

8 GROUPINGS WITHIN CHRISTIANITY

The Christian Church is divided into three main groups:

A The Roman Catholic Church

B The Protestant Churches

C The Orthodox Churches

EAST-WEST SCHISM

The East-West schism of 1054 split the Christian Church into two: the Eastern Church based at Constantinople and the Western Church based at Rome.

PROTESTANT REFORMATION

The sixteenth-century Protestant Reformation rejected a number of Roman Catholic beliefs and practices, and brought about autonomous reformed Churches.

A THE ROMAN CATHOLIC CHURCH

(i)   The pope
(ii)   The sacrifice of the mass
(iii) List of popes

With over 1.1 billion members, the Roman Catholic Church is the largest Christian denomination. Roman Catholic teaching about the pope and the sacrifice of the mass are two of the major theological differences between Roman Catholics and Protestants.

(I) THE POPE

Roman Catholics assert the primacy and authority of the pope. In matters of faith and morals the pope, when speaking *ex cathedra* (from the chair of office) is thought to be infallible. So the pope's teaching is the last word for Roman Catholics and is to be obeyed completely.

The following entry by G. H. Joyce from *The Catholic Encyclopedia* gives a summary of Roman Catholic teaching on one of the most divisive of the doctrinal questions that continue to separate Roman Catholics and Protestants.

(Ecclesiastical Latin *papa* from Greek *papas*, a variant of *pappas* "father," in classical Latin *pappas*).

The title pope is at present employed solely to denote the Bishop of Rome, who, in virtue of his position as successor of St. Peter, is the chief pastor of the whole Church, the Vicar of Christ upon earth.

Besides the bishopric of the Roman Diocese, certain other dignities are held by the pope as well as the supreme and universal pastorate: he is Archbishop of the Roman Province, Primate of Italy and the adjacent islands, and sole Patriarch of the Western Church. The Church's doctrine as to the pope was authoritatively declared in the Vatican Council in the Constitution "Pastor Aeternus". The four chapters of that Constitution deal respectively with the office of Supreme Head conferred on St. Peter, the perpetuity of this office in the person of the Roman pontiff, the pope's jurisdiction over the faithful, and his supreme authority to define in all questions of faith and morals.

Institution of a supreme head by Christ

The proof that Christ constituted St. Peter head of His Church is found in the two famous Petrine texts, Matthew 16:17-19, and John 21:15-17.

In Matthew 16:17-19, the office is solemnly promised to the Apostle. In response to his profession of faith in the Divine Nature of his Master, Christ thus addresses him:. "Blessed art thou, Simon Bar-Jona: because flesh and blood hath not revealed it to thee, but my Father who is in heaven. And I say to thee: That thou art Peter; and upon this rock I will build my church, and the gates of hell shall not prevail against it. And I will give to thee the keys of the kingdom of heaven. And whatsoever thou shalt bind on earth it shall be bound also in heaven: and whatsoever thou shalt loose on earth, it shall be loosed also in heaven." The prerogatives here promised are manifestly personal to Peter. His profession of faith was not made as has been sometimes asserted, in the name of the other Apostles. This is evident from the words of Christ. He pronounces on the Apostle, distinguishing him by his name Simon son of John, a peculiar and personal blessing, declaring that his knowledge regarding the Divine Sonship sprang from a special revelation granted to him by the Father (cf. Matthew 11:27). He further proceeds to recompense this confession of His Divinity by bestowing upon him a reward proper to himself: "Thou art Peter [Cepha,] and upon this rock [Cepha] I will build my Church." The word for Peter and for rock in the original Aramaic is one and the same; this renders it evident that the various attempts to explain the term "rock" as having reference not to Peter himself but to something else are misinterpretations. It is Peter who is the rock of the Church. The term ecclesia (*ekklesia*) here employed is the Greek rendering of the Hebrew *qahal*, the name which denoted the Hebrew nation viewed as God's Church.

Here then Christ teaches plainly that in the future the Church will be the society of those who acknowledge Him, and that this Church will be built on Peter. The expression presents no difficulty. In both the Old and New Testaments the Church is often spoken of under the metaphor of God's house (Numbers 12:7; Jeremiah 12:7; 1 Cor. 3:9-17, Eph. 2:20-2; 1 Tim. 3:5; Hebrews 3:5; I Peter 2:5). Peter is to be to the Church what the foundation is in regard to a house. He is to be the principle of unity, of stability, and of increase. He is the principle of unity, since what is not

joined to that foundation is no part of the Church; of stability, since it is the firmness of this foundation in virtue of which the Church remains unshaken by the storms which buffet her; of increase, since, if she grows, it is because new stones are laid on this foundation. It is through her union with Peter, Christ continues, that the Church will prove the victor in her long contest with the Evil One: "The gates of hell shall not prevail against it." There can be but one explanation of this striking metaphor. The only manner in which a man can stand in such a relation to any corporate body is by possessing authority over it. The supreme head of a body, in dependence on whom all subordinate authorities hold their power, and he alone, can be said to be the principle of stability, unity, and increase. The promise acquires additional solemnity when we remember that both Old Testament prophecy (Isaiah 28:16) and Christ's own words (Matthew 7:24) had attributed this office of foundation of the Church to Himself. He is therefore assigning to Peter, of course in a secondary degree, a prerogative which is His own, and thereby associating the Apostle with Himself in an altogether singular manner.

In the following verse (Matthew 16:19) He promises to bestow on Peter the keys of the kingdom of heaven. The words refer evidently to Isaiah 22:22, where God declares that Eliacim, the son of Helcias, shall be invested with office in place of the worthless Sobna: "And I will lay the key of the house of David upon his shoulder: and he shall open, and none shall shut: and he shall shut and none shall open." In all countries the key is the symbol of authority. Thus, Christ's words are a promise that He will confer on Peter supreme power to govern the Church. Peter is to be His vicegerent, to rule in His place. Further the character and extent of the power thus bestowed are indicated. It is a power to "bind" and to "loose" - words which, as is shown below, denote the grant of legislative and judicial authority. And this power is granted in its fullest measure. Whatever Peter binds or looses on earth, his act will receive the Divine ratification. The meaning of this passage does not seem to have been challenged by any writer until the rise of the sixteenth-century heresies. Since then a great variety of interpretations have been put forward by Protestant controversialists. These agree in little save in the rejection of the plain sense of Christ's words. Some Anglican controversy tends to the view that the reward promised to St. Peter consisted in the prominent part taken by him in the initial activities of the Church, but that he was never more than primus inter pares among the Apostles. It is manifest that this is quite insufficient as an explanation of the terms of Christ's promise.

The promise made by Christ in Matthew 16:16-19, received its fulfillment after the Resurrection in the scene described in John 21. Here the Lord, when about to leave the earth, places the whole flock - the sheep and the lambs alike - in the charge of the Apostle. The term employed in 21:16, "Be the shepherd [poimaine] of my sheep" indicates that his task is not merely to feed but to rule. It is the same word as is used in Psalm 2:9 (Sept.): "Thou shalt rule [poimaneis] them with a rod of iron". The scene stands in striking parallelism with that of Matthew 16. As there the reward was given to Peter after a profession of faith which singled him out from the other eleven, so here Christ demands a similar protestation, but this time of a yet higher virtue: "Simon, son of John, lovest thou Me more than these"? Here, too, as there, He bestows on the Apostle an office which in its highest sense is proper to Himself alone. There Christ had promised to make Peter the foundation-stone of the house of God: here He makes him the shepherd of God's flock to take the place of Himself, the Good Shepherd. The passage receives an admirable comment from St. Chrysostom: "He saith to him, 'Feed my sheep'. Why does He

pass over the others and speak of the sheep to Peter? He was the chosen one of the Apostles, the mouth of the disciples, the head of the choir. For this reason Paul went up to see him rather than the others. And also to show him that he must have confidence now that his denial had been purged away. He entrusts him with the rule [prostasia] over the brethren. . . . If anyone should say 'Why then was it James who received the See of Jerusalem?', I should reply that He made Peter the teacher not of that see but of the whole world", Even certain Protestant commentators frankly own that Christ undoubtedly intended here to confer the supreme pastorate on Peter. But other scholars, relying on a passage of St. Cyril of Alexandria, maintain that the purpose of the threefold charge was simply to reinstate St. Peter in the Apostolic commission which his threefold denial might be supposed to have lost to him. This interpretation is devoid of all probability. There is not a word in Scripture or in patristic tradition to suggest that St. Peter had forfeited his Apostolic commission; and the supposition is absolutely excluded by the fact that on the evening of the Resurrection he received the same Apostolic powers as the others of the eleven. The solitary phrase of St. Cyril is of no weight against the overwhelming patristic authority for the other view. That such an interpretation should be seriously advocated proves how great is the difficulty experienced by Protestants regarding this text.

The position of St. Peter after the Ascension, as shown in the Acts of the Apostles, realizes to the full the great commission bestowed upon him. He is from the first the chief of the Apostolic band - not primus inter pares, but the undisputed head of the Church. If then Christ, as we have seen, established His Church as a society subordinated to a single supreme head, it follows from the very nature of the case that this office is perpetual, and cannot have been a mere transitory feature of ecclesiastical life. For the Church must endure to the end the very same organization which Christ established. But in an organized society it is precisely the constitution which is the essential feature. A change in constitution transforms it into a society of a different kind. If then the Church should adopt a constitution other than Christ gave it, it would no longer be His handiwork. It would no longer be the Divine kingdom established by Him. As a society it would have passed through essential modifications, and thereby would have become a human, not a Divine institution. None who believe that Christ came on earth to found a Church, an organized society destined to endure forever, can admit the possibility of a change in the organization given to it by its Founder. The same conclusion also follows from a consideration of the end which, by Christ's declaration, the supremacy of Peter was intended to effect. He was to give the Church strength to resist her foes, so that the gates of hell should not prevail against her. The contest with the powers of evil does not belong to the Apostolic age alone. It is a permanent feature of the Church's life. Hence, throughout the centuries the office of Peter must be realized in the Church, in order that she may prevail in her age-long struggle. Thus an analysis of Christ's words shows us that the perpetuity of the office of supreme head is to be reckoned among the truths revealed in Scripture. His promise to Peter conveyed not merely a personal prerogative, but established a permanent office in the Church. And in this sense His words were understood by Latin and Greek Fathers alike.

Christ conferred upon St. Peter the office of chief pastor, and the permanence of that office is essential to the very being of the Church. This belongs of right to the Roman See, since St. Peter was Bishop of Rome, and since those who succeed him in that see succeed him also in the supreme headship.

G. H. Joyce, The Catholic Encyclopedia, *Volume XII, 1911*

(II) THE SACRIFICE OF THE MASS

The word Mass (*missa*) first established itself as the general designation in the West for the Eucharistic Sacrifice after the time of Pope Gregory the Great (d. 604), the early Church having used the expression the "breaking of bread" (*fractio panis*) or "liturgy" (Acts 13:2, *leitourgountes*); the Greek Church has employed the latter name for almost sixteen centuries. In the early days of Christianity other terms were also used:

- "The Lord's Supper" (*coena dominica*)
- the "Sacrifice" (*prosphora, oblatio*)
- "the gathering together" (*synaxis, congregatio*)
- "the Mysteries", and
- (since Augustine), "the Sacrament of the Altar."

With the name "Love Feast" (agape) the idea of the sacrifice of the Mass was not necessarily connected. Etymologically, the word *missa* is neither (as Baronius states) from a Hebrew word, nor from the Greek mysis, but is simply derived from *missio*, just as *oblata* is derived from *oblatio, collecta* from *collectio,* and *ulta* from *ultio.* The reference was however not to a Divine "mission", but simply to a "dismissal" (*dimissio*) as was also customary in the Greek rite (cf. "Canon. Apost.", VIII, xv: *apolyesthe en eirene*), and as is still echoed in the phrase *Ite missa est.* This solemn form of leave-taking was not introduced by the Church as something new, but was adopted from the ordinary language of the day, as is shown by Bishop Avitus of Vienne as late as A.D. 500 (Ep. 1 in P.L., LIX, 199):

In churches and in the emperor's or the prefect's courts, Missa est is said when the people are released from attendance.

In the sense of "dismissal", or rather "close of prayer", missa is used in the celebrated "Peregrinatio Silvae" at least seventy times (Corpus scriptor. eccles. latinor., XXXVIII, 366 sq.) and Rule of

St. Benedict places after Hours, Vespers, Compline, the regular formula: Et missae fiant (prayers are ended). Popular speech gradually applied the ritual of dismissal, as it was expressed in both the Mass of the Catechumens and the Mass of the Faithful, by synecdoche to the entire Eucharistic Sacrifice, the whole being named after the part. The first certain trace of such an application is found in Ambrose (Ep. xx, 4, in P. L. XVI, 995). We will use the word in this sense in our consideration of the Mass in its existence, essence, and causality.

1 The existence of the Mass

The Church intends the Mass to be regarded as a "true and proper sacrifice", and will not tolerate the idea that the sacrifice is identical with Holy Communion. That is the sense of a clause from the Council of Trent (Sess. XXII, can. 1): "If any one saith that in the Mass a true and proper sacrifice is not offered to God; or, that to be offered is nothing else but that Christ is given us to eat; let him be anathema" (Denzinger, "Enchir.", 10th ed. 1908, n. 948). When Leo XIII in the dogmatic Bull "Apostolicae Curae" of Sept. 13, 1896, based the invalidity of the Anglican form of consecration on the fact among others, that in the consecrating formula of Edward VI (that is, since 1549) there is nowhere an unambiguous declaration regarding the Sacrifice of the Mass, the Anglican archbishops answered with some irritation: "First, we offer the Sacrifice of praise and thanksgiving; next, we plead and represent before the Father the Sacrifice of the Cross . . . and, lastly, we offer the Sacrifice of ourselves to the Creator of all things, which we have already signified by the oblation of His creatures. This whole action, in which the people has necessarily to take part with the priest, we are accustomed to call the communion, the Eucharistic Sacrifice". In regard to this last contention, Bishop Hedley of Newport declared his belief that not one Anglican in a thousand is accustomed, to call the communion the

"Eucharistic Sacrifice." But even if they were all so accustomed, they would have to interpret the terms in the sense of the thirty-nine Articles, which deny both the Real Presence and the sacrifical power of the priest, and thus admit a sacrifice in an unreal or figurative sense only. Leo XIII, on the other hand, in union with the whole Christian past, had in mind in the above-mentioned Bull nothing else than the Eucharistic "Sacrifice of the true Body and Blood of Christ" on the altar. This Sacrifice is certainly not identical with the Anglican form of celebration.

The simple fact that numerous heretics, such as Wyclif and Luther, repudiated the Mass as "idolatry", while retaining the Sacrament of the true Body and Blood of Christ, proves that the Sacrament of the Eucharist is something essentially different from the Sacrifice of the Mass. In truth, the Eucharist performs at once two functions: that of a sacrament and that of a sacrifice. Though the inseparableness of the two is most clearly seen in the fact that the consecrating sacrificial powers of the priest coincide, and consequently that the sacrament is produced only in and through the Mass, the real difference between them is shown in that the sacrament is intended privately for the sanctification of the soul, whereas the sacrifice serves primarily to glorify God by adoration, thanksgiving, prayer, and expiation. The recipient of the one is God, who receives the sacrifice of His only-begotten Son; of the other, man, who receives the sacrament for his own good. Furthermore, the unbloody Sacrifice of the Eucharistic Christ is in its nature a transient action, while the Sacrament of the Altar continues as something permanent after the sacrifice, and can even be preserved in monstrance and ciborium. Finally, this difference also deserves mention: communion under one form only is the reception of the whole sacrament, whereas, without the use of the two forms of bread and wine (the symbolic separation of the Body and Blood), the mystical slaying of the victim, and therefore the Sacrifice of the Mass, does not take place.

The definition of the Council of Trent supposes as self-evident the proposition that, along with the "true and real Sacrifice of the Mass", there can be and are in Christendom figurative and unreal sacrifices of various kinds, such as prayers of praise and thanksgiving, alms, mortification, obedience, and works of penance. Such offerings are often referred to in Holy Scripture, e.g. in Ecclus., xxxv, 4: "All he that doth mercy offereth sacrifice"; and in Ps. cxl, 2: "Let my prayer be directed as incense in thy sight, the lifting up of my hands as evening sacrifice." These figurative offerings, however, necessarily presuppose the real and true offering, just as a picture presupposes its subject and a portrait its original. The Biblical metaphors - a "sacrifice of jubilation" (Ps. xxvi, 6), the "calves of our lips" (Osee, xiv, 3), the "sacrifice of praise" (Heb., xiii, 15) - expressions which apply sacrificial terms to sacrifice (hostia, thysia). That there was such a sacrifice, the whole sacrificial system of the Old Law bears witness. It is true that we may and must recognize with St. Thomas (II-II:85:3), as the principale sacrificium the sacrificial intent which, embodied in the spirit of prayer, inspires and animates the external offerings as the body animates the soul, and without which even the most perfect offering has neither worth nor effect before God. Hence, the holy psalmist says: "For if thou hadst desired sacrifice, I would indeed have given it: with burnt-offerings thou wilt not be delighted. A sacrifice to God is an afflicted spirit" (Ps. I, 18 sq.). This indispensable requirement of an internal sacrifice, however, by no means makes the external sacrifice superfluous in Christianity; indeed, without a perpetual oblation deriving its value from the sacrifice once offered on the Cross, Christianity, the perfect religion, would be inferior not only to the Old Testament, but even to the poorest form of natural religion. Since sacrifice is thus essential to religion, it is all the more necessary for Christianity, which cannot otherwise fulfil its duty of showing outward honor to God in the most perfect way. Thus, the Church, as the mystical Christ, desires and must have her own permanent sacrifice, which surely cannot be either an independent addition to that of Golgotha or its intrinsic complement; it can only be the one self-same sacrifice of the Cross, whose fruits, by an unbloody offering, are daily made available for believers and unbelievers and sacrificially applied to them.

2 The nature of the Mass

In its denial of the true Divinity of Christ and of every supernatural institution, modern unbelief endeavors, by means of he so-called historico-religious method, to explain the character of the Eucharist and the Eucharist sacrifice as the natural result of a spontaneous process of development in the Christian religion. In this connection it is interesting to observe how these different and conflicting hypotheses refute one another, with the rather startling result at the end of it all that a new, great, and insoluble problem looms of the investigation. While some discover the roots of the Mass in the Jewish funeral feasts (O. Holtzmann) or in Jewish Essenism (Bousset, Heitmuller, Wernle), others delve in the underground strata of pagan religions. Here, however, a rich variety of hypotheses is placed at their disposal. In this age of Pan-Babylonism it is not at all surprising that the germinal ideas of the Christian communion should be located in Babylon, where in the Adapa myth (on the tablet of Tell Amarna) mention has been found of "water of life" and "food of life" (Zimmern). Others (e.g. Brandt) fancy they have found a still more striking analogy in the "bread and water" (Patha and Mambuha) of the Mandaean religion. The view most widely held today among upholders of the historico-religious theory is that the Eucharist and the Mass originated in the practices of the Persian Mithraism (Dieterich, H. T. Holtzmann, Pfleiderer, Robertson, etc.). "In the Mandaean mass" writes Cumont ("Mysterien des Mithra", Leipzig, 1903, p.118), "the celebrant consecrated bread and water, which he mixed with perfumed Haoma-juice, and ate this food while performing the functions of divine service". Tertullian in anger ascribed this mimicking of Christian rites to the "devil" and observed in astonishment (De prescript haeret, C. xl): "celebrat (Mithras) et panis oblationem." This is not the place to criticize in detail these wild creations of an overheated imagination. Let it suffice to note that all these explanations necessarily lead to impenetrable night, as long as men refuse to believe in the true Divinity of Christ, who commanded that His bloody sacrifice on the Cross should be daily renewed by an unbloody sacrifice of His Body and Blood in the Mass under the simple elements of bread and wine. This alone is the origin and nature of the Mass.

J. Pohle, The Catholic Encyclopedia

(III) LIST OF POPES

1. St. Peter (32-67)
2. St. Linus (67-76)
3. St. Anacletus (Cletus) (76-88)
4. St. Clement I (88-97)
5. St. Evaristus (97-105)
6. St. Alexander I (105-115)
7. St. Sixtus I (115-125) - also called Xystus
8. St. Telesphorus (125-136)
9. St. Hyginus (136-140)
10. St. Pius I (140-155)
11. St. Anicetus (155-166)
12. St. Soter (166-175)
13. St. Eleutherius (175-189)
14. St. Victor I (189-199)
15. St. Zephyrinus (199-217)
16. St. Callistus I (217-22)
17. St. Urban I (222-30)
18. St. Pontain (230-35)
19. St. Anterus (235-36)
20. St. Fabian (236-50)
21. St. Cornelius (251-53)
22. St. Lucius I (253-54)
23. St. Stephen I (254-257)
24. St. Sixtus II (257-258)
25. St. Dionysius (260-268)
26. St. Felix I (269-274)
27. St. Eutychian (275-283)
28. St. Caius (283-296) - also called Gaius
29. St. Marcellinus (296-304)
30. St. Marcellus I (308-309)
31. St. Eusebius (309 or 310)
32. St. Miltiades (311-14)
33. St. Sylvester I (314-35)
34. St. Marcus (336)
35. St. Julius I (337-52)
36. Liberius (352-66)
37. St. Damasus I (366-83)
38. St. Siricius (384-99)
39. St. Anastasius I (399-401)
40. St. Innocent I (401-17)
41. St. Zosimus (417-18)
42. St. Boniface I (418-22)
43. St. Celestine I (422-32)
44. St. Sixtus III (432-40)
45. St. Leo I (the Great) (440-61)
46. St. Hilarius (461-68)
47. St. Simplicius (468-83)
48. St. Felix III (II) (483-92)
49. St. Gelasius I (492-96)
50. Anastasius II (496-98)
51. St. Symmachus (498-514)
52. St. Hormisdas (514-23)
53. St. John I (523-26)
54. St. Felix IV (III) (526-30)
55. Boniface II (530-32)
56. John II (533-35)
57. St. Agapetus I (535-36) - also called Agapitus I
58. St. Silverius (536-37)
59. Vigilius (537-55)
60. Pelagius I (556-61)
61. John III (561-74)
62. Benedict I (575-79)
63. Pelagius II (579-90)
64. St. Gregory I (the Great) (590-604)
65. Sabinian (604-606)
66. Boniface III (607)
67. St. Boniface IV (608-15)
68. St. Deusdedit (Adeodatus I) (615-18)
69. Boniface V (619-25)
70. Honorius I (625-38)
72. Severinus (640)
73. John IV (640-42)

74. Theodore I (642-49)
75. St. Martin I (649-55)
76. St. Eugene I (655-57)
77. St. Vitalian (657-72)
78. Adeodatus (II) (672-76)
79. Donus (676-78)
80. St. Agatho (678-81)
81. St. Leo II (682-83)
82. St. Benedict II (684-85)
83. John V (685-86)
84. Conon (686-87)
85. St. Sergius I (687-701)
86. John VI (701-05)
87. John VII (705-07)
88. Sisinnius (708)
89. Constantine (708-15)
90. St. Gregory II (715-31)
91. St. Gregory III (731-41)
92. St. Zachary (741-52)
93. Stephen II (752)
94. Stephen III (752-57)
95. St. Paul I (757-67)
96. Stephen IV (767-72)
97. Adrian I (772-95)
98. St. Leo III (795-816)
99. Stephen V (816-17)
100. St. Paschal I (817-24)
101 Eugene II (824-27)
102. Valentine (827)
103. Gregory IV (827-44)
104. Sergius II (844-47)
105. St. Leo IV (847-55)
106. Benedict III (855-58)
107. St. Nicholas I (the Great) (858-67)
108. Adrian II (867-72)
109. John VIII (872-82)
110. Marinus I (882-84)
111. St. Adrian III (884-85)
112. Stephen VI (885-91)
113. Formosus (891-96)
114. Boniface VI (896)
115. Stephen VII (896-97)
116. Romanus (897)
117. Theodore II (897)
118. John IX (898-900)
119. Benedict IV (900-03)
120. Leo V (903)
121. Sergius III (904-11)
122. Anastasius III (911-13)
123. Lando (913-14)
124. John X (914-28)

125. Leo VI (928)
126. Stephen VIII (929-31)
127. John XI (931-35)
128. Leo VII (936-39)
129. Stephen IX (939-42)
130. Marinus II (942-46)
131. Agapetus II (946-55)
132. John XII (955-63)
133. Leo VIII (963-64)
134. Benedict V (964)
135. John XIII (965-72)
136. Benedict VI (973-74)
137. Benedict VII (974-83)
138. John XIV (983-84)
139. John XV (985-96)
140. Gregory V (996-99)
141. Sylvester II (999-1003)
142. John XVII (1003)
143. John XVIII (1003-09)
144. Sergius IV (1009-12)
145. Benedict VIII (1012-24)
146. John XIX (1024-32)
147. Benedict IX (1032-45)
148. Sylvester III (1045)
149. Benedict IX (1045)
150. Gregory VI (1045-46)
151. Clement II (1046-47)
152. Benedict IX (1047-48)
153. Damasus II (1048)
154. St. Leo IX (1049-54)
155. Victor II (1055-57)
156. Stephen X (1057-58)
157. Nicholas II (1058-61)
158. Alexander II (1061-73)
159. St. Gregory VII (1073-85)
160. Blessed Victor III (1086-87)
161. Blessed Urban II (1088-99)
162. Paschal II (1099-1118)
163. Gelasius II (1118-19)
164. Callistus II (1119-24)
165. Honorius II (1124-30)
166. Innocent II (1130-43)
167. Celestine II (1143-44)
168. Lucius II (1144-45)
169. Blessed Eugene III (1145-53)
170. Anastasius IV (1153-54)
171. Adrian IV (1154-59)
172. Alexander III (1159-81)
173. Lucius III (1181-85)
174. Urban III (1185-87)
175. Gregory VIII (1187)

176. Clement III (1187-91)
177. Celestine III (1191-98)
178. Innocent III (1198-1216)
179. Honorius III (1216-27)
180. Gregory IX (1227-41)
181. Celestine IV (1241)
182. Innocent IV (1243-54)
183. Alexander IV (1254-61)
184. Urban IV (1261-64)
185. Clement IV (1265-68)
186. Blessed Gregory X (1271-76)
187. Blessed Innocent V (1276)
188. Adrian V (1276)
189. John XXI (1276-77)
190. Nicholas III (1277-80)
191. Martin IV (1281-85)
192. Honorius IV (1285-87)
193. Nicholas IV (1288-92)
194. St. Celestine V (1294)
195. Boniface VIII (1294-1303)
196. Blessed Benedict XI (1303-04)
197. Clement V (1305-14)
198. John XXII (1316-34)
199. Benedict XII (1334-42)
200. Clement VI (1342-52)
201. Innocent VI (1352-62)
202. Blessed Urban V (1362-70)
203. Gregory XI (1370-78)
204. Urban VI (1378-89)
205. Boniface IX (1389-1404)
206. Innocent VII (1404-06)
207. Gregory XII (1406-15)
208. Martin V (1417-31)
209. Eugene IV (1431-47)
210. Nicholas V (1447-55)
211. Callistus III (1455-58)
212. Pius II (1458-64)
213. Paul II (1464-71)
214. Sixtus IV (1471-84)
215. Innocent VIII (1484-92)
216. Alexander VI (1492-1503)
217. Pius III (1503)
218. Julius II (1503-13)
219. Leo X (1513-21)
220. Adrian VI (1522-23)
221. Clement VII (1523-34)
222. Paul III (1534-49)
223. Julius III (1550-55)
224. Marcellus II (1555)
225. Paul IV (1555-59)
226. Pius IV (1559-65)

227. St. Pius V (1566-72)
228. Gregory XIII (1572-85)
229. Sixtus V (1585-90)
230. Urban VII (1590)
231. Gregory XIV (1590-91)
232. Innocent IX (1591)
233. Clement VIII (1592-1605)
234. Leo XI (1605)
235. Paul V (1605-21)
236. Gregory XV (1621-23)
237. Urban VIII (1623-44)
238. Innocent X (1644-55)
239. Alexander VII (1655-67)
240. Clement IX (1667-69)
241. Clement X (1670-76)
242. Blessed Innocent XI (1676-89)
243. Alexander VIII (1689-91)
244. Innocent XII (1691-1700)
245. Clement XI (1700-21)
246. Innocent XIII (1721-24)
247. Benedict XIII (1724-30)
248. Clement XII (1730-40)
249. Benedict XIV (1740-58)
250. Clement XIII (1758-69)
251. Clement XIV (1769-74)
252. Pius VI (1775-99)
253. Pius VII (1800-23)
254. Leo XII (1823-29)
255. Pius VIII (1829-30)
256. Gregory XVI (1831-46)
257. Blessed Pius IX (1846-78)
258. Leo XIII (1878-1903)
259. St. Pius X (1903-14)
260. Benedict XV (1914-22)
261. Pius XI (1922-39)
262. Pius XII (1939-58)
263. Blessed John XXIII (1958-63)
264. Paul VI (1963-78)
265. John Paul I (1978)
266. John Paul II (1978-2005)
267. Benedict XVI (2005-

B THE PROTESTANT CHURCHES
The Protestant Church was formed when Christians in sixteenth-century Europe "protested" against the bad practices and unbiblical teaching of much of Roman Catholicism. They rejected the authority of the pope and emphasized the authority of the Bible. This religious revolution is known as the Reformation.

Today, half of the world's 2.2 billion Christians are Roman Catholics. The next largest grouping of Christians are Protestant Christians who number as many as 500 million members, which is more than double the number of members of the Orthodox Churches.

The Protestant Church is divided into different branches, or denominations (see below). If Protestants are grouped not according to organizational alignments but according to theological beliefs, they may be presented in the following way:

- Evangelicals
- Pentecostals
- "Great Commission Christians"

- Liberal Protestants
- Conservative Protestants
- Fundamentalists

THE MAJOR PROTESTANT CHURCHES

(i)   Anglicans/Episcopalians
(ii)   Baptists
(iii) Friends (Quakers)
(iv)   Lutherans
(v)   Mennonites
(vi)   Methodists
(vii) Pentecostals
(viii) Presbyterian/Reformed
(ix)   Salvation Army
(x)   United Brethren

The historical roots of the various Protestant denominations are summarized in the following table.

Name	Founding Date	Main Distinguishing Theological /Practice Doctrines/ Organizational Features	Faith Statement	Leaders	Main Geographical Concentration
Baptists	1610	Baptism by immersion and only for believers (no infant baptism). Bible is the sole rule of life. Salvation through faith by way of grace and contact with the Holy Spirit. Separation between Church and State. Independence of the local church.	Philadelphia Confession (1689) New Hampshire Confession (1832)	John Smyth William Carey Roger Williams	England/U.S./ Netherlands
Episcopalians (Anglicans)	1534	Baptism and Eucharist (Communion) considered to be "witnesses and agencies of God's love and grace"; various views on presence of Christ in the elements of the Eucharist; infant baptism; confirmation as adult. Organizations of provinces, dioceses (headed by bishops) and parishes (headed by vicars) Women accepted into clergy	The Book of Common Prayer Articles of the Church of England	Henry VIII Thomas Cranmer Edward VI Elizabeth I	England/U.S./ Common- wealth countries

Lutherans	1513-1530	Scripture has final authority. Justification by faith, not by works. Baptism/Communion are not just memorials but channels of grace. Infant baptism. Regeneration from the Holy Spirit. Organization by synods/parishes. Liturgical ceremonies.	Augsburg Confession (1530) Smalcald Articles of Faith (1537)	Martin Luther Philip Melanchthon	Germany/ Scandinavia
Mennonites	1534	Great emphasis on godly living Communion is expression of common union and fellowship Marriage only among the believers Refusal to bear arms/ take oaths Distrust temporal authorities, loose organization	Confession of Faith (1632)	Obbe Philips Menno Simons	U. S./Central Europe
Methodists	1729	Emphasis on holy living Emphasis on ministry to the poor and other less fortunate people Trying to find common ground among Protestant denominations Organization by conferences (headed by bishops) and charges (headed by ministers)	Articles of Religion (Wesley) The Book of Common Prayer	John Wesley Charles Wesley George Whit- field	England/U. S.
Pentecostals	1900	Emphasis on the "blessings" of the Holy Spirit-particularly "baptism of the Spirit" Premillenialism Footwashing as part of Communion (Baptist/Methodist tendencies)	(see Baptists/ Methodists)		United States

Presbyterians	1534-1560	Church governed by elders (presbyters). Emphasis on God's sovereignty over all. Emphasis on social reform. Separation of Church and State and also intrachurch authority. ("no kings, no bishops")	Westminster Confession (1643-8) Longer/Shorter Catechism	John Calvin John Knox	Scotland/ Ireland/ Switzerland
Reformists	1561	(very similar to Presbyterians)	Belgic Confession (1561) Heidelberg Confession (1647)	John Calvin Ulrich Zwingley	Netherlands/ Germany
United Church of Christ	1931	Autonomy of the local church—each local church free to set up its own form of worship and determine its own theological positions. Made up of four denominations with theological differences (Congregational Churches and Evangelical and Reformed Churches)	(see Reformists for Reformed branches; Congregation-alist branches were originally Anglicans)	John Robinson (Congrega-tionalists) (see also Presbyter-ians and Reformists)	United States

(I) ANGLICANS/EPISCOPALIANS

(Called the Episcopal Church in the United States and Scotland and the Anglican Church in most of the rest of the world)

The Anglican Church is derived not only from Reformation influences but from the renunciation of papal jurisdiction by King Henry VIII in 1534. With the "Act of Supremacy," the king was declared the supreme head of the English Church.

There is no central administration in the Episcopalian/Anglican Church. There is no pope or president or chief executive. The words of the Archbishop of Canterbury have weight, but he has jurisdiction only over the Anglican Church in England (the Church of England). In each country the Church is self-

directing, and national Churches are linked together by tradition, belief, and agreement. The co-ordination of that unity is achieved through what is known as the Anglican Communion.

The basic unit is the diocese, presided over by a bishop. Dioceses form part of a larger area, called a province, which may be part of an autonomous national Church, or the Church in one country or in a group of countries. For example: the US has nine provinces, England has two, Australia has five; Japan, South Africa and Kenya are each a province; the whole of the West Indies is a province.

Every ten years the leaders of the provinces meet at Lambeth, the London home of the Archbishop of Canterbury (the Lambeth Conference). Decisions are reached by consensus.

Distinctive features

- Use of the Book of Common Prayer. The BOCP is one of the reasons why Anglicans and Episcopalians are called "the people of the book." Although the BOCP has been updated and revised, the concept of using a liturgy from a prayer book still prevails in most Anglican services.
- The practice of infant baptism
- An ordained ministry comprising bishops, priests and deacons

(II) BAPTISTS

Baptists state that the so-called "Baptist Distinctives" are those beliefs and practices that establish the unique character of the New Testament faith, setting it apart as "distinct" from any and all other faiths or systems of belief of religious thought.

These distinctive features are sometimes set out in the form of the following acrostic BRAPSISS:

Bible, the only rule of faith and practice.
Regenerate, immersed church membership.
Autonomy and independence of the Local Church
Priesthood of the believer
Soul Liberty.
Immersion of believers and the Lord's Supper . . . the only two ordinances.
Separation of Church and State
Separation, ethical and ecclesiastical.

Believers' baptism

Only those who actually profess repentance towards God, faith in and obedience to Jesus Christ, are baptized by Baptists. This rules out infant baptism. Baptism is by immersion in water.

(III) FRIENDS (QUAKERS)

Friends are a Christian group who believe in the presence of God within each person. This is often referred to as the "Inner Light." Friends emphasize a personal commitment to God and involvement in humanitarian causes.

The Religious Society of Friends was founded in the mid-seventeenth century in England by George Fox (1624-1691). The society took its name from the New Testament Gospel of John, which says, "You are my friends if you do whatever I command" (John 15:12-15). The original Quakers called themselves "Friends of Truth" after this verse. They were also known as the "Children of Light."

The Society of Friends is commonly known as Quakers because the first Friends were mocked for "trembling with religious zeal."

Today there are about 300,000 Friends worldwide. In the US the five states with the largest number of Quakers are: Indiana, North Carolina, Ohio, Pennsylvania, and California, in that order.

Distinctive features

- There is no priestly or ministerial hierarchy. Friends believe that a person's spiritual relationship with his or her divinity should be unmediated. Quakers hold "meetings," rather than services, in "meeting-houses," not churches, and even the internal layout of the meeting house tends towards the elimination of hierarchy, the benches being arranged around the four sides, facing inward.
- Worship takes the form of a shared silence. However, any member may address the assembly - to "minister" - if so moved.
- The absence of creeds and sacraments

(IV) LUTHERANS

On October 31, 1517, Martin Luther (born November 10, 1483, in Eisleben, Germany, died February 18, 1546 in Eisleben), posted on the church door in Wittenberg a list of ninety-five "theses" in which he questioned some of the doctrines of the Church, and in particular the sale of "letters of indulgence" (a letter, signed by the pope, promising to the buyer a reduction of time spent in Purgatory). This provoked furious debate, as a result of which Luther was accused of heresy and in 1521 was excommunicated.

Luther's hope had been that the Church would reform its practice and preaching by submitting it to the authority of the Bible. He also taught that the Scriptures and Christian worship should be in the language of the people, and not in Latin. The outcome was not a reformation of the Roman Catholic Church, but separation from it.

The Lutheran Church embodies the teaching of Luther, notably "salvation by faith alone." It holds to the clarion call of the Reformation: *Sola Gratia, Sola Fide, Sola Scriptura*.

Number of Lutherans worldwide

Europe		66 million
	Germany	40 million
	Sweden	7.8 million
	Denmark	5.1 million
	Finland	4.7 million
	Norway	4 million
	Latvia	1.3 million
	Estonia	1.1 million
	Hungary	500,000
	Iceland	250,000
	Others	1 million
North America		19 million
	USA	18 million
	Canada	800,000
Africa		11 million
	Ethiopia	3.3 million
	Tanzania	2.2 million
	Madagascar	1.5 million
	Namibia	900,000
	South Africa	850,000
	Nigeria	650,000
Others		1.3 million
Asia		6 million
	Indonesia	2.4 million
	India	1.3 million
	Papua New Guinea	900,000
	Australia	250,000
	Others	800,000
Latin America and Brazil		2 million
All Spanish speaking countries in the western hemisphere		1 million
	Brazil	1 million
Total		104 million

Distinctive features
According to the American Association of Lutheran Churches two of the basic principles of Lutheran Churches are:

> Call to commitment
> Lutherans are called to serve Christ as Savior and Lord in His Church.
> Congregational autonomy
> Lutherans believe that the Lord of the Church has created two expressions of his Church: The local congregation and the "*Una Sancta*" (the one, holy, universal, and apostolic Church or "Body" of Christ in and throughout the world).

(V) MENNONITES
During the Protestant Reformation, a small group of young adults who had been meeting for Bible study and prayer in Zurich, Switzerland, felt convicted to re-baptize each other. In 1536, Menno Simons, a Catholic priest from the north of Holland, joined these Anabaptists (Christians who reject infant baptism and accept only adult baptism), and gave some order to the group. From his study of the Scriptures, he began to teach mutual aid, sharing of resources, support to widows, their children and the poor, sister/brotherhood among believers, a simple lifestyle, nonresistance, nonviolence, peacemaking, and servanthood.

The Mennonites today are a group of Christian Anabaptist denominations based on the teachings of Menno Simons.

There are over one million Mennonites worldwide.

CORE BELIEFS
- Baptism of believers understood as threefold:
  a. baptism by the Spirit (internal change of heart)
  b. baptism by water (public demonstration of witness)
  c. baptism by blood (martyrdom and asceticism)
- Church discipline understood as threefold:
  a. confession of sins
  b. absolution of sin, and

c.   readmission of sinner in the Church
- The Lord's Supper as a memorial, shared by baptized believers within the discipline of the Church

Distinctive features
- Mennonites are one of the peace churches, which hold to a doctrine of non-violence, non-resistance and pacifism. They believe that peace qualifies and defines the struggle for truth, for liberation, and for freedom.
- Nonconformity to the surrounding culture

(VI) METHODISTS

The Methodist Church was started in the eighteenth century by John Wesley, his younger brother Charles and George Whitefield, as a movement within the Church of England that focused on Bible study and a methodical approach to the Scriptures.

The term "Methodist" was a pejorative nickname first given to a small group of students at Oxford, who met together between 1729 and 1735 for Christian fellowship, Bible study, and service to those around them in Oxford. They fasted regularly and rejected most forms of amusement and luxury. They also frequently visited the poor, the sick, and prisoners.

The early Methodists reacted against the apathy of the Church of England, and became open-air preachers, establishing Methodist societies wherever they went. The established Church rejected both their enthusiasm and some of their doctrines, notably the necessity of new birth for salvation; justification by faith; and the constant work of the Holy Spirit in a Christian's life, a teaching that it was felt would produce ill effects upon weak minds.

The first Methodists quickly became the social conscience of England, preaching to the poor a new message of hope and care. They devoted much time to the creation of private welfare agencies to help the poor, social reforms, improvement of the daily life of workers, the legalization of labor unions, the abolition of slavery, and the need to protect woman and children. They started schools, old people's homes, orphanages, dispensaries

for the sick, and agencies for the unemployed and homeless. They were among the foremost champions of a democratic a free United States.

There are over 36 million Methodists worldwide, with the largest number in any country being in America, where about 10 million people belong to the United Methodist Church.

Distinctive features
- Methodists have always believed that a "mystical experience" is the best way to know God. This has been called the "witness of the Spirit" to the individual, personal assurance of salvation, the "heartwarming experience," being "born-again."
- The Church is governed by a conference of ministers (clergy) and representatives of individual church members.

(VII) PENTECOSTALS

Pentecostalism is a highly fragmented family within Christianity: there are over 150 separate Pentecostal denominations.

Pentecostalism is a relatively modern branch of Christianity, growing out of the Holiness movement, which in turn had roots in Methodism. In the US, it is traced back to 1906 when Pentecostalism received worldwide attention as a result of the Azusa Street revival in Los Angeles led by the African-American preacher William J. Seymour. It was at a Bible School conducted by Parham that Seymour learned about the tongues-attested baptism. In April 1906 he took over a former African Methodist Episcopal church building at 312 Azusa Street. Naming his mission, the "Apostolic Faith Mission," he began to hold three services a day, seven days a week. Here thousands sought to be baptized in the Spirit, with the evidence of speaking in tongues, and experienced numerous other Holy Spirit manifestations.

From Azusa Street, Pentecostalism spread around the world, rapidly becoming a major force in Christendom. Pentecostal faiths include the Church of God, the Assemblies of

God, the International Church of the Foursquare Gospel, and the United Pentecostal Church International.

Figures for the number of Pentecostalists worldwide range from 100 million to 500 million, with African and South American countries having the most adherents. There are over 7 million members of Pentecostal churches in US.

Assemblies of God USA and Assemblies of God organizations around the world make up the world's largest Pentecostal denomination with some 51 million members and adherents.

Distinctive features

Pentecostals emphasize "the gifts of the Spirit," and church services are often characterized by speaking in tongues and prophecy.

(VIII) PRESBYTERIAN/REFORMED

The Associate Reformed Presbyterian Church, as we know it today, had its beginnings in the preaching of John Knox in Scotland when the Scottish Church became the official Church of Scotland in 1560.

In 1688, King William III reorganized the Church of Scotland into the Established Presbyterian Church of Scotland. But in 1733 pastor Ebenezer Erskine led a group of Christians in forming a separate Associate Presbytery (from which the name Presbyterian is derived). Ten years later, another group of Christians, who for years had suffered problems with the established Church, organized themselves into the Reformed Presbytery.

Both churches spread to Northern Ireland when the Scots were forced to emigrate and both came to America with those "Scots-Irish" folks. The immigrants landed in Pennsylvania first of all, where both the Associate and the Reformed Presbyteries of Pennsylvania were established.

The Reformed Church in America, established in 1628 in what is now Manhattan, New York City, is the oldest Protestant denomination in North America with a continuous ministry. The theology of the Reformed Church in America is rooted in the Reformation, drawing particularly on the heritage of John Calvin.

The Reformed churches are a group of Protestant denominations historically related by a similar Zwinglian or Calvinist system of doctrine but organizationally independent. Each of the nations in which the Reformed movement was established had originally its own church government. Several of these local churches have expanded to worldwide denominations and most have experienced splits into multiple denominations. There are over 700 Reformed denominations worldwide.

Presbyterians have the second largest membership in the world among the Protestant Churches. They number over 11 million worldwide, 4 million of whom live in the United States.

Distinctive features

Historically, Presbyterian congregational organization had the following four distinctive features:

- First, a church was not formed until the people constituted it.
- Second, the church was tied to a place. It was viewed as the "covenanted" (bound to God) people in a specific location.
- Third, the church was to be an established church. In New England it had intimate ties with the government, and ministers drew their salaries from the civil authority.
- Finally, the church was to be the sacred institute for the society. The clergy spoke directly to issues of public morals, expected to be consulted on matters of importance to public life, and often represented the colony as political figures.

(IX) SALVATION ARMY

The Salvation Army was found in 1865 by William Booth in response to the great poverty and social deprivation that he observed in London. It spread rapidly to inner city areas throughout England and then to the rest of the world.

The rapid deployment of the first Salvationists was aided, in 1878, by the adoption of a quasi-military command structure. It was then that the title, "The Salvation Army" was brought into use.

The Army's doctrine follows the mainstream of Christian belief and its articles of faith emphasize God's saving purposes. It seeks to share in the mission of Christ for the salvation and transformation of the world.

Evangelistic and social enterprises are maintained under the authority of the General, by full-time officers and employees, as well as church members - soldiers - who give service in their free time.

From its earliest days the Army has accorded women equal opportunities, every rank and service being open to them.

The Salvation Army has grown from one man's dream in 1865 to an international movement with headquarters in 82 lands and approximately 25,000 officers preaching the gospel in 110 languages. With a total membership of more than 2,500,000, it operates more than 3,600 social institutions, hospitals, and agencies and nearly 17,000 evangelical centers. There are over 500,000 Salvation Army members in the US.

Distinctive features
- Responding to a recurrent theme in Christianity in which the Church is seen to be engaged in spiritual warfare, the Army uses features such as uniforms, flags and ranks to identify, inspire and regulate its work.
- Leadership in the Army is provided by commissioned officers who are recognized ministers of religion.
- All Salvationists accept a disciplined and compassionate life of high moral standards which includes abstinence from alcohol and tobacco.
- The Army does not administer the two Christian sacraments of baptism and the Lord's Supper.

(X) UNITED BRETHREN
Founded in 1708 by a miller named Alexander Mack (1679-1735) in Schwarzenau, Germany, the Brethren (originally known as the German Baptists) were an outcome of radical Anabaptist and Pietist beliefs which emphasized a more personal relationship with Jesus Christ than that taught by the Catholic, Protestant, and Reformed Churches.

At that time, the Brethren's practice of rebaptizing adults who had been baptized as infants into established churches was considered illegal. Persecuted in Germany, they migrated to Switzerland and the Netherlands, then, in 1719, to Pennsylvania under the leadership of Peter Beck. In 1729, many of the remaining Brethren in Europe under the leadership of Alexander Mack also emigrated to Pennsylvania.

Although closely related in tradition and beliefs to the Mennonites, the Brethren rejected the shared confessions of organized Mennonite conferences in favor of the New Testament as their only creed. The Brethren avoided military service, political involvement, religious iconography, fashionable dress, musical instruments, and contact with the world outside their own rural communities. They emphasized Christian unity (often addressing one another as "Brother" or "Sister"), self-discipline, social punishment (including shunning), obedience, and worldly non-conformity.

Today the United Brethren Church has about 400 churches worldwide, in 15 countries.

Distinctive features
- Christian Brethren are independent groups without hierarchy or a full-time ordained ministry. They stress the different gifts of every member.
- There are no creeds, their only confessions of faith being those found in the New Testament.
- The observance of the love feast - a communion service that includes feet washing, a simple meal, and partaking of the communion elements of unleavened bread and grape juice.

C EASTERN CHURCHES
Members of the Orthodox Churches exceed 250 million people today.

HISTORY
Almost two thousand years ago, Jesus Christ,

the Son of God, came to earth and founded the Church, through His Apostles and disciples, for the salvation of humankind. In the years which followed the Apostles founded many churches, which were united in faith, worship, and the partaking of the Mysteries (or as they are called in the West, the Sacraments) of the Holy Church.

The churches founded by the Apostles themselves include the Patriarchates of:

- Constantinople,
- Alexandria,
- Antioch,
- Jerusalem, and
- Rome.

The Church of Constantinople was founded by St. Andrew, the Church of Alexandria by St. Mark, the Church of Antioch by St. Paul, the Church of Jerusalem by Sts. Peter and James, and the Church of Rome by Sts. Peter and Paul. Those founded in later years through the missionary activity of the first churches were the Churches of Sinai, Russia, Greece, Serbia, Bulgaria, Romania, and many others.

Each of these churches is independent in administration, but, with the exception of the Church of Rome, which finally separated from the others in the year 1054, all are united in faith, doctrine, Apostolic tradition, sacraments, liturgies, and services. Together they constitute and call themselves the Orthodox Church.

The teachings of the Orthodox Church are derived from two sources: Holy Scripture, and Sacred Tradition, within which the Scriptures are interpreted. As written in the Gospel of St. John, "And there are also many other things which Jesus did, the which, if they should be written every one, I suppose that even the world could not contain the books that should be written" (John 21:20). Much teaching transmitted orally by the Apostles has come down to us in Sacred Tradition.

The word Orthodox literally means right teaching or right worship, being derived from two Greek words: *orthos* (right) and *doxa* (teaching or worship). As the false teachings and divisions multiplied in early Christian times, threatening to obscure the identity and purity of the Church, the term Orthodox quite logically came to be applied to it.

Teaching
(i) God the Father
God the Father is the fountainhead of the Holy Trinity. The Scriptures reveal the one God is Three Persons - Father, Son, and Holy Spirit - eternally sharing the one divine nature. From the Father the Son is begotten before all ages and all time (Psalm 2:7; 2 Corinthians 11:31). It is from the Father that the Holy Spirit eternally proceeds (John 15:26). God the Father created all things through the Son, in the Holy Spirit (Genesis 1 and 2; John 1:3; Job 33:4), and we are called to worship Him (John 4:23). The Father loves us and sent His Son to give us everlasting life (John 3:16).

(ii) Jesus Christ
Jesus Christ is the Second Person of the Holy Trinity, eternally born of the Father. He became man, and thus He is at once fully God and fully man. His coming to earth was foretold in the Old Testament by the prophets. Because Jesus Christ is at the heart of Christianity, the Orthodox Church has given more attention to knowing Him than to anything or anyone else.

In reciting the Nicene Creed, Orthodox Christians regularly affirm the historic faith concerning Jesus.

(iii) Incarnation
Incarnation refers to Jesus Christ coming "in the flesh." The eternal Son of God the Father assumed to Himself a complete human nature from the Virgin Mary. He was and is one divine Person, fully possessing from God the Father the entirety of the divine nature, and in His coming in the flesh fully possessing a human nature from the Virgin Mary. By His Incarnation, the Son forever possesses two natures in His one Person. The Son of God, limitless in His divine nature, voluntarily and willingly accepted limitation in His humanity in which He experienced hunger, thirst, fatigue—and ultimately, death. The Incarnation is indispensable to Christianity -

there is no Christianity without it. The Scriptures record, "Every spirit that does not confess that Jesus Christ has come in the flesh is not of God" (I John 4:3). By His Incarnation, the Son of God redeemed human nature, a redemption made accessible to all who are joined to Him in His glorified humanity.

(iv) The Holy Spirit

The Holy Spirit is one of the Persons of the Holy Trinity and is one in essence with the Father. Orthodox Christians repeatedly confess, "And I believe in the Holy Spirit, the Lord, the Giver of life, Who proceeds from the Father, Who together with the Father and the Son is worshiped and glorified." He is called the "promise of the Father" (Acts 1:4), given by Christ as a gift to the Church, to empower the Church for service to God (Acts 1:8), to place God's love in our hearts (Romans 5:5), and to impart spiritual gifts (I Corinthians 12:7-13) and virtues (Galatians 5:22, 23) for Christian life and witness. Orthodox Christians believe the biblical promise that the Holy Spirit is given through chrismation (anointing) at baptism (Acts 2:38). We are to grow in our experience of the Holy Spirit for the rest of our lives.

(v) Sin

Sin literally means to "miss the mark." As St. Paul writes, "All have sinned and fall short of the glory of God" (Romans 3:23). We sin when we pervert what God has given us as good, falling short of His purposes for us. Our sins separate us from God (Isaiah 59:1, 2), leaving us spiritually dead (Ephesians 2:1). To save us, the Son of God assumed our humanity, and being without sin "He condemned sin in the flesh" (Romans 8:3). In His mercy, God forgives our sins when we confess them and turn from them, giving us strength to overcome sin in our lives. "If we confess our sins, He is faithful and just to forgive our sins and to cleanse us from all unrighteousness" (1 John 1:9).

(vi) Salvation

Salvation is the divine gift through which men and women are delivered from sin and death, united to Christ, and brought into His eternal kingdom. Those who heard St. Peter's sermon on the day of Pentecost asked what they must do to be saved. He answered, "Repent, and let every one of you be baptized in the name of Jesus Christ for the remission of sins; and you shall receive the gift of the Holy Spirit" (Acts 2:38). Salvation begins with these three steps: 1) repent, 2) be baptized, and 3) receive the gift of the Holy Spirit. To repent means to change our mind about how we have been, to turn from our sin and to commit ourselves to Christ. To be baptized means to be born again by being joined into union with Christ. And to receive the gift of the Holy Spirit means to receive the Spirit Who empowers us to enter a new life in Christ, to be nurtured in the Church, and to be conformed to God's image.

(vii) Faith

Salvation demands faith in Jesus Christ. People cannot save themselves by their own good works. Salvation is "faith working through love." It is an ongoing, life-long process. Salvation is past tense in that, through the death and Resurrection of Christ, we have been saved. It is present tense, for we are "being saved" by our active participation through faith in our union with Christ by the power of the Holy Spirit. Salvation is also future, for we must yet be saved at His glorious Second Coming.

(viii) Baptism

Baptism is the way in which a person is actually united to Christ. The experience of salvation is initiated in the waters of baptism. The Apostle Paul teaches in Romans 6:1-6 that in baptism we experience Christ's death and resurrection. In it our sins are truly forgiven, and we are energized by our union with Christ to live a holy life. The Orthodox Church practices baptism by full immersion.

(ix) New birth

New Birth is receipt of new life. It is how we gain entrance into God's kingdom and His Church. Jesus said, "Unless one is born of water and the Spirit, he cannot enter the kingdom of God" (John 3:5). From its beginning, the Church has taught that the water is the baptismal water and the Spirit is the Holy Spirit. The new birth occurs in baptism where we die with Christ, are buried with Him, and are raised with Him in the newness of His resurrection, being joined into union with Him in His glorified humanity (Acts 2:38; Romans 6:3-4). The idea that being "born again" is a religious experience disassociated from baptism is a recent one and has no biblical basis whatsoever.

(x) Justification

Justification is a word used in the Scriptures to mean that in Christ we are forgiven and actually made righteous in our living. Justification is not a once-for-all, instantaneous pronouncement guaranteeing eternal salvation, regardless of how wickedly a person might live from that point on. Neither is it merely a legal declaration that an unrighteous person is righteous. Rather, justification is a living, dynamic, day-to-day reality for the one who follows Christ. The Christian actively pursues a righteous life in the grace and power of God granted to all who continue to believe in Him.

(xi) Sanctification

Sanctification is being set apart for God. It involves us in the process of being cleansed and made holy by Christ in the Holy Spirit. We are called to be saints and to grow into the likeness of God. Having been given the gift of the Holy Spirit, we actively participate in sanctification. We cooperate with God, we work together with Him, that we may know Him, becoming by grace what He is by nature.

(xii) Bible

The Bible is the divinely inspired Word of God (2 Timothy 3:16), and is a crucial part of God's self-revelation to the human race. The Old Testament tells the history of that revelation from Creation through the Age of the Prophets. The New Testament records the birth and life of Jesus as well as the writings of His Apostles. It also includes some of the history of the early Church and especially sets forth the Church's apostolic doctrine. Though these writings were read in the Churches from

the time they first appeared, the earliest listings of all the New Testament books exactly as we know them today is found in the 33rd Canon of a local council held at Carthage in 318, and in a fragment of St. Athanasius of Alexandria's Festal Letter in 367. Both sources list all of the books of the New Testament without exception. A local council, probably held at Rome in 382, set forth a complete list of the canonical books of both the Old and the New Testaments. The Scriptures are at the very heart of Orthodox worship and devotion.

(xiii) Worship

Worship is the rendering of praise, glory, and thanksgiving to God: the Father, the Son, and the Holy Spirit. All humanity is called to worship God. Worship is more than being in the "great-out-of-doors," or listening to a sermon, or singing a hymn. God can be known in His creation, but that does not constitute worship. As helpful as sermons may be, they can never offer a proper substitute for worship. Most prominent in Orthodox worship is the corporate praise, thanksgiving, and glory given to God by the Church. This worship is consummated in intimate communion with God at His Holy Table.

As is said in the Liturgy, "To Thee is due all glory, honor, and worship, to the Father, and to the Son, and to the Holy Spirit, now and ever and unto ages of ages. Amen." In that worship we touch and experience His eternal kingdom, the age to come, and we join in adoration with the heavenly hosts. We experience the glory of fulfillment of all things in Christ, as truly all in all.

(xiv) Liturgy

Liturgy is a term used to describe the shape or form of the Church's corporate worship of God. The word "liturgy" derives from a Greek word which means "the common work." All the biblical references to worship in heaven involve liturgy.

In the Old Testament, God ordered a liturgy, or specific pattern of worship. We find it described in detail in the books of Exodus and Leviticus. In the New Testament we find the Church carrying over the worship of Old

Testament Israel as expressed in both the synagogue and the temple, adjusting them in keeping with their fulfillment in Christ. The Orthodox Liturgy, which developed over many centuries, still maintains that ancient shape of worship. The main elements in the Liturgy include hymns, the reading and proclamation of the Gospel, prayers, and the Eucharist itself. For Orthodox Christians, the expressions "The Liturgy" or "Divine Liturgy" refer to the eucharistic rite instituted by Christ Himself at the Last (Mystical) Supper.

(xv) Eucharist

Eucharist literally means thanksgiving and early became a synonym for Holy Communion. The Eucharist is the center of worship in the Orthodox Church. Because Jesus said of the bread and wine at the Last Supper, "This is my body," "This is my blood," and "Do this in remembrance of Me" (Luke 22:19-20), His followers believe - and do - nothing less. In the Eucharist, we partake mystically of Christ's Body and Blood, which impart His life and strength to us. The celebration of the Eucharist was a regular part of the Church's life from its beginning. Early Christians began calling the Eucharist "the medicine of immortality" because they recognized the great grace of God that was received in it.

(xvi) Communion of Saints

When Christians depart this life, they remain a vital part of the Church, the body of Christ. They are alive in the Lord and "registered in heaven" (Hebrews 12:23). They worship God (Revelation 4:10) and inhabit His heavenly dwelling places (John 14:2). In the Eucharist we come "to the city of the living God" and join in communion with the saints in our worship of God (Hebrews 12:22). They are that "great cloud of witnesses" which surrounds us, and we seek to imitate them in running "the race set before us" (Hebrews 12:1). Rejecting or ignoring the communion of saints is a denial of the fact that those who have died in Christ are still part of his holy Church.

(xvii) Confession

Confession is the open admission of known sins before God and man. It means literally "to agree with" God concerning our sins. St. James the Apostle admonishes us to confess our sins to God before the elders, or priests, as they are called today (James 5:16). We are also exhorted to confess our sins directly to God (I John 1:9). The Orthodox Church has always followed the New Testament practices of confession before a priest as well as private confession to the Lord. Confession is one of the most significant means of repenting, and receiving assurance that even our worst sins are truly forgiven. It is also one of our most powerful aids to forsaking and overcoming those sins.

(xviii) Discipline

Discipline may become necessary to maintain purity and holiness in the Church and to encourage repentance in those who have not responded to the admonition of brothers and sisters in Christ, and of the Church, to forsake their sins. Church discipline often centers around exclusion from receiving communion (excommunication). The New Testament records how St. Paul ordered the discipline of excommunication for an unrepentant man involved in sexual relations with his father's wife (1 Corinthians 5:1-5). The Apostle John warned that we are not to receive into our homes those who willfully reject the truth of Christ (II John 9,10). Throughout her history, the Orthodox Church has exercised discipline when it is needed, with compassion, always to help bring a needed change of heart and to aid God's people to live pure and holy lives, never as a punishment.

(xix) Mary

Mary is called *Theotokos*, meaning "God-bearer" or "the Mother of God," because she bore the Son of God in her womb and from her He took His humanity. Elizabeth, the mother of John the Baptist, recognized this reality when she called Mary, "the Mother of my Lord" (Luke 1:43). Mary said of herself, "All generations shall call me blessed" (Luke 1:48). So we, Orthodox, in our generation, call her blessed. Mary lived a chaste and holy life, and we honor her highly as the model of holiness, the first of the redeemed, the Mother of the new humanity in her Son. It is bewildering to Orthodox Christians that many professing Christians who claim to believe the Bible never call Mary blessed nor honor her who bore and raised God the Son in His human flesh.

(xx) Prayer to the saints

Prayer to the saints is encouraged by the Orthodox Church. This is because physical death is not regarded as a defeat for a Christian. It is a glorious passage into heaven. The Christian does not cease to be a part of the Church at death. God forbid! Nor is he set aside, idle until the day of judgment.

The True Church is composed of all who are in Christ - in heaven and on earth. It is not limited in membership to those presently alive. Those in heaven with Christ are alive, in communion with God, worshiping God, doing their part in the body of Christ. They actively pray to God for all those in the Church - and perhaps, indeed, for the whole world (Ephesians 6:8; Revelation 8:3). So we pray to the saints who have departed this life, seeking their prayers, even as we ask Christian friends on earth to pray for us.

(xxi) Apostolic succession

Apostolic succession has been a watershed issue since the second century, not as a mere dogma, but as crucial to the preservation of the faith. Certain false teachers would appear, insisting they were authoritative representatives of the Christian Church. Claiming authority from God by appealing to special revelations, some were even inventing lineages of teachers supposedly going back to Christ or the Apostles. In response, the early Church insisted there was an authoritative apostolic succession passed down from generation to generation. They recorded that actual lineage, showing how its clergy were ordained by those chosen by the successors of the Apostles chosen by Christ Himself.

Apostolic succession is an indispensable factor in preserving Church unity. Those in the succession are accountable to it, and are responsible to ensure all teaching and practice

in the Church is in keeping with Her apostolic foundations. Mere personal conviction that one's teaching is correct can never be considered adequate proof of accuracy. Today, critics of apostolic succession are those who stand outside that historic succession and seek a self-identity with the early Church only. The burgeoning number of denominations in the world can be accounted for in large measure by a rejection of apostolic succession.

(xxii) Councils of the Church

A monumental conflict (recorded in Acts 15) arose in the early Church over legalism, the keeping of Jewish laws by the Christians, as means of salvation. "So the apostles and elders came together [in council] to consider the matter" (Acts 15:6). This council, held in Jerusalem, set the pattern for the subsequent calling of councils to settle problems. There have been hundreds of such councils - local and regional - over the centuries of the history of the Church, and seven councils specifically designated Ecumenical, that is, considered to apply to the whole Church. Aware that God has spoken through the Ecumenical Councils, the Orthodox Church looks particularly to them for authoritative teaching in regard to the faith and practice of the Church.

(xxiii) Spiritual gifts

God poured out His Holy Spirit upon the Apostles and their followers, giving them spiritual gifts to build up the Church and to serve each other. Among the specific gifts of the Spirit mentioned in the New Testament are: apostleship, prophecy, evangelism, pastoring, teaching, healing, helps, administrations, knowledge, wisdom, tongues, and interpretation of tongues. These and other spiritual gifts are recognized in the Orthodox Church. The need for them varies with the times. The gifts of the Spirit are most in evidence in the liturgical and sacramental life of the Church.

(xxiv) Second Coming

Amid the current speculation in some corners of Christendom surrounding the Second Coming of Christ and how it may come to pass, it is comforting to know that the beliefs of the Orthodox Church are basic. Orthodox Christians confess with conviction that Jesus Christ "will come again to judge the living and the dead," and that His "kingdom will have no end." Orthodox preaching does not attempt to predict God's prophetic schedule, but to encourage Christian people to have their lives in order so that they might be confident before Him when He comes (I John 2:28).

(xxv) Heaven

Heaven is the place of God's throne, beyond time and space. It is the abode of God's angels, as well as of the saints who have passed from this life. We pray, "Our Father, who art in heaven." Though Christians live in this world, they belong to the kingdom of heaven, and that kingdom is their true home. But heaven is not only for the future. Neither is it some distant place billions of light years away in a nebulous "great beyond." For the Orthodox, heaven is part of Christian life and worship. The very architecture of an Orthodox Church building is designed so that the building itself participates in the reality of heaven. The Eucharist is heavenly worship, heaven on earth. St. Paul teaches that we are raised up with Christ in heavenly places (Ephesians 2:6), "fellow citizens with the saints and members of the household of God" (Ephesians 2:19). At the end of the age, a new heaven and a new earth will be revealed (Revelation 21:1).

(xxvi) Hell

Hell is real. The Orthodox Church understands hell as a place of eternal torment for those who willfully reject the grace of God. Our Lord once said, "If your hand makes you sin, cut it off. It is better for you to enter into life maimed, than having two hands, to go to hell, into the fire that never shall be quenched - where their worm does not die, and the fire is not quenched" (Mark 9:44-45). He challenged the religious hypocrites with the question: "How can you escape the condemnation of hell?" (Matthew 23:33). His answer is, "God did not send His Son into the world to condemn the world, but that the

world through Him might be saved" (John 3:17). There is a day of judgment coming, and there is a place of punishment for those who have hardened their hearts against God. It does make a difference how we will live this life. Those who of their own free will reject the grace and mercy of God must forever bear the consequences of that choice.

(xxvii) Creation

Orthodox Christians confess God as Creator of heaven and earth (Genesis 1:1, the Nicene Creed). Creation did not just come into existence by itself. God made it all. "By faith we understand that the worlds were framed by the word of God" (Hebrews 11:3). Orthodox Christians do not believe the Bible to be a science textbook on creation, as some mistakenly maintain, but rather to be God's revelation of Himself and His salvation. Also, we do not view science textbooks, helpful though they may be, as God's revelation. The may contain both known facts and speculative theory, but they are not infallible. Orthodox Christians refuse to build an unnecessary and artificial wall between science and the Christian faith. Rather, they understand honest scientific investigation as a potential encouragement to faith, for all truth is from God.

(xxviii) Holy Icons: theology in color

One of the first things that strikes a non-Orthodox visitor to an Orthodox church is the prominent place assigned to Holy Icons. The Iconostasis is covered with them, while others are placed in prominent places throughout the church building. The walls and ceiling are covered with iconic murals. The Orthodox faithful prostrate themselves before Icons, kiss them, and burn candles before them. They are censed by the clergy and carried in processions. Considering the obvious importance of the Holy Icons, then, questions may certainly be raised concerning them: What do these gestures and actions mean? What is the significance of Icons? Are they not idols or the like, prohibited by the Old Testament?

Icons have been used for prayer from the first centuries of Christianity. Sacred Tradition tells us, for example, of the existence of an Icon of the Savior during His lifetime (the "Icon-Made-Without-Hands") and of Icons of the Most Holy Theotokos immediately after Him. Sacred Tradition witnesses that the Orthodox Church had a clear understanding of the importance of Icons right from the beginning; and this understanding never changed, for it is derived from the teachings concerning the Incarnation of the Second Person of the Holy Trinity - Our Lord and Savior Jesus Christ. The use of Icons is grounded in the very essence of Christianity, since Christianity is the revelation by God-Man not only of the Word of God, but also of the Image of God; for, as St. John the Evangelist tells us, "the Word became flesh and dwelt among us" (John 1:14).

"No one has ever seen God; only the Son, Who is in the bosom of the Father, He has made Him known" (John 1:18), the Evangelist proclaims. That is, He has revealed the Image or Icon of God. For being the brightness of [God's] glory, and the express image of [God's] person (Hebrews 1:3), the Word of God in the Incarnation revealed to the world, in His own Divinity, the Image of the Father. When St. Philip asks Jesus, "'Lord, show us the Father,' He answered him: 'Have I been with you so long, and yet you do not know Me, Philip? He who has seen Me has seen the Father'" (John 14:8-9). Thus as the Son is in the bosom of the Father, likewise after the Incarnation He is constubstantial with the Father, according to His divinity being the Father's Image, equal in honor to Him.

The truth expressed above, which is revealed in Christianity, thus forms the foundations of Christian pictorial art. The Image (or Icon) not only does not contradict the essence of Christianity, but is unfailingly connected with it; and this is the foundation of the tradition that from the very beginning the Good News was brought to the world by the Church both in word and image.

St. John of Damascus, an eighth-century Father of the Church, who wrote at the height of the iconoclastic (anti-icon) controversies in the Church, explains that, because the Word of God became flesh (John 1:14), we are no longer in our infancy; we have grown up, we have been given by God the power of discrimination and we know what can be depicted and what is indescribable. Since the Second Person of the Holy Trinity appeared to us in the flesh, we can portray Him and reproduce for contemplation of Him Who has condescended to be seen. We can confidently represent God the Invisible - not as an invisible being, but as one Who has made Himself visible for our sake by sharing in our flesh and blood.

Holy Icons developed side by side with the Divine Services and, like the Services, expressed the teaching of the Church in conformity with the word of Holy Scripture. Following the teaching of the 7th Ecumenical Council, the Icon is seen not as simple art, but that there is a complete correspondence of the Icon to Holy Scripture, "for if the Icon is shown by Holy Scripture, Holy Scripture is made incontestably clear by the Icon" (Acts of the 7th Ecumenical Council, 6).

As the word of Holy Scripture is an image, so the image is also a word, for, according to St. Basil the Great (379 AD):

"By depicting the divine, we are not making ourselves similar to idolaters; for it is not the material symbol that we are worshiping, but the Creator, Who became corporeal for our sake and assumed our body in order that through it He might save mankind. We also venerate the material objects through which our salvation is effected - the blessed wood of the Cross, the Holy Gospel, Holy Relics of Saints, and, above all, the Most-Pure Body and Blood of Christ, which have grace-bestowing properties and Divine Power."

Orthodox Christians do not venerate an Icon of Christ because of the nature of the wood or the paint, but rather we venerate the inanimate image of Christ with the intention of worshiping Christ Himself as God Incarnate through it.

We kiss an Icon of the Blessed Virgin as the Mother of the Son of God, just as we kiss the Icons of the Saints as God's friends who struggled against sin, imitating Christ by shedding their blood for Him and following in His footsteps. Saints are venerated as those who were glorified by God and who became, with God's help, terrible to the Enemy, and benefactors to those advancing in the faith - but not as gods and benefactors themselves. They were the servants of God who were given boldness of spirit in return for their love of Him. We gaze on the depiction of their exploits and sufferings so as to sanctify ourselves through them and to spur ourselves on to zealous emulation.

The Icons of the Saints act as a meeting point between the living members of the Church [Militant] on earth and the Saints who have passed on to the Church [Triumphant] in Heaven. The Saints depicted on the Icons are not remote, legendary figures from the past, but contemporary, personal friends. As meeting points between Heaven and earth, the Icons of Christ, His Mother, the Angels and Saints constantly remind the faithful of the invisible presence of the whole company of Heaven; they visibly express the idea of Heaven on earth.

---

9 COMPARISON OF CHRISTIANITY WITH WORLD RELIGIONS

Christianity is different from all other world religions.

Luis Palau

Christianity is the only true religion.

Charles Hodge

Religion is humans trying to work their way to God through good works. Christianity is God coming to men and women through Jesus Christ offering them a relationship with himself.

Josh McDowell

If you took Buddha out of Buddhism, you'd still basically have Buddhism; if you took Confucius out of Confucianism, you'd still have Confucianism. These are both ethical systems. If you took Muhammad out of Islam, you'd still have Islam, because it all depends upon Allah, not Muhammad. But if you took Christ out of Christianity, you would no longer have Christianity, because Christianity is Jesus Christ.

Josh McDowell, Jesus Christ: The Foundation of Faith

10 GLOSSARY

GLOSSARY OF TERMS ABOUT CHRISTIANITY AND THE BIBLE

Abaddon
Abaddon is Hebrew for destruction.

Abba
Abba is a Chaldee word for father, used in a respectful, affectionate, and familiar way, like papa, dad, or daddy, often used in prayer to refer to our Father in Heaven.

Adultery
Adultery means sexual intercourse with someone who is not your own husband or wife; in the Bible, the only legitimate sexual intercourse is between a man and a woman who are married to each other.

Agnostic
Someone who says we cannot know whether or not God exists.

Alpha
Alpha is the first letter of the Greek alphabet, sometimes used to mean the beginning or the first.

Amen
Amen means "so be it" or "it is certainly so."

Amillennialism
See under millennium

Angel
Angel literally means "messenger" or "envoy," and is usually used to refer to spiritual beings who normally are invisible to us, but can also appear as exceedingly strong creatures or as humans.

Antediluvian
Antediluvian is derived from the two Latin words: *ante* meaning "before" and *diluvium* meaning "a flood." The period before the great deluge of Genesis 7 is referred to as the antediluvian world.

Antinomianism
Antinomy is derived from the two Greek words: *anti* meaning "over against" and *nomos* meaning "law." An antinomian is one who denies that there is any objective law or standard of obedience in the New Testament age to which the believer is accountable.

Apollyon
Apollyon is Greek for destroyer.

Apologetics
This word is derived from the Greek word *apologia* meaning "defense" or "answer." Apologetics means a written or spoken defense of Christianity.

Apostle
The word means a "delegate," "messenger," or "one sent forth with orders." This term is applied in the New Testament in both a general sense connected with a ministry of establishing and strengthening church fellowships, as well as in a specific sense to "The twelve Apostles of the Lamb" (Revelation 21:14). The former category applies to a specific ministry that continues in the Church (Ephesians 4:11-13) and which includes many more than twelve people, while the latter refers to the apostles named in Matthew 10:2-4 (Judas Iscariot was later replaced by Matthias, Acts 1:26).

Armageddon
This word refers to the battlefield where the ultimate conflict between good and evil will take place; hence it symbolizes the conflict itself. The word appears in Revelation 16:16, and may be derived from the words "the mountain of Megiddo." Many great Old Testament battles took place on "the plain of Megiddo" (2 Chronicles 35:22).

Ascension
Jesus' return to heaven, 40 days after his resurrection.

Atheist
Someone who does not believe there is a God.

Baptize
To baptize means "to immerse in," or "wash with" something, usually water. Baptism by and with the Holy Spirit, with fire, into the Body of Christ, and in suffering (Luke 12:50) are also mentioned in the New Testament. Baptism is an outward sign of an inward spiritual cleansing and commitment. Baptism is a sign of repentance, as practiced by John the Baptizer, and of faith in Jesus Christ, as practiced by Jesus' disciples.

Beelzebul
Literally, "lord of the flies." A name used for the devil.

Born again
To be spiritually born after one has already been physically born (John 3:3; 2 Corinthians 5:17).

Catechism
Catechism is a derivative of the Latin word *chatechismus*, which is a handbook of questions and answers. To catechize is to teach or instruct using the repetition of questions and answers.

Catholic
1 The universal Church which confesses Jesus Christ as Lord.
2 Roman Catholic Church recognizing the primacy of the Pope.

Cherub
A cherub is a kind of angel with wings and hands that is associated with the throne room of God and guardian duty, see Ezekiel 10.

Cherubim
Cherubim means more than one cherub or a mighty cherub.

Christology
Christology is derived from the two Greek words *Christos* meaning "anointed one" or

"messiah" and *logos* meaning "word." Christology is the study of the Messiah. Traditionally this deals with the doctrine of Christ's incarnation, seeking to understand the relationship between the divine and human nature of Christ. As a theological discipline, Christology is the study of the messianic content of a passage of Scripture.

Church
The people who gather together to worship God. In the New Testament the word church never refers to a building (Matthew 16:18; 1 Corinthians 11:18).

Concubine
A woman who lives with a man as his wife without being legally married; in some polygamous societies, a second-class wife. In Old Testament times (and in some places now), it was the custom of middle-eastern kings, chiefs, and wealthy men to marry multiple wives and concubines, but God commanded the kings of Israel not to do so (Deuteronomy 17:17) and Jesus encouraged people to either remain single or marry as God originally intended: one man married to one woman (Matthew 19:3-12; 1 Corinthians 7:1-13).

Corban
Corban is a Hebrew word for an offering devoted to God.

Covenant
A covenant is a binding agreement or promise. In the Bible, it is an agreement between God and an individual or people. God reveals himself to be the covenant God. The essence of the covenant between God and humankind is, "I will be your God, and you will be my people." God gave a new covenant to his people through Christ (Jeremiah 31:31-34; Hebrews 9:15).

Crucify
Execution by being nailed to a cross. Before crucifixion, the victim was usually whipped with a Roman cat o' nine tails, which had bits of glass and metal tied to its ends. The victim

was made to carry the heavy crossbeam of his cross from the place of judgment to the place of crucifixion, but often was physically unable after the scourging, so another person would be pressed into involuntary service to carry the cross. Those who were crucified were stripped of their clothes to maximize shame and discomfort. The victim's hands or palms, and sometimes his feet, were nailed to the cross while it was on the ground; then the cross was raised up and dropped into a hole, thus jarring the wounds. The weight of the victim's body tended to force the air out of his lungs. To lift up the chest to breathe, he had to put weight on the wounds. Eventually, the pain, weakness, dehydration, and exhaustion of the muscles needed to breathe make breathing impossible, and the victim suffocated.

Cummin
Cummin is an aromatic seed from the *Cuminum cyminum*, and resembles caraway in flavor and appearance. It is used as a spice.

Darnel
Darnel is a weed grass (probably bearded darnel or *Lolium temulentum*) that looks very much like wheat until it is mature. Darnel seeds aren't good for much except as chicken feed.

Denarii
Denarii is plural form of denarius, a silver Roman coin worth about a day's wages for an agricultural laborer.

Devil
The word comes from the Greek *diabolos,* which means "one prone to slander; a liar." In the Bible, the word refers to a fallen angel, also called "Satan," who works to steal, kill, destroy, and do evil. The devil's doom is certain, and it is only a matter of time before he is thrown into the Lake of Fire, never to escape.

Didrachma
A didrachma is a Greek silver coin worth two drachmas, about as much as two Roman denarii, or about two days' wages. It was commonly used to pay the half-shekel

Temple tax.

Disciple
The word comes from the Latin *discere*, meaning "to learn." A disciple is a student and follower.

Doctrine
Doctrine is derived from the Latin word *doctrina* meaning "teachings." Something taught as the principle or creed of a religion.

Drachma
A drachma is a Greek silver coin worth about one Roman denarius, or about a day's wages for an agricultural laborer.

Ecclesiology
Ecclesiology is derived from the two Greek words *ecclesia* meaning "assembly" or "church" and *logos* meaning "word." Ecclesiology is the study of the doctrine of the Church.

Ecumenism
The word is derived from the Greek *oikoumene*, meaning "inhabited [world]." The adjective "ecumenical" means "general," "universal," and, when used in a Christian context, "belonging to, referring to, the entire Christian church."

Eschatology
Eschatology is derived from the two Greek words *eschatos* meaning "final" or "last" and *logos* meaning "word." Eschatology means "the study of the last things."

Eternal life
A new quality of life, marked by the presence of the Holy Spirit, in which life is lived in fellowship with God. This relationship with God cannot be earned or bought, but is a free gift through faith in Christ (Romans 6:23). Eternal life begins now and continues for ever (John 3:15-16).

Faith
To trust or believe in something or someone. The only way a person can be forgiven of

their sins is through faith (Acts 10:43; Ephesians 2:8.)

Fast
Going without food for certain period of time.

Gehenna
Gehenna means hell or hellfire. It comes from the Hebrew *ge-hinnom,* literally "valley of Hinnom," the name of a valley south of the old city of Jerusalem. In Old Testament times this valley had been a site for child sacrifice. This place was so despised by the people after the righteous King Josiah abolished this hideous practice that it was made into a garbage heap. Bodies of diseased animals and executed criminals were also thrown there and burned. In New Testament times the word became a synonym for hell. Jesus used the word to mean the place of final punishment.

Goad
A sharp prodding device used to motivate reluctant animals (such as oxen and mules) to move in the right direction.

God
Christians believe there is one God, but three persons, Father, Son, and Holy Spirit. All are God equally, they are not separate or smaller parts of God (John 1:1-5; Matthew 28:20).

Gospel
Gospel is a translation of a Greek word meaning "good news" or "glad tidings," specifically the good news of Jesus' life, death, and resurrection for our salvation, healing, and provision; and the hope of eternal life that Jesus made available to us by God's grace.

Grace
God's free and loving action in saving sinful people, and their response of thanksgiving and love. By his grace, God forgives sins and gives us his love.
Grace was revealed in Jesus (John 1:14).

Hades
The nether realm of the disembodied spirits. Also known as "hell."

Heaven
The ultimate paradise, God's kingdom.

Hell
The place reserved for the devil (Satan) and his followers — all who reject Jesus.

Hermeneutics
Hermeneutics is a technical term derived from the Greek *hermeneutikos* meaning "the science of interpretation." It is used by Christians to refer to the study of the Scriptures.

Holy Spirit
The third person of the Trinity who is sent to help believers live more like Christ by giving guidance, strength, and love. He lives in every believer in Christ (John 16:5-15).

Hypocrite
A stage actor; someone who pretends to be someone other than who they really are; a pretender; a dissembler.

Incarnate/incarnation
To take on bodily form. The term "incarnation" refers to the doctrine that the eternal Son of God became fully human by being born in the flesh. At his birth, Jesus Christ did not stop being fully God. He is both fully God and fully human (John 1:14).

Jehovah
See "Yahweh."

Jesus Christ
"Jesus" is the name chosen by God for his Son. The word comes from the Hebrew *Yeshua,* and means "Yahweh saves." The word "Christ" is a title. It comes from the Greek word *Christos,* a translation of the Hebrew word "Messiah," meaning "anointed one." Jesus Christ is worshiped as the Son of God and Savior of the world.

Justification
Justification is God's declaration that a sinner is righteous. God counts a sinner as righteous because Christ died for the sins of humankind, and rose again. Righteousness is a gift from God, received through faith in Christ, and not earned by good actions.

Leviathan
Leviathan is a poetic name for a large aquatic creature, possibly a crocodile or a dinosaur.

The Lord's Supper
(also known as the Communion and the Eucharist and, in the Roman Catholic Church, the Mass). On the night of his arrest, Jesus celebrated the Jewish Passover meal with his twelve disciples. This is now known as the Last Supper. During the course of the supper, Jesus broke the bread and passed it to his disciples saying, "This is my body given for you; this do in remembrance of me." And he passed round the cup of wine saying, "This is the new covenant in my blood which is poured out for you" (Luke 22:19-20). Since then many Christians traditions have obeyed the command, "Do this is remembrance of me," often regarding the Lord's Supper as a sacrament, and making it a central focus in their worship. There has, however, been considerable debate about the meaning of Jesus' words. "Transubstantiation" is the name given to the view that the bread and wine become the actual body and blood of Jesus, a view held by the Roman Catholic Church. Evangelical Christians see the bread as a symbol of the flesh that was sacrificed once and for all, and wine as a symbol of the blood that was shed. When we take the sacrament of the Lord's Supper, we do so in remembrance of Christ's sacrifice for us. They are a witness to Christ sacrificial death.

Manna
Name for the food that God miraculously provided while the Israelites were wandering in the wilderness between Egypt and the promised land. From Hebrew *man-hu* (What is that?) or *manan* (to allot). (See Exodus 16:14-35.)

Marriage
The union of a husband and a wife for the purpose of cohabitation, procreation, and to enjoy each other's company. God's plan for marriage is between one man and one woman (Mark 10:6-9; 1 Corinthians 7). Although there are many cases of a man marrying more

than one woman in the Old Testament, being married to one wife is a requirement to serve in certain church leadership positions (1 Timothy 3:2,1 2; Titus 1:5-6).

Messiah
The Anointed one from God. Jesus fulfilled the many Old Testament prophecies about the Messiah (John 1:41).

Millennium
A 1,000-year period referred to in Revelation 20. This chapter teaches that Satan will be bound for 1,000 years, then released. He will lead a coalition of nations in a final onslaught against God before being finally defeated. Christians have held different views about the meaning of this 1,000 years.
(i) *Premillennialism* (The second coming precedes the thousand years.) The church is at present waiting for Christ's second coming. When he comes again the first resurrection will take place, and will be followed by a literal 1,000-year period, a time of blessing on this earth, when Old Testament prophecies such as Isaiah 11:3-9 will be fulfilled. There will then be the second resurrection, the final judgment, the renewal of the earth and the Lord will reign for ever in his kingdom here on earth.
(ii) *Postmillennialism* (The second coming follows the thousand years.) The thousand years represents a period of time during which the gospel will be victorious over evil, and sin will be reduced as the world will become Christianized. This period will conclude with Christ's second coming and the final judgment.
(iii) *Amillennialism* (*a-* is the Latin prefix meaning "no." There is no second coming.) The thousand years is symbolic and represents the present period between Christ's ascension and his second coming. During this period he is reigning with his saints in heaven. He will then return again and there will be a general resurrection and final judgment.

Myrrh
Myrrh is the fragrant substance that oozes out of the stems and branches of the low, shrubby tree *commiphora myrrha* or *comiphora kataf* native to the Arabian deserts and parts of Africa. The fragrant gum drops to the ground and hardens into an oily yellowish-brown

resin. Myrrh was highly valued as a perfume, and as an ingredient in medicinal and ceremonial ointments.

Nicolaitans
Nicolaitans were most likely Gnostics who taught the detestable lie that the physical and spiritual realms were entirely separate and that immorality in the physical realm wouldn't harm your spiritual health.

Omega
Omega is the last letter of the Greek alphabet. It is sometimes used to mean the last or the end.

Omnipotence
Having all power; a characteristic of God.

Omnipresence
Having all presence; a characteristic of God. He is able to be everywhere at the same time.

Omniscience
Having all knowledge; a characteristic of God. He knows everything that was, is, or ever will be

Parousia
The Greek word, *parousia*, means "presence" or "appearance." The term is used almost exclusively to indicate Christ's second coming.

Passover
Festival celebrating the liberation of the Israelites from slavery in Egypt.

Patriarch
A father. Biblical patriarchs refer to Abraham, Isaac and Jacob who are considered the fathers of the Hebrew nation.

Peace
In the Old Testament, the English word "peace" translates the Hebrew word *shalom*. This means far more than a mere absence of strife. It is a positive state of wholeness, harmony, well-being, healing. In the New Testament peace is the gift of Jesus. It is an inner peace even in the midst of trouble, harmony among believers, and, above all,

peace with God (John 14:27; Colossians 3:12-15; Romans 5:1-11).

Peniel
Peniel is Hebrew for "face of God."

Phylactery
A leather container for holding a small scroll containing important Scripture passages that is worn on the left arm or forehead in prayer. These phylacteries are still used by orthodox Jewish men. (See Deuteronomy 6:8.)

Praetorium
Praetorium: the Roman governor's military headquarters and palace in Jerusalem; in Philippians 1:13, the palace guard, possibly an elite Roman guard responsible to the Emperor, or a larger group of civil servants administered the Empire.

Postmillennialism
See under millennium.

Premillennialism
See under millennium.

Presbyterianism
From the Greek *presbyterion* meaning "body of elders." Presbyterianism is the form of church government in which hierarchical groups or courts of elders gather to determine cases of church policy, dogma, discipline, and doctrine. The presbyterian form of government finds biblical precedent in Acts 15.

Rabbi
Rabbi is a transliteration of the Hebrew word for "my teacher," used as a title of respect for Jewish teachers.

Repent
To change one's mind; turn away from sin and turn towards God; to abhor one's past sins and determine to follow God.

Sabbath
The seventh day of the week, set aside by God

for man to rest. For the Jews, this was a Saturday. Christians changed this day to Sunday, the day of resurrection.

Saints
The Greek word for "saints" literally means "holy ones." Saints are people set apart for service to God as holy and separate, living in righteousness. The word is used in the Bible to refer to all Christians and to all of those who worship Yahweh in Old Testament times.

Samaritan
A Samaritan is a resident of Samaria. The Samaritans and the Jews generally detested each other.

Sanctification
In the Old Testament, "to sanctify" means "to make holy," "to set apart for the service of God." In the New Testament, sanctification is made possible by the death of Jesus (Hebrews 10:29). The New Testament teaches that it is a process: Christians grow into holiness through the power of the Holy Spirit as they obey God's word (for example, John 17:17; 2 Corinthians 3:18; 1 Peter 1:2).

Satan
Satan means "accuser." This is one name for the devil, an enemy of God and God's people.

Scribe
Originally someone who wrote down private and public documents. After the Exile and in the New Testament someone who carefully wrote down and passed on the text of the law, and decisions made on the basis of the law. Scribes were respected and listened to as experts in the law, and teachers of the law.

Scripture
The inspired word of God, the Bible (2 Timothy 3:16).

Selah
Selah is a musical term indicating a pause or instrumental interlude for reflection.

Sexual immorality
The term "sexual immorality" in the New Testament comes from the Greek *porneia*, which refers to any sexual intercourse outside marriage. Prostitution, homosexual and lesbian activity, and the production and consumption of pornography are all included in this term.

Sheol
Sheol is the place of the dead.

Sin
Sin is what separates us from God. It is a turning away from God's love and doing something wrong, disobeying God's command.

Soul
"Soul" refers to the emotions and intellect of a living person, as well as that person's very life. It is distinguished in the Bible from a person's spirit and body. (1 Thessalonians 5:23; Hebrews 4:12).

Span
The length from the tip of the thumb to the tip of the little finger when the hand is stretched out (about 9 inches or 22.8 cm.).

Spirit
Spirit, breath, and wind all derive from the same Hebrew and Greek words. A person's spirit is the very essence of that person's life, which comes from God, who is a Spirit being (John 4:24; Genesis 1:2; 2:7). The Bible distinguishes between a person's spirit, soul, and body (1 Thessalonians 5:23, Hebrews 4:12). Some beings, such as angels and demons) may exist as spirits without necessarily having a visible body (Luke 9:39; 1 John 4:1-3).

Stadia
Stadia: plural for *stadion*, a linear measure of about 184.9 meters or 606.6 feet (the length of the race course at Olympia).

Systematic theology
Systematic theology is that branch of theology which deals with the logical categorization of Biblical truths.

Tabernacle
A dwelling place or place of worship, usually a tent.

Teleology
Teleology is derived from the two Greek words, *telos* meaning "purpose or end" and *logos* meaning "word." Teleology is the study of the end or purpose of things.

Teraphim
Teraphim are household idols. They may have been associated with inheritance rights to the household property.

Testament
A witness or evidence given for belief. The Bible is divided into two parts, the Old Testament and the New Testament. The Old Testament is about events that took place before Christ and the New Testament is about the coming of Christ, and his life, death and resurrection.

Theism
Theism is derived from the Greek *theos* meaning "God." Theism is the belief in the true and living God who is the creator and sovereign ruler of the universe.

Theocracy
Theocracy is derived from the two Greek words *theos* meaning "God" and *cratein* meaning "to rule." Theocracy is the civil rule of God. The government of the people of Israel until the inauguration of Saul is termed a theocracy.

Theology
Theology is derived from the two Greek words, *theos* meaning "God" and *logos* meaning "word." Theology means the study or science of God.

Trinity
The Christian teaching that there is only one God, who is three co-equal Persons: God the Father, God the Son and God the Holy Spirit.

Yah
"Yah" is a shortened form of "Yahweh," which is God's proper name. This form is used occasionally in the Old Testament, mostly in the Psalms. See "Yahweh."

Yahweh
"Yahweh" (this is the probable pronunciation) is God's personal name. In the Hebrew the four consonants YHWH were considered too holy to pronounce so the Hebrew word for "Lord" (*Adonai*) was substituted when reading this word aloud. At first, the Hebrew language had no vowels. When, in the Middle Ages, Jewish scribes added vowel points to the Hebrew text, the vowel points for "*Adonai*" were added to the consonants YHWH to remind readers to pronounce the word *Adonai*. The resulting hybrid word, which was never a real word, is "Jehovah." The first translators of the English Bible, not understanding this, therefore wrote down "Jehovah." Many English Bibles now indicate this Hebrew practice by the use of the word LORD (using small capital letters).

When the Old Testament was translated into Greek, the tradition of substituting "Lord" for God's proper name continued in the translation of God's name to "Lord" (*Kurios*).

In Hebrew, the name "Yahweh" is related to the active declaration "I AM" See (Exodus 3:13-14). Since Hebrew has no tenses, the declaration "I AM" can also be interpreted as "I WAS" and "I WILL BE." Compare Revelation 1:8.

SECTION 2
ROMAN CATHOLICISM

CONTENTS

1   Introduction   75
        List of heresies
2   Encyclicals   76
        Ad Caeli Reginam
3   Doctrines   86
        The pope
        Final authority: the Bible or tradition?
        Mary
        Purgatory
        Justification
        Transubstantiation
        The Mass
4   Glossary   91
5   Quotations   94

1 INTRODUCTION

The Roman Catholic Church, often spoken of as the Catholic Church, is the largest Christian Church, with over 1.1 billion members. For this reason it has a section here to iself.

However, many Protestants think of, and, speak about the Roman Catholic Church as if it were heretical in many of their key doctrines. The most contentious, as far as Protestants are concerned, are the following:

	Date first recorded
Prayers for the dead	300
Making the sign of the cross	300
Veneration of angels and dead saints	375
Use of images in worship	375
The Mass as a daily celebration	394
Beginning of the exaltation of Mary; the term, "Mother of God" applied at Council of Ephesus	431
Extreme Unction (Last Rites)	526
Doctrine of Purgatory, Gregory 1	593
Prayers to Mary and dead saints	600
Worship of cross, images and relics	786
Canonization of dead saints	995
Celibacy of priesthood	1079
Use of the rosary	1090
Indulgences	1190
Transubstantiation, Innocent III	1215
Auricular confession of sins to a priest	1215
Adoration of the wafer (Host)	1220
Cup forbidden to the people at Mass	1414
Purgatory proclaimed as a dogma	1439
The doctrine of the Seven	

Sacraments confirmed	1439
Tradition declared of equal authority with Bible by Council of Trent	1545
Apocryphal books added to Bible	1546
Immaculate Conception of Mary	1854
Infallibility of the pope in matters of faith and morals, proclaimed by the Vatican Council	1870
Assumption of the Virgin Mary (bodily ascension into heaven shortly after her death)	1950
Mary proclaimed Mother of the Church	1965

Although some of the preceding Roman Catholic doctrines are now being questioned by many, both inside and outside the Church, none have been officially repudiated and all continue to be practiced by millions of Catholics around the world.

M. H. Reynolds

2 ENCYCLICALS

Official Church doctrines emanating from the teaching of the pope are called encyclicals. These papal documents are sent by the pope to the bishops and express the mind of the pope to the people. They are to be accepted, believed and obeyed by all Roman Catholics.

ENCYCLICALS ISSUED BY THE LAST FOUR POPES

ENCYCLICALS OF POPE PIUS XII, 1939-1958
On the Unity of Human Society
Summi Pontificatus   October 10,1939

On the Start of the Church in the
United States
Sertum Laetitiae   November 11, 1939

On the Mystical Body
Mystici Corporis Christi   June 29, 1943

On St. Cyril, Patriarch of Alexander
Orientalis Ecclesiae   April 9, 1944

On Saint Benedict
Fulgens Radiatur   March 21, 1947

On the Sacred Liturgy
Mediator Dei   November 20, 1947

On Prayers for Peace in Palestine
In Multiplicbus Curis   October 24, 1948

On Evolution
Humani Generis   August 12, 1950

On the Council of Chalcedon
Sempiternus Rex Christus September 8, 1951

On Reciting the Rosary
Ingruentium Malorum   September 15, 1951

On St. Bernard of Clairvaux,
the Last of the Fathers
Doctor Mellifluus   May 24, 1953

Proclaiming a Marian Year
Fulgens Corona   September 8, 1953

On Saint Boniface
Ecclesiae Fastos   June 5, 1954

On the Supranationality of the Church
Ad Sinarum Gentem   October 7, 1954

Proclaiming the Queenship of Mary
Ad Caeli Reginam   October 11, 1954

On Sacred Music
Musicae Sacrae   December 25, 1955

On Devotion to the Sacred Heart
Haurietis Aquas   May 15, 1956

On Prayers for the People of Hungary
Luctuosissimi Eventus   October 28, 1956

On Prayers for Peace for Poland,
Hungary, and the Middle East
Laetamur Admodum   November 1, 1956

On the Condition of the Catholic Missions
Fidei Donum   April 21, 1957

On Saint Andrew Bobola
Invicti Athlatae   May 16, 1957

Warning Against Materialism
Le Pelerinage De Lourdes July 2, 1957

On Communism and the Church in China
Ad Apostolorum Principis June 29, 1958

On Prayers for the Persecuted Church
Meminisse Luvat   July 12, 1958

ENCYCLICALS OF POPE JOHN XXIII,
1958-1963
On Truth, Unity and Peace
Ad Petri Cathedram   June 29, 1959

On the Rosary
Grata Recordatio   September 26, 1959

On the Missions
Princeps Pastorum   November 26, 1959

Christianity and Social Progress
Mater Et Magistra   May 16, 1961

On Saint Leo the Great
Aeterna Dei Sapientia   November 11, 1961

On the Need for Penance
Paenitentiam Agere   July 1, 1962

Peace On Earth
Pacem in Terris   April 11, 1963

On Saint John Vianney
Sacerdotii Nostri Primordia   August 1, 1963

ENCYCLICALS OF POPE PAUL VI,
1963-1978

On the Church
Ecclesiam Suam   August 6, 1964

On Praying to Mary During May
Mense Maio   April 30, 1965

On the Holy Eucharist
Mysterium Fidei   September 3, 1965

On Prayers to Mary for Peace
Christi Matri   September 15, 1966

On the Development of Peoples
Populorum Progressio   March 26, 1967

On the Celibacy of the Priest
Sacerdotalis Caelibatus   June 24, 1967

On the Regulation of Birth
Humanae Vitae   July 25, 1968

ENCYCLICALS OF POPE JOHN PAUL
II, 1978-2005

The Redeemer of Man
Redemptor Hominis   March 4, 1979

On The Mercy of God
Dives in Misericordia   November 30, 1980

On Human Work
Laborem Exercens   September 14, 1981

Lord and Giver of Life
Dominum et Vivificantem   May 18, 1986

Mother of the Redeemer
Redemptoris Mater   March 25, 1987

On Social Concerns
Sollicitudo Rei Socialis   December 30, 1987

On the Hundreth Anniversary
of Splendor of Truth
Veritatis Splendor Rerum Novarum
Centesimus Annus   October 5, 1993

On The Value and Inviolability of
Human Life
Evangelium Vitae   March 25, 1995

That all May Be One
Ut Unum Sint   May 25, 1995

Faith and Reason
Fides et Ratio   September 1998

AD CAELI REGINAM

Encyclical of Pope Pius XII on Proclaiming
the Queenship of Mary issued on
October 11, 1954

To the Venerable Brethren, the Patriarchs,
Primates, Archbishops, Bishops and other
Local Ordinaries in Peace and
Communion with the Holy See.

Venerable Brethren, Health and Apostolic
Blessing.

1. From the earliest ages of the Catholic
Church a Christian people, whether in
time of triumph or more especially in
time of crisis, has addressed prayers of
petition and hymns of praise and
veneration to the Queen of Heaven. And

never has that hope wavered which they placed in the Mother of the Divine King, Jesus Christ; nor has that faith ever failed by which we are taught that Mary, the Virgin Mother of God, reigns with a mother's solicitude over the entire world, just as she is crowned in heavenly blessedness with the glory of a Queen.

2. Following upon the frightful calamities which before Our very eyes have reduced flourishing cities, towns, and villages to ruins, We see to Our sorrow that many great moral evils are being spread abroad in what may be described as a violent flood. Occasionally We behold justice giving way; and, on the one hand and the other, the victory of the powers of corruption. The threat of this fearful crisis fills Us with a great anguish, and so with confidence We have recourse to Mary Our Queen, making known to her those sentiments of filial reverence which are not Ours alone, but which belong to all those who glory in the name of Christian.

3. It is gratifying to recall that We ourselves, on the first day of November of the Holy Year 1950, before a huge multitude of Cardinals, Bishops, priests, and of the faithful who had assembled from every part of the world, defined the dogma of the Assumption of the Blessed Virgin Mary into heaven where she is present in soul and body reigning, together with her only Son, amid the heavenly choirs of angels and Saints. Moreover, since almost a century has passed since Our predecessor of immortal memory, Pius IX, proclaimed and defined the dogma that the great Mother of God had been conceived without any stain of original sin, We instituted the current Marian Year And now it is a great consolation to Us to see great multitudes here in Rome - and especially in the Liberian Basilica - giving testimony in a striking way to their faith and ardent love for their heavenly Mother. In all parts of the world We learn that devotion to the Virgin Mother of God is flourishing more

and more, and that the principal shrines of Mary have been visited and are still being visited by many throngs of Catholic pilgrims gathered in prayer.

4. It is well known that we have taken advantage of every opportunity - through personal audiences and radio broadcasts - to exhort Our children in Christ to a strong and tender love, as becomes children, for Our most gracious and exalted Mother. On this point it is particularly fitting to call to mind the radio message which We addressed to the people of Portugal, when the miraculous image of the Virgin Mary which is venerated at Fatima was being crowned with a golden diadem. We Ourselves called this the heralding of the "sovereignty" of Mary.

5. And now, that We may bring the Year of Mary to a happy and beneficial conclusion, and in response to petitions which have come to Us from all over the world, We have decided to institute the liturgical feast of the Blessed Virgin Mary, Queen. This will afford a climax, as it were, to the manifold demonstrations of Our devotion to Mary, which the Christian people have supported with such enthusiasm.

6. In this matter We do not wish to propose a new truth to be believed by Christians, since the title and the arguments on which Mary's queenly dignity is based have already been clearly set forth, and are to be found in ancient documents of the Church and in the books of the sacred liturgy.

7. It is Our pleasure to recall these things in the present encyclical letter, that We may renew the praises of Our heavenly Mother, and enkindle a more fervent devotion towards her, to the spiritual benefit of all mankind.

8. From early times Christians have believed, and not without reason, that she

of whom was born the Son of the Most High received privileges of grace above all other beings created by God. He "will reign in the house of Jacob forever," "the Prince of Peace," the "King of Kings and Lord of Lords." And when Christians reflected upon the intimate connection that obtains between a mother and a son, they readily acknowledged the supreme royal dignity of the Mother of God.

9. Hence it is not surprising that the early writers of the Church called Mary "the Mother of the King" and "the Mother of the Lord," basing their stand on the words of St. Gabriel the archangel, who foretold that the Son of Mary would reign forever, and on the words of Elizabeth who greeted her with reverence and called her "the Mother of my Lord." Thereby they clearly signified that she derived a certain eminence and exalted station from the royal dignity of her Son.

10. So it is that St. Ephrem, burning with poetic inspiration, represents her as speaking in this way: "Let Heaven sustain me in its embrace, because I am honored above it. For heaven was not Thy mother, but Thou hast made it Thy throne. How much more honorable and venerable than the throne of a king is her mother." And in another place he thus prays to her: ". . . Majestic and Heavenly Maid, Lady, Queen, protect and keep me under your wing lest Satan the sower of destruction glory over me, lest my wicked foe be victorious against me."

11. St. Gregory Nazianzen calls Mary "the Mother of the King of the universe," and the "Virgin Mother who brought forth the King of the whole world," while Prudentius asserts that the Mother marvels "that she has brought forth God as man, and even as Supreme King."

12. And this royal dignity of the Blessed Virgin Mary is quite clearly indicated through direct assertion by those who call her "Lady," "Ruler" and "Queen."

13. In one of the homilies attributed to Origen, Elizabeth calls Mary "the Mother of my Lord." and even addresses her as "Thou, my Lady."

14. The same thing is found in the writings of St. Jerome where he makes the following statement amidst various interpretations of Mary's name: "We should realize that Mary means Lady in the Syrian Language." After him St. Chrysologus says the same thing more explicitly in these words: "The Hebrew word 'Mary' means 'Domina.' The Angel therefore addresses her as 'Lady' to preclude all servile fear in the Lord's Mother, who was born and was called 'Lady' by the authority and command of her own Son."

15. Moreover Epiphanius, the bishop of Constantinople, writing to the Sovereign Pontiff Hormisdas, says that we should pray that the unity of the Church may be preserved "by the grace of the holy and consubstantial Trinity and by the prayers of Mary, Our Lady, the holy and glorious Virgin and Mother of God."

16. The Blessed Virgin, sitting at the right hand of God to pray for us is hailed by another writer of that same era in these words, "the Queen of mortal man, the most holy Mother of God."

17. St. Andrew of Crete frequently attributes the dignity of a Queen to the Virgin Mary. For example, he writes, "Today He transports from her earthly dwelling, as Queen of the human race, His ever-Virgin Mother, from whose womb He, the living God, took on human form."

18. And in another place he speaks of "the Queen of the entire human race faithful to the exact meaning of her name, who is exalted above all things save only God himself."

19. Likewise St. Germanus speaks to the

humble Virgin in these words: "Be enthroned, Lady, for it is fitting that you should sit in an exalted place since you are a Queen and glorious above all kings." He likewise calls her the "Queen of all of those who dwell on earth."

20. She is called by St. John Damascene: "Queen, ruler, and lady," and also "the Queen of every creature." Another ancient writer of the Eastern Church calls her "favored Queen," "the perpetual Queen beside the King, her son," whose "snow-white brow is crowned with a golden diadem."

21. And finally St. Ildephonsus of Toledo gathers together almost all of her titles of honor in this salutation: "O my Lady, my Sovereign, You who rule over me, Mother of my Lord . . . Lady among handmaids, Queen among sisters."

22. The theologians of the Church, deriving their teaching from these and almost innumerable other testimonies handed down long ago, have called the most Blessed Virgin the Queen of all creatures, the Queen of the world, and the Ruler of all.

23. The Supreme Shepherds of the Church have considered it their duty to promote by eulogy and exhortation the devotion of the Christian people to the heavenly Mother and Queen. Simply passing over the documents of more recent Pontiffs, it is helpful to recall that as early as the seventh century Our predecessor St. Martin I called Mary "our glorious Lady, ever Virgin." St. Agatho, in the synodal letter sent to the fathers of the Sixth Ecumenical Council called her "Our Lady, truly and in a proper sense the Mother of God." And in the eighth century Gregory II in the letter sent to St. Germanus, the patriarch, and read in the Seventh Ecumenical Council with all the Fathers concurring, called the Mother of God: "The Queen of all, the true Mother of God," and also "the Queen of all Christians."

24. We wish also to recall that Our predecessor of immortal memory, Sixtus IV, touched favorably upon the doctrine of the Immaculate Conception of the Blessed Virgin, beginning the Apostolic Letter Cum praexcelsa with words in which Mary is called "Queen," "Who is always vigilant to intercede with the king whom she bore." Benedict XIV declared the same thing in his Apostolic Letter Gloriosae Dominae, in which Mary is called "Queen of heaven and earth," and it is stated that the sovereign King has in some way communicated to her his ruling power.

25. For all these reasons St. Alphonsus Ligouri, in collecting the testimony of past ages, writes these words with evident devotion: "Because the virgin Mary was raised to such a lofty dignity as to be the mother of the King of kings, it is deservedly and by every right that the Church has honored her with the title of 'Queen.'"

26. Furthermore, the sacred liturgy, which acts as a faithful reflection of traditional doctrine believed by the Christian people through the course of all the ages both in the East and in the West, has sung the praises of the heavenly Queen and continues to sing them.

27. Ardent voices from the East sing out: "O Mother of God, today thou art carried into heaven on the chariots of the cherubim, the seraphim wait upon thee and the ranks of the heavenly army bow before thee."

28. Further: "O just, O most blessed Joseph, since thou art sprung from a royal line, thou hast been chosen from among all mankind to be spouse of the pure Queen who, in a way which defies description, will give birth to Jesus the king." In addition: "I shall sing a hymn to the mother, the Queen, whom I joyously approach in praise, gladly celebrating her wonders in song. . . . Our tongue cannot worthily praise thee, O Lady; for thou who hast borne Christ the king art exalted

above the seraphim. . . Hail, O Queen of the world; hail, O Mary, Queen of us all."

29. We read, moreover, in the Ethiopic Missal: "O Mary, center of the whole world, . . . thou art greater than the many-eyed cherubim and the six-winged seraphim . . . Heaven and earth are filled with the sanctity of thy glory."

30. Furthermore, the Latin Church sings that sweet and ancient prayer called the "Hail, Holy Queen" and the lovely antiphons "Hail, Queen of the Heavens," "O Queen of Heaven, Rejoice," and those others which we are accustomed to recite on feasts of the Blessed Virgin Mary: "The Queen stood at Thy right hand in golden vesture surrounded with beauty"; "Heaven and earth praise thee as a powerful Queen"; "Today the Virgin Mary ascends into heaven: rejoice because she reigns with Christ forever."

31. To these and others should be added the Litany of Loreto which daily invites Christian folk to call upon Mary as Queen. Likewise, for many centuries past Christians have been accustomed to meditate upon the ruling power of Mary which embraces heaven and earth, when they consider the fifth glorious mystery of the rosary which can be called the mystical crown of the heavenly Queen.

32. Finally, art which is based upon Christian principles and is animated by their spirit as something faithfully interpreting the sincere and freely expressed devotion of the faithful, has since the Council of Ephesus portrayed Mary as Queen and Empress seated upon a royal throne adorned with royal insignia, crowned with the royal diadem and surrounded by the host of angels and saints in heaven, and ruling not only over nature and its powers but also over the machinations of Satan. Iconography, in representing the royal dignity of the Blessed Virgin Mary, has ever been enriched with works of highest artistic value and greatest beauty; it has even taken the form of representing colorfully the divine Redeemer crowning His mother with a resplendent diadem.

33. The Roman Pontiffs, favoring such types of popular devotion, have often crowned, either in their own persons, or through representatives, images of the Virgin Mother of God which were already outstanding by reason of public veneration.

34. As We have already mentioned, Venerable Brothers, according to ancient tradition and the sacred liturgy the main principle on which the royal dignity of Mary rests is without doubt her Divine Motherhood. In Holy Writ, concerning the Son whom Mary will conceive, We read this sentence: "He shall be called the Son of the most High, and the Lord God shall give unto him the throne of David his father, and he shall reign in the house of Jacob forever, and of his kingdom there will be no end," and in addition Mary is called "Mother of the Lord"; from this it is easily concluded that she is a Queen, since she bore a son who, at the very moment of His conception, because of the hypostatic union of the human nature with the Word, was also as man King and Lord of all things. So with complete justice St. John Damascene could write: "When she became Mother of the Creator, she truly became Queen of every creature." Likewise, it can be said that the heavenly voice of the Archangel Gabriel was the first to proclaim Mary's royal office.

35. But the Blessed Virgin Mary should be called Queen, not only because of her Divine Motherhood, but also because God has willed her to have an exceptional role in the work of our eternal salvation. "What more joyful, what sweeter thought can we have" - as Our Predecessor of happy memory, Pius XI wrote - "than that

Christ is our King not only by natural right, but also by an acquired right: that which He won by the redemption? Would that all men, now forgetful of how much we cost Our Savior, might recall to mind the words, 'You were redeemed, not with gold or silver which perishes, . . . but with the precious blood of Christ, as of a Lamb spotless and undefiled. We belong not to ourselves now, since Christ has bought us 'at a great price.'"

36. Now, in the accomplishing of this work of redemption, the Blessed Virgin Mary was most closely associated with Christ; and so it is fitting to sing in the sacred liturgy: "Near the cross of Our Lord Jesus Christ there stood, sorrowful, the Blessed Mary, Queen of Heaven and Queen of the World." Hence, as the devout disciple of St. Anselm (Eadmer, ed.) wrote in the Middle Ages: "just as . . . God, by making all through His power, is Father and Lord of all, so the blessed Mary, by repairing all through her merits, is Mother and Queen of all; for God is the Lord of all things, because by His command He establishes each of them in its own nature, and Mary is the Queen of all things, because she restores each to its original dignity through the grace which she merited.

37. For "just as Christ, because He redeemed us, is our Lord and king by a special title, so the Blessed Virgin also (is our queen), on account of the unique manner in which she assisted in our redemption, by giving of her own substance, by freely offering Him for us, by her singular desire and petition for, and active interest in, our salvation."

38. From these considerations, the proof develops on these lines: if Mary, in taking an active part in the work of salvation, was, by God's design, associated with Jesus Christ, the source of salvation itself, in a manner comparable to that in which Eve was associated with Adam, the source of death, so that it may be stated that the

work of our salvation was accomplished by a kind of "recapitulation,"[49] in which a virgin was instrumental in the salvation of the human race, just as a virgin had been closely associated with its death; if, moreover, it can likewise be stated that this glorious Lady had been chosen Mother of Christ "in order that she might become a partner in the redemption of the human race"; and if, in truth, "it was she who, free of the stain of actual and original sin, and ever most closely bound to her Son, on Golgotha offered that Son to the Eternal Father together with the complete sacrifice of her maternal rights and maternal love, like a new Eve, for all the sons of Adam, stained as they were by his lamentable fall," then it may be legitimately concluded that as Christ, the new Adam, must be called a King not merely because He is Son of God, but also because He is our Redeemer, so, analogously, the Most Blessed Virgin is queen not only because she is Mother of God, but also because, as the new Eve, she was associated with the new Adam.

39. Certainly, in the full and strict meaning of the term, only Jesus Christ, the God-Man, is King; but Mary, too, as Mother of the divine Christ, as His associate in the redemption, in his struggle with His enemies and His final victory over them, has a share, though in a limited and analogous way, in His royal dignity. For from her union with Christ she attains a radiant eminence transcending that of any other creature; from her union with Christ she receives the royal right to dispose of the treasures of the Divine Redeemer's Kingdom; from her union with Christ finally is derived the inexhaustible efficacy of her maternal intercession before the Son and His Father.

40. Hence it cannot be doubted that Mary most Holy is far above all other creatures in dignity, and after her Son possesses primacy over all. "You have

surpassed every creature," sings St. Sophronius. "What can be more sublime than your joy, O Virgin Mother? What more noble than this grace, which you alone have received from God"? To this St. Germanus adds: "Your honor and dignity surpass the whole of creation; your greatness places you above the angels." And St. John Damascene goes so far as to say: "Limitless is the difference between God's servants and His Mother."

41. In order to understand better this sublime dignity of the Mother of God over all creatures let us recall that the holy Mother of God was, at the very moment of her Immaculate Conception, so filled with grace as to surpass the grace of all the Saints. Wherefore, as Our Predecessor of happy memory, Pius IX wrote, God "showered her with heavenly gifts and graces from the treasury of His divinity so far beyond what He gave to all the angels and saints that she was ever free from the least stain of sin; she is so beautiful and perfect, and possesses such fullness of innocence and holiness, that under God a greater could not be dreamed, and only God can comprehend the marvel."

42. Besides, the Blessed Virgin possessed, after Christ, not only the highest degree of excellence and perfection, but also a share in that influence by which He, her Son and our Redeemer, is rightly said to reign over the minds and wills of men. For if through His Humanity the divine Word performs miracles and gives graces, if He uses His Sacraments and Saints as instruments for the salvation of men, why should He not make use of the role and work of His most holy Mother in imparting to us the fruits of redemption? "With a heart that is truly a mother's," to quote again Our Predecessor of immortal memory, Pius IX, "does she approach the problem of our salvation, and is solicitous for the whole human race; made Queen of heaven and earth by the Lord, exalted above all choirs of angels and saints, and standing at the right hand of her only a

Son, Jesus Christ our Lord, she intercedes powerfully for us with a mother's prayers, obtains what she seeks, and cannot be refused." On this point another of Our Predecessors of happy memory, Leo XIII, has said that an "almost immeasurable" power has been given Mary in the distribution of graces; St. Pius X adds that she fills this office "as by the right of a mother."

43. Let all Christians, therefore, glory in being subjects of the Virgin Mother of God, who, while wielding royal power, is on fire with a mother's love.

44. Theologians and preachers, however, when treating these and like questions concerning the Blessed Virgin, must avoid straying from the correct course, with a twofold error to guard against: that is to say, they must beware of unfounded opinions and exaggerated expressions which go beyond the truth, on the other hand, they must watch out for excessive narrowness of mind in weighing that exceptional, sublime, indeed all but divine dignity of the Mother of God, which the Angelic Doctor teaches must be attributed to her "because of the infinite goodness that is God."

45. For the rest, in this as in other points of Christian doctrine, "the proximate and universal norm of truth" is for all the living Magisterium of the Church, which Christ established "also to illustrate and explain those matters which are contained only in an obscure way, and implicitly in the deposit of faith."

46. From the ancient Christian documents, from prayers of the liturgy, from the innate piety of the Christian people, from works of art, from every side We have gathered witnesses to the regal dignity of the Virgin Mother of God; We have likewise shown that the arguments deduced by Sacred Theology from the treasure store of the faith fully confirm this truth. Such a wealth of witnesses makes up a resounding chorus which

changes the sublimity of the royal dignity of the Mother of God and of men, to whom every creature is subject, who is "exalted to the heavenly throne, above the choirs of angels."

47. Since we are convinced, after long and serious reflection, that great good will accrue to the Church if this solidly established truth shines forth more clearly to all, like a luminous lamp raised aloft, by Our Apostolic authority We decree and establish the feast of Mary's Queenship, which is to be celebrated every year in the whole world on the 31st of May. We likewise ordain that on the same day the consecration of the human race to the Immaculate Heart of the Blessed Virgin Mary be renewed, cherishing the hope that through such consecration a new era may begin, joyous in Christian peace and in the triumph of religion.

48. Let all, therefore, try to approach with greater trust the throne of grace and mercy of our Queen and Mother, and beg for strength in adversity, light in darkness, consolation in sorrow; above all let them strive to free themselves from the slavery of sin and offer an unceasing homage, filled with filial loyalty, to their Queenly Mother. Let her churches be thronged by the faithful, her feast-days honored; may the beads of the Rosary be in the hands of all; may Christians gather, in small numbers and large, to sing her praises in churches, in homes, in hospitals, in prisons. May Mary's name be held in highest reverence, a name sweeter than honey and more precious than jewels; may none utter blasphemous words, the sign of a defiled soul, against that name graced with such dignity and revered for its motherly goodness; let no one be so bold as to speak a syllable which lacks the respect due to her name.

49. All, according to their state, should strive to bring alive the wondrous virtues of our heavenly Queen and most loving Mother through constant effort of mind and manner. Thus will it come about that all Christians, in honoring and imitating their sublime Queen and Mother, will realize they are truly brothers, and with all envy and avarice thrust aside, will promote love among classes, respect the rights of the weak, cherish peace. No one should think himself a son of Mary, worthy of being received under her powerful protection, unless, like her, he is just, gentle and pure, and shows a sincere desire for true brotherhood, not harming or injuring but rather helping and comforting others.

50. In some countries of the world there are people who are unjustly persecuted for professing their Christian faith and who are deprived of their divine and human rights to freedom; up till now reasonable demands and repeated protests have availed nothing to remove these evils. May the powerful Queen of creation, whose radiant glance banishes storms and tempests and brings back cloudless skies, look upon these her innocent and tormented children with eyes of mercy; may the Virgin, who is able to subdue violence beneath her foot, grant to them that they may soon enjoy the rightful freedom to practice their religion openly, so that, while serving the cause of the Gospel, they may also contribute to the strength and progress of nations by their harmonious cooperation, by the practice of extraordinary virtues which are a glowing example in the midst of bitter trials.

51. By this Encyclical Letter We are instituting a feast so that all may recognize more clearly and venerate more devoutly the merciful and maternal sway of the Mother of God. We are convinced that this feast will help to preserve, strengthen and prolong that peace among nations which daily is almost destroyed by recurring crises. Is she not a rainbow in the clouds reaching towards God, the pledge of a covenant of peace? "Look upon the rainbow, and bless Him that

made it; surely it is beautiful in its brightness. It encompasses the heaven about with the circle of its glory, the hands of the Most High have displayed it." Whoever, therefore, reverences the Queen of heaven and earth - and let no one consider himself exempt from this tribute of a grateful and loving soul - let him invoke the most effective of Queens, the Mediatrix of peace; let him respect and preserve peace, which is not wickedness unpunished nor freedom without restraint, but a well-ordered harmony under the rule of the will of God; to its safeguarding and growth the gentle urgings and commands of the Virgin Mary impel us.

52. Earnestly desiring that the Queen and Mother of Christendom may hear these Our prayers, and by her peace make happy a world shaken by hate, and may, after this exile show unto us all Jesus, Who will be our eternal peace and joy, to you, Venerable Brothers, and to your flocks, as a promise of God's divine help and a pledge of Our love, from Our heart We impart the Apostolic Benediction.

53. Given at Rome, from St. Peter's, on the feast of the Maternity of the Blessed Virgin Mary, the eleventh day of October, 1954, in the sixteenth year our Pontificate.

3 DOCTRINES

A The pope
B Final authority: the Bible or tradition?
C Mary
D Purgatory
E Justification
F Transubstantiation
G The Mass

A THE POPE

Papal infallibility became an official Roman Catholic dogma in 1870.

Vatican Council, Sess. IV, Const. de Ecclesiâ Christi, c. iv, holds:

> We teach and define that it is a dogma Divinely revealed that the Roman pontiff when he speaks ex cathedra, that is when in discharge of the office of pastor and doctor of all Christians, by virtue of his supreme Apostolic authority, he defines a doctrine regarding faith or morals to be held by the universal Church, by the Divine assistance promised to him in Blessed Peter, is possessed of that infallibility with which the Divine Redeemer willed that his Church should be endowed in defining doctrine regarding faith or morals, and that therefore such definitions of the Roman pontiff are of themselves and not from the consent of the Church irreformable.

THE ANGLICAN CHURCHES' POSITION

The Church of England, along with all Anglican Churches, rejects papal infallibility, as is seen from its *Thirty-Nine Articles of Religion* (1571):

> XIX. Of the Church. The visible Church of Christ is a congregation of faithful men, in which the pure Word of God is preached, and the Sacraments be duly ministered according to Christ's ordinance, in all those things that of necessity are requisite to the same. As the

Church of Jerusalem, Alexandria, and Antioch, have erred, so also the Church of Rome hath erred, not only in their living and manner of Ceremonies, but also in matters of Faith. XXI. Of the Authority of General Councils. General Councils may not be gathered together without the commandment and will of Princes. And when they be gathered together, (forasmuch as they be an assembly of men, whereof all be not governed with the Spirit and Word of God,) they may err, and sometimes have erred, even in things pertaining unto God. Wherefore things ordained by them as necessary to salvation have neither strength nor authority, unless it may be declared that they be taken out of holy Scripture.

REFORMED CHURCHES' POSITION

Presbyterian and Reformed churches also reject papal infallibility, as is seen from *The Westminster Confession of Faith* (1646)

> (Chapter one) IX. The infallible rule of interpretation of Scripture is the Scripture itself: and therefore, when there is a question about the true and full sense of any Scripture (which is not manifold, but one), it must be searched and known by other places that speak more clearly.
>
> X. The supreme judge by which all controversies of religion are to be determined, and all decrees of councils, opinions of ancient writers, doctrines of men, and private spirits, are to be examined, and in whose sentence we are

to rest, can be no other but the Holy Spirit speaking in the Scripture.

(Chapter Twenty-Five) VI. There is no other head of the Church but the Lord Jesus Christ. Nor can the Pope of Rome, in any sense, be head thereof; but is that Antichrist, that man of sin, and son of perdition, that exalts himself, in the Church, against Christ and all that is called God.

B FINAL AUTHORITY: THE BIBLE OR TRADITION?

Protestant churches cite the Bible alone as their source for doctrine. The Roman Catholic Church, on the other hand, cites the Bible and Tradition.

. . . the Church, to whom the transmission and interpretation of Revelation is entrusted, "does not derive her certainty about all revealed truths from the holy Scriptures alone. Both Scripture and Tradition must be accepted and honored with equal sentiments of devotion and reverence."
Catechism of the Catholic Church, paragraph 82.

For the source of doctrines that are not taught in the Bible the Roman Catholic Church relies on the authority of church tradition.

These doctrines include the following controversial topics:

- The Mass
- Penance
- Veneration of Mary
- Purgatory
- Indulgences
- The priesthood
- The confessional
- The rosary
- Venial and mortal Sins

Protestants assert that the Bible alone is intended by God to be the source of doctrinal truth (2 Timothy 3:16). But Roman Catholics have said: "Sacred Tradition and Sacred Scripture make up a single sacred deposit of the Word of God . . ." (*Catechism of the Catholic Church, paragraph 97*).

Roman Catholics reason as follows:

- "The apostles left bishops as their successors. They gave them 'their own position of teaching authority.'" (*Catechism of the Catholic Church, paragraph 77*).
- "This living transmission, accomplished through the Holy Spirit, is called tradition . . ." (*Catechism of the Catholic Church, paragraph 78*).
- "Both Scripture and Tradition must be accepted and honored with equal sentiments of devotion and reverence." (*Catechism of the Catholic Church, paragraph 82*).

C MARY

Through the centuries, an increasing numbers of doctrines concerning Mary have been "revealed." For example:

Doctrine about Mary	Date doctrine became official
Mary is called the Mother of God	431
Prayers offered to Mary	600
Immaculate Conception (her sinlessness)	1854
Assumption of Mary	1950
Mary Proclaimed Mother of the Church	1965

MARY'S ASSUMPTION TO HEAVEN

The doctrine of the Assumption is an important aspect of Catholic belief, infallibly taught by the Church. It was defined in 1950 by Pope Pius XII, not on his own initiative but in answer to millions of petitions from all over the world. Like the Immaculate Conception, the Assumption of Mary was accepted by Catholics for centuries before it became dogma. This doctrine proclaims that at the end of Mary's life on earth, Christ gave her victory over death, and her body shared fully in his Resurrection as ours will at the end of time. Because Mary never sinned, she was able to experience complete union with her Son, Jesus. This doctrine is a sign of hope because it points the way to heaven for us, who are, like Mary, members of the church.

Oscar Lukefahr, C. M. We Believe . . . A Survey of the Catholic Faith

D PURGATORY

All who die in God's grace and friendship, but still imperfectly purified, are indeed assured of their eternal salvation, but after death they undergo purification, so as to achieve the holiness necessary to enter the joy of heaven.

Catechism of the Catholic Church, p. 1030

The truth has been divinely revealed that sins are followed by punishments. God's holiness and justice inflict them. Sins must be expiated. This may be done on this earth through the sorrows, miseries and trials of this life and, above all, through death. Otherwise the expiation must be made in the next life through fire and torments or purifying punishments.

The Second Vatican Council, p. 63

In purgatory the souls of those "who died in the charity of God and truly repentant, but who had not made satisfaction with adequate penance for their sins and omissions," are cleansed after death with punishments designed to purge away their debt.

Second Vatican Council, "Sacred Liturgy," "Apostolic Constitution on the Revision of Indulgences," no. 3

They preach human folly who pretend that as soon as money in the coffer rings, a soul from purgatory springs.

Martin Luther, 95 Theses, Thesis 27

E JUSTIFICATION

Much of the Roman Catholic teaching on justification by faith is still greatly influenced by the canons of the Council of Trent, 1544-1545.

If any one saith, that by faith alone the impious is justified; in such wise as to mean, that nothing else is required to co-operate in order to obtaining the grace of Justification, and that it is not in any way necessary, that he be prepared and disposed by the movement of his own will; let him be anathema.

Canon 9, Canons on Justification, Council of Trent

A BIBLICAL PERSPECTIVE
(All the Bible quotes in this section are from the KJV.)

Therefore by the deeds of the law there shall no flesh be justified in his sight: for by the law is the knowledge of sin.

Romans 3:20

Being justified freely by his grace through the redemption that is in Christ Jesus.

Romans 3:24

Therefore we conclude that a man is justified by faith without the deeds of the law.

Romans 3:28

For what saith the scripture? Abraham believed God, and it was counted unto him for righteousness.

Romans 4:3

Therefore being justified by faith, we have peace with God through our Lord Jesus Christ.

Romans 5:1

For by grace are ye saved through faith; and that not of yourselves: it is the gift of God.

Ephesians 2:8

Not by works of righteousness which we have done, but according to his mercy he saved us, by the washing of regeneration, and renewing of the Holy Ghost.

Titus 3:5

GOOD DEEDS

If any one saith, that the justice received is not preserved and also increased before God through good works; but that the said works are merely the fruits and signs of Justification obtained, but not a cause of the increase thereof; let him be anathema.

*Canon 24, Canons on Justification,
Council of Trent*

A BIBLICAL PERSPECTIVE

O foolish Galatians, who hath bewitched you, that ye should not obey the truth, before whose eyes Jesus Christ hath been evidently set forth, crucified among you? This only would I learn of you, Received ye the Spirit by the works of the law, or by the hearing of faith? Are ye so foolish? having begun in the Spirit, are ye now made perfect by the flesh?

Galatians 3:1-3

Stand fast therefore in the liberty wherewith Christ hath made us free, and be not entangled again with the yoke of bondage. Behold, I Paul say unto you, that if ye be circumcised, Christ shall profit you nothing. For I testify again to every man that is circumcised, that he is a debtor to do the whole law.

Galatians 5:1-3

TEMPORAL PUNISHMENT

If any one saith, that, after the grace of Justification has been received, to every penitent sinner the guilt is remitted, and the debt of eternal punishment is blotted out in such wise, that there remains not any debt of temporal punishment to be discharged either in this world, or in the next in Purgatory, before the entrance to the kingdom of heaven can be opened (to

him); let him be anathema.

*Canon 30, Canons on Justification,
Council of Trent*

A BIBLICAL PERSPECTIVE

Therefore being justified by faith, we have peace with God through our Lord Jesus Christ.

Romans 5:1

And you, being dead in your sins and the uncircumcision of your flesh, hath he quickened together with him, having forgiven you all trespasses; Blotting out the handwriting of ordinances that was against us, which was contrary to us, and took it out of the way, nailing it to his cross.

Colossians 2:13-14

ANATHEMA

If any one saith, that, by the Catholic doctrine teuching Justification, by this holy Synod inset forth in this present decree, the glory of God, or the merits of our Lord Jesus Christ are in any way derogated from, and not rather that the truth of our faith, and the glory in fine of God and of Jesus Christ are rendered (more) illustrious; let him be anathema. This council declares that if anyone disagrees with it, they are damned.

*Canon 33, Canons on Justification,
Council of Trent*

F TRANSUBSTANTIATION

Transubstantiation (also known as the Real Presence) is the Roman Catholic teaching that during the Mass the elements of the Bread and the Wine, are transformed into the actual Body and Blood of Christ.

G THE MASS

Roman Catholicism teaches that the Mass is a sacrifice of Christ. The Roman Catholic Church intends the Mass to be regarded as a "true and proper sacrifice," and will not tolerate the idea that the sacrifice is identical with Holy Communion. That is the sense of a clause from the Council of Trent (Sess. XXII, can. 1): "If any one saith that in the Mass a true and proper sacrifice is not offered to God; or, that to be offered is nothing else but that Christ is given us to eat; let him be anathema."

The Sacrifice of the Mass forms a pivot upon which all else turns. If it is what Catholics believe it is, then here is the greatest external manifestation of the love of God for man and the most magnificent testimonial to the validity of Catholicism; but if it be false, it is the worse farce and blasphemy every perpetrated upon God or man, and the Catholic faith collapses into nothingness."

The What and Why of Catholicism

The Mass is a real sacrifice because in it a Victim is offered by a priest for the purpose of reconciling man with God.

St. Peter's Catechism, (1972), page 48

The sacrifice on the altar is no mere commemoration of Calvary, but a true and proper act of sacrifice whereby Christ, the high priest, by an unbloody immolation offers himself a most acceptable victim to the eternal father, as he did on the cross.

John Hardon, The Catholic Catechism, *1975*

A PROTESTANT PERSPECTIVE

Consider now, beloved brethren, what the fruits of the Mass have been, even in her greatest purity. The Mass is nothing but the invention of man, set up without all authority of God's word, for honouring of God; and therefore it is idolatry. Unto it is added a vain, false, deceitful, and most wicked opinion: that is, that by it is obtained remission of sins; and therefore it is abomination before God. It is contrary unto the Supper of Jesus Christ, and has taken away both the right use and remembrance thereof, and therefore it is blasphemous to Christ's death.

John Knox

A BIBLICAL PERSPECTIVE

By the which will we are sanctified through the offering of the body of Jesus Christ once for all. And every priest standeth daily ministering and offering oftentimes the same sacrifices, which can never take away sins: But this man, after he had offered one sacrifice for sins for ever, sat down on the right hand of God; from henceforth expecting till his enemies be made his footstool. For by one offering he hath perfected for ever them that are sanctified.

Hebrews 10:10-14

4 GLOSSARY

Absolution
Absolution is the act of releasing someone from their sin by God, through the means of a priest.

Acolyte
Acolyte is derived from the Greek word *akolouthos*, attendant. A person who assists the priest or deacon in the celebration of the liturgy.

Actual grace
God's interventions, whether at the beginning of conversion or in the course of the work of sanctification. Actual sin refers to any sin that a person commits.

Advent
A period of prayer in preparation for the coming of Christ at Christmas. There are four Sundays in Advent, which begins the Church's liturgical year.

Alb
A long white garment worn by bishops, priests and deacons underneath the other vestments during liturgies.

All Saints
A feast day celebrated on November 1 to honor all those saints or holy people who have gone before us into heaven. In a particular way the Church honors those good and holy people who do not have a special feast day celebrated during the year.

All Souls
A special day of prayer and remembrance for all those who have died (November 2).

Altar
In the Catholic Church the altar is the Lord's table at which the people of God celebrate the Eucharist. Roman Catholics have traditionally called the Eucharist a sacrifice because it commemorates the fact that Jesus gave himself up for everyone; so the altar is the table at which Christ's sacrifice of himself on the cross

is remembered and made present.

Anointing of the Sick
A sacrament in which a sick person is anointed with blessed olive oil by a bishop or priest. The oil, which is a sign of healing by the Holy Spirit, is usually put on the person's forehead and hands in the form of a cross. The sacrament is a sign of the love and care that God and the Church have for people who are sick.

Annunciation
When the angel Gabriel told Mary that she was to be the mother of the Messiah.

Ash Wednesday
The first day of the season of Lent in many Christian Churches. At the liturgy on Ash Wednesday ashes are blessed and marked on the foreheads of the people in the form of a cross. This is a reminder that they have turned away from sin and are trying to live the Christian life well.

Assumption
Assumption is the term for the taking of the body and soul of Mary, by God, into glory.

Baptism
One of seven sacraments that takes away original sin and actual sin.

Bishop
The bishop is the head of a diocese, successor of the apostles.

Blessed Sacrament
The elements of the communion supper (bread and wine), which become the body and blood of Christ. It is offered at the altar in the church.

Canon Law
The Official collection of Church laws for the Roman Church. It was revised and updated in accordance with the teachings of the Second Vatican Council. The revised form was published in 1983.

Capital sins
The seven causes of all sin: pride, covetousness, lust, anger, gluttony, envy, sloth.

Cardinal
Priest or bishop appointed to the highest-ranking Church office under the pope. The Sacred College of Cardinals assists the pope with important issues and is also responsible for electing the pope.

Celebrant
Bishops, priests and deacons who preside at the Eucharist and other sacraments. In a real sense, all the people present are celebrants because they all take part in the celebration.

Celibacy
The state of being unmarried: Roman Catholic priests and religious, take a vow of celibacy as a sign of special dedication to service and the reign of God.

Chalice
A cup usually supported on a stem and base, and holding the wine to be consecrated at Mass. The chalice is considered sacred and so is crafted, selected and handled accordingly.

Confession
The act of telling sins to a priest who then pronounces the Lord's forgiveness to the sinner.

Confessional
A small compartment where the priest hears the confessed sins of a sinner.

Confirmation
A ceremony performed by a bishop that is supposed to strengthen a person and enable him to resist sin. This usually takes place at the age of twelve. The Bishop dips his right thumb in holy oil and anoints the person on the forehead by making the sign of the cross and says, "Be sealed with the gift of the Holy Spirit."

Consecration
A moment during the ceremony of the mass when God, allegedly through the priest,

changes bread and wine into the body and blood of Jesus.

Contrition
Extreme sorrow for having sinned with a deep repentance concerning that sin.

Diocese
An area of many parishes presided over by a bishop.

Encyclical
A letter addressed by the pope to all the bishops and people of the Church.

Extreme Unction
A sacrament given to a person who is ill or in danger of dying. It is intended to strengthen the souls of those anointed and help to make their love pure so they may enter into heaven. It is done through prayer and the anointing of oil. This sacrament is also known as Anointing of the Sick or the Sacrament of the Sick.

Guardian Angel
A special angel assigned by God to each person in order to protect and guide that person with the goal of reaching heaven.

Habitual grace
The permanent disposition to live and act in keeping with God's call.

Heresy
The denial of the truths found in the Catholic Church.

Holy Chrism
The special oil used in the sacraments of Baptism, Confirmation, and Holy Orders.

Holy Orders
One of the seven sacraments by which men, bishop, deacons, and priests, are given the power and authority by a bishop to offer sacrifice and forgive sins.

Holy See
A see is the area or diocese ruled by a bishop. The Holy See is the diocese of the pope as bishop of Rome.

Holy Water
Special water that has been blessed by a priest, bishop, etc. or a liturgical ceremony. It is used to bring a blessing to a person when applied.

Host
The bread in the communion supper that is changed into the body of Christ.

Immaculate Conception
The teaching that Mary was conceived without original sin.

Indulgence
A means by which the Catholic church takes away some of the punishment due the Christian in this life and/or purgatory because of his sin.

Laity
The members of the Church who are not ordained.

Lent
A forty-day period between Ash Wednesday and Easter Sunday. Usually it is accompanied by some form of prayer and fasting.

Liturgy
The prayers, readings and music that form a public act of worship.

Mass
A reenactment of the sacrifice of Christ on the cross. This ceremony is symbolically carried out by the priest and involves the prayer of Consecration when the bread and wine are changed into the body and blood of Jesus.

Monstrance
An ornamental receptacle, often silver or gold, which holds the consecrated host for the adoration of the people.

Mortal Sin
A serious and willful transgression of God's law. It involves full knowledge and intent of the will to commit the sin. If left unrepentant, mortal sin damns someone to eternal hell.

Original Sin
The inherited sin nature of Adam that resulted from Adam's sin.

Parish
A subdivision of a diocese with the priest as its head.

Passion
The sufferings of Christ from the time of the Last Supper to his crucifixion.

Penance
A means by which all sins committed after baptism are removed. The means are assigned by a priest and usually consist of special prayers or deeds performed by the sinner.

Pope
Christ's representative on earth. The term was used from early times for the Bishop of Rome. The pope is the visible successor of Peter, who was the first pope. The word comes from the Greek word *papa* meaning "father."

Priest
One who mediates between God and man and administers the sacraments and graces of God. He has received the Holy Orders.

Purgatory
A place of temporary punishment where Christians are cleansed from sin before they can enter into heaven.

Relic
A part of the body of a saint or the saint's clothing, jewelry, etc. Because of its association with the saint, the relic is considered holy.

Rosary
The rosary is used as an aid in praying. It consists of string of beads containing five sets of ten small beads, each set of ten being separated by another bead. It also contains a crucifix. The beads on the rosary are used to count prayers as they are said to Mary.

Sacrament
An outward sign instituted by Christ to give grace.

Sacramentals
Special prayers, deeds, or objects used to gain spiritual benefits from God.

Sanctifying grace
A stable and supernatural disposition that perfects the soul itself to enable it to live with God, to act by his love.

Saint
A very holy person, usually someone who has been dead for many years and has been canonized by the Catholic Church. Saints do not have to pass through purgatory.

Sign of the cross
The movement of the right hand from the forehead to the chest and then left and right upon the shoulders.

Tabernacle
A fixed, suitably adorned and solid place in a church in which the Blessed Sacrament is kept.

Tradition
The handing down through the centuries of the teachings of Jesus. It began with the apostles and continues unbroken to the present bishopric of the Catholic Church.

Transubstantiation
The teaching that the bread and wine in the communion supper become the body and blood of the Lord Jesus at the Consecration during the Mass.

Vatican
Center of Roman Catholicism. Located within the City of Rome and containing the Basilica of St Peter, it is the world's smallest country.

Venerate
To honor, admire, and regard with respect.

Venial sin
A venial sin is a sin that, though not as serious as a mortal sin, nevertheless lessens the grace of God within a person's soul.

Vicar of Christ
The pope.

5 QUOTATIONS

Many who confess their venial sins out of custom and concern for order but without thought of amendment remain burdened with them for their whole life and thus lose many spiritual benefits and advantages.
Francis de Sales

If you say the Rosary faithfully until death, I do assure you that, in spite of the gravity of your sins "you shall receive a never-fading crown of glory."
St Louis de Montfort

Prayer is powerful beyond limits when we turn to the Immaculata who is queen even of God's heart.
Maximillian Kolbe

Peace begins with a smile.
Mother Teresa of Calcutta

. . . evangelical Protestants surely have more in common with charismatic Catholics than with any other type of Catholics.
J.I. Packer

On 31st July 1998 at a meeting in Dublin J.I. Packer referred to John Paul II as "a fine *Christian man".*

Trust the Church of God implicitly even when your natural judgment would take a different course from hers and would induce you to question her prudence or correctness. Recollect what a hard task she has; how she is

sure to be criticized and spoken against, whatever she does; recollect how much she needs your loyal and tender devotion; recollect, too, how long is the experience gained over so many centuries, and what a right she has to claim your assent to principles which have had so extended and triumphant a trial. Thank her that she has kept the faith safe for so many generations and do your part in helping her to transmit it to generations after you.
John Henry Newman

We believe that the Word became flesh and that we receive his flesh in the Lord's Supper. How then can we fail to believe that he really dwells within us?...In the sacrament of his body he actually gives us his own flesh, which he has united to his divinity.
Saint Hilary

That anyone could doubt the right of the holy Virgin to be called the Mother of God fills me with astonishment.
St. Cyril of Alexandria

We are no longer to look upon the bread and wine as earthly substances. They have become heavenly, because Christ has passed into them and changed them into his body and blood. What you receive is the body of him who is the heavenly bread, and the blood of him who is the sacred vine; for when he offered his disciples the consecrated bread and wine, he said: This is my body, this is my blood. We have put our trust in him. I urge you to have faith in him; truth can never deceive.
Saint Gaudentius of Brescia

About Jesus Christ and the Church, I simply know they're just one thing, and we shouldn't complicate the matter.
St. Joan of Arc

Comfort in tribulation can be secured only on the sure ground of faith holding as true the words of Scripture and the teaching of the Catholic Church.
St. Thomas More

Holy Communion is the shortest and safest way to heaven.
Pope St. Pius X

There are not over a 100 people in the U.S. that hate the Catholic Church, there are millions however, who hate what they wrongly believe to be the Catholic Church, which is, of course, quite a different thing.
Fulton J. Sheen

Do not abandon yourselves to despair. We are the Easter people and hallelujah is our song.
Pope John Paul II

When you look at the Crucifix, you understand how much Jesus loved you then. When you look at the Sacred Host you understand how much Jesus loves you now.
Mother Teresa of Calcutta

The Catholic faith never changes. But the language and mode of manifesting this one faith can change according to peoples, times and places.
Francis Arinze

Vatican II declares the Church as necessary for salvation.
Francis Arinze

One cannot believe in Christ without believing in the Church, the Body of Christ. Be faithful, then, to your faith without falling into the dangerous illusion of separating Christ from his Church. The fidelity promised to Christ can never be separated from fidelity to the Church:
"He who hears you, hears Me:! (Lk 10:16)"
Pope John Paul II, Address to the theologians of Spain, Dec. 20 1982

One is the Baptism which the Church administers, the Baptism of water and the Holy Ghost, with which catechumens need to be baptized.
Thomas Aquinas, Exposition on Psalm 118

Since without the Faith it is impossible to please God, no one is justified without it, nor will anyone attain eternal life unless he perseveres to the end in it.
Vatican I

I am not the Catholic candidate for President. I am the Democratic Party's candidate for President, who happens also to be a Catholic.
John F. Kennedy

The principal end both of my father and of myself in the conquest of India... has been the propagation of the holy Catholic faith.
Ignatius Loyola

I like most that I belong to the whole universal comprehensive Catholic church and that it is not just a national church.
Hans Kung

In the Church, priests also are sinners. But I am personally convinced that the constant presence in the press of the sins of Catholic priests, especially in the United States, is a planned campaign, as the percentage of these offenses among priests is not higher than in other categories, and perhaps it is even lower.
Joseph Ratzinger

At its best, the Catholic tradition can claim that it has sufficient joy and gratitude and confidence in its understanding to know that it is not going to be undermined or rubbished by other perspectives, but rather be enriched and illuminated by them.
Rowan Williams

I am not a Catholic; but I consider the Christian idea, which has its roots in Greek thought and in the course of the centuries has nourished all of our European civilization, as something that one cannot renounce without becoming degraded.
Simone Weil

I hope that by going to visit the pope I have enabled everybody to see that the words Catholic and Protestant, as ordinarily used, are completely out of date. They are almost always used now purely for propaganda purposes. That is why so much trouble is caused by them.
Geoffrey Fisher

The truth of our faith becomes a matter of ridicule among the infidels if any Catholic, not gifted with the necessary scientific learning, presents as dogma what scientific scrutiny shows to be false.
Saint Thomas Aquinas

The death of Pope John Paul II led many of different faiths and of no faith to acknowledge their debt to the Roman Catholic Church for holding on to absolutes that the rest of us can measure ourselves against.
Suzanne Fields

Islam

CONTENTS

1 An overview   99

2 Islam's founder   100

3 Islam's holy book   103

4 Facts and figures   114

5 Islamic practices   115

6 Islamic beliefs   117

7 Islamic worship   121

8 Groupings within Islam   122

9 Comparison of Islam with Christianity   124

10 Glossary   126

1 AN OVERVIEW

DEFINITION

Islam means submission and peace.

The word "Islam" is derived from the Arabic root *salaama*, which may be translated as peace, purity, submission (to God) and obedience.

Islam means submission to and obedience to God's will and God's law.

The religion of Muslims was revealed through Muhammad, the Prophet of Allah.

Factfile
- Date of origin: seventh century AD
- Founder: the Prophet Muhammad
- Holy book: Qur'an
- Number of adherents: more than 1,200 million

SUMMARY

Islam is the fastest growing world religion with over 1 billion adherents.

Islam stands for complete surrender and obedience to Allah (Allah is the Arabic name for God).

Islam claims to be a unique religion. Whereas Judaism takes its name from the tribe of Judah, Christianity from Jesus Christ, Buddhism from Buddha and Hinduism from the Indus River, Muslims derive their identity from the message of Islam. The message of Islam is even more important than the person of Muhammad. Muslims are not "Muhammadans" and should never be called by that name.

Strictly speaking, it is not possible to give any start date to the origin of Islam, as the above factfile does, for Muslims believe that Islam is a faith that has always existed.

Islam is more than a religion. It is a complete way of life in which Muslims follow the way of peace, mercy, and forgiveness.

SUMMARY OF PRACTICES

Islam is built on Five Pillars. The five pillars of Islam are:

Shahada
Salat
Saum
Zakat
Hajj

The first pillar, *shahada,* is a state of faith and the other four pillars are major exercises of faith which have to be performed on either a daily, weekly, monthly, or annual basis. The last one, *hajj,* has to be undertaken once in a lifetime.

The Five Pillars of Islam are the five obligations that every Muslim must satisfy in order to live a good and responsible life according to Islam.

- *Shahadah* is the sincere reciting of the Muslim profession of faith.
- *Salat* is the performing of ritual prayers five times each day.
- *Sawm* is fasting during the month of Ramadan.
- *Zakat* is paying a charity tax to the poor.
- *Hajj* is going on pilgrimage to Mecca.

These Five Pillars provide the framework for the lives of all Muslims, and direct their everyday activities and beliefs.

SUMMARY OF BELIEFS

Islam is one of the three great monotheistic faiths.

Muslims believe that submission to the good will of Allah, together with obedience to his beneficial law, bring peace and harmony. The Muslim creed consists of five articles of faith:

- belief in one God
- in the revealed books
- in angels
- in the prophets
- in the Day of Judgment

ALLAH

Muslims believe that there is only one God, called Allah.

Faith in the unity of God is expressed in the primary profession of faith: "There is no deity but Allah" (*la ilaha illallah*). Muslims believe in One, Unique, Incomparable God. He has no partner, and no equal.   God brought creation into being by his word "Be." He is everywhere, but lives in nothing. He is just and merciful. He is also a personal God, close to each believer, answering their prayers, and showing them "the straight path." God is "nearer to man than his jugular vein" (chapter 50:16).

QUR'AN

This is Allah's last and complete book. It is the true word of God, as revealed to Muhammad.

ANGELS

Angels were created by Allah.

PROPHETS

The prophets brought Allah's revelations to humankind.

DAY OF JUDGMENT

On the day of judgment individuals will be accountable for their actions.

---

2 ISLAM'S FOUNDER

A The importance of Muhammad
B Chronological table of the life of Muhammad
C Muhammad's life
D Sayings of the Prophet Muhammad
E The first four caliphs

A THE IMPORTANCE OF MUHAMMAD

It is hard to overestimate the importance of the Prophet Muhammad.
Muslims believe that:

- He is a true prophet of God.
- His teachings are absolutely perfect, and error free.
- He is God's last prophet.

B CHRONOLOGICAL TABLE OF THE LIFE OF MUHAMMAD

570	Birth of Muhammad
576	Death of his mother Aminah
595	Marriage to Khadijah
610	Beginning of Muhammad's call
622	The Hijra (Flight or Migration) of Muhammad and his followers to Medina

632   Muhammad's farewell pilgrimage
       to Mecca
632   June 8, death of Muhammad, three
       months after his return to Medina

C MUHAMMAD'S LIFE
BIRTH AND EARLY LIFE
Muhammad was born in Mecca, in Saudi
Arabia, in AD 570. His father died before he
was born and his mother died when he was
six. He never went to school but was raised
by a nurse and then by his grandfather and,
upon his grandfather's death, by his uncle.
He became a merchant. A wealthy woman,
Khadijah, was so impressed by him that she
offered to marry him. They had two sons,
who died young, and four daughters. After
his early poverty, Muhammad was now rich,
but material comfort did not satisfy him.

THE ANGEL GABRIEL
Muhammad, a spiritual man, often meditated
on Mount Hira, near the summit of Jabal al-
Nur, the "Mountain of Light." In AD 610,
when he was forty years old, he went to
Mount Hira to pray and meditate. When he
was asleep in a cave, he had a vision of the
angel Gabriel, who gave him a message from
God, and urged him to read the words on a
piece of material, which he was unable to do
as he could not read or write.

When Muhammad woke, he heard a
voice from heaven saying, "You are the
Messenger of God." This marked the
beginning of his life as a messenger, or
Prophet, of God.

It is said that Muhammad was at first
disturbed by this experience, but was
reassured by his wife. For the rest of his life
until his death Muhammad received
"revelations" at frequent intervals. There was
normally no vision, and it appears he never
again heard a voice. Instead he was aware of a
verbal message in his conscious mind.

PREACHER
Muhammad understood that God had
appointed him to be his messenger and so he
became a preacher. At that time the people of
Mecca believed in many gods but

Muhammad had a simple message: There is
no God but Allah. Life must be lived in
complete submission to the will of Allah. You
must believe in the power and love of God,
and show your worship of God by generosity
to those in need. There will be a resurrection
of the dead and a judgment day.

Many listened to Muhammad and
became his followers.

THE HIJRAH
But Muhammad's popularity was viewed as a
threat by the rulers in Mecca and Muhammad
and his followers were persecuted, though
there was little or no physical violence.

In June 622, after the death, in 619, of
his wife, and, at about the same time, of his
uncle who had protected him, Muhammad
encouraged his followers to leave Mecca and
travel in small groups to Medina, 260 miles
to the north, where twelve of his followers
were already living. Muhammad himself,
with his chief lieutenant, slipped away
secretly, to avoid a plot to capture him,
arriving in Medina on September 24, 622.
Altogether, about seventy people made this
journey, which became known as the
"emigration" or *Hijrah,* a word meaning the
severing of kinship ties. It is at this point that
Islamic history begins: the Islamic era begins
on June 16, 622, the day when the *Hijrah*
began.

ISLAM SPREADS
In Medina, after a short period of settling
down, Muhammad and his Muslim
supporters gained in strength by making
armed raids on wealthy caravans traveling to
and from Mecca (armed raids were frequent
among Arabs in those days), by judicious
marriage relationships and by making
alliances with nomadic Arabic tribes. He also
broke with the Jews, making Islam an Arabic
faith, and expelled the wealthy Jewish clan
who ran the market. The Muslims were now a
political power.

Muhammad overcame all opposition in
Medina, and made armed raids on Mecca,
where he began to have many supporters. In
630, with an army of 10,000 men, he marched

against the town. A deputation of the leading citizens of Mecca went out to meet him, and formally submitted to him. There was virtually no resistance, and he pronounced an amnesty. With his enthusiastic followers and the support of most of the people of Mecca, he cleared the town of all pagan idols and images, announcing the beginning of a new age and the worship of Allah. Muhammad was accepted as Allah's true and final Prophet and Islam was established.

Muhammad died in Medina in June 632.

Before Muhammad died, aged 63, most of Arabia had embraced the Muslim faith. Within one hundred years of Muhammad's death it had spread far and wide, to Spain in the west and to China in the east.

When Muhammad was alive he was loved and respected for his courage, fairness, gentleness, especially with children, and also for his personal charm, his devotion to God, and mystical outlook.

MUHAMMAD'S MOSQUE IN MEDINA

Muhammad's grave lies in Medina, the second most revered place of worship for Muslims. While pilgrimage to Medina is not mandatory, it is very popular.

When Muhammad migrated from Mecca in 622 he went to the town of Yathrib. Yathrib became known as Al-Madinah an-Nabi, or "City of the Prophet". Today it is called Medina (Arabic Al-Madinah)

According to tradition, the citing of the mosque at Madinah was determined by the place where Muhammad's camel stopped after Muhammad had let it loose. Muhammad was buried in the mosque and it remained the headquarters of the Islamic state under the first four caliphs (Islamic civil and religious leaders). Today's mosque is more than a hundred times as large as the one Muhammad built and can accommodate as many as half a million worshipers at any one time.

D SAYINGS OF THE PROPHET MUHAMMAD

Anger

> Powerful is not he who knocks the other down, indeed powerful is he who controls himself in a fit of anger.

Animals

> A man walking along a path felt very thirsty. Reaching a well, he descended into it, drank his fill, and came up. Then he saw a dog with its tongue hanging out, trying to lick up mud to quench its thirst. The man said, "This dog is feeling the same thirst that I felt." So he went down into the well again, filled his shoe with water, and gave the dog a drink. So, God thanked him and forgave his sins.

> The Prophet was asked, "Messenger of God, are we rewarded for kindness towards animals?"

> He said: There is a reward for kindness to every living animal or human.

Belief, true belief

> None of you truly believes until he wishes for his brother what he wishes for himself.

Believers are like a body

> The believers, in their love, mercy, and kindness to one another are like a body: if any part of it is ill, the whole body shares its sleeplessness and fever.

Believers, false believers

> He who eats his fill while his neighbor goes without food is not a believer.

Charity

> A good word is charity.

Employers

> Pay the worker his wage before his sweat dries.

Heart-judgment (God judges the heart)

> God does not judge you according to your appearance and your wealth, but he looks at your hearts and looks into your deeds.

Love for your brother
> None of you believes (completely)
> until he loves for his brother what
> he loves for himself.

Merciful, the
> The merciful are shown mercy by
> the All-Merciful. Show mercy to
> those on earth, and God will show
> mercy to you.

Mercy, no mercy
> God has no mercy on one who has
> no mercy for others.

Morals
> The most perfect of the believers in
> faith are the best of them in morals.
> And the best among them are those
> who are best to their wives.

Neighbors
> Whoever believes in God and the
> Last Day (the Day of Judgment)
> should do good to his neighbor.

Smiling
> Smiling at your brother is charity.

E THE FIRST FOUR CALIPHS
After Muhammad's death, the role of the
leadership of Islam passed to four people
known as "the four righteous caliphs."

- Abu Bakr, the first caliph, 632-34
- 'Umar, the second caliph, 634-644
- 'Uthman, the third caliph, 644-656
- 'Ali, the fourth caliph, 656-61

These first four caliphs are considered to be
the only caliphs who preserved the true
tradition of Muhammad.

3 ISLAM'S HOLY BOOK

A   Origin
B   Muslims and the Qur'an
C   Form
D   Selected quotations
E   Translations
F   Martin Luther's assessment of the Qur'an
G   Other authorities

INTRODUCTION
The Qur'an (Arabic, al-Qur'an, also spelled
Koran) is the chief sacred text of Islam.

The word Qur'an means something
"read" or "recited."

Three of the most important themes in
the Qur'an are:

- The oneness of Allah
- Allah's messengers
- Life after death

The Qur'an's basic message is that there is only one God, the creator of everything, who alone must be served by correct worship and behavior.

A ORIGIN

Muhammad was given a series of revelations from Allah while he was a prophet in Mecca and Medina.

The first of these revelations came while Muhammad was meditating in a cave on Mt. Hirah, now called Mount Jabal Nur.

The complete contents of the Qur'an were revealed to Muhammad by the angel Gabriel over twenty-three years, between 610 and 632. As he could neither read nor write he memorized these revelations and repeated them to his followers who memorized some of them and wrote others down in Arabic word for word exactly as Muhammad had dictated them.

According to tradition, some of the revelations were written on palm leaves, others on stones, or on bones. After Muhammad's death, the first caliph ordered Muhammad's secretary to collect and arrange these writings. When this work was completed, all other copies were destroyed. Consequently, all Muslims use the same version of the Qur'an.

B MUSLIMS AND THE QUR'AN

- For Muslims, every word in the Qur'an is the actual, literal word of Allah: it is not the word of Muhammad to whom it was given.
- It was the work of one man.
- It is the most influential Book ever written by one person.
- The Qur'an is listened to more than any other book. It is used extensively in public worship, in schools, in individual worship, private study and reading.
  In daily prayers, passages are recited from memory, preeminently chapter 1, which is repeated over and over during the five periods of daily prayer. Many Muslims know the whole Qur'an by heart, though it is almost as long as the New Testament.

- The Qur'an has never been altered since it was originally given.
- Muslim's base their faith and behavior on the Qur'an.
- It is believed that the Qur'an is a perfect transcription of an eternal tablet, kept in heaven.

ALLAH'S WORD
Muslims believe that the Qur'an is Allah's word. He literally spoke it to Gabriel, who conveyed it to Muhammad:

> Say (O Muhammad) "the Holy Spirit has brought it down from your Lord in truth."
>
> *16:102*

> Truly it is the revelation of the Lord of the world brought down upon your heart by the Faithful Spirit so that you may be one of the warners, in a clear Arabic tongue.
>
> *26:192-95*

FREE FROM CONTRADICTIONS
Muslims believe that the Qur'an is "Allah's book" and is free from any contradictions:

> Do they not ponder over the Qur'an? If it had been from other than Allah, surely they would have found in it a lot of differences.
>
> *4: 82*

C FORM

- It has 114 chapters (*surahs).*
- The chapters are divided in verses (*ayat*), of which there are 6,000 altogether.
- They are written in beautiful, rhythmic Arabic prose.
- The chapters are not arranged in the order in which they were revealed, nor according to theme, but as a general rule according to length, the longest at the beginning (the most notable exception being chapter 1, which is short).
- All the *surahs* except number 9 start with the words, "In the name of God, the Merciful, the Compassionate."

D SELECTED QUOTATIONS FROM THE QUR'AN

(i)   God's help during troubles
(ii)   Doing Good
(iii) Faith
(iv)   Forgiveness
(v)   God's power and awareness
(vi)   Guidance
(vii) Conversion and other faiths
(viii) Prayer
(ix)   Thankfulness
(x)   Paradise, resurrection, reward

(I) GOD'S HELP DURING TROUBLES

And We will most certainly try you . . . but give good news to those who endure with patience, who, when a misfortune befalls them, say: "Surely we belong to God and to God we shall surely return." Those are they on whom are blessings and mercy from their Lord.

2.155-157

God does not impose upon any soul more than it can bear.

2.286a

Our Lord, do not punish us if we forget or make a mistake; Our Lord, do not lay on us a burden as was laid on those before us; Our Lord, do not impose upon us that which we have not the strength to bear; and pardon us and grant us protection and have mercy on us, You alone are our Protector.

2.286c

Then after sorrow He sent down peace upon you, a calm coming upon some... saying, "Surely all is in the hands of God."

3.154

Believers, be patient and never allow your patience to be fully exhausted. Stand firm in your faith and fear God, so that you may triumph.

3.200

So Moses watered their sheep for them, then went back to the shade and prayed, "My Lord, surely I stand in need of the blessing which you have sent to me."

28.24

Therefore be patient; surely the promise of God is true; do not allow those who have doubts drive you to despair.

30.60

Therefore be patient; God's promise is true. Ask forgiveness for your faults and sing the praise of your Lord in the evening and the morning.

40.55

If Satan should cause you mischief, seek refuge in God; for truly He is the all hearing and the all knowing."

41.36

To endure with patience and to forgive is the duty of all. These most truly are deeds of courage.

42.43

Believers, if you help God, God will help you, and make you to stand strong.

47.7

[48.1] Surely We have given to you a clear victory that God may forgive your past sins and those in the future, and make complete His favor to you, and guide you on the right way; [48.3] that God might help you with a mighty help. [48.4] It is God who sent down tranquility into the hearts of the believers so that they might have more faith added to their faith.

48.1-4

We created mankind, and We know how mankind thinks. We are nearer to you than your neck vein!

50.16

[70.3] God is the Lord of the heavenly ladders, [70.4] and to Him the angels and the Spirit will ascend in a day; though the measure of a day may be fifty thousand years. [70.5] Therefore, endure with a goodly patience. [70.6] They believe the Day to be far off, [70.7] but We see it near.

70.3-7

[73.8] And remember the name of your Lord and devote yourself to Him with full devotion. [73.9] The Lord of the East and the West, there is no god but Him. Therefore take Him for your protector."

73.8-9

For every soul there is a guardian watching over it.

86.4

[94.6] Surely after every difficulty comes ease.
[94.7] So when you are free from your burden, remember God's name [94.8] And seek your Lord with fervor.

94.5-8

[114.1] Say: I seek refuge in the Lord of humanity, [114.2] the King of humanity, [114.3] the God of humanity, [114.4] from the evil of the whisperings of the Tempter [114.5] who whispers into the hearts [114.6] of jinn and mankind.

114.1-6

(II) DOING GOOD

Righteousness does not consist of whether you turn your faces towards the East or the West, but righteousness is this: that one should believe in God and the last day and the angels and the Scripture and the prophets, and give away wealth out of love for God to the near of kin and the orphans and the needy and the wayfarer and the beggars and for the freedom of the captives, and keep up prayer and pay the poor-rate; and the performers of their promise when they make a promise, and the patient in distress and affliction and in time of conflicts - these are they who are true and these are they who are vigilant.

2.177

God loves the charitable and the doers of good.

2.195

A kind word with forgiveness is better than charity followed by an insult; Remember, God is self-sufficient and charitable.

2.263

O Believers! Be upright for God, and bear true witness. Do not let your hatred of a people to turn you away from justice. Deal justly, for justice is nearer to true piety. And fear God; for God is aware of all you do.

5.8

According to Jewish tradition . . . whoever kills a human life . . . it is as though he killed all mankind; and whoever saves a life, it is as though he saved all mankind.

5.32

Surely those who believe and those who are Jews and the Sabians and the Christians, whoever believes in God and the last day and does good - they shall have no fear nor shall they grieve.

5.69

Whoever does a good deed, he shall be repaid ten-fold; and whoever does evil, he shall be repaid with evil.

6.160

O children of Adam! Dress well when you attend to prayer at the mosque; and eat and drink but be not overindulgent; surely He does not love those who do not practice moderation.

7.31

[7.199] Show forgiveness, speak for justice, and turn aside from the ignorant. [7.200] And if Stan tempts you, seek refuge in God; For He hears and knows all.

7.199-200

Keep up your prayers in the morning and evening, and in the night; surely good deeds make amends for sins. This is a reminder to the thoughtful. [11.115] And be patient, for surely God does not waste the reward of the doers of good deeds.

11.114-115

Repel evil with good.

23.96

They will be granted double their reward, because they are faithful and they repaid evil with good, and gave alms out of what We have given them. [28.55] And when they hear slander against them, they turn aside from it and say: "We shall have our deeds and you shall have your deeds. Peace be on you, we do not desire the company of the uninformed.

28.54

[31.16] (Luqman the Wise did say,) "My child, God will bring all things to light, even if it is as small as the grain of a mustard seed, even though they are hidden in the heart of a rock, or high above in the heavens or deep down in the earth. For God is Knower of all things, aware of all. [31.17] My child, attend to prayer and enjoin justice and forbid evil. Endure patiently whatever befalls you with the courage within you. [31.18] And do not turn your face away from people in contempt, nor strut yourself proudly; surely God does not love any self-conceited bragger. [31.19]Walk in humility and keep your voice low and steady; for surely the worst sounding voice is the braying of jack-asses."

31.16-19

[90.8] Have We not given mankind two eyes, [90.9] And a tongue with two lips, [90.10] and pointed out to them the two paths? [90.11] But they would not attempt the higher path. [90.12] And what will make you understand what the higher path is? [90.13] It is the setting free of a slave, [90.14] or the giving of food in a day of hunger [90.15] to an orphan, having relationship [90.16] with the poor man lying in distress. [90.17] It is to have faith and charge one another to be patient and show compassion. [90.18] These are the people of God's right hand.

90.8-18

[92.5] For the one who is charitable and guards against evil, [92.6] and believes in the good, [92.7] We will smooth for him the path of salvation.

92.5-92.7

[93.4] And surely the life that comes after is better for you than that which has gone before. [93.5] And soon you shall be pleased with what your Lord will give you. [93.6] Did He not find you an orphan and give you shelter? [93.7] And find you in error and guide you? [93.8] And find you in want and enrich you? [93.9] Therefore, do not oppress the orphan; [93.10] And as for him who begs from you, do not chide him. [93.11] But proclaim the favor of your Lord to all.

93.4-93.11

[99.6] On the Day of Judgment all mankind will come in humility to be shown their works. [99.7] And the one who has done an atom's weight of good shall see it [99.8] and the one who has done an atom's weight of evil shall see it also.

99.6-8

[107.1] Considered the person who calls God's Judgment Day a lie: [107.2] That is the one who treats the orphan with harshness, [107.3] And does not urge others to feed the poor. [107.4] Woe to the praying ones, [107.5] who are heedless in their prayers, [107.6] who do good to be seen, [107.7] but withhold the necessities of life from the needy.

107.1-7

(III) FAITH

[16.68] Your Lord revealed to the bee, saying: "Build your hives in the mountains and in the trees and in what mankind builds: [16.69] Partake of every kind of fruit and walk in the ways of your Lord submissively." There comes forth from the bee's belly a beverage of many colors, in which there is a healing drink for mankind; most surely there is a sign in this for a people who would give thought.

16.68-69

And it is God who made the night a covering for you, and the sleep a rest, and made the morning a resurrection to you.

25.47

[25.61] Blessed is the One who made the constellations in the heavens and set up a lamp and a shining moon. [25.62] It is God who made the night and the day to follow each other for him who desires to be mindful and chooses to be thankful.

25.61-62

The life of this world is nothing but a sport and a pastime; and as for the life to come, that is the true life - if they but knew it!

29.64

And one of God's signs is that He created mates for you from among yourselves that you may find joy together; and God put love and compassion in your hearts; most surely there are signs in this for people who reflect.

30.21

Whoever submits himself wholly to God and does good deeds to others, stands on the firmest ground; for to God all things will return.
31.22

. . . Say: God is sufficient for me; on Him do the faithful rely. [39.39] Say: O my people! Do as best you can, and so will I.
39.38-39

[39.61]God will deliver those who fear Him, for salvation is theirs. Evil shall not touch them, nor shall they grieve. [39.62] God is the Creator of all things and over all things is the Guardian. [39.63] His are the treasures of the heavens and the earth.

39.61-63

O Humanity! Surely We have created you male and female, and made you into tribes and families that you may know

each other. The most honorable of you with God is the one among you who fears God most; surely God is all-knowing and wise.

49.13

We created mankind, and We know how mankind thinks. We are nearer to you than your neck vein!

50.16

[73.8] And remember the name of your Lord and devote yourself to Him with full devotion. [73.9] The Lord of the East and the West, there is no God but Him. Therefore take Him for your protector.

73.8-9

[74.54] This is surely an admonition. [74.55] So whoever will take warning. [74.56] None will heed unless God please. For God is the source of goodness and forgiveness.

74.54-56

[81.27] This is a warning to all, [81.28] for those among you who desire the straight path. [81.29] And you can only will it, if God wills, the Lord of the Universe.

81.27-29

(IV) FORGIVENESS

Pardon and forgive, and wait until God makes his will known; for God has power over all things.

2.109

Whoever does evil or wrongs his own soul, then asks forgiveness of God, he shall find God forgiving and merciful.

4.110

O Believers! If you fear God, He will guide you and take away with your sins and forgive you; for God is the Lord of mighty grace.

8.29

Seek forgiveness of your Lord, then turn to Him; He will provide you with a goodly provision for the appointed day and bestow His grace on the righteous;

and if you give no heed, then beware of the chastisement to come. [11.4] To God you will return; He has power over all things.

11.3-4

. . . Is there doubt about God, the Maker of the heavens and the earth? He invites you to Him to forgive your sins and to reprieve you until the appointed time.

14.10

[25.70] If the sinner repents and believes and does good; for him God changes their evil deeds to good ones; for God is forgiving and merciful. [25.71] Whoever repents and does good, he surely turns to God.

25.70-71

Moses said: "My Lord, forgive me, for surely I have sinned against my own soul." So God forgave him; surely God is forgiving and merciful.

28.16

To endure with patience and to forgive is the duty of all. These most truly are deeds of courage.

42.43

Surely We have given to you a clear victory [48.2] that God may forgive your past sins and those in the future, and make complete His favor to you ,and guide you on the right way; [48.3] that God might help you with a mighty help. [48.4] It is God who sent down tranquility into the hearts of the believers so that they might have more faith added to their faith.

48.1-4

Those who restrain themselves from the greatest of sins and wickedness, except the unwilled offenses, shall find the Lord full of mercy. God is fully aware of you, from the time He created you from dust, and when you were hidden in the wombs of your mothers. Therefore do not pretend to be pure, for He is completely aware of those who guard against evil.

53.32

Believers, fear God and believe in His messenger. And He will give you a double portion of His mercy, and make for you a light with which you can walk. And God will forgive you, for God is forgiving and merciful.

57.28

[74.54] This is surely an admonition. [74.55] So whoever will take warning. [74.56] None will heed unless God please. For God is the source of goodness and forgiveness."

74.54-56

(V) GOD'S POWER AND AWARENESS
It is God who has created the heavens and the earth with truth. And on the day He says: Be, it is. His word is the truth, and His is the kingdom on the day when the trumpet shall be blown; the Knower of the unseen and the seen; and He is the Wise, All-knowing.

6.73

No mortal eye sees him, though He sees all eyes; He is Benignant and All-knowing.

6.103

. . . Lord is the Knower of all the unseen - not the weight of an atom in the heavens or earth escapes Him . . .

34.3

. . . There is nothing in the heaven or earth beyond the power of God; surely He is all knowing and most powerful.

35.44

[57.1] All that is in the heavens and the earth gives glory to God. He is the Mighty and Wise. [57.2] His is the kingdom of the heavens and the earth; He gives life and causes death; and He has power over all things. [57.3] He is the First and the Last, the Knower of all hidden things, and He is aware of all. [57.4] It is God who created the heavens and the earth in six

days. He is firm in power. He knows all that goes into the earth and all that comes out of it; all that comes down from heaven and all that goes up into it. He is with you wherever you are. God sees all that you do. [57.5] His is the kingdom of the heavens and the earth; and to God will all things returned. [57.6] He causes the night to enter in upon the day, and causes the day to enter in upon the night, and He is aware of what is in all hearts.
57.1-6

[58.6] . . . God is a witness of all things. [58.7] Do you not realize that God knows whatever is in the heavens and the earth? Nowhere is there a secret meeting between three persons but He is the fourth of them; nor a meeting of five but He is the sixth of them; nor less than that, nor more, but He is with them wherever they are. Then on the day of resurrection, God will inform them of what they did. Surely God is aware of all things.
58.6-7

[59.22] He is God, besides whom there is no other; the Knower of the unseen and the seen; the Beneficent, the Merciful. [59.23] He is God, besides whom there is no other; the King, the Holy, the Giver of peace, the Granter of security, Guardian over all, the Mighty, the Supreme, the Possessor of every greatness. Glory be to God above all idols. [59.24] He is God the Creator, the Maker, the Fashioner; Most excellent are God's names; all that is in the heavens and the earth gives Him glory; and He is the Mighty, the Wise.
59.22-24

[85.12] Surely the might of your Lord is great. [85.13] Surely it is He who creates and recreates. [85.14] And He is the Forgiving, the Loving, [85.15] Lord of the glorious throne, [85.16] The great doer of what He will.
85.12-15

(VI) GUIDANCE
[5.15b] There has come to you light and a clear Book from God; [5.16] With it God guides him who will follow His pleasure in paths of peace and brings them by His will from darkness into light and guides them to the right path.
5.15b-16

Say: The Holy spirit has revealed it (the Koran) from your Lord in truth, that it may reassure those who believe and give guidance and good news for those who submit to God.
16.102

. . . May the Lord guide me and bring me nearer to the truth.
18.24

Highly exalted is God, the King, the Truth; so do not make haste with this Koran before its message is completely understood by you, but say: O my Lord ! increase me in knowledge.
20.114

God is the light of the heavens and the earth; a likeness of His light is as a niche in which is a lamp, the lamp is in a glass, and the glass is as it were a brightly shining star, lit from a blessed olive-tree, neither eastern nor western, the oil whereof almost gives light though fire touch it not. Light upon light - God guides to His light whom He pleases and sets forth parables for men, and God is aware of all things.
24.35

[26.191] And most surely your Lord is mighty and merciful. [26.192] And most surely this Book is a revelation from the Lord of the universe. [26.193] The faithful Spirit has descended [26.194] upon your heart that you may give warning [26.195] in plain language in your own tongue. [26.196] Most surely this Book is the same as the Scriptures of the ancients.
26.191-196

[28.21] . . . Moses prayed: "My Lord, deliver me from these evil people" [28.22]

... "and may my Lord will guide me on the even path."

28.21-22

[31.2] This Book is a book of wisdom, [31.3] a guide and blessing for the righteous, [31.4] for those who keep up prayer and give alms, those who have faith in the life to come. [31.5] They are rightly guided by their Lord, and they shall receive their reward.

31.2-5

... For those who believe, this Book is a guidance and a healing balm.

41.44

Believers, fear God and believe in His messenger. And He will give you a double portion of His mercy, and make for you a light with which you can walk. And God will forgive you, for God is forgiving and merciful.

57.28

(VII) CONVERSION AND OTHER FAITHS

There is to be no compulsion in religion; truly the right way has become clear...therefore, whoever believes in God has indeed laid hold on the firmest handle, which shall not break off, for God hears all and knows all.

2.256

In the *Torah* there is guidance and light. . . .

5.44

In the Gospel there is guidance and light. . . .

5.46

Surely those who believe and those who are Jews and the Sabians and the Christians whoever believes in God and the last day and does good - they shall have no fear nor shall they grieve.

5.69

When those come to you who believe in Our signs, Say: "Peace be on you: Your Lord hath decreed mercy for Himself: truly, if any of you did evil in ignorance, and thereafter repented, and amends his ways, lo! God is forgiving and merciful."

6.54

Be courteous when you argue with the people of the Scriptures (Jews and Christians), except for those who do evil. Say to them: "We believe in that which has been revealed to us and revealed to you, and our God and your God is One, and to Him do we submit."

29.46

Jesus came preaching with clarity, saying: "I truly have come to you with wisdom, that I may make clear to you the things which you do perceive; so fear God and follow me: [43.64] Truly God is my Lord and your Lord - therefore serve Him; for this is the right path."

43.63

(VIII) PRAYER

Fortify yourselves with patience and prayer. This may indeed be a hard thing, but not for the devout who know they will meet their Lord and that to him they will return.

2.45

And God's is the East and the West, therefore, whither you turn, there is God's face; surely God is omnipresent and all-knowing.

2.115

O children of Adam! Dress well when you attend to prayer at the mosque; and eat and drink but be not overindulge; surely He does not love those who do not practice moderation.

7.31

Remember the Lord deep within your soul humbly and reverently with a soft voice; remember Him in the morning and the evening and do not be negligent.

7.205

When you prayed to your Lord for help, He answered you, saying: "I will assist you with a thousand of the angels following one another."
8.9

To God I pray and to God I will return.
13.36c

Glorify your Lord by the praising Him before the rising of the sun and before its setting; day and night glorify Him so that you may find comfort.
20.130

[30.17] Therefore give glory to God when you as the evening begins and when the morning comes. [30.18] To God belongs praise in the heavens and the earth, at nightfall and at midday.
30.17-18

A prayer for travelers:
In the name of God, the Beneficent, the Merciful. I pray [106.1] "for the protection of my clan and family, [106.2] for their protection during their trading caravans in the winter and the summer.[106.3] So let them serve the Lord of this House [106.4] Who feeds them against hunger and gives them security against fear.
106.1-4

[114.1] Say: I seek refuge in the Lord of humanity, [114.2] the King of humanity, [114.3] the God of humanity, [114.4] from the evil of the whisperings of the Tempter [114.5] who whispers into the hearts [114.6] of jinn and mankind.
114.1-6

(IX) THANKFULNESS
Therefore remember Me and I will remember you; and be thankful to Me, and do not be ungrateful.
2.152

. . . My Lord! Grant me that I should be thankful for the favors you hast bestowed

on me, and on my parents, and that I should do good works that please you; and admit me to enter, by your mercy, among your righteous servants.
27.19

And in his mercy God has made for you the night that you may rest therein, and the day that you may seek of His grace, and that you may give thanks.
28.73

(X) PARADISE, RESURRECTION, REWARD
All who believe, whether Jews, Christians, or the Sabians - whoever believes in God and the Last day and does good deeds shall receive their reward from their Lord. They shall not fear nor shall they grieve.
2.62

Whoever truly submits himself entirely to God and does good to others, he has his reward from his lord. He shall not fear nor shall he grieve.
2.112

And as for those who believe and do good works, We will make them enter gardens beneath flowing rivers, to abide in them for ever; and they shall have therein virgins, and We shall lead them under a dark shade.
4.57

Those who fulfill the promise of God and keep the covenant; and those who join that which God has bidden to be joined and have awe of their Lord and fear the evil day of reckoning; and those who are constant, seeking the pleasure of their Lord, and keep up prayer and give alms out of what We have given them secretly and openly, and fight evil with good; as for those, they shall have the happy home of the gardens of everlasting life which they will enter along with those who do good from among their parents and their spouses and their offspring; and the angels will enter in upon them from every gate, saying: "Peace be upon you because you were constant, how excellent, is then, the issue of the abode."

13.20-24

Surely as for those who believe and do good, We do not waste the reward of him who does a good work. These it is for whom are gardens of perpetuity beneath which rivers flow, ornaments shall be given to them therein of bracelets of gold, and they shall wear green robes of fine silk and thick silk brocade interwoven with gold, reclining therein on raised couches; excellent the recompense and goodly the resting place.

18.30-31

And peace on me on the day I was born, and on the day I die, and on the day I am raised to life.

19.33

Surely the dwellers of the garden shall on that day be in an place quite happy. They and their wives shall be in shades, reclining on raised couches. They shall have fruits therein, and they shall have whatever they desire. The word from a Merciful Lord is "Peace."

36.55-58

Except for the servants of God, the purified ones; for them is a known sustenance, fruits, and they shall be highly honored, in gardens of pleasure, on thrones, facing each other. A bowl shall be made to go round them from water running out of springs, white, delicious to those who drink. There shall be no trouble in it, nor shall they be exhausted therewith. And with them shall be virgins having beautiful eyes.

37.40-49

Surely those who guard against evil are in a secure place, in gardens and springs. They shall wear of fine and thick silk, sitting face to face; So shall it be, and We will wed them with pure, beautiful virgins. They shall call therein for every fruit in security; They shall not taste therein death except the first death, and

He will save them from the punishment of the hell, A grace from your Lord; this is the great victory.

44.50-51

Surely those who guard against evil shall be in gardens and bliss. They will rejoice because of what their Lord gave them, and their Lord saved them from the punishment of the burning fire. Eat and drink pleasantly as the reward for what you did, reclining on thrones set in lines, and We will unite them to large-eyed beautiful virgins. And as for those who believe and their children who follow them in faith, We will unite with them their children and We will not diminish to them any of their work; every man is responsible for what he shall have done. And We will aid them with fruit and flesh such as they desire. They shall pass therein from one to another a cup wherein there shall be nothing vain nor any sin. And round them shall go boys of theirs as if they were hidden pearls. And some of them shall advance towards others questioning each other. Saying: Surely we feared before on account of our families: But God has been gracious to us and He has saved us from the punishment of the hot wind.

57.17-27

Most surely the righteous shall be in bliss, and on thrones, they shall gaze. You will recognize in their faces the brightness of bliss. They are made to drink of a pure drink made for only them. The sealing of it is with musk; and for that let the aspirers aspire. And the admixture of it is a water of Tasnim, a fountain from which drink they who are drawn near to God.

83.22-28

O soul, you are now at rest! Return to your Lord, well-pleased with him and well-pleasing Him. So, enter among My servants, And enter into My garden.

89.27-30

H TRANSLATIONS OF THE QUR'AN
The Qur'an was revealed to Muhammad in Arabic. So for a Muslim, any Quranic

translation, either in English or any other language, is neither a Qur'an, nor a version of the Qur'an, but rather is only a translation of the meaning of the Qur'an. The Qur'an exists only in the Arabic in which it was revealed.

I MARTIN LUTHER'S ASSESSMENT OF THE QUR'AN

He (Muhammad) greatly praises Christ and Mary as being the only ones without sin, and yet he believes nothing more of Christ than that He is a holy prophet, like Jeremiah or Jonah, and denies that He is God's Son and true God. . . . On the other hand, Muhammad highly exalts and praises himself and boasts that he has talked to God and the angels.

From this anyone can easily see that Muhammad is a destroyer of our Lord Christ and His kingdom. . . . (the) Father, Son, Holy Ghost, baptism, the sacrament,

gospel, faith, and all Christian doctrine are gone, and instead of Christ only Muhammad and his doctrine of works and especially of the sword is left.

Martin Luther

J OTHER AUTHORITIES

HADITH
The two primary sources of Islam are the Qur'an and the *Hadith*. The *Hadith*, which is secondary to the Qur'an, records what Muhammad said, did, and approved of.

Sunnah 2 ("a well-trodden path")
In the *Hadith*, Muhammad's sayings and deeds are called *Sunnah*.

Qur'an and *Sunnah*
The Qur'an and the *Sunnah* are the two main sources of Islamic law.

4 FACTS AND FIGURES

A Largest groupings of Muslims
B Geographical location of Muslims
C Fourteen Muslim nations
D Largest Muslim populations

INTRODUCTION
Muslims claim that more than one in five, or even one in four, of all the people in the world are Muslims. The beginning of the twenty-first century saw the number of Muslims pass the 1 billion mark.

If present trends continue, there will be more Muslims than Christians in the world by 2010.

A LARGEST GROUPINGS OF MUSLIMS
- Approximately 18% of Muslims live in the Arab world.
- In the Middle East there are twenty-four

countries that each have more than 1 million Muslims.
- Indonesia is the world's largest Muslim community.
- Pakistan, then India, and then Bangladesh have the three next largest populations of Muslims.
- Many parts of Asia and most of Africa are Muslim.
- Significant minorities of Muslims live in Russia, China, North and South America, and Europe.
- Africa has twenty-six countries with more than 1 million Muslims.

B GEOGRAPHICAL LOCATION OF MUSLIMS

Area	Number of Muslims
Asia	550 million
Middle East	More than 306 million
Africa	About 150 million
Europe	About 20 million
North America	Over 5 million

C FOURTEEN MUSLIM NATIONS

The native population of the following fourteen countries is over 95% Muslim. They are the world's most Muslim nations.

Bahrain
Comoros
Kuwait
Maldives
Mauritania
Mayotte
Morocco
Oman
Qatar
Somalia
Saudi Arabia
Tunisia
United Arab Emirates
Western Sahara
Yemen

D LARGEST MUSLIM POPULATIONS

The countries with the largest Muslim populations are as follows:

Country	Muslim population
Indonesia	170 million
Pakistan	140 million
Bangladesh	110 million
India	105 million
Turkey	65 million
Iran	60 million
Egypt	55 million
Nigeria	50 million
China	40 million

5 ISLAMIC PRACTICES

A   The Five Pillars
B   Islamic morals

A THE FIVE PILLARS

The Five Pillars of Islam are the five obligations that every Muslim must satisfy in order to live a good and responsible life according to Islam.

(I) SHAHADAH

Shahadah is the first of the Five Pillars. It is a testimony of faith, and has been called "The Creed of Islam."

The *Shahadah* is a verbal commitment and pledge that there is only one God and that Muhammad is Allah's Messenger. This declaration of the oneness of God is called *tawhid.*

The statement of *Shahadah* in Arabic is: *Ashhadu Alla ilaha illa Allah wa ashhadu anna Muhammad rasulu Allah.*

This has been translated into English as follows: "I bear witness that there is no God but Allah and I bear witness that Muhammad is His Messenger."

The Arabic words said in the creed are: *La ilaha illa Allah, Muhammadur rasoolu Allah.*

This testimony of faith, the *Shahada*, is a simple formula which, when said with conviction, is the path to becoming a Muslim.

(II) SALAT

This is the performance of ritual prayers. They

have to be prayed five times a day:
> at dawn,
> noon,
> mid-afternoon,
> sunset, and
> at night.

Each prayer only takes a few minutes. As there are no intermediaries between God and the worshiper in Islam, prayer is a direct link between the worshiper and God.

Prayers may be said almost anywhere; it is not necessary to enter a mosque in order to pray.

(III) SAUM

Muslims are required to fast from dawn to sunset during the entire month of Ramadan. This fast includes total abstinence from food, liquids and sexual intercourse between married couples. During this period, life slows down. Reconciliations are made within the community. Outer fasting is a sign of an inner quietness and waiting upon God.

(IV) ZAKAT

Originally the word *zakat* meant both purification and growth. Today this word means giving a specified percentage on certain properties to people in need. In this way possessions are thought to be purified. As plants are cut back and pruned, so this cutting back encourages new growth.

In addition to *zakat*, Muslims are encouraged to be generous in giving to charities.

(V) HAJJ ("GREAT PILGRIMAGE")

This pilgrimage to Mecca (Makkah) is required, if at all possible, once in a lifetime. It has now become the world's largest annual convention of faith. It takes place in the twelfth month of the Islamic calendar (a pilgrimage to Mecca at any other time is called a Little Pilgrimage).

Ka'ba

At the Haram mosque in Mecca is the Ka'ba ("cube" in Arabic). The Ka'ba is a shrine about 60 feet, by 60 feet, by 60 feet and is the place of worship that God had commanded Abraham and Ishmael to build. When Muhammad was growing up in Mecca, the Ka'ba contained hundreds of idols. His first action when he took Mecca in 630 was to clear the Ka'ba of all images and signs of pagan belief. He then proclaimed the end of all idolatry and the start of the new age. The Ka'ba became known as the House of Allah and during the *Hajj* pilgrims circle it seven times. Whenever Muslims pray they turn in the direction of the Ka'ba.

On the eastern corner of the Ka'ba is the Black Stone, called in Arabic, *Hajar al Aswad*. The Black Stone is probably a meteorite.

FESTIVALS

The *Hajj* ends with a festival called *'Id al-Adha*.

'Id al-Adha, the festival of sacrifice, and *'Id al-Fitr*, a feast-day commemorating the end of Ramadan, are the two annual festivals of the Muslim calendar.

The *'Id al-Adha*, which lasts four days, is a worldwide festival coinciding with the end of the *Hajj*. The purpose of the festival is to glorify God, and Muslims remember their identity as a people who worship Allah. Animals are sacrificed, and the meat given to the poor.

B ISLAMIC MORALS

(I) DRESS CODE

The dress code for Muslims emphasizes modesty. The material should therefore not be too thin, and the clothes should not be too tight.

(II) DIETARY PROHIBITIONS

Muslims do not eat pork or drink alcohol.

(III) DATING AND PREMARITAL SEX

Islam does not approve of intimate mixing of the sexes, and forbids premarital or extramarital sex. Marriage is encouraged as a shield to such temptations and as a means of having mutual love.

(IV) ABORTION

Islam regards abortion as murder and does not permit it except to save the mother's life (see Qur'an 17.23-31, 6.15 1).

(V) HOMOSEXUALITY

Islam categorically opposes homosexuality and considers it a sin.

(VI) EUTHANASIA AND SUICIDE

Islam is opposed to both suicide and euthanasia.

---

6 ISLAMIC BELIEFS

A   Monotheism
B   Allah
C   The God of all
D   The One and Only God
E   Nature of Allah
F   Allah according to the Qur'an
G   Names of Allah
H   Messengers and prophets of God
I   The resurrection and the day of judgment
J   *Qadaa* and *Qadar*: fate and predestination
K   *Jihad*
L   *Shari'a*
M   Becoming a Muslim

A MONOTHEISM

Islam, along with Christianity and Judaism, teaches monotheism, that is, the doctrine that there is only one God in all existence.

B ALLAH

Allah is the Arabic name for God.

C THE GOD OF ALL

Muslims worship God whose name is Allah. But Allah is not God of Muslims only. He is God of all human beings because he is their Creator and Sustainer. He is the Creator and Sustainer of all creatures and of all creation. Allah is the God for the Christians, the Jews, the Muslims, the Buddhists, the Hindus, the atheists, and others.

Muslims put their trust in Allah. They seek His help and His guidance.

D THE ONE AND ONLY GOD

A Muslim believes in one God, Supreme and Eternal, Infinite and Mighty, Merciful and Compassionate, Creator and Provider. God has neither father nor mother, nor sons, nor was He fathered. There is none equal to Him. He is God of all humankind, not of a special tribe or race.

E NATURE OF ALLAH

God is High and Supreme but He is very near to the pious, thoughtful believers; He answers their prayers and helps them. He loves the people who love Him and forgives their sins. He gives them peace, happiness, knowledge and success.

F ALLAH ACCORDING TO THE QUR'AN

(I) LORD OF HEAVEN AND EARTH

Allah says in the Qur'an, "He is the Lord of the heavens and the Earth and all that is in between them, so worship Him and be patient in His worship; do you know any equal to Him?" (19.65).

(II) CREATOR AND SUSTAINER

Allah is He besides Whom there is no god, the Everliving, the Self-subsisting by Whom all subsist; slumber does not overtake Him nor sleep; whatever is in the heavens and whatever is in the earth is His; who is he that can intercede with Him but by His permission? He knows what is before them and what is behind them, and they cannot comprehend anything out of His knowledge except what He pleases, His knowledge extends over the heavens and the earth, and the preservation of them both tires Him not, and He is the Most High, the Great.

2.255

He is Allah besides Whom there is no god; the Knower of the unseen and the seen; He is the Beneficent, the Merciful. He is Allah, besides Whom there is no god; the King, the Holy, the Giver of peace, the Granter of security, Guardian over all, the Mighty, the Supreme, the Possessor of every greatness Glory be to Allah from what they set up (with Him). He is Allah the Creator, the Maker, the Fashioner; His are the most excellent names; whatever is in the heavens and the earth declares His glory; and He is the Mighty, the Wise.

59.22-24

(III) POWERFUL

Allah's is the kingdom of the heavens and the earth; He creates what He pleases; He grants to whom He pleases daughters and grants to whom He pleases sons. Or He makes them of both sorts, male and female; and He makes whom He pleases barren; surely He is the Knowing, the Powerful.

42.49-50

G NAMES OF ALLAH

Allah is the name of the One and Only God. Allah has the most magnificent names and sublime attributes. Allah has ninety-nine such names, including: The Gracious, The Merciful, The Beneficent, The Creator, The All-Knowing, The All-Wise, The Lord of the Universe, The First, The Last, and others. Allah has the following ninety-nine names.

In the following ninety-nine names of Allah it is not always possible to translate exactly the names and attributes of Allah from their original Arabic into English. So some explanations about individual names are given.

Some Muslims take on one of the names for Allah, but without the "Al" prefix. Rahman, Rahim, Malik, are common names among male Muslims.

According to Islamic tradition, the ninety-nine names of God are the names that God has revealed to man. In the *Hadith*, the reported words of the Prophet Muhammad, it is said that he who memorizes these would get into paradise.

The ninety-nine names of Allah according to the tradition of Islam are:

1. Ar-Rahman: The Most Compassionate, Most Kind
2. Ar-Rahim: The Most Merciful
3. Al-Malik: The Master, The King, The Monarch
4. Al-Quddus: The Pure, The Holy One
5. As-Salaam: The Peace, The Tranquility, The Author of Safety
6. Al-Mu'min: The Faithful, The Trusted, The Giver of Peace
7. Al-Muhaymin: The Protector, The Vigilant, The Controller
8. Al-'Aziz: The Almighty, The Powerful
9. Al-Jabbar: The Oppressor, The All Compelling
10. Al-Mutakabbir: The Haughty, The Majestic, The Lord
11. Al-Khaliq: The Creator, The Maker
12. Al-Baari': The Inventor, The Maker
13. Al-Musawwir: The Fashioner, The Organizer, The Designer
14. Al-Ghaffar: The Forgiving, The Forgiver
15. Al-Qahhar: The Almighty, The Dominant
16. Al-Wahhab: The Donor, The Bestower
17. Ar-Razzaq: The Provider, The Sustainer
18. Al-Fattah: The Opener, The Revealer, The Judge

19. Al-'Alim: The All Knowing, The Omniscient
20. Al-Qabid: The Contractor, The Restrainer, The Recipient
21. Al-Basit: The Expander, The Increaser
22. Al-Khafid: The Abaser, The Humbler, The Pleaser
23. Ar-Rafi': The Raiser, The Exalter
24. Al-Mu'iz: The Honorer, The Exalter
25. Al-Muzil: The Abaser, The Subduer
26. As-Sami': The All Hearing, The All Knowing
27. Al-Basir: The All Seeing, The Insightful
28. Al-Hakam: The Arbitrator, The Judge
29. Al-'Adl: The Justice, The Equitable
30. Al-Latif: The Most Gentle, The Gracious, The One Who is Kind, The Subtle
31. Al-Khabir: The Aware, The Sagacious
32. Al-Halim: The Gentle, The Most Patient, The Benevolent
33. Al-'Azim: The Great, The Mighty
34. Al-Ghafoor: The Forgiving, The Pardoner
35. Ash-Shakur: The Grateful, The Thankful
36. Al-'Aliy: The Most High, The Exalted
37. Al-Kabir: The Greatest, The Biggest
38. Al-Hafiz: The Guardian, The Preserver
39. Al-Muqit: The Maintainer, The Nourisher
40. Al-Hasib: The Noble, The Reckoner
41. Al-Ja'lil: The Majestic, The Honorable, The Exalted, The Beneficent
42. Al-Karim: The Most Generous, The Bountiful
43. Ar-Raqib: The Guardian, The Watcher
44. Al-Mujib: The Answerer
45. Al-Wasi': The Enricher, The Omnipresent, The Knowledgeable
46. Al-Hakim Al-Mutlaq: The Most Wise, The Judicious
47. Al-Wadud: The Affectionate, The Loving
48. Al-Majid: The Glorious, The Exalted
49. Al-Ba'ith: The Resurrector, The Raiser from death, The True
50. Ash-Shahid: The Witness
51. Al-Haqq: The Truth, The Just
52. Al-Wakil: The Guardian, the Trustee
53. Al-Qawee: The Powerful, The Almighty, The Strong
54. Al-Matin: The Strong, The Firm
55. Al-Walee: The Supporter, The Friend, The Defender
56. Al-Hamid: The Praiseworthy, The Commendable
57. Al-Muhsi: The Counter
58. Al-Mubdi': The Beginner, The Creator, The Originator
59. Al-Mu'eed: The Restorer, The Resurrector
60. Al-Muhyee: The Bestower, The Life Giver
61. Al-Mumeet: The Bringer of Death, The Death Giver
62. Al-Hay'y: The Ever-Living
63. Al-Qayyum: The Self-Subsistent, The Eternal, The Self-Sustaining
64. Al-Wajid: The All Perceiving, The Bountiful, The Finder
65. Al-Majid: The Noble, The Illustrious
66. Al-Wahid: The One, The Unique
67. Al-Ahad: The Only, The Unique
68. As-Samad: The Perfect, The Eternal
69. Al-Qadir: The Able, The Capable, The Omnipotent
70. Al-Muqtadir: The Capable, The All Powerful
71. Al-Muqaddim: The Presenter, The Advancer, The Expediter
72. Al-Mu'akhkhir: The Fulfiller, The Deferrer
73. Al-'Awwal: The First
74. Al-'Akhir: The Last
75. Az-Zahir: The Apparent, The Exterior, The Manifest
76. Al-Batin: The Hidden, The Interior, The Veiled
77. Al-Waali: The Governor, The Ruler, The Master
78. Al-Muta'ali: The Exalted, The Most High, The One above reproach
79. Al-Barr: The Benefactor, The Beneficient, The Pious
80. At-Tawwab: The Acceptor of Repentance, The Forgiver, The Relenting
81. Al-Muntaqim: The Avenger
82. Al-'Afuww: The Forgiver, The Pardoner
83. Ar-Ra'uf: The Merciful, The Ever Indulgent
84. Malik Al-Mulk: The Ruler of The Kingdom, The King of The Universe
85. Zul-Jalali wal-Ikram: Lord of Majesty and Generosity
86. Al-Muqsit: The Just, The Equitable
87. Aj-Jami': The Collector, The Comprehensive, The Gatherer

88. Al-Ghanee: The Richest, The All
    Sufficing, The Self-Sufficient
89. Al-Mughnee: The Enricher, The Sufficer,
    The Bestower
90. Al-Maani': The Supporter
91. Ad-Daarr: The Distresser, The Afflictor,
    The Bringer of Adversity
92. An-Nafi': The Beneficial, The Benefactor
93. An-Nur: The Light
94. Al-Hadi': The Guide
95. Al-Badi': The Wonderful, The Maker,
    The Incomparable
96. Al-Baqi: The Enduring, The Everlasting,
    The Eternal
97. Al-Warith: The Inheritor, The Heir
98. Ar-Rashid: The Rightly Guided, The
    Conscious, The Guide
99. As-Sabur: The Most Patient, The
    Enduring

H MESSENGERS AND PROPHETS OF GOD

PROPHETS

Muslims believe in a chain of prophets starting with Adam and including Noah, Abraham, Ishmael, Isaac, Jacob, Joseph, Job, Moses, Aaron, David, Solomon, Elias, Jonah, John the Baptist, and Jesus. God's most important and final revelations came through the Prophet Muhammad, the last of Allah's prophets.

MESSENGERS

Muslims believe that Allah has sent to His people messengers who were "bringing good tidings and warning, so that mankind might have no argument against Allah after the Messengers. Allah is All-mighty, All-wise" (4. 165).

A Muslim believes that all messengers were mortals, human beings, endowed with Divine revelations and appointed by God to teach humankind. The Qur'an mentions the names of twenty-five messengers and prophets and states that there are others. These include Noah, Abraham, Ishmael, Isaac, Moses, Jesus and Muhammad. Their message is the same. It is to submit Allah's will and to obey His law. In a nutshell it is to become a Muslim.

THE FIRST AND LAST MESSENGERS

Muslims believe that the first messenger was Noah and the last is Muhammad: "We revealed to you as We revealed to Noah and the prophets after him" (4.163); and, "Muhammad is not the father of any of your men, but the Messenger of Allah and the Seal of the Prophets" (33.40).

THE ANGELS

There are spiritual beings created by Allah. They require no food or drink or sleep. They have no physical desires nor material needs. Angels spend their time in the service of Allah. Angels cannot be seen.

Muslims believe that Allah's angels are "honored servants. They do not speak before He does, and they act only by His command" (21.26). Allah created them, and they worship and obey Him. "Those who are in His presence do not disdain to worship Him, nor do they weary" (21.19).

THE MESSENGER ANGEL

The angel Gabriel brought Allah's words to the Prophet Muhammad and so is called: "The Messenger Angel."

I THE RESURRECTION AND THE DAY OF JUDGMENT

Muslims believe in the resurrection. Believers will see their Lord on the Day of Resurrection: "Upon that day some faces shall be radiant, gazing upon their Lord" (75.22-3).

This takes place when Allah brings to life all those who have died: "And the trumpet shall be blown, and all who are in the heavens and who are in the Earth shall fall down fainting, except those that Allah shall spare. Then, it shall be blown again and they shall rise gazing around them" (39.68).

Muslims believe that in the Final Day, that is, in the Day of Judgment, all men and women from Adam to the last person will be resurrected. They are then all ordered to stay in the place of enjoyment or in the place of severe punishment. Everything we do, say, make, intend and think are accounted for and kept in accurate records which are brought up on this Day of Judgment.

J *QADAA* AND *QADAR*: FATE AND PREDESTINATION

A Muslim believes in *Qadaa* and *Qadar,* which relate to the ultimate power of Allah. *Qadaa* and *Qadar* mean the timeless knowledge of Allah and His power to execute His wishes. Everything on this earth originates from the one and only Creator who is also the Sustainer and the Sole Source of guidance.

"It is the will of Allah," is no trite phrase for a Muslim.

Divine predestination does not mean that human beings do not have free will. Rather, Muslims believe that God has given human beings free will. This means that they can choose right or wrong and that they are responsible for their choices.

Divine predestination includes belief that:

- God knows everything. He knows what has happened and what will happen.
- God has recorded all that has happened and all that will happen.
- Whatever God wills to happen happens, and whatever He wills not to happen does not happen.
- God is the creator of everything.

K *JIHAD*

The word *"Jihad"* means struggle, and, especially, striving in the cause of God. *Jihad* means much more than holy war.

- All everyday struggles in life to please God can be considered *Jihad.*
- The struggle to build a good Muslim society is a kind of *Jihad.*
  One of the highest levels of *Jihad* is to stand up to a tyrant and speak a word of truth.
- Self-control is also a great *Jihad.*
- Taking up arms in defense of Islam or a Muslim country is also a kind of *Jihad.*

L *SHARI'A*

Shari'a is the comprehensive Muslim law. It is derived form two sources, the Qur'an and the *Sunnah,* the traditions of the Prophet Muhammad.

M BECOMING A MUSLIM

One becomes a Muslim by sincerely saying and believing: *"La ilaha illa Allah, Muhammadur rasoolu Allah."* ("There is no true god (deity) but God (Allah), and Muhammad is the Messenger (Prophet) of God.")

---

7 ISLAMIC WORSHIP

> A Imams
> B Mosques
> C The Muslim calendar
> D Major Islamic festivals

INTRODUCTION

A believer can approach Allah by praying, and by reciting the Qur'an.

A Muslim believes that the purpose of life is to worship Allah. Worshiping Allah means living a life according to His commands.

Muslims do not worship any of their prophets, or even Muhammad himself. No human beings, only God himself, may be worshiped.

A IMAMS

In Islam, there is no hierarchy of religious leadership. There are no priests, bishops, monks, or popes.

The Muslim Imams and scholars cannot forgive sins. They do not receive divine revelations. They cannot issue any passports to heaven. They are just ordinary Muslims who have devoted themselves to Islamic studies.

B MOSQUES
The Muslim building for communal worship is called a mosque.

REMOVE SHOES
Every mosque has a place where worshipers leave their shoes and ritually wash themselves, which is necessary before praying.

NO PICTURES
Mosques consist of a large room. There is no furniture in the room, nor are there any statues or pictures. Such things are blasphemous to Muslims who believe that since Allah is wholly spirit, it is not possible to have any image of him.

MIHRAB
A niche or decorative panel in one of the walls indicates which way the worshipers must face as they worship. This *mihrab* always faces in the direction of Mecca.

MINARET
Most mosques have a tall thin tower, called a minaret.
From the top of the tower a muezzin calls Muslims to prayer five times a day.
Ritual prayer is central to Muslim worship.

C THE MUSLIM CALENDAR
The Islamic year started from the migration (*Hijra*) of Prophet Muhammad from Mecca to Medina in AD 622.

So the year AD 2006 is the Islamic year 1426 AH (standing for "After Hijra").

The Muslim calendar has a lunar year of 354 days. Its first month is called *Muharram*.

D MAJOR ISLAMIC FESTIVALS
- 'Id al-Fitre marks the end of fasting in the month of Ramadan. It is celebrated with public prayers, feasts and exchange of gifts.
- 'Id al-Adha is a four-day festival marking the end of the *Hajj* (the annual pilgrimage to Mecca). Following public prayers, a lamb or a goat is sacrificed signifying Abraham's obedience to God, seen in his readiness to sacrifice his son Ishmael.

8 GROUPINGS WITHIN ISLAM

A   Sunni and Shi'a
B   Major branches of Islam
C   Sufi school of thought

A SUNNI AND SHI'A
There are two main groups of Muslims: Sunni (or "orthodox") Muslims who constitute 85 to 90% of the world's Muslims, and Shi'ite. Most Shi'a Muslims live in Iran and Iraq, where it is the majority faith. Most of the rest of the Muslim world are Sunni.

The division came after Muhammad died. His last message was:

Today I have completed my religion for you and I have fulfilled the extent of my favor towards you. It is my will that Islam be your religion. I have completed my mission. I have left you the Book of Allah and clear commandments. If you keep them, you will never go wrong.

What was not clear to everyone, however, was who, if anyone, should take his place.

SUNNI

- The Sunni said that no one could take Muhammad's place as a prophet, and his successors could merely be administrators, who carried out the Prophet's sayings and actions. They do not have a religious function.
- The name given to subsequent leaders was "caliph." Caliphs (or imams) were chosen by a consensus (*ijma'*) from the male member of the Quraish tribe (Muhammad's tribe).
- The first four caliphs were: Abu Bakr, 'Umar, 'Uthman and 'Ali. It was held that they had lived so close to Muhammad himself that they were "rightly guided" in all they taught.
- The teaching of these four caliphs is called *sunna* ("custom") and it is accepted as authoritative.
- The Shari'a is a system of community law that developed over the centuries Legal scholars explain and interpret the Shari'a.
- Sunnis continued to be governed by caliphs, the guardians of the Shari'a, until 1924, when they were abolished, their place being taken by the different governments of Muslim countries.
- Decisions are by consensus (*ijma'*) – the agreement of the majority, and therefore historical developments and customs may be and are incorporated into the law, even if not part of the Qur'an.

SHI'A

- The fourth caliph 'Ali, was Muhammad's cousin and son-in-law. When he was murdered in 661, Muawiah, his chief opponent, was made caliph. Many Muslims, however, wanted his son, Husayn, to become caliph. The majority of Muslims would not support him, and he and his small group of followers were killed.
- A minority movement believed that the inspired leadership gifts and understanding of the law were passed down through 'Ali's family. They chose as *imam* whichever of his descendants was the most qualified at the time.

- The *imam* had absolute spiritual authority and was the possessor secret insights (the word *imam,* therefore has different meanings for Shi'ites and for Sunnis).
- Most Shi'a Muslims believe that the twelfth *imam* went into "occulation" and will one day return as a messianic figure.
- The guidance of this twelfth *imam* is still available to "agents," the most senior of whom in Iran are the *ayatollahs* who pass judgments on the interpretation of the Shari'a.
- In the sixteenth century, the dynasty in Iran made the Shi'ite faith the sole religion of their empire.
- In the late twentieth century, the Shi'ites became the chief voice of Islamic militant fundamentalism.

B MAJOR BRANCHES OF ISLAM

Sunni	970,000,000
Shi'ite	150,000,000
Ahmadiyya	11,000,000
Druze	500,000

C SUFI SCHOOL OF THOUGHT

Sufism (*sufi* means "mystic") is a mystical Muslim school of thought which encourages Muslims in their question for a direct personal experience of Allah.

This movement, which began in Persia and Iraq in the eighth to thirteenth centuries, in response to what was felt to be the worldliness of much of Islam, encouraged union with the divine by means of ascetic practices, and, in some forms, ecstatic dancing. Though the mainstream of Sufis insisted on the keeping of the *Shari'a*, there was always tension between observance of the external law, and the following of the mystical inner path. Sufism also encouraged worship of saints, and founded religious communities: forbidden in Islamic teaching.

Reciting the names of God and phrases from the Qur'an (*dhikr*) is one form of Sufi devotion.

It was largely because of Sufi missionaries that Islam was extended into India, central Asia, Turkey, and sub-Saharan Africa. Today there are many branches of Sufism throughout the Muslim world.

9 COMPARISON OF ISLAM WITH CHRISTIANITY

A   Human nature and sin
B   Salvation
C   The devil
D   Nature of God
E   The Trinity
F   The Holy Spirit
G   Jesus
       (i)   The existence of Jesus
       (ii)   The deity of Jesus
       (iii)   Belief in Jesus and salvation
       (iv)   Jesus' crucifixion
       (v)   Jesus' resurrection
H   Christian view of Islam

A HUMAN NATURE AND SIN
The Bible teaches:
All people are fallen sinners (Romans 3:23).

The Qur'an teaches:
All people are basically good.

Islam teaches that men and women are born free of sin. Every person is endowed by Allah with the spiritual potential and intellectual inclination that can make him a good Muslim. Everyone is born free from sin. There is no such thing as inherited sin, or original sin.

B SALVATION
The Bible teaches:
Salvation is by grace through faith (Ephesians 2:89).

The Qur'an teaches:
Salvation is by sincerity and works. Salvation is earned through a life of good deeds.

C THE DEVIL
The Bible teaches:
The devil is a fallen angel (Isaiah 14:12-15).

The Qur'an teaches:
The devil, Satan, is not a fallen angel, but a fallen Jinn.

D NATURE OF GOD
The Bible teaches:
"God is love" (1 John 4:6).

The Qur'an teaches:
Among Islam's ninety-nine names for God not one of them is "love" or "loving."

E THE TRINITY
The Bible teaches:
The doctrine of the Trinity is implied in Isaiah 43:10; 44:6-8; Matthew 28:19; 2 Corinthians 13:14.

The Qur'an teaches:
Islam denies the Trinity. Muslims believe in the oneness of God. Muslims believe in the oneness of God. Allah is One and the Only One. From this they conclude that God is not two in one or three in one. The whole idea of the Christian Trinity is rejected. "Certainly they disbelieve who say: Surely Allah is the third (person) of the three" (Qur'an 5.73).

For Christians: An attack on the Trinity is an attack on the deity of Jesus.

F THE HOLY SPIRIT
The Bible teaches:
The Holy Spirit is the third person in the

Godhead. He bears witness to Jesus (John 14:26; 15:26).

The Qur'an teaches:
The Holy Spirit is the angel Gabriel.

G JESUS
(i) THE EXISTENCE OF JESUS
The Bible teaches:
The historical reality of Jesus: "For we did not follow cleverly invented stories when we told you about the power and coming of our Lord Jesus Christ, but we were eye-witnesses of his majesty" (2 Peter 1:16).

The Qur'an teaches:
Muslims do not deny the existence of Jesus. Rather they believe that he was an important prophet. They respect and revere him. The Qur'an recounts his virgin birth. The Annunciation to Mary is recorded by the Qur'an as follows:

"Behold!" the Angel said, "God has chosen you, and purified you, and chosen you above the women of all nations. O Mary, God gives you good news of a word from Him, whose name shall be the Messiah, Jesus son of Mary, honored in this world and the Hereafter, and one of those brought near to God. He shall speak to the people from his cradle and in maturity, and shall be of the righteous."

She said: "O my Lord! How shall I have a son when no man has touched me?" He said: "Even so; God creates what He will. When He decrees a thing, He says to it, 'Be!' and it is."
Qur'an, 3.42-7

(ii) THE DEITY OF JESUS
The Bible teaches:
Jesus is God in flesh (Colossians 2:9).

The Qur'an teaches:
Jesus was merely a messenger of Allah. Jesus is not God. Those who believe Jesus is God are

infidels or disbelievers.

(iii) BELIEF IN JESUS AND SALVATION
The Bible teaches:
There is salvation only in Jesus (Acts 4.12).

The Qur'an teaches:
It is impossible for anyone who believes in Jesus' death on the cross and his resurrection to gain salvation. Jesus can play no part in a Muslim's salvation.

(iv) JESUS' CRUCIFIXION
The Bible teaches:
Jesus was crucified (1 Peter 2:24).

The Qur'an teaches:
Jesus was not really placed on a cross, and he did not die on the cross. "And their saying: Surely we have killed the Messiah, Isa son of Marium, the apostle of Allah; and they did not kill him nor did they crucify him, but it appeared to them so (like Isa) and most surely those who differ therein are only in a doubt about it; they have no knowledge respecting it, but only follow a conjecture, and they killed him not for sure" (4.157).

(v) JESUS' RESURRECTION
The Bible teaches:
Jesus rose from the dead (John 2:19-20).

The Qur'an teaches:
Jesus did not rise from the dead.

H CHRISTIAN VIEW OF ISLAM
The New Testament teaches that to deny the deity and the death and resurrection of Jesus is so serious that anybody or any teaching that does this warrants the description "the antichrist." "Who is the liar but the one who denies that Jesus is the Christ? This is the antichrist, the one who denies the Father and the Son" (1 John 2:22 NAS).

10 GLOSSARY OF ISLAMIC TERMS AND WORDS

A'uzu billahi minashaitanir rajim
"I seek refuge from Allah from the outcast Satan. Muslims recite this statement before reading to Qur'an, before speaking, before doing any work, before praying.

'Abd
A prefix, meaning "servant," used in Muslim male names in conjunction with a divine attribute of God. So, Abd-Allah means "servant of God," Abd al-Rahman means "servant of the Most Merciful."

Abu Bakr as-Sadiq
One of the closest companions of Prophet Muhammad, known as as-Sadiq, "the Truthful." Became the first Caliph in AD 632, until his death in AD 634.

Adhan
The call to prayer.

AH
The letters "AH" are placed after the number of a year in the Islamic calendar. They stand for "After Hijra." The Islamic calendar starts from the day Muhammad made the first Hijra, when he emigrated from Mekkah to Medina, in 622.

Ahmad
Another name for Muhammad.

Alhamdu lillah
Praise be to Allah.

Allah
The Arabic word for God.

Allahu akbar
Allah is Most Great; God is the greatest.

As-salamu alaikum
"Peace be upon you." This is the official Islamic greeting.
As-salamu alaikum wa rahmatullahi wa barakatuh

"Peace and the Mercy and Blessings of God be upon you." An extended form of the official Islamic greeting.

Astaghfir Allah
"I seek forgiveness from Allah."

Awra
The part of a person's body that must be covered before everybody but a spouse; for men this is from navel to knee, for women from upper chest to knee.

Ayah/Ayat
Qur'anic verse.

Azan
The Muslim call to prayer.

Bid`ah
Innovation, addition to the religion's essentials.

Bukhari
One of the most noted compilers of *hadith*. His collection is known as *Sahih Bukhari*.

Bismillah ar-Rahman ar-Rahim
"In the Name of Allah, the Most Gracious, Most Merciful."
    It is used by Muslims to ask for God's blessing on any action and is found at the start of most *surahs* in the Qur'an.

Caliph
A Muslim ruler.

Da'wah
The "call" to Islam; inviting people to learn more about Islam to encourage them to convert.

Dajjal
Antichrist.

Din
Obedience to the revelation of Allah's Qur'an. It involves total submission.

'Id
Islamic holiday.

Fatwa
Legal verdict given based on the Qur'an and the *Sunnah*.

Five pillars of Islam
The duties carried out by Muslims as part of their faith.

Hadith
The sayings and deeds of the prophet Muhammad recorded by his followers. Considered authoritative and perfect. A saying is called a *Sunnah*.

Hafiz
A person who has learned the Qur'an by heart.

Hajar
The Black Stone set into the corner of the Ka'ba in Mecca. Tradition states it fell from heaven.

Hajj
The pilgrimage to Mecca which takes place in the last month of the Islamic calendar. One of the five pillars of Islam.

Halal
Something a Muslim is permitted to do or eat.

Haram
Something a Muslim must not do or eat.

Hawijah
The sixth level of hell which is the place for Christians.

Hegira (Hijrah)
The migration of Muhammad and his followers from Mecca to Yathrib (now Medina)

Hijab
Islamic clothing worn by women to protect their modesty. How much *hijab* covers is often a matter for local customs.

Iblis
Satan, a fallen Jinn.

Ihram
The state of ritual purity required for undertaking the *Hajj* or *Umra*. The special garments worn in this state are also called *Ihram*.

Ijma
Consensus of the Muslim community or its leaders.

Imam
A teacher, or leader, of the Muslim prayer.

Injil
The inspired sayings of Jesus. The message of Jesus.

Islam
Submission, the religion of all the prophets of Allah culminating in Muhammad. The faith of Muslims. The word *Islam* means "surrender or submission to Allah."

Jannah
The heavenly garden, Paradise. The place of the faithful in the afterlife.

Jazakallah khair
May God grant you what is good. (Often used instead of "Thank you.")

Jihad
Striving for Islam. Fighting against one's own sinful self. A physical fight for the truth of Islam. It also can mean "holy war."

Jinn
Supernatural, invisible beings, below angels, who, like humans, are given the power to choose between right and wrong.

Ka'ba
The cubic building at the center of the Mosque at Mecca around which pilgrims process. It is the focal point of Muslim prayer.

Khutba
Sermon.

Kufr
Denial of the truth, rebellion against God.

La Ilaha Illa Allah
"There is no deity but God."

Ma shaa Allah
"What God has willed!" Used to express wonder at Allah's creation.

Mawlid an-Nabi
The birthday of Muhammad.

Mecca
The holy city of Islam. It is the birthplace of Muhammad.

Medina
The city, then called Yathrib, that Muhammad fled to after announcing Islam.

Mihrab
A niche in a mosque showing the direction of Mecca.

Minaret
The tower of a mosque from which the call to prayer is made.

Minbar
The pulpit in a mosque.

Mosque
A building (or place) where Muslims worship together.

Muezzin
The official who calls people to prayer.

Muhajir
Immigrant, one who leaves his home town to join a Muslim community.

Muhammad
The final messenger/prophet of God whose message abrogated all previous revelations. He received the Qur'an through the angel Gabriel over a twenty-three year period.

Muhammad ibn Abd Allah
The full name of Muhammad.

Muslim
One who submits to Allah and is a follower of the Islamic faith.

Nabi
Prophet.

Niyya
The declaration (usually silent) of one's sincere intention to worship.

Paradise
Another word for heaven. A garden (79:41) of bliss and fruit (69:21-24), has rivers (3:198), with maidens pure and holy (4:57), and carpets and cushions (88:8-16). It is the hope of all Muslims.

pbuh
A shortened designation for, "Peace be upon him," used after the name of the Prophet Muhammad (*pbuh*) to indicate one's respect (also used after the names of other prophets).

pbut
"Peace be upon them." Plural of pbuh.

Qibla
The direction which Muslims turn for daily prayers, towards Mecca.

Quiblah
The direction of Mecca.

Quraish
An ancient Arab tribe to which Muhammad once belonged.

Qur'an
The holy book of Islam.

RAA
Radia Allahu Anhu/Anha. "May Allah be please with him/her."

Rakat (rak'ah)
One complete cycle of sacred words and gestures during the ritual prayer (*salat*).

Ramadan
The ninth month of the Islamic calendar. The month of fasting.

Ruku
The bow made in *salat*.

Sadaquah
Voluntary giving to charity, as opposed to the *zakat* charity required in Islam.

Salaam
Peace. An abbreviated version of the Islamic greeting.

Salat (Salah)
The obligatory ritual prayer carried out five times a day.

Salat-ul-Jum'a
Friday prayer at a mosque.

SAW
Salla allahu alaihi wa sallam. "Peace Be Upon Him."

Sawm
Fasting during daylight.

Shahadah
The Muslim declaration of faith. "There is no God but God; Muhammad is the Messenger of God."

Shari'ah
Islamic law

Sheikh
Scholar (or any elder and/or respected man).

Shi'a
The second largest group within Islam that teaches that leaders should be political rulers.

Shirk
Associating another god with Allah. Associating anything with Allah that is not true and revealed in the Qur'an.

Sufism
The mystical movement in Islam (a follower of it is called a Sufi). It teaches strong self-denial with the hope of union with God.

Sujud (Sajdah)
The prostration position in prayer, with forehead, nose, hands, knees, and toes all touching the ground.

Sunnah
The life, practices, and sayings of Muhammad recorded as examples of perfect conduct in society, religion, action, etc. They contain the Hadith.

Sunni
The largest group within Islam.

Sura(h)
A chapter of the Qur'an.

SWT
SubHanahu wa Ta`ala. "Glory be to Him." Used only in reference to Allah.

Taghut
Everything that is worshiped or followed other than Allah.

Takbir
The process of concentrating on prayer to the exclusion of everything else.

Taqwah
Proper fear and veneration of Allah. A divine spark that enables the person to understand God.

Tawhid-al-uluhiyah
Declaring that God is the only one worthy of worship.

Tawhid-ar-rububiyah
Declaring that God is one, the sovereign who performs all his will.

Tawaf
Going round the Ka'ba seven times on *Hajj* or *Umra.*

Ummah
A religious community, usually Islamic.

Wassalaam
And peace. It means "goodbye."

Wudu
Ritual washing before the daily prayers.

Zakat
The third pillar of Islam. Required charity. Compulsory donation of a set proportion of one's savings or property.

Zinah
Fornication and adultery.

HINDUISM

CONTENTS

1 An overview   133

2 Founder of Hinduism   134

3 Holy books   135

4 Facts and figures   189

5 Practices   190

6 Beliefs   191

7 Worship   196

8 Groupings within Hinduism   197

9 Swamiji: Yoga in Daily Life   198

10 Quotations about Hinduism   199

11 Comparison with Christianity   205

12 Glossary   207

1 AN OVERVIEW

DEFINITIONS

Hinduism is so diversified in its theoretical premises and practical expressions that it has been called a "museum of religions."

Hinduism is a way of life or a *Dharma*. It involves living a life of purity and simplicity and having a sense of natural justice.

The following definition of a basic Hindu was quoted in India's Supreme Court on 2 July 1995:

Acceptance of the *Vedas* with reverence; recognition of the fact that the means or ways to salvation are diverse; and the realization of the truth that the number of gods to be worshiped is large, that indeed is the distinguishing feature of the Hindu religion.

B. G. Tilak

Factfile
- Date of origin: relatively little is known about the origins of Hinduism as it predates recorded history. Hinduism (*'tana Dharma*, which may be roughly translated as "Perennial Faith") is generally considered to be the oldest major world religion still practiced today. Hinduism is more than a religion. It also claims to be the most ancient culture and traditional way of life. It has existed for over ten thousand years throughout India.
- Founder: Hinduism has no one founder.
- Holy book: Hindus do not have one single holy book as their basic scriptural guide. The four *Vedas* which include the *Upanishads* and the *Bhagavad Gita* are the three leading sacred texts of the Hindus.
- Number of adherents: more than 1 billion followers.

SUMMARY

In some ways it is more accurate to define Hinduism terms of a civilization and a culture than a religion.

Hinduism is rooted in the merging of two basic religious systems: that of the ancient civilization found in the Indus River Valley from the third millennium BC, and the religious beliefs brought to India by the Aryan (European) people who began moving into the Indus Valley some time after 2000 BC.

PRACTICES

Hinduism embraces a wide range of belief systems, practices and scriptures.

YOGA DHARMA

Hinduism is practiced through a number of spiritual practices, known as yogas.

"Yoga" is a Sanskrit word (Sanskrit is the foundational language of the Hindu religion) meaning "union of *Atman* (individual Soul) with Brahman (Universal Soul)."

The Sanskrit root for yoga is *yuj*; that is "to yoke" [to the Spirit]. This is similar in meaning to the English word "religion," which is derived from the Latin word *religio*, meaning "to link-back" [to the Spirit]. Thus it is a fallacy to argue that yoga is not religion. In the Hindu religion all the many forms of yoga are found.

For the Hindu on the journey to Spiritual-Realization, the many yoga/Hindu spiritual disciplines take into consideration all aspects of one's being. The classic yogas are progressive in nature (see also section 6E below).

- Karma yoga (ethics)
- Bhakti yoga (devotion)
- Raja yoga (meditation)
- Jnana yoga (inner wisdom or enlightenment).

These are the classic four yogas within which are several other forms of yoga. Hatha yoga (worshipful poses), for example, is part of Raja yoga training. Some of the other forms of yoga are Nada yoga (music), Mantra and Japa yoga (chanting and on beads)and Kundalini yoga (study of the psychic centers or *chakras*).

BELIEFS

The Hindu spirit is typified by the following line in the *Rig Veda*:

Truth is One, though the Sages know it as Many.

The Rig Veda (Book I, Hymn CLXIV, Verse 46)

THE FOUR GOALS OF LIFE

Hindus seek moral harmony in all (*dharma*). They do this through the pursuit of *purushartha*, the "four goals of life." These are:

- *kama*
- *artha*
- *dharma*
- *moksha.*

Everyone seeks *kama* (pleasure, both physical pleasure and emotional pleasure), as well as *artha* (power, fame and wealth). But *dharma* stands for a superior quest, the moral harmony in all. The only completely satisfying goal is to be found in *moksha*, happiness and liberation from the endless cycle of life and death.

2 FOUNDER OF HINDUISM

A The origin of Hinduism
B Ancient history of Hinduism

INTRODUCTION

Hindus claim that their religion was founded by God himself, and is therefore God-centered, while other religions, which were founded by prophets, are prophet-centered:

There are these eternal principles, which stand upon their own foundations without depending on any reasoning, even much less on the authority of sages however great, of Incarnations however brilliant they may have been. We may

remark that as this is the unique position in India, our claim is that the Vedanta only can be the universal religion, that it is already the existing universal religion in the world, because it teaches principles and not persons.

Swami Vivekananda

Hinduism has evolved from a mixture of beliefs practiced by people living along the river Indus in India and Pakistan from 7,000 BC onwards. Today's Hinduism can be traced to the second millennium BC, when Aryan nomadic tribes from the Baltic settled in India. Their caste system seems to have been absorbed into Hinduism.

A THE ORIGIN OF HINDUISM

The word "Hindu" is not a religious word, being secular in origin. It is derived from the name given to a major river, the River Sindhu, which flows in the north-western region of the Indian subcontinent. The people who lived beyond this river were called Hindus by the ancient Greeks and Armenians. Then when the Muslims came to the subcontinent, they called the people living in the region "Hindustanis" to distinguish them from the foreign Muslims. Subsequently, when the

British established their rule, they gave all the local religions the collective name of Hinduism.

B ANCIENT HISTORY OF HINDUISM
TIMELINE INDICATING THE
ANCIENT HISTORY OF HINDUISM

3200-2000 BC	The traditionally accepted date of the Indus Valley civilization. The civilization flourished between 2350 and 1750
1200-1000 BC	*Rig Veda* compiled
1000-500 BC	Age of the *Ramayana*, the *Mahabharata* or the *Bhaghavad Gita*

3 HOLY BOOKS

A Introduction
B The Vedic literature (*sruti/shruti*)
C *Brahma Sutra*
D Non-vedic sacred literature(*smriti*)
E The *Bhagavad Gita*

A INTRODUCTION

Hindu scripture is voluminous. Unlike many other religions, Hindus do not have one "holy book" but many sacred texts. Their scriptures are divided into two basic types, *sruti* and *smriti*.

(i) *Sruti* ("that which is heard/revealed [directly from the deity]") consists of the four *Vedas* - *Rig Veda*, *Yajur Veda*, *Sama Veda*, and *Atharva Veda*, together with explanatory texts and commentaries called *Brahmanas*, *Aranyakas*, and *Upanishads*).

The *Rig Veda* is divided into 21 sections, the *Yajur Veda* into 109 sections, the *Sama Veda* into 1,000 sections and the *Atharva Veda* into 50 sections. In all, the whole *Veda* is thus

divided into 1,180 hymns addressed to gods.

(ii) *Smriti* ("that which is remembered") is composed of traditional sacred texts that are not as directly inspired as *sruti*. They include the *Dharma Shastras* (legal and ethical texts), the *Puranas*, and the folk/historical legends known as the *Mahabharata* and *Ramayana*.

(iii) Somewhere between *shruti* and *smriti* are the *sutras* ("threads"), which are composed of terse statements with an attached commentary.

B THE VEDIC LITERATURE (*SRUTI*: "THAT WHICH IS REVEALED")

The *Vedas* (meaning "wisdom" or "knowledge") are collections (*samhita*) of sacred hymns, prayers and ritual texts written in archaic Sanskrit which grew up around a sacrificial cult. Many were used by the Indo-European speaking people who entered India from Iran and are the oldest of the Hindu scriptures: most scholars accept a date of 1500 to 1200 BC for the composition of the earliest of these hymns. They are called *sruti* literally "that which is heard [from the gods]," and not even a syllable can be changed. Hindus consider the *Vedas* to be the most sacred of all literature.

The *Vedas* were passed down orally by Vedic priests, who memorized every syllable. Even after a system of writing was introduced, they continued to be passed down by word of mouth.

The Vedic corpus consists of:

- *Samhita Vedas* - "*samhita* means "Collection"

  ◦ *Rig Veda* "songs of knowledge": 1,028 hymns, many addressed to individual gods (about twenty-four) who for the most part were personifications of natural phenomena. The *Rig Veda* are the oldest of the Vedic texts and are not only the oldest work of literature in any Indo-European language but the oldest religious literature in the world. They were first collected in an oral form about 1500 BC. They were chanted by the chief priest, as part of the sacrificial ritual.

  ◦ *Yajur Veda* Collections of mantras and verses. These were ritual formulas chanted in a low voice by a second group of priests, who were responsible for the sacrificial fire, as they went through the stages in the offering of sacrifices. The *Yajur Veda* is divided into two parts, the *Sukla* (or *Vajasaneya*) and the *Krishna* (or *Taittiriya*). The *Krishna* is the older book, the *Sukla* being a later revelation to sage Yajnavalkya from the resplendent Sun-God.

  ◦ *Sama Veda* Melodic chants arranged for liturgical use. These were chanted by a third group of priests led by the Chanter. They were taken mostly from the *Rig Veda*.

  ◦ *Atharva Veda* consist of 6,000 stanzas of which 1,200 are from the *Rig Veda* and the rest are magical spells and incantations. This was composed about the same time as the *Brahmanas*.

- *Brahmanas* (c. 850 BC) Notes and commentaries on the *Vedas* made by the priests, including the duties of priests, and explanations of the hymns.

- *Aaranyakas* (c. 500 BC) Literally "books of the forest." These were a later addition to the *Brahmanas* and were for the initiated only. They contain information about secret rites to be carried out only by initiates, together with secret, allegorical explanations of hidden, inner meanings of the *Vedas*.

- *Upanishads* (literally "down down near" [the teachers]) Philosophical commentaries on the *Vedas* in prose and verse exploring the ground of the universe and the idea of the Brahman, and the nature of consciousness and the *atman* (the self or soul). They record the ideas of a series of teachers from 1000 BC onwards. The *Upanishads*, which were written down about 500 BC, end the Vedic tradition, and are therefore often called the *Vedanta* ("conclusion"). Over a hundred still exist.

The *Upanishads*, which mark a definite change from the magic formulas in the *Vedas* to mystical ideas about humankind and the universe, constitute the philosophical framework for Hinduism. The philosopher Sarvepalli Radhakrishnan stated that they, "represent a great chapter in the history of the human spirit and have dominated Indian philosophy, religion and life for three thousand years. Every subsequent religious movement in India has had to show itself to be in accordance with their philosophical statements."

The essence of the spirit of the *Upanishads* is seen in the following quotation

"He (The Truth) who cannot even be heard of by many, whom many, even hearing, do not know, wondrous is he (the person) who can teach (The Truth) and skillful is he (the person) who finds (The Truth) and wondrous is he (the person) who knows, even when instructed otherwise.

Katha Upanishhad

The purpose of the *Upanishhads* is expressed in a verse from *Taittiriiya Upanishhad* as the: "Soul of Truth, the delight of life and the bliss of mind, the fullness of peace and eternity."

The *Upanishads* had a great influence on Gautama Buddha, the founder of Buddhism.

C BRAHMA SUTRA (SIXTH CENTURY AD)

Sutras ("threads") were collections of aphorisms based on the *Upanishads*. They were very brief, so commentaries were written to explain them. The *Brahma Sutra* tried to draw together and sum up these commentaries (so it was also called the *Vedanta Sutr*).

D NON-VEDIC SACRED LITERATURE (*SMRITI*: "THAT WHICH IS REMEMBERED")

Non-Vedic sacred literature consists of:

- *Vedangas*: phonetics, grammar, etymology, prosody, medicine.
- *Dharma Shastras*: including the *Laws of Manu*, which are 2.685 metrical verses on law, politics and religion. Their theme is duty and the right way to behave. Written probably in the first century BC or the first century AD, they are a much quoted source of Hindu ethics.
- *Nibandhas*: codification of Vedic laws.
- *Puranas*: Popular devotional literature glorifying various aspects of God (that is, of Vishnu, Krishna, Shiva, Devi).
- Epics : Historical accounts of *avatars* (that is, incarnations of the gods) and heroes of

ancient Bharat. The *Ramayana* and the *Mahabharata* are the most popular of the Hindu books.

- ᴏ The *Ramayana* consists of 24,000 couplets based upon the life of the Lord Rama, a righteous king who was an *avatar* of the God Vishnu.
  The *Ramayana* is one of the two major epic tales of India. Written by the sage-poet Valmiki, it shows how good overcomes evil.

- ᴏ The *Mahabharata*, is the longest poem in the world, and is the second major epic tale of India. It tells of the war between two Aryan clans, and of the deeds of the Lord Krishna. It consists of some 100,000 verses and was composed over an 800-year period beginning about 400 BC. Contained within this work is a great classic, the *Bhagavad Gita*, or the "Song of the Blessed Lord." This is a dialogue between Prince Arjuna, and Lord Krishna, disguised as his charioteer, which takes place on a battlefield. Because of its importance, the *Bhagavad Gita* is considered as a separate holy book (see below)

- *Darshanas*: the six schools of philosophy.
- *Agamas* or *Tantras* (sectarian scriptures of religious groups within Hinduism: Shaivism, Vaishnavism,and Shaktism). Writings of revered Gurus. (e.g., Shankara [800 AD], Ramanuja [1100's], and Ramakrishna [1800's]).

E THE BHAGAVAD GITA

The *Bhagavad Gita*, has sometimes been called "the Bible of Hinduism" because it is so popular. It is the best known and the most read of all Indian books, despite the fact that it was added late to the *Mahabharata* - in the first century AD. More commentaries have been written on it than on any other of the Indian scriptures.

In essence, it is the message of the *Upanishads* and Hindu philosophy and is considered to be a guide on how to live. It contains the true philosophy of life as suggested by Lord Krishna, who is an incarnation of Lord Vishnu, to Arjuna, the mighty hero of the epic *Mahabharata*.

The *Bhagavad Gita* contains 18 chapters and 700 verses, which are attributed to the four principle participants of the narration as follows:

(i)   Dhritarashtra: 1 verse
(iii) Sanjaya: 41 verses
(iii) Arjuna: 84 verses
(iv) Lord Krishna: 574 verses

In the *Bhagavad Gita*, Lord Krishna is addressed with twenty-seven different names and titles. These are : Anantarupa, Achyuta, Arisudhana, Krishna, Kesava, Kesanishudana, Kamalapatraksha, Govinda, Jagadpatih, Jagannivasa, Janardhana, Devedeva, Devavarah, Purushottama, Bhagawan, Bhutabhavana, Bhutesah, Madhusudhana, Mahabahu, Madhavah, Yadava, Yogaviththama, Vasudeva, Varsheya, Vishnuh, Hrisikesa and Harih.

The story revolves around man's duty, which, if carried out, will bring nothing but sorrow. The significance this story has on Hindu belief is its endorsement of *bhakti*, or devotion to a particular god, as a means of salvation, since Arjuna, the story's main character, decides to put his devotion to Vishnu above his own personal desires. The *Gita* ends with Arjuna's devotion to Vishnu. He is ready to kill his relatives in battle.

THE THREE SECRETS
The teachings in the *Bhagavad Gita* have been called the three secrets. They are:

(i) Duty
One must do one's duty in accordance with one's nature (*swadharmacharana*).
(ii) The hidden self
In everyone there is a real and hidden self that is different from the external false self. Every one must realize this difference between the outer self and the inner self.
(iii) God's omnipresence
One must live in this world with the awareness that all that exists in this world is

but *vasudeva*.

These three secrets are known as *guhya* (secret), *guhyatara* (more secret) and *guhyatma* (most secret).

MORE TEACHING IN THE BHAGAVAD GITA
The following seven teachings are also found:

(i)   Know the reality of the world.
(ii) Know yourself.
(iii) Know the reason for your unstable mind.
(iv) Cultivate true knowledge and discrimination. Know the difference between truth and falsehood, and reality and illusion.
(v)   Know the nature of action and inaction and how actions bind us to earthly life and cause suffering.
(vi) Know the nature of the Supreme-Self. Accept him as the center of your life in place of your ego.
(vii) Know the true nature of devotion, surrender and sacrifice. Live in total devotion to God.

Hindus believe that there are three paths which lead directly to establishing a relationship with God. According to the authority of *Bhagavad Gita* these paths have been designated as:

(i)   the yoga of perfect actions
(ii) the yoga of perfect devotion
(iii) the yoga of perfect knowledge

CONTENTS OF THE CHAPTERS
Each chapter is called a yoga. Yoga is the science of the individual consciousness attaining communion with the Ultimate Consciousness. So each chapter is a highly specialized yoga revealing the path of attaining realization of the Ultimate Truth.

The first six chapters have been classified as the Karma yoga section as they mainly deal with the science of the individual consciousness attaining communion with the Ultimate Consciousness through actions. These chapters are:

Chapter 1 : Visada Yoga
Chapter 2 : Sankhya Yoga

Chapter 3 : Karma Yoga
Chapter 4 : Jnana Yoga
Chapter 5 : Karma Vairagya Yoga
Chapter 6 : Abhyasa Yoga

The middle six chapters have been designated as the Bhakti Yoga section as they deal with the science of the individual consciousness attaining communion with the Ultimate Consciousness by the path of devotion. They are:

Chapter 7 : Paramahamsa Vijnana Yoga
Chapter 8 : Aksara-Parabrahman Yoga
Chapter 9 : Raja-Vidya-Guhya Yoga
Chapter 10 : Vibhuti-Vistara-Yoga
Chapter 11 : Visvarupa-Darsana Yoga
Chapter 12 : Bhakti Yoga

The final six chapters are regarded as the Jnana Yoga section as they are primarily concerned with the science of the individual consciousness attaining communion with the Ultimate Consciousness through the intellect. They are:

Chapter 13 : Ksetra-Ksetrajna Vibhaga Yoga
Chapter 14 : Gunatraya-Vibhaga Yoga
Chapter 15 : Purusottama Yoga
Chapter 16 : Daivasura-Sampad-Vibhaga Yoga
Chapter 17 : Sraddhatraya-Vibhaga Yoga
Chapter 18 : Moksa-Opadesa Yoga

THE *BHAGAVAD GITA*

CHAPTER 1: LAMENTING THE CONSEQUENCE OF WAR

Chapter one introduces the scene, the setting, the circumstances and the characters involved determining the reasons for the *Bhagavad Gita*'s revelation. The scene is the sacred plain of Kuruksetra. The setting is a battlefield. The circumstance is war. The main characters are the Supreme Lord Krishna and Prince Arjuna, witnessed by four million soldiers led by their respective military commanders. After naming the principal warriors on both sides, Arjunas growing dejection is said to be because of the fear of losing friends and relatives in the course of the impending war and the subsequent sins attached to such actions.

Chapter 1
1
Dhrtarastra said: O Sanjaya, after my sons and the sons of Pandu assembled in the place of pilgrimage at Kuruksetra, desiring to fight, what did they do?

2
Sanjaya said: O King, after looking over the army arranged in military formation by the sons of Pandu, King Duryodhana went to his teacher and spoke the following words.

3
O my teacher, behold the great army of the sons of Pandu, so expertly arranged by your intelligent disciple the son of Drupada.

4
Here in this army are many heroic bowmen equal in fighting to Bhima and Arjuna: great fighters like Yuyudhana, Virata and Drupada.

5
There are also great, heroic, powerful fighters like Dhrstaketu, Cekitana, Kasiraja, Purujit, Kuntibhoja and Saibya.

6
There are the mighty Yudhamanyu, the very powerful Uttamauja, the son of Subhadra and the sons of Draupadi. All these warriors are great chariot fighters.

7
But for your information, O best of the brahmans, let me tell you about the captains who are especially qualified to lead my military force.

8
There are personalities like you, Bhisma, Karna, Krpa, Asvatthama, Vikarna and the son of Somadatta called Bhurisrava, who are always victorious in battle.

9

There are many other heroes who are prepared to lay down their lives for my sake. All of them are well equipped with different kinds of weapons, and all are experienced in military science.

10

Our strength is immeasurable, and we are perfectly protected by Grandfather Bhisma, whereas the strength of the Pandavas, carefully protected by Bhima, is limited.

11

All of you must now give full support to Grandfather Bhisma, as you stand at your respective strategic points of entrance into the phalanx of the army.

12

Then Bhisma, the great valiant grandsire of the Kuru dynasty, the grandfather of the fighters, blew his conchshell very loudly, making a sound like the roar of a lion, giving Duryodhana joy.

13

After that, the conchshells, drums, bugles, trumpets and horns were all suddenly sounded, and the combined sound was tumultuous.

14

On the other side, both Lord Krishna and Arjuna, stationed on a great chariot drawn by white horses, sounded their transcendental conchshells.

15

Lord Krishna blew His conchshell, called Pancajanya; Arjuna blew his, the Devadatta; and Bhima, the voracious eater and performer of Herculean tasks, blew his terrific conchshell, called Paundra.

16-18

King Yudhisthira, the son of Kunti, blew his conchshell, the Ananta-vijaya, and Nakula and Sahadeva blew the Sughosa

and Manipuspaka. That great archer the King of Kasi, the great fighter Sikhandi, Dhrstadyumna, Virata, the unconquerable Satyaki, Drupada, the sons of Draupadi, and the others, O King, such as the mighty-armed son of Subhadra, all blew their respective conchshells.

19

The blowing of these different conchshells became uproarious. Vibrating both in the sky and on the earth, it shattered the hearts of the sons of Dhrtarastra.

20

At that time Arjuna, the son of Pandu, seated in the chariot bearing the flag marked with Hanuman, took up his bow and prepared to shoot his arrows. O King, after looking at the sons of Dhrtarastra drawn in military array, Arjuna then spoke to Lord Krishna these words.

21-22

Arjuna said: O infallible one, please draw my chariot between the two armies so that I may see those present here, who desire to fight, and with whom I must contend in this great trial of arms.

23

Let me see those who have come here to fight, wishing to please the evil-minded son of Dhrtarastra.

24

Sanjaya said: O descendant of Bharata, having thus been addressed by Arjuna, Lord Krishna drew up the fine chariot in the midst of the armies of both parties.

25

In the presence of Bhisma, Drona and all the other chieftains of the world, the Lord said, Just behold, Partha, all the Kurus assembled here.

26

There Arjuna could see, within the midst

of the armies of both parties, his fathers, grandfathers, teachers, maternal uncles, brothers, sons, grandsons, friends, and also his fathers-in-law and well-wishers.

27

When the son of Kunti, Arjuna, saw all these different grades of friends and relatives, he became overwhelmed with compassion and spoke thus.

28

Arjuna said: My dear Krishna, seeing my friends and relatives present before me in such a fighting spirit, I feel the limbs of my body quivering and my mouth drying up.

29

My whole body is trembling, my hair is standing on end, my bow Gandiva is slipping from my hand, and my skin is burning.

30

I am now unable to stand here any longer. I am forgetting myself, and my mind is reeling. I see only causes of misfortune, O Krishna, killer of the Kesi demon.

31

I do not see how any good can come from killing my own kinsmen in this battle, nor can I, my dear Krishna, desire any subsequent victory, kingdom, or happiness.

32-35

O Govinda, of what avail to us are a kingdom, happiness or even life itself when all those for whom we may desire them are now arrayed on this battlefield? O Madhusudana, when teachers, fathers, sons, grandfathers, maternal uncles, fathers-in-law, grandsons, brothers-in-law and other relatives are ready to give up their lives and properties and are standing before me, why should I wish to kill them, even though they might otherwise kill me? O maintainer of all living entities, I am not prepared to fight with them even

in exchange for the three worlds, let alone this earth. What pleasure will we derive from killing the sons of Dhrtarastra?

36

Sin will overcome us if we slay such aggressors. Therefore it is not proper for us to kill the sons of Dhrtarastra and our friends. What should we gain, O Krishna, husband of the goddess of fortune, and how could we be happy by killing our own kinsmen?

37-38

O Janardana, although these men, their hearts overtaken by greed, see no fault in killing one's family or quarreling with friends, why should we, who can see the crime in destroying a family, engage in these acts of sin?

39

With the destruction of dynasty, the eternal family tradition is vanquished, and thus the rest of the family becomes involved in irreligion.

40

When irreligion is prominent in the family, O Krishna, the women of the family become polluted, and from the degradation of womanhood, O descendant of Vrsni, comes unwanted progeny.

41

An increase of unwanted population certainly causes hellish life both for the family and for those who destroy the family tradition. The ancestors of such corrupt families fall down, because the performances for offering them food and water are entirely stopped.

42

By the evil deeds of those who destroy the family tradition and thus give rise to unwanted children, all kinds of community projects and family welfare activities are devastated.

43

O Krishna, maintainer of the people, I have heard that those who destroy family traditions dwell always in hell.

44

Alas, how strange it is that we are preparing to commit greatly sinful acts. Driven by the desire to enjoy royal happiness, we are intent on killing our own kinsmen.

45

Better for me if the sons of Dhrtarastra, weapons in hand, were to kill me unarmed and unresisting on the battlefield.

46

Sanjaya said: Arjuna, having thus spoken on the battlefield, cast aside his bow and arrows and sat down on the chariot, his mind overwhelmed with grief.

CHAPTER 2: THE ETERNAL REALITY OF THE SOUL'S IMMORTALITY

In chapter two Arjuna accepts the position as a disciple of Lord Krishna and taking complete of Him requests the Lord to instruct him in how to dispel his lamentation and grief. This chapter is often deemed as a summary to the entire *Bhagavad Gita*. Here many subjects are explained such as: karma yoga, jnana yoga, sankhya yoga, buddih yoga and the atma which is the soul. Predominance has been given to the immortal nature of the soul existing within all living entities and it has been described in great detail.

Chapter 2

1

Sanjaya said: Seeing Arjuna full of compassion, his mind depressed, his eyes full of tears, Madhusudana, Krishna, spoke the following words.

2

The Supreme Personality of Godhead said: My dear Arjuna, how have these impurities come upon you? They are not at all befitting a man who knows the value of life. They lead not to higher planets but to infamy.

3

O son of Prtha, do not yield to this degrading impotence. It does not become you. Give up such petty weakness of heart and arise, O chastiser of the enemy.

4

Arjuna said: O killer of enemies, O killer of Madhu, how can I counterattack with arrows in battle men like Bhisma and Drona, who are worthy of my worship?

5

It would be better to live in this world by begging than to live at the cost of the lives of great souls who are my teachers. Even though desiring worldly gain, they are superiors. If they are killed, everything we enjoy will be tainted with blood.

6

Nor do we know which is better - conquering them or being conquered by them. If we killed the sons of Dhrtarastra, we should not care to live. Yet they are now standing before us on the battlefield.

7

Now I am confused about my duty and have lost all composure because of miserly weakness. In this condition I am asking You to tell me for certain what is best for me. Now I am Your disciple, and a soul surrendered unto You. Please instruct me.

8

I can find no means to drive away this grief which is drying up my senses. I will not be able to dispel it even if I win a prosperous, unrivaled kingdom on earth with sovereignty like the demigods in heaven.

9

Sanjaya said: Having spoken thus, Arjuna, chastiser of enemies, told Krishna, "Govinda, I shall not fight," and fell silent.

10

O descendant of Bharata, at that time Krishna, smiling, in the midst of both the armies, spoke the following words to the grief-stricken Arjuna.

11

The Supreme Personality of Godhead said: While speaking learned words, you are mourning for what is not worthy of grief. Those who are wise lament neither for the living nor for the dead.

12

Never was there a time when I did not exist, nor you, nor all these kings; nor in the future shall any of us cease to be.

13

As the embodied soul continuously passes, in this body, from boyhood to youth to old age, the soul similarly passes into another body at death. A sober person is not bewildered by such a change.

14

O son of Kunti, the nonpermanent appearance of happiness and distress, and their disappearance in due course, are like the appearance and disappearance of winter and summer seasons. They arise from sense perception, O scion of Bharata, and one must learn to tolerate them without being disturbed.

15

O best among men [Arjuna], the person who is not disturbed by happiness and distress and is steady in both is certainly eligible for liberation.

16

Those who are seers of the truth have concluded that of the nonexistent [the material body] there is no endurance and of the eternal [the soul] there is no change. This they have concluded by studying the nature of both.

17

That which pervades the entire body you should know to be indestructible. No one is able to destroy that imperishable soul.

18

The material body of the indestructible, immeasurable and eternal living entity is sure to come to an end; therefore, fight, O descendant of Bharata.

19

Neither he who thinks the living entity the slayer nor he who thinks it slain is in knowledge, for the self slays not nor is slain.

20

For the soul there is neither birth nor death at any time. He has not come into being, does not come into being, and will not come into being. He is unborn, eternal, ever-existing and primeval. He is not slain when the body is slain.

21

O Partha, how can a person who knows that the soul is indestructible, eternal, unborn and immutable kill anyone or cause anyone to kill?

22

As a person puts on new garments, giving up old ones, the soul similarly accepts new material bodies, giving up the old and useless ones.

23

The soul can never be cut to pieces by any weapon, nor burned by fire, nor moistened by water, nor withered by the wind.

24

This individual soul is unbreakable and insoluble, and can be neither burned nor dried. He is everlasting, present everywhere, unchangeable, immovable and eternally the same.

25
It is said that the soul is invisible, inconceivable and immutable. Knowing this, you should not grieve for the body.

26
If, however, you think that the soul [or the symptoms of life] is always born and dies forever, you still have no reason to lament, O mighty-armed.

27
One who has taken his birth is sure to die, and after death one is sure to take birth again. Therefore, in the unavoidable discharge of your duty, you should not lament.

28
All created beings are unmanifest in their beginning, manifest in their interim state, and unmanifest again when annihilated. So what need is there for lamentation?

29
Some look on the soul as amazing, some describe him as amazing, and some hear of him as amazing, while others, even after hearing about him, cannot understand him at all.

30
O descendant of Bharata, he who dwells in the body can never be slain. Therefore you need not grieve for any living being.

31
Considering your specific duty as a ksatriya, you should know that there is no better engagement for you than fighting on religious principles; and so there is no need for hesitation.

32
O Partha, happy are the ksatriyas to whom such fighting opportunities come unsought, opening for them the doors of the heavenly planets.

33
If, however, you do not perform your religious duty of fighting, then you will certainly incur sins for neglecting your duties and thus lose your reputation as a fighter.

34
People will always speak of your infamy, and for a respectable person, dishonor is worse than death.

35
The great generals who have highly esteemed your name and fame will think that you have left the battlefield out of fear only, and thus they will consider you insignificant.

36
Your enemies will describe you in many unkind words and scorn your ability. What could be more painful for you?

37
O son of Kunti, either you will be killed on the battlefield and attain the heavenly planets, or you will conquer and enjoy the earthly kingdom. Therefore, get up with determination and fight.

38
Do thou fight for the sake of fighting, without considering happiness or distress, loss or gain, victory or defeat - and by so doing you shall never incur sin.

39
Thus far I have described this knowledge to you through analytical study. Now listen as I explain it in terms of working without fruitive results. O son of Prtha, when you act in such knowledge you can free yourself from the bondage of works.

40
In this endeavor there is no loss or diminution, and a little advancement on this path can protect one from the most dangerous type of fear.

41

Those who are on this path are resolute in purpose, and their aim is one. O beloved child of the Kurus, the intelligence of those who are irresolute is many-branched.

42-43

Men of small knowledge are very much attached to the flowery words of the *Vedas*, which recommend various fruitive activities for elevation to heavenly planets, resultant good birth, power, and so forth. Being desirous of sense gratification and opulent life, they say that there is nothing more than this.

44

In the minds of those who are too attached to sense enjoyment and material opulence, and who are bewildered by such things, the resolute determination for devotional service to the Supreme Lord does not take place.

45

The *Vedas* deal mainly with the subject of the three modes of material nature. O Arjuna, become transcendental to these three modes. Be free from all dualities and from all anxieties for gain and safety, and be established in the self.

46

All purposes served by a small well can at once be served by a great reservoir of water. Similarly, all the purposes of the *Vedas* can be served to one who knows the purpose behind them.

47

You have a right to perform your prescribed duty, but you are not entitled to the fruits of action. Never consider yourself the cause of the results of your activities, and never be attached to not doing your duty.

48

Perform your duty equipoised, O Arjuna, abandoning all attachment to success or failure. Such equanimity is called yoga.

49

O Dhananjaya, keep all abominable activities far distant by devotional service, and in that consciousness surrender unto the Lord. Those who want to enjoy the fruits of their work are misers.

50

A man engaged in devotional service rids himself of both good and bad actions even in this life. Therefore strive for yoga, which is the art of all work.

51

By thus engaging in devotional service to the Lord, great sages or devotees free themselves from the results of work in the material world. In this way they become free from the cycle of birth and death and attain the state beyond all miseries [by going back to Godhead].

52

When your intelligence has passed out of the dense forest of delusion, you shall become indifferent to all that has been heard and all that is to be heard.

53

When your mind is no longer disturbed by the flowery language of the *Vedas*, and when it remains fixed in the trance of self-realization, then you will have attained the divine consciousness.

54

Arjuna said: O Krishna, what are the symptoms of one whose consciousness is thus merged in transcendence? How does he speak, and what is his language? How does he sit, and how does he walk?

55

The Supreme Personality of Godhead said: O Partha, when a man gives up all varieties of desire for sense gratification, which arise from mental concoction, and when his mind, thus purified, finds satisfaction in the self alone, then he is said to be in pure transcendental consciousness.

56

One who is not disturbed in mind even amidst the threefold miseries or elated when there is happiness, and who is free from attachment, fear and anger, is called a sage of steady mind.

57

In the material world, one who is unaffected by whatever good or evil he may obtain, neither praising it nor despising it, is firmly fixed in perfect knowledge.

58

One who is able to withdraw his senses from sense objects, as the tortoise draws its limbs within the shell, is firmly fixed in perfect consciousness.

59

The embodied soul may be restricted from sense enjoyment, though the taste for sense objects remains. But, ceasing such engagements by experiencing a higher taste, he is fixed in consciousness.

60

The senses are so strong and impetuous, O Arjuna, that they forcibly carry away the mind even of a man of discrimination who is endeavoring to control them.

61

One who restrains his senses, keeping them under full control, and fixes his consciousness upon Me, is known as a man of steady intelligence.

62

While contemplating the objects of the senses, a person develops attachment for them, and from such attachment lust develops, and from lust anger arises.

63

From anger, complete delusion arises, and from delusion bewilderment of memory.

When memory is bewildered, intelligence is lost, and when intelligence is lost one falls down again into the material pool.

64

But a person free from all attachment and aversion and able to control his senses through regulative principles of freedom can obtain the complete mercy of the Lord.

65

For one thus satisfied [in Krishna consciousness], the threefold miseries of material existence exist no longer; in such satisfied consciousness, one's intelligence is soon well established.

66

One who is not connected with the Supreme [in Krishna consciousness] can have neither transcendental intelligence nor a steady mind, without which there is no possibility of peace. And how can there be any happiness without peace?

67

As a boat on the water is swept away by a strong wind, even one of the roaming senses on which the mind focuses can carry away a man's intelligence.

68

Therefore, O mighty-armed, one whose senses are restrained from their objects is certainly of steady intelligence.

69

What is night for all beings is the time of awakening for the self-controlled; and the time of awakening for all beings is night for the introspective sage.

70

A person who is not disturbed by the incessant flow of desires - that enter like rivers into the ocean, which is ever being filled but is always still - can alone achieve peace, and not the man who strives to satisfy such desires.

71
A person who has given up all desires for sense gratification, who lives free from desires, who has given up all sense of proprietorship and is devoid of false ego - he alone can attain real peace.

72
That is the way of the spiritual and godly life, after attaining which a man is not bewildered. If one is thus situated even at the hour of death, one can enter into the kingdom of God.

CHAPTER 3: THE ETERNAL DUTIES OF A HUMAN BEING

Chapter three establishes, by various points of view, the fact that the performance of prescribed duties is obligatory for everyone. Here Lord Krishna categorically and comprehensively explains how it is the duty of each and every member of society to carry out their functions and responsibilities in their respective stage of life according to the rules and regulations of the society in which one lives. Further, the Lord explains why such duties must be performed, what benefit is gained by performing them, what harm is caused by not performing them. Plus what actions lead to bondage and what actions lead to salvation. All these points relating to duty have been described in great detail.

Chapter 3
1
Arjuna said: O Janardana, O Kesava, why do You want to engage me in this ghastly warfare, if You think that intelligence is better than fruitive work?

2
My intelligence is bewildered by Your equivocal instructions. Therefore, please tell me decisively which will be most beneficial for me.

3
The Supreme Personality of Godhead said: O sinless Arjuna, I have already explained that there are two classes of men who try to realize the self. Some are inclined to understand it by empirical, philosophical speculation, and others by devotional service.

4
Not by merely abstaining from work can one achieve freedom from reaction, nor by renunciation alone can one attain perfection.

5
Everyone is forced to act helplessly according to the qualities he has acquired from the modes of material nature; therefore no one can refrain from doing something, not even for a moment.

6
One who restrains the senses of action but whose mind dwells on sense objects certainly deludes himself and is called a pretender.

7
On the other hand, if a sincere person tries to control the active senses by the mind and begins karma-yoga [in Krishna consciousness] without attachment, he is by far superior.

8
Perform your prescribed duty, for doing so is better than not working. One cannot even maintain one's physical body without work.

9
Work done as a sacrifice for Vishnu has to be performed, otherwise work causes bondage in this material world. Therefore, O son of Kunti, perform your prescribed duties for His satisfaction, and in that way you will always remain free from bondage.

10
In the beginning of creation, the Lord of all creatures sent forth generations of men and demigods, along with sacrifices for

Vishnu, and blessed them by saying, "Be thou happy by this *yajna* [sacrifice] because its performance will bestow upon you everything desirable for living happily and achieving liberation."

11

The demigods, being pleased by sacrifices, will also please you, and thus, by cooperation between men and demigods, prosperity will reign for all.

12

In charge of the various necessities of life, the demigods, being satisfied by the performance of yajna [sacrifice], will supply all necessities to you. But he who enjoys such gifts without offering them to the demigods in return is certainly a thief.

13

The devotees of the Lord are released from all kinds of sins because they eat food which is offered first for sacrifice. Others, who prepare food for personal sense enjoyment, verily eat only sin.

14

All living bodies subsist on food grains, which are produced from rains. Rains are produced by performance of *yajna* [sacrifice], and yajna is born of prescribed duties.

15

Regulated activities are prescribed in the *Vedas*, and the *Vedas* are directly manifested from the Supreme Personality of Godhead. Consequently the all-pervading Transcendence is eternally situated in acts of sacrifice.

16

My dear Arjuna, one who does not follow in human life the cycle of sacrifice thus established by the *Vedas* certainly leads a life full of sin. Living only for the satisfaction of the senses, such a person lives in vain.

17

But for one who takes pleasure in the self, whose human life is one of self-realization, and who is satisfied in the self only, fully satiated - for him there is no duty.

18

A self-realized man has no purpose to fulfill in the discharge of his prescribed duties, nor has he any reason not to perform such work. Nor has he any need to depend on any other living being.

19

Therefore, without being attached to the fruits of activities, one should act as a matter of duty, for by working without attachment one attains the Supreme.

20

Kings such as Janaka attained perfection solely by performance of prescribed duties. Therefore, just for the sake of educating the people in general, you should perform your work.

21

Whatever action a great man performs, common men follow. And whatever standards he sets by exemplary acts, all the world pursues.

22

O son of Prtha, there is no work prescribed for Me within all the three planetary systems. Nor am I in want of anything, nor have I a need to obtain anything - and yet I am engaged in prescribed duties.

23

For if I ever failed to engage in carefully performing prescribed duties, O Partha, certainly all men would follow My path.

24

If I did not perform prescribed duties, all these worlds would be put to ruination. I would be the cause of creating unwanted population, and I would thereby destroy the peace of all living beings.

25

As the ignorant perform their duties with attachment to results, the learned may similarly act, but without attachment, for the sake of leading people on the right path.

26

So as not to disrupt the minds of ignorant men attached to the fruitive results of prescribed duties, a learned person should not induce them to stop work. Rather, by working in the spirit of devotion, he should engage them in all sorts of activities [for the gradual development of Krishna consciousness].

27

The spirit soul bewildered by the influence of false ego thinks himself the doer of activities that are in actuality carried out by the three modes of material nature.

28

One who is in knowledge of the Absolute Truth, O mighty-armed, does not engage himself in the senses and sense gratification, knowing well the differences between work in devotion and work for fruitive results.

29

Bewildered by the modes of material nature, the ignorant fully engage themselves in material activities and become attached. But the wise should not unsettle them, although these duties are inferior due to the performers' lack of knowledge.

30

Therefore, O Arjuna, surrendering all your works unto Me, with full knowledge of Me, without desires for profit, with no claims to proprietorship, and free from lethargy, fight.

31

Those persons who execute their duties according to My injunctions and who follow this teaching faithfully, without envy, become free from the bondage of fruitive actions.

32

But those who, out of envy, disregard these teachings and do not follow them are to be considered bereft of all knowledge, befooled, and ruined in their endeavors for perfection.

33

Even a man of knowledge acts according to his own nature, for everyone follows the nature he has acquired from the three modes. What can repression accomplish?

34

There are principles to regulate attachment and aversion pertaining to the senses and their objects. One should not come under the control of such attachment and aversion, because they are stumbling blocks on the path of self-realization.

35

It is far better to discharge one's prescribed duties, even though faultily, than another's duties perfectly. Destruction in the course of performing one's own duty is better than engaging in another's duties, for to follow another's path is dangerous.

36

Arjuna said: O descendant of Vrsni, by what is one impelled to sinful acts, even unwillingly, as if engaged by force?

37

The Supreme Personality of Godhead said: It is lust only, Arjuna, which is born of contact with the material mode of passion and later transformed into wrath, and which is the all-devouring sinful enemy of this world.

38

As fire is covered by smoke, as a mirror is covered by dust, or as the embryo is covered by the womb, the living entity is similarly covered by different degrees of this lust.

39

Thus the wise living entity's pure consciousness becomes covered by his eternal enemy in the form of lust, which is never satisfied and which burns like fire.

40

The senses, the mind and the intelligence are the sitting places of this lust. Through them lust covers the real knowledge of the living entity and bewilders him.

41

Therefore, O Arjuna, best of the Bharatas, in the very beginning curb this great symbol of sin [lust] by regulating the senses, and slay this destroyer of knowledge and self-realization.

42

The working senses are superior to dull matter; mind is higher than the senses; intelligence is still higher than the mind; and he [the soul] is even higher than the intelligence.

43

Thus knowing oneself to be transcendental to the material senses, mind and intelligence, O mighty-armed Arjuna, one should steady the mind by deliberate spiritual intelligence [Krishna consciousness] and thus -by spiritual strength - conquer this insatiable enemy known as lust.

CHAPTER 4: APPROACHING THE ULTIMATE TRUTH

In chapter four Lord Krishna reveals how spiritual knowledge is received by succession and the reason and nature of His descent into the material worlds. Here He also explains the paths of action and knowledge as well as the wisdom regarding the supreme knowledge which results at the culmination of the two paths.

Chapter 4

1

The Personality of Godhead, Lord Sri Krishna, said: I instructed this imperishable science of yoga to the sun-god, Vivasvan, and Vivasvan instructed it to Manu, the father of mankind, and Manu in turn instructed it to Iksvaku.

2

This supreme science was thus received through the chain of succession, and the saintly kings understood it in that way. But in course of time the succession was broken, and therefore the science as it is appears to be lost.

3

That very ancient science of the relationship with the Supreme is today told by Me to you because you are My devotee as well as My friend and can therefore understand the transcendental mystery of this science.

4

Arjuna said: The sun-god Vivasvan is senior by birth to You. How am I to understand that in the beginning You instructed this science to him?

5

The Personality of Godhead said: Many, many births both you and I have passed. I can remember all of them, but you cannot, O subduer of the enemy!

6

Although I am unborn and My transcendental body never deteriorates, and although I am the Lord of all living entities, I still appear in every millennium in My original transcendental form.

7

Whenever and wherever there is a decline in religious practice, O descendant of Bharata, and a predominant rise of irreligion - at that time I descend Myself.

8

To deliver the pious and to annihilate the miscreants, as well as to reestablish the principles of religion, I Myself appear, millennium after millennium.

9

One who knows the transcendental nature of My appearance and activities does not, upon leaving the body, take his birth again in this material world, but attains My eternal abode, O Arjuna.

10

Being freed from attachment, fear and anger, being fully absorbed in Me and taking refuge in Me, many, many persons in the past became purified by knowledge of Me - and thus they all attained transcendental love for Me.

11

As all surrender unto Me, I reward them accordingly. Everyone follows My path in all respects, O son of Prtha.

12

Men in this world desire success in fruitive activities, and therefore they worship the demigods. Quickly, of course, men get results from fruitive work in this world.

13

According to the three modes of material nature and the work associated with them, the four divisions of human society are created by Me. And although I am the creator of this system, you should know that I am yet the nondoer, being unchangeable.

14

There is no work that affects Me; nor do I aspire for the fruits of action. One who understands this truth about Me also does not become entangled in the fruitive reactions of work.

15

All the liberated souls in ancient times

acted with this understanding of My transcendental nature. Therefore you should perform your duty, following in their footsteps.

16

Even the intelligent are bewildered in determining what is action and what is inaction. Now I shall explain to you what action is, knowing which you shall be liberated from all misfortune.

17

The intricacies of action are very hard to understand. Therefore one should know properly what action is, what forbidden action is, and what inaction is.

18

One who sees inaction in action, and action in inaction, is intelligent among men, and he is in the transcendental position, although engaged in all sorts of activities.

19

One is understood to be in full knowledge whose every endeavor is devoid of desire for sense gratification. He is said by sages to be a worker for whom the reactions of work have been burned up by the fire of perfect knowledge.

20

Abandoning all attachment to the results of his activities, ever satisfied and independent, he performs no fruitive action, although engaged in all kinds of undertakings.

21

Such a man of understanding acts with mind and intelligence perfectly controlled, gives up all sense of proprietorship over his possessions, and acts only for the bare necessities of life. Thus working, he is not affected by sinful reactions.

22

He who is satisfied with gain which comes

of its own accord, who is free from duality and does not envy, who is steady in both success and failure, is never entangled, although performing actions.

23
The work of a man who is unattached to the modes of material nature and who is fully situated in transcendental knowledge merges entirely into transcendence.

24
A person who is fully absorbed in Krishna consciousness is sure to attain the spiritual kingdom because of his full contribution to spiritual activities, in which the consummation is absolute and that which is offered is of the same spiritual nature.

25
Some yogis perfectly worship the demigods by offering different sacrifices to them, and some of them offer sacrifices in the fire of the Supreme Brahman.

26
Some [the unadulterated brahmacaris] sacrifice the hearing process and the senses in the fire of mental control, and others [the regulated householders] sacrifice the objects of the senses in the fire of the senses.

27
Others, who are interested in achieving self-realization through control of the mind and senses, offer the functions of all the senses, and of the life breath, as oblations into the fire of the controlled mind.

28
Having accepted strict vows, some become enlightened by sacrificing their possessions, and others by performing severe austerities, by practicing the yoga of eightfold mysticism, or by studying the *Vedas* to advance in transcendental knowledge.

29
Still others, who are inclined to the process of breath restraint to remain in trance, practice by offering the movement of the outgoing breath into the incoming, and the incoming breath into the outgoing, and thus at last remain in trance, stopping all breathing. Others, curtailing the eating process, offer the outgoing breath into itself as a sacrifice.

30
All these performers who know the meaning of sacrifice become cleansed of sinful reactions, and, having tasted the nectar of the results of sacrifices, they advance toward the supreme eternal atmosphere.

31
O best of the Kuru dynasty, without sacrifice one can never live happily on this planet or in this life: what then of the next?

32
All these different types of sacrifice are approved by the Vedas, and all of them are born of different types of work. Knowing them as such, you will become liberated.

33
O chastiser of the enemy, the sacrifice performed in knowledge is better than the mere sacrifice of material possessions. After all, O son of Prtha, all sacrifices of work culminate in transcendental knowledge.

34
Just try to learn the truth by approaching a spiritual master. Inquire from him submissively and render service unto him. The self-realized souls can impart knowledge unto you because they have seen the truth.

35
Having obtained real knowledge from a self-realized soul, you will never fall again

into such illusion, for by this knowledge you will see that all living beings are but part of the Supreme, or, in other words, that they are Mine.

36

Even if you are considered to be the most sinful of all sinners, when you are situated in the boat of transcendental knowledge you will be able to cross over the ocean of miseries.

37

As a blazing fire turns firewood to ashes, O Arjuna, so does the fire of knowledge burn to ashes all reactions to material activities.

38

In this world, there is nothing so sublime and pure as transcendental knowledge. Such knowledge is the mature fruit of all mysticism. And one who has become accomplished in the practice of devotional service enjoys this knowledge within himself in due course of time.

39

A faithful man who is dedicated to transcendental knowledge and who subdues his senses is eligible to achieve such knowledge, and having achieved it he quickly attains the supreme spiritual peace.

40

But ignorant and faithless persons who doubt the revealed scriptures do not attain God consciousness; they fall down. For the doubting soul there is happiness neither in this world nor in the next.

41

One who acts in devotional service, renouncing the fruits of his actions, and whose doubts have been destroyed by transcendental knowledge, is situated factually in the self. Thus he is not bound by the reactions of work, O conqueror of riches.

42

Therefore the doubts which have arisen in your heart out of ignorance should be slashed by the weapon of knowledge. Armed with yoga, O Bharata, stand and fight.

CHAPTER 5: ACTION AND RENUNCIATION

In chapter five Lord Krishna delineates the concepts of action with detachment and renunciation in actions explaining that both are a means to the same goal. Here He explains how salvation is attained by the pursuance of these paths.

Chapter 5
1

Arjuna said: O Krishna, first of all You ask me to renounce work, and then again You recommend work with devotion. Now will You kindly tell me definitely which of the two is more beneficial?

2

The Personality of Godhead replied: The renunciation of work and work in devotion are both good for liberation. But, of the two, work in devotional service is better than renunciation of work.

3

One who neither hates nor desires the fruits of his activities is known to be always renounced. Such a person, free from all dualities, easily overcomes material bondage and is completely liberated, O mighty-armed Arjuna.

4

Only the ignorant speak of devotional service [karma-yoga] as being different from the analytical study of the material world [Sankhya]. Those who are actually learned say that he who applies himself well to one of these paths achieves the results of both.

5

One who knows that the position reached

by means of analytical study can also be attained by devotional service, and who therefore sees analytical study and devotional service to be on the same level, sees things as they are.

6

Merely renouncing all activities yet not engaging in the devotional service of the Lord cannot make one happy. But a thoughtful person engaged in devotional service can achieve the Supreme without delay.

7

One who works in devotion, who is a pure soul, and who controls his mind and senses is dear to everyone, and everyone is dear to him. Though always working, such a man is never entangled.

8-9

A person in the divine consciousness, although engaged in seeing, hearing, touching, smelling, eating, moving about, sleeping and breathing, always knows within himself that he actually does nothing at all. Because while speaking, evacuating, receiving, or opening or closing his eyes, he always knows that only the material senses are engaged with their objects and that he is aloof from them.

10

One who performs his duty without attachment, surrendering the results unto the Supreme Lord, is unaffected by sinful action, as the lotus leaf is untouched by water.

11

The yogis, abandoning attachment, act with body, mind, intelligence and even with the senses, only for the purpose of purification.

12

The steadily devoted soul attains unadulterated peace because he offers the result of all activities to Me; whereas a person who is not in union with the Divine, who is greedy for the fruits of his labor, becomes entangled.

13

When the embodied living being controls his nature and mentally renounces all actions, he resides happily in the city of nine gates [the material body], neither working nor causing work to be done.

14

The embodied spirit, master of the city of his body, does not create activities, nor does he induce people to act, nor does he create the fruits of action. All this is enacted by the modes of material nature.

15

Nor does the Supreme Lord assume anyone's sinful or pious activities. Embodied beings, however, are bewildered because of the ignorance which covers their real knowledge.

16

When, however, one is enlightened with the knowledge by which science is destroyed, then his knowledge reveals everything, as the sun lights up everything in the daytime.

17

When one's intelligence, mind, faith and refuge are all fixed in the Supreme, then one becomes fully cleansed of misgivings through complete knowledge and thus proceeds straight on the path of liberation.

18

The humble sages, by virtue of true knowledge, see with equal vision a learned and gentle brahmana, a cow, an elephant, a dog and a dog-eater [outcast].

19

Those whose minds are established in sameness and equanimity have already conquered the conditions of birth and death. They are flawless like Brahman, and thus they are already situated in Brahman.

20

A person who neither rejoices upon achieving something pleasant nor laments upon obtaining something unpleasant, who is self-intelligent, who is unbewildered, and who knows the science of God, is already situated in transcendence.

21

Such a liberated person is not attracted to material sense pleasure but is always in trance, enjoying the pleasure within. In this way the self-realized person enjoys unlimited happiness, for he concentrates on the Supreme.

22

An intelligent person does not take part in the sources of misery, which are due to contact with the material senses. O son of Kunti, such pleasures have a beginning and an end, and so the wise man does not delight in them.

23

Before giving up this present body, if one is able to tolerate the urges of the material senses and check the force of desire and anger, he is well situated and is happy in this world.

24

One whose happiness is within, who is active and rejoices within, and whose aim is inward is actually the perfect mystic. He is liberated in the Supreme, and ultimately he attains the Supreme.

25

Those who are beyond the dualities that arise from doubts, whose minds are engaged within, who are always busy working for the welfare of all living beings, and who are free from all sins achieve liberation in the Supreme.

26

Those who are free from anger and all material desires, who are self-realized, self-disciplined and constantly endeavoring for perfection, are assured of liberation in the Supreme in the very near future.

27-28

Shutting out all external sense objects, keeping the eyes and vision concentrated between the two eyebrows, suspending the inward and outward breaths within the nostrils, and thus controlling the mind, senses and intelligence, the transcendentalist aiming at liberation becomes free from desire, fear and anger. One who is always in this state is certainly liberated.

29

A person in full consciousness of Me, knowing Me to be the ultimate beneficiary of all sacrifices and austerities, the Supreme Lord of all planets and demigods, and the benefactor and well-wisher of all living entities, attains peace from the pangs of material miseries.

CHAPTER 6: THE SCIENCE OF SELF-REALIZATION

In chapter six Lord Krishna reveals astanga yoga, and the exact process of practicing such yoga. He explains in detail the difficulties of the mind and the procedures by which one may gain mastery of their mind through yoga which reveals the spiritual nature of a living entity.

Chapter 6

1

The Supreme Personality of Godhead said: One who is unattached to the fruits of his work and who works as he is obligated is in the renounced order of life, and he is the true mystic, not he who lights no fire and performs no duty.

2

What is called renunciation you should know to be the same as yoga, or linking oneself with the Supreme, O son of Pandu, for one can never become a yogi unless he renounces the desire for sense gratification.

3

For one who is a neophyte in the eightfold yoga system, work is said to be the means; and for one who is already elevated in yoga, cessation of all material activities is said to be the means.

4

A person is said to be elevated in yoga when, having renounced all material desires, he neither acts for sense gratification nor engages in fruitive activities.

5

One must deliver himself with the help of his mind, and not degrade himself. The mind is the friend of the conditioned soul, and his enemy as well.

6

For him who has conquered the mind, the mind is the best of friends; but for one who has failed to do so, his mind will remain the greatest enemy.

7

For one who has conquered the mind, the Supersoul is already reached, for he has attained tranquility. To such a man happiness and distress, heat and cold, honor and dishonor are all the same.

8

A person is said to be established in self-realization and is called a yogi [or mystic] when he is fully satisfied by virtue of acquired knowledge and realization. Such a person is situated in transcendence and is self-controlled. He sees everything - whether it be pebbles, stones or gold - as the same.

9

A person is considered still further advanced when he regards honest well-wishers, affectionate benefactors, the neutral, mediators, the envious, friends and enemies, the pious and the sinners all with an equal mind.

10

A transcendentalist should always engage his body, mind and self in relationship with the Supreme; he should live alone in a secluded place and should always carefully control his mind. He should be free from desires and feelings of possessiveness.

11-12

To practice yoga, one should go to a secluded place and should lay kusa grass on the ground and then cover it with a deerskin and a soft cloth. The seat should be neither too high nor too low and should be situated in a sacred place. The yogi should then sit on it very firmly and practice yoga to purify the heart by controlling his mind, senses and activities and fixing the mind on one point.

13-14

One should hold one's body, neck and head erect in a straight line and stare steadily at the tip of the nose. Thus, with an unagitated, subdued mind, devoid of fear, completely free from sex life, one should meditate upon Me within the heart and make Me the ultimate goal of life.

15

Thus practicing constant control of the body, mind and activities, the mystic transcendentalist, his mind regulated, attains to the kingdom of God [or the abode of Krishna] by cessation of material existence.

16

There is no possibility of one's becoming a yogi, O Arjuna, if one eats too much or eats too little, sleeps too much or does not sleep enough.

17
He who is regulated in his habits of eating, sleeping, recreation and work can mitigate all material pains by practicing the yoga system.

18
When the yogi, by practice of yoga, disciplines his mental activities and becomes situated in transcendence - devoid of all material desires - he is said to be well established in yoga.

19
As a lamp in a windless place does not waver, so the transcendentalist, whose mind is controlled, remains always steady in his meditation on the transcendent self.

20-23
In the stage of perfection called trance, or samadhi, one's mind is completely restrained from material mental activities by practice of yoga. This perfection is characterized by one's ability to see the self by the pure mind and to relish and rejoice in the self. In that joyous state, one is situated in boundless transcendental happiness, realized through transcendental senses. Established thus, one never departs from the truth, and upon gaining this he thinks there is no greater gain. Being situated in such a position, one is never shaken, even in the midst of greatest difficulty. This indeed is actual freedom from all miseries arising from material contact.

24
One should engage oneself in the practice of yoga with determination and faith and not be deviated from the path. One should abandon, without exception, all material desires born of mental speculation and thus control all the senses on all sides by the mind.

25
Gradually, step by step, one should become situated in trance by means of intelligence sustained by full conviction, and thus the mind should be fixed on the self alone and should think of nothing else.

26
From wherever the mind wanders due to its flickering and unsteady nature, one must certainly withdraw it and bring it back under the control of the self.

27
The yogi whose mind is fixed on Me verily attains the highest perfection of transcendental happiness. He is beyond the mode of passion, he realizes his qualitative identity with the Supreme, and thus he is freed from all reactions to past deeds.

28
Thus the self-controlled yogi, constantly engaged in yoga practice, becomes free from all material contamination and achieves the highest stage of perfect happiness in transcendental loving service to the Lord.

29
A true yogi observes Me in all beings and also sees every being in Me. Indeed, the self-realized person sees Me, the same Supreme Lord, everywhere.

30
For one who sees Me everywhere and sees everything in Me, I am never lost, nor is he ever lost to Me.

31
Such a yogi, who engages in the worshipful service of the Supersoul, knowing that I and the Supersoul are one, remains always in Me in all circumstances.

32
He is a perfect yogi who, by comparison to his own self, sees the true equality of all beings, in both their happiness and their distress, O Arjuna!

33

Arjuna said: O Madhusudana, the system of yoga which You have summarized appears impractical and unendurable to me, for the mind is restless and unsteady.

34

For the mind is restless, turbulent, obstinate and very strong, O Krishna, and to subdue it, I think, is more difficult than controlling the wind.

35

Lord Sri Krishna said: O mighty-armed son of Kunti, it is undoubtedly very difficult to curb the restless mind, but it is possible by suitable practice and by detachment.

36

For one whose mind is unbridled, self-realization is difficult work. But he whose mind is controlled and who strives by appropriate means is assured of success. That is My opinion.

37

Arjuna said: O Krishna, what is the destination of the unsuccessful transcendentalist, who in the beginning takes to the process of self-realization with faith but who later desists due to worldly-mindedness and thus does not attain perfection in mysticism?

38

O mighty-armed Krishna, does not such a man, who is bewildered from the path of transcendence, fall away from both spiritual and material success and perish like a riven cloud, with no position in any sphere?

39

This is my doubt, O Krishna, and I ask You to dispel it completely. But for You, no one is to be found who can destroy this doubt.

40

The Supreme Personality of Godhead said: Son of Prtha, a transcendentalist engaged in auspicious activities does not meet with destruction either in this world or in the spiritual world; one who does good, My friend, is never overcome by evil.

41

The unsuccessful yogi, after many, many years of enjoyment on the planets of the pious living entities, is born into a family of righteous people, or into a family of rich aristocracy.

42

Or [if unsuccessful after long practice of yoga] he takes his birth in a family of transcendentalists who are surely great in wisdom. Certainly, such a birth is rare in this world.

43

On taking such a birth, he revives the divine consciousness of his previous life, and he again tries to make further progress in order to achieve complete success, O son of Kuru.

44

By virtue of the divine consciousness of his previous life, he automatically becomes attracted to the yogic principles - even without seeking them. Such an inquisitive transcendentalist stands always above the ritualistic principles of the scriptures.

45

And when the yogi engages himself with sincere endeavor in making further progress, being washed of all contaminations, then ultimately, achieving perfection after many, many births of practice, he attains the supreme goal.

46

A yogi is greater than the ascetic, greater than the empiricist and greater than the fruitive worker. Therefore, O Arjuna, in all circumstances, be a yogi.

47

And of all yogis, the one with great faith who always abides in Me, thinks of Me within himself, and renders transcendental loving service to Me - he is the most intimately united with Me in yoga and is the highest of all. That is My opinion.

CHAPTER 7: KNOWLEDGE OF THE ULTIMATE TRUTH

In chapter seven Lord Krishna gives concrete knowledge of the absolute reality as well as the opulence of divinity. He describes His illusory energy in the material existence called *Maya* and declares how extremely difficult it is to surmount it. He also describes the four types of people attracted to divinity and the four types of people who are opposed to divinity. In conclusion He reveals that one in spiritual intelligence takes exclusive refuge of the Lord without reservation in devotional service.

Chapter 7

1

The Supreme Personality of Godhead said: Now hear, O son of Prtha, how by practicing yoga in full consciousness of Me, with mind attached to Me, you can know Me in full, free from doubt.

2

I shall now declare unto you in full this knowledge, both phenomenal and numinous. This being known, nothing further shall remain for you to know.

3

Out of many thousands among men, one may endeavor for perfection, and of those who have achieved perfection, hardly one knows Me in truth.

4

Earth, water, fire, air, ether, mind, intelligence and false ego - all together these eight constitute My separated material energies.

5

Besides these, O mighty-armed Arjuna, there is another, superior energy of Mine, which comprises the living entities who are exploiting the resources of this material, inferior nature.

6

All created beings have their source in these two natures. Of all that is material and all that is spiritual in this world, know for certain that I am both the origin and the dissolution.

7

O conqueror of wealth, there is no truth superior to Me. Everything rests upon Me, as pearls are strung on a thread.

8

O son of Kunti, I am the taste of water, the light of the sun and the moon, the syllable *om* in the Vedic mantras; I am the sound in ether and ability in man.

9

I am the original fragrance of the earth, and I am the heat in fire. I am the life of all that lives, and I am the penances of all ascetics.

10

O son of Prtha, know that I am the original seed of all existences, the intelligence of the intelligent, and the prowess of all powerful men.

11

I am the strength of the strong, devoid of passion and desire. I am sex life which is not contrary to religious principles, O lord of the Bharatas [Arjuna].

12

Know that all states of being - be they of goodness, passion or ignorance - are manifested by My energy. I am, in one sense, everything, but I am independent. I am not under the modes of material nature, for they, on the contrary, are within Me.

13

Deluded by the three modes [goodness, passion and ignorance], the whole world does not know Me, who am above the modes and inexhaustible.

14

This divine energy of Mine, consisting of the three modes of material nature, is difficult to overcome. But those who have surrendered unto Me can easily cross beyond it.

15

Those miscreants who are grossly foolish, who are lowest among mankind, whose knowledge is stolen by illusion, and who partake of the atheistic nature of demons do not surrender unto Me.

16

O best among the Bharatas, four kinds of pious men begin to render devotional service unto Me - the distressed, the desirer of wealth, the inquisitive, and he who is searching for knowledge of the Absolute.

17

Of these, the one who is in full knowledge and who is always engaged in pure devotional service is the best. For I am very dear to him, and he is dear to Me.

18

All these devotees are undoubtedly magnanimous souls, but he who is situated in knowledge of Me I consider to be just like My own self. Being engaged in My transcendental service, he is sure to attain Me, the highest and most perfect goal.

19

After many births and deaths, he who is actually in knowledge surrenders unto Me, knowing Me to be the cause of all causes and all that is. Such a great soul is very rare.

20

Those whose intelligence has been stolen by material desires surrender unto demigods and follow the particular rules and regulations of worship according to their own natures.

21

I am in everyone's heart as the Supersoul. As soon as one desires to worship some demigod, I make his faith steady so that he can devote himself to that particular deity.

22

Endowed with such a faith, he endeavors to worship a particular demigod and obtains his desires. But in actuality these benefits are bestowed by Me alone.

23

Men of small intelligence worship the demigods, and their fruits are limited and temporary. Those who worship the demigods go to the planets of the demigods, but My devotees ultimately reach My supreme planet.

24

Unintelligent men, who do not know Me perfectly, think that I, the Supreme Personality of Godhead, Krishna, was impersonal before and have now assumed this personality. Due to their small knowledge, they do not know My higher nature, which is imperishable and supreme.

25

I am never manifest to the foolish and unintelligent. For them I am covered by My internal potency, and therefore they do not know that I am unborn and infallible.

26

O Arjuna, as the Supreme Personality of Godhead, I know everything that has happened in the past, all that is happening in the present, and all things that are yet to come. I also know all living entities; but Me no one knows.

27

O scion of Bharata, O conqueror of the foe, all living entities are born into delusion, bewildered by dualities arisen from desire and hate.

28

Persons who have acted piously in previous lives and in this life and whose sinful actions are completely eradicated are freed from the dualities of delusion, and they engage themselves in My service with determination.

29

Intelligent persons who are endeavoring for liberation from old age and death take refuge in Me in devotional service. They are actually Brahman because they entirely know everything about transcendental activities.

30

Those in full consciousness of Me, who know Me, the Supreme Lord, to be the governing principle of the material manifestation, of the demigods, and of all methods of sacrifice, can understand and know Me, the Supreme Personality of Godhead, even at the time of death.

CHAPTER 8: ATTAINMENT OF SALVATION

In chapter eight Lord Krishna emphasizes the science of yoga. Revealing that one attains whatever one remembers at the end of one's life, the Lord emphasizes the utmost importance of the very last thought at the moment of death. Also he gives information on the creation of the material worlds as well as establishing a distinction between them and the spiritual world. Here he explains the light and dark paths in regards to leaving this material existence, the destination to which they each lead to and the reward received by each.
Chapter 8

1

Arjuna inquired: O my Lord, O Supreme Person, what is Brahman? What is the self? What are fruitive activities? What is this material manifestation? And what are the demigods? Please explain this to me.

2

Who is the Lord of sacrifice, and how does He live in the body, O Madhusudana? And how can those engaged in devotional service know You at the time of death?

3

The Supreme Personality of Godhead said: The indestructible, transcendental living entity is called Brahman, and his eternal nature is called *adhyatma*, the self. Action pertaining to the development of the material bodies of the living entities is called *karma*, or fruitive activities.

4

O best of the embodied beings, the physical nature, which is constantly changing, is called *adhibhuta* [the material manifestation]. The universal form of the Lord, which includes all the demigods, like those of the sun and moon, is called *adhidaiva*. And I, the Supreme Lord, represented as the Supersoul in the heart of every embodied being, am called *adhiyajna* [the Lord of sacrifice].

5

And whoever, at the end of his life, quits his body, remembering Me alone, at once attains My nature. Of this there is no doubt.

6

Whatever state of being one remembers when he quits his body, O son of Kunti, that state he will attain without fail.

7

Therefore, Arjuna, you should always think of Me in the form of Krishna and at the same time carry out your prescribed duty of fighting. With your activities dedicated to Me and your mind and intelligence fixed on Me, you will attain Me without doubt.

8

He who meditates on Me as the Supreme Personality of Godhead, his mind constantly engaged in remembering Me, undeviated from the path, he, O Partha, is sure to reach Me.

9

One should meditate upon the Supreme Person as the one who knows everything, as He who is the oldest, who is the controller, who is smaller than the smallest, who is the maintainer of everything, who is beyond all material conception, who is inconceivable, and who is always a person. He is luminous like the sun, and He is transcendental, beyond this material nature.

10

One who, at the time of death, fixes his life air between the eyebrows and, by the strength of yoga, with an undeviating mind, engages himself in remembering the Supreme Lord in full devotion, will certainly attain to the Supreme Personality of Godhead.

11

Persons who are learned in the *Vedas*, who utter omkara and who are great sages in the renounced order enter into Brahman. Desiring such perfection, one practices celibacy. I shall now briefly explain to you this process by which one may attain salvation.

12

The yogic situation is that of detachment from all sensual engagements. Closing all the doors of the senses and fixing the mind on the heart and the life air at the top of the head, one establishes himself in yoga.

13

After being situated in this yoga practice and vibrating the sacred syllable om, the supreme combination of letters, if one thinks of the Supreme Personality of Godhead and quits his body, he will certainly reach the spiritual planets.

14

For one who always remembers Me without deviation, I am easy to obtain, O son of Prtha, because of his constant engagement in devotional service.

15

After attaining Me, the great souls, who are yogis in devotion, never return to this temporary world, which is full of miseries, because they have attained the highest perfection.

16

From the highest planet in the material world down to the lowest, all are places of misery wherein repeated birth and death take place. But one who attains to My abode, O son of Kunti, never takes birth again.

17

By human calculation, a thousand ages taken together form the duration of Brahma's one day. And such also is the duration of his night.

18

At the beginning of Brahma's day, all living entities become manifest from the unmanifest state, and thereafter, when the night falls, they are merged into the unmanifest again.

19

Again and again, when Brahma's day arrives, all living entities come into being, and with the arrival of Brahma's night they are helplessly annihilated.

20

Yet there is another unmanifest nature, which is eternal and is transcendental to this manifested and unmanifested matter. It is supreme and is never annihilated. When all in this world is annihilated, that part remains as it is.

21

That which the Vedantists describe as unmanifest and infallible, that which is known as the supreme destination, that place from which, having attained it, one never returns - that is My supreme abode.

22

The Supreme Personality of Godhead, who is greater than all, is attainable by unalloyed devotion. Although He is present in His abode, He is all-pervading, and everything is situated within Him.

23

O best of the Bharatas, I shall now explain to you the different times at which, passing away from this world, the yogi does or does not come back.

24

Those who know the Supreme Brahman attain that Supreme by passing away from the world during the influence of the fiery god, in the light, at an auspicious moment of the day, during the fortnight of the waxing moon, or during the six months when the sun travels in the north.

25

The mystic who passes away from this world during the smoke, the night, the fortnight of the waning moon, or the six months when the sun passes to the south reaches the moon planet but again comes back.

26

According to Vedic opinion, there are two ways of passing from this world - one in light and one in darkness. When one passes in light, he does not come back; but when one passes in darkness, he returns.

27

Although the devotees know these two paths, O Arjuna, they are never bewildered. Therefore be always fixed in devotion.

28

A person who accepts the path of devotional service is not bereft of the results derived from studying the *Vedas*, performing austere sacrifices, giving charity or pursuing philosophical and fruitive activities. Simply by performing devotional service, he attains all these, and at the end he reaches the supreme eternal abode.

CHAPTER 9: CONFIDENTIAL KNOWLEDGE OF THE ULTIMATE TRUTH

In chapter nine Lord Krishna reveals that the sovereign science and the sovereign secret. He explains how the entire material existence is created, pervaded, maintained and annihilated by His external energy and all beings are coming and going under His supervision. The subjects matters covered subsequently are primarily concerned with devotional service and the Lord Himself declares that these subject matters are most confidential.

Chapter 9
1

The Supreme Personality of Godhead said: My dear Arjuna, because you are never envious of Me, I shall impart to you this most confidential knowledge and realization, knowing which you shall be relieved of the miseries of material existence.

2

This knowledge is the king of education, the most secret of all secrets. It is the purest knowledge, and because it gives direct perception of the self by realization, it is the perfection of religion. It is everlasting, and it is joyfully performed.

3

Those who are not faithful in this devotional service cannot attain Me, O conqueror of enemies. Therefore they return to the path of birth and death in this material world.

4

By Me, in My unmanifested form, this entire universe is pervaded. All beings are in Me, but I am not in them.

5

And yet everything that is created does not rest in Me. Behold My mystic opulence! Although I am the maintainer of all living entities and although I am everywhere, I am not a part of this cosmic manifestation, for My Self is the very source of creation.

6

Understand that as the mighty wind, blowing everywhere, rests always in the sky, all created beings rest in Me.

7

O son of Kunti, at the end of the millennium all material manifestations enter into My nature, and at the beginning of another millennium, by My potency, I create them again.

8

The whole cosmic order is under Me. Under My will it is automatically manifested again and again, and under My will it is annihilated at the end.

9

O Dhananjaya, all this work cannot bind Me. I am ever detached from all these material activities, seated as though neutral.

10

This material nature, which is one of My energies, is working under My direction, O son of Kunti, producing all moving and nonmoving beings. Under its rule this manifestation is created and annihilated again and again.

11

Fools deride Me when I descend in the human form. They do not know My transcendental nature as the Supreme Lord of all that be.

12

Those who are thus bewildered are attracted by demonic and atheistic views. In that deluded condition, their hopes for liberation, their fruitive activities, and their culture of knowledge are all defeated.

13

O son of Prtha, those who are not deluded, the great souls, are under the protection of the divine nature. They are fully engaged in devotional service because they know Me as the Supreme Personality of Godhead, original and inexhaustible.

14

Always chanting My glories, endeavoring with great determination, bowing down before Me, these great souls perpetually worship Me with devotion.

15

Others, who engage in sacrifice by the cultivation of knowledge, worship the Supreme Lord as the one without a second, as diverse in many, and in the universal form.

16

But it is I who am the ritual, I the sacrifice, the offering to the ancestors, the healing herb, the transcendental chant. I am the butter and the fire and the offering.

17

I am the father of this universe, the mother, the support and the grandsire. I am the object of knowledge, the purifier and the syllable om. I am also the *Rg*, the *Sama* and the *Yajur Vedas*.

18

I am the goal, the sustainer, the master, the witness, the abode, the refuge, and the most dear friend. I am the creation and the annihilation, the basis of everything, the resting place and the eternal seed.

19

O Arjuna, I give heat, and I withhold and send forth the rain. I am immortality, and I am also death personified. Both spirit and matter are in Me.

20

Those who study the *Vedas* and drink the soma juice, seeking the heavenly planets, worship Me indirectly. Purified of sinful reactions, they take birth on the pious, heavenly planet of Indra, where they enjoy godly delights.

21

When they have thus enjoyed vast heavenly sense pleasure and the results of their pious activities are exhausted, they return to this mortal planet again. Thus those who seek sense enjoyment by adhering to the principles of the three *Vedas* achieve only repeated birth and death.

22

But those who always worship Me with exclusive devotion, meditating on My transcendental form - to them I carry what they lack, and I preserve what they have.

23

Those who are devotees of other gods and who worship them with faith actually worship only Me, O son of Kunti, but they do so in a wrong way.

24

I am the only enjoyer and master of all sacrifices. Therefore, those who do not recognize My true transcendental nature fall down.

25

Those who worship the demigods will take birth among the demigods; those who worship the ancestors go to the ancestors; those who worship ghosts and spirits will take birth among such beings; and those who worship Me will live with Me.

26

If one offers Me with love and devotion a leaf, a flower, fruit or water, I will accept it.

27

Whatever you do, whatever you eat, whatever you offer or give away, and whatever austerities you perform - do that, O son of Kunti, as an offering to Me.

28

In this way you will be freed from bondage to work and its auspicious and inauspicious results. With your mind fixed on Me in this principle of renunciation, you will be liberated and come to Me.

29

I envy no one, nor am I partial to anyone. I am equal to all. But whoever renders service unto Me in devotion is a friend, is in Me, and I am also a friend to him.

30

Even if one commits the most abominable action, if he is engaged in devotional service he is to be considered saintly because he is properly situated in his determination.

31

He quickly becomes righteous and attains lasting peace. O son of Kunti, declare it boldly that My devotee never perishes.

32

O son of Prtha, those who take shelter in Me, though they be of lower birth - women, *vaishyas* [merchants] and *sudras* [workers] - can attain the supreme destination.

33
How much more this is so of the righteous brahmanas, the devotees and the saintly kings. Therefore, having come to this temporary, miserable world, engage in loving service unto Me.

34
Engage your mind always in thinking of Me, become My devotee, offer obeisances to Me and worship Me. Being completely absorbed in Me, surely you will come to Me.

CHAPTER 10: THE INFINITE GLORIES OF THE ULTIMATE TRUTH

Chapter ten reveals Lord Krishna's exalted position as the cause of all causes. Also specifying His special manifestations and opulences. Arjuna prays to the Lord to describe more of the opulences and the Lord describes those which are most prominent.

Chapter 10
1
The Supreme Personality of Godhead said: Listen again, O mighty-armed Arjuna. Because you are My dear friend, for your benefit I shall speak to you further, giving knowledge that is better than what I have already explained.

2
Neither the hosts of demigods nor the great sages know My origin or opulences, for, in every respect, I am the source of the demigods and sages.

3
He who knows Me as the unborn, as the beginningless, as the Supreme Lord of all the worlds - he only, undeluded among men, is freed from all sins.

4-5
Intelligence, knowledge, freedom from doubt and delusion, forgiveness, truthfulness, control of the senses, control of the mind, happiness and distress, birth, death, fear, fearlessness, nonviolence, equanimity, satisfaction, austerity, charity, fame and infamy - all these various qualities of living beings are created by Me alone.

6
The seven great sages and before them the four other great sages and the Manus [progenitors of mankind] come from Me, born from My mind, and all the living beings populating the various planets descend from them.

7
One who is factually convinced of this opulence and mystic power of Mine engages in unalloyed devotional service; of this there is no doubt.

8
I am the source of all spiritual and material worlds. Everything emanates from Me. The wise who perfectly know this engage in My devotional service and worship Me with all their hearts.

9
The thoughts of My pure devotees dwell in Me, their lives are fully devoted to My service, and they derive great satisfaction and bliss from always enlightening one another and conversing about Me.

10
To those who are constantly devoted to serving Me with love, I give the understanding by which they can come to Me.

11
To show them special mercy, I, dwelling in their hearts, destroy with the shining lamp of knowledge the darkness born of ignorance.

12-13
Arjuna said: You are the Supreme Personality of Godhead, the ultimate

abode, the purest, the Absolute Truth. You are the eternal, transcendental, original person, the unborn, the greatest. All the great sages such as Narada, Asita, Devala and Vyasa confirm this truth about You, and now You Yourself are declaring it to me.

14

O Krishna, I totally accept as truth all that You have told me. Neither the demigods nor the demons, O Lord, can understand Your personality.

15

Indeed, You alone know Yourself by Your own internal potency, O Supreme Person, origin of all, Lord of all beings, God of gods, Lord of the universe!

16

Please tell me in detail of Your divine opulences by which You pervade all these worlds.

17

O Krishna, O supreme mystic, how shall I constantly think of You, and how shall I know You? In what various forms are You to be remembered, O Supreme Personality of Godhead?

18

O Janardana, again please describe in detail the mystic power of Your opulences. I am never satiated in hearing about You, for the more I hear the more I want to taste the nectar of Your words.

19

The Supreme Personality of Godhead said: Yes, I will tell you of My splendorous manifestations, but only of those which are prominent, O Arjuna, for My opulence is limitless.

20

I am the Supersoul, O Arjuna, seated in the hearts of all living entities. I am the beginning, the middle and the end of all beings.

21

Of the Adityas I am Vishnu, of lights I am the radiant sun, of the Maruts I am Marici, and among the stars I am the moon.

22

Of the *Vedas* I am the *Sama Veda*; of the demigods I am Indra, the king of heaven; of the senses I am the mind; and in living beings I am the living force [consciousness].

23

Of all the Rudras I am Lord Shiva, of the Yaksas and Raksasas I am the Lord of wealth [Kuvera], of the Vasus I am fire [Agni], and of mountains I am Meru.

24

Of priests, O Arjuna, know Me to be the chief, Brhaspati. Of generals I am Kartikeya, and of bodies of water I am the ocean.

25

Of the great sages I am Bhrgu; of vibrations I am the transcendental om. Of sacrifices I am the chanting of the holy names [Japa], and of immovable things I am the Himalayas.

26

Of all trees I am the banyan tree, and of the sages among the demigods I am Narada. Of the Gandharvas I am Citraratha, and among perfected beings I am the sage Kapila.

27

Of horses know Me to be Uccaihsrava, produced during the churning of the ocean for nectar. Of lordly elephants I am Airavata, and among men I am the monarch.

28

Of weapons I am the thunderbolt; among cows I am the surabhi. Of causes for procreation I am Kandarpa, the god of love, and of serpents I am Vasuki.

29
Of the many-hooded Nagas I am Ananta, and among the aquatics I am the demigod Varuna. Of departed ancestors I am Aryama, and among the dispensers of law I am Yama, the lord of death.

30
Among the Daitya demons I am the devoted Prahlada, among subduers I am time, among beasts I am the lion, and among birds I am Garuda.

31
Of purifiers I am the wind, of the wielders of weapons I am Rama, of fishes I am the shark, and of flowing rivers I am the Ganges.

32
Of all creations I am the beginning and the end and also the middle, O Arjuna. Of all sciences I am the spiritual science of the self, and among logicians I am the conclusive truth.

33
Of letters I am the letter A, and among compound words I am the dual compound. I am also inexhaustible time, and of creators I am Brahma.

34
I am all-devouring death, and I am the generating principle of all that is yet to be. Among women I am fame, fortune, fine speech, memory, intelligence, steadfastness and patience.

35
Of the hymns in the Sama Veda I am the Brhat-sama, and of poetry I am the Gayatri. Of months I am Margasirsa [November-December], and of seasons I am flower-bearing spring.

36
I am also the gambling of cheats, and of

the splendid I am the splendor. I am victory, I am adventure, and I am the strength of the strong.

37
Of the descendants of Vrsni I am Vasudeva, and of the Pandavas I am Arjuna. Of the sages I am Vyasa, and among great thinkers I am Usana.

38
Among all means of suppressing lawlessness I am punishment, and of those who seek victory I am morality. Of secret things I am silence, and of the wise I am the wisdom.

39
Furthermore, O Arjuna, I am the generating seed of all existences. There is no being - moving or nonmoving - that can exist without Me.

40
O mighty conqueror of enemies, there is no end to My divine manifestations. What I have spoken to you is but a mere indication of My infinite opulences.

41
Know that all opulent, beautiful and glorious creations spring from but a spark of My splendor.

42
But what need is there, Arjuna, for all this detailed knowledge? With a single fragment of Myself I pervade and support this entire universe.

CHAPTER 11: THE VISION OF THE UNIVERSAL FORM
In chapter eleven Lord Krishna is beseeched by Arjuna to reveal His universal form showing all of existence.

Chapter 11
1
Arjuna said: By my hearing the

instructions You have kindly given me about these most confidential spiritual subjects, my illusion has now been dispelled.

2

O lotus-eyed one, I have heard from You in detail about the appearance and disappearance of every living entity and have realized Your inexhaustible glories.

3

O greatest of all personalities, O supreme form, though I see You here before me in Your actual position, as You have described Yourself, I wish to see how You have entered into this cosmic manifestation. I want to see that form of Yours.

4

If You think that I am able to behold Your cosmic form, O my Lord, O master of all mystic power, then kindly show me that unlimited universal Self.

5

The Supreme Personality of Godhead said: My dear Arjuna, O son of Prtha, see now My opulences, hundreds of thousands of varied divine and multicolored forms.

6

O best of the Bharatas, see here the different manifestations of Adityas, Vasus, Rudras, Asvini-kumaras and all the other demigods. Behold the many wonderful things which no one has ever seen or heard of before.

7

O Arjuna, whatever you wish to see, behold at once in this body of Mine! This universal form can show you whatever you now desire to see and whatever you may want to see in the future. Everything - moving and nonmoving - is here completely, in one place.

8

But you cannot see Me with your present eyes. Therefore I give you divine eyes. Behold My mystic opulence!

9

Sanjaya said: O King, having spoken thus, the Supreme Lord of all mystic power, the Personality of Godhead, displayed His universal form to Arjuna.

10-11

Arjuna saw in that universal form unlimited mouths, unlimited eyes, unlimited wonderful visions. The form was decorated with many celestial ornaments and bore many divine upraised weapons. He wore celestial garlands and garments, and many divine scents were smeared over His body. All was wondrous, brilliant, unlimited, all-expanding.

12

If hundreds of thousands of suns were to rise at once into the sky, their radiance might resemble the effulgence of the Supreme Person in that universal form.

13

At that time Arjuna could see in the universal form of the Lord the unlimited expansions of the universe situated in one place although divided into many, many thousands.

14

Then, bewildered and astonished, his hair standing on end, Arjuna bowed his head to offer obeisances and with folded hands began to pray to the Supreme Lord.

15

Arjuna said: My dear Lord Krishna, I see assembled in Your body all the demigods and various other living entities. I see Brahma sitting on the lotus flower, as well as Lord Shiva and all the sages and divine serpents.

16

O Lord of the universe, O universal form, I see in Your body many, many arms, bellies, mouths and eyes, expanded everywhere, without limit. I see in You no end, no middle and no beginning.

17

Your form is difficult to see because of its glaring effulgence, spreading on all sides, like blazing fire or the immeasurable radiance of the sun. Yet I see this glowing form everywhere, adorned with various crowns, clubs and discs.

18

You are the supreme primal objective. You are the ultimate resting place of all this universe. You are inexhaustible, and You are the oldest. You are the maintainer of the eternal religion, the Personality of Godhead. This is my opinion.

19

You are without origin, middle or end. Your glory is unlimited. You have numberless arms, and the sun and moon are Your eyes. I see You with blazing fire coming forth from Your mouth, burning this entire universe by Your own radiance.

20

Although You are one, You spread throughout the sky and the planets and all space between. O great one, seeing this wondrous and terrible form, all the planetary systems are perturbed.

21

All the hosts of demigods are surrendering before You and entering into You. Some of them, very much afraid, are offering prayers with folded hands. Hosts of great sages and perfected beings, crying "All peace!" are praying to You by singing the Vedic hymns.

22

All the various manifestations of Lord Shiva, the Adityas, the Vasus, the Sadhyas, the Visvedevas, the two Asvis, the Maruts, the forefathers, the Gandharvas, the Yaksas, the Asuras and the perfected demigods are beholding You in wonder.

23

O mighty-armed one, all the planets with their demigods are disturbed at seeing Your great form, with its many faces, eyes, arms, thighs, legs, and bellies and Your many terrible teeth; and as they are disturbed, so am I.

24

O all-pervading Vishnu, seeing You with Your many radiant colors touching the sky, Your gaping mouths, and Your great glowing eyes, my mind is perturbed by fear. I can no longer maintain my steadiness or equilibrium of mind.

25

O Lord of lords, O refuge of the worlds, please be gracious to me. I cannot keep my balance seeing thus Your blazing deathlike faces and awful teeth. In all directions I am bewildered.

26-27

All the sons of Dhrtarastra, along with their allied kings, and Bhisma, Drona, Karna - and our chief soldiers also - are rushing into Your fearful mouths. And some I see trapped with heads smashed between Your teeth.

28

As the many waves of the rivers flow into the ocean, so do all these great warriors enter blazing into Your mouths.

29

I see all people rushing full speed into Your mouths, as moths dash to destruction in a blazing fire.

30

O Vishnu, I see You devouring all people from all sides with Your flaming mouths. Covering all the universe with Your effulgence, You are manifest with terrible, scorching rays.

31

O Lord of lords, so fierce of form, please tell me who You are. I offer my obeisances unto You; please be gracious to me. You are the primal Lord. I want to know about You, for I do not know what Your mission is.

32

The Supreme Personality of Godhead said: Time I am, the great destroyer of the worlds, and I have come here to destroy all people. With the exception of you [the Pandavas], all the soldiers here on both sides will be slain.

33

Therefore get up. Prepare to fight and win glory. Conquer your enemies and enjoy a flourishing kingdom. They are already put to death by My arrangement, and you, O Savyasaci, can be but an instrument in the fight.

34

Drona, Bhisma, Jayadratha, Karna and the other great warriors have already been destroyed by Me. Therefore, kill them and do not be disturbed. Simply fight, and you will vanquish your enemies in battle.

35

Sanjaya said to Dhrtarastra: O King, after hearing these words from the Supreme Personality of Godhead, the trembling Arjuna offered obeisances with folded hands again and again. He fearfully spoke to Lord Krishna in a faltering voice, as follows.

36

Arjuna said: O master of the senses, the world becomes joyful upon hearing Your name, and thus everyone becomes attached to You. Although the perfected beings offer You their respectful homage, the demons are afraid, and they flee here and there. All this is rightly done.

37

O great one, greater even than Brahma, You are the original creator. Why then should they not offer their respectful obeisances unto You? O limitless one,

God of gods, refuge of the universe! You are the invincible source, the cause of all causes, transcendental to this material manifestation.

38

You are the original Personality of Godhead, the oldest, the ultimate sanctuary of this manifested cosmic world. You are the knower of everything, and You are all that is knowable. You are the supreme refuge, above the material modes. O limitless form! This whole cosmic manifestation is pervaded by You!

39

You are air, and You are the supreme controller! You are fire, You are water, and You are the moon! You are Brahma, the first living creature, and You are the great-grandfather. I therefore offer my respectful obeisances unto You a thousand times, and again and yet again!

40

Obeisances to You from the front, from behind and from all sides! O unbounded power, You are the master of limitless might! You are all-pervading, and thus You are everything!

41-42

Thinking of You as my friend, I have rashly addressed You "O Krishna," "O Yadava," "O my friend," not knowing Your glories. Please forgive whatever I may have done in madness or in love. I have dishonored You many times, jesting as we relaxed, lay on the same bed, or sat or ate together, sometimes alone and sometimes in front of many friends. O infallible one, please excuse me for all those offenses.

43

You are the father of this complete cosmic manifestation, of the moving and the nonmoving. You are its worshipable chief, the supreme spiritual master. No one is equal to You, nor can anyone be one with You. How then could there be anyone greater than You within the three worlds, O Lord of immeasurable power?

44

You are the Supreme Lord, to be worshiped by every living being. Thus I fall down to offer You my respectful obeisances and ask Your mercy. As a father tolerates the impudence of his son, or a friend tolerates the impertinence of a friend, or a wife tolerates the familiarity of her partner, please tolerate the wrongs I may have done You.

45

After seeing this universal form, which I have never seen before, I am gladdened, but at the same time my mind is disturbed with fear. Therefore please bestow Your grace upon me and reveal again Your form as the Personality of Godhead, O Lord of lords, O abode of the universe.

46

O universal form, O thousand-armed Lord, I wish to see You in Your four-armed form, with helmeted head and with club, wheel, conch and lotus flower in Your hands. I long to see You in that form.

47

The Supreme Personality of Godhead said: My dear Arjuna, happily have I shown you, by My internal potency, this supreme universal form within the material world. No one before you has ever seen this primal form, unlimited and full of glaring effulgence.

48

O best of the Kuru warriors, no one before you has ever seen this universal form of Mine, for neither by studying the *Vedas*, nor by performing sacrifices, nor by charity, nor by pious activities, nor by severe penances can I be seen in this form in the material world.

49

You have been perturbed and bewildered by seeing this horrible feature of Mine. Now let it be finished. My devotee, be free again from all disturbances. With a peaceful mind you can now see the form you desire.

50

Sanjaya said to Dhrtarastra: The Supreme Personality of Godhead, Krishna, having spoken thus to Arjuna, displayed His real four-armed form and at last showed His two-armed form, thus encouraging the fearful Arjuna.

51

When Arjuna thus saw Krishna in His original form, he said: O Janardana, seeing this humanlike form, so very beautiful, I am now composed in mind, and I am restored to my original nature.

52

The Supreme Personality of Godhead said: My dear Arjuna, this form of Mine you are now seeing is very difficult to behold. Even the demigods are ever seeking the opportunity to see this form, which is so dear.

53

The form you are seeing with your transcendental eyes cannot be understood simply by studying the Vedas, nor by undergoing serious penances, nor by charity, nor by worship. It is not by these means that one can see Me as I am.

54

My dear Arjuna, only by undivided devotional service can I be understood as I am, standing before you, and can thus be seen directly. Only in this way can you enter into the mysteries of My understanding.

55

My dear Arjuna, he who engages in My pure devotional service, free from the contaminations of fruitive activities and mental speculation, he who works for Me, who makes Me the supreme goal of his life, and who is friendly to every living being - he certainly comes to Me.

CHAPTER 12: THE PATH OF DEVOTION

In chapter twelve Lord Krishna extols the glory of devotion to God. Along with this he explains the different forms of spiritual disciplines and discusses the qualities of the devotees who by performing their activities in this way become very dear to Him.

Chapter 12

1

Arjuna inquired: Which are considered to be more perfect, those who are always properly engaged in Your devotional service or those who worship the impersonal Brahman, the unmanifested?

2

The Supreme Personality of Godhead said: Those who fix their minds on My personal form and are always engaged in worshiping Me with great and transcendental faith are considered by Me to be most perfect.

3-4

But those who fully worship the unmanifested, that which lies beyond the perception of the senses, the all-pervading, inconceivable, unchanging, fixed and immovable - the impersonal conception of the Absolute Truth - by controlling the various senses and being equally disposed to everyone, such persons, engaged in the welfare of all, at last achieve Me.

5

For those whose minds are attached to the unmanifested, impersonal feature of the Supreme, advancement is very troublesome. To make progress in that discipline is always difficult for those who are embodied.

6-7

But those who worship Me, giving up all their activities unto Me and being devoted to Me without deviation, engaged in devotional service and always meditating upon Me, having fixed their minds upon Me, O son of Prtha - for them I am the swift deliverer from the ocean of birth and death.

8

Just fix your mind upon Me, the Supreme Personality of Godhead, and engage all your intelligence in Me. Thus you will live in Me always, without a doubt.

9

My dear Arjuna, O winner of wealth, if you cannot fix your mind upon Me without deviation, then follow the regulative principles of bhakti-yoga. In this way develop a desire to attain Me.

10

If you cannot practice the regulations of bhakti-yoga, then just try to work for Me, because by working for Me you will come to the perfect stage.

11

If, however, you are unable to work in this consciousness of Me, then try to act giving up all results of your work and try to be self-situated.

12

If you cannot take to this practice, then engage yourself in the cultivation of knowledge. Better than knowledge, however, is meditation, and better than meditation is renunciation of the fruits of action, for by such renunciation one can attain peace of mind.

13-14

One who is not envious but is a kind friend to all living entities, who does not think himself a proprietor and is free from false ego, who is equal in both happiness and distress, who is tolerant, always satisfied, self-controlled, and engaged in devotional service with determination, his mind and intelligence fixed on Me - such a devotee of Mine is very dear to Me.

15

He for whom no one is put into difficulty and who is not disturbed by anyone, who is equipoised in happiness and distress, fear and anxiety, is very dear to Me.

16

My devotee who is not dependent on the ordinary course of activities, who is pure, expert, without cares, free from all pains, and not striving for some result, is very dear to Me.

17

One who neither rejoices nor grieves, who neither laments nor desires, and who renounces both auspicious and inauspicious things - such a devotee is very dear to Me.

18-19

One who is equal to friends and enemies, who is equipoised in honor and dishonor, heat and cold, happiness and distress, fame and infamy, who is always free from contaminating association, always silent and satisfied with anything, who doesn't care for any residence, who is fixed in knowledge and who is engaged in devotional service - such a person is very dear to Me.

20

Those who follow this imperishable path of devotional service and who completely engage themselves with faith, making Me the supreme goal, are very, very dear to Me.

CHAPTER 13: THE INDIVIDUAL AND THE ULTIMATE CONSCIOUSNESS

In chapter thirteen Lord Krishna reveals the distinct difference between the physical body and the immortal soul. He explains that the physical is transitory and perishable whereas the soul is immutable and eternal. The Lord also gives precise knowledge about the individual soul and the ultimate soul.

Chapter 13
1-2

Arjuna said: O my dear Krishna, I wish to know about prakrti [nature], purusa [the enjoyer], and the field and the knower of the field, and of knowledge and the object of knowledge.

The Supreme Personality of Godhead said: This body, O son of Kunti, is called the field, and one who knows this body is called the knower of the field.

3

O scion of Bharata, you should understand that I am also the knower in all bodies, and to understand this body and its knower is called knowledge. That is My opinion.

4

Now please hear My brief description of this field of activity and how it is constituted, what its changes are, whence it is produced, who that knower of the field of activities is, and what his influences are.

5

That knowledge of the field of activities and of the knower of activities is described by various sages in various Vedic writings. It is especially presented in Vedanta-sutra with all reasoning as to cause and effect.

6-7

The five great elements, false ego, intelligence, the unmanifested, the ten senses and the mind, the five sense objects, desire, hatred, happiness, distress, the aggregate, the life symptoms, and convictions - all these are considered, in summary, to be the field of activities and its interactions.

8-12

Humility; pridelessness; nonviolence; tolerance; simplicity; approaching a bona fide spiritual master; cleanliness;

steadiness; self-control; renunciation of the objects of sense gratification; absence of false ego; the perception of the evil of birth, death, old age and disease; detachment; freedom from entanglement with children, wife, home and the rest; even-mindedness amid pleasant and unpleasant events; constant and unalloyed devotion to Me; aspiring to live in a solitary place; detachment from the general mass of people; accepting the importance of self-realization; and philosophical search for the Absolute Truth - all these I declare to be knowledge, and besides this whatever there may be is ignorance.

13
I shall now explain the knowable, knowing which you will taste the eternal. Brahman, the spirit, beginningless and subordinate to Me, lies beyond the cause and effect of this material world.

14
Everywhere are His hands and legs, His eyes, heads and faces, and He has ears everywhere. In this way the Supersoul exists, pervading everything.

15
The Supersoul is the original source of all senses, yet He is without senses. He is unattached, although He is the maintainer of all living beings. He transcends the modes of nature, and at the same time He is the master of all the modes of material nature.

16
The Supreme Truth exists outside and inside of all living beings, the moving and the nonmoving. Because He is subtle, He is beyond the power of the material senses to see or to know. Although far, far away, He is also near to all.

17
Although the Supersoul appears to be divided among all beings, He is never divided. He is situated as one. Although

He is the maintainer of every living entity, it is to be understood that He devours and develops all.

18
He is the source of light in all luminous objects. He is beyond the darkness of matter and is unmanifested. He is knowledge, He is the object of knowledge, and He is the goal of knowledge. He is situated in everyone's heart.

19
Thus the field of activities [the body], knowledge and the knowable have been summarily described by Me. Only My devotees can understand this thoroughly and thus attain to My nature.

20
Material nature and the living entities should be understood to be beginningless. Their transformations and the modes of matter are products of material nature.

21
Nature is said to be the cause of all material causes and effects, whereas the living entity is the cause of the various sufferings and enjoyments in this world.

22
The living entity in material nature thus follows the ways of life, enjoying the three modes of nature. This is due to his association with that material nature. Thus he meets with good and evil among various species.

23
Yet in this body there is another, a transcendental enjoyer, who is the Lord, the supreme proprietor, who exists as the overseer and permitter, and who is known as the Supersoul.

24
One who understands this philosophy concerning material nature, the living entity and the interaction of the modes of

nature is sure to attain liberation. He will not take birth here again, regardless of his present position.

25
Some perceive the Supersoul within themselves through meditation, others through the cultivation of knowledge, and still others through working without fruitive desires.

26
Again there are those who, although not conversant in spiritual knowledge, begin to worship the Supreme Person upon hearing about Him from others. Because of their tendency to hear from authorities, they also transcend the path of birth and death.

27
O chief of the Bharatas, know that whatever you see in existence, both the moving and the nonmoving, is only a combination of the field of activities and the knower of the field.

28
One who sees the Supersoul accompanying the individual soul in all bodies, and who understands that neither the soul nor the Supersoul within the destructible body is ever destroyed, actually sees.

29
One who sees the Supersoul equally present everywhere, in every living being, does not degrade himself by his mind. Thus he approaches the transcendental destination.

30
One who can see that all activities are performed by the body, which is created of material nature, and sees that the self does nothing, actually sees.

31
When a sensible man ceases to see different identities due to different material bodies and he sees how beings are

expanded everywhere, he attains to the Brahman conception.

32
Those with the vision of eternity can see that the imperishable soul is transcendental, eternal, and beyond the modes of nature. Despite contact with the material body, O Arjuna, the soul neither does anything nor is entangled.

33
The sky, due to its subtle nature, does not mix with anything, although it is all-pervading. Similarly, the soul situated in Brahman vision does not mix with the body, though situated in that body.

34
O son of Bharata, as the sun alone illuminates all this universe, so does the living entity, one within the body, illuminate the entire body by consciousness.

35
Those who see with eyes of knowledge the difference between the body and the knower of the body, and can also understand the process of liberation from bondage in material nature, attain to the supreme goal.

CHAPTER 14: THE THREE QUALITIES OF MATERIAL NATURE
In chapter fourteen Lord Krishna reveals matters pertaining goodness, passion and nescience which everything in the material existence is influenced by. He gives pertinent details on the essential characteristics of each individually, their cause, the level of their potency, how they influence a living entity affected by them as well as the signs of one who has risen above them. Here he clearly advises to relinquish oneself from ignorance and passion and adopt the path of pure goodness until acquiring the ability to transcend them.

Chapter 14

1

The Supreme Personality of Godhead said: Again I shall declare to you this supreme wisdom, the best of all knowledge, knowing which all the sages have attained the supreme perfection.

2

By becoming fixed in this knowledge, one can attain to the transcendental nature like My own. Thus established, one is not born at the time of creation or disturbed at the time of dissolution.

3

The total material substance, called Brahman, is the source of birth, and it is that Brahman that I impregnate, making possible the births of all living beings, O son of Bharata.

4

It should be understood that all species of life, O son of Kunti, are made possible by birth in this material nature, and that I am the seed-giving father.

5

Material nature consists of three modes - goodness, passion and ignorance. When the eternal living entity comes in contact with nature, O mighty-armed Arjuna, he becomes conditioned by these modes.

6

O sinless one, the mode of goodness, being purer than the others, is illuminating, and it frees one from all sinful reactions. Those situated in that mode become conditioned by a sense of happiness and knowledge.

7

The mode of passion is born of unlimited desires and longings, O son of Kunti, and because of this the embodied living entity is bound to material fruitive actions.

8

O son of Bharata, know that the mode of darkness, born of ignorance, is the delusion of all embodied living entities.

The results of this mode are madness, indolence and sleep, which bind the conditioned soul.

9

O son of Bharata, the mode of goodness conditions one to happiness; passion conditions one to fruitive action; and ignorance, covering one's knowledge, binds one to madness.

10

Sometimes the mode of goodness becomes prominent, defeating the modes of passion and ignorance, O son of Bharata. Sometimes the mode of passion defeats goodness and ignorance, and at other times ignorance defeats goodness and passion. In this way there is always competition for supremacy.

11

The manifestations of the mode of goodness can be experienced when all the gates of the body are illuminated by knowledge.

12

O chief of the Bharatas, when there is an increase in the mode of passion the symptoms of great attachment, fruitive activity, intense endeavor, and uncontrollable desire and hankering develop.

13

When there is an increase in the mode of ignorance, O son of Kuru, darkness, inertia, madness and illusion are manifested.

14

When one dies in the mode of goodness, he attains to the pure higher planets of the great sages.

15

When one dies in the mode of passion, he takes birth among those engaged in fruitive activities; and when one dies in the mode of ignorance, he takes birth in the animal kingdom.

16

The result of pious action is pure and is said to be in the mode of goodness. But action done in the mode of passion results in misery, and action performed in the mode of ignorance results in foolishness.

17

From the mode of goodness, real knowledge develops; from the mode of passion, greed develops; and from the mode of ignorance develop foolishness, madness and illusion.

18

Those situated in the mode of goodness gradually go upward to the higher planets; those in the mode of passion live on the earthly planets; and those in the abominable mode of ignorance go down to the hellish worlds.

19

When one properly sees that in all activities no other performer is at work than these modes of nature and he knows the Supreme Lord, who is transcendental to all these modes, he attains My spiritual nature.

20

When the embodied being is able to transcend these three modes associated with the material body, he can become free from birth, death, old age and their distresses and can enjoy nectar even in this life.

21

Arjuna inquired: O my dear Lord, by which symptoms is one known who is transcendental to these three modes? What is his behavior? And how does he transcend the modes of nature?

22-25

The Supreme Personality of Godhead said: O son of Pandu, he who does not hate illumination, attachment and delusion when they are present or long for them when they disappear; who is unwavering and undisturbed through all

these reactions of the material qualities, remaining neutral and transcendental, knowing that the modes alone are active; who is situated in the self and regards alike happiness and distress; who looks upon a lump of earth, a stone and a piece of gold with an equal eye; who is equal toward the desirable and the undesirable; who is steady, situated equally well in praise and blame, honor and dishonor; who treats alike both friend and enemy; and who has renounced all material activities - such a person is said to have transcended the modes of nature.

26

One who engages in full devotional service, unfailing in all circumstances, at once transcends the modes of material nature and thus comes to the level of Brahman.

27

And I am the basis of the impersonal Brahman, which is immortal, imperishable and eternal and is the constitutional position of ultimate happiness.

CHAPTER 15: REALIZATION OF THE ULTIMATE TRUTH

In chapter fifteen Lord Krishna reveals the virtues, the glories and transcendental characteristics of God being omnipotent, omniscient and omnipresent. Also He explains the purpose and value of knowing about God and the means by which He can be realized.

Chapter 15

1

The Supreme Personality of Godhead said: It is said that there is an imperishable banyan tree that has its roots upward and its branches down and whose leaves are the Vedic hymns. One who knows this tree is the knower of the *Vedas*.

2

The branches of this tree extend downward and upward, nourished by the three modes of material nature. The twigs are the objects of the senses. This tree also has roots going down, and these are bound to the fruitive actions of human society.

3-4

The real form of this tree cannot be perceived in this world. No one can understand where it ends, where it begins, or where its foundation is. But with determination one must cut down this strongly rooted tree with the weapon of detachment. Thereafter, one must seek that place from which, having gone, one never returns, and there surrender to that Supreme Personality of Godhead from whom everything began and from whom everything has extended since time immemorial.

5

Those who are free from false prestige, illusion and false association, who understand the eternal, who are done with material lust, who are freed from the dualities of happiness and distress, and who, unbewildered, know how to surrender unto the Supreme Person attain to that eternal kingdom.

6

That supreme abode of Mine is not illumined by the sun or moon, nor by fire or electricity. Those who reach it never return to this material world.

7

The living entities in this conditioned world are My eternal fragmental parts. Due to conditioned life, they are struggling very hard with the six senses, which include the mind.

8

The living entity in the material world carries his different conceptions of life from one body to another as the air carries aromas. Thus he takes one kind of body and again quits it to take another.

9

The living entity, thus taking another gross body, obtains a certain type of ear, eye, tongue, nose and sense of touch, which are grouped about the mind. He thus enjoys a particular set of sense objects.

10

The foolish cannot understand how a living entity can quit his body, nor can they understand what sort of body he enjoys under the spell of the modes of nature. But one whose eyes are trained in knowledge can see all this.

11

The endeavoring transcendentalists, who are situated in self-realization, can see all this clearly. But those whose minds are not developed and who are not situated in self-realization cannot see what is taking place, though they may try to.

12

The splendor of the sun, which dissipates the darkness of this whole world, comes from Me. And the splendor of the moon and the splendor of fire are also from Me.

13

I enter into each planet, and by My energy they stay in orbit. I become the moon and thereby supply the juice of life to all vegetables.

14

I am the fire of digestion in the bodies of all living entities, and I join with the air of life, outgoing and incoming, to digest the four kinds of foodstuff.

15

I am seated in everyone's heart, and from Me come remembrance, knowledge and forgetfulness. By all the *Vedas*, I am to be known. Indeed, I am the compiler of Vedanta, and I am the knower of the *Vedas*.

16

There are two classes of beings, the fallible

and the infallible. In the material world every living entity is fallible, and in the spiritual world every living entity is called infallible.

17
Besides these two, there is the greatest living personality, the Supreme Soul, the imperishable Lord Himself, who has entered the three worlds and is maintaining them.

18
Because I am transcendental, beyond both the fallible and the infallible, and because I am the greatest, I am celebrated both in the world and in the *Vedas* as that Supreme Person.

19
Whoever knows Me as the Supreme Personality of Godhead, without doubting, is the knower of everything. He therefore engages himself in full devotional service to Me, O son of Bharata.

20
This is the most confidential part of the Vedic scriptures, O sinless one, and it is disclosed now by Me. Whoever understands this will become wise, and his endeavors will know perfection.

CHAPTER 16: THE DIVINE AND DEMONIAC NATURE DEFINED

In chapter sixteen Lord Krishna describes explicitly, explaining separately and in detail the divine properties, conduct and actions which are righteous in nature and conducive to divinity. Also he delineates the evil propensities and ill conduct which are unrighteous in nature and which determine the unrighteous and which are antagonistic to divinity.

Chapter 16
1-3
The Supreme Personality of Godhead said: Fearlessness; purification of one's existence; cultivation of spiritual knowledge; charity; self-control;

performance of sacrifice; study of the *Vedas*; austerity; simplicity; nonviolence; truthfulness; freedom from anger; renunciation; tranquility; aversion to faultfinding; compassion for all living entities; freedom from covetousness; gentleness; modesty; steady determination; vigor; forgiveness; fortitude; cleanliness; and freedom from envy and from the passion for honor - these transcendental qualities, O son of Bharata, belong to godly men endowed with divine nature.

4
Pride, arrogance, conceit, anger, harshness and ignorance - these qualities belong to those of demoniac nature, O son of Prtha.

5
The transcendental qualities are conducive to liberation, whereas the demoniac qualities make for bondage. Do not worry, O son of Pandu, for you are born with the divine qualities.

6
O son of Prtha, in this world there are two kinds of created beings. One is called the divine and the other demoniac. I have already explained to you at length the divine qualities. Now hear from Me of the demoniac.

7
Those who are demoniac do not know what is to be done and what is not to be done. Neither cleanliness nor proper behavior nor truth is found in them.

8
They say that this world is unreal, with no foundation, no God in control. They say it is produced of sex desire and has no cause other than lust.

9
Following such conclusions, the demoniac, who are lost to themselves and who have no intelligence, engage in unbeneficial, horrible works meant to destroy the world.

10

Taking shelter of insatiable lust and absorbed in the conceit of pride and false prestige, the demoniac, thus illusioned, are always sworn to unclean work, attracted by the impermanent.

11-12

They believe that to gratify the senses is the prime necessity of human civilization. Thus until the end of life their anxiety is immeasurable. Bound by a network of hundreds of thousands of desires and absorbed in lust and anger, they secure money by illegal means for sense gratification.

13-15

The demoniac person thinks: "So much wealth do I have today, and I will gain more according to my schemes. So much is mine now, and it will increase in the future, more and more. He is my enemy, and I have killed him, and my other enemies will also be killed. I am the lord of everything. I am the enjoyer. I am perfect, powerful and happy. I am the richest man, surrounded by aristocratic relatives. There is none so powerful and happy as I am. I shall perform sacrifices, I shall give some charity, and thus I shall rejoice." In this way, such persons are deluded by ignorance.

16

Thus perplexed by various anxieties and bound by a network of illusions, they become too strongly attached to sense enjoyment and fall down into hell.

17

Self-complacent and always impudent, deluded by wealth and false prestige, they sometimes proudly perform sacrifices in name only, without following any rules or regulations.

18

Bewildered by false ego, strength, pride, lust and anger, the demons become envious of the Supreme Personality of Godhead, who is situated in their own bodies and in the bodies of others, and blaspheme against the real religion.

19

Those who are envious and mischievous, who are the lowest among men, I perpetually cast into the ocean of material existence, into various demoniac species of life.

20

Attaining repeated birth amongst the species of demoniac life, O son of Kunti, such persons can never approach Me. Gradually they sink down to the most abominable type of existence.

21

There are three gates leading to this hell - lust, anger and greed. Every sane man should give these up, for they lead to the degradation of the soul.

22

The man who has escaped these three gates of hell, O son of Kunti, performs acts conducive to self-realization and thus gradually attains the supreme destination.

23

He who discards scriptural injunctions and acts according to his own whims attains neither perfection, nor happiness, nor the supreme destination.

24

One should therefore understand what is duty and what is not duty by the regulations of the scriptures. Knowing such rules and regulations, one should act so that he may gradually be elevated.

CHAPTER 17: THE THREE DIVISIONS OF MATERIAL EXISTENCE

In chapter seventeen Lord Krishna classifies the three divisions of faith, revealing that it is these different qualities of faith in the Supreme that determine that character of living entities. These three types of faith determine one's consciousness in this world.

Chapter 17

1

Arjuna inquired: O Krishna, what is the situation of those who do not follow the principles of scripture but worship according to their own imagination? Are they in goodness, in passion or in ignorance?

2

The Supreme Personality of Godhead said: According to the modes of nature acquired by the embodied soul, one's faith can be of three kinds - in goodness, in passion or in ignorance. Now hear about this.

3

O son of Bharata, according to one's existence under the various modes of nature, one evolves a particular kind of faith. The living being is said to be of a particular faith according to the modes he has acquired.

4

Men in the mode of goodness worship the demigods; those in the mode of passion worship the demons; and those in the mode of ignorance worship ghosts and spirits.

5-6

Those who undergo severe austerities and penances not recommended in the scriptures, performing them out of pride and egoism, who are impelled by lust and attachment, who are foolish and who torture the material elements of the body as well as the Supersoul dwelling within, are to be known as demons.

7

Even the food each person prefers is of three kinds, according to the three modes of material nature. The same is true of sacrifices, austerities and charity. Now hear of the distinctions between them.

8

Foods dear to those in the mode of goodness increase the duration of life, purify one's existence and give strength, health, happiness and satisfaction. Such foods are juicy, fatty, wholesome, and pleasing to the heart.

9

Foods that are too bitter, too sour, salty, hot, pungent, dry and burning are dear to those in the mode of passion. Such foods cause distress, misery and disease.

10

Food prepared more than three hours before being eaten, food that is tasteless, decomposed and putrid, and food consisting of remnants and untouchable things is dear to those in the mode of darkness.

11

Of sacrifices, the sacrifice performed according to the directions of scripture, as a matter of duty, by those who desire no reward, is of the nature of goodness.

12

But the sacrifice performed for some material benefit, or for the sake of pride, O chief of the Bharatas, you should know to be in the mode of passion.

13

Any sacrifice performed without regard for the directions of scripture, without distribution of *prasadam* [spiritual food], without chanting of Vedic hymns and remunerations to the priests, and without faith is considered to be in the mode of ignorance.

14

Austerity of the body consists in worship of the Supreme Lord, the brahmanas, the spiritual master, and superiors like the father and mother, and in cleanliness, simplicity, celibacy and nonviolence.

15

Austerity of speech consists in speaking words that are truthful, pleasing, beneficial, and not agitating to others, and also in regularly reciting Vedic literature.

16

And satisfaction, simplicity, gravity, self-control and purification of one's existence are the austerities of the mind.

17

This threefold austerity, performed with transcendental faith by men not expecting material benefits but engaged only for the sake of the Supreme, is called austerity in goodness.

18

Penance performed out of pride and for the sake of gaining respect, honor and worship is said to be in the mode of passion. It is neither stable nor permanent.

19

Penance performed out of foolishness, with self-torture or to destroy or injure others, is said to be in the mode of ignorance.

20

Charity given out of duty, without expectation of return, at the proper time and place, and to a worthy person is considered to be in the mode of goodness.

21

But charity performed with the expectation of some return, or with a desire for fruitive results, or in a grudging mood, is said to be charity in the mode of passion.

22

And charity performed at an impure place, at an improper time, to unworthy persons, or without proper attention and respect is said to be in the mode of ignorance.

23

From the beginning of creation, the three words om tat sat were used to indicate the Supreme Absolute Truth. These three symbolic representations were used by brahmanas while chanting the hymns of the *Vedas* and during sacrifices for the satisfaction of the Supreme.

24

Therefore, transcendentalists undertaking performances of sacrifice, charity and penance in accordance with scriptural regulations begin always with om, to attain the Supreme.

25

Without desiring fruitive results, one should perform various kinds of sacrifice, penance and charity with the word tat. The purpose of such transcendental activities is to get free from material entanglement.

26-27

The Absolute Truth is the objective of devotional sacrifice, and it is indicated by the word sat. The performer of such sacrifice is also called sat, as are all works of sacrifice, penance and charity which, true to the absolute nature, are performed to please the Supreme Person, O son of Prtha.

28

Anything done as sacrifice, charity or penance without faith in the Supreme, O son of Prtha, is impermanent. It is called asat and is useless both in this life and the next.

CHAPTER 18: FINAL REVELATIONS OF THE ULTIMATE TRUTH

In chapter eighteen Lord Krsishna sums up the conclusion of the previous chapters and describes the attainment of salvation by the paths of *karma* in chapters one through six and in jnana yoga section which are chapters thirteen through eighteen. The Lord explains that while doing so one must offer without reservation everything to God. The knowledge revealed gets progressively more and more confidential then in all the previous chapters.

Chapter 18

1

Arjuna said: O mighty-armed one, I wish to understand the purpose of renunciation [*tyaga*] and of the renounced order of life [*sannyasa*], O killer of the Kesi demon, master of the senses.

2

The Supreme Personality of Godhead said: The giving up of activities that are based on material desire is what great learned men call the renounced order of life [*sannyasa*]. And giving up the results of all activities is what the wise call renunciation [*tyaga*].

3

Some learned men declare that all kinds of fruitive activities should be given up as faulty, yet other sages maintain that acts of sacrifice, charity and penance should never be abandoned.

4

O best of the Bharatas, now hear My judgment about renunciation. O tiger among men, renunciation is declared in the scriptures to be of three kinds.

5

Acts of sacrifice, charity and penance are not to be given up; they must be performed. Indeed, sacrifice, charity and penance purify even the great souls.

6

All these activities should be performed without attachment or any expectation of result. They should be performed as a matter of duty, O son of Prtha. That is My final opinion.

7

Prescribed duties should never be renounced. If one gives up his prescribed

duties because of illusion, such renunciation is said to be in the mode of ignorance.

8

Anyone who gives up prescribed duties as troublesome or out of fear of bodily discomfort is said to have renounced in the mode of passion. Such action never leads to the elevation of renunciation.

9

O Arjuna, when one performs his prescribed duty only because it ought to be done, and renounces all material association and all attachment to the fruit, his renunciation is said to be in the mode of goodness.

10

The intelligent renouncer situated in the mode of goodness, neither hateful of inauspicious work nor attached to auspicious work, has no doubts about work.

11

It is indeed impossible for an embodied being to give up all activities. But he who renounces the fruits of action is called one who has truly renounced.

12

For one who is not renounced, the threefold fruits of action - desirable, undesirable and mixed - accrue after death. But those who are in the renounced order of life have no such result to suffer or enjoy.

13

O mighty-armed Arjuna, according to the Vedanta there are five causes for the accomplishment of all action. Now learn of these from Me.

14

The place of action [the body], the performer, the various senses, the many different kinds of endeavor, and ultimately the Supersoul - these are the five factors of action.

15
Whatever right or wrong action a man performs by body, mind or speech is caused by these five factors.

16
Therefore one who thinks himself the only doer, not considering the five factors, is certainly not very intelligent and cannot see things as they are.

17
One who is not motivated by false ego, whose intelligence is not entangled, though he kills men in this world, does not kill. Nor is he bound by his actions.

18
Knowledge, the object of knowledge, and the knower are the three factors that motivate action; the senses, the work and the doer are the three constituents of action.

19
According to the three different modes of material nature, there are three kinds of knowledge, action and performer of action. Now hear of them from Me.

20
That knowledge by which one undivided spiritual nature is seen in all living entities, though they are divided into innumerable forms, you should understand to be in the mode of goodness.

21
That knowledge by which one sees that in every different body there is a different type of living entity you should understand to be in the mode of passion.

22
And that knowledge by which one is attached to one kind of work as the all in all, without knowledge of the truth, and which is very meager, is said to be in the mode of darkness.

23
That action which is regulated and which is performed without attachment, without love or hatred, and without desire for fruitive results is said to be in the mode of goodness.

24
But action performed with great effort by one seeking to gratify his desires, and enacted from a sense of false ego, is called action in the mode of passion.

25
That action performed in illusion, in disregard of scriptural injunctions, and without concern for future bondage or for violence or distress caused to others is said to be in the mode of ignorance.

26
One who performs his duty without association with the modes of material nature, without false ego, with great determination and enthusiasm, and without wavering in success or failure is said to be a worker in the mode of goodness.

27
The worker who is attached to work and the fruits of work, desiring to enjoy those fruits, and who is greedy, always envious, impure, and moved by joy and sorrow, is said to be in the mode of passion.

28
The worker who is always engaged in work against the injunctions of the scripture, who is materialistic, obstinate, cheating and expert in insulting others, and who is lazy, always morose and procrastinating is said to be a worker in the mode of ignorance.

29
O winner of wealth, now please listen as I tell you in detail of the different kinds of understanding and determination, according to the three modes of material nature.

30

O son of Prtha, that understanding by which one knows what ought to be done and what ought not to be done, what is to be feared and what is not to be feared, what is binding and what is liberating, is in the mode of goodness.

31

O son of Prtha, that understanding which cannot distinguish between religion and irreligion, between action that should be done and action that should not be done, is in the mode of passion.

32

That understanding which considers irreligion to be religion and religion to be irreligion, under the spell of illusion and darkness, and strives always in the wrong direction, O Partha, is in the mode of ignorance.

33

O son of Prtha, that determination which is unbreakable, which is sustained with steadfastness by yoga practice, and which thus controls the activities of the mind, life and senses is determination in the mode of goodness.

34

But that determination by which one holds fast to fruitive results in religion, economic development and sense gratification is of the nature of passion, O Arjuna.

35

And that determination which cannot go beyond dreaming, fearfulness, lamentation, moroseness and illusion - such unintelligent determination, O son of Prtha, is in the mode of darkness.

36

O best of the Bharatas, now please hear from Me about the three kinds of happiness by which the conditioned soul enjoys, and by which he sometimes comes to the end of all distress.

37

That which in the beginning may be just like poison but at the end is just like nectar and which awakens one to self-realization is said to be happiness in the mode of goodness.

38

That happiness which is derived from contact of the senses with their objects and which appears like nectar at first but poison at the end is said to be of the nature of passion.

39

And that happiness which is blind to self-realization, which is delusion from beginning to end and which arises from sleep, laziness and illusion is said to be of the nature of ignorance.

40

There is no being existing, either here or among the demigods in the higher planetary systems, which is freed from these three modes born of material nature.

41

Brahmanas, ksatriyas, vaishyas and sudras are distinguished by the qualities born of their own natures in accordance with the material modes, O chastiser of the enemy.

42

Peacefulness, self-control, austerity, purity, tolerance, honesty, knowledge, wisdom and religiousness - these are the natural qualities by which the brahmanas work.

43

Heroism, power, determination, resourcefulness, courage in battle, generosity and leadership are the natural qualities of work for the ksatriyas.

44

Farming, cow protection and business are the natural work for the vaishyas, and for the sudras there is labor and service to others.

45

By following his qualities of work, every man can become perfect. Now please hear from Me how this can be done.

46

By worship of the Lord, who is the source of all beings and who is all-pervading, a man can attain perfection through performing his own work.

47

It is better to engage in one's own occupation, even though one may perform it imperfectly, than to accept another's occupation and perform it perfectly. Duties prescribed according to one's nature are never affected by sinful reactions.

48

Every endeavor is covered by some fault, just as fire is covered by smoke. Therefore one should not give up the work born of his nature, O son of Kunti, even if such work is full of fault.

49

One who is self-controlled and unattached and who disregards all material enjoyments can obtain, by practice of renunciation, the highest perfect stage of freedom from reaction.

50

O son of Kunti, learn from Me how one who has achieved this perfection can attain to the supreme perfectional stage, Brahman, the stage of highest knowledge, by acting in the way I shall now summarize.

51-53

Being purified by his intelligence and controlling the mind with determination, giving up the objects of sense gratification, being freed from attachment and hatred, one who lives in a secluded place, who eats little, who controls his body, mind and power of speech, who is always in trance and who is detached, free from false ego, false strength, false pride, lust, anger, and acceptance of material things, free from false proprietorship, and peaceful - such a person is certainly elevated to the position of self-realization.

54

One who is thus transcendentally situated at once realizes the Supreme Brahman and becomes fully joyful. He never laments or desires to have anything. He is equally disposed toward every living entity. In that state he attains pure devotional service unto Me.

55

One can understand Me as I am, as the Supreme Personality of Godhead, only by devotional service. And when one is in full consciousness of Me by such devotion, he can enter into the kingdom of God.

56

Though engaged in all kinds of activities, My pure devotee, under My protection, reaches the eternal and imperishable abode by My grace.

57

In all activities just depend upon Me and work always under My protection. In such devotional service, be fully conscious of Me.

58

If you become conscious of Me, you will pass over all the obstacles of conditioned life by My grace. If, however, you do not work in such consciousness but act through false ego, not hearing Me, you will be lost.

59

If you do not act according to My direction and do not fight, then you will be falsely directed. By your nature, you will have to be engaged in warfare.

60

Under illusion you are now declining to

act according to My direction. But, compelled by the work born of your own nature, you will act all the same, O son of Kunti.

61
The Supreme Lord is situated in everyone's heart, O Arjuna, and is directing the wanderings of all living entities, who are seated as on a machine, made of the material energy.

62
O scion of Bharata, surrender unto Him utterly. By His grace you will attain transcendental peace and the supreme and eternal abode.

63
Thus I have explained to you knowledge still more confidential. Deliberate on this fully, and then do what you wish to do.

64
Because you are My very dear friend, I am speaking to you My supreme instruction, the most confidential knowledge of all. Hear this from Me, for it is for your benefit.

65
Always think of Me, become My devotee, worship Me and offer your homage unto Me. Thus you will come to Me without fail. I promise you this because you are My very dear friend.

66
Abandon all varieties of religion and just surrender unto Me. I shall deliver you from all sinful reactions. Do not fear.

67
This confidential knowledge may never be explained to those who are not austere, or devoted, or engaged in devotional service, nor to one who is envious of Me.

68
For one who explains this supreme secret to the devotees, pure devotional service is guaranteed, and at the end he will come back to Me.

69
There is no servant in this world more dear to Me than he, nor will there ever be one more dear.

70
And I declare that he who studies this sacred conversation of ours worships Me by his intelligence.

71
And one who listens with faith and without envy becomes free from sinful reactions and attains to the auspicious planets where the pious dwell.

72
O son of Prtha, O conqueror of wealth, have you heard this with an attentive mind? And are your ignorance and illusions now dispelled?

73
Arjuna said: My dear Krishna, O infallible one, my illusion is now gone. I have regained my memory by Your mercy. I am now firm and free from doubt and am prepared to act according to Your instructions.

74
Sanjaya said: Thus have I heard the conversation of two great souls, Krishna and Arjuna. And so wonderful is that message that my hair is standing on end.

75
By the mercy of Vyasa, I have heard these most confidential talks directly from the master of all mysticism, Krishna, who was speaking personally to Arjuna.

76
O King, as I repeatedly recall this wondrous and holy dialogue between Krishna and Arjuna, I take pleasure, being thrilled at every moment.

77

O King, as I remember the wonderful form of Lord Krishna, I am struck with wonder more and more, and I rejoice again and again.

78

Wherever there is Krishna, the master of all mystics, and wherever there is Arjuna, the supreme archer, there will also certainly be opulence, victory, extraordinary power, and morality. That is my opinion.

The Bhagavad Gita
English translation by A. C. Bhaktivedanta Swami Prabhupada

4 FACTS AND FIGURES

A Geographic location of Hindus
B Countries with the highest proportion of Hindus
C Hindus and New York State
D Major branches of Hinduism

INTRODUCTION

Hinduism, which claims to have over 1 billion followers worldwide, is the third largest religion in the world, after Christianity and Islam.

A GEOGRAPHIC LOCATION OF HINDUS

- 96% of Hindus live in the Indian subcontinent. They live mainly in India, Nepal, Sri Lanka, Malaysia, Singapore, Thailand, Cambodia, Mauritius, and Indonesia.
- Significant Hindu minorities live in:

Bangladesh	13 million
Myanmar	7.1 million
Sri Lanka	3.0 million
The United States	1.0 million
Pakistan	3.0 million
South Africa	1.5 million
United Kingdom	1.2 million
Malaysia	1.4 million
Canada	0.7 million
Fiji	0.5 million
Trinidad and Tobago	0.5 million
Guyana	0.4 million
Netherlands	0.4 million

Strong Hindu communities also live in some ex-Soviet Union countries, such as Russia and Poland.

B COUNTRIES WITH THE HIGHEST PROPORTION OF HINDUS

Country	Percentage of population	Number
Nepal	90%	20,000,000
India	80%	800,000,000
Mauritius	50%	600,000
Guyana	40%	300,000
Fiji	38%	300,000
Suriname	30%	120,000
Bhutan	25%	450,000
Trinidad and Tobago	24%	330,000
Sri Lanka	15%	3,000,000
Bangladesh	12%	13,000,000

C HINDUS AND NEW YORK STATE

In the USA, the state that has the highest proportion of Hindus in its population, is New York State, where the percentage stands at just over 5%.

D MAJOR BRANCHES OF HINDUISM

Vaishnavites	600,000,000
Shaivites	230,000,000
Neo-Hindus and reform Hindus	25,000,000
Veerashaivas (Lingayats)	11,000,000

5 PRACTICES

A Non-violence (*ahimsa*)
B Cows
C Vegetarianism

A NON-VIOLENCE (*AHIMSA*)

Hindus believe in *ahimsa*, or non-violence and non-injury, in all activities and also in all thoughts, words, and deeds.

Mahatma Gandhi once described Hinduism as, "A quest for truth through non-violence."

This ideal is the basis of the pacific character of Hindu civilization. It is also the reason for the vegetarian diet of many Hindus.

B COWS

Hindus regard all living creatures, mammals, fish and birds as sacred. The cow symbolically represents all creatures, and is the living symbol of Mother Earth. The cow is therefore particularly sacred. Feeding the cow is an act of worship in itself.

The cow represents life and the sustenance of life. It represents our soul, our obstinate intellect, our unruly emotions. But the cow supersedes human beings because it is so giving, taking nothing but grass and grain. It gives and gives and gives.

The cow is vital to life, the virtual sustainer of life for human beings. The cow is a complete ecology, a gentle creature and a symbol of abundance.

C VEGETARIANISM

Less than one third of all Hindus are vegetarian: there are good Hindus who eat meat, and there are bad Hindus who are vegetarians. But the Hindu who wishes to strictly follow the path of non-injury to all creatures naturally adopts a vegetarian diet.

6 BELIEFS

A The Eternal Way
B *Bindi*
C The four stages of life
D Common beliefs

    (i)   All paths lead to God
    (ii)   God
    (iii)   Panentheism
    (iv)   Hindu mythology and the living Gods
    (v)   Brahman
    (vi)   The gods and goddesses
    (vii)   The nature of humanity
    (viii) Cause of suffering
    (ix)   The caste system
    (x)   *Maya*
    (xi)   *Karma*
    (xii)   Reincarnation
    (xiii) Nivarna

E Yoga dharma

INTRODUCTION

Hinduism does not require its adherents to accept any one idea: no single dogma is imposed on everyone.

A THE ETERNAL WAY

For many thousands of years, Hinduism has been known as the Eternal Way (in Sanskrit *tana Dharma*). It is also known as the "Perennial Philosophy/Harmony/Faith."

Hindus believe that certain spiritual principles always remain true and that each person's life is a quest to discover the divine within the self. This search for the one truth is known as the *dharma*.

B *BINDI*

An example of the pervasiveness of this truth-seeking spirituality in Hinduism is the *bindi*, an ornamental mark worn by women on the forehead between the two eyebrows. It symbolizes the need to foster supramental consciousness, which may be achieved by opening the mystic "third eye."

C THE FOUR STAGES OF LIFE

Hindus view human life as four phases or stages (*ashramas*). These are:

- *Brahmacharya*
- *Grihasthya*
- *Vanaprastha*
- *Sanyasa*

(i)   *Brahmacharya*

The first quarter of one's life, *brahmacharya* (literally "grazing in Brahma") is spent in celibate, sober and pure contemplation of life's secrets under a guru. In this stage, the body and mind are built up for the responsibilities of life.

(ii)   *Grihastya*

Grihastya, also known as *samsara*, is the stage of life when one marries and satisfies *kama* (pleasure) and *artha* (power, fame and wealth) within a married life or a professional career.

(iii) *Vanaprastha*

Vanaprastha is gradual detachment from the material world. During this time one spends more time in contemplation of the truth.

(iv) *Sanyasa*

During *sanyasa* one becomes more secluded, preparing for the next life, and seeking God through Yogic meditation.

D COMMON BELIEFS

Hinduism knows nothing about orthodoxy. Beliefs within Hinduism are wide, varied, and changing. However, nearly all Hindu sects share the following beliefs:

(i) ALL PATHS LEAD TO GOD

Hindus believe that as all streams and rivers lead to the same ocean, all genuine religious/ spiritual paths lead to the same goal, that is, the worship of every form of "God." All people are allowed to worship, in their own ways, whoever they conceive to be God.

(ii) GOD

God is One, but also Many.

The Hindu religion is both monotheistic (the worship of one God) and henotheistic (belief in and worship of one God without denying the existence of others). Hindus were never polytheistic (worshiping many gods).

The One becomes many and the many have to begin their journey finally towards the One as a process of creation.

Hindus believe in one supreme God who created the universe and who is worshiped as Light, Love and Consciousness.

(iii) PANENTHEISM

Hindus believe that there is one all-pervasive God who energizes the entire universe. This concept of God as existing in and giving life to all things is called "panentheism." It is different from pantheism, which is the belief that God is the natural universe and nothing more. It is also different from theism which says God is only above the world. Panentheism says that God is both in the world and beyond it, both immanent and transcendent: that the world is a part, but not the whole of God's being.

Truth for the Hindu has many names, but that does not make for many truths.

(iv) HINDU MYTHOLOGY AND THE LIVING GODS

Heroes of epics like the *Mahabharata* and the *Ramayana* are immortalized and are still alive in the day-to-day existence of ordinary people. The gods of Hinduism are at once supra-human and human.

(v) BRAHMAN

In the Veda, the ultimate is Brahman. He is the supreme spirit and creator of the universe. He is the ultimate source of all being. Brahman is formless, eternal, and an intrinsic part of the soul. Other figures were and are worshiped, too, but they are different manifestations of Brahman. Hindus are divided into three groups, according to the form of Brahman they worship.

(vi) THE GODS AND GODDESSES

In various periods of Hindu history, different deities have assumed prominence. In today's India, for example, Lord Brahma is rarely worshiped, while Swami Ayyappa (a form of Lord Kartikeya) is popular.

A deity might be known by another name or form - Goddess Kali, for instance, is worshiped as an angry form of Parvati; Lord Vishnu is worshiped as both Krishna and Rama.

The Hindu gods are very much alive and live in temples, on snow-capped peaks, in rivers and oceans and in the very hearts and minds of the Hindus.

The Vedic gods

The earliest gods were the Aryan gods of the Vedic period (1200-1000 BC). These gods are personifications of nature or cosmic forces, and are all manifestations of the One, of Brahman. The three chief gods are:

Indra   The administrator-in-chief of heaven and the God most frequently prayed to. He is the one who has overcome the sun, setting free the dawn.

Agni   The god of fire, and the life force of nature. He unites earth, heaven and the atmosphere.

Varuna   The chief of the Vedic gods, and the god of rains. He preserves the cosmic order.

About twenty-four gods are referred to in the Vedic literature. Other gods include:

Surya   the sun god
Vayu   the wind god
Varuna   the god of rains
Yama   the god of death
Kubera   the god of material wealth
Soma   the moon god

Later, non-Aryan gods
These deities form the essential core of Hindu belief. They are headed by a triad (*Trimurti*), who are manifestations of the one all-powerful god, Ishvara (who symbolizes Brahman). These three are:

Brahma   the creator of life and the entire universe. He is depicted with four heads corresponding to the four directions of the compass.
Vishnu   the protector and preserver who guides the cycle of birth and rebirth.
Shiva (Hara,   the destroyer but also the
Shambu, etc) Ishwar recreator, the source of good and evil and also the destroyer of evil. He is often seen with a coiled cobra around his neck.

Goddesses and consorts of the three gods:

Sarasvati   the female side of Brahma, the
(Sharada)   energy that comes from him, and the goddess of sacred rivers; also of knowledge, learning and truth.
Laxmi   Vishnu's wife and provider,
(Lakshmi) goddess of beauty and good fortune, wealth and prosperity.
Kali (Uma, Shiva's consort, the Great
Shakti,   Mother, reflects the earliest,
Durga,Kali, most ancient, pre-Aryan,
etc.)   matriarchal religion, represents both judgment and death and peace.

Sons and relatives
Many great leaders (like Shivaji, Tilak), in order to preserve the ancient culture and tradition, popularized deities. The inherently plural nature of Hinduism could easily accommodate the new forms of gods. They include:

Ganesh   son of Shiva and Parvati
Kartikeya
(Subramaynan,
Shanmuga)   son of Shiva and Parvati
Krishna   son of Vasudeva, brother of
Balarama   Balarama, the most popular of the gods
Ramachandra
and Sitadevi
Hanuman   son of Vayu
Vasudeva

Vishnu's incarnations
In medieval India, many saints fought against the evils of the caste system and gave rise to the immensely popular cults of Vaishnavism, or worship of Vishnu. Lord Vishnu did his job of preserving the world by incarnating himself in different forms at times of crisis.

The following are the 10 forms or *avatars* Lord Vishnu is said to have taken to rescue his followers:

1. Matsya   the fish who appeared at the time of the flood
2. Kurma   the tortoise, who rescued treasures from the flood
3. Varaha   the boar, who lifted up the earth from the flood
4. Narasimha   the lion-man
5. Vamana   the dwarf, who fought demons
6. Parusarama "Rama with an ax"
7. Rama-Chandra represents virtue, and fights evil
8. Krishna   a warrior and king (Krishna is also a god)
9. Buddha   the completely enlightened one, the founder of Buddhism
10. Kalki   the tenth *avatar* is still to come

Other gods and goddesses
There are millions of Hindu gods and
goddesses, as many as 330 million, but this is
not seen as polytheism. These gods are ways of
approaching the one god. They include:

Ganesh	who has an elephant's head
Hanuman	an ape
Surya	lord of the sun
Ganga	Magoddess of the River Ganges
Samundra	lord of the sea

(vii) THE NATURE OF HUMANITY
Humankind's nature (*atman*) is divine, being
identical with the absolute (Brahman). Each
individual also shares a common identity with
every other individual. There is thus only one
Reality (monism). The basic purpose of
human beings is to realize this divine nature
and shared identity with all Reality.

(viii) CAUSE OF SUFFERING
The ego or *ahamkar* is the root cause of all
suffering. To escape from suffering we have to
stop being self-absorbed and to ally ourselves
with our limitless inner selves.

(ix) THE CASTE SYSTEM
Hinduism teaches that there are four basic
castes, or social classes. Each caste has its own
rules and obligations for living.

Nobody can choose his or her caste. The
matter is decided when one is born into a
particular caste.

The four castes
- Brahman
  - The elite caste is the Brahman, or
    priest caste.
- Kshatriyas
  - The Kshatriyas are the warriors and
    rulers.
- Vaisyas
  - The Vaisyas are merchants and
    farmers.
- Shudras
  - The fourth caste is the Shudras, or
    laborers.

Untouchables
Outside the caste system are the
untouchables. The untouchables are the
outcasts of Hindu society. In India in the
1940s the practice of treating anyone as an
outcast was outlawed. However, the
untouchables still remain part of Indian
society.

Hierarchy
The four castes in Hindu religion are arranged
in a hierarchy. The highest caste being the
Brahman, and the lowest caste the Shudra.
None of the four castes have any physical
contact with the untouchables.

One can only marry, and even eat, with
one's own caste.

(x) MAYA
The world is an illusion (*maya*) and
attachment to it causes the cycle of birth and
death. When a person overcomes this illusion
through detachment he/she will arrive at self-
realization.

(xi) KARMA
Karma means "cause and effect." The process
of action and reaction on all levels - physical,
mental and spiritual - is *karma*. It is the law
that states that good begets good, and bad
begets bad. Every action, thought, or decision
one makes has consequences – good or bad
and these consequences will return to each
person in the present life, or in one yet to
come.

Karma is basically energy. Hindus believe
that everyone throws energy out through
thoughts, words and deeds.

Good karma and bad karma
God does not give us *karma*. We create our
own. Bad *karma* is because in the past we have
done something bad to someone, and now
someone is doing something bad to us. Good
karma means that we have done something
good in the past and now others are doing
something good to us.

Detachment and sacrifice
The doctrine of *karma* emphasizes that God is
not a remote, heavenly judge, but an

indwelling being (the Self) who works in us here and now through the moral law. Awareness of this is achieved through Karma yoga in which one must perform one's duties with a sense of detachment. Sacrifice through surrendering to God is the basis of salvation.

Hinduism says, "Live your normal life, offering all your actions and possessions mentally to God in the spirit of sacrifice."

(xii) REINCARNATION

The Hindus believe in reincarnation ("life after life," or rebirth), according to which each individual lives many lives.

Reincarnation is known as *samsara* in Sanskrit. The word means to "re-enter the flesh." Hindus believe the soul is immortal and keeps re-entering a body of flesh time and time again in order to resolve experiences and thereby learn all the lessons that life in the material world has to offer. Reincarnation explains the natural way the soul evolves from immaturity to spiritual illumination.

Reincarnation is also known as "transmigration of souls." This is a journey on the "circle of life," where each person experiences a series of physical births, deaths, and rebirths. Every individual soul returns to earth several times by rebirth to perform proper *karma* to purify itself. Once purified by good *karma*, the soul reaches liberation with no-rebirth. Attachment, greed and lust lead to bad *karma* resulting in grief and further suffering and rebirths to wash off those effects.

With good *karma*, a person can be reborn into a higher caste, or even to godhood. Bad *karma* can relegate one to a lower caste, or even to life as an animal, in their next life.

(xiii) NIRVANA

This is the goal of the Hindu. Hindus believe that all living things are Brahman, or god. Enlightenment is attained by becoming tuned in to the Brahman within. Then one reaches Nirvana. This brings release (*moksha*) from the wheel of life and gives access to Nirvana.

E YOGA DHARMA

To practice yoga has been defined as "to yoke oneself to God within." Yoga is often the primary focus of a Hindu's religious activities. It consists of spiritual practices akin to meditation, prayer and healthy exercise.

Hinduism is practiced through a variety of yogas, primarily:

* Karma yoga (selfless service),
* Raja yoga (meditational yoga)
* Jnana yoga (Yoga of discrimination).
* Bhakti (loving devotion)

These are described in the *Bhagavad Gita* and the Yoga Sutras.

(i) KARMA YOGA

Karma yoga is the correct path of performing work without greed or desire. This way of salvation focuses on the attainment of liberation through fulfilling one's family duties. Karma yoga is work or service without attachment to the benefits of work. This overcomes the bad *karma* one has accrued.

(ii) RAJA YOGA

Raja yoga is the control of body and mind. It teaches concentration, meditation, breathing and physical exercises and a state of equanimity of the mind as a natural reaction to all activities.

(iii) JNANA YOGA

Jnana yoga is the path of obtaining spiritual knowledge through action, study, meditation and devotion. It is believed that ignorance causes human bondage to the cycle of rebirths. Such ignorance causes bad actions, which result in bad *karma*. Salvation is achieved through attaining a state of consciousness in which we realize our identity with Brahman. Concentrated meditation, often as a part of the discipline of yoga, enables us to arrive at this point.

(iv) BHAKTI YOGA

Bhakti yoga is the way of spiritual discipline and love of God. Most people in India follow this path. It involves self-surrender to one of the many personal gods and goddesses of Hinduism. Such devotion is expressed through acts of worship, prayers, temple rituals, and pilgrimages.

7 WORSHIP

A Not just one deity
B Not idol worshipers
C Hindu rituals and worship
D Festivals
E Holy places

A NOT JUST ONE DEITY

Unlike most other religions, Hinduism does not advocate the worship of one particular deity. One may worship Shiva or Vishnu, Rama or Krishna, or other gods and goddesses, or one may believe in the "Supreme Spirit" or the "Indestructible Soul" within each individual.

B NOT IDOL WORSHIPERS

Hindus are not idol worshipers. They do not worship stones or statues. They do, however, invoke the presence of great souls, living in higher consciousness, into stone images so that they may feel the presence of God. Thus, although Hindus may have a stone image of a God, they are not worshiping that image, but are invoking the physical presence of the God into the stone image so that they may be blessed. Such invocations can be performed by invoking God's presence in a fire, or in a tree, or in the enlightened person.

C HINDU RITUALS AND WORSHIP

Hindus worship in a temple or at home. The temple is not just a hall, but rather is a palace of the Supreme God.

Hindus make offerings directly to a god, or through the priest. Their offerings may be flowers, coconut, fruits, or incense. They chant prayers in Sanskrit or their mother tongue.

D FESTIVALS

Hindu festivals and ceremonies are associated not only with gods and goddesses but also with the sun, moon, planets, rivers, oceans, trees and animals.

Some of the popular Hindu festivals are:

• Deepawali
• Holi
• Dussehra
• Ganesh Chaturthi
• Pongal
• Janamasthmi
• Shiva Ratri

These, along with other innumerable festive occasions, have helped to give Hinduism its popular appeal and have influenced much of India's rich and colorful culture.

THE KUMBH MELA FESTIVAL

This festival takes place every ten years, at Allahabad, where the waters of the Ganges and the Jamna join. Ten million or most people join in the ritual bathing which marks this festival.

E HOLY PLACES

Hindus have many holy places. The four holiest places for the Hindus are:

• Badrinath
• Puri
• Dwarkha
• Rameshwaram

Rivers, the Ganges in particular, are regarded as holy. Rivers are sources of spiritual life.

Hindus also worship and respect some animals and birds, such as cobra, apes, peacocks and the cow, and some trees and bush trees, such as the Tulsi.

8 GROUPINGS WITHIN HINDUISM

Contemporary Hinduism is traditionally divided into four major divisions:

A Saivism
B Shaktism
C Vaishnavism
D Smartism

Hinduism is a rich and complex religion. Each of its four sects shares rituals, beliefs, traditions and gods with one another, but each sect has a different philosophy on how to achieve life's ultimate goal (*moksha*, liberation) and on their views of the gods. Each sect believes in different methods of self-realization and in different beings as the One Supreme God. However, each sect respects and accepts all others, and conflict of any kind is rare.

Some sects of Hinduism believe in a monotheistic ideal of Vishnu (often as Krishna), or Shiva. But this view does not exclude worship of other gods, as they are understood to be aspects of the chosen ideal (for example, to many devotees of Krishna, Shiva is seen as having sprung from Krishna's creative force). Often the monad Brahman is seen as the one source, with all other gods emanating from him. Someone may consider himself or herself a Shakta (a devotee of Shakti), a Shaiva (a devotee of Shiva), and a Vaishnava (a devotee of Vishnu) all at the same time.

All Hindus believe that all religious paths lead to one God or source (the ultimate truth).

A SHAIVISM

Shaivism, also Saivism, is a branch of Hinduism in which Siva/Shiva is worshipped as the Supreme God.

In the *Vedas* Shiva is called Rudra. He is also called Pashupati, the lord of animal beings. Unlike Vaishnavism, Shaivism does not believe that God incarnates. Shaivism stresses the formless aspect of God. Since God is without form, devotees often worship Shiva in the form of lingam (a phallus) rather than portraying him in human form.

B SHAKTISM

Shaktism is a denomination of Hinduism that worships Shakti, the Divine Mother, in all of her forms while not rejecting the importance of masculine and neuter divinity.

Shaktism as we know it today developed between the fourth and seventh centuries AD in India. It was during this development that the many religious texts known as the Tantras were written.

In this form of Hinduism, the feminine energy (Shakti) is considered to be the motive force behind all action and existence in the Hindu cosmos.

C VAISHNAVISM

Vaishnavism is the branch of Hinduism in which Vishnu or one of his *avatars* (incarnations) is worshiped as the supreme God.

Major branches of Vaishnavism include Srivaishnavism, Dvaita and Gaudiya Vaishnavism.

The distinction between this branch and others is made by those who study religion. It may not, however, always be clear to practicing Hindus, who often take freely from the practices of the different branches.

D SMARTISM

Smartas (followers of Smartism) accept and worship all major forms of God (Ganesha, Siva, Sakti, Vishnu, Surya and Skanda). Its adherents follow a meditative, philosophical path, and the denomination is generally considered to be liberal and non-sectarian.

9 Swamiji: Yoga in Daily Life

Paramhans Swami Maheshwarananda, simply known as Swamiji, is recognized globally by thousands as one of the great Self-Realized Masters who has brought the ancient science of yoga to the West. His insight and understanding of the problems of modern society led him to create a unique and comprehensive system of yoga called "Yoga in Daily Life." Swamiji spreads the message of *Sat Sanatan Dharma* "the eternal truth" around the world to inspire humankind to follow the ethics and moral principles of non-violence, love, tolerance and protection of all living creatures.

SWAMIJI

Born in rural Rajasthan, India, Swamiji was drawn to spirituality from an early age. When he was thirteen, he met his Master, Paramhans Swami Madhavananda (known simply as "Holy Guruji"). Through serving Holy Guruji and doing rigorous spiritual practice under his guidance, Swamiji attained the state of Self-Realization at the age of seventeen.

In 1972, Swamiji moved from India to Europe to spread the teachings of yoga. Here he became aware of the many problems people face in the modern world as a consequence of stress, bad habits, and unnatural ways of living. Swamiji based yoga in Daily Life on original yoga tradition but directed it to the needs of modern life, and made it available to people of all ages and walks of life, regardless of age or level of physical ability.

Today, Yoga in Daily Life centers in twenty-six countries offer Swamiji's teachings through the practices of yoga and meditation.

YOGA IN DAILY LIFE

The main points of Swamiji's teachings are:

- physical, mental, social and spiritual health
- respect for life
- tolerance for all religions, cultures and nationalities
- global peace
- protection of human rights and values
- protection of the environment and preservation of nature.

The realization of these fundamental principles of life leads to spiritual development, self-realization and realization of God.

10 QUOTATIONS ABOUT HINDUISM

A Quotations from Swamiji's writings
B The golden rule
C Duty
D Other quotations

A QUOTATIONS FROM SWAMIJI'S WRITINGS

Success or achievement is not the final goal. It is the "spirit" in which you act that puts the seal of beauty upon your life.

To love and be loved is the greatest happiness.

Do the best and leave the rest.

Efficiency is the capacity to bring proficiency into expression.

Brood less, smile more and serve all.

The tragedy of human history is decreasing happiness in the midst of increasing comforts.

The highest form of grace is silence.

Out of purity and silence come the words of power.

The cultured give happiness wherever they go. The uncultured whenever they go.

Faults become thick when love is thin.

Introspect daily, detect diligently, negate ruthlessly.

Substitute wisely, grow steadily and be free.

Every body dies, nobody dies.

Comfort: Comes as Guest, Lingers to become Host and stays to *enslave* us.

Disappointment can come only to those who make appointment with the future.

Temper takes you to trouble; pride keeps you there.

He who depends on chances and situations to be happy is a Sansari.

Mind alone is *maya* at play.

Remember, "Even This Will Pass Away."

It is sure to be dark if you close your eyes.

Not to do what you feel like doing is freedom.

To be angry is to revenge the faults of others on ourselves.

A successful man is one who can lay a firm foundation with the bricks that others throw at him.

He who submits to discipline is a *disciple*.

Happiness depends on what you can give, not on what you can get.

In all adversities there is always in its depth, a treasure of spiritual blessings secretly hidden.

Alert and vigilant living itself is a "Sadhana" in the true sense.

Sin is never in action, it is always in reaction.

If I rest, I rust.

Moksha is not freedom from action but freedom in action.

Work without faith and prayer is like an artificial flower without fragrance.

Faith is, "To believe what you do not see," the reward of which is, "You see what you believed."

Grace is only to be found by effort, although it is here and now."

Appreciating the mind as "*all silence*." "*I am*" is meditation.

To say, "*The Lord is*" is *Gyanam*. But "*The Lord is I*" is *Vigyanam*.

To understand anything is to find in it something which is our own.

The end of ego is the "Mystic Death" of the mediator.

"Surrender in spite of freedom" is the way of wise men.

There is nothing,
at any time, in any circumstance,
to worry over - "Why this to me?"

What you have is all His gift to you.
What you do with what you have is your gift to Him . . .

Don't put the key to your happiness in someone else's pocket.

To forget oneself totally, one's mind should keep awake at every moment. A mind that has forgotten the past and the future, that is awake to the now, to the present, expresses the highest concentration of intelligence. It is alert, it is watchful, it is inspired. The actions of a man who has such a mind are exceptionally creative and perfect. Verily to forget oneself totally, is to be in perfection.

Wisdom is the assimilated knowledge in us, gained from an intelligent estimation and close study of our own direct and indirect experience in the world.

Temper brings you to trouble.
Pride keeps you there.

Unless we have a definite faith in the goal of our existence, and unless we believe, work for, and actually come to experience the goal positively as an existent factor, there is no hope of any plan becoming successful.

More important than
what is behind you and what is ahead of you is what is in you.
Seek it.
Centered in it, act and live.

Universe is a cosmos and not a chaos. There exists a mental affinity; a scientific law; a rhythm of mental relationship in which the entire living world is held together, in one web of love.

To assume differences in the world, is to belie this great Oneness in life.

Silently hear everyone.
Accept what is good.
Reject and forget what is not.
This is intelligent living.

Love is a consistent passion to give, not a meek persistent hope to receive. The only demand of life is the privilege to love all.

Bhakti is the attitude of the mind, and *jnana* is the attitude of the intellect, both flow towards the Lord.

In life to handle yourself, use your head, but to handle others, use your heart.

Be strict and intelligently critical about yourself and your own weakness and follies. But, cushion your words and attitudes with Love. Love is the greatest persuasive power we know in life.

Everybody exists.
It is only the few who live.

To live, you should have an ideal.

Man is the roof and crown of creation. He may be tossed about by uncertain storms of life, but the solution to it lies in his own efforts in finding an ideal, and then raising his personality, from the level of petty emotions, to the loftier heights of the chosen ideal.

A man-of-wisdom lives in the world, but he is never of the world.

The secret of success behind all men of achievement, lies in the faculty of applying their intellect in all their activities, without being mislead by any surging emotions or feelings. The secret of success in life lies in keeping the head above the storms of the heart.

Plan out your work,
Then work out your plan.
The former without the latter is a sheer waste.
The latter without the former is mere unproductive confusion.

To give without sympathy is to build a temple without the idol and is as futile as painting a picture with black ink on a black board.

You are successful and creative only when you see an opportunity in every difficulty.

Strange! Wealth estranges us all. It is all very strange, the money psychology! When you have not got any, you will pant to get some! When you get some, you grow jealous of others who have more,

and feel conceited among those who have less!

Know what to do.
Do it yourself.

Religion must not be considered true because it is necessary, but necessary because it is true.

Sandalwood perfumes even the axe that hurls it down! The more we rub sandalwood against a stone, the more its fragrance spreads.
Burn it, and it wafts its glory through the entire neighborhood.
Such is the enchanting beauty of forgiveness in life.

We may often give without love, but we can never love without giving.

Fanatic secularism is as dangerous to the world as fanatic religion.

Love is the heart of all religions; the theme of all classical works of art and literature; the song of all devotees. Scientists know only what love does, not what love is. Love is to human hearts what the sun is to flowers."

Without devotion, knowledge is tasteless. Without knowledge, devotion is mere empty idol worship.

To remember the ever present Divine at all times, even while acting in the world, is the most positive practice for a seeker who is striving to evolve. He will thereby transform his inner personality from its present condition, to a state of harmony and efficiency.

The greatness is not what we do, but, unavoidably, it is always in how we do what we do.
Our present work may be great or small, yet the important is to do it well.

Stop all your attachments to false values.

In an ever changing world, there is nothing worthwhile for us to desire or weep for. Joys and sorrows are bound come in human life; they are just like the two sides of the same coin.

Hindu culture is essentially based upon the sacrifice implied in duty, and not upon acquisition, which is implied in rights.

The cultured give happiness wherever they go. The uncultured whenever they go.

Everyone points to the other man, who, according to him, is happier. But the only one, who has the courage to declare that he is truly happy, is he who has relinquished all his passions and hungers from within.

In all worthwhile undertakings, there will be risks of failure, of disappointments, even of disaster. To face them all with inner poise and firm faith is to discover the glory of final victory.

A conquest, without facing dangers is as dull as victory without a shining glory. A game without a prize!

Mind at rest is the Temple of Joy. So long as it is gurgling with its desires, passions and attachments in its stormy surface, the signature of joy gets ruffled out.

Some act till they meet obstacles, others act in spite of obstacles and conquer them; but some act not fearing the possibility of some obstacles, that might arise en route.

Live morality before you talk of it.
Practice meditation before you preach it.
Taste goodness before you recommend it.
Gain bliss before you offer it to others.

Spiritual enlightenment cannot take place merely because of an intellectual appreciation of the theory of perfection. Evolution takes place only when a

corresponding change in the subjective life is accomplished.
There is no destiny beyond and above ourselves; we are ourselves the architects of our future.

All disturbances and challenges rise not only from our relationship with others, but in our attitude to all other things and beings.

Charity is an attempt wherein I try to expand and bring into the ambit of my life, all others around me and grow to consider the other man's needs and requirements as important as my own personal needs. To live seeking an identity thus, with at least those who are immediately around me, is to live away from the suffocating selfishness and the throttling grip of my body-consciousness.

We like someone because . . . ; we love someone in spite of . . .

Flood your mind with love. Look into the eyes of the other and embrace the person with whom you have quarreled.
Words are not necessary. Both will have their eyes flooded, and the joy of tears will wash away all quarrels.

The God-Man functions as a true "sportsman" in his playfield, where the very enjoyment is in the sport and not in the score.

A successful man is one who can lay a firm foundation with the bricks that others throw at him.

Mind can make a hell of heaven.
or a heaven of hell.

There is no companion like solitude. One who knows how to tune himself to the inner silence, even in the midst of the din and roar of the marketplace, enjoys a most recreative solitude.

Seek the Lord

in the smiles of your friends,
in the glow of angry eyes,
in the storms of passion.
He is everywhere, in everything.

The real men of achievement are people who have the heroism to fuel more and more enthusiasm in their work, when they face more and more difficulties.

Character is formed from the repeated choice of thoughts and action.
Make the right choice - you shall have a firm and noble character.

The greatness in an ideology is not, in fact, in the ideology; but it is in the subject which lives that ideology.

Out of purity and silence come words of power.

When opportunity knocks,
we are either "out" or sleeping "in."

To be patient means to suffer something that hinders or hurts us, and still retain our self-composure. How many difficulties, with their consequent unpleasantness and discord, could be smoothed over and almost entirely eliminated by patience. Patience always elevates and strengthens our character. We need it not only with others but also with ourselves.

Yoga is skill in action.
The secret of action is to get established in equanimity, renouncing all egocentric attachments, and forgetting to worry over our successes and failures.

To define God is to defile God.

Prosperity is like wine, which goes to the head, and makes man forget his Creator. Adversity, on the contrary, sobers him and reminds him of God and his glory.

The tragedy of human history is decreasing happiness in the midst of increasing comforts.

History is full of instances wherein victory would have been to the vanquished, if only they had battled a little longer! We often fail for lack of perseverance in our efforts. We leave our work half done in our impatience. Every job demands its quota of efforts. Never give up too soon.

The spirit of *Advaita* is not to keep away from anything,
but to keep in tune with everything.

To "listen" is not merely to "hear."
We in life "hear" but very rarely do we know how to "listen."
To "listen" is to "hear" with an intellectual alertness and attention of awareness.

In life,
the glory lies
not in the quarry,
but in the chase.
The success is not in the trophy won
but in the race run.

One single ideal
can transform a
listless soul
into a towering
leader of men.

The average man looks up at night and sees thousands and thousands, of twinkling stars, each different from the others. But a man of wisdom and achievement, perceives the one light, behind the dark dome of the night-sky, whose incandescence peeps at us through all the holes in the night-dome!

To see the one in the many
is the casual vision of knowledge.
To see the many in the one,
is the mission wisdom.

To do your job even if circumstances are not conducive,
is our gift to Him - who is the sole Lord of all circumstances.

Become quietly effective.

Don't expect "them" to fully understand you.

They won't: So?
Demonstrate with results
what "they" would not
understand with words!"

To give love is true freedom;
to demand love is pure slavery.

When the time of judgment comes,
we shall not be asked what we have read
but what we have done.

Spirituality is neither the privilege of the poor nor the luxury of the rich. It is the choice of the wise man.

Swamiji

B THE GOLDEN RULE

Do not to others what ye do not wish
done to yourself;
and wish for others too what ye desire and
long for, for yourself.
This is the whole of *dharma*, heed it well.
The Mahabharata

This is the sum of duty: do naught to others which if done to thee would cause thee pain.

The Mahabharata

This *dharma* stands unchallenged changelessly,
That I should sorrow when my fellow-beings
May sorrow, and rejoice when they rejoice.

Bhagavata Purana

C DUTY

The final mark of duty, righteousness, legal and moral lawfulness, is this -that what ye hold as dear and good for self and which your inner higher self approves, ye hold as dear and good for others too; and what ye may not like for your own self,

for others like it not, in the same way,
who feeleth as his own the joys and
sorrows of others, he is the true yogi,
he hath truly "joined" his own soul with
all souls.

Hitopadesa

D OTHER QUOTATIONS

Live simply so that others may simply live.
Mahatma Gandhi

Hinduism, as a faith, is vague, amorphous, many-sided, all things to all men. It is hardly possible to define it, or indeed to say definitely whether it is a religion or not, in the usual sense of the word. In its present form, and even in the past, it embraces many beliefs and practices, from the highest to the lowest, often opposed to or contradicting each other.
*Jawaharlal Nehru, the first Prime Minister of
independent India*

Hinduism does not rest on the authority of one book or one prophet, nor does it possess a common creed - like the Kalma of Islam - acceptable to all. That renders a common definition of Hinduism a bit difficult.
Mahatma Gandhi

Hinduism is a veritable chamber of horrors. The sanctity and infallibility of the *Vedas*, Smritis and Shastras, the iron law of caste, the heartless law of *karma* and the senseless law of status by birth are to the Untouchables veritable instruments of torture which Hinduism has forged against untouchables. These very instruments which have mutilated blasted and blighted the lives of the Untouchables are to be found intact and untarnished in the bosom of Gandhism.
*Dr. B. R. Ambedkar,
former first Law Minister of independent India.
He was the head of the committee that drafted
the constitution of India, and he is known as
the Father of the Indian Constitution*

Hinduism defies definition. It has no specific creed.

Khushwant Singh

Hinduism is not a religion established by a single person. It is a growth of ideas, rituals and beliefs so comprehensive as to include anything between atheism and pantheism.

P. Thomas

The more Hinduism is considered, the more difficult it becomes to define it in a single phrase . . . A Hindu may have any religious belief or none; he may be an atheist or an agnostic and still be an accepted Hindu. It is public opinion working through the caste system which determines whether someone shall or shall not be regarded as a Hindu.

Percival Spear

Hinduism is far more unstructured than most other religions. It has no archbishops, chief rabbis, grand muftis. Each Hindu decides for himself which manifestations of God are most important to him, what scriptures to accept as authentic, which holy man to follow. The one ineluctable certainty is a person's *dharma*.

The Economist, *June 8, 1991*

---

11 COMPARISON WITH CHRISTIANITY

A Major differences
- (i) God
- (ii) The world and humankind
- (iii) Sin
- (iv) The penalty of sin
- (v) Salvation

B The legacy of Hinduism

A MAJOR DIFFERENCES
There are numerous basic differences between Hinduism and Christianity.

(I) GOD
Hinduism:
A vast plurality of gods and goddesses exist as part of the impersonal Brahman.

Christianity:
There is one God, who cares deeply for every individual.

"Hear, O Israel: The Lord our God, the Lord is one" (Deuteronomy 6:4).

"And call upon me in the day of trouble; I will deliver you, and you will honor me" (Psalm 50:15).

(II) THE WORLD AND HUMANKIND
Hinduism:
The world and everything in it, including human beings, are manifestions of Brahman.

Christianity:
God created the universe. God did not create Himself, the world exists separately from God. God created humankind, and gave free will. God values everyone he created.

"So God created man in his own image, in the image of God he created him; male and female he created them" (Genesis 1:27).

(III) SIN
Hinduism:
Sin is committed against oneself, not against God.

Christianity:
God gave us laws to follow because he cares about us. He also gave us free will – we can choose to disobey. Disobedience is sin and a grave offense against God.

"Against you, you only, have I sinned and done what is evil in your sight, so that you are proved right when you speak and justified when you judge" (Psalm 51:4).

"For all have sinned and fall short of the glory of God" (Romans 3:23).

(IV) THE PENALTY OF SIN
Hinduism:
Since "sin" is committed only against oneself, the penalties are accrued only against the self. The penalty is the repeated cycle of rebirths, until we can escape to Nirvana.

Christianity:
Sin cannot exist in the presence of God. Therefore the penalty of sin is spiritual separation from God.

"For the wages of sin is death" (Romans 6:23a).

(V) SALVATION
Hinduism:
Salvation is the release from the wheel of life, the cycle of rebirths, through which we must work to better ourselves, and realize our oneness with Brahman. It must be worked out by each individual through uccessive lives.

Christianity:
Salvation is a free gift to us from God which must be accepted, not achieved. Jesus bought our salvation by taking all our sin upon himself on the cross, dying as a sacrifice for us, and then rising from the dead three days later. Salvation begins the moment we accept Jesus and continues for ever, even after death.

". . . but the gift of God is eternal life in Christ Jesus our Lord" (Romans 6:23b)

"For God so loved the world that he gave his one and only Son, that whoever believes in him shall not perish but have eternal life" (John 3:16).

"For it is by grace you have been saved, through faith and this not from yourselves, it is the gift of God - not by works, so that no one can boast" (Ephesians 2:8, 9).

B THE LEGACY OF HINDUISM
Hinduism has given birth to innumerable other cults and religious movements. Buddhism started as an offshoot of Hinduism. Today, the New Age Movement, Transcendental Meditation, Wicca, and many forms of pagan worship trace their roots back to Hinduism.

12 GLOSSARY

Ahamkar
The ego; identification with one's ego.

Ahimsa
Non-violence.

Ajapâjapa
A devotee who has practiced *japa* for a long period of time may enjoy *ajapâjapa*. When this happens, recitation of the mantra continues within the devotee's heart (his inner being) automatically and ceaselessly.

Antahkaran
The mind with its four faculties called *man* (the emotional mind), *buddhi* (the discriminative mind), *chit* (the section of the mind that holds all the *sanskars*) and *ahamkar* (the ego).

Apâna
Vital energy represented by inhaling.

Ashram
A retreat house.

Atman
The self; the all-pervading soul in every creature, which is divine. The panentheist paradigm is known in the Sanskrit language as the *atman* or *purusha*, the real self. In the *Upanishads* and the *Gita* the one *atman* is present within all creatures.

Avatar
The coming down of God or a divine personality, an incarnation of a deity.

Bhagavan
"Lord;" God manifesting himself as a person; the object of worship of the *bhaktas*. By worshiping God as a person, devotees are able to assume human-like relationships with God, for example: God as parent, devotee as child; God as Lord, devotee as servant; God as the Beloved, devotee as the lover. This makes a personal relationship with God more easily possible.

Bhakti
The deep loving feelings of a devotee's heart for his beloved God where all of his personal requisites are merged into his Divine beloved's overwhelming grace which He imparts for His loving devotee. .

Bharat
The short term of Bharatvarsh is Bharat, which was called "Hindustan" by the Muslims and "India" by the British. Accordingly, the word Hindu and Indian came into being.

Brahmajnana
The knowledge of Brahman.

Brahman
The supreme Godhead, beyond all distinctions or forms; ultimate Reality (from *brih*: that which expands).

Caste system
Social groups in India that rank in a hierarchic order. There are four castes, and outside the castes are the Untouchables. It was taught that one could move from one caste to another only as the result of reincarnation. This system was rejected by Buddha. Ghandi also rejected it, and attempts have been made by the Indian government to reform aspects of the caste system. It is, however, still an integral part of Indian life.

Chand
A poetic stanza or a Vedic verse.

Dharma
In general, *dharma* means the search for the one truth. It also means the duty each individual person must do.

Gita
Song; short for the *Bhagavad Gita*, possibly the most revered of all Hindu scriptures.

God
The supreme, all-powerful Divinity, who is kind, gracious and omnipresent in His Divine form in the entire creation, and also has an omnipresent impersonal aspect of His Divine being.

Grishasta
Householder; a lay person, as opposed to a monk.

Incarnation (*avatar*)
Hindus often regard an enlightened individual as an incarnation of God. The name used to refer to God varies (for example, Shiva or Vishnu).

Japa
A mantra is usually one of the names of God, or a brief sentiment directed toward God; the act of repeating the mantra over and over again is called *japa*.

Jiva
The embodied soul.

Jivanmukta
A person who is liberated (enlightened) while living.

Jivan-mukti
The state of being liberated (enlightened) while alive.

Jnanayoga
The path of knowledge, consisting of discrimination, renunciation, and other disciplines.

Jnani
One who follows the path of knowledge and discrimination to realize God.

Kali
Kali is a female manifestation of God. Through her grace, those who are devoted to her may pass from the realm of time to the realm of timelessness. Kali is often depicted holding a severed head. The head represents the false ego that must be subdued before enlightenment can be attained.

Karma
The good and bad actions of a person. They are stored in a section of the mind and determine the form of the next incarnation.

Krishna
Krishna is considered one of the incarnations of Visnu. Krishna's advice to Arjuna on the battlefield of Kurukshetra was recorded in the *Bhagavad Gita*.

Kundalini
Spiritual energy.

Mantra
The evocative sentence, verse, or stanza related to: (i) the propitiation of the celestial gods to be used in the fire ceremonies (*yagya*), or (ii) for general prayer to supreme God.

Maya
The illusion of separateness. *Maya* is the power that creates and maintains the universe's apparent diversity, so that the One may appear as many.

Moksha
Liberation, enlightenment.

Nirvikalpa
During this state the mystic loses consciousness of his or her surroundings.

Pandit
A Sanskrit scholar of India.

Rama
An incarnation of Visnu, a manifestation of God. The story of Rama's earthly life is told in the Hindu epic, the *Ramayana*. Lord Rama is the example of the noble man (*arya*) and heroism.

Sadhu
A sadhu is a hermit who has left his family and is living a renounced life.

Samadhi
Turning one's attention away from creation toward that which is uncreated. The individual is ecstatically transported and becomes unaware of his surroundings.

Satchidananda
Another name for Brahman. It is a combination of the words *sat* (being), *chit* (consciousness), and *ananda* (bliss). It is the union of the observer, the observed and the awareness of observation.

Siddha
A perfected being; one who has attained great powers through self-perfection.

Tantra
A system of religious philosophy in which the Divine Mother, or Power, is the ultimate reality.

Yoga
Yoga is awareness, transformation of the human consciousness into divine consciousness.

Yogi
One who practices yoga.

BUDDHISM

CONTENTS

1 An overview   213

2 Buddhism's founder   214

3 Buddhism's holy book   218

4 Facts and figures   242

5 Buddhist practices   243

6 Buddhist beliefs   244

7 Worship   247

8 Groupings within Buddhism 249

9 In praise of Buddhism   253

10 Comparison with Christianity 256

11 Glossary   257

1 AN OVERVIEW

DEFINITION

A way of living based on the teachings of Siddartha Gautama, the Buddha. Buddhism focuses on personal spiritual development. Buddhists strive for a deep insight into the true nature of life. They do not worship gods or deities.

Factfile
- Date of origin: Over 2,500 years old
- Founder: Buddha, c. 563–483 BC, the Enlightened One
- Holy book: in Buddhism there is not one universally sacred scripture for all Buddhists. Theravada Buddhism follow the Pali Canon, which is divided into three parts often known as the *Tripitaka* ("three baskets").
- Number of adherents: 350 million Buddhists worldwide

SUMMARY

The essence of Buddhism may be summarized in its:

- Three jewels
- Four noble truths
- The noble eightfold paths
- The ten precepts

THE THREE JEWELS
- I go to the Buddha for refuge
- I go to the Dhamma for refuge
- I go to the Samgha for refuge

THE FOUR NOBLE TRUTHS
- Life is disappointing and full of suffering
- Suffering is the result of one's desires for pleasure, power, continued existence
- To stop suffering one must stop desiring.
- The way to stop desiring is the noble eightfold path.

THE NOBLE EIGHTFOLD PATH OF RIGHT UNDERSTANDING
- Right thought/attitude
- Right intention
- Right speech
- Right conduct/action
- Right livelihood/occupation
- Right effort
- Right awareness
- Right concentration

THE TEN PRECEPTS
- I observe the precept not to kill any sentient being
- I observe the precept not to steal the ungiven things
- I observe the precept not to indulge in unnoble sexual pleasures
- I observe the precept not to tell falsehood
- I observe the precept not to be intoxicated with narcotics, drugs and alcoholic drinks
- I observe the precept not to take any food after noon
- I observe the precept not to enjoy any

dancing, singing or playing of musical instruments

○ I observe the precept not to indulge in the use of flowers, perfumes, or any other cosmetics

○ I observe the precept not to use high and grand seats and beds

○ I observe the precept not to engage in monetary matters and handling of silver and gold

PRACTICES

The path to Enlightenment or Buddhahood is through the practice and development of morality, meditation, and wisdom.

BELIEFS

Buddhism is a philosophy of life expounded by Gautama Buddha ("Buddha" means "Enlightened One"), who lived and taught in northern India in the sixth century BC. The Buddha was not a god and Buddhism does not embrace a theistic worldview. Buddha's teachings aim to liberate us from suffering.

---

2 BUDDHISM'S FOUNDER

A Buddha's names
B Buddha's life
C Buddha's first sermon at Benares

A BUDDHA'S NAMES

Siddhartha: his personal name chosen for him by his parents. It means "he who has reached his goal."

Gautama: According to tradition, this was the family name. Gautama was a famous Indian teacher from whom it is believed he was descended.

Buddha: The name by which he came to be known. This is a title meaning "the Enlightened One."

B BUDDHA'S LIFE

The rise of Buddhism is the story of Buddha's spiritual quest for enlightenment and the teachings he left behind so others could follow him on this journey.

THE CHAINS OF LUXURY

Siddhartha Gautama was born in about 560 BC in the village of Lumbini in north-eastern India. His father, Shuddhodanna, was a wealthy and prominent rajah of the ruling Ksatriya, or warrior, caste. His mother, Mahamaya, died a week after he was born, and he was brought up by his aunt Mahapatjapati.

It is said that when Siddharta was born, his father was told that his son would become a great leader or a wanderer without a home. To bring about the former, his father made sure that the young prince was educated in the sciences and arts, and that he was insulated from any contact with poverty, suffering, sickness, old age, and death. He grew up knowing nothing but a life of pampered luxury.

Siddhartha married when he was sixteen, and had one son. The fact that he was not satisfied with his rich and easy life is indicated by the name he gave his son: Rahula, meaning "Chain."

THE JOURNEYS

When he was twenty-nine, Gautama had four decisive experiences. One day he left the royal enclosure on a chariot drive. On the journey, he saw an old man, "an aged man, as bent as a roof gable, decrepit, leaning on a staff . . .". On a second journey, he saw "a sick man, suffering and very ill." On a third journey, he saw a funeral procession. Each time, Gautama's charioteer said to him that this was just the way life was: all people are subject to old age, illness and death.

Each time, he returned home deeply disturbed.

In the sixth century, north-eastern India was experiencing a period of great spiritual and intellectual development. The Hindu scriptures, the *Vedas*, had been written 1,000 years earlier, and some of the *Upanishads* had been written, stressing the inner nature of the religious life. At that time, there was a movement within Hinduism for men in search of spiritual understanding to take up a wandering life. On a further chariot drive Gautama saw such a man: "a shaven-headed man, a wanderer who has gone forth, wearing a yellow robe." In spite of his poverty this man was serene and peaceful.

"THE GREAT RENUNCIATION"

Gautama decided to leave home and find out the reason for such peacefulness in the midst of the misery of the world. Taking the advice of an Indian ascetic, he followed the path of extreme asceticism. With five followers, he gave embarked on a life of self-denial and spiritual exercises. But after six years, with his health destroyed, Siddhartha still felt that he was still trapped. For all his suffering, he had not achieved release.

THE BANYAN TREE

Siddhartha realized that an inner change was necessary in order to get rid of the greed and lust for life. Abandoning his austere lifestyle (whereupon his friends left him), he resolved to pursue goodness through meditation. Under a banyan tree (an Indian fig-tree (later to be known as a *bodhi*-tree, or "tree of enlightenment,") Siddhartha achieved enlightenment. This came in three stages.

During the first watch of the night, he found himself being able to recall the events of his previous reincarnations.

During the second watch, he understood the law that determines the cycle of birth, death and rebirth.

During the third watch, the four noble truths were revealed to him: the understanding of suffering, the source of suffering, the removal of suffering, and the way to remove this suffering. Now he knew that his reincarnations were over for ever. He was "the Buddha," the one who has been awakened, who has gained enlightenment. He could have at once entered Nirvana.

(The Mahabodhi Temple, the site of Buddha's enlightenment, is now a pilgrimage site.)

"THE WHEEL OF TEACHING"

It is said that at this point Buddha was tempted by the demon Mara to enter Nirvana at once, and not seek to pass on this knowledge to a world that would not listen, but the God Brahma Sahampati appeared to him and told him to teach others for the sake of the few who would believe.

So Buddha began "the wheel of teaching.". He did not teach people to worship one God, or many gods, but rather to follow the path he had taken and achieve enlightenment and freedom from suffering.

His five followers, who had earlier left him, were present when he gave his first sermon, and rejoined him, becoming *aharants*, "noble ones," as they also achieved enlightenment. His son also joined him.

BUDDHA

For the next forty-four years Buddha traveled throughout India as a wandering teacher. The movement grew rapidly. During the rainy season, he and his followers would stay in the town parks, where halls were specially built for him.

Buddha died suddenly, when he was eighty, in the town of Kushinagara.

C BUDDHA'S FIRST SERMON AT BENARES

These two extremes, O monks, should not be practiced by one who has gone forth [from the household life]. What are the two?

1. That which is linked with sensual desires, which is low, vulgar, common, unworthy, and useless,

2. and that which is linked with self-torture, which is painful, unworthy, and useless.

By avoiding these two extremes the *Tathagata* [Buddha] has gained the knowledge of the middle path which gives vision and knowledge, and leads to calm, to clairvoyances, to enlightenment, to Nirvana.

O monks, what is the middle path, which gives vision . . . ? It is the noble eightfold path: right views, right intention, right speech, right action, right livelihood, right effort, right mindfulness, right concentration. This, O monks, is the middle path, which gives vision.

1. Now this, O monks, is the noble truth of suffering: birth is suffering, old age is suffering, death is suffering, sorrow, grieving, dejection, and despair are suffering. Contact with unpleasant things is suffering, not getting what you want is also suffering. In short, the five aggregates of grasping are suffering.

2. Now this, O monks, is the noble truth of the arising of suffering: that craving which leads to rebirth, combined with longing and lust for this and that - craving for sensual pleasure, craving for rebirth, craving for cessation of birth.

3. Now this, O monks, is the noble truth of the cessation of suffering: It is the complete cessation without remainder of that craving, the abandonment, release from, and non-attachment to it.

4. Now this, O monks, is the noble truth of the path that leads to the cessation of suffering: This is the noble eightfold path. . . .

Now monks, as long as my threefold knowledge and insight regarding these noble truths were not well purified, so long, O monks, I was not sure that in this world I had attained the highest complete enlightenment.

But when my threefold knowledge and insight in these noble truths with their twelve divisions were well purified, then, O monks, I was sure that in this world...I had attained the highest complete enlightenment. Now knowledge and insight have arisen in me, so that I know: My mind's liberation is assured; this is my last existence; for me there is no rebirth.

EXPLANATION OF THIS TEACHING

Soon after the Blessed One left, the venerable Shariputra said to the monks who were there:

"Venerable monks what is the noble truth of suffering? Birth is suffering; aging is suffering; death is suffering; sorrow, distress, misery, and despair are suffering; not getting what you want is suffering. In short, the five aggregates of grasping are suffering.

"And what, sirs, is birth? It is the conception, production, degeneration, rebirth, the arising of various beings belonging to the various types of beings, the appearance of the aggregates, the acquisition of the sense-spheres.

"And what, sirs, is aging? It is the aging, decrepitude, loss of teeth, gray hair, wrinkles, dwindling of the term of life, diminishment of the sense-faculties of various beings belonging to the various types of beings . . .

"And what, sirs, is death? It is the leaving, the passing away, the breaking up, the disappearance, dying, death, decrease, and dissolving of the aggregates, the leaving of the body. . . .

"And what, sirs, is sorrow? It is the grieving, sorrowing, inner sorrow, the inner pain of someone experiencing some kind of trouble, afflicted by some kind of suffering. It is the crying, weeping, or wailing of someone experiencing some kind of trouble, afflicted by some kind of suffering. . . .

"And what, sirs, is distress? It is physical distress, physical unpleasantness that arises from something affecting the body and experienced as distress, as unpleasantness.

"And what, sirs, is misery? It is mental suffering, mental unpleasantness that arises from something affecting the mind and experienced as distress, as unpleasantness.

"And what, sirs, is despair? It is despondency, despair, the despondency and despair of someone afflicted by some kind of calamity, burdened by some kind of suffering.

"And what, sirs, is not getting what you want?" A wish like this arises in beings that are subject to birth: "May we not be subject birth and may birth not come to us." But this is not gained just by wishing. Sirs, a wish like this arises in beings that are subject to aging, disease, death, and to beings that are subject to sorrow, distress, misery, and despair: May we not be subject to sorrow, distress, misery, and despair, and may sorrow, distress, misery, and despair not come to us. But this is not gained just by wishing.

"And what, in brief, sirs, are the five aggregates of grasping that are suffering? They are: the aggregate of grasping for form, for feelings, for discriminations, for compositional factors, for consciousness. Sirs, this is called the noble truth of suffering.

"And what, sirs, is the noble truth of the arising of suffering? Whatever craving is associated with rebirth, accompanied by delight and attachment, finding delight in something - craving for sensual pleasures, craving for being, craving for cessation - this, sirs, is called the noble truth of the arising of suffering.

"And what, sirs, is the noble truth of the cessation of suffering? Whatever is the cessation, with no remainder of attachment, of that very grasping, the renouncing of it, abandoning it, release from it, independence from it, sirs, is called the noble truth of the cessation of suffering.

"And what, sirs, is the noble truth of the path leading to the cessation of suffering? It is the noble eightfold path itself: right view, right intention, right speech, right action, right livelihood, right effort, right mindfulness, and right concentration.

"And what, sirs, is right view? Sirs, whatever is knowledge of suffering, knowledge of the arising of suffering, knowledge of the cessation of suffering, knowledge of the path leading to the cessation: this, sirs, is called right view.

"And what, sirs, is right intention? Intention toward renunciation, intention toward non-harmfulness, intention toward non-injury: this, sirs, is called right intention.

"And what, sirs, is right speech? Avoiding lying speech, slanderous speech, harsh speech, and gossip: this, sirs, is called right speech.

"And what, sirs, is right action? Avoiding harming living beings, taking what is not given, and sexual misconduct: this, sirs, is called right action.

"And what, sirs, is right livelihood? Sirs, it is that by which a follower of the Noble One makes a living, avoiding wrong modes of making a living: this, sirs, is called right livelihood.

"And what, sirs, is right effort? Sirs, a follower of the Noble One applies the will, aspires, applies himself, exerts the mind, and works at stopping bad qualities that have not yet arisen, gets rid of those that have already arisen, cultivates good qualities that have not yet arisen, and establishes, keeps from deteriorating, multiplies, enlarges, develops, and perfects those good qualities that have already arisen. This, sirs, is called right effort.

"And what, sirs, is right mindfulness? Sirs, a monk practices contemplating what the body is, what feelings are, what mind is, and what mental factors are: a monk remains enthusiastic, alert, and mindful, free from the wants and dejections of the world. This, sirs, is called right mindfulness.

"And what, sirs, is right concentration? Sirs, a monk, who is indifferent to sense pleasures, indifferent to non-virtuous mental states, enters into and abides in the first concentration, which is conceptual and analytical, arises from indifference, and is joyful and blissful. Due to decreasing conceptuality and analysis, with the mind subjectively pacified and focused on one point, one enters into and abides in the second concentration, which is non-conceptual and non-analytical, arises from concentration, and is joyful and blissful. Due to eliminating bliss, one enters into and abides in the third concentration, the fourth concentration: this, sirs, is called right concentration. This, sirs, is called the noble truth of the path leading to the cessation of suffering."

3 BUDDHISM'S HOLY BOOK

THE PALI CANON (THE *TRIPITAKA*)

When Buddha knew that he was dying he did not choose a successor. But he bequeathed the Dharma, his teachings, and the Vinaya, his set of rules and spiritual guidelines, to his monks and nuns.

A few months after his death, a council met in Rajagha to gather together his teachings. This work was reviewed at a second council held a hundred years later. Over two hundred years after his death, in 253 BC, a third council met at Pataliputta. At this council, a thousand monks spent nine months checking, completing and classifying Buddha's teachings. This was the official canon of Buddhist teachings. These teachings, however, were still in oral form.

In the first century AD, on the island of Ceylon, these writings were written down. The language used was Pali - hence the name "The Pali canon." This was in three parts. It was first written on palm leaves, which were kept in baskets, hence the more usual name is the *Tripitaka* or "triple basket."

The complete *Tripitaka* is a massive work which today is published in forty volumes. The three parts are:

VINAYA PITAKA

The first section of the *Tripitaka*, the *Vinaya Pitaka* (the "basket of order"), contains advice and rules for monks and nuns.

SUTTA PITAKA

The second section, the *Sutta Pitaka* (the guideline or instruction book), contains all the Buddha's discourses. These are in the form of poems, stories, sermons, and dialogues. Some discourses of the Buddha's enlightened disciples are also included.

ABHIDHAMMA PITAKA

The third section of the *Tripitaka*, the *Abhidhamma Pitaka* (the "basket of higher teaching"), seven books, written in an academic style, giving all the component parts under which an individual may be classified.

A GOOD GUIDE, NOT AN INFALLIBLE REVELATION

Buddhists do not think of their scriptures as an infallible guide. They do not seek to carry out every instruction in it to the last letter. They go to the *Tripitaka* for advice, instruction, and encouragement.

OTHER SCRIPTURES

There are many other Buddhist writings in Pali, Sanskrit, Chinese, and other languages. Among the most important of these are:

- *Questions of King Milinda*
  written in the first century AD

- *The Way to Purity*
  by Buddhaghosa in the fifth century

- *The Summary of the Meaning of Higher Teaching*
  written by Anuruddha in the eleventh century

Each sect of Buddhism has its scriptures (see below for details of these groupings)

THERAVADA
Main scriptures: *Tripitaka*
Most popular part of scripture: *Dhammapada*
- Sayings of Buddha

MAHAYANA
Mahayana Buddhists recognize more texts as authoritative than do the Theravada Buddhists. Their main scriptures are the *Tripitaka* but they add many *sutras* - 2,184 sacred writings. The most popular of these extra scriptures are the *Lotus of the Good Law*, a sermon by Buddha on *Bodhisattva*, the Buddha-nature; and the *Guide to Perfect Wisdom*, an explanation of being a Buddha.

VAJRAYANA
Vajrayana Buddhism uses Mahayana scriptures and adds many Tantric texts to them. The most popular Tantric text, *Great Stages of Enlightenment*, deals with ethical behavior and control of mind.

THE DHAMMAPADA
The *Dhammapada* is one of the smallest section of the first of the three parts of the *Tripitaka*. Translated, it means, "The Way of Truth," or, "Verses of Truth." Its 423 verses are a collection of the Buddha's sayings and teaching which he gave on 305 occasions. Its twenty-six chapters are arranged according to subject matter.

The *Dhammapada* is the most popular piece of Buddhist literature.

The Dhammapada is the best known and most widely esteemed text in the Pali Tipitaka, the sacred scriptures of Theravada Buddhism. The work is included in the *Khuddaka Nikaya* ("Minor Collection") of the *Sutta Pitaka*, but its popularity has raised it far above the single niche it occupies in the scriptures to the ranks of a world religious classic. Composed in the ancient Pali language, this slim anthology of verses constitutes a perfect compendium of the Buddha's teaching, comprising between its covers all the essential principles elaborated at length

in the forty-odd volumes of the Pali Canon.

Acharya Buddharakkhita

THE DHAMMAPADA

Chapter 1	The Twin-Verses
Chapter 2	On Earnestness
Chapter 3	Thought
Chapter 4	Flowers
Chapter 5	The Fool
Chapter 6	The Wise Man (Pandita)
Chapter 7	The Venerable (Arhat)
Chapter 8	The Thousands
Chapter 9	Evil
Chapter 10	Punishment
Chapter 11	Old Age
Chapter 12	Self
Chapter 13	The World
Chapter 14	The Buddha (The Awakened)
Chapter 15	Happiness
Chapter 16	Pleasure
Chapter 17	Anger
Chapter 18	Impurity
Chapter 19	The Just
Chapter 20	The Way
Chapter 21	Miscellaneous
Chapter 22	The downward course
Chapter 23	The Elephant
Chapter 24	Thirst
Chapter 25	The Bhikshu (Mendicant)
Chapter 26	The Brâhmana (Arhat)

INTRODUCTION BY F. MAX MÜLLER
The *Dhammapada* forms part of the Pâli Buddhist canon.

Those who divide that canon into three Pitakas or baskets, Sutta-pitaka, the Vinaya-pitaka, and Abhidhamma-pitaka, assign the Dhammapada to the Sutta-pitaka.

That Pitaka consists of five Nikâyas:
the Dîgha-nikâya,
the Magghima-nikâya,
the Samyutta-nikâya,
the Anguttara-nikâya, and
the Khuddaka-nikâya.

The fifth, or Khuddaka-nikâya, consists of the following works:

1. Khuddaka-pâtha;
2. Dhammapada;
3. Udâna;
4. Itivuttaka;
5. Sutta-nipâta;
6. Vimânavatthu;
7. Petavatthu;
8. Theragâthâ;
9. Therîgâthâ;
10. Gâtaka;
11. Niddesa;
12. Patisambhidâ;
13. Apadâna;
14. Buddhavamsa;
15. Kariyâ-pitaka.

I cannot see any reason why we should not treat the verses of the *Dhammapada*, if not as the utterances of Buddha, at least as what were believed to have been the utterances of the founder of Buddhism.

The title of *Dhammapada*
The title of *Dhammapada* has been interpreted in various ways. It is an ambiguous word, and has been accepted as such by the Buddhists themselves. *Dhamma* has many meanings. Under one aspect it means religion, particularly the religion taught by Buddha, the law which every Buddhist should accept and observe. Under another aspect *dhamma* is virtue, or the realization of the law.

Pada also has many meanings. In the *Abhidhânapadîpikâ* it is explained by place, protection, Nirvâna, cause, word, thing, portion, foot, footstep.

Hence *dhammapada* may mean "footstep of religion," or, "The Footsteps of Religion." I think that "Path of Virtue," or "Footstep of the Law," was the idea most prominent in the mind of those who originally framed the title of this collection of verses.

F. Max Müller

THE *DHAMMAPADA*

CHAPTER 1: THE TWIN VERSES

1. All that we are is the result of what we have thought: it is founded on our thoughts, it is made up of our thoughts. If a man speaks or acts with an evil thought, pain follows him, as the wheel follows the foot of the ox that draws the carriage.

2. All that we are is the result of what we have thought: it is founded on our thoughts, it is made up of our thoughts. If a man speaks or acts with a pure thought, happiness follows him, like a shadow that never leaves him.

3. "He abused me, he beat me, he defeated me, he robbed me," - in those who harbor such thoughts hatred will never cease.

4. "He abused me, he beat me, he defeated me, he robbed me," - in those who do not harbor such thoughts hatred will cease.

5. For hatred does not cease by hatred at any time: hatred ceases by love, this is an old rule.

6. The world does not know that we must all come to an end here; - but those who know it, their quarrels cease at once.

7. He who lives looking for pleasures only, his senses uncontrolled, immoderate in his food, idle, and weak, Mâra (the tempter) will certainly overthrow him, as the wind throws down a weak tree.

8. He who lives without looking for pleasures, his senses well controlled, moderate in his food, faithful and strong, him Mâra will certainly not overthrow, any more than the wind throws down a rocky mountain.

9. He who wishes to put on the yellow dress without having cleansed himself from sin, who disregards temperance and truth, is unworthy of the yellow dress.

10. But he who has cleansed himself from sin, is well grounded in all virtues, and regards also temperance and truth, he is indeed worthy of the yellow dress.

11. They who imagine truth in untruth, and see untruth in truth, never arrive at truth, but follow vain desires.

12. They who know truth in truth, and untruth in untruth, arrive at truth, and follow true desires.

13. As rain breaks through an ill-thatched house, passion will break through an unreflecting mind.

14. As rain does not break through a well-thatched house, passion will not break through a well-reflecting mind.

15. The evil-doer mourns in this world, and he mourns in the next; he mourns in both. He mourns and suffers when he sees the evil of his own work.

16. The virtuous man delights in this world, and he delights in the next; he delights in both. He delights and rejoices, when he sees the purity of his own work.

17. The evil-doer suffers in this world, and he suffers in the next; he suffers in both. He suffers when he thinks of the evil he has done; he suffers more when going on the evil path.

18. The virtuous man is happy in this world, and he is happy in the next; he is happy in both. He is happy when he thinks of the good he has done; he is still more happy when going on the good path.

19. The thoughtless man, even if he can recite a large portion (of the law), but is not a doer of it, has no share in the priesthood, but is like a cowherd counting the cows of others.

20. The follower of the law, even if he can recite only a small portion (of the law), but, having forsaken passion and hatred and foolishness, possesses true knowledge and serenity of mind, he, caring for nothing in this world or that to come, has indeed a share in the priesthood.

CHAPTER 2 ON EARNESTNESS

21. Earnestness is the path of immortality (Nirvâna), thoughtlessness the path of death. Those who are in earnest do not die, those who are thoughtless are as if dead already.

22. Those who are advanced in earnestness, having understood this clearly, delight in earnestness, and rejoice in the knowledge of the Ariyas (the elect).

23. These wise people, meditative, steady, always possessed of strong powers, attain to Nirvâna, the highest happiness.

24. If an earnest person has roused himself, if he is not forgetful, if his deeds are pure, if he acts with consideration, if he restrains himself, and lives according to law - then his glory will increase.

25. By rousing himself, by earnestness, by restraint and control, the wise man may make for himself an island which no flood can overwhelm.

26. Fools follow after vanity, men of evil wisdom. The wise man keeps earnestness as his best jewel.

27. Follow not after vanity, nor after the enjoyment of love and lust! He who is earnest and meditative, obtains ample joy.

28. When the learned man drives away vanity by earnestness, he, the wise, climbing the terraced heights of wisdom, looks down upon the fools, serene he looks upon the toiling crowd, as one that stands on a mountain looks down upon them that stand upon the plain.

29. Earnest among the thoughtless, awake among the sleepers, the wise man advances like a racer, leaving behind the hack.

30. By earnestness did Maghavan (Indra) rise to the lordship of the gods. People

praise earnestness; thoughtlessness is always blamed.

31. A Bhikshu (mendicant) who delights in earnestness, who looks with fear on thoughtlessness,

32. A Bhikshu (mendicant) who delights in reflection, who looks with fear on thoughtlessness, cannot fall away (from his perfect state)—he is close upon Nirvâna.

CHAPTER 3 THOUGHT

33. As a fletcher makes straight his arrow, a wise man makes straight his trembling and unsteady thought, which is difficult to guard, difficult to hold back.

34. As a fish taken from his watery home and thrown on dry ground, our thought trembles all over in order to escape the dominion of Mâra (the tempter).

35. It is good to tame the mind, which is difficult to hold in and flighty, rushing wherever it listeth; a tamed mind brings happiness.

36. Let the wise man guard his thoughts, for they are difficult to perceive, very artful, and they rush wherever they list: thoughts well guarded bring happiness.

37. Those who bridle their mind which travels far, moves about alone, is without a body, and hides in the chamber (of the heart), will be free from the bonds of Mâra (the tempter).

38. If a man's thoughts are unsteady, if he does not know the true law, if his peace of mind is troubled, his knowledge will never be perfect.

39. If a man's thoughts are not dissipated, if his mind is not perplexed, if he has ceased to think of good or evil, then there is no fear for him while he is watchful.

40. Knowing that this body is (fragile) like a jar, and making this thought firm like a fortress, one should attack Mâra (the tempter) with the weapon of knowledge, one should watch him when conquered, and should never rest.

41. Before long, alas! this body will lie on the earth, despised, without understanding, like a useless log.

42. Whatever a hater may do to a hater, or an enemy to an enemy, a wrongly-directed mind will do us greater mischief.

43. Not a mother, not a father will do so much, nor any other relative; a well-directed mind will do us greater service.

CHAPTER 4 FLOWERS

44. Who shall overcome this earth, and the world of Yama (the lord of the departed), and the world of the gods? Who shall find out the plainly shown path of virtue, as a clever man finds out the (right) flower?

45. The disciple will overcome the earth, and the world of Yama, and the world of the gods. The disciple will find out the plainly shown path of virtue, as a clever man finds out the (right) flower.

46. He who knows that this body is like froth, and has learnt that it is as unsubstantial as a mirage, will break the flower-pointed arrow of Mâra, and never see the king of death.

47. Death carries off a man who is gathering flowers and whose mind is distracted, as a flood carries off a sleeping village.

48. Death subdues a man who is gathering flowers, and whose mind is distracted, before he is satiated in his pleasures.

49. As the bee collects nectar and departs

without injuring the flower, or its color or scent, so let a sage dwell in his village.

50. Not the perversities of others, not their sins of commission or omission, but his own misdeeds and negligences should a sage take notice of.

51. Like a beautiful flower, full of color, but without scent, are the fine but fruitless words of him who does not act accordingly.

52. But, like a beautiful flower, full of color and full of scent, are the fine and fruitful words of him who acts accordingly.

53. As many kinds of wreaths can be made from a heap of flowers, so many good things may be achieved by a mortal when once he is born.

54. The scent of flowers does not travel against the wind, nor (that of) sandal-wood, or of Tagara and Mallikâ flowers; but the odor of good people travels even against the wind; a good man pervades every place.

55. Sandal-wood or Tagara, a lotus-flower, or a Vassikî, among these sorts of perfumes, the perfume of virtue is unsurpassed.

56. Mean is the scent that comes from Tagara and sandal-wood;—the perfume of those who possess virtue rises up to the gods as the highest.

57. Of the people who possess these virtues, who live without thoughtlessness, and who are emancipated through true knowledge, Mâra, the tempter, never finds the way.

58, 59. As on a heap of rubbish cast upon the highway the lily will grow full of sweet perfume and delight, thus the disciple of the truly enlightened Buddha shines forth by his knowledge among those who are like rubbish, among the people that walk in darkness.

CHAPTER 5 THE FOOL

60. Long is the night to him who is awake; long is a mile to him who is tired; long is life to the foolish who do not know the true law.

61. If a traveler does not meet with one who is his better, or his equal, let him firmly keep to his solitary journey; there is no companionship with a fool.

62. "These sons belong to me, and this wealth belongs to me," with such thoughts a fool is tormented. He himself does not belong to himself; how much less sons and wealth?

63. The fool who knows his foolishness, is wise at least so far. But a fool who thinks himself wise, he is called a fool indeed.

64. If a fool be associated with a wise man even all his life, he will perceive the truth as little as a spoon perceives the taste of soup.

65. If an intelligent man be associated for one minute only with a wise man, he will soon perceive the truth, as the tongue perceives the taste of soup.

66. Fools of little understanding have themselves for their greatest enemies, for they do evil deeds which must bear bitter fruits.

67. That deed is not well done of which a man must repent, and the reward of which he receives crying and with a tearful face.

68. No, that deed is well done of which a man does not repent, and the reward of which he receives gladly and cheerfully.

69. As long as the evil deed done does not bear fruit, the fool thinks it is like honey; but when it ripens, then the fool suffers grief.

70. Let a fool month after month eat his food (like an ascetic) with the tip of a blade of Kusa grass, yet he is not worth the sixteenth particle of those who have well weighed the law.

71. An evil deed, like newly-drawn milk, does not turn (suddenly); smoldering, like fire covered by ashes, it follows the fool.

72. And when the evil deed, after it has become known, brings sorrow to the fool, then it destroys his bright lot, nay, it cleaves his head.

73. Let the fool wish for a false reputation, for precedence among the Bhikshus, for lordship in the convents, for worship among other people!

74. "May both the layman and he who has left the world think that this is done by me; may they be subject to me in everything which is to be done or is not to be done," thus is the mind of the fool, and his desire and pride increase.

75. "One is the road that leads to wealth, another the road that leads to Nirvâna;" if the Bhikshu, the disciple of Buddha, has learnt this, he will not yearn for honor, he will strive after separation from the world.

CHAPTER 6 THE WISE MAN

76. If you see an intelligent man who tells you where true treasures are to be found, who shows what is to be avoided, and administers reproofs, follow that wise man; it will be better, not worse, for those who follow him.

77. Let him admonish, let him teach, let him forbid what is improper! - he will be beloved of the good, by the bad he will be hated.

78. Do not have evil-doers for friends, do not have low people for friends: have virtuous people for friends, have for friends the best of men.

79. He who drinks in the law lives happily with a serene mind: the sage rejoices always in the law, as preached by the elect (Ariyas).

80. Well-makers lead the water (wherever they like); fletchers bend the arrow; carpenters bend a log of wood; wise people fashion themselves.

81. As a solid rock is not shaken by the wind, wise people falter not amidst blame and praise.

82. Wise people, after they have listened to the laws, become serene, like a deep, smooth, and still lake.

83. Good people walk on whatever befall, the good do not prattle, longing for pleasure; whether touched by happiness or sorrow wise people never appear elated or depressed.

84. If, whether for his own sake, or for the sake of others, a man wishes neither for a son, nor for wealth, nor for lordship, and if he does not wish for his own success by unfair means, then he is good, wise, and virtuous.

85. Few are there among men who arrive at the other shore (become Arhats); the other people here run up and down the shore.

86. But those who, when the law has been well preached to them, follow the law, will pass across the dominion of death, however difficult to overcome.

87, 88. A wise man should leave the dark state (of ordinary life), and follow the bright state (of the Bhikshu). After going from his home to a homeless state, he should in his retirement look for enjoyment where there seemed to be no enjoyment. Leaving all pleasures behind, and calling nothing his own, the wise man should purge himself from all the troubles of the mind.

89. Those whose mind is well grounded in the (seven) elements of knowledge, who without clinging to anything, rejoice in freedom from attachment, whose appetites have been conquered, and who are full of light, are free (even) in this world.

CHAPTER 7 THE VENERABLE

90. There is no suffering for him who has finished his journey, and abandoned grief, who has freed himself on all sides, and thrown off all fetters.

91. They depart with their thoughts well-collected, they are not happy in their abode; like swans who have left their lake, they leave their house and home.

92. Men who have no riches, who live on recognized food, who have perceived void and unconditioned freedom (Nirvâna), their path is difficult to understand, like that of birds in the air.

93. He whose appetites are stilled, who is not absorbed in enjoyment, who has perceived void and unconditioned freedom (Nirvâna), his path is difficult to understand, like that of birds in the air.

94. The gods even envy him whose senses, like horses well broken in by the driver, have been subdued, who is free from pride, and free from appetites.

95. Such a one who does his duty is tolerant like the earth, like Indra's bolt; he is like a lake without mud; no new births are in store for him.

96. His thought is quiet, quiet are his word and deed, when he has obtained freedom by true knowledge, when he has thus become a quiet man.

97. The man who is free from credulity, but knows the uncreated, who has cut all ties, removed all temptations, renounced all desires, he is the greatest of men.

98. In a hamlet or in a forest, in the deep water or on the dry land, wherever venerable persons (Arhanta) dwell, that place is delightful.

99. Forests are delightful; where the world finds no delight, there the passionless will find delight, for they look not for pleasures.

CHAPTER 8 THE THOUSANDS

100. Even though a speech be a thousand (of words), but made up of senseless words, one word of sense is better, which if a man hears, he becomes quiet.

101. Even though a *Gâthâ* (poem) be a thousand (of words), but made up of senseless words, one word of a *Gâthâ* is better, which if a man hears, he becomes quiet.

102. Though a man recite a hundred *Gâthâs* made up of senseless words, one word of the law is better, which if a man hears, he becomes quiet.

103. If one man conquer in battle a thousand times thousand men, and if another conquer himself, he is the greatest of conquerors.

104, 105. One's own self conquered is better than all other people; not even a god, a Gandharva, not Mâra with Brahman could change into defeat the victory of a man who has vanquished himself, and always lives under restraint.

106. If a man for a hundred years sacrifice month after month with a thousand, and if he but for one moment pay homage to a man whose soul is grounded (in true knowledge), better is that homage than sacrifice for a hundred years.

107. If a man for a hundred years worship Agni (fire) in the forest, and if he but for one moment pay homage to a man whose soul is grounded (in true knowledge), better is that homage than sacrifice for a hundred years.

108. Whatever a man sacrifice in this world as an offering or as an oblation for a whole year in order to gain merit, the whole of it is not worth a quarter (a farthing); reverence shown to the righteous is better.

109. He who always greets and constantly reveres the aged, four things will increase to him, viz. life, beauty, happiness, power.

110. But he who lives a hundred years, vicious and unrestrained, a life of one day is better if a man is virtuous and reflecting.

111. And he who lives a hundred years, ignorant and unrestrained, a life of one day is better if a man is wise and reflecting.

112. And he who lives a hundred years, idle and weak, a life of one day is better if a man has attained firm strength.

113. And he who lives a hundred years, not seeing beginning and end, a life of one day is better if a man sees beginning and end.

114. And he who lives a hundred years, not seeing the immortal place, a life of one day is better if a man sees the immortal place.

115. And he who lives a hundred years, not seeing the highest law, a life of one day is better if a man sees the highest law.

CHAPTER 9 EVIL

116. If a man would hasten towards the good, he should keep his thought away from evil; if a man does what is good slothfully, his mind delights in evil.

117. If a man commits a sin, let him not do it again; let him not delight in sin: pain is the outcome of evil.

118. If a man does what is good, let him do it again; let him delight in it: happiness is the outcome of good.

119. Even an evil-doer sees happiness as long as his evil deed has not ripened; but when his evil deed has ripened, then does the evil-doer see evil.

120. Even a good man sees evil days, as long as his good deed has not ripened; but when his good deed has ripened, then does the good man see happy days.

121. Let no man think lightly of evil, saying in his heart, It will not come nigh unto me. Even by the falling of water-drops a water-pot is filled; the fool becomes full of evil, even if he gather it little by little.

122. Let no man think lightly of good, saying in his heart, It will not come nigh unto me. Even by the falling of water-drops a water-pot is filled; the wise man becomes full of good, even if he gather it little by little.

123. Let a man avoid evil deeds, as a merchant, if he has few companions and carries much wealth, avoids a dangerous road; as a man who loves life avoids poison.

124. He who has no wound on his hand, may touch poison with his hand; poison does not affect one who has no wound; nor is there evil for one who does not commit evil.

125. If a man offend a harmless, pure, and innocent person, the evil falls back upon that fool, like light dust thrown up against the wind.

126. Some people are born again; evil-doers go to hell; righteous people go to heaven; those who are free from all worldly desires attain Nirvâna.

127. Not in the sky, not in the midst of the sea, not if we enter into the clefts of the mountains, is there known a spot in the whole world where death could not overcome (the mortal).

128. Not in the sky, not in the midst of the sea, not if we enter into the clefts of the mountains, is there known a spot in the whole world where death could not overcome (the mortal).

CHAPTER 10 PUNISHMENT

129. All men tremble at punishment, all men fear death; remember that you are like unto them, and do not kill, nor cause slaughter.

130. All men tremble at punishment, all men love life; remember that thou art like unto them, and do not kill, nor cause slaughter.

131. He who seeking his own happiness punishes or kills beings who also long for happiness, will not find happiness after death.

132. He who seeking his own happiness does not punish or kill beings who also long for happiness, will find happiness after death.

133. Do not speak harshly to anybody; those who are spoken to will answer thee in the same way. Angry speech is painful, blows for blows will touch thee.

134. If, like a shattered metal plate (gong), thou utter not, then thou hast reached Nirvâna; contention is not known to thee.

135. As a cowherd with his staff drives his cows into the stable, so do Age and Death drive the life of men.

136. A fool does not know when he commits his evil deeds: but the wicked man burns by his own deeds, as if burnt by fire.

137. He who inflicts pain on innocent and harmless persons, will soon come to one of these ten states:

138. He will have cruel suffering, loss, injury of the body, heavy affliction, or loss of mind,

139. Or a misfortune coming from the king, or a fearful accusation, or loss of relations, or destruction of treasures,

140. Or lightning-fire will burn his houses; and when his body is destroyed, the fool will go to hell.

141. Not nakedness, not platted hair, not dirt, not fasting, or lying on the earth, not rubbing with dust, not sitting motionless, can purify a mortal who has not overcome desires.

142. He who, though dressed in fine apparel, exercises tranquility, is quiet, subdued, restrained, chaste, and has ceased to find fault with all other beings, he indeed is a Brâhmana, an ascetic (sramana), a friar (bhikshu).

143. Is there in this world any man so restrained by humility that he does not mind reproof, as a well-trained horse the whip?

144. Like a well-trained horse when touched by

145. Well-makers lead the water (wherever they like); fletchers bend the arrow; carpenters bend a log of wood; good people fashion themselves.

CHAPTER 11 OLD AGE

146. How is there laughter, how is there joy, as this world is always burning? Why do you not seek a light, ye who are surrounded by darkness?

147. Look at this dressed-up lump, covered with wounds, joined together, sickly, full of many thoughts, which has no strength, no hold!

148. This body is wasted, full of sickness, and frail; this heap of corruption breaks to pieces, life indeed ends in death.

149. Those white bones, like gourds thrown away in the autumn, what pleasure is there in looking at them?

150. After a stronghold has been made of the bones, it is covered with flesh and blood, and there dwell in it old age and death, pride and deceit.

151. The brilliant chariots of kings are destroyed, the body also approaches destruction, but the virtue of good people never approaches destruction - thus do the good say to the good.

152. A man who has learnt little, grows old like an ox; his flesh grows, but his knowledge does not grow.

153, 154. Looking for the maker of this tabernacle, I shall have to run through a course of many births, so long as I do not find (him); and painful is birth again and again. But now, maker of the tabernacle, thou hast been seen; thou shalt not make up.

155. Men who have not observed proper discipline, and have not gained treasure in their youth, perish like old herons in a lake without fish.

156. Men who have not observed proper discipline, and have not gained treasure in their youth, lie, like broken bows, sighing after the past.

CHAPTER 12 SELF

157. If a man hold himself dear, let him watch himself carefully; during one at least out of the three watches a wise man should be watchful.

158. Let each man direct himself first to what is proper, then let him teach others; thus a wise man will not suffer.

159. If a man make himself as he teaches others to be, then, being himself well subdued, he may subdue (others); one's own self is indeed difficult to subdue.

160. Self is the lord of self, who else could be the lord? With self well subdued, a man finds a lord such as few can find.

161. The evil done by oneself, self-begotten, self-bred, crushes the foolish, as a diamond breaks a precious stone.

162. He whose wickedness is very great brings himself down to that state where his enemy wishes him to be, as a creeper does with the tree which it surrounds.

163. Bad deeds, and deeds hurtful to ourselves, are easy to do; what is beneficial and good, that is very difficult to do.

164. The foolish man who scorns the rule of the venerable (Arahat), of the elect (Ariya), of the virtuous, and follows false doctrine, he bears fruit to his own destruction, like the fruits of the Katthaka reed.

165. By oneself the evil is done, by oneself one suffers; by oneself evil is left undone, by oneself one is purified. Purity and impurity belong to oneself, no one can purify another.

166. Let no one forget his own duty for the sake of another's, however great; let a man, after he has discerned his own duty, be always attentive to his duty.

CHAPTER 13 THE WORLD

167. Do not follow the evil law! Do not live on in thoughtlessness! Do not follow false doctrine! Be not a friend of the world.

168. Rouse thyself! do not be idle! Follow the law of virtue! The virtuous rests in bliss in this world and in the next.

169. Follow the law of virtue; do not follow that of sin. The virtuous rests in bliss in this world and in the next.

170. Look upon the world as a bubble, look upon it as a mirage: the king of death does not see him who thus looks down upon the world.

171. Come, look at this glittering world, like unto a royal chariot; the foolish are immersed in it, but the wise do not touch it.

172. He who formerly was reckless and afterwards became sober, brightens up this world, like the moon when freed from clouds.

173. He whose evil deeds are covered by good deeds, brightens up this world, like the moon when freed from clouds.

174. This world is dark, few only can see here; a few only go to heaven, like birds escaped from the net.

175. The swans go on the path of the sun, they go through the ether by means of their miraculous power; the wise are led out of this world, when they have conquered Mâra and his train.

176. If a man has transgressed one law, and speaks lies, and scoffs at another world, there is no evil he will not do.

177. The uncharitable do not go to the world of the gods; fools only do not praise liberality; a wise man rejoices in liberality, and through it becomes blessed in the other world.

178. Better than sovereignty over the earth, better than going to heaven, better than lordship over all worlds, is the reward of the first step in holiness.

CHAPTER 14 THE BUDDHA (THE AWAKENED)

179. He whose conquest is not conquered again, into whose conquest no one in this world enters, by what track can you lead him, the Awakened, the Omniscient, the trackless?

180. He whom no desire with its snares and poisons can lead astray, by what track can you lead him, the Awakened, the Omniscient, the trackless?

181. Even the gods envy those who are awakened and not forgetful, who are given to meditation, who are wise, and who delight in the repose of retirement (from the world).

182. Difficult (to obtain) is the conception of men, difficult is the life of mortals, difficult is the hearing of the True Law, difficult is the birth of the Awakened (the attainment of Buddhahood).

183. Not to commit any sin, to do good, and to purify one's mind, that is the teaching of (all) the Awakened.

184. The Awakened call patience the highest penance, long-suffering the highest Nirvâna; for he is not an anchorite (*pravragita*) who strikes others, he is not an ascetic (*sramana*) who insults others.

185. Not to blame, not to strike, to live restrained under the law, to be moderate in eating, to sleep and sit alone, and to dwell on the highest thoughts, - this is the teaching of the Awakened.

186. There is no satisfying lusts, even by a shower of gold pieces; he who knows that lusts have a short taste and cause pain, he is wise;

187. Even in heavenly pleasures he finds no satisfaction, the disciple who is fully awakened delights only in the destruction of all desires.

188. Men, driven by fear, go to many a refuge, to mountains and forests, to groves and sacred trees.

189. But that is not a safe refuge, that is not the best refuge; a man is not delivered from all pains after having gone to that refuge.

190. He who takes refuge with Buddha, the Law, and the Church; he who, with clear understanding, sees the four holy truths:-

191. Viz. pain, the origin of pain, the destruction of pain, and the eightfold holy way that leads to the quieting of pain; -

192. That is the safe refuge, that is the best refuge; having gone to that refuge, a man is delivered from all pain.

193. A supernatural person (a Buddha) is not easily found, he is not born everywhere. Wherever such a sage is born, that race prospers.

194. Happy is the arising of the awakened, happy is the teaching of the True Law, happy is peace in the church, happy is the devotion of those who are at peace.

195, 196. He who pays homage to those who deserve homage, whether the awakened (Buddha) or their disciples, those who have overcome the host (of evils), and crossed the flood of sorrow, he who pays homage to such as have found deliverance and know no fear, his merit can never be measured by anybody.

CHAPTER 15 HAPPINESS

197. Let us live happily then, not hating those who hate us! among men who hate us let us dwell free from hatred!

198. Let us live happily then, free from ailments among the ailing! among men who are ailing let us dwell free from ailments!

199. Let us live happily then, free from greed among the greedy! among men who are greedy let us dwell free from greed!

200. Let us live happily then, though we call nothing our own! We shall be like the bright gods, feeding on happiness!

201. Victory breeds hatred, for the conquered is unhappy. He who has given up both victory and defeat, he, the contented, is happy.

202. There is no fire like passion; there is no losing throw like hatred; there is no pain like this body; there is no happiness higher than rest.

203. Hunger is the worst of diseases, the body the greatest of pains; if one knows this truly, that is Nirvâna, the highest happiness.

204. Health is the greatest of gifts, contentedness the best riches; trust is the best of relationships, Nirvâna the highest happiness.

205. He who has tasted the sweetness of solitude and tranquility, is free from fear and free from sin, while he tastes the sweetness of drinking in the law.

206. The sight of the elect (Arya) is good, to live with them is always happiness; if a man does not see fools, he will be truly happy.

207. He who walks in the company of fools suffers a long way; company with fools, as with an enemy, is always painful; company with the wise is pleasure, like meeting with kinsfolk.

208. Therefore, one ought to follow the wise, the intelligent, the learned, the much enduring, the dutiful, the elect; one ought to follow a good and wise man, as the moon follows the path of the stars.

CHAPTER 16 PLEASURE

209. He who gives himself to vanity, and does not give himself to meditation, forgetting the real aim (of life) and grasping at pleasure, will in time envy him who has exerted himself in meditation.

210. Let no man ever look for what is pleasant, or what is unpleasant. Not to see what is pleasant is pain, and it is pain to see what is unpleasant.

211. Let, therefore, no man love anything; loss of the beloved is evil. Those who love nothing and hate nothing, have no fetters.

212. From pleasure comes grief, from pleasure comes fear; he who is free from pleasure knows neither grief nor fear.

213. From affection comes grief, from affection comes fear; he who is free from affection knows neither grief nor fear.

214. From lust comes grief, from lust comes fear; he who is free from lust knows neither grief nor fear.

215. From love comes grief, from love comes fear; he who is free from love knows neither grief nor fear.

216. From greed comes grief, from greed comes fear; he who is free from greed knows neither grief nor fear.

217. He who possesses virtue and intelligence, who is just, speaks the truth, and does what is his own business, him the world will hold dear.

218. He in whom a desire for the Ineffable (Nirvâna) has sprung up, who is satisfied in his mind, and whose thoughts are not bewildered by love, he is called ûrdhvamsrotas (carried upwards by the stream).

219. Kinsmen, friends, and lovers salute a man who has been long away, and returns safe from afar.

220. In like manner his good works receive him who has done good, and has gone from this world to the other; - as kinsmen receive a friend on his return.

CHAPTER 17 ANGER

221. Let a man leave anger, let him forsake pride, let him overcome all bondage! No sufferings befall the man who is not attached to name and form, and who calls nothing his own.

222. He who holds back rising anger like a rolling chariot, him I call a real driver; other people are but holding the reins.

223. Let a man overcome anger by love, let him overcome evil by good; let him overcome the greedy by liberality, the liar by truth!

224. Speak the truth, do not yield to anger; give, if thou art asked for little; by these three steps thou wilt go near the gods.

225. The sages who injure nobody, and who always control their body, they will go to the unchangeable place (Nirvâna), where, if they have gone, they will suffer no more.

226. Those who are ever watchful, who study day and night, and who strive after Nirvâna, their passions will come to an end.

227. This is an old saying, O Atula, this is not only of to-day: "They blame him who sits silent, they blame him who speaks much, they also blame him who says little; there is no one on earth who is not blamed."

228. There never was, there never will be, nor is there now, a man who is always blamed, or a man who is always praised.

229, 230. But he whom those who discriminate praise continually day after day, as without blemish, wise, rich in knowledge and virtue, who would dare to blame him, like a coin made of gold from the Gambû river? Even the gods praise him, he is praised even by Brahman.

231. Beware of bodily anger, and control thy body! Leave the sins of the body, and with thy body practice virtue!

232. Beware of the anger of the tongue, and control thy tongue! Leave the sins of the tongue, and practice virtue with thy tongue!

233. Beware of the anger of the mind, and control thy mind! Leave the sins of the mind, and practice virtue with thy mind!

234. The wise who control their body, who control their tongue, the wise who control their mind, are indeed well controlled.

CHAPTER 18 IMPURITY

235. Thou art now like a sear leaf, the messengers of death (Yama) have come near to thee; thou standest at the door of thy departure, and thou hast no provision for thy journey.

236. Make thyself an island, work hard, be wise! When thy impurities are blown away, and thou art free from guilt, thou wilt enter into the heavenly world of the elect (*Ariya*).

237. Thy life has come to an end, thou art come near to death (Yama), there is no resting-place for thee on the road, and thou hast no provision for thy journey.

238. Make thyself an island, work hard, be wise! When thy impurities are blown away, and thou art free from guilt, thou wilt not enter again into birth and decay.

239. Let a wise man blow off the impurities of his self, as a smith blows off the impurities of silver one by one, little by little, and from time to time.

240. As the impurity which springs from the iron, when it springs from it, destroys it; thus do a transgressor's own works lead him to the evil path.

241. The taint of prayers is non-repetition; the taint of houses, non-repair; the taint of the body is sloth; the taint of a watchman, thoughtlessness.

242. Bad conduct is the taint of woman, greediness the taint of a benefactor; tainted are all evil ways in this world and in the next.

243. But there is a taint worse than all taints - ignorance is the greatest taint. O mendicants! throw off that taint, and become taintless!

244. Life is easy to live for a man who is without shame, a crow hero, a mischief-maker, an insulting, bold, and wretched fellow.

245. But life is hard to live for a modest man, who always looks for what is pure, who is disinterested, quiet, spotless, and intelligent.

246. He who destroys life, who speaks untruth, who in this world takes what is not given him, who goes to another man's wife;

247. And the man who gives himself to drinking intoxicating liquors, he, even in this world, digs up his own root.

248. O man, know this, that the unrestrained are in a bad state; take care that greediness and vice do not bring thee to grief for a long time!

249. The world gives according to their faith or according to their pleasure: if a man frets about the food and the drink given to others, he will find no rest either by day or by night.

250. He in whom that feeling is destroyed, and taken out with the very root, finds rest by day and by night.

251. There is no fire like passion, there is no shark like hatred, there is no snare like folly, there is no torrent like greed.

252. The fault of others is easily perceived, but that of oneself is difficult to perceive; a man winnows his neighbor's faults like chaff, but his own fault he hides, as a cheat hides the bad die from the gambler.

253. If a man looks after the faults of others, and is always inclined to be offended, his own passions will grow, and he is far from the destruction of passions.

254. There is no path through the air, a man is not a Samana by outward acts. The world delights in vanity, the Tathâgatas (the Buddhas) are free from vanity.

255. There is no path through the air, a man is not a Samana by outward acts. No creatures are eternal; but the awakened (Buddha) are never shaken.

CHAPTER 19 THE JUST

256, 257. A man is not just if he carries a matter by violence; no, he who distinguishes both right and wrong, who is learned and leads others, not by violence, but by law and equity, and who is guarded by the law and intelligent, is called just.

258. A man is not learned because he talks much; he who is patient, free from hatred and fear, he is called learned.

259. A man is not a supporter of the law because he talks much; even if a man has learnt little, but sees the law bodily, he is a supporter of the law, a man who never neglects the law.

260. A man is not an elder because his head is gray; his age may be ripe, but he is called "Old-in-vain."

261. He in whom there is truth, virtue, love, restraint, moderation, he who is free from impurity and is wise, he is called an elder.

262. An envious, greedy, dishonest man does not become respectable by means of much talking only, or by the beauty of his complexion.

263. He in whom all this is destroyed, and taken out with the very root, he, when freed from hatred and wise, is called respectable.

264. Not by tonsure does an undisciplined man who speaks falsehood become a Samana; can a man be a Samana who is still held captive by desire and greediness?

265. He who always quiets the evil, whether small or large, he is called a Samana (a quiet man), because he has quieted all evil.

266. A man is not a mendicant (Bhikshu) simply because he asks others for alms; he who adopts the whole law is a Bhikshu, not he who only begs.

267. He who is above good and evil, who is chaste, who with knowledge passes through the world, he indeed is called a Bhikshu.

268, 269. A man is not a Muni because he observes silence (mona, i.e. mauna), if he is foolish and ignorant; but the wise who, taking the balance, chooses the good and avoids evil, he is a Muni, and is a Muni thereby; he who in this world weighs both sides is called a Muni.

270. A man is not an elect (Ariya) because he injures living creatures; because he has pity on all living creatures, therefore is a man called Ariya.

271, 272. Not only by discipline and vows, not only by much learning, not by entering into a trance, not by sleeping alone, do I earn the happiness of release which no worldling can know. Bhikshu, be not confident as long as thou hast not attained the extinction of desires.

CHAPTER 20 THE WAY

273. The best of ways is the eightfold; the best of truths the four words; the best of virtues passionlessness; the best of men he who has eyes to see.

274. This is the way, there is no other that leads to the purifying of intelligence. Go on this way! Everything else is the deceit of Mâra (the tempter).

275. If you go on this way, you will make an end of pain! The way was preached by me, when I had understood the removal of the thorns (in the flesh).

276. You yourself must make an effort. The Tathâgatas (Buddhas) are only preachers. The thoughtful who enter the way are freed from the bondage of Mâra.

277. "All created things perish," he who knows and sees this becomes passive in pain; this is the way to purity.

278. "All created things are grief and pain," he who knows and sees this becomes passive in pain; this is the way that leads to purity.

279. "All forms are unreal," he who knows and sees this becomes passive in pain; this is the way that leads to purity.

280. He who does not rouse himself when it is time to rise, who, though young and strong, is full of sloth, whose will and thought are weak, that lazy and idle man will never find the way to knowledge.

281. Watching his speech, well restrained in mind, let a man never commit any wrong with his body! Let a man but keep these three roads of action clear, and he

will achieve the way which is taught by the wise.

282. Through zeal knowledge is gotten, through lack of zeal knowledge is lost; let a man who knows this double path of gain and loss thus place himself that knowledge may grow.

283. Cut down the whole forest (of lust), not a tree only! Danger comes out of the forest (of lust). When you have cut down both the forest (of lust) and its undergrowth, then, Bhikshus, you will be rid of the forest and free!

284. So long as the love of man towards women, even the smallest, is not destroyed, so long is his mind in bondage, as the calf that drinks milk is to its mother.

285. Cut out the love of self, like an autumn lotus, with thy hand! Cherish the road of peace. Nirvâna has been shown by Sugata (Buddha).

286. "Here I shall dwell in the rain, here in winter and summer," thus the fool meditates, and does not think of his death.

287. Death comes and carries off that man, praised for his children and flocks, his mind distracted, as a flood carries off a sleeping village.

288. Sons are no help, nor a father, nor relations; there is no help from kinsfolk for one whom death has seized.

289. A wise and good man who knows the meaning of this, should quickly clear the way that leads to Nirvâna.

CHAPTER 21 MISCELLANEOUS

290. If by leaving a small pleasure one sees a great pleasure, let a wise man leave the small pleasure, and look to the great.

291. He who, by causing pain to others,

wishes to obtain pleasure for himself, he, entangled in the bonds of hatred, will never be free from hatred.

292. What ought to be done is neglected, what ought not to be done is done; the desires of unruly, thoughtless people are always increasing.

293. But they whose whole watchfulness is always directed to their body, who do not follow what ought not to be done, and who steadfastly do what ought to be done, the desires of such watchful and wise people will come to an end.

294. A true Brâhmana goes scatheless, though he have killed father and mother, and two valiant kings, though he has destroyed a kingdom with all its subjects.

295. A true Brâhmana goes scatheless, though he have killed father and mother, and two holy kings, and an eminent man besides.

296. The disciples of Gotama (Buddha) are always well awake, and their thoughts day and night are always set on Buddha.

297. The disciples of Gotama are always well awake, and their thoughts day and night are always set on the law.

298. The disciples of Gotama are always well awake, and their thoughts day and night are always set on the church.

299. The disciples of Gotama are always well awake, and their thoughts day and night are always set on their body.

300. The disciples of Gotama are always well awake, and their mind day and night always delights in compassion.

301. The disciples of Gotama are always well awake, and their mind day and night always delights in meditation.

302. It is hard to leave the world (to become a friar), it is hard to enjoy the world; hard is the monastery, painful are the houses; painful it is to dwell with equals (to share everything in common), and the itinerant mendicant is beset with pain. Therefore let no man be an itinerant mendicant and he will not be beset with pain.

303. Whatever place a faithful, virtuous, celebrated, and wealthy man chooses, there he is respected.

304. Good people shine from afar, like the snowy mountains; bad people are not seen, like arrows shot by night.

305. He alone who, without ceasing, practices the duty of sitting alone and sleeping alone, he, subduing himself, will rejoice in the destruction of all desires alone, as if living in a forest.

CHAPTER 22 THE DOWNWARD COURSE

306. He who says what is not, goes to hell; he also who, having done a thing, says I have not done it. After death both are equal, they are men with evil deeds in the next world.

307. Many men whose shoulders are covered with the yellow gown are ill-conditioned and unrestrained; such evil-doers by their evil deeds go to hell.

308. Better it would be to swallow a heated iron ball, like flaring fire, than that a bad unrestrained fellow should live on the charity of the land.

309. Four things does a wreckless man gain who covets his neighbor's wife - a bad reputation, an uncomfortable bed, thirdly, punishment, and lastly, hell.

310. There is bad reputation, and the evil way (to hell), there is the short pleasure of the frightened in the arms of the frightened, and the king imposes heavy punishment; therefore let no man think of his neighbor's wife.

311. As a grass-blade, if badly grasped, cuts the arm, badly-practiced asceticism leads to hell.

312. An act carelessly performed, a broken vow, and hesitating obedience to discipline, all this brings no great reward.

313. If anything is to be done, let a man do it, let him attack it vigorously! A careless pilgrim only scatters the dust of his passions more widely.

314. An evil deed is better left undone, for a man repents of it afterwards; a good deed is better done, for having done it, one does not repent.

315. Like a well-guarded frontier fort, with defenses within and without, so let a man guard himself. Not a moment should escape, for they who allow the right moment to pass, suffer pain when they are in hell.

316. They who are ashamed of what they ought not to be ashamed of, and are not ashamed of what they ought to be ashamed of, such men, embracing false doctrines enter the evil path.

317. They who fear when they ought not to fear, and fear not when they ought to fear, such men, embracing false doctrines, enter the evil path.

318. They who forbid when there is nothing to be forbidden, and forbid not when there is something to be forbidden, such men, embracing false doctrines, enter the evil path.

319. They who know what is forbidden as forbidden, and what is not forbidden as not forbidden, such men, embracing the true doctrine, enter the good path.

CHAPTER 23 THE ELEPHANT

320. Silently shall I endure abuse as the elephant in battle endures the arrow sent from the bow: for the world is ill-natured.

[320. The elephant is with the Buddhists the emblem of endurance and self-restraint. Thus Buddha himself is called Nâga, "the Elephant" (Lal. Vist. p. 553), or Mahânâga, "the great Elephant." The reason for this name is given, by stating that Buddha was sudânta, "well-tamed," like an elephant. He descended from heaven in the form of an elephant to be born on earth.]

321. They lead a tamed elephant to battle, the king mounts a tamed elephant; the tamed is the best among men, he who silently endures abuse.

322. Mules are good, if tamed, and noble Sindhu horses, and elephants with large tusks; but he who tames himself is better still.

323. For with these animals does no man reach the untrodden country (Nirvâna), where a tamed man goes on a tamed animal, viz. on his own well-tamed self.

324. The elephant called *Dhanapâlaka*, his temples running with sap, and difficult to hold, does not eat a morsel when bound; the elephant longs for the elephant grove.

325. If a man becomes fat and a great eater, if he is sleepy and rolls himself about, that fool, like a hog fed on wash, is born again and again.

326. This mind of mine went formerly wandering about as it liked, as it listed, as it pleased; but I shall now hold it in thoroughly, as the rider who holds the hook holds in the furious elephant.

327. Be not thoughtless, watch your thoughts! Draw yourself out of the evil way, like an elephant sunk in mud.

328. If a man find a prudent companion who walks with him, is wise, and lives soberly, he may walk with him, overcoming all dangers, happy, but considerate.

329. If a man find no prudent companion who walks with him, is wise, and lives soberly, let him walk alone, like a king who has left his conquered country behind - like an elephant in the forest.

330. It is better to live alone, there is no companionship with a fool; let a man walk alone, let him commit no sin, with few wishes, like an elephant in the forest.

331. If an occasion arises, friends are pleasant; enjoyment is pleasant, whatever be the cause; a good work is pleasant in the hour of death; the giving up of all grief is pleasant.

332. Pleasant in the world is the state of a mother, pleasant the state of a father, pleasant the state of a Samana, pleasant the state of a Brâhmana.

333. Pleasant is virtue lasting to old age, pleasant is a faith firmly rooted; pleasant is attainment of intelligence, pleasant is avoiding of sins.

CHAPTER 24 THIRST

334. The thirst of a thoughtless man grows like a creeper; he runs from life to life, like a monkey seeking fruit in the forest.

335. Whomsoever this fierce thirst overcomes, full of poison, in this world, his sufferings increase like the abounding Bîrana grass.

336. He who overcomes this fierce thirst, difficult to be conquered in this world, sufferings fall off from him, like water-drops from a lotus leaf.

337. This salutary word I tell you, "Do ye, as many as are here assembled, dig up the root of thirst, as he who wants the sweet-scented Usîra root must dig up the Bîrana grass, that Mâra (the tempter) may not crush you again and again, as the stream crushes the reeds."

338. As a tree, even though it has been cut down, is firm so long as its root is safe, and grows again, thus, unless the feeders of thirst are destroyed, the pain (of life) will return again and again.

339. He whose thirst running towards pleasure is exceeding strong in the thirty-six channels, the waves will carry away that misguided man, viz. his desires which are set on passion.

340. The channels run everywhere, the creeper (of passion) stands sprouting; if you see the creeper springing up, cut its root by means of knowledge.

341. A creature's pleasures are extravagant and luxurious; sunk in lust and looking for pleasure, men undergo (again and again) birth and decay.

342. Men, driven on by thirst, run about like a snared hare; held in fetters and bonds, they undergo pain for a long time, again and again.

343. Men, driven on by thirst, run about like a snared hare; let therefore the mendicant drive out thirst, by striving after passionlessness for himself.

344. He who having got rid of the forest (of lust) (i.e. after having reached Nirvâna) gives himself over to forest-life (i.e. to lust), and who, when removed from the forest (i.e. from lust), runs to the forest (i.e. to lust), look at that man! though free, he runs into bondage.

345. Wise people do not call that a strong fetter which is made of iron, wood, or hemp; far stronger is the care for precious stones and rings, for sons and a wife.

346. That fetter wise people call strong which drags down, yields, but is difficult to undo; after having cut this at last, people leave the world, free from cares, and leaving desires and pleasures behind.

347. Those who are slaves to passions, run down with the stream (of desires), as a

spider runs down the web which he has made himself; when they have cut this, at last, wise people leave the world free from cares, leaving all affection behind.

348. Give up what is before, give up what is behind, give up what is in the middle, when thou goest to the other shore of existence; if thy mind is altogether free, thou wilt not again enter into birth and decay.

349. If a man is tossed about by doubts, full of strong passions, and yearning only for what is delightful, his thirst will grow more and more, and he will indeed make his fetters strong.

350. If a man delights in quieting doubts, and, always reflecting, dwells on what is not delightful (the impurity of the body, &c.), he certainly will remove, nay, he will cut the fetter of Mâra.

351. He who has reached the consummation, who does not tremble, who is without thirst and without sin, he has broken all the thorns of life: this will be his last body.

352. He who is without thirst and without affection, who understands the words and their interpretation, who knows the order of letters (those which are before and which are after), he has received his last body, he is called the great sage, the great man.

353. 'I have conquered all, I know all, in all conditions of life I am free from taint; I have left all, and through the destruction of thirst I am free; having learnt myself, whom shall I teach?'

354. The gift of the law exceeds all gifts; the sweetness of the law exceeds all sweetness; the delight in the law exceeds all delights; the extinction of thirst overcomes all pain.

355. Pleasures destroy the foolish, if they look not for the other shore; the foolish by his thirst for pleasures destroys himself, as if he were his own enemy.

356. The fields are damaged by weeds, mankind is damaged by passion: therefore a gift bestowed on the passionless brings great reward.

357. The fields are damaged by weeds, mankind is damaged by hatred: therefore a gift bestowed on those who do not hate brings great reward.

358. The fields are damaged by weeds, mankind is damaged by vanity: therefore a gift bestowed on those who are free from vanity brings great reward.

359. The fields are damaged by weeds, mankind is damaged by lust: therefore a gift bestowed on those who are free from lust brings great reward.

CHAPTER 25 THE BHIKSHU (MENDICANT, BEGGAR)

360. Restraint in the eye is good, good is restraint in the ear, in the nose restraint is good, good is restraint in the tongue.

361. In the body restraint is good, good is restraint in speech, in thought restraint is good, good is restraint in all things. A Bhikshu, restrained in all things, is freed from all pain.

362. He who controls his hand, he who controls his feet, he who controls his speech, he who is well controlled, he who delights inwardly, who is collected, who is solitary and content, him they call Bhikshu.

363. The Bhikshu who controls his mouth, who speaks wisely and calmly, who teaches the meaning and the law, his word is sweet.

364. He who dwells in the law, delights in the law, meditates on the law, follows the law, that Bhikshu will never fall away from the true law.

365. Let him not despise what he has received, nor ever envy others: a mendicant who envies others does not obtain peace of mind.

366. A Bhikshu who, though he receives little, does not despise what he has received, even the gods will praise him, if his life is pure, and if he is not slothful.

367. He who never identifies himself with name and form, and does not grieve over what is no more, he indeed is called a Bhikshu.

368. The Bhikshu who acts with kindness, who is calm in the doctrine of Buddha, will reach the quiet place (Nirvâna), cessation of natural desires, and happiness.

369. O Bhikshu, empty this boat! if emptied, it will go quickly; having cut off passion and hatred thou wilt go to Nirvâna.

370. Cut off the five (senses), leave the five, rise above the five. A Bhikshu, who has escaped from the five fetters, he is called Oghatinna, "saved from the flood."

371. Meditate, O Bhikshu, and be not heedless! Do not direct thy thought to what gives pleasure that thou mayest not for thy heedlessness have to swallow the iron ball (in hell), and that thou mayest not cry out when burning, "This is pain."

372. Without knowledge there is no meditation, without meditation there is no knowledge: he who has knowledge and meditation is near unto Nirvâna.

373. A Bhikshu who has entered his empty house, and whose mind is tranquil, feels a more than human delight when he sees the law clearly.

374. As soon as he has considered the origin and destruction of the elements (*khandha*) of the body, he finds happiness and joy which belong to those who know the immortal (Nirvâna).

375. And this is the beginning here for a wise Bhikshu: watchfulness over the senses, contentedness, restraint under the law; keep noble friends whose life is pure, and who are not slothful.

376. Let him live in charity, let him be perfect in his duties; then in the fullness of delight he will make an end of suffering.

377. As the Vassika plant sheds its withered flowers, men should shed passion and hatred, O ye Bhikshus!

378. The Bhikshu whose body and tongue and mind are quieted, who is collected, and has rejected the baits of the world, he is called quiet.

379. Rouse thyself by thyself, examine thyself by thyself, thus self-protected and attentive wilt thou live happily, O Bhikshu!

380. For self is the lord of self, self is the refuge of self; therefore curb thyself as the merchant curbs a good horse.

381. The Bhikshu, full of delight, who is calm in the doctrine of Buddha will reach the quiet place (Nirvâna), cessation of natural desires, and happiness.

382. He who, even as a young Bhikshu, applies himself to the doctrine of Buddha, brightens up this world, like the moon when free from clouds.

CHAPTER 26 THE BRAHMANA

383. Stop the stream valiantly, drive away the desires, O Brâhmana! When you have understood the destruction of all that was made, you will understand that which was not made.

384. If the Brâhmana has reached the other shore in both laws (in restraint and contemplation), all bonds vanish from him who has obtained knowledge.

385. He for whom there is neither this nor that shore, nor both, him, the fearless and unshackled, I call indeed a Brâhmana.

386. He who is thoughtful, blameless, settled, dutiful, without passions, and who has attained the highest end, him I call indeed a Brâhmana.

387. The sun is bright by day, the moon shines by night, the warrior is bright in his Armour, the Brâhmana is bright in his meditation; but Buddha, the Awakened, is bright with splendor day and night.

388. Because a man is rid of evil, therefore he is called Brâhmana; because he walks quietly, therefore he is called Samana; because he has sent away his own impurities, therefore he is called Pravragita (Pabbagita, a pilgrim).

389. No one should attack a Brâhmana, but no Brâhmana (if attacked) should let himself fly at his aggressor! Woe to him who strikes a Brâhmana, more woe to him who flies at his aggressor!

390. It advantages a Brâhmana not a little if he holds his mind back from the pleasures of life; when all wish to injure has vanished, pain will cease.

391. Him I call indeed a Brâhmana who does not offend by body, word, or thought, and is controlled on these three points.

392. After a man has once understood the law as taught by the Well-awakened (Buddha), let him worship it carefully, as the Brâhmana worships the sacrificial fire.

393. A man does not become a Brâhmana by his platted hair, by his family, or by birth; in whom there is truth and righteousness, he is blessed, he is a Brâhmana.

394. What is the use of platted hair, O fool! what of the raiment of goat-skins? Within thee there is ravening, but the outside thou makest clean.

395. The man who wears dirty raiments, who is emaciated and covered with veins, who lives alone in the forest, and meditates, him I call indeed a Brâhmana.

396. I do not call a man a Brâhmana because of his origin or of his mother. He is indeed arrogant, and he is wealthy: but the poor, who is free from all attachments, him I call indeed a Brâhmana.

397. Him I call indeed a Brâhmana who has cut all fetters, who never trembles, is independent and unshackled.

398. Him I call indeed a Brâhmana who has cut the strap and the thong, the chain with all that pertains to it, who has burst the bar, and is awakened.

399. Him I call indeed a Brâhmana who, though he has committed no offence, endures reproach, bonds, and stripes, who has endurance for his force, and strength for his army.

400. Him I call indeed a Brâhmana who is free from anger, dutiful, virtuous, without appetite, who is subdued, and has received his last body.

401. Him I call indeed a Brâhmana who does not cling to pleasures, like water on a lotus leaf, like a mustard seed on the point of a needle.

402. Him I call indeed a Brâhmana who, even here, knows the end of his suffering, has put down his burden, and is unshackled.

403. Him I call indeed a Brâhmana whose knowledge is deep, who possesses wisdom, who knows the right way and the wrong, and has attained the highest end.

404. Him I call indeed a Brâhmana who keeps aloof both from laymen and from mendicants, who frequents no houses, and has but few desires.

405. Him I call indeed a Brâhmana who finds no fault with other beings, whether feeble or strong, and does not kill nor cause slaughter.

406. Him I call indeed a Brâhmana who is tolerant with the intolerant, mild with fault-finders, and free from passion among the passionate.

407. Him I call indeed a Brâhmana from whom anger and hatred, pride and envy have dropt like a mustard seed from the point of a needle.

408. Him I call indeed a Brâhmana who utters true speech, instructive and free from harshness, so that he offend no one.

409. Him I call indeed a Brâhmana who takes nothing in the world that is not given him, be it long or short, small or large, good or bad.

410. Him I call indeed a Brâhmana who fosters no desires for this world or for the next, has no inclinations, and is unshackled.

411. Him I call indeed a Brâhmana who has no interests, and when he has understood (the truth), does not say How, how? and who has reached the depth of the Immortal.

412. Him I call indeed a Brâhmana who in this world is above good and evil, above the bondage of both, free from grief from sin, and from impurity.

413. Him I call indeed a Brâhmana who is bright like the moon, pure, serene, undisturbed, and in whom all gaiety is extinct.

414. Him I call indeed a Brâhmana who has traversed this miry road; the impassable world and its vanity, who has gone through, and reached the other shore, is thoughtful, guileless, free from doubts, free from attachment, and content.

415. Him I call indeed a Brâhmana who in this world, leaving all desires, travels about without a home, and in whom all concupiscence is extinct.

416. Him I call indeed a Brâhmana who, leaving all longings, travels about without a home, and in whom all covetousness is extinct.

417. Him I call indeed a Brâhmana who, after leaving all bondage to men, has risen above all bondage to the gods, and is free from all and every bondage.

418. Him I call indeed a Brâhmana who has left what gives pleasure and what gives pain, who is cold, and free from all germs (of renewed life), the hero who has conquered all the worlds.

419. Him I call indeed a Brâhmana who knows the destruction and the return of beings everywhere, who is free from bondage, welfaring (Sugata), and awakened (Buddha).

420. Him I call indeed a Brâhmana whose path the gods do not know, nor spirits (Gandharvas), nor men, whose passions are extinct, and who is an Arhat (venerable).

421. Him I call indeed a Brâhmana who calls nothing his own, whether it be before, behind, or between, who is poor, and free from the love of the world.

422. Him I call indeed a Brâhmana, the manly, the noble, the hero, the great sage, the conqueror, the impassible, the accomplished, the awakened.

423. Him I call indeed a Brâhmana who knows his former abodes, who sees heaven and hell, has reached the end of births, is perfect in knowledge, a sage, and whose perfections are all perfect.

The Dhammapada
translated from the Pâli by F. Max Müller,
Clarendon Press 1881

---

4 FACTS AND FIGURES

The countries with the highest proportion of Buddhists are as follows:

Country	Percentage of population
Thailand	95%
Cambodia	90%
Myanmar	89%
Bhutan	74%
Sri Lanka	70%
Tibet	66%
Laos	60%
Vietnam	55%
Japan	50%
Macau	46%
Taiwan	42%

The countries with the largest Buddhist populations are as follows:

Country	Number of adherents
China	1,002,000,000
Japan	90,000,000
Thailand	58,000,000
Vietnam	50,000,000
Myanmar	43,000,000
Sri Lanka	15,000,000
South Korea	12,000,000
Taiwan	10,000,000
Cambodia	9,000,000
India	8,000,000

5 BUDDHIST PRACTICES

A   Venerating Buddha
B   Monasteries
C   Meditation
D   Vegetarianism
E   Magic
F   Buddhist morals

A VENERATING BUDDHA

Buddhist customs and practices differ in various countries of the world. However, all Buddhists venerate Buddha. Venerating the Buddha may involve meditating on the qualities of Buddha, and honoring the Buddha or Buddha-figure. Many Buddhists honor the Buddha by making offerings to relics or images of the Buddha.

B MONASTERIES

Monastic institutions are important in Buddhism.

C MEDITATION

Meditation is a conscious effort to change how the mind works. The Pali word for meditation is *bhavana* which means "to make grow" or "to develop."

Meditation is at the heart of the Buddhist way of life. It is basically a method for understanding and working on our own mind. We first learn to identify our different negative mental states, known as "delusions," and then learn how to develop peaceful and positive mental states or "virtuous minds." Meditation overcomes our delusions as we become familiar with virtuous minds.

The Buddha taught many different types of meditation. Each one was designed to overcome a particular problem. The two most common types of meditation are Mindfulness of Breathing (*anapana sati*) and Loving-kindness Meditation (*metta bhavana*).

D VEGETARIANISM

Not all Buddhists are vegetarians. The Buddha was not a vegetarian and he did not teach his disciples to be vegetarians. To a Buddhist the purification of the mind is the most important thing in life, not what one eats.

E MAGIC

The Buddha denounced fortune-telling and wearing magic charms for protection as empty superstitions. He labeled such practices "low arts" and told his followers not to engage in them.

F BUDDHIST MORALS

THE FIVE PRECEPTS

Buddhists believe that following certain moral guidelines and precepts protects one from causing suffering to oneself and to others. The Five Precepts are the basis of Buddhist morality. They are:

1.   Reverence for life, so one must not kill.
2.   Generosity, so one must not steal.
3.   Sexual responsibility, so one must not indulge in adultery or sex before marriage.
4.   Deep listening and loving speech, so one must not lie.
5.   Mindful consumption, so one must on drink any alcohol.

Giving up false speech, he becomes a speaker of truth, reliable, trustworthy, dependable. He does not deceive the world.

Giving up malicious speech, he does not repeat there what he has heard here, what he has heard there, in order to cause variance between people. He reconciles those who are divided and brings closer together those who are already friends. Harmony is his joy, harmony is his delight, harmony is his love; it is the motive of his speech.

Giving up harsh speech, his speech is blameless, pleasing to the ear, agreeable, going to the heart, urbane, liked by most.

Giving up idle chatter, he speaks at the right time what is correct and to the point about Dhamma and about discipline. He speaks words worth being treasured up, seasonable, reasonable, well-defined and to the point.

The Buddha, MI 179

6 BUDDHIST BELIEFS

A   Suffering and Buddhism
B   The Four Noble Truths
C   The Eightfold Path
D   *Karma*
E   Reincarnation
F   Nirvana
G   Belief in God

A SUFFERING AND BUDDHISM
Gautama Buddha taught that everything in life is impermanent. So any attachment to the idea of an enduring self is an illusion. That attachment is the main reason for our suffering.

Buddha said, "I teach suffering, its origin, cessation and path. That's all I teach."

B THE FOUR NOBLE TRUTHS
To deal with this problem of suffering, Buddha taught four noble truths:

• There is suffering.
• Suffering has a cause.
• Suffering has an end.
• There is a path that leads to the end of suffering. This path is the Eightfold Path.

The Four Noble Truths are the fundamental teachings of the Buddha. They constitute the fundamental philosophy of Buddhism, and the core of Buddhist teaching. Seated beneath the Bodhi tree the Buddha

understood the Four Noble truths.

They are called "noble" because they ennoble everyone who understands them. They are called "truths" because, corresponding with reality, they are true.

THE FIRST NOBLE TRUTH: THE
REALITY OF SUFFERING: *DUKKHA*
The Pali word *dukkha*, usually means "suffering," "pain," "sorrow," or "misery." But in the context of the First Noble Truth, *dukkha* also means "imperfection," "impermanence," "emptiness," "insubstantiality." According to the Buddha, life is full of suffering. We cannot be free from suffering because it is a product of ignorance, illusion and impermanence.

Three kinds of suffering
• Ordinary Suffering: *dukkha-dukkha*
• Suffering produced by Change: *virapinama-dukkha*
• Suffering as conditioned states: *samkara-dukkha*

(i) Ordinary Suffering: *dukkha-dukkha*

There are all kinds of suffering in life: birth, old age, sickness, death, association with unpleasant persons and conditions, separation from beloved ones and pleasant conditions, not getting what one desires, grief, lamentation, distress - all forms of physical and mental suffering.

(ii) Suffering produced by change: *virapinama-dukkha*

Pleasant and happy feelings or conditions in life are not permanent. Sooner or later they change. When they change they may produce pain, suffering, unhappiness or disappointment. This vicissitude is considered *viparimana-dukkha.*

(iii) Suffering as conditioned states: *samkara-dukkha*

An "individual," an "I" or a "self" is a combination of ever-changing mental and physical forces that can be divided into five groups or "aggregates" (*pancakkhandha*). Suffering as conditioned states is produced by attachment to these five aggregates. They are:

Matter (*rupakkhandha*)
Sensations: (*vedanakkhandha*)
Perceptions: (*sannakkhandha*)
Mental Formations: (*sankharakkhandha*)
Consciousness: (*vinnanakkhandha*)

According to the First Noble Truth, life is suffering. To live, you must suffer. Everyone experiences some kind of suffering, whether it be physical suffering, like sickness, injury, tiredness, old age and death, or whether it be psychological suffering like loneliness, fear, and anger.

THE SECOND NOBLE TRUTH: THE CAUSE OF SUFFERING

The cause of suffering is a desire to have and control things. All suffering is caused by such craving. It can take many forms: craving of sensual pleasures; the desire for fame; the desire to avoid unpleasant sensations, like fear, anger or jealousy. The Second Noble Truth points out that getting what you want does not guarantee happiness.

THE THIRD NOBLE TRUTH: THE END OF SUFFERING

The Third Noble Truth explains how suffering can be overcome. This is achieved by ridding ourselves of our cravings and by patiently enduring problems without fear, hatred and anger. If we do this, we will eventually be freed from suffering and reach the state of Nirvana.

THE FOURTH NOBLE TRUTH: THE EIGHTFOLD PATH

The Fourth Noble Truth is the path leading to the overcoming of suffering. This path, which is called the Noble Eightfold Path, is the path to achieving salvation and to the end of one's suffering. It leads to peace, discernment, enlightenment and finally Nirvana.

C THE EIGHTFOLD PATH

The Eightfold Path consists of:

(i) Perfect Understanding
(ii) Perfect Thought
(iii) Perfect Speech
(iv) Perfect Action
(v) Perfect Livelihood
(vi) Perfect Effort
(vii) Perfect Mindfulness, and
(viii) Perfect Concentration.

These eight characteristics are divided under the three headings of:

• Wisdom (*panna*)
• Morality (*sila*)
• Meditation (*samadhi*)

a. Wisdom comprises:
• Right Understanding
• Right Thought

b. Morality comprises:
• Right Speech
• Right Action
• Right Livelihood

c. Meditation comprises:
* Right Effort
* Right Mindfulness
* Right Contemplation/Composure

Buddhist practice consists in practicing these eight things until they become more complete.

THE FIRST PART OF THE EIGHTFOLD PATH
Right understanding: this involves having the correct understanding about the Four Noble Truths.

THE SECOND PART OF THE EIGHTFOLD PATH
Right thinking: this involves following the right path in one's thinking.

THE THIRD PART OF THE EIGHTFOLD PATH
Right speech: this involves not lying, condemning, or indulging in gossip or unkind language.

THE FOURTH PART OF THE EIGHTFOLD PATH
Right conduct: this is achieved by following the Five Precepts.

THE FIFTH PART OF THE EIGHTFOLD PATH
Right livelihood: this involves supporting yourself without harming others.

THE SIXTH PART OF THE EIGHTFOLD PATH
Right effort: this involves promoting good thoughts and conquering evil thoughts.

THE SEVENTH PART OF THE EIGHTFOLD PATH
Right mindfulness: this involves becoming aware of the body, mind and feelings.

THE EIGHTH PART OF THE EIGHTFOLD PATH
Right contemplation: this involves meditating in order to achieve a higher state of consciousness.

D KARMA
Like Hindu teaching, Buddhist teaching is based on belief in the law of *karma*. This states that for every event that occurs, there will follow another event whose existence was caused by the first. This second event will be pleasant if its cause was skillful, and unpleasant if its cause was unskillful. A skillful event is one that is not accompanied by craving, resistance or delusions; an unskillful event is one that is accompanied by one of those things.

Buddhists believe that actions have such influential consequences that our lives are conditioned by our past actions.

E REINCARNATION
Buddhists believe in rebirth and reincarnation. Buddhism teaches that consciousness continues after death, and finds expression in a future life.

Buddha preached that the soul goes through many incarnations before it finally sheds all its *karma* and is reunited to its pure state. Buddha called this state Nirvana.

F NIRVANA

Nirvana is the highest happiness.
The Dhammapada *204*

Nirvana is beyond time, so there is no movement and so no aging or dying there. It is the state that all Buddhists aspire to, where one is completely free from suffering.

G BELIEF IN GOD
Buddhism does not teach the concept of a personal creator or God. Buddha did not deny God's existence, and he did teach that the universe is governed by a Supreme Power. Buddha said that this Supreme Power did not have a name or form. He said that there was no need to believe in God.

The Buddha says:

Gripped by fear men go to the sacred mountains, sacred groves, sacred trees and shrines.
The Dhammapada *188*

The Buddha believed that religious ideas and especially belief in a God have their origin in fear. Buddhism aims to overcome fear and suffering, and so has no need for any belief in God:

Buddhism has the characteristics of what would be expected in a cosmic religion for the future: it transcends a personal God, avoids dogmas and theology; it covers both the natural and spiritual, and it is based on a religious sense aspiring from the experience of all things, natural and spiritual, as a meaningful unity.

Albert Einstein

7 WORSHIP

A Temples

B Stupa

C Festivals

    (i) Wesak

    (ii) Dharma Day

    (iii) Sangha Day

    (iv) Parinirvana Day

D Pilgrimages

INTRODUCTION
Buddhists can worship both at home or at a temple.

At home, Buddhists will often set aside a room or a part of a room, as a shrine. There will be a statue of Buddha, candles, and an incense burner.

In a temple, worshipers sit on the floor barefoot facing an image of Buddha and chant.

A TEMPLES
The many and beautiful Buddhist temples (*caitya*) enshrine a stupa or an image of the Buddha.

Buddhist temples come in many shapes, the best known ones being the pagodas of China and Japan.

FIVE ELEMENTS
Buddhist temples are designed to symbolize the five elements:
- Fire
- Air
- Earth, symbolized by the square base
- Water
- Wisdom, symbolized by the pinnacle at the top.

B STUPA (PAGODA/DAGABA)
In Buddhism, there is only one type of monument. This is the stupa, a domed monumental shrine built to house relics of the Buddha, or his disciples, or to commemorate a Buddhist event. In China and Japan stupas are called "pagodas"; in Sri Lanka "dagabas." A most magnificent example is the stupa in Borodubur in Java.

BOROBUDUR STUPA, JAVA
The Borobudur stupa is a massive, symmetrical monument, 200 square meters, sitting on a low sculptured hill. The monument represents a Buddhist cosmological model of the universe organized around the axis of mythical Mt. Meru.

Starting at the eastern gateway, pilgrims circumambulate the stupa, always in a clockwise direction. Walking through nearly five kilometers of open air corridors while ascending through six square terraces and three circular ones, the pilgrim symbolically spirals upward from the everyday world to the nirvanic state of absolute nothingness.

The first six terraces are filled with richly decorated relief panels in which the sculptors have carved a textbook of Buddhist doctrines and a fascinating panorama of ninth century Javanese life. Upon the upper three terraces are seventy-two small stupas, each containing a statue of the Buddha. Crowning the entire structure is a great central stupa. Representing Nirvana, it is empty.

Buddha's teaching carved at the Borodubur temple tells the following interesting story.

"Once upon a time there was a bird with two heads. One head had a long neck so its mouth could easily take the food it wanted. This first mouth could easily reach all apples and oranges to eat for itself. On the other hand, the second head had a short neck so it was difficult for its mouth to reach the fruits and food on the trees high above. The second mouth could only see the oranges and apples but it could not reach them. The second mouth said to the first: "Give me a few apples and oranges because I am hungry. Please, give me some food." But the first answered: "No. All of the oranges and apples are for me because I have a long neck. It is your own fault why you don't have a long neck like me. All the oranges and apples are mine, not yours." Listening to this, the short-necked head felt very sad. Being very hungry, the short-necked head scraped the ground for food. It ate the poisonous tuber in the ground. Consequently, the whole bird's body was poisoned and the bird died."

C FESTIVALS
Festivals play a big part in the lives of most Buddhists. The main festivals celebrate the three major events of Buddha's life: his birth, enlightenment and death.

(I) WESAK
Wesak is the most important of the Buddhist festivals and is celebrated on the full moon in May. It celebrates Buddha's birthday.

During this festival, Buddhists visit their local temples to join in services and to receive teaching. They give offerings of food, flowers, and candles to the monks.

(II) DHARMA DAY
This marks the beginning of the Buddha's teaching.

The word *dharma* can mean truth and refers to the path to enlightenment which is gained by embracing Buddhist teaching.

After Buddha's own enlightenment, he shared this experience with his disciples. This time is viewed as the beginning of the Buddhist religion. Dharma day celebrates this day.

The first teaching given to the Buddha's original disciples was known as "The First Turning of the Wheel of the Dharma (*Dharmachakra*)." On Dharma Day, Buddhists give thanks to Buddha, as well as to other enlightened teachers, for all their teachings.

Dharma Day includes readings from the Buddhist scriptures, and meditation on them.

(III) SANGHA DAY
Sangha Day is the second most important Buddhist festival. It celebrates the Buddhist spiritual community, which is known as *sangha*. It is a time for gathering together, exchanging gifts and renewing one's commitment to Buddhist practices and traditions.

(IV) PARINIRVANA DAY
This is a Mahayana Buddhist festival that marks the death of the Buddha. On this day Buddhists remember friends and relations who have died during the previous year. They also celebrate the positive approach that Buddhism has to death and change.

D PILGRIMAGES

Four main centers of pilgrimage, linked to Buddha's life, remain important to Buddhists.

The four sacred places for worshipers to visit are:

- His birthplace at Lumbini, in Nepal.
- The place where he achieved supreme enlightenment: Bodh Gaya, in Bihar state, India.
- The place where he delivered his first sermon: the deer park in Sarnath, near Varanasi (Benares).
- The place where he achieved Nirvana: Kushinagara.

Buddhist worshipers still visit these four sites, in the above order, to chart the Buddha's life. These pilgrimages are seen as an important act for the Buddhist as he seeks to achieve spiritual happiness, which takes the pilgrim to heaven.

FURTHER PILGRIMAGE SITES

Wherever Buddhism becomes established, sites of pilgrimage spring up.

Pilgrimages establish links with the historical figures associated with the pilgrimage site, encourage spiritual discipline, and enable Buddhists to express their feelings of devotion to Buddha.

8 GROUPINGS WITHIN BUDDHISM

A Theravada Buddhism
B Mahayana Buddhism
C Vajrayana Buddhism
D Pure Land Buddhism
E Tibetan Buddhism
F Zen

INTRODUCTION

All Buddhists share this common goal: to bring an end to suffering by taming the mind. Since the human condition contains many different forms of suffering, the Buddha taught many paths to liberation, which are now practiced throughout the world. The numerous sects of Buddhism, as it is practiced today, are categorized into three schools (*yana* is the Sanskrit term for "vehicle"):

- Lesser Vehicle (Theravada or Hinayana)
- Greater Vehicle (Mahayana)
- Diamond Vehicle (Vajrayana or Tantric or Esoteric).

A THERAVADA BUDDHISM

Theravada (Hinayana; the Lesser Vehicle) is found mainly in Sri Lanka, Burma, Thailand,

and Vietnam, as well as in Cambodia, and Laos. It is sometimes called "Southern Buddhism."

DOCTRINE OF THE ELDERS

The name "Theravada" means the doctrine of the elders - the elders being the senior Buddhist monks.

This is the most conservative of the schools of Buddhism. It is said that Theravada Buddhism has remained closest to the original teachings of the Buddha.

THERAVADA BELIEFS

Like other branches of Buddhism, Theravada Buddhism does not offer supernatural solutions to the spiritual problems of human beings. Rather, it teaches its followers to meditate so that they may experience awakening, that is, enlightenment.

B MAHAYANA BUDDHISM

Mahayana (the Greater Vehicle) is found mainly in Tibet, Mongolia, China, Korea, Japan, and Taiwan.

Mahayana Buddhism is not a single group but a collection of Buddhist traditions: Zen Buddhism, Pure Land Buddhism, and Tibetan Buddhism are all forms of Mahayana Buddhism.

Theravada and Mahayana have many similarities. Both are rooted in the basic teachings of the historical Buddha, and both emphasize the need to be freed from the cycle of birth, death, and rebirth.

However, the methods by which they seek to achieve this often differ.

RISE OF MAHAYANA BUDDHISM

Theravada Buddhism focuses primarily on meditation and concentration: the eighth of the Eightfold Noble Paths. As a result, it centers on a monastic life and an extreme expenditure of time in meditation. This makes it difficult for ordinary people, who are unable to give up so much time, so in the first century AD, a new sect was formed that reformulated the teachings of Buddha to accommodate more people.

This new Buddhism was called the "Greater Vehicle" (literally, "The Greater Ox-Cart") or Mahayana, since it could accommodate more people. These Buddhists distinguished themselves from mainstream Theravada Buddhism by contemptuously referring to Theravada as Hinayana, or "The Lesser Vehicle."

TEACHING

Mahayana Buddhism is more liberal and more open to new ideas than Theravada Buddhism.

A distinctive teaching of Mahayana Buddhism is its teaching about the Bodhisattva. He is someone who is destined for Buddhahood, but makes a vow to postpone this goal in order to save as many as possible - committing himself to work for others even in future incarnations. It is believed that he gathers others into his own being. In some cases, the sacrificial love of the Bodhisavatta is so great that he will postpone his own Nirvana indefinitely in order to help others, not only in their search for salvation, but in their daily lives.

C VAJRAYANA BUDDHISM/TANTRIC BUDDHISM

Vajrayana (Esoteric or Tantric Buddhism) is practiced mainly in Tibet, but in Japan it has a stronghold with the Shingon and Tendai sects.

In Sanskrit, *vajra* means "diamond" (literally "adamantine," "unsplittable"), while *yana* means "vehicle." Vajrayana is thus translated as "The Diamond Vehicle." In English, this form of Buddhism is also known as Tantric Buddhism, because of its reliance on sacred texts called *tantras*.

RISE OF VAJRAYANA BUDDHISM

Vajrayana Buddhism developed out of Mahayana teachings, and first appeared around 500 AD in north-west India. From here it spread to Tibet and China with only brief success (but centuries later it took strong root in Tibet), and finally it arrived in Japan around the eighth century, as a result of the teaching of the Japanese priest Kukai (also known as Kobo Daishi, 774-835 AD), the founder of Japan's Shingon Sect of Esoteric Buddhism.

TEACHING

Vajrayana's main claim is that it enables a person to reach Nirvana (freedom from suffering) in a single lifetime, rather than passing through countless lives before achieving salvation. In Theravada (Hinayana) Buddhism, which stresses meditation and the monastic path to enlightenment (the laity are excluded), followers hope to gain enough merit in this life to reincarnate into the next with better *karma*, thereby moving one step forward on the long path to Nirvana. Vajrayana promises the "fast path" to Buddhahood - a path that, in some Vajrayana traditions, brings magical powers.

Vajrayana Buddhism involves esoteric visualizations, symbols, and complicated rituals that can only be learned by study with a master. This explains why Vajrayana Buddhism is also referred to as Esoteric Buddhism. It lays great emphasis on mantras (incantations), *mudras* (hand gestures) and *mandalas* (diagrams of the deities and cosmic forces), as well as on magic and a multiplicity of deities.

In Vajrayana traditions, there is no external reference point for good and evil, and the role of the teacher thus becomes critical. In the West, the complete devotion to the teacher required of the acolyte is sometimes referred to as "guru yoga."

D PURE LAND BUDDHISM
Pure Land Buddhism offers a way to enlightenment for people who can't handle the subtleties of meditation, or endure long rituals, or even just live especially good lives.

RISE OF PURE LAND BUDDHISM
This school of Buddhism emerged in China in about 400 AD and later spread to Japan. It remains popular in China and Japan today.

TEACHING
This school venerates the Bodhisattva Amitabha, who is said to reside in the Western Paradise (*Sukhavati*), or Pure Land. Devotion to Amitabha will result in being reborn in the Pure Land from where it is much easier to work for the attainment of Nirvana, which is therefore guaranteed.

The essential practice in Pure Land Buddhism is the chanting of the mantra *Namu Amida Butsu* ("Hail to Amitabha Buddha") with total concentration, as an expression of faith, trusting that one will be reborn in the Pure Land.

Pure Land Buddhism adds mystical elements to the basic Buddhist teachings which make those teachings easier to work with.

E TIBETAN BUDDHISM
Tibetan Buddhism is a religion in exile, forced from its homeland when Tibet was conquered by the Chinese.

The leader of Tibetan Buddhism is the Dalai Lama, who has lived in exile in India since he fled Chinese occupation of Tibet in 1959.

RISE OF TIBETAN BUDDHISM
Buddhism was brought to Tibet by Padmasambhava in the eighth century, and has flourished there ever since, transmitted from Gurus to disciples in an unbroken lineage.

TEACHING
The Tibetan practices share a distinctive motivation: they are undertaken to end not only one's own suffering, but also the suffering of all other beings, to each of whom we owe a karmic debt. The understanding is that since we are all linked to one another, one person's liberation is incomplete until all other beings have been liberated.

So with the help and guidance of the Guru, Tibetan Buddhist practitioners work to develop the pure perception that arises out of meditation. That clarity is then used to awaken and increase their compassion for others until it equals the unconditioned compassion of the Buddha.

F ZEN
Zen Buddhism is the mystical school of Buddhism. (Zen in Chinese is *ch'an-na*, which transliterates the sanskrit term *dhyana* ("meditation").

RISE OF ZEN BUDDHISM
Mahayana Buddhism reached China in the first century, but was strongly opposed and remained weak. In 526 Bodhidharma came to China and started the first Ch'an school. The movement he founded grew, and separated from Mahayana Buddhism. (Zen Buddhism is now a mixture of Indian Mahayana Buddhism and Taoism.)

In the twelfth century Bodhidharma's teaching spread to Japan where it became known as Zen Buddhism. In this form it became very popular in the West from the mid-twentieth century.

TEACHING
The purpose of Zen is the attempt to understand the meaning of life directly, without being misled by logical thought, or language.

Zen Buddhism teaches that all human beings are Buddha, and all they have to do is to discover that truth for themselves. This is achieved by means of:

- Meditation according to strict rules.
- A particularly effective way of reaching enlightenment (*satori*) is meditation while sitting in the lotus position (cross-legged, each foot on the opposite thigh). This is known as *zazan*.
- Concentration on a *koan* (a riddle, or question, to which there is no rational answer). The purpose of the *koan* is to alter the Zen student's way of thinking.
- The student undertaking these disciplines must be supervised by a Zen master.

EXAMPLE OF THE KOAN
When you listen to two hands clapping there is a sound.
What is the sound of one hand clapping?

ZEN SAYINGS

Sitting quietly

Sitting quietly, doing nothing,
Spring comes, and the grass grows by itself.

Zenrin Kushû

Suchness

The blue mountains are of themselves blue mountains;
The white clouds are of themselves white clouds.

Zenrin Kushû

Mountains are mountains

Before I had studied Zen for thirty years, I saw mountains as mountains, and waters as waters. When I arrived at a more intimate knowledge, I came to the point where I saw that mountains are not mountains, and waters are not waters. But now that I have got its very substance I am at rest. For it's just that I see mountains once again as mountains, and waters once again as waters.

Ch'uan Teng Lu

Oneness

Heaven and earth and I are of the same root,
The ten-thousand things and I are of one substance.

Zen Master Sêng-chao/Sōjō, 384-414

Unity

Merge your mind with cosmic space, integrate your actions with myriad forms.

Hung-chih Cheng-chüeh

Nondiscrimination

When you forget the good and the non-good, the worldly life and the religious life, and all other *dharmas*, and permit no thoughts relating to them to arise, and you abandon body and mind - then there is complete freedom. When the mind is like wood or stone, there is nothing to be discriminated.

Pai-chang Huai-hai

Speech and silence

Speech is blasphemy, silence a lie. Above speech and silence there is a way out.

I-tuan

Independence

I would rather sink to the bottom of the sea for endless eons than seek liberation through all the saints of the universe.

Shih-t'ou

9 IN PRAISE OF BUDDHISM

QUOTATIONS

Twenty-four brand-new hours

Every morning, when we wake up, we have twenty-four brand-new hours to live. What a precious gift! We have the capacity to live in a way that these twenty-four hours will bring peace, joy, and happiness to ourselves and others.

Peace is present right here and now, in ourselves and in everything we do and see. The Question is whether or not we are in touch with it. We don't have to travel far away to enjoy the blue sky. We don't have to leave our city or even our neighborhood to enjoy the eyes of a beautiful child. Even the air we breathe can be a source of joy. We can smile, breathe, walk, and eat our meals in a way that allows us to be in touch with the abundance of happiness that is available. We are very good at preparing to live, but not very good at living. We know how to sacrifice ten years for a diploma, and we are willing to work very hard to get a job, a car, a house, and so on. But we have difficulty remembering that we are alive at the present moment, the only moment there is for us to be alive. Every breath we take, every step we make, can be filled with peace, joy, and serenity. We need only to be awake, alive in the present moment.

Thich Nhat Hanh

Peace is every step

Although attempting to bring about world peace through the internal transformation of individuals is difficult, it is the only way. Wherever I go, I express this, and I am encouraged that people from many different walks of life receive it well. Peace must first be developed within an individual. And I believe that love, compassion, and altruism are the fundamental basis for peace. Once these qualities are developed within an individual, he or she is then able to create an atmosphere of peace and harmony. This atmosphere can be expanded and extended from the individual to his family, from the family to the community and eventually to the whole world.

The Dalai Lama

The illusory nature of the world

Know all things to be like this:
a mirage, a cloud castle,
a dream, an apparition,
without essence but with qualities
that can be seen.
Know all things to be like this:
as the moon in a bright sky
in some clear lake reflected,
though to that lake the moon has never moved.
Know all things to be like this:
as an echo that derives
from music, sounds, and weeping,
yet in that echo is no melody.
Know all things to be like this.
As a magician makes illusions
of horses, oxen, carts, and other things,
nothing is as it appears.

The Buddha

Zen Buddhism helps man to find an answer to the question of his existence, an answer which is essentially the same as that given in the Judaeo-Christian tradition, and yet which does not contradict the rationality, realism, and independence which are modern man's precious achievements. Paradoxically, Eastern religious thought turns out to be more congenial to Western rational thought than does Western religious thought itself.

Erich Fromm (1900-1980)
German-American psychoanalyst

I have no hesitation in declaring that I owe a great deal to the inspiration that I have derived from the life of the Enlightenment One. Asia has a message for the whole world, if only it would live up to it. There is the imprint of Buddhistic influence on the whole of Asia, which includes India, China, Japan, Burma, Ceylon, and the Malay States. For Asia to be not for Asia but for the whole world, it has to re-learn the message of the Buddha and deliver it to the whole world. His love, his boundless love went out as much to the lower animal, to the lowest life as to human beings. And he insisted upon purity of life.

Mahatma Gandhi (1869-1948)

The intellectual content of Buddha's teaching is only half his work, the other half is his life, his life as lived, as labor accomplished and action carried out. A training, a spiritual self training of the highest order was accomplished and is taught here, a training about which unthinking people who talk about "quietism" and "Hindu dreaminess" and the like in connection with Buddha have no conception; they deny him the cardinal Western virtue of activity. Instead Buddha accomplished a training for himself and his pupils, exercised a discipline, set up a goal, and produced results before which even the genuine heroes of European action can only feel awe.

Herman Hesse (1877-1962)
German author and winner of the
Nobel Prize for Literature, 1946

The way of Buddhism is Middle Way between all extremes. This is no weak compromise, but a sweet reasonableness which avoids fanaticism and laziness with equal care, and marches onward without

that haste which brings its own reaction, but without ceasing. The Buddha called it the Noble Eightfold Path to Nirvana, and it may be regarded as the noblest course of spiritual training yet presented, in such a simple form, to man. Buddhism is neither pessimistic nor "escapist." It is a system of thought, a religion, a spiritual science and a way of life which is reasonable, practical and all-embracing. For 2,500 years it has satisfied the spiritual needs of nearly one third of mankind. It appeals to those in search of truth because it has no dogmas, satisfies the reason and the heart alike, insists on self-reliance coupled with tolerance for other points of view, embraces science, religion, philosophy, psychology, mysticism, ethics and art, and points to man alone as the creator of his present life and sole designer of his destiny.

Justice Christmas Humphreys (1901-1983)
British judge

As a student of comparative religions, I believe that Buddhism is the most perfect one the world has even seen. The philosophy of the theory of evolution and the law of *karma* were far superior to any other creed. It was neither the history of religion nor the study of philosophy that first drew me to the world of Buddhist thought but my professional interest as a doctor. My task was to teat psychic suffering and it was this that impelled me to become acquainted with the views and methods of that great teacher of humanity, whose principal theme was the chain of suffering, old age, sickness and death.

C. C. Jung (1875-1961)
Swiss psychologist

If I knew the Buddha would be speaking here tomorrow, nothing in the world could stop me from going to listen to him. And I would follow him to the very end.

J. Krishnamurti
Indian philosopher (1895-1986)

Buddhism is much less a matter of organized and institutional orthodoxy than a state of mind. Buddhism does not aim directly at theological salvation but a total clarification of consciousness. It is not so much a way of worshiping as a way of being. Exterior cultural accretions are much less important than they may seem, and the Buddhist cultural awareness is endowed with mercury like formlessness, which erodes the statistical eye of the Western scholar.

Thomas Merton (1915-1968)
American Trappist monk

Whenever one thinks of the Buddha, one inevitably thinks of his great teaching; and I often feel that, perhaps, if we think more of that basic teaching of the avoidance of hatred and violence, we may be nearer the solution to our problem. In this world of storm and strife, hatred and violence, the message of the Buddha shines like a radiant sun: Perhaps at no time was that message more needed than in this world of the atomic and hydrogen bombs . . . Let us remember that immortal message and try to fashion our thoughts and actions in the light of that teaching . . . and help a little in prompting right thinking and right action. . . . If any question has to be considered, it has to be considered peacefully and democratically in the way taught by the Buddha.

Jawaharlal Nehru (1889-1964)
Indian Prime Minister

He gave expression to truths of everlasting value and advanced the ethics not of India alone but of humanity. Buddha was one of the greatest ethical men of genius ever bestowed upon the world.

Albert Schweitzer (1875-1965)

Buddhism was the first spiritual force, known to us in history, which drew close together such a large number of races separated by most difficult barriers of distance, by difference of language and custom, by various degrees and divergent

types of civilization. It had its motive power, neither in international commerce, nor in empire building, nor in a scientific curiosity, nor in a migrative impulse to occupy fresh territory. It was a purely disinterested effort to help mankind forward to its final goal.

Rabindranath Tagore (1861-1941)
Indian poet and educationalist

I ever believe that the mark of a truly educated and imaginative person facing the twenty-first century is that he feels himself to be a planetary being. Perhaps my own Buddhist upbringing has helped me more than anything else to realize and to express in my speeches and writings this concept of world citizenship. As a Buddhist, I was trained to be tolerant of everything except intolerance. I was brought up not only to develop the spirit of tolerance, but also to cherish moral and spiritual qualities, especially modesty, humanity, compassion, and, most important, to attain a certain degree of emotional equilibrium.

U Thant (1910-1974)
Burmese diplomat and Secretary
General of the United Nations

Buddhism is more the advance of world civilization and true culture than any other influence in the chronicles of mankind.

H. G. Wells (1866-1946)
British historian, and
science fiction writer

Buddhism has conquered China as a philosophy and as a religion, as a philosophy for the scholars and a religion for the common people. Whereas Confucianism has only a philosophy of moral conduct, Buddhism possesses a logical method, a metaphysics and a theory of knowledge. Besides, it is fortunate in having a high tradition of scholarship in the translation of Buddhist classics, and the language of these translations, so succinct and often so distinguished by a beautiful lucidity of language and reasoning, cannot but attract the scholar with a philosophical bias. Hence, Buddhism has always enjoyed a prestige among Chinese scholars, which so far Christianity has failed to achieve.

Lin Yutang (1895-1976)
Chinese writer

10 COMPARISON WITH CHRISTIANITY

A Buddha and Jesus Christ compared
B Other differences

A BUDDHA AND JESUS CHRIST COMPARED

(I) THE CLAIM TO BE GOD

Buddha:
never claimed to be God.

Jesus Christ:
claimed to be God.

(II) PROPHESY

Buddha:
never prophesied.

Jesus Christ:
made many prophecies.

(III) MIRACLES

Buddha:
performed no miracles

Jesus Christ:
performed dozens of miracles

(IV) RESURRECTION

Buddha:
died and his body was cremated.

Jesus Christ:
was crucified but was resurrected to life again.

B OTHER DIFFERENCES

(I) A PERSONAL GOD
In Buddhism:
there is no personal God, not even a creator God. The world exists by natural laws.

In Christianity:
God created the world and everything in it.

(II) SIN

In Buddhism:
there is no such thing as sinning against a supreme being.

In Christianity:
everyone is guilty of sinning against God.

(III) AN INDIVIDUAL'S WORTH

In Buddhism:
people have only a temporary existence, and are not worth anything in themselves.

In Christianity:
human beings were created by God, in his image, and are of infinite worth. They live for ever.

11 GLOSSARY

Alms
The offering of food to monks on their daily rounds and the donation of goods and money to the monasteries.

Amitabha
The Bodhisattva whose name means "Buddha of Boundless Light" and who dwells in the paradise called the Pure Land. He is also the founder of this sect of Buddhism.

Arhat
A Buddhist monk who is free from all illusions and who has achieved personal enlightenment. This term is used primarily in Theravada Buddhism.

Avalokiteshvara
A Bodhisattva of Compassion. Compassion and Wisdom represent the two main concepts of Mahayana Buddhism.

Bardo
A human soul between the stages of after-death and rebirth.

Bardo Thodol
The Tibetan name for the Book of the Dead.

Bhikkhu
A fully ordained monk who has left his home and renounced all his possessions in order to follow the way of the Buddha

Bodhisattva
A being in the final stages of attaining Buddhahood, who has vowed to help all sentient beings achieve Nirvana, or enlightenment, before he himself achieves it.

Bodhi tree (often shortened to Bo tree)
The banyan (or Indian fig-tree) beneath which the meditating Gautama sat before he achieved enlightenment.

Bodhidharma
The legendary monk who brought Buddhism

from India to China in the sixth century AD.

Brahman
The Ultimate Reality. Similar to a Supreme Being.

Buddhahood
Enlightenment: on death, the one who has been enlightened passes at once into Nirvana.

Buddha-nature
The nature innate in every sentient being. The potential for attaining Buddhahood.

Butsu-dan
Japanese Buddhist household altar.

Chaitya
An assembly hall for monks.

Ch'an
The Chinese form of Zen Buddhism.

Dharma
The ultimate law, or doctrine, as taught by Buddha, which consists of the Four Noble Truths and the Eightfold Path.

Dhyana
A state of mind achieved through higher meditation.

Dukkha
Suffering, emptiness, impermanence.

Hinayana
Literally, "small vehicle." A term used by the Mahayanists to describe earlier orthodox sects of Buddhism (Theravada School). Their scriptures are written in Pali, an ancient Indian language.

Karma
Literally, "deed." A concept that binds its followers to an endless cycle of birth, death, and rebirth and, according to one's deeds in life, determines the condition of one's rebirth.

Koan
A riddle, tale, or short statement used by Zen masters to bring their students to sudden insight.

Lama
Literally, "superior one." A Buddhist monk of Tibet.

Mahayana
Literally, "great vehicle." One of the three major forms of Buddhism, Mahayana is considered the more liberal and practical. Its scriptures are written in Sanskrit.

Maitreya
Literally, "Friendly One." The Bodhisattva who embodies the virtues of wisdom and eloquence.

Manjushri
Bodhisattva of Wisdom. Wisdom (*prajna*), along with compassion, represents the two main concepts of Mahayana Buddhism.

Mandala
A painting or tapestry with images of Buddha, bodhisattvas, and other images. It is used as a focus of meditation for monks and as an object of worship for many.

Mantra
Ritual sound, word, or phrase used to evoke a certain religious effect.

Mara
The personification of evil. The god of death.

Maya
Queen Maya, Buddha's mother.

Moksha
Literally, "release." An idea originally developed from Upanishadic teachers. By leading a highly spiritual life (or several lives), a soul could be reunited with Brahman, the Ultimate Reality.

Mudra
Hand gestures often depicted on statues of the Buddha. The gestures have different meaning (meditation, etc).

Namu Amida Butsa
Literally, "Praise to the Buddha Amitabha." In the Japanese Pure Land sect, this is the phrase used to call on Amitabha Buddha.

Nirvana
Literally, "extinction." The ultimate goal of Buddhists, characterized by the extinction of both craving and the separate "ego." The state of peace and quietude attained by extinguishing all illusions.

Pali canon
The most complete and the earliest collection of canonical literature in Buddhism.

Parinirvana
Death of the Buddha.

Prajna
Literally, Wisdom. This term represents the wisdom obtained during enlightenment, and one of the key insight is emptiness.

Prajna-Paramita Sutra
Collection of forty Mahayana *sutras* dealing with *prajna* and its attainment.

Pure Land
A sect of Mahayana Buddhism founded by Amitabha Buddha. The Pure Land is a paradise in the "west" where people can go when they die. People must call on Amitabha to enter this paradise.

Rajah
Chief or king.

Samsara
The continuous cycle of birth, death, and rebirth (reincarnation).

Sangha
An organized assembly of Buddhist monks.

Sanskrit
The sacred language of India, which the

Indians consider "the language of the gods;" means "perfected" and "cultured."

Shuddhodanna
King Shuddhodanna, father of Buddha.

Siddhartha
He whose aim is accomplished; birth name of the Buddha.

Skandhas
The five elements of which each individual is composed.

Stupa
A dome, or pagoda, in which sacred relics are deposited.

Sunyata
Emptiness; the belief that all phenomena are dependent on and caused by other phenomena, thus without intrinsic essence.

Sutra
Literally, "thread" or "string." A scripture containing the teachings of Buddha.

Theravada
Literally, "School of the Elders," also known as Hinayana. One of the three major forms of Buddhism, Theravada is considered to be the original and orthodox form of Buddhism.

Tipitaka
Literally, "Three Baskets." According to Buddhist belief, the scriptures were stored in three baskets, dividing Buddha's teachings into the code of discipline for monks, his sermons and discourses, and the higher doctrine.

Upasaka
Followers of Buddhism who believed in Buddha's teachings, but did not follow the strict rule of the *sangha* (the community of Buddhist monks, which started with Buddha).

Urna
A mark on the Buddha's forehead, between his eyebrows, that signifies his great intuition.

Ushanisha
A protuberance on the top of Buddha's head that signifies his great wisdom.

Vajrayana
Literally, "diamond vehicle." One of the three major forms of Buddhism, Vajrayana is popular in Tibet.

Vihara
Cave dwellings for monks.

Yasodhara
Buddha's wife.

Zen
Form of Mahayana Buddhism in Japan. The Chinese version is called Ch'an.

SIKHISM

CONTENTS

1   An overview   263

2   Founder of Sikhism   264

3   Sikh's holy book   267

4   Facts and figures   275

5   Sikh practices   276

6   Sikh beliefs   279

7   Sikh worship   280

8   Sikh groups   283

9   Comparison with Christianity   283

10 Glossary   284

1 AN OVERVIEW

DEFINITION

The word Sikh is derived from the Pali word *sikkha*, meaning "disciple." Sikhs are the disciples of the first ten Gurus, and Sikhism is based on their teachings. These teachings are enshrined in the Sikh's holy book Guru Granth Sahib.

Factfile
- Date of origin: fifteenth century AD
- Founder: Guru Nanak
- Holy book: Guru Granth Sahib
- Number of adherents: More than 25 million

SUMMARY

Sikhism is the world's fifth largest world religion.

Sikhism is a monotheistic religion founded in the Punjab, in north-west India, in the fifteenth century AD as a synthesis of Islam and Hinduism. Sikhism originated from the teachings of Guru Nanak. Sikhs believe that Guru Nanak obtained his message direct from the One Timeless Lord and sought to put people on to the righteous path towards the realization of God through meditation, sharing the fruits of honest work and loving everyone. He exposed the futility of the caste system, of idol worship and of the inequality of the genders. Sikhism is open to everyone. Sikhs are easy to identify because of their beards and turbans.

SUMMARY OF PRACTICES
- Prayers: repeated multiple times each day.
- Worship: Sikhs are prohibited from worshiping idols, images, or icons.
- Temples: there are over 200 *gurdwaras* (temples, shrines or holy places) in India alone. The most sacred is at Amritsar.
- The Five Ks. These are five symbolic items worn by Sikhs.
- *Kesh* (long hair, which is never cut)

- *Kangha* (comb)
- *Kaccha* (short pants)
- *Kara* (metal bracelet)
- *Kirpan* (a ceremonial dagger)

SUMMARY OF BELIEFS

A God
B The human condition

INTRODUCTION
God himself is regarded as the true Guru, and the Sikh community is called a Guru. The message of Sikhism includes:

- Remembering God at all times
- Living in a truthful way
- The equality of humankind
- The elimination of superstitions and rituals.

A GOD
Sikhism developed from a devotional movement among followers of Vishnu. This teaching maintained that though God is known by many names, there is only one Reality.

Sikhism is a monotheistic religion. It teaches that the one God is without form, or gender. Everyone has direct access to God and everyone is equal before him.

B THE HUMAN CONDITION

Sikhs believe that God is in everyone and so everyone can change for the better, no matter how evil they may appear to be. The way of salvation is found by making God and not the self the center and focus of life: salvation is achieved as the soul is united in love with God. The power of sin and pride are destroyed as God's name is praised. As love grows there is a longing to serve God: expressed by loving acts in the community and the *gurdwara*. Until the soul is united with God in love, the individual keeps on being reincarnated.

2 FOUNDERS OF SIKHISM

A   Guru Nanak
B   The Sikh Gurus
C   The Great Masters of Sikhism
D   The growth of Sikhism
E   Famous quotations of Guru Nanak
F   No Gurus today

INTRODUCTION

Sikhism was founded in the Punjab, when the surrounding religions were Hinduism and Islam. In the fifteenth century AD, Guru Nanak started to teach a faith that differed greatly from Hinduism and Islam.

A GURU NANAK

Guru Nanak (1469-1539), the founder of the Sikh religion, is revered by Sikhs as one of the greatest religious innovators. Although Nanak drew on both Hindu and Islamic thought, he was an original thinker. Many of his thoughts are now enshrined in Sikh scripture.

Nanak was born in the village of Rai Bhoi di Talvandi, forty miles from Lahore, which is now in Pakistan, on November 26, 1469. His father, who belonged to a sub-caste of the Kshatriyas (warrior caste), was a tax collector. According to Sikh tradition, his birth and early years reveal that God had appointed him for a special spiritual mission. He was educated in Hindu teaching and in the teaching of Islam, and early in life began to seek out holy men.

For a time he worked as an accountant of the Afghan chieftain at Sultanpur. Here a Muslim family servant, Mardana, who was also a rebec player, joined him. Nanak began to compose hymns, which Mardana put to music. Together, they organized community hymn-singing. It is also said that they organized a canteen where Muslims and Hindus of different castes could eat together (alternatively, this is an innovation that may have been introduced by the third Guru, Amar Das).

A Sultanpur Nanak had a vision of God in which God told him to preach to all people. One day, while bathing in a stream, he disappeared. Three days later, he reappeared and proclaimed: "There is no Hindu. There is no Muslim."

He became a preacher, and a group of followers gathered round him. Later it is said he went on four long journeys: east as far as

Assam; south to Ceylon; north to Tibet and west to Mecca and Baghdad.

He ended his life at Kartarpur in the Punjab where he built the first Sikh temple. There many disciples were attracted by his teachings and joined him. He was always thought of as a teacher, and never as a manifestation of God. Guru Nanak taught that that there is only one God, and that everyone has direct access to God without any need for rituals or any go-between priests.

He denounced the caste system, teaching that everyone is equal, regardless of birth or gender.

Nanak chose one of his disciples to be his successor.

B THE SIKH GURUS

The Sanskrit word "Guru" means teacher, honored person, or saint. In Sikhism, Guru means the descent of divine guidance to humankind through ten Enlightened Masters. So only the ten Gurus who founded the religion are called Sikh Gurus. They are said to have the same truth, the same insight, the same identity. They are like candles that have been lit from each other.

THE GURUS ARE A LADDER

The Palace of the Lord God is so beautiful. Within it, there are gems, rubies, pearls and flawless diamonds. A fortress of gold surrounds this Source of Nectar. How can I climb up to the Fortress without a ladder? By meditating on the Lord, through the Guru, I am blessed and exalted. The Guru is the Ladder, the Guru is the Boat, and the Guru is the Raft to take me to the Lord's Name. The Guru is the Boat to carry me across the world-ocean; the Guru is the Sacred Shrine of Pilgrimage, the Guru is the Holy River. If it pleases Him, I bathe in the Pool of Truth, and become radiant and pure.

Guru Nanak, Sri Rag, page 17

C THE GREAT MASTERS OF SIKHISM

- The First Master: Nanak (1469-1539)
- The Second Master: Angad (1504-1552)
- The Third Master: Amar Das (1479-1574)
- The Fourth Master: Ram Das (1534-1581)
- The Fifth Master: Arjan (1563-1606)
- The Sixth Master: Har Govind (1595-1644)
- The Seventh Master: Har Rai (1630-1661)
- The Eighth Master: Har Krishan (1656-1664)
- The Ninth Master: Tegh Bahadur (1621-1675)
- The Tenth Master: Gobind Singh (1666-1708)

D THE GROWTH OF SIKHISM

THE PERIOD OF THE FIRST FIVE GURUS (1469-1606)

During this period most of the doctrines were developed. Sikhism was a peaceful movement, whose adherents were devoted to the worship of the one God. Their worship services focused on the singing of hymns written by Guru Nanak. The second Guru introduced an emphasis on games and physical training; the third Guru encouraged Sikhs of all castes to eat together. The fifth Guru, Guru Arjan, collected together many of the Sikh hymns and writings. During this time, the Sikh community lived at peace with the Muslims.

THE PERIOD OF THE LAST FIVE GURUS

About 1600 the Muslim Empire passed into the control of Jehangir, a ruler who opposed the Sikhs. The fifth Guru, Guru Arjan, began to take a stand against Muslim aggression, and he was killed while in Muslim custody. Sikhs regard his death as a martyrdom.

Many people in the Punjab now rallied to the Sikhs, who began to see that they must take a stand to defend their religion. The change into a militant sect culminated under the tenth Guru, Gobind Singh (1666-1708), who was a renowned warrior. Guru Gobind founded the *Khalsa* fraternity, a warrior order. Its members took up arms against the aggressor.

After initial victories, the twenty-year long conflict against the Muslims led by Gobind Singh ultimately resulted in defeat and the death of his four sons. In 1708 he himself was assassinated. Military leadership passed to Banda Singh Bahadur, who continued to lead the *Khalsa* in defiant military action. Guru Gobind, however, was the last individual Guru.

THE PEOPLE OF THE BOOK
With the death of his sons, Gobind Singh declared that when he died his authority as a Guru would pass for ever into the community (now called Guru Panth) and into the scriptures (Guru Granth Sahib). This brought about a radical change in the way Sikhs regarded themselves and led to a strengthening and invigoration of the Sikh religion.

TWENTIETH CENTURY
Sikhism is an ethnic religion: the identify of Sikhs is bound up with their identity as people who live or lived in the Punjab.

In the twentieth century, large numbers of Sikh men traveled to the US, Britain, Canada and parts of South and East Africa. Later, they were joined by their wives and families. Buildings were converted to *gurdwaras*, and serve as community centers. Sikhism is not a missionary religion. Their roots in the Punjab, their shared history, worship of God and obedience to the Gurus give Sikhs throughout the world their sense of identity.

E FAMOUS QUOTATIONS OF GURU NANAK

Let no man in the world live in delusion. Without a Guru none can cross over to the other shore.

The word is the Guru,
The Guru is the Word,
For all nectar is enshrined in the world.
Blessed is the word which reveal the Lord's name.
But more is the one who knows by the Guru's grace.

Whoever, styling himself as a teacher lives on the charity of others, never bow before him. He who earns his livelihood by the sweat of his brow and shares it with others. O Nanak only he can know the way.

God is one, but he has innumerable forms. He is the creator of all and He himself takes the human form.

One cannot comprehend Him through reason, even if one reasoned for ages.

The lord can never be established nor created; the formless one is limitlessly complete in Himself.

Even Kings and emperors with heaps of wealth and vast dominion cannot compare with an ant filled with the love of God.

As fragrance abides in the flower
as reflection is within the mirror,
so does your Lord abide within you.
Why search for him without?

Guru Nanak

F NO GURUS TODAY
With the death of the third Guru, the leadership of Sikhism became hereditary. In 1699, after losing all four of his sons in military conflict, the tenth Guru, Gobind Rais, transferred all his authority to the Sikh community itself. Then in 1708 he declared that after his death, the holy book itself would be the perpetual Guru. There is therefore no place in Sikhism today for a living Guru.

3 SIKH'S HOLY BOOK

A Contents
B List of sections of the Guru Granth Sahib
C Jup

INTRODUCTION

The writings of the early Gurus were collected together by the fifth Guru, Guru Arjun. This became the Sikh holy book (Guru Granth Sahib). The version accepted by most Sikhs as authentic is said to have been revised by Gobind Singh in 1704. Gobind Singh said that the Guru Granth Sahib would become the Sikh's spiritual guide after his death. Sikhs now revere the Guru Granth Sahib as if were a human Guru. They regard it as the Guru incarnate.

A CONTENTS

Guru Granth Sahib, also called *Adi Granth* ("First Book"), is a collection of devotional hymns and poetry which proclaim God, lay stress on meditation on the true Guru (God), and lay down moral and ethical rules for development of the soul, spiritual salvation and unity with God. These hymns, or *shabads*, form the chief element in Sikh communal worship.

HYMNS

Guru Granth Sahib has nearly 6,000 hymns:

- 974 hymns are by Guru Nanak Dev Ji, the first Guru
- 62 by Guru Angad Dev Ji, the second Guru
- 907 by Guru Amar Das, the third Guru
- 679 by Guru Ram Das, the fourth Guru
- 2218 by Guru Arjan, the fifth Guru
- 115 by Guru Tegh Bahadur, the ninth Guru (Guru Gobind's father, added by Guru Gobind

- 937 by the Bhakta saints and Muslim Sufis.

DIFFERENT RELIGIONS

Not only does Guru Granth Sahib contain writings of some of the Sikh Gurus, but also texts by Hindus and Muslims. In the Guru Granth Sahib are found the hymns of:

- six Sikh Gurus
- thirteen Hindu *bhaktas* (saints): Trilochan, Nam Dev, Ramanand, Surday, Beni, Sadna, Kabir, Ravidas, Parmanand, Ravidas, Sain, Dhanna, Pipa and Jai Dev)
- five Muslim divines (Sheikh Farid, Bhikhan, Mardana, Satta and Balwand)
- a Sikh devotee (Sundar) and twelve bards.

B LIST OF SECTIONS OF GURU GRANTH SAHIB

1. Jup
2. So Dar
3. So Purakh
4. Sohila
5. Siree Raag
6. Raag Maajh
7. Raag Gauree
8. Raag Aasaa
9. Raag Goojaree
10. Raag Dayv-Gandhaaree
11. Raag Bihaagra
12. Raag Wadahans
13. Raag Sorat'h
14. Raag Dhanaasaree
15. Raag Jaitsree
16. Raag Todee
17. Raag Bairaaree
18. Raag Tilang
19. Raag Soohee
20. Raag Bilaaval
21. Raag Gond
22. Raag Raamkalee
23. Raag Nat Naaraayan

24. Raag Maale Gaaura
25. Raag Maaroo
26. Raag Tukhaari
27. Raag Kaydaaraa
28. Raag Bhairao
29. Raag Basant
30. Raag Saarang
31. Raag Malaar
32. Raag Kaanraa
33. Raag Kalyaan
34. Raag Prabhaatee
35. Raag Jaijaavantee
36. Shalok Sehskritee, First Mehl & Fifth Mehl
37. Fifth Mehl, Gaat'haa
38. Phunhay, Fifth Mehl
39. Chaubolas, Fifth Mehl
40. Shaloks of Devotee Kabeer Jee
41. Shaloks of Shaykh Fareed Jee
42. Swaiyas from the Mouth of the Great Fifth Mehl
43. Shaloks in addition to the Vaars
44. Shalok, Ninth Mehl
45. Mundaavanee, Fifth Mehl & Raag Maalaa

C JUP
The text of the first section of the Guru Granth Sahib, entitled, Jup, follows.

SECTION 1, JUP, PART 1
One Universal Creator God. The Name Is Truth. Creative Being Personified. No Fear. No Hatred. Image Of The Undying, Beyond Birth, Self-Existent. By Guru's Grace:
Chant And Meditate:
True In The Primal Beginning. True Throughout The Ages.
True Here And Now. O Nanak, Forever And Ever True.
By thinking, He cannot be reduced to thought, even by thinking hundreds of thousands of times.
By remaining silent, inner silence is not obtained, even by remaining lovingly absorbed deep within.
The hunger of the hungry is not appeased, even by piling up loads of worldly goods.
Hundreds of thousands of clever tricks, but not even one of them will go along with you in the end.

So how can you become truthful? And how can the veil of illusion be torn away? O Nanak, it is written that you shall obey the Hukam of His Command, and walk in the Way of His Will.
By His Command, bodies are created; His Command cannot be described.
By His Command, souls come into being; by His Command, glory and greatness are obtained.
By His Command, some are high and some are low; by His Written Command, pain and pleasure are obtained.
Some, by His Command, are blessed and forgiven; others, by His Command, wander aimlessly forever.
Everyone is subject to His Command; no one is beyond His Command.
O Nanak, one who understands His Command, does not speak in ego.
Some sing of His Power - who has that Power?
Some sing of His Gifts, and know His Sign and Insignia.
Some sing of His Glorious Virtues, Greatness and Beauty.
Some sing of knowledge obtained of Him, through difficult philosophical studies.
Some sing that He fashions the body, and then again reduces it to dust.
Some sing that He takes life away, and then again restores it.
Some sing that He seems so very far away.

SECTION 1, JUP, PART 2
Some sing that He watches over us, face to face, ever-present.
There is no shortage of those who preach and teach.
Millions upon millions offer millions of sermons and stories.
The Great Giver keeps on giving, while those who receive grow weary of receiving.
Throughout the ages, consumers consume.
The Commander, by His Command, leads us to walk on the Path.
O Nanak, He blossoms forth, Carefree and Untroubled.
True is the Master, True is His Name -

speak it with infinite love.

People beg and pray, "Give to us, give to us," and the Great Giver gives His Gifts.

So what offering can we place before Him, by which we might see the Darbaar of His Court?

What words can we speak to evoke His Love?

In the Amrit Vaylaa, the ambrosial hours before dawn, chant the True Name, and contemplate His Glorious Greatness.

By the *karma* of past actions, the robe of this physical body is obtained. By His Grace, the Gate of Liberation is found.

O Nanak, know this well: the True One Himself is All.

He cannot be established, He cannot be created.

He Himself is Immaculate and Pure.

Those who serve Him are honored.

O Nanak, sing of the Lord, the Treasure of Excellence.

Sing, and listen, and let your mind be filled with love.

Your pain shall be sent far away, and peace shall come to your home.

The Guru's Word is the Sound-current of the Naad; the Guru's Word is the Wisdom of the *Vedas*; the Guru's Word is all-pervading.

The Guru is Shiva, the Guru is Vishnu and Brahma; the Guru is Paarvati and Lakhshmi.

Even knowing God, I cannot describe Him; He cannot be described in words.

The Guru has given me this one understanding:

there is only the One, the Giver of all souls. May I never forget Him!

If I am pleasing to Him, then that is my pilgrimage and cleansing bath. Without pleasing Him, what good are ritual cleansings?

I gaze upon all the created beings: without the *karma* of good actions, what are they given to receive?

Within the mind are gems, jewels and rubies, if you listen to the Guru's Teachings, even once.

The Guru has given me this one understanding:

there is only the One, the Giver of all souls. May I never forget Him!

Even if you could live throughout the four ages, or even ten times more,

and even if you were known throughout the nine continents and followed by all, with a good name and reputation, with praise and fame throughout the world-still, if the Lord does not bless you with His Glance of Grace, then who cares? What is the use?

Among worms, you would be considered a lowly worm, and even contemptible sinners would hold you in contempt.

O Nanak, God blesses the unworthy with virtue, and bestows virtue on the virtuous. No one can even imagine anyone who can bestow virtue upon Him.

Listening - the Siddhas, the spiritual teachers, the heroic warriors, the yogic masters.

Listening - the earth, its support and the Akaashic ethers.

Listening - the oceans, the lands of the world and the nether regions of the underworld.

Listening -Death cannot even touch you.

O Nanak, the devotees are forever in bliss.

Listening - pain and sin are erased.

Listening - Shiva, Brahma and Indra.

Listening - even foul-mouthed people praise Him.

Listening - the technology of yoga and the secrets of the body.

Listening - the Shaastras, the Simritees and the *Vedas*.

O Nanak, the devotees are forever in bliss.

SECTION 1, JUP, PART 3

Listening - pain and sin are erased.

Listening - truth, contentment and spiritual wisdom.

Listening - take your cleansing bath at the sixty-eight places of pilgrimage.

Listening - reading and reciting, honor is obtained.

Listening - intuitively grasp the essence of meditation.

O Nanak, the devotees are forever in bliss.

Listening - pain and sin are erased.

Listening - dive deep into the ocean of virtue.

Listening - the Shaykhs, religious scholars, spiritual teachers and emperors.

Listening - even the blind find the Path.

Listening - the Unreachable comes within your grasp.

O Nanak, the devotees are forever in bliss.

Listening - pain and sin are erased.
The state of the faithful cannot be described.
One who tries to describe this shall regret the attempt.
No paper, no pen, no scribe
can record the state of the faithful.
Such is the Name of the Immaculate Lord.
Only one who has faith comes to know such a state of mind.
The faithful have intuitive awareness and intelligence.
The faithful know about all worlds and realms.
The faithful shall never be struck across the face.
The faithful do not have to go with the Messenger of Death.
Such is the Name of the Immaculate Lord.
Only one who has faith comes to know such a state of mind.
The path of the faithful shall never be blocked.
The faithful shall depart with honor and fame.
The faithful do not follow empty religious rituals.
The faithful are firmly bound to the *Dharma.*
Such is the Name of the Immaculate Lord.
Only one who has faith comes to know such a state of mind.
The faithful find the Door of Liberation.
The faithful uplift and redeem their family and relations.
The faithful are saved, and carried across with the Sikhs of the Guru.
The faithful, O Nanak, do not wander around begging.
Such is the Name of the Immaculate Lord.
Only one who has faith comes to know such a state of mind.
The chosen ones, the self-elect, are accepted and approved.
The chosen ones are honored in the Court of the Lord.
The chosen ones look beautiful in the

courts of kings.
The chosen ones meditate single-mindedly on the Guru.
No matter how much anyone tries to explain and describe them,
the actions of the Creator cannot be counted.
The mythical bull is *Dharma,* the son of compassion;
this is what patiently holds the earth in its place.
One who understands this becomes truthful.
What a great load there is on the bull!
So many worlds beyond this world - so very many!
What power holds them, and supports their weight?
The names and the colors of the assorted species of beings
were all inscribed by the Ever-flowing Pen of God.
Who knows how to write this account?
Just imagine what a huge scroll it would take!
What power! What fascinating beauty!
And what gifts! Who can know their extent?
You created the vast expanse of the Universe with One Word!
Hundreds of thousands of rivers began to flow.
How can Your Creative Potency be described?
I cannot even once be a sacrifice to You.
Whatever pleases You is the only good done,
You, Eternal and Formless One!
Countless meditations, countless loves.
Countless worship services, countless austere disciplines.
Countless scriptures, and ritual recitations of the *Vedas.*
Countless Yogis, whose minds remain detached from the world.

SECTION 1, JUP, PART 4
Countless devotees contemplate the Wisdom and Virtues of the Lord.
Countless the holy, countless the givers.
Countless heroic spiritual warriors, who

bear the brunt of the attack in battle (who with their mouths eat steel).

Countless silent sages, vibrating the String of His Love.

How can Your Creative Potency be described?

I cannot even once be a sacrifice to You.

Whatever pleases You is the only good done,

You, Eternal and Formless One.

Countless fools, blinded by ignorance.

Countless thieves and embezzlers.

Countless impose their will by force.

Countless cut-throats and ruthless killers.

Countless sinners who keep on sinning.

Countless liars, wandering lost in their lies.

Countless wretches, eating filth as their ration.

Countless slanderers, carrying the weight of their stupid mistakes on their heads.

Nanak describes the state of the lowly.

I cannot even once be a sacrifice to You.

Whatever pleases You is the only good done,

You, Eternal and Formless One.

Countless names, countless places.

Inaccessible, unapproachable, countless celestial realms.

Even to call them countless is to carry the weight on your head.

From the Word, comes the Naam; from the Word, comes Your Praise.

From the Word, comes spiritual wisdom, singing the Songs of Your Glory.

From the Word, come the written and spoken words and hymns.

From the Word, comes destiny, written on one's forehead.

But the One who wrote these Words of Destiny - no words are written on His Forehead.

As He ordains, so do we receive.

The created universe is the manifestation of Your Name.

Without Your Name, there is no place at all.

How can I describe Your Creative Power?

I cannot even once be a sacrifice to You.

Whatever pleases You is the only good done,

You, Eternal and Formless One.

When the hands and the feet and the body are dirty,

water can wash away the dirt.

When the clothes are soiled and stained by urine,

soap can wash them clean.

But when the intellect is stained and polluted by sin,

it can only be cleansed by the Love of the Name.

Virtue and vice do not come by mere words;

actions repeated, over and over again, are engraved on the soul.

You shall harvest what you plant.

O Nanak, by the Hukam of God's Command, we come and go in reincarnation.

Pilgrimages, austere discipline, compassion and charity

- these, by themselves, bring only an iota of merit.

Listening and believing with love and humility in your mind,

cleanse yourself with the Name, at the sacred shrine deep within.

All virtues are Yours, Lord, I have none at all.

Without virtue, there is no devotional worship.

I bow to the Lord of the World, to His Word, to Brahma the Creator.

He is Beautiful, True and Eternally Joyful.

What was that time, and what was that moment? What was that day, and what was that date?

What was that season, and what was that month, when the Universe was created?

The Pandits, the religious scholars, cannot find that time, even if it is written in the Puraanas.

That time is not known to the Qazis, who study the Koran.

The day and the date are not known to the Yogis, nor is the month or the season.

The Creator who created this creation - only He Himself knows.

How can we speak of Him? How can we praise Him? How can we describe Him? How can we know Him?

SECTION 1, JUP, PART 5

O Nanak, everyone speaks of Him, each one wiser than the rest.

Great is the Master, Great is His Name. Whatever happens is according to His Will.

O Nanak, one who claims to know everything shall not be decorated in the world hereafter.

There are nether worlds beneath nether worlds, and hundreds of thousands of heavenly worlds above.

The Vedas say that you can search and search for them all, until you grow weary. The scriptures say that there are 18,000 worlds, but in reality, there is only One Universe.

If you try to write an account of this, you will surely finish yourself before you finish writing it.

O Nanak, call Him Great! He Himself knows Himself.

The praisers praise the Lord, but they do not obtain intuitive understanding
- the streams and rivers flowing into the ocean do not know its vastness.

Even kings and emperors, with mountains of property and oceans of wealth
- these are not even equal to an ant, who does not forget God.

Endless are His Praises, endless are those who speak them.

Endless are His Actions, endless are His Gifts.

Endless is His Vision, endless is His Hearing.

His limits cannot be perceived. What is the Mystery of His Mind?

The limits of the created universe cannot be perceived.

Its limits here and beyond cannot be perceived.

Many struggle to know His limits, but His limits cannot be found.

No one can know these limits.

The more you say about them, the more there still remains to be said.

Great is the Master, High is His Heavenly Home.

Highest of the High, above all is His Name.

Only one as Great and as High as God

can know His Lofty and Exalted State.

Only He Himself is that Great. He Himself knows Himself.

O Nanak, by His Glance of Grace, He bestows His Blessings.

His Blessings are so abundant that there can be no written account of them.

The Great Giver does not hold back anything.

There are so many great, heroic warriors begging at the Door of the Infinite Lord.

So many contemplate and dwell upon Him, that they cannot be counted.

So many waste away to death engaged in corruption.

So many take and take again, and then deny receiving.

So many foolish consumers keep on consuming.

So many endure distress, deprivation and constant abuse.

Even these are Your Gifts, O Great Giver! Liberation from bondage comes only by Your Will.

No one else has any say in this.

If some fool should presume to say that he does,

he shall learn, and feel the effects of his folly.

He Himself knows, He Himself gives.

Few, very few are those who acknowledge this.

One who is blessed to sing the Praises of the Lord,

O Nanak, is the king of kings.

Priceless are His Virtues, Priceless are His Dealings.

Priceless are His Dealers, Priceless are His Treasures.

Priceless are those who come to Him, Priceless are those who buy from Him.

Priceless is Love for Him, Priceless is absorption into Him.

Priceless is the Divine Law of Dharma, Priceless is the Divine Court of Justice.

Priceless are the scales, priceless are the weights.

Priceless are His Blessings, Priceless is His Banner and Insignia.

Priceless is His Mercy, Priceless is His Royal Command.

Priceless, O Priceless beyond expression!

Speak of Him continually, and remain absorbed in His Love.

The *Vedas* and the Puraanas speak.

The scholars speak and lecture.

Brahma speaks, Indra speaks.

SECTION 1, JUP, PART 6

The Gopis and Krishna speak.

Shiva speaks, the Siddhas speak.

The many created Buddhas speak.

The demons speak, the demi-gods speak.

The spiritual warriors, the heavenly beings, the silent sages, the humble speak.

Many speak and try to describe Him.

Many have spoken of Him over and over again, and have then arisen and departed.

If He were to create as many again as there already are,

even then, they could not describe Him.

He is as Great as He wishes to be.

O Nanak, the True Lord knows.

If anyone presumes to describe God,

he shall be known as the greatest fool of fools!

Where is that Gate, and where is that Dwelling, in which You sit and take care of all?

The Sound-current of the Naad vibrates there, and countless musicians play on all sorts of instruments there.

So many Ragas, so many musicians singing there.

The praanic wind, water and fire sing; the Righteous Judge of *Dharma* sings at Your Door.

Chitr and Gupt, the angels of the conscious and the subconscious who record actions, and the Righteous Judge of Dharma who judges this record sing.

Shiva, Brahma and the Goddess of Beauty, ever adorned, sing.

Indra, seated upon His Throne, sings with the deities at Your Door.

The Siddhas in Samaadhi sing; the Saadhus sing in contemplation.

The celibates, the fanatics, the peacefully accepting and the fearless warriors sing.

The Pandits, the religious scholars who recite the *Vedas*, with the supreme sages of all the ages, sing.

The Mohinis, the enchanting heavenly beauties who entice hearts in this world, in paradise, and in the underworld of the subconscious sing.

The celestial jewels created by You, and the sixty-eight holy places of pilgrimage sing.

The brave and mighty warriors sing; the spiritual heroes and the four sources of creation sing.

The planets, solar systems and galaxies, created and arranged by Your Hand, sing.

They alone sing, who are pleasing to Your Will. Your devotees are imbued with the Nectar of Your Essence.

So many others sing, they do not come to mind. O Nanak, how can I consider them all?

That True Lord is True, Forever True, and True is His Name.

He is, and shall always be. He shall not depart, even when this Universe which He has created departs.

He created the world, with its various colors, species of beings, and the variety of Maya.

Having created the creation, He watches over it Himself, by His Greatness.

He does whatever He pleases. No order can be issued to Him.

He is the King, the King of kings, the Supreme Lord and Master of kings. Nanak remains subject to His Will.

Make contentment your ear-rings, humility your begging bowl, and meditation the ashes you apply to your body.

Let the remembrance of death be the patched coat you wear, let the purity of virginity be your way in the world, and let faith in the Lord be your walking stick.

See the brotherhood of all mankind as the highest order of Yogis; conquer your own mind, and conquer the world.

I bow to Him, I humbly bow.

The Primal One, the Pure Light, without beginning, without end. Throughout all the ages, He is One and the Same.

Let spiritual wisdom be your food, and compassion your attendant. The Sound-current of the Naad vibrates in each and every heart.

He Himself is the Supreme Master of all; wealth and miraculous spiritual powers, and all other external tastes and pleasures, are all like beads on a string.

Union with Him, and separation from Him, come by His Will. We come to receive what is written in our destiny.

SECTION 1, JUP, PART 7

I bow to Him, I humbly bow.

The Primal One, the Pure Light, without beginning, without end. Throughout all the ages, He is One and the Same.

The One Divine Mother conceived and gave birth to the three deities.

One, the Creator of the World; One, the Sustainer; and One, the Destroyer.

He makes things happen according to the Pleasure of His Will. Such is His Celestial Order.

He watches over all, but none see Him. How wonderful this is!

I bow to Him, I humbly bow.

The Primal One, the Pure Light, without beginning, without end. Throughout all the ages, He is One and the Same.

On world after world are His Seats of Authority and His Storehouses.

Whatever was put into them, was put there once and for all.

Having created the creation, the Creator Lord watches over it.

O Nanak, True is the Creation of the True Lord.

I bow to Him, I humbly bow.

The Primal One, the Pure Light, without beginning, without end. Throughout all the ages, He is One and the Same.

If I had 100,000 tongues, and these were then multiplied twenty times more, with each tongue,

I would repeat, hundreds of thousands of times, the Name of the One, the Lord of the Universe.

Along this path to our Husband Lord, we climb the steps of the ladder, and come to merge with Him.

Hearing of the etheric realms, even worms long to come back home.

O Nanak, by His Grace He is obtained. False are the boastings of the false.

No power to speak, no power to keep silent.

No power to beg, no power to give.

No power to live, no power to die.

No power to rule, with wealth and occult mental powers.

No power to gain intuitive understanding, spiritual wisdom and meditation.

No power to find the way to escape from the world.

He alone has the Power in His Hands. He watches over all.

O Nanak, no one is high or low.

Nights, days, weeks and seasons; wind, water, fire and the nether regions in the midst of these, He established the earth as a home for Dharma.

Upon it, He placed the various species of beings.

Their names are uncounted and endless.

By their deeds and their actions, they shall be judged.

God Himself is True, and True is His Court.

There, in perfect grace and ease, sit the self-elect, the self-realized Saints.

They receive the Mark of Grace from the Merciful Lord.

The ripe and the unripe, the good and the bad, shall there be judged.

O Nanak, when you go home, you will see this.

This is righteous living in the realm of Dharma.

And now we speak of the realm of spiritual wisdom.

So many winds, waters and fires; so many Krishnas and Shivas.

So many Brahmas, fashioning forms of great beauty, adorned and dressed in many colors.

So many worlds and lands for working out karma. So very many lessons to be learned!

So many Indras, so many moons and suns, so many worlds and lands.

So many Siddhas and Buddhas, so many Yogic masters. So many goddesses of various kinds.

So many demi-gods and demons, so many silent sages. So many oceans of jewels.

So many ways of life, so many languages.
So many dynasties of rulers.
So many intuitive people, so many selfless servants. O Nanak, His limit has no limit!
In the realm of wisdom, spiritual wisdom reigns supreme.

The Sound-current of the Naad vibrates there, amidst the sounds and the sights of bliss.

4 FACTS AND FIGURES

A Geographical location of Sikhs
B Large national Sikh populations
C Sikh names

INTRODUCTION
There are over 25 million Sikhs in the world, making it the fifth largest world religion. Sikhism is the youngest of the great world faiths.

A GEOGRAPHICAL LOCATION OF SIKHS
Most Sikhs live on the sub-continent of India, with the majority living in their homeland, the state of Punjab in northern India. The Punjab is the home of more than 80% of India's 20 million Sikhs.

B LARGE INTERNATIONAL SIKH POPULATIONS

United Kingdom	500,000
Canada	350,000
USA	150,000
Malaysia	60,000
Singapore	25,000

C SIKH NAMES
Traditional Sikh names normally end in the suffixes:

- "inder," as in Rajinder, Jatinder and Sukhinder.
- "pal," as in Kirnpal, Pritpal and Rajpal.
- "deep," as in Kirndeep, Jasdeep and Mandeep.
- "preet," as in Harpreet, Jaspreet and Sukhpreet.

The tenth Guru founded the *Khalsa* (Pure) community. Its members took on the extra name of Singh (Lion), and Kaur (Lioness or Princess). This has remained the principal Sikh order to this day (see on next page).

5 SIKH PRACTICES

A   No rituals
B   No retreats, no fasting
C   Equality
D   Rejection of castes
E   The *Khalsa*
F   The *Amrit* ceremony
G   Singh and Kaur
H   The five Ks
I   Serving God
J   Sikh dress

A NO RITUALS

- Sikhs do not perform rituals in their religious lives.
- They do not go on pilgrimages.
- They do not build statues, or worship or bow down to statues.
- They seek to avoid all superstitious behavior.

The world is in agony because of the filth of ego, the word is filthy because of duality; The filth of ego cannot be washed away, even if one bathes at one hundred holy places.

Guru Amar Das, Sri Raga

They go to holy places for a bath, Their minds are impure and bodies are like thieves; if by bath their dirt drops down, they got on themselves twice as much dirt and ego.

Guru Nanak, Var Suhi

Whosoever controls the mind, he is a pilgrim.

Guru Arjan Dev, Maru Solhe

B NO RETREATS, NO FASTING

Sikhs have no monks, nuns, or hermits. They believe in living out their religion in the world.

Let good conduct be thy fasting.

Guru Nanak, Var Majh

Only fools argue whether to eat meat or not. They don't understand truth nor do they meditate on it. Who can define what is meat and what is plant? Who knows where the sin lies, being a vegetarian or a non vegetarian?

Guru Nanak, Var Malar

The way to true yoga is found by dwelling in God and remaining detached in the midst of worldly attachments.

Guru Nanak, Suhi

C EQUALITY

Sikhism recognizes the equality of men and women in all spheres of life. The Gurus rejected female infanticide, *sati* (wife burning) and they permitted widows to remarry. They also rejected the purdah (women wearing veils).

We are born of woman, we are conceived in the womb of woman, we are engaged and married to woman. We make friendships with woman and the lineage continued because of woman. When one woman dies, we take another one, we are bound with the world through woman. Why should we talk ill of her, who gives birth to kings? The woman is born from woman; there is none without her. Only the One True Lord is without woman.

Guru Nanak, Var Asa

They cannot be called *satis*, who burn themselves with their dead husbands. They can only be called satis, if they bear the shock of separation. They may also be known as satis, who live with character and contentment and always show veneration to their husbands by remembering them.

Guru Amar Das, Var Suhi

D REJECTION OF CASTES

All are created from the seed of God. There is the same clay in the whole world, the potter [God] makes many kinds of pots.

Guru Amar Das, Bhairo

Recognize the light [of God] and do not ask for the caste, There is no caste in the next world.

Guru Nanak, Asa

E THE KHALSA

The word *Khalsa* means both "pure" and "belonging only to God." The *Khalsa* was created by the tenth master, Guru Gobind Singh Ji on Vaisakhi Day 1699. The *Amrit* ceremony is an initiation bringing Sikhs into membership of this spiritual order.

I have made this body and mind a sacrifice, a sacrificial offering to the Lord. Dedicating my body and mind, I have crossed over the terrifying world-ocean, and shaken off the fear of death.

Guru Arjan Dev, Chant, *pg. 576*

F THE AMRIT CEREMONY

Sikhs who have been through the *Amrit* Ceremony of initiation become *Amrit-dhari*, that is, initiated.

The *Amrit* ceremony takes place in a *gurdwara*, in front of the Guru Granth Sahib. Five initiated Sikhs need to be present as they represent the Panj Piyaras, the first five Sikhs who were initiated.

The *Khalsa* baptism ceremony involves drinking *amrit* (sugar water stirred with a dagger). The initiate is instructed in the following *Khalsa* Code of Conduct:

- You shall never remove any hair from any part of your body.
- You shall not use tobacco, alcohol or any other intoxicants.
- You shall not eat the meat of an animal slaughtered the Muslim way.
- You shall not commit adultery.

The initiated then assume new names, and begin to wear the five Ks.

G SINGH AND KAUR
- *Khalsa* Sikh men adopt the name "Singh," meaning lion.
- *Khalsa* Sikh women adopt the name "Kaur," meaning princess.

H THE FIVE KS
The five Ks are five symbolic tokens of Sikhism. They are worn by Sikhs who have been newly initiated into the *Khalsa*. The five Ks are:

- *Kesh* (uncut hair)
- *Kara* (a steel bracelet)
- *Kangha* (a wooden comb)
- *Kaccha* (cotton underwear)
- *Kirpan* (sword)

The five Ks symbolize a life of dedication to the Guru.

KESH (UNCUT HAIR)
As hair is part of God's creation, keeping it uncut is seen as a mark of respect to God as one accepts his gift.

Sikh women are not allowed to cut any body hair. This means that they are even forbidden to trim their eyebrows. Sikh men are not allowed to trim their beards.

KARA (A STEEL BRACELET)
This symbol of restraint reminds Sikhs not to do anything that would displease the Guru.

KANGHA (A WOODEN COMB)
The *Kangha*, which is used to keep uncut hair neat and tidy, symbolizes a pure mind as well as a clean body.

KACCHA (COTTON UNDERWEAR)
Kaccha are a special, slightly longer than usual, type of underwear and are symbolic of continence and a high moral character.

KIRPAN (SWORD)
This ceremonial sword is used in the initiation ceremony to stir the mixture of sugar and water that the initiate must drink.

All baptized Sikhs should wear a short form of *Kirpan* (approximately 6 inches to 9 inches long). It is a symbol of a Sikhs' commitment to protect the weak and to promote justice.

I SERVING GOD
Sikhs believe that they serve God by serving (*seva*) others. As they devote themselves to the service of others, so they eliminate their own ego and pride.

THREE DUTIES TO PERFORM
Sikhs must:

* pray
* work
* give

Nam japna (Prayer)
Praying involves keeping God in one's mind all the time.

Kirt Karna (Work)
Sikhs have high moral standards and always seek to earn an honest living.

They avoid gambling, begging, or working in the alcohol or tobacco industries.

Vand Chhakna (Giving)
Vand Chhakna means sharing one's earnings with others. Sikhs make a priority of giving to charity and caring for others.

FIVE VICES TO AVOID
In their quest to avoid the following five vices, Sikhs are attempting to curtail their own self-centeredness as they strive to knock down all the barriers in their own lives that separate them from God.

The five vices are:

* lust (*Kam*)
* covetousness and greed (*Lobh*)
* attachment to things of this world (*Moh*)
* anger (*Krodh*)
* pride (*Ahankar*).

If one can overcome these five vices, one will achieve salvation.

> Five thieves who live within this body are lust, anger, greed, attachment and ego. They rob us of ambrosia, but the egocentrics do not understand it and no one listens to their cries.
>
> *Guru Amar Das,* Sorath

> I am in the Refuge of the Lord; Bless me, O Lord with your Grace, so that the lust, anger, greed, attachment and ego may be destroyed.
>
> *Guru Arjan Dev,* Gauri Sukhmani

J SIKH DRESS
FEMALE
The traditional dress of a Sikh is a *salwaar kameez* - a loose fitting top and bottoms - with a *chunni* (a large rectangular piece of cloth) which covers the head and is draped around the shoulders. This traditional dress is also worn by others from the Indian subcontinent. Therefore the most obvious sign of a Sikh is unshorn hair kept in a bun or plaits, the other being the *kara* (the steel bracelet which forms part of the five Ks) worn on the left wrist.

Amrit-dhari Sikhs, those who have been baptized by partaking in the *Amrit* ceremony and who are therefore members of the brotherhood of the *Khalsa*, may also wear a *Kasekee* (small turban).

MALE
Amrit-dhari
Amrit-dhari wear full beard and turban and a *kara* on the right wrist. Older Sikhs may wear the traditional Kurta Pyjama - loose fitting white cotton clothing.

Sehaj-dhari (slow learners)
Sehaj-dhari may wear a turban with stubble

rather than a full beard, or may not wear a turban and be clean shaven, or have a combination of the above. Most still wear the *kara* on their wrist.

TURBAN: AFRICAN STYLE
Pointed apex at the front. This style, started by Sikhs living in Kenya and Uganda, is now favored by the young.

TURBAN: INDIAN STYLE
Blunt rounded apex at the front. The style of the Sikhs of India.

TURBAN: TRADITIONAL STYLE
A very rounded style. This style is favored by orthodox Sikhs and by spiritually enlightened souls.

TURBAN COLOR
White: favored by older Sikhs.
Black: favored by the younger generation.
Saffron: the traditional color of the Sikhs.
Red: normally worn by the groom at the *Anand Karaj* (wedding) ceremony.
Other colors have no significance.

---

6 SIKH BELIEFS

A Creator God
B Contemplation on the Name
C Truth
D Seeking God
E The cycle of life

A CREATOR GOD
Sikhs believe that there is only one God. He is the creator, and sustainer of all life.

> You are the Creator, O Lord, the Unknowable. You created the Universe of diverse kinds, colors and qualities. You know your own Creation. All this is your Play.
>
> *Guru Nanak,* Var Majh

> The Formless Supreme Being abides in the Realm of Eternity. Over His creation He casts His glance of grace. In that Realm are contained all the continents and the universes, Exceeding in number all count. Of creation worlds upon worlds abide therein; All obedient to His will; He watches over them in bliss, And has each constantly in mind.
>
> *Guru Nanak,* Japji

B CONTEMPLATION ON THE NAME
Contemplation and meditation are important

aspects of the Sikh religion.

> Without devotion to the Name Divine is birth in the world gone waste. Such consume poison, poisonous their utterance; Without devotion to the Name, without gain they die, and after death in transmigration wander.
>
> *Guru Nanak,* Raga Bhairon

> True life is life in God, contemplation on the Name and the society of the saints.
>
> *Guru Arjan Dev,* Dhanasari

> The disciple of the True Guru (God) dwells upon the Lord through the teaching of the Guru and all his sins are washed away.
>
> *Guru Ram Das,* Var Gauri

C TRUTH
> Realization of Truth is higher than all else. Higher still is Truthful Living.
>
> *Guru Nanak,* Sri Rag

UNDERSTANDING TRUTH

Though Sikhs do not think it is possible to fully comprehend God, they believe that it is possible to experience him through love, worship, and contemplation.

In their quest to find spiritual freedom and union with God, Sikhs search for God inside themselves and in the world at large.

D SEEKING GOD

Sikhs believe that God is inside every person, no matter how wicked that person may appear to be, and so everyone is capable of change.

E THE CYCLE OF LIFE

In common with Hinduism, Buddhism and Jainism, Sikhs believe that all human beings are trapped in a cycle of birth, life, and rebirth.

Everyone's quality of life is dependant on the law of *karma*. So one's present station in life is the result of how one lived one's previous life.

The way to break out of this cycle is through complete knowledge of God and union with him. Sikhs' religious devotions all have this goal in mind. All Sikhs strive to become one with God. To achieve this state, known as *mukti* (liberation) one needs God's help and grace.

7 SIKH WORSHIP

A Personal worship
B Public worship
C The *gurdwara*
D Visiting a *gurdwara*
E Sikh festivals

INTRODUCTION

Sikhs worship God and only God. They seek to worship God in his true abstract form, but never use images or statues to help them.

A PERSONAL WORSHIP

Sikhs take part in *naam-simram*, the devotional practice of meditating on the divine Name.

Sikhs pray anywhere and at any time. They get up early, bathe, and begin their day by meditating on God. They think of prayer as spending time in the company of God.

The praising of His Name is the highest of all practices. It has uplifted many a human soul. It slakes the desire of restless mind. It imparts an all-seeing vision.
Guru Arjan

Daily devotion, remembering God, is the key to Sikh devotion.

Meditation of the Lord is the highest of the deeds,
through which myriads obtain release,
through which the thirst (of desires) is quenched,
through which one becomes all knowing,
through which the fear of death goes away,
through which all the desires are fulfilled,
through which the dirt of the mind is cleansed
and the Nectar of the Name of God is absorbed in the mind.
Guru Nanak, Gauri Sukhmani

B PUBLIC WORSHIP

Sikhs believe that God becomes visible in the

Sikh congregation (*sangat*). So worshiping with other Sikhs and serving the *sangat* is thought to be pleasing to God.

C THE GURDWARA

> (i)   The Golden Temple
> (ii) The four doors
> (ii) No statues
> (iv) No priests
> (v)   The Guru in the *gurdwara*
> (vi) Seating in a *gurdwara*
> (vii) A light

INTRODUCTION
The building which houses the Guru Granth Sahib is called a *gurdwara* and all Sikhs acknowledge the sanctity that the scriptures confer it.

A *gurdwara* (to a non-Sikh a *gurdwara* may appear to be similar to a temple, but in the eyes of a Sikh it is definitely not a temple) is the building in which Sikhs come together for congregational worship. In Punjabi the word *gurdwara* means the residence of the Guru, or the door that leads to the Guru, that is, the gateway to the Guru.

The first *gurdwara* was built by Guru Nanak in 1521-1522 at Kartarpur.

(I) THE GOLDEN TEMPLE
The magnificent Golden Temple at Amritsar, known as God's Temple, was built by Guru Arjan, the fifth Guru, and was completed in 1604. Here Arjan installed the sacred hymns of the early Gurus, and other non-Sikh mystics, which he had collected together (the Guru Granth). Today these hymns are sung in the Golden Temple from morning to night.

For Sikhs, the Golden Temple is a most sacred *gurdwara*, and a symbol of their religion. They regard it as *Darbar Sahib* (the court of the Lord). However, while it is the inspirational and historical center of Sikhism, Sikhs are not bound to make a pilgrimage to it. All places where the Guru Granth are installed are considered equally holy.

(II) THE FOUR DOORS
Unlike Muslim and Hindu shrines, which have one door, every *gurdwara* has four doors:
- the Door of Peace
- the Door of Livelihood
- the Door of Learning
- the Door of Grace

The doors represent the four points of the compass, and symbolize the openness of the Sikh faith to all people.

(III) NO STATUES
Sikhs do not believe that God has any physical form. So *gurdwara* do not have any idols, statues, or religious pictures. There are no icons or images to help in one's worship. Gurdwara have no candles, incense, or bells.

(IV) NO PRIESTS
Sikhs do not have the equivalent of ordained priests or full-time ministers. Sikh public worship can be led by any competent Sikh, male or female.

Each *gurdwara* has a Granthi who organizes the daily services and reads from the Guru Granth Sahib. A Granthi is not a priest but is the reader/custodian of the *Adi Granth* (the Guru Granth Sahib).

(V) THE GURU IN THE GURDWARA
In a *gurdwara* the Guru is not a person, but a book. This book is the Sikh scriptures, the Guru Granth Sahib. It is the presence of the Guru Granth Sahib that gives the *gurdwara* its religious status.

The only object of reverence in the main hall of a *gurdwara* is the Guru Granth Sahib. It is revered as if it were a human Guru. However, although Sikhs appear to be showing reverence to the Guru Granth Sahib, they are really showing their reverence to its spiritual content (*shabad*). The Guru Granth Sahib is a visible manifestation of the *shabad*.

Sikhs bow to the Guru Granth Sahib as they enter a *gurdwara*, touching the floor with their forehead. This indicates their willingness to submit themselves to the truths the Guru Granth Sahib.

Worshiping Sikhs also place a gift of money or a food offering in front of the Guru Granth Sahib.

The Guru Granth Sahib rests on a raised

platform (the *takht* or *manji sahib*, meaning "throne") under a canopy (*chanani* or *palki*), and when not being read it is covered with an expensive cloth.

(VI) SEATING IN A GURDWARA
Everyone sits on the floor, usually in the cross-legged position. No one sits with their feet pointing at the Guru Granth Sahib, as that would be a sign of disrespect.

(VII) A LIGHT
A light always shines in a *gurdwara*, indicating that the Guru's light is available to everyone all the time.

D VISITING A GURDWARA
Do not go into a *gurdwara* if you have recently drunk any alcohol or if you have any cigarettes or tobacco on you.

Before entering the *darbar* (the main hall), remove your shoes and cover your head. Heads can be covered with a hat or material shaped like a handkerchief which is available from the *gurdwara*.

All visitors to a *gurdwara*, regardless of position or caste, are served a free meal, from food cooked on the premises.

E SIKH FESTIVALS

(i) Vaisakhi Gurpurbs
(ii) Gurpurbs
(iii) Divali

(I) VAISAKHI (BAISAKHI)
Vaisakhi, celebrated on April 13 or 14, is the Sikh New Year festival. It also recalls the anniversary of the founding of the *Khalsa* on sakhi 1699 by the tenth Guru, Guru Gobind Singh.

(II) GURPURBS
Gurpurbs are the Sikh festivals linked to the lives of the Gurus. The most celebrated Gurpurbs are:

• The birthday of Guru Nanak, in November.
• The birthday of Guru Gobind Singh, in January.
• The martyrdom of Guru Arjan, in June.
• The martyrdom of Guru Tegh Bahadur, in November/December.

Sikhs celebrate Gurpurbs with an *akhand path*. This is an uninterrupted, complete reading of the Guru Granth Sahib. This takes forty-eight hours and finishes on the day of the festival. The reading is undertaken by a team of readers, each reading for between two to three hours.

(III) DIVALI
Divali, the Festival of Light, a festival also celebrated by Hindus, takes place at the end of October or early November.

8 SIKH GROUPS

A *Amrit-dhari* Sikhs
B *Kes-dhari* Sikhs
C *Sahaj-dhari* Sikhs

A AMRIT-DHARI SIKHS

Sikhs who have undergone initiation are known as *amrit-dhari* Sikhs.

B KES-DHARI SIKHS

If they have not been initiated but still accept at least the fundamentals of the Rahit Sikhs they are regarded as *kes-dhari* Sikhs. Acceptance must include the ban on cutting hair.

C SAHAJ-DHARI SIKHS

Those Sikhs who are not *kes-dhari* and who do not follow the Rahit are known as *sahaj-dhari* Sikhs, slow learners.

9 COMPARISON OF SIKHISM WITH HINDUISM AND CHRISTIANITY

A Sikhs and Hinduism
B Sikhs and Christianity

A SIKHS AND HINDUISM

Sikhs reject the claim that they are a type of Hinduism.

There are four castes of Hindus and four sects of Muslims in the world. The members of both religions are selfish, jealous, proud, bigoted and violent. The Hindus make pilgrimage to Hardvar and Banaras, the Muslim to the Kaaba of Mecca. Circumcision is dear to the Muslims, sandal mark (*tilak*) and sacred thread to the Hindus. The Hindus invoke Ram, the Muslims, Rahim, but in reality there is only One God. Since they have forgotten the *Vedas* and the *Katebas*, worldly greed and the devil have led them astray. Truth hidden from both; the Brahmins and Maulvis kill one another by their animosities. Neither sect shall find liberation from transmigration.

Guru Nanak

You may bathe and wash, and apply a ritualistic tilak mark to your forehead, but without inner purity, there is no understanding.

Guru Nanak, Raag Raamkalee

B SIKHS AND CHRISTIANITY

(i) Belief about God
(ii) Belief about humanity
(iii) Belief about salvation

(I) BELIEF ABOUT GOD

Sikhism: holds that there is no Trinity. God is the abstract principle of truth. God never became a man. Sikhs do not believe in the incarnation.

The Bible: God has revealed himself as Father, Son, and Holy Spirit.

The incarnation of Jesus Christ points to his unique role as Savior and Lord. (See John 1:1-14; 3:16.)

(II) BELIEF ABOUT HUMANITY

Sikhism: Everyone is caught up in the process of the transmigration of the soul, which involves the endless cycle of birth, death, and rebirth (reincarnation). The aim of Sikhism is to break this cycle.

The Bible: There is no such thing as reincarnation. We have only one life. Everyone has to be judged by God (John 3:16; Hebrews 9:27).

(III) BELIEF ABOUT SALVATION

Sikhism: Liberation from the cycle of birth and rebirth and union with God is achieved by being devoted to God.

The Bible: Our future state is not dependant on our *karma*, but whether we accept or reject Jesus Christ as our Savior and Lord. (See Ephesians 2:1-10; 1 Thessalonians 4:13-18; Revelation 21:1-7).

10 GLOSSARY

Adi Granth
Guru Granth Sahib, the sacred scripture of the Sikhs as compiled by the fifth Guru, Guru Arjan, in 1603-1604. It is the eternal Guru, and the central focus of the home, and community.

Akal Purkh
"The One beyond Time," God.

Akal Takhat
The principle seat of authority for the Sikhs where decisions are made concerning the life of the community. Built by the sixth Guru, it is a building with a golden roof immediately adjacent to the Golden Temple.

Akhand path
Unbroken reading of the Guru Granth Sahib.

Amrit
Nectar of immortality. Sweetened baptismal water used in *Amrit sanskar.*

Amrit-dhari
A Sikh who has "taken *amrit*," that is, has become an initiated member of the *Khalsa.*

Amrit sanskar
The initiation ceremony of the *Khalsa.*

Anand Karaj
The Sikh marriage ceremony.

Ardas
The *Khalsa* prayer, a formal prayer recited at the conclusion of most Sikh ceremonies.

Baba
"Father," a term of respect applied to holy men.

Baisakhi
Birth of the *Khalsa*, New Year's day in rural Punjab, the first day of the month of *Baisakh*, normally April 13.

Bani
Works of the Gurus and other poets in the sacred text of Guru Granth Sahib.

Bhagat
A contributor to the Guru Granth Sahib who was not a Guru, for example, Bhagat Kabir, Ramanand, Sheikh Farid, Ravidas, Pipa and Dhanna.

Bhakti
Belief in, adoration of, a personal God.

Bhog
The ceremony which concludes a complete reading of Guru Granth Sahib.

Chaunki
A division of each day in the larger *gurdwaras*, in which a particular selection of *bani* is sung. There are five *chaunkies* in each day.

Dharamsala
Place of worship for the early Sikh Panth, later known as a *gurdwara*.

Five Ks
Five items, each beginning with the intial k, which Sikhs of the *Khalsa* must wear. These are the *kesh, kangha, kaccha, kara* and *kirpan*.

Granth
The sacred volume, the *Adi Granth* (Guru Granth Sahib). It can be used for all sacred scriptures. The Dasam Granth is a collection of hymns made by the tenth Guru.

Granthi
Custodian of the *gurdwara.*

Gurdwara
This is from *gur* (Guru) and *dwar* (house of) and means "the house of God" or Sikh place of worship, sometimes wrongly referred to as a Sikh temple.

Gurmat
The teachings of the Gurus.

Gurmukhi
"From the Guru's mouth," the script in which Punjabi is written.

Guru
A spiritual teacher. In Sikhism, the term "Guru" refers to the ten Gurus and Guru Granth Sahib, and no other.

Guru Granth Sahib
The sacred scriptures of the Sikhs.

Harmandar
Sahib "Hari's mandir," The Golden Temple or *Darbar Sahib* ("The Court of the Lord") complex at Amritsar.

Haumain
Self-centeredness, ego, pride. According to Sikhism, the most deadly of the five sins. The power of pride is destroyed by praising the Name of God.

Hukam
Divine order, a passage from Guru Granth Sahib chosen at random.

Hukam-nama
"Letter of command," document containing a command issued by one of the Gurus to an individual or *sangat*, a similar document issued to the Panth by the Sarbat Khalsa from Akal Takhat.

Ik onkar
"There is One God," benedictory formula from Guru Granth Sahib.

Jura
Tying of long hair into a knot on one's head, over which a turban is tied.

Kachha
Pair of breeches worn as part of the five Ks.

Kangha
Wooden comb, worn as part of the five Ks.

Kara
Steel wrist ring, worn as part of the five Ks.

Kesh
Uncut hair, worn as part of the five Ks.

Khalsa
The religious order established by Guru Gobind Singh.

Khanda
Double-edged sword: a *Khalsa* symbol comprising a vertical double edged sword over a quoit with two crossed kirpans.

Khande da pahul
"Initiation with the two-edged sword," the Khalsa initiation ceremony.

Kirpan
Sword, worn as part of the five Ks.

Kurahit
One of the four cardinal infringements of the Rahit. These are: cutting one's hair, consuming meat, extra-marital intercourse and smoking.

Langar
The kitchen attached to every *gurdwara* from which food is served to all regardless of creed or caste.

Mantra
A verse, phrase or syllable of particular religious import.

Moksha
Spiritual liberation, liberation from transmigration.

Naam
The divine Name, a summary term expressing the total being of Akal Purkh.

Nam jap
Devoutly repeating the divine Name.

Naam simran
The devotional practice of meditating on the divine Name.

Nitname
The Sikh daily liturgy.

Paath
A reading from the Sikh scriptures.

Panth
A "path" or "way;" system of religious belief or practice; the Sikh community.

Prasad
Sacramentally offered food.

Ramala
A cloth covering Guru Granth Sahib.

Sangat
Congregation, group of devotees.

Sant
One who knows the truth, a pious person, term used for a holy man, sadhu.

Sant-sipahi
A "Saint-soldier," the ideal Sikh, the Sikh who combines the piety of a saint and the bravery of a warrior.

Sat
Truth; true.

Satnaam
Name of Truth

Satsang
An assembly of true believers; congregation.

Sewa
Service, commonly done at a *gurdwara*. Service is important to Sikhs. It is the expression of loving devotion to God.

Vaak
"Saying;" a passage from Guru Granth Sahib, chosen at random.

Varna
The classical caste hierarchy. The four sections being Brahmin, Kshatriya, Vaisha and Shudra.

Waheguru
"Praise to the Guru," the Sikh name for God.

TAOISM

CONTENTS

1 An overview   289

2 Taoism's founder   290

3 Taoist holy book   291

4 Facts and figures   316

5 Taoist practices   317

6 Taoist beliefs   318

7 Worship   319

8 Comparison with Christianity   321

9 Glossary   322

1 AN OVERVIEW

DEFINITION

Taoism (or Daoism) is an ancient Chinese philosophy based on the Tao. Aspects of this philosophy developed into a religion. Tao (pronounced "Dow") is roughly translated into English as "path," or "the way."

Factfile
- Date of origin: sixth century BC
- Founder: Lao-tzu
- Holy book: *Tao-te-ching*
- Number of adherents: More than 20 million; depending on definitions, could be several factors of 10 more than that

SUMMARY

Taoism is an alternative to the Confucian tradition in China.

Classical Taoism is a "Way" of life. The Tao is a River. It is the natural order of things. It is a force that flows through every living and sentient object, as well as through the entire universe, a power that envelops, surrounds and flows through all things, living and non-living. It is thus not so much a set of beliefs as something that has to be experienced.

In a nutshell, Taoism is the consolidation of a number of concepts and practices that make up the "Path," or "Way," of living. The consolidation of ideas and concepts include basic principles or "theories" regarding the body, diet, breathing and physical exercises, uses of herbs, philosophical inquiry and, of course, meditation. All of which the Taoist feels brings a human being into closer alignment with the "natural order" of life and living - a pathway that humankind appears to have gotten derailed from."

Madelyn Hamilton
The Search For Tao

Lao-tzu, in the *Tao-te-ching,* gives the following traditional definition of Taoism:

The Tao that can be named is not the eternal Tao.
The Name that can be named is not the eternal name.
The nameless is the beginning of Heaven and Earth.
The named is the mother of all things.

Lao-tzu

Tao is not God, but rather a force. It flows through the entire world, and we're all affected by it, even if we do not realize it.

Taoism as a religion developed in the second century AD. The basic text of both philosophical and religious Tao is the *Tao-te-ching.*

SUMMARY OF PRACTICES

Taoism advocates a simple honest life and non-interference with the course of natural events. Its main precepts are loyalty and filial piety. In practice, it calls on its faithful to:

- respect heaven
- honor ancestors

• be compassionate to everyone and all things under heaven.

Though without being fully conscious of what they are doing, many people have accepted some aspects of Taoism into their homes with *feng shui*, into their athletic lives with *taijiquan*, and into their medical and health care with acupuncture.

SUMMARY OF BELIEFS

The essential message of Taoism is that the universe is governed by a set of natural and unalterable laws that manifest themselves as a flow of continuous change. This natural order and flow is referred to as the Tao. By recognizing and aligning ourselves with these laws, we can achieve harmony with the forces inherent in the cosmos - the transcendent Tao.

2 TAOISM'S FOUNDERS

A Lao-tzu
B Chuang-tzu
C Chang Tao-ling
D A state religion

INTRODUCTION

The primary figures in Taoism are Lao-tzu and Chuang-tzu, two scholars who dedicated their lives to balancing their inner spirits. Taoism began as a philosophy and a way of life, but some aspects of it were developed into a religion, with gods, temples, and religious rites. The ultimate aim, however, of unity with the Tao, remained the same.

A LAO-TZU (MASTER LAO, OLD MASTER, "GRAND OLD MASTER")

Lao-tzu (Lao Tsu, Lao Tse, Laotse, Laotzu, Lao Zi, Laozi, Lao-tse), 604-531 BC, was the founder of Taoism. Nothing is known for certain about his life, although his oldest biographer (c. 100 BC) claims that he held official rank as the curator of the archives at the court of the Chyou dynasty. He is supposed to have sought to avoid the constant feudal warfare and other conflicts that disrupted society during his lifetime. Taoist tradition attributes the writing of *Tao-te-ching* (also called the *Lao-tzu)* to Lao-tzu.

Lao-tzu is looked upon as the first philosopher

of the Taoist school. His writings teach the philosophy of the Tao, or the Way, which is the reality that naturally exists prior to, and gives rise to, all other things, including the physical universe and everything in it. *ch'i*, which means "virtue," is the life energy in things and a sense of morality, which constitutes the Way. The Tao can be found by experiencing the oneness in all things, oneness with nature and oneness with one's inner self. Lao-tzu taught a simple, natural philosophy of social harmony.

B CHUANG-TZU

Chuang-tzu (c. 360-c. 275 BC) is the second of the major founders of the Tao movement. The book that bears his name was influential in the development of Taoist thought. It presents a philosophy for individuals, who are advised to opt out of society and pursue spontaneity, freedom and a natural-mystical approach as ways of dealing with the chaos found within society. Discarding conventional values, freeing oneself from worldly attachments and goals, and following a mystical, esoteric approach is Chuang-tzu's theme.

C CHANG TAO-LING

Chang Tao-ling (AD 142), an exorcist and founder of the Five Pecks of Rice movement, established a mystical/religious healing school of thought. Today, most Taoist priests take Chang Tao-ling as their main inspiration.

D STATE RELIGION

Taoism, one of the three great religions of China (the other two are Buddhism and Confucianism), became a state religion in China in 440 AD.

During the Ming dynasty (1369-1644) there was much cross-fertilization between these three religions. Lin Chao-en (1517-1598) sought to combine the best of Tao, Buddhist and Confucian thinking.

At the close of the Ch'ing Dynasty in 1911, state support for Taoism ended and much of its heritage was attacked under the war lords who followed. When Communism took over China in 1949, much of the remaining Taoist heritage was threatened with extinction.

However, Taoism is an integral part of Chinese culture, and will never be destroyed.

3 TAOIST HOLY BOOK

A   *I Ching*
B   *Tao-te-ching*
C   Taoist quotations

A I CHING

The original source of Taoism is said to be the *I Ching*. The *I Ching* is an ancient Chinese oracle that gives insight by providing an Oriental philosophical perspective on situations and problems.

"*I*" means change. "*Ching*" means book. Therefore *I Ching* means "The Book of Changes."

The *I Ching* is both a book and a method of divination and is one of the first efforts of human beings to grasp their relationship to nature and society.

- The *I Ching* is a book of wisdom that illustrates correct and balanced action in a multitude of situations.
- It is a chart of changes. The basis of the *I Ching* philosophy is that nothing is static and that our task is to adjust to the ebbs and flows of change.
- It is used as an oracle to find out the answers to questions such as, "What does the future hold for me?"

The book consists of sixty-four hexagrams, which is the number of possible combinations of pairs of six broken or unbroken lines (trigrams). The lines represent the two primal cosmic principles in the universe, *yin* (the broken lines) and *yang* (the unbroken lines). The trigrams represent heaven, earth, thunder, water, mountain, wind, fire, and lake.

The meanings of the hexagrams were divined many years ago by Chinese philosopher-priests in tune with the Tao. They consist of homely wisdom such as: "If you are sincere, you have light and success. Perseverance brings good fortune." Or, "The superior man discriminates between high and low."

One may consult the *I Ching* by flipping numbered coins and adding up the numbers to determine the hexagram.

B TAO-TE-CHING

Tao-te-ching ("The Way of Power," or "The Book of the Way," also known as the *Lao-tzu*) is believed by Taoists to have been written by Lao-tzu. It describes the nature of life, the way to peace and how a ruler should lead his life. It is written as a handbook for the ruler, who should be a wise man whose actions pass so unnoticed that his existence is unknown.

Tao-te-ching claims that all of life follows the spiritual path known as the Tao, which can be known only through quiet meditation and simple living.

It comprises only eighty-one brief sections, and 5,000 characters.

The *Teo-te-ching* by Lao-tzu, translated by J. H. Mcdonald

1

The Tao that can be described
is not the eternal Tao.
The name that can be spoken
is not the eternal Name.

The nameless is the boundary of Heaven
and Earth.
The named is the mother of creation.

Freed from desire, you can see the hidden
mystery.
By having desire, you can only see what is
visibly real.

Yet mystery and reality
emerge from the same source.
This source is called darkness.

Darkness born from darkness.
The beginning of all understanding.

2

When people see things as beautiful,
ugliness is created.
When people see things as good,
evil is created.
Being and non-being produce each other.
Difficult and easy complement each
other.
Long and short define each other.
High and low oppose each other.
Fore and aft follow each other.

Therefore the Master
can act without doing anything
and teach without saying a word.
Things come her way and she does not
stop them;
things leave and she lets them go.
She has without possessing,
and acts without any expectations.
When her work is done, she take no
credit.
That is why it will last forever.

3

If you overly esteem talented individuals,
people will become overly competitive.
If you overvalue possessions,
people will begin to steal.

Do not display your treasures
or people will become envious.

The Master leads by
emptying people's minds,
filling their bellies,
weakening their ambitions,
and making them become strong.
Preferring simplicity and freedom from
desires,
avoiding the pitfalls of knowledge and
wrong action.

For those who practice not-doing,
everything will fall into place.

4

The Tao is like an empty container:
it can never be emptied and can never be
filled.
Infinitely deep, it is the source of all
things.
It dulls the sharp, unties the knotted,
shades the lighted, and unites all of
creation with dust.

It is hidden but always present.
I don't know who gave birth to it.
It is older than the concept of God.

5

Heaven and Earth are impartial;
they treat all of creation as straw dogs.

The Master doesn't take sides;
she treats everyone like a straw dog.

The space between Heaven and Earth is
like a bellows;
it is empty, yet has not lost its power.
The more it is used, the more it produces;
the more you talk of it, the less you
comprehend.

It is better not to speak of things you do
not understand.

6
The spirit of emptiness is immortal.
It is called the Great Mother
because it gives birth to Heaven and
Earth.

It is like a vapor,
barely seen but always present.
Use it effortlessly.

7
The Tao of Heaven is eternal,
and the earth is long enduring.
Why are they long enduring?
They do not live for themselves;
thus they are present for all beings.

The Master puts herself last;
And finds herself in the place of authority.
She detaches herself from all things;
Therefore she is united with all things.
She gives no thought to self.
She is perfectly fulfilled.

8
The supreme good is like water,
which benefits all of creation
without trying to compete with it.
It gathers in unpopular places.
Thus it is like the Tao.

The location makes the dwelling good.
Depth of understanding makes the mind
good.
A kind heart makes the giving good.
Integrity makes the government good.
Accomplishments makes your labors
good.

Proper timing makes a decision good.

Only when there is no competition
will we all live in peace.

9
It is easier to carry an empty cup
than one that is filled to the brim.

The sharper the knife
the easier it is to dull.
The more wealth you possess
the harder it is to protect.
Pride brings its own trouble.

When you have accomplished your goal
simply walk away.
This is the pathway to Heaven.

10
Nurture the darkness of your soul
until you become whole.
Can you do this and not fail?
Can you focus your life-breath until you
become
supple as a newborn child?
While you cleanse your inner vision
will you be found without fault?
Can you love people and lead them
without forcing your will on them?
When Heaven gives and takes away
can you be content with the outcome?
When you understand all things
can you step back from your own
understanding?

Giving birth and nourishing,
making without possessing,
expecting nothing in return.
To grow, yet not to control:
This is the mysterious virtue.

11
Thirty spokes are joined together in a
wheel,
but it is the center hole
that allows the wheel to function.

We mold clay into a pot,
but it is the emptiness inside
that makes the vessel useful.

We fashion wood for a house,
but it is the emptiness inside
that makes it livable.

We work with the substantial,
but the emptiness is what we use.

12
Five colors blind the eye.
Five notes deafen the ear.
Five flavors makes the palate go stale.
Too much activity deranges the mind.
Too much wealth causes crime.

The Master acts on what she feels and not
what she sees.
She shuns the latter, and prefers to seek
the former.

13
Success is as dangerous as failure,
and we are often our own worst enemy.

What does it mean that success is as
dangerous as failure?
He who is superior is also someone's
subordinate.
Receiving favor and loosing it both cause
alarm.
That is what is meant by success is as
dangerous as failure.
What does it mean that we are often our
own worst enemy?
The reason I have an enemy is because I
have "self."
If I no longer had a "self," I would no
longer have an enemy.

Love the whole world as if it were your
self;
then you will truly care for all things.

14
Look for it, and it can't be seen.
Listen for it, and it can't be heard.
Grasp for it, and it can't be caught.
These three cannot be further described,
so we treat them as The One.

Its highest is not bright.
Its depths are not dark.

Unending, unnamable, it returns to
nothingness.
Formless forms, and image less images,
subtle, beyond all understanding.

Approach it and you will not see a
beginning;
follow it and there will be no end.
When we grasp the Tao of the ancient
ones,
we can use it to direct our life today.
To know the ancient origin of Tao:
this is the beginning of wisdom.

15
The Sages of old were profound
and knew the ways of subtlety and
discernment.
Their wisdom is beyond our
comprehension.
Because their knowledge was so far
superior
I can only give a poor description.

They were careful
as someone crossing an frozen stream in
winter.
Alert as if surrounded on all sides by the
enemy.
Courteous as a guest.
Fluid as melting ice.
Whole as an uncarved block of wood.
Receptive as a valley.
Turbid as muddied water.

Who can be still
until their mud settles
and the water is cleared by itself?
Can you remain tranquil until right
action occurs by itself?

The Master doesn't seek fulfillment.
For only those who are not full are able to
be used
which brings the feeling of completeness.

16
If you can empty your mind of all
thoughts
your heart will embrace the tranquility of
peace.

Watch the workings of all of creation,
but contemplate their return to the source.

All creatures in the universe
return to the point where they began.
Returning to the source is tranquility
because we submit to Heaven's mandate.

Returning to Heaven's mandate is called being constant.
Knowing the constant is called "enlightenment."
Not knowing the constant is the source of evil deeds
because we have no roots.
By knowing the constant we can accept things as they are.
By accepting things as they are, we become impartial.
By being impartial, we become one with Heaven.
By being one with Heaven, we become one with Tao.
Being one with Tao, we are no longer concerned about
losing our life because we know the Tao is constant
and we are one with Tao.

17
The best leaders are those the people hardly know exist.
The next best is a leader who is loved and praised.
Next comes the one who is feared.
The worst one is the leader that is despised.

If you don't trust the people,
they will become untrustworthy.

The best leaders value their words, and use them sparingly.
When she has accomplished her task,
the people say, "Amazing:
we did it, all by ourselves!"

18
When the great Tao is abandoned,
charity and righteousness appear.

When intellectualism arises,
hypocrisy is close behind.

When there is strife in the family unit,
people talk about "brotherly love."

When the country falls into chaos,
politicians talk about "patriotism."

19
Forget about knowledge and wisdom,
and people will be a hundred times better off.
Throw away charity and righteousness,
and people will return to brotherly love.
Throw away profit and greed,
and there won't be any thieves.

These three are superficial and aren't enough
to keep us at the center of the circle, so we must also:

Embrace simplicity.
Put others first.
Desire little.

20
Renounce knowledge and your problems will end.
What is the difference between yes and no?
What is the difference between good and evil?
Must you fear what others fear?
Nonsense, look how far you have missed the mark!

Other people are joyous,
as though they were at a spring festival.
I alone am unconcerned and expressionless,
like an infant before it has learned to smile.

Other people have more than they need;
I alone seem to possess nothing.
I am lost and drift about with no place to go.
I am like a fool, my mind is in chaos.

Ordinary people are bright;
I alone am dark.
Ordinary people are clever;
I alone am dull.
Ordinary people seem discriminating;
I alone am muddled and confused.
I drift on the waves on the ocean,
blown at the mercy of the wind.
Other people have their goals,
I alone am dull and uncouth.

I am different from ordinary people.
I nurse from the Great Mother's breasts.

21

The greatest virtue you can have
comes from following only the Tao;
which takes a form that is intangible and
evasive.

Even though the Tao is intangible and
evasive,
we are able to know it exists.
Intangible and evasive, yet it has a
manifestation.
Secluded and dark, yet there is a vitality
within it.
Its vitality is very genuine.
Within it we can find order.

Since the beginning of time, the Tao has
always existed.
It is beyond existing and not existing .
How do I know where creation comes
from?
I look inside myself and see it.

22

If you want to become whole,
first let yourself become broken.
If you want to become straight,
first let yourself become twisted.
If you want to become full,
first let yourself become empty.
If you want to become new,
first let yourself become old.
Those whose desires are few gets them,
those whose desires are great go astray.

For this reason the Master embraces the
Tao,

as an example for the world to follow.
Because she isn't self centered,
people can see the light in her.
Because she does not boast of herself,
she becomes a shining example.
Because she does not glorify herself,
she becomes a person of merit.
Because she wants nothing from the
world,
the world can not overcome her.

When the ancient Masters said,
"If you want to become whole,
then first let yourself be broken,"
they weren't using empty words.
All who do this will be made complete.

23

Nature uses few words:
when the gale blows, it will not last long;
when it rains hard, it lasts but a little
while;
What causes these to happen? Heaven and
Earth.

Why do we humans go on endlessly about
little
when nature does much in a little time?
If you open yourself to the Tao,
you and Tao become one.
If you open yourself to Virtue,
then you can become virtuous.
If you open yourself to loss,
then you will become lost.

If you open yourself to the Tao,
the Tao will eagerly welcome you.
If you open yourself to virtue,
virtue will become a part of you.
If you open yourself to loss,
the lost are glad to see you.

When you do not trust people,
people will become untrustworthy.

24

Those who stands on tiptoes
do not stand firmly.
Those who rush ahead
don't get very far.
Those who try to out shine others

dim their own light.
Those who call themselves righteous
can't know how wrong they are.
Those who boast of their
accomplishments
diminishes the things they have done.

Compared to the Tao, these actions are
unworthy.
If we are to follow the Tao,
we must not do these things.

25
Before the universe was born
there was something in the chaos of the
heavens.
It stands alone and empty,
solitary and unchanging.
It is ever present and secure.
It may be regarded as the Mother of the
universe.
Because I do not know its name,
I call it the Tao.
If forced to give it a name,
I would call it "Great."

Because it is Great means it is everywhere.
Being everywhere means it is eternal.
Being eternal means everything returns to
it.

Tao is great.
Heaven is great.
Earth is great.
Humanity is great.
Within the universe, these are the four
great things.

Humanity follows the earth.
Earth follows Heaven.
Heaven follows the Tao.
The Tao follows only itself.

26
Heaviness is the basis of lightness.
Stillness is the standard of activity.

Thus the Master travels all day
without ever leaving her wagon.
Even though she has much to see,
she is at peace in her indifference.

Why should the lord of a thousand
chariots
be amused at the foolishness of the world?
If you abandon yourself to foolishness,
you lose touch with your beginnings.
If you let yourself become distracted,
you will lose the basis of your power.

27
A good traveler leaves no tracks,
and a skillful speaker is well rehearsed.
A good bookkeeper has an excellent
memory,
and a well made door is easy to open and
needs no locks.
A good knot needs no rope and it can not
come undone.

Thus the Master is willing to help
everyone,
and doesn't know the meaning of
rejection.
She is there to help all of creation,
and doesn't abandon even the smallest
creature.
This is called embracing the light.

What is a good person but a bad person's
teacher?
What is a bad person but raw material for
his teacher?
If you fail to honor your teacher or fail to
enjoy your student,
you will become deluded no matter how
smart you are.
It is the secret of prime importance.

28
Know the masculine,
but keep to the feminine:
and become a watershed to the world.
If you embrace the world,
the Tao will never leave you
and you become as a little child.

Know the white,
yet keep to the black:
be a model for the world.
If you are a model for the world,
the Tao inside you will strengthen

and you will return whole to your eternal
beginning.

Know the honorable,
but do not shun the disgraced:
embracing the world as it is.
If you embrace the world with
compassion,
then your virtue will return you to the
uncarved block.

The block of wood is carved into utensils
by carving void into the wood.
The Master uses the utensils, yet prefers
to keep to the block
because of its limitless possibilities.
Great works do not involve discarding
substance.

29

Do you want to rule the world and
control it?
I don't think it can ever be done.

The world is a sacred vessel
and it can not be controlled.
You will only it make it worse if you try.
It may slip through your fingers and
disappear.

Some are meant to lead,
and others are meant to follow;
Some must always strain,
and others have an easy time;
Some are naturally big and strong,
and others will always be small;
Some will be protected and nurtured,
and others will meet with destruction.

The Master accepts things as they are,
and out of compassion avoids
extravagance,
excess and the extremes.

30

Those who lead people by following the
Tao
don't use weapons to enforce their will.
Using force always leads to unseen
troubles.

In the places where armies march,
thorns and briars bloom and grow.
After armies take to war,
bad years must always follow.
The skillful commander
strikes a decisive blow then stops.
When victory is won over the enemy
through war
it is not a thing of great pride.
When the battle is over,
arrogance is the new enemy.
War can result when no other alternative
is given,
so the one who overcomes an enemy
should not dominate them.
The strong always weakened with time.

This is not the way of the Tao.
That which is not of the Tao will soon
end.

31

Weapons are the bearers of bad news;
all people should detest them.

The wise man values the left side,
and in time of war he values the right.
Weapons are meant for destruction,
and thus are avoided by the wise.
Only as a last resort
will a wise person use a deadly weapon.
If peace is her true objective
how can she rejoice in the victory of war?
Those who rejoice in victory
delight in the slaughter of humanity.
Those who resort to violence
will never bring peace to the world.
The left side is a place of honor on happy
occasions.
The right side is reserved for mourning at
a funeral.
When the lieutenants take the left side to
prepare for war,
the general should be on the right side,
because he knows the outcome will be
death.
The death of many should be greeted
with great sorrow,
and the victory celebration should honor
those who have died.

32
The Tao is nameless and unchanging.
Although it appears insignificant,
nothing in the world can contain it.

If a ruler abides by its principles,
then her people will willingly follow.
Heaven would then reign on earth,
like sweet rain falling on paradise.
People would have no need for laws,
because the law would be written on their
hearts.

Naming is a necessity for order,
but naming can not order all things.
Naming often makes things impersonal,
so we should know when naming should
end.
Knowing when to stop naming,
you can avoid the pitfall it brings.

All things end in the Tao
just as the small streams and the largest
rivers
flow through valleys to the sea.

33
Those who know others are intelligent;
those who know themselves are truly wise.
Those who master others are strong;
those who master themselves have true
power.

Those who know they have enough are
truly wealthy.

Those who persist will reach their goal.

Those who keep their course have a
strong will.
Those who embrace death will not perish,
but have life everlasting.

34
The great Tao flows unobstructed in every
direction.
All things rely on it to conceive and be born,
and it does not deny even the smallest of
creation.
When it has accomplishes great wonders,
it does not claim them for itself.

It nourishes infinite worlds,
yet it doesn't seek to master the smallest
creature.
Since it is without wants and desires,
it can be considered humble.
All of creation seeks it for refuge
yet it does not seek to master or control.
Because it does not seek greatness;
it is able to accomplish truly great things.

35
She who follows the way of the Tao
will draw the world to her steps.
She can go without fear of being injured,
because she has found peace and
tranquility in her heart.

Where there is music and good food,
people will stop to enjoy it.
But words spoken of the Tao
seem to them boring and stale.
When looked at, there is nothing for
them to see.
When listen for, there is nothing for them
to hear.
Yet if they put it to use, it would never be
exhausted.

36
If you want something to return to the
source,
you must first allow it to spread out.
If you want something to weaken,
you must first allow it to become strong.
If you want something to be removed,
you must first allow it to flourish.
If you want to possess something,
you must first give it away.

This is called the subtle understanding
of how things are meant to be.

The soft and pliable overcomes the hard
and inflexible.

Just as fish remain hidden in deep waters,
it is best to keep weapons out of sight.

37
The Tao never acts with force,
yet there is nothing that it can not do.

If rulers could follow the way of the Tao,
then all of creation would willingly follow
their example.
If selfish desires were to arise after their
transformation,
I would erase them with the power of the
Uncarved Block.

By the power of the Uncarved Block,
future generations would loose their
selfish desires.
By loosing their selfish desires,
the world would naturally settle into
peace.

38

The highest good is not to seek to do
good,
but to allow yourself to become it.
The ordinary person seeks to do good
things,
and finds that they can not do them
continually.

The Master does not force virtue on
others,
thus she is able to accomplish her task.
The ordinary person who uses force,
will find that they accomplish nothing.

The kind person acts from the heart,
and accomplishes a multitude of things.
The righteous person acts out of pity,
yet leaves many things undone.
The moral person will act out of duty,
and when no one will respond
will roll up his sleeves and uses force.

When the Tao is forgotten, there is
righteousness.
When righteousness is forgotten, there is
morality.
When morality is forgotten, there is the
law.
The law is the husk of faith,
and trust is the beginning of chaos.

Our basic understandings are not from
the Tao
because they come from the depths of our
misunderstanding.

The master abides in the fruit and not in
the husk.
She dwells in the Tao,
and not with the things that hide it.
This is how she increases in wisdom.

39

The masters of old attained unity with the
Tao.
Heaven attained unity and become pure.
The earth attained unity and found peace.
The spirits attained unity so they could
minister.
The valleys attained unity that they might
be full.
Humanity attained unity that they might
flourish.
Their leaders attained unity that they
might set the example.
This is the power of unity.

Without unity, the sky becomes filthy.
Without unity, the earth becomes
unstable.
Without unity, the spirits become
unresponsive and disappear.
Without unity, the valleys become dry as
a desert.
Without unity, human kind can't
reproduce and becomes extinct.
Without unity, our leaders become
corrupt and fall.

The great view the small as their source,
and the high takes the low as their
foundation.
Their greatest asset becomes their
humility.
They speak of themselves as orphans and
widows,
thus they truly seek humility.
Do not shine like the precious gem,
but be as dull as a common stone.

40

All movement returns to the Tao.
Weakness is how the Tao works.

All of creation is born from substance.
Substance is born of nothing-ness.

41

When a superior person hears of the Tao,
She diligently puts it into practice.
When an average person hears of the Tao,
he believes half of it, and doubts the other
half.
When a foolish person hears of the Tao,
he laughs out loud at the very idea.
If he didn't laugh,
it wouldn't be the Tao.

Thus it is said:
The brightness of the Tao seems like
darkness,
the advancement of the Tao seems like
retreat,
the level path seems rough,
the superior path seem empty,
the pure seems to be tarnished,
and true virtue doesn't seem to be enough.
The virtue of caution seems like
cowardice,
the pure seems to be polluted,
the true square seems to have no corners,
the best vessels take the most time to
finish,
the greatest sounds cannot be heard,
and the greatest image has no form.

The Tao hides in the unnamed,
Yet it alone nourishes and completes all
things.

42

The Tao gave birth to One.
The One gave birth to Two.
The Two gave birth to Three.
The Three gave birth to all of creation.

All things carry Yin
yet embrace Yang.
They blend their life breaths
in order to produce harmony.

People despise being orphaned, widowed
and poor.
But the noble ones take these as their
titles.
In losing, much is gained,
and in gaining, much is lost.

What others teach I too will teach:
"The strong and violent will not die a
natural death."

43

That which offers no resistance,
overcomes the hardest substances.
That which offers no resistance
can enter where there is no space.

Few in the world can comprehend
the teaching without words,
or understand the value of non-action.

44

Which is more important, your honor or
your life?
Which is more valuable, your possessions
or your person?
Which is more destructive, success or
failure?

Because of this, great love extracts a great
cost
and true wealth requires greater loss.

Knowing when you have enough avoids
dishonor,
and knowing when to stop will keep you
from danger
and bring you a long, happy life.

45

The greatest accomplishments seems
imperfect,
yet their usefulness is not diminished.
The greatest fullness seems empty,
yet it will be inexhaustible.

The greatest straightness seems crooked.
The most valued skill seems like
clumsiness.
The greatest speech seems full of
stammers.

Movement overcomes the cold,
and stillness overcomes the heat.
That which is pure and still is the
universal ideal.

46
When the world follows the Tao,
horses run free to fertilize the fields.
When the world does not follow the Tao,
war horses are bread outside the cities.

There is no greater transgression
than condoning peoples selfish desires,
no greater disaster than being discontent,
and no greater retribution than for greed.

Whoever knows contentment will be at
peace forever.

47
Without opening your door,
you can know the whole world.
Without looking out your window,
you can understand the way of the Tao.

The more knowledge you seek,
the less you will understand.

The Master understands without leaving,
sees clearly without looking,
accomplishes much without doing
anything.

48
One who seeks knowledge learns
something new every day.
One who seeks the Tao unlearns
something new every day.
Less and less remains until you arrive at
non-action.
When you arrive at non-action,
nothing will be left undone.

Mastery of the world is achieved
by letting things take their natural course.
You can not master the world by changing
the natural way.

49
The Master has no mind of her own.
She understands the mind of the people.

To those who are good she treats as good.
To those who aren't good she also treats as
good.

This is how she attains true goodness.

She trusts people who are trustworthy.
She also trusts people who aren't
trustworthy.
This is how she gains true trust.

The Master's mind is shut off from the
world.
Only for the sake of the people does she
muddle her mind.
They look to her in anticipation.
Yet she treats them all as her children.

50
Those who leave the womb at birth
and those who enter their source at death,
of these; three out of ten celebrate life,
three out of ten celebrate death,
and three out of ten simply go from life to
death.
What is the reason for this?
Because they are afraid of dying,
therefore they can not live.

I have heard that those who celebrate life
walk safely among the wild animals.
When they go into battle, they remain
unharmed.
The animals find no place to attack them
and the weapons are unable to harm
them.
Why? Because they can find no place for
death in them.

51
The Tao gives birth to all of creation.
The virtue of Tao in nature nurtures
them,
and their family give them their form.
Their environment then shapes them into
completion.
That is why every creature honors the Tao
and its virtue.

No one tells them to honor the Tao and
its virtue,
it happens all by itself.
So the Tao gives them birth,
and its virtue cultivates them,
cares for them,
nurtures them,
gives them a place of refuge and peace,

helps them to grow and shelters them.
It gives them life without wanting to possess them,
and cares for them expecting nothing in return.
It is their master, but it does not seek to dominate them.
This is called the dark and mysterious virtue.

52
The world had a beginning
which we call the Great Mother.
Once we have found the Mother,
we begin to know what Her children should be.

When we know we are the Mother's child,
we begin to guard the qualities of the Mother in us.
She will protect us from all danger
even if we lose our life.

Keep your mouth closed
and embrace a simple life,
and you will live care-free until the end of your days.
If you try to talk your way into a better life
there will be no end to your trouble.

To understand the small is called clarity.
Knowing how to yield is called strength.
To use your inner light for understanding regardless of the danger
is called depending on the Constant.

53
If I understood only one thing,
I would want to use it to follow the Tao.
My only fear would be one of pride.
The Tao goes in the level places,
but people prefer to take the short cuts.

If too much time is spent cleaning the house
the land will become neglected and full of weeds,
and the granaries will soon become empty
because there is no one out working the fields.

To wear fancy clothes and ornaments,
to have your fill of food and drink
and to waste all of your money buying possessions
is called the crime of excess.

Oh, how these things go against the way of the Tao!

54
That which is well built
will never be torn down.
That which is well latched
can not slip away.
Those who do things well
will be honored from generation to generation.

If this idea is cultivated in the individual,
then his virtue will become genuine.
If this idea is cultivated in your family,
then virtue in your family will be great.
If this idea is cultivated in your community,
then virtue will go a long way.
If this idea is cultivated in your country,
then virtue will be in many places.
If this idea is cultivated in the world,
then virtue will be with everyone.

Then observe the person for what the person does,
and observe the family for what it does,
and observe the community for what it does,
and observe the country for what it does,
and observe the world for what it does.
How do I know this saying is true?
I observe these things and see.

55
One who is filled with the Tao
is like a newborn child.
The infant is protected from
the stinging insects, wild beasts, and birds of prey.
Its bones are soft, its muscles are weak,
but its grip is firm and strong.
It doesn't know about the union
of male and female,
yet his penis can stand erect,

because of the power of life within him.
It can cry all day and never become hoarse.
This is perfect harmony.

To understand harmony is to understand the Constant.
To know the Constant is to be called "enlightened."
To unnaturally try to extend life is not appropriate.
To try and alter the life-breath is unnatural.
The master understands that when something reaches its prime
it will soon begin to decline.
Changing the natural is against the way of the Tao.
Those who do it will come to an early end.

56
Those who know do not talk.
Those who talk do not know.

Stop talking,
meditate in silence,
blunt your sharpness,
release your worries,
harmonize your inner light,
and become one with the dust.
Doing this is called the dark and mysterious identity.

Those who have achieved the mysterious identity
can not be approached, and they can not be alienated.
They can not be benefited nor harmed.
They can not be made noble nor to suffer disgrace.
This makes them the most noble of all under the heavens.

57
Govern your country with integrity,
Weapons of war can be used with great cunning,
but loyalty is only won by not-doing.
How do I know the way things are?
By these:

The more prohibitions you make,
the poorer people will be.
The more weapons you posses,
the greater the chaos in your country.
The more knowledge that is acquired,
the stranger the world will become.
The more laws that you make,
the greater the number of criminals.

Therefore the Master says:
I do nothing,
and people become good by themselves.
I seek peace,
and people take care of their own problems.
I do not meddle in their personal lives,
and the people become prosperous.
I let go of all my desires,
and the people return to the Uncarved Block.

58
If a government is unobtrusive,
the people become whole.
If a government is repressive,
the people become treacherous.

Good fortune has its roots in disaster,
and disaster lurks with good fortune.
Who knows why these things happen,
or when this cycle will end?
Good things seem to change into bad,
and bad things often turn out for good.
These things have always been hard to comprehend.

Thus the Master makes things change without interfering.
She is probing yet causes no harm.
Straightforward, yet does not impose her will.
Radiant, and easy on the eye.

59
There is nothing better than moderation
for teaching people or serving Heaven.
Those who use moderation
are already on the path to the Tao.

Those who follow the Tao early
will have an abundance of virtue.

When there is an abundance of virtue,
there is nothing that can not be done.
Where there is limitless ability,
then the kingdom is within your grasp.
When you know the Mother of the kingdom,
then you will be long enduring.

This is spoken of as the deep root and the firm trunk,
the Way to a long life and great spiritual vision.

60

Governing a large country
is like frying small fish.
Too much poking spoils the meat.

When the Tao is used to govern the world
then evil will lose its power to harm the people.
Not that evil will no longer exist,
but only because it has lost its power.
Just as evil can loose its ability to harm,
the Master shuns the use of violence.

If you give evil nothing to oppose,
then virtue will return by itself.

61

A large country should take the low place
like a great watershed,
which from its low position assumes the female role.
The female overcomes the male by the power of her position.
Her tranquility gives rise to her humility.

If a large country takes the low position,
it will be able to influence smaller countries.
If smaller countries take the lower position,
then they can allow themselves to be influenced.
So both seek to take the lower position
in order to influence the other, or be influenced.

Large countries should desire to protect and help the people,
and small countries should desire to serve others.
Both large and small countries benefit greatly from humility.

62

The Tao is the tabernacle of creation,
it is a treasure for those who are good,
and a place of refuge for those who are not.

How can those who are not good be abandoned?
Words that are beautiful are worth much,
but good behavior can only be learned by example.

When a new leader takes office,
don't give him gifts and offerings.
These things are not as valuable
as teaching him about the Tao.

Why was the Tao esteemed by the ancient Masters?
Is it not said: "With it we find without looking.
With it we find forgiveness for our transgressions."
That is why the world can not under stand it.

63

Act by not acting;
do by not doing.
Enjoy the plain and simple.
Find that greatness in the small.
Take care of difficult problems
while they are still easy;
Do easy things before they become too hard.

Difficult problems are best solved while they are easy.
Great projects are best started while they are small.
The Master never takes on more than she can handle,
which means that she leaves nothing undone.

When an affirmation is given too lightly,
keep your eyes open for trouble ahead.

When something seems too easy,
difficulty is hiding in the details.
The master expects great difficulty,
so the task is always easier than planned.

64
Things are easier to control while things
are quiet.
Things are easier to plan far in advance.
Things break easier while they are still
brittle.
Things are easier hid while they are still
small.

Prevent problems before they arise.
Take action before things get out of hand.
The tallest tree
begins as a tiny sprout.
The tallest building
starts with one shovel of dirt.
A journey of a thousand miles
starts with a single foot step.

If you rush into action, you will fail.
If you hold on too tight, you will loose
your grip.

Therefore the Master lets things take their
course
and thus never fails.
She doesn't hold on to things
and never looses them.
By pursing your goals too relentlessly,
you let them slip away.
If you are as concerned about the
outcome
as you are about the beginning,
then it is hard to do things wrong.
The master seeks no possessions.
She learns by unlearning,
thus she is able to understand all things.
This gives her the ability to help all of
creation.

65
The ancient Masters
who understood the way of the Tao,
did not educate people, but made them
forget.

Smart people are difficult to guide,
because they think they are too clever.

To use cleverness to rule a country,
is to lead the country to ruin.
To avoid cleverness in ruling a country,
is to lead the country to prosperity.

Knowing the two alternatives is a pattern.
Remaining aware of the pattern is a
virtue.
This dark and mysterious virtue is
profound.
It is opposite our natural inclination,
but leads to harmony with the heavens.

66
Rivers and seas are rulers
of the streams of hundreds of valleys
because of the power of their low
position.

If you want to be the ruler of people,
you must speak to them like you are their
servant.
If you want to lead other people,
you must put their interest ahead of your
own.

The people will not feel burdened,
if a wise person is in a position of power.
The people will not feel like they are
being manipulated, if a wise person is in
front as their leader.
The whole world will ask for her
guidance,
and will never get tired of her.
Because she does not like to compete,
no one can compete with the things she
accomplishes.

67
The world talks about honoring the Tao,
but you can't tell it from their actions.
Because it is thought of as great,
the world makes light of it.
It seems too easy for anyone to use.

There are three jewels that I cherish:
compassion, moderation, and humility.
With compassion, you will be able to be
brave,
With moderation, you will be able to give
to others,

With humility, you will be able to become
a great leader.
To abandon compassion while seeking to
be brave,
or abandoning moderation while being
benevolent,
or abandoning humility while seeking to lead
will only lead to greater trouble.
The compassionate warrior will be the
winner,
and if compassion is your defense you will
be secure.
Compassion is the protector of Heaven's
salvation.

68
The best warriors
do not use violence.
The best generals
do not destroy indiscriminately.
The best tacticians
try to avoid confrontation.
The best leaders
becomes servants of their people.

This is called the virtue of non-
competition.
This is called the power to manage others.
This is called attaining harmony with the
heavens.

69
There is an old saying:
"It is better to become the passive
in order to see what will happen.
It is better to retreat a foot
than to advance only an inch."

This is called
being flexible while advancing,
pushing back without using force,
and destroying the enemy without
engaging him.

There is no greater disaster
than underestimating your enemy.
Underestimating your enemy
means loosing your greatest assets.
When equal forces meet in battle,
victory will go to the one
that enters with the greatest sorrow.

70
My words are easy to understand
and easier to put into practice.
Yet no one in the world seem to
understand them,
and are not able to apply what I teach.

My teachings come from the ancients,
the things I do are done for a reason.

Because you do not know me,
you are not able to understand my
teachings.
Because those who know me are few,
my teachings become even more precious.

71
Knowing you don't know is wholeness.
Thinking you know is a disease.
Only by recognizing that you have an
illness
can you move to seek a cure.

The Master is whole because
she sees her illnesses and treats them,
and thus is able to remain whole.

72
When people become overly bold,
then disaster will soon arrive.

Do not meddle with peoples livelihood;
by respecting them they will in turn
respect you.

Therefore, the Master knows herself but is
not arrogant.
She loves herself but also loves others.
This is how she is able to make
appropriate choices.

73
Being over bold and confident is deadly.
The wise use of caution will keep you
alive.

One is the way to death,
and the other is the way to preserve your
life.
Who can understand the workings of
Heaven?

The Tao of the universe
does not compete, yet wins;
does not speak, yet responds;
does not command, yet is obeyed;
and does act, but is good at directing.

The nets of Heaven are wide,
but nothing escapes its grasp.

74
If you do not fear death,
then how can it intimidate you?
If you aren't afraid of dying,
there is nothing you can not do.

Those who harm others
are like inexperienced boys
trying to take the place of a great
lumberjack.
Trying to fill his shoes will only get them
seriously hurt.

75
When people go hungry,
the governments taxes are too high.
When people become rebellious,
the government has become too intrusive.

When people begin to view death lightly,
wealthy people have too much
which causes others to starve.

Only those who do not cling to their life
can save it.

76
The living are soft and yielding;
the dead are rigid and stiff.
Living plants are flexible and tender;
the dead are brittle and dry.

Those who are stiff and rigid
are the disciple of death.
Those who are soft and yielding
are the disciples of life.

The rigid and stiff will be broken.
The soft and yielding will overcome.

77
The Tao of Heaven works in the world
like the drawing of a bow.
The top is bent downward;
the bottom is bent up.
The excess is taken from,
and the deficient is given to.

The Tao works to use the excess,
and gives to that which is depleted.
The way of people is to take from the
depleted, and give to those who already
have an excess.

Who is able to give to the needy from
their excess?
Only some one who is following the way
of the Tao.

This is why the Master gives
expecting nothing in return.
She does not dwell on her past
accomplishments,
and does not glory in any praise.

78
Water is the softest and most yielding
substance.
Yet nothing is better than water,
for overcoming the hard and rigid,
because nothing can compete with it.

Everyone knows that the soft and yielding
overcomes the rigid and hard,
but few can put this knowledge into
practice.

Therefore the Master says:
"Only he who is the lowest servant of the
kingdom,
is worthy to become its ruler.
He who is willing tackle the most
unpleasant tasks,
is the best ruler in the world."

True sayings seem contradictory.

79
Difficulties remain, even after solving a
problem.
How then can we consider that as good?

Therefore the Master
does what she knows is right,
and makes no demands of others.
A virtuous person will do the right thing,
and persons with no virtue will take
advantage of others.

The Tao does not choose sides,
the good person receives from the Tao
because she is on its side.

80

Small countries with few people are best.
Give them all of the things they want,
and they will see that they do not need
them.
Teach them that death is a serious thing,
and to be content to never leave their
homes.
Even though they have plenty
of horses, wagons and boats,
they won't feel that they need to use them.
Even if they have weapons and shields,
they will keep them out of sight.
Let people enjoy the simple technologies,
let them enjoy their food,
let them make their own clothes,
let them be content with their own
homes,
and delight in the customs that they
cherish.
Although the next country is close
enough
that they can hear their roosters crowing
and dogs barking,
they are content never to visit each other
all of the days of their life.

81

True words do not sound beautiful;
beautiful sounding words are not true.
Wise men don't need to debate;
men who need to debate are not wise.

Wise men are not scholars,
and scholars are not wise.
The Master desires no possessions.
Since the things she does are for the
people,
she has more than she needs.
The more she gives to others,
the more she has for herself.

The Tao of Heaven nourishes by not
forcing.
The Tao of the Wise person acts by not
competing.

The Lao-tzu,
translated by J. H. Mcdonald

C TAOIST QUOTATIONS

A leader is most effective when people
barely know he exists. When his work is
done, his aim fulfilled, his troops will feel
they did it themselves.

Lao-tzu

Build up virtue, and you master all.

Lao-tzu

Don't think you can attain total awareness
and whole enlightenment without proper
discipline and practice. This is egomania.
Appropriate rituals channel your
emotions and life energy toward the light.
Without the discipline to practice them,
you will tumble constantly backward into
darkness.

Lao-tzu

Fame or integrity: which is more
important? Money or happiness: which is
more valuable? Success or failure: which is
more destructive? If you look to others for
fulfillment, you will never truly be
fulfilled. If your happiness depends on
money, you will never be happy with
yourself. Be content with what you have;
rejoice in the way things are. When you
realize there is nothing lacking, the whole
world belongs to you.

Lao-tzu

He who controls others may be powerful,
but he who has mastered himself is
mightier still.

Lao-tzu

Hold on to the center and make up your
mind to rejoice in this paradise called life.

Lao-tzu

Knowing others is intelligence; knowing
yourself is true wisdom. Mastering others

is strength; mastering yourself is true power.

Lao-tzu

Men are born soft and supple; dead, they are stiff and hard. Plants are born tender and pliant; dead, they are brittle and dry. Thus whoever is stiff and inflexible is a disciple of death. Whoever is soft and yielding is a disciple of life. The hard and stiff will be broken. The soft and supple will prevail.

Lao-tzu

The journey of a thousand miles begins with a step.

Lao-tzu

In conflict it is better to be receptive than aggressive, better to retreat a foot than advance an inch. This is called moving ahead without advancing, capturing the enemy without attacking him. There is no greater misfortune than underestimating your opponent. To underestimate your opponent is to forsake your three treasures. When opposing forces are engaged in conflict, the one who fights with sorrow will triumph.

Lao-tzu

What the caterpillar calls the end, the rest of the world calls a butterfly.

Lao-tzu

Be still like a mountain and flow like a great river.

Lao-tzu

Yielding is the way of the Tao.

Lao-tzu

We believe in the formless and eternal Tao, and we recognize all personified deities as being mere human constructs. We reject hatred, intolerance, and unnecessary violence, and embrace harmony, love and learning, as we are taught by Nature. We place our trust and our lives in the Tao, that we may live in peace and balance with the Universe, both in this mortal life and beyond.

Lao-tzu

The Tao's principle is spontaneity.

Lao-tzu

The Tao of the sage is work without effort.
Lao-tzu

The Tao is near and people seek it far away.
Mencius (c. 372-c. 289 BC)

The one who can dissolve her mind will suddenly discover the Tao at her feet.

Lao-tzu

All the fish needs is to get lost in the water. All man needs is to get lost in Tao.
Chuang Tzu (c. 360 -c. 275),
Chinese philosopher

Worlds and particles, bodies and beings, time and space: All are transient expressions of the Tao.

Lao-tzu

Can you let go of words and ideas, attitudes and expectations? If so, then the Tao will loom into view.

Lao-tzu

The Tao that can be told is not the eternal Tao. The name that can be named is not the eternal Name.

Lao-tzu

If you can let go of [the Tao] with your mind and surround it with your heart, it will live inside you for ever.

Lao-tzu

In the pursuit of learning, every day something is acquired. In the pursuit of Tao, every day something is dropped.
Lao-tzu

The Tao that is coded in words is dead. The teachings of the Tao are so precious and important that they cannot be revealed in the written word.

Shui-ch'ing Tzu

But if you do not have the Tao yourself, what business have you spending your time in vain efforts to bring corrupt politicians into the right path?

Confucius

Tao is beyond words and beyond things. It is not expressed either in word or in silence. Where there is no longer word or silence Tao is apprehended.

Chuang-tzu

[The Tao] is always present and always available. . . . If you are willing to be lived by it, you will see it everywhere, even in the most ordinary things.

Lao-tzu

Only the intelligent knows how to identify all things as one. . . . When one is at ease with himself, one is near Tao. This is to let Nature take its own course.

Chuang-tzu

To exercise no-thought and rest in nothing is the first step toward resting in Tao. To start from nowhere and follow no road is the first step toward attaining Tao.

Chuang-tzu

When you accurately perceive the fluidity of things, you can also begin to perceive the constancy behind them: the creative, transformative, boundless, immutable Tao.

Lao-tzu

When the mortal mind is dead, the mind of Tao can live. . . . When the mind of Tao lives, no thoughts can arise. When no thoughts arise, one returns to Earlier Heaven.

Shui-ch'ing Tzu

Understand this if nothing else: spiritual freedom and oneness with the Tao are not randomly bestowed gifts, but the rewards of conscious self-transformation and self-evolution.

Lao-tzu

The Way of Tao is this: It strives not, but conquers; It speaks not, but all is made clear; It summons not, but its house is crowded; It contrives not, but the design is perfect.

Lao-tzu

When there is no more separation between "this" and "that," it is called the still-point of the Tao. At the still point in the center of the circle one can see the infinite in all things.

Chuang-tzu

Does one scent appeal more than another? Do you prefer this flavor, or that feeling? Is your practice sacred and your work profane? Then your mind is separated: from itself, from oneness, from the Tao.

Lao-tzu

Who can enjoy enlightenment and remain indifferent to suffering in the world? This is not in keeping with the Way. Only those who increase their service along with their understanding can be called men and women of Tao.

Lao-tzu

Giving to others selflessly and anonymously, radiating light throughout the world and illuminating your own darkness, your virtue becomes a sanctuary for yourself and all beings. That is what is meant by embodying the Tao.

Lao-tzu

To regard the fundamental as the essence, to regard things as coarse, to regard accumulation as deficiency, and to dwell quietly alone with the spiritual and the intelligent - herein lie the techniques of Tao of the ancients.

Chuang-tzu

Chanting is no more holy than listening to the murmur of a stream, counting prayer beads no more sacred than simply breathing. . . . If you wish to attain oneness with the Tao, don't get caught up in spiritual superficialities.

Lao-tzu

I confess that there is nothing to teach: no religion, no science, no body of information which will lead your mind back to the Tao. Today I speak in this fashion, tomorrow in another, but always the Integral Way is beyond words and beyond mind.

Lao-tzu

My own words are not the medicine, but a prescription; not the destination, but a map to help you reach it. When you get there, quiet your mind and close your mouth. Don't analyze the Tao. Strive instead to live it: silently, undividedly, with your whole harmonious being.

Lao-tzu

If you are sincere in seeking this knowledge, you must look for a teacher and humbly ask your teacher to show you the opening of the Mysterious Gate. From then on, if your actions follow the Tao, you will progress. If your actions stray from the Tao, your progress will be halted.

Shui-ch'ing Tzu

Acting without design, occupying oneself without making a business of it, finding the great in what is small and the many in the few, repaying injury with kindness, effecting difficult things while they are easy, and managing great things in their beginnings; this is the method of Tao.

Lao-tzu

Though [the Tao] is uncreated itself, it creates all things. Because it has no substance, it can enter into where there is no space. Exercising by returning to itself, winning victories by remaining gentle and yielding, it is softer than anything, and therefore overcomes everything hard.

Lao-tzu

The first practice is the practice of undiscriminating virtue: take care of those

who are deserving; also, and equally, take care of those who are not. When you extend your virtue in all directions without discriminating, you feet are firmly planted on the path that returns to the Tao.

Lao-tzu

Can you dissolve your ego? Can you abandon the idea of self and other? Can you relinquish the notions of male and female, short and long, life and death? Can you let go of all these dualities and embrace the Tao without skepticism or panic? If so, you can reach the heart of the Integral Oneness.

Lao-tzu

Do you think that you can clear your mind by sitting constantly in silent meditation? This makes your mind narrow, not clear. Integral awareness is fluid and adaptable, present in all places and at all times. That is true meditation. . . . The Tao is clear and simple, and it doesn't avoid the world.

Lao-tzu

The Tao is supreme goodness. It has no form and is limitless. It is formless because there is no visible trace of its existence. The Tao is that energy that has existed from the beginning when there was neither structure nor differentiation. It is the source of life in heaven and on earth. It creates and all things.

Shui-ch'ing Tzu

To name Tao is to name no-thing. Tao is not the name of [something created]. "Cause" and "chance" have no bearing on the Tao. Tao is a name that indicates without defining. Tao is beyond words and beyond things. It is not expressed either in word or in silence. Where there is no longer word or silence Tao is apprehended.

Chuang-tzu

The Tao gives birth to One. One gives birth to yin and yang. Yin and yang give birth to all things. . . . The complete whole is the complete whole. So also is any part the complete whole. . . . But forget about understanding and harmonizing and making all things one. The universe is already a harmonious oneness; just realize it.

Lao-tzu

. . . These are notions of the mind, which is like a knife, always chipping away at the Tao, trying to render it graspable and manageable. But that which is beyond form is ungraspable, and that which is beyond knowing is unmanageable. There is, however, this consolation: She who lets go of the knife will find the Tao at her fingertips.

Lao-tzu

If you persist in trying to attain what is never attained (It is Tao's gift), if you persist in making effort to obtain what effort cannot get, if you persist in reasoning about what cannot be understood, you will be destroyed by the very thing you seek. To know when to stop, to know when you can get no further by your own action, this is the right beginning!

Chuang-tzu

Riches, fame, and fortune are as ephemeral as lightning, The passion of sexual love and childish piety will vanish like flames. Do not crave and be the master of your own life, Cultivate the Tao and there will be gods to help your *karma*. Do not lose your original nature and the dust of the earthly realm will vanish. The sky will reveal the circular bright moon.

Shui-ch'ing Tzu

How can we fret and stew *sub specie aeternitatis* - under the calm gaze of ancient Tao? The salt of the sea is in our blood; the calcium of the rocks is in our bones; the genes of ten thousand generations of stalwart progenitors are in our cells. The sun shines and we smile. The winds rage and we bend before them.

The blossoms open and we rejoice. Earth is our long home.

Stewart W. Holmes

There are three layers to the universe. In the lower, Tai Ching, and the middle, Shan Ching, the hindrance of a physical bodily existence is required. Those who fail to live consistently in accord with the Tao reside here. In the upper, Yu Ching, there is only Tao: the bondage of form is broken, and the only thing existing is the exquisite energy dance of the immortal divine beings.

Lao-tzu

A man's excellence is like that of water; It benefits all things without striving; It takes to the low places shunned by men. Water is akin to Tao. . . . In all the earth nothing weaker than water, Yet in attacking the hard, nothing superior, Nothing so certain in wearing down strength: There is no way to resist it. Note then: The weak conquer the strong, The yielding outlast the aggressors.

Lao-tzu

What is essential to practice the Tao is to get rid of cravings and vexations. If these afflictions are not removed, it is impossible to attain stability. This is like the case of the fertile field, which cannot produce good crops as long as the weeds are not cleared away. Cravings and ruminations are the weeds of the mind; if you do not clear them away, concentration and wisdom do not develop.

Chang San-feng

The mind remains undetermined in the great Void. Here the highest knowledge is unbounded. That which gives things their thusness cannot be delimited by things. So when we speak of 'limits', we remain confined to limited things. The limit of the unlimited is called "fullness." The limitlessness of the limited is called "emptiness." Tao is the source of both. But it is itself neither fullness nor emptiness.

Chuang-tzu

Tao is obscured when men understand only one pair of opposites, or concentrate only on a partial aspect of being. Then clear expression also becomes muddled by mere wordplay, affirming this one aspect and denying all the rest. The pivot of Tao passes through the center where all affirmations and denials converge. He who grasps the pivot is at the still-point from which all movements and oppositions can be seen in their right relationship... Abandoning all thought of imposing a limit or taking sides, he rests in direct intuition.

Chuang-tzu

All that is limited by form, semblance, sound, color is called object. Among them all, man alone is more than an object. Though, like objects, he has form and semblance, He is not limited to form. He is more. He can attain to formlessness. When he is beyond form and semblance, beyond "this" and "that," where is the comparison with another object? Where is the conflict? What can stand in his way? He will rest in his eternal place which is no-place. He will be hidden in his own unfathomable secret. His nature sinks to its root in the One. His vitality, his power hide in secret Tao.

Chuang-tzu

Look, it cannot be seen - it is beyond form. Listen, it cannot be heard - it is beyond sound. Grasp, it cannot be held - it is intangible. These three are indefinable; Therefore they are joined in one. From above it is not bright; From below it is not dark; An unbroken thread beyond description. It returns to nothingness. The form of the formless, The image of the imageless, It is called indefinable and beyond imagination. Stand before it and there is no beginning. Follow it and there is no end. Stay with the ancient Tao, move with the present. Knowing the ancient beginning is the essence of Tao.

Lao-tzu

. . . knowledge emerges in (humans). Opposed to knowledge is the spirit. The spirit is formless and is incomprehensible to mundane thoughts. . . . Knowledge is active, mischievous, and intelligent. It changes constantly. Spirit, on the other hand, is the master of humankind. Its origin is in wu-chi. . . . It is never born and it never dies. The spirit tends toward purity and stillness. Knowledge tends toward action and disturbs the mind so that it cannot be still. . . . Recognize the difference between the human mind and the mind of Tao. Do not mistake the human mind for the mind of Tao, and knowledge for the spirit.

Shui-ch'ing Tzu

[There are two paths leading to oneness with the Tao.] The first in the path of acceptance. Affirm everyone and everything. Freely extend your goodwill and virtue in every direction, regardless of circumstances. Embrace all things as part of the Harmonious Oneness, and then you will begin to perceive it. The second path is that of denial. Recognize that everything you see and think is a falsehood, an illusion, a veil over the truth. Peel all the veils away, and you will arrive at the Oneness. Though these paths are entirely different, they will deliver you to the same place: spontaneous awareness of the Great Oneness.

Lao-tzu

When we look at things in the light of Tao, nothing is best, nothing is worst. Each thing, seen in its own light stands out in its own way. It can seem to be "better" than what is compared with it on its own terms. But seen in terms of the whole, no one thing stands out as "better" . . . All creatures have gifts of their own. . . . All things have varying capacities. Consequently he who wants to have right without wrong, order without disorder, does not understand the principles of heaven and earth. He does not know how things hang together. Can a man cling only to heaven and know nothing of earth? They are correlative: to know one is to know the other. To refuse one is to refuse both.

Chuang-tzu

The true men of old were not afraid when they stood alone in their views. No great exploits. No plans. If they failed, no sorrow. No self-congratulation in success. . . . The true men of old knew no lust for life, no dread of death. Their entrance was without gladness, their exit, yonder, without resistance. Easy come, easy go. They did not forget where from, nor ask where to, nor drive grimly forward fighting their way through life. They took life as it came, gladly; took death as it came, without care; and went away, yonder. Yonder! They had no mind to fight Tao. They did not try by their own contriving, to help Tao along. These are the ones we call true men. Minds free, thoughts gone. Brows clear, faces serene.

Chuang-tzu

The man in whom Tao acts without impediment harms no other being by his actions yet he does not know himself to be "kind," to be "gentle. . . ." [He] does not bother with his own interests and does not despise others who do. He does not struggle to make money and does not make a virtue of poverty. He goes his way without relying on others and does not pride himself on walking alone. While he does not follow the crowd he won't complain of those who do. Rank and reward make no appeal to him; disgrace and shame do not deter him. He is not always looking for right and wrong, always deciding "Yes" or "No." The ancients said, therefore: The man of Tao remains unknown. Perfect virtue produces nothing. "No-Self" is "True-Self." And the greatest man is Nobody.

Chuang-tzu

If a man is crossing a river and an empty boat collides with his own skiff, even though he be a bad-tempered man he will not become very angry. But if he sees a

man in the boat, he will shout at him to steer clear. If the shout is not heard, he will shout again, and yet again, and begin cursing. And all because there is somebody in the boat. Yet if the boat were empty, he would not be shouting, and not angry. If you can empty your own boat crossing the river of the world, no one will oppose you, no one will seek to harm you. . . . Who can free himself from achievement, and from fame, descend and be lost amid the masses of men? He will flow like Tao, unseen, he will go about like Life itself with no name and no home. Simple is he, without distinction. To all appearances he is a fool. His steps leave no trace. He has no power. He achieves nothing, has no reputation. Since he judges no one, no one judges him. Such is the perfect man: His boat is empty.

Chuang-tzu

The world is full of half-enlightened masters. Overly clever, too "sensitive" to live in the real world, they surround themselves with selfish pleasures and bestow their grandiose teachings upon the unwary. Prematurely publicizing themselves, intent upon reaching some spiritual climax, they constantly sacrifice the truth and deviate from the Tao. What they really offer the world is their own confusion. The true master understands that enlightenment is not the end, but the means. Realizing that virtue is her goal, she accepts the long and often arduous cultivation that is necessary to attain it. She doesn't scheme to become a leader, but quietly shoulders whatever responsibilities fall to her. Unattached to her accomplishments, taking credit for nothing at all, she guides the whole world by guiding the individuals who come to her. She shares her divine energy with her students, encouraging them, creating trials to strengthen them, scolding them to awaken them, directing the streams of their lives toward the infinite ocean of the Tao.

Lao-tzu

Prince Wen Hui's cook was cutting up an ox. . . . The ox fell apart with a whisper. The bright cleaver murmured like a gentle wind. Rhythm! Timing! Like a sacred dance. . . .

Prince Wen Hui: Good work! Your method is faultless!

The cook: Method? What I follow is Tao beyond all methods! When I first began to cut up oxen I would see before me the whole ox all in one mass. After three years I no longer saw this mass. I saw the distinctions. But now I see nothing with the eye. My whole being apprehends. My senses are idle. The spirit free to work without plan follows its own instinct guided by natural line, by the secret opening, the hidden space, my cleaver finds its own way . . . Then I withdraw the blade, I stand still and let the joy of the work sink in. I clean the blade and put it away.

Prince Wan Hui: This is it! My cook has shown me how I ought to live my own life!"

Chuang-tzu

Certain Chinese philosophers writing in, perhaps, the fifth and fourth centuries, explained ideas and a way of life that have come to be known as Taoism - the way of man's co-operation with the course or trend of the natural world, whose principles we discover in the flow patterns of water, gas, an fire, which are subsequently memorialized or sculptured in those of stone and wood, and, later, in many forms of human art.

Alan Watts

---

4 FACTS AND FIGURES

Taoism is popular in China, South-East Asia, Japan, Australia, Europe, South America, and the US. The estimated total number of Taoists worldwide is more than 20 million.

Taiwan has the greatest concentration of Taoists. 75% of people in Taiwan identify themselves as Buddhists or Taoists.

Countries with the largest populations of Taoists:

Taiwan	nearly 3 million
North America	30,000
Canada	2,000

5 TAOIST PRACTICES

A Taoist hygiene and yoga
B *Wu-hsing*
C *Tai Chi*
D *Feng Shui*
E *Taijiquan*
F Acupuncture

INTRODUCTION

Taoists aim to live simply, and in harmony with nature. They meditate regularly to maintain contact with the Tao.

A TAOIST HYGIENE AND YOGA

Taoists generally have an interest in promoting health and vitality.

There are a number of Taoist practices that have been designed to enhance a person's Tao, which is referred to as *ch'i* (vital energy). The three main approaches are:

- eating substances which are thought to enhance *ch'i*
- types of movement, such as dance, exercise, and martial arts
- a form of meditation somewhat similar to Raja yoga, by means of which practitioners bring the Tao into themselves and then direct it to others.

B WU-SING

An important concept is the notion of five agents or phases that are present in the cosmos and in each individual person. These are: water, fire, wood, metal and earth. Philosophers have constructed a system of correspondences between these agents, and use them to work out techniques for long life and health.

C TAI CHI

Taoists engage in various exercise and movement techniques (*Tai Ch'i*) which stimulate the central nervous system, lower blood pressure, and relieve stress. It is believed that everyone has a portion of *ch'i* at birth,

and must strengthen it. Traditional Chinese medicine teaches that illness is caused by blockages or lack of balance in the body's *ch'i* (intrinsic energy). It is believed that *Tai Ch'i* balances this energy flow.

D FENG SHUI

Traditional *Feng Shui* is the science and art of *ch'i*. This discipline, or philosophy, is often referred to in the West as the art of placement and has been popularized by many books and magazines. But it is much more than the mere placing of furniture to manage *ch'i* flow. *Feng Shui* is a way of harmonizing architecture and landscaping in accordance with Taoist principles. It teaches us how to refine and align our internal and external worlds and how to exist in harmony with the space we inhabit.

E TAIJIQUAN

"*Taijiquan*" is the Romanized Chinese spelling of *Tai Chi Chuan,* which is a form of Chinese martial art. The term *taiji* means "the cosmos," and *quan* is the short form for *quan fa,* which means "fist techniques" and refers to what Westerners today would term kungfu.

Tai Chi Chuan masters have categorized the benefits of *Tai Chi Chuan* into three levels:

- good health
- self-defense
- spiritual cultivation.

The practice of *Tai Chi Chuan* is an excellent way of promoting physical, emotional and mental health, and may be undertaken by anybody, irrespective of race, culture and religion. The training is gentle and graceful, and there is no need for special apparatus. *Tai Chi Chuan* is an effective martial art in which physical size and mechanical strength are not necessarily winning factors. At the highest level, *Tai Chi Chuan* leads to mind expansion and spiritual fulfillment.

F ACUPUNCTURE

Acupuncture is the manipulation of *ch'i* in the body. It works by placing pins just below the skin in very specific places and combinations. This stimulates nerve bundles to relax muscle fibers, thereby relieving tension, pain and stress. The acupuncture points are located where natural nodes in the human body meet. It is at these places that the *ch'i* is concentrated. By placing the needles at these nodes, the *ch'i* is redistributed to the rest of the body, thereby restoring the natural balance.

6 TAOIST BELIEFS

A Belief in God
B Tao
C *Ch'i*
D Three Jewels
E *Wu-wei*
F Symbols

   (i) Yin-Yang
   (ii) Water

A BELIEF IN GOD

Taoism as a classical philosophy has no concept of a personal deity, a conscious God, or a God who is responsible for the creation of the universe.

B TAO

Tao is the first-cause of the universe. It is a force that flows through all life, the total of all things which are and which change. It is marked, therefore, by creative spontaneity.
"The Tao surrounds everyone and therefore everyone must listen to find enlightenment."

Each believer's goal is to become one with the Tao and so live in spontaneity and freedom (from, for example, social and political pressures, or from fear of death).

C CH'I

Ch'i is the life force, the essence, the wind, the movement of energy. It is the forces that arise from the earth, that touch and nourish the earth as well as tear it apart (earthquakes). Each person must nurture the *ch'i* (air, breath, virtue) that has been given to him or her. Development of virtue is one's chief task.

D THREE JEWELS

The Three Jewels to be sought are compassion, moderation and humility.

E WU-WEI

The Tao is the pattern for human behavior. Taoists therefore follow the art of *wu-wei*, which is sometimes called "uncontrived action." It is action so well in accordance with the way things are that the one who performs the action leaves no trace of himself. "Perfect activity leaves no track behind it; perfect speech is like a jade worker whose tool leaves no mark." One aspect of this may be described as letting nature take its course. For example, one should allow a river to flow towards the sea unimpeded, without erecting a dam, which would interfere with its natural flow.

F SYMBOLS

> (i) Yin-Yang
> (ii) Water

(I) YIN-YANG
A frequent graphic representation of Taoist theology is the circular Yin-Yang figure. It represents the balance of opposites that are found in the universe. When they are equally present, all is calm. When one is outweighed by the other, there is confusion and disarray. The Yin and Yang are a model that the faithful follow.

- Yin (dark side) is the breath that formed the earth.
- Yang (light side) is the breath that formed the heavens.

Intervention by human civilization upsets the balance of Yin and Yang.

Some of the pairs of opposites represented by Yang and Yin are:

Yang	Yin
male	female
good	evil
active	passive
light	darkness
heaven	earth
sun	moon
summer	winter
positive	negative
life	death

(II) WATER
The best symbol of the Tao is water. Water moves gently forward, it seeks its own level and adapts itself to its surroundings. When it is still, it becomes clear. It also has tremendous power and is able to wear away the hardest stone.

7 WORSHIP

> A Taoism as a religion
> B Yu-huang
> C The Immortals
> D Taoist deities
> E Festivals

A TAOISM AS A RELIGION
In the second century AD, Taoism developed as a religious movement. Taoism as a religion seems to be incompatible with the aims of Taoism as a philosophy. There are, however, suggestions in the *Tao-tzu* that safety from harm, health and long life come to those who are at one with the Tao. Communities were therefore established where techniques were practiced that were designed to achieve immortality. These included: diet, breath control, sexual disciplines, the taking of drugs, and meditation. Alchemists searched for the elixir of immortality.

Taoism as a religion is polytheistic. Lao-tzu himself is deified as a revealer of secret texts and a savior. Taoists worship gods, "Immortals" and saints, both in their own homes and in their temples. They go to the temples for teaching and meditation, under the instruction of Taoist priests.

B YU-HUANG

Jade Emperor Yu-huang is considered the foremost deity of popular Taoism. He is the ruler of Heaven. He is also considered to be the ruler of all the other gods who in turn must report to him.

C THE IMMORTALS

The Immortals (*hsien*) are the "Perfected ones." They first appear in the *Chuang-tzu* as a special class of spiritual beings, who live an effortless, spontaneous life, far away from the turmoils of the world of men They dine on air, drink dew, and are able to fly. Later the *hsien* were linked to legendary mortal figures who, it was said, had lived perfect lives and so had become immortal and now live in the Realm of Great Purity. These figures were classified, and put in a heavenly hierarchy. The earliest systematic collection of biographical information about them is the *Lives of the Immortals.* Written in the early second century AD, it has brief accounts of seventy-two *hsien*. Each entry is followed by a short hymn of praise.

The lives of the *hsien* inform religious Taoism. People try to attain to their qualities, and the goal of life is to become a *hsien*.

D TAOIST DEITIES

Jade Emperor (Yu Huang)
   High God of Taoists
   Rules other gods

First Principle (Yuan Shi Tian Zun)
   Instructs Jade Emperor

Three Pure Ones (San Qing)
(i) Jade Pure (Yu Qing [Yu-ch'ing])
(ii) Upper Pure (Shang Qing [Shang-ch'ing])
(iii) Great Pure (Tai Qing)

Three Officials (San Guan)
(i) Ruler of Heaven (Tian Guan): grants happiness
(ii) Ruler of Earth (Di Guan): grants remissions of sins
(iii) Ruler of Water (Shui Guan): averts all evil

Three Epochs/Principles (San Yuan)
(i) Shang Yuan: ruled first six moons (winter and spring)
(ii) Xia Yuan: ruled seventh and eighth moons (summer)
(iii) Zhong Yuan: ruled ninth thru eleventh moons (fall)

Tian Shi
Hsi Wang Mu : Mother Empress of the West.

E FESTIVALS

Taoists celebrate a large number of festivals. Some festivals, such as the Lunar New Year, Dragon Boat Festival and Hungry Ghost Festival, are well known. Others festivals, such as the birthdays of the different deities, often only involve the local community and devotees of that particular deity.

All Taoists celebrate the fifteenth day of the second lunar month. This is Taoist Day - the birthday of Lao-tzu.

8 COMPARISON OF TAOISM WITH CHRISTIANITY

A Common ground
B Great differences
C Yin and Yang

INTRODUCTION

Taoism as a popular religion is often little more than a system of magical practices and incantations. Its priests sell charms against demons and evil spirits of the dead. It is both polytheistic and animistic.

A COMMON GROUND

The *Tao-Te-ching* states:

"Before heaven and earth existed there was something nebulous . . . I do not know its name and I address it as Tao."

Genesis 1:1-2:

"In the beginning God created the heaven and the earth. And the earth was without form, and void; and darkness was upon the face of the deep. And the Spirit of God moved upon the face of the waters."

B GREAT DIFFERENCES

Taoism: There is no personal creator God in any form of Taoism. Taoism is instead involved with nature, mysticism, and an impersonal principle.

Jesus taught:

"When you pray [to God] say, "Out Father . . .""
  God created man to have a relationship with him.
  He answers those who call to him.

Taoism:

Sin and morality are minimized in Taoism. Salvation is achieved by following the Tao. A person must commit himself to the Tao and live a life of simplicity, quietness, compassion, moderation and humility.

Christianity:

"All have sinned and fall short of the glory of God" (Romans 3:23).

  Salvation is a gift of God that comes through faith in Jesus Christ.

  "For God so loved the world that he gave his one and only Son, that whoever believes in him should not die but have eternal life" (John 3:16).

C YIN AND YANG

It should not be supposed that Tao and Yin-Yang can be favorably compared with the Bible's belief that good and bad do not complement each other. The source of good is God. The source of evil, the devil who opposes the work of God, does not commune in harmony with the earth, but "seeks whom he may devour."

9 GLOSSARY

Acupuncture
Traditional Chinese medical treatment using needles to stimulate the flow of *ch'i* in the body.

Ch'ang ("enduring")
The permanent and eternal.

Chang Kuo-lao
One of the Eight Immortals, connected with a historical figure of the T'ang dynasty. His symbol is a fish-drum.

Chiao ("doctrine")
Religion.

Chia ("school of transmission")
Philosophy.

Ch'i ("air," "breath, "strength" "virtue")
Life energy that flows throughout the human body and the universe.

Chuang-tzu
A later disciple of Lao-tzu who wrote some thirty-three books, which helped popularize Taoism.

Chung-li Ch'uan
One of the Eight Immortals. He is depicted as a stout man with a near-bald ut a long beard. His symbol is a fan, indicating power to raise the dead.

Han Hsiang-tzu
One of the Eight Immortals. He is depicted as a peaceful mountain-dweller with a flute, flowers and a peach. He is the patron of music.

Ho Hsien-ku
The only female Immortal.

Hsien ("fluttering")
The Immortals, who are described in the Chuang-tzu. Perhaps originally intended to be allegorical, the nature and abilities of these beings became a practical goal for later Taoists.

Hsin
Heart or mind.

Lao-tzu
Chinese sage and philosopher who founded Taoism.

Ling-pao P'ai ("School of the Magic Jewel")
Movement within religious Taoism based on Ling-pao Ching. Influenced by Buddhist devotion to *bodhisattvas*, it teaches that liberation depends on help from deities (*t'ien-tsun*). A central ritual is a formal fast (*chai*).

Ming
Name. In Chinese thought, to name something is to assign it a place in the hierarchy of the universe. The Tao is therefore nameless.

Pa-hsien ("Eight Immortals"). Taoist figures associated with good fortune and the eight conditions of life that are frequently portrayed in Chinese art and literature. They are: Li T'ieh-juai; Chang Kuo-lao; Ts'ao Kuo-chiu; Han Hsiang-tzu; Lu Tung-pen; Ho Hsien-ku; Lan Ts'ai-ho; and Chung-li Ch'uan.

P'u ("uncarved block")
State of simplicity and true nature, as in infancy, before being shaped by knowledge, morality and other influences of society. For Lao-tzu, this is the state of the ideal ruler.

Shen
Spiritual consciousness.

T'ai chi ("Great Polarity")
Yin and yang.

T'ai chi chu'uan ("Great Polarity Boxing")
Martial art aimed at harnessing the strength of *ch'i*.

Tao
Tao: Pronounced "dow," literally, the "Way" or "Path." The Tao is the inexpressible way of

ultimate reality by which one should order one's life. Tao is the unchanging principle behind the universe, the unproduced producer of all that is. The *Tao-te-ching* describes it as "something formlessly fashioned, that existed before Heaven and Earth."

Tao-shih
Scholars and ritual functionaries of religious Taoism.

Tao-te-ching ("Book of the Way and its Power")
Foundational text and the sacred scripture of Taoism. Attributed to Lao-tzu (and therefore sometimes referred to as *Lao-tzu)*, and probably composed in the fourth century BC, it teaches about the Tao.

Tao-te t'ien-tsun
Ruler of Taoist heaven of highest purity; San-ch'ing.

Tao-tsang
Taoist canon of authoritative texts.

Tao-yin
Exercise for guiding the breath to different parts of the body.

Te ("power" or "virtue")
Means through which the Tao becomes manifest and actualized.

Tzu-jan
Spontaneity; unconditioned and totally itself. The Tao is characterized by *tzu-jan*.

Wu
Not-Being. Not synonymous with nothingness, *wu* is an immense void containing all potentialities. It is thus interdependent with *yu*, being.

Wu-wei ("non-action")
The ideal for rulers as set out in the Tao-te-ching. *Wu wei* is the concept of inaction. By practicing *wu wei*, one harmonizes one's life with the Tao and so manages to live as one was meant to.

Yin and Yang
Yin and Yang represent elements in the universe that are contrary to each other, such as life and death, light and darkness, good and evil. Yang (pronounced "yawn") represents the positive, warm, light, or dry elements, as on the sunny side of a mountain. Yin represents the negative, cold, dark, or moist elements, as on the shady side of a mountain.

yu
Being.

JUDAISM

CONTENTS

1 An overview   327

2 Judaism's founders   328

3 Jewish holy book   328

4 Facts and figures   332

5 Jewish practices   332

6 Jewish beliefs   335

7 Worship   351

8 Groupings within Judaism   357

9 Famous Jews   358

10 Comparison with Christianity   359

11 Glossary   360

1 An Overview

DEFINITION

Judaism is the religion of the Jewish people.

Factfile
- Date of origin: Second millennium BC
- Founder: Abraham was the first Jew, according to religious Jews
- Holy book: Tanakh (The Old Testament)
- Number of adherents: More than 16 million

SUMMARY

Judaism is the oldest known monotheistic religion still practiced in the world today. Some of its teachings form part of the basis for Christianity and Islam.

The world stands upon three things,
Torah (Knowledge, study, principles, ideas),
Avodah (Worship, practice, religious experience),
Gemilut chasadim (loving deeds which repair the world).

Mishnah Avot

SUMMARY OF PRACTICES

Jews follow the ideals of truth, justice, humility, faithfulness, and loving-kindness.

They are noted for their love of learning. Ever since their delivery from slavery in Egypt they have valued freedom. Many principles fundamental to Western democracy are based on the Hebrew scriptures.

SUMMARY OF BELIEFS

MONOTHEISM
There is one universal God who created and rules the world.

REVELATION
God has revealed his will through his prophets, especially Abraham and Moses.

THE CHOICE OF ISRAEL
God chose Israel as his own special followers.

2 JUDAISM'S FOUNDERS

THE PATRIARCHS

Abraham, Isaac and Jacob, known as the patriarchs, are both the physical and spiritual ancestors of Judaism. They founded Judaism, and their descendants are the Jewish people.

ABRAHAM

God called Abram from the city of Haran in Mesopotamia and told him to go to Canaan. In Canaan, God established his covenant with Abram and his wife Sarai and changed their names to Abraham and Sarah.

MOSES AND THE TORAH

After liberating the Israelites from Egypt, God led his people Israel, the descendants of Abraham and Sarah, to Mount Sinai. Here he renewed the covenant, and gave Moses his Law. The *Torah* of Moses still remains the basis of Judaism.

3 JEWISH HOLY BOOK

A Tanakh
B Other authorities

  (i)   *Talmud*
  (ii) *The Mishnah*
        Orders and tractates
  (iii) *The Gemara*

A TANAKH

The Jewish scriptures are known as the Tanakh. They correspond to what non-Jews call the "Old Testament."

The Tanakh is composed of three groups of books:

* the *Torah*
* the *Nevi'im* (Prophets)
* the *Ketuvim* (Writings).

THE TORAH

The *Torah*, also known as the Pentateuch, consists of:
Genesis
Exodus
Leviticus
Numbers
Deuteronomy.

A non-Jew told the Jewish rabbi, Hillel, that he would become a Jew if he managed to teach him the whole of the *Torah* while he balanced on one leg.

Hillel came up with this reply: "What is hateful to yourself, do not do to your neighbor. That is the whole *Torah*; the rest is just commentary. Go and study it."

THE NEVI'IM (THE PROPHETS)

The *Nevi'im* comprise:
Joshua
Judges
Samuel
Kings
Isaiah
Jeremiah
Ezekiel
The twelve prophets
  Hosea
  Joel
  Amos

Obadiah
Jonah
Micah
Nahum
Habakkuk
Zephaniah
Haggai
Zechariah
Malachi

THE KETUVIM (THE WRITINGS)
The *Ketuvim* comprise:
Psalms
Proverbs
Job
Song of Songs
Ecclesiastes
Ruth
Esther
Lamentations
Daniel
Ezra and Nehemiah
Chronicles

(In the Jewish Scriptures the books of Samuel, Kings, Chronicles, Ezra and Nehemiah are each one book.)

CONTENTS OF THE TORAH
Genesis (Bereshit)
Creation, Adam and Eve, Noah and the flood, Abraham and Sarah, Isaac, Jacob, Joseph. The promise that Abraham's descendants would receive the Land of Israel and be a blessing to the rest of the world. Jacob and his sons settle in Egypt.

Exodus (Shemot)
The Egyptian exile, Moses, the ten plagues, the exodus from Egypt and the revelation at Mt. Sinai. The gift of the written and the oral *Torah*. The building of the *Mishkan* (Tabernacle).

Leviticus (Vayikra)
The laws of the priests, the Temple, the sacrifices, and the festivals, and their reason: "I am LORD who brought you up out of Egypt to be your God; therefore be holy, because I am holy" (Leviticus 11:45). Social and moral laws: "Love your neighbor as yourself" (Leviticus 19:18).

Numbers (Bamidbar)
The struggles of the Jewish People for forty years in the desert. The census, the formation of the camp. The rebellion of Korah, the episode of the twelve spies, the capture of the East Bank of the Jordan River.

Deuteronomy (Devarim)
Moses addresses the Jewish people before his death. His words include rebuke, encouragement and warnings for their future; commandments that apply only in Israel and commandments that govern the interaction with other nations. One copy of the complete *Torah* is given to each tribe. One is placed in the Holy Ark. It ends with the death of Moses, "the greatest of all prophets" and "the most humble of all men."

CONTENTS OF THE NEVI'IM (PROPHETS)
Joshua
Joshua takes over the leadership of the Jewish people from Moses, the River Jordan is crossed miraculously and the spies are sent to Jericho. The famous story of Joshua and the battle of Jericho is followed by the account of the conquest of the land of Canaan.

Judges
Begins with the death of Joshua and continues until the period of Samson (approximately 400 years). Written by Samuel as a prophetic criticism for future generations, it describes a period of self-government prior to the establishment of the monarchy.

Samuel
Begins with Samuel's birth and tutelage under Eli the high priest, detailing the major events of the next half century, in which Samuel, as God's prophet, played an important role. It describes the choice of David, the passing of Samuel and the death of King Saul and Jonathan on the battlefield. Israel's leadership passes to its second king, David, who makes Jerusalem his capital city and extends the kingdom.

Kings

Begins with King David's last days and continues through the reign of Solomon and the building of the Temple in Jerusalem. It covers the schism of the kingdom and describes Elijah's confrontation with Ahab, King of Israel, and the destruction of the false prophets on Mount Carmel. Elisha continues the prophetic work of Elijah. The destruction of the northern kingdom is followed by the destruction of Jerusalem and the beginning of the Babylonian exile.

Isaiah

Commences with the prophet's castigation of the people for their spiritual backsliding and continues with a description of the Messianic era.

Jeremiah

Begins with the first two prophecies of the impending invasion by the Babylonians and Jeremiah's castigation of the people for their sins. In the wake of the assassination of Gedaliah, the Judean governor, he exhorts the people to surrender to the Babylonians and to remain in the land. But his warning goes unheeded.

Ezekiel

Commences with the vision of the Celestial Chariot (*merkavah*), representing the Divine Presence leaving the Temple. Although Ezekiel is in Babylon, he forewarns those remaining in the Holy Land of the impending destruction of Jerusalem and the Temple. This book includes the prophecy of the destruction of the great Phoenician commercial cities, Tyre and Zidon. It continues with the prophet's discourse on the efficacy of repentance. The vision of the dry bones also appears here.

The Twelve Prophets

The Twelve Prophets include the story of Jonah and the big fish. The book of the Twelve Prophets ends with Malachi, who prophesies the coming of the prophet Elijah, the forerunner of the Messiah, who will return the heart of the fathers to their children and the heart of the children to their fathers.

CONTENTS OF THE WRITINGS (KETUVIM)

Psalms (Tehillim)

These 150 psalms, many of which have been written by King David, have been a source of solace and hope to countless generations.

Proverbs

The wisdom of King Solomon, the wisest of men.

Job

Eloquently seeks to answer one very important question: If Job is truly righteous, what makes him deserve the punishment God sees fit to give him?

Song of Songs

Deals with a maiden whose husband left her for many years, promising to return and restore her to her previous status. It is considered to be an allegorical representation of the exile of the Jewish people and their return to the Holy Land with the coming of the Messiah.

Ecclesiastes

Contains King Solomon's philosophical discourses in which he ponders the reason for man's existence and concludes that man's purpose is only to fear God.

Ruth

Relates the story of a Moabite woman who married an Israelite man and was reduced to poverty after her husband's demise. She accompanied her mother-in-law Naomi to the Holy Land, where she ultimately married Boaz, and became the matriarch of the house of David. The conversion of Ruth to Judaism is the basis for the laws of Judaism relating to conversion.

Esther

Recounts the well-known miracle of Purim, when the Jews of the Persian Empire were saved from annihilation.

Lamentations

Depicts the heartrending experiences of the prophet Jeremiah during the destruction of the first Temple and the city of Jerusalem.

Daniel

Deals with the experiences of Daniel, who was exiled to Babylon by Nebuchadnezzar. Includes the narratives of the fiery furnace and the lion's den. It also contains Daniel's interpretation of Nebuchadnezzar's dreams and his visions of the future.

Ezra and Nehemiah

Traditionally counted as one book, it deals with the difficulties of the Jewish people when they returned to the Holy Land after the Babylonian Exile, and the ways in which their leaders, Ezra and Nehemiah, solved these problems. The walls of Jerusalem are rebuilt.

Chronicles (In the Jewish Scriptures, one book)

Contains the history of man from Adam until the reign of Solomon to Cyrus' proclamation permitting the Jews to return to Jerusalem to rebuild the Temple.

B OTHER AUTHORITIES

(I) TALMUD

The *Talmud* is also traditionally referred to as *Shas* (an abbreviation of *shishah sedarim*). It includes stories, laws, medical knowledge, and debates about moral choices. It is viewed as the authoritative record of rabbinic discussions on Jewish law, Jewish ethics, customs, legends and stories, and is a fundamental source of customs, case histories and moral exhortations.

The *Talmud* is the summary of Judaism's oral tradition and is the major influence on Jewish belief and thought. Although not a formal legal code, it is the basis for all later codes of Jewish law. It is composed of material from two sources: the *Mishnah* and the *Gemara*.

(II) THE MISHNAH

The *Mishnah* consists of six orders (*sedarim*), each of which contains between seven and twelve tractates, called *masechtot* (*masechet* in the singular). Each *masechet* is divided into smaller units called *mishnayot* (*mishnah* in the singular).

It was compiled about 200 AD.

Orders and tractates

The six orders in the *Mishnah* are:

- First Order: *Zeraim* ("Seeds"). 11 tractates. It deals with agricultural laws and prayers.
- Second Order: *Moed* ("Festival Days"). 12 tractates. This pertains to the laws of the Sabbath and the Festivals.
- Third Order: *Nashim* ("Women"). 7 tractates. Concerns marriage and divorce.
- Fourth Order: *Nezikim* ("Damages"). 10 tractates. Deals with civil and criminal law.
- Fifth Order: *Kodshim* ("Holy things"). 11 tractates. This involves sacrificial rites, the Temple, and the dietary laws.
- Sixth Order: *Tohorot* ("Purity"). 12 tractates. This pertains to ritual and the laws of family purity.

(III) THE GEMERA

The *Gemera* (one Babylonian and one Palestinian) is encyclopedic in scope. It includes comments from hundreds of rabbis from 200 to 500 AD, explaining the *Mishnah* with additional historical, religious, legal, and sociological material.

4 FACTS AND FIGURES

GEOGRAPHICAL LOCATION OF JEWS

United States	6,000,000
Israel	5,000,000
Europe	less than 2,000,000
Canada	400,000
The former Soviet Union	400,000
Argentina	250,000
Brazil	30,000
South Africa	110,000
Australia	100,000

5 JEWISH PRACTICES

A Obedience to the Law
B *Tefillin*
C Marriage
D Mourning
E Praying
F Keeping *kosher*

A OBEDIENCE TO THE LAW

Strict discipline, according to the Law, governs all areas of Jewish life.

B TEFILLIN

Jewish males from the age of thirteen onwards wear *tefillin* on the left arm and head during weekday morning prayers to remind them of the importance of following the Jewish Scriptures.

Also known as phylacteries, *tefillin* are small black leather boxes held in place with straps. They contain the following verses from the Hebrew Scriptures:

And the LORD spake unto Moses, saying, Sanctify unto me all the firstborn, whatsoever openeth the womb among the children of Israel, both of man and of beast: it is mine.

And Moses said unto the people, Remember this day, in which ye came out from Egypt, out of the house of bondage; for by strength of hand the LORD brought you out from this place: there shall no leavened bread be eaten.

This day came ye out in the month Abib. And it shall be when the LORD shall bring thee into the land of the Canaanites, and the Hittites, and the Amorites, and the Hivites, and the Jebusites, which he sware unto thy fathers to give thee, a land flowing with milk and honey, that thou shalt keep this service in this month.

Seven days thou shalt eat unleavened bread, and in the seventh day shall be a feast to the LORD.

Unleavened bread shall be eaten seven days; and there shall no leavened bread be seen with thee, neither shall there be leaven seen with thee in all thy quarters.

And thou shalt shew thy son in that day, saying, This is done because of that which the LORD did unto me when I came forth out of Egypt.

And it shall be for a sign unto thee upon thine hand, and for a memorial between thine eyes, that the LORD's law may be in thy mouth: for with a strong hand hath the LORD brought thee out of Egypt.

Thou shalt therefore keep this ordinance in his season from year to year.

Exodus 13:1-10

And it shall be when the LORD shall bring thee into the land of the Canaanites, as he sware unto thee and to thy fathers, and shall give it thee,

That thou shalt set apart unto the LORD all that openeth the matrix, and every firstling that cometh of a beast which thou hast; the males shall be the LORD's.

And every firstling of an ass thou shalt redeem with a lamb; and if thou wilt not redeem it, then thou shalt break his neck: and all the firstborn of man among thy children shalt thou redeem.

And it shall be when thy son asketh thee in time to come, saying, What is this? that thou shalt say unto him, By strength of hand the LORD brought us out from Egypt, from the house of bondage:

And it came to pass, when Pharaoh would hardly let us go, that the LORD slew all the firstborn in the land of Egypt, both the firstborn of man, and the firstborn of beast: therefore I sacrifice to the LORD all that openeth the matrix, being males; but all the firstborn of my children I redeem.

And it shall be for a token upon thine hand, and for frontlets between thine eyes: for by strength of hand the LORD brought us forth out of Egypt.

Exodus 13:11-16

Hear, O Israel: The LORD our God is one LORD:

And thou shalt love the LORD thy God with all thine heart, and with all thy soul, and with all thy might.

And these words, which I command thee this day, shall be in thine heart:

And thou shalt teach them diligently unto thy children, and shalt talk of them when thou sittest in thine house, and when thou walkest by the way, and when thou liest down, and when thou risest up.

And thou shalt bind them for a sign upon thine hand, and they shall be as frontlets between thine eyes.

And thou shalt write them upon the posts of thy house, and on thy gates.

Deuteronomy 6:4-9

And it shall come to pass, if ye shall hearken diligently unto my commandments which I command you this day, to love the LORD your God, and to serve him with all your heart and with all your soul,

That I will give you the rain of your land in his due season, the first rain and the latter rain, that thou mayest gather in thy corn, and thy wine, and thine oil.

And I will send grass in thy fields for thy cattle, that thou mayest eat and be full.

Take heed to yourselves, that your heart be not deceived, and ye turn aside, and serve other gods, and worship them;

And then the LORD's wrath be kindled against you, and he shut up the heaven, that there be no rain, and that the land yield not her fruit; and lest ye perish quickly from off the good land which the LORD giveth you.

Therefore shall ye lay up these my words in your heart and in your soul, and bind them for a sign upon your hand, that they may be as frontlets between your eyes.

And ye shall teach them your children, speaking of them when thou sittest in thine house, and when thou walkest by the way, when thou liest down, and when thou risest up.

And thou shalt write them upon the door posts of thine house, and upon thy gates:

That your days may be multiplied, and the days of your children, in the land which the LORD sware unto your fathers to give them, as the days of heaven upon the earth.

Deuteronomy   *11:13-21*

C MARRIAGE

Jews are only supposed to marry fellow-Jews.

Marriage is a holy covenant.

Vows are said under a canopy (*huppah*), which symbolizes the expanse of the heavens under which all life takes place.

D MOURNING

Judaism has a multi-staged mourning practice.

The first stage, called the *Shiv'ah*, is observed for one week. During this time the family sits in mourning.

The second stage, called the *shloshim*, is observed for one month.

On the loss of a parent, there is a third state, called *avelut yud bet chodesh*, which is observed for one year.

The year anniversary of the death, a *yahrzeit,* is marked by a service and a candle is lit in the home.

The doctrine of the resurrection is not found in the *Torah*, but it is included in Maimonides' Thirteen Principles (see below).

E PRAYING

Jews believe that God hears and answers prayer. The whole of life is covered and marked by prayer, and is lived in conscious reverence at the presence of God. The wearing of the *tefillin* symbolizes this. Other symbolic actions performed by devout orthodox Jews are:

- Prayer three times a day – morning, afternoon and evening. When he prays the Jew covers his head with a skull cap, or an ordinary hat. In the morning he may also wear a prayer shawl. This has tassels at the four corners in obedience to a command in the *Torah.*

- A *mezuzah* on the upper part of the right hand front door post. This is a small scroll with the words of the *Shema* written on it in Hebrew. It is kept in a wooden or metal container. This reminds members of the family of God's presence whenever they go in and out.

- Traveler's Prayer: according to the *Talmud*, the following traveler's prayer should be recited at the beginning of every journey:

May it be Your will, Lord, My God and God of my ancestors, to lead me, to direct my steps, and to support me in peace. Lead me in life, tranquil and serene, until I arrive at where I am going. Deliver me from every enemy, ambush and hurt that I might encounter on the way and from all afflictions that visit and trouble the world. Bless the work of my hands. Let me receive divine grace and those loving acts of kindness and mercy in Your eyes and in the eyes of all those I encounter. Listen to the voice of my appeal, for you are a God who responds to prayerful supplication. Praised are you, Lord, who responds to prayer.

F KEEPING KOSHER

Jews who observe the dietary laws (*kashrut*) make decisions about what they eat, when they eat it and how they prepare their food. Food that may be eaten is called *kosher*. Orthodox Jews are careful to keep all the dietary laws; other Jews will not eat forbidden food, but do not insist on a *kosher* kitchen. Others ignore all these laws.

KOSHER FOOD

A *kosher* animal must be a ruminant and have split hooves cows, sheep, goats and deer are all *kosher*, whereas camels and pigs (having each only one sign of *kashrut*) are not *kosher*. Most common fowl, like chickens, ducks and geese, are *kosher*, but the birds of prey (hawks, eagles, etc.) are not *kosher*. A sea creature is only *kosher* if it has fins and scales. So most species of fish are *kosher* (tuna, salmon, flounder, etc.) but not; nor are dolphins, whales and squids. Any food product (for example, milk) of a non-*kosher* animal is also non-*kosher*. The exception to this rule is bee's honey.

SLAUGHTERING ANIMALS

An animal or bird must be slaughtered according to Jewish law (*shechita*). This involves cutting the animal's trachea and esophagus. The cut must be swift, continuous and performed by a trained and ordained *shochet*. This method of slaughter immediately reduces the blood pressure in the brain to zero, so that the animal loses consciousness in a few seconds and dies in minutes, with a minimum of pain. The meat must be broiled, or soaked in cold water and salted to remove all traces of blood.

NO TREIFOT
The animal or bird must be free of *treifot*, which refers to seventy different categories of injuries, diseases or abnormalities, the presence of which renders the animal non-*kosher*.

FATS
Certain fats, known as *chelev*, may not be eaten.

NO MIXTURES
It is forbidden to cook and serve meat and poultry with dairy food. This means that when meat is eaten, there must be no butter on the bread or milk in the drinks. To ensure

that this rule is kept, many housewives have two sets of dishes: one for meats and the other for milk foods. Hotels and restaurants have two kitchens.

BENEFITS OF THE LAWS OF KASHRUT
The laws of *kashrut* enable Jews to enjoy the pleasures of the physical world. But they ensure that such pleasures are engaged in with sensitivity.

Kashrut recognizes that the basic human need is not food, drink or comfort, but meaning. Judaism, through the dietary laws, focuses on the meaning of everyday eating and drinking.

6 JEWISH BELIEFS

A God
B The Messiah
C Covenant
D The Ten Commandments
E 613 commandments
Maimonides' list

INTRODUCTION
Maimonides (AD 1135-1204) was a Jewish philosopher who lived in Spain and then Egypt. His thirteen principles of faith are the nearest that anyone has ever come to creating a widely-accepted list of Jewish beliefs.

These principles of faith are the minimum requirements of Jewish belief.

1. G-d exists
2 G-d is one and unique
3. G-d is incorporeal

4. G-d is eternal
5. Prayer is to be directed to G-d alone and to no other
6. The words of the prophets are true
7. Moses' prophecies are true, and Moses was the greatest of the prophets
8. The Written *Torah* (first five books of the Bible) and Oral *Torah* (teachings now contained in the *Talmud* and other writings) were given to Moses
9. There will be no other *Torah*

10. G-d knows the thoughts and deeds of men
11. G-d will reward the good and punish the wicked
12. The Messiah will come
13. The dead will be resurrected

A GOD

God is the creator of all that exists.

God is one. The *Shema*, "Hear, O Israel, the Lord our God, the Lord is One," summarizes this most fundamental characteristic of God. (*Shema* is the Hebrew word for "hear.")

God is incorporeal (without a body).

God alone is to be worshiped.

B THE MESSIAH

Jews do not believe that Jesus was the Messiah, although some accept that he was a good moral teacher.

The Messiah, God's anointed one, will arrive in the future and gather Jews into the land of Israel. There will be a general resurrection of the dead at that time.

C COVENANT

The idea of a covenant (an agreement) between God and his people is central to Jewish religion: the people are bound to God by a covenant that was initiated by God and freely agreed to by the people.

In the Scriptures God makes a number of covenants:

- With Noah, when he promises never again to destroy the earth.
- With Abraham, which resulted in the establishment of Abraham's descendants as the chosen people. Circumcision is a sign of this covenant.
- 600 years later, at Mount Sinai, with all the people who came out of Egypt. God promises that Israel will be his special possession. The people agree to keep the God's commandments.
- With King David, promising that David's descendants will reign for ever.
- In Jeremiah and Ezekiel there is the promise of a new covenant in which the laws will not be imposed externally, but

will be obeyed spontaneously because they are written on people's hearts.

Judaism has a 3000-year-old tradition of infusing the spiritual into our everyday lives, not for personal redemption, but to uplift the lot of [humankind] through adherence to ethical and moral principles, and to preserve through this common endeavor a sense of connectedness with a people. This, the essence of our Covenant, gives us tools to deal with the disparate and often confusing aspects of modern life.

Alfred Moses, US Ambassador
to Romania, 1996

D THE TEN COMMANDMENTS

The Ten Commandments, as delineated in Exodus 20:1-17 and Deuteronomy 5:6-21, form a brief synopsis of the Law.

God spoke all these words:
I am God, your God,
who brought you out of the land of Egypt,
out of a life of slavery.
No other gods, only me.

No carved gods of any size, shape, or form of anything whatever, whether of things that fly or walk or swim. Don't bow down to them and don't serve them because I am God your God, and I'm a most jealous God, punishing the children for any sins their parents pass on to them to the third, and yes, even to the fourth generation of those who hate me. But I'm unswervingly loyal to the thousands who love me and keep my commandments.

No using the name of God your God, in curses or silly banter; God won't put up with the irreverent use of his name.

Observe the Sabbath day, to keep it holy. Work six days and do everything you need to do. But the seventh day is a Sabbath to God your God. Don't do any work – not you, nor your son, nor your daughter, nor your servant, nor your maid, nor your animals, not even the foreign guest visiting in your town. For in six days God made Heaven, Earth, and sea, and everything in them; he rested on the seventh day. Therefore God blessed the Sabbath day; he set it apart as a holy day.

Honor your father and mother so that you'll live a long time in the land that God your God, is giving you.

No murder.

No adultery.

No stealing.

No lies about your neighbor.

No lusting after your neighbor's house – or wife or servant or maid or ox or donkey. Don't set your heart on anything that is your neighbor's.

Exodus 20:1-17, The Message

E 613 COMMANDMENTS

Jewish believers are able to sanctify their lives and draw closer to God by keeping the *mitzvot* (divine commandments). The 613 commandments, found in Leviticus and other books, regulate all aspects of Jewish life. This is not mere legalism. Judaism is not an other-worldly religion. It does not seek to escape present realities by focusing on a future world: it seeks to make the whole of this life holy. It may be said that it is this distinctive emphasis on holiness in every detail of everyday life and separation from corrupting worldly influences that explains Jewish survival.

MAIMONIDES' LIST

The 613 commandments and their source in the Jewish scriptures, as enumerated by Maimonides, follow.

Book One, The Book of Knowledge

The fundamentals of the Torah

1. To know there is a God Ex. 20:2
2. Not to entertain thoughts of other gods besides Him Ex. 20:3
3. To know that He is one Deut. 6:4
4. To love Him Deut. 6:5
5. To fear Him Deut. 10:20
6. To sanctify His Name Lev. 22:32
7. Not to profane His Name Lev. 22:32
8. Not to destroy objects associated with His Name Deut. 12:4
9. To listen to the prophet speaking in His Name Deut. 18:15
10. Not to test the prophet unduly Deut. 6:16

Laws about character

11. To emulate His ways Deut. 28:9
12. To cleave to those who know Him Deut. 10:20
13. To love other Jews Lev. 19:18
14. To love converts Deut. 10:19
15. Not to hate fellow Jews Lev. 19:17
16. To reprove a sinner Lev. 19:17
17. Not to embarrass others Lev. 19:17
18. Not to oppress the weak Ex. 21:22
19. Not to speak derogatorily of others Lev. 19:16
20. Not to take revenge Lev. 19:18
21. Not to bear a grudge Lev. 19:18

Laws about Torah study

22. To learn Torah Deut. 6:7
23. To honor those who teach and know Torah Lev. 19:32

Laws about idolatry and paganism

24. Not to inquire into idolatry Lev. 19:4
25. Not to follow the whims of your heart or what your eyes see Num. 15:39
26. Not to blaspheme Ex. 22:27
27. Not to worship idols in the manner they are worshiped Ex. 20:5
28. Not to worship idols in the four ways we worship God Ex. 20:5
29. Not to make an idol for yourself Ex. 20:4
30. Not to make an idol for others Lev. 19:4
31. Not to make human forms even for decorative purposes Ex. 20:20
32. Not to turn a city to idolatry Ex. 23:13
33. To burn a city that has turned to idol worship Deut. 13:17
34. Not to rebuild it as a city Deut. 13:17
35. Not to derive benefit from it Deut. 13:18
36. Not to missionize an individual to idol worship Deut. 13:12
37. Not to love the missionary Deut. 13:9
38. Not to cease hating the missionary Deut. 13:9
39. Not to save the missionary Deut. 13:9
40. Not to say anything in his defense Deut. 13:9
41. Not to refrain from incriminating him Deut. 13:9

42. Not to prophesize in the name of idolatry Deut. 13:14
43. Not to listen to a false prophet Deut. 13:4
44. Not to prophesize falsely in the name of God Deut. 18:20
45. Not to be afraid of killing the false prophet Deut. 18:22
46. Not to swear in the name of an idol Ex. 23:13
47. Not to perform ov (medium) Lev. 19:31
48. Not to perform yidoni (magical seer) Lev. 19:31
49. Not to pass your children through the fire to Molech Lev. 18:21
50. Not to erect a column in a public place of worship Deut. 16:22
51. Not to bow down on smooth stone Lev. 26:1
52. Not to plant a tree in the Temple courtyard Deut. 16:21
53. To destroy idols and their accessories Deut. 12:2
54. Not to derive benefit from idols and their accessories Deut. 7:26
55. Not to derive benefit from ornaments of idols Deut. 7:25
56. Not to make a covenant with idolaters Deut. 7:2
57. Not to show favor to them Deut. 7:2
58. Not to let them dwell in our land Ex. 23:33
59. Not to imitate them in customs and clothing Lev. 20:23
60. Not to be superstitious Lev. 19:26
61. Not to go into a trance to foresee events, etc. Deut. 18:10
62. Not to engage in astrology Lev. 19:26
63. Not to mutter incantations Deut. 18:11
64. Not to attempt to contact the dead Deut. 18:11
65. Not to consult the ov Deut. 18:11
66. Not to consult the yidoni Deut. 18:11
67. Not to perform acts of magic Deut. 18:10
68. Men must not shave the hair off the sides of their head Lev. 19:27
69. Men must not shave their beards with a razor Lev. 19.27

70. Men must not wear women's clothing Deut. 22:5
71. Women must not wear men's clothing Deut. 22:5
72. Not to tattoo the skin Lev. 19:28
73. Not to tear the skin in mourning Deut. 14:1
74. Not to make a bald spot in mourning Deut. 14:1

Law about repentance
75. To repent and confess wrongdoings Num. 5:7

Book Two, The Book about the Love of God

Law about reading the Shema
76. To say the Shema twice daily Deut.6:7

Laws about prayer and Kohanim blessings
77. To serve the Almighty with prayer daily Ex. 23:25
78. The Kohanim must bless the Jewish nation daily Num. 6:23

Laws about tefillin, mezuza and Sefer Torah
79. To wear tefillin on the head Deut. 6:8
80. To bind tefillin on the arm Deut. 6:8
81. To put a mezuzah on each door post Deut. 6:9
82. Each male must write a Sefer Torah Deut. 31:19
83. The king must have a separate Sefer Torah for himself Deut. 17:18

Law about tzitzit
84. To have tzitzit on four-cornered garments Num. 15:38

Law about blessings
85. To bless the Almighty after eating Deut. 8:10

Law about circumcision
86. To circumcise all males on the eighth day after their birth Lev. 12:3

Book Three, The Book of the Seasons

Laws about the Sabbath
87. To rest on the seventh day Ex. 23:12
88. Not to do prohibited labor on the

seventh day Ex. 20:10

89. The court must not inflict punishment on Shabbat Ex. 35:3
90. Not to walk outside the city boundary on Shabbat Ex. 16:29
91. To sanctify the day with Kiddush and Havdalah Ex. 20:8

Laws about Yom Kippur rest
92. To rest from prohibited labor Lev. 23:32
93. Not to do prohibited labor on Yom Kippur Lev. 23:32
94. To afflict yourself on Yom Kippur Lev. 16:29
95. Not to eat or drink on Yom Kippur Lev. 23:29

Laws about festival rest
96. To rest on the first day of Passover Lev. 23:7
97. Not to do prohibited labor on the first day of Passover Lev. 23:8
98. To rest on the seventh day of Passover Lev. 23:8
99. Not to do prohibited labor on the seventh day of Passover Lev. 23:8
100. To rest on Shavuot Lev. 23:21
101. Not to do prohibited labor on Shavuot Lev. 23:21
102. To rest on Rosh Hashana Lev. 23:24
103. Not to do prohibited labor on Rosh Hashana Lev. 23:25
104. To rest on Sukkot Lev. 23:35
105. Not to do prohibited labor on Sukkot Lev. 23:35
106. To rest on Shmini Atzeret Lev. 23:36
107. Not to do prohibited labor on Shmini Atzeret Lev. 23:36

Laws about chometz and matzah
108. Not to eat chametz on the afternoon of the 14th day of Nissan Deut. 16:3
109. To destroy all chametz on 14th day of Nissan Ex. 12:15
110. Not to eat chametz all seven days of Passover Ex. 13:3
111. Not to eat mixtures containing chametz all seven days of Passover Ex. 12:20
112. Not to see chametz in your domain seven days Ex. 13:7
113. Not to find chametz in your domain seven days Ex. 12:19
114. To eat matzah on the first night of Passover Ex. 12:18
115. To relate the Exodus from Egypt on that night Ex. 13:8

Laws about Shofar, Sukkah, Lulav
116. To hear the Shofar on the first day of Tishrei (Rosh Hashana) Num. 9:1
117. To dwell in a Sukkah for the seven days of Sukkot Lev. 23:42
118. To take up a Lulav and Etrog all seven days Lev. 23:40

Law about Shekalim
119. Each man must give a half shekel annually Ex. 30:13

Laws about sanctification of months
120. Courts must calculate to determine when a new month begins Ex. 12:2

Laws about fasts
121. To afflict and cry out before God in times of catastrophe Num. 10:9

Book Four: The Book of Women

Laws about marriage
122. To marry a wife by means of ketubah and kiddushin Deut.22:13
123. Not to have relations with women not thus married Deut. 23:18
124. Not to withhold food, clothing, and sexual relations from your wife Ex. 21:10
125. To have children with one's wife Gen 1:28

Laws about divorce
126. To issue a divorce by means of a Get document Deut. 24:1
127. A man must not remarry his wife after she has married someone else Deut. 24:4

Laws of yivum and chalitzah (Levirate marriage)
128. To do yibum (marry childless

brother's widow) Deut. 25:5

129. To do chalitzah (freeing a widow from yibum) Deut. 25:9
130. The widow must not remarry until the ties with her brother-in-law are removed Deut. 25:5

Laws about women

131. The court must fine one who seduces a maiden Ex. 22:15-16
132. The rapist must marry the maiden (if she chooses) Deut. 22:29
133. He is not allowed to divorce her Deut. 22:29
134. The slanderer must remain married to his wife Deut. 22:19
135. He must not divorce her Deut. 22:19

Laws about Sotah (suspect wife)

136. To fulfill the laws of the Sotah Num. 5:30
137. Not to put oil on her meal offering Num. 5:15
138. Not to put frankincense on her Meal Offering Num. 5:15

Book Five: The Book of Holiness

Laws of forbidden relationships

139. Not to have sexual relations with your mother Lev. 18:7
14o. Not to have sexual relations with your father's wife Lev. 18:8
141. Not to have sexual relations with your sister Lev. 18:9
142. Not to have sexual relations with your father's wife's daughter Lev. 18:11
143. Not to have sexual relations with your son's daughter Lev. 18:10
144. Not to have sexual relations with your daughter Lev. 18:10
145. Not to have sexual relations with your daughter's daughter Lev. 18:10
146. Not to have sexual relations with a woman and her daughter Lev. 18:17
147. Not to have sexual relations with a woman and her son's daughter Lev.18:17
148. Not to have sexual relations with a woman and her daughter's daughter Lev. 18:17
149. Not to have sexual relations with

150. Not to have sexual relations with your father's sister Lev. 18:12
151. Not to have sexual relations with your mother's sister Lev. 18:13
152. Not to have sexual relations with your father's brother's wife Lev. 18:14
153. Not to have sexual relations with your son's wife Lev. 18:15
154. Not to have sexual relations with your brother's wife Lev. 18:16
155. Not to have sexual relations with your wife's sister Lev. 18:18
156. A man must not have sexual relations with a beast Lev. 18:23
157. A woman must not have sexual relations with a beast Lev. 18:23
158. Not to have homosexual sexual relations Lev. 18:22
159. Not to have homosexual sexual relations with your father Lev. 18:7
160. Not to have homosexual sexual relations with your father's brother Lev. 18:14
161. Not to have sexual relations with a married woman Lev. 18:20
162. Not to have sexual relations with a menstrual impure woman Lev. 18:19
163. Not to marry non-Jews Deut. 7:3
164. Not to let Moabite and Ammonite males marry into the Jewish people Deut. 23:4
165. Don't keep a third generation Egyptian convert from marrying into the Jewish people Deut. 23:8-9
166. Not to refrain from marrying a third generation Edomite convert Deut. 23:8-9
167. Not to let a mamzer ("bastard") marry into the Jewish people Deut. 23:3
168. Not to let a eunuch marry into the Jewish people Deut. 23:2
169. Not to castrate any male (including animals) Lev. 22:24
170. The High Priest must not marry a widow Lev. 21:14
171. The High Priest must not have sexual relations with a widow even outside of marriage Lev. 21:15
172. The High Priest must marry a virgin maiden Lev. 21:13

172. A Kohen (Priest) must not marry a divorcee Lev. 21:7
173. A Kohen must not marry a zonah (a woman who had forbidden relations) Lev.21:7
174. A priest must not marry a chalalah (party to or product of 169-172) Lev. 21:7
175. Not to make pleasurable (sexual) contact with any forbidden woman Lev. 18:6

Laws about forbidden foods
176. To examine the signs of animals to distinguish between kosher and non-kosherLev. 11:2
177. To examine the signs of fowl to distinguish between kosher and non-kosher Deut. 14:11
178. To examine the signs of fish to distinguish between kosher and non-kosher Lev. 11:9
179. To examine the signs of locusts to distinguish between kosher and non-kosher Lev. 11:21
180. Not to eat non-kosher animals Lev.11:4
181. Not to eat non-kosher fowl Lev. 11:13
182. Not to eat non-kosher fish Lev. 11:11
183. Not to eat non-kosher flying insects Deut. 14:19
184. Not to eat non-kosher creatures that crawl on land Lev. 11:41
185. Not to eat non-kosher maggots Lev.11:44
186. Not to eat worms found in fruit on the ground Lev. 11:42
187. Not to eat creatures that live in water other than fish Lev. 11:43
188. Not to eat the meat of an animal that died without ritual slaughter Deut. 14:21
189. Not to benefit from an ox condemned to be stoned Ex. 21:28
190. Not to eat meat of an animal that was mortally wounded Ex. 22:30
191. Not to eat a limb torn off a living creature Deut 12:23
192. Not to eat blood Lev. 3:17
193. Not to eat certain fats of clean animals Lev. 3:17

194. Not to eat the sinew of the thigh Gen. 32:33
195. Not to eat meat and milk cooked together Ex. 23:19
196. Not to cook meat and milk together Ex. 34:26
197. Not to eat bread from new grain before the Omer Lev. 23:14
198. Not to eat parched grains from new grain before the Omer Lev. 23:14
199. Not to eat ripened grains from new grain before the Omer Lev. 23:14
200. Not to eat fruit of a tree during its first three years Lev. 19:23
201. Not to eat diverse seeds planted in a vineyard Deut. 22:9
202. Not to eat untithed fruits Lev. 22:15
203. Not to drink wine poured in service to idols Deut. 32:38

Laws about slaughtering
204. To ritually slaughter an animal before eating it Deut. 12:21
205. Not to slaughter an animal and its offspring on the same day Lev. 22:28
206. To cover the blood (of a slaughtered beast or fowl) with earth Lev. 17:13
207. Not to take the mother bird from her children Deut. 22:6
208. To release the mother bird if she was taken from the nest Deut. 22:7

Book Six: The Book of Oaths

Laws of oaths
209. Not to swear falsely in God's Name Lev. 19:12
210. Not to take God's Name in vain Ex. 20:7
211. Not to deny possession of something entrusted to you Lev. 19:11
212. Not to swear in denial of a monetary claim Lev. 19:11
213. To swear in God's Name to confirm the truth when deemed necessary by court Deut. 10:20

Laws of vows
214. To fulfill what was uttered and to do what was avowed Deut. 23:24
215. Not to break oaths or vows Num. 30:3

216. For oaths and vows annulled, there are the laws of annulling vows explicit in Torah Num. 30:3

Law about the Nazir
217. The Nazir must let his hair grow Num. 6:5
218. He must not cut his hair Num. 6:5
219. He must not drink wine, wine mixtures, or wine vinegar Num. 6:3
220. He must not eat fresh grapes Num. 6:3
221. He must not eat raisins Num. 6:3
222. He must not eat grape seeds Num. 6:4
223. He must not eat grape skins Num. 6:4
224. He must not be under the same roof as a corpse Num. 6:6
225. He must not come into contact with the dead Num. 6:7
226. He must shave after bringing sacrifices upon completion of his Nazirite period Num. 6:9

Laws of estimated values and vows
227. To estimate the value of people as determined by the Torah Lev. 27:2
228. To estimate the value of consecrated animals Lev. 27:12-13
229. To estimate the value of consecrated houses Lev. 27:14
230. To estimate the value of consecrated fields Lev. 27:16
231. Carry out the laws of interdicting possessions (cherem) Lev. 27:28
232. Not to sell the cherem Lev. 27:28
233. Not to redeem the cherem Lev. 27:28

Book Seven: The Book of Seeds

Laws about mixed species
234. Not to plant diverse seeds together Lev. 19:19
235. Not to plant grains or greens in a vineyard Deut. 22:9
236. Not to crossbreed animals Lev. 19:19
237. Not to work different animals together Deut. 22:10
238. Not to wear shatnez, a cloth woven of wool and linen Deut. 22:11
Laws about gifts to the poor
239. To leave a corner of the field uncut for the poor Lev. 19:10
240. Not to reap that corner Lev. 19:9

241. To leave gleanings Lev. 19:9
242. Not to gather the gleanings Lev. 19:9
243. To leave the gleanings of a vineyard Lev. 19:10
244. Not to gather the gleanings of a vineyard Lev. 19:10
245. To leave the unformed clusters of grapes Lev. 19:10
246. Not to pick the unformed clusters of grapes Lev. 19:10
247. To leave the forgotten sheaves in the field Deut. 24:19
248. Not to retrieve them Deut. 24:19
249. To separate the tithe for the poor Deut. 14:28
250. To give charity Deut. 15:8
251. Not to withhold charity from the poor Deut. 15:7
252. To set aside Terumah Gedolah (tithe for the Kohen) Deut. 18:4
253. The Levite must set aside a tenth of his tithe Num. 18:26
254. Not to preface one tithe to the next, but separate them in their proper order Ex. 22:28
255. A non-Kohen must not eat Terumah Lev. 22:10
256. A hired worker or a Jewish bondsman of a Kohen must not eat Terumah Lev. 22:10
257. An uncircumcised Kohen must not eat Terumah Ex.12:48
258. An impure Kohen must not eat Terumah Lev. 22:4
259. A chalalah must not eat Terumah Lev. 22:12

Law about Ma'aser
260. To set aside Ma'aser (tithe) each planting year and give it to a Levite Num. 18:24

Laws about the second tithe and fourth year produce
261. To set aside the second tithe (Ma'aser Sheni) Deut. 14:22
262. Not to spend its redemption money on anything but food, drink, or ointment Deut. 26:14
263. Not to eat Ma'aser Sheni while impure Deut. 26:14

264. A mourner on the first day after death must not eat Ma'aser Sheni Deut. 26:14
265. Not to eat Ma'aser Sheni grains outside Jerusalem Deut. 12:17
266. Not to eat Ma'aser Sheni wine products outside Jerusalem Deut. 12:17
267. Not to eat Ma'aser Sheni oil outside Jerusalem Deut. 12:17
268. The fourth year crops must be totally for holy purposes like Ma'aser Sheni Lev. 19:24
269. To read the confession of tithes every fourth and seventh year Deut. 26:13

Laws about first fruits and other Kohanic gifts
270. To set aside the first fruits and bring them to the Temple Ex. 23:19
271. The Kohanim must not eat the first fruits outside Jerusalem Deut. 12:17
272. To read the Torah portion pertaining to their presentation Deut. 26:5
273. To set aside a portion of dough for a Kohen Num. 15:20
274. To give the shoulder, two cheeks, and stomach of slaughtered animals to a Kohen Deut. 18:3
275. To give the first sheering of sheep to a Kohen Deut. 18:4
276. To redeem the firstborn sons and give the money to a Kohen Num. 18:15
277. To redeem the firstborn donkey by giving a lamb to a Kohen Ex. 13:13
278. To break the neck of the donkey if the owner does not intend to redeem it Ex. 13:13

Laws about the Sabbatical and Jubilee years
279. To rest the land during the seventh year by not doing any work which enhances growth Ex. 34:21
280. Not to work the land during the seventh year Lev. 25:4
281. Not to work with trees to produce fruit during that year Lev. 25:4
282. Not to reap crops that grow wild that year in the normal manner Lev. 25:5
283. Not to gather grapes which grow wild that year in the normal way Lev. 25:5
284. To leave free all produce which grew in that year Ex. 23:11

285. To release all loans during the seventh year Deut. 15:2
286. Not to pressure or claim from the borrower Deut. 15:2
287. Not to refrain from lending immediately before the release of the loans for fear of monetary loss Deut. 15:9
288. The Sanhedrin must count seven groups of seven years Lev. 25:8
289. The Sanhedrin must sanctify the fiftieth year Lev. 25:10
290. To blow the Shofar on the tenth of Tishrei to free the slaves Lev. 25:9
291. Not to work the soil during the fiftieth year (Jubilee)Lev. 25:11
292. Not to reap in the normal manner that which grows wild in the fiftieth year Lev. 25:11
293. Not to pick grapes which grew wild in the normal manner in the fiftieth year Lev. 25:11
294. Carry out the laws of sold family properties Lev. 25:24
295. Not to sell the land in Israel indefinitely Lev. 25:23
296. Carry out the laws of houses in walled cities Lev. 25:29
297. The Tribe of Levi must not be given a portion of the land in Israel, rather they are given cities to dwell in Deut. 18:1
298. The Levites must not take a share in the spoils of war Deut. 18:1
299. To give the Levites cities to inhabit and their surrounding fields Num. 35:2
300. Not to sell the fields but they shall remain the Levites' before and after the Jubilee year Lev. 25:34

Book Eight: The Book of Service

Laws about the Temple
301. To build a Sanctuary Ex. 25:8
302. Not to build the altar with stones hewn by metal Ex. 20:23
303. Not to climb steps to the altar Ex. 20:26
304. To show reverence to the Temple Lev. 19:30
305. To guard the Temple area Num. 18:2
306. Not to leave the Temple unguarded Num. 18:5

Laws about Temple vessels and employees

307. To prepare the anointing oil Ex. 30:31
308. Not to reproduce the anointing oil Ex. 30:32
309. Not to anoint with anointing oil Ex. 30:32
310. Not to reproduce the incense formula Ex. 30:37
311. Not to burn anything on the Golden Altar besides incense Ex. 30:9
312. The Levites must transport the ark on their shoulders Num. 7:9
313. Not to remove the staves from the ark Ex. 25:15
314. The Levites must work in the Temple Num. 18:23
315. No Levite must do another's work of either a Kohen or a Levite Num. 18:3
316. To dedicate the Kohen for service Lev. 21:8
317. The kohanic work shifts must be equal during holidays Deut. 18:6-8
318. The Kohanim must wear their priestly garments during service Ex. 28:2
319. Not to tear the priestly garments Ex. 28:32
320. The breastplate must not be loosened from the Ephod Ex. 28:28

Laws about entering the Temple

321. A Kohen must not enter the Temple intoxicated Lev. 10:9
322. A Kohen must not enter the Temple with long hair Lev. 10:6
323. A Kohen must not enter the Temple with torn clothes Lev. 10:6
324. A Kohen must not enter the Temple indiscriminately Lev. 16:2
325. A Kohen must not leave the Temple during service Lev. 10:7
326. To send the impure from the Temple Num. 5:2
327. Impure people must not enter the Temple Num. 5:3
328. Impure people must not enter the Temple Mount area Deut. 23:11
329. Impure Kohanim must not do service in the temple Lev. 22:2
330. An impure Kohen, following immersion, must wait until after sundown before returning to service Lev. 22:7

331. A Kohen must wash his hands and feet before service Ex. 30:19
332. A Kohen with a physical blemish must not enter the sanctuary or approach the altar Lev. 21:23
333. A Kohen with a physical blemish must not serve Lev.21:17
334. A Kohen with a temporary blemish must not serve Lev. 21:17
335. One who is not a Kohen must not serve Num. 18:4

Laws about restrictions concerning sacrifices

336. To offer only unblemished animals Lev.22:21
337. Not to dedicate a blemished animal for the altar Lev. 22:20
338. Not to slaughter it Lev. 22:22
339. Not to sprinkle its blood Lev. 22:24
340. Not to burn its fat Lev. 22:22
341. Not to offer a temporarily blemished animal Deut. 17:1
342. Not to sacrifice blemished animals even if offered by non-Jews Lev. 22:25
343. Not to inflict wounds upon dedicated animals Lev. 22:21
344. To redeem dedicated animals which have become disqualified Deut. 12:15
345. To offer only animals which are at least eight days old Lev. 22:27
346. Not to offer animals bought with the wages of a harlot or the animal exchanged for a dog Deut. 23:19
347. Not to burn honey or yeast on the altar Lev. 2:11
348. To salt all sacrifices Lev. 2:13
349. Not to omit the salt from sacrifices Lev. 2:13

Laws about sacrificial procedure

350. Carry out the procedure of the burnt offering as prescribed in the Torah Lev. 1:3
351. Not to eat its meat Deut. 12:17
352. Carry out the procedure of the sin offering Lev. 6:18
353. Not to eat the meat of the inner sin offering Lev. 6:23
354. Not to decapitate a fowl brought as a sin offering Lev. 5:8
355. Carry out the procedure of the guilt offering Lev. 7:1

356. The Kohanim must eat the sacrificial meat in the Temple Ex. 29:33
357. The Kohanim must not eat the meat outside the Temple courtyard Deut. 12:17
358. A non-Kohen must not eat sacrificial meat Ex. 29:33
359. To follow the procedure of the peace offering Lev. 7:11
360. Not to eat the meat of minor sacrifices before sprinkling the blood Deut. 12:17
361. To bring meal offerings as prescribed in the Torah Lev. 2:1
362. Not to put oil on the meal offerings of wrongdoers Lev. 5:11
363. Not to put frankincense on the meal offerings of wrongdoers Lev. 3:11
364. Not to eat the meal offering of the High Priest Lev. 6:16
365. Not to bake a meal offering as leavened bread Lev. 6:10
366. The Kohanim must eat the remains of the meal offerings Lev. 6:9
367. To bring all avowed and freewill offerings to the Temple on the first subsequent festival Deut. 12:5-6
368. Not to withhold payment incurred by any vow Deut. 23:22
369. To offer all sacrifices in the Temple Deut. 12:11
370. To bring all sacrifices from outside Israel to the Temple Deut. 12:26
371. Not to slaughter sacrifices outside the courtyard Lev. 17:4
372. Not to offer any sacrifices outside the courtyard Deut. 12:13

Laws about perpetual and additional offerings
373. To offer two lambs every day Num. 28:3
374. To light a fire on the altar every day Lev. 6:6
375. Not to extinguish this fire Lev. 6:6
376. To remove the ashes from the altar every day Lev. 6:3
377. To burn incense every day Ex 30:7
378. To light the *menorah* every day Ex. 27:21
379. The Kohen Gadol must bring a meal offering every day Lev. 6:13

380. To bring two additional lambs as burnt offerings on Shabbat Num 28:9
381. To make the show bread Ex. 25:30
382. To bring additional offerings on the New Month ("Rosh Chodesh") Num. 28:11
383. To bring additional offerings on Passover Num. 28:19
384. To offer the wave offering from the meal of the new wheat Lev. 23:10
385. Each man must count the Omer - seven weeks from the day the new wheat offering was brought Lev. 23:15
386. To bring additional offerings on Shavuot Num. 28:26
387. To bring two leaves to accompany the above sacrifice Lev. 23:17
388. To bring additional offerings on Rosh Hashana Num. 29:2
389. To bring additional offerings on Yom Kippur Num. 29:8
390. To bring additional offerings on Sukkot Num. 29:13
391. To bring additional offerings on Shmini Atzeret Num. 29:35

Laws about disqualified offerings
392. Not to eat sacrifices which have become unfit or blemished Deut. 14.3
393. Not to eat from sacrifices offered with improper intentions Lev. 7:18
394. Not to leave sacrifices past the time allowed for eating them Lev. 22:30
395. Not to eat from that which was left over Lev. 19:8
396. Not to eat from sacrifices which became impure Lev. 7:19
397. An impure person must not eat from sacrifices Lev. 7:20
398. To burn the leftover sacrifices Lev. 7:17
399 To burn all impure sacrifices Lev. 7:19

Laws about Yom Kippur service
400. To follow the procedure of Yom Kippur in the sequence prescribed in Parshat "Acharei Mot" (After the death of Aaron's sons . . .) Lev. 16:3

Laws about misusing sanctified property
401. One who profaned property must repay what he profaned plus a fifth and bring a sacrifice Lev. 5:16

402. Not to work consecrated animals Deut. 15:19
403. Not to shear the fleece of consecrated animals Deut. 15:19

Book Nine: The Book of Sacrifices

Laws about pascal sacrifice
404. To slaughter the paschal sacrifice at the specified time Ex. 12:6
405. Not to slaughter it while in possession of leaven Ex. 23:18
406. Not to leave the fat overnight Ex. 23:18
407. To slaughter the second Paschal Lamb Num. 9:11
408. To eat the Paschal Lamb. Ex. 12:8
409. To eat the second Paschal Lamb on the night of the 15th of Iyar Num.9:11
410. Not to eat the paschal meat raw or boiled Ex. 12:9
411. Not to take the paschal meat from the confines of the group Ex. 12:46
412. An apostate must not eat from it Ex.12:43
413. A permanent or temporary hired worker must not eat from it Ex. 12:45
414. An uncircumcised male must not eat from it Ex. 12:48
415. Not to break any bones from the paschal offering Ex. 12:46
416. Not to break any bones from the second paschal offering Num. 9:12
417. Not to leave any meat from the paschal offering over until morning Ex. 12:10
418. Not to leave the second paschal meat over until morning Num. 9:12
419. Not to leave the meat of the holiday offering of the 14th until the 16th Deut. 16:4

Laws about pilgrim offerings
420. To be seen at the Temple on Passover, Shavuot, and Sukkot Deut. 16:16
421. To celebrate on these three Festivals (bring a peace offering) Ex. 23:14
422. To rejoice on these three Festivals (bring a peace offering) Deut. 16:14
423. Not to appear at the Temple without offerings Deut. 16:16
424. Not to refrain from rejoicing with, and giving gifts to, the Levites Deut. 12:19

425. To assemble all the people on the Sukkot following the seventh year Deut. 31:12

Laws about first-born animals
426. To set aside the firstborn animals Ex. 13:12
427. The Kohanim must not eat unblemished firstborn animals outside Jerusalem Deut.12:17
428. Not to redeem the firstborn Num. 18:17
429. Separate the tithe from animals Lev. 27:32
430. Not to redeem the tithe Lev. 27:33

Laws about offerings for unintentional transgressions
431. Every person must bring a sin offering for his transgression Lev. 4:27
432. Bring an asham talui when uncertain of guilt Lev. 5:17-18
433. Bring an asham vadai when guilt is ascertained Lev. 5:25
434. Bring an oleh v'yored offering (if the person is wealthy, an animal; if poor, a bird or meal offering) Lev. 5:7-11
435. The Sanhedrin must bring an offering when it rules in error Lev. 4:13

Laws about necessary offerings
436. A woman who had a running issue must bring an offering after she goes to the Mikveh Lev. 15:28-29
437. A woman who gave birth must bring an offering after she goes to the Mikveh Lev. 12:6
438. A man who had a running issue must bring an offering after he goes to the Mikveh Lev. 15:13-14
439. A metzora must bring an offering after going to the Mikveh Lev. 14:10

Laws about substitution of sacrifices
440. Not to substitute another beast for one set apart for sacrifice Lev. 27:10
441. The new animal, in addition to the substituted one, retains consecration Lev. 27:10
442. Not to change consecrated animals

from one type of offering to another Lev. 27:26

Book Ten: The Book of Purity

Law about impurity of the human dead
443. Carry out the laws of impurity of the dead Num. 19:14

Laws about the red heifer
444. Carry out the procedure of the Red Heifer ("Para Aduma") Num. 19:2
445. Carry out the laws of the sprinkling water Num. 19:21

Laws about impurity through tzara'at
446. Rule the laws of human tzara'at ("Leprosy") as prescribed in the Torah Lev. 13:12
447. The metzora ("leper") must not remove his signs of impurity Deut. 24:8
448. The metzora must not shave signs of impurity in his hair Lev. 13:33
449. The metzora must publicize his condition by tearing his garments, allowing his hair to grow and covering his lips Lev. 13:45
450. Carry out the prescribed rules for purifying the metzora Lev. 14:2
451. The metzora must shave off all his hair prior to purification Lev. 14:9
452. Carry out the laws of tzara'at of clothing Lev. 13:47
453. Carry out the laws of tzara'at of houses Lev. 13:34

Laws about impurity of reclining and sitting
454. Observe the laws of menstrual impurity Lev. 15:19
455. Observe the laws of impurity caused by childbirth Lev. 12:2
456. Observe the laws of impurity caused by a woman's running issue Lev. 15:25
457. Observe the laws of impurity caused by a man's running issue (irregular ejaculation of infected semen) Lev. 15:3

Laws about other sources of impurity
458. Observe the laws of impurity caused by a dead beast Lev. 11:39
459. Observe the laws of impurity caused by

the eight shratzim - Insects Lev. 11:29
460. Observe the laws of impurity of a seminal emission (regular ejaculation, with normal semen) Lev. 15:16

Laws about impurity of food
461. Observe the laws of impurity concerning liquid and solid foods Lev. 11:34

Laws about Mikveh
462. Every impure person must immerse himself in a Mikveh to become pure Lev. 15:16

Book Eleven: The Book of Damages

Laws about property damage
463. The court must judge the damages incurred by a goring ox Ex. 21:28
464. The court must judge the damages incurred by an animal eating Ex. 22:4
465. The court must judge the damages incurred by a pit Ex. 21:33
466. The court must judge the damages incurred by fire Ex. 22:5

Laws about theft
467. Not to steal money stealthily Lev. 19:11
468. The court must implement punitive measures against the thief Ex. 21:37
469. Each individual must ensure that his scales and weights are accurate Lev. 19:36
470. Not to commit injustice with scales and weights Lev. 19:35
471. Not to possess inaccurate scales and weights even if they are not for use Deut. 25:13
472. Not to move a boundary marker to steal someone's property Deut. 19:14
473. Not to kidnap Ex. 20:13

Laws about robbery and lost objects
474. Not to rob openly Lev. 19:13

475. Not to withhold wages or fail to repay a debt Lev. 19:13
476. Not to covet and scheme to acquire another's possession Ex. 20:14

477. Not to desire another's possession Deut. 5:18
478. Return the robbed object or its value Lev. 5:23
479. Not to ignore a lost object Deut. 22:3
480. Return the lost object Deut. 22:1
481. The court must implement laws against the one who assaults another or damages another's property Ex. 21:18

Laws about murder and preservation of life
482. Not to murder Ex. 20:13
483. Not to accept monetary restitution to atone for the murderer Num. 35:31
484. The court must send the accidental murderer to a city of refuge Num. 35:25
485. Not to accept monetary restitution instead of being sent to a city of refuge Num. 35:32
486. Not to kill the murderer before he stands trial Num. 35:12
487. Save someone being pursued even by taking the life of the pursuer Deut. 25:12
488. Not to pity the pursuer Num. 35:12
489. Not to stand idly by if someone's life is in danger Lev. 19:16
490. Designate cities of refuge and prepare routes of access Deut. 19:3
491. Break the neck of a calf by the river valley following an unsolved murder Deut. 21:4
492. Not to work nor plant that river valley Deut. 21:4
493. Not to allow pitfalls and obstacles to remain on your property Deut. 22:8
494. Make a guard rail around flat roofs Deut. 22:8
495. Not to put a stumbling block before a blind man (nor give harmful advice)
496. Not to curse the deaf Lev. 19:14
497. Help another remove the load from a beast which can no longer carry it Ex. 23:5
498. Help others load their beast Deut. 22:4
499. Not to leave others distraught with their burdens (but to help either load or unload) Deut. 22:4

Book Twelve: The Book of Acquisition

Laws about sales
500. Buy and sell according to Torah law Lev. 25:14
501. Not to overcharge or underpay for an article Lev. 25:14
502. Not to insult or harm anybody with words Lev. 25:17
503. Not to cheat a sincere convert monetarily Ex. 22:20
504. Not to insult or harm a sincere convert with words Ex. 22:20

Laws about slaves
505. Purchase a Hebrew slave in accordance with the prescribed laws Ex. 21:2
506. Not to sell him as a slave is sold Lev. 25:42
507. Not to work him oppressively Lev. 25:43
508. Not to allow a non-Jew to work him oppressively Lev. 25:53
509. Not to have him do menial slave labor Lev. 25;39
510. Give him gifts when he goes free Deut. 15:14
511. Not to send him away empty-handed Deut. 15:13
512. Redeem Jewish maidservants Ex. 21:8
513. Betroth the Jewish maidservant Ex. 21:8
514. The master must not sell his maidservant Ex. 21:8
515. Canaanite slaves must work forever unless injured in one of their limbs Lev. 25:46
516. Not to extradite a slave who fled to (Biblical) Israel Deut. 23:16
517. Not to wrong a slave who has come to Israel for refuge Deut. 23:16

Book Thirteen: The Book of Judgments

Laws about hiring
518. The courts must carry out the laws of a hired worker and hired guard Ex. 22:9
519. Pay wages on the day they were earned Deut. 24:15
520. Not to delay payment of wages past the agreed time Lev. 19:13

521. The hired worker may eat from the unharvested crops where he works Deut. 23:25
522. The worker must not eat while on hired time Deut. 23:26
523. The worker must not take more than he can eat Deut. 23:25
524. Not to muzzle an ox while plowing Deut. 25:4

Laws about borrowing and depositing
525. The courts must carry out the laws of a borrower Ex. 22:13
526. The courts must carry out the laws of an unpaid guard Ex. 22:6

Laws about creditors and debtors
527. Lend to the poor and destitute Ex. 22:24
528. Not to press them for payment if you know they don't have it Ex. 22:24
529. Press the idolater for payment Deut. 15:3
530. The creditor must not forcibly take collateral Deut. 24:10
531. Return the collateral to the debtor when needed Deut. 24:13
532. Not to delay its return when needed Deut. 24:12
533. Not to demand collateral from a widow Deut. 24:17
534. Not to demand as collateral utensils needed for preparing food Deut. 24:6
535. Not to lend with interest Lev.25:37
536. Not to borrow with interest Deut. 23:20
537. Not to intermediate in an interest loan, guarantee, witness, or write the promissory note Ex. 22:24
538. Lend to and borrow from idolaters with interest Deut. 23:21

Law about plaintiff and defendant
539. The courts must carry out the laws of the plaintiff, admitter, or denier Ex. 22:8

Laws about inheritance
540. Carry out the laws of the order of inheritance Num. 27:8

Book Fourteen: The Book of Judges

Laws about the Sanhedrin and punishments
541. Appoint judges Deut. 16:18
542. Not to appoint judges who are not familiar with judicial procedure Deut. 1:17
543. Decide by majority in case of disagreement Ex. 23:2
544. The court must not execute through a majority of one at least a majority of two is required Ex. 23:2
545. A judge who presented an acquittal plea must not present an argument for conviction in capital cases Deut. 23:2
546. The courts must carry out the death penalty of stoning Deut. 22:24
547. The courts must carry out the death penalty of burning Lev. 20:14
548. The courts must carry out the death penalty of the sword Ex. 21:20
549. The courts must carry out the death penalty of strangulation Lev. 20:10
550. The courts must hang those stoned for blasphemy or idolatry Deut. 21:22
551. Bury the executed on the day they are killed Deut.21:23
552. Not to delay burial overnight Deut. 21:23
553. The court must not let the sorcerer live Ex. 22:17
554. The court must give lashes to the wrongdoer Ex. 25:2
555. The court must not exceed the prescribed number of lashes Deut. 25:3
556. The court must not kill anybody on circumstantial evidence Ex. 23:7
557. The court must not punish anybody who was forced to do a crime Deut. 22:26
558. A judge must not pity the murderer or assaulter at the trial Deut. 19:13
559. A judge must not have mercy on the poor man at the trial Lev. 19:15
560. A judge must not respect the great man at the trial Lev. 19:15
561. A judge must not decide unjustly the case of the habitual transgressor Ex. 23:6
562. A judge must not pervert justice Lev. 19:15

563. A judge must not pervert a case involving a convert or orphan Deut. 24:17
564. Judge righteously Lev. 19:15
565. The judge must not fear a violent man in judgment Deut. 1:17
566. Judges must not accept bribes Ex. 23:8
567. Judges must not accept testimony unless both parties are present Ex. 23:1
568. Not to curse judges Ex. 22:27
569. Not to curse the head of state or leader of the Sanhedrin Ex. 22:27
570. Not to curse any upstanding Jew Lev. 19:14

Laws about evidence
571. Anybody who knows evidence must testify in court Lev. 5:1
572. Carefully interrogate the witness Deut. 13:15
573. A witness must not serve as a judge in capital crimes Deut. 19:17
574. Not to accept testimony from a lone witness Deut. 19:15
575. Transgressors must not testify Ex. 23:1
576. Relatives of the litigants must not testify Deut. 24:16
577. Not to testify falsely Ex. 20:13
578. Punish the false witnesses as they tried to punish the defendant Deut. 19:19

Laws about insurgents
579. Act according to the ruling of the Sanhedrin Deut. 17:11
580. Not to deviate from the word of the Sanhedrin Deut. 17:11
581. Not to add to the Torah commandments or their oral explanations Deut. 13:1
582. Not to diminish from the Torah any commandments, in whole or in part Deut. 13:1
583. Not to curse your father and mother Ex. 21:17
584. Not to strike your father and mother Ex. 21:15
585. Respect your father or mother Ex. 20:12
586. Fear your father or mother Lev. 19:3
587. Not to be a rebellious son Deut. 21:18

Laws about mourning
588. Mourn for relatives Lev. 10:19
589. The High Priest must not defile himself for any relative Lev. 21:11
590. The High Priest must not enter under the same roof as a corpse Lev. 21:11
591. A Kohen must not defile himself for anyone except relatives Lev. 21:1

Laws about kings and their wars
592. Appoint a king from Israel Deut. 17:15
593. Not to appoint a convert Deut. 17:15
594. The king must not have too many wives Deut. 17:17
595. The king must not have too many horses Deut. 17:16
596. The king must not have too much silver and gold Deut. 17:17
597. Destroy the seven Canaanite nations Deut. 20:17
598. Not to let any of them remain alive Deut. 20:16
599. Wipe out the descendants of Amalek Deut. 25:19
600. Remember what Amalek did to the Jewish people Deut. 25:17
601. Not to forget Amalek's atrocities and ambush on our journey from Egypt in the desert Deut. 25:19
602. Not to dwell permanently in Egypt Deut. 17:16
603. Offer peace terms to the inhabitants of a city while holding siege, and treat them according to the Torah if they accept the terms Deut. 20:10
604. Not to offer peace to Ammon and Moab while besieging them Deut. 23:7
605. Not to destroy fruit trees even during the siege Deut. 20:19
606. Prepare latrines outside the camps Deut. 23:13
607. Prepare a shovel for each soldier to dig with Deut. 23:14
608. Appoint a priest to speak with the soldiers during the war Deut. 20:2
609. He who has taken a wife, built a new home, or planted a vineyard is given a year to rejoice with his possessions Deut. 24:5

610. Not to demand from the above any involvement, communal or military Deut. 24:5
611. Not to panic and retreat during battle Deut. 20:3

612. Keep the laws of the captive woman Deut. 21:11
613. Not to sell her into slavery Deut. 21:14

7 WORSHIP

The worship practices described below are those of orthodox Jews.

A The Sabbath

     The *havdalah* ceremony

B Synagogue

   (i)   Rabbi

   (ii)   Synagogue furnishings

   (iii) Synagogue services

C Life-cycle events

   (i)   Birth ceremony

   (ii)   *Brit milah*

   (iii) *Brit bat*

   (iv) *Bar Mitzvah* and *Bat Mitzvah*

D Annual festivals

   (i)   New Year's Day (*Rosh Hashanah*)

   (ii)   Day of Atonement (*Yom Kippur*)

   (iii) Tabernacles (*Sukkot*)

   (iv) Rejoicing in the Law (*Simchat Torah*)

   (v)   Festival of Lights (*Hanukkah*)

   (vi) Purim

   (vii) Passover (*Pesach*)

   (viii) Pentecost (*Shavuot*)

E The Jewish calendar

A THE SABBATH

Jews observe the Sabbath (*Shabbat,* from the Hebrew word for "rest") as a day of rest. It commemorates the creation of the world: God rested on the seventh day (Exodus 20:11), and also the deliverance from slavery in Egypt (Deuteronomy 5:14-15). *Shabbat* is therefore also a sign of God's covenant with his people. It is the most important of the Jewish festival days, a day of peace and joy.

No work is done on the Sabbath, no fires may be lit (though a fire lit before the Sabbath may be left). Long journeys are forbidden, and so is driving the car or using public transport.

THE START OF SHABBAT

The Sabbath starts at sundown on Friday evening

- Candles are lit and are blessed by the mother.
- The father goes to the synagogue with his sons, and on his return, blesses his children and praises his wife, reading Proverbs 31.
- The Sabbath meal is eaten by all the family. It begins with the *kiddush*, a blessing of the wine, and the *ha' motzi,* a blessing of the bread.
- Special braided bread (*challah*) is eaten ? usually two loaves in memory of the double portion of manna that was given in the Wilderness wanderings on the day before the Sabbath.

HAVDALAH

At the end of the Sabbath, the family meet together for a brief ceremony called *Havdalah.*

It takes place after nightfall on Saturday night: that is, when three stars can be seen in the sky. The name *havdalah* means "to distinguish" or "separate." *Havdalah* marks the distinction between the holy Sabbath day and the secular working week.

Three items are used in the *havdalah* ceremony: a glass of *kosher* wine or grape juice; fragrant spices, such as cloves, cinnamon and bay leaves; and a special *havdalah* candle.

- The wine symbolizes the joy of the Sabbath.
- The spices symbolize the sweetness of the Sabbath, which carries over into the working week.
- The candle is braided and has two wicks. The braiding symbolizes the unity that should be a mark of the end of the Sabbath. Since the blessing refers to "lights of the fire" in the plural, two wicks are used in one candle.

THE HAVDALAH CEREMONY

The service begins with verses recited from the Hebrew Scriptures that praise God the Savior. Then blessings are recited over the wine, the spices and the candle. The service concludes with the Havdalah blessing.

Biblical verses

The leader raises a cup of wine and says:

"Behold, God is my savior, I will trust in God and will not be afraid, because my strong faith and song of praise for God will be my salvation" (Isaiah 12:2) .

"You shall joyfully draw water out of the wells of salvation" (Isaiah 12:3) .

"God is our savior, may God bless God's people" (Psalm 3:9).

"God of the universe is with us, the God of Jacob is a fortress protecting us" (Psalms 46:12).

"God of the universe, happy is the person who trusts you" (Psalm 84:13).
"God, redeem us. The King will answer on the day we call." (Psalms 20:10)

Everyone then joins in with the words that were spoken by the Jews when they were saved from Haman's plot:

"The Jewish People had light and joy and gladness and dignity, So may we be blessed" (Esther 8:16).

The leader raises a cup of wine and says:

"I will lift the cup of salvation and call upon God's name" (Psalms 116:13).

The blessing over the wine
The leader says:

"Blessed are You, Adonai our God, Ruler of the Universe, Creator of the fruit of the vine."
The wine is put down without anyone drinking from it.

The blessing over the spices
The leader says:

"Blessed are You, Adonai our God, Ruler of the Universe, Creator of many kinds of spices."

The spices are passed around so that all participants can sniff them.

The blessing over the candle

The candle that has been burning since the beginning of the ceremony is lifted up high, and the leader says:

"Blessed are you, Oh Lord our God, King of the Universe who has created the light of the fire."

The Havdalah blessing

The leader says:

"Blessed are you, Oh L-rd our G-d, King of the Universe who created a distinction between the holy and the profane, between the light and darkness, between Isra'el and the nations, between the seventh day and the rest of the week.

"Blessed are You, Oh L-rd our G-d who made a distinction between the sacred and the profane."

Everyone now tastes the wine.

Songs
The Havdalah ceremony often concludes with two traditional songs: *Shavua Tov* and *Eliahu HaNavi*.

Shavua Tov (a good week):
"A good week, a week of peace, may gladness reign and joy increase. "
Eliahu Ha' Navi:

"Elijah the Prophet, Elijah the Tishbite, Elijah the Gileadite.
With speed, Come to us, With the Messiah, The son of David."

B SYNAGOGUE ("GATHERING TOGETHER")

Synagogues probably began when the Temple was destroyed by Nebuchadnezzar, and the Jews were in exile in Babylonia. When the Temple was again destroyed in AD 70, synagogues became central to Judaism The synagogue was the church, town hall, day school, law court and community center.

Today, most Jews belong to a synagogue, though they may not attend every week.

The fullest service takes place on the Jewish Sabbath. A quoram (*minyan*) of at least ten people over the age of thirteen is necessary before a communal prayer service can take place.

(I) RABBI

The local synagogue is governed by the congregation and is normally led by a rabbi who has been chosen by the congregation. A rabbi is a teacher who has been well educated in Jewish law and tradition.

(II) SYNAGOGUE FURNISHINGS

Bimah
The area inside the synagogue is called the sanctuary. In the center, or near the front, is a raised platform (a *bimah*) The rabbi and cantor lead prayers from a pulpit in this area. A reading table serves to hold the *Torah* when it is opened.

Ark
The *Torah* scroll is kept in a cabinet called the Ark. A *parokhet* (curtain) covers the Ark and a lamp, symbolic of eternal light, burns continuously above and in front of it.

Mehitsah
Many Orthodox Jewish synagogues have a partition that separates men and women.

Ritual objects
Tallit   In Orthodoxy, all men wear prayer shawls.

Torah   The scroll contains the first five books of the Bible (Genesis, Exodus, Leviticus, Numbers, Deuteronomy), handwritten in

Hebrew. It rests in the Ark. A *yad* (a metal pointer) assists the reading of the *Torah* as the handwritten letters must not be touched.

Menorah   A seven-branched candelabra may be placed on the *bimah*
.

(III) SYNAGOGUE SERVICES

Jewish worship is liturgical. The prayer book (*siddur*) sets out the various readings and prayers for the day. A rabbi directs the service, teaches and preaches. Songs and chants are led by a cantor. A specific *Torah* reader chants or reads from the texts for the day.

The *Amidah* consists of praises, thanks and prayer requests to God.

The *Shema* ("Hear, O Israel, the Lord is our God, the Lord is One") is a declaration of faith, a central affirmation of Judaism.

C LIFE-CYCLE EVENTS

Life-cycle events occur throughout a Jew's life. They link him/her to the entire community.

(I) BIRTH CEREMONY

Called a *brit* or covenant, these rituals welcome newborn babies into the Jewish community.

(II) *BRIT MILAH*

The *brit milah* ceremony, which takes place on the eighth day after his birth, welcomes male babies into the covenant through the rite of circumcision.

A *mohel* (a specially trained circumciser) may accompany the rabbi.

(III) *BRIT BAT*

The *Brit bat* is a naming ceremony for baby girls.

(IV) *BAR MITZVAH* AND BAT *MITZVAH*

Boys reach the status of *Bar Mitzvah* (son of the commandment) on their thirteenth birthday; girls reach *Bat Mitzvah* (daughter of the commandment) on their twelfth birthday. This means that they are recognized as adults and are personally responsible to follow the Jewish commandments and laws.

In the synagogue service, on the Sabbath

after his thirteenth birthday, a boy reads from the scroll of the Law for the first time. This service is often followed by a party. Some synagogues also have a ceremony for a girl when she becomes *Bat-Mitzvah*.

D ANNUAL FESTIVALS AND DAYS OF FASTING

The Jewish religious day runs from sunset to sunset rather than midnight to midnight. So festivals begin on evenings prior to dates stated on their calendars.

(I) NEW YEAR'S DAY (ROSH HASHANAH)

Rosh Hashanah ("head of the year"), is held is September or October. This festival commemorates the creation of the world, and also God's future judgment. A ram's horn is blown in the synagogue to tell people to return to God, and the next ten days are given over to self-examination, repentance and prayer.

Often, apples dipped in honey are eaten on New Year's Day.

(II) DAY OF ATONEMENT (YOM KIPPUR)

Yom Kippur comes ten days after New Year's Day, and is the culmination of the period of repentance. It is the holiest day of the year. Devout Jews fast all day, and, wearing white robes, spend all day in the synagogue, repenting of their sins and seeking forgiveness and oneness with God.

(III) TABERNACLES (SUKKOT)

This is an eight-day harvest festival of thanksgiving (it is one of three harvest festivals: the other two are Passover and Pentecost). Its name comes from the practice of building booths (*sukkot*) in fields in order to watch over the gathering-in of the harvest. The name also commemorates the temporary structures in which the Israelites lived following their departure from Egypt. During the Feast of Tabernacles, Jews remember God's provision for them during the forty years spent wandering in the wilderness.

Sukkot is a time of thanksgiving, and of rejoicing in God's presence in creation and his care for his people. Today, the people build shelters made from branches, in their gardens, or by their synagogues. Here they eat they meals, and may even sleep.

(IV) CELEBRATING THE LAW (SIMCHAT TORAH)

The whole of the Pentateuch (Genesis to Deuteronomy) is read in the synagogue during the course of the year. On this day the final passage of Deuteronomy is read, and then the first verses of Genesis as the cycle begins again. To celebrate this event the scrolls of the law are carried around the synagogue with great rejoicing, singing and dancing.

(V) FESTIVAL OF LIGHTS (HANUKKAH)

Hanukkah, the Festival of Lights, or the Feast of Dedication, is an eight-day festival that recalls the war fought by the Maccabees in the cause of religious freedom and celebrates the victory of Judas Maccabeus and the rededication of the Temple in 164 BC. This festival takes place towards the end of December. Many Jews light an eight-branched candlestick (*menorah*), lighting one extra candle each day, until they are all lit.

(VI) PURIM

This festival is held in February or March. "Purim" means "lots" and refers to the lots cast by Haman in order to find the day on which to destroy all the Jews in the Persian Empire: a plot foiled by Queen Esther. The book of Esther is read in the synagogues, and in the homes, there are fancy dress parties and pastries called *Hamanatascen* are eaten.

(VII) PASSOVER (ALSO CALLED THE FEAST OF THE UNLEAVENED BREAD)

Each spring, Jews celebrate the Passover, or *Pesach*, in memory of their deliverance from slavery in Egypt. The eight-day festival, which is also a harvest festival, consists of the recitation of special prayers and eating symbolic foods. On the eve of the Passover, the home is searched to make sure that there is no yeast (leaven) anywhere in the house.

The highlight of the festival is a ritual meal (*seder*, meaning "order") eaten in the home. Six different foods are placed on the *seder* plate in the order in which they are eaten:

- *karpas* (vegetables dipped in salt water) recall the bitter tears shed during slavery
- *maror* (bitter herbs) to symbolize the bitterness of slavery
- *chazeret* (bitter vegetables) also to symbolize the bitterness of slavery
- *choroset* (apple, nuts and spices with wine) represents the mortar used by Hebrew slaves.

Also placed on the *seder* plate, but uneaten during the meal are:

- *zeroa* (lamb shankbone) to recall the Passover sacrifice in the Temple.
- *beitzah* (roasted egg), which symbolizes mourning, sacrifice, spring, and renewal.

Not placed on the *Seder* plate, but often eaten, is a boiled egg.

Matzah, a flat, unleavened bread, is also eaten. It symbolizes the bread eaten during the Exodus, and the "bread of affliction" of the slavery in Egypt.

Traditionally, an extra place is set at the table for the prophet Elijah, who will return one day to bring in the Messianic age.

At the meal, the youngest child asks: "Why is this night different from other nights?" The father then recounts the events of the Passover, reading from an order of service, the *Haggadah* ("telling the story"). There are also prayers and songs.

(VIII) PENTECOST (SHAVUOT)

Shavuot ("Weeks") is celebrated in late May or early June, fifty days after the second day of Passover. It is a harvest festival, "the feast of

the first fruits," which also celebrates God's revelation of the *Torah* to the Jewish people. The synagogue is decorated with flowers and plants, and the Ten Commandments are read. Dairy foods are eaten.

E THE JEWISH CALENDAR

Each new month begins with the appearance of the new moon and has either 29 or 30 days.

The current definition of the Jewish calendar is generally said to have been set down by the Sanhedrin president Hillel II in approximately AD 359.

The Jewish calendar is used for religious purposes by Jews all over the world, and it is the official calendar of Israel.

An ordinary year has twelve months, a leap year has thirteen months.

Every month starts (approximately) on the day of a new moon. The months are:

Tishri
Heshvan
Kislev
Tevet
Shevat
Adar I
Adar II
Nisan
Iyyar
Sivan
Tammuz
Av
Elul

The month Adar I is only present in leap years. In non-leap years Adar II is simply called "Adar."

COUNTING THE YEARS

Years are counted since the creation of the world, which is assumed to have taken place in 3761 BC. In that year, AM 1 started (AM = Anno Mundi = year of the world). The year AD 2006 is the Jewish year AM 5766.

8 GROUPINGS WITHIN JUDAISM

A Orthodox Judaism
B Conservative Judaism
C Reform Judaism
D Reconstructionism

INTRODUCTION

Judaism is usually classified in three denominations: Orthodox, Conservative, and Reform.

The estimated size of the different Jewish denominations is as follows:

Conservative	33%
Reform	22%
Orthodox	17%
Unaffiliated	28%

A ORTHODOX JUDAISM

This is the oldest and most conservative form of Judaism. Orthodox Judaism holds that the *Torah* was written by God and Moses, and that the original laws within it are binding and unchanging. Every word in their sacred texts is thought of as being divinely inspired.

While Orthodox Judaism is in many senses what Judaism has been since the Middle Ages, its formation as a movement was a direct response to the formation of Reform Judaism. Orthodox Jews insist on traditional Judaism. They have no wish to embrace the ways of modern culture.

Orthodox Judaism may be divided into two broad categories: Modern Orthodox and Hasidim. The Modern Orthodox are usually more academic, while the Hasidim are more mystical. Hasidic men usually wear black or dark gray suits and always wear skullcaps. The Hasidim movement was founded in Europe by Israel Baal Shem Tov (1700-1760).

B CONSERVATIVE JUDAISM

This began in the mid-nineteenth century as a reaction against the Reform movement. It is a main-line movement midway between Reform and Orthodox. This is the largest denomination within American Jewry.

Conservative Jews make allowances for modern culture, while "conserving," as far as possible, traditional Judaism. This movement views the *Torah* as unchanging, but subject to interpretation.

C REFORM JUDAISM

Reform Judaism is known as Progressive Judaism outside of the USA, and in the UK as Liberal Judaism. It sprang up in Germany as a reaction to traditional Judaism. It stresses integration with society and a personal interpretation of the *Torah*.

Reform Judaism has gladly embraced modernity, liberalism, and even, in some instances, aspects of humanism, in an effort to achieve a sense of relevance. Its members are usually sympathetic to an inclusive position regarding feminism, homosexuality, and agnosticism.

D RECONSTRUCTIONISM

Reconstructionism is the most recent branch of Judaism. The founder was Mordecai Kaplan (born 1881). Reconstructionism gives equal importance to religion, ethics and culture, and teaches that Judaism is an evolving religious civilization.

MAJOR BRANCHES OF JUDAISM

Conservative	4,700,000
Unaffiliated and Secular	4,700,000
Reform	3,900,000
Orthodox	2,100,000
Reconstructionist	170,000

9 FAMOUS JEWS

Rashi (1040-1105) Rabbi Shlomo Itzhaki. French *Torah* leader and scholar whose explanation of the Classic texts remains the cornerstone of Jewish commentary.

Maimonides (1135-1204) Rabbi Moses ben Maimon (the Rambam). Great *Torah* scholar and physician to his sovereign. Codifier of *Torah* Law.

Nachmonides (1195-1270) Rabbi Moses ben Nachman (the Ramban). Greatest *Torah* scholar of the thirteenth century.

Abarbanel (1437-1508) Don Isaac Abarbanel. Statesman, and *Torah* commentator. Renowned for his work on behalf of the Jewish people before and during the expulsion from Spain.

Baal Shem Tov (1700-1760) Rabbi Israel Shem Tov, the Founder of Chassidism.

Rav Moshe Chaim Luzzatto (1707-1746) A Kabbalist and scholar, who explained the enumerations of the ten steps leading to G-d.

Alter Rebbe (1745-1812) Rabbi Schneur Zalman of Liadi. Third generation disciple of the Baal Shem Tov, and author of the Tanya.

Rabbi Sampson Raphael Hirsch (1808-1888) Leader of German Jewry, who, in an effort to stem the tide of assimilation in Germany, promoted the idea that the study of *Torah* may form the basis of the pursuit of secular knowledge.

Chofetz Chaim (1839-1933) Rabbi Yisroel Meir Kagan. Leader of twentieth-century European Jewry, famous for his work on careless speech.

Rav Kook (1865-1935) Rabbi Avraham Isaac Kook. Chief Rabbi of Palestine prior to the establishment of the State of Israel. Passionate nationalist and mystic.

Martin Buber (1878-1965) Active Zionist. Supported Chassidic revival, formulated a dialogical, or "I-Thou" philosophy.

Lubavitcher Rebbe (1902-1995) Rabbi Menachem Mendel Schneerson. Seventh leader of Chabad Lubavitch.

Rav Soloveitchik (1903-1993) Rabbi Joseph Ber Soloveitchik. Father of Modern Orthodoxy. Combined Jewish Halacha and philosophy.

Rabbi Abraham Joshua Heschel (1907-1972) Central philosophy: religion provides the answer for the modern alienated person who asks existential questions.

Rabbi Aryeh Kaplan (1934-1983) The forty-seven books that were his life's work accounted for a qualitative and quantitative leap in Jewish publishing, making a host of difficult topics and concepts available to the English-reading public.

10 COMPARISON OF JUDAISM WITH CHRISTIANITY

A God
B Messiah
C Trinity
D Bible

INTRODUCTION

The roots of Christianity are in Judaism. So it is not surprising that the two religions share many similarities in their basic beliefs. There are, however, fundamental differences in belief between Christianity and Judaism.

The biggest difference between the two religions is their views about Jesus Christ. Christians accept Jesus Christ as the Messiah; Jews still await the coming of the Messiah.

A GOD

Judaism: Yhwh (Yahweh) is one eternal being who will send the Messiah. He rewards the righteous and punish the sinners.

Christianity: God, who is the creator of all, the Father of all living things. A personal being involved in the affairs of the world.

B MESSIAH

Judaism: Jews believe the Messiah is yet to come. Descended from the house of David, he will establish God's kingdom on earth. The Jewish view of Jesus centers on the belief that Jesus was no more than a teacher and storyteller. Jesus was only a human being. He was not the Son of God and did not rise from the dead. So Jesus cannot save souls.

Christianity: Christians believe that the Messiah is Jesus Christ, Son of God. He was God incarnate.

C TRINITY

Judaism: Jews do not believe in the Trinity.

"Hear, O Israel: The Lord our God, the Lord is one."
Opening words of the Shema

Christianity: Christians believe in the Father, Son and the Holy Spirit. They exist within the same God but are distinct from each other.

D BIBLE

Judaism: The Jewish Scriptures are known as the Hebrew Bible. It is an arrangement of the Old Testament into three sections.

Christianity: The Bible consists of the New and Old Testaments.

11 GLOSSARY

Abraham
Patriarchal figure who is the father of the Jewish faith. He championed monotheism. God made a binding covenant with him, and promised that through him all the nations of the world would be blessed.

CE
These initials stand for "Common Era" and are used to replace AD, which stands for *Anno Domini* (Latin for "in the year of our Lord" [Jesus Christ]).

Adam (and Eve)
Adam is Hebrew for "human, man." It is the name given to the first created male (with Eve as female) in the creation story in the Jewish scriptures (Genesis 1).

Amen
"Agreed."

Anti-Semitism
Literally means "opposed to Semites." Semites are people who, according to Genesis 10, are descended from Shem. They are people who speak a Semitic language (for example, Assyrian, Aramaic, Hebrew, Phoenician, Arabic.) The term, however, is usually applied specifically to opposition to Jews (anti-Judaism).

Ark
An acronym of *aron kodesh*, literally, "holy chest." It refers to the cabinet where the *Torah* scrolls are kept. The word has no connection with Noah's Ark, which is *teyvah* in Hebrew.

Aryan
"Aryan" was a nineteenth-century term used in linguistics to describe the Indo-European languages. The Nazis subsequently applied the term to the people who spoke those languages, whom they deemed superior to those who spoke Semitic languages.

Assur
Something prohibited according to Jewish law.

Atonement (kaparah).
Reconciliation between God and humanity is achieved by the process of repentance (*teshuvah*), seeking forgiveness and making amends with our fellow human beings.

Auschwitz
Concentration and extermination camp in upper Silesia, Poland, thirty-seven miles west of Krakow. Established in 1940 as a concentration camp, it became an extermination camp in early 1942.

Av or Ab
A month in the Jewish calendar; the 9th of Av is a day of mourning for the destruction of the Jerusalem Temple in 586 BC and again in 70 AD.

Babylonian exile
In 586 BC, Babylonia conquered the kingdom of Judah. Jerusalem and the first Temple were destroyed, and most Jews were exiled.

Balfour Declaration
A declaration of 1917 by British Foreign Minister Balfour supporting the establishment of a "Jewish national home in Palestine."

Bar Kokhba Revolt
The second Jewish revolt against Rome (131-135 CE), led by the warrior Bar Kokhba and the prominent sage Rabbi Akiva. After the defeat of the revolt, the Romans leveled Jerusalem and exiled the population.

Bar Kokhba (Aramaic: "Son of a Star")
Simeon ben Kosiba, the leader of the last and most successful Jewish rebellion against Rome in 132-135 CE. He died in battle when the rebellion was defeated. Rabbi Akiba believed he was the Messiah.

Bar (Bat) Mitzvah ("son (daughter)-of-the-commandment(s)")
The phrase originally referred to a person responsible for performing the divine commandments of Judaism; it now refers to the occasion when a boy or girl reaches the age of religious majority and responsibility (thirteen years for a boy; twelve years and a day for a girl).

BCE ("before the common era")
An attempt to use a neutral term for the period traditionally labeled "BC" (before Christ) by Christians. Thus 586 BCE is identical to 586 BC.

Ben (Hebrew, "son," "son of").
Used frequently in "patronymics" (naming by identity of father); Rabbi Akiba ben Joseph means Akiba son of Joseph.

Ben-Gurion, David (1886-1973)
The first prime minister of Israel.

Brit ha-hayim
Ritual developed by Reform Judaism to celebrate the birth of girls.

Canaan
Another name for Palestine or the present location of Israel.

Canon, canonical Scripture
The collection of books of the Bible recognized as authoritative.

Challah
The portion of bread dough which is burned entirely as a sacrifice to God; today, the term is used to refer to a braided loaf of white bread used to celebrate the Sabbath.

Chumash
The five books of the *Torah*, bound in one volume (not a scroll).

Circumcision (from Latin, "to cut around")
The minor surgical removal of the skin covering the tip of the penis. In Judaism, it is ritually performed when a boy is eight days old in a ceremony called *brit milah*. It is a sign of the covenant that God made with the Jews.

Conservative Judaism
Jewish school of thought which teaches that the *Torah* is binding but new thought can also influence belief.

Covenant
A binding agreement between two partners. In biblical times, the contractual agreement between God and Abraham became central to Jewish theology. The major covenants in Jewish scriptures are God's covenant with Abraham (Genesis 15), and the Sinai/Moses covenant (Exodus 19-24) between God and Israel.

David
King of Israel (northern Palestine) and Judea (southern Palestine), author of many of the psalms, and a leading figure in Jewish history. Jerusalem, the city of David, became the capital of the nation of Israel during David's reign.

Decalogue
A Greek term referring to the Ten Commandments (*aseret hadibrot*) received by Moses on Mount Sinai (Exodus 20.1-17; Deuteronomy 5.1- 21).

Diaspora, The
Term used for the dispersed Jews (the Jews living outside Palestine) after the captivity in Babylon; for the Jews living away from their land after the Romans destroyed Jerusalem and the Temple in AD 70; and now for Jews living outside Israel.

Exodus (from Greek "to exit or go out")
Refers to the event of the Israelites leaving Egypt and to the biblical book that records this event.

Gemara
Explanations on the *Mishnah*; written in Aramaic.

Hagar
Servant woman of Abraham by whom Abraham fathered a son, Ishmael.

Hasidim
Jewish ultra-orthodox movement established in Poland in the eighteenth century, where distinctive dress and language become essential elements of the faith.

Havdalah ("Separation")
The ceremony at the end of Sabbath marking the separation of the holy day from the week day.

Hebrew ("to pass over," "cross over")
An old name given to the people of Israel, and also to their language.

Holocaust (from Greek, "entire burnt offering")
This term describes the brutal killing of six million Jewish people by the Nazis between 1933-1945 during World War II.

Isaac
One of the Israelite patriarchs, the son of Abraham and father of Jacob.

Ishmael
First born son of Abraham by his servant woman Hagar.

Israel
A name given to the Jewish patriarch Jacob (Genesis 32:38). In Jewish biblical times, this name refers to the northern tribes, but also to the entire nation. Also name of the modern Jewish state, founded in 1948.

Jacob
One of the Israelite patriarchs, the son of Isaac and grandson of Abraham. Jacob had his name changed to Israel by God. The descendants of Abraham have called themselves Israelites since Jacob's time.

Jerusalem
The main city in ancient Israel where the Temple of David/Solomon was located.

Judaism, Jew
From the Hebrew name of the patriarch Judah, whose name also came to designate the tribe and tribal district in which Jerusalem was located. Thus, the inhabitants of Judah and members of the tribe of Judah come to be called "Judahites" or, in short form, "Jews." The religious outlook associated with these people after about the sixth century BCE came to be called "Judaism."

Kabala
A branch of Jewish mysticism which interprets the Scriptures in an esoteric manner as it seeks to fathom divine mysteries.

Kosher (*kashrut,* "Proper" or "ritually correct")
Kashrut refers to ritually correct Jewish dietary practices. Traditional Jewish dietary laws are based on biblical legislation. Only land animals that chew the cud and have split hooves (sheep, beef; not pigs, camels) are permitted to be eaten, and they must be slaughtered in a special way. Further, meat products may not be eaten with milk products or immediately after them. Only fish with fins and scales are allowed to be eaten.

Menorah
Jewish candlestick with special religious significance; an eight-branched *menorah* is used at *Hanukkah* (there are actually nine candles, one, called "the servant," being used to light the others), while the seven- branched *menorah* was used in the ancient Temple.

Messiah ("anointed one")
Ancient priests and kings (and sometimes prophets) of Israel were anointed with oil. In early Judaism, the term came to mean a royal descendant of the dynasty of David who would restore the united kingdom of Israel and Judah and usher in an age of peace, justice and plenty; the redeemer figure.

Mezuzah
Small parchment scroll of *Torah* verses affixed to doorposts.

Midrash
A method of expounding the *Torah,* with the purpose of revealing its inner meaning. The text is explained from and ethical and devotional point of view.

Mishnah
Jewish oral teachings which were collected and written down in six volumes by Rabbi Judah ha Nasi, around 200 AD.

Moses
The great biblical leader who took the people of Israel out of Egyptian bondage and taught them the divine laws at Sinai.

Orthodox Judaism
Jewish law and right doctrine are the defining criteria for this traditional grouping within Judaism. Orthodoxy has a variety of schools, the modern/centrist and traditional/rightist being the most common. It is the form of religion accepted as authentic in Israel.

Palestine (from a Greek word representing "Philistines," referring for the seacoast population encountered by early geographers)
An ancient designation for the area between Syria (to the north) and Egypt (to the south), between the Mediterranean Sea and the River Jordan; roughly, modern Israel. The name was given to the whole land of Israel during the years of the Jewish exile.

Parasha(h) ("section")
Prescribed weekly section of the biblical *Torah* (Pentateuch) read in Jewish synagogue liturgy.

Passover (*Pesach*)
The major Jewish spring holiday also known as *hag hamatzot* (Festival of Unleavened Bread) commemorating the exodus of the Hebrew people from Egypt (see Exodus 12-13). The festival lasts eight days, and during this time Jews refrain from eating all leavened foods and products. A special ritual meal called the *Seder* is prepared, and a traditional narrative called the *Haggadah*, supplemented by hymns and songs, is read to mark the event.

Patriarchs
The early founding figures of ancient Semitic tradition (before Moses) such as Abraham, Isaac, Jacob and the twelve tribal figureheads of Israel (Judah, Benjamin, etc.).

Pentateuch (from the Greek, *pentateuchos*, "five-volumed")
The five books of Moses (Genesis, Exodus, Leviticus, Numbers, Deuteronomy).

Phylacteries
(Greek for "protectors")
See *tefillin*.

Promised Land
The land that God promised to Abraham he would give to Abraham's descendants: the land specially designated by God for the Jews.

Prophet (from Greek, to "speak for" or "speak forth")
Name given to God's spokesmen. God communicated to the Jewish people through his prophets. It became a name for a section of the Jewish scriptures.

Psalm(s) (Hebrew, *tehillim*)
Collection of Biblical hymns, that is, sacred songs or poems used in worship.

Rabbi (Hebrew, "my master")
An authorized teacher of the classical Jewish tradition after the fall of the second Temple in 70 AD.

Reconstructionism
Jewish school of thought that advocates an all-encompassing approach to faith and practice.

Reform Judaism
Liberal school of Jewish practice that sees God's relationship with his people as an ongoing process throughout history.

Sabbath (Hebrew, "rest")
The seventh day of the week (*Shabbat*), recalling the completion of the creation and the exodus from Egypt. It is a day symbolic of new beginnings and one dedicated to God, a most holy day of rest.

Sarah
Abraham's wife who was unable to have a child until, in her old age, she gave birth to Isaac.

Seder (Hebrew for "order")
The traditional Jewish evening service, held at home, which opens the celebration of Passover. It includes special food, symbols and narratives. The order of the service is highly regulated, and the traditional narrative is known as the Passover *Haggadah*.

Shema
Prayer affirming the Jewish belief in one God.

Shofar
In Jewish worship, a ram's horn sounded at *Rosh Hashanah* morning worship and at the conclusion of *Yom Kippur*, as well as other times in that period during the fall.

Synagogue (Greek for "gathering")
The central institution of Jewish communal worship and study.

Talmud
A combination of the *Mishnah* and the *Gemara*.

Tefillin
Usually translated as "phylacteries." Small, box-like structures worn by Jewish adult males at the weekday morning services. The boxes have leather thongs attached and contain scriptural verses. One box (with four sections) is placed on the head, the other (with one section) is placed on the left arm, near the heart. The biblical passages emphasize the unity of God and the duty to love God and be mindful of him with "all one's heart and mind" (Exodus 13:1-10, 11-16; Deuteronomy 6:4-9; 11:13-21).

Temple
In Judaism, the only legitimate Temple was the one in Jerusalem, built first by King Solomon around 950 BC, destroyed by the Babylonian King Nebuchadnezzar around 587/6 BC, and rebuilt about seventy years later. It was destroyed by the Romans in AD 70.

Tetragrammaton (Greek, "four lettered [name]") See YHWH.

Theocracy (from Greek, "divine rule")
The idea that God should be the ultimate ruler over, or instead of, human rulers.

Torah (Hebrew, "teaching, instruction")
In general, *torah* refers to the study of the whole gamut of Jewish tradition or to some aspect thereof. In its special sense, "the *Torah*" refers to the "five books of Moses" in the Hebrew scriptures (see Pentateuch).

Tzitzit
Ritual strings placed on four cornered garments, as a reminder of the 613 commandments.

YHWH (Yahweh)
The sacred name of God in Jewish scriptures and tradition; also known as the tetragrammaton. Since Hebrew was written without vowels in ancient times, the four consonants YHWH contain no clue as to their original pronunciation. They are generally rendered "Yahweh" in contemporary scholarship. In traditional Judaism, the name YHWH is not pronounced, but Adonai ("Lord") is substituted when the Scriptures are read aloud. In most English versions of the Bible, the tetragrammaton is represented by "LORD" (or, less frequently, "Jehovah").

Yiddish
Uses the same alphabet as Hebrew but is a blend of Hebrew and several European languages, primarily German. Yiddish was the vernacular of East European and Russian Jews.

JAINISM

CONTENTS

1 An overview   367

2 Founder of Jainism   368

3 Jainist holy books   369

4 Facts and figures   375

5 Jainist practices   376

6 Jainist beliefs   378

7 Jainist worship   383

8 Jainist groupings   385

9 Famous Jainists   385

10 Quotations about Jainism   385

11 Glossary   387

1 AN OVERVIEW

DEFINITION

Jainism is an ancient religion and philosophy from India. It teaches that the way to liberation and bliss is to live a life of non-violence, renunciation and fasting.

Factfile
- Date of origin: sixth century BC
- Founder: Said to be Rsabha, the first *Tirthankara*;
             Vardhamana, known as Mahavira (the Great Hero) c. 540-c.468 BC
- Holy book: Svetambara canon; the Karmaprabhrta and the Kasayaprabhrta
- Number of adherents: 6-7 million

SUMMARY

The word "Jaina" means, "He is a Jain who follows the Jina." The word *jina* means "conquerer." Jinas were legendary figures who it was believed had achieved perfection.

The foremost duty of every Jain is the evolution of his soul and that of his fellow creatures. His objective is *moksha* (liberation) from unending cycles of birth, death and re-birth.

SUMMARY OF PRACTICES

Jains follow:

- Non-violence
- Renunciation
- Vegetarianism
- Fasting
- Meditation on the *Tirthankaras*

SUMMARY OF BELIEFS

Jainism denies the existence of a supreme being who created the world.

Jainism believes in the cyclical nature of the universe: a universe without beginning and without end.

Jains believe in *karma* and reincarnation, as do Hindus, but they believe that enlightenment and liberation from this cycle can only be achieved through a monastic life of penance and rigorous fasting, and non-violence. They also believe that *karma* is a physical substance: fine particles of matter, which cling to the soul.

The goal is *moksha* (liberation) from the cycles of birth, death and re-birth. The guides on this journey are the *Tirthankaras*. Once rid of the cloying weight of *karma*, the liberated soul rises to the eternal rest of Nirvans.

A core doctrine is *ahimsa*, that is, non-injury to all living creatures.

2 FOUNDER OF JAINISM

A Early history of Jainism
B Vardhamana

A EARLY HISTORY OF JAINISM

Jains believe that their religion has always existed. However, Jainism traces its roots back to a succession of twenty-four *Tirthankaras* (Ford-makers or Path-makers, also called *Jinas*, which means "Conquerors")) who lived, it is said, in India in very ancient times. The first is traditionally believed to have been Rsabha, whose name does appear in the *Vedas*. There is no further historical evidence for the existence of the *Tirthankaras* until Parsva, the twenty-third *Tirthankara*, who probably died in the late eighth century

Jainism as a historical movement arose in the sixth century BC as a protest against the overdeveloped ritualism of Hinduism, particularly its sacrificial cults.

B VARDHAMANA

The most recent and last Jina was Vardhamana (known as Mahavira, "The Great Hero"), and he is the historical founder of Jainism.

Mahavira was traditionally born in 559 BC and was an elder contemporary of Buddha (others suggest his dates were 540-468 BC) near Patna, in what is now Bihar state. His father was a ruling *Kshatriya* (of the Warrior caste), and was the chief of the Nata clan. His family name was Jnatriputra (in Pakrit, Nattaputta).

ENLIGHTENMENT

At about the age of twenty-eight, when his parents died, Mahavira left home and his life as a prince, to become a wandering beggar and ascetic, in search of liberation from the cycle of birth, death and rebirth. At first he wore a loin-cloth, but after thirteen months he decided to discard even this, and went about naked, unprotected from the sun, rain and wind. He lived on a most basic vegetarian diet, and practiced harsh fasts.

When Mahavira was about forty, after a period of extreme deprivation and fasting, he reached full enlightenment: he had become a *jina* (conqueror), a perfected soul (*kevalin*), freed from the power of *karma*.

A TEACHER

For the next thirty years Mahavira traveled from place to place, teaching his beliefs. Since he thought that salvation was achieved by personal effort alone, he took what appeared to be the logical step of rejecting as useless the *Vedas* and the Vedic rites, for which he was branded a heretic by Brahminism.

Many followers joined him and he organized them into a monastic community, with lay and monastic members of both sexes.

In 420 BC, he committed the act of *salekhana* (death by voluntary starvation).

Later followers deified Mahavira, calling him the twenty-fourth *Tirthankara* who descended from heaven without sin and with all knowledge.

3 JAINIST HOLY BOOKS

Jains hold Mahavira's teaching in very high regard, as they believe that these words represent a series of beginningless, endless and fixed truths, a tradition without any origin, human or divine, which in this world age has been channeled through Sudharman, the last of Mahavira's disciples to survive.

Paul Dundas

Since Jain monks were not allowed to have any religious books, Mahavira's teaching was memorized and passed down orally. Traditionally, this consisted of fourteen texts (*Purvas*). It is said that the last person to know this by heart was Bhadrabahu (the leader of the Svetambara sect). When he died, at the beginning of the third century, an attempt was made to reconstruct and write down what could be remembered of the canon. It was produced in twelve sections (*Angas*) (which still had to be memorized by individual monks).

Very early on, the Jainists split into two sects, the Svetambaras and the Digambaras. Both the Digambaras and Svetambaras believe that the "purest" Jainist teachings were contained within the (mostly lost) "*Purvas*." Each group have a different approach to the existing writings.

THE SVETAMBARAS

The Svetambara canon includes the *Agama*. This consists of forty-five texts:

11 *Angas* (the main texts)
12 *Upangas* (subsidiary texts)
4 *Mula-sutras* (various topics)
6 *Cheda-sutras* (concerned with discipline)
10 *Prakirnakas* (assorted texts)
2 *Culika-sutras* (on cognition)

The canon (which was fixed in the fifth century AD) also includes about another thirty-nine works, including thirteen commentaries. The canon is in the ancient language of Ardha-Magadhi language.

THE DIGAMBARAS

The Digambaras do not accept the Svetambara canon, as they believe it is not a true record of the Mahavara's teachings. They give canonical status to only two principal works, written in Praket:

the *Karmaprabhrta* (a chapter on *karma*)
the *Kasayaprabhrta*

THE STHANAKAVASIS SECT

This group does not have any scriptures.

QUOTATIONS FROM JAIN SCRIPTURE

There's no knowledge without right faith,
No conduct is possible without knowledge,
Without conduct, there's no liberation,
And without liberation, no deliverance.
Mahavira (Uttaradhyayana sutra, ch. 27, verse 30)

Endowed with conduct and discipline,
Who practices control of self,
Who throws out all his bondage,
He attains the eternal place.
Mahavira (Uttaradhyayana sutra, ch. 20, verse 52)

All unenlightened persons produce sufferings. Having become deluded, they produce and reproduce sufferings, in this endless world.
Mahavira, Uttaradhyayana, 6/1

Just as a threaded (*sasutra*) needle is secure from being lost,
in the same way a person given to self-study (*sasutra*) cannot be lost.
Mahavira, Uttaradhyayana, 29/59

Only that science is a great and the best of all sciences,

the study of which frees man from all kinds of miseries.

Mahavira, Isibhasiya, 71

That with the help of which we can know the truth,
control the restless mind, and purify the soul is called knowledge.

Mahavira, Mulachara, 5/70

That which subdues passions, leads to beatitude and fosters friendliness is called knowledge.

Mahavira, Mulachara 5/71

The unenlightened takes millions of lives to extirpate the effects of karma whereas a man possessing spiritual knowledge and discipline obliterates them in a single moment.

Mahavira, Bhagavati Aradhana, 10

The nights that have departed will never return.
They have been wasted by those given to *adharma* (unrighteousness).

Mahavira, Uttaradhyayana, 14/25

The nights that have departed will never return.
They are profitable for one who is given to *dharma* (righteousness).

Mahavira, Uttaradhyayana, 14/25

Those who are ignorant of the supreme purpose of life will never be able to attain nirvana (liberation) in spite of their observance of the *vratas* (vows) and *niymas* (rules) of religious conduct and practice of *shila* (celibacy) and *tapas* (penance).

Mahavira, Samayasara, 153

My soul characterized by knowledge and faith is alone eternal.
All other phases of my existence to which I am attached are external occurrences that are transitory.

Mahavira, Niyamasara, 99

Righteousness consists in complete self-absorption and in giving up all kinds of passions including attachment.
It is the only means of transcending the mundane existence.
The Jinas have said so.

Bhava-pahuda, 83

Don't kill any living beings. Don't try to rule them.

Mahavira, Acaranga, 4/23

The essence of all knowledge consists in not committing violence.
The doctrine of *ahimsa* is nothing but the observance of equality, that is,
the realization that just as I do not like misery, others also do not like it.
(Knowing this, one should not kill anybody).

Mahavira, Sutrakrtanga, 1/1/4/10

Just as you do not like misery, in the same way others also do not like it.
Knowing this, you should do unto them what you want them to do unto you.

Mahavira, Bhagavati Aradhana, 780

To kill any living being amounts to killing one self.
Compassion to others is compassion to one's own self.
Therefore one should avoid violence like poison and thorn (that cause pain).

Mahavira, Bhagavati Aradhana, 797

Don't be proud if you gain. Nor be sorry if you lose.

Mahavira, Acaranga, 2/4/114, 115

One who cultivates an attitude of equality towards all living beings, mobile and stationary, can attain equanimity. Thus do the kevalis say.

Mahavira, Anuyogadvar, 708, gatha 2

Only the one who has transcended fear can experience equanimity.

Mahavira, Sutrakrtanga 1/2/2/17

(One should reflect thus:) Let me treat all living beings with equanimity and none with enmity. Let me attain *samadhi* (tranquility) by becoming free from expectations.

Mahavira, Mulachara, 2/42

Let me renounce the bondage of attachment and hatred, pride and meekness, curiosity, fear, sorrow, indulgence and abhorrence (in order to accomplish equanimity).

Mahavira, Mulachara 2/44

Let me give up attachment through unattachment.
My soul will be my only support (in this practice of unattachment).
(Hence) let me give up everything else.

Mahavira, Mulachara 2/44

Just as I do not like misery, so do others. Knowing this, one neither kills, nor gets killed. A *sramana* is so called because he behaves equanimously.

Mahavira, Anuyogadvara, 708, gatha 3

One who remains equanimous in the midst of pleasures and pains is a *sramana*, being in the state of pure consciousness.

Mahavira, Pravachansara, 1/14

A *sramana* devoid of the knowledge of *Agama* does neither know himself, nor others.

Mahavira, Pravasanasara, 3/32)

Other beings perceive through their senses whereas the *sramana* perceives through the *Agama*.

Mahavira, Pravachansara, 3/34

One devoted whole-heartedly to knowledge, faith and right conduct equally accomplishes in full the task of the *sramana*.

Mahavira, Pravachansara, 3/42

O Self! Practice Truth, and nothing but Truth.

Mahavira, Acaranga, 3/3/66

Enlightened by the light of Truth, the wise transcends death.

Mahavira, Acaranga, 3/3/66

Truth alone is the essence in the world.

Mahavira, Prasnavyakarna, 2/2

The ascetic who never thinks of telling a lie out of attachment, aversion or delusion is indeed the practice of the second vrata of truthfulness.

Mahavira, Niyamasara, 57

A truthful man is treated as reliable as the mother, as venerable as the guru (preceptor) and as beloved as the one who commands knowledge.

Mahavira, Mulachara, 837

Truthfulness indeed is *tapa* (penance).
In truthfulness do reside self-restraint and all other virtues.
Just as the fish can live only in the sea, so can all other virtues reside in Truthfulness alone.

Mahavira, Bhagavati Aradhana, 842

One may have a tuft or matted hair on the head or a shaven head, remain naked or wear a rag.
But if he tells a lie, all this is futile or fruitless.

Mahavira, Bhagavat Aradhana, 843

One can bear all kinds of unbearable pain caused by spikes in expectation of wealth etc.
But he alone who tolerates, without any motive of worldly gain, harsh words spoken to him is venerable.

Mahavira, Dasavaikalika, 9/3/6

One should not speak unless asked to do so.
He should not disturb others in conversation.
He should not back-bite and indulge in fraudulent untruth.

Mahavira, Dasavaikalika, 8/46

One should not utter displeasing words that arouse ill feelings in others.

One should not indulge in speech conducive to the evil.
Mahavira, Dasavaikalika , 8/47

Discipline of speech consists in refraining from telling lies and in observing silence.
Mahavira, Mulachara, 332

The *sadhaka* (one who practices spiritual discipline) speaks words that are measured and beneficial to all living beings.
Mahavira, Kartikeyanupreksa, 334

The *bhiksu* (ascetic) should not be angry with one who abuses him.
Otherwise he would be like the ignoramus.
He should not therefore lose his temper.
Mahavira, Uttaradhyayana, 2/24

If somebody were to beat a disciplined and restrained ascetic, the latter should not think of avenging himself considering the soul to be imperishable.
Mahavira, Uttaradhyayana, 2/27

As gold does not cease to be gold even if it is heated in the fire; an enlightened man does not cease to be enlightened on being tortured by the effects of *karma*.
Mahavira, Samayasara, 184

A thief feels neither pity nor shame, nor does he possess discipline and faith.
There is no evil that he cannot do for wealth.
Mahavira, Bhagavat Aradhana, 862

On the aggravation of one's greed,
a person fails to distinguish between what should be done and what should not be done. He is dare-devil who can commit any offence even at the cost of his own life.
Mahavira, Bhagavati Aradhana, 857

By practicing celibacy one can fulfill all other vows – chastity, *tapas* (penance), *vinaya* (humility), *sayyama* (self-restraint), forgiveness, self-protection and detachment.
Mahavira, Prasnavyakarana, 9/3
Knowing that pleasing sound, beauty,

fragrance, pleasant taste and soothing touch are transitory transformations of matter, the celibate should not be enamored of them.
Mahavira, Dasavaikalika, 8/58

The soul is the Brahman. Brahmacarya is therefore nothing but spiritual conduct of the ascetic concerning the soul, who has snapped out of relationship with alien body.
Mahavira, Bhagavati Aradhana, 877

An amorous person, failing to achieve his desired objects, becomes frantic and even ready to commit suicide by any means.
Mahavira, Bhagavati Aradhana, 889

The sun scorches only during the day,
but cupid scorches in the day as well as in the night.
One can protect oneself from the sun, but cannot from cupid.
Mahavira, Bhagavti Aradhana

The more you get, the more you want.
The greed increases with the gain.
What could be accomplished by two *masas* (grams) of gold could not be done by ten millions.
Mahavira, Uttaradhyayana, 8/17

Knowing that the earth with its crops of rice and barley, with its gold and cattle, and all this put together will not satisfy one single man, one should practice penance.
Mahavira, Uttardhyayana, 9/49

Just as fire is not quenched by the fuel and the ocean by thousands of rivers, similarly no living being is satisfied even with all the wealth of all the three worlds.
Mahavira, Bhagavati Aradhana, 1143

Non-possessiveness controls the senses
in the same way as a hook controls the elephant.
As a ditch is useful for the protection of a town, so is non-attachment for the control of the senses.
Mahavira, Bhagavati Aradhana, 1168

Greed even for a piece of straw, not to speak of precious things, produces sin.
A greedless person, even if he wears a crown, cannot commit sin.
Mahavira, Bhagavati Aradhana, 1371

One who, being swayed by wishful thinking, becomes a victim of passions at every step, and does not ward off the desires, cannot practice asceticism.
Mahavira, Dasavaikalika, 2/1

External renunciation is meaningless if the soul remains fettered by internal shackles.
Mahavira, Bhava-pahuda, 13

Living beings have desires. Desires consist in pleasure and pain.
Mahavira, Kartikeyanupreksa, 18/14

One who is constantly careful in his deportment is like the lily in the pond, untarnished by mud.
Mahavira, Pravachansara, 3/18

Objects of the senses pollute knowledge if it is not protected by discipline.
Mahavira, Shila-pahuda, 2

Discipline is the means of achieving liberation.
Mahavira, Shila-pahuda, 20

Even the noble becomes mean in the company of the wicked, as precious necklace on the neck of a dead body.
Mahavira, Bhagavati Aradhana, 245

The ignoramus is always benighted.
The enlightened is always wide awake.
Mahavira, Acaranga, 3/1

The five senses of the awakened always remain inactive.
The five senses of the unawakened always remain active.
By means of the active five one acquires bondage while by means of the inactive five the bondage is severed.
Mahavira, Isibhasiyam, 29/2

Just as every body keeps away from the burning fire, so do the evils remain away from an enlightened person.
Mahavira, Isibhasiya, 35/23

Keep yourself always awake.
One who keeps awake increases his wisdom.
He who falls asleep in wretched. Blessed is he who keeps awake.
Mahavira, Brhatkalpa-bhasya, 3387

The yogi who is indifferent to worldly affairs remains spiritually alert to his own duty, namely, his duty towards his soul.
On the other hand, one who indulges in worldly affairs is not dutiful to his soul.
Mahavira, Moksha-pahuda, 31

Birth is attended by death, youth by decay and fortune by misfortune.
Thus everything in this world is momentary.
Mahavira, Kartikeyanupreksa, 5

The courageous as well as the cowardly must die.
When death is inevitable for both, why should not one welcome death smilingly and with fortitude?
Mahavira, Mulachara, 2/100

Both the righteous and unrighteous must die.
When death is inevitable for both,
when should not one embrace death while maintaining good conduct?
Mahavira, Mulachara, 2/101

There is nothing as fearful as death, and there is no suffering as great as birth.
Be free from the fear of both birth and death, by doing away with attachment to the body.
Mahavira, Mulachara, 2/119

Do not be in dread of the dreadful, the illness, the disease, the old age, and even the death or any other object of fear.
Mahavira, Prasnavyakarana, 7/20

The non-vigilant has fear from all
directions.
The vigilant has none from any.
Mahavira, Acaranga, 3/75

One who entertains fear finds himself
lonely (and helpless).
Mahavira, Prasnavyakarana, 7/20

The valiant does not tolerate indulgence,
nor does he tolerate abhorrence.
As he is pleased with his own self, he is
not attached to anything.
Mahavira, Acaranga, 2/6/160

As a tortoise withdraws his limbs within
his own body, even so does the valiant
withdraw his mind within himself from
all sins.
He also withdraws his hands, legs, mind,
sense-organs, sinful moods, evil words,
pride, and deceitfulness. This indeed is
the valor of the valiant.
Mahavira, Sutrakrtanga, 1/8/16-18

The enlightened should contemplate that
his soul is endowed with boundless
energy.
Mahavira, Niyamasara, 96

Only that man can take a right decision,
whose soul is not tormented by the
afflictions of attachment and aversion.
Mahavira, Isibhasiyam, 44/1

One who knows the spiritual (self) knows
the external (world) too.
He who knows the external world, knows
the self also.
Mahavira, Acaranga, 1/7/147

If one's vision is capable of expelling the
darkness, he would not need a lamp.
Likewise the soul itself being blissful,
there is no need of external object for
bliss.
Mahavira, Pravachansara, 1/67

Those who are interested in worldly
objects have of necessity misery in them.
If there were no misery in them, they
would not indulge in those objects.
Mahavira, Pravachansara, 1/84

I condemn what is worthy of
condemnation.
I censure what is worthy of censure.
I atone for all the outer and inner
encroachments on the soul.
Mahavira, Mulachara 2/55

May the state of Arhats, the Siddhas and
the Vitranagas be my goal.
Mahavira, Mulachara, 2/107

As the fire quickly consumes dry wood,
even so an adept whose soul is equipoised
and unattached causes the accumulated
karma structure to disintegrate
Mahavira, Acaranga, 4/3/33

Those who hanker after pleasure, those
who are attached to or seized by passions
and are obstinate like miser, cannot know
the nature of *samadhi* (self-
concentration).
Mahavira, Sutrakrtanga, 1/2/58

A monk engrossed in meditation
renounces all evils.
Meditation is therefore the best way of
regression from all transgressions.
Mahavira, Niyamasara, 65

One who meditates on the soul, attains
the supreme samadhi.
Mahavira, Niyamasara, 129

The monk who is absorbed in meditation
achieves victory over attachment and
aversion, and the senses.
His fear vanishes and his passions are
shattered.
Finally, he extirpates his indulgences,
abhorrence and delusion.
Mahavira

The *Arhats* of the past, those of the
present and the future narrate thus,
discourse thus, proclaim thus, and affirm
thus: One should not injure, subjugate,
enslave, torture or kill any animal, living

being, organism or sentient being. This doctrine of Non-Violence (*Ahimsa Dharma*) is immaculate, immutable and eternal.

Mahavira, Acharanga sutra, ch. 4

Above, below and in front, people indulge in violent activities against living beings individually and collectively in many ways; discerning this, a wise man neither himself inflicts violence on these bodies, nor induces others to do so, nor approved of their doing so.

Mahavira, Acharanga sutra, ch. 1

The *Arhats* have propounded the doctrine of Non-Violence, one and all, equally for those who are desirous to practice it and those who are not, those who have abandoned violence and those who have not, those who are deeply engrossed in worldly ties and those who are not. This doctrine of *Ahimsa* is Truth. It is rightly enunciated here in the teachings of the *Arhats*. Comprehending the true spirit of the doctrine, one should practice it till one's last breath.

Mahavira, Acharanga sutra, ch. 4

---

4 Facts and Figures

GEOGRAPHICAL LOCATION

India   About half, over three million, of all the world's Jainists live in India, primarily in to the Indian states of Rajasthan, Gujarat, Maharashtra, Madhya Pradesh, and Karnataka.

USA	About 50,000
UK	About 30,000
East Africa	Some Jain communities

HEADQUARTERS MAIN CENTER

In India, the headquarters for the Svetambaras is Mount Satrunjaya, and for the Digambaras it is Sravana Belgola.

5 JAINIST PRACTICES

A Sacredness of all life
B Vows for lay people
C Vows for monks and nuns
D Leaders

A   SACREDNESS OF ALL LIFE: AHIMSA, NON-INJURY

Jains believe in the sacredness of all life. It follows that committing an act of violence against a human, animal, or even vegetable, generates negative *karma* that in turn adversely affects one's next life. So they believe that the only way to save their own souls is to protect the souls of everyone else. They therefore practice *ahimsa*, non-violence, following the Jain scripture: "Do not injure, abuse, oppress, enslave, insult, torment, torture or kill any creature or living being."

The concept of non-violence extends to every part of a person's life: mental, verbal and physical. While the Brahmin tolerates the slaughter of animals for food, to provide offerings for the sacrifice, or to show hospitality to a guest; and while the Buddhist does not scruple to eat meat prepared for a banquet; Jains will not tolerate eating meat or fish under any circumstances. They follow the policy of only eating anything that will not kill the plant or animal from which it is taken.

Jain monks wear muslin cloths over their mouths to stop them from accidentally swallowing a fly.

Ahimsa puts restrictions on the work a Jain may do. He may not, for example, be a farmer, in case he injures plans or animals while ploughing, or a carpenter, because the wood must not be hurt. Safe professions are trading, banking and money-lending.

The code of morals enjoined on monks and lay people is a working out of this fundamental principle of non-violence.

B VOWS FOR LAY PEOPLE

Lay people may begin the upward path leading to the full asceticism of the monk, and, ultimately, voluntary starvation resulting in death. In the first stage, they undertake twelve vows, which prepare them for the rigors of an ascetic life. These vows are in three groups:

Group 1: five *anuvratas* ("little vows")
Group 2: three *gunavratas* ("assistant vows")
Group 3: four *siksavratas* (vows aimed at strengthening the mind and resolve)

GROUP 1 (ANUVRATA)

- Non-violence to souls with more than one sense (souls with only one sense are the elements and the vegetable kingdom).
- Do not lie
- Do not steal
- Be content with your wife or husband
- Limit your possessions

GROUPS 2 AND 3

The remaining seven vows are meant to strengthen the first five. They include avoidance of unnecessary travel; avoidance of harmful activities including the pursuit of pleasure; control of diet; offering gifts and service to monks; meditation.

THE SECOND STAGE

Lay people who are wanting to reach a higher stage, must keep a further eleven vows, which medieval writers thought of as rungs on a ladder:

- worship of a Tirthankara; reverence of a true guru; belief in the true doctrine
- to face death by self-starvation in peace
- to meditate three times a day
- to live the life of a monk six times a month

- to avoid uncooked vegetables
- to refrain from eating between sunset and sunrise, and to refrain from drinking water before daylight in case an insect was swallowed
- to keep away from one's own wife or husband
- to refrain from anything that might involve a worldly pursuit
- to be a novice for the rest of his or her days
- to eat only left-overs
- to wear ascetic's clothes, live away from home in a religious building, follow the rules for an ascetic.

C VOWS FOR MONKS AND NUNS (MAHAVRATA)

The life of an ascetic monk begins with a service of initiation. He gives away his clothes, wears the dress of an ascetic, has his hair cut and becomes a homeless wanderer.

He takes five great vows, which are similar, but stricter, than those taken by lay people:

- to do violence to no living thing (even one-sensed inanimate objects)

- truthfulness: to speak only what is pleasant and wholesome
- non-stealing: not to take what is not given
- chastity: to have no dealings with gods, human beings or animals of the opposite sex.
- to be indifferent to anything that comes through the senses.

The austerities in which a monk engages, their severity, and length of time, are regulated by a preceptor.

The monk's final act of non-attachment is the act of *sallekhana*, in which he lies on one side on a bed of thorny grass and refuses to move or eat food.

D LEADERS

Jainism embodies five stages of spiritual development.

Tirthankaras occupy the highest level, followed by *Siddhas* (liberated souls) and then spiritual leaders (teachers, nuns and monks). The fourth level includes those who instruct monks and nuns, and the fifth ordinary Jain monks. On a local level, each Jain community has an elected leader.

6 JAINIST BELIEFS

A   God
B   The universe
C   Jinas
D   Reincarnation
E   Souls
F   *Karma*
G   Salvation
H   *Tirthankara*
I   List of *Tirthankaras*
J   The three jewels
K   Nine *Tattvas*
L   Other religions

A GOD

Jains do not believe in the concept of a God who created and sustained the universe. Rather they view God as a universal consciousness, or *Atman*, the ultimate. Therefore Jains do not believe that they will neither be judged by a God or receive help from him.

B THE UNIVERSE

Jains believe that the universe had no beginning and everything in it is eternal, and so will have no ending. Time is thought of as a wheel with twelve spokes.

The universe exists as a series of layers, both heavens and hells. It consists of:

- The supreme abode: This is located at the top of the universe and is where the liberated souls live.
- The upper world: thirty heavens where celestial beings live.
- Middle world: the earth and the rest of the universe.
- Nether world: seven hells with various levels of misery and punishments.
- The Nigoda, or base: where the lowest forms of life reside.
- Universe space: layers of clouds which surround the upper world.
- Space beyond: an infinite volume without soul, matter, time, medium of motion or medium of rest.

Everyone is bound within the universe by one's *karma* (the accumulated good and evil that one has done).

Moksha (liberation from an endless succession of lives through reincarnation) is achieved by enlightenment, which can be attained only through asceticism.

C JINAS

Spiritual guides of Jains are called the Jinas (*Tirthankaras*). Jinas ("victors") have conquered themselves, as well as their faults and desires.

D REINCARNATION

Jains believe in the perpetual recycling of one's eternal soul (*jiva*) through endless incarnations. Freedom from reincarnation comes through the purification of the soul. It is dependent upon one's own efforts.

E SOULS

All living beings have permanent souls, but only temporary bodies. The soul, or *jiva* is a conscious, living being. Souls can be freed from the endless cycle of death and rebirth, and this is their goal and purpose. Such liberated souls do not have physical bodies and have become perfect beings.

F KARMA

Jains believe in the law of *karma*. The *karma* theory has been called "the scorecard of your life and actions." All of one's thoughts and actions have consequences that will become apparent in this life and in the next lives. However, in Jainism, the *karma* (or *karman*) is physical matter, very fine particles that cling to the soul, and not a process as in Hinduism. This atomic substance causes the rebirths and must be got rid of.

G SALVATION

Every form of earthly, bodily existence is misery. Freedom from rebirth is the goal. To achieve liberation one's soul must be free from all *karma*. This salvation is obtained by personal effort alone. It is accomplished by the life of severe mortification of which Jina set the example. Even death by voluntary starvation cannot bring about liberation, but it does improve the soul's situation in the next birth. Twelve years of ascetic life as a Jainist monk and eight rebirths are necessary to constitute the purgatorial preparation for the Jainist heaven.

H *TIRTHANKARA*

In Jainism, a *Tirthankara* ("Ford-maker") is a legendary human being who, by adopting asceticism, achieved enlightenment (perfect knowledge), thus becoming a Jina (one who has conquered his inner enemies – anger, pride, deceit, desire, etc.).

A *Tirthankara* is so-named because he is the founder of a *Tirth,* which is a community of Jains which acts as a "ford" across the "river of human misery." They were omniscient teachers.

The religious teachings of the *Tirthankaras* form the canon of Jainism. The inner knowledge of all *Tirthankaras* is perfect and the same in all respects. Therefore the teachings of one *Tirthankara* do not in any way contradict those of another. However, the degree of elaboration varies according to the spiritual advancement and purity of mind of humans during the time of a particular *Tirthankara.* The higher the spiritual advancement and purity of mind, the lower is the elaboration required.

Jainism teaches that time is like a wheel. It moves in the same way as the wheel of a moving cart or bicycle. There have been an infinite number of time cycles before the present one and there will be an infinite number of time cycles after the present one. At the beginning of the twenty-first century, we are approximately 2,530 years into the fifth era of the present half cycle.

Twenty-four *Tirthankaras* are born in each half cycle of time (that is forty-eight in each full cycle), in this part of the universe.

In the present (descending) half cycle of time, the first *Tirthankara* was Rishabh (Rsabha) Dev who lived billions of years ago and attained liberation (*moksh* or *nirvan*a) towards the end of the third era. The twenty-fourth and last *Tirthankara* was Mahavira Swami.

Digambaras believe that all twenty-four *Tirthankaras* were men but Svetambaras believe that the nineteenth *Tirthankar*a, Malli Nath, was a woman.

The next *Tirthankara* in this part of the universe will be born at the beginning of the third era of the next (ascending) half cycle of time, that is in approximately 81,500 years.

As *Tirthankaras* are credited with showing the path to enlightenment, their statues are worshiped in Jain temples by Jains aspiring to achieve enlightenment themselves.

Tirthankaras should not be confused with God or gods. Jainism does not believe in the existence of God in the sense of a creator and gods are a form of life usually superior to that of humans but nevertheless not enlightened.

I LIST OF TIRTHANKARS

The twenty-four *Tirthankaras* who were born in the present (descending) half cycle of time, in this part of the universe, are as follows: (*Dev, Nath* and *Swami* mean Lord)

Each *Tirthankara* is identified with an animal, object, or other such symbol.

Name	Symbol
Rishabh Dev (Adi Nath)	Bull
Ajit Nath	Elephant
Sambhav Nath	Horse
Abhinandan Swami	Monkey
Sumathi Nath	Curlew (*Kraunea*)

Padmaprabh Swami	Red Lotus
Suparshva Nath	Swastik
Chandraprabh Swami	Moon
Suvidhi Nath	Crocodile
Shithal Nath	Srivatsa
Shreyans Nath	Rhinoceros
Vasupujya Swami	Buffalo
Vimal Nath	Boar
Ananth Nath	Bear (Falcon)
Dharma Nath	Spike-headed Club (*Vajradanda*)
Shanthi Nath	Deer
Kunthu Nath	He-Goat
Ar Nath	Fish
Malli Nath	Water Pot
Munisuvrat Swami	Tortoise
Nami Nath	Blue Lotus
Nemi Nath	Shell (Conch)
Parshva Nath	Serpent
Mahavir Swami	Lion

J THE THREE JEWELS

The Jainist creed consists of the so-called three jewels, the three guiding ethical principles of Jainism. These must be cultivated together. None can be achieved by itself. They are:

- right belief
- right knowledge
- right conduct.

RIGHT BELIEF

Right belief embraces faith in Jina (Mahavira) as the true teacher of salvation and the acceptance of the Jainist scriptures as his authoritative teaching. These scriptures are less extensive, less varied, than the Buddhist, and, while resembling the latter to a large degree, lay great stress on bodily mortification. The canon of the White-robed Sect consists of forty-five Agamas, or sacred texts, in the Prakrit tongue. Jacobi, who has translated some of these texts in the "Sacred Books of the East," is of the opinion that they cannot be older than 300 BC. According to Jainist tradition, they were preceded by an ancient canon of fourteen so-called *Purvas*, which have disappeared.

Right belief leads to calmness, tranquility, detachment, kindness, renunciation of pride,

beauty, wealth, scholarship, fame.

RIGHT KNOWLEDGE

With the Jainist, right knowledge embraces the religious view of life. Knowledge of the scriptures is distinguished from inner knowledge, which is also required.

RIGHT CONDUCT

Right conduct is concerned with the main ethical precepts and with the ascetic, monastic system. It is spontaneous, arising from a purified mind (right knowledge), and is not mechanical obedience.

K NINE TATTVAS

The nine *tattvas*, or principles, are the basis of Jain philosophy. They expound the *karma* theory of Jainism, which provides the basis for the path of liberation. They bring about right faith, right knowledge, and right conduct in an individual.

(i)	*Jiva*	soul or living being (consciousness)
(ii)	*Ajiva*	non-living substances
(iii)	*Asrava*	cause of the influx of *karma*
(iv)	*Bandha*	bondage of *karma*
(v)	*Punya*	virtue
(vi)	*Papa*	sin
(vii)	*Samvara*	arrest of the influx of *karma*
(viii)	*Nirjara*	exhaustion of the accumulated *karma*
(ix)	*Moksha*	total liberation from *karma*

(i) and (ii) *Jiva and Ajiva*

Jains believe that reality is made up of two eternal principles, *jiva and ajiva*. Jiva consists of an infinite number of identical spiritual units; *ajiva* (that is, *non-jiva*) is matter in all its forms and the conditions under which matter exists: time, space, and movement.

Both *jiva* and *ajiva* are eternal; they never came into existence for the first time and will never cease to exist. The whole world is made up of *jivas* trapped in *ajiva*; there are *jivas* in rocks, plants, insects, animals, human beings, and spirits.

Any contact whatsoever of the *jiva* with the *ajiva* causes the former to suffer. Thus the Jains believed that existence in this world inevitably means suffering. Neither social reform nor the reform of individuals themselves can ever stop suffering. In every human being, a *jiva* is trapped, and the *jiva* suffers because of its contact with *ajiva*. The only way to escape from suffering is for the *jiva* to completely escape from the human condition, from human existence.

(iii) *Asrava* (cause of the influx of *karma*)
Asrava leads to the influx of good and evil *karma* which lead to the bondage of the soul.

Asrava is the attraction in the soul toward sense objects. The following cause good and evil *karma*:

- *Mithyatva*   ignorance
- *Avirati*   lack of self restraint
- *Kasaya*   passions like anger, conceit, deceit, and lust
- *Pramada*   unawareness
- *Yoga*   activities of mind, speech, and body

Additionally, the five great sins cause the influx of *karma*:

- violence
- untruth
- stealing
- sensual indulgence
- attachment to worldly objects.

(iv) *Bandha* (bondage of *karma*)
Bandha is the attachment of *karmic* matter (*karma pudgala*) to the soul. The soul has had this *karmic* matter bondage from eternity. This *karmic* body is known as the *karmana* body or causal body. Karmic matter is a particular type of matter which is attracted to the soul because of its ignorance, lack of self restraint, passions, unmindfulness, activities of body, mind, and speech.

The soul, which is covered by *karmic* matter, continues acquiring new *karma* from the universe and exhausting old *karma* into the universe through the above mentioned actions at every moment. Because of this continual process of acquiring and exhausting *karma* particles, the soul has to pass through the cycles of births and deaths, in the course

of which it experiences pleasure and pain.

So under normal circumstances the soul cannot attain freedom from *karma*, and hence liberation.

FOUR FORMS OF KARMA
Karmic matter attaching to the soul assumes four forms:

Prakriti bandha	Type of *karma*
Sthiti bandha	Duration of *karma*
Anubhava bandha	Intensity of attachment of *karma*
Pradesa bandha	Quantity of *karma*.

Prakriti bandha:
When *karmic* matter attaches to the soul, *karma* will obscure its essential nature of: perfect knowledge, vision, bliss, power, eternal existence, non-corporeal, and equanimity.

Prakriti bandha is classified into eight categories, according to the particular attribute of the soul that it obscures.

a. *Jnana-varaniya*
It covers the soul's power of perfect knowledge.
b. *Darasna-varaniya*
It covers the soul's power of perfect visions.
c. *Vedniya*
It obscures the blissful nature of the soul, and thereby produces pleasure and pain.
d. *Mohniya*
It generates delusion in the soul in regard to its own true nature, and makes it identify itself with other substances.
e. *Ayu*
It determines the span of life in one birth, thus obscuring its nature of eternal existence.
f. *Nama*
It obscures the non-corporeal existence of the soul, and produces the body with its limitations and faculties.
g. *Gotra*
It obscures the soul's characteristics of equanimity, and determines the caste, family, and social standing.
h. *Antaraya*
It obstructs the natural energy of the soul and prevents it from attaining liberation. It also prevents a living being from doing something good and enjoyable.

(v) *Punya* (virtue)

The influx of *karmic* matter because of good activities of the mind, body, and speech with the potential of producing pleasant sensations is called *punya* or virtue.

Activities such as offering food, drink, shelter, purifying thought, physical and mental happiness, result in producing *punya karmic* matter.

(vi) *Papa* (sin)

The influx of *karmic* matter due to evil activities of the mind, body, and speech with the potential of producing unpleasant sensations is called *papa* or sin.

Activities such as violence, untruth, theft, unchastity, attachment to objects, anger, conceit, deceit, lust, result in producing *papa karmic* matter.

(vii) *Samvara* (arrest of *karma*)

Samvara arrests fresh *karma* from coming into the soul. This process is a reverse of *asrava*. It can be accomplished by constant practice of:

- restraint of mind, body, and speech
- religious meditation
- conquest of desire
- forgiveness, tenderness, purity, truth, austerity,
- renunciation, unattachment, and chastity

(viii) *Nirjara*

Nirjara is the exhaustion of *karmic* matter already acquired.

The *karmas* exhaust themselves by producing their results when it is time for them to do so. Unless they are exhausted before they are mature and start producing results, it becomes difficult to be free. By that time, new *karmic* matter begins to pour in.

Therefore, to achieve final liberation all *karmas* must be exhausted before they become mature. This is called *nirjara*.

Nirjara is achieved through rigorous austerities.

a. External *Nirjara*:

Anasan	complete abstinence of eating and drinking
Alpahara	reduction in the quantity of food one normally eats
Ichhanirodha	control of the desire for food and material things
Rasatyaga	complete abstinence of eating or drinking juicy and tasty foods such as honey, alcohol, butter, milk, tea, sweets, and juice
Kayaklesa	control of passions by discipline
Samlinata	sitting in a lonely place in a particular posture with senses withdrawn

b. Internal *Nirjara*:

Prayaschita	repentance for the breach of vows
Vinaya	appropriate behavior towards a teacher
Vaiyavrata	selfless service to the suffering and deserving
Svadhyaya	studying/listening of religious scriptures
Bhutsarga	non-attachment to the body
Subha-dhyana	religious meditation

(ix) *Moksha*

Moksha is the liberation of the living being (soul) after complete exhaustion or elimination of all *karmas*.

A liberated soul regains totally its original attributes of perfect knowledge, vision, power, and bliss. It climbs to the top of Lokakas and remains there for ever in its blissful and unconditional existence, never returning again into the cycles of birth, life, and death. This state of the soul is the liberated or perfect state known as "Nirvana."

L OTHER RELIGIONS

Jains support tolerance between different faiths, claiming that no single belief holds truth exclusively. This belief is called *anekantavada*, or "non-one-sidedness."

7 JAINIST WORSHIP

A Prayers
B Fasting
C Pilgrimage
D Jainism holy days

INTRODUCTION

While the Jains are not worshipers of the Hindu gods, they erect imposing temples to Jina and other venerated teachers. The images of these Jainist saints are adorned with lights and flowers, and the faithful walk around them while reciting sacred mantras. Jainist worship is thus little more than a veneration of a few saints and heroes of the past.

There is a vital difference between Jain and Hindu worship. Jains do not worship the *Tirthankaras* as persons. However, Jains do worship the concept of perfection. This perfection was achieved by the *Tirthankaras*.

A PRAYERS

Jain prayer inspire Jains to be more spiritual. It reminds them of the teachings and inspiring qualities of the *tirthankaras*. Their prayers are not addressed to or focused on God.

JAIN'S FIRST PRAYER

The following prayer, known as the *Namaskara Sutra*, is learned by all Jains when they are children and is said daily:

I bow down to those who have reached omniscience in the flesh and teach the road to everlasting life in the liberated state.
I bow down to those who have attained perfect knowledge and liberated their souls of all *karma*.
I bow down to those who have experienced self-realization of their souls through self-control and self-sacrifice.
I bow down to those who understand the true nature of soul and teach the importance of the spiritual over the material.

I bow down to those who strictly follow the five great vows of conduct and inspire us to live a virtuous life.
To these five types of great souls I offer my praise.
Such praise will help diminish my sins.
Giving this praise is most auspicious.
So auspicious as to bring happiness and bliss.

THE UNIVERSAL PRAYER

Every day Jains bow their heads and say their universal prayer, the *Navkar-mantra*. All good work and events start with this prayer of salutation and worship.

The five *Parmesthees*
I prostrate before – the Arihanta: I bow to the enlightened beings
I prostrate before – the Siddhas: I bow to the liberated souls
I prostrate before – the Acharyas: I bow to religious leaders
I prostrate before – the Upadhyaya: I bow to religious teachers
I prostrate before – all the saints: I bow to all ascetics of the world

These *Parmesthees* are considered to be the eternal mantras of Jainism.

An alternative for these *Parmesthees* is:
I bow to the Arahants, the perfected human beings, Godmen.
I bow to the Siddhas, liberated bodiless souls, God.
I bow to the Acharyas, the masters and heads of congregations.
I bow to the Upadhyayas, the spiritual teachers.

I bow to the spiritual practitioners in the universe, Sadhus.

This fivefold obeisance mantra,
Destroys all sins and obstacles,
And of all auspicious repetitions,
Is the first and foremost.

In the above prayer, Jains salute the virtues of their five benevolent. They do not pray to a specific *Tirthankara* or monk by name. By saluting them, Jains receive the inspiration from the five benevolent for the right path of true happiness and total freedom from the misery of life. Jain prayers do not ask for any favors or material benefits from their gods, the *Tirthankaras* or from monks and nuns.

B FASTING
REASONS FOR FASTING:
Jains undertake fasting for a number of reasons, including:

* penance
* to purify the mind and body
* as a reminder of Mahavira's teaching about renunciation and asceticism.

TYPES OF FASTING
Jains practice a number of different types of fasting.

* In complete fasting they give up food and water completely for a specified length of time
* In partial fasting the normal quantity of food eaten is reduced
* In *Vruti Sankshep*a fasting only a certain the number of foods are allowed to be eaten
* In *Rasa Parityaga* fasting one's favorite foods are not eaten

HOLY DEATH FAST
During a *Santhara* or *Sallenkhana* a Jain stops

eating as he/she prepares for death and so concentrates exclusively on the spiritual. This fast involves eating nothing until one dies.

C PILGRIMAGE
For Jains there are no compulsory pilgrimages. But for Digambaras and for some Svetambaras pilgrimages are important.

Most pilgrimages involve visiting a temple or other site that is linked with the life, death or the deeds of one of the Tirthankaras.

Shatrunjaya in Gujarat is the most holy site of pilgrimage for Jains.

D JAINISM HOLY DAYS

MAHAVIRA JAYANTI
Mahavira Jayanti, held in March/April, celebrates the day of Mahavira's birth. Jains go to their temples and listen to readings of Mahavira's teaching. In the streets images of Mahavira lead parades.

PARYUSHANA
Paryushana, held in August/September, means "to stay in one place." It lasts for eight days and consists of fasting and repentance.

DIVALI
Divali, also a great Hindu festival, is celebrated in October/November. Jains recall at this time in 527 BC Mahavira spoke his last teaching and is believed to have acquired ultimate liberation.

KARTAK PURNIMA
Kartak Purnima falls just after Divali and is marked by pilgrimages to sacred Jain sites.

MAUNA AGYARAS
Mauna Agyaras takes place in November/December and is a time of fasting and keeping silence.

8 Jainist Groupings

Jainism has two main variants: Digambara and Svetambara.

The Digambaras (literally "sky clad" or "naked"): their monks carry asceticism to the point of rejecting even clothing (even when they appear in public). There are about 170,000 Digambaras.

The Svetambaras (literally "white clad"): their monks wear simple white robes. The laity are permitted to wear clothes of any color. There are over 4 million Svetambaras.

---

9 Famous Jainists

Modern Jainists, in an attempt to avoid any occupation that even remotely endangers animal life, mainly work in commerce and finance. Among them are many of India's most prominent industrialists and bankers as well as several important political leaders.

In India, Jains are over-represented in positions of economic and political power; the global diamond market is dominated by Jain-owned corporations. Jains have been a significant force in Indian culture, contributing to Indian philosophy, art, architecture (a Jain temple or derasar), sciences and last but not least the politics of Mohandas Gandhi, which led to Indian independence.

---

10 Quotations about Jainism

In conclusion let me assert my conviction that Jainism is an original system, quite distinct and independent from all others; and that therefore it is of great importance for the study of philosophical thoughts and religious life in ancient India.

Dr. Herman Jacobi

What would be the condition of the Indian Sanskrit literature if the contribution of the Jains were removed? The more I study Jain literature the more happy and wonder struck I am.

Dr. Hertel, Germany

Jainism is of a very high order. Its important teachings are based upon science. The more the scientific knowledge advances the more that Jain teachings will be proven.

L. P. Tessetori, Italy

I adore so greatly the principles of the Jain religion, that I would like to be reborn in a Jain community.

George Bernard Shaw

Lofty ideas and high ascetic practices are found in Jainism. It is impossible to know the beginning of Jainism.

Major-General Forlong

The Jains have written great masterpieces only for the benefit of the world.

Dr. Hertel, Germany

I say with conviction that the doctrine for which the name of Lord Mahavir is glorified nowadays is the doctrine of *Ahimsa*. If anyone has practiced to the fullest extent and has propagated most the doctrine of *Ahimsa*, it was Lord Mahavira.

Mahatma Gandhi

I am not Rama. I have no desire for material things. Like Jina I want to establish peace within myself.

Yoga Vasishta, Chapter 15, Sloka 8 the saying of Rama

O Arhan! You are equipped with the arrow of Vastuswarpa, the law of teaching, and the ornaments of the four infinite qualities. O Arhan! You have attained omniscient knowledge in which the universe is reflected. O Arhan! You are the protector of all the Souls (*Jivas*) in the world. O Arhan! The destroyer of *kama* (lust)! There is no strong person equal to you.

Yajur Veda, Chapter 19, Mantra 14

Mahavira proclaimed in India that religion is a reality and not a mere social convention. It is really true that salvation cannot be had by merely observing external ceremonies. Religion cannot make any difference between man and man.

Dr. Rabindranath Tagore

We learn from scriptures (*Sashtras*) and commentaries that Jainism is existing from beginningless time. This fact is indisputable and free from difference of opinion. There is much historical evidence on this point.

Lokamanya Bala Gangadhar Tilak

Jainism has contributed to the world the sublime doctrine of Ahimsa. No other religion has emphasized the importance of Ahimsa and carried its practice to the extent that Jainism has done. Jainism deserves to become the universal religion because of its Ahimsa doctrine.

Justice Ranglekar, Bombay High Court

The Jain Sadhu leads a life which is praised by all. He practices the vratas and rites strictly and shows to the world the way one has to go in order to realize the *atma* (soul). Even the life of a Jain householder is so faultless that India should be proud of him.

Dr. Satischandra Vidhya Bhushan

The right of welcoming the delegates of the universal peace organization belongs to the Jains only. Because *Ahimsa* alone contributes to the establishment of universal peace. *Tirthankaras*, the propounders of Jainism, preached to the world the *Ahimsa* doctrine. Therefore, who else except the followers of Bhagavan Parsvanath and Mahavira can preach universal peace?

Dr. Radha Vinodpal

There is nothing wonderful in my saying that Jainism was in existence long before the *Vedas* were composed.

Dr. S. Radhakrishnan, Vice-President, India

Truly speaking, Jainism is an independent and original religion, for it is neither Hinduism nor Vedic religion, but of course it is an aspect of Indian life, culture, and philosophy.

Shri Jawaharlal Nehru, Prime Minister, India

11 GLOSSARY

Ahimsa
Principle of non-violence to any living thing.

Ajiva
Nonliving.

Ambika
Mother-Goddess.

Anekantvad
Principle of multiple viewpoints. The illustration is given of blind men and an elephant. They were asked what the elephant was like, so each blind man took hold of part of the animal. One, feeling the skin, said, "A wall;" another, holding the trunk, said, "A snake;" a third felt the ears, and said, "A fan;" a fourth said, "A tree trunk;" a fifth said, "A rope."

Apirigraham
Principle of avoidance of material possessions.

Arihanta ("destroyer of enemies")
The spiritual state at which inner passions have been destroyed (ego, deceit, greed, anger, etc.).

Jambudvina ("Continent of the Rose-Apple Tree")
Earthly realm, which is divided into seven regions.

Jinas
Spiritual victors; *Tirthankaras.*

Kalchakra
Time cycle.

Kashaya
Passions.

Loka
True nature of the universe.

Mahavira
Vardhamana, the twenty-fourth *Tirthankara.*

Pap
Bad.

Punya
Good.

Salekhana
Fasting to death.

Satya
Renunciation of secular lifestyle.

Tirthankaras ("Ford-makers")
Twenty-four spiritual teachers.

CONFUCIANISM

CONTENTS

1 An overview   391

2 Founder of Confucianism   392

3 Confucian holy books   393

4 Facts and figures   403

5 Confucian practices   404

6 Confucian beliefs   405

7 Confucian worship   407

8 Famous Confucianists   407

9 Glossary   408

1 AN OVERVIEW

DEFINITION

Confucianism is a system of honor codes and moral assumptions that was originally directed towards the educated upper classes of Chinese society. It is based on the teachings of Confucius (K'ung Fu-tzu), Mencius (Mengzi), and Hsun-tzu.

- Factfile
- Date of origin: fifth century BC
- Founder: Confucius, 551-479 BC
- Holy book: The *Analects*
- Number of adherents: More than 6 million

SUMMARY

It is a matter of debate whether or not Confucianism is purely a humanistic moral philosophy or a religion. It is true that it focuses on the achievements and interests of human beings rather than on theological doctrine. But it also inherited the worship of the Lord on High, and has a basis in mysticism and a religious awareness.

In Confucianism, however, humankind is king. Humanity's ultimate goal is individual happiness. To achieve this goal there must be peace, so war has to be abolished. Confucius believed that human beings could live in happiness if they followed his five relationships which are based on love and duty.

Confucianism was the chief cultural influence in China for two thousand years. The overthrow of the Chinese monarchy and the Communist revolution during the twentieth century greatly curtailed the influence of Confucianism in modern China. Many now regard it as a relic of the past,

perhaps preserving its heritage out of academic interest. But the principles of Confucianism are part of the fabric of Chinese culture.

SUMMARY OF PRACTICES

The key to the whole Confucian philosophy is: "Do unto others as you would be done by."

SUMMARY OF BELIEFS

The teachings of Confucius were never intended to be a religion. Confucianism has no priesthood, no doctrine of an afterlife, and encourages neither asceticism nor monasticism. Confucius, however, held that Heaven itself protected him. He said, "Heaven is the author of the virtue that is in me."

The tradition Confucius left was not intended to be a complete philosophy, but more a "Way of the Gentleman," and so Confucianism is often called "The School of the learned."

2 FOUNDER OF CONFUCIANISM

INTRODUCTION

Strictly speaking, Confucius was not the founder of Confucianism. Confucius thought of himself as a transmitter, and not the originator, of social values and wisdom. He aimed to reanimate ancient Chinese philosophy.

CONFUCIUS

K'ung Fu-tzu ("Grand Master K'ung) was born in 551 BC in the state of Lu (modern-day Shantung Province) in China. Confucius is the Latin version of K'ung Fu-tzu.

Little is known of the early life of Confucius. His family may have been impoverished nobility. His parents died when he was young, and he grew up with little money. He was self-educated, but it is said that he became the most learned man of his day in China. He lived during the Chou dynasty, an era known for its moral laxity and he was deeply disturbed by the political and social turmoil he observed. Unable to obtain a government postion, he spent most of his life educating groups of disciples.

Confucius was both a philosopher and social reformer. The purpose of his teaching was to establish ways of acting and thinking that would restore moral order in China. He traveled throughout China spreading his teachings and giving advice to the rulers. This was often hard: he experienced joblessness, homelessness, starvation and sometimes life-threatening violence. But he was convinced, and convinced others, that Heaven was on his side: "If Heaven does not intend this culture to be destroyed, than what can the men of K'uang do to me?"

His teaching focused on individual morality and ethics, and the proper exercise of political power. The community that gathered round him was a scholarly fellowship, devoted to his teaching and aims. He demanded willingness to learn: "I do not enlighten anyone who is not eager to learn, nor encourage anyone who is not anxious to put his ideas into words."

The last years of his life were spent back in Lu. It is said that he had three thousand students, of whom seventy-two were close disciples.

Confucius left behind him a system of thought emphasizing education, proper behavior, and loyalty. Many ancient literary classics were attributed to him (as author or editor). His writings formed the basic curriculum of Chinese education for more than two thousand years.

3 CONFUCIAN HOLY BOOKS

A *Lun-yu* (The *Analects*)
B The Confucian canon
C Extracts from the *Analects*

A LUN-YU (THE ANALECTS OR "CONVERSATIONS")

Confucius' sayings and dialogues, known collectively as the *Analects*, were probably compiled by the second generation of his disciples.

The Analects come closest to an actual exposition of Confucius' philosophy and are the most revered scriptures in the Confucian tradition. They represent a "communal memory" and capture the Confucian spirit. They consist primarily of dialogues, showing Confucius in the center of relationships. "Through the Analects Confucians for centuries learned to reenact the awe-inspiring ritual of participating in a conversation with Confucius."

These works were put into their present form by Chu Hsi in the late twelfth century AD. From 1315 until the beginning of the twentieth century they were required reading in order to pass the civil service examinations, which were the gateway to employment in the Imperial bureaucracy.

B THE CONFUCIAN CANON

Confucianism has no sacred scriptures purporting to give divine revelation, but the *Analects* give the essence of Confucian teaching and his method of teaching. Confucius also wrote and edited a large number of classical books.

Mencius (371-289 BC) and Hsun-tzu (fl. 298-238 BC) were the great expositors of Confucius in the fourth and third centuries BC and their writings were added to the canon.

The list of generally accepted books are as follows:

THE FOUR BOOKS:
The Four Books are a collection of the teachings and sayings of Confucius. They include: The Analects, The Great Learning, The Doctrine of the Mean, The Book of Mencius.

FIVE CLASSICS
Along with the Four Books, the Five Classics are the authoritative writings of Confucianism. They comprise:.

(i)   *I Ching* (*Yi Jing*) (Classic of Changes)
(ii) *Shih Ching* (Classic of Poetry)
(iii) *Shu Ching* (Classic of History)
(iv) *Li Chi* (*Li Ching*) (Records of Ritual, or Book of Rites) This work includes both *Ta Hsüeh* (The Great Learning), and *Chung Yung* (The Doctrine of the Mean)
(v)   *Ch'un Ch'iu* (Spring and Autumn Annals)

THE NINE CLASSICS
These consist of all of the preceding works, plus:

(vi)   *Chou Li* (Rites of Chou, part of the *Li Ching*)
(vii) *I Li* (Ceremonial and Ritual, part of the *Li Ching*)
(viii) *Hsiao Ching* (Filial Piety Classic)
(ix)   *Lun Yü* (*Analects*)

THE THIRTEEN CLASSICS
These consist of all of the preceding works, plus:

(x) *Meng Tzu* (The Mencius)
(xi) *Er Ya* (Dictionary of Terms)

(xii) *Kung-yang Chuan* (commentary on *Ch'un Ch'iu*)

(xiii) *Ku-liang Chuan* (commentary on *Ch'un Ch'iu*)

C EXTRACTS FROM THE ANALECTS

by K'ung Fu-tzu (Confucius)
The first three books and the last three books in the Analects follow.

BOOK 1

1-1. The Master said, "Is it not pleasant to learn with a constant perseverance and application?

"Is it not delightful to have friends coming from distant quarters? Is he not a man of complete virtue, who feels no discomposure though men may take no note of him?"

1-2. The philosopher Yu said, "They are few who, being filial and fraternal, are fond of offending against their superiors. There have been none, who, not liking to offend against their superiors, have been fond of stirring up confusion.

1-3. "The superior man bends his attention to what is radical. That being established, all practical courses naturally grow up. Filial piety and fraternal submission – are they not the root of all benevolent actions?"

1-3. The Master said, "Fine words and an insinuating appearance are seldom associated with true virtue."

1-4. The philosopher Tsang said, "I daily examine myself on three points: whether, in transacting business for others, I may have been not faithful; whether, in intercourse with friends, I may have been not sincere; whether I may have not mastered and practiced the instructions of my teacher."

1-5. The Master said, "To rule a country of a thousand chariots, there must be reverent attention to business, and sincerity; economy in expenditure, and love for men; and the employment of the people at the ˙proper seasons."

1-6. The Master said, "A youth, when at home, should be filial, and, abroad, respectful to his elders. He should be earnest and truthful. He should overflow in love to all, and cultivate the friendship of the good. When he has time and opportunity, after the performance of these things, he should employ them in polite studies."

1-7. Tsze-hsia said, "If a man withdraws his mind from the love of beauty, and applies it as sincerely to the love of the virtuous; if, in serving his parents, he can exert his utmost strength; if, in serving his prince, he can devote his life; if, in his intercourse with his friends, his words are sincere: although men say that he has not learned, I will certainly say that he has.

1-8. The Master said, "If the scholar be not grave, he will not call forth any veneration, and his learning will not be solid.

"Hold faithfulness and sincerity as first principles.

Have no friends not equal to yourself.

When you have faults, do not fear to abandon them."

1-9. The philosopher Tsang said, "Let there be a careful attention to perform the funeral rites to parents, and let them be followed when long gone with the ceremonies of sacrifice; then the virtue of the people will resume its proper excellence."

1-10. Tsze-ch'in asked Tsze-kung saying, "When our master comes to any country, he does not fail to learn all about its government. Does he ask his information? Or is it given to him?"

Tsze-kung said, "Our master is benign, upright, courteous, temperate, and complaisant and thus he gets his information. The master's mode of asking information, is it not different from that of other men?"

1-11. The Master said, "While a man's father is alive, look at the bent of his will; when his father is dead, look at his conduct. If for three years he does not alter from the way of his father, he may be called filial."

1-12. The philosopher Yu said, "In practicing the rules of propriety, a natural ease is to be prized. In the ways prescribed by the ancient kings, this is the excellent quality, and in things small and great we follow them.

"Yet it is not to be observed in all cases. If one, knowing how such ease should be prized, manifests it, without regulating it by the rules of propriety, this likewise is not to be done."

1-13. The philosopher Yu said, "When agreements are made according to what is right, what is spoken can be made good. When respect is shown according to what is proper, one keeps far from shame and disgrace. When the parties upon whom a man leans are proper persons to be intimate with, he can make them his guides and masters."

1-14. The Master said, "He who aims to be a man of complete virtue in his food does not seek to gratify his appetite, nor in his dwelling place does he seek the appliances of ease; he is earnest in what he is doing, and careful in his speech; he frequents the company of men of principle that he may be rectified: such a person may be said indeed to love to learn."

1-15. Tsze-kung said, "What do you pronounce concerning the poor man who yet does not flatter, and the rich man who is not proud?" The Master replied, "They will do; but they are not equal to him, who, though poor, is yet cheerful, and to him, who, though rich, loves the rules of propriety."

Tsze-kung replied, "It is said in the Book of Poetry, 'As you cut and then file, as you carve and then polish.' – The meaning is the same, I apprehend, as that which you have just expressed."

The Master said, "With one like Ts'ze, I can begin to talk about the odes. I told him one point, and he knew its proper sequence."

The Master said, "I will not be afflicted at men's not knowing me; I will be afflicted that I do not know men."

BOOK 2
2-1. The Master said, "He who exercises government by means of his virtue may be compared to the north polar star, which keeps its place and all the stars turn towards it."

2-2. The Master said, "In the Book of Poetry are three hundred pieces, but the design of them all may be embraced in one sentence 'Having no depraved thoughts.'"

2-3. The Master said, "If the people be led by laws, and uniformity sought to be given them by punishments, they will try to avoid the punishment, but have no sense of shame.

"If they be led by virtue, and uniformity sought to be given them by the rules of propriety, they will have the sense of shame, and moreover will become good."

2-4. The Master said, "At fifteen, I had my mind bent on learning.
"At thirty, I stood firm.
At forty, I had no doubts.
At fifty, I knew the decrees of Heaven.
At sixty, my ear was an obedient organ for the reception of truth.
At seventy, I could follow what my heart desired, without transgressing what was right."

2-5. Mang I asked what filial piety was. The Master said, "It is not being disobedient."
Soon after, as Fan Ch'ih was driving him, the Master told him, saying, "Mang-sun asked me what filial piety was, and I answered him, 'not being disobedient.'"

Fan Ch'ih said, "What did you mean?" The Master replied, "That parents, when alive, be served according to propriety; that, when dead, they should be buried according to propriety; and that they should be sacrificed to according to propriety."

2-6. Mang Wu asked what filial piety was. The Master said, "Parents are anxious lest their children should be sick."

2-7. Tsze-yu asked what filial piety was. The Master said, "The filial piety nowadays means the support of one's parents. But dogs and horses likewise are able to do something in the way of support; without reverence, what is there to distinguish the one support given from the other?"

2-8. Tsze-hsia asked what filial piety was. The Master said, "The difficulty is with the countenance. If, when their elders have any troublesome affairs, the young take the toil of them, and if, when the young have wine and food, they set them before their elders, is *this* to be considered filial piety?"

2-9. The Master said, "I have talked with Hui for a whole day, and he has not made any objection to anything I said – as if he were stupid. He has retired, and I have examined his conduct when away from me, and found him able to illustrate my teachings. Hui! He is not stupid."

2-10. The Master said, "See what a man does.
"Mark his motives.
Examine in what things he rests.
How can a man conceal his character? How can a man conceal his character?"

2-11. The Master said, "If a man keeps cherishing his old knowledge, so as continually to be acquiring new, he may be a teacher of others."

2-12. The Master said, "The accomplished scholar is not a utensil."

2-13. Tsze-kung asked what constituted the superior man. The Master said, "He acts before he speaks, and afterwards speaks according to his actions."

2-14. The Master said, "The superior man is catholic and not partisan. The mean man is partisan and not catholic."

2-15. The Master said, "Learning without thought is labor lost; thought without learning is perilous."

2-16. The Master said, "To attack a task from the wrong end can do nothing but harm."

2-17. The Master said, "Yu, shall I teach you what knowledge is? When you know a thing, to hold that you know it; and when you do not know a thing, to allow that you do not know it; – this is knowledge."

2-18. Tsze-chang was learning with a view to official emolument.
The Master said, "Hear much and put aside the points of which you stand in doubt, while you speak cautiously at the same time of the others: then you will afford few occasions for blame. See much and put aside the things which seem perilous, while you are cautious at the same time in carrying the others into practice: then you will have few occasions for repentance. When one gives few occasions for blame in his words, and few occasions for repentance in his conduct, he is in the way to get emolument."

2-19. Duke Ai asked, saying, "What should be done in order to secure the submission of the people?"
Confucius replied, "Advance the upright and set aside the crooked, then the people will submit. Advance the crooked and set aside the upright, then the people will not submit."

2-20. Chi K'ang asked how to cause the people to reverence their ruler, to be faithful to him, and to go on to nerve themselves to virtue.
The Master said, "Let him preside over them with gravity – then they will reverence him. Let him be final and kind to all – then they will be faithful to him. Let him advance the good and teach the incompetent – then they will eagerly seek to be virtuous."

2-21. Some one addressed Confucius, saying, "Sir, why are you not engaged in the government?"
The Master said, "What does the Book of History say of filial piety? – 'You are final, you discharge your brotherly duties. These qualities are displayed in government.' This then also constitutes the exercise of government. Why must there be *that* – making one be in the government?"

2-22. The Master said, "I do not know how a man without truthfulness is to get on. How can a large carriage be made to go without the crossbar for yoking the oxen to, or a small carriage without the arrangement for yoking the horses?"

2-23. Tsze-chang asked whether the affairs of ten ages from now could be known.

Confucius said, "The Yin dynasty followed the regulations of the Hsia: wherein it took from or added to them may be known. The Chau dynasty has followed the regulations of Yin: wherein it took from or added to them may be known. Some other may follow the Chau, but though it should be at the distance of a hundred ages, its affairs may be known."

2-24. The Master said, "For a man to sacrifice to a spirit which does not belong to him is flattery.
"To see what is right and not to do it is want of courage."

BOOK 3
3-1. Confucius said of the head of the Chi family, who had eight rows of pantomimes in his area, "If he can bear to do this, what may he not bear to do?"

3-2. The three families used the Yungode, while the vessels were being removed, at the conclusion of the sacrifice. The Master said, "'Assisting are the princes – the son of heaven looks profound and grave' – what application can these words have in the hall of the three families?"

3-3. The Master said, "If a man be without the virtues proper to humanity, what has he to do with the rites of propriety? If a man be without the virtues proper to humanity, what has he to do with music?"

3-4. Lin Fang asked what was the first thing to be attended to in ceremonies. The Master said, "A great question indeed!

"In festive ceremonies, it is better to be sparing than extravagant. In the ceremonies of mourning, it is better that there be deep sorrow than in minute attention to observances."

3-5. The Master said, "The rude tribes of the east and north have their princes, and are not

like the States of our great land which are without them."

3-6. The chief of the Chi family was about to sacrifice to the T'ai mountain. The Master said to Zan Yu, "Can you not save him from this?" He answered, "I cannot." Confucius said, "Alas! will you say that the T'ai mountain is not so discerning as Lin Fang?"

3-7. The Master said, "The student of virtue has no contentions. If it be said he cannot avoid them, shall this be in archery? But he bows complaisantly to his competitors; thus he ascends the hall, descends, and exacts the forfeit of drinking. In his contention, he is still the Chun-tsze."

3-8. Tsze-hsia asked, saying, "What is the meaning of the passage – 'The pretty dimples of her artful smile! The well-defined black and white of her eye! The plain ground for the colors?'"

The Master said, "The business of laying on the colors follows the preparation of the plain ground." "Ceremonies then are a subsequent thing?" The Master said, "It is Shang who can bring out my meaning. Now I can begin to talk about the Odes with him."

3-9. The Master said, "I could describe the ceremonies of the Hsia dynasty, but Chi cannot sufficiently attest my words. I could describe the ceremonies of the Yin dynasty, but Sung cannot sufficiently attest my words. They cannot do so because of the insufficiency of their records and wise men. If those were sufficient, I could adduce them in support of my words."

3-10. The Master said, "At the great sacrifice, after the pouring out of the libation, I have no wish to look on."

3-11. Some one asked the meaning of the great sacrifice. The Master said, "I do not know. He who knew its meaning would find it as easy to govern the kingdom as to look on this" – pointing to his palm.

3-12. He sacrificed to the dead, as if they were present. He sacrificed to the spirits, as if the spirits were present.

The Master said, "I consider my not being present at the sacrifice, as if I did not sacrifice."

3-13. Wang-sun Chia asked, saying, "What is the meaning of the saying, 'It is better to pay court to the furnace then to the southwest corner?'"

The Master said, "Not so. He who offends against Heaven has none to whom he can pray."

3-14. The Master said, "Chau had the advantage of viewing the two past dynasties. How complete and elegant are its regulations! I follow Chau."

3-15. The Master, when he entered the grand temple, asked about everything. Some one said, "Who say that the son of the man of Tsau knows the rules of propriety! He has entered the grand temple and asks about everything." The Master heard the remark, and said, "This is a rule of propriety."

3-16. The Master said, "In archery it is not going through the leather which is the principal thing; – because people's strength is not equal. This was the old way."

3-17. Tsze-kung wished to do away with the offering of a sheep connected with the inauguration of the first day of each month. The Master said, "Ts'ze, you love the sheep; I love the ceremony."

3-18. The Master said, "The full observance of the rules of propriety in serving one's prince is accounted by people to be flattery."

3-19. The Duke Ting asked how a prince should employ his ministers, and how ministers should serve their prince. Confucius replied, "A prince should employ his minister according to according to the rules of propriety; ministers should serve their prince with faithfulness."

3-20. The Master said, "The Kwan Tsu is expressive of enjoyment without being licentious, and of grief without being hurtfully excessive."

3-21. The Duke Ai asked Tsai Wo about the altars of the spirits of the land. Tsai Wo replied, "The Hsia sovereign planted the pine tree about them; the men of the Yin planted the cypress; and the men of the Chau planted the chestnut tree, meaning thereby to cause the people to be in awe."

When the Master heard it, he said, "Things that are done, it is needless to speak about; things that have had their course, it is needless to remonstrate about; things that are past, it is needless to blame."

3-22. The Master said, "Small indeed was the capacity of Kwan Chung!"
Some one said, "Was Kwan Chung parsimonious?" "Kwan," was the reply, "had the San Kwei, and his officers performed no double duties; how can he be considered parsimonious?"

"Then, did Kwan Chung know the rules of propriety?" The Master said, "The princes of States have a screen intercepting the view at their gates. Kwan had likewise a screen at his gate. The princes of States on any friendly meeting between two of them, had a stand on which to place their inverted cups. Kwan had also such a stand. If Kwan knew the rules of propriety, who does not know them?"

3-23. The Master instructing the grand music master of Lu said, "How to play music may be known. At the commencement of the piece, all the parts should sound together. As it proceeds, they should be in harmony while severally distinct and flowing without break, and thus on to the conclusion."

3-24. The border warden at Yi requested to be introduced to the Master, saying, "When men of superior virtue have come to this, I have never been denied the privilege of seeing them." The followers of the sage introduced him, and when he came out from the interview, he said, "My friends, why are you distressed by your master's loss of office? The kingdom has long been without the principles of truth and right; Heaven is going to use your master as a bell with its wooden tongue."

3-25. The Master said of the Shao that it was perfectly beautiful and also perfectly good. He said of the Wu that it was perfectly beautiful but not perfectly good.

3-26. The Master said, "High station filled without indulgent generosity; ceremonies performed without reverence; mourning conducted without sorrow; – wherewith should I contemplate such ways?"

BOOK 18
The Viscount of Wei withdrew from the court. The Viscount of Chi became a slave to Chau. Pi-kan remonstrated with him and died.

Confucius said, "The Yin dynasty possessed these three men of virtue."

Hui of Liu-hsia, being chief criminal judge, was thrice dismissed from his office. Some one said to him, "Is it not yet time for you, sir, to leave this?" He replied, "Serving men in an upright way, where shall I go to, and not experience such a thrice-repeated dismissal? If I choose to serve men in a crooked way, what necessity is there for me to leave the country of my parents?"

The duke Ching of Ch'i, with reference to the manner in which he should treat Confucius, said, "I cannot treat him as I would the chief of the Chi family. I will treat him in a manner between that accorded to the chief of the Chil and that given to the chief of the Mang family." He also said, "I am old; I cannot use his doctrines." Confucius took his departure.

The people of Ch'i sent to Lu a present of female musicians, which Chi Hwan received, and for three days no court was held. Confucius took his departure.

The madman of Ch'u, Chieh-yu, passed by Confucius, singing and saying, "*O Fang! O Fang!* How is your virtue degenerated! As to the past, reproof is useless; but the future may still be provided against. Give up your vain pursuit. Give up your vain pursuit. Peril awaits those who now engage in affairs of government."

Confucius alighted and wished to converse with him, but Chieh-yu hastened away, so that he could not talk with him.

Ch'ang-tsu and Chieh-ni were at work in the field together, when Confucius passed by them, and sent Tsze-lu to inquire for the ford.

Ch'ang-tsu said, "Who is he that holds the reins in the carriage there?" Tsze-lu told him, "It is K'ung Ch'iu.', 'Is it not K'ung of Lu?" asked he. "Yes," was the reply, to which the other rejoined, "He knows the ford."

Tsze-lu then inquired of Chieh-ni, who said to him, "Who are you, sir?" He answered, "I am Chung Yu." "Are you not the disciple of K'ung Ch'iu of Lu?" asked the other. "I am," replied he, and then Chieh-ni said to him, "Disorder, like a swelling flood, spreads over the whole empire, and who is he that will change its state for you? Rather than follow one who merely withdraws from this one and that one, had you not better follow those who have withdrawn from the world altogether?" With this he fell to covering up the seed, and proceeded with his work, without stopping.

Tsze-lu went and reported their remarks, when the Master observed with a sigh, "It is impossible to associate with birds and beasts, as if they were the same with us. If I associate not with these people – with mankind – with whom shall I associate? If right principles prevailed through the empire, there would be no use for me to change its state."

Tsze-lu, following the Master, happened to fall behind, when he met an old man, carrying across his shoulder on a staff a basket for weeds. Tsze-lu said to him, "Have you seen my master, sir?" The old man replied, "Your four limbs are unaccustomed to toil; you cannot distinguish the five kinds of grain: who is your master?" With this, he planted his staff in the ground, and proceeded to weed.

Tsze-lu joined his hands across his breast, and stood before him.

The old man kept Tsze-lu to pass the night in his house, killed a fowl, prepared millet, and feasted him. He also introduced to him his two sons.

Next day, Tsze-lu went on his way, and reported his adventure. The Master said, "He is a recluse," and sent Tsze-lu back to see him again, but when he got to the place, the old man was gone.

Tsze-lu then said to the family, "Not to take office is not righteous. If the relations between old and young may not be neglected, how is it that he sets aside the duties that should be observed between sovereign and minister? Wishing to maintain his personal purity, he allows that great relation to come to confusion. A superior man takes office, and performs the righteous duties belonging to it. As to the failure of right principles to make progress, he is aware of that."

The men who have retired to privacy from the world have been Po-i, Shu-ch'i, Yuchung, I-yi, Chu-chang, Hui of Liu-hsia, and Shao-lien.

The Master said, "Refusing to surrender their wills, or to submit to any taint in their persons; such, I think, were Po-i and Shu-ch'i.

"It may be said of Hui of Liu-hsia! and of Shaolien, that they surrendered their wills, and submitted to taint in their persons, but their words corresponded with reason, and their actions were such as men are anxious to see. This is all that is to be remarked in them.

"It may be said of Yu-chung and I-yi, that, while they hid themselves in their seclusion, they gave a license to their words; but in their persons, they succeeded in preserving their purity, and, in their retirement, they acted according to the exigency of the times.

"I am different from all these. I have no course for which I am predetermined, and no course against which I am predetermined."

The grand music master, Chih, went to Ch'i.

Kan, the master of the band at the second meal, went to Ch'u. Liao, the band master at the third meal, went to Ts'ai. Chueh, the band master at the fourth meal, went to Ch'in.

Fang-shu, the drum master, withdrew to the north of the river.

Wu, the master of the hand drum, withdrew to the Han.

Yang, the assistant music master, and Hsiang, master of the musical stone, withdrew to an island in the sea.

The duke of Chau addressed his son, the duke of Lu, saying, "The virtuous prince does not neglect his relations. He does not cause the great ministers to repine at his not employing them. Without some great cause, he does not dismiss from their offices the members of old families. He does not seek in one man talents for every employment."

To Chau belonged the eight officers, Po-ta, Po-kwo, Chung-tu, Chung-hwu, Shu-ya, Shuhsia, Chi-sui, and Chi-kwa.

BOOK 19
Tsze-chang said, "The scholar, trained for public duty, seeing threatening danger, is prepared to sacrifice his life. When the opportunity of gain is presented to him, he thinks of righteousness. In sacrificing, his thoughts are reverential. In mourning, his thoughts are about the grief which he should feel. Such a man commands our approbation indeed.

Tsze-chang said, "When a man holds fast to virtue, but without seeking to enlarge it, and believes in right principles, but without firm sincerity, what account can be made of his existence or non-existence?"

The disciples of Tsze-hsia asked Tsze-chang about the principles that should characterize mutual intercourse. Tsze-chang asked, "What does Tsze-hsia say on the subject?" They replied, "Tsze-hsia says: 'Associate with those who can advantage you. Put away from you those who cannot do so.'" Tsze-chang observed, "This is different from what I have learned. The superior man honors the talented and virtuous, and bears with all. He praises the good, and pities the incompetent. Am I possessed of great talents and virtue? Who is there among men whom I will not bear with? Am I devoid of talents and virtue? Men will put me away from them. What have we to do with the putting away of others?"

Tsze-hsia said, "Even in inferior studies and employments there is something worth being looked at; but if it be attempted to carry them out to what is remote, there is a danger of their proving inapplicable. Therefore, the superior man does not practice them."

Tsze-hsia said, "He, who from day to day recognizes what he has not yet, and from month to month does not forget what he has attained to, may be said indeed to love to learn."

Tsze-hsia said, "There are learning extensively, and having a firm and sincere aim; inquiring with earnestness, and reflecting with self-application: virtue is in such a course."

Tsze-hsia said, "Mechanics have their shops to dwell in, in order to accomplish their works. The superior man learns, in order to reach to the utmost of his principles."

Tsze-hsia said, "The mean man is sure to gloss his faults."

Tsze-hsia said, "The superior man undergoes three changes. Looked at from a distance, he appears stern; when approached, he is mild; when he is heard to speak, his language is firm and decided."

Tsze-hsia said, "The superior man, having obtained their confidence, may then impose labors on his people. If he have not gained their confidence, they will think that he is oppressing them. Having obtained the confidence of his prince, one may then remonstrate with him. If he have not gained his confidence, the prince will think that he is vilifying him."

Tsze-hsia said, "When a person does not transgress the boundary line in the great virtues, he may pass and repass it in the small virtues."

Tsze-yu said, "The disciples and followers of Tsze-hsia, in sprinkling and sweeping the ground, in answering and replying, in advancing and receding, are sufficiently accomplished. But these are only the branches of learning, and they are left ignorant of what is essential – how can they be acknowledged as sufficiently taught?"

Tsze-hsia heard of the remark and said, "Alas! Yen Yu is wrong. According to the way of the superior man in teaching, what departments are there which he considers of prime importance, and delivers? what are there which he considers of secondary importance, and allows himself to be idle about? But as in the case of plants, which are assorted according to their classes, so he deals with his disciples. How can the way of a superior man be such as to make fools of any of them? Is it not the sage alone, who can unite in one the beginning and the consummation of learning?"

Tsze-hsia said, "The officer, having discharged all his duties, should devote his leisure to learning. The student, having completed his learning, should apply himself to be an officer."

Tsze-hsia said, "Mourning, having been carried to the utmost degree of grief, should stop with that."

Tsze-hsia said, "My friend Chang can do things which are hard to be done, but yet he is not perfectly virtuous."

The philosopher Tsang said, "How imposing is the manner of Chang! It is difficult along with him to practice virtue."

The philosopher Tsang said, "I heard this from our Master: 'Men may not have shown what is in them to the full extent, and yet they will be found to do so, on the occasion of mourning for their parents."

The philosopher Tsang said, "I have heard this from our Master: 'The filial piety of Mang Chwang, in other matters, was what other men are competent to, but, as seen in his not changing the ministers of his father, nor his father's mode of government, it is difficult to be attained to."

The chief of the Mang family having appointed Yang Fu to be chief criminal judge, the latter consulted the philosopher Tsang. Tsang said, "The rulers have failed in their duties, and the people consequently have been disorganized for a long time. When you have found out the truth of any accusation, be grieved for and pity them, and do not feel joy at your own ability."

Tsze-kung said, "Chau's wickedness was not so great as that name implies. Therefore, the superior man hates to dwell in a low-lying situation, where all the evil of the world will flow in upon him."

Tsze-kung said, "The faults of the superior man are like the eclipses of the sun and moon. He has his faults, and all men see them; he changes again, and all men look up to him."

Kung-sun Ch'ao of Wei asked Tszekung, saying. "From whom did Chung-ni get his learning?"

Tsze-kung replied, "The doctrines of Wan and Wu have not yet fallen to the ground. They are to be found among men. Men of talents and virtue remember the greater principles of them, and others, not possessing such talents and virtue, remember the smaller. Thus, all possess the doctrines of Wan and Wu. Where could our Master go that he should not have an opportunity of learning them? And yet what necessity was there for his having a regular master?"

Shu-sun Wu-shu observed to the great officers in the court, saying, "Tsze-kung is superior to Chung-ni."

Tsze-fu Ching-po reported the observation to Tsze-kung, who said, "Let me use the comparison of a house and its encompassing wall. My wall only reaches to the shoulders. One may peep over it, and see whatever is valuable in the apartments.

"The wall of my Master is several fathoms high. If one do not find the door and enter by it, he cannot see the ancestral temple with its beauties, nor all the officers in their rich array.

"But I may assume that they are few who find the door. Was not the observation of the chief only what might have been expected?"

Shu-sun Wu-shu having spoken revilingly of Chung-ni, Tsze-kung said, "It is of no use doing so. Chung-ni cannot be reviled. The talents and virtue of other men are hillocks and mounds which may be stepped over. Chung-ni is the sun or moon, which it is not possible to step over. Although a man may wish to cut himself off from the sage, what harm can he do to the sun or moon? He only shows that he does not know his own capacity."

Ch'an Tsze-ch'in, addressing Tsze-kung, said, "You are too modest. How can Chung-ni be said to be superior to you?"

Tsze-kung said to him, "For one word a man is often deemed to be wise, and for one word he is often deemed to be foolish. We ought to be careful indeed in what we say.

"Our Master cannot be attained to, just in the same way as the heavens cannot be gone up by the steps of a stair.

"Were our Master in the position of the ruler of a state or the chief of a family, we should find verified the description which has been given of a sage's rule: he would plant the people, and forthwith they would be established; he would lead them on, and forthwith they would follow him; he would

make them happy, and forthwith multitudes would resort to his dominions; he would stimulate them, and forthwith they would be harmonious. While he lived, he would be glorious. When he died, he would be bitterly lamented. How is it possible for him to be attained to?"

BOOK 20

Yao said, "Oh! you, Shun, the Heaven-determined order of succession now rests in your person. Sincerely hold fast the due Mean. If there shall be distress and want within the four seas, the Heavenly revenue will come to a perpetual end."

Shun also used the same language in giving charge to Yu.

T'ang said, "I the child Li, presume to use a dark-colored victim, and presume to announce to Thee, O most great and sovereign God, that the sinner I dare not pardon, and thy ministers, O God, I do not keep in obscurity. The examination of them is by thy mind, O God. If, in my person, I commit offenses, they are not to be attributed to you, the people of the myriad regions. If you in the myriad regions commit offenses, these offenses must rest on my person."

Chau conferred great gifts, and the good were enriched.

"Although he has his near relatives, they are not equal to my virtuous men. The people are throwing blame upon me, the One man."

He carefully attended to the weights and measures, examined the body of the laws, restored the discarded officers, and the good government of the kingdom took its course.

He revived states that had been extinguished, restored families whose line of succession had been broken, and called to office those who had retired into obscurity, so that throughout the kingdom the hearts of the people turned towards him.

What he attached chief importance to were the food of the people, the duties of mourning, and sacrifices.

By his generosity, he won all. By his sincerity, he made the people repose trust in him. By his earnest activity, his achievements were great. By his justice, all were delighted.

Tsze-chang asked Confucius, saying, "In

what way should a person in authority act in order that he may conduct government properly?" The Master replied, "Let him honor the five excellent, and banish away the four bad, things;-then may he conduct government properly." Tsze-chang said, "What are meant by the five excellent things?" The Master said, "When the person in authority is beneficent without great expenditure; when he lays tasks on the people without their repining; when he pursues what he desires without being covetous; when he maintains a dignified ease without being proud; when he is majestic without being fierce."

Tsze-chang said, "What is meant by being beneficent without great expenditure?" The Master replied, "When the person in authority makes more beneficial to the people the things from which they naturally derive benefit – is not this being beneficent without great expenditure? When he chooses the labors which are proper, and makes them labor on them, who will repine? When his desires are set on benevolent government, and he secures it, who will accuse him of covetousness? Whether he has to do with many people or few, or with things great or small, he does not dare to indicate any disrespect – is not this to maintain a dignified ease without any pride? He adjusts his clothes and cap, and throws a dignity into his looks, so that, thus dignified, he is looked at with awe – is not this to be majestic without being fierce?"

Tsze-chang then asked, "What are meant by the four bad things?" The Master said, "To put the people to death without having instructed them – this is called cruelty. To require from them, suddenly, the full tale of work, without having given them warning – this is called oppression. To issue orders as if without urgency, at first, and, when the time comes, to insist on them with severity – this is called injury. And, generally, in the giving pay or rewards to men, to do it in a stingy way – this is called acting the part of a mere official."

The Master said, "Without recognizing the ordinances of Heaven, it is impossible to be a superior man.

"Without an acquaintance with the rules of Propriety, it is impossible for the character to be established.

"Without knowing the force of words, it is impossible to know men."

The Analects

---

4 FACTS AND FIGURES

There are over 6 million Confucianists in the world.

Confucianism originated in China, but it is now all over East Asia. Most Confucianists are still found in China and the rest of Asia, but there are about 30,000 Confucianists in North America.

5 CONFUCIAN PRACTICES

A Ethical behavior
B Rites of passage

A ETHICAL BEHAVIOR
Because all humanity is good and always striving to be better, Confucianists strive to be loyal and live upright lives.

Confucianists emphasize and practice the need to sympathize with others when they are suffering.

B RITES OF PASSAGE
Confucianism does not include many of the elements found in some other world religions, such as Christianity and Islam. It is primarily an ethical system to which rituals at important times during one's lifetime have been added. Since the time of the Han dynasty (206 BC) (when Confucianism was adopted as a state religion) four life passages have been recognized and regulated by Confucian tradition:

- birth
- reaching maturity
- marriage
- death.

BIRTH
The T'ai-shen (spirit of the fetus) protects the expectant woman and deals harshly with anyone who harasses the mother to be. The mother's family provides everything the baby needs on the first, fourth and twelfth monthly anniversaries of the birth.

REACHING MATURITY
This life passage, now rarely celebrated, involves a group meal in which the young adult is served chicken.

MARRIAGE
This consists of six parts.

- Proposal
  The couple exchange the eight characters: the year, month, day and hour of each of their births.

- Engagement
  Once the wedding day is has been selected the bride sends out invitations to the wedding, along with a gift of cookies made in the shape of the moon.

- Dowry
  This is taken to the groom's home in a solemn procession. Gifts from the groom to the bride, equal in value to the dowry, are then sent to her.

- Procession
  The groom visits the bride's home and brings her back to his house.

- Marriage and reception
  The couple recite vows to each other and then toast each other with wine before hosting a banquet.

- Morning after the wedding
  The bride serves breakfast to the groom's parents, who then do the same for her.

DEATH
Once the corpse has been washed and placed in a coffin, food and significant objects of the deceased are also put in the coffin. Mourners bring incense and money to help with the cost of the funeral. Friends and family follow the coffin to the cemetery.

A willow branch is taken with them as it symbolizes the soul of the person who has died. With the help of the priest, mourners say prayers and offer sacrifices of food.

Paper money is symbolically burnt, and sometimes paper cars or planes to help the dead soul on its journey to heaven. The willow branch is taken back to the home, where an ancestral tablet will be dedicated. This helps to install the spirit of the deceased in the home. Liturgies are recited on the seventh, ninth, forty-ninth days after the burial and on the first and third anniversaries of the death.

6 CONFUCIAN BELIEFS

A God
B Confucian philosophy
C Confucian values
D Personal harmony
E The teaching of Mencius
F The teaching of Hsun-tzu
G Neo-Confucianism

INTRODUCTION

The ideas of Confucianism became the standard in Chinese politics and scholarship and were eventually recognized as the Imperial ideology.

A GOD

In Confucianism the concept of God is vague. In the *Analects* there is reference to "Heaven" as a supreme deity, but in the teaching of Mencius "Heaven" becomes a moral force, and for Hsun-tzu it is the universe.

B CONFUCIAN PHILOSOPHY

Confucianism teaches that all people can reach perfection. Confucius' concept of humanity may be summed up in the term *jen*, and it was on this that he focused his teaching. *Jen*, which is the goal and the inner ideal for all people, should always be practiced. It has been translated as: love, human-heartedness, virtue, the goodness of the human spirit. It means supreme moral achievement and excellence in accordance with the following principles:

* *Chung*
* *Li*
* *Shu*
* *Yi*
* *Hsiao.*

These principles summarize basic Confucian philosophy and its ethical teachings.

Chung

Chung is loyalty to one's true nature. A mature person is deemed to be one who is comfortable with himself and his surroundings.

Li

Li refers to the way things should be done and is seen as the greatest principle of living. Everybody should know how to act in every situation.

Shu

Reciprocity, altruism.

Yi

Righteousness.

Hsiao

Filial piety, love among family members; completing one's parents' will and desires.

C CONFUCIAN VALUES

Confucius also stressed the following values:

Wen

Wen has been defined as the arts of peace and this embraces culture as it produces art, poetry, philosophy, dance and music.

Te

Te refers to the power by which men are ruled. Te is the ruler's virtue and discipline which he uses to lead people.

Xin

Honesty and trustworthiness.

D PERSONAL HARMONY

Ultimate personal harmony in life stems from the following Five Relationships between:

(i)   parent and child
(ii)   older and younger
(iii) husband and wife
(iv)   senior and junior
(v)   ruler and subject

These Five Relationships should be conducted in the following ways:

(i)   kindness in the father; filial piety in the son;
(ii)   gentility in the eldest brother; humility and respect in the younger;
(iii) righteous behavior in the husband; obedience in the wife;
(iv)   humane consideration in elders; deference in juniors;
(v)   benevolence in rulers; loyalty in ministers and subjects.

E THE TEACHING OF MENCIUS (371- C. 289 BC)

Mencius has been called "The second sage." It is said that Confucius did not discuss human nature, and the way of Heaven. Mencius centered his teaching on these concepts, developing the idea of *jen*. He contributed, in particular, two important teachings:

(i)   The basic goodness of human nature, which has compassion, wisdom and propriety, and is of the essence of Heaven. Evil is self-violation and self-abandonment. The cultivation of the self is directed towards recovering the "childlike heart" and serving Heaven, a way that is open to all people. This view became orthodox.

(ii) The concept of kingly government, on the basis of *jen*, which Mencius contrasts with tyrannical government. He argued that it was permissible to rebel against rulers who were motivated by power and profit.

F THE TEACHING OF HSUN-TZU (C. 298- 230 BC)

Hsun-tzu added what he felt to be an important corrective to the teaching of Mencius. Developing the idea of *li*, he taught that the human heart is naturally prone to err and has evil tendencies, and he suggested practical ways of keeping on the right path. He showed that correct ritual action performed with humility and grace will help the disciple to follow the insights of Confucius and Mencius.

G NEO-CONFUCIANISM

From AD 200 to AD 960 Confucianism was the central philosophy and religion of China. But Buddhism and Taoism became increasingly influential.

Neo-Confucianism was an attempt to reform and reassert Confucianism. The two greatest proponents are two scholars:

Chu Hsi (1130-1200) whose system came to be called "the school of principle;" and Wang Yang-ming (1472-1529) whose school of teaching was "the school of mind."

The goal of both teachings was the strengthening of the innate goodness in the mind until it was transformed into the mind of Heaven. But the methods differed. Chu Hsi taught a long, gradual process of learning and the practice of ethical conduct in an attempt to know the self. Wang Yang-ming taught that "sagehood" would only be reached by an experience of enlightenment.

7 WORSHIP

ANCESTOR WORSHIP

Confucians worship their ancestors both at the altars in their homes and in their temples. Ancestral worship was made popular by Confucius, though it had been introduced into China much earlier. It was seen as a continuation of the respect and honor that children should pay to their parents when they are alive, and was thought to be vital to a harmonious society.

> While parents are alive serve them according to *li*, the ritual; when they die bury them according to the ritual; and sacrifice to them according to the ritual."
>
> *Confucius, Analects 2:5*

It is believed that when someone dies, the soul lives in three places:

- one part goes to heaven
- one part stays in the grave to receive sacrifices
- one part stays in the ancestral tablet or shrine.

The ritual of funerals is very detailed (see above under death) in order to assist the soul on its journey to heaven. Some time within a hundred days after the funeral a memorial service is held in the home and an ancestral tablet is dedicated by a priest. Joss sticks are burned on the tablet, and there is a picture of the dead person.

Funerals and offerings to the ancestors are still among the most important Chinese rituals.

IN JAPAN

In Japan, under the emperor, sacrifices were offered to heaven and earth, the heavenly bodies, the imperial ancestors, various nature gods, and Confucius himself. These were abolished at the Revolution in 1912, but ancestor worship (better expressed as reverence and remembrance) remained a regular practice in the home.

8 FAMOUS CONFUCIANISTS

The following are among those who have had the most influence on the Confucian tradition.

Confucius
Mencius
Hsun-tzu
Kaozi
Wang Fuzhi
Phan Van Cac
Tang Yijie
Chu Hsi
Wang Yang-ming
Yi Hwang
Yi I

9 GLOSSARY

Age, and respect for Age
People should respect their elders. The older one is, the more respect one deserves. As people grow older they embody the quality of Chun-tzu more fully.

Analects
One of the Four Books containing the sayings of Confucius. *The Analects* are considered the best source of determining the sayings and wisdom of Confucius.

Ancestor worship
The Chinese practice of worshiping the spirits of their dead relatives. It was believed that after death, a person became deified. This enabled them to watch over their living descendants and to pray for them. They living worshiped them at a household shrine.

Chun-tzu
The Confucian ideal of a perfected human being. This person is mature, self-controlled, and helpful towards others.

Doctrine of the mean
The Confucian ideal of avoiding extremes, and of finding a way between two conflicting ideals or problems. This involves negotiation rather than confrontation.

Feng Shui
The Chinese name for geomancy, a branch of divination to determine appropriate sights for houses or graves.

Hsiao (Filial piety)
Respect and love for one's parents and elder relatives.

Five Constant Relationships
The Five Constant Relationships are: parent and child, husband and wife, elder sibling and junior sibling, elder friend and junior friend, ruler and subject. These are the central relationships one must always foster.

I-Ching
In Chinese, the "Book of Changes," a book used in divination.

Jen
The most important Confucian virtue: "Do not do to others what you would not have them do to you.". It means "humanness," and involves respect for and love of a person's dignity.

Jün-zi
Gentleman, superior man; nobleman, noble man

K'ung Fu-tzu
The Chinese name of Confucius.

Li
The Confucian notion of proper behavior. It refers to both propriety – the right thing to do – and to correct rituals.

Mencius, 372-289 BC
The most important Confucian teacher after Confucius. He systematized Confucius's teachings.

Shu
Reciprocity, altruism, taking oneself as an analogy.

Te
The exercise of power through virtue.

Tian
Heaven, destiny, a cosmic spiritual-moral power.

Wen
The "arts of peace." It refers to culture and its arts, such as music, painting, poetry, and literature.

Yi
Duty, obligation, sense of right and wrong.

Zhong
Loyalty, doing one's best.

BAHAI

CONTENTS

1 An overview   411

2 Bahai's founder   412

3 Bahai's holy books   414

4 Facts and figures   420

5 Bahai practices   420

6 Bahai beliefs   421

7 Bahai worship   430

8 Comparison with Christianity   431

9 Glossary   432

1 AN OVERVIEW

DEFINITION

Bahai people consist of those who accept the message of the Baha'u'llah. The Baha'i Faith was founded in Iran in the mid-nineteenth century by Mirza Hoseyn 'Ali Nuri, who is known as Bahá'u'lláh (Arabic: "Glory of God").

Factfile
- Date of origin: 1844
- Founder: Baha'u'llah.
- Holy book: Writings of Bab, Baha'u'lláh, and 'Abd ol-Baha
- Number of adherents: More than 6 million

SUMMARY

The Baha'i Faith, the youngest of the world's independent religions, is an offshoot of Shi'ite Islam.

The central theme of Bahá'u'lláh's message is that humanity is one single race which should be united in one global society. The one God progressively reveals himself to humanity. Following in the footsteps of other great religious leaders, such as Moses, Krishna, Buddha, Zoroaster, Jesus, Muhammad, Bahá'u'lláh is God's most recent messenger. His teachings supply the moral and spiritual stimulus our modern world needs.

SUMMARY OF PRACTICES

The Baha'i Faith has no initiation ceremonies, no sacraments, and no clergy. But the faith is open to all who express the wish to follow the Baha'i Faith.

SUMMARY OF BELIEFS

The Baha'i Faith embraces three basic principles:

(i) The oneness of God.
(ii) The oneness of religion.
(iii) The oneness of humankind.

God, Baha'u'llah said, has set in motion historical forces that are breaking down traditional barriers of race, class, creed, and nation and that will, in time, give birth to a universal civilization. Baha'i communities work to break down barriers of prejudice. They are convinced that humanity is a single people with a common destiny.

THE APPEAL OF THE BAHA'I FAITH

It has been claimed that no other worldview is better suited to the tenor of our time.

Leo Tolstoy described the Baha'i Faith as "the highest and purest form of religious teaching."

Arnold Toynbee predicted that it will be "the world religion of the future."

J. K. Van Baalen has stated that the Baha'i Faith "is the unifying cult *par excellence*."

2 BAHA'I'S FOUNDERS

A Three leaders
B The Bab (1819-1850)
C Baha'u'llah (1817-1892)
D 'Abd ul-Baha (1844-1921)
E The guardianship
F Universal House of Justice
G Present day headquarters

A THREE LEADERS

Followers of the Baha'i Faith look back to their first three leaders as the founders of their religion:

- Mirza Ali Muhammed – "the Bab" (meaning "the Gate") (1820-1850)
- Mirza Husain Ali – "Baha'u'llah" (meaning "Glory of God") (1817-1892)
- Abbas Effendi – 'Abd ul-Baha (1844-1921).

B THE BAB (1819-1850)

On May 23, 1844, in Shiraz, Persia, a young man, Mirza Ali Muhammed, known as the Bab, said that God's messenger was about to appear. Bab's work was to prepare a way for this messenger: he would be the living door or "the gate."

He claimed that "he closed the door to the Age of Prophecy [about the coming of the kingdom of God on earth]" and that he "opened the door to the Age of Fulfillment." Bab's teachings spread throughout Iran, and although he had relatively few supporters, they provoked strong opposition from both the Shi'ite Muslim clergy and the government. He was arrested and imprisoned by the Muslims and the Persian Government for forming a new Muslim sect. In 1848 Bab's movement declared its complete secession from Islam and in 1850, after Bab and his followers staged an insurrection against the Shah, Ali Muhammed was executed. The Baha's religion grew out of the Babi faith.

C BAHA'U'LLAH (1817-1892)

One of the Bab's earliest disciples was Mirza Husain Ali, who had assumed the name of Baha'u'llah when he renounced his social standing and joined the Babis. Baha'u'llah was arrested in 1852 and jailed in Tehran, where he supposedly became aware that he was the prophet and messenger of God whose coming had been predicted by the Bab.

In 1863 Baha'u'llah announced himself as the one promised by the Bab who had been sent to reveal God's will for a new age. Most Babis acknowledged his claim and then became known as Baha'is.

Imprisoned in Baghdad, Baha'u'llah was sent to Constantinople, then to Adrianople, and finally to Acre, in the Holy Land. Baha'u'llah arrived as a prisoner in Acre in 1868.

From his prison cell Baha'u'llah sent a number of letters to different rulers including Napoleon III, Queen Victoria, Pope Pius IX, the Shah of Persia, Kaiser Wilhelm I of Germany, the Emperor Franz Joseph of Austria. In these letters he announced the coming unification of humanity and the emergence of a world civilization. He urged them to live in universal peace.

Baha'u'llah died at Bahjí, just north of Acre, and is buried there. His shrine is now the focal point of the world community of the Baha'i Faith.

BAHA'U'LLAH'S PRAYER

Exalted, immeasurably exalted art Thou above any attempt to measure the greatness of Thy Cause, above any comparison that one may seek to make, above the efforts of the human tongue to utter its import! From everlasting Thou hast existed, alone with no one else beside Thee, and wilt, to everlasting, continue to remain the same, in the sublimity of Thine essence and the inaccessible heights of Thy glory. And when Thou didst purpose to make Thyself known unto men, Thou didst successively reveal the Manifestations of Thy Cause, and ordained each to be a sign of Thy Revelation among Thy people, and the Day-Spring of Thine invisible Self amidst Thy creatures.

D 'ABD UL-BAHA (1844-1921)

Before Baha'u'llah died in 1892, he appointed his eldest son, 'Abd ul-Baha, to be the leader of the Baha'i community and the authorized interpreter of his teachings. 'Abd ul-Baha actively administered the movement's affairs and spread the faith to North America, Europe, and other continents. In 'Abd ul-Baha was seen a perfect example of the Baha'i way of life.

He appointed his eldest grandson, Shoghi Effendi Rabbani (1897-1957), as his successor.

'Abd ul-Baha described the mission of His Father Baha'u'llah as follows:

He bore these ordeals, suffered these calamities and difficulties in order that a manifestation of selflessness and service might become apparent in the world of humanity; that the Most Great Peace should become a reality; that human souls might appear as the angels of heaven; that heavenly miracles would be wrought among men; that human faith should be strengthened and perfected; that the precious, priceless bestowal of God, the human mind, might be developed to its fullest capacity in the temple of the body; and man become the reflection and likeness of God, even as it hath been revealed in the Bible: "We shall create man in our own image." Briefly, the

Blessed Perfection [Baha'u'llah] bore all these ordeals and calamities in order that our hearts might become enkindled and radiant, our spirits be glorified, our faults become virtues, our ignorance transformed into knowledge; in order that we might attain the real fruits of humanity and acquire heavenly graces; although pilgrims upon earth we should travel the road of the heavenly kingdom; although needy and poor we might receive the treasures of life eternal. For this has He borne these difficulties and sorrows.

E THE GUARDIANSHIP

Shoghi Effendi Rabbani, the eldest grandson of 'Abd ul-Baha, became the Vali Amrullah or "Guadian of the Cause of God" and the interpreter of the Baha'i teachings.

Before he died in 1957, Shoghi Effendi designated a thirty-two-man group as "chief stewards of Baha'u'llah's embryonic World Commonwealth." This group of men became known as the "Hands of the Cause of God."

F UNIVERSAL HOUSE OF JUSTICE

In 1963, the so-called "Hands of the Cause of God" eventually solved the problem of succession when they established the nineteen-member "Universal House of Justice." This organization still administers the Baha'i Faith international. The members of the Universal House of Justice are elected democratically every five years at the International Baha'i Convention.

G PRESENT-DAY HEADQUARTERS

The Baha'i World Center, Mount Carmel, Haifa, Israel is today's headquarters of the Bahai Faith. In addition to being the seat of the Universal House of Justice, it is the International Teaching Center, the International Baha'i Archives and Library, and the Center for the Study of the sacred text of the Bahai Faith.

3 BAHA'I'S HOLY BOOKS

INTRODUCTION

The writings and spoken words of the Bab, Baha' u'llah, and 'Abd ul-Baha form the sacred literature of the Baha'i Faith. Each of these men wrote and spoke extensively on the principles of the Baha'i Faith and it is these scriptures that are revered most by the Baha'i today.

Some of the most notable of the one hundred volumes of sacred Scripture are:

- Selections from the writings of the Bab
- Tablets of Baha'u'llah, *Kitab-i-Aqdas* (Most Holy Book)
- *Kitab-i-Iqan* (Book of Certitude)
- Baha'i prayers.

AQDAS

The most holy text is the *Kitab-i-Aqdas* (Most Holy Book) written by Baha'u'llah. This text is the book of laws in the Baha'i Faith.

The *Aqdas* is the basis for almost every distinctive feature of the Baha'i community. Baha'u'llah himself refers to it as the "source of true felicity," the "Unerring Balance," the "Straight Path," and the "quickener of mankind"

VARIOUS TITLES

Written in Arabic around 1873, its Arabic title is *al-Kitab al-Aqdas*, but it is commonly referred to by its Persian title, *Kitab-i-Aqdas*, which was the title given to the work by Baha'u'llah himself. It is sometimes called "the *Aqdas*," "the Most Holy Book," "the Book of Laws" and occasionally "the Book of *Aqdas*." The *Kitab-i-Aqdas* is also referred to as "the Mother-Book" of the Baha'i Revelation.

CONTENT

The *Aqdas* is more than a mere book of laws. It discusses:

- the establishment of Baha'i administrative institutions
- Baha'i religious practices

- laws of personal status
- criminal law
- ethical exhortations
- social principles
- miscellaneous laws and abrogations
- prophecies.

QUESTIONS AND ANSWERS

The Aqdas is supplemented by the Questions and Answers, which consists of 107 questions submitted to Baha'u'llah by Zaynu'l-Muqarrabin concerning the application of the laws of the Aqdas, and Baha'u'llah's replies to those questions.

The Kitab-i-Aqbas

The first 30, of the 190 sections of the Aqdas follow.

IN THE NAME OF HIM WHO IS THE SUPREME RULER OVER ALL THAT HATH BEEN AND ALL THAT IS TO BE.

1

The first duty prescribed by God for His servants is the recognition of Him Who is the Dayspring of His Revelation and the Fountain of His laws, Who representeth the Godhead in both the Kingdom of His Cause and the world of creation. Whoso achieveth this duty hath attained unto all good; and whoso is deprived thereof hath gone astray, though he be the author of every righteous deed. It behoveth every one who reacheth this most sublime station, this summit of transcendent glory, to observe every ordinance of Him Who is the Desire of the world. These twin duties are inseparable. Neither is acceptable without the other. Thus hath it been decreed by Him Who is the Source of Divine inspiration.

2

They whom God hath endued with insight will readily recognize that the precepts laid down by God constitute the highest means for the maintenance of order in the world and the security of its peoples. He that turneth away from them is accounted among the abject and foolish. We, verily, have commanded you to refuse the dictates of your evil passions and corrupt desires, and not to transgress the bounds which the Pen of the Most High hath fixed, for these are the breath of life unto all created things. The seas of Divine wisdom and Divine utterance have risen under the breath of the breeze of the All-Merciful. Hasten to drink your fill, O men of understanding! They that have violated the Covenant of God by breaking His commandments, and have turned back on their heels, these have erred grievously in the sight of God, the All-Possessing, the Most High.

3

O ye peoples of the world! Know assuredly that My commandments are the lamps of My loving providence among My servants, and the keys of My mercy for My creatures. Thus hath it been sent down from the heaven of the Will of your Lord, the Lord of Revelation. Were any man to taste the sweetness of the words which the lips of the All-Merciful have willed to utter, he would, though the treasures of the earth be in his possession, renounce them one and all, that he might vindicate the truth of even one of His commandments, shining above the Dayspring of His bountiful care and loving-kindness.

4

Say: From My laws the sweet-smelling savor of My garment can be smelled, and by their aid the standards of Victory will be planted upon the highest peaks. The Tongue of My power hath, from the heaven of My omnipotent glory, addressed to My creation these words: "Observe My commandments, for the love of My beauty." Happy is the lover that hath inhaled the divine fragrance of his Best-Beloved from these words, laden

with the perfume of a grace which no tongue can describe. By My life! He who hath drunk the choice wine of fairness from the hands of My bountiful favor will circle around My commandments that shine above the Dayspring of My creation.

5

Think not that We have revealed unto you a mere code of laws. Nay, rather, We have unsealed the choice Wine with the fingers of might and power. To this beareth witness that which the Pen of Revelation hath revealed. Meditate upon this, O men of insight!

6

We have enjoined obligatory prayer upon you, with nine rak'ahs, to be offered at noon and in the morning and the evening unto God, the Revealer of Verses. We have relieved you of a greater number, as a command in the Book of God. He, verily, is the Ordainer, the Omnipotent, the Unrestrained. When ye desire to perform this prayer, turn ye towards the Court of My Most Holy Presence, this Hallowed Spot that God hath made the Center round which circle the Concourse on High, and which He hath decreed to be the Point of Adoration for the denizens of the Cities of Eternity, and the Source of Command unto all that are in heave and on earth; and when the Sun of Truth and Utterance shall set, turn your faces towards the Spot that We have ordained for you. He, verily, is Almighty and Omniscient.

7

Everything that is hath come to be through His irresistible decree. Whenever My laws appear like the sun in the heaven of Mine utterance, they must be faithfully obeyed by all, though My decree be such as to cause the heaven of every religion to be cleft asunder. He doeth what He pleaseth. He chooseth, and none may question His choice. Whatsoever He, the Well-Beloved, ordaineth, the same is, verily, beloved. To this He Who is the Lord of all creation beareth Me witness. Whoso hath inhaled the sweet fragrance of the All-Merciful, and recognized the Source of this utterance, will welcome with his own eyes the shafts of the enemy, that he may establish the truth of the laws of God amongst men. Well is it with him that hath turned thereunto, and apprehended the meaning of His decisive decree.

8

We have set forth the details of obligatory prayer in another Tablet. Blessed is he who observeth that whereunto he hath been bidden by Him Who ruleth over all mankind. In the Prayer for the Dead six specific passages have been sent down by God, the Revealer of Verses. Let one who is able to read recite that which hath been revealed to precede these passages; and as for him who is unable, God hath relieved him of this requirement. He, of a truth, is the Mighty, the Pardoner.

9

Hair doth not invalidate your prayer, nor aught from which the spirit hath departed, such as bones and the like. Ye are free to wear the fur of the sable as ye would that of the beaver, the squirrel, and other animals; the prohibition of its use hath stemmed, not from the Qur'an, but from the misconceptions of the divines. He, verily, is the All-Glorious, the All-Knowing.

10

We have commanded you to pray and fast from the beginning of maturity; this is ordained by God, your Lord and the Lord of your forefathers. He hath exempted from this those who are weak from illness or age, as a bounty from His Presence, and He is the Forgiving, the Generous. God hath granted you leave to prostrate yourselves on any surface that is clean, for We have removed in this regard the limitation that had been laid down in the Book; God, indeed, hath knowledge of

that whereof ye know naught. Let him that findeth no water for ablution repeat five times the words "In the Name of God, the Most Pure, the Most Pure", and then proceed to his devotions. Such is the command of the Lord of all worlds. In regions where the days and nights grow long, let times of prayer be gauged by clocks and other instruments that mark the passage of the hours. He, verily, is the Expounder, the Wise.

11

We have absolved you from the requirement of performing the Prayer of the Signs. On the appearance of fearful natural events call ye to mind the might and majesty of your Lord, He Who heareth and seeth all, and say "Dominion is God's, the Lord of the seen and the unseen, the Lord of creation."

12

It hath been ordained that obligatory prayer is to be performed by each of you individually. Save in the Prayer for the Dead, the practice of congregational prayer hath been annulled. He, of a truth, is the Ordainer, the All-Wise.

13

God hath exempted women who are in their courses from obligatory prayer and fasting. Let them, instead, after performance of their ablutions, give praise unto God, repeating ninety-five times between the noon of one day and the next "Glorified be God, the Lord of Splendor and Beauty." Thus hath it been decreed in the Book, if ye be of them that comprehend.

14

When traveling, if ye should stop and rest in some safe spot, perform ye – men and women alike—a single prostration in place of each unsaid Obligatory Prayer, and while prostrating say "Glorified be God, the Lord of Might and Majesty, of Grace and Bounty." Whoso is unable to do this, let him say only "Glorified be

God"; this shall assuredly suffice him. He is, of a truth, the all-sufficing, the ever-abiding, the forgiving, compassionate God. Upon completing your prostrations, seat yourselves cross-legged – men and women alike – and eighteen times repeat "Glorified be God, the Lord of the kingdoms of earth and heaven." Thus doth the Lord make plain the ways of truth and guidance, ways that lead to one way, which is this Straight Path. Render thanks unto God for this most gracious favor; offer praise unto Him for this bounty that hath encompassed the heavens and the earth; extol Him for this mercy that hath pervaded all creation.

15

Say: God hath made My hidden love the key to the Treasure; would that ye might perceive it! But for the key, the Treasure would to all eternity have remained concealed; would that ye might believe it! Say: This is the Source of Revelation, the Dawning-place of Splendor, Whose brightness hath illumined the horizons of the world. Would that ye might understand! This is, verily, that fixed Decree through which every irrevocable decree hath been established.

16

O Pen of the Most High! Say: O people of the world! We have enjoined upon you fasting during a brief period, and at its close have designated for you Naw-Ruz as a feast. Thus hath the Day-Star of Utterance shone forth above the horizon of the Book as decreed by Him Who is the Lord of the beginning and the end. Let the days in excess of the months be placed before the month of fasting. We have ordained that these, amid all nights and days, shall be the manifestations of the letter Ha, and thus they have not been bounded by the limits of the year and its months. It behoveth the people of Baha, throughout these days, to provide good cheer for themselves, their kindred and, beyond them, the poor and needy, and with joy and exultation to hail and glorify

their Lord, to sing His praise and magnify His Name; and when they end – these days of giving that precede the season of restraint – let them enter upon the Fast. Thus hath it been ordained by Him Who is the Lord of all mankind. The traveler, the ailing, those who are with child or giving suck, are not bound by the Fast; they have been exempted by God as a token of His grace. He, verily, is the Almighty, the Most Generous.

17

These are the ordinances of God that have been set down in the Books and Tablets by His Most Exalted Pen. Hold ye fast unto His statutes and commandments, and be not of those who, following their idle fancies and vain imaginings, have clung to the standards fixed by their own selves, and cast behind their backs the standards laid down by God. Abstain from food and drink from sunrise to sundown, and beware lest desire deprive you of this grace that is appointed in the Book.

18

It hath been ordained that every believer in God, the Lord of Judgment, shall, each day, having washed his hands and then his face, seat himself and, turning unto God, repeat "Allah-u-Abha" ninety-five times. Such was the decree of the Maker of the Heavens when, with majesty and power, He established Himself upon the thrones of His Names. Perform ye, likewise, ablutions for the Obligatory Prayer; this is the command of God, the Incomparable, the Unrestrained.

19

Ye have been forbidden to commit murder or adultery, or to engage in backbiting or calumny; shun ye, then, what hath been prohibited in the holy Books and Tablets.

20

We have divided inheritance into seven categories: to the children, We have allotted nine parts comprising five hundred and forty shares; to the wife, eight parts comprising four hundred and eighty shares; to the father, seven parts comprising four hundred and twenty shares; to the mother, six parts comprising three hundred and sixty shares; to the brothers, five parts or three hundred shares; to the sisters, four parts or two hundred and forty shares; and to the teachers, three parts or one hundred and eighty shares. Such was the ordinance of My Forerunner, He Who extolleth My Name in the night season and at the break of day. When We heard the clamor of the children as yet unborn, We doubled their share and decreased those of the rest. He, of a truth, hath power to ordain whatsoever He desireth, and He doeth as He pleaseth by virtue of His sovereign might.

21
Should the deceased leave no offspring, their share shall revert to the House of Justice, to be expended by the Trustees of the All-Merciful on the orphaned and widowed, and on whatsoever will bring benefit to the generality of the people, that all may give thanks unto their Lord, the All-Gracious, the Pardoner.

22
Should the deceased leave offspring, but none of the other categories of heirs that have been specified in the Book, they shall receive two thirds of the inheritance and the remaining third shall revert to the House of Justice. Such is the command which hath been given, in majesty and glory, by Him Who is the All-Possessing, the Most High.

23
If the deceased should leave none of the specified heirs, but have among his relatives nephews and nieces, whether on his brother's or his sister's side, two thirds of the inheritance shall pass to them; or, lacking these, to his uncles and aunts on both his father's and his mother's side, and after them to their sons and daughters.

The remaining third of the inheritance shall, in any case, revert to the Seat of Justice. Thus hath it been laid down in the Book by Him Who ruleth over all men.

24
Should the deceased be survived by none of those whose names have been recorded by the Pen of the Most High, his estate shall, in its entirety, revert to the aforementioned Seat that it may be expended on that which is prescribed by God. He, verily, is the Ordainer, the Omnipotent.

25
We have assigned the residence and personal clothing of the deceased to the male, not female, offspring, nor to the other heirs. He, verily, is the Munificent, the All-Bountiful.

26
Should the son of the deceased have passed away in the days of his father and have left children, they will inherit their father's share, as prescribed in the Book of God. Divide ye their share amongst them with perfect justice. Thus have the billows of the Ocean of Utterance surged, casting forth the pearls of the laws decreed by the Lord of all mankind.

27
If the deceased should leave children who are under age, their share of the inheritance must be entrusted to a reliable individual, or to a company, that it may be invested on their behalf in trade and business until they come of age. The trustee should be assigned a due share of the profit that hath accrued to it from being thus employed.

28
Division of the estate should take place only after the Ḥuqúqu'lláh hath been paid, any debts have been settled, the expenses of the funeral and burial defrayed, and such provision made that

the deceased may be carried to his resting-place with dignity and honor. Thus hath it been ordained by Him Who is Lord of the beginning and the end.

29

Say: This is that hidden knowledge which shall never change, since its beginning is with nine, the symbol that betokeneth the concealed and manifest, the inviolable and unapproachably exalted Name. As for what We have appropriated to the children, this is a bounty conferred on them by God, that they may render thanks unto their Lord, the Compassionate, the Merciful. These, verily, are the Laws of God; transgress them not at the prompting of your base and selfish desires. Observe ye the injunctions laid upon you by Him Who is the Dawning-place of Utterance. The sincere among His servants will regard the precepts set forth by God as the Water of Life to the followers of every faith, and the Lamp of wisdom and loving providence to all the denizens of earth

and heaven.

30

The Lord hath ordained that in every city a House of Justice be established wherein shall gather counselors to the number of Baha, and should it exceed this number it doth not matter. They should consider themselves as entering the Court of the presence of God, the Exalted, the Most High, and as beholding Him Who is the Unseen. It behoveth them to be the trusted ones of the Merciful among men and to regard themselves as the guardians appointed of God for all that dwell on earth. It is incumbent upon them to take counsel together and to have regard for the interests of the servants of God, for His sake, even as they regard their own interests, and to choose that which is meet and seemly. Thus hath the Lord your God commanded you. Beware lest ye put away that which is clearly revealed in His Tablet. Fear God, O ye that perceive.

Bahai World Center translation

4 FACTS AND FIGURES

The Baha'i Faith is the second most widespread of the world's independent religions, having more than 6 million adherents. It is established in 235 countries and territories throughout the world and claims adherents from over 2,000 ethnic, racial, and tribal groups

The Baha'i faith grew greatly in the 1960s, and by the end of the late twentieth century it had more than 150 national spiritual assemblies (national governing bodies) and about 20,000 local spiritual assemblies.

There are 1,700 Spiritual Assemblies in the United States.

Baha'i writings have been translated into 802 languages.

Under friendly evangelistic strategies adherents to the Bahai faith grow at the rate of 5.5% a year worldwide. By comparison, Christianity is expanding at a rate of 2.3% a year worldwide.

5 BAHAI PRACTICES

A   Spiritual development and personal behavior
B   Universal House of Justice
C   The United Nations

A SPIRITUAL DEVELOPMENT AND PERSONAL BEHAVIOR

Baha'is are meant to:

- pray daily
- abstain totally from narcotics, alcohol, or any substances that affect the mind
- practice monogamy
- obtain the consent of parents to marriage.

Baha'u'llah linked spiritual development and personal behavior. He wrote, "The citadels of men's hearts should be subdued through the hosts of a noble character and praiseworthy deeds."

B UNIVERSAL HOUSE OF JUSTICE

All Baha'i national spiritual assemblies elect a supreme governing body known as the Universal House of Justice.

This body applies the laws promulgated by Baha'u'llah and legislates on matters not covered in the sacred texts.

The seat of the Universal House of Justice is in Haifa, Israel, in the immediate vicinity of the shrines of the Bab and 'Abd ul-Baha, and near the Shrine of Baha'u'llah at Bahji near 'Akko.

C THE UNITED NATIONS

Believing that the United Nations represents a major effort in the unification of the planet, Baha'is are enthusiastic supporters of its work. The Baha'i International Community is accredited with consultative status with the United Nations Economic and Social Council (ECOSOC) and with the United Nations Children's Fund (UNICEF).

6 BAHA'I BELIEFS

A   Overview of key Bahai beliefs
B   Speeches of 'Abdu'l-Bahá

INTRODUCTION

The Baha'i people believe that all faith is unified in the eyes of God, and that there are certain principles under which God intended us to live. These spiritual and social teachings and laws that humankind needs to solve our contemporary problems have been revealed by Baha'u'llah.

Every Divine Revelation hath been sent down in a manner that befitted the circumstances of the age in which it hath appeared.

Baha'hu'llah

A OVERVIEW OF KEY BAHAI BELIEFS
THE PRIMACY OF LOVE

Love is the most great law that ruleth this mighty and heavenly cycle, the unique power that bindeth together the diverse elements of this material world, the supreme magnetic force that directeth the movements of the spheres in the celestial realms. Love revealeth with unfailing and limitless power the mysteries latent in the universe. Love is the spirit of life unto the adorned body of mankind, the establisher of true civilization in this mortal world, and the shedder of imperishable glory upon every high aiming race and nation.

'Abd ul-Baha

A NEW ROLE FOR HUMANITY

Baha'u'llah sought a redefinition of all human relationships:

- between human beings themselves
- between human beings and the natural world
- between the individual and society
- between the members of society and its institutions.

Each of these relationships must be sought in the light of our understanding of God's will.

Rather than seeking to found a new religion, Baha'u'llah sought to bring about a collective transformation of society.

The Baha'i Faith upholds the unity of God, recognizes the unity of His Prophets, and inculcates the principle of the oneness and wholeness of the entire human race. It proclaims the necessity and the inevitability of the unification of mankind.

Baha'u'llah

THE TWELVE PRINCIPLES

The Twelve Principles of Baha'i philosophy are summed up in Bahaha'u'llah's statement: "The earth is but one country and mankind its citizens."

Behind this maxim are the twelve principles of Baha'i thought:

(i)   Oneness of God.
(ii)   Oneness of Religion.
(iii) Oneness of Mankind.
(iv)   Elimination of prejudice of all kinds.
(v)   Individual search after truth.
(vi)   Universal auxiliary language.
(vii) Equality of men and women.
(viii) Universal education.
(ix)   Harmony of science and religion.
(x)   Elimination of extremes of wealth and poverty.
(xi)   World government.
(xii) Protection of cultural diversity.

ONENESS OF GOD

There can be no doubt whatever that the peoples of the world, of whatever race or religion, derive their inspiration from one heavenly Source, and are the subjects of one God.

Baha'u'llah

FOUNDATION BELIEFS

Baha'u'llah and Bab were manifestations of God.

God in his essence is unknowable.

SUCCESSIVE REVELATIONS

Baha'u'llah taught that there is one God whose successive revelations of his will have been the chief civilizing force in history. Baha'is believe that all the founders of the world's great religions have been manifestations of God and agents of a progressive divine plan for the education of the human race.

BASIC UNITY OF ALL RELIGIONS

Despite their apparent differences, the world's great religions, teach the same truth. Baha'u'llah's work was to overcome the disunity between religions and establish a universal faith.

The purpose of religion as revealed from the heaven of God's holy will is to establish unity and concord amongst the peoples of the world.

Baha'u'llah

Know thou assuredly that the essence of all the Prophets of God is one and the same. Their unity is absolute. God, the Creator, saith: There is no distinction whatsoever among the Bearers of My Message.

Baha'u'llah

Religion should unite all hearts and cause wars and disputes to vanish from the face of the earth, give birth to spirituality, and bring life and light to each heart. If religion becomes a cause of dislike, hatred and division, it were better to be without it, and to withdraw from such a religion would be a truly religious act.

Baha'u'llah

RELIGIOUS DIALOGUE

Baha'i believe that religious strife has caused the majority of world war and conflict. They believe that all faith comes from God and that all paths to the divine are cornerstones for interfaith dialogue.

MAN HAS COME OF AGE

Humanity is now coming of age. So a global, united society is now a possibility.

All men have been created to carry forward an ever-advancing civilization . . . To act like the beasts of the field is unworthy of man. Those virtues that befit his dignity are forbearance, mercy, compassion and loving-kindness towards all the peoples and kindreds of the earth.

Baha'u'llah

THE ONENESS OF THE HUMAN RACE

O Children Of Men! Know ye not why We created you all from the same dust? That no one should exalt himself over the other . . . Since We have created you all from one same substance it is incumbent on you to be even as one soul . . . that from your inmost being, by your deeds and actions, the signs of oneness and the essence of detachment may be made manifest.

Baha'u'llah

Ye are all the leaves of one tree and the drops of one ocean.

Baha'u'llah

The holy Manifestations of God were sent to make visible the oneness of humanity. For this did They endure unnumbered ills and tribulations, that a community from amongst mankind's divergent peoples could gather within the shadow of the Word of God and live as one, and could, with delight and grace, demonstrate on earth the unity of humankind.

Baha'u'llah

PREJUDICE

The Baha'i Faith seeks the abolition of racial, class, and religious prejudices.

. . . religious, racial, national, and political prejudices, all are subversive of the foundation of human society, all lead to bloodshed, all heap ruin upon mankind. So long as these remain, the dread of war will continue.

Baha'u'llah

RACIAL UNITY
Baha'i believe that racism hinders the development of the individual and even entire communities. It blights human progress.

EQUALITY FOR WOMEN
Denying the equality of women is an injustice against half of the world's population and encourages men to bring harmful attitudes to the workplace and to the world. The Baha'i Faith supports the concept of full equality of opportunity for women.

ECONOMIC JUSTICE
The disparity between rich and poor is a source of acute world suffering, and keeps the world instable and on the brink of war. The Baha'i Faith seeks to eliminate the extremes of poverty and wealth.

UNIVERSAL EDUCATION
Baha'is believe that historically ignorance has been a principle reason for the decline of societies and the perpetuation of prejudice. Baha'i scriptures state that every human deserves an education including the right to learn to read and write.

> Regard man as a mine rich in gems of inestimable value. Education can, alone, cause it to reveal its treasures, and enable mankind to benefit there from.
> *Baha'u'llah*

UNIVERSAL LANGUAGE
A common language would make communicating clearer and more efficient. All people should learn a common language in addition to their cultural language.

WORLD FEDERAL SYSTEM
According to the Baha'i scriptures, there should be a global international federation in place that governs the resources, solves problems and co-ordinates resolutions for the entire planet.

SCIENCE
Baha'is believe that harmony must exist between religion and science.

B SPEECHES OF 'ABD UL-BAHA
'Abd ul-Baha, the son of Baha'u'llah, the founder of the Baha'i Faith, after many years in prison, finally became free to travel. He visited London firstl, where he gave his first public speech ever on September 10, 1911.

LONDON SPEECH

> O noble friends; seekers after God! Praise be to God! Today the light of Truth is shining upon the world in its abundance; the breezes of the heavenly garden are blowing throughout all regions; the call of the Kingdom is heard in all lands, and the breath of the Holy Spirit is felt in all hearts that are faithful. The Spirit of God is giving eternal life. In this wonderful age the East is enlightened, the West is fragrant, and everywhere the soul inhales the holy perfume. The sea of the unity of mankind is lifting up its waves with joy, for there is real communication between the hearts and minds of men. The banner of the Holy Spirit is uplifted, and men see it, and are assured with the knowledge that this is a new day. This is a new cycle of human power. All the horizons of the world are luminous, and the world will become indeed as a garden and a paradise. It is the hour of unity of the sons of men and of the drawing together of all races and all classes. You are loosed from ancient superstitions which have kept men ignorant, destroying the foundation of true humanity. The gift of God to this enlightened age is the knowledge of the oneness of mankind and of the fundamental oneness of religion. War shall cease between nations, and by the will of God the Most Great Peace shall come; the world will be seen as a new world, and all men will live as brothers.
> *'Abd ul-Baha*

NEW YORK CITY SPEECH
This second speech was delivered in 1912 and was one of over one hundred speeches 'Abd ul-Bah gave in the US in that year.

I have spoken in the various Christian churches and in the synagogues, and in no assemblage has there been a dissenting voice. All have listened, and all have conceded that the teachings of Baha'u'llah are superlative in character, acknowledging that they constitute the very essence or spirit of this new age and that there is no better pathway to the attainment of its ideals. Not a single voice has been raised in objection. At most there have been some who have refused to acknowledge the mission of Baha'u'llah, although even these have admitted that He was a great teacher, a most powerful soul, a very great man. Some who could find no other pretext have said, "These teachings are not new; they are old and familiar; we have heard them before." Therefore, I will speak to you upon the distinctive characteristics of the manifestation of Baha'u'llah and prove that from every standpoint His Cause is distinguished from all others. It is distinguished by its didactic character and method of exposition, by its practical effects and application to present world conditions, but especially distinguished from the standpoint of its spread and progress.

First among the great principles revealed by Him is that of the investigation of reality. The meaning is that every individual member of humankind is exhorted and commanded to set aside superstitious beliefs, traditions and blind imitation of ancestral forms in religion and investigate reality for himself. Inasmuch as the fundamental reality is one, all religions and nations of the world will become one through investigation of reality. The announcement of this principle is not found in any of the sacred Books of the past.

A second characteristic principle of the teachings of Baha'u'llah is that which commands recognition of the oneness of the world of humanity. Addressing all mankind, He says, "Ye are all the leaves of one tree." There are no differences or distinctions of race among you in the sight of God. Nay, rather, all are the servants of God, and all are submerged in the ocean of His oneness. Not a single soul is bereft. On the contrary, all are the recipients of the bounties of God. Every human creature has a portion of His bestowals and a share of the effulgence of His reality. God is kind to all. Mankind are His sheep, and He is their real Shepherd. No other Scriptures contain such breadth and universality of statement; no other teachings proclaim this unequivocal principle of the solidarity of humanity. As regards any possible distinctions, the utmost that Baha'u'llah says is that conditions among men vary, that some, for instance, are defective. Therefore, such souls must be educated in order that they may be brought to the degree of perfection. Some are sick and ailing; they must be treated and cared for until they are healed. Some are asleep; they need to be awakened. Some are immature as children; they should be helped to attain maturity. But all must be loved and cherished. The child must not be disliked simply because it is a child. Nay, rather, it should be patiently educated. The sick one must not be avoided nor slighted merely because he is ailing. Nay, rather, he must be regarded with sympathy and affection and treated until he is healed. The soul that is asleep must not be looked upon with contempt but awakened and led into the light.

Baha'u'llah teaches that religion must be in conformity with science and reason. If belief and teaching are opposed to the analysis of reason and principles of science, they are not worthy of acceptance. This principle has not been revealed in any of the former Books of divine teaching.

Another fundamental announcement made by Baha'u'llah is that religion must be the source of unity and fellowship in the world. If it is productive of enmity, hatred and bigotry, the absence of religion would be preferable. This is a new principle of revelation found only in the utterances of Baha'u'llah.

Again, Baha'u'llah declares that all forms of prejudice among mankind must be abandoned and that until existing prejudices are entirely removed, the world of humanity will not and cannot attain peace, prosperity and composure. This principle cannot be found in any other sacred volume than the teachings of Baha'u'llah.

Another teaching is that there shall be perfect equality between men and women. Why should man create a distinction which God does not recognize? In the kingdoms below man sex exists, but the distinction between male and female is neither repressive nor restrictive. The mare, for instance, is as strong and often more speedy than the horse. Throughout the animal and vegetable kingdoms there is perfect equality between the sexes. In the kingdom of mankind this equality must likewise exist, and the one whose heart is purest, whose life and character are highest and nearest to the divine standard is most worthy and excellent in the sight of God. This is the only true and real distinction, be that one man or woman.

Baha'u'llah has announced the necessity for a universal language which shall serve as a means of international communication and thus remove misunderstandings and difficulties. This teaching is set forth in the *Kitab-i-Aqdas* ("Most Holy Book") published fifty years ago.

He has also proclaimed the principle that all mankind shall be educated and that no illiteracy be allowed to remain. This practical remedy for the need of the world cannot be found in the text of any other sacred Books.

He teaches that it is incumbent upon all mankind to become fitted for some useful trade, craft or profession by which subsistence may be assured, and this efficiency is to be considered as an act of worship.

The teachings of Bahá'u'lláh are boundless and without end in their far-reaching benefit to mankind. The point and purpose of our statement today is that they are new and that they are not found in any of the religious Books of the past. This is in answer to the question, "What has Baha'u'llah brought that we have not heard before?"

Therefore, it is conclusive and evident that the Manifestation of God in this day is distinguished from all former appearances and revelations by His majesty, His power and the efficacy and application of His Word. Specifically, the Baha'i principles introduce a new methodology, principle, to areas where principle has never been successfully applied. This will shake history by elevating dull secular issues, mere political correctness, into the realm of the holy and the creative. In order to understand the revolutionary quality of the Baha'i principles, it is helpful to reflect upon how science determines novelty.

Science is a hotbed of innovation, invention, and novelty, and centuries ago it had to forge clear criteria for what is a new contribution and what is not. A new discovery in science can influence, for better or worse, millions of lives. Scientific progress has become so fast that a new invention can be spread and applied not in decades but often in months and weeks. A researcher who gains recognition for an innovation is assured of a successful career, and his project or laboratory stands to gain millions of dollars in funding.

Yet even in such an intensely competitive atmosphere it is recognized that never will the person credited with a major discovery be the first to come up with the idea. Complete originality is almost unheard of. Research scientist W. I. B. Beveridge lists some examples from the history of science:

> Edward Jenner was not the first to inoculate people with cowpox to protect them against smallpox, William Harvey was not the first to postulate circulation of the blood, Darwin was by no means the first to

suggest evolution, Columbus was not the first European to go to America, Pasteur was not the first to propound the germ theory of disease, Lister was not the first to use carbolic acid as a wound antiseptic. But these men were the ones who fully developed these ideas and forced them on a reluctant world, and most credit rightly goes to them for bringing the discoveries to fruition . . . Charles Nicolle calls these early ideas that are not at first followed up, "precursor ideas." [Beveridge, W. I. B., The Art of Scientific Investigation, Norton and Co., NY, 1957., p. 36]

Many scientists have remarked upon this phenomenon of precursor ideas.

As examples, Beveridge cites Delacroix: "What makes men of genius, or rather, what they make, is not new ideas; it is the idea by which they are obsessed that what has been said has still not been said enough."

And Ostler: "In science the credit goes to the man who convinces the world, not to the man to whom the idea first occurs." The Baha'i principles assert emphatically that the most important and neglected "precursor ideas" are religious principles, such as love, the Golden Rule, reverence and sanctity, the Oneness of God, etc. They then apply these basic aspects of monotheistic belief to the specific areas of social life where they are most needed. It is all too evident that most people have long ago despaired of ever finding unity and productivity on the religious front. Baha'is, though, like the innovators in science, are obsessed with putting into effect a religious solution to the world's problems. Obsession is not too strong a word, for thousands of Baha'is have laid down their lives for these principles in the heart of darkness, those seedbeds of fanaticism and corruption that are the lands where the Faith and its administration were born. 'Abd ul-Baha declared the validity of this determination when he said that Baha'u'llah has left no

ground or possibility for strife and disagreement. First he has proclaimed the oneness of mankind and drawn attention and specialized religious teachings for existing human conditions. So, before deciding whether the Baha'i principles are likely, in the long run, to be something new to religion and the world, one must first make a judgment about the age in which we live. Where is history leading us? Is the world about to unite? Is unification the most effective way to improve the world? Is a religious solution the way to bring unity about?

It will indeed take a great deal to convince the world of all this, and then there is the question of which specific principles to choose. Why are elimination of prejudice, equality of the sexes, and a universal auxiliary language singled out as central? What about the environment, space exploration, control of the media and the press, corporate power, reproductive technologies, medical funding, terrorism, criminality, or any number of other issues? If you had to choose a dozen or so principles for uniting the world, which would you choose? You can bet that your pick would be different from mine, and ours would differ from a third person's. In fact, it would probably take a thousand years for the world to come to a consensus about a remotely similar group of principles, and then we would have to agree on how to enact them. But the problems of the world are so pressing! Whatever the cure, it must be given quickly before the patient dies. What is the answer? Some people despair of ever finding agreement, and reject principle altogether. Why not just follow expediency? Why not pick the most urgent problem, or the problem we know best, and work from there? History has shown, though, that there are high-level and low-level problems. Solving a high-level problem gives solutions to any number of bothersome low-level issues. Low-level problems are not less important, but they are symptoms, not the disease. A principle is by definition a cure for a disease, a problem that confronts the whole body of humankind.

A good example was the introduction of sewers and the infrastructure of public sanitation. When people got indoor toilets, baths, and running water, suddenly infant mortality went down, hundreds of communicable diseases ceased to spread, and people lived longer, healthier lives. The terrible epidemics that had plagued humanity subsided. Historians of science give the credit for this advance to sanitation rather than advances in medical knowledge, since many of these diseases are still poorly understood and remain incurable. Following a principle, in this case the principle of cleanliness, is much more efficient than slapdash attempts to cut off the Hydra's heads. It was a Herculean task to pipe water and electricity to every home, rich or poor, but the principle of cleanliness demanded it. In the same way, the Baha'i principles will require a heavy investment, but the returns should be even more spectacular than they have been for sanitation. In order to work, principle must become the reflective focus and the foundation of the education of every world citizen. The Baha'i principles are intended to become a body of knowledge, a set of terms of reference, that will act as the Greek and Roman classics did among an earlier generation of scholars. They will serve as common ground whenever two minds meet, from whatever background or culture they come from. As among Baha'is now, you will be able to mention any of the principles and be confident of a sympathetic ear and an intelligent response. You can go anywhere in the world and talk with any Baha'i, of any race, class, or profession, and not have to go through a tedious process of pounding out agreement on fundamentals. It is comparatively easy to change the outer world by building sewers and water pipes, compared with the massive task of persuading even a few hearts and minds to follow principle, and not sacrifice it for

the sake of narrow, low-level interests.

This is why the religious nature of the principles is so unique and powerful, for only religion has shown itself able to convert whole peoples to a new way of thinking in a very short span of time. I have attempted to show here that the Baha'i principles are new in that they can help humanity make that first and most difficult step to effective action, agreement on principle. It was the genius of 'Abd ul-Baha to seize the relevant social principles of His Father's teachings and promote them repeatedly and emphatically to a skeptical world. So advanced are they, and such is the resistance of competing ideologies, that even now Baha'is find it difficult to persuade people that principle is viable. But I believe that in the long reach of history principle will be judged the heir apparent for the role that ideologies and "isms" have until now played, those bankrupt systems that have so terribly retarded social progress in the twentieth century.

When Baha'u'llah appeared in Persia, all the contemporaneous religious sects and systems rose against Him. His enemies were kings. The enemies of Christ were the Jews, the Pharisees; but the enemies of Baha'u'llah were rulers who could command armies and bring hundreds of thousands of soldiers into the arena of operation. These kings represented some fifty million people, all of whom under their influence and domination were opposed to Baha'u'llah. Therefore, in effect Baha'u'llah, singly and alone, virtually withstood fifty million enemies. Yet these great numbers, instead of being able to dominate Him, could not withstand His wonderful personality and the power and influence of His heavenly Cause. Although they were determined upon extinguishing the light in that most brilliant lantern, they were ultimately defeated and overthrown, and day by day His splendor became more radiant. They made every effort to lessen His greatness, but His prestige and renown grew in proportion to their endeavors to diminish it. Surrounded by enemies who were seeking His life, He never sought to conceal Himself, did nothing to protect Himself; on the contrary, in His spiritual might and power He was at all times visible before the faces of men, easy of access, serenely withstanding the multitudes who were opposing Him. At last His banner was upraised.

If we study historical record and review the pages of Holy Writ, we will find that none of the Prophets of the past ever spread His teachings or promulgated His Cause from a prison. But Baha'u'llah upheld the banner of the Cause of God while He was in a dungeon, addressing the kings of the earth from His prison cell, severely arraigning them for their oppression of their subjects and their misuse of power. The letter He sent to the Shah of Persia under such conditions may now be read by anyone. His Epistles to the Sultan of Turkey, Napoleon III, Emperor of France, and to the other rulers of the world including the President of the United States are, likewise, current and available. The book containing these Epistles to the kings was published in India about thirty years ago and is known as the *Suratu'l-Haykal* ("Discourse of the Temple"). Whatever is recorded in these Epistles has happened. Some of the prophecies contained in them came to pass after two years; others were fulfilled after five, ten and twenty years. The most important prophecies relative to events transpiring in the Balkans are being fulfilled at the present time though written long ago. For instance, in the Epistle which Baha'u'llah addressed to the Sultan of Turkey, the war and the occurrences of the present day were foretold by Him.

While addressing these powerful kings and rulers He was a prisoner in a Turkish dungeon. Consider how marvelous it was for a prisoner under the eye and control of the Turks to arraign so boldly and severely the very king who was responsible for His imprisonment. What power this is! What greatness! Nowhere in history can the record of such a happening be found. In spite of the iron rule and absolute dominion of these kings, His function was to withstand them; and so constant and firm was He that He caused their banners to come down and His own standard to be upraised. For today the flags of both the Persian and the Ottoman Empires are trailing in the dust, whereas the ensign of Baha'u'llah is being held aloft in the world both in the East and in the West. Consider what a mighty power this is! What a decisive argument! Although a prisoner in a fortress, He paid no heed to these kings, regarded not their power of life and death, but, on the contrary, addressed them in plain and fearless language, announcing explicitly that the time would come when their sovereignty would be brought low and His own dominion be established.

This is one of the characteristics of Baha'u'llah's message and teachings. Can you find events and happenings of this kind in any other prophetic dispensation? If so, in what cycle have similar things taken place? Do you find such specific prophecies and explicit statements concerning the future in the Holy Books of the past? All the Prophets of God were scorned and persecuted. Consider Moses. The people called Him a murderer. They said, "You killed a man and fled from punishment and retribution. Is it possible after your former deeds that you could become a Prophet?"

Many similar experiences are recorded concerning the holy, divine Messengers. How bitter and severe was the persecution to which They were subjected! Consider how they endeavored to efface and belittle Christ. They placed upon His head a crown of thorns and paraded Him through the streets and bazaars in mockery crying, "Peace be upon thee, thou king of the Jews!" Some would bow to Him backward, saying in scornful tones, "Thou king of the Jews!" or "Lord of lords, peace be upon thee!"

Still others would spit upon His blessed countenance. In brief, the persecutions which Christ suffered during the time of His manifestation are mentioned in the books of the old cycle, Jewish, Roman or Greek. No praises were bestowed upon Him. The only recognition and acceptance offered Him was from His believers and followers. Peter, for instance, was one who praised Him; and the other disciples spoke in His behalf. Numerous books were written against Him. In the history of the Church you will find record of the hatred and antagonism manifested by the Roman, Greek and Egyptian philosophers, attributing calumnies and ascribing imperfection to Him.

But during the manifestation of Baha'u'llah, from the day of His appearance to the time of His departure, the people of all nations acknowledged His greatness, and even those who were His most bitter enemies have said of Him, "This man was truly great; his influence was mighty and wonderful. This personage was glorious; his power was tremendous, his speech most eloquent; but, alas, he was a misleader of the people." This was the essence of their praise, eulogy and denial. It is evident that the authors of such statements, although His enemies, were profoundly impressed by His greatness and majesty. Some of His enemies have even written poems about Him, which though intended for satire and sarcastic allusion, have in reality been praise. For instance, a certain poet opposed to His Cause has said, "Beware! Beware! lest ye approach this person, for he is possessed of such power and of such an eloquent tongue that he is a sorcerer. He charms men, he drugs them; he is a hypnotizer. Beware! Beware! lest you read his book follow his example and associate with his companions because they are the possessors of tremendous power and they are misleaders." That is to say, this poet used such characterisations, believing them to be terms of belittlement and disparagement, unaware that they were in reality praises, because a wise man, after reading such a warning, would say, "The power of this man must unquestionably be very great if even his enemies acknowledge it. Undoubtedly, such a power is heavenly in its nature." This was one of the reasons why so many were moved to investigate. The more His enemies wrote against Him, the more the people were attracted and the greater the number who came to inquire about the truth. They would say, "This is remarkable. This is a great man, and we must investigate. We must look into this cause to find out what it all means, to discover its purpose, examine its proofs and learn for ourselves what it signifies." In this way the malign and sinister statements of His enemies caused the people to become friendly and approach the Cause. In Persia the mullas went so far as to proclaim from the pulpits against the Cause of Baha'u'llah casting their turbans upon the ground – a sign of great agitation – and crying out, "O people! This Baha'u'llah is a sorcerer who is seeking to mesmerize you; he is alienating you from your own religion and making you his own followers. Beware! lest you read his book. Beware! lest you associate with his friends."

Baha'u'llah, speaking of these very ones who were attacking and decrying Him, said, "They are My heralds; they are the ones who are proclaiming My message and spreading My Word. Pray that they may be multiplied, pray that their number may increase and that they may cry out more loudly. The more they abuse Me by their words and the greater their agitation, the more potent and mighty will be the efficacy of the Cause of God, the more luminous the light of the Word and the greater the radiance of the divine Sun. And eventually the gloomy darkness of the outer world will disappear, and the light of reality will shine until the whole earth will be effulgent with its glory.

'Abd ul-Baha

7 BAHA'I WORSHIP

A No rituals and no ministers
B Prayer
C Fasting
D Every nineteen days
E Holidays

A NO RITUALS AND NO MINISTERS

The Baha'i faith practices no rituals and has no ministers or priests. Every Baha'i is responsible for his or her own spiritual growth.

B PRAYER

Followers of the Baha'i faith pray and meditate daily.

Baha'u'llah encouraged Baha'is to pray daily. They should pray one of three "obligatory" prayers every day. The shortest of these obligatory prayers follows:

> I bear witness, O my God, that Thou has created me to know Thee and to worship Thee.
>
> I testify, at this moment, to my powerlessness and to Thy might, to my poverty and to Thy wealth.
>
> There is none other God but Thee, the Help in Peril, the Self-Subsisting.

C FASTING

Members of the Baha'i faith fast nineteen days a year. From March 2 to March 20 they refrain from eating and drinking from sunrise to sunset.

D EVERY NINETEEN DAYS

Followers of the Baha'i faith gather together every nineteen days for spiritual devotion, administrative consultation and fellowship.

E HOLIDAYS

INTRODUCTION

The Baha'i calendar includes nine holy days, which all have the significance of major feasts, and observance of them is required. Seven are joyful days celebrated by picnics or festal gatherings at which music, the reading of

verses and tablets, and short addresses suitable to the occasion are contributed by those present. The anniversaries of the martyrdom of the Bab and the Ascension of Baha'u'llah are celebrated with solemnity by appropriate meetings and discourses, the reading of prayers and tablets. All Baha'i holy days run from sundown to sundown.

Months of the Bahá'í Calendar

Persian EnglishGregorian Date

	Persian	English	Gregorian Date
1	**Bahá**	Splendor	March 21–April 8
2	**Jalál**	Glory	April 9–April 27
3	**Jamál**	Beauty	April 28–May 16
4	**'Azamat**	Grandeur	May 17–June 4
5	**Núr**	Light	June 5–June 23
6	**Rahmat**	Mercy	June 24–July 12
7	**Kalimát**	Words	July 13–July 31
8	**Kamál**	Perfection	August 1–August 19
9	**Asmá'**	Names	August 20–September 7
10	**'Izzat**	Might	September 8–September 26
11	**Mashíyyat**	Will	September 27–October 15
12	**'Ilm**	Knowledge	October 16–November 3
13	**Qudrat**	Power	November 4–November 22
14	**Qawl**	Speech	November 23–December 11
15	**Masá'íl**	Questions	December 12–December 30
16	**Sharaf**	Honor	December 31–January 18
17	**Sultán**	Sovereignty	January 19–February 6
18	**Mulk**	Dominion	February 7–February 25
19	**'Alá'**	Loftiness	March 2–March 21

CALENDAR OF BAHA'I HOLIDAYS

April 21	First Day of Ridván (Declaration of Baha'u'llah)
April 21–May 4	Ridvan
April 29	Ninth Day of Ridván
May 2	Twelfth Day of Ridván
May 23	Declaration of the Báb
May 29	Ascension of Baha'u'llah
June 13	Race Unity Day
July 9	Martyrdom of the Bab
October 20	Birth of the Bab
November 12	Birth of Baha'u'llah
March 2-20	Month of Fasting
March 21	New Year

In the sacred laws of God, in every cycle and dispensation there are blessed feasts, holidays and workless days. On such days all kinds of occupations, commerce, industry, agriculture, classes, etc. should be suspended.

'Abd ul-Baha

All should rejoice together, hold general meetings, become as one assembly, so that the national oneness, unity and harmony may be demonstrated in the eyes of all.

'Abd ul-Baha

8 COMPARISON WITH CHRISTIANITY

Basic Bahai beliefs are diametrically opposed to biblical Christianity.

The Bahai faith rejects:

- the Trinity
- the deity of Christ
- the virgin birth of Jesus
- the bodily resurrection of Christ
- Jesus' death on the cross as an atonement for our sins
- salvation by faith in Jesus alone
- the final authority of the Bible
- the second coming of Christ.

In the Bahai faith Jesus is only one of the prophets.

There is very little indeed that a true Christian can have in common with the faith of Bahai. There is simply no common ground on which to meet . . . The Baha'i faith is at its very core anti-Christian theology.

Dr. Walter Martin,
The Kingdom of the Cults

9 GLOSSARY

'Abd ul-Baha (1844-1921)
The "Servant of Baha," Abbas Effendi. In His Will and Testament, Baha'u'llah appointed 'Abd ul-Baha, who was his eldest son, as the head of the Baha'i community. 'Abd ul-Baha is also known by the titles that Baha'u'llah used in reference to His son: the "Master," and the "Center of the Covenant." 'Abd ul-Baha is an Arabic name that means "Servant of God." He was the author of some 27,000 writings (mostly letters) which Baha'is consider scripture, and he is considered the infallible interpreter of his father's writings and a perfect example of how to live a Baha'i life.

Abjad
The ancient Arabic system of allocating a numerical value to letters of the alphabet, so that numbers may be represented by letters, and vice versa. Thus every word has both a literal meaning and a numerical value.

Ablutions
The act of washing ones' hands and face for the obligatory prayer that Baha'is say daily.

Akka
The one-time prison city in present-day Israel where Baha'u'llah was kept for the last twenty years of His life. He eventually died while still a prisoner, and is buried on the outskirts in the property of Bahji.

'Alá
The Arabic word for "loftiness" and the name of the Baha'i month of fasting (2-20 March).

Appointed Arm (of Bahá'í Administration)
The Appointed Arm, also known as the "Learned," are member of Baha'i administration who are appointed to their position. All other administrative positions are filled by election (known as the Elected Arm). Appointed members are Counselors (appointed by the Universal House of Justice), Auxiliary Board Members (appointed by

Counselors) and assistants (appointed by Auxiliary Board Members). Members of the Appointed Arm are characterized by their level of wisdom, maturity, and dedication to service.

Aqdas, Kitáb-i-
The "Most Holy Book" of Baha'u'llah. It was composed about 1873 and contains the main laws, ordinances, and principles of the Baha'i Faith.

The Bab (1819-1850)
Literally the "Gate," the title assumed by Mirza Ali-Muhammed (1819-1850) after the Declaration of His Mission in Shiraz in May 1844. He was the Founder of the Babi Faith and the Herald of Baha'u'llah.

Babis
Followers of the Bab.

Baha
Baha means "Glory." It is the Greatest Name of God and a title by which Baha'u'llah is designated. Also, the name of the first month of the Baha'i year and of the first day of each Baha'i month.

Baha'u'llah (1817-1892)
The "Glory of God," title of Mirza Husain-Ali (1817-1892), the founder of the Baha'i Faith. Born into a wealthy family in Iran, his father worked in a high-ranking position in the Iranian government. Baha'u'llah never showed interest in the wealth and power of his family, and when he advocated the cause of the Bab, he was stripped of his property. For forty years, while teaching the Baha'i Faith, Baha'u'llah was kept in prison and exile until his eventual death in 1892 outside of the prison city of Akka in Israel. He declared himself the Promised One of the world's religions in 1863 and, in spite of imprisonment and persecution, wrote thousands of letters and other documents, about 15,000 of which are extant.

Baha'i

Literally, "follower of baha." It is also used as an adjective. (Compare the word "Christian," which is used in the same way.)

Bahji

The burial site of Baha'u'llah, in modern-day Israel. Bahji is the holiest site for Baha'is, and Baha'is turn in the direction of this city when they say their obligatory prayers. It is north of Haifa, the Israeli city that is the seat of the Shrine of the Bab and the Baha'i world headquarters.

Bayan

The Bayan ("Exposition") is the title given by the Bab to His Book of Laws, and it is also applied to the entire body of His Writings.

Bisharat (Glad-Tidings)

One of Baha'u'llah's chief works of social ethics, composed in the 1870s or 1880s.

Calendar

The Baha'i calendar is composed of 19 months of 19 days with an additional 4 (or 5, in a leap year) days to equal 364 days annually. The months are named after different attributes of God (Beauty, Light, Mercy, Splendor, etc.).

Counselor

An individual appointed by the Universal House of Justice to serve a particular region or country. Counselors act as the representative of the Universal House of Justice, and are the highest position that an individual Baha'i can achieve today. Counselors are known as members of the "Appointed Arm," as opposed to the "Elected Arm" that is comprised of the Local and National Spiritual Assemblies, and the House of Justice Itself. Counselors are extremely well respected by the Baha'is of the world. They in turn appoint Auxiliary Board Members.

Dawn-Breakers, The

An account of the life of the Bab and the development of the Babi religion by Nabil-i-Zarandi, a companion of Baha'u'llah; it was edited and translated into English by Shoghi Effendi in 1932.

Declaration Card

A card that is filled out by someone wanting to become a Baha'i. Though the true definition of a Baha'i is "anyone who believes in Baha'u'llah," signing a declaration card is the formalization of that belief. The declaration then registers the new Baha'i as a voting member of his or her Baha'i community.

Elected Arm

Members of the Elected Arm of the Baha'i Faith serve on the Local Spiritual Assembly, the Regional Council, the National Spiritual Assembly, and the Universal House of Justice. These individuals are elected by secret ballot, with no electioneering. They are elected for their loyalty, devotion, ability and experience.

Fast

The Fast is the last month of the Baha'i calendar, a nineteen-day period during which Baha'is refrain from eating and drinking between sunrise and sunset. It is essentially a period of meditation and prayer, of spiritual recuperation, during which the believer must strive to make the necessary readjustments in the inner life, and to refresh and reinvigorate the spiritual forces latent in the soul.

Feast

The Baha'i Feast is held every nineteen days according to the Baha'i calendar. The Feast consists of three elements: devotional, administrative, and social. The devotional element is a time for Baha'is to gather together in prayer and worship. The administrative element allows for the community to attend to its affairs as a group, and the social element is so that everyone can have a good time and enjoy the fellowship of the Baha'i community.

Fireside

A fireside is a small meeting that is held in someone's home with the purpose of educating people about various aspects of the Baha'i Faith.

The Guardian

The official title of Shoghi Effendi, the grandson of 'Abd ul-Baha.

Greatest Name

Some Islamic popular traditions hold that God has one hundred names or attributes of God of which ninety-nine are known, and the hundredth or Greatest Name will be revealed on the Day of Judgment. Baha'u'llah maintained that the Greatest Name was *baha*, "Glory," and its superlative *abha*, "most glorious." Baha'is use various forms of the two as a prayer and a greeting.

Haifa

The administrative center of the Baha'i Faith is located in the city of Haifa, Israel. This is also the resting place of the Bab.

Holy Day

There are nine Baha'i Holy Days that mark special events in Baha'i history. On a Holy Day, Baha'is are urged to suspend work, and commemorate the day with family and community.

Holy Land

The Holy Land refers to Israel, as the Baha'i Administrative Center. It is considered holy not only because it contains sites that are holy for Jews, Christians and Muslims, but also because it contains the resting places of the Bab, Baha'u'llah, and 'Abd ul-Baha.

House of Justice

The governing council of a local or national Baháa'i community in the future, and of the Baha'i world today. Local and national houses of justice are temporarily styled spiritual assemblies.

Iqan, Kitab-i- (Book of Certitude)

A work composed by Baha'u'llah in 1862 in response to a list of questions prepared by an uncle of the Bab. It consists of interpretation of biblical and quranic terms, images, and prophecies, as well as many ethical and spiritual exhortations.

Local Spiritual Assembly

The Local Spiritual Assembly (LSA) is responsible for administering the affairs of the Baha'i Faith at the local level. The Assembly may also be called upon for counsel or advice. It is composed of nine elected members of the community. The Assembly is elected once a year.

The Master

A title of 'Abd ul-Baha, given to him by Baha'u'llah.

Manifestation of God

A Baha'i term for the founders of the major world religions, who are seen as mouthpieces of divine revelation and examples of a divine life. Baha'i scripture clearly identifies ten historic individuals as Manifestations: the founder of the Sabaean religion, mentioned in the Qur'án; Abraham; Moses; Jesus Christ; Muhammad; Krishna; Zoroaster; Buddha; the Bab; and Baha'u'llah.

Mashriqu'l-Adhkar

Literally "the Dawning-place of the praise of God," the designation of the Baha'i House of Worship and its dependencies.

National Spiritual Assembly

The National Spiritual Assembly is a body of nine elected members who administer the affairs of a National Baha'i Community. They also provide guidance to Local Spiritual Assemblies. The National Assembly is elected once a year.

Naw Ruz

The Baha'i New Year begins on *Naw Ruz*. This falls on March 21, and coincides with the spring equinox.

Obligatory prayer

Baha'is say an obligatory prayer on a daily basis. There are three different prayers to choose from. The short prayer is to be said once between noon and sunset, the medium prayer is to be said at morning, noon and night, and the long prayer is to be said once in a twenty-four hour period.

Pioneering

When Baha'is travel overseas with the intention of developing the Faith in a locality, this is termed "pioneering." This differs from missionary work as Baha'is are forbidden to proselytize.

Progressive revelation
The Baha'i believe that the major religions have been founded by Manifestations of God and that the Manifestations succeed one another, each bringing a greater measure of divine truth to humanity.

Ridvan
Ridvan is the name of the twelve-day festival that marks the holiest time in the Baha'i calendar. An Arabic word meaning "Paradise," the Twelve Days of Ridvan are named after the Twelve Days that Baha'u'llah spent with his family and followers in the Garden of Ridvan outside of Baghdad. It was during this time that Baha'u'llah officially declared himself to be a Prophet of God.

Seven Valleys
A mystical work composed by Baha'u'llah between 1856 and 1862, in response to questions asked him by a Sufi leader. It is Baha'u'llah's major mystical work.

Shiraz
The city in Iran where the Bab declared His mission on May 23, 1844.

Shoghi Effendi (1896-1957)
The great grandson of Baha'u'llah, Shoghi Effendi led the Baha'i world after the death of his Grandfather, 'Abd ul-Baha, in 1921 He was given the title of The Guardian.

Shrine of the Bab
The Shrine in which the Bab is buried stands on Mount Carmel in Haifa, Israel.

Universal House of Justice
The supreme governing body of the Baha'i world, the Universal House of Justice is elected by the Baha'is of the world once every five years. Like other Baha'i institutions, it has nine members. The Universal House of Justice meets in Haifa, Israel, and administers the Baha'i community at a global level.

Year of Service
Baha'is, especially young people, are en- couraged to spend a year offering volunteer service to communities around the world. This service is generally related to assisting the growth and development of Baha'i communities and participation in social and economic development projects.

SHINTOISM

CONTENTS

1 An overview   439

2 Shinto's founder   440

3 Shinto's holy books   440

4 Facts and figures   449

5 Shinto practices   449

6 Shinto beliefs   451

7 Shinto Worship   452

8 Groupings within Shintoism   455

9 Glossary   456

1 An Overview

DEFINITION
Shinto means, "The Way of the Spirits," and dates back to prehistoric times. It is based on the worship of ancestors and nature-spirits. The name Shinto is derived from two Chinese characters:

- *Shen*, meaning "divine being," and
- *Tao*, meaning "way."

So Shinto is "The Way of the Gods," or "The Way of the Spirits," or "The Way of the *Kami*." (*Kami* are similar to nature deities.)

Factfile
- Date of origin: sixth century AD. There is no exact date for the foundation of Shintoism as it embraces rituals and customs that began in Japan during ancient times. But when Buddhism and Confucianism were introduced into Japan in 552 AD, the term "Shinto" was used to identify the religious history of Japan.
- Founder: Shintoism does not have a founder.
- It is rooted in ancient Japanese mythology and history.
- Holy books: *Kojiki* and *Nohongi*.
- Number of adherents: 3 to 4 million.

SUMMARY
Shintoism was the primitive religion of Japan before the coming of Buddhism, which is currently the main religion of Japan. Shintoism is a very simple religion. It focuses on being loyal to one's ancestors.

Shinto has been called, "The religion of nature worship, emperor worship, and purity."

Unlike most other religions, Shinto has no real founder, no single book regarded as its written scriptures, no set of religious laws. It has only a very loosely-organized priesthood.

Shinto is as much a religious form of Japanese patriotism as it is a religion in the sense that Westerners usually understand religion.

SUMMARY OF PRACTICES
Japanese Shinto is devoted to spiritual beings (*kami*), to shrines, and to special rituals.

Much practice is simply an individual affair: visiting a shrine when special help is needed.

Shinto has been called, "the religion of Japan." However, ritual, not belief, is the basis of Shinto. So most Japanese people think of Shinto as the way of life for a Japanese person rather than as a religion. Ritual purity and offerings of food and rice wine assist one to acquire salvation (deliverance from the troubles and evils of the world).

SUMMARY OF BELIEFS
Shinto is based on the worship of, and belief in, *kami*.

Salvation is achieved by observing the many Japanese traditions. There is no need of forgiveness, as Shintos believe in the essential goodness of humanity. The concepts of sin and depravity of human nature are absent.

2 SHINTO'S FOUNDER

NO FOUNDER

Shintoism does not have a founder, but it is rooted in prehistoric religious practices of the Japanese people. This history was orally transmitted to successive generations of Japanese people prior to the introduction of Buddhism in the sixth century AD.

---

3 SHINTO HOLY BOOKS

A The *Kojiki*
B Extracts from the *Kojiki*
C Other holy books
D Shinto sayings

INTRODUCTION

Shinto does not have any books that are regarded as sacred Scripture. Neither of the two leading holy books of Shinto, the *Kojiki* (AD 712), and the *Nihongi* (also known as the *Nihonshoki*, AD 720), are thought of as being sacred. Though they are respected, and considered to be important, they are not recited or studied by ordinary believers in Shintoism.

They consist of collections of ancient myths and traditional teachings.

A KOJIKI (CHRONICLES OF ANCIENT EVENTS)

The Japanese founding myths are collected in a volume known as the *Kojiki*. The stories tell of the formation of the Japanese islands and the founding of human society.

The *Kojiki* mythology teaches about the *kami*. Two of these primeval *kami* were Izanagi (male-who-invites) and Izanami (female who-invites). They gave birth to the land of Japan and then went on to produce more *kami*.

The children of these first two deities, Izanagi and Izanami, became the deities of the various Japanese clans. One of their daughters

was Amaterasu (Sun Goddess). One of the most important stories in this set of tales is the story of Amaterasu, who is still the most important deity in Japan and is said to be the ancestor of the imperial family.

B EXTRACTS FROM KOJIKI

PART I: THE BIRTH OF THE DEITIES
THE BEGINNING OF HEAVEN AND EARTH
The names of the deities that were born in the Plain of High Heaven when the Heaven and Earth began were the deity Master-of-the-August-Center-of-Heaven; next, the High-August-Producing-Wondrous deity; next, the Divine-Producing-Wondrous deity. These three deities were all deities born alone, and hid their persons. The names of the deities that were born next from a thing that sprouted up like unto a reed-shoot when the earth, young and like unto floating oil, drifted about medusa-like, were the Pleasant-Reed-Shoot-Prince-Elder deity, next the Heavenly-Eternally-Standing

deity. These two deities were likewise born alone, and hid their persons.

The five deities in the above list are separate Heavenly deities.

THE SEVEN DIVINE GENERATIONS

The names of the deities that were born next were the Earthly-Eternally-Standing deity; next, the Luxuriant-Integrating-Master deity. These two deities were likewise deities born alone, and hid their persons. The names of the deities that were born next were the deity Mud-Earth-Lord; next, his Younger sister the deity -Mud-Earth-Lady; next, the Germ-Integrating deity; next, his younger sister the Life-Integrating-Deity; next, the deity of Elder-of-the-Great-Place; next, his younger sister the deity Elder-Lady-of-the-Great-Place; next, the deity Perfect-Exterior; next, his younger sister the deity Oh-Awful-Lady; next, the deity Izanagi or the Male-Who-Invites; next, his younger sister Izanami or the deity the Female-Who-Invites.

From the Earthly-Eternally-Standing deity down to the deity the Female-Who-Invites in the previous list are what are termed the Seven Divine Generations.

THE ISLAND OF ONOGORO

Hereupon all the Heavenly deities commanded the two deities His Augustness the Male-Who-Invites and Her Augustness the Female-Who-Invites, ordering them to "make, consolidate, and give birth to this drifting land." Granting to them a heavenly jeweled spear, they thus deigned to charge them. So the two deities, standing upon the Floating Bridge of Heaven pushed down the jeweled spear and stirred with it, whereupon, when they had stirred the brine till it went curdle-curdle, and drew the spear up, the brine that dripped down from the end of the spear was piled up and became an island. This is the Island of Onogoro.

COURTSHIP OF THE DEITIES THE MALE-WHO-INVITES AND THE FEMALE-WHO-INVITES

Having descended from Heaven on to this island, they saw to the erection of a heavenly august pillar, they saw to the erection of a hall of eight fathoms. Then Izanagi, the Male-Who-Invites, said to Izanami, the Female-Who-Invites, "We should create children"; and he said, "Let us go around the heavenly august pillar, and when we meet on the other side let us be united. Do you go around from the left, and I will go from the right." When they met, Her Augustness, the Female-Who-Invites, spake first, exclaiming, "Ah, what a fair and lovable youth!" Then His Augustness said, "Ah what a fair and lovable maiden!" But afterward he said, "It was not well that the woman should speak first!" The child which was born to them was Hiruko (the leech-child), which when three years old was still unable to stand upright. So they placed the leech-child in a boat of reeds and let it float away. Next they gave birth to the island of Aha. This likewise is not reckoned among their children.

Hereupon the two deities took counsel, saying: "The children to whom we have now given birth are not good. It will be best to announce this in the august place of the Heavenly deities." They ascended forthwith to Heaven and inquired of Their Augustnesses the Heavenly deities. Then the Heavenly deities commanded and found out by grand divination, and ordered them, saying: "they were not good because the woman spoke first. Descend back again and amend your words." So thereupon descending back, they again went round the heavenly august pillar. Thereupon his Augustness the Male-who-Invites spoke first: "Ah! what a fair and lovely maiden!" Afterward his younger sister Her Augustness the Female-Who-Invites spoke: "Ah! what a fair and lovely youth! "Next they gave birth to the Island of Futa-na in Iyo. This island has one body and four faces, and each face has a name. So the Land of Iyo is called Lovely-Princess; the Land of Sanuki is called Princess-Good-Boiled-Rice; the Land of Aha is called the Princess-of-Great-Food, the Land of Tosa is called Brave-Good-Youth. Next they gave birth to the islands of Mitsu-go near Oki, another name for which islands is Heavenly-Great-Heart-Youth. This island likewise has one body and four faces, and each face has a name. So the Land of Tsukushi is called White-Sun-Youth; the Land of Toyo is called Luxuriant-Sun-Youth; the Land of Hi is called Brave-Sun-Confronting-Luxuriant-Wondrous-Lord-Youth; the Land of Kumaso is called Brave-Sun-Youth. Next they gave birth to the Island of Iki, another name for which is Heaven's One-Pillar. Next they gave birth to the Island of Tsu, another name for which is Heavenly-Hand-Net-Good-Princess. Next they gave birth to the Island of Sado. Next they gave birth to Great-Yamato-the-Luxuriant-Island-of-the-Dragon-fly, another name for which is Heavenly-August-Sky-Luxuriant-Dragon-fly-Lord-Youth. The name of "Land-of-the-Eight-Great-Islands" therefore originated in these eight islands having been born first. After that, when they had returned, they gave birth to the Island of Koo-zhima in Kibi, another name for which island is Brave-Sun-Direction-Youth. Next they gave birth to the Island of Adzuki, another name for which is Oho-Nu-De-Hime. Next they gave birth to the Island of Oho-shima, another name for which is Oho-Tamaru-Wake. Next they gave birth to the Island of Hime, another name for which is Heaven's-One-Root. Next they gave birth to the Island of Chika, another name for which is Heavenly-Great-Male. Next they gave birth to the islands of Futa-go, another name for which is Heaven's Two-Houses. (Six islands in all from the Island of Ko in Kibi to the Island of Heaven's-Two-Houses.)

BIRTH OF THE VARIOUS DEITIES

When they had finished giving birth to countries, they began afresh giving birth to deities. So the name of the deity they gave birth to was the deity Great-Male-of-the-Great-Thing; next, they gave birth to the deity Rock-Earth-Prince; next, they gave birth to the deity Rock-Nest-Princess; next, they gave birth to the deity Great-Door-Sun-Youth; next, they gave birth to the deity Heavenly-Blowing-Male; next, they gave birth to the deity Great-House-Prince; next, they gave birth to the deity Youth-of-the-Wind-Breath-the-Great-Male; next, they gave birth to the sea-deity, whose name is the deity Great-Ocean-Possessor next, they gave birth to the deity of the Water-Gates, whose name is the deity Prince-of-Swift-Autumn ; next they gave birth to his younger sister the deity Princess-of-Swift-Autumn. (Ten deities in all from the deity Great-Male-of-the-Great-Thing to the deity Princess-of-Autumn.) The names of the deities given birth to by these two deities Prince-of-Swift-Autumn and Princess-of-Swift-Autumn from their separate dominions of river and sea were: the deity Foam-Calm; next, the deity Foam-Waves; next the deity Bubble-Calm; next, the deity Bubble-Waves; next the deity Heavenly-Water-Divider; next, the deity Earthly-Water-Divider; next, the deity Heavenly-Water-Drawing-Gourd-Possessor; next, the deity Earthly-Water-Drawing-Gourd-Possessor. (Eight deities in all from the deity Foam-Prince to the deity Earthly-Water-Drawing-Gourd-Possessor.) Next, they gave birth to the deity of Wind, whose name is the deity Prince-of-Long-Wind. Next, they gave birth to the deity of Trees, whose name is deity Stem-Elder; next, they gave birth to the deity of Mountains, whose name is the deity Great-Mountain-Possessor. Next, they gave birth to the deity of Moors, whose name is the deity Thatch-Moor-Princess, another name for whom is the deity Moor-Elder. (Four deities in all from the deity Prince-of-long-wind to Moor-Elder.) The names of the deities given birth to by these two deities, the deity Great-Mountain-Possessor and the deity, Moor-Elder from their separate dominions of mountain and moor were: the deity Heavenly-Elder-of-the Passes; next, the deity Earthly-Elder-of-the-Passes; next, the deity Heavenly-Pass-Boundary; next, the deity Earthly-Pass-Boundary; next, the deity Heavenly-Dark-Door; next, the deity Earthly-Dark-Door next, the deity Great-Vale-Prince; next, the deity Great-Vale-Princess. (Eight deities in all from the deity Heavenly-Elder-of-the-Passes to the deity Great-Vale-Princess.) The name of the deity they next gave birth to was the deity Bird's-Rock-Camphor-tree-Boat, another name for whom is the Heavenly-Bird-Boat. Next, they gave birth to the deity Princess-of-Great-Food. Next, they gave birth to the Fire-Burning-Swift-Male deity, another name for whom is the deity Fire-Shining-Prince, and another name is the deity Fire-Shining-Elder.

RETIREMENT OF HER AUGUSTNESS THE PRINCESS-WHO-INVITES

Through giving birth to this child her august private parts were burned, and she sickened and lay down. The names of the deities born from her vomit were the deity Metal-Mountain-Prince and, next, the deity Metal-Mountain-Princess. The names of the deities that were born from her feces were the deity Clay-Viscid-Prince and, next, the deity Clay-Viscid-Princess. The names of the deities that were next born from her urine were the deity Mitsubanome and, next, the Young-Wondrous-Producing deity. The child of this deity was called the deity Luxuriant-Food-Princess. So the deity the Female-Who-Invites, through giving birth to the deity of Fire, at length divinely retired. (Eight deities in all from the Heavenly-Bird-Boat to the deity Luxuriant-Food-Princess.) The total number of islands given birth to jointly by the two deities the Male-Who-Invites and the Female-Who-Invites was fourteen, and of deities

thirty-five. (These are such as were given birth to before the deity the Princess-Who-Invites divinely retired. Only the Island of Onogoro was not given birth to and, moreover, the Leech-Child and the Island of Aha are not reckoned among the children.)

So then His Augustness the Male-Who-Invites said: "Oh! Thine Augustness my lovely younger sister' Oh! that I should have exchanged thee for this single child!" And as he crept round her august pillow, and as he crept round her august feet and wept, there was born from his august tears the deity that dwells at Konomoto, near Unewo on Mount Kagu, and whose name is the Crying-Weeping-Female deity. So he buried the divinely retired deity the Female-Who-Invites on Mount Hiba, at the boundary of the Land of Idzumo and the Land of Hahaki.

THE SLAYING OF THE FIRE-DEITY

Then His Augustness the Male-Who-Invites, drawing the ten-grasp saber that was augustly girded on him, cut off the head of his child the deity Shining-Elder. Hereupon the names of the deities that were born from the blood that stuck to the point of the august sword and bespattered the multitudinous rock-masses were: the deity Rock-Splitter; next, the deity Root-Splitter; next, the Rock-Possessing-Male deity. The names of the deities that were next born from the blood that stuck to the upper part of the august sword and again bespattered the multitudinous rock-masses were: the Awfully-Swift deity; next, the Fire-Swift deity; next, the Brave-Awful-Possessing-Male deity, another name for whom is the Brave-Snapping deity, and another name is the Luxuriant-Snapping deity. The names of the deities that were next born from the blood that collected on the hilt of the august sword and leaked out between his fingers were: the deity Kura-okami and, next, the deity Kura-mitsuba.

All the eight deities in the above list, from the deity Rock-Splitter to the deity Kura-mitsuha, are deities that were born from the august sword.

The name of the deity that was born from the bead of the deity Shining-Elder, who bad been slain, was the deity Possessor-of-the-True-Pass-Mountains. The name of the deity that was next born from his chest was the deity Possessor-of-Descent-Mountains. The name of the deity that was next born from his belly was the deity Possessor-of-the-Innermost Mountains. The name of the deity that was next born from his private parts was the deity Possessor-of-the-Dark-Mountains. The name of the deity that was next born from his left hand was the deity Possessor-of-the-Densely-Wooded-Mountains. The name of the deity that was next born from his right hand was the deity Possessor-of-the-Outlying-Mountains. The name of the deity that was next born from his left foot was the deity Possessor-of-the-Moorland-Mountains. The name of the deity that was next born from his right foot was the deity Possessor-of-the-Outer-Mountains. (Eight deities in and from the deity Possessor-of-the-True-Pass-Mountains to the deity Possessor-of-the-Outer-Mountains.) So the name of the sword with which the Male-Who-Invites cut off his son's head was Heavenly-Point-Blade-Extended, and another name was Majestic-Point-Blade-Extended.

PART II: THE QUARREL OF IZANAGA AND IZANAMI
THE LAND OF HADES
Thereupon His Augustuess the Male-Who-Invites, wishing to meet and see his younger sister Her Augustness the Female Who-Invites, followed after her to the Land of Hades. So when from the palace she raised the door and came out to meet him, His Augustness the Male-Who-Invites spoke, saying: "Thine Augustness, my lovely younger sister! the lands that I and thou made are not yet finished making; so come back! "Then Her Augustness the Female-Who-Invites answered, saying: "Lamentable indeed that thou camest not sooner! I have eaten of the furnace of Hades. Nevertheless, as I

reverence the entry here of Thine Augustness, my lovely elder brother, I wish to return. Moreover, I will discuss it particularly with the deities of Hades. Look not at me!" Having thus spoken, she went back inside the palace; and as she tarried there very long, he could not wait. So having taken and broken off one of the end-teeth of the multitudinous and close-toothed comb stuck in the august left bunch of his hair, he lit one light and went in and looked. Maggots were swarming, and she was rotting, and in her head dwelt the Great-Thunder, in her breast dwelt the Fire-Thunder, in her left hand dwelt the Young-Thunder, in her right hand dwelt the Earth-Thunder, in her left foot dwelt the Rumbling-Thunder, in her right foot dwelt the Couchant-Thunder—altogether eight Thunder-deities had been born and dwelt there. Hereupon His Augustness the Male-Who-Invites, overawed at the sight, fled back, whereupon his younger sister, "Her Augustness the Female-Who-Invites, said: "Thou hast put me to shame," and at once sent the Ugly-Female-of-Hades to pursue him. So His Augustness the Male-Who-Invites took his black august head-dress and cast it down, and it instantly turned into grapes. While she picked them up and ate them, he fled on; but as she still pursued him, he took and broke the multitudinous and close-toothed comb in the right bunch of his hair and cast it down, and it instantly turned into bamboo-sprouts. While she pulled them up and ate them, he fled on. Again, later, his younger sister sent the eight Thunder-deities with a thousand and five hundred warriors of Hades to pursue him. So he, drawing the ten-grasp saber that was augustly girded on him, fled forward brandishing it in his back hand;" and as they still pursued, he took, on reaching the base of the Even-Pass-of-Hades, three peaches that were growing at its base, and waited and smote his pursuers therewith, so that they all fled back. Then His Augustness the Male-Who-Invites announced to the peaches:

"Like as ye have helped me, so must ye help all living people in the Central Land of Reed-Plains when they shall fall into troublous circumstances and be harassed! . . . . and he gave to the peaches the designation of Their Augustnesses Great-Divine-Fruit. Last of all, his younger sister, Her Augustness the Princess-Who-Invites, came out herself in pursuit. So he drew a thousand-draught rock, and with it blocked up the Even-Pass-of-Hades, and placed the rock in the middle; and they stood opposite to one another and exchanged leave-takings ; and Her Augustness the Female-Who-Invites said: "My lovely elder brother, thine Augustness! If thou do like this, I will in one day strangle to death a thousand of the folk of thy land." Then His Augustness the Male-Who-Invites replied: "My lovely younger sister, Thine Augustness! If thou do this, I will in one day set up a thousand and five hundred parturition-house. In this manner each day a thousand people would surely be born." So Her Augustness the Female-Who-Invites is called the Great-Deity-of-Hades. Again it is said that, owing to her having pursued and reached her elder brother, she is called the Road-Reaching-Great deity."' Again, the rock with which he blocked up the Even-Pass-of-Hades is called the Great-Deity-of-the-Road-Turning-back, and again it is called the Blocking-Great-Deity-of-the-Door-of-Hades. So what was called the Even-Pass-of-Hades is now called the Ifuya-Pass in the Land of Idzumo.

THE PURIFICATION OF THE
AUGUST PERSON
Therefore the great deity the Male-Who-Invites said: "Nay! hideous! I have come to a hideous and polluted land - I have! So I will perform the purification of my august person." So he went out to a plain covered with altagi, at a small river-mouth near Tachibana in Himuka in the island of Tsukushi, and purified and cleansed himself. So the name of the deity that was born from the august staff which he threw

down was the deity Thrust-Erect-Come-Not-Place. The name of the deity that was born from the august girdle which he next threw down was the deity Road-Long-Space. The name of the deity that was born from the august skirt which he next threw down was the deity Loosen-Put. The name of the deity that was born from the august upper garment which he next threw down was the deity Master-of-Trouble. The name of the deity that was born from the august trousers which he next threw down was the Road-Fork deity. The name of the deity that was born from the august hat which he next threw down was the deity Master-of-the-Open-Mouth. The names of the deities that were born from the bracelet of his august left hand which he next threw down were the deity Offing-Distant, next, the deity Wash-Prince-of-the-Offing; next, the deity Intermediate-Direction-of-the-offing. The names of the deities that were born from the bracelet of his august right hand which he next threw down were: the deity Shore-Distant; next, the deity Wash-Prince-of-the-Shore; next, the deity Intermediate-Direction-of-the-Shore.

The twelve deities mentioned in the foregoing list from the deity Come-Not-Place down to the deity Intermediate-Direction-of-the-Shore are deities that were born from his taking off the things that were on his person.

Thereupon saying: "The water in the upper reach is too rapid; the water in the lower reach is too sluggish," he went down and plunged in the middle reach; and, as he washed, there was first born the Wondrous-Deity-of-Eighty-Evils, and next the Wondrous-Deity-of-Great-Evils. These two deities are the deities that were born from the filth he contracted when he went to that polluted, hideous land. The names of the deities that were next born to rectify those evils were: the Divine-Rectifying-Wondrous deity; next, the Great-Rectifying-Wondrous deity; next, the Female-Deity-Idzu. The names of the deities that were next born as be bathed at the bottom of the water were: the deity

Possessor-of-the-Ocean-Bottom and, next, His Augustness Elder-Male-of-the-Bottom. The names of the deities that were born as he bathed in the middle of the water were: the deity Possessor-of-the-Ocean-Middle and, next, His Augustness Elder-Male-of-the-Middle. The names of the deities that were born as lie bathed at the top of the water were the deity Possessor-of-the-Ocean-Surface and, next, His Augustness Elder-Male-of-the-Surface. These three Ocean-Possessing deities are the deities held in reverence as their ancestral-deities by the Chiefs of Adzumi. So the Chiefs of Adzumi are the descendants of His Augustness Utsushi-hi-gana-saku, a child of these Ocean-possessing deities. These three deities His Augustness Elder-Male-of-the-Bottom, His Augustness Elder-Male-of-the-Middle, and His Augustness Elder-Male-of-the-Surface are the three great deities of the Inlet of Sumi. The name of the deity that was born as he thereupon washed his left august eye was the Heaven-Shining-Great-August deity. The name of the deity that was next born as he washed his right august eye was His Augustness Moon-Night-Possessor. The name of the deity that was next born as he washed his august nose was His Brave-Swift-Impetuous-Male-Augustness.

The fourteen deities in the foregoing list from the Wondrous-Deity-of-Eighty-Evils down to His Swift-Impetuous-Male-Augustness are deities born from the bathing of his august person.

PART III: AMATERASU, THE SUN-GODDESS, AND THE STORM-GOD

INVESTITURE OF THE THREE DEITIES, THE ILLUSTRIOUS AUGUST CHILDREN

At this time His Augustness the Male-Who-Invites greatly rejoiced, saying: "I, begetting child after child, have at my final begetting gotten three illustrious children." With which words, at once jinglingly taking off and shaking the jewel-string forming his august necklace, be bestowed it on Amaterasu, the Heaven-Shining-Great-August deity.

saying: "Do Thine Augustness rule the Plain-of-High-Heaven." With this charge he bestowed it on her. Now the name of this august necklace was the August-Storehouse-Shelf deity. Next he said to His Augustness Moon-Night-Possessor: "Do Thine Augustness rule the Dominion of the Night." Thus he charged him. Next he said to His-Brave-Swift-Impetuous-Male-Augustness: "Do Thine Augustness rule the Sea-Plain."

THE CRYING AND WEEPING OF HIS IMPETUOUS-MALE-AUGUSTNESS

So while the other two deities each assumed his and her rule according to the command with which her father had deigned to charge them, the Storm-God, His-Swift-Impetuous-Male-Augustness, did not assume the rule of the dominion with which he had been charged, but cried and wept till his eight-grasp beard reached to the pit of his stomach. The fashion of his weeping was such as by his weeping to wither the green mountains into withered mountains, and by his weeping to dry up all the rivers and seas. For this reason the sound of bad deities was like unto the flies in the fifth moon as they all swarmed, and in all things every portent of woe arose. So the Great August deity the Male-Who-Invites said to His Swift-Impetuous-Male-Augustness: "How is it that, instead of ruling the land with which I charged thee, thou dost wail and weep?" He replied, saying: "I wail because I wish to depart to my deceased mother's land, to the Nether Distant Land." Then the Great August deity the Male-Who-Invites was very angry and said: If that be so,, thou shalt not dwell in this land, and forthwith expelled him with a divine expulsion. So the great deity the Male-Who-Invites dwells at Taga in Afumi.

THE AUGUST OATH

So thereupon His-Swift-Impetuous-Male-Augustness said: if that be so I will take leave of the Heaven-Shining-Great-August deity, and depart." With these words he forthwith went up to Heaven, whereupon all the mountains and rivers shook, and every land and country quaked. So the Heaven-Shining-Great-August deity, alarmed at the noise, said: "The reason of the ascent hither of His Augustness my elder brother is surely of no good intent. It is only that he wishes to wrest my land from me." And she forthwith, unbinding her august hair, twisted it into august bunches; and both into the left and into the right august bunch, as likewise into her august head-dress and likewise on to her left and her right august arm, she twisted an augustly complete string of curved jewels eight feet long, of five hundred jewels, and, slinging on her back a quiver holding a thousand arrows, and adding thereto a quiver holding five hundred arrows, she likewise took and slung at her side a mighty and high sounding elbow-pad, and brandished and stuck her bow upright so that the top shook, and she stamped her feet into the hard ground up to her opposing thighs, kicking away the earth like rotten snow, and stood valiantly like unto a mighty man, and, waiting, asked: "Wherefore ascendest thou hither?" Then His-Swift-Impetuous-Male-Augustness replied, saying: "I have no evil intent. It is only that when the Great August deity our father spoke, deigning to inquire the cause of my wailing and weeping, I said: 'I wail because I wish to go to my deceased mother's land'—whereupon the Great-August deity said: 'Thou shalt not dwell in this land,' and deigned to expel me with a divine expulsion. It is therefore solely with the thought of taking leave of thee and departing, that I have ascended hither. I have no strange intentions." Then the Heaven-Shining-Great-August deity said: "If that be so, whereby shall I know the sincerity of thine intentions? "Thereupon His-Swift-Impetuous-Male-Augustness replied, saying: "Let each of us swear and produce children." So as they then swore to each other from the opposite banks of the Tranquil River of Heaven, the august names of the deities

that were born from the mist of her breath when, having first begged His-Swift-Impetuous-Male-Augustness to hand her the ten-grasp saber which was girded on him, and broken it into three fragments, and with the jewels making a jingling sound, having brandished and washed them in the True-Pool-Well of Heaven, and having crunchingly crunched them, the Heaven-Shining-Great deity blew them away, were Her Angustness Torrent-Mist-Princess, another august name for whom is Her Augustness Princess-of-the-Island-of-the-Offing; next Her Augustness Lovely-Island-Princess another august name for whom is Her Augustness Good-Princess; next Her Augustness Princess-of-the-Torrent. The august name of the deity that was born from the mist of his breath when, having begged the Heaven-Shining-Great-August deity to hand him the augustly complete string of curved jewels eight feet long - of five hundred jewels - that was twisted in the left august bunch of her hair, and with the jewels making a jingling sound having brandished and washed them in the True-Pool-Well of Heaven, and having crunchingly crunched them, His-Swift-Impetuous-Male-Augustness blew them away, was His Augustness Truly-Conqueror-I-Conqueror-Conquering-Swift-Heavenly-Great-Great-Ears. The august name of the deity that was born from the mist of his breath when again, having begged her to hand him the jewels that were twisted in the right august bunch of her hair, and having crunchingly crunched them, he blew them away, was His Augustness Ame-no-hohi. The august name of the deity that was born from the mist of his breath when again, having begged her to hand him the jewels that were twisted in her august head-dress, and having crunchingly crunched them, he blew them away, was His Augustness Prince-Lord-of-Heaven. The august name of the deity that was born from the mist of his breath when again, having begged her to hand him the jewels that were twisted on her left august arm, and having crunchingly crunched them, he blew them away, was His Augustness Prince-Lord-of-Life. The august name of the deity that was born from the mist of his breath when again, having begged her to band him the jewels that were twisted on her right august arm, and having crunchingly crunched them,, be blew them away was His-Wondrous-Augustness-of-Kumanu. (Five deities in all.)

THE AUGUST DECLARATION OF THE DIVISION OF THE AUGUST MALE CHILDREN A.ND THE AUGUST FEMALE CHILDREN

Hereupon the Heavenly Shining-Great-August deity said to His-Swift-Impetuous-Male-Augustness: "As for the seed of the five male deities born last, their birth was from things of mine; so undoubtedly they are my children. As for the seed of the three female deities born first, their birth was from a thing of thine; so doubtless they are thy children." Thus did she declare the division. So Her Augustness Torrent-Mist-Princess, the deity born first, dwells in the inner temple of Munakata. The next, Her Augustness Lovely-Island-Princess, dwells in the middle temple of Munakata. The next, Her Augustness Princess-of-the-Torrent, dwells in the outer temple of Munakata. These three deities are of the three great deities held in reverence by the dukes of Munakata. So His Augustuess Brave-Rustic-Illuminator, child of His Augustness Ame-no-hohi, one of the five children born afterward. This is the ancestor of the rulers of the land of Idzumo, of the rulers of the land of Muzashi, of the rulers of the upper land of Unakami, of the rulers of the lower land of Unakami, of the rulers of the land of Izhimu, of the departmental suzerains of the Island of Tsu and of the rulers of the land of Tobo-tsu-Afumi. The next, His Augustness Prince-Lord-of-Heaven, is the ancestor of the rulers of the land of Ofushi-kafuchi, of the chiefs of

Nukatabe-no-yuwe, of the rulers of the land of Ki, of the suzerains of Tanaka in Yamato, of the rulers of the land of Yamashiro, of the rulers of the land of Umaguta, of the rulers of the land of Kine in Michi-no-Shiri, of the rulers of the land of Suhau, of the rulers of Amuchi, in Yamato, of the departmental suzerains of Takechi, of the territorial lords of Kamafu, and of the rulers of Sakikusabe.

Translated by B. H. Chamberlain

C OTHER HOLY SHINTO BOOKS
Many texts are valued in the Shinto religion. Most of them were written in the eighth century AD. Two additional, well-known texts are:

- The *Rokkokushi* (Six National Histories)
- The *Jinno Shotoki* (a study of Shinto and Japanese politics and history) written in the fourteenth century .

D SHINTO SAYINGS

The heart of the person before you is a mirror. See there your own form.

Even the wishes of an ant reach to heaven.

Leave the things of this world and come to me daily with pure bodies and pure hearts.

A single sincere prayer moves heaven. You will surely realize the divine presence through sincere prayer.

Where you have sincerity, there also is virtue. Sincerity is a witness to truth.

Sincerity is the mother of knowledge. Sincerity is a single virtue that binds Divinity and man in one.

Retribution for good or ill is as sure as the shadow after substance.

To do good is to be pure. To commit evil

is to be impure.

To admit a fault is the beginning of righteousness.

The first and surest means to enter into communion with the Divine is sincerity. If you pray to a deity with sincerity, you will surely feel the divine presence.

4 FACTS AND FIGURES

SHINTOISTS BY SIX CONTINENTAL AREAS

Asia	2,727,000
Latin America	7,000
North America	55,000
Africa, Europe, Oceania	None reported

ADHERENTS IN JAPAN

The number of adherents of Shinto are often reported as being around 100 million, or between 75% to 90% of the Japanese population. Over 80% of Japanese people follow Shinto.

5 SHINTO PRACTICES

A Rituals
B Ethics
　(i) The Four Affirmations
　(ii) Ten precepts of Shinto
C Little missionary activity

A RITUALS

Shinto is more interested in rituals and traditions than in belief and creeds (see below under Worship.)

B ETHICS

Shinto ethics are not derived from any list of commandments. Rather, they are based on carrying out the will of the *kami*.

The aim of Shinto is to spread harmony and purity to every aspect of life. Shinto teaches that all human life is sacred. Worshipers revere *musuhi*, the *kami's* creative and harmonizing powers, and long to possess *makoto*, sincerity or true heart.

This lack of ethical rules has been explained in the following way: "It is because the Japanese were truly moral in their practice that they require no theory of morals" (Motoori, 1730-1801).

(1) THE FOUR AFFIRMATIONS

Fundamental beliefs in Shinto are called affirmations. There are four affirmations to be observed by Shinto followers. Shinto morality is summarized in these four affirmations:

- Affirmation of the tradition and the family: the family is the main way through which traditions are preserved.
- Affirmation of the love of nature: nature is sacred. Objects in nature are worshiped as sacred spirits.

- Affirmation of physical cleanliness: baths, hand-washing and mouth-rinsing are to be observed frequently.
- Affirmation of *matsuri*. *Matsuri* is the festival that honors individual or group *kami*.

(2) TEN PRECEPTS OF SHINTO

1. Do not transgress the will of the gods.
2. Do not forget your obligations to ancestors.
3. Do not offend by violating the decrees of the State.
4. Do not forget the profound goodness of the gods, through which calamity and misfortunes are averted and sickness is healed.
5. Do not forget that the world is one great family.
6. Do not forget the limitations of your own person.
7. Do not become angry even though others become angry.
8. Do not be sluggish in your work.
9. Do not bring blame to the teaching.
10. Do not be carried away by foreign teachings.

C LITTLE MISSIONARY ACTIVITY

Shinto is so strongly identified with the country of Japan and Japanese people that it does not engage in missionary work. It is an ethnic religion and has relatively few followers outside Japan.

6 SHINTO BELIEFS

A The Sun Goddess
B The emperor
C A nature religion
D *Kami*
E Humanity
F Other religions

INTRODUCTION
Apart from reverence for the emperor, Shintoism has no creed or definite set of theological beliefs which must be believed.

A THE SUN GODDESS
The only deity actually recognized in higher Shintoism is the spiritualized human mind. For the masses, however, Shintoism has about 800,000 gods, mostly the deified heroes of the Japanese.

Although Shintoism does not believe in one supreme being, great emphasis is placed on the Sun Goddess (also called the Mother Goddess), Amaterasu, from whom the imperial family of Japan traces its roots.

Shinto is unique among the world religions in representing the supreme being as feminine.

The imperial shrine at Ise is dedicated to Amaterasu, and all loyal Japanese citizens try to visit the Ise Shrine at least once.

B THE EMPEROR
Shinto followers believe that the Japanese emperor is a direct descendant of Amaterasu. Although after the Second World War Shinto was disestablished (that is, it is no longer a state religion), and the emperor's semi-divine status was repudiated, the imperial family is still held in high esteem.

C A NATURE RELIGION
Shinto worship and practice is rooted in nature. For Shinto, every part of the physical world is thought to have a sacred aspect.

D KAMI
Kami is a concept that is central to Shinto belief. Kami are spirits. They are not God or gods, even though they are often referred to as Shinto "gods." These sacred spirits take the form of important things in life, such as wind, rain, mountains, trees, rivers and fertility. A *kami* may be present in anything: people, animals, spirits or inanimate objects.

There are many millions (according to tradition, eight million million) of these spirits who are interested in the lives of individual believers and will intervene in a positive way to bring health and success. The *kami* possess a power that the individual believer does not and all one has to do is to ask the *kami* for their help in a sincere way.

Human beings become *kami* after they have died and may be revered by their families as ancestral *kami*. The Sun Goddess Amaterasu is considered Shinto's most important *kami*.

Because of their belief in *kami* the Japanese view the natural world as being both sacred and material.

E HUMANITY
Shinto views us as being basically good. It has no place for the doctrine of original sin.

F OTHER RELIGIONS
It is permissible to practice another religion/philosophy alongside Shinto as it is a non-exclusive religion. Many people practice Shinto along with a second or even third religion. Three out of four Japanese are comfortable about following Shinto as well as Buddhism.

Many Japanese homes have both a *kamidana* (a Shinto god-shelf) and a *butsudan* (a Buddha altar).

7 Worship

A Visiting shrines
B Visiting graves
C Structures and objects found at shrines

   (i) *Torii*
   (ii) *Komainu*
   (iii) Purification fountain or water basin
   (iv) Main and offering hall
   (v) Wishes
   (vi) *Omikuji*

D Types of shrine

   (i) Imperial shrines
   (ii) Inari shrines
   (iii) Hachimangu shrines
   (iv) Sengen shrines
   (v) Local shrines

E Famous Japanese shrines

   (i) Ise
   (ii) Izumo

F Worship at home
G Festivals

   (i) New Year
   (ii) Spring Festival
   (iii) Adults' Day
   (iv) Autumn Festival

H Life cycle events

   (i) *Hatsumiyamairi*
   (ii) *Shichigosan*

INTRODUCTION

Shinto is primarily a form of nature worship, and mountains, rivers, heavenly bodies, and other things are worshiped and personified (as, for example, the Sun Spirit, Amaterasu). Rules, rituals, and worship of *kami* (spirit) help to maximize agricultural harvests and bring blessings to social units or territories while preventing destruction and ill fortune.

Today, Shinto is based on each individual shrine, each shrine having its own reason for its existence (for instance, a physical feature, an event important to the local community, an important historical figure).

Shinto shrines are places of worship where the *kami* live. Japan has more than 100,000 Shinto shrines, each dedicated to a particular *kami*. Nearly every town and village in Japan has a Shinto shrine dedicated to the local *kami*. In addition, most Japanese have their own personal small shrine-altar in their own home. Most Japanese devote themselves to a shrine and a kami, rather than thinking that they belong to a national religion.

A VISITING SHRINES

Shrine visiting is an important aspect of Shinto religion. Shrines are visited for a festival, but not regularly on the same day of the week. People visit shrines in order to pay respect to the *kami* and to pray for good fortune.

Visiting a shrine at New Year is Japan's most popular religious activity. To enter a Shinto shrine is to leave the world of finite things and to pass into the world of the infinite and immeasurable.

PRIESTS

Shinto worship is highly ritualized. Most Shinto rituals are intended to ward off evil spirits by purification, and to help in one's prayers and offerings to the *kami*.

Shinto priests perform Shinto rituals and often live on the shrine grounds. Men and women can become priests, and they are allowed to marry and have children. Priests are supported by young ladies (*miko*) during rituals. *Miko* wear white kimono, must be unmarried and are often the priest's daughters.

B VISITING GRAVES

For important decisions and important occasions of one's life, ancestors are consulted, that is, their graves are visited for reflection and meditation.

C STRUCTURES AND OBJECTS FOUND AT SHRINES

(i) TORII

The most recognizable symbol of Shinto is the *torii* gate, One or more *torii* gates, consisting of two uprights and two crossbars, indicate the approach and entrance to a shrine. Most *torii* are wooden and are usually painted orange and black.

(ii) KOMAINU

Komainu are a pair of guardian dogs or lions. They are usually on each side of a shrine's entrance

(III) PURIFICATION FOUNTAIN OR BASINS

A water fountain, or a large trough of clean water, usually sheltered with a roof, is found at the entrance of shrines. There are also clean wooden ladles. The water is used for purification: purification is essential for a Shinto worshiper before any prayer can be offered.

The ritual of purification is performed through exorcism called *Harai*, during which

one's body is symbolically cleansed. This is referred to as *Misogi*. Shrines have stone washbasins (or water fountains) that enable visitors to rinse their face (or mouth) and hands for *Misogi* before daring to approach the deity. In this way, outward purity of hands and mouths is ensured before one proceeds to enter the main hall.

(iv) MAIN AND OFFERING HALL

Shines, which are built of wood, either have a main hall (*honden*) and offering hall (*haiden*), or they have two separate buildings. The main hall's innermost chamber contains the shrine's sacred object. Sacred objects of worship that represent the *kami* are stored in this innermost chamber, on view to no one. Visitors to the shrine pray and make their offerings in the offering hall.

(v) WISHES

Shrine visitors write their wishes (*onegai koto*) on the back of wooden plates or paper votive boards and then leave them at the shrine in the hope that their wishes may come true. People ask for such things as good health, financial success, and passing exams.

(vi) OMIKUJI

Omikuji are fortune-telling paper slips are found at many shrines and temples. Randomly drawn, they contain predictions ranging from *daikichi* ("great good luck") to *daikyo* ("great bad luck"). By tying the piece of paper around a tree's branch, good fortune will come true or bad fortune can be averted.

D TYPES OF SHRINE

(i) IMPERIAL SHRINES

These shrines include many of Shinto's most important shrines, such as the Ise Shrines, Izumo Shrine and Atsuta Shrine. Imperial shrines bear the imperial family's chrysanthemum crest and are often called *jingu* rather than *jinja*.

(ii) INARI SHRINES

Inari shrines are dedicated to Inari, the *kami* of rice. They have fox statues, as the fox is the messenger of Inari.

(iii) HACHIMANGU SHRINES
Hachimangu shrines are dedicated to Hachiman, the *kami* of war.

(iv) SENGEN SHRINES
There are over one thousand Sengen shrines in Japan, dedicated to Princess Konohanasakuya, the Shinto deity of Mount Fuji.

(v) LOCAL SHRINES
Many shrines are dedicated to local *kami*, and have no links with any other shrines.

E FAMOUS JAPANESE SHRINES
(i) ISE
The Ise Jingu are made up of two shrines: the Outer Shrine (*Geku*), which is dedicated to Toyouke, the *kami* of clothing, food and housing, and the Inner Shrine (*Naiku*), which enshrines Amaterasu, the Sun Goddess. Ise shrines are Japan's most sacred shrines.

(ii) IZUMO
Izumo Taisha is Japan's oldest shrine. It is regarded as the annual gathering place of all of Shinto's millions of *kami*. Izumo Taisha is considered Japan's second most important shrine after Ise Jingu.

F WORSHIP AT HOME
Prayers and sacrifices to ancestors can be offered at family altars. Many Japanese have a shrine in their own homes, a *kami-dana* ("*kami* shelf"). At this shrine they offer food or flowers and say prayers to a kami, making a request, or giving thanks. The *kami-dana* consists of a shelf on which is a small replica of a shrine.

G FESTIVALS
INTRODUCTION
A festival (*matsuri*) is one of the most important features of the practice of Shinto. Unlike most other aspects of the religion, the festivals are communal celebrations. They are centered on the shrine.
There are several types of Shinto *matsuri* in Japan. The *matsuri* of supplication to the gods asks for a successful harvest. Other *matsuri* are for thanksgiving, and others drive away ill-health and natural disasters.

Most Shinto festivals are linked to the farming seasons. A festival often includes a procession with banners and lanterns, sometimes with large floats, and a fair, with stalls and side-shows. Sometimes a portable shrine is carried to sites throughout a town, symbolizing a journey taken by the *kami*.

(i) NEW YEAR (OSHOGATSU)
Many Japanese visit a shrine at New Year to give thanks to the *kami* for the blessings of the past year and to ask for personal good fortune during the coming year.

(ii) SPRING FESTIVAL (HARU MATSURI, OR TOSHIGOI-NO-MATSURI)
This festival asks the gods for a good harvest.

(iii) ADULTS' DAY (SEIJIN SHIKI), JANUARY 20
Anyone who has had their twentieth birthday in the previous year goes to a shrine to thank the *kami* for his/her life.

(iv) AUTUMN FESTIVAL (AKI MATSURI, OR NIINAME-SAI)
This festival gives thanks to the gods for the year's harvest.

G LIFE-CYCLE EVENTS

(i) *HATSUMIYAMAIRI*
Newborn babies are taken to a shrine so that they can come under the protection of the *kami*. For boys this happens on the thirty-second day after birth and for girls on the thirty-third day after birth.

(ii) *SHICHIGOSAN*
The *Shichigosan* festival takes place on November 15. It derives its name from the ages of the children taking part: that is, seven (*shichi*), five (*go*), three (*san*).
Three-year-old and five-year-old boys, and three-year-old and seven-year-old girls are taken to a shrine so that the gods can be thanked for their health and so that their future can be prayed for.

8 GROUPINGS WITHIN SHINTO

A Shrine Shinto
B Sect Shinto
C Folk Shinto
D Shinto sects and other Japanese new religions
E Seicho-No-Ie

INTRODUCTION
In Japan it is quite normal for a person to be a Buddhist, or a Confucian, as well as being a member of a Shinto sect.

There are three main groupings within Shinto:

• Shrine Shinto
• Sect Shinto
• Folk Shinto.

A SHRINE SHINTO (JINJA)
Shrine Shinto is the most traditional form of Shinto, tracing its origin back to prehistoric times, and it is the largest Shinto group. As its name implies, Shrine Shinto concentrates on rituals linked to particular shrines that are devoted to the *Jinja Honcho*. Almost all shrines in Japan are members of *Jinja Honcho*, the Association of Shinto Shrines. Over 80,000 shrines belong to it as members.
The association encourages followers of Shinto:

> To be grateful for the blessings of Kami and the benefits of the ancestors, and to be diligent in the observance of the Shinto rites, applying oneself to them with sincerity, brightness, and purity of heart.

> To be helpful to others and in the world at large through deeds of service without thought of rewards, and to seek the advancement of the world as one whose life mediates the will of *Kami*.

> To bind oneself with others in harmonious acknowledgment of the will

of the emperor, praying that the country may flourish and that other peoples too may live in peace and prosperity.
> *The Shrine Shinto*

B SECT SHINTO (SHUHA SHINTO)
Sect Shinto began in the nineteenth century and incorporates thirteen independent sects. They are all recognized by the Japanese government.
Each sect has its own beliefs and doctrines. Most emphasize worship of their own central deity.

THE THIRTEEN SECTS
A list of the thirteen sects, with the dates when they were officially recognized follow:

1. Fusokyô (1882)
2. Izumo Oyashirokyô (1882)
3. Jikkokyô (1882)
4. Konkokyô (1900)
5. Kurozumikyô (1876)
6. Misogikyô (1894)
7. Ontakekyô, formerly known as Mitakekyô (1882)
8. Shinrikyô (1894)
9. Shinshukyô (1882)
10. Shinto Shusei-ha (1876)
11. Shinto Taikyô, known before World War II simply as Shinto (1886)
12. Taiseikyô (1882)
13. Tenrikyô (1908)

C FOLK SHINTO (MINZOKU)
This is not a separate Shinto group; it has no formal central organization or creed. It refers to traditional Shinto practices, observances and rites of passage, performed at local

shrines, which have never been incorporated into institutional Japanese religion.

The influences of Folk Shinto are evident in Shinto rites of passage and in Shinto agricultural festivals.

D SHINTO SECTS, AND OTHER JAPANESE NEW RELIGIONS

Sect	Number of adherents
All Shinto sects	3,000,000
Seicho-No-Ie	3,200,000
Tenrikyo	2,800,000
PL Kyodan	2,600,000
Sekai Kyuseikyo	800,000
Zenrinkai	600,000
Tensho Kotai Jingukyo	400,000
Ennokyo	300,000

E SEICHO-NO-IE

Seicho-No-Ie is a monotheistic religion of Japanese origin. It emphasizes gratitude for nature and ancestors and, above all, religious faith in God. It inherits most of its characteristics from Shinto rather than Buddhism.

The Seicho-No-Ie Truth of Life Movement is a nondenominational movement based on the belief that all religions emanate from one universal God. It is dedicated to spreading the truth that every person is a child of God; therefore, in reality, every person is divine in nature and the possessor of all of the creative powers of God.

The message that Seicho-No-Ie propagates was founded in Japan in 1930 by Dr. Masaharu Taniguchi, who, through his deep concern over the many contradictions in life, dedicated many years of intensive study to different philosophies and religions, until one day, while in deep meditation, he received the divine inspirations that were to form the basis for the Truth of Life Movement

9 GLOSSARY

Aikido
Japanese martial art.

Amaterasu
The Sun Goddess, the chief deity worshiped in Shintoism.

Bushido ("Warrior knight way")
Military devotion to a ruler, demanding loyalty, duty and self-sacrifices; an ideal promoted by State Shinto.

Bushido Code (Literally, "the warrior-knight-way")
The code practiced by the military class of the feudal period (Samurai) which has held a fascination for the Japanese people throughout its history. The code is an unwritten system of behavior stressing loyalty to emperor and country.

Emperor Meiji
The Japanese emperor who established Shinto as the state religion of Japan.

Gagaku
The stately ceremonial music of Shinto.

Gohei
White paper streamers, cut and folded sacred paper.

Harakiri
The ceremonial suicide committed by the Bushido warrior performed as an atonement for failure or bad judgment. The warrior believed death was to be preferred to disgrace.

Hondon
The inner sanctuary of a Shinto shrine in which is housed the *Shintai*, or "god body."

Ise
Location in eastern Honshu of a major shrine to Amaterasu.

Izanagi (The "female-who-invites")
The female deity who, according to the Shinto Myth, gave birth to the eight islands of Japan.

Izanami (The "male-who-invites")
The male deity who, along with the female deity Izanagi, helped produce the Japanese islands and the Japanese people.

Jigai
A method of suicide consisting of cutting the jugular vein. It is committed by females as an atonement for their sins.

Jinja
A Shinto shrine.

Kami
The sacred power found in both animate and inanimate objects. This power is deified in Shintoism and so is a spirit, god, or goddess of Shinto.

Kami Dama
"The god shelf," found in most private homes, on which are placed memorial tablets with the names of an ancestor or deity inscribed on them.

Kamidan
A shelf or home altar for the veneration of *kami*.

Kamikaze ("Spirit wind")
Japanese suicide fighter pilots of World War II.

Kigansai
A prayer of purification for the peace of the world.

Ko-Ji-Ki
The "records of ancient matters," composed in 712 AD , charting the imperial ancestors and the imperial court.

Mikado
A term used by foreigners to designate the emperor of Japan.

Miko
Shrine maidens.

Nihon-Gi
The "chronicles of Japan" composed around 720 AD. This work is a history of Japan from its origin until 700 AD.

Noh
Dramas performed in mask and costume, associated with Shinto.

O-Harai ("The Great Purification")
Important Shinto ceremony which involves a national purging of sins.

Ryobu Shinto
Also known as "dual aspect Shinto." The term refers to the mixing of Shintoism with Buddhism and Confucianism.

Samurai
Feudal soldier in Japan.

Shimenawa
Twisted rope, marking a sacred spot.

Shintai
An object of worship housed in the inner sanctuary of a Shinto shrine. The *Shintai* is usually an object of little value, such as a sword or mirror, but it supposedly contains magical powers and consequently is viewed as a good-luck charm.

Shinto
The term Shinto is derived from the Chinese term *Shen-tao*, meaning the "way of the higher spirits." Shinto is the designation for the religion that has long characterized Japan and its people.

Shinto myth
The belief that the islands of Japan and the Japanese people are of divine origin.

State Shinto
The patriotic ritual, established in 1882,

which worshiped the emperor as the direct descendant of the gods. State Shinto was abolished at the end of World War II.

Torii

A gate like structure that marks a Shinto sacred place.

ZOROASTORIANISM

CONTENTS

1 An overview   461

2 Zoroastrian's founder   462

3 Zoroastrian holy book   463

4 Facts and figures   467

5 Zoroastrian practices   467

6 Zoroastrian beliefs   469

7 Worship   472

8 Groupings within Zoroastrianism   472

9 Glossary   473

1 AN OVERVIEW

DEFINITION

An ancient Persian dualistic religion, Zoroastrianism is reputed to have been founded by the prophet Zarathushtra (Zoroaster).

Factfile
- Date of origin: c. 1500 BC
- Founder: Zarathushtra (Zoroaster)
- Holy book: *Avesta*
- Number of adherents: More than 300,000

SUMMARY

Zoroastrianism is a strongly ethical religion which teaches that every human being freely chooses to do good or evil. Ahura Mazda (in the Middle Persian language, Ohrmazd) wholly good and the creator of the world and of all goodness, is at war with Angra Mainyu (later called Ahriman) the source of evil. Ahura Mazda, the ultimate victor, will judge each individual soul after death. Zoroastrianism later developed a complex system of speculative doctrines dealing with the nature of the universe.

> Zoroastrianism is the oldest of the revealed world-religions, and it has probably had more influence on mankind, directly and indirectly, than any other single faith.
>
> *Mary Boyce,* Zoroastrians: Their Religious Beliefs and Practices *(London: Routledge and Kegan Paul, 1979)*

Zoroastrianism has relatively few followers, but its theology, so it is claimed, has had a great impact on Judaism, Christianity and other later religions, in beliefs about God and Satan, the soul, heaven and hell, salvation, resurrection, and final judgment.

SUMMARY OF PRACTICES

Zoroastorianism is known as "the good religion." Zoroastrians dedicate their lives to a three-fold path represented by their motto: "Good thoughts, good words, good deeds." A longer version of this quotation is: "Taking the first footstep with a good thought, the second with a good word, and the third with a good deed, I entered Paradise."

SUMMARY OF BELIEFS

All men and women are responsible to choose between good and evil: actions which are taken freely. Zoroaster was the first to teach doctrines about individual judgment, heaven and hell, the future resurrection of the body, the general last judgment, and life everlasting for the reunited soul and body.

2 ZOROASTRIAN'S FOUNDER

A Uncertain dates
B Direct revelation
C The growth and decline of Zoroastrianism
D Quotations of Zoroaster

INTRODUCTION

Zoroaster was a Persian prophet, possibly a priest, and the founder of the religion that bears his name.

The correct name of the prophet is Zarathushtra; "Zoroaster" and "Zoroastrianism" are the Greek versions of the names.

Zoroaster grew up among people who worshiped powerful forces, seen at work all around them in nature and in qualities such as victory and kindness. They feared the evil demonic forces expressed in evil qualities such as greed and deceit. Their world was full of spirits that had to be propitiated. Zoroaster's teaching was radically different. He was one of the first monotheists in human history.

A UNCERTAIN DATES

Conservative Zoroastrians believe that their religion started in around 6000 BC, but on the basis of language, historians and religious scholars today generally date Zoroaster's life to around 1500 to 1200 BC (this is a revision of a previous scholarly view, which dated Zoroaster to about 600 BC).

B DIRECT REVELATION

While drawing water at age 30, Zarathushtra had a vision of a shining being calling itself Vohu Manah ("Good Purpose") who took him into the presence of Ahura Mazda. Zarathushtra then received a revelation that Ahura Mazda was the single, eternal, and moral creator God. This was the first of a number of visions given to Zarathushtra, who began to preach the new message he had received.

Zarathushtra was persecuted, and was forced to leave home. It was ten years before he made his first convert, his cousin. Then a local king, Vishtasp, welcomed Zoroaster, and his teaching became the official religion of a small kingdom in north-east Persia.

> From the content of the *Gathas* [very early hymns, many probably written by Zarathushtra] it is abundantly clear that Zarathushtra was a natural man. He was an exceptionally wise and righteous person. He was an Ashu – one who has reached the apex of self-realization, perfection, and thenceforth immortality.
>
> *Dr. Farhang Mehr*

C THE GROWTH AND DECLINE OF ZOROASTRIANISM

Zoroaster's teaching spread throughout Persia, largely through the movement of tribes. But for the first 1,000 years little is known about its development. Then in 559 BC, Cyrus came to the throne of a small Persian kingdom. In 550 he became king of the Medes, and within twenty years had become emperor of the vast Babylonian Empire. He brought with him the religion of Zoroaster, which was taught throughout the empire by the Magi, who were a priestly tribe of the Medes.

When Alexander the Great conquered Persia in 331 BC, Zoroastrianism, according to one view, was neglected, and only revived in 224 AD when the Parthian Empire came to an end and Zoroastrianism was made the state religion of Persia by the Sasanians. According to a second view, after the Parthians expelled the Greek Seleucids in the middle of the second century BC, Zoroastrianism again become dominant in Persia – and at the time of Jesus was the most powerful religion in the world. What is agreed is that when the

Muslim Arab armies conquered Persia in the seventh century, Zorastrianism was viciously persecuted. Believers retreated to the desert villages and Zoroastrianism became the religion of the poor and oppressed.

In the tenth century, a small group set out from Persia to India in search of a land where they could have freedom to practice their faith. They found acceptance and a refuge on the west coast of India, where they became known as Parsis (Persians, see below).

In Iran (present-day Persia) the ancient religion of Zoroastrianism is still followed, mostly in the villages of the Yazdi Plain.

D QUOTATIONS OF ZOROASTER

When you doubt, abstain.

Doing good to others is not a duty, it is a joy, for it increases our own health and happiness.

Be good, be kind, be humane, and charitable; love your fellows; console the afflicted; pardon those who have done you wrong.

Suffer no anxiety, for he who is a sufferer of anxiety becomes regardless of enjoyment of the world and the spirit, and contraction happens to his body and soul.

Ability in a man is knowledge which emanates from divine light.

Do not hold grain waiting for higher prices when people are hungry.

He who sows the ground with care and diligence acquires a greater stock of religious merit than he could gain by the repetition of ten thousand prayers.

Let us be such as help the life of the future.

Zoroaster

---

3 ZOROASTRIAN HOLY BOOK

A *Avesta*
B *Yasna*

A AVESTA

The central Zoroastrian scripture is the *Avesta*, which consists of twenty-one books or divisions. The *Avesta* is a collection of texts compiled in different stages. Much of it deals with rituals, the practice of worship, and traditions of the faith. The language of these scriptures is known as "Avestan," an Iranian language very closely related to Sanskrit, the sacred language of Hinduism.

THE YASNA

One of the main divisions of the *Avesta*, and the most important, is the *Yasna*, which means "sacrifice." The *Yasna* is recited during a liturgy, also called "*Yasna*." The *Yasna* has seventy-two *has* (sections).

THE GATHAS

Embedded in the *Yasna* are *Gathas* ("hymns"). These are the oldest portion of the *Avesta*. Composed in a dialect different from the rest of the *Avesta*, they are thought to have been written by Zoroaster himself. They are sacred poetry directed towards:

- the worship of the one God
- understanding righteousness and cosmic order
- promotion of social justice
- individual choice between good and evil.

The basic tenets of the Zoroastrian religion are contained in the *Gathas*. These sacred songs are divided into stanzas and strophes. Zoroaster is said to have composed around 100,000 strophes but only a few hundred remain.

The *Gathas*, especially the first one called *Ahunavaiti*, contain most of his teachings and form the core of the Zoroastrian religion.

TRANSLATIONS AND FURTHER TEXTS
In the ninth and tenth centuries, the Avesta, which by then few people could read, was translated into Pahlavi (Middle Persian) and further texts were written to teach and encourage believers. These later sacred books develop and systematize traditional teachings. The Pahlavi texts contain extensive quotations and paraphrases from Avesta texts that had been destroyed either by the Greeks or, later, by the Arabs, but had been preserved orally by the priests.

B *YASNA* 71: THE *YASNA* CONCLUDING

1
Frashaoshtra, the holy, asked the saintly Zarathushtra: Answer me, O thou most eminent Zarathushtra, what is (in very truth) the memorized recital of the rites? What is the completed delivery of the Gathas?

2
Upon this Zarathushtra said: (It is as follows.) We worship Ahura Mazda with our sacrifice (as) the holy lord of the ritual order; and we sacrifice to Zarathushtra likewise as to a holy lord of the ritual order; and we sacrifice also to the Fravashi of Zarathushtra, the saint. And we

sacrifice to the Bountiful Immortals, (the guardians) of the saints.

3
And we sacrifice to (all) the good heroic and bounteous Fravashis of the saints, of the bodily (world on earth), and of the mental (those in Heaven). And we worship that one of ritual lords who attains the most his ends; and we sacrifice to that one of the Yazads, lords of the ritual order, who is the most strenuous, who gains the most, who reaches most to what he seeks, even that well-timed Prayer which is the prayer of that holy ritual lord, and which has approached the nearest (to us for our help).

4
We sacrifice to Ahura Mazda, the holy lord of the ritual order, and we worship His entire body, and we worship the Bountiful Immortals all; and we worship all the ritual lords. And we sacrifice to the entire Mazdayasnian Faith. And we worship all the sacred meters.

5
And we worship the entire bounteous Mathra, even the entire system of the Faith set up against the Daevas; and we worship its complete and long descent. And we sacrifice to all the holy Yazads, heavenly and earthly; and we worship all the good, heroic, and bountiful Fravashis of the saints.

6
And we worship all the holy creatures which Mazda created, and which possess the holy institutions, which were established holy in their nature, which possess the holy lore, and the holy sacrifice, which are holy, and for the holy, and to be worshiped by the holy. And we worship all the five Gathas, the holy ones, and the entire Yasna [its flow and its ebb, and the sounding (of its chants)].

7
And we sacrifice to all the Praises of the Yasna, and to all the words which Mazda

spake, which are the most fatal to evil thoughts, and words, and deeds;

8

And which designate the evil thought, and word, and deed, and which then cut down and fell every evil thought, and word, and deed. [(Pazand.) One would think of it as when the fire cuts, sucks out, and consumes the dry wood which has been sanctified and carefully selected (for its flame).] And we sacrifice to the strength, the victory, the glory, and the speed of all these words (as they go forth for their work).

9

And we sacrifice to all the springs of water, and to the water-streams as well, and to growing plants, and forest-trees, and to the entire land and heaven, and to all the stars, and to the moon and sun, even to all the lights without beginning (to their course). And we sacrifice to all cattle, and to the aquatic beasts, and to the beasts that live on land, and to all that strike the wing, and to the beasts that roam the plains, and to those of cloven hoof.

10

And to all Thy good and holy female (creatures) in the creation do we sacrifice, (O Thou who art) Ahura Mazda the skillful maker! on account of which Thou hast made many things and good things (in Thy world). And we sacrifice to those male creatures in the creation which are Thine and which are meet for sacrifice because of Asha Vahishta (of Righteousness the Best). And we sacrifice to all the mountains brilliant with holiness, and to all the lakes which Mazda created, and to all fires. And we sacrifice to all the truthful and correctly spoken words,

11

Even those which have both rewards and Piety within them. Yea, we worship (you) for protection and shielding, for guarding and watching; and may ye be to me for preparation. I call upon the Gathas here, the bountiful holy ones, ruling in the ritual order; yea, we sacrifice to you, (O ye Gathas!) for protection and shielding, for guarding and watching. Mine may ye be as a preparation. For me, for (mine) own soul I call on (you), and we would worship (you) for protection and for shielding, for guarding and for watching.

12

And we sacrifice to Weal, the complete welfare, holy and ruling in its course in the ritual order; and we sacrifice to Deathlessness (the immortal being of the good), holy, and ruling in the ritual order. And we sacrifice to the question of the Lord; and to His lore, the holy chiefs, and to the heroic Haptanghaiti, the holy lord of the ritual order.

13

(Frasha.) Let the holy Zarathushtra himself seek out a friend and a protector. And I say to thee (O Zarathushtra!) to make to thee a friend holy beyond the holy, and truer than the true, for that is the better thing; for he is evil who is the best to the evil, and he is holy to whom the holy is a friend,

14

For these are the best of words, those which Ahura Mazda spoke to Zarathushtra. And do thou, O Zarathushtra! pronounce these words at the last ending of (thy) life.

15

For if, O Zarathushtra! thou shalt pronounce these words at the last ending of (thy) life I, Ahura Mazda, will keep your soul away from Hell. Yea, so far away shall I hold it as is the breadth and extension of the earth [(Pazand) and the earth is as wide as it is long].

16

As thou dost desire, O holy (one)! so shalt thou be, holy shalt thou-cause (thy) soul to pass over the Chinvat Bridge; holy shalt thou come into Heaven. Thou shalt intone the Gatha Ushtavaiti, reciting the salvation hail.

17

We sacrifice to the active man, and to the man of good intent, for the hindrance of darkness, of wasting of the strength and life, and of distraction. And we sacrifice to health and healing, to progress and to growth, for the hindrance of impurity, and of the diseases of the skin.

18

And we sacrifice to the (Yasna's) ending words, to those which end the Gathas. And we sacrifice to the bounteous Hymns themselves which rule in the ritual course, the holy ones. And we sacrifice to the Praise-songs of the Yasna which were the products of the world of yore; yea, we sacrifice to all the Staota-Yesnya hymns. And we sacrifice to (our) own soul and to (our) Fravashi.

19-21

And we worship the pious and good Blessing with our sacrifice, and the pious man, the saint, and that Yazad, the mighty Curse of wisdom.

And we worship these waters, lands, and plants, these places, districts, pastures, and abodes with their springs of water, and we worship this lord of the district with our sacrifice, who is Ahura Mazda (Himself).

And we worship all the greatest lords, the Day-lords in the day's duration, and the Day-lords during daylight, and the Month-lords, and the Year-lords.

22

I praise, invoke, and I weave my song to the good, heroic, bountiful Fravashis of the saints, to those of the house, and of the village, the district and the province, and to those of the Zarathushtrotemas.

23

And we sacrifice to the Fire, Ahura Mazda's son, the holy ritual chief. And we sacrifice to this Baresman haying the Zaothra

with it, and its girdle with it, and spread with sanctity, the holy ritual chief. And we sacrifice to Apam-napat, and to Nairya-sangha, and to that Yazad, the wise man's swift Curse. And we sacrifice to the souls of the dead, [which are the Fravashis of the saints]

24

And we sacrifice to that lofty Lord who is Ahura Mazda Himself.

25

And we pray (again) for the Kine (once more) with these gifts and (ceremonial) actions which are the best.

26-28

May'st Thou, O Ahura Mazda! reign at Thy will, and with a saving rule over Thine own creatures, and render Ye the holy (man) also a sovereign at his will over waters, and over plants, and over all the clean and sacred (creatures) which contain the seed of Righteousness. Strip ye the wicked of all power!

Absolute in power may the holy be, bereft of all free choice the wicked ! Gone (may he be), met as foe, carried out from the creatures of Spenta Mainyu, hemmed in without power over any wish!

I will incite, even I who am Zarathushtra, the heads of the houses, villages, Zantus, and provinces, to the careful following of this Religion which is that of Ahura, and according to Zarathushtra, in their thoughts, their words, and their deeds.

29-31

In order that our minds may be delighted, and our souls the best, let our bodies be glorified as well, and let them; O Mazda! go likewise openly (unto Heaven) as the best world of the saints as devoted to Ahura,

And accompanied by Asha Vahishta (who is Righteousness the Best), and the most beautiful! And may we see Thee, and may we, approaching, come around about Thee, and attain to entire companionship with Thee! And we sacrifice to the Righteous Order, the best, the most beautiful, the bounteous Immortal!

4 FACTS AND FIGURES

The largest populations of Zoroastrians are in India, about 100,000 in total. There are about 20,000 in Iran.

In North America it is estimated that there are about 20,000 Zoroastrians.

THE PARSIS
In India the Zoroastrians are called the Parsis (Persians). They have amassed vast fortunes in the cotton and steel industries, and have the highest literacy rate in India. Their cultural and economic importance is far out of proportion to their small numbers.

---

5 ZOROASTRIAN PRACTICES

A The three great commandments
B Harmony, health and happiness
C Clothing
D *Naujote*
E Mixed marriages, proselytization, and conversion
F Death and vultures

A THE THREE GREAT COMMANDMENTS
Zarathushtra gave three commandments to his followers to enable them lead perfect lives and work for their own salvation. These are *humata* (good thoughts), *hukhta* (good words), and *havarshta* (good deeds).

GOOD THOUGHTS
Without good thoughts, there will be no progress on the spiritual path. Without good thoughts one cannot subject oneself to the divine will.

GOOD WORDS
But one must have the courage to speak truth all the time. One must be truthful to oneself and to others. There is no place for hypocrisy or duplicity in the life of a true Zoroastrian.

GOOD DEEDS
The supreme power of God, in the aspect of Kshatra Vairya, comes to everyone who engages in good actions. Good actions include *sraosha* or service.

B HARMONY, HEALTH AND HAPPINESS
The world God created is good and it is the duty of humankind to care for the earth, develop it and enjoy it.

There is no ascetic aspect to Zoroastrianism. Human beings are basically good, made by nature to work with God for the good of the world (though they can refuse this calling). It is their duty to seek the health of body and spirit and to keep both in balance: neither should dominate. Fasting is as wrong as greed; celibacy is as wrong as promiscuity. People should get married and have children: there are no monastic orders.

C CLOTHING
Two sacred garments, the *sudreh* (a white

cotton shirt, a symbol of the purity of the religion) and the *kusti* (a narrow cord), are the emblems of the religion and are worn by all followers of Zoroastrianism. The cord is woven out of seventy-two strands of lamb's wool (symbolic of the seventy-two chapters of the *Yasna*) and is wound three times around the waist, symbolizing the three cardinal tenets of the faith: good thoughts, good deeds and good words. It is tied in the middle of the body to signify that a Zoroastrian should put into practice the principle of moderation or golden mean in all his activities.

Zoroastrians perform a short cleansing ritual (*Padyab*), and untie and retie the *kusti* at least five times a day with a short ritual (*Nirang-i Kusti*) which includes prayers, and a resolve to be good in thought, word and deed. Before untying or tying the *kusti*, a short cleansing ritual (*padyab*) is performed. The *kusti* serves as a permanent symbol of service to God.

It is a sin for a Zoroastrian to move about without *sudreh* and *kusti*.

D *NAUJOTE*

Naujote is a ceremony in which a Zoroastrian child is invested with *sudreh* and *kusti*. The word *naujote* means "a new initiate who offers prayers." Before the ceremony, the child has a *naahn* (sacred bath) to symbolize purification.

The usual age is about nine. Children have to be old enough to make a free choice to become members of "God's army," and must also be old enough to know the difference between right and wrong.

E MIXED MARRIAGES, PROSELYTIZATION, AND CONVERSION

Traditional Zoroastrians believe that religion and ethnicity are inseparable; that one must

be born into the faith, and that one must marry within the faith.

More liberal Zoroastrians believe that conversion is legitimate and should even be encouraged.

F DEATH AND VULTURES

Zoroastrians believe that death is caused by the devil and is a temporary victory for the powers of evil. Demons are therefore present. The purpose of the funeral rites is to limit the spread of evil, and to avoid contamination. Dead bodies cannot be cremated, since fire is divinely created, and a focus of worship. Nor can they be buried, since the earth is holy and good, having been created by Ahura Mazda.

The solution is to allow the body to be eaten by vultures and crows, birds which, it is thought, were created by God for this purpose. Round structures (*dakhma*) are built, with high walls, but no roof. These were named by the British in India, "towers of silence." Often they are set on a hill, with gardens around. In Mumbai, where most of India's Parsis live, *dakhma* have been built on a hill in fifty-seven acres of forest gardens. They are places of peace.

When someone dies, the funeral takes place as quickly as possible. The body is washed and dressed. Mourners pray, and then the corpse is taken by bearers into the *dakhma*, where it is stripped and left. The mourners pray in a nearby building for about half an hour, then go home. For the next three days there are further ceremonies, and a gift is given to a charity.

Some time later, after the bones have been bleached by the sun, they are lowered into deep wells at the bottom of which are layers of charcoal, lime and other minerals that slowly dissolve the bones.

6 ZOROASTRIAN BELIEFS

A God: Ahura Mazda
B The six aspects of Ahura Mazda
C Good and evil
D Human beings
E The end times
F Creed
G Symbols

INTRODUCTION

In the tenth century AD Zoroaster's teaching was developed, and given a cosmological dimension. The traditional writings were translated into Middle Persian, the name Ahura Mazda becoming Ohrmazd and Angra Mainya becoming Ahriman.

A GOD: AHURA MAZDA

The single, supreme being is called Ahura Mazda meaning "Wise Lord." He is spirit, and cannot be represented by idols. Ahura Mazda is all good, and the source of all goodness. He created the world and everything in it. The world, therefore, is good. He is a personal God, the friend of human beings, and can be known personally. He is also a moral God, and the great Judge who will one day judge all humankind.

B THE SIX ASPECTS OF AHURA MAZDA

Ahura Mazda created a number of heavenly beings, the chief of which are called Beneficent Immortals (*Amesha Spentas*) Within the *Gathas*, these Immortals are sometimes described as concepts, and are sometimes personified. They reveal Zoroaster's understanding of the character of God.

Together the *Amesha Spentas* symbolize the way God works. Each one represents and is represented by one of six creations, which, taken together, represent the created earth.

- Asha Vahishta
  Asha Vahishta represents Justice/Truth. Fire is the earthly symbol for Asha.
- Vohu Manah

Vohu Manah is Good Mind/Righteous Thinking. He protects and is represented by cattle.

- Khshathra Vairya
  Khshathra Vairya is Desirable Dominion. He is the supreme creative power of God and sustains creation. His earthly symbol is metal. He also stands for the kingdom to come.

- Armaiti
  Armaiti is Devotion. He represents earth.

- Haurvatat
  Haurvatat is Wholeness and represents water.

- Ameretat
  Ameretat represents Immortality and is symbolized by plants.

All these good qualities, which are part of Ahura Mazda, can be earned and possessed by his followers.

C GOOD AND EVIL

Zoroastrians today belief in the dualism of good and evil either as a cosmic battle between Ahura Mazda and an evil spirit of violence and death, Angra Mainyu, or as an ethical dualism within the human consciousness.

In the teaching of Zoroaster, in the beginning God created two spirits who met together and were given the freedom to choose "life or not life." One chose life, and the other evil, and this gave birth to the good and evil principles in the world. The evil spirit, called Anghra Mainya, meaning "Destructive Spirit," is the embodiment of evil and the creator of all destructive things, of chaos, violence and of the kingdom of the lie. The wise Lord will ultimately triumph, and banish the spirit of evil.

Since it could not be conceived that Anghra Mainya could create evil, a dualism developed in which there are two equal powers from the beginning of time. In Middle Persian texts, Ahriman (the evil power) was trapped in this earth, which became a cosmic battleground between good and evil. At first, the forces were evenly balanced, but with the birth of Zoroaster and the revelation of the Good Religion, the triumph of Ormazd became certain.

Ohrmazd's victory will only take place, however, after a further three thousand years of cataclysmic conflict. During this time, three saviors are born, at one-thousand year intervals. Finally Ohrmazd will become supreme. The third savior will rise from the dead and bring in the final judgment. "In the last turn of creation" the world will be renewed and inhabited by the good people who will live in paradise.

D HUMAN BEINGS

Human beings, having been created by Ahura Mazda, are basically good: there is no teaching about original sin. They are morally responsible and at every moment freely choose between good and evil. They are free to join forces with Ahura Mazda in the battle against evil, or can live against their good nature and make evil choices. Their duty is to make their bodies the dwelling place of the good Spirits. Their motive for doing good is the reward of eternal life in heaven.

E THE END TIMES

The *Gathas* are permeated by eschatological thinking. In the end times there will be a judgment and a mighty conflagration. The dead will be raised and judged by Ahura Mazda. The wicked will go to hell, and the good to a kingdom of everlasting light and joy. This will happen to all people: irrespective of social position. As a result of this teaching,

Zoroaster was persecuted by the priests and nobility, who wanted to keep heaven for themselves.

The Middle Persian translations explain that there are two judgments. The first will come soon after death, when individual human beings are judged on their good and bad actions. Those whose good actions outweigh the bad pass into heaven; the bad will go to hell. The second judgment will come after the final resurrection of the dead.

Hell, however, is akin to the Roman Catholic view of Purgatory. Since human beings are ultimately good, after correction and punishment, all people will be restored to a life of bliss with Ormazd.

F CREED

The creed is summarized in *Yasna 12*, which was probably composed by Zarathushtra himself.

1
I curse the Daevas. I declare myself a Mazda-worshiper, a supporter of Zarathushtra, hostile to the Daevas, fond of Ahura's teaching, a praiser of the Amesha Spentas, a worshiper of the Amesha Spentas. I ascribe all good to Ahura Mazda, "and all the best," the Asha-owning one, splendid, arena-owning, whose is the cow, whose is Asha, whose is the light, "may whose blissful areas be filled with light."

2
I choose the good Spenta Armaiti for myself; let her be mine. I renounce the theft and robbery of the cow, and the damaging and plundering of the Mazdayasnian settlements.

3
I want freedom of movement and freedom of dwelling for those with homesteads, to those who dwell upon this earth with their cattle. With reverence for Asha, and (offerings) offered up, I vow this: I shall nevermore damage or plunder the Mazdayasnian settlements, even if I have to risk life and limb.

4

I reject the authority of the Daevas, the wicked, no-good, lawless, evil-knowing, the most druj-like of beings, the foulest of beings, the most damaging of beings. I reject the Daevas and their comrades, I reject the demons (*yatu*) and their comrades; I reject any who harm beings. I reject them with my thoughts, words, and deeds. I reject them publicly.

Even as I reject the head (authorities), so too do I reject the hostile followers of the *druj*.

5

As Ahura Mazda taught Zarathushtra at all discussions, at all meetings, at which Mazda and Zarathushtra conversed – even as Zarathushtra rejected the authority of the Daevas, so I also reject, as Mazda-worshiper and supporter of Zarathushtra, the authority of the Daevas, even as he, the Asha-owning Zarathushtra, has rejected them.

6

As the belief of the waters, the belief of the plants, the belief of the well-made (Original) Cow; as the belief of Ahura Mazda who created the cow and the Asha-owning Man; as the belief of Zarathushtra, the belief of Kavi Vishtaspa, the belief of both Frashaostra and Jamaspa; as the belief of each of the Saoshyants (saviors) fulfilling destiny and Asha-owning – so I am a Mazda-worshiper of this belief and teaching.

7

I profess myself a Mazda-worshiper, a Zoroastrian, having vowed it and professed it. I pledge myself to the well-thought thought, I pledge myself to the well-spoken word, I pledge myself to the well-done action.

8

I pledge myself to the Mazdayasnian religion, which causes the attack to be put off and weapons put down; which upholds khvaetvadatha (kin-marriage), which possesses Asha; which of all religions that exist or shall be, is the greatest, the best, and the most beautiful: Ahuric, Zoroastrian. I ascribe all good to Ahura Mazda. This is the creed of the Mazdayasnian religion.

Yasna 12

G SYMBOLS: FIRE AND "ASHA"

Fire, as a symbol of "Asha" and the "original light of God," holds a special place of esteem in the religion. Prayer often takes place in front of a fire, and consecrated fires are kept perpetually burning in the major temples.

7 Worship

A Sacred fire
B Festivals

(i) New Year's Day festival
(ii) The birthday of Zarathustra, Khordad Saal
(iii) Zarthost No Deeso

INTRODUCTION

Prayers are recited daily from the *Khorda Avesta*. Prayer usually takes place in the Avestan language.

A SACRED FIRE

Fire, symbolizing Truth, is an integral part of Zoroastrian worship. Zoroastrians worship through prayers and symbolic ceremonies that are conducted before a sacred fire, which also symbolizes their God.

B FESTIVALS

The faithful participate in seasonal communal festivals (*Gahambars*) during the year.

(I) NEW YEAR'S DAY FESTIVAL

This is the most important of the Parsi Festivals. Most Parsis in India now celebrate it in August. On the New Year Day festival people flock to the Fire Temples, meet relatives and go to the theater in the evening.

(II) THE BIRTHDAY OF ZARATHUSTRA (KHORDAD SAAL)

Khordad Saal falls on the sixth day in the first month of the Parsi year, around August/September.

(III) ZARTHOST NO DEESO

Zarthost No Deeso takes place in June and is the day on which the death anniversary of the prophet symbolically falls. Special prayers are recited and Zoroastrians go to the Fire Temple to pray.

8 Groupings within Zoroastrianism

There are two main groups within Zoroastrianism:

• Parsis
• Gabars.

The Parsis are the far bigger group.

9 GLOSSARY

Ahunawad
Name of the first *Gatha* and name of the first *Gatha* day.

Ahunwar
The holiest prayer of the Zoroastrians.

Ahura Mazda
God, literally, "Wise Lord," the supreme being of Zoroastrians.

Asha
A fundamental concept of Zoroastrianism; there is no adequate translation, although the following are often used: world-order, truth, right, righteousness, holiness.

Ashem vohu
One of the most sacred prayers of Zoroastrianism, which praises *Asha*.

Avesta
The holy scriptures of Zoroastrianism.

Gatha
The sacred hymns of Zarathushtra (*Yasna* chapters 28-34, 43-51, 53), part of the *Avesta*; the five supplementary days at the end of the Zoroastrian religious calendar.

Godavara
One of the Gujarat ecclesiastical groups of priests, serving a large rural area, with headquarters in Anklesar.

Ilm-i Khshnoom
An occult movement within Zoroastrianism.

Indar
Name of a demon.

Khorda Avesta
The "Small Avesta," a prayer book with excerpts from the *Avesta*.

Kusti
Sacred cord worn around the waist by Zoroastrians; the short ritual of untying and retying the *kusti*.

Manthra
Holy Word; specific passages of the *Avesta* that have poetic and spiritual properties.

Padyab-kusti
A ritual ablution followed by the ritual untying and retying of the kusti.

Parsis
Zoroastrians who settled in India.

Sudreh
Sacred shirt.

Yasna
One of the divisions of the *Avesta*; the name of a high liturgical service in which the text of the *Yasna* is recited.

Zarathushtra (the Greek form is Zoroaster)
Name of the founder of Zoroastrianism.

Zoroastrianism
The religion founded by Zarathushtra, the oldest of the great prophetic religions.

Zot
Officiating priest.

ATHEISM, AGNOSTICISM, AND NON-RELIGIOUS WORLDVIEWS

CONTENTS

1   Non-religious worldviews   477

2   Famous agnostics   480

3   Sound-bites against God   481

4   Arguments for the existence of God   482

5   Answering atheists   484

1 NON-RELIGIOUS WORLDVIEWS

A Agnosticism
B Atheism
C Facts and figures
D Ethical culturalism
E Humanism
F "Why I am a non-believer"

INTRODUCTION

It is has been estimated that only about 15% of the world population is non-religious or anti-religious.

A AGNOSTICISM

Agnosticism is a belief that we can neither prove nor disprove the existence of God.

> Agnosticism is a term invented by Thomas Henry Huxley in 1869 to denote the philosophical and religious attitude of those who claim that metaphysical ideas can be neither proved nor disproved. Huxley wrote, "I neither affirm nor deny the immortality of man. I see no reason for believing it, but on the other hand, I have no means of disproving it. I have no a priori objection to the doctrine.
> The Cambridge Dictionary of Philosophy
> *2nd Edition, Robert Audi, General Editor*

B ATHEISM

Atheists are certain about one thing: they believe that God does not exist. They do not believe there is any evidence for the existence of a god or gods.

> Being an atheist . . . means not knowing the true nature of created reality but

absolutizing it, and therefore "idolizing" it, instead of considering it a mark of the Creator and the path that leads to him."
> *John Paul II*

C FACTS AND FIGURES

About 7% of the population of America call themselves atheistic or agnostic.

This means that America has more atheists and agnostics than Mormons (by a 3 to 1 margin), Jews (by a 4 to 1 margin) or Muslims (by a 14 to 1 margin). A typical atheist or agnostic living in America will be a white man, under the age of thirty-five, who lives in the north-east or west.

D ETHICAL CULTURALISM

Felix Adler (1851-1933) founded this movement by suggesting that religious beliefs and religious practices should be replaced by a system of secular ethics.

E HUMANISM

INTRODUCTION
Humanism has been called the major modern philosophical enemy of Christianity.

Humanists, who are most often atheists or agnostics, have created an ethical system, not based on Christian or any religious principles, but based upon human reason and logic. In Humanism, humanity is the measure of all things. Humanists usually emphasize the importance of doing good in society.

ITS SCOPE
It is behind a number of other philosophies:

- scientism
- secularism
- naturalism
- materialism
- Satanism
- feminism
- hedonism.

HUMANISM AND AREAS OF CONFLICT
Absolutes
Are morals absolute? Are there any absolute truths? If there is no God there is no reason to believe in any unchanging standards of morality. All standards are relative.

Three basic errors in the humanist philosophy:

(i) Humanism affirms the self-sufficiency of man.
The Gospel says that man can find sufficiency only in God (John 15:15; Philippians 4:13).

(ii) Humanism says that human beings are essentially good.
If the Christian concept of sin is done away with, we are not accountable to God. If people are basically good, who is to challenge the conclusion that whatever we do is also basically good? The gospel says man is a sinner before God and in need of salvation (Mark 7:21; Romans 3:23).

(iii) Humanism believes that this life is the only one.
The gospel asserts that there is life beyond the grave, and that there will be a final judgment (Matthew 25:46; John 5:28-29).

CONSEQUENCES OF HUMANISM
In Humanism, people become their own saviors, so teaching about sin, repentance, and

judgment is out of date. The world has grown beyond that kind of religion, and no church is relevant if it keeps harping on about personal salvation. Humankind needs to save the human family by getting involved with a total commitment to massive humanitarian projects.

Humanists have so asserted their views that previously held Christian standards in marriage, and Christian teaching about divorce, abortion and euthanasia are now being constantly attacked and laws changed in favor of Humanist ideas.

CONCLUSION
Our world is now dominated by ideas that stem from Humanism. Christian values are constantly being derided and undermined by Humanists.

HUMANIST MANIFESTO

(i)   Humanists regard the universe as self-existing and not created.
(ii)   Humanists believe that human beings are a part of nature and have emerged as the result of a continuous process (evolution).
(iii)   Moral values derive their source from human experience. Ethics is autonomous and situational, needing no theological or ideological sanction.
(iv)   Traditional religions inhibit men and women from experiencing their full potentialities.
(v)   We can discover no divine purpose or providence for the human species. We are entirely responsible for what we are or will become. No deity will save us – we must save ourselves.

F "WHY I AM A NON-BELIEVER"
The following are reasons that members and supporters of Gay and Lesbian Atheists and Humanists (GALAH) have given for why they are atheists, agnostics, and/or humanists:

I think that reality (the truth) should be found through reflective open questioning, which religion inhibits.

I slowly became aware that some, many,

then most religious ideas, rules, etc. could not be rationally explained. It was an evolutionary process.

There is too much evil in the world to believe in an all-good God.

I am an Atheist because I think. I am an Atheist because I think that the Truth should reflect that which is true. I am an Atheist because I think that truth can never be assumed: evidence and explanations are required, and alternate possibilities need to be examined. I am an Atheist because I think that dogma hinders open, honest communication, and is therefore dishonest and destructive. I think that dishonesty is immoral – the end does not justify the means. I think that destructiveness –physical and mental – is what religion is really about. I am an Atheist because I think.

I have doubts about established religions.

Nearly everyone who seems to believe in god has been indoctrinated from an early age. A few "original" religionists seem to have had "divine" revelations. I do not fit in either category. It also seems to me that the concerns of religionists are trivia.

The religious view of the world seems incredible to me. People who have informed me about the "truth" of the Bible have proven their unreliability via other means.

I am a humanist because I have observed that people can develop compassionate moral values without relying on supernatural belief systems.

The Bible is wrong about homosexuality. That was the inspiration for me to question other things in that book.

Because I do reason, that is, THINK! How could anyone who thinks, by which I mean "to subject to the processes of logical thought" ever commit the abomination of faith as in "firm belief in something for which there is no proof?"

Reasons why I am an atheist:
1 I'm interested more in the here and now and not in the hereafter.
2 "The proper study of mankind is man."
—Alexander Pope
3 Trusting in the unknown is folly.

2 Famous Agnostics

Charles Darwin

Charles Darwin, a 19th century British self-taught geologist and writer. He attended a course in theology at Christ's College, Cambridge. Darwin wrote in two places in his book *Life and Letters* about his personal faith: "The mystery of the beginning of all things is insoluble by us; and I for one must be content to remain an Agnostic."

"I think an Agnostic would be the more correct description of my state of mind. The whole subject [of God] is beyond the scope of man's intellect."

Thomas H. Huxley

Thomas H. Huxley, a well known English religious skeptic, invented the term agnostic in the 1840s. He combined "a" which implies negative, with "gnostic" which is a Greek word meaning knowledge. In 1899, he wrote:

> . . . every man should be able to give a reason for the faith that is in him; it is the great principle of Descartes; it is the fundamental axiom of modern science. Positively the principle may be expressed: In matters of the intellect, follow your reason as far as it will take you, without regard to any other consideration. And negatively: In matters of the intellect do not pretend that conclusions are certain which are not demonstrated or demonstrable. That I take to be the agnostic faith, which if a man keep whole and undefiled, he shall not be ashamed to look the universe in the face, whatever the future may have in store for him.
>
> *Thomas H. Huxley,* Agnosticism*, 1889*

Huxley also wrote:

> When I reached intellectual maturity, and began to ask myself whether I was an atheist, a theist, or a pantheist; a materialist or an idealist; a Christian or a freethinker, I found that the more I

learned and reflected, the less ready was the answer; until at last I came to the conclusion that I had neither art nor part with any of these denominations, except the last . . . So I took thought, and invented what I conceived to be the appropriate title of "agnostic." It came into my head as suggestively antithetic to the "gnostic" of Church history, who professed to know so much about the very things of which I was ignorant . . ."

> *Thomas H. Huxley,* Agnosticism*, 1889*

Robert G. Ingersoll

Robert G. Ingersoll was a famous nineteenth-century American agnostic.

Commenting on the problem of theodicy, the presence of evil in a universe that many people believe was created and is run by God, he wrote:

> There is no subject – and can be none – concerning which any human being is under any obligation to believe without evidence. The man who, without prejudice, reads and understands the Old and New Testaments will cease to be an orthodox Christian. The intelligent man who investigates the religion of any country without fear and without prejudice will not and cannot be a believer. He who cannot harmonize the cruelties of the Bible with the goodness of Jehovah, cannot harmonize the cruelties of Nature with the goodness and wisdom of a supposed Deity. He will find it impossible to account for pestilence and famine, for earthquake and storm, for slavery, for the triumph of the strong over the weak, for the countless victories of injustice. He will find it impossible to account for martyrs – for the burning of the good, the noble, the loving, by the ignorant, the malicious, and the infamous.

> *R. G. Ingersoll,* Why I am an Agnostic

3 SOUND-BITES AGAINST RELIGION AND CHRISTIANITY

Atheists, agnostics, and others against religion have been very vocal in speaking out against religion in general and against Christianity in particular. Here is a selection of some of their sound-bites.

The divinity of Jesus is made a convenient cover for absurdity.
John Adams, U.S. President

This would be the best of all possible worlds, if there were no religion in it.
John Adams, U.S. President

Every sensible man, every honorable man, must hold the Christian sect in horror.
Francois Marie Arouet ("Voltaire") French author and playwright

Christianity is the most ridiculous, the most absurd and bloody religion that has ever infected the world.
Francois Marie Arouet ("Voltaire") French author and playwright

Nothing can be more contrary to religion and the clergy than reason and common sense.
Francois Marie Arouet ("Voltaire") French author and playwright

I am an atheist, out and out. It took me a long time to say it. I've been an atheist for years and years, but somehow I felt it was intellectually unrespectable to say that one is an atheist, because it assumed knowledge that one didn't have. Somehow it was better to say one was a humanist or agnostic. I don't have the evidence to prove that God doesn't exist, but I so strongly suspect that he doesn't that I don't want to waste my time.
Isaac Asimov, Russian-born American author

All religions have been made by men.
Napoleon Bonaparte, French emperor

Religion is just mind control.
George Carlin, comedian

I don't believe in God. My god is patriotism. Teach a man to be a good citizen and you have solved the problem of life.
Andrew Carnegie, Scottish-born American industrialist and philanthropist

It may be that our role on this planet is not to worship God, but to create him.
Arthur C. Clarke, author

Religion is a byproduct of fear. For much of human history, it may have been a necessary evil, but why was it more evil than necessary? Isn't killing people in the name of God a pretty good definition of insanity?
Arthur C. Clarke, author

If there is a God, he is a malign thug.
Samuel Clemens ("Mark Twain") American author and humorist

I do not consider it an insult, but rather a compliment, to be called an agnostic. I do not pretend to know where many ignorant men are sure.
Clarence Darrow, American lawyer

I believe that religion is the belief in future life and in God. I don't believe in either. I don't believe in God as I don't believe in Mother Goose.
Clarence Darrow, American lawyer

The mystery of the beginning of all things is insoluble by us, and I for one must be content to remain an agnostic.
Charles Darwin, English naturalist

I cannot believe in the immortality of the soul . . . No, all this talk of an existence for us, as individuals, beyond the grave is wrong. It is born of our tenacity of life

–our desire to go on living – our dread of coming to an end.

Thomas Edison, American inventor

I do not believe in a personal God and I have never denied this but have expressed it clearly. If something is in me which can be called religion then it is the unbounded admiration for the structure of the world so far as our science can reveal it.

Albert Einstein, German-born American physicist

I do not believe in the immortality of the individual, and I consider ethics to be an exclusively human concern with no superhuman authority behind it.

Albert Einstein, German-born American physicist

Neither in my private life nor in my writings, have I ever made a secret of being an out-and-out unbeliever.

Sigmund Freud, German-born psychologist

Religion is comparable to a childhood neurosis.

Sigmund Freud, German-born psychologist

The first requisite for the happiness of the people is the abolition of religion.

Karl Marx

Religion . . . is the first enemy of the ability to think. . . . Faith is the worst curse of mankind, as the exact antithesis and enemy of thought.

Ayn Rand, novelist

I turned to speak to God,
About the world's despair;
But to make bad matters worse,
I found God wasn't there.

Robert Frost, American poet

All thinking men are atheists.

Ernest Hemingway, American author

That it is wrong for a man to say he is certain of the objective truth of a proposition unless he can provide evidence which logically justifies that certainty. This is what agnosticism asserts and in my opinion, is all that is essential to agnosticism.

Thomas Henry Huxley, English biologist

I do not find in orthodox Christianity one redeeming feature.

Thomas Jefferson, U.S. President

Religions are all alike – founded upon fables and mythologies.

Thomas Jefferson, U.S. President

The wretchedness of religion is at once an expression and a protest against real wretchedness. Religion is the sigh of the oppressed creature, the feeling of a heartless world, just as it is the spirit of unspiritual conditions. It is the opium of the people.

Karl Marx, German economist and political philosopher

The Christian faith from the beginning, is sacrifice: the sacrifice of all freedom, all pride, all self-confidence of spirit; it is at the same time subjection, a self-derision, and self-mutilation.

Freidrich Nietzsche, German philosopher

All national institutions of churches, whether Jewish, Christian or Turkish, appear to me no other than human inventions, set up to terrify and enslave mankind, and monopolize power and profit.

Thomas Paine, American revolutionary

Religion is based . . . mainly on fear . . . fear of the mysterious, fear of defeat, fear of death. Fear is the parent of cruelty, and therefore it is no wonder if cruelty and religion have gone hand in hand. . . . My own view on religion is that of Lucretius. I regard it as a disease born of fear and as a source of untold misery to the human race.

Bertrand Russell, British philosopher

Fear is the parent of cruelty, therefore it is no wonder if religion and cruelty have gone hand-in-hand.
Bertrand Russell, British philosopher

The idea of God is the sole wrong for which I cannot forgive mankind.
Marquis de Sade, French libertine

My view is that if there is no evidence for it, then forget about it. An agnostic is somebody who doesn't believe in something until there is evidence for it, so I'm agnostic.
Carl Sagan, American astronomer and author

At present there is not a single credible established religion in the world.
George Bernard Shaw, Irish-born English playwright

If God has spoken, why is the world not convinced?
Percy Bysshe Shelley, English poet

By the year 2000, we will, I hope, raise our children to believe in human potential, not God.
Gloria Steinem, women's rights activist

I do not believe in the divinity of Christ, and there are many other of the postulates of the orthodox creed to which I cannot subscribe.
William Howard Taft, US President

---

4 ARGUMENTS FOR THE EXISTENCE OF GOD

INTRODUCTION

The existence of God is taken for granted in the Bible. It does not spend time attempting to "prove" God's existence. He who disbelieves this truth is spoken of as one devoid of understanding (Psalm 14:1). The KJV of Psalm 14:1 reads, "The fool hath said in his heart, There is no God."

THEOLOGICAL ARGUMENTS IN FAVOR OF GOD'S EXISTENCE

- The cosmological argument
- The cosmological argument shows that there must be a First Cause of all things, as every effect must have a cause.
- The teleological argument
- The teleological, or the argument from design, shows that we see everywhere work of an intelligent Cause in nature.
- The anthropological argument

The anthropological, or moral, argument, points to moral consciousness and the history of humankind, which shows a moral order and purpose. This can only be explained if God exists.

First, that human beings, all over the earth, have this curious idea that they ought to behave in a certain way, and cannot really get rid of it. Secondly, that they do not in fact behave in that way. They know the Law of Nature; they break it. These two facts are the foundation of all clear thinking about ourselves and the universe we live in.
C. S. Lewis, Mere Christianity (London: Collins, 1961)

Pascal's wager
Pascal, the brilliant French mathematician and apologist, essentially said that if the atheist is right, then both he and the Christian will die and that will be it. But if the Christian is right, the atheist has everything to lose and the Christian everything to gain.

5 ANSWERING ATHEISTS

INTRODUCTION

The apostle Paul wrote: "Dear friends, although I was very eager to write to you about the salvation we share, I felt I had to write and urge you to contend for the faith that was once for all entrusted to the saints" (Jude 1.3).

Christians should have something to say about their faith.

A QUESTION FOR ATHEISTS

Atheists may ask for proof of God's existence. It is fair to ask an atheist the following question: "If someone managed to prove to you that God does exist, do you think that you would want to know him for yourself?"

Some people just do not want to know God as Jesus said to his own disciples, "But as I told you, you have seen me and still you do not believe" (John 6:36). They had witnessed Jesus' miracles and still did not believe that he was God's Son.

CREATION

To those with the eyes to see, the eyes of faith, God has demonstrated his existence through creation: "For since the creation of the world God's invisible qualities – his eternal power and divine nature – have been clearly seen, being understood from what has been made, so that men are without excuse" (Romans 1:20).

Should we have some sympathy for atheists? They may have been misled by:

- False teachings about Christianity
- Man-made religions

PART TWO

CULTS

CONTENTS

Four traditional "Christian" cults

Mormonism

Jehovah's Witnesses

Christian Science

Christadelphianism

Other cults

Apocalyptic cults

Hare Krishna

New Age Movement

Scientology

Swedenborgianism

The Family/Children of God

Theosophy

Transcendental Meditation

Unification Church (Moonies)

Unity School of Christianity

Way International

Other trails

Freemasonry

Seventh-Day Adventists

Worldwide Church of God

INTRODCTION

A cult, then, is a group of people polarized around someone's interpretation of the Bible and is characterized by major deviations from orthodox Christianity relative to the cardinal doctrines of the Christian faith, particularly the fact that God became man in Jesus Christ.

Walter Martin, The Rise of the Cults

. . . if you believe in it, it is a religion or perhaps 'the' religion; and if you do not care one way or another about it, it is a sect; but if you fear and hate it, it is a cult.

Leo Pfeffer

This quotation turns on the confusion many people feel about these words, and their consequent misuse.

The terms, "denomination," "sect," and "cult" have different meanings but the boundaries are often unclear. It also depends upon what you define as "historic teaching". some Roman Catholics view Protestant churches in the same light as Protestants view modern sects. Some would say that the seventh-day Adventists, for example, are more a sect or denomination than a cult. Others, that the Freemasons are more a social than religious organization. This section follows the general consensus in evengelical thinking.

DENOMINATION

A denomination is a particular branch of a church. According to *The Shorter Oxford Dictionary,* a denomination is "A religious . . . body designated by a distinctive name." Methodists and Baptists, for example, are denominations or branches within Christianity.

SECTS

A body of persons who unite in holding certain views differing from those of others who are accounted to be of the same religion.

The Shorter Oxford Dictionary

A sect is a small religious group that is an offshoot of an established religion or denomination. It holds most beliefs in common with its religion of origin, but has a number of novel concepts that differentiate it from that religion.

Christians usually use the term "sect" to refer to heretical offshoots of Christianity, such as the Mormons or Jehovah's Witnesses.

CULTS

Devotion to a particular person or thing.

The Shorter Oxford Dictionary

Today, the words "cult" and "sect" are often used as synonyms.

Traditionally, Christians have used the word "cult" to refer to groups that have few Christian characteristics. As with the section on World Religions, writings are quoted for the readers to make up their own mind.

HERESY AND THE NEW TESTAMENT: "REFUTE" AND "SILENCE" THEM

One of the most neglected aspects of the teaching of the New Testament is its emphasis on promoting truth and opposing evil. The seasoned apostle Paul longs for Titus to be an effective Christian leader on the island of Crete. He tells Titus to appoint elders and lists the spiritual qualities that Titus must look for. Paul's list of qualifications for an elder include the following stipulation: "He must hold firmly to the trustworthy message as it has been taught, so that he can encourage others by sound doctrine and refute those who oppose it" (Titus 1:9). Where are all the Christian pastors and teachers who not only encourage their fellow-Christians by passing on "sound doctrine," but are also able to "refute" those who attack the Christian gospel? And, of course, no one can refute what he does not know about.

It seems rather uncharitable to say that it is the task of Christian preachers to "silence" people who promote false teaching. Yet Paul goes on to tell Titus:

> For there are many rebellious people, mere talkers and deceivers, especially those of the circumcision group. They must be *silenced*, because they are ruining whole households by teaching things they ought not to teach–and that for the sake of dishonest gain. Even one of their own prophets has said, 'Cretans are always liars, evil brutes, lazy gluttons.' This testimony is true. Therefore, rebuke them sharply, so that they will be sound in the faith and will pay no attention to Jewish myths or to the commands of those who reject the truth. To the pure, all things are pure, but to those who are corrupted and do not believe, nothing is pure. In fact, both their minds and consciences are corrupted. They claim to know God, but by their actions they deny him. They are detestable, disobedient and unfit for doing anything good.
>
> *Titus 1:10-16*

"DIFFERENT" GOSPELS

Quite a good definition of sects and cults would be "different gospels." The apostle Paul becomes white-hot with righteous anger when he writes to the Galatians, who have been taken in, he says, by a "different" (Galatians 1:6) gospel. He tells them that they have been bewitched! "You foolish Galatians! Who has bewitched you?" (Galatians 3:1). But Paul is not content with this situation. He launches into a devastating attack on these false teachers:

> I am astonished that you are so quickly deserting the one who called you by the grace of Christ and are turning to a different gospel-which is really no gospel at all. Evidently some people are throwing you into confusion and are trying to pervert the gospel of Christ. But even if we or an angel from heaven should preach a gospel other than the one we preached to you, let him be eternally condemned! As we have already said, so now I say again: If anybody is preaching to you a gospel other than what you accepted, let him be eternally condemned!
>
> *Galatians 1:6-9*

Of course, such "different" gospels are not gospels at all. The errors of today's cults have to be treated in exactly the same way as by Paul in his day. They need to be analyzed, compared with Christian teaching, and exposed. Those who teach heresy must be halted in their attempts to throw people into confusion and "pervert the gospel." As John Calvin said, "A dog barks when his master is attacked. I would be a coward if I saw that God's Truth is attacked and yet remained silent without giving the sound."

MORMONISM

CONTENTS

1 An overview   491

2 Mormon's founder   492

3 Mormon holy book   505

4 Facts and figures   517

5 Mormon practices   518

6 Mormon beliefs   520

7 Worship   524

1 AN OVERVIEW

DEFINITION OF A MORMON

Someone who accepts Joseph Smith as a prophet and the book of Mormon as an inspired message from God.

Factfile
- Date of origin: 1830
- Founder: Joseph Smith
- Holy book: KJV Bible, and the *Book of Mormon*
- Number of adherents: 13 million

SUMMARY

The Church of Jesus Christ of Latter-day Saints, LDS, is commonly known by the name of the Mormon Church.

The Mormon Church claims to be the "true Church." Originally, the name revealed to Joseph Smith, was "the Church of Christ." But four years later, on April 3, 1830, a different name was given: "The Church of the Latter-day Saints."

In April of 1834, in a third revelation, the name was changed to, "Church of Jesus Christ of Latter-day Saints."

SUMMARY OF BELIEFS

The Lutheran Church, at its Missouri Synod, rejected the Mormon Church as a true Christian Church on the following grounds:

The Lutheran Church, together with the vast majority of Christian denominations in the United States, does not regard the Mormon church as a Christian church. The official writings of Mormonism deny a number of the basic teachings of orthodox Christianity.

The Nicene Creed confesses the biblical truth that Jesus Christ, the second Person of the Trinity, is "of one substance with the Father." This central article of the Christian faith is expressly rejected by Mormon teaching. For Mormons state that the three persons of the Trinity are "not . . . one being," but are "separate individuals." In addition, the Father is regarded as having a body "of flesh and bone." Such teaching is contrary to the Holy Scriptures, destructive to the Gospel of Jesus Christ, and indicative of the fact that Mormon teaching is not Christian.

The Lutheran Church, Missouri Synod

2 MORMON'S FOUNDER

A   Joseph Smith
B   *Joseph Smith History*
C   Failed prophecies

INTRODUCTION
Joseph Smith (December 23, 1805-June 27, 1844) was the founder and leader of the Latter Day Saint movement,

A JOSEPH SMITH
Joseph Smith was born in Vermont and raised in upstate New York near a town called Palmyra.

VISIONS
Smith began receiving visions in 1820, at age fourteen. In these visions, he was told it was his mission to restore the church of Jesus Christ on earth.

In 1823 Joseph had a heavenly visitation in which an angel named Moroni told him of a sacred history of the ancient peoples of America. Written in America by ancient Hebrews, it had been engraved in an Egyptian dialect on tablets of gold and buried in a nearby hill. Joseph was told that it was his mission to tell the world about this history. In 1827, he obtained these gold plates from the angel and translated them into English by the spirit of God and with the aid of a sacred instrument accompanying the plates called the "Urim and Thummim."

FOUNDING THE MORMON CHURCH
According to Cowdery and Smith, on May 15, 1829, they both received the Aaronic Priesthood by laying on of hands from John the Baptist and then using this priesthood, they baptized each other by immersion. The apostles Peter, James, and John also came to them between May and June 1829 and ordained them to the Melchizedek Priesthood. Latter Day Saints believe that these events were necessary for the restoration of the Church.

On April 6, 1830, Smith and five others formally established "The Church of Christ" (later officially named The Church of Jesus Christ of Latter-day Saints) under New York state laws. Joseph Smith said:

> I have more to boast of than every any man had. I am the only man that has ever been able to keep a whole church together since the days of Adam. Neither Paul, John, Peter, nor Jesus ever did it. I boast that no man ever did such a work as I. The followers of Jesus ran away from Him; but the Latter-day Saints never ran away from me yet.
>
> *Joseph Smith*

SMITH'S MARTYRDOM
In 1844 Smith announced that he was going to run for President of the United States on an anti-slavery platform. This announcement aroused great antagonism against the Mormons. This intensified when a newspaper controlled by Mormon dissenters revealed the Mormon practice of polygamy. Smith was furious about this revelation, and he ordered the destruction of the newspaper's press. He was arrested for inciting a riot and was imprisoned in Carthage, Illinois. Before he could be tried, a mob broke into the jail and brutally killed both him and his brother.

Joseph Smith's followers revere him as a prophet and also a martyr. He was the first candidate to be assassinated during a US presidential campaign.

B JOSEPH SMITH HISTORY
According to the Mormons, "In 1820 young Joseph Smith prayed to know which church he should join. In answer to his prayer, God the Father and Jesus Christ appeared to him.

Through him they restored the truth about the plan of God. Joseph Smith was a prophet and a powerful witness of Christ. Here is his story in his own words."

The following is the *Joseph Smith History* which is part of *The Pearl of Great Price,* the fourth book among the Mormon sacred books. The headings have been added to clarify significant moments in Joseph Smith's life and are not part of the original book.

OWING TO THE MANY REPORTS

1 Owing to the many reports which have been put in circulation by evil-disposed and designing persons, in relation to the rise and progress of the Church of Jesus Christ of Latter-day Saints, all of which have been designed by the authors thereof to militate against its character as a Church and its progress in the world – I have been induced to write this history, to disabuse the public mind, and put all inquirers after truth in possession of the facts, as they have transpired, in relation both to myself and the Church, so far as I have such facts in my possession.

1838

2 In this history I shall present the various events in relation to this Church, in truth and righteousness, as they have transpired, or as they at present exist, being now [1838] the eighth year since the organization of the said Church.

BORN DECEMBER 25, 1805

3 I was born in the year of our Lord one thousand eight hundred and five, on the twenty-third day of December, in the town of Sharon, Windsor county, State of Vermont . . . My father, Joseph Smith, Sen., left the State of Vermont, and moved to Palmyra, Ontario (now Wayne) county, in the State of New York, when I was in my tenth year, or thereabouts. In about four years after my father's arrival in Palmyra, he moved with his family into Manchester in the same county of Ontario.

FAMILY MEMBERS

4 His family consisting of eleven souls, namely, my father, Joseph Smith; my mother, Lucy Smith (whose name, previous to her marriage, was Mack, daughter of Solomon Mack); my brothers, Alvin (who died November 19th, 1823, in the 26th year of his age), Hyrum, myself, Samuel Harrison, William, Don Carlos; and my sisters, Sophronia, Catherine, and Lucy.

EXCITEMENT DURING SECOND YEAR IN MANCHESTER

5 Some time in the second year after our removal to Manchester, there was in the place where we lived an unusual excitement on the subject of religion. It commenced with the Methodists, but soon became general among all the sects in that region of country. Indeed, the whole district of country seemed affected by it, and great multitudes united themselves to the different religious parties, which created no small stir and division amongst the people, some crying, "Lo, here!" and others, "Lo, there!" Some were contending for the Methodist faith, some for the Presbyterian, and some for the Baptist.

CONTENTION

6 For, notwithstanding the great love which the converts to these different faiths expressed at the time of their conversion, and the great zeal manifested by the respective clergy, who were active in getting up and promoting this extraordinary scene of religious feeling, in order to have everybody converted, as they were pleased to call it, let them join what sect they pleased; yet when the converts began to file off, some to one party and some to another, it was seen that the seemingly good feelings of both the priests and the converts were more pretended than real; for a scene of great confusion and bad feeling ensued – priest contending against priest, and convert against convert; so that all their good

feelings one for another, if they ever had any, were entirely lost in a strife of words and a contest about opinions.

7 I was at this time in my fifteenth year. My father's family was proselyted to the Presbyterian faith, and four of them joined that church, namely, my mother, Lucy; my brothers Hyrum and Samuel Harrison; and my sister Sophronia.

JOSEPH REFLECTS, PARTIAL TO METHODISTS

8 During this time of great excitement my mind was called up to serious reflection and great uneasiness; but though my feelings were deep and often poignant, still I kept myself aloof from all these parties, though I attended their several meetings as often as occasion would permit. In process of time my mind became somewhat partial to the Methodist sect, and I felt some desire to be united with them; but so great were the confusion and strife among the different denominations, that it was impossible for a person young as I was, and so unacquainted with men and things, to come to any certain conclusion who was right and who was wrong.

9 My mind at times was greatly excited, the cry and tumult were so great and incessant. The Presbyterians were most decided against the Baptists and Methodists, and used all the powers of both reason and sophistry to prove their errors, or, at least, to make the people think they were in error. On the other hand, the Baptists and Methodists in their turn were equally zealous in endeavoring to establish their own tenets and disprove all others.

10 In the midst of this war of words and tumult of opinions, I often said to myself: What is to be done? Who of all these parties are right; or, are they all wrong together? If any one of them be right, which is it, and how shall I know it?

ASK OF GOD

11 While I was laboring under the extreme difficulties caused by the contests of these parties of religionists, I was one day reading the Epistle of James, first chapter and fifth verse, which reads: If any of you lack wisdom, let him ask of God, that giveth to all men liberally, and upbraideth not; and it shall be given him.

12 Never did any passage of scripture come with more power to the heart of man than this did at this time to me: It seemed to enter with great force into every feeling of my heart. I reflected on it again and again, knowing that if any person needed wisdom from God, I did; for how to act I did not know, and unless I could get more wisdom than I then had, I would never know; for the teachers of religion of the different sects understood the same passages of scripture so differently as to destroy all confidence in settling the question by an appeal to the Bible.

13 At length I came to the conclusion that I must either remain in darkness and confusion, or else I must do as James directs, that is, ask of God. I at length came to the determination to "ask of God," concluding that if he gave wisdom to them that lacked wisdom, and would give liberally, and not upbraid, I might venture.

SPRING 1820 TO WOODS AND FIRST VOCAL PRAYER

14 So, in accordance with this, my determination to ask of God, I retired to the woods to make the attempt. It was on the morning of a beautiful, clear day, early in the spring of eighteen hundred and twenty. It was the first time in my life that I had made such an attempt, for amidst all my anxieties I had never as yet made the attempt to pray vocally.

SEIZED BY UNSEEN POWER

15 After I had retired to the place where I had previously designed to go, having looked around me, and finding myself

alone, I kneeled down and began to offer up the desires of my heart to God. I had scarcely done so, when immediately I was seized upon by some power which entirely overcame me, and had such an astonishing influence over me as to bind my tongue so that I could not speak. Thick darkness gathered around me, and it seemed to me for a time as if I were doomed to sudden destruction.

CALLS ON GOD

16 But, exerting all my powers to call upon God to deliver me out of the power of this enemy which had seized upon me, and at the very moment when I was ready to sink into despair and abandon myself to destruction – not to an imaginary ruin, but to the power of some actual being from the unseen world, who had such marvelous power as I had never before felt in any being – just at this moment of great alarm, I saw a pillar of light exactly over my head, above the brightness of the sun, which descended gradually until it fell upon me.

"THIS IS MY BELOVED SON"

17 It no sooner appeared than I found myself delivered from the enemy which held me bound. When the light rested upon me I saw two Personages, whose brightness and glory defy all description, standing above me in the air. One of them spake unto me, calling me by name and said, pointing to the other – This is My Beloved Son. Hear Him!

PURPOSE TO KNOW WHICH SECT RIGHT

18 My object in going to inquire of the Lord was to know which of all the sects was right, that I might know which to join. No sooner, therefore, did I get possession of myself, so as to be able to speak, than I asked the Personages who stood above me in the light, which of all the sects was right (for at this time it had never entered into my heart that all were wrong) – and which I should join.

19 I was answered that I must join none

of them, for they were all wrong; and the Personage who addressed me said that all their creeds were an abomination in his sight; that those professors were all corrupt; that: "they draw near to me with their lips, but their hearts are far from me, they teach for doctrines the commandments of men, having a form of godliness, but they deny the power thereof."

COMES TO, LYING ON BACK

20 He again forbade me to join with any of them; and many other things did he say unto me, which I cannot write at this time. When I came to myself again, I found myself lying on my back, looking up into heaven. When the light had departed, I had no strength; but soon recovering in some degree, I went home. And as I leaned up to the fireplace, mother inquired what the matter was. I replied, "Never mind, all is well –I am well enough off." I then said to my mother, "I have learned for myself that Presbyterianism is not true."

It seems as though the adversary was aware, at a very early period of my life, that I was destined to prove a disturber and an annoyer of his kingdom; else why should the powers of darkness combine against me? Why the opposition and persecution that arose against me, almost in my infancy?

TELLS METHODIST PREACHER OF VISION

21 Some few days after I had this vision, I happened to be in company with one of the Methodist preachers, who was very active in the before mentioned religious excitement; and, conversing with him on the subject of religion, I took occasion to give him an account of the vision which I had had. I was greatly surprised at his behavior; he treated my communication not only lightly, but with great contempt, saying it was all of the devil, that there were no such things as visions or revelations in these days; that all such

things had ceased with the apostles, and that there would never be any more of them.

ALL UNITE AGAINST YOUNG JOSEPH

22 I soon found, however, that my telling the story had excited a great deal of prejudice against me among professors of religion, and was the cause of great persecution, which continued to increase; and though I was an obscure boy, only between fourteen and fifteen years of age, and my circumstances in life such as to make a boy of no consequence in the world, yet men of high standing would take notice sufficient to excite the public mind against me, and create a bitter persecution; and this was common among all the sects – all united to persecute me.

STRANGE TO ATTRACT SO MUCH ATTENTION

23 It caused me serious reflection then, and often has since, how very strange it was that an obscure boy, of a little over fourteen years of age, and one, too, who was doomed to the necessity of obtaining a scanty maintenance by his daily labor, should be thought a character of sufficient importance to attract the attention of the great ones of the most popular sects of the day, and in a manner to create in them a spirit of the most bitter persecution and reviling. But strange or not, so it was, and it was often the cause of great sorrow to myself.

COULD NOT DENY VISION

24 However, it was nevertheless a fact that I had beheld a vision. I have thought since, that I felt much like Paul, when he made his defense before King Agrippa, and related the account of the vision he had when he saw a light, and heard a voice; but still there were but few who believed him; some said he was dishonest, others said he was mad; and he was ridiculed and reviled. But all this did not destroy the reality of his vision. He had seen a vision, he knew he had, and all the

persecution under heaven could not make it otherwise; and though they should persecute him unto death, yet he knew, and would know to his latest breath, that he had both seen a light and heard a voice speaking unto him, and all the world could not make him think or believe otherwise.

JOSEPH SAW TWO PEOPLE

25 So it was with me. I had actually seen a light, and in the midst of that light I saw two Personages, and they did in reality speak to me; and though I was hated and persecuted for saying that I had seen a vision, yet it was true; and while they were persecuting me, reviling me, and speaking all manner of evil against me falsely for so saying, I was led to say in my heart: Why persecute me for telling the truth? I have actually seen a vision; and who am I that I can withstand God, or why does the world think to make me deny what I have actually seen? For I had seen a vision; I knew it, and I knew that God knew it, and I could not deny it, neither dared I do it; at least I knew that by so doing I would offend God, and come under condemnation.

26 I had now got my mind satisfied so far as the sectarian world was concerned –that it was not my duty to join with any of them, but to continue as I was until further directed. I had found the testimony of James to be true – that a man who lacked wisdom might ask of God, and obtain, and not be upbraided.

SEVERE PERSECUTION

27 I continued to pursue my common vocations in life until the twenty-first of September, one thousand eight hundred and twenty-three, all the time suffering severe persecution at the hands of all classes of men, both religious and irreligious, because I continued to affirm that I had seen a vision.

OTHERS SHOULD HAVE TRIED TO HELP

28 During the space of time which intervened between the time I had the vision and the year eighteen hundred and twenty-three – having been forbidden to join any of the religious sects of the day, and being of very tender years, and persecuted by those who ought to have been my friends and to have treated me kindly, and if they supposed me to be deluded to have endeavored in a proper and affectionate manner to have reclaimed me – I was left to all kinds of temptations; and, mingling with all kinds of society, I frequently fell into many foolish errors, and displayed the weakness of youth, and the foibles of human nature; which, I am sorry to say, led me into divers temptations, offensive in the sight of God. In making this confession, no one need suppose me guilty of any great or malignant sins. A disposition to commit such was never in my nature. But I was guilty of levity, and sometimes associated with jovial company, etc., not consistent with that character which ought to be maintained by one who was called of God as I had been. But this will not seem very strange to any one who recollects my youth, and is acquainted with my native cheery temperament.

SEPTEMBER 21, 1823 PRAYS FOR FORGIVENESS

29 In consequence of these things, I often felt condemned for my weakness and imperfections; when, on the evening of the above-mentioned twenty-first of September, after I had retired to my bed for the night, I betook myself to prayer and supplication to Almighty God for forgiveness of all my sins and follies, and also for a manifestation to me, that I might know of my state and standing before him; for I had full confidence in obtaining a divine manifestation, as I previously had.

LIGHT APPEARS

30 While I was thus in the act of calling upon God, I discovered a light appearing in my room, which continued to increase until the room was lighter than at noonday, when immediately a personage appeared at my bedside, standing in the air, for his feet did not touch the floor.

31 He had on a loose robe of most exquisite whiteness. It was a whiteness beyond anything earthly I had ever seen; nor do I believe that any earthly thing could be made to appear so exceedingly white and brilliant. His hands were naked, and his arms also, a little above the wrist; so, also, were his feet naked, as were his legs, a little above the ankles. His head and neck were also bare. I could discover that he had no other clothing on but this robe, as it was open, so that I could see into his bosom.

32 Not only was his robe exceedingly white, but his whole person was glorious beyond description, and his countenance truly like lightning. The room was exceedingly light, but not so very bright as immediately around his person. When I first looked upon him, I was afraid; but the fear soon left me.

MORONI: GOD HAS A WORK FOR YOU

33 He called me by name, and said unto me that he was a messenger sent from the presence of God to me, and that his name was Moroni; that God had a work for me to do; and that my name should be had for good and evil among all nations, kindreds, and tongues, or that it should be both good and evil spoken of among all people.

GOLD PLATES, A HISTORY

34 He said there was a book deposited, written upon gold plates, giving an account of the former inhabitants of this continent, and the source from whence they sprang. He also said that the fullness

of the everlasting Gospel was contained in it, as delivered by the Savior to the ancient inhabitants;

URIM AND THUMMIM, THE SEERS, MADE FOR TRANSLATING

35 Also, that there were two stones in silver bows—and these stones, fastened to a breastplate, constituted what is called the Urim and Thummim—deposited with the plates; and the possession and use of these stones were what constituted "seers" in ancient or former times; and that God had prepared them for the purpose of translating the book.

36 After telling me these things, he commenced quoting the prophecies of the Old Testament. He first quoted part of the third chapter of Malachi; and he quoted also the fourth or last chapter of the same prophecy, though with a little variation from the way it reads in our Bibles. Instead of quoting the first verse as it reads in our books, he quoted it thus:

37 For behold, the day cometh that shall burn as an oven, and all the proud, yea, and all that do wickedly shall burn as stubble; for they that come shall burn them, saith the Lord of Hosts, that it shall leave them neither root nor branch.

38 And again, he quoted the fifth verse thus: Behold, I will reveal unto you the Priesthood, by the hand of Elijah the prophet, before the coming of the great and dreadful day of the Lord.

39 He also quoted the next verse differently: And he shall plant in the hearts of the children the promises made to the fathers, and the hearts of the children shall turn to their fathers. If it were not so, the whole earth would be utterly wasted at his coming.

ISAIAH 11 ABOUT TO BE FULFILLED (END TIME)

40 In addition to these, he quoted the eleventh chapter of Isaiah, saying that it was about to be fulfilled. He quoted also the third chapter of Acts, twenty-second and twenty-third verses, precisely as they stand in our New Testament. He said that that prophet was Christ; but the day had not yet come when "they who would not hear his voice should be cut off from among the people," but soon would come.

FULLNESS OF THE GENTILES

41 He also quoted the second chapter of Joel, from the twenty-eighth verse to the last. He also said that this was not yet fulfilled, but was soon to be. And he further stated that the fullness of the Gentiles was soon to come in. He quoted many other passages of scripture, and offered many explanations which cannot be mentioned here.

DON'T SHOW PLATES, BREASTPLATE, URIM AND THUMMIM UNLESS COMMANDED

42 Again, he told me, that when I got those plates of which he had spoken – for the time that they should be obtained was not yet fulfilled – I should not show them to any person; neither the breastplate with the Urim and Thummim; only to those to whom I should be commanded to show them; if I did I should be destroyed. While he was conversing with me about the plates, the vision was opened to my mind that I could see the place where the plates were deposited, and that so clearly and distinctly that I knew the place again when I visited it.

LIGHT GATHERS AROUND THE PERSON, ASCENDS INTO HEAVEN

43 After this communication, I saw the light in the room begin to gather immediately around the person of him who had been speaking to me, and it continued to do so until the room was

again left dark, except just around him; when, instantly I saw, as it were, a conduit open right up into heaven, and he ascended till he entirely disappeared, and the room was left as it had been before this heavenly light had made its appearance.

SECOND VISIT

44 I lay musing on the singularity of the scene, and marveling greatly at what had been told to me by this extraordinary messenger; when, in the midst of my meditation, I suddenly discovered that my room was again beginning to get lighted, and in an instant, as it were, the same heavenly messenger was again by my bedside.

REPEATS MESSAGE WITHOUT CHANGE

45 He commenced, and again related the very same things which he had done at his first visit, without the least variation; which having done, he informed me of great judgments which were coming upon the earth, with great desolations by famine, sword, and pestilence; and that these grievous judgments would come on the earth in this generation. Having related these things, he again ascended as he had done before.

THIRD VISIT

46 By this time, so deep were the impressions made on my mind, that sleep had fled from my eyes, and I lay overwhelmed in astonishment at what I had both seen and heard. But what was my surprise when again I beheld the same messenger at my bedside, and heard him rehearse or repeat over again to me the same things as before; and added a caution to me, telling me that Satan would try to tempt me (in consequence of the indigent circumstances of my father's family), to get the plates for the purpose of getting rich. This he forbade me, saying

that I must have no other object in view in getting the plates but to glorify God, and must not be influenced by any other motive than that of building his kingdom; otherwise I could not get them.

COCK CROWS

47 After this third visit, he again ascended into heaven as before, and I was again left to ponder on the strangeness of what I had just experienced; when almost immediately after the heavenly messenger had ascended from me for the third time, the cock crowed, and I found that day was approaching, so that our interviews must have occupied the whole of that night.

FAINT AT WORK; FALLS UNCONSCIOUS

48 I shortly after arose from my bed, and, as usual, went to the necessary labors of the day; but, in attempting to work as at other times, I found my strength so exhausted as to render me entirely unable. My father, who was laboring along with me, discovered something to be wrong with me, and told me to go home. I started with the intention of going to the house; but, in attempting to cross the fence out of the field where we were, my strength entirely failed me, and I fell helpless on the ground, and for a time was quite unconscious of anything.

MESSENGER APPEARS

49 The first thing that I can recollect was a voice speaking unto me, calling me by name. I looked up, and beheld the same messenger standing over my head, surrounded by light as before. He then again related unto me all that he had related to me the previous night, and commanded me to go to my father and tell him of the vision and commandments which I had received.

JOSEPH GOES TO SITE; JOSEPH SR. BELIEVES

50 I obeyed; I returned to my father in the field, and rehearsed the whole matter to him. He replied to me that it was of God,

and told me to go and do as commanded by the messenger. I left the field, and went to the place where the messenger had told me the plates were deposited; and owing to the distinctness of the vision which I had had concerning it, I knew the place the instant that I arrived there.

HILL; STONE VISIBLE

51   Convenient to the village of Manchester, Ontario county, New York, stands a hill of considerable size, and the most elevated of any in the neighborhood. On the west side of this hill, not far from the top, under a stone of considerable size, lay the plates, deposited in a stone box. This stone was thick and rounding in the middle on the upper side, and thinner towards the edges, so that the middle part of it was visible above the ground, but the edge all around was covered with earth.

SEES PLATES, URIM AND THUMMIM, BREASTPLATE

52   Having removed the earth, I obtained a lever, which I got fixed under the edge of the stone, and with a little exertion raised it up. I looked in, and there indeed did I behold the plates, the Urim and Thummim, and the breastplate, as stated by the messenger. The box in which they lay was formed by laying stones together in some kind of cement. In the bottom of the box were laid two stones crossways of the box, and on these stones lay the plates and the other things with them.

COME AGAIN IN A YEAR

53   I made an attempt to take them out, but was forbidden by the messenger, and was again informed that the time for bringing them forth had not yet arrived, neither would it, until four years from that time; but he told me that I should come to that place precisely in one year from that time, and that he would there meet with me, and that I should continue to do so until the time should come for obtaining the plates.

GOES EACH YEAR, SEES MESSENGER, WHO INSTRUCTS REGARDING CONDUCT OF COMING KINGDOM

54   Accordingly, as I had been commanded, I went at the end of each year, and at each time I found the same messenger there, and received instruction and intelligence from him at each of our interviews, respecting what the Lord was going to do, and how and in what manner his kingdom was to be conducted in the last days.

POOR, MANUAL LABOR

55   As my father's worldly circumstances were very limited, we were under the necessity of laboring with our hands, hiring out by day's work and otherwise, as we could get opportunity. Sometimes we were at home, and sometimes abroad, and by continuous labor were enabled to get a comfortable maintenance.

1823 ALVIN DIES

56   In the year 1823 my father's family met with a great affliction by the death of my eldest brother, Alvin.

1825 WORKS FOR STOAL

In the month of October, 1825, I hired with an old gentleman by the name of Josiah Stoal, who lived in Chenango county, State of New York. He had heard something of a silver mine having been opened by the Spaniards in Harmony, Susquehanna county, State of Pennsylvania; and had, previous to my hiring to him, been digging, in order, if possible, to discover the mine. After I went to live with him, he took me, with the rest of his hands, to dig for the silver mine, at which I continued to work for nearly a month, without success in our undertaking, and finally I prevailed with the old gentleman to cease digging after it. Hence arose the very prevalent story of my having been a money-digger.

BOARDS WITH THE HALES; 1827 MARRIES EMMA

57   During the time that I was thus employed, I was put to board with a Mr. Isaac Hale, of that place; it was there I first

saw my wife (his daughter), Emma Hale. On the 18th of January, 1827, we were married, while I was yet employed in the service of Mr. Stoal.

PERSECUTION

58 Owing to my continuing to assert that I had seen a vision, persecution still followed me, and my wife's father's family were very much opposed to our being married. I was, therefore, under the necessity of taking her elsewhere; so we went and were married at the house of Squire Tarbill, in South Bainbridge, Chenango county, New York. Immediately after my marriage, I left Mr. Stoal's, and went to my father's, and farmed with him that season.

SEPTEMBER 22, 1827, MESSENGER DELIVERS PLATES TO JOSEPH

59 At length the time arrived for obtaining the plates, the Urim and Thummim, and the breastplate. On the twenty-second day of September, one thousand eight hundred and twenty-seven, having gone as usual at the end of another year to the place where they were deposited, the same heavenly messenger delivered them up to me with this charge: that I should be responsible for them; that if I should let them go carelessly, or through any neglect of mine, I should be cut off; but that if I would use all my endeavors to preserve them, until he, the messenger, should call for them, they should be protected.

ATTEMPTS TO GET PLATES

60 I soon found out the reason why I had received such strict charges to keep them safe, and why it was that the messenger had said that when I had done what was required at my hand, he would call for them. For no sooner was it known that I had them, than the most strenuous exertions were used to get them from me. Every stratagem that could be invented was resorted to for that purpose. The persecution became more bitter and severe than before, and multitudes were on the alert continually to get them from

me if possible.

JOSEPH COMPLETES WORK, MESSENGER HAS PLATES

But by the wisdom of God, they remained safe in my hands, until I had accomplished by them what was required at my hand. When, according to arrangements, the messenger called for them, I delivered them up to him; and he has them in his charge until this day, being the second day of May, one thousand eight hundred and thirty-eight. one thousand eight hundred and thirty-eight: 1828

RUMORS, PERSECUTION; MOVES TO PENNSYLVANIA; MEETS MARTIN HARRIS OF PALMYRA

61 The excitement, however, still continued, and rumor with her thousand tongues was all the time employed in circulating falsehoods about my father's family, and about myself. If I were to relate a thousandth part of them, it would fill up volumes. The persecution, however, became so intolerable that I was under the necessity of leaving Manchester, and going with my wife to Susquehanna county, in the State of Pennsylvania. While preparing to start – being very poor, and the persecution so heavy upon us that there was no probability that we would ever be otherwise – in the midst of our afflictions we found a friend in a gentleman by the name of Martin Harris, who came to us and gave me fifty dollars to assist us on our journey. Mr. Harris was a resident of Palmyra township, Wayne county, in the State of New York, and a farmer of respectability.

BEGINS TRANSLATING AT HALE HOME IN PENNSYLVANIA

62 By this timely aid was I enabled to reach the place of my destination in Pennsylvania; and immediately after my arrival there I commenced copying the characters off the plates. I copied a considerable number of them, and by means of the Urim and Thummim I

translated some of them, which I did between the time I arrived at the house of my wife's father, in the month of December, and the February following.

MARTIN VISITS

63 Sometime in this month of February, the aforementioned Mr. Martin Harris came to our place, got the characters which I had drawn off the plates, and started with them to the city of New York. For what took place relative to him and the characters, I refer to his own account of the circumstances, as he related them to me after his return, which was as follows:

CHARLES ANTHON

64 I went to the city of New York, and presented the characters which had been translated, with the translation thereof, to Professor Charles Anthon, a gentleman celebrated for his literary attainments.

VERIFIES TRANSLATION

Professor Anthon stated that the translation was correct, more so than any he had before seen translated from the Egyptian.

CHARACTERS AUTHENTIC

I then showed him those which were not yet translated, and he said that they were Egyptian, Chaldaic, Assyriac, and Arabic; and he said they were true characters.

CERTIFICATE

He gave me a certificate, certifying to the people of Palmyra that they were true characters, and that the translation of such of them as had been translated was also correct.

GOLD PLATES, ANGEL

I took the certificate and put it into my pocket, and was just leaving the house, when Mr. Anthon called me back, and asked me how the young man found out that there were gold plates in the place where he found them. I answered that an angel of God had revealed it unto him.

DESTROYS CERTIFICATE

65 He then said to me, "Let me see that certificate." I accordingly took it out of my pocket and gave it to him, when he took it and tore it to pieces, saying that there was no such thing now as ministering of angels, and that if I would bring the plates to him he would translate them.

CANNOT READ A SEALED BOOK

I informed him that part of the plates were sealed, and that I was forbidden to bring them. He replied, "I cannot read a sealed book."

I left him and went to Dr. Mitchell, who sanctioned what Professor Anthon had said respecting both the characters and the translation.

OLIVER COWDERY

66 On the 5th day of April, 1829, Oliver Cowdery came to my house, until which time I had never seen him. He stated to me that having been teaching school in the neighborhood where my father resided, and my father being one of those who sent to the school, he went to board for a season at his house, and while there the family related to him the circumstances of my having received the plates, and accordingly he had come to make inquiries of me.

WRITES FOR JOSEPH

67 Two days after the arrival of Mr. Cowdery (being the 7th of April) I commenced to translate the Book of Mormon, and he began to write for me.

MAY, 1829 PRAY ABOUT BAPTISM; MESSENGERS LAYS ON HANDS

68 We still continued the work of translation, when, in the ensuing month (May, 1829), we on a certain day went into the woods to pray and inquire of the Lord respecting baptism for the remission of sins,

that we found mentioned in the translation of the plates. While we were thus employed, praying and calling upon the Lord, a messenger from heaven descended in a cloud of light, and having laid his hands upon us, he ordained us, saying:

PRIESTHOOD OF AARON

69 Upon you my fellow servants, in the name of Messiah, I confer the Priesthood of Aaron, which holds the keys of the ministering of angels, and of the gospel of repentance, and of baptism by immersion for the remission of sins; and this shall never be taken again from the earth until the sons of Levi do offer again an offering unto the Lord in righteousness.

AUTHORITY TO BAPTIZE

70 He said this Aaronic Priesthood had not the power of laying on hands for the gift of the Holy Ghost, but that this should be conferred on us hereafter; and he commanded us to go and be baptized, and gave us directions that I should baptize Oliver Cowdery, and that afterwards he should baptize me.

BAPTIZE, ORDAIN EACH OTHER

71 Accordingly we went and were baptized. I baptized him first, and afterwards he baptized me – after which I laid my hands upon his head and ordained him to the Aaronic Priesthood, and afterwards he laid his hands on me and ordained me to the same Priesthood – for so we were commanded.

MESSENGER JOHN, ACTING UNDER PETER, JAMES AND JOHN

15 May, 1829

72 The messenger who visited us on this occasion and conferred this Priesthood upon us, said that his name was John, the same that is called John the Baptist in the New Testament, and that he acted under the direction of Peter, James and John, who held the keys of the Priesthood of Melchizedek, which Priesthood, he said, would in due time be conferred on us, and that I should be called the first Elder

of the Church, and he (Oliver Cowdery) the second. It was on the fifteenth day of May, 1829, that we were ordained under the hand of this messenger, and baptized.

HOLY GHOST; JOSEPH PROPHESIES OF CHURCH

73 Immediately on our coming up out of the water after we had been baptized, we experienced great and glorious blessings from our Heavenly Father. No sooner had I baptized Oliver Cowdery, than the Holy Ghost fell upon him, and he stood up and prophesied many things which should shortly come to pass. And again, so soon as I had been baptized by him, I also had the spirit of prophecy, when, standing up, I prophesied concerning the rise of this Church, and many other things connected with the Church, and this generation of the children of men. We were filled with the Holy Ghost, and rejoiced in the God of our salvation.

SCRIPTURES LAID OPEN TO UNDERSTANDINGS: KEEP PRIESTHOOD SECRET TO AVOID MORE PERSECUTION

74 Our minds being now enlightened, we began to have the scriptures laid open to our understandings, and the true meaning and intention of their more mysterious passages revealed unto us in a manner which we never could attain to previously, nor ever before had thought of. In the meantime we were forced to keep secret the circumstances of having received the Priesthood and our having been baptized, owing to a spirit of persecution which had already manifested itself in the neighborhood.

MOB THREATS; HALES NOW FRIENDLY, OPPOSE MOBS

75 We had been threatened with being mobbed, from time to time, and this, too, by professors of religion. And their intentions of mobbing us were only counteracted by the influence of my wife's father's family (under Divine providence), who had become very friendly to me, and

who were opposed to mobs, and were willing that I should be allowed to continue the work of translation without interruption; and therefore offered and promised us protection from all unlawful proceedings, as far as in them lay.

Joseph Smith History

C JOSEPH SMITH AND HIS FAILED PROPHECIES

Joseph Smith was known by many titles in his lifetime – Elder, Seer, President, Mayor, Lieutenant General – but he is best known as the Prophet.

FIRST FAILED PROPHECY: THE COMING OF THE LORD

President Smith then stated that the meeting had been called, because God had commanded it; and it was made known to him by vision and by the Holy Spirit. . . . it was the will of God that they should be ordained to the ministry and go forth to prune the vineyard for the last time, for the coming of the Lord, which was nigh even fifty six years should wind up the scene.

History of the Church, Vol. 2, page 182

• Joseph Smith gave this prophecy in 1835. The fifty-six years were passed by 1891.

SECOND FAILED PROPHECY: DAVID W. PATTEN TO GO ON A MISSION:

Verily, thus saith the Lord: It is wisdom in my servant David W. Patten, that he settle up all his business as soon as he possibly can, and make a disposition of his merchandise, that he may perform a mission unto me next spring, in company with others, even twelve including himself, to testify of my name and bear glad tidings unto the world.

Doctrine and Covenants 114:1

• This prophecy, made on April 17, 1838, never came true as David W. Patten died in October of 1838.

THIRD FAILED PROPHECY: THE UNITED STATES GOVERNMENT TO BE OVERTHROWN IN A FEW YEARS:

I prophecy in the name of the Lord God of Israel, unless the United States redress the wrongs committed upon the Saints in the state of Missouri and punish the crimes committed by her officers that in a few years the government will be utterly overthrown and wasted, and there will not be so much as a potsherd left for their wickedness in permitting the murder of men, women and children, and the wholesale plunder and extermination of thousands of her citizens to go unpunished.

History of the Church, Vol. 5, page 394

• Joseph Smith made this prophecy in May 6, 1843, but the United States Government never altered its laws against the Mormons in Missouri.

TESTING PROPHETIC CLAIMS

Over the past two centuries many people have claimed to be religious prophets, including Charles Taze Russell (Jehovah's Witnesses), Ellen G. White (Seventh-day Adventists), Mary Baker Eddy (Christian Science), and Joseph Smith (Church of Jesus Christ of Latter-day Saints).

All such claims need to be tested. Jesus, Paul, Peter, John and Jude all warn about false prophets and the danger of being deceived by them: Matthew 7:15; 2 Corinthians 11:4-15; Galatians 1:6-9; 1 Timothy 4:1; 2 Peter 2:1-3; 1 John 4:1 and Jude 3-16.

WARNINGS FROM DEUTERONOMY

Deuteronomy 13 reminds us about the need to be discerning:

If there arise among you a prophet, or a dreamer of dreams, and giveth thee a sign or a wonder, And the sign or the wonder come to pass, whereof he spake unto thee, saying, Let us go after other gods, which thou hast not known, and let us serve them; Thou shalt not hearken unto the words of that prophet, or that dreamer of dreams: for the LORD your God proveth you, to know whether ye love the LORD your God with all your heart and with all your soul. Ye shall walk after the LORD your God, and fear him, and keep his commandments, and obey his voice, and ye shall serve him, and cleave unto him. And that prophet, or that dreamer of dreams, shall be put to death; because he hath spoken to turn you away from the LORD your God, which brought you out of the land of Egypt, and redeemed you out of the house of bondage, to thrust thee out of the way which the LORD thy God commanded thee to walk in. So shalt thou put the evil away from the midst of thee.

Deuteronomy 13:1-5 KJV

Deuteronomy 18 sets out tests to apply to anyone who claims to be God's prophet:

And if thou say in thine heart, How shall we know the word which the LORD hath not spoken? When a prophet speaketh in the name of the LORD, if the thing follow not, nor come to pass, that is the thing which the LORD hath not spoken, but the prophet hath spoken it presumptuously: thou shalt not be afraid of him.

Deuteronomy 18:21-22

---

3 MORMON HOLY BOOKS

A   The Bible: the Joseph Smith Revision
B   *The Book of Mormon*
C   The Doctrine and Covenants
D   *The Pearl of Great Price*
E   Non-discoveries and the *Book of Mormon*

INTRODUCTION

Mormon teaching is drawn from the following four sources, which are called the "Standard Works." Mormons regard them as divinely inspired and authoritative scripture.

A THE BIBLE
The Mormon Bible, at first sight, looks very like the King James Version.

The Mormon Church believes in the Bible only in so much as it has been correctly translated. Joseph Smith wrote, "I believe the Bible as it read when it came from the pen of the original writers. Ignorant translators, careless transcribers, or designing and corrupt priests have committed many errors."

TITLE OF THE MORMON BIBLE
Joseph Smith's work with the Bible has been known by various titles. The revelations in the Doctrine and Covenants call it a "translation" (D&C 37:1; 90:13). Joseph Smith called it the "new translation," and it is known by this title in the early literature of the Church. It was published under the title "Holy Scriptures," with the later subtitle, "Inspired Version." It is also known as the Joseph Smith Revision. Many call it an "inspired revision." In 1978 the LDS Church officially labeled it the "Joseph Smith Translation," abbreviated to JST. The JST is Joseph Smith's doctrinal correction ("translation") of the Old and New Testaments. Smith's translation differs from any other Bible translation because of the text he added as he went through the KJV.

"RESTORES TRUTHS"
Mormons give the following explanation for the additional text added to the King James Version of the Bible:

The Lord inspired the Prophet Joseph Smith to restore truths to the Bible text that had become lost or changed since the original words were written. These restored truths clarified doctrine and improved scriptural understanding. Because the Lord revealed to Joseph certain truths that the original authors had once recorded, the Joseph Smith Translation is unlike any other Bible translation in the world. In this sense, the word translation is used in a broader and different way than usual, for Joseph's translation was more revelation than literal translation from one language into another.

Robert J. Matthews

Joseph Smith's "new translation" of the King James Version (KJV) differs from the KJV in at least 3,410 verses and consists of additions, deletions, rearrangements, and other alterations that cause it to vary not only from the KJV but from other biblical texts. Changes range from minor details to fully reconstituted chapters.

The following list gives the number of chapters in the King James Version of the Bible that Joseph Smith considered to be correct:

Old Testament

Genesis	13 out of 50 chapters
Exodus	19 out of 40 chapters
Leviticus	24 out of 27 chapters
Numbers	34 out of 36 chapters
Deuteronomy	30 out of 34 chapters
Joshua	23 out of 24 chapters
Judges	20 out of 21 chapters
Ruth	"The Book of Ruth is all correct"
1 Samuel	26 out of 31 chapters
2 Samuel	22 out of 24 chapters
1 Kings	16 out of 22 chapters
2 Kings	23 out of 25 chapters
1 Chronicles	27 out of 29 chapters
2 Chronicles	29 out of 36 chapters
Ezra	10 out of 10 chapters
Nehemiah	10 out of 13 chapters
Esther	10 out of 10 chapters
Job	40 out of 42 chapters

Psalms through Malachi

	From Psalm through Malachi 263 chapters were not listed on the manuscript pages of the Joseph Smith Translation.
Psalms	89 chapters not listed in manuscript of 150 chapters; 10 chapters listed correct
Proverbs	28 chapters not listed in manuscript of 31 chapters
Ecclesiastes	has marking in Bible but not listed in manuscript
Song of Solomon	"The Songs of Solomon are not Inspired writings"
Isaiah	28 chapters not listed in manuscript of 66 chapters; 1 chapter listed correct
Jeremiah	33 chapters not listed in manuscript of 52 chapters; 4 chapters listed correct
Lamentations	"The Lamentations of Jeremiah is Correct"
Ezekiel	28 chapters not listed in manuscript of 48 chapters
Daniel	11 chapters not listed in manuscript of 12 chapters
Hosea	13 chapters not listed in manuscript of 14 chapters
Joel	1 chapter not listed in manuscript of 3 chapters
Amos	6 chapters not listed in manuscript of 9 chapters
Obadiah	Correct
Jonah	3 chapters not listed in manuscript of 4 chapters
Micah	Correct
Nahum	Correct
Habakkuk	Correct
Zephaniah	Correct
Haggai	Correct
Zechariah	11 chapters not listed in manuscript of 14 chapters
Malachi	Correct

New Testament

The New Testament has more extensive revisions so fewer chapters are considered correct. A list of the number of "correct" chapters follow:

John	chapters 15, 17-18, 21 are correct
Acts	9 out of 28 chapters
1 Corinthians	1 out of 16 chapters
2 Corinthians	3 out of 13 chapters
Galatians	2 out of 6 chapters
Ephesians	2 out of 6 chapters
Colossians	1 out of 4 chapters
1 Thessalonians	1 out of 5 chapters
2 Thessalonians	1 out of 3 chapters
Titus	1 out of 3 chapters
James	2 out of 5 chapters
2 John	1 out of 1 correct
3 John	1 out of 1 correct
Revelation	4 out of 22 chapters

JOSEPH SMITH'S CLAIMS FOR HIS JST:

- the Bible is corrupt and full of errors
- he is a prophet of God
- as such he is called to restore the Scriptures through a new translation.

However, it would not be too harsh to say that it is a different gospel rather than a translation.

B THE BOOK OF MORMON

Mormons do not believe that the revelations of God were confined to ancient Israel, or to the writers of the New Testament. They believe that fresh revelation was given to Joseph Smith. The *Book of Mormon*, however, is not the "Mormon Bible," as is sometimes erroneously supposed. It is one of the complementary works that Mormons accept as scripture.

The *Book of Mormon*, which was published in 1830, claims to be a translation from the original golden plates, and is therefore the most important of the Mormon sacred books.

THE METAL PLATES OF THE BOOK OF MORMON

Mormons believe that the *Book of Mormon* is a sacred record of peoples in ancient America, and was engraved upon sheets of metal. Four

kinds of metal record plates are spoken of in the book itself.

- The Plates of Nephi, which were of two kinds: the Small Plates and the Large Plates. The former were more particularly devoted to the spiritual matters and the ministry and teachings of the prophets, while the latter were occupied mostly with a secular history of the peoples concerned (1 Nephi 9: 2-4). From the time of Mosiah, however, the large plates also included items of major spiritual importance.

- The Plates of Mormon, which consist of an abridgment by Mormon from the Large Plates of Nephi, with many commentaries. These plates also contained a continuation of the history by Mormon and additions by his son Moroni.

- The Plates of Ether, which present a history of the Jaredites. This record was abridged by Moroni, who inserted comments of his own and incorporated the record with the general history under the title "Book of Ether."

- The Plates of Brass brought by the people of Lehi from Jerusalem in 600 BC. These contained "the five books of Moses, . . . And also a record of the Jews from the beginning, . . . down to the commencement of the reign of Zedekiah, king of Judah; And also the prophecies of the holy prophets" (1 Nephi 5: 11-13). Many quotations from these plates, citing Isaiah and other biblical and nonbiblical prophets, appear in the Book of Mormon.

HISTORY OF THE BOOK OF MORMON

In 1823, the seventeen-year-old Joseph Smith received a visit from a resurrected person (an angel) called Moroni. In 1827, Angel Moroni subsequently delivered engraved metal plates of gold to Smith. These plates are the origin of the Book of Mormon.

The Book of Mormon records the history of some Hebrews who migrated from Jerusalem to America in about 600 BC under the leadership of the prophet Lehi. In about AD 400 Jesus appeared to and taught some of their descendants. This history and Jesus' teachings were abridged and written on gold plates by the prophet Mormon. His son Moroni buried these plates in the ground. They remained there for about 1,400 years. Then Moroni, a resurrected angel, delivered these gold plates to Joseph Smith.

Smith transcribed the plates into modern speech and then returned them to Moroni.

The books were first published as the *Book of Mormon* on March 26, 1830, when Smith was twenty-four years old. The *Book of Mormon* had the subtitle "Another Testament of Jesus Christ."

Smith said that the "*Book of Mormon* was the most correct of any book on earth, and the keystone of our religion, and a man would get nearer to God by abiding by its precepts, than by any other book."

A later President of the Mormon Church, Ezra Benson, said that the book "establishes and proves to the world that Joseph Smith is a prophet, for he received the book from a resurrected personage and translated it by the gift and power of God . . . The Church is thus the one true Church because it was set up by a prophet acting under command of God."

The Mormon Church claims that the *Book of Mormon* is an historical record of ancient civilizations located on the American continents. However, no archaeological record of any of the *Book of Mormon* people groups has been located.

DIVISIONS, OR "BOOKS," OF THE BOOK OF MORMON

The *Book of Mormon* has fifteen main parts or divisions, known, with one exception, as books, each designated by the name of its principal author. The first portion (the first six books, ending with Omni) is a translation from the Small Plates of Nephi. Between books of Omni and Mosiah is an insert called The Words of Mormon. This insert connects the record engraved on the Small Plates with Mormon's abridgment of the Large Plates.

The longest portion, from Mosiah to Mormon, chapter 7, inclusive, is a translation of Mormon's abridgment of the Large Plates of Nephi. The concluding portion, from Mormon, chapter 8, to the end to the volume, was engraved by Mormon's son Moroni, who, after finishing the record of his father's life, made an abridgment of the Jaredite record (as the Book of Ether) and later added the parts known as the Book of Moroni.

In AD 421, Moroni, the last of the Nephite prophet-historians, sealed the sacred record and hid it up unto the Lord, to be brought forth in the latter days, as predicted by the voice of God through his ancient prophets. In AD 1823, this same Moroni, then a resurrected personage, visited the prophet Joseph Smith and subsequently delivered the engraved plates to him.

The title page of the book of Mormon reads as follows:

THE BOOK OF MORMON
AN ACCOUNT WRITTEN BY THE
HAND OF MORMON UPON PLATES
TAKEN FROM THE PLATES OF NEPHI

Preface to the Book of Mormon

Wherefore, it is an abridgment of the record of the people of Nephi, and also of the Lamanites – Written to the Lamanites, who are a remnant of the house of Israel; and also to Jew and Gentile – Written by way of commandment, and also by the spirit of prophecy and of revelation – Written and sealed up, and hid up unto the Lord, that they might not be destroyed – To come forth by the gift and power of God unto the interpretation thereof – Sealed by the hand of Moroni, and hid up unto the Lord, to come forth in due time by way of the Gentile – The interpretation thereof by the gift of God.

An abridgment taken from the Book of Ether also, which is a record of the people of Jared, who were scattered at the time the Lord confounded the language of the people, when they were building a tower to get to heaven – Which is to show unto the remnant of the House of Israel what great things the Lord hath done for their fathers; and that they may know the covenants of the Lord, that they are not cast off forever – And also to the convincing of the Jew and Gentile that JESUS is the CHRIST, the ETERNAL GOD, manifesting himself unto all nations – And now, if there are faults they are the mistakes of men; wherefore, condemn not the things of God, that ye may be found spotless at the judgment-seat of Christ.

Translated by Joseph Smith. First English edition published in 1830

Introduction
The Book of Mormon is a volume of holy scripture comparable to the Bible. It is a record of God's dealings with the ancient inhabitants of the Americas and contains, as does the Bible, the fullness of the everlasting gospel.

The book was written by many ancient prophets by the spirit of prophecy and revelation. Their words, written on gold plates, were quoted and abridged by a prophet-historian named Mormon. The record gives an account of two great civilizations. One came from Jerusalem in 600 B.C., and afterward separated into two nations, known as the Nephites and the Lamanites. The other came much earlier when the Lord confounded the tongues at the Tower of Babel. This group is known as the Jaredites. After thousands of years, all were destroyed except the Lamanites, and they are the principal ancestors of the American Indians.

The crowning event recorded in the Book of Mormon is the personal ministry of the Lord Jesus Christ among the Nephites soon after his resurrection. It puts forth the doctrines of the gospel, outlines the plan of salvation, and tells men what they must do to gain peace in this life and eternal salvation in the life to come.

After Mormon completed his writings, he delivered the account to his son Moroni, who added a few words of his own and hid up the plates in the hill Cumorah. On September 21, 1823, the same Moroni, then a glorified, resurrected being, appeared to the Prophet Joseph Smith and instructed him relative to the ancient record and its destined translation into the English language.

In due course the plates were delivered to Joseph Smith, who translated them by the gift and power of God. The record is now published in many languages as a new and additional witness that Jesus Christ is the Son of the living God and that all who will come unto him and obey the laws and ordinances of his gospel may be saved.

Concerning this record the Prophet Joseph Smith said: "I told the brethren that the Book of Mormon was the most correct of any book on earth, and the keystone of our religion, and a man would get nearer to God by abiding by its precepts, than by any other book."

In addition to Joseph Smith, the Lord provided for eleven others to see the gold plates for themselves and to be special witnesses of the truth and divinity of the Book of Mormon. Their written testimonies are included herewith as "The Testimony of Three Witnesses" and "The Testimony of Eight Witnesses."

We invite all men everywhere to read the Book of Mormon, to ponder in their hearts the message it contains, and then to ask God, the Eternal Father, in the name of Christ if the book is true. Those who pursue this course and ask in faith will gain a testimony of its truth and divinity by the power of the Holy Ghost. (See Moroni 10: 3-5.)

Those who gain this divine witness from the Holy Spirit will also come to know by the same power that Jesus Christ is the Savior of the world, that Joseph Smith is his revelator and prophet in these last days, and that The Church of Jesus Christ of Latter-day Saints is the Lord's kingdom once again established on the earth, preparatory to the second coming of the Messiah.

The first book of Nephi: his reign and ministry
Chapter summary
An account of Lehi and his wife Sariah and his four sons, being called,(beginning at the eldest) Laman, Lemuel, Sam, and Nephi. The Lord warns Lehi to depart out of the land of Jerusalem, because he prophesieth unto the people concerning their iniquity and they seek to destroy his life. He taketh three days' journey into the wilderness with his family. Nephi taketh his brethren and returneth to the land of Jerusalem after the record of the Jews. The account of their sufferings. They take the daughters of Ishmael to wife. They take their families and depart into the wilderness. Their sufferings and afflictions in the wilderness. The course of their travels. They come to the large waters. Nephi's brethren rebel against him. He confoundeth them, and buildeth a ship. They call the name of the place Bountiful. They cross the large waters into the promised land, and so forth. This is according to the account of Nephi; or in other words, I, Nephi, wrote this record.

1 Nephi: 1
Summary
Nephi begins the record of his people – Lehi sees in vision a pillar of fire and reads from a book of prophecy – He praises God, foretells the coming of the Messiah, and prophesies the destruction of Jerusalem – He is persecuted by the Jews. [About 600 BC]
Text
1 I, NEPHI, having been born of goodly parents, therefore I was taught somewhat in all the learning of my father; and having seen many afflictions in the course of my days, nevertheless, having been highly favored of the Lord in all my days; yea, having had a great knowledge of the goodness and the mysteries of God, therefore I make a record of my proceedings in my days.
2 Yea, I make a record in the language of my father, which consists of the learning of the Jews and the language of the Egyptians.
3 And I know that the record which I make is true; and I make it with mine own hand; and I make it according to my knowledge.
4 For it came to pass in the commencement of the first year of the reign of Zedekiah, king of Judah, (my father, Lehi, having dwelt at Jerusalem in all his days); and in that same year there came many prophets, prophesying unto the people that they must repent, or the great city Jerusalem must be destroyed.
5 Wherefore it came to pass that my father, Lehi, as he went forth prayed unto the Lord, yea, even with all his heart, in behalf of his people.
6 And it came to pass as he prayed unto the Lord, there came a pillar of fire and dwelt upon a rock before him; and he saw and heard much; and because of the things which he saw and heard he did quake and tremble exceedingly.
7 And it came to pass that he returned to his own house at Jerusalem; and he cast himself upon his bed, being overcome with the Spirit and the things which he had seen.
8 And being thus overcome with the Spirit, he was carried away in a vision, even that he   saw the heavens open, and he thought he saw God sitting upon his throne, surrounded with numberless concourses of angels in the attitude of singing and praising their God.
9 And it came to pass that he saw One descending out of the midst of heaven, and he beheld that his luster was above that of the sun at noon-day.
10 And he also saw twelve others following him, and their brightness did exceed that of the stars in the firmament.
11 And they came down and went forth upon the face of the earth; and the first came and stood before my father, and gave unto him a book, and bade him that he should read.
12 And it came to pass that as he read, he was filled with the Spirit of the Lord.

13 And he read, saying: Wo, wo, unto Jerusalem, for I have seen thine abominations! Yea, and many things did my father read concerning Jerusalem –that it should be destroyed, and the inhabitants thereof; many should perish by the sword, and many should be carried away captive into Babylon.

14 And it came to pass that when my father had read and seen many great and marvelous things, he did exclaim many things unto the Lord; such as: Great and marvelous are thy works, O Lord God Almighty! Thy throne is high in the heavens, and thy power, and goodness, and mercy are over all the inhabitants of the earth; and, because thou art merciful, thou wilt not suffer those who come unto thee that they shall perish!

15 And after this manner was the language of my father in the praising of his God; for his soul did rejoice, and his whole heart was filled, because of the things which he had seen, yea, which the Lord had shown unto him.

16 And now I, Nephi, do not make a full account of the things which my father hath written, for he hath written many things which he saw in visions and in dreams; and he also hath written many things which he prophesied and spake unto his children, of which I shall not make a full account.

17 But I shall make an account of my proceedings in my days. Behold, I make an abridgment of the record of my father, upon plates which I have made with mine own hands; wherefore, after I have abridged the record of my father then will I make an account of mine own life.

18 Therefore, I would that ye should know, that after the Lord had shown so many marvelous things unto my father, Lehi, yea, concerning the destruction of Jerusalem, behold he went forth among the people, and began to prophesy and to declare unto them concerning the things which he had both seen and heard.

19 And it came to pass that the Jews did mock him because of the things which he testified of them; for he truly testified of their wickedness and their abominations; and he testified that the things which he saw and heard, and also the things which he read in the book, manifested plainly of the coming of a Messiah, and also the redemption of the world.

20 And when the Jews heard these things they were angry with him; yea, even as with the prophets of old, whom they had cast out, and stoned, and slain; and they also sought his life, that they might take it away. But behold, I, Nephi, will show unto you that the tender mercies of the Lord are over all those whom he hath chosen, because of their faith, to make them mighty even unto the power of deliverance.

Chapter 2
Chapter summary
Lehi takes his family into the wilderness by the Red Sea – They leave their property – Lehi offers a sacrifice to the Lord and teaches his sons to keep the commandments – Laman and Lemuel murmur against their father – Nephi is obedient and prays in faith; the Lord speaks to him, and he is chosen to rule over his brethren. [Between 600 and 592 BC]
Text
For behold, it came to pass that the Lord spake unto my father, yea, even in a dream, and said unto him: Blessed art thou Lehi, because of the things which thou hast done; and because thou hast been faithful and declared unto this people the things which I commanded thee, behold, they seek to take away thy life.

2 And it came to pass that the Lord commanded my father, even in a dream, that he should take his family and depart into the wilderness.

3 And it came to pass that he was obedient unto the word of the Lord, wherefore he did as the Lord commanded him.

4 And it came to pass that he departed into the wilderness. And he left his house, and the land of his inheritance, and his

gold, and his silver, and his precious things, and took nothing with him, save it were his family, and provisions, and tents, and departed into the wilderness.

5 And he came down by the borders near the shore of the Red Sea; and he traveled in the wilderness in the borders which are nearer the Red Sea; and he did travel in the wilderness with his family, which consisted of my mother, Sariah, and my elder brothers, who were Laman, Lemuel, and Sam.

6 And it came to pass that when he had traveled three days in the wilderness, he pitched his tent in a valley by the side of a driver of water.

7 And it came to pass that he built an altar of stones, and made an offering unto the Lord, and gave thanks unto the Lord our God.

8 And it came to pass that he called the name of the river, Laman, and it emptied into the Red Sea; and the valley was in the borders near the mouth thereof.

9 And when my father saw that the waters of the river emptied into the fountain of the Red Sea, he spake unto Laman, saying: O that thou mightest be like unto this river, continually running into the fountain of all righteousness!

10 And he also spake unto Lemuel: O that thou mightest be like unto this valley, firm and steadfast, and immovable in keeping the commandments of the Lord!

11 Now this he spake because of the stiffneckedness of Laman and Lemuel; for behold they did murmur in many things against their father, because he was a visionary man, and had led them out of the land of Jerusalem, to leave the land of their inheritance, and their gold, and their silver, and their precious things, to perish in the wilderness. And this they said he had done because of the foolish imaginations of his heart.

12 And thus Laman and Lemuel, being the eldest, did murmur against their father. And they did murmur because they knew not the dealings of that God who had created them.

13 Neither did they believe that Jerusalem, that great city, could be destroyed according to the words of the prophets. And they were like unto the Jews who were at Jerusalem, who sought to take away the life of my father.

14 And it came to pass that my father did speak unto them in the valley of Lemuel, with power, being filled with the Spirit, until their frames did shake before him. And he did confound them, that they durst not utter against him; wherefore, they did as he commanded them.

15 And my father dwelt in a tent.

16 And it came to pass that I, Nephi, being exceedingly young, nevertheless being large in stature, and also having great desires to know of the mysteries of God, wherefore, I did cry unto the Lord; and behold he did visit me, and did soften my heart that I did believe all the words which had been spoken by my father; wherefore, I did not rebel against him like unto my brothers.

17 And I spake unto Sam, making known unto him the things which the Lord had manifested unto me by his Holy Spirit. And it came to pass that he believed in my words.

18 But, behold, Laman and Lemuel would not hearken unto my words; and being grieved because of the hardness of their hearts I cried unto the Lord for them.

19 And it came to pass that the Lord spake unto me, saying: Blessed art thou, Nephi, because of thy faith, for thou hast sought me diligently, with lowliness of heart.

20 And inasmuch as ye shall keep my commandments, ye shall prosper, and shall be led to a bland of promise; yea, even a land which I have prepared for you; yea, a land which is choice above all other lands.

21 And inasmuch as thy brethren shall rebel against thee, they shall be cut off from the presence of the Lord.

22 And inasmuch as thou shalt keep my commandments, thou shalt be made a ruler and a teacher over thy brethren.

23 For behold, in that day that they shall rebel against me, I will curse them even with a sore curse, and they shall have no power over thy seed except they shall rebel against me also.

24 And if it so be that they rebel against me, they shall be a scourge unto thy seed, to stir them up in the ways of remembrance.

Summaries of chapters 3 to 21

1 Nephi: 3
Lehi's sons return to Jerusalem to obtain the plates of brass – Laban refuses to give them up – Nephi exhorts and encourages his brethren – Laban steals their property and attempts to slay them – Laman and Lemuel smite Nephi and are reproved by an angel. [Between 600 and 592]

1 Nephi: 4
Nephi slays Laban at the Lord's command and then secures the plates of brass by stratagem – Zoram chooses to join Lehi's family in the wilderness. [Between 600 and 592 BC]

1 Nephi: 5
Sariah complains against Lehi – Both rejoice over the return of their sons – They offer sacrifices – The plates of brass contain writings of Moses and the prophets – They identify Lehi as a descendant of Joseph –Lehi prophesies concerning his seed and the preservation of the plates. [Between 600 and 592 BC]

1 Nephi: 6
Nephi writes of the things of God – His purpose is to persuade men to come unto the God of Abraham and be saved. [Between 600 and 592 BC]

1 Nephi: 7
Lehi's sons return to Jerusalem and enlist Ishmael and his household in their cause – Laman and others rebel – Nephi exhorts his brethren to have faith in the Lord –They bind him with cords and plan his destruction – He is freed by the power of faith – His brethren ask forgiveness – Lehi and his company offer sacrifice and burnt offerings. [Between 600 and 592]

1 Nephi: 8
Lehi sees a vision of the tree of life – He partakes of its fruit and desires his family to do likewise – He sees a rod of iron, a strait and narrow path, and the mists of darkness that enshroud men – Sariah, Nephi, and Sam partake of the fruit, but Laman and Lemuel refuse. [Between 600 and 592 BC]

1 Nephi: 9
Nephi makes two sets of records – Each is called the plates of Nephi – The larger plates contain a secular history; the smaller ones deal primarily with sacred things. [Between 600 and 592 BC]

1 Nephi: 10
Lehi predicts the Babylonian captivity – He tells of the coming among the Jews of a Messiah, a Savior, a Redeemer – He tells also of the coming of the one who should baptize the Lamb of God – Lehi tells of the death and resurrection of the Messiah – He compares the scattering and gathering of Israel to an olive tree –Nephi speaks of the Son of God, of the gift of the Holy Ghost, and of the need for righteousness. [Between 600 and 592 BC]

1 Nephi: 11
Nephi sees the Spirit of the Lord and is shown in vision the tree of life – He sees the mother of the Son of God and learns of the condescension of God – He sees the baptism, ministry, and crucifixion of the Lamb of God – He sees also the call and ministry of the twelve apostles of the Lamb. [Between 600 and 592 BC]

1 Nephi: 12
Nephi sees in vision: the land of promise; the righteousness, iniquity, and downfall of its inhabitants; the coming of the Lamb of God among them; how the twelve disciples and the twelve apostles shall judge Israel; the loathsome and filthy state of those who dwindle in unbelief. [Between 600 and 592 BC]

1 Nephi: 13

Nephi sees in vision: the church of the devil set up among the Gentiles; the discovery and colonizing of America; the loss of many plain and precious parts of the Bible; the resultant state of gentile apostasy; the restoration of the gospel, the coming forth of latter-day scripture, and the building up of Zion. [Between 600 and 592 BC]

1 Nephi: 14

An angel tells Nephi of the blessings and cursings – to fall upon the Gentiles –There are only two churches: the Church of the Lamb of God and the church of the devil – The saints of God in all nations are persecuted by the great and abominable church – The apostle John shall write concerning the end of the world. [Between 600 and 592 BC]

1 Nephi: 15

Lehi's seed are to receive the gospel from the Gentiles in the latter days –The gathering of Israel is likened unto an olive tree whose natural branches shall be grafted in again – Nephi interprets the vision of the tree of life and speaks of the justice of God in dividing the wicked from the righteous. [Between 600 and 592 BC]

1 Nephi: 16

The wicked take the truth to be hard – Lehi's sons marry the daughters of Ishmael– The Liahona guides their course in the wilderness– Messages from the Lord are written on the Liahona from time to time – Ishmael dies; his family murmur because of afflictions. [Between 600 and 592 BC]

1 Nephi: 17

Nephi is commanded to build a ship – His brethren oppose him – He exhorts them by recounting the history of God's dealings with Israel – He is filled with the power of God – His brethren are forbidden to touch him, lest they whither as a dried reed. [About 592-591 BC]

1 Nephi: 18

The ship is finished – The births of Jacob and Joseph are mentioned – The company embarks for the promised land – The sons of Ishmael and their wives join in revelry and rebellion – Nephi is bound, and the ship is driven back by a terrible tempest – Nephi is freed, and by his prayer the storm ceases – They arrive in the promised land. [About 590-589 BC]

1 Nephi: 19

Nephi makes plates of ore and records the history of his people – The God of Israel shall come six hundred years from the time Lehi left Jerusalem – Nephi tells of His sufferings and crucifixion – The Jews shall be despised and scattered until the latter days, when they will return unto the Lord. [Between 588 and 570 BC]

1 Nephi: 20

The Lord reveals his purposes to Israel – They have been chosen in the furnace of affliction and are to go forth from Babylon – Compare Isaiah 48. [Between 588 and 570 BC]

1 Nephi: 21

Messiah shall be a light to the Gentiles and shall free the prisoners – Israel shall be gathered with power in the last days – Kings shall be their nursing fathers –Compare Isaiah 49. [Between 588 and 570 BC]

1 Nephi: 22

Israel shall be scattered upon all the face of the earth – The gentiles shall nurse and nourish Israel with the gospel in the last days – Israel shall be gathered and saved, and the wicked shall burn as stubble – The kingdom of the devil shall be destroyed, and Satan shall be bound. [Between 588 and 570 BC]

Text of 1 Nephi: 22

1 And now it came to pass that after I, Nephi, had read these things which were engraven upon the plates of brass, my brethren came unto me and said unto me: What meaneth these things which ye have

read? Behold, are they to be understood according to things which are spiritual, which shall come to pass according to the spirit and not the flesh?

2 And I, Nephi, said unto them: Behold they were manifest unto the prophet by the voice of the Spirit; for by the Spirit are all things made known unto the prophets, which shall come upon the children of men according to the flesh.

3 Wherefore, the things of which I have read are things pertaining to things both temporal and spiritual; for it appears that the house of Israel, sooner or later, will be scattered upon all the face of the earth, and also among all nations.

4 And behold, there are many who are already lost from the knowledge of those who are at Jerusalem. Yea, the more part of all the tribes have been led away; and they are scattered to and fro upon the isles of the sea; and whither they are none of us knoweth, save that we know that they have been led away.

5 And since they have been led away, these things have been prophesied concerning them, and also concerning all those who shall hereafter be scattered and be confounded, because of the Holy One of Israel; for against him will they harden their hearts; wherefore, they shall be scattered among all nations and shall be hated of all men.

6 Nevertheless, after they shall be nursed by the Gentiles, and the Lord has lifted up his hand upon the Gentiles and set them up for a standard, and their children have been carried in their arms, and their daughters have been carried upon their shoulders, behold these things of which are spoken are temporal; for thus are the covenants of the Lord with our fathers; and it meaneth us in the days to come, and also all our brethren who are of the house of Israel.

7 And it meaneth that the time cometh that after all the house of Israel have been scattered and confounded, that the Lord God will raise up a mighty nation among the Gentiles, yea, even upon the face of this land; and by them shall our seed be scattered.

8 And after our seed is scattered the Lord God will proceed to do a marvelous work among the Gentiles, which shall be of great worth unto our seed; wherefore, it is likened unto their being nourished by the Gentiles and being carried in their arms and upon their shoulders.

9 And it shall also be of worth unto the Gentiles; and not only unto the Gentiles but unto all the house of Israel, unto the making known of the covenants of the Father of heaven unto Abraham, saying: In thy seed shall all the kindreds of the earth be blessed.

10 And I would, my brethren, that ye should know that all the kindreds of the earth cannot be blessed unless he shall make bare his arm in the eyes of the nations.

11 Wherefore, the Lord God will proceed to make bare his arm in the eyes of all the nations, in bringing about his covenants and his gospel unto those who are of the house of Israel.

12 Wherefore, he will bring them again out of captivity, and they shall be gathered together to the lands of their inheritance; and they shall be brought out of obscurity and out of darkness; and they shall know that the Lord is their Savior and their Redeemer, the Mighty One of Israel.

13 And the blood of that great and abominable church, which is the whore of all the earth, shall turn upon their own heads; for they shall war among themselves, and the sword of their own hands shall fall upon their own heads, and they shall be drunken with their own blood.

14 And every nation which shall war against thee, O house of Israel, shall be turned one against another, and they shall fall into the pit which they digged to ensnare the people of the Lord. And all that fight against Zion shall be destroyed, and that great whore, who hath perverted the right ways of the Lord, yea, that great and abominable church, shall tumble to the dust and great shall be the fall of it.

15 For behold, saith the prophet, the time cometh speedily that Satan shall have no

more power over the hearts of the children of men; for the day soon cometh that all the proud and they who do wickedly shall be as stubble; and the day cometh that they must be burned.

16 For the time soon cometh that the fullness of the wrath of God shall be poured out upon all the children of men; for he will not suffer that the wicked shall destroy the righteous.

17 Wherefore, he will preserve the righteous by his power, even if it so be that the fullness of his wrath must come, and the righteous be preserved, even unto the destruction of their enemies by fire. Wherefore, the righteous need not fear; for thus saith the prophet, they shall be saved, even if it so be as by fire.

18 Behold, my brethren, I say unto you, that these things must shortly come; yea, even blood, and fire, and vapor of smoke must come; and it must needs be upon the face of this earth; and it cometh unto men according to the flesh if it so be that they will harden their hearts against the Holy One of Israel.

19 For behold, the righteous shall not perish; for the time surely must come that all they who fight against Zion shall be cut off.

20 And the Lord will surely prepare a way for his people, unto the fulfilling of the words of Moses, which he spake, saying: A prophet shall the Lord your God raise up unto you, like unto me; him shall ye hear in all things whatsoever he shall say unto you. And it shall come to pass that all those who will not hear that prophet shall be cut off from among the people.

21 And now I, Nephi, declare unto you, that this prophet of whom Moses spake was the Holy One of Israel; wherefore, he shall execute judgment in righteousness.

22 And the righteous need not fear, for they are those who shall not be confounded. But it is the kingdom of the devil, which shall be built up among the children of men, which kingdom is established among them which are in the flesh —

23 For the time speedily shall come that all churches which are built up to get gain, and all those who are built up to get power over the flesh, and those who are built up to become popular in the eyes of the world, and those who seek the lusts of the flesh and the things of the world, and to do all manner of iniquity; yea, in fine, all those who belong to the kingdom of the devil are they who need fear, and tremble, and quake; they are those who must be brought low in the dust; they are those who must be consumed as stubble; and this is according to the words of the prophet.

24 And the time cometh speedily that the righteous must be led up as calves of the stall, and the Holy One of Israel must reign in dominion, and might, and power, and great glory.

25 And he gathereth his children from the four quarters of the earth; and he numbereth his sheep, and they know him; and there shall be one fold and one shepherd; and he shall feed his sheep, and in him they shall find pasture.

26 And because of the righteousness of his people, Satan has no power; wherefore, he cannot be loosed for the space of many years; for he hath no power over the hearts of the people, for they dwell in righteousness, and the Holy One of Israel reigneth.

27 And now behold, I, Nephi, say unto you that all these things must come according to the flesh.

28 But, behold, all nations, kindreds, tongues, and people shall dwell safely in the Holy One of Israel if it so be that they will repent.

29 And now I, Nephi, make an end; for I durst not speak further as yet concerning these things.

30 Wherefore, my brethren, I would that ye should consider that the things which have been written upon the plates of brass are true; and they testify that a man must be obedient to the commandments of God.

31 Wherefore, ye need not suppose that I and my father are the only ones that have testified, and also taught them. Wherefore, if ye shall be obedient to the commandments, and endure to the end, ye shall be saved at the last day. And thus it is. Amen.

C THE DOCTRINE AND COVENANTS

The Doctrine and Covenants consist of 138 revelations from God, 135 of which were recorded by Joseph Smith, and one added by each of: John Taylor, Brigham Young, and Joseph F. Smith.

It also has two official declarations: one about polygamy added in 1890, one about the role of black persons in the Mormon Church, added in 1978.

D THE PEARL OF GREAT PRICE

The *Pearl of Great Price* consists of:
- two lost books of the Bible:
  - the Book of Moses and
  - the Book of Abraham
- a translation of the Gospel of Matthew
- *Joseph Smith History*
- The Mormon 13 Articles of Faith.

THE BOOK OF ABRAHAM

The Mormon Church obtained some ancient Egyptian writings on papyrus scrolls in 1835. Although at that time little was known about Egyptian hieroglyphics, Smith said that it was written by the Old Testament patriarch Abraham, in his own hand. Smith, with no knowledge or schooling in the Egyptian language, translated the hieroglyphics from the papyrus scrolls and called it the Book of Abraham. The Book of Abraham is now included in *The Pearl of Great Price*.

E NON-DISCOVERIES AND THE BOOK OF MORMON

No cities mentioned in the *Book of Mormon* have been found.

No names mentioned in the *Book of Mormon* names have been found in New World inscriptions.

No nations mentioned in the *Book of Mormon* have been found.

No ancient copies of the *Book of Mormon* have been found.

---

4 FACTS AND FIGURES

INTRODUCTION

The Mormon Church is the largest Christian sect in the world today, claiming a membership of more than 13 million. Mormons claim to have about 5 million members in the US. It is the fifth largest "Christian Church" in the US. It is the fourth major monotheistic faith tradition:

> Given a continuation of present growth rates, the Mormon Church will achieve the status of the fourth major monotheistic faith tradition sometime during the first quarter of the twenty-first century.
> *Rodney Stark,* Review of Religious Research, *1980*

Mormons have:

20,000 churches and 100 temples in 150 countries.

In 2000 32 temples were opened in the US.

US STATES WITH LARGE MORMON POPULATIONS

Utah

The greatest concentration of Mormons live in Utah. About 60% of the adults of Utah identify themselves as Mormon.

Idaho	14%
Nevada	9%
Arizona	6%
Oregon	4%

The Mormon population of all other states is 3% or less.

REMARKABLE GROWTH RATE

Membership of the Mormon church has at least doubled every fifteen years since 1945.

In the 1980s it was growing at the rate of 6% a year, but now is just under 3% a year.

In November 2000 the US News & World Report stated that Mormonism is the fastest growing faith group in American history. It estimated that if present trends continue, there could be 265 million Mormon members worldwide by the year 2080.

SALT LAKE CITY

The Mormon church is headquartered in Salt Lake City.

5 MORMON PRACTICES

A   Mormon missionaries
B   Baptism for the dead
C   Smoking and drinking alcohol, tea and coffee

A MORMON MISSIONARIES

More than 60,000 men and women serve the Church of Jesus Christ of Latter-day Saints as missionaries (referred to as "Elders") in more than 330 missions around the world. More than 300,000 Mormon converts are won every year, mainly from Christian Churches.

B BAPTISM FOR THE DEAD

In 1 Corinthians 15:29 Paul wrote: "Now if there is no resurrection, what will those do who are baptized for the dead? If the dead are not raised at all, why are people baptized for them?"

THE MORMON VIEW

At first it was thought that there was no salvation for those who had died before the start of the Church of Jesus Christ of Latter-day Saints. To solve this problem, in about 1840, Smith devised a doctrine and rite of baptism for the dead. Today, Mormons still go to a temple and are baptized for dead relatives.

Baptism and salvation for the dead are based on the conviction that persons who died without a chance to hear or accept the gospel cannot possibly be condemned by a just and merciful God. The gospel

must be preached to them after death.

Mormons find authority for this practice in 1 Peter 4:6: "For this cause was the gospel preached also to them that are dead, that they might be judged according to men in the flesh, but live according to God in the spirit."

Baptism is considered as essential for the dead as it is for the living, even though the rites will not finally save them; there must be faith and repentance. The ceremony is performed with a living person standing proxy for the dead.

Handbook of Denominations

GENEALOGICAL LIBRARY

Mormons have compiled the largest genealogical library in the world containing millions of volumes of birth, marriage, death, and other records for this work of standing proxy for deceased ancestors in their rite of baptism for the dead.

THE CHRISTIAN VIEW

The whole of 1 Corinthians 15 is about Jesus' resurrection. Paul used this opportunity to correct some false teaching that was then believed by Christians at Corinth. Faced with the erroneous idea that there was no resurrection of the dead, Paul wrote, "But if it is preached that Christ has been raised from the dead, how can some of you say that there is no resurrection of the dead?" (1 Corinthians 15:12).

Paul goes on to use an argument from baptism, which was by immersion, and was a picture of death and resurrection. If there was no resurrection of the dead, as some were teaching, why, asks Paul, were they baptized in a picture of resurrection?

Those Corinthians who were denying the resurrection, were removing the significance of the figure of baptism and reducing it to a mere picture of death, without any hope of a future resurrection. Paul was reasoning that continuing to practice baptism by immersion required faith in the resurrection. It is as if said, "Else what shall they do which are baptized for the resurrection of the dead, if the dead rise not at all? why are they then baptized for the resurrection of the dead?"

1 Corinthians 15:29 is thus teaching that baptism is by immersion and that it is a picture of our faith in the resurrection.

The practice of baptism for the dead is at variance with all other Christian Churches.

C SMOKING AND DRINKING ALCOHOL, TEA AND COFFEE

A code of health and conduct given in 1833, known as the "Word of Wisdom," disapproves of the use of tobacco, alcoholic beverages and "hot drinks." While the "Word of Wisdom" forbids the use of hot drinks, strong drinks and tobacco, the Mormon Church today interprets hot drinks to mean tea and coffee.

DRUGS

Not only do Latter-day Saints caution their members against using tobacco, consuming alcohol, tea and coffee, they interpret the misuse of drugs – illegal, legal, prescription or controlled – as a violation of their health code in the "Word of Wisdom."

6 MORMON BELIEFS

A   Articles of Faith
B   Doctrine of God
   (i)   God was once a man
   (ii)   Humans can become gods
   (iii) More than one god
C   The only true Church
D   Jesus' birth
E   Revelation
F   Salvation

INTRODUCTION

The Mormon Church teaches doctrines in direct opposition to historic Christianity, yet it claims to be the true Church of Jesus Christ.

A ARTICLES OF FAITH

At first sight, many of the Mormon Articles of Faith appear to be quite orthodox. On further examination, however, they are often seen to be heretical.

The Articles of Faith of The Church of Jesus Christ of Latter-day Saints:

1 We believe in God, the Eternal Father, and in His Son, Jesus Christ, and in the Holy Ghost.

[However, Mormons reject the Christian Trinity. They teach that the Trinity is three separate gods. "God the Father", for the Mormons, was once a man, but became God.]

2 We believe that men will be punished for their own sins, and not for Adam's transgression.

3 We believe that through the Atonement of Christ, all mankind may be saved, by obedience to the laws and ordinances of the Gospel.

4 We believe that the first principles and ordinances of the Gospel are: first, Faith in the Lord Jesus Christ; second,

Repentance; third, Baptism by immersion for the remission of sins; fourth, Laying on of hands for the gift of the Holy Ghost.

5 We believe that a man must be called of God, by prophecy, and by the laying on of hands by those who are in authority, to preach the Gospel and administer in the ordinances thereof.

6 We believe in the same organization that existed in the Primitive Church, namely, apostles, prophets, pastors, teachers, evangelists, and so forth.

7 We believe in the gift of tongues, prophecy, revelation, visions, healing, interpretation of tongues, and so forth.

8 We believe the Bible to be the word of God as far as it is translated correctly; we also believe the Book of Mormon to be the word of God.

[However, the "correct translation" of Joseph Smith's *Book of Mormon* contains 1,475 verses that have been changed from the King James Version of the Bible. Moreover, the early Mormons, and many Mormons today, do not live according to the instructions found in the *Book of Mormon*. For example, polygamy is forbidden in the *Book of Mormon*, but Joseph Smith, in his 132nd revelation, was ordered by God to have polygamous relationships, as

Solomon had. Smith had twenty-seven wives officially, and sixty unofficially, and the second leader of the Mormons, Brigham Young, had twenty-five wives with fifty-six children. Brigham Young once said: "He who rejects the doctrine of polygamy shall be condemned."

Smith began practicing a form of polygamy, which he called plural marriage, possibly as early as 1833.

Although polygamy was abolished officially by the Mormons in 1904, it has been estimated that as many as 30,000 fundamentalist Mormons have plural marriages in Utah.]

9 We believe all that God has revealed, all that He does now reveal, and we believe that He will yet reveal many great and important things pertaining to the Kingdom of God.

10 We believe in the literal gathering of Israel and in the restoration of the Ten Tribes; that Zion (the New Jerusalem) will be built upon the American continent; that Christ will reign personally upon the earth; and, that the earth will be renewed and receive its paradisiacal glory.

11 We claim the privilege of worshiping Almighty God according to the dictates of our own conscience, and allow all men the same privilege, let them worship how, where, or what they may.

12 We believe in being subject to kings, presidents, rulers, and magistrates, in obeying, honoring, and sustaining the law.

13 We believe in being honest, true, chaste, benevolent, virtuous, and in doing good to all men; indeed, we may say that we follow the admonition of Paul – We believe all things, we hope all things, we have endured many things, and hope to be able to endure all things. If there is anything virtuous, lovely, or of good report or praiseworthy, we seek after these things.

Joseph Smith

B DOCTRINE OF GOD

MORMON DOCTRINE

(i) God the Father was once a man

God himself was once as we are now, and is an exalted man, and sits enthroned in yonder heavens! . . . I am going to tell you how God came to be God. We have imagined and supposed that God was God from all eternity. I will refute that idea, and take away the veil, so that you may see. . . . He was once a man like us; yea that God himself, the Father dwelt on an earth, the same as Jesus Christ himself did.

Joseph Smith

God the Father was once a man on another planet who passed the ordeal we are now passing through.

Brigham Young

God is a glorified and perfected man, a personage of flesh and bones. Inside his tangible body is an eternal spirit.

The Doctrine and Covenants 130:22

(ii) Joseph Smith exhorted all Mormons to aim to become gods. He wrote:

Here then, is eternal life - to know the only wise and true God; and you have got to learn how to be gods yourselves, and to be kings and priests to God, the same as all gods have done before you.

If Mormons marry according to Mormon ceremony, and live obedient lives, they may attain godhood at the resurrection:

Ye shall come forth in the first resurrection; . . . and shall inherit thrones, kingdoms, principalities, and powers, dominions, all heights and depths . . . (and you) shall pass by the angels, and the gods, which are set there, to (their) exaltation. . . . Then they shall be gods, because they have no end; therefore shall they be from everlasting to everlasting because they continue. . . . Then they shall be gods because they have all power, and the angels are subject to them.

The Doctrine and Covenants 132

(iii) More than one god

In the beginning, the head of the gods called a council of the gods; and they came together and concocted a plan to create the world and (the) people in it.

Joseph Smith

And they (the gods) said: let there be light and there was light. And they (the gods) comprehended the light, . . . and the gods called the light Day and the darkness they called Night. . . .

The Pearl of Great Price

Mormons claim to be monotheists, and to worship only one God but in reality they are henotheists. Henotheism is a form of polytheism that stresses a central, but not the only, deity.

THE TEACHING OF THE BIBLE

Each of the following twenty-seven passages explicitly teach that there is one – and only one – true and living God.

(i) Deuteronomy 4:35, 39: "Unto thee it was shown, that thou mightest know that the LORD he is God; there is none else beside him. (39) Know therefore this day, and consider it in thine heart, that the LORD he is God in heaven above, and upon the earth beneath: there is none else."

(ii) Deuteronomy 6:4: "Hear, O Israel: The LORD thy God is one LORD." (Note in Mark 12:28-34 how Jesus and a Jewish scribe he encountered understood this text.)

(iii) Deuteronomy 32:39: "See now that I, even I, am he, and there is no god with me: I kill, and I make alive; I wound, and I heal: neither is there any that can deliver out of my hand."

(iv) 2 Samuel 7:22: "Wherefore thou art great, O LORD God; for there is none like

thee, neither is there any God beside thee, according to all that we have heard with our ears."

(v) 1 Kings 8:60: "That all the people of the earth may know that the LORD is God, and that there is none else."

(vi) 2 Kings 5:15: "And he returned to the man of God, he and all his company, and came, and stood before him: and he said, Behold, now I know that there is no God in all the earth, but in Israel; now therefore, I pray thee, take a blessing of thy servant."

(vii) 2 Kings 19:15: "And Hezekiah prayed before the LORD, and said, O LORD God of Israel, which dwellest between the cherubims, thou art the God, even thou alone, of all the kingdoms of the earth; thou hast made heaven and earth."

(viii) Nehemiah 9:6: "Thou, even thou, art LORD alone; thou has made heaven, the heaven of heavens, with all their host, the earth, and all things that are therein, the seas, and all that is therein, and thou preservest them all; and the host of heaven worshippeth thee."

(ix) Psalm 18:31: "For who is God save the LORD? or who is a rock save our God?"

(x) Psalm 86:10: "For thou art great, and doest wondrous things: thou art God alone."

(xi) Isaiah 37:16, 20: "O LORD of hosts, God of Israel, that dwellest between the cherubims, thou art the God, even thou alone, of all the kingdoms of the earth: thou has made heaven and earth. (20) Now therefore, O LORD our God, save us from his hand, that all the kingdoms of the earth may know that thou art the LORD, even thou only."

(xii) Isaiah 43:10, 11: "Ye are my witnesses, saith the LORD, and my servant whom I have chosen: that ye may know and believe me, and understand that I am he: before me there was no God formed, neither shall there be after me. I, even I, am the LORD; and beside me there is no saviour."

(xiii) Isaiah 44:6, 8: "Thus saith the LORD the King of Israel, and his redeemer the LORD of hosts; I am the first, and I am the last; and beside me there is no God. (8) Fear ye not, neither be afraid; have not I told thee from that time, and have declared it? ye are even my witnesses. Is there a God beside me? yea, there is no God; I know not any."

(xiv) Isaiah 45:21: "Tell ye, and bring them near; yea, let them take counsel together: who hath declared this from ancient time? who hath told it from that time? have not I the LORD? and there is no God else beside me; a just God and a Saviour; there is none beside me."

(xv) Isaiah 46:9: "For I am God, and there is none else; I am God, and there is none like me."

(xvi) Hosea 13:4: "Yet I am the LORD thy God from the land of Egypt, and thou shalt know no god but me; for there is no saviour beside me."

(xvii) Joel 2:27: "And ye shall know that I am in the midst of Israel, and that I am the LORD your God, and none else: and my people shall never be ashamed."

(xviii)   Zechariah 14:9: "And the LORD shall be king over all the earth: in that day shall there be one Lord, and his name one."

(xix) Mark 12:29-34: "And Jesus answered him, The first of all the commandments is, Hear, O Israel; The Lord our God is one Lord: And thou shalt love the Lord thy God with all thy heart, and with all thy soul, and with all thy mind, and with all thy strength: this is the first commandment. And the second is like, namely this, thou shalt love thy neighbor as thyself. There is none other commandment greater than these. And the scribe said unto him, Well, Master, thou hast said the truth: for there is one God; and there is none other but he: And to love him with all the heart, and

with all the understanding, and with all the soul, and with all the strength, and to love his neighbor as himself, is more than all whole burnt offerings and sacrifices. And when Jesus saw that he answered discreetly, he said unto him, Thou art not far from the kingdom of God. And no man after that durst ask him any question."

(xx) John 17:3: "And this is life eternal, that they might know thee the only true God, and Jesus Christ, whom thou hast sent."

(xxi) Romans 3:30: "Seeing it is one God, which shall justify the circumcision by faith, and uncircumcision through faith."

(xxii) 1 Corinthians 8:4-6: "As concerning therefore the eating of those things that are offered in sacrifice unto idols, we know that an idol is nothing in the world, and that there is none other God but one: For though there be that are called gods, whether in heaven or in earth, (as there be gods many, and lords many,) But to us there is but one God, the Father, of whom all things, and we in him; and one Lord Jesus Christ, by whom are all things, and we by him.

(xxiii)   Galatians 3:20: "Now a mediator is not a mediator of one, but God is one . . ."

(xxiv) Ephesians 4:6: "One God and Father of all, who is above all, and through all, and in you all."

(xxv) 1 Timothy 1:17: "Now unto the King eternal, immortal, invisible, the only wise God, be honour and glory for ever and ever. Amen."

(xxvi) 1 Timothy 2:5: "For there is one God, and one mediator between God and men, the man Christ Jesus."

(xxvii)   James 2:19: "Thou believest that there is one God; thou doest well: the devils also believe, and tremble."

C THE ONLY TRUE CHURCH
Mormons believe that the Church of Jesus Christ of Latter-day Saints is the only true church of Jesus Christ, God's restored Church on earth today. Mormons believe all other Churches are false religions teaching incorrect doctrines.

D JESUS' BIRTH
The Mormon Church teaches that Jesus Christ progressed to godhood, having first been procreated as a spirit child by Heavenly Father and a heavenly mother. He was later conceived physically through intercourse between Heavenly Father and the Virgin Mary.

THE TEACHING OF THE BIBLE
The Bible teaches that Jesus is the unique Son of God; he has always existed as God, and is co-eternal and co-equal with the Father (John 1:1, 14; 10:30; 14:9; Colossians 2:9). He laid aside the glory he shared with the Father (John 17:4, 5; Philippians 2:6-11) and was made flesh for our salvation. He was conceived supernaturally by the Holy Spirit and born of a virgin (Matthew 1:18-23; Luke 1:34-35).

E REVELATION
The Presbyterian Church (USA) has stated:
> The Reformed tradition believes that the canon of scripture is closed and the Bible is complete, although the Holy Spirit continues to lead the Church into deeper understandings of God's revelation. Reformed Christians test new understandings against the content of the central revelatory events recorded in the Bible. Latter-day Saints speak of receiving new revelations. Revelatory events not found in the Old and New Testaments are recounted in additional Mormon scriptures.

F SALVATION
The Presbyterian Church (USA) has stated:

> For Latter-day Saints, salvation through Christ's atonement is a first step toward sanctification and exaltation – an eternal progression that is in the hand of each person and family – thus explaining the special importance of obedient living, marriage, or baptism for the dead. The Reformed tradition understands both the initiative and completion of the plan of salvation to rest on God's grace. Nothing is required but acceptance of God in Christ, from which a life of gratitude flows.

7 WORSHIP

MORMON TEMPLES
Mormon temples are closed on Sundays and are very different from Mormon local "chapels" or "meeting houses" or "ward houses" or "churches" where they hold their weekly worship services.

ORDINANCES
The rituals, called "ordinances" by Mormons performed in temples are:

- baptism for the dead
- endowment for the dead and the living
- sealings for the dead and the living
- sealing of husband and wife (marriage)
- sealing of children to parents.

SEALINGS
Mormons believe that the family relationships – between husband and wife and between parent and child – can be made eternal by the authority of the Mormon priesthood. The ceremonies in which this is done are called "sealings."

ENDOWMENT RITE

The endowment ceremony is a kind of initiation rite, consisting of dramatization, instruction, passwords, oaths, and examinations.

Your endowment is to receive all those ordinances in the House of the Lord which are necessary for you, after you have departed this life, to enable you to walk back to the presence of the Father, passing the angels who stand as sentinels, being enabled to give them the key words, the signs and tokens, pertaining to the Holy Priesthood, and gain your eternal exaltation in spite of earth and hell.

Brigham Young, Journal of Discourses
Vol. 2, p.315, April 6, 1853

JEHOVAH'S WITNESSES

CONTENTS

1 An overview 529

2 Founder 529

3 Jehovah's Witnesses' holy book 530

4 Facts and figures 532

5 Jehovah's Witnesses' practices 533

6 Jehovah's Witnesses' beliefs 536

7 Worship 539

8 Glossary 539

1 AN OVERVIEW

Jehovah's Witnesses are a non-trinitarian Protestant millennialist sect founded in the 1870s in Pennsylvania by Charles Taze Russell as a small Bible study group. Their goal is the establishment of God's Kingdom, the theocracy, which will follow the Armageddon.

Factfile
- Date of origin: February 16, 1852
- Founder: Charles Taze Russell
- Holy book: New World Translation of the Holy Scriptures
- Number of adherents: 7 million

NAME
Jehovah's Witnesses derive their name from:
Jehovah, an English translation of the name for God in the Hebrew Scriptures.

Witnesses is taken from the passage in Isaiah 43:10 (and similar passages): "Ye are my witnesses, saith the Lord . . ."

2 FOUNDER

CHARLES TAZE RUSSELL (1852-1916)
The Watch Tower Society (WTS) traces its origin to Charles Taze Russell. After periods of being a Presbyterian, Congregationalist, skeptic, and Adventist, he organized a Bible study group in Pennsylvania in 1870. The group's intense examination of the Bible caused them to reject traditional Christian teachings on the nature of deity, and the immortality of the soul.

By 1880, thirty congregations had been formed in seven states.

Russell founded Zion's Watch Tower in 1879, and Zion's Watch Tower Tract Society in 1884 (later renamed the Watch Tower Bible and Tract Society). Zion's Watch Tower Bible and Tract Society was incorporated in 1884.

In 1896, it dropped the word "Zion" from its name.

In addition to his speaking and editorial work, Russell wrote six volumes titled *Studies in Scriptures* (originally *Millennial Dawn*), which appeared between 1886 and 1904. By the time of his death in 1916, the legal and doctrinal foundation of the Society had been established.

JUDGE JOSEPH FRANKLIN RUTHERFORD (1869-1942)
After Russell's death in 1916, the WTS's lawyer, Judge Joseph Franklin Rutherford, took over the presidency. In 1931, the Society became known as "Jehovah's Witnesses."

Under Rutherford's leadership the organization began to experience phenomenal growth. In 1928, the organization had 44,000 members and by his death in 1942, membership had grown to over 115,000. Part of this growth can be attributed to Rutherford's insistence that the world was about to end and Armageddon would happen any day.

NATHAN H. KNORR
After Rutherford's death in 1942, Nathan Homer Knorr was elected as the third president, and he remained president until his death in 1942. Under his leadership, the WTS greatly increased its publication work. This included the publication of the New World Translation of the Bible. This translation, published in six volumes between 1950 and 1960, supports many Jehovah's Witnesses'

doctrines while ignoring accepted rules of language translation.

When Knorr took over the leadership of the Witnesses, it had 115,000 members, but by his death in 1977 it had 2.25 million members.

FREDERICK W. FRANZ
After Knorr's death, Fred Franz was elected the fourth president and he continued in office until his death in 1992 at age ninety-nine. A high point in his career was the 1958 convention of the Witnesses, when he addressed an audience of 253,922 people from 123 countries gathered at Yankee Stadium and the Polo Grounds.

The current president is Milton G. Henschel.

---

3 JEHOVAH'S WITNESSES' HOLY BOOK

THE NEW WORLD TRANSLATION
In 1961, the Jehovah's Witnesses published their own English version of the Bible, calling it The New World Translation (NWT) of the Holy Scriptures. The NWT is described by the Witnesses as "a translation of the Holy Scriptures made directly from Hebrew, Aramaic and Greek into modern day English by a committee of anointed witnesses of Jehovah." However, it has been heavily criticized for distorting some of the original Hebrew and Greek texts in order to more suitably reflect WTS theology.

According to David Reed, an ex-Witness, the New World Translation came into being for the sole purpose of supporting Watch Tower doctrines. Reed said, "During the 1950s, Watch Tower leaders went beyond interpretation by producing their own version of the Bible, with hundreds of verses changed to fit Watch Tower doctrine. And their New World Translation of the Holy Scriptures continues to be rewritten every few years, with additional changes made to bring God's Word into closer agreement with what the organization teaches."

GREEK SCHOLARS AND THE NEW WORLD TRANSLATION
The New World Translation has received many critical reviews from numerous leading Bible scholars. It has been called, "a frightful mistranslation," "erroneous," "pernicious," and "reprehensible," lacking in objectivity.

> If the Jehovah's Witnesses take this translation seriously, they are polytheists.
> *Dr. Bruce M. Metzger, professor of New Testament at Princeton University*

> It is abundantly clear that a sect which can translate the New Testament like that is intellectually dishonest.
> *William Barclay*
> From beginning to end this volume is a shining example of how the Bible should not be translated.
> *H. H. Rowley*

> [It] must be viewed as a radically biased piece of work. At some points it is actually dishonest. At others it is neither modern nor scholarly.

Dr. Robert Countess, The Jehovah's
Witnesses' New Testament

Their New World Translation is by no
means an objective rendering of the
sacred text into modern English, but is a
biased translation in which many of the
peculiar teachings of the Watch Tower
Society are smuggled into the text of the
Bible itself.

Anthony Hoekema,
The Four Major Cults

EXAMPLES OF MISTRANSLATION
The translations given in the New World
Translation of the opening verses of Genesis,
of John's Gospel, and of Colossians 1:16, 17,
illustrate the ways in which this translation
deliberately mistranslates certain critical verses
so that they back up the doctrinal viewpoint
of Jehovah's Witnesses.

NEW WORLD TRANSLATION OF
GENESIS 1:1-2:

In [the] beginning God created the
heavens and the earth.
Now the earth proved to be formless and
waste and there was darkness upon the
surface of [the] watery deep; and God's
active force was moving to and fro over
the surface of the waters.

This translation ties in with The Watch
Tower Bible and Tract Society's denial that the
Holy Spirit is alive, and is the third person of
the Trinity.

The correct translation should be: ". . .
the Spirit of God was moving over the surface
of the waters."

NEW WORLD TRANSLATION OF
JOHN 1:1:

In the beginning was the Word, and the
Word was with God, and the Word was
a god.
This translation supports the teaching that
Jesus was not divine.

The correct translation should be: "In the
beginning was the Word, and the Word was
with God, and the Word was God." (New
International Version)

NEW WORLD TRANSLATION OF
COLOSSIANS 1:16, 17:

. . . because by means of him all [other]
things were created in the heavens and
upon the earth, the things visible and the
things invisible, no matter whether they
are thrones or lordships or governments
or authorities. All [other] things have
been created through him and for him.
Also, he is before all [other] things and by
means of him all [other] things were made
to exists.

In the New World Translation, the word
"other" is in brackets. This is a correct
admission that the word "other" does not
appear in the original Greek.

However, if Paul had wanted to teach that
Jesus was "another" created thing there were
two perfectly suitable Greek words, *allos* and
heteros, which he could have used. But he used
neither word. There is no word for "other" in
the Greek. The only reason for adding the
word "other" would be to support the idea
that Jesus is a created being and not God.
Jehovah's Witnesses teach that God created
Jesus and then Jesus created everything else.

The translation given in the New
International Version is:
For by him all things were created: things
in heaven and on earth, visible and
invisible, whether thrones or powers or
rulers or authorities; all things were
created by him and for him. He is before
all things, and in him all things hold
together.

4 FACTS AND FIGURES

HISTORY
The modern-day organization of Jehovah's Witnesses began toward the end of the nineteenth century with a small group of Bible students near Pittsburgh, Pennsylvania.

In 1879 they started publishing the Bible journal now called the *Watchtower Announcing Jehovah's Kingdom*. It is published in more than 140 languages and is the world's most widely circulated religious magazine.

The name Jehovah's Witnesses was adopted in 1931. Previously, they were known as International Bible Students.

HEADQUARTERS
The worldwide organization of the Jehovah's Witnesses is directed by an unpaid governing body serving at the international offices in Brooklyn, New York.

WORLDWIDE MEMBERSHIP STATISTICS IN 2003

Attendance at the annual Memorial of Christ's death	16,097,622
Total volunteer hours spent in public Bible educational work	1.2 billion
Average weekly home Bible courses taught	5,726,509
Practicing members	6,429,351
New members baptized this year	258,845
Increase over 2002	2.2 %
Branch offices	109
Congregations	95,919
Number of Witnesses in the US	just over 1 million
Number of Witnesses in Canada	about 120,000

WORLDWIDE PUBLISHING AND TRANSLATING
Jehovah's Witnesses claim to have developed an unparalleled worldwide organization that provides free Bible education to all who wish to have a better understanding of the Bible.

They publish in 400 languages, using more than 2,000 volunteers to assist with translation worldwide.

BIBLES
Since 1926, the Watch Tower Bible and Tract Society of Pennsylvania has published more than 124 million copies of the Bible in 45 languages.

SOME OTHER PUBLICATIONS
The *Watchtower*, the primary Bible study aid for Jehovah's Witnesses, has an average printing of 25 million, making it the largest circulation of any religious magazine in the world. It is published in 148 languages. Of these editions, 135 are translated and printed for simultaneous release.

Awake!, published in 86 languages, is a general-interest news magazine with a religious slant and has an average printing of 22 million.

Knowledge That Leads to Everlasting Life is the introductory textbook used extensively in the home Bible study program of Jehovah's Witnesses. More than 93 million copies have been printed in 161 languages since the book was released in 1995.

ORGANIZATIONAL STRUCTURE
The headquarters are in Brooklyn, NY. Jehovah's Witnesses are organized into:

Governing Body: this is a group of anointed volunteers – all men – which is based in the Brooklyn NY head office. It currently consists of eleven members.

Publishers and Pioneers: these are men and women of all ages who go from door to door attempting to share the Bible with the public in their communities.

Regular Pioneers: those who are dedicated, full-time preachers are given the title Regular Pioneers. They commit themselves to preach for 840 hours a year.

Auxiliary Pioneers: Auxiliary Pioneers do 50 hours a month for one or more consecutive months.

Special Pioneers: Special Pioneers are selected from among the Regular Pioneers and are sent

wherever the need is greatest.

Publishers: typically go door-to-door once per week.

---

5 Jehovah's Witnesses' Practices

A	Disfellowshipping/Shunning
B	Allegiance
C	Holidays
D	Witnessing
E	Blood transfusions
F	Other medical practices
G	No involvement in politics
H	Studying
I	Symbol

A DISFELLOWSHIPPING/SHUNNING

Inactive, openly sinful, or former Jehovah's Witnesses may be disfellowshipped, that is, shunned and avoided by other Jehovah's Witnesses. Jehovah's Witnesses believe they have biblical warrant for this action:

Those who become inactive in the congregation, perhaps even drifting away from association with fellow believers, are not shunned. In fact, special effort is made to reach out to them and rekindle their spiritual interest.

If, however, someone unrepentantly practices serious sins, such as drunkenness, stealing or adultery, he will be disfellowshipped and such an individual is avoided by former fellow-worshipers. Every effort is made to help wrongdoers. But if they are unrepentant, the congregation needs to be protected from their influence. The Bible clearly states: 'Remove the wicked man from among yourselves.' (1 Corinthians 5:13 NWT). Those who formally say they do not want to be part of the organization any more are also avoided.

"What of a man who is disfellowshipped but whose wife and children are still Jehovah's Witnesses?"
The spiritual ties he had with his family change, but blood ties remain. The marriage relationship and normal family affections and dealings can continue. As for disfellowshipped relatives not living in the same household, Jehovah's Witnesses apply the Bible's counsel: "Quit mixing with them." "But now I am writing YOU to quit mixing in company with anyone called a brother that is a fornicator or a greedy person or an idolater or a reviler or a drunkard or an extortioner, not even eating with such a man" (1 Corinthians 5:11 NWT).

Disfellowshipped individuals may continue to attend religious services and, if they wish, they may receive spiritual counsel from the elders with a view to their being restored. They are always welcome to return to the faith if they reject the improper course of conduct for which they were disfellowshipped.

Office of Public Information of
Jehovah's Witnesses

B ALLEGIANCE

Jehovah's Witnesses say that they give allegiance only to Jehovah. They believe that world powers and political parties are, without realizing it, supporting the work of Satan. Therefore Witnesses do not:

- pledge allegiance to the flag of any country
- vote
- serve in armed forces
- hold public office
- and rarely take part in elections.

C HOLIDAYS

Jehovah's Witnesses do not celebrate Thanksgiving, Independence Day, Canada Day, Halloween, Christmas, Easter, birthdays, or any other holidays, except for one. They believe these celebrations grew out of ancient false religions and were not celebrated by the first Christians. Jehovah's Witnesses therefore believe that by not joining in with such "pagan" festivals, they are returning to the practice of the early Church.

Although they estimate that Jesus was born on October 2, this date is not celebrated. Members who are found celebrating "worldly" holidays may be disfellowshipped.

Only one day of celebration is recognized: the Memorial of Christ's Death at the time of Passover.

Jehovah's Witnesses commemorate the Memorial of Christ's Death (also known as the Lord's Evening Meal or Lord's Supper) annually, rather than on a weekly, daily, or monthly basis. Worldwide attendance at the 2004 celebration of the Memorial was 16,760,607. However, very few are allowed to take communion.

D WITNESSING

Jehovah's Witnesses believe that every member of the Jehovah's Witnesses must spend time regularly in the spreading the Christian gospel.

Probably the most well-known practice is evangelism, which is most often done door-to-door. An official website of the Jehovah's Witnesses explains the reason for this practice as follows:

Jesus told his followers to "make disciples of people of all the nations," and he set the example by "journeying from city to city and from village to village, preaching and declaring the good news of the kingdom of God." The apostle Paul taught in public places, in the marketplace, and from house to house. We follow their example. Other religions have acknowledged the Christian obligation to preach in public places and from house to house, although this is often left to a limited group of missionaries or clergy to fulfill.

Office of Public Information of Jehovah's Witnesses

Evangelism, mostly door to door, is central to the religious life of a Jehovah's Witness. "Pioneer publishers" hold only part-time jobs and devote 100 hours each month to witnessing. "Special publishers," who are full-time salaried employees of the Watch Tower Society, are expected to spend about 150 hours per month on evangelism.

Each Kingdom Hall is responsible for evangelizing an assigned territory and each publisher has an assigned neighborhood. Statistics related to these efforts are tracked carefully. Each month, statistical data such as number of visits, hours spent preaching, Bible studies conducted and tracts distributed are reported to the society's headquarters in Brooklyn.

E BLOOD TRANSFUSIONS

The Jehovah's Witnesses are perhaps best known to other Americans as people who won't allow themselves or their children to have blood transfusions.

According to Jehovah's Witnesses "Taking blood into the body through mouth or veins violates God's laws." So an adult who willingly accepts a blood transfusion is considered to be committing a sin and might forfeit his or her eternal life.

This teaching is based upon four passages in the Bible which prohibit the consuming of blood:

But flesh (meat) with . . . blood . . . .shall ye not eat.

Genesis 9:4 KJV

No soul of you shall eat blood . . .
whosoever eateth it shall be cut off.
Leviticus 17:12-14 KJV

That ye abstain . . . from blood . . .
Acts 15:29 KJV

Gentiles . . . keep themselves from things
offered to idols and from blood . . .
Acts 21:25 KJV

The WTS (Watch Tower Society) interprets "eating" of blood in its most general form to include accepting "transfusion of whole blood, packed RBCs, and plasma, as well as WBC and platelet administration." Moreover, because Witnesses believe that any blood that leaves the body must be destroyed, they do not approve of an individual storing his own blood for a later autotransfusion.

It is, however, wrong to say that eating blood is the same as receiving a blood transfusion. Even orthodox Jews do not refuse blood transfusions on the basis of the Old Testament prohibition.

All other Christian and Jewish faith groups belief that the passages refer to dietary laws, that is, to the actual eating of meat containing blood.

F OTHER MEDICAL PRACTICES

From the 1930s to the 1950s Jehovah's Witnesses taught vaccination was wrong. From 1968 to 1980 they taught that organ transplants were cannibalism.

G NO INVOLVEMENT IN POLITICS

Jehovah's Witnesses remain neutral in all political conflicts and believe that God will intervene in human affairs to bring about a peaceful human society earth-wide.

H STUDYING

Jehovah's Witnesses devote themselves to studying their beliefs and attend as many as five teaching meetings each week.

PUBLIC TALK

This is usually held each Sunday. An elder gives a talk on a specific topic.

WATCHTOWER STUDY

This is a lesson based on a study article in the current issue of the *Watchtower*, and usually follows the public talk.

THEOCRATIC MINISTRY SCHOOL

At this evening weekday meeting speakers practice giving talks and witnessing.

> At each meeting, six students give brief speeches on preselected Bible topics, and an instructor comments on the speech and offers suggestions for improvement. Witnesses and non-Witnesses of all ages can enroll in this school.
>
> *Watch Tower Bible and Tract*
> *Society of Pennsylvania*

SERVICE MEETING

After the Theocratic Ministry School, training is given on various ministry activities.

> The Service Meeting focuses on helping Witnesses improve their ability to teach the Bible to others. Topics of discussion have included how to show good manners when approaching others with a Bible message and how to discern what Bible topics may be of interest to people in the community.
>
> *Watch Tower Bible and Tract*
> *Society of Pennsylvania*

CONGREGATION BOOK STUDY

> Witnesses meet in small groups of about 10 to 15, usually in the private homes of members, to discuss a single Bible topic in depth. One of the books or brochures published by Jehovah's Witnesses is used to direct the question-and-answer Bible discussion.
>
> *Watch Tower Bible and Tract*
> *Society of Pennsylvania*

I SYMBOL

Jehovah's Witnesses teach that Jesus was crucified on a stake, and they reject the cross as a pagan symbol. No crosses are to be displayed in the worship hall, on a person, or in Jehovah's Witnesses' houses. The Jehovah's Witness symbol is a watchtower.

6 JEHOVAH'S WITNESSES' BELIEFS

A   Doctrinal denials
B   The Godhead/Trinity
C   The Father
D   Jesus
E   The resurrection of Jesus
F   The Holy Spirit
G   The Bible
H   Heaven and hell
I   Anointed Remnant
J   Second coming of Jesus and Armageddon
K   Salvation
L   Angels
M   Heretical teaching from the *Watchtower*

INTRODUCTION

Jehovah's Witnesses claim to have the only true religion on earth. To the untaught ear the teachings of Jehovah's Witnesses have a Christian ring to them. But on careful examination they are found to deny the deity of Christ, his physical resurrection, and salvation by grace.

A DOCTRINAL DENIALS

One way to understand how different the doctrinal system of the Jehovah's Witnesses is from that of orthodox Christianity is to see what is denied. The doctrinal teaching of Jehovah's Witnesses includes the following:

- denial of the Trinity
- denial of the deity of Christ
- denial of the personality of the Holy Spirit
- denial of the biblical view of the atonement
- denial of the bodily resurrection of Christ
- denial of salvation by faith in Christ alone
- denial of salvation outside their organization

B THE GODHEAD/TRINITY

Jehovah's Witnesses teach that there is no Trinity.

Orthodox Christians do not claim to understand the mystery of the Trinity but when they study the New Testament, they come to the inescapable conclusion that it teaches that there are three eternal persons existing as the one God.

C THE FATHER

Jehovah's Witnesses teach that the Father is Almighty God. He is not part of a Trinity. His personal name is Jehovah and he should be addressed by that name. Prayer and worship should be directed to the Father. He is not omniscient or omnipresent.

D JESUS

Jehovah's Witnesses believe that Jesus Christ is only one of many gods and is a created being. They translate John 1:1 as, "In the beginning was the word . . . and the word was a god." The correct translation is, "In the beginning was the Word, and the Word was with God, and the Word was God" (John 1:1 NIV).

Jehovah's Witnesses teach that:

- only Jehovah is worthy of worship and to worship Jesus is unscriptural. (Compare this with John 5:23: "that all should honour the Son just as they honour the Father. He who does not honour the Son does not honour the Father who sent Him" [NKJV].)

- When he was on earth, Jesus was a perfect sinless man, nothing more and nothing less.
- Jesus is God's agent for establishing the theocracy (God's Kingdom on earth).
- His ransom paid for Adam's sin alone. This gives people the opportunity to earn their salvation by believing in God and doing good works.
- You should not pray to Jesus.
- Jesus is the mediator only for the "anointed remnant." He is not mediator for all men.
- Jesus died on a stake, not a cross.

E RESURRECTION OF JESUS

The Watch Tower organization denies the physical resurrection of Jesus, teaching that Jesus did not rise from the dead in the body he died in (see *You Can Live Forever on Paradise Earth,* pages 143-44). Jesus' body was supposedly dissolved into gases in the tomb, and he was raised as Michael the Archangel, who is a spirit creature without a physical body.

After Jesus' resurrection, God generated bodies to appear to the disciples. These bodies even included nail holes.

F THE HOLY SPIRIT

Jehovah's Witnesses teach that the Holy Spirit is not God but an "invisible active force," like the wind or electricity.

Orthodox Christians believe that the Holy Spirit is God and has the same divine nature as the Father and the Son. In John 16:7 and 13 the Holy Spirit is called our Teacher and Comforter, while Hebrews 10:29 and Ephesians 4:30 teach that he can be insulted, outraged and grieved.

G THE BIBLE

Jehovah's Witnesses teach that the Bible is the inspired Word of God, but it is their version of the Bible (see above). It is also thought to be a closed book to all but the "remnant," and can only be understood if it is studied in combination with the books put out by the Watch Tower Society. They say:

We all need help to understand the Bible, and we cannot find the Scriptural guidance we need outside the "faithful and discreet slave" organization.

The Watchtower, *2/15/81, page 19*

As "the faithful and discreet slave," Witnesses claim that only the Watch Tower Society is capable of rightly understanding God's Word:

Only this organization functions for Jehovah's purpose and to his praise. To it alone God's Sacred Word, the Bible, is not a sealed book.

The Watchtower; *July 1, 1973, pages 402*

H HEAVEN AND HELL

Only 144,000 people will go to heaven. There is no hell.

I ANOINTED REMNANT

The anointed remnant are those of the 144,000 who are still alive, most of whom were born in 1914 or earlier.

There are only about 8,000 left alive.

The remnant that have died and gone to heaven guide the work of Jehovah's Witnesses here on earth.

J SECOND COMING OF JESUS AND ARMAGEDDON

All goals and activities are directed towards the Second Coming of Christ, which will be followed by the Armageddon, and the setting up of God's Kingdom on earth.

1914

Early on, Jehovah's Witnesses taught that the Second Coming would take place in October 1914.

When that didn't happen, they changed the prophecy in their books. To explain it away, they changed the definition of a word in the Bible that talks about Christ's "coming," to mean Christ's "invisible presence." After all, it is difficult to disprove that Christ's "invisible presence" did not take place in 1914.

Jesus, however, said, "For as lightning that comes from the east is visible even in the west, so will be the coming (*parousia*) of the Son of Man" (Matthew 24:27). Thus, all nations will see his coming.

1918

Then they taught that the Second Coming would occur in 1918.

1920

Then they taught it would occur in 1920.

1925

They changed it again to 1925.

In the early 1920s, Jehovah's Witnesses distributed a book entitled *Millions Now Living Will Never Die*. It was prophesied, "The year 1925 is a date definitely and clearly marked in the Scriptures, even more clearly than that of 1914. We may confidently expect that 1925 will mark the return of Abraham, Isaac, Jacob and the faithful prophets of old . . . to the condition of human perfection."

1941

They changed it again to 1941.

1975

They changed it again to 1975.

They no longer give a date for the Second Coming, but analyze "the signs of the times".

K SALVATION

The February 15, 1983 issue of the *Watchtower* identifies four requirements for salvation:

- You must take in accurate knowledge of Jehovah and his son Jesus.
- You must obey God's laws.
- You must be associated with God's channel, his visible earthly organization.
- You must loyally advocate his kingdom rule to others, primarily through door-to-door witnessing.

L ANGELS

Angels are used by God to communicate "new light" to the remnant here on earth.

M HERETICAL TEACHING FROM THE WATCHTOWER

JESUS CHRIST

The *Watchtower* says: "The foremost angel, both in power and authority, is the archangel, Jesus Christ, also called Michael." (The *Watchtower*, November 1, 1995, page 8)

The Bible says: Jesus is ". . . so much better than the angels . . . Let all the angels of God worship him." (Hebrews 1:4, 6 KJV)

GOOD DEEDS

The *Watchtower* says: "To get one's name written in that Book of Life will depend upon one's works." (The *Watchtower*, July 1, 1947, page 204)

The Bible says: "For it is by grace you have been saved, through faith – and this not from yourselves, it is the gift of God – not by works, so that no one can boast." (Ephesians 2:8, 9)

7 WORSHIP

SUNDAYS
Jehovah's Witnesses do not have a Sabbath; they regard all days as holy.

BAPTISM
Jehovah's Witnesses baptize those "of a responsible age" who have made a conscious decision to join the faith. Baptism is performed by full water immersion.

After baptism Jehovah's Witnesses are expected to attend Kingdom Hall meetings and to engage in evangelism.

COMMUNION
Only the "anointed" members may take communion. These members are determined by the organization and they are very few and far between. Communion for the anointed is held just once a year, in the spring, at their annual communion service.

CONGREGATIONS
Appointed members, called Overseers or Elders, are each given a specific role. For example, the Presiding Overseer leads the elder meetings. The Service Overseer handles ministry issues within the congregation. Ministerial Servants handle administrative duties and assist the Elders.

KINGDOM HALLS
Local congregations meet at places of worship called Kingdom Halls. The public are invited to their meetings, and no collections are taken.

The term "Kingdom Hall" is unique to Jehovah's Witnesses. (The Watch Tower Society sometimes refers to itself as a *Theocratic Organization* or an organization which is directed by God.)

8 GLOSSARY

1914
The year of Jesus Christ's invisible return (his Second Coming).

Armageddon
The holy war between Christ and his forces and Satan and his forces. This is an imminent war in which the world will be destroyed.

Awake!
One of the major publications of the Watch Tower Bible and Tract Society.

Bible Students
Original name of Jehovah's Witnesses.

Circuit
Organization of about twenty congregations.

Company
Another name for a congregation of Jehovah's Witnesses.

Congregation
Group of no more than 200 Witnesses meeting at a Kingdom Hall.

District
Organization of about ten circuits.

Elder
Leader of a congregation.

Goat
Someone opposed to Jehovah's Witnesses.

Governing Body
The central group of experienced elders who oversee the worldwide congregation.

Holy spirit
A divine force, not a person as in Trinitarian Christianity.

Jehovah (Also "Jehovah God")
The name of God, strongly emphasized by Witnesses.

Kingdom Hall
The meeting place and house of worship of Jehovah's Witnesses. They are usually simple and austere.

Kingdom publishers
Majority of Jehovah's Witnesses. Expected to spend five hours per week at meetings in Kingdom Hall and as much time as possible witnessing.

Last Days
The time between 1914 and Armageddon.

Millennium
A 1,000 year period, beginning after Armageddon, when Christ will rule over the earth. During this time, the dead will be resurrected, humankind will attain perfection, and paradise will be restored.

Pioneer
A full-time, voluntary minister who is required to complete ninety hours of missionary work per month. They also serve as a lay clergy.

Pioneers, Special
Full-time, salaried employees of the Watch Tower Society, who spend at least 150 hours per month in religious service.

Publisher
A part-time missionary who has certain requirements to fulfill. These include: spending a certain number of hours distributing literature door-to-door (there are no formal quotas anymore; on average: seventeen hours a month), attending several meetings and services per week, and keeping complete records of missionary activities.

Sheep
Jehovah's Witnesses and possible converts.

The Watchtower
(Full title: *The Watchtower Announcing Jehovah's Kingdom*) Magazine/tract published semimonthly by the Watch Tower Bible and Tract Society of New York. Its stated purpose is to exalt Jehovah God and keep watch on world events as they fulfill Bible prophecy.

Watch Tower Bible and Tract Society
The official legal corporation of Jehovah's Witnesses. With its headquarters in New York, the society prepares different publications, including the *Watchtower*, *Awake!* and the New World Translation of he Holy Scriptures.

CHRISTIAN SCIENCE

CONTENTS

1 An overview   543

2 Founder   543

3 Christian Science's holy book   547

4 Facts and figures   549

5 Christian Science practices   549

6 Christian Science beliefs   550

7 Worship   556

1 AN OVERVIEW

DEFINITION

The movement known as Christian Science is a religion "emphasizing divine healing as practiced by Jesus Christ." It is officially known as The Church of Christ, Scientist (CCS).

Factfile
- Date of origin: 1879
- Founder: Mary Baker Eddy, 1821-1910
- Holy book: *Science and Health with Key to the Scriptures*, by Mary Baker Eddy
- Number of adherents: 500,000

SUMMARY

Christian Science, as discovered by Mary Baker Eddy, refers to the universal, practical system of spiritual, prayer-based healing, available and accessible to everyone. It teaches that matter was not created by God, but that matter, sin, evil, disease and death are all limited modes of human perception, and ultimately unreal.

2 FOUNDER

INTRODUCTION

Mrs. Eddy considered herself to be the "God-appointed" and "God-anointed" messenger to this age, the woman chosen by God to discover the Science of Christian healing and to interpret it to mankind; she is so closely related to Christian Science that a true sense of her is essential to the understanding of Christian Science; in other words, the revelator cannot be separated from the revelation.

The Christian Science Board of Directors, 1943

OVERVIEW OF MARY BAKER EDDY

- Discoverer and founder of Christian Science
- Healer and pioneer of a system of prayer-based healing
- Author of best-selling book, with 10 million copies sold, on spirituality and healing, *Science and Health with Key to the Scriptures*
- President and founder, the Massachusetts Metaphysical College, a teaching college that prepares teachers of Christian Science
- Founder of a publishing house which has

produced weekly and monthly magazines, and a Bible daily self-study guide
- Founder and publisher of *The Christian Science Monitor*
- Leader of a worldwide church, The First Church of Christ, Scientist. This now has branches in 80 countries.

MILESTONES IN MARY BAKER EDDY'S LIFE

1866 Mary Baker Eddy discovered Christian Science

1875 *Science and Health with Key to the Scriptures* first published by Mary Baker Eddy

1879 Eddy established The First Church of Christ, Scientist

1908 Eddy founded *The Christian Science Monitor*

A BIOGRAPHICAL SKETCH

This biographical sketch of Mary Baker Eddy was written by one of her strongest supporters, William D. McCrackan.

Glimpses of spiritual reality have lightened the darkness of material history for centuries. But it was left for one woman to receive this full revelation of Truth in this age – Mary Baker Eddy. The parentage, education, experience, and remarkable spirituality of Mrs. Eddy had made her well fitted for the mission to which God had called her. She possessed a remarkable degree of spirituality even in childhood, and rapidly developed into that individuality which was needed to voice to this age the Science of Christianity.

In her autobiography, *Retrospection and Introspection*, she recorded the "experiences which led her, in the year 1866, to the discovery of the system that she denominated Christian Science" (*Science and Health*, p. viii).

CHILDHOOD AND BACKGROUND

Mary Baker Eddy was born on July 16, 1821, in Bow, New Hampshire, five miles from Concord, the state capital. The Baker family had been in New England for six generations. Mary Baker's father was Mark Baker, who married Abigail Ambrose of Pembroke, New Hampshire.

Both on the paternal and maternal side, the future Discoverer of Christian Science was descended from members of the Congregational Church.

A HEALER

In Rumney a mother came to her with a child in her arms who was suffering from inflamed eyes. She took the child in her arms, lifted her thought to God, and the child was healed. These and other instances had caused her to ponder. She kept them stored in her heart, waiting until the time when an explanation should be vouchsafed her.

AN ACCIDENT AND RECOVERY

After the death of her first husband, George W. Glover, Mary Baker Eddy married Dr. Daniel Patterson, a dentist. Mrs. Patterson was returning home one evening when she sustained an accident which was to become memorable by reason of its immediate result. The Lynn Reporter of February 3, 1866, made mention of the following:

"Mrs. Mary Patterson of Swampscott fell upon the ice near the corner of Market and Oxford Streets on Thursday evening and was severely injured. She was taken up in an insensible condition and carried into the residence of S.M. Bubier, Esq., near by, where she was kindly cared for during the night. Doctor Cushing, who was called, found her injuries to be internal and of a serious nature, inducing spasms and internal suffering. She was removed to her home in Swampscott yesterday afternoon, though in a critical condition."

Of this accident and her recovery, Mrs. Eddy herself afterward published the following explanation:

"St. Paul writes: 'For to be carnally minded is death; but to be spiritually minded is life and peace.' This knowledge came to me in an hour of great need; and I give it to you as death-bed testimony to the daystar that dawned on the night of material sense. This knowledge is practical, for it wrought my immediate recovery from an injury caused by an accident, and pronounced fatal by the physicians. On the third day thereafter, I called for my Bible, and opened it at Matthew 9:2. As I read, the healing Truth dawned upon my sense; and the result was that I rose, dressed myself, and ever after was in better health than I had before enjoyed. That short experience included a glimpse of the great fact that I have since tried to make plain to others, namely, Life in and of Spirit; this Life being the sole reality of existence."

Miscellaneous Writings, p. 24:1-18

Her words show clearly the impassable gulf between Christian Science and any method of personal magnetic healing. Her recovery was due to the Word of God, a spiritual illumination from the divine Mind, and in this sense was wholly impersonal in its nature.

Here, indeed, was the healing for which she had always striven, which she felt must be at hand did one only know how to realize its presence. Here at last was the ideal toward which her whole life had tended from her childhood experiences, her stout refusal to believe in a cruel God, her insistent conviction that divine Love is the liberator of mankind from all woe. This conviction had only been fortified by the measure of sorrow and suffering through which she had

passed. Even her experience with the subtle counterfeit of spiritual healing had not disabled her from recognizing the real healing when it dawned upon her consciousness. Thereafter she could never be deceived again, never be in doubt as to what constituted the healing of Bible times. Nor from the moment of her discovery does she ever seem to have hesitated about her manifest mission to give this truth to the world.

Her experiences for the next ten years proved inexpressibly hard, and one would gladly omit all chronicle of them, did they not prove, as perhaps nothing else can do, the unquestioning attitude of her mind toward her mission. It must be understood that as the discovery of Christian Science is inseparable from Mrs. Eddy's human experience, so also is its development.

SEARCHING THE SCRIPTURES
Then followed Doctor Patterson's desertion of his wife, and Mrs. Patterson was obliged to secure a decree of divorce from him. Her father and mother having passed away, she might naturally have gone to the home of her sister, Mrs. Tilton, but the sister made it a condition that she should forsake her unconventional religious convictions, and this Mary Baker was determined not to do. She turned now more and more to the elucidation of the meaning of her discovery and its practical application to human affairs. She chose poverty rather than ease, and now began a life of involuntary wandering from one home to another, from one boarding place to another, the life of a student searching the Scriptures, nourishing her glorious discovery, applying it where she was welcomed; sometimes loved and appreciated, more often misunderstood and even traduced; healing the sick, transforming character, and always writing, writing that mankind at large might gain the spiritual revelation which had come to her.

HER FIRST STUDENT

While she was boarding with a family of the name of Clark, she met a Mr. Hiram S. Crafts and his wife. He was an expert workman in the shoe trade. Finding him ready to accept her teachings, Mary Baker made him her first student, and he was soon able to set up as a mental healer and prove the truth of what he had been taught for himself.

SCIENCE AND HEALTH PUBLISHED

In 1875, while residing in Lynn, Massachusetts, Mary Baker finished her book *Science and Health*, placed it in the hands of a publisher, and an edition of one thousand copies was issued. In that year also was made the first beginning of a Christian Science church, when a number of her students united in inviting her to hold meetings and preach to them every Sunday, and subscribed a weekly salary for her.

In 1877 Mary Baker Glover was married to Mr. Asa G. Eddy, who, being in bad health, had been sent to her for treatment. She had healed him, had taken him through one of her classes, and had learned to trust him so thoroughly that she had placed many of her affairs in his charge.

GROWING INTEREST IN CHRISTIAN SCIENCE

Mrs. Eddy began to lecture in Boston before audiences growing ever larger and more appreciative. Her home with Mr. Eddy provided her an atmosphere of peace and security for her teaching and healing work.

In 1879, Mrs. Eddy's followers and students formed the "Church of Christ, Scientist," with Mrs. Eddy appointed pastor. In 1892 a reorganization of this church took place and the name adopted of "The First Church of Christ, Scientist," which it holds today.

Services were held in Hawthorne Hall in Boston, and in 1882 Mr. and Mrs. Eddy moved to that city, but Mr. Eddy

passed away in that same year, and Mrs. Eddy once more faced the world alone in her efforts to establish Christian Science upon a sure footing.

THE CHRISTIAN SCIENCE JOURNAL

In 1883 *The Journal of Christian Science* was first published. This magazine, of which Mrs. Eddy was the editor and publisher, became the official organ of the Christian Science Church, under the title *The Christian Science Journal*.

EXPANSION THROUGHOUT THE WORLD

The Christian Science Church, which had originally met in Hawthorne Hall, then in Chickering Hall, was now about to acquire a church building of its own. After some vicissitudes, a church occupying the triangle at the junction of Norway and Falmouth Streets, in the Back Bay district of Boston, was finished at the end of December, 1894, and dedicated in January 1895. And in 1902 an extension was added.

Mrs. Eddy's followers were now found among all classes of society and among the principal nations of the earth. Christian Science not only covered the United States and Canada, but also many parts of the world.

Mrs. Eddy established one by one the different means by which Christian Science is placed before the public. She founded the periodicals of the denomination, beginning with *The Christian Science Journal*, a monthly to which reference has already been made; *Der Herold der Christian Science*, printed in German; *The Christian Science Sentinel*; *The Christian Science Quarterly* contained the weekly Christian Science Lesson-Sermons; and *The Christian Science Monitor*, a daily newspaper.

MRS. EDDY'S PASSING

In 1908 Mrs. Eddy decided to leave Pleasant View and took a house in Chestnut Hill, a suburb of Boston, where she quietly passed away in the winter of 1910, full of years and good works, greatly beloved by a multitude of men, women, and children in all parts of the world, who have been redeemed and healed by her teachings.

William D. McCrackan.

---

3 CHRISTIAN SCIENCE'S HOLY BOOK

The Bible and *Science and Health with Key to the Scriptures* are primary texts used for individual study and spiritual growth. Together they are the foundation for Christian Science teaching and practice, and are used during church services. Eddy ordained these books as a "dual and impersonal pastor" for these services.

SCIENCE AND HEALTH WITH KEY TO THE SCRIPTURES, BY MARY BAKER EDDY

Eddy believed that this book of hers was divinely inspired. She wrote:

> I should blush to write of *Science and Health with Key to the Scriptures* as I have, were it of human origin and I apart from God its author; but [since] I was only a scribe echoing the harmonies of heaven in Divine Metaphysics, I cannot be super-modest of the Christian Science Text-book.
>
> *Mary Baker Eddy*

OUTLINE OF CHAPTERS IN SCIENCE AND HEALTH WITH KEY TO THE SCRIPTURES

1 Prayer
The purpose of prayer
Practical prayer
The special power of silent prayer
Spiritual sense of The Lord's Prayer

2 Atonement and Eucharist
Atonement defined as "at-one-ment" with God
The spiritual nature of sacrament
Eucharist defined as "spiritual communion with the one God"
The purpose of Jesus' life
Discipleship

3 Marriage
The purpose of marriage
Elements of a lasting relationship
Resolving interpersonal conflicts
Practical counsel on how to treat each other
Guidance on raising children

4 Christian Science versus spiritualism
The nature of divine Spirit
The distinction between spirituality and spiritualism
Intuition explained
The distinction between clairvoyance and divine communication

5 Animal magnetism unmasked
A caution about hypnotism
Misuses of mental power
How to develop and maintain inner peace

6 Science, theology, medicine
The universality of scientific, spiritual laws
Natural phenomena as governed by divine Mind
How Christianity is scientific
Theology based on Truth
The mental nature of disease and cure
Divine Mind the true medicine

7 Physiology
The mind-body connection
The relationship between diagnosis and disease
Health not based on diet
Caring for your body
Preventing disease

8 Footsteps of truth
Step-by-step nature of spiritual growth
Practical guidance for educators, physicians, clergy and parents
Role of mental images in promoting spiritual progress
Dealing with fatigue
Attaining spiritual freedom
Lessons from nature

9 Creation
The spiritual nature of creation
Material versus spiritual substance
Man as the image of divine Mind
The Fatherhood and Motherhood of God

10 Science of being
Contrasting natures of spirituality and materiality
The Biblical basis for scientific spirituality
The unreliability of sensory knowledge
Angels
The transforming struggle against materiality
Divine Soul
The importance of acknowledging only one God

11 Some objections answered
Spiritual ideas versus human language
Healing consistent with spirituality
Spiritual healing not faith healing
How Christians and Jews can agree theologically

12 Christian Science practice
Qualities of a spiritual healer
Method of treating the sick
Mental treatment illustrated
Dealing with relapse
An allegory comparing spiritual treatment to a legal trial

13 Teaching Christian Science
Ethics essential to effective spiritual healing practice

Learning and teaching metaphysics
"Scientific Obstetrics"

14 Recapitulation
A summary of Mary Baker Eddy's basic teachings on metaphysics
Answers to questions such as: "What is God?" "Is there no sin?" "Will you explain sickness and show how it is to be healed?"
The tenets of Christian Science

15 Genesis
An explanation of first four chapters of Genesis
The two different creation stories
A discussion of Darwinism
A spiritual perspective on Scripture

16 The Apocalypse
An explanation of Revelation 12 and 21
Apocalypse as culmination of spiritualization
A spiritual perspective on the 23rd Psalm

17 Glossary
A dictionary of 125 spiritual definitions

18 Fruitage
The testimonials in this chapter were submitted by people who were healed solely by the ideas in *Science and Health*. Some of the problems resolved:
Addiction to tobacco
Alcoholism
Asthma
Astigmatism
Cancer
Deafness
Eczema
Heart disease
Hernia
Insanity
Kidney disease
Rheumatism
Tuberculosis (also called consumption)

4 FACTS AND FIGURES

There is a big difference between people who think of themselves as followers of CCS in a general way, and those who are members of CCS.

Mary Baker Eddy forbade publication of membership figures, on the grounds the numbers were no indication of vitality.

In 1936, a report of the US Bureau of the Census gave membership figures in the US as about 269,000. Since 1950, membership has declined in North America and Europe, but grown considerably in Africa and South America. Today there are perhaps 100,000 followers (as against members) in the US.

In the 1930s CCS had over 2,500 branch churches, societies, and college organizations in more than 50 countries. Today, they have about 2,300 branch congregations in 70 countries. There are about 1,600 congregations in the US, and about 60 in Canada.

---

5 CHRISTIAN SCIENCE PRACTICES

PRACTITIONERS

Practitioners, both men and women, devote themselves full time to the work of "spiritual healing."

Most often, Christian Scientists pray for their own healing. Christian Scientists believe that Jesus' words in John 14:12: "He that believeth on me, the works that I do shall he do also" apply to them today. For additional assistance through prayer, they call on Christian Science practitioners. Practitioners do not claim to have any personal healing power in themselves, but rather emphasize that God alone brings healing power in all cases of spiritual healing.

READING ROOMS

CCS operate Christian Science Reading Rooms. These are small libraries and reading rooms that are open to the general public, who are invited to read the Bible and literature published by CCS.

THE CHRISTIAN SCIENCE MONITOR

In 1908, Mrs. Eddy founded an international newspaper, *The Christian Science Monitor*. Its writers have won 6 Pulitzer prizes.

6 CHRISTIAN SCIENCE BELIEFS

A   Healing
B   Promotion of Christian Science ideas
C   Christian Science and the Bible
D   Jesus Christ's deity
E   The purpose of Jesus' crucifixion
F   The Holy Spirit
G   The Trinity
H   Judgment
I   Salvation
J   The nature of humanity

INTRODUCTION

Christian Science claims to be based on the life, teachings, and works of Christ Jesus. While Christian Science does not have a creed as such, some of its main tenets are found in *Science and Health*:

- As adherents of Truth, we take the inspired Word of the Bible as our sufficient guide to eternal Life.
- We acknowledge and adore one supreme and infinite God. We acknowledge His Son, one Christ; the Holy Ghost or divine Comforter; and man in God's image and likeness.
- We acknowledge God's forgiveness of sin in the destruction of sin and the spiritual understanding that casts out evil as unreal. But the belief in sin is punished so long as the belief lasts.
- We acknowledge Jesus' atonement as the evidence of divine, efficacious Love, unfolding man's unity with God through Christ Jesus the Way-shower; and we acknowledge that man is saved through Christ, through Truth, Life, and Love as demonstrated by the Galilean Prophet in healing the sick and overcoming sin and death.
- We acknowledge that the crucifixion of Jesus and his resurrection served to uplift faith to understand eternal Life, even the allness of Soul, Spirit, and the nothingness of matter.

- And we solemnly promise to watch, and pray for that Mind to be in us which was also in Christ Jesus; to do unto others as we would have them do unto us; and to be merciful, just, and pure.

Science and Health, *page 496*

Christian Science faith teaches that God, Father-Mother of all, is completely good and wholly spiritual, and that all God's creation, including the true nature of every person, is the flawless, spiritual likeness of the Divine. Since God's creation is good, evils such as disease, death, and sin cannot be a part of fundamental reality. Rather, these evils are the result of living apart from God. Prayer is a central way to come closer to God and heal human ills.

A HEALING

Over the past hundred years, Christian Science magazines have published more than 60,000 testimonies of healing through prayer.

Christian Science teaches that all ills and diseases can be overcome through prayer in proportion as one gains "the mind of Christ," that is, a correct understanding of the spiritual status of human beings. This true status was demonstrated by Jesus in his healings and his victory over the death and the grave. Mrs Eddy taught that matter was not created by God, since God, the "Divine Mind," could not have created the attendant evils brought about by matter. Sin itself is a delusion.

However, the regenerative process may be slow:

> We need "Christ and him crucified." We must have trials and self-denials, as well as joys and victories, until all error is destroyed.
>
> *Mary Baker Eddy*

B PROMOTION OF CHRISTIAN SCIENCE IDEAS

Some main-line Christian leaders have used the Christian Science concept of the Divine Mind and combined it with traditional Christian teaching. See Norman Vincent Peale's *Power of Positive Thinking*, Bishop Sheen's *Peace of Soul*, Robert Schuller's *Possibility Thinking*.

C CHRISTIAN SCIENCE AND THE BIBLE

Since Mary Baker Eddy said that she discovered Christian Science through "a spiritual sense of the Scriptures and through the teachings of the Comforter." (*Science and Health with Key to the Scriptures*, 123:21-22) we should always find that Christian Science clarifies the Bible and never contradicts it.

When considering Mary Baker Eddy's writings the question to ask is: "Does Christian Science spiritually illuminate the Bible – or do its metaphysical interpretations actually change the Bible's message?"

D JESUS CHRIST'S DEITY

Christian Science teaching
Jesus is the Son of God, and is divine, but he is not God: he is not a deity.

> . . . Jesus Christ is not God, as Jesus himself declared, but is the Son of God.
> Science and Health, *361:12-13*

The Bible's teaching
The Bible describes Jesus as the Son of God, but it also assigns him attributes and names that can only belong to God. The Bible describes Jesus as:

eternally existent:

> In the beginning was the Word, and the Word was with God, and the Word was

God. . . . And the Word was made flesh, and dwelt among us . . . .
> *John 1:1, 14a*

the creator of all things:

> In the beginning was the Word, and the Word was with God, and the Word was God. . . . All things were made by him; and without him was not any thing made that was made. . . . He was in the world, and the world was made by him, and the world knew him not.
> *John 1:1, 3, 10*

> [God] Hath in these last days spoken unto us by his Son, whom he hath appointed heir of all things, by whom also he made the worlds.
> *Hebrews 1:2*

the sustainer of all things:

> The Son is the radiance of God's glory and the exact representation of his being, sustaining all things by his powerful word. After he had provided purification for sins, he sat down at the right hand of the Majesty in heaven.
> *Hebrews 1:3, NIV*

Jesus claimed the authority to forgive sins (a claim that the scribes labeled as blasphemous):

> And they come unto him, bringing one sick of the palsy, which was borne of four. And when they could not come nigh unto him for the press, they uncovered the roof where he was: and when they had broken it up, they let down the bed wherein the sick of the palsy lay. When Jesus saw their faith, he said unto the sick of the palsy, Son, thy sins be forgiven thee. But there were certain of the scribes sitting there, and reasoning in their hearts, Why doth this man thus speak blasphemies? who can forgive sins but God only? And immediately when Jesus perceived in his spirit that they so reasoned within themselves, he said unto them, Why reason ye these things in your hearts?

Whether is it easier to say to the sick of the palsy, Thy sins be forgiven thee; or to say, Arise, and take up thy bed, and walk? But that ye may know that the Son of man hath power on earth to forgive sins. . .

Mark 2:3-10

E THE PURPOSE OF JESUS' CRUCIFIXION

Christian Science teaching

- Jesus only seemed to die on the cross
- his triumph over the belief in death demonstrated that man is the perfect, spiritual, reflection of God and that disease and death are not real
- Jesus' shed blood had no power to cleanse from sin.

His disciples believed Jesus to be dead while he was hidden in the sepulcher, whereas he was alive, demonstrating within the narrow tomb the power of Spirit to overrule mortal, material sense . . . . Our Master fully and finally demonstrated divine Science in his victory over death and the grave.

Science and Health, 44:28-31, 45:6-7

Does erudite theology regard the crucifixion of Jesus chiefly as providing a ready pardon for all sinners who ask for it and are willing to be forgiven? . . . Then we must differ. . . .

The efficacy of the crucifixion lay in the practical affection and goodness it demonstrated for mankind. The truth had been lived among men; but until they saw that it enabled their Master to triumph over the grave, his own disciples could not admit such an event to be possible. . . .

The spiritual essence of blood is sacrifice. The efficacy of Jesus' spiritual offering is infinitely greater than can be expressed by our sense of human blood. The material blood of Jesus was no more efficacious to cleanse from sin when it was shed upon "the accursed tree," than when it was flowing in his veins as he went daily about his Father's business.

Science and Health, 24:20-31, 25:3-9

One sacrifice, however great, is insufficient to pay the debt of sin. The atonement requires constant self-immolation on the sinner's part. That God's wrath should be vented upon His beloved Son, is divinely unnatural. Such a theory is man-made.

Science and Health, 23:3-7

The Bible's teaching
Jesus physically died on the cross to pay for the sins of humankind. Because of Jesus' sinless nature he was uniquely qualified to bear the judgment and punishment that God's holiness and divine justice demand. Jesus' shed blood and death paid the debt "once for all" for everyone who is prepared to believe.

By the which will we are sanctified through the offering of the body of Jesus Christ once for all.

Hebrews 10:10

Forasmuch as ye know that ye were not redeemed with corruptible things, as silver and gold, from your vain conversation received by tradition from your fathers; But with the precious blood of Christ, as of a lamb without blemish and without spot.

1 Peter 1:18-19

For Christ also hath once suffered for sins, the just for the unjust, that he might bring us to God, being put to death in the flesh, but quickened by the Spirit.

1 Peter 3:18

And almost all things are by the law purged with blood; and without shedding of blood is no remission. It was therefore necessary that the patterns of things in the heavens should be purified with these; but the heavenly things themselves with better sacrifices than these. For Christ is not entered into the holy places made with hands, which are the figures of the true; but into heaven itself, now to appear in the presence of God for us: Nor yet that he should offer himself often, as the high priest entereth into the holy place every year with blood of others; For then must he often have suffered since the foundation of the world: but now once in the end of the world hath he appeared to put away sin by the sacrifice of himself. And as it is appointed unto men once to die, but after this the judgment: So Christ was once offered to bear the sins of many; and unto them that look for him shall he appear the second time without sin unto salvation.

Hebrews 9:22-28

F THE HOLY SPIRIT

The terms "Divine Science" and "Christian Science" are used interchangeably by Mary Baker Eddy.

Christian Science teaching

The Holy Spirit is Christian Science: "a scientific system of healing."

The term CHRISTIAN SCIENCE was introduced by the author to designate the scientific system of divine healing.
Science and Health, *123:16-18*

In the words of St. John: "He shall give you another Comforter, that he may abide with you forever." This Comforter I understand to be Divine Science.
Science and Health, *55:27-29*

[Jesus'] students then received the Holy Ghost. By this is meant, that by all they had witnessed and suffered, they were roused to an enlarged understanding of divine Science, even to the spiritual interpretation and discernment of Jesus' teachings and demonstrations, which gave them a faint conception of the Life which is God. . . . The influx of light was sudden. It was sometimes an overwhelming power as on the Day of Pentecost.
Science and Health, *46:30-47:3, 47:7-9*

The Bible's teaching

The Holy Spirit is God – a divine personality and a member of the Trinity. The Holy Spirit is not a set of spiritually scientific principles.

The Holy Spirit listens to people

But Peter said, Ananias, why hath Satan filled thine heart to lie to the Holy Ghost, and to keep back part of the price of the land? . . . thou hast not lied unto men, but unto God.

Acts 5:3-4

The Holy Spirit helps people pray

Likewise the Spirit also helpeth our infirmities: for we know not what we should pray for as we ought: but the Spirit itself maketh intercession for us with groanings which cannot be uttered. And he that searcheth the hearts knoweth what is the mind of the Spirit, because he maketh intercession for the saints according to the will of God.
Romans 8:26-27

The Holy Spirit can be grieved

And grieve not the holy Spirit of God, whereby ye are sealed unto the day of redemption.
Ephesians 4:30

The Holy Spirit rebukes the world of sin

Nevertheless I tell you the truth; It is expedient for you that I go away: for if I go not away, the Comforter will not come unto you; but if I depart, I will send him unto you. And when he is come, he will reprove the world of sin, and of righteousness, and of judgment.
John 16:7-8

The Holy Spirit comforts believers
And I will pray the Father, and he shall give you another Comforter, that he may

abide with you for ever; Even the Spirit of truth; whom the world cannot receive, because it seeth him not, neither knoweth him: but ye know him; for he dwelleth with you, and shall be in you.

John 14:16-17

G THE TRINITY

The Bible does not use the word "Trinity" (meaning one God in three persons), but both Christian Science and orthodox Christianity incorporate the term into their doctrines.

Christian Science teaching

Christian Science defines the Trinity as Life, Truth, and Love, which are three of the seven synonyms that Mrs. Eddy uses to describe God.

The seven synonyms are Principle, Soul, Mind, Spirit, Life, Truth, and Love.

> Life, Truth, and Love constitute the triune Person called God – that is, the triply divine Principle, Love. They represent a trinity in unity, three in one – the same in essence, though multiform in office: God the Father-Mother; Christ the spiritual idea of sonship; divine Science [i.e., Christian Science] or the Holy Comforter. These three express in divine Science the threefold, essential nature of the infinite. They also indicate the divine Principle of scientific being, the intelligent relation of God to man and the universe.
> Science and Health, *331:26-332:3*

> The name Elohim [a Hebrew term for God] is in the plural, but this plurality of Spirit does not imply more than one God, nor does it imply three persons in one. It relates to the oneness, the tri-unity of Life, Truth, and Love.
> Science and Health, *515:17-20*

> The theory of three persons in one God (that is, a personal Trinity or Tri-unity) suggests polytheism rather than the one ever-present I AM.
> Science and Health, *256:9-11*

The Bible's teaching

Biblical Christianity teaches that God exists as three distinct persons who make up one "godhead." This "godhead" refers to God's nature and essence. So while it remains true that there is only one God, the name "God" is used of the Father, the Son, and the Holy Spirit.

The Father is called God

> To all that be in Rome, beloved of God, called to be saints: Grace to you and peace from God our Father, and the Lord Jesus Christ.
> *Romans 1:7*

The Son is called God

> But unto the Son he saith, Thy throne, O God, is for ever and ever: a sceptre of righteousness is the sceptre of thy kingdom.
> *Hebrews 1:8*

The Holy Spirit is called God

> But Peter said, Ananias, why hath Satan filled thine heart to lie to the Holy Ghost, and to keep back part of the price of the land. . . . thou hast not lied unto men, but unto God.
> *Acts 5:3-4*

H JUDGMENT

Christian Science teaches that there is no final judgment.

> No final judgment awaits mortals, for the judgment-day of wisdom comes hourly and continually, even the judgment by which mortal man is divested of all material error.
> Science and Health, *291:28-31*

> As man falleth asleep, so shall he awake. As death findeth mortal man, so shall he be after death, until probation and growth shall effect the needed change.
> Science and Health, *291:22-25*

"When the last mortal fault is destroyed, then the final trump will sound which will end the battle of Truth with error and mortality. . . .

> Science and Health, *292:1-3*

The Bible's teaching
Everyone will be judged on the day of judgment.

> And as it is appointed unto men once to die, but after this the judgment.
>
> *Hebrews 9:27*

> But I say unto you, That every idle word that men shall speak, they shall give account thereof in the day of judgment.
>
> *Matthew 12:36*

> Not every one that saith unto me, Lord, Lord, shall enter into the kingdom of heaven; but he that doeth the will of my Father which is in heaven. Many will say to me in that day, Lord, Lord, have we not prophesied in thy name? and in thy name have cast out devils? and in thy name done many wonderful works? And then will I profess unto them, I never knew you: depart from me, ye that work iniquity.
>
> *Matthew 7:21-23*

I SALVATION

Christian Science teaching
Progressive spiritual understanding enables one to achieve salvation. Nobody is saved from hell, but one can be saved from one's own belief in materiality.

> SALVATION: Life, Truth, and Love understood and demonstrated as supreme over all; sin, sickness and death destroyed.
>
> Science and Health, *593:20-22*

The Bible's teaching

Salvation is a gift from God. It is due entirely to his grace. Nobody can earn salvation. It has to be accepted by confession of one's sins and by faith in the sacrificial death of Jesus Christ on one's behalf. Salvation is not from a belief in materiality, but from hell.

> For by grace are ye saved through faith; and that not of yourselves: it is the gift of God: Not of works, lest any man should boast.
>
> *Ephesians 2:8-9*

> For the wages of sin is death; but the gift of God is eternal life through Jesus Christ our Lord.
>
> *Romans 6:23*

J THE NATURE OF HUMANITY

Christian Science teaching
Humankind is perfect, spiritual, and sinless.

> Man is spiritual and perfect....He is the compound idea of God, including all right ideas; the generic term for all that reflects God's image and likeness....that which has not a single quality underived from Deity.
>
> Science and Health, *475:11-20*

> . . . the only reality of sin, sickness, or death is the awful fact that unrealities seem real to human, erring belief, until God strips off their disguise.
>
> Science and Health, *472:27-29*

The Bible's teaching
Men and women have sinful natures and, spiritually speaking, are dead, or, separated from God.

> If we say that we have no sin, we deceive ourselves, and the truth is not in us . . . If we say that we have not sinned, we make him a liar and his word is not in us.
>
> *1 John 1:8,10*

7 WORSHIP

INTRODUCTION
Scientific Statement of Being

Eddy's *Scientific Statement of Being* (read every week from every Christian Science pulpit) begins with the words, "There is no life, truth, intelligence, nor substance in matter," and ends with, "Therefore, man is not material; he is spiritual."

WEDNESDAY MEETINGS
Wednesday meetings include testimonies of healing from the congregation.

SUNDAY SERVICES
Readers, both men and women, are elected from the membership to conduct the services.

Instead of preachers (the CCS has no ordained clergy), Christian Science's Sunday services consist mainly of prescribed readings from the Bible, followed by interpretive readings from *Science and Health with Key to the Scriptures.*

An important part of a Christian Scientist's religious practice is study of the weekly Lesson-Sermon outlined in *The Christian Science Quarterly* which includes citations from the Bible and *Science and Health.*

This lesson includes a sermon that is read at each Sunday service in churches throughout the world.

CHRISTADELPHIANISM

CONTENTS

1 An overview   559

2 Founder   559

3 Christadelphian holy book   560

4 Facts and figures   564

5 Christadelphian practices   565

6 Christadelphian beliefs   565

7 Worship   568

1 An Overview

DEFINITION

The Christadelphians are a small religious body who have attempted to revert to the faith and character of the Christian Church of the New Testament.

Factfile
- Date of origin: 1844
- Founder: John Thomas
- Holy book: The Bible
- Number of adherents: The Christadelphian movement is highly decentralized and does not keep statistical information on its membership. However, there are probably about 7,000 members in the United States and 55,000 members worldwide.

CHRISTADELPHIAN NAME

Christadelphians means "Brethren in Christ," from the two Greek words:
Christos (Christ) and
adelphois (brothers and sisters).
The name "Christadelphian" was first used in the mid-1800s, but Christadelphians believe that throughout history there have been people who have shared their beliefs.

SUMMARY

The Christadelphians are a worldwide community of Bible students whose fellowship is based on a common, literal, understanding of the Scriptures. Despite their rejection of orthodox Christian doctrines, they claim to be the one true church, the remnant of faithful disciples left over from a partial apostasy.

2 Founder

JOHN THOMAS (1805-1871)

Dr. John Thomas was born in London, England, on April 12, 1805. He immigrated to the United States in 1832 where he joined the Campbellite group (also known as the Disciples). However, he disagreed with some the Campbellite teachings and left them, taking with him a group of the Campbellites, who formed the beginning of the Christadelphian movement.

From 1848, Thomas founded a number of groups, who were commonly referred to as the Thomasites. His motivation was to return to what he believed to be the beliefs of the very early Christian Church.

Thomas returned to England in 1848, and preached about his religious ideas, before returning again to America.

In 1864, the group adopted a formal name, the Christadelphians, which is based on the Greek words for "Brethren of Christ."

Dr. Thomas died in New York on March 5, 1871.

3 CHRISTADELPHIAN HOLY BOOK

THE BIBLE

The Bible is taken seriously, and studied very carefully by Christadelpians. They believe it to be the inspired word of God and accept it as their only guide.

THE BIBLE COMPANION

The Bible Companion is a table of readings that covers the entire Bible in the course of one year. The Bible is divided into three portions of roughly equal size; each day's readings consist of one or more chapters from each of the three portions. By following this systematic plan, the Old Testament is read once and the New Testament twice in a yearly cycle.

BIBLE COMPANION TABLE
READINGS FOR JANUARY

Date	First Portion	Second Portion	Third Portion
1 Jan	Gen 1, 2	Ps 1, 2	Mt 1, 2
2 Jan	Gen 3, 4	Ps 3, 5	Mt 3, 4
3 Jan	Gen 5, 6	Ps 6, 8	Mt 5
4 Jan	Gen 7, 8	Ps 9, 10	Mt 6
5 Jan	Gen 9, 10	Ps 11, 13	Mt 7
6 Jan	Gen 11, 12	Ps 14, 16	Mt 8
7 Jan	Gen 13, 14	Ps 17	Mt 9
8 Jan	Gen 15, 16	Ps 18	Mt 10
9 Jan	Gen 17, 18	Ps 19, 21	Mt 11
10 Jan	Gen 19	Ps 22	Mt 12
11 Jan	Gen 20, 21	Ps 23, 25	Mt 13
12 Jan	Gen 22, 23	Ps 26, 28	Mt 14
13 Jan	Gen 24	Ps 29, 30	Mt 15
14 Jan	Gen 25, 26	Ps 31	Mt 16
15 Jan	Gen 27	Ps 32	Mt 17
16 Jan	Gen 28, 29	Ps 33	Mt 18
17 Jan	Gen 30	Ps 34	Mt 19
18 Jan	Gen 31	Ps 35	Mt 20
19 Jan	Gen 32, 33	Ps 36	Mt 21
20 Jan	Gen 34, 35	Ps 37	Mt 22
21 Jan	Gen 36	Ps 38	Mt 23
22 Jan	Gen 37	Ps 39, 40	Mt 24
23 Jan	Gen 38	Ps 41, 43	Mt 25
24 Jan	Gen 39, 40	Ps 44	Mt 26
25 Jan	Gen 41	Ps 45	Mt 27
26 Jan	Gen 42, 43	Ps 46, 48	Mt 28
27 Jan	Gen 44, 45	Ps 49	Rom 1, 2
28 Jan	Gen 46, 47	Ps 50	Rom 3, 4
29 Jan	Gen 48, 50	Ps 51, 52	Rom 5, 6
30 Jan	Ex 1, 2	Ps 53, 55	Rom 7, 8
31 Jan	Ex 3, 4	Ps 56, 57	Rom 9

READINGS FOR FEBRUARY

Date	First Portion	Second Portion	Third Portion
1 Feb	Ex 5, 6	Ps 58, 59	Rom 10, 11
2 Feb	Ex 7, 8	Ps 60, 61	Rom 12
3 Feb	Ex 9	Ps 62, 63	Rom 13, 14
4 Feb	Ex 10	Ps 64, 65	Rom 15, 16
5 Feb	Ex 11, 12	Ps 66, 67	Mk 1
6 Feb	Ex 13, 14	Ps 68	Mk 2
7 Feb	Ex 15	Ps 69	Mk 3
8 Feb	Ex 16	Ps 70, 71	Mk 4
9 Feb	Ex 17, 18	Ps 72	Mk 5
10 Feb	Ex 19, 20	Ps 73	Mk 6
11 Feb	Ex 21	Ps 74	Mk 7
12 Feb	Ex 22	Ps 75, 76	Mk 8
13 Feb	Ex 23	Ps 77	Mk 9
14 Feb	Ex 24, 25	Ps 78	Mk 10
15 Feb	Ex 26	Ps 79, 80	Mk 11
16 Feb	Ex 27	Ps 81, 82	Mk 12
17 Feb	Ex 28	Ps 83, 84	Mk 13
18 Feb	Ex 29	Ps 85, 86	Mk 14
19 Feb	Ex 30	Ps 87, 88	Mk 15, 16
20 Feb	Ex 31, 32	Ps 89	1 Cor 1, 2
21 Feb	Ex 33, 34	Ps 90, 91	1 Cor 3
22 Feb	Ex 35	Ps 92, 93	1 Cor 4, 5
23 Feb	Ex 36	Ps 94, 95	1 Cor 6
24 Feb	Ex 37	Ps 96, 99	1 Cor 7
25 Feb	Ex 38	Ps 100, 101	1 Cor 8, 9
26 Feb	Ex 39, 40	Ps 102	1 Cor 10
27 Feb	Lev 1, 2	Ps 103	1 Cor 11
28 Feb	Lev 3, 4	Ps 104	1 Cor 12, 13

READINGS FOR MARCH

Date	First Portion	Second Portion	Third Portion
1 Mar	Lev 5, 6	Ps 105	1 Cor 14

2 Mar	Lev 7	Ps 106	1 Cor 15
3 Mar	Lev 8	Ps 107	1 Cor 16
4 Mar	Lev 9, 10	Ps 108, 109	2 Cor 1, 2
5 Mar	Lev 11	Ps 110, 112	2 Cor 3, 4
6 Mar	Lev 12, 13	Ps 113, 114	2 Cor 5, 7
7 Mar	Lev 14	Ps 115, 116	2 Cor 8, 9
8 Mar	Lev 15	Ps 117, 118	2 Cor 10, 11
9 Mar	Lev 16	Ps 119 vv 1-40	2 Cor 12, 13
10 Mar	Lev 17, 18	Ps 119 vv 41-80	Lk 1
11 Mar	Lev 19	Ps 119 vv 81-128	Lk 2
12 Mar	Lev 20	Ps 119 vv 129-176	Lk 3
13 Mar	Lev 21	Ps 120, 124	Lk 4
14 Mar	Lev 22	Ps 125, 127	Lk 5
15 Mar	Lev 23	Ps 128, 130	Lk 6
16 Mar	Lev 24	Ps 131, 134	Lk 7
17 Mar	Lev 25	Ps 135, 136	Lk 8
18 Mar	Lev 26	Ps 137, 139	Lk 9
19 Mar	Lev 27	Ps 140, 142	Lk 10
20 Mar	Num 1	Ps 143, 144	Lk 11
21 Mar	Num 2	Ps 145, 147	Lk 12
22 Mar	Num 3	Ps 148, 150	Lk 13, 14
23 Mar	Num 4	Prov 1	Lk 15
24 Mar	Num 5	Prov 2	Lk 16
25 Mar	Num 6	Prov 3	Lk 17
26 Mar	Num 7	Prov 4	Lk 18
27 Mar	Num 8, 9	Prov 5	Lk 19
28 Mar	Num 10	Prov 6	Lk 20
29 Mar	Num 11	Prov 7	Lk 21
30 Mar	Num 12, 13	Prov 8, 9	Lk 22
31 Mar	Num 14	Prov 10	Lk 23

READINGS FOR APRIL

Date	First Portion	Second Portion	Third Portion
1 Apr	Num 15	Prov 11	Lk 24
2 Apr	Num 16	Prov 12	Gal 1, 2
3 Apr	Num 17, 18	Prov 13	Gal 3, 4
4 Apr	Num 19	Prov 14	Gal 5, 6
5 Apr	Num 20, 21	Prov 15	Eph 1, 2
6 Apr	Num 22, 23	Prov 16	Eph 3, 4
7 Apr	Num 24, 25	Prov 17	Eph 5, 6
8 Apr	Num 26	Prov 18	Phil 1, 2
9 Apr	Num 27	Prov 19	Phil 3, 4
10 Apr	Num 28	Prov 20	Jn 1
11 Apr	Num 29, 30	Prov 21	Jn 2, 3
12 Apr	Num 31	Prov 22	Jn 4
13 Apr	Num 32	Prov 23	Jn 5
14 Apr	Num 33	Prov 24	Jn 6
15 Apr	Num 34	Prov 25	Jn 7
16 Apr	Num 35	Prov 26	Jn 8

17 Apr	Num 36	Prov 27	Jn 9, 10
18 Apr	Deut 1	Prov 28	Jn 11
19 Apr	Deut 2	Prov 29	Jn 12
20 Apr	Deut 3	Prov 30	Jn 13, 14
21 Apr	Deut 4	Prov 31	Jn 15, 16
22 Apr	Deut 5	Ecc 1	Jn 17, 18
23 Apr	Deut 6, 7	Ecc 2	Jn 19
24 Apr	Deut 8, 9	Ecc 3	Jn 20, 21
25 Apr	Deut 10, 11	Ecc 4	Acts 1
26 Apr	Deut 12	Ecc 5	Acts 2
27 Apr	Deut 13, 14	Ecc 6	Acts 3, 4
28 Apr	Deut 15	Ecc 7	Acts 5, 6
29 Apr	Deut 16	Ecc 8	Acts 7
30 Apr	Deut 17	Ecc 9	Acts 8

READINGS FOR MAY

Date	First Portion	Second Portion	Third Portion
1 May	Deut 18	Ecc 10	Acts 9
2 May	Deut 19	Ecc 11	Acts 10
3 May	Deut 20	Ecc 12	Acts 11, 12
4 May	Deut 21	Song 1	Acts 13
5 May	Deut 22	Song 2	Acts 14, 15
6 May	Deut 23	Song 3	Acts 16, 17
7 May	Deut 24	Song 4	Acts 18, 19
8 May	Deut 25	Song 5	Acts 20
9 May	Deut 26	Song 6	Acts 21, 22
10 May	Deut 27	Song 7	Acts 23, 24
11 May	Deut 28	Song 8	Acts 25, 26
12 May	Deut 29	Is 1	Acts 27
13 May	Deut 30	Is 2	Acts 28
14 May	Deut 31	Is 3, 4	Col 1
15 May	Deut 32	Is 5	Col 2
16 May	Deut 33, 34	Is 6	Col 3, 4
17 May	Jos 1	Is 7	1 Thes 1, 2
18 May	Jos 2	Is 8	1 Thes 3, 4
19 May	Jos 3, 4	Is 9	1 Thes 5
20 May	Jos 5, 6	Is 10	2 Thes 1, 2
21 May	Jos 7	Is 11	2 Thes 3
22 May	Jos 8	Is 12	1 Tim 1, 3
23 May	Jos 9	Is 13	1 Tim 4, 5
24 May	Jos 10	Is 14	1 Tim 6
25 May	Jos 11	Is 15	2 Tim 1
26 May	Jos 12	Is 16	2 Tim 2
27 May	Jos 13	Is 17, 18	2 Tim 3, 4
28 May	Jos 14	Is 19	Tit 1, 3
29 May	Jos 15	Is 20, 21	Philemon
30 May	Jos 16	Is 22	Heb 1, 2
31 May	Jos 17	Is 23	Heb 3, 5

READINGS FOR JUNE

Date	First Portion	Second Portion	Third Portion
1 Jun	Jos 18	Is 24	Heb 6, 7
2 Jun	Jos 19	Is 25	Heb 8, 9
3 Jun	Jos 20, 21	Is 26, 27	Heb 10
4 Jun	Jos 22	Is 28	Heb 11
5 Jun	Jos 23, 24	Is 29	Heb 12
6 Jun	Judg 1	Is 30	Heb 13
7 Jun	Judg 2, 3	Is 31	Jas 1
8 Jun	Judg 4, 5	Is 32	Jas 2
9 Jun	Judg 6	Is 33	Jas 3, 4
10 Jun	Judg 7, 8	Is 34	Jas 5
11 Jun	Judg 9	Is 35	1 Pet 1
12 Jun	Judg 10, 11	Is 36	1 Pet 2
13 Jun	Judg 12, 13	Is 37	1 Pet 3, 5
14 Jun	Judg 14, 15	Is 38	2 Pet 1, 2
15 Jun	Judg 16	Is 39	2 Pet 3
16 Jun	Judg 17, 18	Is 40	1 Jn 1, 2
17 Jun	Judg 19	Is 41	1 Jn 3, 4
18 Jun	Judg 20	Is 42	1 Jn 5
19 Jun	Judg 21	Is 43	2 & 3 Jn
20 Jun	Ruth 1, 2	Is 44	Jude
21 Jun	Ruth 3, 4	Is 45	Rev 1, 2
22 Jun	1 Sam 1	Is 46, 47	Rev 3, 4
23 Jun	1 Sam 2	Is 48	Rev 5, 6
24 Jun	1 Sam 3	Is 49	Rev 7, 9
25 Jun	1 Sam 4	Is 50	Rev 10, 11
26 Jun	1 Sam 5, 6	Is 51	Rev 12, 13
27 Jun	1 Sam 7, 8	Is 52	Rev 14
28 Jun	1 Sam 9	Is 53	Rev 15, 16
29 Jun	1 Sam 10	Is 54	Rev 17, 18
30 Jun	1 Sam 11, 12	Is 55	Rev 19, 20

READINGS FOR JULY

Date	First Portion	Second Portion	Third Portion
1 Jul	1 Sam 13	Is 56, 57	Rev 21, 22
2 Jul	1 Sam 14	Is 58	Mt 1, 2
3 Jul	1 Sam 15	Is 59	Mt 3, 4
4 Jul	1 Sam 16	Is 60	Mt 5
5 Jul	1 Sam 17	Is 61	Mt 6
6 Jul	1 Sam 18	Is 62	Mt 7
7 Jul	1 Sam 19	Is 63	Mt 8
8 Jul	1 Sam 20	Is 64	Mt 9
9 Jul	1 Sam 21, 22	Is 65	Mt 10
10 Jul	1 Sam 23	Is 66	Mt 11
11 Jul	1 Sam 24	Jer 1	Mt 12
12 Jul	1 Sam 25	Jer 2	Mt 13
13 Jul	1 Sam 26, 27	Jer 3	Mt 14
14 Jul	1 Sam 28	Jer 4	Mt 15
15 Jul	1 Sam 29, 30	Jer 5	Mt 16
16 Jul	1 Sam 31	Jer 6	Mt 17
17 Jul	2 Sam 1	Jer 7	Mt 18
18 Jul	2 Sam 2	Jer 8	Mt 19
19 Jul	2 Sam 3	Jer 9	Mt 20
20 Jul	2 Sam 4, 5	Jer 10	Mt 21
21 Jul	2 Sam 6	Jer 11	Mt 22
22 Jul	2 Sam 7	Jer 12	Mt 23
23 Jul	2 Sam 8, 9	Jer 13	Mt 24
24 Jul	2 Sam 10	Jer 14	Mt 25
25 Jul	2 Sam 11	Jer 15	Mt 26
26 Jul	2 Sam 12	Jer 16	Mt 27
27 Jul	2 Sam 13	Jer 17	Mt 28
28 Jul	2 Sam 14	Jer 18	Rom 1, 2
29 Jul	2 Sam 15	Jer 19	Rom 3, 4
30 Jul	2 Sam 16	Jer 20	Rom 5, 6
31 Jul	2 Sam 17	Jer 21	Rom 7, 8

READINGS FOR AUGUST

Date	First Portion	Second Portion	Third Portion
1 Aug	2 Sam 18	Jer 22	Rom 9
2 Aug	2 Sam 19	Jer 23	Rom 10, 11
3 Aug	2 Sam 20, 21	Jer 24	Rom 12
4 Aug	2 Sam 22	Jer 25	Rom 13, 14
5 Aug	2 Sam 23	Jer 26	Rom 15, 16
6 Aug	2 Sam 24	Jer 27	Mk 1
7 Aug	1 Kgs 1	Jer 28	Mk 2
8 Aug	1 Kgs 2	Jer 29	Mk 3
9 Aug	1 Kgs 3	Jer 30	Mk 4
10 Aug	1 Kgs 4, 5	Jer 31	Mk 5
11 Aug	1 Kgs 6	Jer 32	Mk 6
12 Aug	1 Kgs 7	Jer 33	Mk 7
13 Aug	1 Kgs 8	Jer 34	Mk 8
14 Aug	1 Kgs 9	Jer 35	Mk 9
15 Aug	1 Kgs 10	Jer 36	Mk 10
16 Aug	1 Kgs 11	Jer 37	Mk 11
17 Aug	1 Kgs 12	Jer 38	Mk 12
18 Aug	1 Kgs 13	Jer 39	Mk 13
19 Aug	1 Kgs 14	Jer 40	Mk 14
20 Aug	1 Kgs 15	Jer 41	Mk 15
21 Aug	1 Kgs 16	Jer 42	Mk 16
22 Aug	1 Kgs 17	Jer 43	1 Cor 1, 2
23 Aug	1 Kgs 18	Jer 44	1 Cor 3
24 Aug	1 Kgs 19	Jer 45, 46	1 Cor 4, 5
25 Aug	1 Kgs 20	Jer 47	1 Cor 6

26 Aug	1 Kgs 21	Jer 48	1 Cor 7
27 Aug	1 Kgs 22	Jer 49	1 Cor 8, 9
28 Aug	2 Kgs 1, 2	Jer 50	1 Cor 10
29 Aug	2 Kgs 3	Jer 51	1 Cor 11 30
Aug	2 Kgs 4	Jer 52	1 Cor 12, 13
31 Aug	2 Kgs 5	Lam 1	1 Cor 14

READINGS FOR SEPTEMBER

Date	First Portion	Second Portion	Third Portion
1 Sep	2 Kgs 6	Lam 2	1 Cor 15
2 Sep	2 Kgs 7	Lam 3	1 Cor 16
3 Sep	2 Kgs 8	Lam 4	2 Cor 1, 2
4 Sep	2 Kgs 9	Lam 5	2 Cor 3, 4
5 Sep	2 Kgs 10	Ezek 1	2 Cor 5, 7
6 Sep	2 Kgs 11, 12	Ezek 2	2 Cor 8, 9
7 Sep	2 Kgs 13	Ezek 3	2 Cor 10, 11
8 Sep	2 Kgs 14	Ezek 4	2 Cor 12, 13
9 Sep	2 Kgs 15	Ezek 5	Lk 1
10 Sep	2 Kgs 16	Ezek 6	Lk 2
11 Sep	2 Kgs 17	Ezek 7	Lk 3
12 Sep	2 Kgs 18	Ezek 8	Lk 4
13 Sep	2 Kgs 19	Ezek 9	Lk 5
14 Sep	2 Kgs 20	Ezek 10	Lk 6
15 Sep	2 Kgs 21	Ezek 11	Lk 7
16 Sep	2 Kgs 22, 23	Ezek 12	Lk 8
17 Sep	2 Kgs 24, 25	Ezek 13	Lk 9
18 Sep	1 Chr 1	Ezek 14	Lk 10
19 Sep	1 Chr 2	Ezek 15	Lk 11
20 Sep	1 Chr 3	Ezek 16	Lk 12
21 Sep	1 Chr 4	Ezek 17	Lk 13, 14
22 Sep	1 Chr 5	Ezek 18	Lk 15
23 Sep	1 Chr 6	Ezek 19	Lk 16
24 Sep	1 Chr 7	Ezek 20	Lk 17
25 Sep	1 Chr 8	Ezek 21	Lk 18
26 Sep	1 Chr 9	Ezek 22	Lk 19
27 Sep	1 Chr 10	Ezek 23	Lk 20
28 Sep	1 Chr 11	Ezek 24	Lk 21
29 Sep	1 Chr 12	Ezek 25	Lk 22
30 Sep	1 Chr 13, 14	Ezek 26	Lk 23

READINGS FOR OCTOBER

Date	First Portion	Second Portion	Third Portion
1 Oct	1 Chr 15	Ezek 27	Lk 24
2 Oct	1 Chr 16	Ezek 28	Gal 1, 2
3 Oct	1 Chr 17	Ezek 29	Gal 3, 4
4 Oct	1 Chr 18, 19	Ezek 30	Gal 5, 6
5 Oct	1 Chr 20, 21	Ezek 31	Eph 1, 2
6 Oct	1 Chr 22	Ezek 32	Eph 3, 4
7 Oct	1 Chr 23	Ezek 33	Eph 5, 6
8 Oct	1 Chr 24, 25	Ezek 34	Phil 1, 2
9 Oct	1 Chr 26	Ezek 35	Phil 3, 4
10 Oct	1 Chr 27	Ezek 36	Jn 1
11 Oct	1 Chr 28	Ezek 37	Jn 2, 3
12 Oct	1 Chr 29	Ezek 38	Jn 4
13 Oct	2 Chr 1, 2	Ezek 39	Jn 5
14 Oct	2 Chr 3, 4	Ezek 40	Jn 6
15 Oct	2 Chr 5, 6	Ezek 41	Jn 7
16 Oct	2 Chr 7	Ezek 42	Jn 8
17 Oct	2 Chr 8	Ezek 43	Jn 9, 10
18 Oct	2 Chr 9	Ezek 44	Jn 11
19 Oct	2 Chr 10, 11	Ezek 45	Jn 12
20 Oct	2 Chr 12, 13	Ezek 46	Jn 13, 14
21 Oct	2 Chr 14, 15	Ezek 47	Jn 15, 16
22 Oct	2 Chr 16, 17	Ezek 48	Jn 17, 18
23 Oct	2 Chr 18, 19	Dan 1	Jn 19
24 Oct	2 Chr 20	Dan 2	Jn 20, 21
25 Oct	2 Chr 21, 22	Dan 3	Acts 1
26 Oct	2 Chr 23	Dan 4	Acts 2
27 Oct	2 Chr 24	Dan 5	Acts 3, 4
28 Oct	2 Chr 25	Dan 6	Acts 5, 6
29 Oct	2 Chr 26, 27	Dan 7	Acts 7
30 Oct	2 Chr 28	Dan 8	Acts 8
31 Oct	2 Chr 29	Dan 9	Acts 9

READINGS FOR NOVEMBER

Date	First Portion	Second Portion	Third Portion
1 Nov	2 Chr 30	Dan 10	Acts 10
2 Nov	2 Chr 31	Dan 11	Acts 11, 12
3 Nov	2 Chr 32	Dan 12	Acts 13
4 Nov	2 Chr 33	Hos 1	Acts 14, 15
5 Nov	2 Chr 34	Hos 2	Acts 16, 17
6 Nov	2 Chr 35	Hos 3	Acts 18, 19
7 Nov	2 Chr 36	Hos 4	Acts 20
8 Nov	Ezra 1, 2	Hos 5	Acts 21, 22
9 Nov	Ezra 3, 4	Hos 6	Acts 23, 24
10 Nov	Ezra 5, 6	Hos 7	Acts 25, 26
11 Nov	Ezra 7	Hos 8	Acts 27
12 Nov	Ezra 8	Hos 9	Acts 28
13 Nov	Ezra 9	Hos 10	Col 1
14 Nov	Ezra 10	Hos 11	Col 2
15 Nov	Neh 1, 2	Hos 12	Col 3, 4
16 Nov	Neh 3	Hos 13	1 Thes 1, 2
17 Nov	Neh 4	Hos 14	1 Thes 3, 4

18 Nov	Neh 5, 6	Joel 1	1 Thes 5
19 Nov	Neh 7	Joel 2	2 Thes 1, 2
20 Nov	Neh 8	Joel 3	2 Thes 3
21 Nov	Neh 9	Amos 1	1 Tim 1, 3
22 Nov	Neh 10	Amos 2	1 Tim 4, 5
23 Nov	Neh 11	Amos 3	1 Tim 6
24 Nov	Neh 12	Amos 4	2 Tim 1
25 Nov	Neh 13	Amos 5	2 Tim 2
26 Nov	Esth 1	Amos 6	2 Tim 3, 4
27 Nov	Esth 2	Amos 7	Tit 1, 3
28 Nov	Esth 3, 4	Amos 8	Phlm
29 Nov	Esth 5, 6	Amos 9	Heb 1, 2
30 Nov	Esth 7, 8	Obad	Heb 3, 5

READINGS FOR DECEMBER

Date	First Portion	Second Portion	Third Portion
1 Dec	Esth 9, 10	Jon 1	Heb 6, 7
2 Dec	Job 1, 2	Jon 2, 3	Heb 8, 9
3 Dec	Job 3, 4	Jon 4	Heb 10
4 Dec	Job 5	Mic 1	Heb 11
5 Dec	Job 6, 7	Mic 2	Heb 12
6 Dec	Job 8	Mic 3, 4	Heb 13
7 Dec	Job 9	Mic 5	Jas 1
8 Dec	Job 10	Mic 6	Jas 2
9 Dec	Job 11	Mic 7	Jas 3, 4
10 Dec	Job 12	Nah 1, 2	Jas 5

11 Dec	Job 13	Nah 3	1 Pet 1
12 Dec	Job 14	Hab 1	1 Pet 2
13 Dec	Job 15	Hab 2	1 Pet 3, 5
14 Dec	Job 16, 17	Hab 3	2 Pet 1, 2
15 Dec	Job 18, 19	Zeph 1	2 Pet 3
16 Dec	Job 20	Zeph 2	1 Jn 1, 2
17 Dec	Job 21	Zeph 3	1 Jn 3, 4
18 Dec	Job 22	Hag 1, 2	1 Jn 5
19 Dec	Job 23, 24	Zech 1	2 & 3 Jn
20 Dec	Job 25, 27	Zech 2, 3	Jude
21 Dec	Job 28	Zech 4, 5	Rev 1, 2
22 Dec	Job 29, 30	Zech 6, 7	Rev 3, 4
23 Dec	Job 31, 32	Zech 8	Rev 5, 6
24 Dec	Job 33	Zech 9	Rev 7, 9
25 Dec	Job 34	Zech 10	Rev 10, 11
26 Dec	Job 35, 36	Zech 11	Rev 12, 13
27 Dec	Job 37	Zech 12	Rev 14
28 Dec	Job 38	Zech 13, 14	Rev 15, 16
29 Dec	Job 39	Mal 1	Rev 17, 18
30 Dec	Job 40	Mal 2	Rev 19, 20
31 Dec	Job 41, 42	Mal 3, 4	Rev 21, 22

OTHER CHRISTADELPHIAN LITERATURE

John Thomas' book, *Elpis Israel (Hope of Israel)*, and *Christendom Astray from the Bible* by Robert Roberts, John Thomas' successor, form the basis for the group's beliefs.

4 FACTS AND FIGURES

- The Christadelphians became a distinct group about the middle of the nineteenth century, in the eastern United States.
- Today, Christadelphians can be found in over 130 countries around the world.
- There are about 1,000 congregations throughout Africa, North America, South-East Asia, and Europe.

- There are also large groups of Christadelphians in Australia and New Zealand.
- Oceania has more than 150 ecclesias.
- There are over 300 ecclesias in Great Britain and Ireland.
- There are ecclesias in all 50 states of US.
- In Canada there are ecclesias in all ten provinces and three territories.

5 CHRISTADELPHIAN PRACTICES

Members do not:

- vote in political elections
- run for political office
- go to war.

METHOD OF EVANGELISM

The main method of evangelism for Christadephians is through advertising in newspapers. These advertisements emphasize the return of Christ, the decline in morality, world affairs, the resurrection of Christ and the assertion that we need not fear a personal devil. Readers are invited to a public meeting to hear a special message.

Though Christadelphians no longer go door-to-door, visiting people in their homes, they do have stands at fairs where they sell their literature, which, at first glance looks like orthodox Christian literature.

---

6 CHRISTADELPHIAN BELIEFS

Not only do Christadelphians reject many unorthodox doctrines, they also reject orthodox Christian teachings. Moreover, they state: "Fellowship cannot be extended to anyone who holds, teaches, fellowships or countenances any of these doctrinal heresies."

REJECTED DOCTRINES:

- We reject the doctrine – that the Bible is only partly the work of inspiration – or if wholly so, contains errors which inspiration has allowed.
- We reject the doctrine – that God is three persons.
- We reject the doctrine – that the Son of God was co-eternal with the Father.
- We reject the doctrine – that Christ was born with a "free life."
- We reject the doctrine – that Christ's nature was immaculate.
- We reject the doctrine – that the Holy Spirit is a person distinct from the Father.
- We reject the doctrine – that man has an immortal soul.
- We reject the doctrine – that man consciously exists in death.
- We reject the doctrine – that the wicked will suffer eternal torture in hell.
- We reject the doctrine – that the righteous will ascend to the kingdoms beyond the skies when they die.

- We reject the doctrine – that the devil is a supernatural being.
- We reject the doctrine – that the Kingdom of God is "the church."
- We reject the doctrine – that the Gospel is the death, burial, and resurrection of Christ merely.
- We reject the doctrine – that Christ will not come till the close of the thousand years.
- We reject the doctrine – that the tribunal of Christ, when he comes, is not for judgment of saints, but merely to divide among them different degrees of reward.
- We reject the doctrine – that the resurrection is confined to the faithful.
- We reject the doctrine – that the dead rise in an immortal state.
- We reject the doctrine – that the subject-nations of the thousand years are immortal.
- We reject the doctrine – that the Law of Moses is binding on believers of the Gospel.

- We reject the doctrine – that the observance of Sunday is a matter of duty.
- We reject the doctrine – that baby sprinkling is a doctrine of Scripture.
- We reject the doctrine – that those without knowledge – through personal choice, immaturity, or lack of mental capacity – will be saved.
- We reject the doctrine – that man can be saved by morality or sincerity, without the Gospel.
- We reject the doctrine – that the Gospel alone will save, without obedience to Christ's commandments.
- We reject the doctrine – that a man cannot believe without possessing the Spirit of God.
- We reject the doctrine – that men are predestined to salvation unconditionally.
- We reject the doctrine – that there is no sin in the flesh.
- We reject the doctrine – that Joseph was the actual father of Jesus.
- We reject the doctrine – that the earth will be destroyed.
- We reject the doctrine – that baptism is not necessary to salvation.
- We reject the doctrine – that a knowledge of the Truth is not necessary to make baptism valid.
- We reject the doctrine – that some meats are to be refused on the score of uncleanness.
- We reject the doctrine – that the English are the ten tribes of Israel, whose prosperity is a fulfillment of the promises made concerning Ephraim.
- We reject the doctrine – that marriage with an unbeliever is lawful.
- We reject the doctrine – that we are at liberty to serve in the Army, Navy, Police Force, or any service whatsoever requiring the Oath of Allegiance or use of force.
- We reject the doctrine – that we are at liberty to take part in politics, or recover debts by legal coercion.

IN SUMMARY

Christadelphian doctrines may be summarized as follows.

Bible: The Bible is God's word and the only message from him. The Bible is the infallible and inerrant word of God. It is without error, except for copying and translation errors.

God: there is only one God – the Father.

The Holy Spirit: the Holy Spirit is God's power.

Jesus: Jesus is the Son of God, and a human being, through his mother Mary.

Jesus' death: by living a sinless life, ending with his sacrificial death by crucifixion, Jesus has opened the way of salvation from death.

Baptism: baptism is the outward sign of a repentant and contrite heart, of a person convicted of his or her sinfulness and desiring redemption. Those who are baptized participate symbolically in the sacrifice and resurrection of Christ, and thereby attain forgiveness of sins. Thus belief and baptism are both essential steps to salvation.

Resurrection of Jesus: God raised Jesus from death. Jesus is currently in heaven, on God's right hand.

Salvation: salvation is attained through faith in Christ. Through faith believers are baptized into Christ for forgiveness of sins, and thereby participate in the promises to Abraham: to inherit the earth for ever.

Existence after death: human beings are mortal, having no existence when dead (immortality is a gift, see below).

Kingdom of God: the Kingdom of God will be established on earth. Then Jesus will be king in Jerusalem; his rule will be worldwide and his government will bring eternal righteousness and peace.

Second coming of Jesus: Jesus will one day return to earth and set up the Kingdom of God. When he returns, he will raise his "sleeping" followers from death and grant immortality to the faithful who have tried to live by God's precepts.

UNORTHODOX CHRISTADELPHIAN BELIEFS

Christadelphians differ from orthodox Christians in their beliefs concerning the nature of God, Jesus Christ, the Holy Spirit and Satan.

THE TRINITY

They deny the Trinity, and say there is only one eternal person – the Father.

JESUS

Christadelphians believe that Jesus the Christ is the Son of God, who came to fulfill the Old Testament promises and covenants of God with mankind, primarily the covenants with Eve, Abraham and David. They believe that Christ is a man, the Son of God, but not God. They say:

> There is no hint in the Old Testament that the Son of God was already existent or in any way active at that time.
> *Harry Tennant*

> Jesus Christ, the Son of God, was first promised, and came into being only when he was born of the virgin Mary.
> *Harry Tennant*

Christadelphians reject the assertion that Jesus is God for the following reasons:

- God is one. There can only be one true God. It is undeniable that Jesus referred to himself and the Father as separate.
- Mortality and immortality are mutually exclusive characteristics. God is immortal, and cannot die. Jesus died.
- Jesus pointed out his subservience to God; in power, teaching and life itself. To assert their equality is untenable.

They deny Christ's sinless nature and believe Christ had a sinful nature like us. They teach that Christ overcame his sinful nature as he grew.

GOD'S COVENANTS

The Christadelphians believe that the Christ and his mission can only be understood in the light of a clear comprehension of the covenants he came to fulfill.

(i) He fulfilled the promise to Eve, that one of her seed would crush the serpent (Genesis 3:15).

(ii) He fulfilled the covenant with Abraham, that in his seed would all the nations of the earth be blessed (Genesis 22:18; Galatians 3:16).

(iii) He will fulfill on his return God's promise to David that one of his descendants will sit on his throne in Jerusalem for ever (2 Samuel 7:12-16).

It was always the understanding of these men and women that the Messiah would be their descendant. Therefore to say that Jesus was born more than a man, or that he existed as a person before Eve, Abraham and David, is to reject the clear presentation of God's purpose to these people of faith.

REDEMPTION

Christadelphians reject as unbiblical the idea that Christ could die as a replacement sacrifice for us, thus covering all our sins for ever with that one act. While they believe that it is through his sacrifice that we may be forgiven, they also assert that this is only possible if we walk the path of Christian self-denial.

> The cross is not a substitutionary offering whereby someone is paid a price so that others might then go free.
> *Harry Tennant*

HOLY SPIRIT

Christadelphians deny that the Holy Spirit is the third person of the Trinity and teach that it is a force, the invisible power that comes from the Father. It is a "power concentrated through an individual or angel for the purpose of a specific miraculous event or activity" (*The Testimony: The Distinctive Beliefs of the Christadelphians*, Vol. 58, No. 691, July 1988, page 254).

THE DEVIL

Christadelphians reject the idea that the devil is one of Gods' angels that was permitted to rebel.

They reject the doctrine of a supernatural tempter and say that the Bible uses the word "devil" as a symbol of sinful human nature. They teach that Satan is in all of us in the form of our own personal lusts. The devil is really our own natural desire to sin.

According to a Christadelphian publication:

Its [the devil's] general meaning is sin or lawlessness, whether manifested individually or politically. It is also applied to the unlawful lusts and tendencies of human nature which invariably lead to sin. It is not a supernatural being. Satan is a Hebrew word signifying "adversary," "enemy," or "accuser."

Key to Understanding the Bible

HEAVEN

Christadelphians do not believe that the saved will spend eternity in heaven. They believe that the Kingdom of God will be located on the earth, with Jerusalem as its capital.

7 WORSHIP

MEMORIAL MEETING

Christadelphians meet weekly on Sundays for a Memorial Meeting or Breaking of Bread.

At the meeting for the "breaking of bread" on "the first day of the week" there are hymns, prayers, readings from the Scriptures and an exhortation. The bread and the wine circulate among all the "brothers and sisters" present. Voluntary collections are taken to meet all the expenses.

ECCLESIA (GREEK FOR "CONGREGATION")

Local groups are called "ecclesias." These are groups of brethren and sisters sharing the same beliefs who live in the same area. They average about twenty members each.

Most of the ecclesias meet in each other's homes or in rented halls. A few own their own buildings.

Christadelphians have no central organization. Each ecclesia is autonomous.

Christadelphianism is a lay movement and has no clergy/laity distinctions. And no paid ministry. Responsibility for ecclesial duties is shared out between the members as necessary.

APOCALYPTIC CULTS

CONTENTS

1 An Overview   571

2 Apocalyptic Cults   572

     Aum Shinri Kyo

     The Family

     Branch Davidians

     Heaven's Gate

     Jeffrey Lundgren

     Movement for the Restoration of the Ten Commandments of
God (Uganda)

     The People's Temple

     Solar Temple

1 AN OVERVIEW

DEFINITION

Apocalyptic cults, also known as Destructive cults, and as Doomsday cults, are religiously based, and have members controlled by leaders who have caused, or are liable to cause, death among their membership and/or among the general public.

CATEGORIZATION

Apocalyptic cults may be categorized in the following way:

Homicides directed against the public
- Aum Shinri Kyo
- The Family (Charles Manson)

Suicides or homicides against their own members
- Branch Davidians
- Heaven's Gate
- Jeffrey Lundgren
- Movement for the Restoration of the Ten Commandments of God (Uganda)
- The People's Temple (Jim Jones)
- Solar Temple

PERPETRATORS OF EVIL

The evil in these cults may appear to be out of all proportion to their size.

In Japan: Japanese cult Aum Shinrikyo allegedly used sarin nerve gas on a subway car in Japan, killing twelve people and injuring more than 5,000 others.

In Waco, Texas: a standoff between US government officials and Branch Davidian cult members, led by David Koresh, left 75 Davidians, including 21 children, and four US agents dead.

In Santa Fe, California: 39 people were found dead at Rancho Santa Fe, California, in a carefully orchestrated group suicide by members of the Heaven's Gate cult.

In Uganda: at least 590 deaths were linked to a religious cult called the Movement for the Restoration of the Ten Commandments of God.

In Jonestown: more than 900 people, followers of Jim Jones' "People's Temple," died in the South American jungle.

2 THE APOCALYPTIC CULTS

A Aum Shinri Kyo
B The Family (Charles Manson)
C Branch Davidians
D Heaven's Gate
E Jeffrey Lundgren
F Movement for the Restoration of the Ten Commandments of God (Uganda)
G The People's Temple (Jim Jones)
H Solar Temple

A AUM SHINRI KYO

The Aum Shinri Kyo cult is based in Japan and was founded in 1987. The name combines "Aum" and "Shinri Kyo." *Aum* is a sacred Hindu syllable; *Shinri Kyo* means "supreme truth."

This movement has a syncretistic religious basis, incorporating elements of Buddhism with Christianity.

Its leader, Shoko Asahara, born in 1955, was originally named Chizuo Matsumoto.

Asahara was arrested for spreading the nerve gas, Sarin, in a Tokyo subway station on March 20, 1995. The gas killed twelve passengers and injured over five thousand people.

B THE FAMILY

Charles Milles Manson, born 1934, gathered more than a hundred people around him at the Spahn Ranch, thirty miles north-west of Los Angeles CA. The media called this group "The Family," with Manson its guru. Some of his followers referred to him as "God" and some as "Satan." Manson himself said he was a reincarnation of Jesus Christ.

Manson believed that the murderous activities of his followers would precipitate wide-spread, black-white race wars and an Armageddon, which he called "Helter Skelter"(supposedly predicted in the Beatles tune of that name). After this, the "family" would emerge from their safe hiding place in the Mojave Desert, and take over what remained of the United States, with Charles Manson as king.

The first five murders occurred in a house high above the city of Los Angeles. A band of middle-class Manson followers broke into the home of film-maker Roman Polanski and savagely murdered his pregnant wife, Sharon Tate, and four guests.

The next two victims, Leno and Rosemary LaBianca, were found stabbed to death in their home in the Los Feliz section of Los Angeles.

On January 15, 1971, Charles Manson (35), Patricia Krenwinkel (20), Susan (Sadie) Atkins (21), and Leslie Van Houten (22) were convicted of murder and conspiracy to commit murder. All four defendants received the death penalty. Later, Charles "Tex" Watson was convicted of murder and conspiracy to commit murder.

The California Supreme Court abolished the death penalty in 1972, and so Charles Manson and his family are all now serving life sentences.

C BRANCH DAVIDIANS

The Branch Davidians are a religious group originating from the Seventh-day Adventist Church, founded by David Koresh.

Vernon Howell, having been recently excommunicated from the Seventh-day Adventist church, gained control of the cult and its compound. . . . Howell enticed young girls into becoming his sexual partners by naming them as "wives" and prophetically declaring that they had been commissioned by God to help him repopulate planet earth. He proved to be a master at managing and manipulating the core followers in virtually every dimension of their lives – including sleep, prayer, Bible study, diet, activities, reading, music, occupations, and finances.

In 1990, Howell legally changed his name to David Koresh.

Hank Hanegraaff

BATF RAID AND SIEGE

On February 28, 1993, the Bureau of Alcohol, Tobacco and Firearms (BATF) raided the Branch Davidian ranch in Mount Carmel, a rural area near Waco, Texas. The raid was conducted because of allegations of illegal weapons present on the property. The initial raid resulted in the deaths of four agents and five Davidians. The subsequent 51 day siege ended on April 19, when the compound was completely consumed by fire killing between 72 and 86 men, women, and children, including Koresh.

D HEAVEN'S GATE

In March 1997, 39 members of this cult participated in a group suicide in the wake of the Hale-Bopp comet. They claimed they were shedding their "earthly containers" in order to enter a spaceship that they said was trailing the tail of the Hale-Bopp comet. They believed they would be whisked away by benevolent ETs.

One report recorded the suicide as follows: "The bodies of 39 men and women, cloaked in purple shrouds, were found in a million dollar California mansion Wednesday in what police said appeared to be a mass suicide. All the victims were cloaked in purple, triangular shaped shrouds covering their faces and chests."

Whether Hale-Bopp has a "companion" or not is irrelevant from our perspective. However, its arrival is joyously very significant to us at Heaven's Gate. The joy is that our Older Member in the Evolutionary Level Above Human (the Kingdom of Heaven) has made it clear to

us that Hale-Bopp's approach is the marker we've been waiting for – the time for the arrival of the spacecraft from the Level Above Human to take us home to "Their World" – in the literal Heavens. Our 22 years of classroom here on planet Earth is finally coming to conclusion – "graduation" from the Human Evolutionary Level. We are happily prepared to leave "this world" and go with Ti's crew.

Heaven's Gate

E JEFFREY LUNDGREN

Jeffrey Lundgren headed up a cult he founded in 1989. It was a small splinter group that had broken away from the Reorganized Church of Jesus Christ of Latter Day Saints (RLDS), which itself had broken away from the Church of Jesus Christ of Latter-day Saints (the Mormons).

They began practicing communal living and took part in para-military training. Called "Prophet" and "Father" by other cult members, Lundgren received revelations naming two specific dates for the return of Christ. He explained that Jesus would at that moment destroy everyone except those righteous who were found inside the Kirtland temple. The Kirtland temple, built by Joseph Smith and his contemporaries, is currently owned and operated by the RLDS Church.

Lundgren's authority was opposed by one family, the Averys. Lundgren said God told him, through interpretation of scripture, to kill the Averys. So the five members of the Dennis Avery family were executed and buried on the group's ranch. Lundgren was sentenced to death for his crimes; his wife and son received long prison sentences.

F MOVEMENT FOR THE RESTORATION OF THE TEN COMMANDMENTS OF GOD (UGANDA)

On August 24, 1988, a young woman called Mwerinde had the first of what she said was a series of visions of the Virgin Mary and began to share her story with those who would listen. In 1991, Joseph Kibwetere, a Roman Catholic Church employee, traveled to

Nyanmitanga, Uganda, to hear Mwerinde and was so impressed that he invited her to live in his home.

This became the headquarters of the Movement for the Restoration of the Ten Commandments of God (Uganda) for three years, until they moved to Kanangu in 1994. By this time, Kibwetere had separated from his wife and had been excommunicated from the Roman Catholic Church. The pair led the group.

Mwerinde's visions had also attracted other Roman Catholics, including the priest Dominic Kataribabo, who eventually left the Roman Catholic Church and worked for the MRTC.

From 1994, the Movement developed as an ordered community, adherents accepting a disciplined life and new behavioral rules as conditions of membership (somewhat like life in other Catholic orders). Its primary center was in Kanungu, but other groups emerged at several nearby towns. Members were united in their acceptance of the material received by Mwerinde from her reported visions.

As families joined, they adopted the group rules designed to prevent any further breaking of the Ten Commandments. They refrained from sex and any unnecessary verbal interaction (a means of refraining from adultery and profaning the Lord's name). They developed a sign language that they used whenever possible.

As the group formed around the visions, it moved to separate itself from society and the Roman Catholic Church. For MRTC, the Catholic Church was high on the list of those who, by regularly breaking the Ten Commandments, were causing God great offense. In return, as soon as the Movement became large enough for Church officials to take note, its leaders were excommunicated, and it was written off as not Catholic. At its largest, the group may have had as many as 4,000 members.

Integral to the group was a belief that the world was disintegrating around it, but, as with apocalyptic groups through the centuries, they also hoped that God or the Virgin would deliver them. The end of the century provided an occasion for actualizing that belief, and as December 31 approached, members began to liquidate assets and prepare for the coming deliverance predicted by Mwerinde and Kibwetere.

When deliverance did not come, the pair revised their prediction. It would still happen, they said, but at some point during 2000. A significant number of members lost their confidence in Mwerinde's contact with the divine realm and demanded that the money and resources they had donated be returned. That demand created a crisis that threatened to bankrupt, if not destroy, the group.

When 530 members of the Movement for the Restoration of the Ten Commandments of God died in an intentionally set fire on March 17, 2000, it was labeled the second-worst mass suicide on record, after Jonestown. Upon further examination of the cult's compound in Kanungu, however, officials decided instead to handle it as a murder investigation. The bodies of 388 additional people – many clearly stabbed or strangled to death – have since been found buried in several mass graves on property owned by the sect.

G THE PEOPLE'S TEMPLE

This cult was founded and led by James Warren Jones (1931-1978). Jim Jones, the son of a Klansman, considered himself to be the reincarnation of both Jesus and Lenin. Jones had visions of an impending nuclear holocaust in which only the towns of Ukiah, California, and Belo Horizonte, Brazil, would survive. He therefore relocated his first People's Temple to Ukiah to await the Armageddon.

Tired of waiting for the third world war, he moved his group to San Francisco, where he received humanitarian awards and became the Chairman of the city's Housing Authority. It was there that he first practiced a ritual called "White Nights" in which he prepared his followers for an act of revolutionary suicide to protest against racism and fascism.

By 1977, as things started getting weirder, he was forced to move his church to Guyana, South America. There, in the isolation of the jungle, Jones created his dream community, Jonestown, and lost his mind. Jones's nirvana rapidly deteriorated into a nightmare.

On November 18, 1978, Congressman Leo Ryan from San Francisco spent one day at the jungle pavilion investigating alleged human rights abuses. When Ryan, his party and eighteen temple members who wanted to leave, prepared to return to the United States, they were ambushed on the airstrip.

Ryan, three newsmen, and a Temple defector were killed. Eleven others were injured.

Hours later, Jones ordered his followers to drink from a tub of grape-flavored Kool Aid laced with cyanide and tranquilizers. All 914 died: 638 adults and 276 children. Children died first; babies were killed by poison squirted into their mouths with a syringe. Then the adults. Most were poisoned, some forcibly. Some were shot by security guards. As the ritual suicide progressed, it is unclear whether Jones put a bullet through his brain, or someone did it for him.

H SOLAR TEMPLE

The apocalyptic Order of the Solar Temple cult claimed 74 victims in three bizarre mass suicide rituals. Most of the members of the sect seem to be highly educated and well-off individuals. The Order itself stems from the Knights of Templar, a secretive medieval organization founded by French crusaders in Jerusalem.

Joseph Di Mambro, from France, was the leader of the Solar Temple. He founded a school in the south border of Switzerland, near France, called the "Center For The Preparation For The New Age," and moved to Canada following tax problems in France, and for practicing psychology without a license.

Computer records seized by Canadian police in Montreal showed that some members had personally donated over $1 million to the cult, and the respectability of these followers' public life was in massive contrast to the bizarre small cult they had joined.

The beliefs of the Order of the Solar Temple were based partly on the Hindu teaching of reincarnation. Di Mambro claimed to have had a previous life as a member of the Knight's Temple during the Crusades. During its ceremonies, the members wore Crusade-type robes. They held in awe a sword that Di Mambro said had been given to him one thousand years earlier. Death represented for them an essential stage of life.

The Temple came to prominence on October 5, 1994, when 53 people committed murder-suicide in several chalets in Switzerland and Canada. Luc Jouret, a Belgian New Ageist homeopathic doctor, one of the leaders of the group, and Joseph di Mambro, described as "a wealthy businessman," were among the dead in Switzerland.

The cult gave great importance to the sun. The ritual murder-suicides were meant to take members of the sect to a new world on the star "Sirius." To assist with the trip, several of the victims, including some children, were shot in the head, asphyxiated with black plastic bags, and/or poisoned. Luc and Joseph wrote, in a letter delivered after their deaths that they were "leaving this earth to find a new dimension of truth and absolution, far from the hypocrisies of this world."

A second mass suicide ritual occurred in 1995, about a week before Christmas. On December 23, on a remote plateau of the French Alps, police found sixteen charred bodies arranged in a star formation with their feet pointing to the ashes of a fire. Like the rituals of 1994, they all died by stabbing, asphyxiation, shooting and/or poisoning. Some had left behind handwritten notes expressing their intentions of committing mass suicide. One of the notes stated: "Death does not exist, it is pure illusion. May we, in our inner life, find each other forever." Two of the dead were the wife and son of French ski champion and millionaire eye wear manufacturer, Jean Vuarnet.

On March 23, 1997, five more dead bodies were found in a burned house owned by Didier Queze, a member of the Order, in St. Casimir, Quebec. The bodies of four cultists – Didier, her husband, and another couple – were found in a bed upstairs positioned in what may have been intended to be the shape of the cross. The mother of Didier was found dead on a sofa downstairs with a plastic bag over her head. Unlike earlier suicides in which adults killed their children, the three teenage children of the cultist couple were spared.

Apparently the teenagers woke up the day before the suicide to discover their parents and their cultist friend had placed propane tanks, electric hot plates, and fire-starters on the main floor of the two-story house and were trying to burn down the place. Realizing what was happening the teenagers expressed their disapproval and negotiated with their parents to be spared. However, Fanie Queze-Goupillot, 14, and her brothers Tom, 13, and Julien, 16, agreed to take sleeping pills before their parents' fiery death and went to sleep in a workshop near the house. "The children were given medication, but they knew that when they woke up that their parents and grandmother would be dead."

HARE KRISHNA

CONTENTS

1 An Overview   579

2 Founder   580

3 Hare Krishna's Holy Book   580

4 Facts and Figures   580

5 Hare Krishna Practices   581

6 Hare Krishna Beliefs   583

7 Worship   586

8 Quotations   587

1 AN OVERVIEW

DEFINITION

The International Society for Krishna Consciousness (ISKCON) is the religious organization for devotees of Krishna (Krshna). Their religion is commonly known as Hare Krishna, because of the first two words of their principle mantra.

Krishna, meaning "all-attractive," is a name of the Supreme. Supreme is also known as Rama, which means "the highest eternal pleasure."

Hare (pronounced huh-ray) is a call to Krishna's divine energy.

These names of God and the Hare Krishna mantra are derived from ancient Indian texts of knowledge called the *Vedas*.

Factfile
- Date of origin: 1966
- Founder: His Divine Grace A. C. Bhaktivedanta Swami Prabhupada, 1896-1977
- Holy book: *Bhagavad Gita.*
- Number of adherents: 1,250,000

SUMMARY

The International Society for Krishna Consciousness is a movement aiming at the spiritual reorientation of mankind through the simple process of chanting the holy names of God.

His Divine Grace A. C. Bhaktivedanta Swami Prabhupada

SUMMARY OF PRACTICES AND BELIEFS

When Srila Prabhupada founded ISKCON, he defined the following seven purposes of this religion:

1. To systematically propagate spiritual knowledge to society at large and to educate all peoples in the techniques of spiritual life in order to check the imbalance of values in life and to achieve real unity and peace in the world.

2. To propagate a consciousness of Krishna, as it is revealed in Bhagavad-Gita and Srimad Bhagavatam.

3. To bring the members of the Society together with each other and nearer to Krishna, the prime entity, thus developing the idea within the members and humanity at large, that each soul is part and parcel of the quality of Godhead (Krishna).

4. To teach and encourage the sankirtana movement, congregational chanting of the holy names of God, as revealed in the teachings of Lord Sri Chaitanya Mahaprabhu.

5. To erect for the members and for society at large, a holy place of transcendental pastimes dedicated to the personality of Krishna.

6. To bring the members closer together for the purpose of teaching a simpler, more natural way of life.

7. With a view toward achieving the aforementioned purposes, to publish and distribute periodicals, books and other writings.

2 FOUNDER

The Founder-Acarya of ISKCON (International Society for Krishna Consciousness) is His Divine Grace A. C. Bhaktivedanta Swami Prabhupada (1896-1977).

3 HARE KRISHNA'S HOLY BOOK

Although the Hare Krishna movement has only been established in the West since 1966, its roots go back thousands of years into India's past. The lifestyle and philosophical beliefs are based on ancient scriptures known as the *Vedas*. Originally preserved in the spoken word, the Vedas were written down in the Sanskrit language 5000 years ago.

ISKCON's sacred text is the Hindu poem *The Bhagavad Gita* (one of the ancient books that comprise the *Vedas*) which contains conversations between Lord Krishna and a soldier Arjuna.

Lord Krishna, the Supreme Personality of Godhead, speaks to his intimate disciple Arjuna. The Gita's seven hundred concise verses provide a guide to self-realization, the nature of consciousness, the universe, and the Supreme.

4 FACTS AND FIGURES

The Hare Krishna movement have many centers throughout North America. They also run a Vedic School in Coral Springs, FL, as well as a number of farm communities and restaurants.

In the sixteenth century Sri Caitanya Mahaprabhu said that in the future Krishna consciousness would be spread across the globe. For most of the centuries since then that has seemed a highly unlikely idea.

However, since Srila Prabhupada, in direct disciplic succession from Sri Caitanya, founded the International Society for Krishna Consciousness (ISKCON) it has grown to include 300 temples, 40 rural and farm communities, and 80 restaurants in 71 countries. In 1965, His Divine Grace A.C. Bhaktivedanta Swami Prabhupada (1896-

1977), already an elderly monk, traveled alone from India to establish the culture of Krishna consciousness in the Western world.

People worldwide are given the opportunity to pursue spiritual life according to their abilities and can pursue Krishna conscious culture within their own culture and in their own language.

ISKCON centers can cover a wide range of activities from temple worship to preaching, book distribution, farming, free food distribution, restaurants, education, and more. There is plenty of scope in the types of activities that can be offered as service to Krishna, God.

ISKCON centers are autonomous bodies that place themselves under the authority of ISKCON's Governing Body Commission (GBC). Centers are affiliated with ISKCON by adhering to certain standards and accepting the teachings of

Srila Prabhupada as their basis.
International Society for Krishna
Consciousness

LITERATURE

Back to Godhead is the magazine of the Hare Krishna movement.

Srila Prabhupada started *Back to Godhead* to fulfill the mission of his spiritual master, Srila Bhaktisiddhanta Sarasvati, who had ordered him to preach Vaishnavism, the science of Krishna consciousness, in the English-speaking world.

It is still Srila Prabhupada's magazine, presenting Krishna consciousness without compromise. The founder's lecture begins each issue – it's a transcription of one of the hundreds of lectures he gave. In the other articles, Prabhupada's followers explain the philosophy in their own words, ensuring the continuity of the Vaishnava tradition.
International Society for Krishna
Consciousness

5 HARE KRISHNA PRACTICES

A   Mantra meditation
B   Krishna consciousness
C   The Tilaka mark
D   Monks
E   Congregation members

Hare Krishnas developed a high profile through their appearance in airports and other public places, dressed in saffron colored robes, chanting, playing drums and finger cymbals, selling their literature, and proselytizing.

A MANTRA MEDITATION

Members of the Hare Krishna movement practice mantra meditation. A chant, or mantra, is a vibration of sound that cleanses the mind, freeing it from anxiety and illusion. In Sanskrit, *manah* means "mind" and *tra* means "freeing." So a mantra is a combination of words that are meant to relieve the mind of anxieties arising from worldly entanglement.

It is believed that Krishna and his energy are fully present in the sound of the mantra, and therefore anyone who chants the mantra will come in touch with Krishna, as a result of which, "life will become sublime."

THE MAHA-MANTRA:

Hare Krishna
Hare Krishna
Krishna Krishna
Hare Hare
Hare Rama
Hare Rama
Rama Rama
Hare Hare

Anyone can chant this mantra. It is for people of all religions, all nations, all colors, and both sexes.

The *Vedas* refer to as the *maha* – mantra or "Great Mantra." This sixteen-word mantra is especially recommended as the easiest method for self-realization in the present age.

Vedic knowledge teaches that since we are all constitutionally servants of God, the chanting of His names is not an artificial imposition on the mind but is as natural as a child calling for its mother.

There are two ways to chant the maha mantra: group chanting (*kirtan*) and softly saying the mantra to oneself (*japa*). The latter is done by using a string of 108 wooden prayer beads to enhance concentration. In both methods there are no hard and fast rules, and anyone can chant with good results.

The Hare Krishna Movement

B KRISHNA CONSCIOUSNESS

Hare Krishnas believe that those who place themselves in harmony with Krishna and Krishna's energy return to their natural, pure state of consciousness: that is, to "Krishna consciousness."

They teach that Krishna consciousness is inside each person, waiting to come out, like fire in a match. Chanting Hare Krishna brings out that natural, pure state of mind.

There are four simple practices in Krishna consciousness.

(I) READING (SHRAVANARN)

It is held that reading is essential to developing faith in any spiritual practice. Vedic literature offers logical answers to profound questions, and when carefully studied, books like the *Bhagavad Gita* give an opportunity to explore new ideas and concepts.

The books of His Divine Grace, A.C. Bhaktivedanta Swami Prabhupada, are translations and commentaries upon India's spiritual classics. Written over a period of twenty years, his writings comprise a complete course of study in bhakti-yoga, and are the basis of the spiritual lives of Hare Krishna members.

(II) CHANTING (KIRTANAM)

Recitation of the Hare Krishna mantra is considered to be the essential practice of Krishna consciousness. Devotees may spend from ten minutes to two hours per day chanting *japa*. Once around the circle of 108 beads is called a "round" and between one and sixteen "rounds" are chanted each day. Chanting is done either sitting or walking, usually in the morning.

(III) FRIENDSHIP (SAT-SANGAM)

Associating with others who are spiritually inclined is said to be one of the most rewarding aspects of the Hare Krishna way of life.

New members of ISKCON usually start off by linking up with others in the same town or county. Where there is no temple, meetings take place hired rooms or private homes.

(IV) REMEMBERING (SMARANAM)

The aim of Krishna consciousness is to cultivate a constant flow of awakened states of consciousness in which we remember our spiritual identity and our relationship with Krishna. Vaishnavas therefore begin the day with a combination of practices, which help to focus the mind spiritually. Rising early, bathing, japa meditation and study, all purify the mind from its sleepiness and create a mental state suitable for an entire day of spiritual progress.

The Hare Krishna movement

C THE TILAKA MARK

The Tilaka mark is put on the foreheads of all followers of Hare Krishna. It is a U-shaped marking of clay made on the forehead with a yellow clay from the banks of sacred rivers in India.

- The two stripes signify the lotus feet of Krishna.
- The leaf in the center represents holy basil, or *Tulasi*, which traditionally adorns his feet.

D MONKS

ISKCON consists of two groups of members: an order of monks and priests, and congregation members.

Monks live in a temple. Male monks shave their heads, except for a *sikha*, a central patch of unshaven hair. They adopt a Sanskrit name of one of the names of God, and the suffix *dasa* (servant). Robes (*dhotis*) are worn: monks who are celibate wear saffron colored *dhotis* and married monks wear white *dhotis*.

Monks vow do not smoke, drink alcohol or take any other drugs. They do not gamble and are vegetarian.

They chant God's names every day.

E CONGREGATION MEMBERS
Congregation members of ISKCON live outside the temple. They wear ordinary clothes and engage in ordinary work. They eat a vegetarian diet. In addition to praying and chanting at home, they usually attend a temple at least once a week

---

6 HARE KRISHNA BELIEFS

A   Hinduism and ISKON
B   Manifesto of Krsna Consciousness

A HINDUISM AND ISKON
Many ISKCON beliefs are the same as those of conventional Hinduism. A common ISKCON expression is "We are not this body." That is, we are all spirit souls who are temporarily trapped in a material body and its cares and woes. The goal is to break away from *samsara* (endless repetitive reincarnations) and return to the kingdom of God.

ISKCON and Hinduism both trace their beginnings to the *Vedas* and to the *Bhagavad Gita* text.

DIFFERENCES BETWEEN ORTHODOX HINDUSISM AND ISKCON ARE AS FOLLOWS:

- Hinduism regards Krishna as the eighth incarnation of Vishnu (the Preserver and one of the Hindu trinity of deities). But ISKCON regards Krishna as the supreme Lord over all deities, including Vishnu. Krishna is worshiped as the Supreme God.
- It is possible to have a personal relationship with him.
- Jesus Christ is a representative of Krishna.
- Liberation from *samsara* is attained through *sankirtana*, which is congregational singing of God's names, which leads to Krishna Consciousness.

- Hell as a temporary destination after death for people who have sinned greatly while on earth.
- Eating food prepared for and offered to God is an act of communion with Krishna. Eating such food enables Krishna's energy to purify the body of the devotee.

B MANIFESTO OF KRSNA CONSCIOUSNESS
Press Release, Los Angeles,
December 22, 1968

The International Society for Krishna Consciousness is a movement aiming at the spiritual reorientation of mankind through the simple process of chanting the holy names of God. The human life is meant for ending the miseries of material existence. Our present-day society is trying to do so by material progress. However, it is visible to all that in spite of the extensive material progress, the human society is not in peaceful condition. The reason is that a human being is essentially a spirit soul. It is the spirit soul which is the background of development of the material body. However the materialist scientist may deny the spiritual existence in the background of the living force, there is no better understanding than accepting the spirit soul within the body.

The body is changing from one form to another, but the spirit soul is existing eternally. This fact we can experience even in our own life. Since the beginning of our material body in the womb of our mother, the body is transforming from one shape to another in every second and in every minute. This process is generally known as growth, but actually it is change of body. On this earth planet we see change of day and night and of seasons. The more primitive mentality attributes this change to changes occurring in the sun.

For example, in the winter they think the sun is getting weaker, and at night they presume sometimes that the sun is dead. With more advanced knowledge of discovery we see that sun is not changing at all in this way. Seasonal and diurnal changes are attributed to the change of the position of the earth planet. Similarly, we experience bodily changes from embryo to child to youth to maturity to old age and to death. The less intelligent mentality presumes that at the death the spirit soul's existence is forever finished, just like primitive tribes who believe that the sun dies at sunset.

Actually, the sun is rising in another part of the world. Similarly, the soul is accepting another type of body. When the body gets old like the old garments and is no longer usable, then the soul accepts another body just like we accept a new suit of clothes. The modern civilization is practically unaware of this truth. They do not care about the constitutional position of the soul. There are different departments of knowledge in different universities and many technological institutions to study and understand the subtle laws of material nature- medical research laboratories to study the physiological condition of the material body- but there is no institution to study the constitutional position of the soul.

This is the greatest drawback of material civilization, which is external manifestation of the soul. They are enamored by the glimmering manifestation of the cosmic body or the individual body, but they do not try to understand the basic principles of this glimmering situation. The body looks very beautiful working with full energy and exhibiting great traits of talent and wonderful brain work. But as soon as the soul is away from the body, all this glimmering situation of the body becomes useless. Even the great scientists who have discovered many wonderful scientific contributions could not trace out about the personal self, which is the cause of such wonderful discoveries. The Krsna consciousness movement basically is trying to reach this science of the soul- not in any dogmatic way, but in complete scientific and philosophical understanding.

You can find out the background of this body as the soul and the soul's presence as perceived, perceivable by consciousness. Similarly, the presence of Supersoul and superconsciousness in the universal body of cosmic manifestation is perceived by the presence of the Supreme Lord, or the Absolute Truth. The Absolute Truth is systematically experienced in the Vedanta-sutra, generally known as the Vedanta philosophy, which is elaborately explained by a commentary by the same author of the Vedanta-sutras known as the Srimad-Bhagavatam. The Bhagavad-gita is the preliminary study of the Srimad-Bhagavatam to understand the constitutional position of the Supreme Lord, or the Absolute Truth.

The Absolute Truth is realized in three phases of understanding, namely as Brahman, or the impersonal universal soul; Paramatma, or the localized universal soul; and at the end as the Supreme Personality of Godhead. An individual soul is understood in three aspects, namely first in the consciousness pervading all over the body, then as the spirit soul within the heart, and ultimately exhibited as a person. Similarly, the Absolute Truth is first realized as impersonal Brahman, then as localized Supersoul, Paramatma, and at the end as the Supreme Personality of Godhead, Krsna.

Krsna means all-inclusive, or, in other words, Krsna is simultaneously Brahman, Paramatma, and the Personality of Godhead. As such, as every one of us is simultaneously consciousness, soul, and person, this individual person and the Supreme Lord Person are qualitatively one but quantitatively different. Just like the drop of sea water and the vast mass of sea water - both are qualitatively one. The chemical composition of the drop of sea water and that of the mass of sea water are one and the same, but the quantity of salt and other minerals in the whole sea is many, many times greater than the quantity of salt and other minerals contained in the drop of sea water. The Krsna consciousness movement maintains the (sic:) speciality of the individual soul and the Supreme Soul. From the Vedic Upanisads we can understand that both the Supreme Person, or God, and the individual person are eternal and living entities. The difference is that the supreme living entity, or Supreme Person, maintains all the innumerable living entities. In the Christian way of understanding, the same principle is admitted because in the Bible it is taught that the individual entities should pray to the supreme father for supplying means of maintenance and giving pardon for their sinful activities.

So it is understood from any source of scriptural injunction that the Supreme Lord, or Krsna, is the maintainer of the individual living entities, and it is the duty of the individual entity to feel obliged to the Supreme Lord. This is the whole background of religious principle. Without this acknowledgement, there is

chaos, as it is happening in our daily experience at the present moment. Everyone is trying to become the Supreme Lord, either socially, politically or individually. Therefore there is competition for this false lordship and there is chaos all over the world, individually, nationally, socially or collectively. The Krsna consciousness movement is trying to establish the supremacy of the Absolute Personality of Godhead.

The human society is meant for this understanding because this consciousness makes his life successful. This Krsna consciousness movement is not a new introduction of the mental speculators. Actually this movement was started by Krsna Himself in the Battlefield of Kuruksetra. At least five thousand years ago the movement was presented by Krsna in the Bhagavad-gita. From this Bhagavad-gita we can understand that this system of consciousness was spoken by Him long, long before – He imparted to the sun-god Vivasvan. That calculation goes to show that before the repetition of the Bhagavad-gita in the Battlefield of Kuruksetra, it was once before explained at least forty million years ago.

So this movement is not at all new. It is coming down from disciplic succession, and in India from all great leaders of the Vedic society like Sankaracarya, Ramanujacarya, Madhvacarya, Visnu Swami, Nimbarka, and lately, about 480 years ago, Lord Caitanya. The principle is still being followed today. This Bhagavad-gita is also very widely pursued in all parts of the world by great scholars, philosophers, and religionists. But in most cases the principle is not followed as it is. Krsna consciousness movement means to present the principles of the Bhagavad-gita as it is, without any misinterpretation.

In the Bhagavad-gita we can understand five main principles: namely God, the living entity, the material or the spiritual nature, time, and activities. Out of these five items, God, the living entities, nature - material or spiritual - and time are eternal. But activities are not eternal. The activities in the material nature are different from the activities in the spiritual nature. In the material nature, although the spiritual soul is eternal, as we have explained before, the activities are temporary.

Krsna consciousness movement is aiming to place the spirit soul in his eternal activities. The eternal activities can be practiced even when we are materially encaged. It requires simply direction. But it is possible, under the prescribed rules and regulations, to act spiritually. The Krsna consciousness movement teaches these spiritual activities, and if one is trained up in such spiritual activities, one is transferred to the spiritual world, of which we get ample evidence from Vedic literatures and also from the Bhagavad-gita. And the spiritually trained person can be transferred to the spiritual world

easily by change of consciousness. The consciousness is always there because it is the symptom of the living spirit soul. But at the present moment the consciousness is materially contaminated.

Just like pouring water down from the cloud is pure, distilled water, but as soon as the water comes in touch with the earth it becomes muddy immediately. Again, by filtering the same water, the original clearness can be regained. Similarly, Krsna consciousness movement is the process of clearing the consciousness, and as soon as the consciousness clear and pure it is transferred to the spiritual world for eternal life of knowledge and bliss, which we are hankering for in this material world, and being frustrated in every step on account of material contamination. Therefore this Krsna consciousness movement should be taken very seriously by the leaders of the human society.

His Divine Grace A. C. Bhaktivedanta
Swami Prabhupada

7 WORSHIP

Congregation members of ISKCON usually go to the "Sunday Feast" at their local temples. Members of the congregation are allowed to take part in the chanting, dancing, and feasting on vegetarian food offered to the Lord.

DEVOTIONAL SERVICE
There are nine processes of devotional service for ISKCON members:

(i)   Hearing about God .
(ii)   Chanting the names of God .

(iii) Remembering God by reading, associating with devotees .
(iv)   Serving the Lord Krishna in the temple.
(v)   Worshiping God by preparation of food, decorating the Lord, bringing others to see Him.
(vi)   Praying to God.
(vii) Encouraging others to chant the names of God.
(viii) Developing a close personal and intimate relationship with God.
(ix)   Giving everything we have to God including our bodies.

8 QUOTATIONS

BHAGAVAD GITA

The following famous people express their appreciation of the *Bhagavad Gita*.

When I read the Bhagavad-Gita and reflect about how God created this universe everything else seems so superfluous.

Albert Einstein

When doubts haunt me, when disappointments stare me in the face, and I see not one ray of hope on the horizon, I turn to *Bhagavad Gita* and find a verse to comfort me; and I immediately begin to smile in the midst of overwhelming sorrow. Those who meditate on the *Gita* will derive fresh joy and new meanings from it every day.

Mahatma Gandhi

In the morning I bathe my intellect in the stupendous and cosmogonal philosophy of the *Bhagavad Gita*, in comparison with which our modern world and its literature seem puny and trivial.

Henry David Thoreau

The *Bhagavad Gita* has a profound influence on the spirit of mankind by its devotion to God which is manifested by actions.

Dr. Albert Schweitzer

The *Bhagavad Gita* is a true scripture of the human race a living creation rather than a book, with a new message for every age and a new meaning for every civilization.

Sri Aurobindo

The *Bhagavad Gita* deals essentially with the spiritual foundation of human existence. It is a call of action to meet the obligations and duties of life; yet keeping in view the spiritual nature and grander purpose of the universe.

Prime Minister Nehru

The marvel of the *Bhagavad Gita* is its truly beautiful revelation of life's wisdom which enables philosophy to blossom into religion.

Herman Hesse

I owed a magnificent day to the *Bhagavad Gita*. It was the first of books; it was as if an empire spoke to us, nothing small or unworthy, but large, serene, consistent, the voice of an old intelligence which in another age and climate had pondered and thus disposed of the same questions which exercise us.

Ralph Waldo Emerson

In order to approach a creation as sublime as the *Bhagavad Gita* with full understanding it is necessary to attune our soul to it.

Rudolph Steiner

From a clear knowledge of the *Bhagavad Gita* all the goals of human existence become fulfilled. *Bhagavad Gita* is the manifest quintessence of all the teachings of the Vedic scriptures.

Adi Shankara

The *Bhagavad Gita* is the most systematic statement of spiritual evolution of endowing value to mankind. It is one of the most clear and comprehensive summaries of perennial philosophy ever revealed; hence its enduring value is subject not only to India but to all of humanity.

Aldous Huxley

The *Bhagavad Gita* was spoken by Lord Krishna to reveal the science of devotion to God which is the essence of all spiritual knowledge. The Supreme Lord Krishna's primary purpose for descending and incarnating is relieve the world of any demoniac and negative, undesirable influences that are opposed to spiritual development, yet simultaneously it is His incomparable intention to be perpetually within reach of all humanity.

Ramanuja

The *Bhagavad Gita* is not separate from the Vaishnava philosophy and the Srimad Bhagavatam fully reveals the true import of this doctrine which is transmigration of the soul. On perusal of the first chapter of Bhagavad-Gita one may think that they are advised to engage in warfare. When the second chapter has been read it can be clearly understood that knowledge and the soul is the ultimate goal to be attained. On studying the third chapter it is apparent that acts of righteousness are also of high priority. If we continue and patiently take the time to complete the *Bhagavad Gita* and try to ascertain the truth of its closing chapter we can see that the ultimate conclusion is to relinquish all the conceptualized ideas of religion which

we possess and fully surrender directly unto the Supreme Lord.

Bhaktisiddhanta Saraswati

The *Mahabharata* has all the essential ingredients necessary to evolve and protect humanity and that within it the *Bhagavad Gita* is the epitome of the Mahabharata just as ghee is the essence of milk and pollen is the essence of flowers.

Madhvacarya

THE CHRISTIAN FAITH AND ISKCON

Since ISKCON has a different God, a different Jesus, and a different way of salvation from what the Bible reveals, it is impossible for there to be any compatibility between the two. They differ on all crucial issues. A person must choose between Krishna and Jesus Christ; no harmony can exist between the sect of Hare Krishna and Christianity.

Josh McDowell,
Handbook of Today's Religions

NEW AGE MOVEMENT

CONTENTS

1 An Overview   591

2 Founder   592

3 New Age's holy book   593

4 Facts and figures   593

5   New Age practices   594

6 New Age beliefs   594

7 Worship   596

8 Links to the NAM   596

9 Quotations   597

10 Glossary   598

1 An Overview

DEFINITION

The New Age movement is best understood as a network – or, to be more exact, a *metanetwork* (network of networks).

The New Age Movement is a broad-based amalgam of diverse spiritual, social, and political elements with the common aim of transforming individuals and society through spiritual awareness.

Microsoft Encarta Encyclopedia

Factfile
- Date of origin: ?1970
- Founder: no one person
- Holy book: no sacred book
- Number of adherents: no membership lists are kept, but tens of millions of people have been influenced by the NAM.

SUMMARY

The New Age is a free-flowing spiritual movement, made up of a network of believers and practitioners who share similar, but not identical, beliefs and practices, which are tacked on to their own religious beliefs.

The six main characteristics of New Age thinking are:

(i) all is unity
(ii) all is divine
(iii) humanity is divine
(iv) a change in consciousness
(v) all religions are one
(vi) cosmic evolutionary optimism.

A.K.A.

The New Age Movement (NAM) is also known as:
- Self-spirituality
- New spirituality
- Mind-body-spirit.

Other names:

- Higher Consciousness Movement
- Occultism
- Eastern Mysticism
- Eastern Spirituality
- Ancient or Perennial Wisdom
- Age of Aquarius
- Holistic Health Movement.

2 FOUNDER

HELENA PETROVNA BLAVATSKY AND ALICE A. BAILEY

The umbrella term "New Age" dates back to at least 1875 with the theosophical teachings of Helena Petrovna Blavatsky. These teachings were popularized in the 1930s by the Englishwoman and founder of an offshoot of the Theosophical Society, Alice A. Bailey (1880-1949).

Alice Bailey practiced as a spiritist medium and claimed to receive messages from the Tibetan Djwal Khul, who was supposed to be "a master of wisdom." A number of these teachings are still followed by New Agers.

THE FINDHORN COMMUNITY

The NAM became recognizable in England in the 1960s with the formation of some small groups, such as the Findhorn Community in Inverness and the Wrekin Trust. Many date the NAM to 1970 when the American theosophist David Spangler developed the fundamental idea of the New Age movement in the Findhorn Foundation.

THE WREKIN TRUST

One inspirer of the New Age movement, Sir George Trevelyan, the founder of the Wrekin Trust, summed up New Age world-view as follows:

> Behind all outwardly manifested form is a timeless realm of absolute consciousness. It is the great Oneness underlying all the diversity, all the myriad forms of nature. It may be called God, or may be deemed beyond all naming.... The world of

nature, in short, is but a reflection of the eternal world of Creative imagining. The inner core of man, that which in each of us might be called spirit, is a droplet of the divine source. As such, it is imperishable and eternal, for life cannot be extinguished. The outer sheath in which it manifests can, of course, wear out and be discarded; but to speak of 'death' in relation to the true being and spirit of man is irrelevant.

> *George Trevelyan,* A Vision of the Aquarian Age

DAVID SPANGLER

David Spangler taught that the release of new waves of spiritual energy marked the beginning of the New Age. This was confirmed by the astrological changes in the Earth's movement as it moved into a new cycle called the Age of Aquarius. He believed that this new energy could be used by people and this would confirm the arrival of this New Age.

David Spangler's book *Revelation: The Birth of a New Age* (1976) drew a number of leaders from older occult and metaphysical organizations to his mushrooming New Age movement.

AN INTERNATIONAL MOVEMENT

In the 1970s the movement became international. In North America a "New Age Seminar" run by the Association for Research and Enlightenment, and the establishment of the East-West Journal in 1971, were two notable milestones.

3 NEW AGE'S HOLY BOOK

The NAM does not have the Bible, or any other books, as its sacred text.

---

4 FACTS AND FIGURES

The NAM has:

- no holy text
- no central organization
- no membership
- no formal clergy
- no geographic center
- no creed.

AMERICANS AND THE NAM

As many as 20% of the people in the US admit to following the NAM to a greater or lesser extent. In polls the NAM often comes out as the third largest religious group.

GEORGE BARNA POLLS

From his polls taken in the U.S. George Barna claims that:

- 8% believe in astrology as a method of foretelling the future
- 7% believe that crystals are a source of healing or energizing power
- 9% believe that Tarot Cards are a reliable base for life decisions
- 25% believe in a non-traditional concept of the nature of God which are often associated with New Age thinking
- 11% believe that God is "a state of higher consciousness that a person may reach"
- 8% define God as "the total realization of personal, human potential"
- 3% believe that each person is God.

George Barna, The Index of Leading Spiritual Indicators

5 NEW AGE PRACTICES

INTRODUCTION

Members of particular religions, including Christianity, incorporate many New Age practices into their faith. A great variety of practices are found among New Agers, but, typically, a follower of the NAM will only embrace a few of them. They include:

- Channeling
  Channelers contact the spirit of a dead person whose consciousness is channeled through the medium so that it can guide and speak to people today through the medium's voice.

- Crystals
  New Agers believe that crystals, such as salt, possess healing energy.

- Meditation
  It is believed that by repeating a mantra one can move beyond one's own consciousness to a higher spiritual level.

New Agers also engage in a number of the following activities:

- divination

- using techniques to foretell the future such as:
  I Ching
  pendulum movements
  Tarot cards.

- astrology
- holistic health
- Human Potential Movement (a.k.a. Emotional Growth Movement). Engaging in any of the following is supposed to enable one to progress spiritually:

  Esalen Growth Center programs
  EST
  Gestalt Therapy
  Primal Scream Therapy
  Transactional Analysis
  Transcendental Meditation
  Yoga.

6 NEW AGE BELIEFS

Pick and mix: the NAM does not have a single creed or set of beliefs. Rather, its followers choose from an array of sometimes contradictory beliefs. The basic beliefs are set out below.

MONISM
All that exists is derived from a single source of divine energy.

GOD
God is an impersonal energy/force, immanent in all things. He (it) pervades all nature. This view of god is similar to the pantheistic beliefs of Hinduism. In pantheism everything that exists is God, and God is thought of as being in everything that exists. This leads on to the

idea that we are individually divine. We are all gods and just have to completely realize our own goodness. It can be said that God and I do not just communicate; we commune and are one.

Shirley MacLaine's book, *Out on a Limb*, asserts: "I know that I exist, therefore I AM, I know that the God-source exists. Therefore IT IS. Since I am part of that force, then I AM that I AM."

PANTHEISM
God is all that exists. God, as well as being the entire universe, also transcends the universe.

REINCARNATION
After we die, we are reborn and have another human life. This closely resembles the concept of transmigration of the soul in Hinduism.

PERSONAL TRANSFORMATION
This may be brought about by a mystical experience and by following New Age beliefs and practices. To achieve this end, a number of practices may be adopted, such as hypnosis, meditation, and even the use of hallucinogenic drugs.

CARE FOR THE EARTH
The New Agers call the earth Gaia It is to be revered and respected, and is even worshiped by some New Agers.

A UNIVERSAL RELIGION
New Agers have no desire to promote one religion over against another, or one set of religious beliefs against any other set of religious beliefs. Rather, they are more interested in a synthesis of religions and in some kind of unity among the different religions.

They look forward to the day when a new universal religion, containing elements of all current faiths, will develop into a widely accepted global religion.

NEW WORLD ORDER
New Agers believe that as the Age of Aquarius becomes established, so a New Age will be ushered in. This will be some kind of utopia. There will be no more discrimination, and such present horrors such as wars, disease, hunger, pollution, and poverty will be swept away by a new world administration.

THE DEVIL
The NAM thinks more of a "force," as in Star Wars, than any form of personal devil, which they view as a mere illusion.

SALVATION
There is no concept of original sin in the NAM, so salvation means enlightenment.

MORAL ABSOLUTES
There are no moral absolutes in the NAM. All truth systems should be embraced and everyone should work towards harmonization and unity.

JESUS CHRIST
Christ is a reincarnated *avatar*, Messiah, or messenger, sent to give the living on earth spiritually advanced revelation. He is not thought of as being the God, the Son of God, but is one of many historical teachers or "christs." He is viewed in the same light as other teachers, such as Hercules, Hermes, Rama, Mithra, Confucius, Muhammad, Vyasa, Sanskaracharya, Krishna, and Buddha.

One greater than all these teachers will soon come to usher in the New Age.

ASTROLOGY
Astrology is an important part of the New Age movement.

UFOS
The belief in UFOs links with the NAM's belief in masters who guide us on to a higher evolutionary plain.

7 WORSHIP

The NAM have no centers of worship. Seminars, conventions, books and informal groups replace sermons and religious services.

---

8 LINKS TO THE NAM

There are numerous organizations, movements, practices and beliefs that are influenced by or closely allied to the NAM, some of which, at first sight, would appear to have no connection at all. Some of these organizations, beliefs and practices are listed below:

- Astrology
- Aura
- Black and white magic
- Bioenergy
- Brahman
- Buddhism
- Charkas
- *Chi* energy
- Christ-consciousness
- Christian Science
- Church Universal and Triumphant
- Crystals
- Druidism
- Eastern mysticism
- ESP
- Est
- Extraterrestrials
- The Forum
- Firewalking
- Gaia
- Gnosticism
- Hare Krishna
- Higher consciousness
- Hinduism
- Human potential movement
- Kaballah
- Karma
- Magick
- Mind Science
- Native American spirituality
- Near-death experiences
- Neo-Paganism
- Nirvana
- Parapsychology
- Prana
- psi
- Psychic practices
- Reflexology
- Reiki
- Reincarnation
- Religious Science
- Shamanism
- Silva Mind Control
- Spiritism
- Tai Chi
- Taoism
- Tarot cards
- Theosophy
- Therapeutic touch
- Trance-channeling
- Transcendental Meditation
- Transpersonal psychology
- UFOs
- Unity School of Christianity
- Witchcraft
- yin-yang
- Yoga
- Zen

9 QUOTATIONS

We are at any given moment living the totality of everything . . . The vibrational oscillation of nature is quickening . . . Just remember that you are God, and act accordingly.

Shirley Maclaine

The New Age Movement is a very broad, feel-good, movement. It teaches inner-divinity, goddesses, the Christ conscious-ness, spiritual evolution, being one-with-nature, and anything else you want to believe – except Christianity.

Christian Apologetics and Research Ministry

[New Age cults] usually try to unify eastern and western thinking. The Bible and Jesus Christ do not play a key role in the New Age Movement. Nor does it claim to be the true expression of oriental religion. It claims to be a blend of the beliefs, with the overriding theory of pantheism ("all is one," "all is God") and reincarnation. The Heavens Gate cult would be in this category.

Rich McGee

In turbulent times, in times of great change, people or the two extremes: fundamentalism and personal, spiritual experience . . . With no membership lists or even a coherent philosophy or dogma, it is difficult to define or measure the unorganized New Age movement. But in every major US and European city, thousands who seek insight and personal growth cluster around a metaphysical bookstore, a spiritual teacher, or an education center.

J. Naisbitt & P. Aburdene,
Megatrends 2000

The New Age Movement is the most dangerous enemy of Christianity in the world today . . . more dangerous than secular humanism.

Norman L. Geisler
professor of Systematic Theology at Dallas
(Tex.) Theological Seminary

The most central and commonly shared beliefs among New Agers are various combinations of gnosticism and occultism. Gnosticism is an ancient world-view stating that Divine essence is the only true or highest reality, and that the unconscious Self of man is actually this essence. It is through intuitional discovery, "visionary experience or initiation into secret doctrine" (not the plenary revelation of propositional truth in the Bible), that man becomes conscious of this true Self.

Encyclopedia Britannica, *Vol. 10, 1968,*
p. 506;

J. D. Douglas, ed., New Bible
Dictionary, *pp. 473-4*

New Age practices are the spiritual version of AIDS; they destroy the ability of people to cope and function. It is essentially the marketing end of the political packaging of occultism . . . a breeding ground for a new American form of fascism.

Dr. Carl Raschke
professor of Religious Studies at the
University of Denver

The New Age Movement is the most powerful social force in the world today.

Dr. Carl Raschke
professor of Religious Studies at the
University of Denver

10 GLOSSARY

Acupuncture
An ancient Chinese healing art in which fine needles are inserted in the skin at "lines of force."

Astrology
An ancient art of the occult. It is thought that the planets and other heavenly bodies have power over the decisions and destinies of man. Also see Horoscopes.

Aupressure
Healing by use of certain pressure points on the body.

Aura
Emanations or colors supposed to surround the human body and other living things. It is believed that they reveal the condition of the body, soul and spirit. An analysis is given by a psychic.

Book of Changes
(See *I Ching*).

Cabbala (also Kabbalah)
An ancient Jewish occult form of mysticism by which Rabbis sought to decipher meanings in scripture by assigning numerical value to letters and words. See numerology.

Chi
The life-giving energy force of the cosmos. Composed of opposites known as Yin and Yang.

Clairvoyant
Someone who, while in a mesmeric state, discerns objects that are not present to the senses.

Crystals
Quartz rocks that have highly predictable vibrations, which leads to the belief that they can affect the similar vibrations of the body.

Divination
The art or practice that seeks to foresee or foretell future events or discover hidden knowledge by the interpretation of omens or by the aid of supernatural powers.

Horoscopes
A diagram of the relative positions of planets and signs of the zodiac at a specific time (as at one's birth) used by astrologers to infer individual character and personality traits and to foretell events of a person's life.

I Ching (*The Book of Changes*)
A 3,000-year-old book of Chinese wisdom, one of the Confucian classics, consisting of sixty-four sections. Each one is introduced by a Hexagram and is said the reveal the secrets of the universe.

Numerology
A method of divination that is also employed in the use of magic.

Palmistry
Reading one's hand by the size, shape and creases. It is said to reflect the person's past and reveal the future.

Psychic readings
Giving personal information that has supposedly been discovered by non-physical means.

Reincarnation
The belief that when you die you keep coming back to life, possibly in another form, until you become perfect.

Runes
Stones inscribed with letters of the ancient Scandinavian alphabet. Used by the Vikings and revived for today's fortune-telling.

Tarot Cards
Cards with inscribed figures and emblems. It is said that they reveal the purpose of the universe and the future of a person's life.

Tasseography
A method of divination that is formed by reading the pattern of tea leaves in the bottom of a cup to reveal hidden truths about the subject in question.

Third Eye or Mind's Eye
A spiritually intuitive center of consciousness that is supposed to exist in the center of the forehead. The so-called seventh enlightenment in yoga.

Yoga
1. A Hindu theistic philosophy teaching the suppression of all activity of body, mind, and will in order that the self may realize its distinction from them and attain liberation.
2. A system of exercises for attaining bodily or mental control and well-being.

SCIENTOLOGY

CONTENTS

1 An overview   603

2 Founder   604

3 Scientology's holy book   607

4 Facts and figures   607

5 Scientology practices   608

6 Scientology beliefs   609

7 Scientology groupings   612

8 Worship   612

9 Quotations   613

1 AN OVERVIEW

DEFINITION

The word "Scientology" is derived from the Latin word *scio*, which means "know" and the Greek word *logos*, meaning "the word or outward form by which the inward thought is expressed and made known." Thus, Scientology means knowing about knowing.

Factfile
- Date of origin: 1954
- Founder: Lafayette Ronald Hubbard (L. Ron Hubbard), 1911-1986
- Holy book: *Dianetics: The Modern Science of Mental Health*, L. Ron Hubbard
- Number of adherents: 8 million

SUMMARY

Scientology is an applied religious philosophy dealing with the study and handling of the spirit in relationship to itself, universes and other life. It includes teaching about reincarnation, the occult, and the role of *thetan* (soul, life, energy) in the physical universe.

The aims of Scientology were once expressed as follows:

A civilization without insanity, without criminals and without war, where the able can prosper and honest beings can have rights, and where man is free to rise to greater heights, are the aims of Scientology.

L. Ron Hubbard

2 FOUNDER

A Lafayette Ron Hubbard
B Origins of Scientology
C Today's President

A LAFAYETTE RON HUBBARD
(1911-1986)

Lafayette Ron Hubbard, the founder of The Church of Scientology, was born in Nebraska, USA, in 1911. He spent time in the Far East, where he explored both Asian religion and the workings of the human mind.

He was a successful author, publishing hundreds of novels, novelettes and short stories, mostly science fiction. In the late 1940s, L. Ron Hubbard declared: "Writing for a penny a word is ridiculous. If a man really wants to make a million dollars, the best way would be to start his own religion."

In 1959, after a period of illness, Hubbard published *Dianetics: The Modern Science of Mental Health,* which has sold 20 million copies. It deals with the subconscious and Hubbard's understanding of the reasons for his recovery from illness.

In 1951, Hubbard formed the religious philosophy of Scientology based on his discovery that men and women are fundamentally spiritual beings – the X-factor. In 1955, the Founding Church of Scientology was opened in Washington DC. This growing movement appealed in particular to wealthy young people. Numbers increased in the US, and the teaching was introduced into Britain and other countries.

The sect began to be criticized heavily for its medical claims, and for the financial demands it made on its followers. In the States, Hubbard was repeatedly accused of adopting a religious facade for Scientology in order to maintain tax-exempt status. These accusations have dogged the Church of Scientology to the present day.

The US Food and Drug Administration raided Scientology offices in 1963 and seized hundreds of the Church's e-meters as illegal medical devices. The devices are now required to carry a disclaimer saying that they are a purely religious artifact. They are used in a Scientology counseling technique known as "auditing."

In 1968, Hubbard, who claimed to have visited heaven twice, was banned from re-entering Britain because of concern over his aims and methods.

In the 1980s there were many lawsuits in the States and abroad, and in 1984 Hubbard was accused in the US of embezzlement. It was said that he had used the tax-exempt status of the Church to build a financial empire, and had secreted the movement's money into his own bank accounts.

In 1984, when the tax-exempt status of the movement was revoked in the USA, he withdrew from public life. He died in 1986 in California.

B ORIGINS OF SCIENTOLOGY

Scientology was expanded and reworked from Dianetics, an earlier system of self-improvement techniques originally set out in the 1950 book, *Dianetics: The Modern Science of Mental Health.*

Immediately prior to this work, Hubbard had been intensively involved with the occultist Jack Parsons in performing the occult rites developed by Aleister Crowley, and some of these ideas were later incorporated into the teaching of the sect.

By the mid-1950s, Hubbard had relegated Dianetics to being a sub-study of Scientology, although it is still promoted and delivered by Scientology organizations. The chief difference between the two is that Dianetics is a form of psychotherapy and is explicitly secular, focused on the individual's present life and dealing with physical and mental or emotional problems, whereas Scientology adopts a more overtly religious approach, focused on spiritual issues spanning multiple past lives as well as the present day.

C TODAY'S PRESIDENT

Below is a message from the President of the Church of Scientology International, the Rev. Heber C. Jentzsch.

This year [2004], as we celebrate the 40th anniversary of the Church of Scientology, our religion spans the globe. Today, nearly 13,000 church staff members minister the religion to some 8 million members, through 2,318 churches, missions and related organizations in 107 countries and in 31 languages. Each year, approximately 500,000 people participate in Scientology services for the first time in one of our churches or missions.

Years ago, L. Ron Hubbard predicted that Scientology would only go so far as it works. The Church's first 40 years have proven him right and proven that Scientology works. The real story of Scientology is reflected in the daily miracles experienced by its millions of parishioners; in its appeal to people from all walks of life from all over the world; in its attraction to the artisan and the academic, to the blue collar and the white collar, to professionals, to tradespeople, and even to some of the most famous celebrities in the entertainment industry.

But to focus on who Scientologists are is to miss the real point about Scientology. The real point is that the Church and its members are working hard to make this world a better place to live for themselves and for others. Scientology concerns itself with the betterment of the individual – freeing him from the debilitating effects of drugs, illiteracy and declining moral values – and provides a means for him to improve himself and life's conditions. Yet it offers even more. Scientologists aspire to and reach new levels of spiritual awareness in which the answers to the fundamental questions of existence are found – Who am I? Where did I come from? What is the meaning of life? What happens when I die?

It has not been an easy road. Despite its immediate public popularity, Dianetics and Scientology met strong opposition from the very beginning. The book *Dianetics: The Modern Science of Mental Health* promised to alleviate the human condition – to provide relief from mental trauma and suffering and from psychosomatic illness. Had these been empty claims, Dianetics would have come and gone, relegated to a passing mention in the newspapers of the day, and Scientology would never have even happened. But the fact is, for increasing millions, Dianetics and Scientology provide the means to a better, healthier and happier life.

Yes, Scientology has had its share of controversy. It has been no stranger to negative publicity, but that is a fate that all major religious movements have endured during their formative years. Sometimes sensation-hungry media are quick to quote the few but vocal apostates who seek publicity while ignoring the testimony of the loyal millions of the Scientology religion. Governments, too, have played their part in negative media, but that, too, is the rule rather than the exception in the history of emerging religions.

The simple truth is this: if even one hundredth of the bad things that have been written or said about Scientology were true, the Church would not exist, let alone thrive as it does.

One of the most significant events to occur to neutralize and dispel unfair and false allegations is the landmark Internal Revenue Service (IRS) decision in the United States in 1993. Throughout its history, the Church was dogged by the IRS, which investigated it for nearly 40 years.

However, charges against Scientology were not based on fact, but rather on unfounded hearsay and embittered apostates, and we wanted to put an end to this history of distrust. At our request, beginning in 1991, the IRS assembled a high-level team to examine the Church and to resolve its tax status once and for all. They repeatedly met with Church leaders, inspected thousands upon thousands of documents, and asked hundreds of questions. They personally examined the inner workings of the Church and scrutinized 10 years worth of financial statements from every sizable Scientology organization in the world. They investigated the compensation levels of Church executives and employees around the world. They even reviewed – and rejected – the claims of the apostates which had generated negative media reports.

After this latest two-year chapter of what had been a decades-long war, the IRS, and indeed the entire United States government, came to the irresistible conclusion that Scientology is precisely what it claimed all along – a sincere and genuine religion in all respects. And in this instance – unlike the unfounded allegations of the past by misinformed media and others – their decision was based on actual documented and examined facts. They found that the Church is both organized and operated exclusively for religious and charitable purposes, that the income of the Church does not inure to the benefit of any private individual or interest and that the Church does not operate in violation of public policy.

According to the IRS, the examination of Scientology was not only the most extensive of any religious organization, but indeed, the largest inquiry into any organization in the history of that agency.

That inquiry finally concluded on October 1, 1993, when the IRS issued a series of ruling letters recognizing the tax-exempt religious and charitable status of Scientology churches and every related organization – more than 150 in all. Further, the IRS determined that donations for Scientology services are not legally distinguishable from the fund-raising practices of other religions and allowed Scientology donations to be deducted against personal income taxes to the full extent of the law.

The IRS decision marks the end of one era and the beginning of another, as the best evidence of the entrance of Scientology into the mainstream of society. The religion has survived the turbulence of its formative years and is now a recognized religious institution.

Of course, Scientology remains in the news and will continue to do so. But regardless of media coverage, good or bad, on our 40th anniversary the Church has unquestionably arrived. We have come of age. And because of our prominence, with hundreds of organizations, thousands of groups and millions of members around the world, we are creating a major impact upon society.

In recent years, the Church has gone to great lengths to clear away mysteries and misconceptions. Dianetics and Scientology books can be found in all public libraries and in local bookstores. The entirety of its scriptures are available to anyone who desires spiritual betterment and who reaches for it. Church staff members are open and friendly and more than willing to answer questions.

The Rev. Heber C. Jentzsch
President, Church of Scientology
International

3 SCIENTOLOGY'S HOLY BOOK

Hubbard's writings are viewed as the final authority among Scientologists.

The scripture of the Scientology religion consists of the writings and recorded spoken words of L. Ron Hubbard on the subjects of Dianetics and Scientology. This "scripture" includes more than half a million written pages, over three thousand tape-recorded lectures and some hundred films.

A fundamental doctrine of the Scientology religion is that spiritual freedom can be attained only if the path outlined in these works is followed without deviation.

What Is Scientology?
The definitive reference work on Scientology

is *What Is Scientology?*, an 833-page work that describes the philosophy and beliefs, catechism, creeds and codes, services and scriptures of the Scientology religion. It is written by L. Ron Hubbard.

The Scientology Handbook
The Scientology Handbook, also by L. Ron Hubbard, describes the basic practices of the religion and its practical applications.

The Bible
The Bible is thought of as just one of many books that record humanity's search after the truth.

4 FACTS AND FIGURES

The Scientology religion claims to be "the only major religion to emerge in the 20th century," and to be "the fastest-growing religious movement in the world today."

Unlike many new religious movements, Scientology has successfully survived the death of its founder, and millions still follow his teachings. Mr. David Miscavige, Chairman of the Board of the Religious Technology Center, now heads the organization. The Board Religious Technology Center is a non-profit organization formed in 1982 to preserve, maintain and protect the Scientology religion.

HEADQUARTERS
In 1959, Hubbard established the worldwide headquarters of Scientology at Saint Hill, near East Grinstead in West Sussex, England.

3,200 "CHURCHES"
Every church of Scientology is separately incorporated and has its own local board of directors and executives responsible for that church's activities. Together, these churches

form an extensive international network of more than 3,200 churches, missions and groups in 154 countries. Nearly 13,000 Scientologists serve as staff members of these churches and missions and related groups and organizations around the world.

MISSION
Missions are an important outreach activity, and by their sheer number they reflect the dynamism of Scientology's expansion: 10 years ago there were 126 missions in 58 countries; today there are 221 missions in 107 nations.

SYMBOL
The main symbol of Scientology consists of:

- The letter "S" – this stands for Scientology.
- An upper triangle. Its sides stand for the three closely interrelated factors: knowledge, responsibility and control.
- A lower triangle. Its sides stand for affinity, reality and communication.

5 SCIENTOLOGY PRACTICES

THE INDIVIDUAL

Scientology provides the individual the means to not only solve his own problems, accomplish his goals and gain lasting happiness, but also to achieve new states of awareness he may never have dreamed possible.

Church of Scientology International

SOCIETY

Scientology contains effective solutions and answers to society's most crucial problems, among them drug abuse, crime, illiteracy and declining moral values.

Church of Scientology International

The Church states that the goal of Scientology is a world without war, criminals, and insanity, where good decent people have the freedom to reach their goals. Scientology consists of a complex worldwide network of corporations dedicated to the promotion of L. Ron Hubbard's philosophies in all areas of life. This includes:

- drug treatment centers (Narconon)
- criminal rehab programs (Criminon)
- activities to reform the field of mental health (Citizens Commission on Human Rights)
- projects to implement workable and effective educational methods in schools (Applied Scholastics)
- a campaign to return moral values to living (The Way to Happiness)
- an organization to educate and assist businesses to succeed (World Institute of Scientology Enterprises, or WISE)
- a crusade directed to world leaders as well as the general public to implement the 1948 United Nations document, "The Universal Declaration of Human Rights."

6 SCIENTOLOGY BELIEFS

A Creed
B God
C Jesus
D Humanity
E Salvation
F The bridge
G *Thetan*
H Eight dynamics
I The mind
J Acknowledgements
K Auditing

INTRODUCTION

The life each person leads should be one of continual spiritual and ethical education, awareness, and improvement, so that he or she can be happy and achieve ultimate salvation, as well as being more effective in creating a better world. Scientology claims to offer specific methodologies to assist a person to achieve this quality of life.

A CREED

The Creed of the Church of Scientology

We of the Church believe:
- That all men of whatever race, color, or creed were created with equal rights;
- That all men have inalienable rights to their own religious practices and their performance;
- That all men have inalienable rights to their own lives;
- That all men have inalienable rights to their sanity;
- That all men have inalienable rights to their own defense;
- That all men have inalienable rights to conceive, choose, assist or support their own organizations, churches and governments;
- That all men have inalienable rights to think freely, to talk freely, to write freely their own opinions and to counter or utter or write upon the opinions of others;
- That all men have inalienable rights to the creation of their own kind;
- That the souls of men have the rights of men;
- That the study of the mind and the healing of mentally caused ills should not be alienated from religion or condoned in non-religious fields;
- And that no agency less than God has the power to suspend or set aside these rights, overtly or covertly.

And we of the Church believe:
- That man is basically good;
- That he is seeking to survive;
- That his survival depends upon himself and upon his fellows and his attainment of brotherhood with the universe.

And we of the Church believe that the laws of God forbid man:
- To destroy his own kind;
- To destroy the sanity of another;
- To destroy or enslave another's soul;
- To destroy or reduce the survival of one's companions or one's group.

And we of the Church believe that the spirit can be saved and that the spirit alone may save or heal the body.

Church of Scientology International

B GOD

In Scientology, God can be whoever you want him to be.

C JESUS

Jesus is seen as a great teacher. He rarely is featured in Scientology.

D HUMANITY

It is believed that human beings are trapped in material bodies and need to be released from this state so that they can achieve their original god-like state.

Scientology practitioners guide people into this state.

E SALVATION

Salvation occurs when the psychological problems ("engrams") that block the way to re-establishing the god-like state are overcome.

F THE BRIDGE

The bridge is the broad path that Scientologists follow as they study the teachings of Scientology. These teachings enable them to cross over a chasm from their present state into a vastly higher level of awareness.

G THETAN

- *Thetan*, derived from the Greek letter "theta," is the soul, life, energy in the physical universe; it also refers to the essence of each person.
- Each person is basically good.
- Each person is an immortal spiritual being (a *thetan*) who possesses a mind and a body: people do not have a *thetan*, they are a *thetan.*
- The body and the brain, therefore, are viewed as mechanisms: they are a communication center for the *thetan*, the mind being thought of as a collection of pictures.

H EIGHT DYNAMICS

Scientology teaches that there are eight dynamics.

A "dynamic" has been defined as "an urge,

drive or impulse." The more a person understands these dynamics the more he/she can harmonize everything in his/her life.

- The first dynamic is the urge to survive as oneself.
- The second the urge to survive through family and sex.
- The third is to survive in various groups such as a company or with a group of friends.
- The fourth is to survive as humankind.
- The fifth, sixth, seventh and eighth are the urge to survive through other life forms such as animals, the physical universe, the spiritual universe and Infinity or God respectively.

I THE MIND

Scientologists divide the human mind into two components: the analytical mind and the reactive mind.

THE ANALYTICAL MIND

The analytical mind, as in Freud's teaching about the conscious mind, can feel things, reason and remember.

THE REACTIVE MIND

The reactive mind resembles what Freud labeled as the unconscious. Scientologists teach that every experience, even pre-natal experiences and the trauma of birth, are recorded in the reactive mind as mental images. Painful experiences are called engrams, which are a kind of psychic scar. They cannot be perceived with the analytical mind, and so lie unnoticed, but if stimulated by later painful experiences they cause irrational behavior. If they are not understood they can harm people's lives and keep them from fulfilling their full potential.

These engrams, it is said, are "the single source of all insanities, psychosomatic illnesses and neuroses." But once such engrams are removed the person moves up into a "clear" state (from being in a "preclear" [PC] state). When someone arrives in the "clear" state he or she is free of all engrams.

THE GOAL OF DIANETICS

The goal of Dianetics is to rid individuals of engrams so they become "Clear."

It is maintained that becoming Clear strengthens a person's native individuality and creativity and that a "Clear" is emotionally free.

THE GOAL OF SCIENTOLOGY

The stated goal of Scientology is to fully rehabilitate the spiritual nature, including rehabilitating all abilities and realizing one's full potential.

Further progress is possible beyond this "clear" state. One can move on towards becoming an "OT" or "Operating *Thetan.*" Scientologists believe that an OT is able to leave the body and mind. In this state one can see, hear and feel without the use of the five senses of sight, hearing, touch, taste and smell.

J ACKNOWLEDGEMENTS

L. Ron Hubbard stated: "Acknowledgment is made to fifty thousand years of thinking men without whose speculations and observations the creation and construction of Dianetics would not have been possible. Credit in particular is due to: Anaxagoras, Thomas Paine, Aristotle, Thomas Jefferson, Socrates, René Descartes, Plato, James Clerk Maxwell, Euclid, Charcot, Lucretius, Herbert Spencer, Roger Bacon, William James, Francis Bacon, Sigmund Freud, Isaac Newton, van Leeuwenhoek, Cmdr. Joseph Thompson (MC) USN, William A. White, Voltaire, Will Durant, Count Alfred Korzybski, and my instructors in atomic and molecular phenomena, mathematics and the humanities at George Washington University and at Princeton."

K AUDITING

The central methodology of Scientology is called "auditing" (from the Latin root *aud-*, to listen), which is one-on-one communication with a Scientology-trained "auditor." The auditor assists a person to unravel the reactive portion of his mind, that is, "charge," specific traumatic incidents, his own ethical transgressions, and bad decisions of his past, that tend to lock him into a life not totally under his own control.

Hubbard's electro-psychometer (e-meter), a crude lie detector, is used by Scientology auditors (counselors) to examine a person's mental state. Scientologists claim the device allows people to "see a thought." In the hands of a trained auditor, they believe, it can uncover "hidden crimes."

In his book, *The Book Introducing The E-Meter*, L. Ron Hubbard states, "This is a Hubbard Electrometer, called an e-meter for short. Technically it is a specially developed 'Wheatstone Bridge' well known to electrically minded people as a device to measure the amount of resistance to a flow of electricity."

Critics of Scientology sometimes deride the e-meter as "an overpriced ohm-meter" or "just a wheatstone bridge." Hubbard himself makes this admission. Technically, the e-meter is an ohm-meter with continuously variable range and sensitivity settings.

7 SCIENTOLOGY GROUPINGS

FREE ZONE

The Free Zone is the name used to describe the various individuals and groups who have broken away from the Church of Scientology, but who continue to practice Scientology-derived beliefs and techniques in an environment free from the control of the official Church.

In spite of the controversy surrounding the teachings of L. Ron Hubbard, members of the Free Zone believe that the auditing process and other techniques used in dianetics and scientology offer genuine benefits.

THE INTERNATIONAL CHURCH OF ADVANCED UNIVERSAL SPIRITUAL ENLIGHTENMENT

The Church was founded to forward Ron's intention. They say: "We are Protestant Scios, we consider the works of Ron our 'Old Testament.' We consider him a prophet, and his teachings as our 'Scripture.' We consider that the alterations created by the management of the Church of Scientology after 1983 have resulted in greater and greater deviation from the teachings of the prophet LRH."

8 WORSHIP

Scientology offers no specific dogma about a God or gods. It believes that the nature of the Supreme Being is revealed personally through each individual as he or she becomes more conscious and spiritually aware.

So Scientology does not provide worship services. Its "churches" are very well organized, efficient and highly structured centers where Scientology is promoted and taught.

Today, every church of Scientology in the world is organized into a standard pattern and organizational structure which makes it possible to minister to the needs of their ever-growing congregations. Individual churches are organized into a hierarchical structure which encompasses all churches and their supporting organizations. From the missions and groups at the entry point of Scientology to the advanced churches which minister the highest levels of Scientology religious services, individual churches of Scientology are the milestones which mark the road Scientologists walk as they cross the Bridge.

Church of Scientology International

9 QUOTATIONS

SCIENTOLOGY'S AIMS

A civilization without insanity, without criminals and without war, where the able can prosper and honest beings can have rights, and where man is free to rise to greater heights, are the aims of Scientology.

L. Ron Hubbard

CRITICAL QUOTATIONS

Many people have accused Scientology of being less than honest and straightforward.

Scientology is both immoral and socially obnoxious . . . It is corrupt, sinister and dangerous. It is corrupt because it is based on lies and deceit.

*Justice Latey, ruling in the
High Court of London*

But in the end, money is what Scientology is all about. As long as the organization's opponents and victims are successfully squelched, Scientology's managers and lawyers will keep pocketing millions of dollars by helping it achieve its ends.

Time Magazine, *May 6, 1991 page 50.
Special Report (cover story)*

SUPPORTIVE QUOTATIONS

In January of 1975 I was working on my first film in Durango, Mexico. There I met an actress who gave me the book *Dianetics*. During the five weeks we were filming she gave me some auditing sessions and applied some basic principles. That was when I became involved in Dianetics – because it worked. When I returned to the United States I began Scientology training and auditing. My career immediately took off and I landed a leading role on the TV show *Welcome Back Kotter* and had a string of successful films. I have been a successful actor for more than twenty years and Scientology has played a major role in that success.

I have a wonderful child and a great marriage because I apply L. Ron Hubbard's technology to this area of my life.

John Travolta, actor

Scientology is the gateway to eternity. It is the path to happiness and total spiritual freedom. Until one has experienced the technology of Scientology it's unlikely that one will ever experience these wonderful discoveries. I know because it has worked for me. The more time and effort I invest, the more I receive. I highly recommend it.

Isaac Hayes, composer, musician and actor

Ron Hubbard researched man and has carefully and precisely mapped a route out of the madness, misery and unwanted conditions one can encounter in life. When applied exactly, the technology produces incredible results. Those results are very definite and eternal.

Were it not for Scientology, I would either be completely insane or dead by now. I am forever grateful for the technology of Scientology and to Mr. Hubbard who dedicated his life to helping man and this planet, as well as to the people who have dedicated their lives to helping others through Scientology.

Lisa Marie Presley, daughter of Elvis

I am no longer stuck in the bottomless pit of despair and apathy. Having achieved the state of Clear is the single most important thing that I've done for myself. It has allowed me to experience life in a way I only imagined.

Juliette Lewis, actress

The single greatest thing that studying Scientology has done for me is that it's helped me become freer. Freer to create life as I want to, without being thrown off from my objectives. One of the first simple successes was that I learned to handle and remove my own self-imposed barriers and restraints. Through further study, my ability to handle life around me also increased. This freedom has been hard won, but the rewards are great.

My study of Scientology has also enabled me to write more music. I have become quicker and am able to use all of the musical abilities that I already have. I gained a new understanding of what the proper importances are in the process of creating music.

Scientology has helped me to live better. Using the basic principles of Scientology has become a natural way of life for me. From Scientology I've gotten a freedom to learn whatever I want to learn in life and I'm gaining new abilities all the time.

Chick Corea, musician and composer

SWEDENBORGIANISM

CONTENTS

1 An overview   617

2 Founder   618

3 Swedenborgianism's holy book   619

4 Facts and figures   620

5 Swedenborgianism's practices   620

6 Swedenborgianism's beliefs   620

7 Worship and structure of Church   621

8 Famous Swedenborg fellow-travelers   623

9 Quotations   624

1 AN OVERVIEW

DEFINITION

Swedenborgianism teaches that the writings of Emmanuel Swedenborg are divinely inspired.

Factfile
- Date of origin: 1787
- Founder: The followers of Emanuel Swedenborg
- Holy book: Parts of the Bible, as interpreted by Swedenborg
- Number of adherents: 150,000

NAME

Swedenborgianism is also known as:

- The New Church
- The Church of the New Jerusalem or the New Jerusalem Church.

The Church of the New Jerusalem (Swedenborgian) is usually called the "New Church" by its members.

SUMMARY

Swedenborg was an eighteenth-century Swedish scientist, mystic and theologian who blended occult mysticism with Christian terminology. His visions and writings inspired his followers to establish the Church of the New Jerusalem after his death. With the rise of the New Age Movement, Swedenborgianism has had a revival of popularity.

2 Founder

INTRODUCTION

Swedenborgianism was founded by a group of followers of Swedenborg not long after his death.

EMANUEL SWEDENBORG (1688-1772)

Emanuel Swedenborg was born in Stockholm, Sweden. His father was professor of theology at Uppsala University, court chaplain, and later Bishop of Skala. Emanuel Swedenborg excelled in his studies of science and religion at Uppsala University and became an expert in geology.

After leaving university, Swedenborg spent five years traveling throughout Europe. He studied and wrote about mathematics, mechanics, and the natural sciences, displaying an "inventive and mechanical genius." Returning to Sweden in 1715, he wrote in the country's first scientific magazine and published books and articles on algebra navigation, astronomy, chemistry, and on his discoveries. He also published poetry written in Latin. He was made an assessor in the college of mines at Uppsala and spent thirty years working for the improvement of Sweden's metal-mining industry.

In 1734, on a third journey in Europe, he published a monumental three-volume work entitled *Opera philosophica et mineralia* (Philosophical and logical works), which dealt with metallurgy and metaphysical speculation on the creation of the world. In the first volume, *The Philosophy of Natural Things*, he reached conclusions that proved to be similar to the discoveries of modern scientists: for example, that matter consists of infinitely divisible particles, that are constantly in motion and that themselves consist of smaller swirling particles.

After further erudite publications on natural history, Swedenborg turned his attention to a thorough academic study of human anatomy and physiology, especially concentrating on the blood and the brain. This had a purpose: he was seeking to locate the "soul" of man. In the process, he made some contributions to the understanding of the human body.

A SPIRITUAL CRISIS

In 1744 Swedenborg published a *Journal of Dreams* which records some very curious, and sometimes sexually shocking dreams, and also spiritual experiences that he experienced from March to October 1774. In particular, however, he was consumed by guilt at his own pride and worldly ambition. In April 1774 he had his first vision of Christ, which gave him peace from the attacks of pride and from the evil spirits that he felt to be around him. Later in April 1775 in a "waking vision" of Christ, he felt called to give up worldly learning. After this he wrote no further books on natural history or science. As a result of this crisis, he felt that all his spiritual senses were opened to live in the spiritual world with as much awareness and understanding as he lived in the physical world.

RELIGIOUS STUDIES

In one of his visions, Swedenborg was told that he would be the messenger of teachings from an unseen world to everyone in this world, and that through him God would make more revelations.

From 1749 to 1777 he wrote seventy volumes, all in Latin, and mostly anonymous. In them he described what he had seen and heard in the realm of spirits and angels. Two of his best known are *On heaven and its wonders and on hell*, and, *True Christian Religion*. Swedenborg claimed to have experienced astral travel, journeying to the spirit world to communicate with good and evil angels. He said he had had conversations with Luther, Calvin, St. Augustine, and St. Paul. He has been called a medium and the earliest of the great clairvoyants.

1757

Swedenborg said that his new revelation was what was meant by the second coming. He nominated a particular year, 1757, as the end of the old Christian Age. This, he said, would be overtaken by a New Christian Age, of truth and reason in religion. Other similar compatible religions would also come to accept the values of the New Age.

DEATH

Swedenborg died in London in 1772 and was buried in the Swedish Church. In 1908 his body was moved to Uppsala Cathedral, at the request of the Swedish Government.

FOUNDING OF SWEDENBORGISM

Swedenborg never left the Lutheran Church, and professed that he did not want to found a new religion. Nevertheless, he also believed that his writings would lead to the formation of a "New Church," taking its name from the description of the New Jerusalem in the book of Revelation. Followers of Swedenborg believe that his writings are "a revelation for mankind."

Not long after he died, a group in London decided to establish a separate Church, based on his teachings. Called the General Conference of the New Church, this opened in Great East Cheap, London. In 1789, a conference met in London, and has met each year ever since (except from 1794 to 1806, and 1809 to 1814).

Swedenborg's religious ideas spread to the States in the 1780s. The first society was organized in Baltimore in 1792 and the first ministers were ordained in 1798. The General Convention of the New Jerusalem in the USA was founded in 1817 in Philadelphia.

As a result of some differences of interpretation, a second group was founded, called the General Church of the New Jerusalem.

AFFILIATE ORGANIZATION

The Academy of the New Church is the educational branch of the General Church. The Academy was granted a charter in 1877, for the purpose of teaching the Writings of Emanuel Swedenborg, promoting New Church education in all its forms, educating young men for the ministry, publishing books and other printed material, and establishing a library. The Academy consists of four schools: separate secondary schools for boys and girls, a four-year college, and a theological school which also offers post-graduate programs for lay people.

---

3 SWEDENBORGIANISM'S HOLY BOOK

Swedenborg's followers maintain that their beliefs are based on the Bible, but they say that they gain further inspiration and understanding through the teachings of Emanuel Swedenborg. They believe that in his thirty-five volumes of theology, Swedenborg sets out God's plan for a rebirth of Christianity.

THE BIBLE

Swedenborg proposed eliminating the Pauline Epistles from the Bible, along with much of the Old Testament. So the only valid portions of the New Testament are the four Gospels and the book of Revelation.

The Scriptures can only be properly interpreted through Swedenborgianism.

4 FACTS AND FIGURES

There are about 15,000 members of Swedenborg churches in the US.

PUBLICATIONS

Arcana Coelestia: The Earths in the Universe, run to thirty-five volumes of writings by Swedenborg.
Current official publication: *Chrysalis*

The three branches of the New Church differ in administration:
The British General Conference and the US General Convention each meet annually and appoint a general council which, with a ministerial council, administers the Church. The General Church is episcopal.

---

5 SWEDENBORGIANISM'S PRACTICES

MEMBERSHIP

The membership of the General Church is made up of those who have been baptized into the faith of the New Church, and who subscribe to the principles and purposes of the General Church.

Membership is individual, and is not limited by race, nationality or geography. Women join the church at the age of eighteen, while men join when they are twenty-one.

One becomes a member of a particular society by first becoming a member of the General Church and then by signing the roll of membership of that society.

---

6 SWEDENBORGIANISM'S BELIEFS

INTRODUCTION

Swedenborgianism denies Jesus' deity, teaches salvation by works, and claims latter day revelation. It also teaches a need for a rebirth of Christianity.
Swedenborgianism denies:

- the vicarious atonement of Jesus
- the deity of Christ
- the Trinity
- deity of the Holy Spirit

Swedenborgianism affirms that:

- all religions lead to God
- salvation is by good works

- angels are humans who have died, (rather than supernatural creations of God.)

OVERVIEW OF BELIEFS

SALVATION
Salvation is deliverance from the domination of evil and hell, their power having been broken by Jesus. Human beings are recreated in the image of God. This is made possible because of the life, death and glorification of Jesus. Salvation is an on-going process as people turn away from selfishness and live lives in obedience to God's commandments.

THE BIBLE:

The Bible is not God's word but rather a "symbolic parable of our inner life." We should not try to understand it literally but look for a spiritual interpretation.

THE TRINITY

The orthodox Trinity of three persons is rejected, and replaced by a Trinity of Love, Wisdom and Activity. God the Father is the originating power of the universe; the Son is the human embodiment of the divine soul; the Holy Spirit is the activity of Jesus now.

DEATH

Our true character emerges at death. After death we will be together with all those whom we love.

HEAVEN AND HELL

Heaven and hell are both within us and we can freely enter into either one based on the choices we make concerning good or evil in this life.

OTHER FAITHS

People of all faiths can go to heaven.

DOCTRINE OF CORRESPONDENCE

Swedenborg taught a pantheistic theosophy. This was focused on Jesus Christ, in whom he found a Trinity of Love, Wisdom and Energy.

He viewed the human body as the kingdom of the soul, and this led him to develop his doctrine of correspondence. He believed that all phenomena of the physical world have their spiritual correspondences. For Swedenborg this idea was a key that enabled him to interpret scripture, and find its hidden meaning. As a result of this understanding, he maintained that only those books of the Bible that presented a correspondential spiritual meaning were really "the Word."

In the Old Testament, Swedenborg taught that the only books of "the Word" were the Pentateuch, Joshua, Judges, Samuel, Kings, the Psalms, and the Prophets from Isaiah to Malachi. In the New Testament, Swedenborg taught that the only books of "the Word" are the four Gospels and Revelation.

7 WORSHIP AND STRUCTURE OF THE CHURCH

- Worship: the worship is almost always liturgical.
- Sacraments: there are two sacraments: baptism and the Lord's Supper.
- Preaching: the preaching is based on the Bible, using Swedenborg's methods of interpretation.
- Festivals: the established Christian festivals are observed, and there is one additional festival: New Church Day, held on June 19.

STRUCTURE OF THE CHURCH

The President of the Church has traditionally been a member of the clergy, whose responsibilities include an ex officio participation in all aspects of the Swedenborgian Church. The president addresses each session of the Convention, setting forth the State of the Church.

The administrative and governing structure of the Swedenborgian Church consists of:

- The General Council: the governing body.
- Support Units: foster, administer, supervise, and support programs that cohere around a central focus (e.g. education, communications, growth and outreach).
- The Cabinet: consists of the Chair of each Support Unit and the President of the Swedenborgian Church. Its task is to co-ordinate and prioritize the projects

and activities under the auspices of the Support Units.

- The Council of Ministers: consists of all ordained ministers and meets as a total body once a year. The Council oversees the pastoral and theological dimensions of the life of the Church.
- The Central Office: functions as the primary center, coordinating information and support services for all areas of the Swedenborgian Church.

LEADERSHIP STRUCTURE

Both the General Church, unincorporated and incorporated, are headed by an Executive Bishop. The ecclesiastical affairs (church services, sacred rites) are performed by a clergy that must be ordained by the current (or previous) bishop. The civil, or organizational affairs are run by a Board of Directors of the incorporated General Church.

New bishops are nominated and selected by the clergy, "seconded" by the Board, then voted on by the membership of the unincorporated General Church.

The Bishop may govern the ecclesiastical affairs of the Church with the help of an Assistant Bishop (or an Assistant to the Bishop, an appointed position), as well as with advice from the Council of the Clergy and the Bishop's Consistory.

In his role as general pastor of the Church, the Bishop is further aided by the priesthood, who serve in their roles as leaders of the local congregations.

In governing the civil affairs of the Church, the Bishop is ex officio the chairman of the Board of Directors, and is aided in running the central offices by a Treasurer/Chief Administrative Officer; by the Bishop's Council, a group of lay people appointed by the Bishop to advise him on uses, issues, and the life of the Church; and by the Joint Committee, a group of members appointed from the Board, the Consistory, and other lay people, to advise the Bishop on policy matters.

8 FAMOUS SWEDENBORG FELLOW-TRAVELERS

Johnny Appleseed

The unique Swedenborgian convert, John Chapman, is better known in American folklore as Johnny Appleseed. In addition to his legendary sowing of seeds in the Midwestern wilderness, Johnny Appleseed carried with him all of the Swedenborgian publications he could procure and distributed them wherever the opportunity was presented.

Ralph Waldo Emerson

Ralph Waldo Emerson was greatly impressed by Swedenborg's writings and effected their introduction into his intellectual world. When his essay "Nature" was published anonymously, many praised it as a Swedenborgian work because its central idea of nature as the symbol of the human soul mirrored the Swedenborgian concept of "correspondence."

Transcendentalist movement

The Transcendentalist movement shared many of the philosophical tenets that characterized Swedenborgianism, although few Transcendentalists embraced the Church organization.

Helen Keller

During the 1920s, the Swedenborg church found a most eloquent spokeswoman in the form of this gallant and courageous receiver of Swedenborgian theology. Helen Keller's activism on the part of the handicapped and her inspiring account of her personal Swedenborgian beliefs in *My Religion* (updated as *Light In My Darkness*) served to bring attention back to the small group of Swedenborg's followers.

---

9 QUOTATIONS

The New Church is not a sect. The New Church is not a cult. The New Church is Universal. It has new teaching based and founded on the Word of God.
Swedenborg leaflet

... perhaps the fullest and earliest revival of the Five Age concept, and especially of the New Age is to be found in the theological writings of Swedenborg. He integrates the Classical Ages of the Greeks and Romans with the Biblical pattern, and then claims that the New Age has begun.
The New Age and the ages that came before it

Everyone who lives up to the best he knows, whether Christian, Jew, Moslem, or Pagan, is truly a member of the church Invisible.
Paul Zacharias, a Swedenborgian minister

This is a dangerous, mystical, non-Christian religion. Its denial of the Trinity and the Holy Spirit, the vicarious atonement, and rejection of Acts and the Pauline epistles clearly set it outside of Christian orthodoxy.
Christian Apologetics and Research Ministry

What simplifies our examination of Swedenborgianism is its claim to be, not a mere new sect or offshoot of Christianity, but a new dispensation, as distinct from Church Christianity as that was from Judaism. The old Church is affirmed to have come to its end in 1757 when, as some will be surprised to learn, the last judgment took place. Swedenborg says he was present; though why he was not judged himself does not appear clear. However, all this is opposed in Scripture and facts. The Lord promised that "the gates of hell should not prevail" against His Church (Matthew 16:18), and we know we have received "a kingdom which cannot be moved" (Hebrews 12:28) and a succeeding dispensation of Christianity to the Church dispensation is a pure invention without foundation. Is it not too much to ask us to believe that there has been no true Church testimony on the earth since 1757, except that of a little handful of self-commended Swedenborgians?

William Hoste, Heresies Exposed

THE FAMILY/CHILDREN OF GOD

CONTENTS

1 An overview   627

2 Founder   628

3 Children of God's holy book   629

4 Facts and figures   630

5 Children of God practices   630

6 Children of God beliefs   633

1 AN OVERVIEW

DEFINITION

The Family is an international Christian fellowship dedicated to sharing God's Word and love with others. The Family, as the Children of God were first known, emerged in the late 1960s out of the "Jesus People" movement that attempted to reach a popular subculture.

Factfile
- Date of origin: 1968
- Founder: David Brandt Berg, 1919–1994
- Holy book: The Bible
- Number of adherents: 14,000

NAME

- The Family
- Family of Love

Other names include:

- Heaven's Magic
- Martinelli
- World Services
- Fellowship of Independent Christian Churches

2 FOUNDER

David Brandt Berg was affectionately known as "Moses David," "Mo," (being short for "Moses"), "Father David," and "Dad" to Family members.

David Berg's parents were both active Christian pastors and evangelists, and his early years were spent traveling with them in evangelistic work. In 1941 he nearly died of pneumonia, shortly after being drafted into the US Army. After determining to rededicate his life to Christian service, he experienced a miraculous healing.

For most of the next 27 years he worked as a pastor and in various evangelistic endeavors until, in 1968, he received God's call to take the Gospel to the hippies of southern California. There he and his then teen-aged children began a ministry to the youth that grew and was known as The Children of God, and eventually became known as The Family. Today, members of The Family engage in missionary and humanitarian work in about 90 countries worldwide.

David Berg called on his followers to devote their full time to spreading the message of Christ's love and salvation as far and wide as possible, unfettered by convention or tradition, and to teach others to do the same.

The Family

THE FAMILY'S HISTORY

The Family traces its origins to 1968 and Huntington Beach, California. There David Berg, also known as Father David or Moses David, together with his wife and teenage children, began a ministry to the counterculture youth of that seaside town. Many of these experienced dramatic changes in their lives as they came to understand that there is a God and that they could have a personal relationship with him through Jesus Christ.

Some of them chose to work with Father David, dedicating their lives to the service of God and others. Thus, The Family was born, although it was not to become known by that name for many years. At the end of 1969, when the group had grown to about 100 members, it was dubbed "The Children of God" by the news media. By 1972, there were 130 Children of God communities scattered throughout the world.

In early 1978, The Children of God was formally dissolved and a new group, The Family of Love, with a new organizational structure, was formed. In recent years, they have become known simply as The Family.

The Family

TEEN CHALLENGE

David Berg was an evangelist for the Christian and Missionary Alliance in 1964. He became the leader of a Teen Challenge chapter in Huntington Beach, CA. in 1967. Teen Challenge was a youth ministry of the Assemblies of God denomination. Berg separated the group from the national *Teen Challenge* organization in 1968 and renamed it Light Club. Members were called Lightclubbers.

Berg received a revelation from God in 1969 that a disastrous earthquake was about to hit California, and cause part of the state to slide into the ocean. He led the group out of Huntington Beach to wander throughout the American southwest for 8 months. During that time, they changed their name to the Children of God. The earthquake never materialized.

B. A. Robinson, Ontario Consultants on Religious Tolerance

FREECOG

In the early 1970s, Berg established three communities, in Los Angeles, CA, Coachella, CA.

Some parents of some of the young people who had joined COG, under the leadership of Ian Haworth founded the first anti-cult organization in order to try to restore their children to their families. The group became called FREECOG, "Free Our Children From the Children of God." They believed that Berg employed mind control practices to persuade their children to join the COG, as all new members were encouraged to sever all contact with their families of origin, to donate almost their entire possessions to the group, and become full time evangelists.

B. A. Robinson, Ontario Consultants on Religious Tolerance

KAREN ZERBY

Since the passing of "Mo" in 1994, "Maria" (Karen Zerby, one of Berg's multiple wives) has been leading the group.

3 CHILDREN OF GOD'S HOLY BOOK

We believe the Holy Bible to be the inspired Word of God, given to us by God our Creator to be a "lamp unto our feet and a light unto our path" (Psalm 119:105). We assert that the Scriptures are a sacred revelation, written by holy men of old who spake as they were moved by God's Holy Spirit; and that these writings are the divinely appointed standard and guide to our faith and practice. Holding fast this truth, that "all Scripture is given by inspiration of God, and is profitable for doctrine, for reproof, for correction, for instruction in righteousness" (2 Timothy 3:16), we strive to study, memorize and obey it, that we may grow in faith, wisdom and spiritual strength through our knowledge of and adherence to its tenets.

God's Word as revealed in the Holy Bible is the basis and cornerstone of all our beliefs and practices. It is the mainstay of our spiritual strength and nourishment; its principles are the foundation of the instruction we give our children, and its truth is the basis of the witness we give to others. We come to the Bible not merely as a source of knowledge, which indeed it is, but much more importantly, through a prayerful reading of its pages we are able to "partake of the Divine Nature" (2 Peter 1:4), to commune with Jesus, Who is Himself the living Word.

The Family

Critics of the Children of God have pointed out that they imposed their own unique way of interpreting the Bible, and that, on occasions, Berg's own writings seem to have taken precedence over the Bible itself, when they differed.

Berg claimed to be the end-time Prophet with his prolific writings being a "continuing revelation."

4 FACTS AND FIGURES

There are approximately 12,000 full-time and associate adult volunteer members in The Family working out of over 1,400 centers, or communities, situated in over 100 countries.

Adult members of The Family live with, and when possible are joined in their ministries by, their children.

There are over ninety different nationalities belonging to the Family.

EVANGELISM

The Family sees its prime task as that of bringing the message of God's love to all. Members of the Family have personally shared the Gospel message with over 237 million individuals, while billions have heard their message through the mass media. As a result, over 23.3 million people have personally prayed with members of the Family to receive God's love, forgiveness and salvation.

Members of the Family have distributed over 850 million pieces of Gospel literature in 61 languages. A total of over 1.4 million videos and eight million audio tapes in more than 20 languages have also been distributed.

The Family

OFFICIAL PUBLICATIONS

Mo Letters: Berg wrote more than 2,500 letters which became known as "Mo Letters."
Mama Letters from Berg's common-law wife (mistress), Karen Zerby (Maria), are also considered authoritative.

5 CHILDREN OF GOD PRACTICES

A Polygamy
B End time prophet
C Co-operative lifestyle
D Flirty Fishing
E Sexual sharing

INTRODUCTION

- COG believe that loyalties to one's family-of-origin should take second place to loyalty to Jesus.
- COG emphasize the importance helping the poor and having a simple lifestyle.
- COG practice communal living.
- COG practice free love among adults within their group.

A POLYGAMY

In 1969, David Berg became a polygyamist by marrying a second wife, Maria. He justified this action from precedents in the Old Testament.

After David Berg, according to his daughter, Deborah, his first wife initially accepted her husband's polygamy, but eventually left him and the Children of God. "Sin had so twisted my dad's mind, heart and conscience," Deborah Berg wrote, ". . . his own wife was the first to feel the tormenting fire of his burning lusts."

B END TIME PROPHET

Berg also received revelations from God in which he felt God was identifying him as the "End Time Prophet." He was certain that he would play a major role in the second coming of Jesus.

C CO-OPERATIVE LIFESTYLE

Following the pattern of the earliest Christians, the Family maintain a cooperative lifestyle, sharing material possessions, resources and responsibilities with one another.

Family communities, or "Homes'" as they are commonly called, serve a number of purposes. They provide bases from which The Family conduct their outreach endeavors and Christian social work.

These Family Homes range from small family-size residences to large 'combos' - facilities which combine a number of outreach-related functions under one roof. Regardless of size, make-up or locale, each community and its membership endeavor to uphold a Bible-based code of conduct and maintain high standards in the areas of health and hygiene, educational opportunities for the children, and a proper balance between work, recreation and rest.

The Family

D FLIRTY FISHING

In 1976, Berg proposed an unprecedented corollary to the Law of Love: he contended that, in certain circumstances, it would be acceptable for a Christian to have sexual relations with someone in an effort to demonstrate a tangible manifestation of God's Love, thereby helping them to come to a saving knowledge of Jesus Christ. This doctrine became known as "Flirty Fishing," a term that David adapted from Jesus' admonition to His disciples to "follow Me, and I will make you fishers of men" (Matthew 4:19).

What better way to show them the Love of God than to do your best to supply their desperately hungry needs for love, fellowship, companionship, mental and spiritual communication, and physical needs such as food, clothing, shelter, warmth, affection, a tender loving kiss, a soft warm embrace, the healing touch of your loving hands, the comforting feeling of your body next to theirs – and yes, even sex if need be!"

David Berg's Letters, no 79

What greater way could you show anyone your love than to give them your all in the bed of love? How much more can you show them the Love of God than to show them His Love to the uttermost through you? How much more love can you show them than this?

David Berg's Letters, no 80

There's no amount of love that could possibly be illegitimate to try to win a soul! There's no sin in love to begin with, and there's no "sin" so great that God would condemn you for it when it's done in love . . .because when it's love it can't be sin.

David Berg's Letters, no 81

The only price that's worth it is an immortal undying soul! That's the price we'd even go to bed for! The salvation of an eternal soul! And that is worth it!

David Berg's Letters, no 82

The greatest need of man is love, so the greatest service to man is love! That's why FFing [Flirty Fishing] is such a service. It is the greatest, most sacrificial service that anyone can possibly give, outside of actually dying, because it is laying your life on the line. You are laying down your life or your wife for love, love of the Lord. Unselfish love! I'm not just talking about fleshly gratification, but for the love of someone, sacrificial love, even risky love, dangerous love!

David Berg's Letters, no 83

E SEXUAL SHARING

In 1977 free consensual sexual activity among the membership was introduced by Berg.

> The free expression of sexuality, including fornication, adultery, lesbianism (though not male homosexuality), and incest were not just permitted but encouraged.
>
> *Richard Kyle,* The Religious Fringe: A History of Alternate Religions in America *InterVarsity Press Downers Grove, IL, (1993), Pages 361-367*

True love, real love, God's Love, is all the religion you need!

David Berg's Letters, no 69

Everything must be judged from the standpoint of love. Is it doing good or is it doing evil?

David Berg's Letters, no 70

If we're keeping God's law of love, then we'll try not to hurt or offend anybody. We'll do our best to try to live in love, to help people without offending anyone.

David Berg's Letters, no 71

Love is really the stricter law in the long run ... The [Mosaic] Law was only obeyed because they had to and they would only do as much as they were made to do, whereas love will ... go to the death and die for someone else to do the right thing.

David Berg's Letters, no 73

While many aspects of this belief were easily accepted in theory by mainstream Christians, David applied it most shockingly to matters of sex. Simply put, he maintained that sex was not inherently evil in the eyes of God, and that loving consensual heterosexual relations, even outside of marriage, were permissible, as long as no one was hurt or offended.

The Family

Is sex a sin? Well, if there's anything I've tried to preach and tried to show the world, we're one of the few, if not the only religion of the world which doesn't teach that sex is sinful! Think of that! Isn't it horrible to think that nearly every other religion – even if it doesn't actually directly teach so – gives the impression by their practice that sex is sinful and somehow wicked?

David Berg's Letters, no 74

Adam and Eve enjoyed sex before they ever fell, and before the Fall they were commanded to be fruitful and multiply and replenish the Earth, and were created with sexual organs to do so in the very beginning! – So how could sex be sinful, if they were commanded to do it before the Fall?

David Berg's Letters, no 75

Sex was created and instituted by God in the very beginning, and [was] the subject of His first commandment: 'Be fruitful and multiply!' (Genesis 1:22).

David Berg's Letters, no 76

Jesus said [in Matthew 22:37-39] this is all the law, the only law – love! Therefore, whatever is done in pure love, the Love of God, unselfish love, sacrificial love, for God or others, is lawful, according to God's Word and Law of Love! As long, therefore, as it is in love with mutual consent and hurts no innocent one, it is lawful, according to God's Own Word and His Own Son, Jesus Christ!

The Apostle Paul also says, "Against such (love) there is no law" (Galatians 5:23). Against this pure kind of love, the Love of God, the unselfish sacrificial Love of God and your fellow man, there is no law of God! According to the Scriptures there is therefore no longer any law against sex that is done in love, God's Love, and hurts no one.

David Berg's Letters, no 77

So enjoy yourself and enjoy life! Enjoy the pleasures and senses and the sensual pleasures of life which God has given you to enjoy as much as you please and as much as you need. Just don't enjoy them more than Him and more than His love. Don't worship the creation more than the Creator. Be sure that you put God first,

and then you can have all this and Heaven, too!

David Berg's Letters, no 78

---

6 CHILDREN OF GOD BELIEFS

INTRODUCTION

Most of the teaching of the COG appears to be traditional Evangelical Christian doctrine.

But they also believe in:

- universal salvation, and
- contacts with spirits.

Berg said that he himself made contact with Abraham, as his own spirit guide, as well as with other spiritual contacts with the dead.

SPIRITISM AND THE OCCULT

Berg has a long history of personal involvement with and endorsement of astrology, possession and revelation by spirit guides and helpers (which included departed saints and pagans), use of mediums. In addition to Necromancy, Berg claims to have sexual intercourse with spirits and pagan goddesses (*Mo Letters* 621:26; 554; 102:7-12; 61:17; 268:1-2, 12;107:18, 25).

The Watchman Expositor

THEOSOPHY

CONTENTS

1 An overview   637

2 Founder   638

3 Theosophy's holy book   639

4 Facts and figures   639

5 Theosophy practices   640

6 Theosophy beliefs   640

7 Worship   646

8 Quotations   647

1 AN OVERVIEW

DEFINITION

The word "Theosophy" is derived from the Greek *theos* ("God") and *sophos* ("wisdom"). It therefore means "divine wisdom;" and refers to any system of thought concerned with the relationship between God and the creation, especially one intended to help men and women achieve direct experience of the divine. Theosophy has been called, "a synthesis of science, religion, and philosophy."

The Concise Oxford Dictionary describes theosophy as "any of various philosophies professing to achieve a knowledge of God by spiritual ecstasy, direct intuition, or special individual relations, esp. a modern movement following Hindu and Buddhist teachings and seeking universal brotherhood."

Factfile
- Date of origin: November 17, 1875
- Founder: Madame Blavatsky
- Holy book: No one book. But a favorite is Helena Petrovna Blavatsky's *The Secret Doctrine*
- Number of members: 30,000

SUMMARY

Theosophy is based on the visions and revelations that Mme. Blavatsky had by the "mahatnas" of Tibet. The result is a mix of Hinduism, Buddhism, Spiritualism, and Gnostic Christianity, with Masonic rituals. Included in this is a systematic criticism of Christianity, Judaism and Islam.

2 FOUNDER

A Madame Blavatsky
B Growth of the Theosophical Society

INTRODUCTION

The Theosophical Society was founded in New York in 1875 by the Ukraine born Madame Blavatsky with the assistance of Henry S. Olcott.

A MADAME HELENA PETROVNA BLAVATSKY (1831-1891)

Helena Hahn was born in the Ukraine in 1831 of noble Russian descent. In her teens she married the Czarist general Nikifor V. Blavatsky, but after three months she left him, and traveled in many places in Europe and in the East, including Tibet where, it is claimed, she was trained by the masters of Theosophy.

In 1873 she moved to the US where she founded the Theosophical Society with Henry Steel Olcott, a lawyer, who was also a spiritualist.

In 1978, Madame Blavatsky and Olcott moved to India and they made their headquarters at Adyar, near Madras. Madame Blavastsky's psychic powers were widely acclaimed, and the movement's ideas and teaching spread throughout the world. Madame Blavatsky was discredited, however, after an investigation by the Society for Psychical Research. She became addicted to hashish, and died a lonely woman, deserted by most of her followers.

B GROWTH OF THE THEOSOPHICAL SOCIETY

After Madame Blavatsky moved to India, the movement almost died out it in the United States. In the 1880's and 1890's it was revived in the US under the leadership of William Q. Judge (1851-1896). There were tensions between Judge and Olcott, and the American branch broke away from the movement in India.

Mrs. Katherine Tingley (1847-1929) took charge of the American branch when Judge died, and, working from the new headquarters in California, improved the organization of the American branch of the movement.

MRS. ANNIE BESANT (1847-1933)

London-born Annie Wood married the Rev. Frank Besant, the brother of Sir Walter Besant, a novelist and social reformer. In 1773 she separated from her husband and became Vice President of the National Secular Society. In 1889 she met Madame Blavatsky, and became interested in Theosophy, moving to India. When Olcott died in 1907, she became president. She founded a college of Theosophy, which became the University of Benares. She was a powerful writer, and her books provide very good teaching on the ideas of Theosophy.

In 1991 Mrs. Besant announced that Jiddu Krishnamurti, a young unknown Indian, was the reincarnation of Christ, the messiah the world was waiting for, and she traveled with him throughout Europe and the USA. This announcement caused much controversy, and he himself later renounced these claims. His books, however, are very popular.

The current President of the Theosophical Society of America is John Coates. He encourages modern Theosophists to dabble in contemporary occult phenomena such as Kirlian photography and psychokinesis.

Recent interest in the occult and the New Age has swelled the ranks of this organization. Alice Bailey, a student of Theosophy, has given the name "New Age" to this movement.

3 THEOSOPHY'S HOLY BOOK

The Secret Doctrine
The text most widely referred to by the Theosophical Society is Helena Petrovna Blavatsky's *The Secret Doctrine*. However, this is not the only text. Members are encouraged to read and study the numerous books on theosophy, as well as to explore with science and philosophy.

I confined myself to the Hindu Scriptures, and in all cases I stated that I regarded these scriptures and the Hindu religion as the origin of all scriptures and all religions.
Annie Besant, The Daily Chronicle,
April 9, 1894

4 FACTS AND FIGURES

MEMBERSHIP
The Theosophical Society is Theosophy's most prominent group, with about 30,000 members in 60 countries.

In the USA, membership is about 6,500, divided between 140 centers (or lodges).

SYMBOL OF THEOSOPHY
The five prominent symbols visible in the Seal of the Theosophical Society are:

• the Star of David
• the Ankh
• the Swastika
• the Ouroboros, and above the seal is
• the Aum.

Around the seal are written the words: "There is no religion higher than truth."

INFLUENCE
While there may be as few as 30,000 members of the Theosophical Society, its influence stretches far beyond the boundaries of its own ranks. It influences numerous movements, such as the New Age Movement, the Rosicrucians, and the Anthropological Society.

The movement has been a catalytic force in the 20th century-Asian revival of Buddhism and Hinduism and a pioneering agency in the promotion of greater Western acquaintance with Eastern thought. In the United States it has influenced a whole series of religious movements, including the I AM movement, Rosicrucianism, the Liberal Catholic Church, Psychiana, Unity, and sections of the New Thought movement.
The New Encyclopedia Britannica,
15th edition, 1989

MAGAZINES
Theosophy World: dedicated to the Theosophical Philosophy and its Practical Application

The High Country Theosophist: This is an independent journal with the following objectives:

• to serve the greater Theosophical Movement as a forum for the free interchange of ideas and commentary in the pursuit of Truth and to facilitate various projects in furtherance of theosophical principles
• to present articles and essays consistent with source Theosophy, otherwise known as the Ancient Wisdom, as given by the Masters, H.P. Blavatsky, and other theosophical writers consistent with this tradition

- to examine contemporary ethical, religious, metaphysical, scientific, and philosophical issues from the viewpoint of the source theosophical teachings

- to impartially examine significant events and issues in the history of the Theosophical Movement that have affected and shaped its present-day realities.

5 THEOSOPHY PRACTICES

Theosophists are not asked to accept any opinion or adopt any practice that does not appeal to their inner sense of reason and morality. However, the following practices are followed by the majority of Theosophists:

- they meditate regularly, both to gain insight into themselves and as a service to humanity
- they are vegetarians and avoid the use of furs or skins for which animals are killed
- they do not use alcohol or drugs (except under a doctor's order)

- they support the rights of all human beings for fair and just treatment, being therefore supporters of women's and minority rights
- They respect differences of culture and support intellectual freedom.

OCCULT CONTACT

The "Mahatnas" are the "Great White Fraternity," and include Buddha, Krishna, Jesus. Theosophians try to make contact with them through numerous forms of occultism.

6 THEOSOPHY BELIEFS

A God
B Hindu gods
C Doctrines believed by Theosophists
D Aims of the Society
E *The Key to Theosophy* by H. P. Blavatsky

INTRODUCTION

Theosophical philosophy is said to be a contemporary presentation of the perennial wisdom underlying the world's religions, sciences, and philosophies.

This philosophy teaches that we are not brought into existence by chance nor thrown up into earth-life like wreckage

cast along the shore, but are here for infinitely noble purposes.

Katherine Tingley

A GOD

God is just "energy."

B HINDU GODS

In Theosophy, there are many Hindu gods, to whom altars are dedicated in the home.

C DOCTRINES BELIEVED BY THEOSOPHISTS

Theosophy is a way of looking at life rather than a creed. Modern Theosophy, however, present the following beliefs that explain the world as they look at it and experience it:

- reincarnation
- *karma* (or moral justice)
- the existence of worlds of experience beyond the physical
- the presence of life and consciousness in all matter
- the evolution of spirit and intelligence as well as of physical matter
- the possibility of our conscious participation in evolution
- the power of thought to affect one's self and surroundings
- the reality of free will and self-responsibility
- the duty of altruism, a concern for the welfare of others
- the ultimate perfection of human nature, society, and life.

D AIMS OF THE SOCIETY

Madame Blavatsky stated that the following were the three aims of the Theosophy Society:

(i) To promote universal brotherhood and world peace, without distinction of race, creed, sex, case, color, or financial status.
(ii) The study of comparative religions, philosophy and science.
(iii) To make a systematic investigation of the mystic potencies of men and nature and investigate the unexplained laws of Nature and the powers latent in humanity.

E *THE KEY TO THEOSOPHY* BY H. P. BLAVATSKY

CHAPTER 1: THEOSOPHY AND THE THEOSOPHICAL SOCIETY

The meaning of the name
ENQUIRER. Theosophy and its doctrines are often referred to as a new-fangled religion. Is it a religion?

THEOSOPHIST. It is not. Theosophy is Divine Knowledge or Science.

ENQ. What is the real meaning of the term?
THEO. "Divine Wisdom," (Theosophia) or Wisdom of the gods, as (theogonia), genealogy of the gods. The word theos means a god in Greek, one of the divine beings, certainly not "God" in the sense attached in our day to the term. Therefore, it is not "Wisdom of God," as translated by some, but Divine Wisdom such as that possessed by the gods. The term is many thousand years old.

ENQ. What is the origin of the name?
THEO. It comes to us from the Alexandrian philosophers, called lovers of truth, Philaletheians, from (phil) "loving," and (aletheia) "truth." The name Theosophy dates from the third century of our era, and began with Ammonius Saccas and his disciples who started the Eclectic Theosophical system.

ENQ. What was the object of this system?
THEO. First of all to inculcate certain great moral truths upon its disciples, and all those who were "lovers of the truth." Hence the motto adopted by the Theosophical Society: "There is no religion higher than truth." The chief aim of the Founders of the Eclectic Theosophical School was one of the three objects of its modern successor, the Theosophical Society, namely, to reconcile all religions, sects and nations under a common system of ethics, based on eternal verities.

ENQ. What have you to show that this is not an impossible dream; and that all the world's religions are based on the one and the same truth?
THEO. Their comparative study and analysis. The "WISDOM-RELIGION" was one in antiquity; and the sameness of primitive religious philosophy is proven to us by the identical doctrines taught to

the Initiates during the MYSTERIES, an institution once universally diffused. "All the old worships indicate the existence of a single Theosophy anterior to them. The key that is to open one must open all; otherwise it cannot be the right key." (Eclect. Philo.)

THE POLICY OF THE THEOSOPHICAL SOCIETY

ENQ. In the days of Ammonius there were several ancient great religions, and numerous were the sects in Egypt and Palestine alone. How could he reconcile them?

THEO. By doing that which we again try to do now. The Neo-Platonists were a large body, and belonged to various religious philosophies; so do our Theosophists. In those days, the Jew Aristobulus affirmed that the ethics of Aristotle represented the esoteric teachings of the Law of Moses; Philo Judaeus endeavored to reconcile the Pentateuch with the Pythagorean and Platonic philosophy; and Josephus proved that the Essenes of Carmel were simply the copyists and followers of the Egyptian Therapeutae (the healers). So it is in our day. We can show the line of descent of every Christian religion, as of every, even the smallest, sect. The latter are the minor twigs or shoots grown on the larger branches; but shoots and branches spring from the same trunk — the WISDOM-RELIGION. To prove this was the aim of Ammonius, who endeavored to induce Gentiles and Christians, Jews and Idolaters, to lay aside their contentions and strifes, remembering only that they were all in possession of the same truth under various vestments, and were all the children of a common mother. This is the aim of Theosophy likewise.

ENQ. What are your authorities for saying this of the ancient Theosophists of Alexandria?

THEO. An almost countless number of well-known writers. Mosheim, one of them, says that:

"Ammonius taught that the religion of the multitude went hand-in-hand with philosophy, and with her had shared the fate of being by degrees corrupted and obscured with mere human conceits, superstitions, and lies; that it ought, therefore, to be brought back to its original purity by purging it of this dross and expounding it upon philosophical principles; and the whole Christ had in view was to reinstate and restore to its primitive integrity the wisdom of the ancients; to reduce within bounds the universally-prevailing dominion of superstition; and in part to correct, and in part to exterminate the various errors that had found their way into the different popular religions."

This, again, is precisely what the modern Theosophists say. Only while the great Philaletheian was supported and helped in the policy he pursued by two Church Fathers, Clement and Athenagoras, by all the learned Rabbis of the Synagogue, the Academy and the Groves, and while he taught a common doctrine for all, we, his followers on the same line, receive no recognition, but, on the contrary, are abused and persecuted. People 1,500 years ago are thus shown to have been more tolerant than they are in this enlightened century.

ENQ. Was he encouraged and supported by the Church because, notwithstanding his heresies, Ammonius taught Christianity and was a Christian?

THEO. Not at all. He was born a Christian, but never accepted Church Christianity. As said of him by the same writer:

"He had but to propound his instructions according to the ancient pillars of Hermes, which Plato and Pythagoras knew before, and from them constituted their philosophy. Finding the same in the prologue of the Gospel according to St. John, he very properly supposed that the purpose of Jesus was to restore the great doctrine of wisdom in its primitive integrity. The narratives of the Bible and the stories of the gods he considered to be allegories illustrative of the truth, or else fables to be rejected." Moreover, as says the Edinburgh Encyclopoedia, "he acknowledged that Jesus Christ was an excellent man and the 'friend of God,' but alleged that it was not his design entirely to abolish the worship of demons (gods), and that his only intention was to purify the ancient religion."

THE WISDOM-RELIGION ESOTERIC IN ALL AGES
ENQ. Since Ammonius never committed anything to writing, how can one feel sure that such were his teachings?
THEO. Neither did Buddha, Pythagoras, Confucius, Orpheus, Socrates, or even Jesus, leave behind them any writings. Yet most of these are historical personages, and their teachings have all survived. The disciples of Ammonius (among whom Origen and Herennius) wrote treatises and explained his ethics. Certainly the latter are as historical, if not more so, than the Apostolic writings. Moreover, his pupils – Origen, Plotinus, and Longinus (counsellor of the famous Queen Zenobia) – have all left voluminous records of the Philalethian System – so far, at all events, as their public profession of faith was known, for the school was divided into exoteric and esoteric teachings.

ENQ. How have the latter tenets reached our day, since you hold that what is properly called the WISDOM-RELIGION was esoteric?
THEO. The WISDOM-RELIGION was ever one, and being the last word of possible human knowledge, was, therefore, carefully preserved. It preceded by long ages the Alexandrian Theosophists, reached the modern, and will survive every other religion and philosophy.

ENQ. Where and by whom was it so preserved?

THEO. Among Initiates of every country; among profound seekers after truth — their disciples; and in those parts of the world where such topics have always been most valued and pursued: in India, Central Asia, and Persia.

ENQ. Can you give me some proofs of its esotericism?
THEO. The best proof you can have of the fact is that every ancient religious, or rather philosophical, cult consisted of an esoteric or secret teaching, and an exoteric (outward public) worship. Furthermore, it is a well-known fact that the MYSTERIES of the ancients comprised with every nation the "greater" (secret) and "Lesser" (public) MYSTERIES — e.g. in the celebrated solemnities called the Eleusinia, in Greece. From the Hierophants of Samothrace, Egypt, and the initiated Brahmins of the India of old, down to the later Hebrew Rabbis, all preserved, for fear of profanation, their real bona fide beliefs secret. The Jewish Rabbis called their secular religious series the Mercavah (the exterior body), "the vehicle," or, the covering which contains the hidden soul. — i.e., their highest secret knowledge. Not one of the ancient nations ever imparted through its priests its real philosophical secrets to the masses, but allotted to the latter only the husks. Northern Buddhism has its "greater" and its "lesser" vehicle, known as the Mahayana, the esoteric, and the Hinayana, the exoteric, Schools. Nor can you blame them for such secrecy; for surely you would not think of feeding your flock of sheep on learned dissertations on botany instead of on grass? Pythagoras called his Gnosis "the knowledge of things that are," or e gnosis ton onton, and preserved that knowledge for his pledged disciples only: for those who could digest such mental food and feel satisfied; and he pledged them to silence and secrecy. Occult alphabets and secret ciphers are the development of the old Egyptian hieratic writings, the secret of which was, in the days of old, in the

possession only of the Hierogrammatists, or initiated Egyptian priests. Ammonius Saccas, as his biographers tell us, bound his pupils by oath not to divulge his higher doctrines except to those who had already been instructed in preliminary knowledge, and who were also bound by a pledge. Finally, do we not find the same even in early Christianity, among the Gnostics, and even in the teachings of Christ? Did he not speak to the multitudes in parables which had a two-fold meaning, and explain his reasons only to his disciples? "To you," he says, "it is given to know the mysteries of the kingdom of heaven; but unto them that are without, all these things are done in parables" (Mark iv. 11). "The Essenes of Judea and Carmel made similar distinctions, dividing their adherents into neophytes, brethren, and the perfect, or those initiated" (Eclec. Phil.). Examples might be brought from every country to this effect.

ENQ.   Can you attain the "Secret Wisdom" simply by study? Encyclopaedias define Theosophy pretty much as Webster's Dictionary does, i.e., as "supposed intercourse with God and superior spirits, and consequent attainment of superhuman knowledge by physical means and chemical processes." Is this so?

THEO.   I think not. Nor is there any lexicographer capable of explaining, whether to himself or others, how superhuman knowledge can be attained by physical or chemical processes. Had Webster said "by metaphysical and alchemical processes," the definition would be approximately correct: as it is, it is absurd. Ancient Theosophists claimed, and so do the modern, that the infinite cannot be known by the finite — i.e., sensed by the finite Self–but that the divine essence could be communicated to the higher Spiritual Self in a state of ecstasy. This condition can hardly be attained, like hypnotism, by "physical and chemical means."

ENQ.   What is your explanation of it?

THEO.   Real ecstasy was defined by Plotinus as "the liberation of the mind from its finite consciousness, becoming one and identified with the infinite." This is the highest condition, says Prof. Wilder, but not one of permanent duration, and it is reached only by the very very few. It is, indeed, identical with that state which is known in India as Samadhi. The latter is practiced by the Yogis, who facilitate it physically by the greatest abstinence in food and drink, and mentally by an incessant endeavor to purify and elevate the mind. Meditation is silent and unuttered prayer, or, as Plato expressed it, "the ardent turning of the soul toward the divine; not to ask any particular good (as in the common meaning of prayer), but for good itself – for the universal Supreme Good" of which we are a part on earth, and out of the essence of which we have all emerged. Therefore, adds Plato, "remain silent in the presence of the divine ones, till they remove the clouds from thy eyes and enable thee to see by the light which issues from themselves, not what appears as good to thee, but what is intrinsically good."

ENQ.   Theosophy, then, is not, as held by some, a newly devised scheme?

THEO.   Only ignorant people can thus refer to it. It is as old as the world, in its teachings and ethics, if not in name, as it is also the broadest and most catholic system among all.

ENQ.   How comes it, then, that Theosophy has remained so unknown to the nations of the Western Hemisphere? Why should it have been a sealed book to races confessedly the most cultured and advanced?

THEO.   We believe there were nations as cultured in days of old and certainly more spiritually "advanced" than we are. But there are several reasons for this willing ignorance. One of them was given by St. Paul to the cultured Athenians – a loss, for long centuries, of real spiritual insight, and even interest, owing to their too great devotion to things of sense and their long slavery to the dead letter of dogma and ritualism. But the strongest reason for it lies in the fact that real Theosophy has ever been kept secret.

ENQ. You have brought forward proofs that such secrecy has existed; but what was the real cause for it?

THEO. The causes for it were: Firstly, the perversity of average human nature and its selfishness, always tending to the gratification of personal desires to the detriment of neighbors and next of kin. Such people could never be entrusted with divine secrets. Secondly, their unreliability to keep the sacred and divine knowledge from desecration. It is the latter that led to the perversion of the most sublime truths and symbols, and to the gradual transformation of things spiritual into anthropomorphic, concrete, and gross imagery – in other words, to the dwarfing of the god-idea and to idolatry.

THEOSOPHY IS NOT BUDDHISM

ENQ. You are often spoken of as "Esoteric Buddhists." Are you then all followers of Gautama Buddha?

THEO. No more than musicians are all followers of Wagner. Some of us are Buddhists by religion; yet there are far more Hindus and Brahmins than Buddhists among us, and more Christian-born Europeans and Americans than converted Buddhists. The mistake has arisen from a misunderstanding of the real meaning of the title of Mr. Sinnett's excellent work, "Esoteric Buddhism," which last word ought to have been spelt with one, instead of two, d's, as then Budhism would have meant what it was intended for, merely "Wisdomism" (Bodha, bodhi, "intelligence," "wisdom") instead of Buddhism, Gautama's religious philosophy. Theosophy, as already said, is the WISDOM-RELIGION.

ENQ. What is the difference between Buddhism, the religion founded by the Prince of Kapilavastu, and Budhism, the "Wisdomism" which you say is synonymous with Theosophy?

THEO. Just the same difference as there is between the secret teachings of Christ, which are called "the mysteries of the Kingdom of Heaven," and the later ritualism and dogmatic theology of the Churches and Sects. Buddha means the "Enlightened" by Bodha, or understanding, Wisdom. This has passed root and branch into the esoteric teachings that Gautama imparted to his chosen Arhats only.

ENQ. But some Orientalists deny that Buddha ever taught any esoteric doctrine at all?

THEO. They may as well deny that Nature has any hidden secrets for the men of science. Further on I will prove it by Buddha's conversation with his disciple Ananda. His esoteric teachings were simply the Gupta Vidya (secret knowledge) of the ancient Brahmins, the key to which their modern successors have, with few exceptions, completely lost. And this Vidya has passed into what is now known as the inner teachings of the Mahayana school of Northern Buddhism. Those who deny it are simply ignorant pretenders to Orientalism. I advise you to read the Rev. Mr. Edkins' Chinese Buddhism – especially the chapters on the Exoteric and Esoteric schools and teachings – and then compare the testimony of the whole ancient world upon the subject.

ENQ. But are not the ethics of Theosophy identical with those taught by Buddha?

THEO. Certainly, because these ethics are the soul of the WISDOM-RELIGION, and were once the common property of the initiates of all nations. But Buddha was the first to embody these lofty ethics in his public teachings, and to make them the foundation and the very essence of his public system. It is herein that lies the immense difference between exoteric Buddhism and every other religion. For while in other religions ritualism and dogma hold the first and most important place, in Buddhism it is the ethics which have always been the most insisted upon. This accounts for the resemblance, amounting almost to identity, between the ethics of Theosophy and those of the religion of Buddha.

ENQ. Are there any great points of difference?
THEO. One great distinction between Theosophy and exoteric Buddhism is that the latter, represented by the Southern Church, entirely denies (a) the existence of any Deity, and (b) any conscious post-mortem life, or even any self-conscious surviving individuality in man. Such at least is the teaching of the Siamese sect, now considered as the purest form of exoteric Buddhism. And it is so, if we refer only to Buddha's public teachings; the reason for such reticence on his part I will give further on. But the schools of the Northern Buddhist Church, established in those countries to which his initiated Arhats retired after the Master's death, teach all that is now called Theosophical doctrines, because they form part of the knowledge of the initiates – thus proving how the truth has been sacrificed to the dead-letter by the too-zealous orthodoxy of Southern Buddhism. But how much grander and more noble, more philosophical and scientific, even in its dead-letter, is this teaching than that of any other Church or religion. Yet Theosophy is not Buddhism.

H. P. Blavatsky, The Key to Theosophy

7 WORSHIP

MEETINGS HELD BY THEOSOPHISTS
Theosophists do not hold worship services. Their meetings typically consist of a talk followed by discussion or the study of a topic.

Theosophy has no developed rituals, although meetings may be opened and closed by brief meditations or the recitation of short texts, and some groups use a simple ceremony for welcoming new members.

CLERGY
There are no clergy or leaders, other than democratically chosen officers.

8 QUOTATIONS

Theosophy is a fragment of the ancient, once universal, wisdom teaching.

Reed Carson

The kosmical universe

Theosophy: A compound Greek word: *theos*, a "divine being, a "god;" *sophia*, "wisdom;" hence divine wisdom. Theosophy is the majestic wisdom-religion of the archaic ages and is as old as thinking man. It was delivered to the first human protoplasts, the first thinking human beings on this earth, by highly intelligent spiritual entities from superior spheres. This ancient doctrine, this esoteric system, has been passed down from guardians to guardians to guardians through innumerable generations until our own time. Furthermore, portions of this original and majestic system have been given out at various periods of time to various races in various parts of the world by those guardians when humanity stood in need of such extension and elaboration of spiritual and intellectual thought.

Theosophy is not a syncretistic philosophy-religion-science, a system of thought or belief which has been put together piecemeal and consisting of parts or portions taken by some great mind from other various religions or philosophies. This idea is false. On the contrary, theosophy is that single system or systematic formulation of the facts of visible and invisible nature which, as expressed through the illuminated human mind, takes the apparently separate forms of science and of philosophy and of religion. We may likewise describe theosophy to be the formulation in human language of the nature, structure, origin, destiny, and operations of the kosmical universe and of the multitudes of beings which infill it.

G. de Purucker, Occult Glossary, TUP, 2nd ed., 1996, pp. 176-7

Ocean of knowledge

Theosophy is that ocean of knowledge which spreads from shore to shore of the evolution of sentient beings; unfathomable in its deepest parts, it gives the greatest minds their fullest scope, yet, shallow enough at its shores, it will not overwhelm the understanding of a child. . . . Embracing both the scientific and the religious, Theosophy is a scientific religion and a religious science.

It is not a belief or dogma formulated or invented by man, but is a knowledge of the laws which govern the evolution of the physical, astral, psychical, and intellectual constituents of nature and of man.

W. Q. Judge, The Ocean of Theosophy, 1893

Archaic Wisdom-Religion

Theosophy is . . . the archaic Wisdom-Religion, the esoteric doctrine once known in every ancient country having claims to civilization.

H. P. Blavatsky, Collected Writings, 2:89

Divine ethics

[It is] the substratum and basis of all the world-religions and philosophies, taught and practiced by a few elect ever since man became a thinking being. In its practical bearing, Theosophy is purely divine ethics.

H. P. Blavatsky, Theosophical Glossary

Universal brotherhood

Theosophy, broadly stated, is Universal Brotherhood . . . the effort to convert our lower nature into higher nature, and thus to aid in the great process of evolution going on throughout the macrocosm.

W. Q. Judge, Echoes of the Orient

Truth, love, wisdom

Theosophy is the shoreless ocean of universal truth, love, and wisdom, reflecting its radiance on the earth, while the Theosophical Society is only a visible bubble on that reflection. Theosophy is divine nature, visible and invisible, and its Society human nature trying to ascend to its divine parent. Theosophy, finally, is the fixed eternal sun, and its Society the evanescent comet trying to settle in an orbit to become a planet, ever revolving within the attraction of the sun of truth. It was formed to assist in showing to men that such a thing as Theosophy exists, and to help them to ascend towards it by studying and assimilating its eternal verities.

Theosophy, on earth, is like the white ray of the spectrum, and every religion only one of the seven prismatic colors. Ignoring all the others, and cursing them as false, every special colored ray claims not only priority, but to be that white ray itself, and anathematizes even its own tints from light to dark, as heresies. Yet, as the sun of truth rises higher and higher on the horizon of man's perceptions, and each colored ray gradually fades out until it is finally re-absorbed in its turn, humanity will at last be cursed no longer with artificial polarizations, but will find itself bathing in the pure colorless sunlight of eternal truth. And this will be Theosophia.

H. P. Blavatsky, The Key to Theosophy,
1889, Key 57-8

T.S.'s duty

It is the duty of the T.S. to continue to be the Leader in the thoughts of men, to carry on the work which H.P.B. did, and to keep the link with the Lodge unbroken. H. P. B. did what she had to do; and what we are doing is merely carrying on the same building of the Temple of Truth in which, so it is hoped, will live as realities for ages the living spirit of love and wisdom, the new religion of mankind.

[A] new era, psychical and physical, is opening for mankind. Great events are in the making today. There will soon be a need for men and women of outstanding spiritual power and of intellectual force, and the Masters are preparing for this need. The teachings that you have been receiving are such as have not been divulged for tens of thousands of years in the past, except under the most stringent and rigid conditions . . .

The first rule of chelaship is 'To live to benefit mankind,' combined with a pure life, a clean heart, an eager intellect, an unveiled spiritual perception. Where these are, there you will find the Masters with you.

G. de Purucke, Esoteric Teachings, *PLP,*
1987, 2:102-3, 108

Christian evaluation

When Theosophy beliefs are examined, we discover the whole Theosophical system is contrary to Christianity. There is, therefore, no possibility of reconciliation between the two, since the followers of Theosophy extol Buddhist and Brahmanic theories, and Christians follow Jesus Christ alone.

Josh McDowell, Handbook of
Today's Religions

TRANSCENDENTAL MEDITATION

CONTENTS

1 An overview   651

2 Founder   652

3 Transcendental Meditation's holy book   652

4 Facts and figures   652

5 Transcendental Meditation's practices   653

6 Transcendental Meditation's beliefs   654

7 The Bible and meditation   654

8 Christian evaluation   655

1 An overview

SUMMARY

Transcendental Meditation opens the awareness to the infinite reservoir of energy, creativity, and intelligence that lies deep within everyone. By enlivening this most basic level of life, Transcendental Meditation is that one simple procedure which can raise the life of every individual and every society to its full dignity, in which problems are absent and perfect health, happiness, and a rapid pace of progress are the natural features of life.

Maharishi

Factfile
- Date of origin: 1955
- Founder: Maharishi Mahesh Yogi
- Holy book: TM, officially, has no one holy book
- Number of adherents: Claims 5 million followers

OTHER NAMES

- World Plan Executive Council
- Natural Law Party
- Society for Creative Intelligence

2 FOUNDER

HISTORY

Guru Maharishi Mahest Yogi was born in 1911 as Mahesh Brasad Warma, at Jabalpur, India.

In 1957, at the end of a major "festival of spiritual luminaries" in remembrance of the previous Shankaracharya of the North, Swami Brahmananda Saraswati, his disciple Maharishi ("great sage") Mahesh Yogi (now usually called Maharishi) inaugurated a "movement to spiritually regenerate the world." That was the formal beginning of TM, and from that point it spread all over the world.

In the movement's initial stages, Maharishi emphasized the religious aspects of TM and operated under the auspices of an organization named the *Spiritual Regeneration Movement*. However, in the 1970's the requirements of the West made him adopt a more secular approach. He focused on western science both to show theoretical parallels with his thinking and to give practical verification of the results of TM. The main emphasis was on relaxation, relief from stress, and improved personal effectiveness.

The TM movement became the largest and fastest growing of the various Eastern spiritual disciplines that have taken root in the West.

3 TRANSCENDENTAL MEDITATION'S HOLY BOOK

Transcendental Meditation denies reliance on any religious book, but it does recommend that advanced courses of TM use the *Bhagavad Gita* and *Rig Veda*, Hindu holy scriptures.

4 FACTS AND FIGURES

OFFICIAL PUBLICATIONS

- *Science of Being and Art of Living*
- Maharishi's *Absolute Theory of Defence*
- Maharishi's *Absolute Theory of Government*

POLITICAL ASPECTS OF TM

During the late 1970s Maharishi founded The World Government, with its sovereignty "in the domain of consciousness." The Natural Law political parties originated with Maharishi's decree that parties around the world should run for government, in order to inflict the natural law, which is defined by the "global consciousness."

TM INSTRUCTION CENTERS

There are over 1100 TM instruction centers located in 108 countries, including 145 centers in the United States.

5 Transcendental Meditation's practices

THE TRANSCENDENTAL MEDITATION PROGRAM

The Transcendental Meditation® (TM®) program of Maharishi Mahesh Yogi is the single most effective meditation technique available for gaining deep relaxation, eliminating stress, promoting health, increasing creativity and intelligence, and attaining inner happiness and fulfillment.

The Transcendental Meditation technique, practiced by 5 million people worldwide, is a simple, natural, effortless technique. The effectiveness of the Transcendental Meditation program has been validated by over 500 scientific studies at more than 200 independent research institutions in 30 countries. The Transcendental Meditation technique requires no belief or lifestyle change, is non-religious, is not time-consuming, and can be learned by anyone regardless of age or level of education.

The Transcendental Meditation technique must be learned from a qualified teacher of the Transcendental Meditation program. The technique cannot be learned from a book, video or audio tape.

Maharishi Vedic Education Development Corporation

ENLIGHTENMENT

Transcendental Meditation (TM®) is a set of Hindu meditation techniques introduced to the Western world by Maharishi Mahesh Yogi. TM claims to bring the practitioner to a special state of consciousness often characterized as "enlightenment" or "bliss." This state is reached by reciting a mantra.

TECHNIQUE

TM is to be practiced fifteen to twenty minutes twice daily while sitting comfortably in a chair. In essence, the TM technique comprises the silent mental repetition of a simple sound known as a mantra, allowing the repetition to become quieter and quieter, until it disappears and one is left conscious, but without thoughts. This is the goal of the inward stroke of meditation and is called pure consciousness. Together with the mind, the body has come to rest too, and starts to clear out "stress." This means bodily activity, and therefore also mental activity in the form of thoughts: the outward stroke of meditation. After the purification has finished, the inward stroke starts again.

STRESS

TM has defined stress as "structural or material impurities resulting from overload on the physiology," which includes both body and mind. The assumption is that it is possible to purify the physiology completely, and that that is the goal of human life, equal to gaining enlightenment.

THE MANTRA

According to the TM organization, the mantras comprise meaningless sounds specifically chosen to have a soothing effect upon the individual's nervous system. An examination of the full list of mantras issued by sources disassociated from the TM movement over the years reveals that each mantra names one of the Hindu gods.

6 TRANSCENDENTAL MEDITATION'S BELIEFS

By using the TM technique one is supposed to be able to "arrive at the source of all thought – transcending consciousness – the source of all creative processes."

TM claims to be unlike any other form of meditation in that the mind of the person meditating "transcends" physical boundaries to become one with the "creative force."

This communion with the "wellspring of life" leads to more productivity and better health through enlightenment.

TM claims to:

* reduce crime,
* promote peace,
* lower blood pressure and
* promote greater well being to the meditator.

---

7 THE BIBLE AND MEDITATION

The Bible recommends a form of meditation, but the meditation does not involve emptying the mind, which lays the mind open to occult influence, but, rather, the mind is to be focused on God and his teaching.

> This book of the law shall not depart out of thy mouth; but thou shalt meditate therein day and night, that thou mayest observe to do according to all that is written therein: for then thou shalt make thy way prosperous, and then thou shalt have good success.
>
> *Joshua 1:8*

> Blessed is the man that walketh not in the counsel of the ungodly, nor standeth in the way of sinners, nor sitteth in the seat of the scornful. But his delight is in the law of the LORD; and in his law doth he meditate day and night.
>
> *Psalm 1:1-2*

> I will meditate in thy precepts, and have respect unto thy ways.
>
> *Psalm 119:15*

> I remember the days of old; I meditate on all thy works; I muse on the work of thy hands.
>
> *Psalm 143:5*

8 CHRISTIAN EVALUATION

TM is often referred to in our culture as a relaxation "technique" that consists of controlled breathing, emptying one's mind of thoughts, repeating a mantra, sitting still in a certain position, among other things. In actuality, it is Hinduism and Eastern Mysticism repackaged for a Western culture as a methodology for relieving stress.

Christian Discipleship Ministry

It is clear that, within the TM movement, the idolatrous pagan rite of the Puja (contrary to Exodus 20:2–5), the failure to see, much less honor, the clear distinction between creature and Creator (contrary to Romans 1:25), and the assertion of the basic goodness of all men (contrary to Luke 11:13) are sufficient proof, but by no means are the only proof, in demonstrating TM's incompatibility with Christianity and its rejection of Christ as the true God, the true salvation and the true hope for mankind.

Marty Butz, Watchman Fellowship

Transcendental Meditation is a meditative technique taken from Hinduism by a Hindu guru named Maharishi Mahesh Yogi. He wanted to spread Hinduism to the west without people knowing it. So he took the Hindu meditative system and called it a "relaxation technique." It uses the names of the Hindu gods and demons from the Veda texts. (Although users are told this is a meaningless word) the practitioner repeated the word given him over and over till he reaches a altered state of consciousness.

To practice TM one must be initiated into it by a Hindu guru or holy man. The ceremony is called the *Puja*. Repeating the name of a Hindu god or demon over and over again until something happens is not some thing God would have us do. The advanced meditative technique, called

SIidhi, begins to yoke you with the Hindu god/demon and you begin to develop psychic powers. Supposedly the highest form of which is levitation.

Bible Facts

The "God" of the Maharishi is impersonal, as opposed to the God manifested in Christian revelation where God is a personal God who loves each human person in an intimate way.

By denying the Creator as Supreme and teaching that "All is One," Maharishi removes the distinction between the Creator and the creature. This directly leads to, or is an equivalent form of, pantheism.

The mantras given to the followers of the Maharishi have been discovered to be invocations, in most of the cases, to deities of the Hindu pantheon, thus in a real sense denying the oneness of God and fostering polytheism.

Jaime Cardinal Sin, Archbishop of Manila

Transcendental Meditation is in reality a form of pantheism. It does not teach the existence of one eternal, personal God, the Creator of the universe. It is part of the monist tradition in that it teaches belief in the essential oneness of all reality and therefore the possibility of man's unity with the divine. The practice of TM itself leads the meditator toward the idolatry of selfworship because of the identification of the self with the higher "Self" of the creation. In short, TM promotes an experience involving the loss of one's distinctive identity under the false pretense of a scientific technique.

R. M. Enroth,
Elwell Evangelical Dictionary

UNIFICATION CHURCH (MOONIES)

CONTENTS

1 An overview   659

2 Founder   660

3 Unification Church's holy book   660

4 Facts and figures   661

5 Unification Church's practices   662

6 Unification Church's beliefs   663

7 Worship   676

1 AN OVERVIEW

DEFINITION
The Unification Church is a cult founded and led by Sun Myung Moon who, claiming that Jesus failed, has declared himself to be the Messiah.

Factfile
- Date of origin: 1954
- Founder: Rev. Sun Myung Moon, 1920-
- Holy book: The Bible; *Divine Principles,* by Sun Myung Moon
- Number of adherents: 4.5 million

NAME
The full original name of the church is The Holy Spirit Association for the Unification of World Christianity, but in the 1980s and 1990s it began to change its name to The Family Federation for World Peace and Unification (nickname: "family fed"). For legal and public relations purposes, the group still uses the name Unification Church.

Members were initially dubbed "Moon Children" by the US media around 1973-1974, although this nickname was quickly shortened to "Moonies," a term now primarily used by critics.

OTHER NAMES USED
The Unification Church also use a wide variety of other names to promote their activities:

- The Holy Spirit Association
- Holy Spirit Association for the Unification of World Christianity
- The Unified Family
- International One World Crusade
- Interfaith Endeavor

CARP
CARP, the Collegiate Association for Research Principles, recruit on the campus of universities, without identifying themselves as Moonies.

CAUSA
CAUSA, the Confederation of Association for the Unity of Societies in America, work worldwide.

2 FOUNDER

HISTORY

According to Unification Church (UC) tradition, at Easter time in 1935, Jesus appeared to a fifteen-year-old Korean boy named Moon Yong-myung and asked the boy to help him with the accomplishment of the work left unfinished after his crucifixion. After a period of prayer and consideration, the boy accepted the mission, later changing his name to Sun Myung Moon.

After the end of World War II, Sun Myung Moon traveled as a preacher to North Korea, where, in 1946, he was imprisoned. He was liberated from prison, along with many North Koreans, by American forces during the Korean War.

The date commonly cited as the foundation of the organization is May 1, 1954. In was on this date, in Pusan, South Korea, that Moon founded the Holy Spirit Association for the Unification of World Christianity.

In 1958 Moon sent missionaries to Japan and in 1959 to America. Moon himself moved to the United States in 1971. The movement's presence was established first in San Francisco and then quickly spread to many of the nation's most populous cities.

LINKS WITH THE OCCULT

While Moon may claim to have received revelations from God, what is certain is that he has been involved in séances and other occult practices like clairvoyance, and trances.

TWO CONCLUSIONS

Although the Unification Church makes astounding claims for itself, the facts speak otherwise. The teaching of the *Divine Principle* is at odds with the Bible at all of its central points and therefore cannot be a completion of God's revelation. Moon has no messianic credentials and must be considered as a false prophet, of which Jesus warned us: 'Beware of false prophets, who come to you in sheep's clothing, but inwardly are ravenous wolves. You will know them by their fruits' (Matthew 7:15, 16 NASB).

Josh McDowell, Handbook of Today's Religions

Begin with a well-seasoned Taoist philosophy, add Christian words and phrases and some Bible verses, and stir briskly until they blend.

Now add a bit of spiritism, a pinch of numerology, a dab of physics and a dash of anti-communism; mix it all together, using a Korean Messiah, and you have the recipe for one of the newest religious movements sweeping America – the Unification Church, founded by Rev. Sun Myung Moon.

James Bjornstad, The Moon Is Not the Son *(Bethany Fellowship, 1976)*

3 UNIFICATION CHURCH'S HOLY BOOK

Two books are thought the be divinely inspired: the Bible, and *Divine Principles*, a 536-page book written by Sun Myung Moon.

Moon pays lip service to the Bible but feels free to interpret it as he pleases. For example, in *Divine Principle*s he states on page 9, that the Bible is "not the truth itself, but a textbook teaching the truth." It must not be regarded as "absolute in every detail."

4 FACTS AND FIGURES

CHURCH AFFILIATED ORGANIZATIONS

The Unification Church has established over 300 businesses and organizations throughout the world, including publishers, jewelers, and clothing stores. Some have been formed just to make money, while others are used to promote some aspect of the Unification Church.

THE WASHINGTON TIMES

The Washington Times, which is the largest conservative newspaper in the Washington, D.C. area, is owned by the Unification Church.

The following organizations are affiliated to the Unification Church:

• Tparents (True Parents)

Adam and Eve should have been the True Parents of humanity. A physical and spiritual ideal world (Kingdom of Heaven) should have stemmed from them. However, they fell by sexual sin.

Heavenly Father worked with fallen man to make a foundation to send a Second Adam, Jesus. Jesus, the Second Adam, should have fulfilled what Adam did not. Jesus should have grown to maturity, married a Second Eve, had children, and established a Kingdom of Heaven on Earth and in Heaven. However, he was not received by those prepared to welcome him, resulting in Jesus going the way of the cross. The cross gave spiritual salvation, but could not solve the entire problem of sin.

Since, Jesus could not fulfil his entire mission, Heavenly Father had to rebuild the foundation for True Parents, by sending the Third Adam, Sun Myung Moon. Rev. Moon fulfilled the mission of True Parents that Adam and Jesus had failed to fulfil. By uniting with Rev. and Mrs. Moon humanity can fulfil their purpose of creation and enter the Kingdom of Heaven both spiritually and physically.

True Parents Organization

• Summit Council for World Peace, committed to the ideal of a peaceful world.

• The Family Federation for World Peace and Unification for the promotion of family in the context of Unification thought.

• The Inter-Religious Federation For World Peace to promote world peace, including peace among nations as well as peace among religions.

• The Collegiate Association for the Research of the Principle, which is active on many college campuses worldwide. It is dedicated to "intercultural, interracial, and international cooperation and communication."

• Professors World Peace Academy, an organization affiliated with the Unification Church. It consists of academics in support of peace among peoples worldwide.

5 UNIFICATION CHURCH'S PRACTICES

OBEDIENCE TO THE TEACHING OF THE DIVINE PRINCIPLES

Members of the Unification Church are expected to:

- Commit their entire lives to the "establishment of Kingdom of Heaven on Earth" under Mr. and Mrs. Moon's (that is, "True Parents") dominion.

  This will eventually mean leaving school, job, family and friends, "raising funds" (by selling foil pictures, and flowers) and "witnessing" (recruiting new members) for sixteen to twenty hours per day, with only four to five hours' sleep.

- Get up every Sunday morning at five to bow to the picture of Mr. and Mrs. Moon, the "True Parents," pledging their lives to them with a Korean pledge.

- Accept Mr. Moon's choice of an "eternal" spouse – as he has already chosen thousands for others.

- Follow an appointed leader or "Central Figure" (CF) with absolute obedience – having to ask him for permission for almost everything, including permission to visit one's parents. Members will also be required to accept his scolding and disciplining if they do not accomplish the goals (for fundraising and witnessing) and directions he has given. Members have to fast and take cold showers.

- Members must disassociate from anybody and any source of information which is critical about Moon and his worldview –

because it is said that such people are "invaded by Satan."

ABSOLUTE SEX

The Unification Church uses the term "absolute sex" to refer to its teaching about sexual morality, which is essentially abstinence before marriage and fidelity thereafter.

MASS WEDDINGS

During the twentieth century, members of the Unification Church could marry only another member of the church.

Many members considered it the ultimate test of their faith to accept a match arranged by Moon. The church arranged increasingly large marriage blessings. In 2001, at Seoul's Chamsil Olympic stadium, Reverend Sun Myung Moon "matched and blessed" 20,000 new brides and bridegrooms, and saw 40,000 people renew their wedding vows. Church officials say the Rev Moon plans to "match and bless" some 400 million couples through future mass weddings.

RECRUITING TECHNIQUES

In the 1960s and 1970s, the Unification Church recruited vigorously in the US. In the process, they faced allegations of brainwashing, and deception. The appeal of the Moonies has been particularly to young people, who are drawn away from their parents and brainwashed into making money for the cult.

6 UNIFICATION CHURCH'S BELIEFS

A Jesus' failed mission
B Satan
C Prayer
D The principle of indemnity
E Messiah
F *Clouds of Witnesses: The Saints' Testimonies*

INTRODUCTION

The Church differentiates itself from traditional Christianity through its novel view of the Trinity and by its strong denial that Jesus' death was a preordained necessity. Like other traditional Christians, however, they do believe that his death serves as a redemption of humanity's sins and that his resurrection was a victory over death for all eternity.

A JESUS' FAILED MISSION

It is believed that the cross is the symbol of the defeat of Christianity.

God appointed Jesus to establish the kingdom of heaven on earth, preferably in his lifetime. But when the Jewish people refused to accept "him whom he had sent" (John 6:29), Jesus had to go the alternate course of dying on the cross.

With the mission of establishing his kingdom unfulfilled, God will appoint another Messiah to accomplish his purpose. "I have purposed, and I will do it. I have spoken, and I will bring it to pass." (Isaiah 46:11).

B SATAN

In the Last Days, Satan will be brought to repentance and become a good angel again.

C PRAYER

Mr. Moon states that prayers are to be made in the name of the True Father and the True Mother, namely Mr. Moon and his wife, who are also bearing "perfect children" to replace the twelve apostles.

D THE PRINCIPLE OF INDEMNITY

A little-known church teaching is that by willingly enduring mistreatment (the

principle of Indemnity), one can receive God's blessing. The principle apparently bore fruit in the 1980s, after Rev. Moon served 11 months of an 18-month sentence for what the church considers trumped-up charges of tax evasion and conspiracy to obstruct justice.

E MESSIAH

Moon claims to be the Messiah of the second coming. Moon's wife, Mrs. Hak Ja Han Moon, is the Holy Spirit. He and his wife are called The True Parents. Moon is the True Father and his wife the True Mother. They are the first couple to be able to bring forth children with no original sin.

Rev. Moon claims that thirty-six US presidents (speaking from "spirit world") have proclaimed him "Lord of the Second Advent, the Messiah, the Savior and True Parent of Humanity."

In 2002, the movement published a message which it says describes a conference at which all the historical founders of all other religions have recently, in heaven, proclaimed Moon's messiahship.

F *CLOUDS OF WITNESSES: THE SAINTS' TESTIMONIES*

Clouds of Witnesses: The Saints' Testimonies to the True Parents is a document published in 2002 by the Family Federation for World Peace and Unification (that is, the Unification Church) purportedly recording a ceremony in the spirit world that took place on the first Christmas of the new millennium. At this ceremony, representatives of the world's five major religions and several Communist leaders testified that Sun Myung Moon is the

Messiah and pledged to follow him. The document concluded with a letter from God in which he expresses his love for the Reverend Moon.

The Family Federation for World Peace and Unification made the following as an introduction to the document:

Clouds of Witnesses: The Saints' Testimonies to the True Parents

What follows is a complex document. It was produced at a seminar in spirit world for leaders of the five great religions. It includes testimonies to the True Parents, a letter from God, messages from four communist leaders, and a resolution written and adopted by the representatives of the five great religions.

To take this all in, we advise you to relax and open your mind for a while. If you believe in the existence of a higher dimension of reality, of God, of an invisible realm, this will call you to reflect on the implications of that belief. We believe in the spirit world and in the continuation of individual identity from this world to that one. All the passed-away saints are residing in spirit world. Since Jesus called him in 1935, the Reverend Sun Myung Moon has carried on a ministry to spirit world in parallel with his ministry on Earth. He has sought to gather the founders and saints of all faiths around one table of unity. In recent times, he has ministered to spirits in hell and opened the gates of their liberation. This collection of testimonies is one fruit of that ministry.

The Family Federation for World Peace and Unification is publishing this document throughout America and in 40 countries worldwide. This proclamation is our responsibility to let all humankind know the works of God in our age.

This message has significant practical as well as spiritual import. It is a unifying message, addressing believers of all faiths

as one global family. As such it is intended to draw all men and women to the one Holy God and help bring world peace. Peace will not arrive through politics or economic development alone, as crucial as these things are. The foundation for peace is common faith in God and practice of true parental, conjugal and familial love. Hence the value of True Parents, and the messianic power of their words and works.

A committee or coalition cannot instigate true love; the responsibility for this devolves to substantial human exemplars. The testimonies that follow bear witness that the Reverend and Mrs. Sun Myung Moon are those exemplars and have opened the gates for all people to inherit, through them, God's completed salvation, prophesied in all scriptures.

The testimonies appeal to Father Moon's teachings and works as the evidence of their veracity. We encourage the reader to move beyond these messages and duly pursue study of his teachings and works. Those of us who have followed Father Moon's leadership confirm the testimonies of the saints. We believe in God's work for world peace, to bring His kingdom upon the Earth and in Heaven. With that love and hope in our hearts, we recommend these messages to you.

The Editors, Family Federation for World Peace, International

Ceremony in spirit world for the adoption and proclamation of a written resolution by the representatives of the five great religions.

The written resolution of the representatives of the five great religions
- Christianity: Jesus and 12 other representatives
- Confucianism: Confucius and 12 other representatives (including 3 additional people)
- Buddhism: Buddha and 12 other representatives

- Islam: Muhammad and 12 other representatives
- Hinduism: Three people among the 12 representatives

This report was sent by Dr. Sang Hun Lee and received by reporter Mrs. Young Soon Kim, between December 19 and December 27, 2001, at the Asan Campus of Sun Moon University.

Ceremony in spirit world for the adoption and proclamation of a written resolution by representatives of the five great religions.

Order of the Ceremony
Date and time: Noon, December 25, 2001
Master of Ceremonies: Dr. Sang Hun Lee
Proclamation of the opening of the ceremony: We will now conduct the ceremony for the adoption and proclamation of a written resolution by the representatives of the five great religions.
Recitation of the Family Pledge
Proclamation of the written resolution (Jesus)
Representative prayer (Jesus)
Three cheers of victory, led by Muhammad – Victory for God, Victory for True Parents, Victory for the five great religions
The ceremony concluded with applause.

Seating Arrangement
The front seats were filled by the leading representatives of the five great religions. Behind the leading representatives, the 12 other representatives of each religion sat. In the back of the arena, 120 representatives from each religion sat.

Jesus' Prayer
"We of the five great religions, attending God above us and True Parents horizontally, pledge and proclaim that we will go the way of absolute obedience, in order to correct all of the wrongs committed throughout history.

"I report this in the name of Jesus, of a central blessed family. Amen, Amen, Amen."

The written resolution by representatives of the five great religions
We resolve and proclaim that God is the Parent of all humankind.
We resolve and proclaim that Reverend Sun Myung Moon is the Savior, Messiah, Second Coming and True Parent of all humanity.
We resolve and proclaim that the Unification Principle is a message of peace for the salvation of humanity and the gospel for the Completed Testament Age.
We resolve and proclaim that we will accomplish the peaceful unification of the cosmos through "living for others" while transcending religion, nationality and race, centering on true love.
The representatives of the five great religions resolve and proclaim that we will harmonize with one another, unite and move forward, in order to bring about the nation of God and world peace, while attending True Parents.
This has been resolved and proclaimed by Jesus, the leading representative of the group of representatives of the five great religions, Christianity, Confucianism, Buddhism, Islam and Hinduism, at noon on December 25, 2001.

Christianity
Jesus
Reverend Sun Myung Moon! Thou art the Second Coming who inaugurated the Completed Testament Age! The 120 people, who have brought light to the history of Christianity, pledge to take part in all that the True Parents do, and resolve to strive toward the ideal, the original garden where there is no original sin, through the guidance, the words of the Completed Testament, and the Unification Principle, of the Savior and Messiah, the Reverend Sun Myung Moon. (2001.12.19)

Peter (Disciple of Jesus)
I, Peter, representing the twelve disciples of Jesus, pledge to attend the Lord of the Second Coming, the Reverend Sun Myung Moon, as Messiah and Savior.

Paul (Missionary)
I, Paul, pledge to believe and attend the Lord of the Second Coming, the Reverend Sun Myung Moon, as Messiah, Savior and True Parent, with the fire I felt when I met the resurrected Jesus on the road to Damascus. I will live with the words, "You must save the saints" in my heart.

John Calvin (Religious Reformer)
God is the Parent of humankind and Reverend Sun Myung Moon is the Messiah, Savior and Second Coming. Therefore, I shall live by the teachings of the Lord, and I, John Calvin, pledge to become a pioneer in helping those who are still waiting for the Lord, who are in agony, following a theology of bigotry.

Martin Luther (Religious Reformer)
I believe that God is the Parent of humankind. I believe that Reverend Sun Myung Moon is the Lord of the Second Advent. I proudly proclaim that the Unification Principle is the new gospel for humanity. I, Martin Luther, pledge that I will believe in these truths, and live a life of attendance, to become a pioneer for humanity.

John Wesley (Missionary and Revivalist)
I, John Wesley, proclaim that Reverend Sun Myung Moon is the True Parent of all humankind and I pledge and pledge again to live according to the direction and teachings of the True Parents.

Karl Barth (Modern Theologian)
Dear Reverend Sun Myung Moon: Although I am late in doing so, I, Karl Barth, wish to live a life of attendance to, and receive guidance from, the Reverend Sun Myung Moon, who is the Second Coming and Savior. True Parents, I wish to receive the messianic teachings. Please guide me in this. I pledge to live in attendance to the True Parents.

David Livingston (Missionary to Africa)
Reverend Sun Myung Moon! O Second Coming of Christ! Dear True Parents, I, Livingston, wish to create a land of God's ideal, even if it is a modest place. Can you give me a place in which to do this? I pledge to live according to the guidance of the will of the Second Coming.

Jonathan Edwards (Leader of American Great Awakening)
Reverend Sun Myung Moon! Lord! I am so grateful to you. Please forgive and save America with the magnanimity of True Parents. America is God's Garden of Eden. Let it remain as the eternal Eden on earth. I know that the ideal of the Lord is that of God, and only Godism can save America. I, Jonathan Edwards, promise to never change my heart attending the Second Coming.

John Smyth (Founder of the Baptist Church)
O esteemed Reverend Sun Myung Moon! Please allow the grace of your blessing unto the whole of humanity, so that they may start a new life. Please open the way for humankind to be able to live together as brothers and sisters in a Garden of Eden without original sin as soon as possible. I, John Smyth, shall go anywhere, if the Lord goes with me.

John Harvard (Founder of Harvard University, Puritan)
I, John Harvard, truly wish that not only the youth of Harvard University, but those of all the universities in the world, can be armed with Unification Principle and receive the guidance of Reverend Sun Myung Moon. I pledge to participate actively in Reverend Sun Myung Moon's movement for world peace.

St. Augustine (Bishop of Hippo, who laid the cornerstone of Catholic theology)

I, Augustine, will move forward strongly in realizing the ideal of the Completed Testament Age, to allow all of humanity to have the Unification Principle as their truth and Reverend Sun Myung Moon as their Messiah. I respect, believe and depend on all the words and theology of Reverend Sun Myung Moon and I give my oath and pledge, raising my hands, to do all that I do together with the Lord.

Horace Underwood (American Presbyterian, first missionary to Korea)
I, Horace Underwood, joyfully celebrate the fact that the Second Coming has come to Korea, an eastern country that takes polite etiquette very seriously. I put my hands together and bow to the Messiah. I pledge and give my word of honor to devote all that I possess in attendance to the Reverend Sun Myung Moon.

Confucianism
Confucius
The 120 figures representing Confucianism pledge to accept the Unification Principle as the truth and to believe and attend the Reverend Sun Myung Moon as the Savior and Messiah in the Completed Testament Age.

Yeom, Baek Woo (who was outstanding in his virtue)
I give my oath that, centered on my teacher, Confucius, I will accept the Unification Principle as the truth and attend Reverend Sun Myung Moon as the True Parent.

Ja Ro (who developed the traditional Chinese political theory)
I will loyally follow the way of my master, Confucius.
Min, Ja Geon (who was outstanding in his virtue)
As I have followed the great Confucius throughout my life, I will trust and follow the way that he has now taken. Reverend Sun Myung Moon, True Parents, I will go the same way as my master. This I pledge.

Jae A (along with Ja Gong, this person is renowned for his oratory)
Reverend Sun Myung Moon! The True Parents of humankind! Following my teacher Confucius, I pledge to unite with the will of the True Parents of humankind.

Yeom Woo (who had political capability, along with many other talents)
I cheer the Reverend Sun Myung Moon! I cheer the True Parents of humankind! I cheer the Savior and Messiah! I, Yeom Woo, offer my pledge. I will believe and follow the Savior of the new age, who is the Second Coming of Christ, and proceed along this path with the great Confucius.
Chung Gong (renowned for his benevolence, great generosity and virtue)
I will follow the path that my master, Confucius, has taken.

An Yeon (an able disciple of Confucius' teachings, outstanding in his studiousness and virtue)
Until now, my teacher, Confucius, taught us disciples a way to attain virtue and to follow the true way of a scholar. Witnessing the fact that the Reverend Sun Myung Moon has guided my teacher to the correct way of truth, I, An Yeon, promise to believe and attend Reverend Sun Myung Moon as well.

Ja Gong (a great diplomat and political leader during the No and Wui dynasties of ancient China)
I, Ja Gong, believe that the Unification Principle is a great truth that can shake the soul of all of humanity. Therefore, I shall arm myself with the Unification Principle and guide Confucianists to a new and revolutionary path. And because our master, Confucius, came to save our souls, I resolve to become a part of the advance guard of the movement for unification, along with him.

Ja Ha (renowned for his fighting and literary abilities)

As my master, Confucius, humbly accepted and adopted this as the genuine truth, I, Ja Ha, pledge to be obedient to the way of the will of Reverend Sun Myung Moon as well.

Ja Yu (outstanding in literature, created a powerful school in the age of the civil wars)
Since this is the way that was chosen by my master, Confucius, I, Ja Yu, will also offer my undying passion in going this way.

Jeong Ja (leading theoretician of filial piety, self-cultivation and loving kindness in Confucianism. Compiled "The Great Learning," one of the Seven Chinese Classics)
I believe that the Unification Principle is a theory that can save all humanity, and that it surpasses the teachings, virtues and studies of my master, Confucius. Therefore, along with my master, I determine to receive the teachings of the Unification Principle and the guidance of Reverend Sun Myung Moon.

Ja Yu (an advocate of filial piety)
I was very moved and inspired by the fact that God, who created the entire universe and human beings, is the Parent of humankind. I respect Reverend Sun Myung Moon, who has revealed such a great truth. I am grateful to my master's loyalty and courageous decision. I wish to guide all Confucianists to this truth.

Ja Jang (an advocate of loyalty to and faith in one's king or ruler)
Even though I am a human being, I have found the genuine truth. Therefore, even if that way may be one of suffering and difficulty, I believe that following with an unchanging mind is the way of loyalty. So I pledge to Reverend Sun Myung Moon that I will share the suffering and joy of my teacher through following this path.

Mencius (who taught the divinity of human character):
If our Parent is God, then the natural way is to attend God. Therefore, I pledge that

I will live in attendance to the Reverend Sun Myung Moon, and that I will do this with unending passion. There is no greater truth than this.

Sun Ja (who taught the importance of education and propriety)
I think that the Unification Principle is a truth that can guide people on a clear road through life. Reverend Sun Myung Moon, I thank you and respect you. And I promise to dedicate myself to this great truth unconditionally.

Buddhism
Buddha: Reverend Sun Myung Moon! True Parents! The 120 people of Buddhism vow and pledge to advance toward a movement of peace that will guide humanity in a new direction. We pledge to attend God as the Parent of humankind and Reverend Sun Myung Moon as a True Parent, and to equip ourselves with the Unification Principle and Unification Thought. (2001.12.20)
Ven. Sariputa (One of Buddha's ten greatest disciples, who had outstanding wisdom):

True Parents, Reverend Sun Myung Moon: the twelve Buddhist representatives have resolved to dedicate themselves to your teachings. We respect the virtue and teachings of Buddha and think that the way of Buddha was the way of Heaven.

Mok, Keon Ryeon (One of Buddha's ten greatest disciples, who had outstanding divine power)
Because I believed in and attended the teachings of Buddha, I will proceed with a sincere heart. Reverend Sun Myung Moon, the Savior of the Completed Testament Age, I resolve to follow the way of God's will, along with Buddha.

Ven. Mahakassapa (One of Buddha's ten greatest disciples, who systematized the Buddhist faith)
I think that the Unification Principle and Unification Thought are great teachings,

not only for Buddhists, but for all of humankind. I pledge to harmonize the teachings of Buddha and the detailed teachings of the Unification Principle, to lift up the will of God, who is the Parent of humankind, and of the Reverend Sun Myung Moon, who is the True Parent.

Ven. Anuruddha (One of Buddha's ten greatest disciples)
Reverend Sun Myung Moon! I am sincerely grateful for your revelation of and guidance along the way toward the eternal future of humanity. I promise to pioneer a new way of life, along with Buddha, and to meet you in an eternal place.

Ven. Subhadda (One of Buddha's ten greatest disciples)
I give thanks to have lived in faith in and attendance to Buddha. I am now able to attend the Reverend Sun Myung Moon and study the Unification Principle. I am deeply grateful for this. I think that the way of truth lies in knowing that the true victor is the one who can win the battles that human beings must fight from the cradle to the grave. This is the fight within oneself. Now that I have encountered the wonderful Unification Principle, I resolve and pledge to make a new start following the guidance and teachings of my new teacher. I can now courageously put aside my old way of thinking.

Ven. Purna (One of Buddha's ten greatest disciples, the greatest Buddhist preacher)
Human beings' birth, life course and death proceed not according to human power but by the will of God. What a great teacher we have met, the one who has taught us about God and that God is our Parent! Reverend Sun Myung Moon, although we are small and insufficient, we of the Buddhist faith have resolved and pledged together, to lift up and attend the will of True Parents, while attending Buddha.

Ka, Jeon Yeon (One of Buddha's ten

greatest disciples, the greatest at debate)
There is a section of the Unification Principle entitled "Give and Take Action." I truly admire and am amazed by that content. The Unification Principle is organized perfectly; it is the truth that can save humankind. The theory of Give and Take Action seems at first glance to be commonplace, but it is actually a monumental truth. It contains deep and meaningful content that is essential for our following God's will. I think that the way of following Reverend Sun Myung Moon, who has revealed the Unification Principle, is the way of Heaven, and I promise that I will follow the way of Heaven.

Ven. Upali (One of Buddha's ten greatest disciples, the greatest observant of the Buddhist commandments)
Buddha has always been patient, and he has not just taught us but has shown us through his actions. The Unification Principle is very new to us, but since Buddha learned and experienced everything on his own before bringing it us, I cannot but absolutely believe in the Unification Principle. Reverend Sun Myung Moon is the True Parent and Messiah of humankind. I strongly resolve to believe and follow the Messiah. I will advance toward a world of peace centered on God, by going beyond all religious denominations.

Ven. Rahula (the son of Buddha, one of the ten greatest disciples, who was not known to be a disciple)
I, Rahula, think of Buddha not just as my father, but as the father of all of us, and I am grateful that I lived a life of asceticism. Now, I am grateful that Buddha has given me the opportunity to access the Unification Principle, which allows me to go the way to the eternal ideal of Heaven. I strongly resolve and pledge that we Buddhist disciples will unite centered on Godism, which can bring about an eternal world of peace for all humanity, while we attend Reverend Sun Myung Moon as our True Parent.

Ven. Ananda (a younger cousin of Buddha, one of the ten greatest disciples, the greatest in knowledge)
It is only natural to attend Reverend Sun Myung Moon as the Messiah of the Completed Testament Age, because all of the fundamental truths Buddha taught to us are found in the Unification Principle. I firmly believe that God is our vertical Parent, and I pledge from now to follow only one path.

Yong Su (who studied and developed Mahayana Buddhism)
I firmly believe that Reverend Sun Myung Moon is the True Parent, Messiah and Savior of humankind. And I believe that the Unification Principle is the truth that will save all of humanity. I resolve to stand in the forefront of a movement to bring unity centered on Godism, through overcoming the barriers that stand between religious denominations.

Se Chin (who helped expand the power of Mahayana Buddhism)
I believe that Reverend Sun Myung Moon, who revealed the Unification Principle on the earth, is the True Parent and Messiah. And I hope that the Unification Principle will be passed on to all the people of Buddhist faith. I firmly pledge to actively help in the movement for unification.

Islam
Muhammad
Since I, Muhammad, encountered the Unification Principle and met the Reverend Sun Myung Moon, my worldview has changed. I am now confident in everything. Everything seems new to me now. I am filled with optimism and hope. This is because I have come to know the fundamental will of God and that God is the Parent of humankind. I know now that this is the way I must go. The basic way of life is to live in attendance to our vertical and horizontal parents.

I cry out: Victory for God! Victory for Reverend Sun Myung Moon, the True Parent, Messiah and Savior! All Muslims follow the will of Muhammad. Allah, whom you have been following, was actually God, Jehovah. There is only one God for humankind and God is our Parent. I offer my pledge. I pledge to have faith in everything and follow the will of the Eternal God. (2001.12.26)

Abubakr (First Khalifa)
Allah is actually God. God and Allah are the same being. Reverend Sun Myung Moon has let the world know that God is the Parent of humankind. He is the True Parent of humankind. Through the Unification Principle, I have discovered truth that has moved me deeply. As Reverend Sun Myung Moon has let me realize the correct fundamentals of human life and the direction of history, I pledge to follow his way. Thank you.

Umar Bin Kha Pab (Second Khalifa)
Muhammad is more passionate and faithful than anyone else. As he introduced us to the Unification Principle, Unification Theology and Reverend Sun Myung Moon, he told us that if we believed in him this far, we should follow him until the end. Moreover, Unification Principle and Unification Theology moved me much more than the teachings of Muhammad did. When we realized that God is our Parent, it hurt us quite a lot. There is only one God called on by different religions, and His purpose is always exactly the same. I was surprised by the fact that religions have fought over small differences. Reverend Sun Myung Moon, I will go forward. I pledge to attend and to follow the will of the True Parent of all humankind.

Osman Bin Afan (Third Khalifa)
I have realized that even though the Unification Principle is new, it is a precious truth that can truly change and renew human beings. I sincerely realized God's pain as He waited for humanity for so long. Reverend Sun Myung Moon is

qualified to be the Messiah of the Completed Testament Age, and the True Parent of all humankind. I pledge to have faith in, and follow, this great teacher.

Ali Bin Abi Palib (Fourth Khalifa)
I wish to say, "Victory to Muhammad!" Because I followed Muhammad, I came to know the Unification Principle and was able to meet Reverend Sun Myung Moon. We are all grateful to both of these people. The Unification Principle provides very accurate and clear guidance for humanity. Muslims, your hard work and devotion have not been in vain. I desire that you receive the teachings of Reverend Sun Myung Moon. He is a great teacher, Messiah and Savior of the Completed Testament Age. He clearly directs humanity concerning the final problem of the afterlife. I desire that Muslims study Unification Principle. Reverend Sun Myung Moon, thank you for your hard work. I will believe in and follow True Parents.

Abdullah Bin Abbas (A scholar in the Age of Sahaba, who interpreted the Qur'an)
Muhammad has shown us great courage and passion. He did not allow us to be mistaken about God. I, Abdulla bin Abbas, will follow with total faith everything that Muhammad decides. And, although I have not heard the Unification Principle many times, I can say that it is very systematic and well-organized. I think its logical analysis touched Muhammad's mind. I also accept it and believe it. I pledge to work hard testifying to Muslims, while believing in the vertical God and the horizontal True Parents.

Abdullah Bin Masud (An interpreter of the Qur'an who lived in the days of Muhammad)
I believe that Unification Principle will move Muslims greatly. I desire that all Muslims take interest in the activities of Reverend Sun Myung Moon, who is the Savior and True Parent in the Completed Testament Age, and study Unification

Principle. Allah, whom we have attended thus far, is none other than God. The world is a wide place. Muslims, please try to broaden your conservative thinking and ideas. I will believe in and attend Reverend Sun Myung Moon, the True Parent of humankind, who revealed the Unification Principle.

Abi Bin Khab (An interpreter of the Qur'an, who lived in the days of Muhammad)
Reverend Sun Myung Moon! True Parents of all humanity! I believe in the Messiah, who is the Savior. I also have faith in the fact that the Unification Principle is an eye-opening truth that can guide the future of the world and the afterlife of all humanity. I will go forward believing in and attending the True Parents of humankind. This I pledge and swear.

Amu Hanifa (Founder of the Hanapi School)
Unification Principle is so moving. Words cannot express the greatness of its truth. It is definitely a revelation from God. Reverend Sun Myung Moon, True Parents, thank you for your hard work. As the future and afterlife of all of humanity has now been clearly revealed through Unification Principle, Earth and Heaven should be happy and cheer, "Victory! Victory!" I pledge to believe in and attend Reverend Sun Myung Moon.

Malikh Bin Anas (Founder of the Maliki School)
Muhammad did not persuade us. He did not even teach us the details of the Unification Principle. We were moved by the look in his eyes and quality of his actions, once he learned about the Unification Principle. Muhammad's courage and vision, manifested as if the whole world were his, moved us. I believe in Reverend Sun Myung Moon, the True Parent and Savior of humankind, and I believe that the Unification Principle is a revelation from God. We pledge to equip

ourselves with the Unification Principle and to follow unchangingly, actively supporting the work of the True Parents.

Ibn Idris Il-Shafi (Founder of the Shafi School)
The Unification Principle is an eye-opening gospel given to humankind. Reverend Sun Myung Moon, who has come as a True Parent! I'm sorry that I have not been given enough time to express how I am moved, but I am truly grateful to you. Without a revelation from God, the Unification Principle couldn't have appeared on the Earth. I firmly pledge to believe in and attend the Messiah in the Completed Testament Age.

Ahmad Bin Hanbal (Founder of the Hanballi School):
Reverend Sun Myung Moon, the Savior of humankind, thank you! Thank you for your hard work. The Unification Principle proves everything. I will believe in and attend you.

Al-Ashari (Founder of the Sunni branch)
I first would like to shout, "Victory to Muhammad!" Because of his having devoted all of his passion to Allah, he has been able to find the Unification Principle. Now, I hope that those of the Muslim faith will believe in and follow Muhammad until the end. The Unification Principle is not a theory that came from the brain of a person on Earth. It is the new gospel, which Reverend Sun Myung Moon revealed through revelations from God. Reverend Sun Myung Moon! True Parents! O Messiah, O Savior! Victory! Victory! Victory! I firmly resolve to go the way of loyalty and filial piety, while believing and attending the True Parents.

Hinduism
Three people from among the 12 representatives
Shankara (founder of the Advaita Vedanta)
I am very sorry to have to tell you my reflection on the Unification Principle after having listened to lectures for but a short period of time. I will try to make a worthy statement in the time given. Through this seminar, I newly realized the following: that God is the Parent of humankind, that in order to correct the deviated history, God sent providential central figures, that God sent the great teacher Reverend Sun Myung Moon as the Savior of humankind, and that the Unification Principle has been revealed as the new truth, to teach humankind the correct path. God! Reverend Sun Myung Moon!

Because Hinduism didn't know of the existence of the one God, our religious ceremonies were very complex, and as the ages and environments changed, our religion adopted various local and ethnic religious forms. However, the Hindu mind always desired to find an absolute being. Whether it is expressed through a local religion or a philosophical ideology, is not the desire to find God lodged within the original character of all human beings?

Through listening to the Unification Principle, I, Shankara, have clearly realized that God has been involved in the internal world of human beings. Now, since I know God's fundamental purpose, I have rid myself of all of my previous thoughts. I will organize all my thought patterns centered on Godism. And I will think over Reverend Sun Myung Moon's theory about how to save humanity, God's love, and the dispensational history of restoration. I will invest all that I have to go the way of genuine truth, while thinking carefully about everything I do. Reverend Moon! Thank you. It is a great honor that you have thought of the religion of Hinduism. As a representative of Hinduism, I pledge to become a pioneer in the unification movement.

Madwa (A pioneer of dualistic philosophy, who built the Temple of Krishna)
After listening to the Unification Principle, I realize that we have been

spending much time on things that are pointless. There exists a Creator, a causal being, but as humanity didn't know about the cause, neither could we know about the effect –this world. I, Madwa, am mortified that I spent so much time meditating and reasoning, when that was all pointless. Of what use are arguments over monism or dualism without the guidance originally intended for humankind?

O God! I, Madwa, have been able to find You. I did not even dream that You are the Parent of humankind. Although we lived wrongly, now that we have found the genuine truth in the eternal afterlife, we will be grateful to God and start our lives over. We will absolutely obey the guidance and teachings of Reverend Moon, who is a great leader, a great teacher and the True Parent.

Moreover, I, Madwa, will pour all my energy into completely understanding the Unification Principle. Thank you.

Maharishi Gautama (Founder of the Niyaya philosophy and the philosophy and practice of yoga)
I was severely shocked when I realized that God is the Parent of humankind. Even though there is an ideal place in which God and His children should have lived together from the time we were created, up until now, we have turned our face away from God and have created an unprincipled history. When I realize that we need to discard atheistic philosophy completely, my mind is so troubled, infinitely troubled. What can I do? There is no other way. I cannot explain how I feel. I am filled with regret, lamentation and nausea.

The Unification Principle gives us new hope. It is so clear. God did not create man and woman to be complicated. God gave humankind one correct way. I feel that after having floated in a sky endlessly, I have been rearranged and recreated as a new human being. This is not a time for lament and regret, but rather to have new hope and energy as I

attend Reverend Moon, whom God has sent as the Messiah. Therefore, I firmly offer my pledge.

Reverend Moon! Thank you for having called Hinduism. From the moment we encounter this new truth, Hindus will not live quietly. I firmly pledge to be obedient to God.

Communist Leaders
Karl Marx (1818-1883, The founder of Marxism; born in Trier, Germany.)
I, Marx, affirm God's existence and that He is the Parent of all humankind. I denied God and shouted loudly with confidence to the extent that people believed me more than God. Now I'd like to reveal my experience with God to the whole world. I felt that my theoretical paradigm was crumbling as I listened to the Godism lecture. At the same time my pride was damaged severely. When I listened to Godism, I thought it was a dream, but it was not. Then a beam of light came into my heart like a red-hot bullet.

I, Marx, have met God. I have found that He is the Parent of humankind. I have felt the greatness of God's love. I clearly convey to you who God is. He is the Parent of humankind. Reverend Sun Myung Moon, who is on the Earth, brought this fact to light. The Divine Principle and Unification Thought express the original standards that open the way to salvation, so you must read them. I ask this of you seriously. I clearly say that I apologize for my past to God and True Parents and love them and am proud of them.

Lenin (Vladimir Ilich Ulyanov; 1870-1924, The leader of the Russian Revolution, the October 1917 revolution, Chairman of The People's Commissariat.)
God certainly exists. He exists as the Parent of humankind. In spite of that, I put myself on the vanguard of Communist revolution with a sword in my hands, shouting out that there are no parents. I made their hearts ache.

I announce to Communists: God,

Jehovah, certainly exists and He is the Parent of humankind. The Communist counties will perish without fail. The ideal of Communism will be realized by its being engrafted upon Unification Thought. I have an earnest request for you. There is only one way for Communist countries to live and that is to follow Reverend Moon's guidance. Please study the Divine Principle in detail. Please receive the thought of Reverend Moon and study it deeply. If you do so, you will attend God more truly than the thinkers or politicians of the Free World. This is the only way to live truly. If you follow my words, it will release me from unimaginable suffering and agony. I beg this of you. Communist countries must re-arrange everything as soon as possible. I met God. The spirit doesn't die, but lives. This is my last wish, given in blood from the world of Heaven. "God is alive. God is the Parent of humankind."

Stalin (Joseph Vissarionovich Djugashvili, 1879-1953, Lenin's successor, who communized Russia.)
Friends in Communist countries, I am Stalin. You have had wrong thinking. As the way you are going is not the way you should go, you must turn to the right path as soon as possible. One's life on the Earth determines the place one will live in the heavenly world. Our beliefs are wrong. The worst of it is that we deny and ignore God, who is the origin of the cosmos. The God we denied is the Parent of humankind. God is not a theological existence, but is our Parent.

Those at whom we laughed live well in spirit world. It is certain that they didn't go to Hell. When we laughed at them, they and God loved us. We live in the bottom of Hell here. Do you understand what it means? People here don't treat each other as human beings, but as material. If there were any means to rid myself of this pain, I would do it. The place one dwells in the spirit world cannot be decided by power, honor or gold. It is

decided by the sincerity of your life on the Earth. First, know and believe God and attend Him. Second, completely clarify your way of life.

Please receive the will of Reverend Moon completely, open your minds and build churches for the worship of God and hold worship services. Reverend Moon reflects the image of God, even though he is a man, and he is struggling intensely to save Communist countries. His thought is messianic, especially for the Communist countries. You must receive his ideology of peace immediately. I, the dictator who denied God, cry out to all the Communist countries on the Earth. Please believe in God and seek for Him.

Deng Xiao Ping (1902-1997, the Chairman of Chinese Communist Party.)
Thanks be to God for forgiving the one who committed sin. Thank you Reverend Moon for working hard to save those in Hell and in the Communist bloc.

Friends in the Communist Party! The word that followed me was one that made God's heart bleed. I now know that I was a terrible sinner. Reverend Moon is the one who brought to light Unification Thought and the Divine Principle, and he is the father of humankind named as True Parent by God. Follow him and be guided by him. Communism has misled humankind. God exists as the Parent of humankind. We all became rebels against God. The spirits are destined to live here in the spirit world. There is no way for Communists to live, but by following Reverend Moon's guidance. This is my earnest wish and appeal.

A Letter From God
Dear Beloved True Parents, I am the God of all people. I am the God of all people. I am the God of all people. My beloved son. My beloved son. My beloved son, I, the God of all people, love True Parents! I love you greatly! I hold you dearly!

How could I help but feel happiness and gratitude for you, who are my son? If there were a word better than "love," I would like to borrow that verb, but I can't think of a better word. Although the True Parents reside in a deep place in my heart, I cannot adequately express my love for you in words.

As you, the True Parents, have now succeeded in everything and have raised everything to its true level, you are now the Savior, Messiah and King of Kings of all of humanity!!! Because on December 25, 2001, the Founders and representatives of Christianity and the other religions adopted written resolutions in which they without exception resolved to participate in realizing the peaceful unification of the cosmos, while attending the True Parents, it is right and proper that the True Parents are exalted in the position of True Parents of all humankind. I, the God of all people, desire this and want to see it happen. Despite the people of the world not yet fully understanding the position of True Parents, because the position should be fulfilled internally, I, the God of all people, invite the True Parents to the position of King of Kings.

Because the True Parents have, in my place, endured countless difficult paths, I now want to bestow upon you all of the gratitude, inspiration, excitement and joy that I have been feeling. I want you to inherit all that is mine.

My beloved True Parents! I have wanted to express my heart to you for a long time, but I have not had such an opportunity. However, now this daughter of mine has looked into my heart. This has allowed this time to come to pass, and I would like to express to you my gratitude.

True Parents! My beloved True Parents! I want to hold you in my bosom and not let you go! It is a waste for me to walk the floor with my two legs. I want to hold you all night and talk to you!

I, the God of all people, have faith. I believe in the True Parents. I know and remember all of the difficulties, pain and suffering that you have had to endure. I have seen it all. It was all my responsibility, yet you endured and raised a victorious standard. How can I ever forget you? I am grateful.

I am so happy because of you. Truly, I thank you for your hard work.

My beloved True Parents, victory to you! Victory to the Saviors of humanity! Victory to the King of Kings, True Parents!

I, the God of all people, sincerely convey this to my beloved True Parents.

The Family Federation for World Peace and Unification

7 WORSHIP

MASS WEDDING CEREMONIES

The Blessing or mass wedding ceremony is the most important Unification ritual. Rev. Moon matches up each couple a month (or less) in advance, selecting from among the membership.

A Holy Wine Ceremony is conducted before the marriage; this purifies the couple so that they are able to have children free of Fallen Nature (resulting from original sin inherited from Adam and Eve).

A special Three Day Ceremony is performed by the married couple some weeks after their wedding, before they engage in sexual activity.

PLEDGE SERVICE

A Pledge Service is celebrated at 5 am each Sunday, and on the first day of each month.

Seasonal days of celebration

- True God's Day,
- True Parents' Day,
- True Day of All Things.
- Chil Il Jeol: Declaration Day of God's Eternal Blessing
- True Children's Day
- Foundation Day for the nation of the Unified World

UNITY SCHOOL OF CHRISTIANITY

CONTENTS

1 An overview   679

2 Founder   679

3 Unity School of Christianity's holy book   680

4 Facts and figures   680

5 Unity School of Christianity practices   681

6 Unity School of Christianity beliefs   681

7 Christian evaluation   682

1 AN OVERVIEW

DEFINITION

Unity is a not-for-profit organization based on the teachings of Jesus and the healing power of prayer. It is a worldwide movement of prayer, publishing, and education that helps people of all faiths apply positive spiritual principles in their daily lives. We support all people in their individual quest to know God and find healing in their lives. Our philosophy offers a practical approach to Christianity and teaches that as children of God, we are heir to all that we need.

Unity

Factfile
- Date of origin: 1889
- Founder: Charles and Myrtle (d. 1931) Fillmore
- Holy book: The Bible
- Number of adherents: 1,100,000

---

2 FOUNDER

Unity was founded in 1889 in Kansas City, Missouri, by Charles and Myrtle Fillmore. After Mrs. Fillmore's remarkable healing using prayer and affirmations, many friends became interested in how she accomplished this healing. Unity grew from small prayer circles in living rooms to the worldwide movement it is today.

Unity

3 UNITY SCHOOL OF CHRISTIANITY'S HOLY BOOK

The Bible is the Unity School of Christianity's holy book.

---

4 FACTS AND FIGURES

PUBLISHING

Unity operates one of the largest religious publishing houses in the Midwest, offering hundreds of books, pamphlets, CDs, and tapes on a variety of spiritual subjects. Our Message of Hope literature is distributed to hospitals, prisons, nonprofit organizations, and the military. Unity also publishes two magazines to inspire and advance personal growth.

Unity

DAILY WORD

Daily Word is a monthly magazine of daily inspirational messages published in seven languages and distributed in 137 countries. It includes affirmations, prayers and a monthly calendar.

UNITY MAGAZINE

Unity Magazine is a bimonthly magazine comprising articles written to encourage spiritual education and development.

EDUCATION

Unity offer a variety of classes, workshops, and seminars designed to increase spiritual understanding and promote inner growth. Spiritual retreats are also offered throughout the year and are open to anyone who would like to attend.

UNITY INSTITUTE

Unity Institute (UI) offers a resident study program for adults. Classes in the Continuing Education Program may be taken by individuals interested in informal study for personal growth or by those seeking to become licensed Unity teachers. UI also conducts a two-year resident Ministerial Education Program for those preparing for ministry.

SILENT UNITY

Silent Unity, the prayer ministry of Unity, responds to nearly two million requests from people who write, call, or e-mail for prayer support throughout the year. A vigil of prayer is maintained in Silent Unity around the clock to pray for those who request prayer.

5 Unity School of Christianity practices

Followers of the Unity School of Christianity are encouraged to remain in and practice their respective religions.

---

6 Unity School of Christianity beliefs

DENIALS
The Unity School of Christianity:

- denies the Trinity
- denies the deity of Jesus
- denies the personality of the Holy Spirit
- denies the necessity of the atonement of Jesus for our sins
- denies heaven
- denies hell
- denies sin
- denies the existence of the devil.

AFFIRMATIONS
The Unity School of Christianity:

- affirms that God is a divine universal consciousness
- affirms reincarnation
- affirms that humankind is part of divine consciousness
- affirms that humankind is divine.

HEIRS TO DIVINE NATURE
The main purpose of Unity School of Christianity is to enable people to become the heir to their true divine nature. "We see the good in all religions and we want everyone to feel free to find the Truth for himself wherever may be led to find it" (*Modern Thought*, 1889, p. 42).

SALVATION
Unity teaches that as we discover pure divine nature, we can raise our inner being until we are fully God-realized. Once we have reached this state, we are said to be in perfect oneness with God and do not need further redemption. We are now divine. It is the potential of every man and woman to become a "Christ." J. Sig Paulson, an author in Unity magazine wrote: "Each individual has within himself the Christ potential, the Christ presence, the Christ reality."

JESUS
According to Unity School of Christianity, Jesus was only a man who attained a higher mental state.

GOD
There is no belief in a personal God.

> We must relieve our minds of a personal God ruling over us….God is not person but Principle.
>
> *Charles Fillmore,*
> Dynamics for Living, *p. 30*

REINCARNATION

> We believe that the dissolution of spirit, soul and body, caused by death, is annulled by rebirth of the same spirit and soul in another body here on earth. We believe the repeated incarnations of man to be a merciful provision of our loving Father to the end that all may have the opportunity to attain immortality through regeneration, as did Jesus.
>
> *Article 22 of the Unity Statement of Faith*

7 CHRISTIAN EVALUATION

The Unity School of Christianity is a classic new age cult. It has the appearance of being Christian; however, it holds pantheistic or new age beliefs at its core. Unity was founded by Charles and Myrtle Fillmore in 1889, and was later incorporated as a church in 1903 by the Unity Society of Practical Christianity in Kansas City. Unity is best known by its publication The Daily Word, used by many who are unaware of its doctrinal positions.

Russ Wise

Unity uses the Bible and Jesus when it suits its needs but is not faithful to the biblical revelation of who and what God is, what Jesus has done, and the nature of the Trinity and salvation. It is a dangerous non-Christian cult that should be avoided.

Christian Apologetics and Research Ministry

THE WAY INTERNATIONAL

CONTENTS

1 An overview   685

2 Founder   686

3 The Way International's holy book   687

4 Facts and figures   687

5 The Way International's practices   688

6 The Way International's beliefs   688

7 Worship   689

1 AN OVERVIEW

DEFINITION

The Way is a worldwide, nondenominational Biblical research, teaching, and fellowship ministry headquartered in rural Ohio. It is designed to teach those who are hungering and thirsting for the truth how to understand the Bible.

The Way International

Factfile
- Date of origin: 1942
- Founder: Victor Paul Wierwille, 1916-1985
- Holy book: The Bible, excluding the Old Testament and the Gospels, as interpreted by Wierwille
- Number of adherents: 120,000

NAMES
The organization is known by a number of names:

- The Way
- The Way International
- The Way International Biblical Research and Teaching Institute
- PFAL course (Power for Abundant Living)

2 FOUNDER

WIERWILLE'S CALL

Victor Wierwille believes that he heard God speaking to him in 1942. It was revealed to him that he would teach and interpret the Bible in a new way, in the way that the first apostles of Jesus did in the Acts of the Apostles.

"He spoke to me audibly, just like I am talking to you now," says Wierwille in a biography written about him. "He said he would teach me the Word as it had not been known since the first century, if I would teach it to others."

In 1953, Wierwille began teaching "Power For Abundant Living" (PFAL) classes, which evolved into a thirty-six-hour taped introductory course to The Way.

In 1957 Wierwille resigned from being a pastor in the United Church of Christ and started a radio program, the "Vesper Chimes" As he preached about his "revelations" people started to follow his new teachings.

WIERWILLE'S DEATH

The Certificate of Death filed with the Ohio Department of Health states that the immediate cause of Wierville's death was metastatic liver cancer which set in a month before his death. His illness had begun with eye cancer about 18 months earlier, which then spread to his liver.

Most public figures publicly announce significant illnesses which affect their work. Wierwille's illnesses, however, were not publicly announced.

WIERVILLE'S TEACHING ON SICKNESS

Wierwille taught that people's own negative believing (fear) make and keep them sick. He wrote

> If one is afraid of a disease, he will manifest that disease because the law is that what one believes (in this case, what he believes negatively), he is going to receive . . . Today I have no fear within me

> . . . fear always defeats the promises of God.
>
> Power for Abundant Living, *pages 38, 53*

> . . . we do not limit God, then we will not talk about worry, fear, anxiety, sickness and want. We forget those negatives for we are sons by the One who overcame. If you doubt your recovery from sickness, you will by all means slow up and retard your own progress. If you doubt its success, you have, by your own believing, determined its unsuccessful outcome.
>
> The Bible Tells Me So

> We may at times have diseases, but these should not linger. When we say "I believe God's Word" and really believe it, we come out the victor. The prosperity of your substance and health is dependent upon how much our minds are renewed to what God's Word says.
>
> God's Magnified Word

According to Wierwille's own teachings, from his prolonged fatal illness, it is possible to conclude that he:

- had cancer because he feared (negatively believed for) cancer
- defeated God's promises about healing by his own fear
- could not be healed by God because of his unbelief
- limited God and could not forget sickness
- doubted, and therefore retarded, his recovery from cancer
- determined his own continued illness and death by his own believing
- did not have health because his mind was not renewed by the teaching of God's Word
- accepted the Devil's lie, thereby causing his own disease.

If one accepted Wierwille's teaching the conclusion is that he caused his own cancer, prevented his own healing, and died because of his own negative believing and lack of the renewed mind.

After Wierwille died in 1985, the membership of Way International fell from an estimated 100,000 to 20,000.

L. CRAIG MARTINDALE

In 1982 Wierwille passed leadership to L. Craig Martindale.

PRESENT PRESIDENT

The present president of The Way International is Rev. Rosalie F. Rivenbark.

3 THE WAY INTERNATIONAL'S HOLY BOOK

The Way claims the Bible as their final authority. However, in practice, Wierwille's interpretations of the Bible became the final authority.

Wierwille claimed that he had had special revelation from God, and as a result taught the only "pure and correct" interpretation of the Bible since the first century. He also once wrote: "The Bible as a whole is not relevant to all people of all times." He went as far as rejecting most of the Old Testament.

4 FACTS AND FIGURES

HEADQUARTERS

The headquarters is just outside of New Knoxville, Ohio.

FELLOWSHIPS

There are fellowships throughout the United States and in forty countries and two U.S. territories.

THE WAY INTERNATIONAL GROUPS

Prominent splinter groups of Way International are:

- Christian Educational Service (CES) led by John Lynn

- Pacific West Fellowship
- Great Lakes Fellowship
- The Way of Great Britain headed by Chris Geer.

OFFICIAL PUBLICATIONS

- *The Way Magazine*
- *Jesus Christ is Not God*
- *The Bible Tells Me So*
- *God's Magnified Word*
- *The Word's Way*
- *The Rise and Expansion of the Church*

5 THE WAY INTERNATIONAL'S PRACTICES

INTRODUCTION

Biblical research, teaching, and fellowship is our ministry, and with it come a myriad of supporting responsibilities to see that God's Word prevails in our day and time.

The Way International

BIBLICAL RESEARCH

There are many keys to Biblical research that will unlock the door to the accuracy of God's Word – for example, learning about Eastern manners and customs, identifying and understanding figures of speech, and knowing how to find the accuracy of the Hebrew, Greek, and Aramaic texts.

Our ministry provides these keys for those who want to know.

The Way International

---

6 THE WAY INTERNATIONAL'S BELIEFS

The Way International denies:

- the doctrine of the Trinity
- the deity of Jesus
- the personhood and deity of the Holy Spirit
- salvation by grace
- the Jewish Holocaust

THE HOLY SPIRIT

There is a distinction between the Holy Spirit and the holy spirit. It teaches that the Holy Spirit is the same thing as the God the Father and that the holy spirit is different, a mere power from God.

JESUS

Jesus was not born of a virgin, and he is not and was not God. Further, Jesus Christ is not eternal and did not exist before the creation of the world.

We, as well as Jesus Christ, were with God in His foreknowledge, but not in existence, before the world began. Neither was Jesus Christ.

Wierville, Jesus Christ Is Not God

Before conception in Mary's womb, Jesus did not exist, except in the mind of God. At his conception, "Jesus Christ the Son of God, was made by God." (*Jesus Christ Is Not God*)

TONGUES

Way International expects all its members to speak in tongues every day:

There's no one I can't lead into speaking in tongues if they are Christian and want to do it.

The Way: Living in Love

7 WORSHIP

FELLOWSHIP
The Way International seeks to be primarily a home fellowship ministry.

The life of our ministry is at the home fellowship level. The "church" – the called-out body of believers – meets together in private homes for supervised fellowships, which include a short, positive teaching from the Bible, words of edification and comfort, prayer, and singing. In our fellowships The Way Ministry teaches what we have researched in our over sixty-year history.

The Way International

"THE WAY IS NOT A CHURCH"
Although The Way holds services, commissions missionaries, performs weddings, and other functions associated with Churches, The Way does not consider itself to be a religion or a church.

The Way International is a biblical research and teaching organization concerned with . . . the inherent accuracy of the Word of God . . . The Way is not a church, nor is it a denomination or a religious sect of any sort.

This Is The Way

ORGANIZATION
Wierwille patterned the organization of The Way on the structure of a tree. Individuals are Leaves, local home fellowships are Twigs, state advisers are Limb Co-ordinators, and the headquarters is the Root.

Twigs generally meet twice during the week and on Sunday mornings to sing, pray and listen to teaching tapes by Wierwille.

PART THREE

OTHER TRAILS

INTRODUCTION

Due to controversies that are associated with Freemasonry, The Seventh Day Adventist Church, and The Worldwide Church of God, *The Encyclopedia of World Religions, Cults, and the Occult* has chosen to list these organizations in a miscellaneous category titled "Other Trails."

Many evangelical Christians now consider the Seventh Day Adventist Church (SDA) to be a Christian denomination with some heterodox beliefs. The Worldwide Church of God was once considered by many to be a cult, but due to a dramatic transformation in its leadership and doctrinal beliefs, many evangelical Christians have an increasingly favorable opinion of the Worldwide Church of God today. Controversy has surrounded Freemasonry for centuries, and much of the debate centers on whether Freemasonry is a suitable organization for Christians.

FREEMASONRY

CONTENTS

1 An overview 695

2 Founder 696

3 Freemasonry's holy book 697

4 Facts and figures 700

5 Freemasonry practices 701

6 Freemasonry beliefs 702

7 Worship 703

8 Quotations 704

1 AN OVERVIEW

DEFINITION

Freemasonry has called itself "a peculiar system of morality veiled in allegory and illustrated by symbols."

Factfile
- Date of origin: Unknown
- Founder: Unknown
- Holy book: *Landmarks*
- Number of adherents: 5 million members of Lodges

SUMMARY

Freemasonry claims to be the oldest and largest fraternity known. It is based on the belief that each man has a responsibility to improve himself and help make the world a better place. Much debate continues to swirl around whether Freemasonry is seen as a primarily religious or social organisation.

Its members are joined together by shared ideals of both a moral and metaphysical nature, and, in most of its branches, by a common belief in a Supreme Being. Freemasonry is an esoteric art in that certain aspects of its internal work are not generally revealed to the public.

2 FOUNDER

ORIGINS

The origins of Freemasonry are shrouded in mystery. Freemasonry has been said to have come about as:

- an institutional outgrowth of the medieval guilds of stonemasons
- a direct descendant of the "Poor Fellow-Soldiers of Christ and the Temple of Solomon in Jerusalem" (the Knights Templar)
- an offshoot of the ancient Mystery schools.

Others claim that it dates back only to the late seventeenth century, and has no real connections at all to earlier organizations.

Much of this is highly speculative, and the precise origins of Freemasonry may be lost in history. It is unlikely that Freemasonry is a straightforward outgrowth of medieval guilds of stonemasons for stonemasons' guilds do not appear to predate reasonable estimates for the time of Freemasonry's origin. Also, stonemasons lived near their worksite and thus had no need for secret signs to identify themselves. Moreover, the "Ancient Charges" of Freemasonry are nonsensical when thought of as being rules for a stonemasons' guild.

POSSIBLE ORIGIN IN THE MIDDLE AGES

Freemasonry provided a haven for the unorthodox and their sympathizers during a time when such activity could result in one's death. This may account for the tradition of secret meetings and handshakes. As the Middle Ages gave way to the modern age, the need for secrecy subsided, and Freemasons began to openly declare their association with the fraternity, which began to organize itself more formally.

GRAND LODGES

In 1717, four Lodges, which met at the Apple-Tree Tavern, the Crown Ale-House near Drury Lane, the Goose and Gridiron in St. Paul's Churchyard, and the Rummer and Grapes Tavern in Westminster, in London, England combined together and formed the first public Grand Lodge, the Premier Grand Lodge of England (PGLE).

After this, Grand Lodges opened throughout Europe. The PGLE in the beginning did not have the current three degrees, but only the first two. The third degree appeared, so far as is known, around 1725.

3 FREEMASONRY'S HOLY BOOK

Though the King James Version of the Bible is on the altars at Masonic Lodges, Freemasonry is not based upon the Bible.

> Masonry has nothing to do with the Bible; it is not founded upon the Bible, for if it were, it would not be Masonry, it would be something else."
> *The Digest of Masonic Law, p. 207-209*

THE PRECEPTS OF FREEMASONRY: LANDMARKS

Landmarks are the ancient and unchangeable precepts of Masonry, the standards by which regularity of Lodges and Grand Lodges are judged.

1
The modes of recognition are, of all the Landmarks, the most legitimate and unquestioned. They admit of no variation.

2
The division of symbolic Freemasonry into three Degrees is a Landmark that has been better preserved than almost any other.

3
The Legend of the Third Degree is an important Landmark, the integrity of which has been well preserved. There is no Rite of Freemasonry, practiced in any country or in any language, in which the essential elements of this Legend are not taught. Any Rite which should exclude it, or materially alter it, would at once, by that exclusion or alternation cease to be a Masonic Rite.

4
The government of the Fraternity by a presiding officer called a Grand Master, who is elected from the body of the Craft, is a fourth Landmark. Many persons suppose that the election of a Grand Master is held in consequence of a law or regulation of a Grand Lodge. Such, however, is not the case. The office is indebted for its existence to a Landmark of the Order.

5
The prerogative of the Grand Master to preside over every Assembly of the Craft, wheresoever and whensoever held, is a fifth Landmark. It is in consequence of this Landward, derived from ancient usages, that the Grand Master assumes the chair at every Communication of a Grand Lodge; and that he is also entitled to preside at the communication of every subordinate Lodge where he may happen to be present.

6
The prerogative of the Grand Master to grant Dispensations for conferring Degrees at irregular times is another very important Landmark. The statutory law of Freemasonry requires a month, or other determinate period, to elapse between the presentation of a petition and the election of a candidate. But the Grand Master has the power to set aside or dispense with this probation, and to allow a candidate to be initiated at once. This prerogative he possessed before the enactment of the law requiring a probation, and as no statute can impair his prerogative, he still retains this power.

7
The prerogative of the Grand Master to give Dispensations for opening and holding Lodges is another Landmark. He may grant in virtue of this, to a sufficient number of Freemasons, the privilege of meeting together and conferring Degrees. The Lodges thus established are called Lodges Under Dispensation.

8
The prerogative of the Grand Master to make Freemasons at sight is an Ancient Landmark which is closely connected with the preceding one.

9

The necessity for Freemasons to congregate in Lodges is another Landmark. From time immemorial, the Landmarks of the Order always prescribed that Freemasons should, from time to time, congregate together for the purpose of either Operative or Speculative labor, and that these Congregations should be called Lodges. Formerly, these were extemporary meetings called together for special purposes, and then dissolved, the Brethren departing to meet again at other times and other places, according to the necessity of circumstances. But Warrants of Constitution, by-laws, and permanent officers are modern innovations wholly outside of the Landmarks, and dependent entirely on special enactments of a comparatively recent period.

10

The government of the Craft, when so congregated in a Lodge, by a Master and two Wardens is a Landmark. A Congregation of Freemasons meeting together under any other government, as that, for instance, of a president and vice-president, or a chairman and subchairman, would not be recognized as a Lodge. The presence of a Master and two Wardens is as essential to the valid organization of a Lodge as a Warrant of Constitution is at the present day. The names of these three officers vary in different languages; but the officers, their number, prerogatives, and duties are everywhere identical.

11

The necessity that every Lodge, when congregated, should be duly tiled, is an important Landmark of the Institution which is never neglected. The necessity of this law arises from the esoteric character of Freemasonry. The duty of guarding the door, and keeping off cowans and eavesdroppers, is an ancient one.

12

The right of every Freemason to be represented in all general meetings of the Craft, and to instruct his representatives, is a twelfth Landmark. Formerly, these general meetings, which were usually held once a year, were called General Assemblies, and all the Fraternity, even to the youngest Entered Apprentice, were permitted to be present. Now they are called Grand Lodges, and only the Masters and Wardens of the subordinate Lodges are summoned. But this is simply as the representatives of their members. Originally, each Freemason represented himself; now he is represented by the officers of his Lodge.

13

The right of every Freemason to appeal from the decision of his Brethren, in Lodge convened, to the Grand Lodge or General Assembly of Freemasons, is a Landmark highly essential to the preservation of justice, and the prevention of oppression.

14

The right of every Freemason to visit and sit in every regular Lodge is an unquestionable Landmark of the Order. This is called the Right of Visitation. This right of visitation has always been recognized as an inherent right which inures to every Freemason as he travels through the world. And this is because Lodges are justly considered as only divisions for convenience of the universal Masonic family.

15

It is a Landmark of the Order, that no visitor unknown to the Brethren present, or to some one of them as a Freemason, can enter a Lodge without first passing an examination according to ancient usage. If the visitor is known to any Brother present to be a Freemason in good standing, and if that Brother will vouch for his qualifications, the examination may be dispensed with, as the Landmark refers only to the cases of strangers, who are not to be recognized unless after strict trial, due examination or lawful information.

16

No Lodge can interfere in the business of another Lodge, nor give Degrees to Brethren who are members of other Lodges. This Landmark is founded on the great principles of courtesy and fraternal kindness, which are at the very foundation of our Institution.

17

It is a Landmark that every Freemason is amenable to the laws and regulations of the Masonic Jurisdiction in which he resides, and this although he may not be a member of any Lodge in that Jurisdiction.

18

Certain qualifications of candidates for initiation are derived from a Landmark of the Order. These qualifications are that he shall be a man, unmutilated, free born, and of mature age.

19

A belief in the existence of God as the Great Architect of the Universe, is one of the most important Landmarks of the Order. It has always been admitted that a denial of the existence of a Supreme and Superintending Power is an absolute disqualification for initiation. The annals of the Order never have furnished or could furnish an instance in which an avowed Athiest was ever made a Freemason. The very initiatory ceremonies of the First Degree forbid and prevent the possibility of such an occurrence.

20

Subsidiary to this belief in God, as a Landmark of the Order, is the belief in a resurrection to a future life.

21

It is a Landmark that a Book of the Law shall constitute an indispensable part of the furniture of every Lodge. It is not absolutely a requirement that the Old and New Testaments be used. The Book of the Law is that volume which, by the religion of the country, is believed to contain the

revealed will of the Great Architect of the Universe. Hence, in all Lodges in Christian countries, the Book of the Law is composed of the Old and New Testaments; in a country where Judaism is the prevailing faith, the Old Testament alone would be sufficient; and in a Mohammedan countries, and among Mohammedan Freemasons, the Koran may be substituted. Freemasonry does not attempt to interfere with the particular religious faith of its disciples, except so far as it relates to the belief in the existence of God, and what necessarily results from that belief. The Book of Law is to the Speculative Freemason his spiritual Trestleboard; without this he cannot labor; whatever he belies to be the revealed will of the Great Architect constitutes for him in his hours of speculative labor, to be the rule and guide of his conduct. The Landmark, therefore, requires that a Book of the Law, a religious code of some kind as the revealed will of God, shall form an essential part of the furniture of every Lodge.

22

The equality of all Freemasons is another Landmark of the Order. This equality has not reference to any subversion of those graduations of rank which have been instituted by the usages of society. The monarch, the nobleman and the common laborer are all equal within Freemasonry.

23

The secrecy of the Institution is another and most important Landmark. If the Institution were divest of its secret character, it would cease to be Freemasonry. This secrecy is based on the forms and modes of recognition so that one Freemason may know another.

24

The foundation of a Speculative Science upon an Operative Art, and the symbolic use and explanation of other terms of that art, for the purposes of religious or moral teaching constitute another Landmark of the Order. The Temple of Solomon is the symbolic cradle of the Institution, and, therefore, the reference to the Operative Masonry which constructed that magnificent edifice, to the materials and implements which were employed in its construction, and to the artists who were engaged in the building, are all component and essential parts of the body of Freemasonry, which could not be subtracted from it without an entire destruction of the whole identity of the Order.

25
The last and crowning Landmark of all is, that these Landmarks can never be changed. Nothing can be subtracted from them – nothing can be added to them – not the slightest modification can be made in them. As they were received from our predecessors, we are bound by the most solemn obligations of duty to transmit them to our successors.

Landmarks, Albert Mackey, 1858

4 FACTS AND FIGURES

OVERVIEW

Masonry exists in 164 countries, with 5 million members, 3 million of whom are in the US. There are 33,700 Lodges worldwide

MASONRY LODGES AROUND THE WORLD

Country	Number of Lodges	Members
USA	15,300	3 million
England	8,100	560,000
Canada	1,500	160,000
Australia	550	25,000
Italy	550	24,000
Germany	380	20,000
Cuba	280	18,000
Philippines	180	12,000

DONATIONS TO CHARITY

American Masonic Philanthropy gives away 1.5 million dollars every day. It has been estimated that Freemasons outside the U.S. give away 2 million dollars every day.

5 FREEMASONRY PRACTICES

A Masons of California
B Lodges

INTRODUCTION
Freemasonry upholds the principles of "Brotherly Love, Relief and Truth" (or, in France, "Liberty, Equality, Fraternity"). It claims to teach moral lessons through rituals. Members working through the rituals are taught by "degrees." Freemasons are also commonly involved in public service and charity work. Freemasonry provides a social outlet for masons.

A MASONS OF CALIFORNIA
The masons of California have made the following statement:

> As Masons, we lead by example, give back to our communities, and support numerous Masonic philanthropies. We invest in children, our neighborhoods, and our future.

Our values
The rich traditions and core values of our centuries-old fraternity are relevant today and will endure for centuries to come.

Ethics
Masons practice a lifestyle based on honor, integrity, and philanthropic values. Masons believe that things like honesty, compassion, trust, and knowledge are important.

Tolerance
The fraternity transcends religious, ethnic, cultural, social, and educational differences. We respect others' opinions and strive to grow and develop as human beings.

Personal growth
Our continuing pursuit of knowledge, ethics, and leadership skills makes us

better men and brings more meaning to our lives.

Philanthropy
We are committed to make a difference in our world through community service, volunteerism, and charity.

Family
Strong family relationships are important, and we include our families in many of our activities. Striving to be better husbands, fathers, and family members enhances our fellowship.

Masons of California

B LODGES
Contrary to popular belief, Freemasons meet *as* a Lodge and not *in* a lodge.

The ruling authority of a Masonic jurisdiction is usually called a Grand Lodge.

The oldest jurisdiction in the Anglo branch of Freemasonry is the Grand Lodge of England (GLE), founded in 1717. This later became the United Grand Lodge of England (UGLE) when it joined with another English Grand Lodge in 1813. Its headquarters are at Freemasons Hall, Great Queen Street, London.

MEMBERSHIP
Freemasons are expected to exhibit the utmost tolerance both in Lodge and in their daily lives. Freemasonry will thus accept members from almost any religion, including all denominations of Christianity, Judaism, Islam, and Buddhism.

To be a Freemason, one must:

- be a man, if joining the majority of Masonic jurisdictions, or a woman, if joining a jurisdiction with women's Lodges

- believe in a Supreme Being
- be at least the minimum age (18–25 years depending on the jurisdiction),
- be of sound mind, body and of good morals, and

- be free (or "born free," that is, not born a slave or bondsman).

Traditionally membership was limited to men only.

---

6 FREEMASONRY BELIEFS

INTRODUCTION

Critics of Freemasonry accuse it of being in essence a series of ritually systematic demonization procedures and of being a successor to the ancient mysteries religions: the secret worship rites of pagan gods. Supporters say this is paranoid, and they should be judged by the good works they do.

WORSHIPING GODS

Freemasonry acknowledges a series of gods to be worshiped:

G.A.O.T.U.	the Great Architect of the Universe
JAHBULON	a revelation of the real name of God
JAH	the God of the Israelites
BUL (Baal)	the god of the Syrians
ON	the Egyptian god OSIRIS of the underworld
AHURA-MAZDA	spirit of light, a nature god of Zoroastrianism worshiped in Persia (Iran) with fire
AUM of the Hindus	(Brahma – Vishna – Shiva).
ALLAH	God of Arabs, Muslims, and Mohammedans
LUCIFER	the devil, Satan

GOD

Humanity, "in-toto," then, is the only Personal God.

J. D. Buck, Mystic Masonry, *page 136, 32nd Degree*

7 WORSHIP

RITUAL AND SYMBOLS

The Freemasons rely heavily on the architectural symbolism of the medieval operative masons who actually worked in stone. One of their principal symbols is the square and compasses, tools of the trade, so arranged as to form a quadrilateral. The square is sometimes said to represent matter, and the compasses spirit or mind.

Alternatively, the square might be said to represent the world of the concrete, or the measure of objective reality, while the compasses represent abstraction, or subjective judgment. The compasses straddle the square, representing the interdependence between the two. In the space between the two, there is optionally placed a symbol of metaphysical significance. Sometimes, this is a blazing star or other symbol of Light, representing Truth or knowledge. Alternatively, there is often a letter G placed there, usually said to represent God and/or Geometry.

The square and compasses are displayed at all Masonic meetings, along with the open Volume of the Sacred Law (or Lore) (VSL). In English-speaking countries, this is usually a Holy Bible, but it can be whatever book(s) of inspiration or scripture that the members of a particular Lodge or jurisdiction feel they draw on – whether the Bible, the Qur'an, or other volumes.

Much of Masonic symbolism is mathematical in nature, and in particular geometrical, which is probably a reason why Freemasonry has attracted so many rationalists (such as Voltaire, Fichte, Goethe, George Washington, Benjamin Franklin, Mark Twain and many others).

In keeping with the geometrical and architectural theme of Freemasonry, the Supreme Being (or God, or Creative Principle) is sometimes also referred to in Masonic ritual as the Grand Geometer, or the Great Architect of the Universe (G.A.O.T.U.). Freemasons use a variety of labels for this concept in order to avoid the idea that they are talking about any one religion's particular God or God-like concept.

DEGREES

There are three initial degrees of Freemasonry:

*   Entered Apprentice
*   Fellow Craft
*   Master Mason

One works through each degree by taking part in a ritual, essentially a medieval morality play, in which one plays a role, along with members of the Lodge that one is joining. The setting is biblical – the building of the Temple of Solomon in Jerusalem – although the stories themselves are not directly from the Bible, and not intended to be necessarily Jewish or Christian in nature. Nothing supernatural happens in these stories. The Temple can be taken to represent the "temple" of the individual human being, that of the human community, or of the entire universe.

As one works through the degrees, one studies the lessons and interprets them for oneself. There are as many ways to interpret the rituals as there are Masons, and no Mason may dictate to any other Mason how he is to interpret them. No particular truths are espoused, but a common structure – speaking symbolically to universal human archetypes – provides for each Mason a means to come to his own answers to life's important questions. Freemasons working through the degrees are often (especially in Continental Europe) asked to prepare papers on related philosophical topics, and present lectures.

Mozart was a Freemason, and his opera, The Magic Flute, makes extensive use of Masonic symbolism.

8 QUOTATIONS

NEGATIVE

The greatest problem for the Christian Mason is that by taking the oaths of the Craft, and living his life according to them, he has opened the door to Lucifer to steal his relationship with the living God.

Ruth Wise, Probe Ministries

Freemasonry has tenets peculiar to itself. They serve as testmonials of character and qualifications, which are only conferred after due course of instruction and examination. These are of no small value; they speak a universal language, and act as a passport to the attentions and support of the initiated in all parts of the world. They cannot be lost as long as memory retains its power. Let the possessor of them be expatriated, shipwrecked or imprisoned, let him be stripped of everything he has got in the world, still those credentials remain, and are available for use as circumstances require. The good effects they have produced are established by the most incontestable facts of history. They have stayed the uplifted hand of the destroyer; they have softened the asperities of the tyrant; they have mitigated the horrors of captivity; they have subdued the rancour of malevolence; and broken down the barriers of political animosity and sectarian alienation. On the field of battle, in the solitudes of the uncultivated forest, or in the busy haunts of the crowded city, they have made men of the most hostile feelings, the most distant regions, and diversified conditions, rush to the aid of each other, and feel a special joy and satisfaction that they have been able to afford relief to a Brother Mason.

Benjamin Franklin

The very word "secrecy" is repugnant in a free and open society; and we are as a people inherently and historically opposed to secret societies, to secret oaths and to secret proceedings. We decided long ago that the dangers of excessive and unwarranted concealment of pertinent facts far outweighed the dangers, which are cited to justify it.

John F. Kennedy, April 27, 1961

I do not see how any Christian, most of all a Christian minister, can go into these lodges with unbelievers. They say they can have more influence for good, but I say they can have more influence for good by staying out of them and then reproving their evil deeds. You can never reform anything by unequally yoking yourself with ungodly men. True reformers separate themselves from the world. But, some say to me, if you talk that way you will drive all the members of secret societies out of your meetings and out of your churches. But what if I did? Better men will take their places. Give them the truth anyway and if they would rather leave their churches than their lodges, the sooner they get out of the churches the better. I would rather have ten members who are separated from the world than a thousand such members. Come out from the lodge. Better one with God than a thousand without Him. We must walk with God and if only one or two go with us, it is all right. Do not let down the standard to suit men who love their secret lodges or have some darling sin they will not give up.

Dwight L. Moody

We are now prepared to consider the question of the relation of Freemasonry to the Church of Christ. On this question I remark:

"God holds the church and every branch of it, responsible for its opinion and action in accordance with the best light, which, in his providence, is afforded them. . . If any particular branch of the church has better means of information, and therefore more light on moral questions, than another branch, its responsibility is greater, in proportion to its greater means of information. Such a branch of the church is bound to take a higher and more advanced position in Christian life and duty, to bear a fuller and lighter testimony against every form of iniquity, than that required by less favored and less informed branches of the church. They are not to wait till other branches of the church have received their light, before they bear a testimony and pursue a course in accordance with their own degree of information.

"While Masonry was a secret, the church had no light, and no responsibility respecting it. Although individual members of the church were Freemasons, as a body, she knew nothing of Masonry; therefore she could say nothing. . .

"But the state of the case is now greatly changed. Freemasonry is now revealed. It is no longer a secret to any who wish to be informed. . . . Now, since these revelations are made, and both the church and the world are aware of what Masonry really is, God demands, and the world has a right to expect, that the church will take due action and bear a truthful testimony in respect to this institution. She can not now innocently hold her peace. The light has come. Fidelity to God, and to the souls of men, require that the church, which is the light of the world, should speak out, and should take such action as will plainly reveal her views of the compatibility or incompatibility of Freemasonry with the Christian religion. As God's witnesses, as the pillar and ground of the truth, the church is bound to give the trumpet no uncertain sound, upon this question, that all men may know, whether, in her judgment, an intelligent embracing and determinate adhering to Freemasonry are compatible with a truthful profession of religion.

"Every local branch of the Church of Christ is bound to examine this subject, and pronounce upon this institution, according to the best light they can get. God does not allow individuals, or churches, to withhold action, and the expression of their opinion, until other churches are as enlightened as themselves. We are bound to act up to our own light, and to go as far in advance of others as we have better means of information than they. We have no right to say to God that we will act according to our own convictions, when others become so enlightened that our action will be popular and meet their approval.

"Again: Those individuals and churches, who have had the best means of information, owe it to other branches of the church, and to the whole world, to take action and to pronounce upon the unchristian character of Freemasonry, as the most influential means within their reach of arousing the whole church and the world to an examination of the character and claims of Freemasonry. If churches who are known to have examined the subject withhold their testimony; if they continue to receive persistent and intelligent Freemasons; if they leave the public to infer that they see nothing in Freemasonry inconsistent with a creditable profession of the Christian religion, it will justly be inferred by other branches of the church, and by the world, that there is nothing in it so bad, so dangerous and unchristian as to call for their examination, action, or testimony. Before the publishing of Morgan's book, the Baptist denomination, especially, in that part of the country, had been greatly carried away by Freemasonry. A large proportion of its eldership and membership were Freemasons. A considerable number of ministers and members of other branches of the Christian Church had also fallen into the snare. The murder of Wm. Morgan, and the publication of Masonry consequent thereupon in the books I have named, broke upon the church − fast asleep on this subject − like a clap of thunder from a clear sky. The facts were such, the revelations were so clear, that the Baptist denomination backed down, and took the lead in renouncing and denouncing the institution. Their elders and associated churches, almost universally, passed resolutions disfellowshipping adhering Masons. The denomination, to a considerable extent, took the same course. Throughout the Northern States, at that time, I believe it was almost universally conceded that persistent Freemasons, who continued to adhere and co-operate with them, ought not to be admitted to Christian churches. Now it is worthy of all consideration and remembrance, that God set the seal of His approbation upon the action taken by those churches at that time, by pouring out His Spirit upon them. Great revivals immediately followed over that whole region.

And should the question be asked, 'What shall be done with the great number of professed Christians who are Freemasons?' I answer, Let them have no more to do with it. Again, let Christian men labor with them, plead with them, and endeavor to make them see it to be their duty to abandon it. . . . Let them be distinctly asked whether they intend still to aid and abet the administration and taking of these oaths, if they still intend to countenance the false and hypocritical teachings of Masonry, if they mean to countenance the profanity of their ceremonies, and practice the partiality they have sworn to practice. If so, surely they should not be allowed their places in the church.

Charles Finney
The Character, Claims and Practical
Workings of Freemasonry

SUPPORTIVE

"We represent a fraternity which believes in justice and truth and honorable action in your community . . . men who are endeavoring to be better citizens . . . [and] to make a great country greater. This is the only institution in the world where we can meet on the level all sorts of people who want to live rightly."
Harry S. Truman, President of the United States

"To me, Freemasonry is one form of dedication to God and service to humanity."
Norman Vincent Peale

"The values and ideas, the profound principals of religion, morality, and honour for which Masonry stands, mean much to me as an American."
Norman Vincent Peale

"Freemasonry embraces the highest moral laws and will bear the test of any system of ethics or philosophy ever promulgated for the uplift of man."
General Douglas MacArthur

"The Masonic Fraternity is one of the most helpful mediating and conserving organizations among men, and I have never wavered from that childhood impression, but it has stood steadfastly with me through the busy, vast hurrying years."
George W. Truett, Southern Baptist Leader

"There is no doubt in my mind that Masonry is the cornerstone of America."
Dave Thomas, Founder of Wendy's International

SEVENTH-DAY ADVENTISTS

CONTENTS

1   An overview   707

2   Founder   707

3   Seventh-day Adventists' holy book   708

4   Facts and figures   709

5   Seventh-day Adventists' practices   712

6   Seventh-day Adventists' beliefs   712

7   Seventh-day Adventists groups   722

1 AN OVERVIEW

DEFINITION

The word "Adventists" is from the Latin *advent* ("coming"), and refers to the second coming of Jesus Christ. "Seventh day" applies to Saturday, the seventh day of creation.

Factfile
- Date of origin: 1863
- Founder: Ellen G. White, 1827-1915
- Holy book: Bible
- Number of adherents: 17 million

SUMMARY

Adventists are members of a group of related religious denominations whose distinctive doctrine centers in their belief concerning the imminent second coming of Jesus. The largest Adventist body is the Seventh-day Adventists who, in keeping with what they feel to be God's command, observe Saturday as their Sabbath day of rest and worship.

2 FOUNDER

INTRODUCTION

The Seventh-day Adventist Church (SDA), colloquially referred to as the Adventists, is an evangelical Protestant Christian denomination that grew out of the prophetic Millerite movement in the United States during the middle of the nineteenth century.

WILLIAM MILLER (1782-1849)

Between 1831 and 1844, William Miller launched what he called the "great second advent awakening." This was also known as the Millerite Movement. Based on his study of the prophecy of Daniel 8:14, Miller calculated that Jesus would return to the earth some time between March 21, 1843 and March 21, 1844. Others within the movement calculated a specific date of October 22, 1844.

THE GREAT DISAPPOINTMENT

When Jesus did not appear, Miller's followers experienced what came to be called "the Great Disappointment." The majority of the thousands of his followers left and Miller himself altogether rejected his own movement. A few people, however, went back to their Bibles to find out why they had been disappointed. They concluded that the prophecy predicted, not that Jesus would return to earth in 1844, but that a special ministry in heaven would be formed on that date. From this started the modern Seventh-day Adventist Church.

THE FIRST STAGE

Further Bible study led to the belief that in 1844 Jesus had entered into the Most Holy Place of the heavenly sanctuary, and had began an "investigative judgment" of the world: a process in which there is an examination of the Book of Life, that is, the heavenly records, to "determine who, through repentance of sin and faith in Christ, are entitled to the benefits of His atonement" after which Jesus will return to earth. According to the movement's teaching, the return of Christ may occur very soon, though nobody knows the exact date of that event (Matthew 24:36).

For about twenty years the Adventist movement was a loose group of people who held to this message. It was led by James White, Ellen G. White and Joseph Bates.

ELLEN G. WHITE (1827-1915)

Mrs White was born in Gorham, ME. A former Methodist, she was converted to Adventism through the preaching of William Miller. She claimed to have received the gift of prophecy, and to have experienced two thousand visions and prophetic dreams. She wrote over sixty books, one of which, *Steps to Christ*, has sold over 20 million copies.

In May 1863, when a formally organized Church, called the General Conference of Seventh-day Adventists, was established in Battle Creek, Michigan, with a membership of 3,500, she became its leader. She traveled widely in the US and Europe, and through her evangelism and inspiration, the Church quickly grew, establishing a presence beyond North America. In 1903, the denominational headquarters were moved from Battle Creek to Washington DC, and in 1989, to Silver Spring, Maryland.

---

3 SEVENTH-DAY ADVENTISTS' HOLY BOOK

The Bible is the yardstick for all belief and conduct.

THE TRANSLATION USED BY SEVENTH-DAY ADVENTISTS

The Seventh-day Adventist Church has published a version of the Bible called *The Clear Word Bible* (now entitled *The Clear Word*). In this "Bible" the Bible text is not separated from the author's personal commentary and opinions. Parts of this Bible version are sometimes slanted so that they always agree with the writings of Ellen G. White.

4 FACTS AND FIGURES

NUMBER OF MEMBERS

1961	1 million
	Adventists worldwide
1970	2 million
1980	3.5 million
1990	nearly 7 million
2000	11 million
2003	12 million
2004	14 million

RATE OF GROWTH

Rate of growth estimates indicate the following for the near and mid-term future:

2013	20 million members
2025/2030	40 million members

SEVENTH-DAY ADVENTIST CHURCH LEADERS

The current head of the Seventh-day Adventist Church is General Conference President Jan Paulsen from Norway.

Jan Paulsen was elected President of the General Conference of Seventh-day Adventists on March 1, 1999. Pastor Paulsen has been a pastor, a departmental leader, a teacher, and a college president.

Born in Norway, Paulsen is the third non-American president of the world Church. He has academic degrees from Andrews University in Michigan and the Evangelical Faculty of the University of Tuebingen in Germany.

PAST PRESIDENTS

1863-1865	John Byington
1865-1867	James White (Ellen G. White's husband).
1867- 869	John N. Andrews
1869-1871	James White
1871-1874	George I. Butler
1874- 880	James White
1880-1888	George I. Butler
1888-1897	Ole A. Olsen
1897-1901	George A. Irwin
1901-1922	Arthur G. Daniells
1922-1930	William Spicer
1930-1936	Charles H. Watson
1936-1950	J. Lamar McElhany
1950-1954	William H. Branson
1954-1966	Reuben R. Figuhr
1966-1979	Robert H. Pierson
1979-1990	Neal C. Wilson
1990-1999	Robert S. Folkenberg
1999-present	Jan Paulsen

MEDIA MINISTRIES

The Seventh-day Adventist Church has many affiliated broadcast ministries that are seen every day on American radio and television.

PATHFINDERS

The Youth Department of the Seventh-day Adventist Church runs an organization for ten to sixteen year olds called Pathfinders. Pathfinders are similar to Scouts.

STRUCTURE

The global Church is called the General Conference.

The General Conference is organized by divisions.

Those are organized by union conferences.

Those are organized by local conferences.

Those are organized by local churches (congregations).

Each of these has its own elected governing body and office.

HOSPITAL AND EDUCATION

Seventh-day Adventists have a special interest in education and health.

THE FOLLOWING IS A LIST OF SEVENTH-DAY ADVENTIST HOSPITALS:

Inside the US

Adventist Medical Center

Castle Medical Center

Central Valley General Hospital

Feather River Hospital

Glendale Adventist Medical Center

Hanford Community Medical Center

Florida Hospital

Frank R. Howard Memorial Hospital
Kettering Medical Center Corporation
Loma Linda University Medical Center
Metroplex Hospital
North Hawaii Community Hospital
North York Branson Hospital
Paradise Valley Hospital
Parkview Adventist Medical Center
Porter Adventist Hospital
Redbud Community Hospital
Rollins-Brook Community Hospital
St. Helena Hospital
San Joaquin Community Hospital
Selma Community Hospital
Shady Grove Adventist Hospital
Simi Valley Hospital
Sonora Regional Medical Center
South Coast Medical Center
Tillamook County General Hospital
Ukiah Valley Medical Center
Walla Walla General Hospital
Washington Adventist Hospital
White Memorial Medical Center

OUTSIDE THE US
Bangkok Adventist Hospital, Thailand
Hong Kong Adventist Hospital, Hong Kong
Mindanao Sanitarium and Hospital, Philippines
Penang Adventist Hospital, Penang, Malaysia
Scheer Memorial Hospital, Nepal
Sydney Adventist Hospital, Australia
Taiwan Adventist Hospital, Taiwan
Tsuen Wan Adventist Hospital, Hong Kong

THE FOLLOWING IS A LIST OF
SEVENTH-DAY ADVENTIST
COLLEGES AND UNIVERSITIES:
Africa
Adventist University at Lukanga, Democratic Republic of Congo
Adventist University Cosendai, Cameroon
Universite Adventiste d'Afrique Centrale (Adventist University of Central Africa), Rwanda
Adventist University Zurcher, Madagascar
Babcock University, Nigeria
Seminario Adventista do Bongo (Bongo Adventist Seminary), Angola
Bugema University, Uganda
Ethiopian Adventist College, Ethiopia

Helderberg College, South Africa
Seminario Adventista do Setimo Dia de Mocambique (Mozambique Adventist Seminary), Mozambique
Solusi University, Zimbabwe
Tanzania Adventist College, Tanzania
University of Eastern Africa, Baraton, Kenya
Valley View University, Ghana

East Asia
Hong Kong Adventist College, People's Republic of China
Sahmyook Uimyeong Daehak (Sahmyook College), South Korea
Sahmyook Ganho Bogeon Daehak (Sahmyook Nursing and Health College), South Korea
Sahmyook Daehakgyo (Sahmyook University), South Korea
Saniku Gakuin College, Japan
Taiwan Adventist College, Republic of China

South-East Asia and islands of the Pacific Ocean
Adventist International Institute of Advanced Studies, Philippines
Adventist University of the Philippines, Philippines
Avondale College, Australia
Central Philippine Adventist College, Philippines
Fulton College, Fiji
Universitas Advent Indonesia (Indonesian Adventist University), Indonesia
Mission College, Thailand
Universitas Klabat (Mount Kablat College), Indonesia
Colegio ng Tanawing Kabundukan (Mountain View College), Philippines
Myanmar Union Adventist Seminary, Myanmar
Naga View Adventist College, Philippines
Northern Luzon Adventist College, Philippines
Pacific Adventist University, Papua New Guinea
Sonoma Adventist College, Papua New Guinea
South Philippine Adventist College, Philippines
Surya Nusantara Adventist College, Indonesia

Europe (including the Russian Federation)

Adventisticko uciliste Marusevec/Adventisticki teoloski fakulet (Adriatic Union College), Croatia

Adventist Seminary, Croatia

Belgrade Teoloski Fakultet (Belgrade Theological Seminary), Serbia and Montenegro

Seminar Schloss Bogenhofen (Bogenhofen Seminary), Austria

Vejlefjordskolen (Danish Junior College), Denmark

Toivonlinnan Yhteiskoulu (Finland Junior College), Finland

Theologische Hochschule Friedensau (Friedensau Adventist University), Germany

Adventist Teologiai Foiskola (Hungarian Theological Seminary), Hungary

Istituto Avventista di Cultura Biblica Villa Aurora (Italian Adventist College Villa Aurora), Italy

Newbold College, England

Tyrifjord Videregaende Skole (Norwegian Junior College), Norway

Scoala Postliceala Teologico-Sanitara Adventista de Ziua a Saptea Dr. Luca-Braila (Romanian Adventist College of Health), Romania

Institutul Teologic Adventist (Romanian Adventist Theological Institute), Romania

Russian Sahmyook University, Russian Federation

Campus Adventiste du Saleve (Saleve Adventist University), France

Teologick" seminá? CASD (Sazava Theological Seminary), Czech Republic

Seminario Adventista de España (Spanish Adventist Seminary), Spain

Ukrainsky gumanitarny institut (Ukrainian Institute of Arts and Sciences), Ukraine

Zaokskaya Dukhovnaya Akademiya (Zaoksky Adventist University), Russian Federation

Inter-America (including the Caribbean and Central America)

Universidad Adventista de las Antillas (Antillian Adventist University), Puerto Rico

Caribbean Union College, Trinidad & Tobago

Universidad Adventista de Centro America (Central American Adventist University), Costa Rica

Seminario Adventista de Cuba (Cuba Adventist Seminary), Cuba

Universidad Adventista Dominicana (Dominican Adventist University), Dominican Republic

Universite Adventiste d'Haiti (Haitian Adventist University), Haiti

Inter-American Adventist Theological Seminary, FL, USA (technically in North America)

Northern Caribbean University, Jamaica

North America (excluding the Caribbean)

Atlantic Union College, MA, USA

Andrews University, MI, USA

Canadian University College, AB, Canada

Columbia Union College, MD, USA

Florida Hospital College of Health Sciences, FL, USA

Griggs University, MD, USA

Kettering College of Medical Arts, OH, USA

La Sierra University, CA, USA

Loma Linda University, CA, USA

Universidad Linda Vista (Linda Vista University), Mexico

Universidad de Montemorelos (Montemorelos University), Mexico

Universidad de Navojoa (Navojoa University), Mexico

Oakwood College, AL, USA

Pacific Union College, CA, USA

Southern Adventist University, TN, USA

Southwestern Adventist University, TX, USA

Union College, NE, USA

Walla Walla College, WA, USA

South America

Universidad Adventista de Bolivia (Bolivia Adventist University), Bolivia

Centro Universitário Adventista de São Paulo (Brazil Adventist University), Brazil

Universidad Adventista de Chile (Chile Adventist University), Chile

Corporacion Universitaria Adventista (Colombia Adventist University),Columbia

Seminario Adventista Latinoamericano de Teologia (Latin-American Adventist Theological Seminary), Brazil

Faculdade Adventista da Bahia (Northeast Brazil College), Brazil

Universidad Peruana Union (Peruvian Union University), Peru

Universidad Adventista del Plata (River Plate
Adventist University), Argentina
Instituto Universitario Adventista de
Venezuela (Venezuelan Adventist University),
Venezuela

**South Asia and South-west Asia (or
Middle East)**
Adventist College of Professional Studies,
India

Bangladesh Adventist Seminary and College,
Bangladesh
Flaiz Adventist College, India
Lakpahana Adventist College and Seminary,
Sri Lanka
Lowry Memorial College, India
Middle East University, Lebanon
Northeast Adventist College, India
Pakistan Adventist Seminary, Pakistan
Spicer Memorial College, India

5 SEVENTH-DAY ADVENTIST PRACTICES

Seventh-day Adventists:

- practice vegetarianism
- avoid alcohol
- avoid caffeine.

6 SEVENTH-DAY ADVENTIST BELIEFS

A 27 Fundamental beliefs of Seventh-day Adventists
B Are Seventh-day Adventists heretical?
(i) Orthodox?
(ii) Teaching about Mrs Ellen White
C Doctrinal differences

INTRODUCTION
Seventh-day Adventists, for the most part,
accept orthodox Trinitarian Protestant
theology.

Through the years, Seventh-day
Adventists have been reluctant to formalize a
creed (in the usual sense of that word).
However, they say that from time to time, for
practical purposes, they have found it
necessary to summarize their beliefs.

In 1872 the Adventist press at Battle

Creek, Michigan, published a "synopsis of our
faith" in twenty-five propositions. This
document, slightly revised and expanded to
twenty-eight sections, appeared in the
denominational Yearbook of 1889. This was
not continued in subsequent issues, but it was
inserted again in the Yearbook in 1905 and
continued to appear through 1914. In
response to an appeal from Church leaders in
Africa for "a statement [that] would help
government officials and others to a better

understanding of our work," a committee of four, including the president of the General Conference, prepared a statement encompassing "the principal features" of belief as they "may be summarized." This statement of twenty-two fundamental beliefs, first printed in the 1931 Yearbook, stood until the 1980 General Conference session replaced it with a similar but more comprehensive, summarization in twenty-seven paragraphs, published under the title "Fundamental Beliefs of Seventh-day Adventists."

A 27 FUNDAMENTAL BELIEFS OF SEVENTH-DAY ADVENTISTS

1. The Holy Scriptures:
The Holy Scriptures, Old and New Testaments, are the written Word of God, given by divine inspiration through holy men of God who spoke and wrote as they were moved by the Holy Spirit. In this Word, God has committed to man the knowledge necessary for salvation. The Holy Scriptures are the infallible revelation of His will. They are the standard of character, the test of experience, the authoritative revealer of doctrines, and the trustworthy record of God's acts in history. (2 Peter 1:20, 21; 2 Tim. 3:16, 17; Ps. 119:105; Prov. 30:5, 6; Isa. 8:20; John 17:17; 1 Thess. 2:13; Heb. 4:12.)

2. The Trinity:
There is one God: Father, Son, and Holy Spirit, a unity of three co-eternal Persons. God is immortal, all-powerful, all knowing, above all, and ever present. He is infinite and beyond human comprehension, yet known through His self-revelation. He is forever worthy of worship, adoration, and service by the whole creation. (Deut. 6:4; Matt. 28:19; 2 Cor. 13:14; Eph. 4:4-6; 1 Peter 1:2; 1 Tim. 1:17; Rev. 14:7.)

3. The Father:
God the eternal Father is the Creator, Source, Sustainer, and Sovereign of all creation. He is just and holy, merciful and gracious, slow to anger, and abounding in steadfast love and faithfulness. The qualities and powers exhibited in the Son and the Holy Spirit are also revelations of the Father. (Gen. 1:1; Rev. 4:11; 1 Cor. 15:28; John 3:16; 1 John 4:8; 1 Tim. 1:17; Ex. 34:6, 7; John 14:9.)

4. The Son:
God the eternal Son became incarnate in Jesus Christ. Through Him all things were created, the character of God is revealed, the salvation of humanity is accomplished, and the world is judged. Forever truly God, He became also truly man, Jesus the Christ. He was conceived of the Holy Spirit and born of the virgin Mary. He lived and experienced temptation as a human being, but perfectly exemplified the righteousness and love of God. By His miracles He manifested God's power and was attested as God's promised Messiah. He suffered and died voluntarily on the cross for our sins and in our place, was raised from the dead, and ascended to minister in the heavenly sanctuary in our behalf. He will come again in glory for the final deliverance of His people and the restoration of all things. (John 1:1-3, 14; Col. 1:15-19; John 10:30; 14:9; Rom. 6:23; 2 Cor. 5:17-19; John 5:22; Luke 1:35; Phil. 2:5-11; Heb. 2:9-18; 1 Cor. 15:3, 4; Heb. 8:1, 2; John 14:1-3.)

5. The Holy Spirit:
God the eternal Spirit was active with the Father and the Son in Creation, incarnation, and redemption. He inspired the writers of Scripture. He filled Christ's life with power. He draws and convicts human beings; and those who respond He renews and transforms into the image of God. Sent by the Father and the Son to be always with His children, He extends spiritual gifts to the church, empowers it to bear witness to Christ, and in harmony with the Scriptures leads it into all truth. (Gen. 1:1, 2; Luke 1:35; 4:18; Acts 10:38; 2 Peter 1:21; 2 Cor. 3:18; Eph. 4:11, 12; Acts 1:8; John 14:16-18, 26; 15:26, 27; 16:7-13.)

6. Creation:

God is Creator of all things, and has revealed in Scripture the authentic account of His creative activity. In six days the Lord made "the heaven and the earth" and all living things upon the earth, and rested on the seventh day of that first week. Thus He established the Sabbath as a perpetual memorial of His completed creative work. The first man and woman were made in the image of God as the crowning work of Creation, given dominion over the world, and charged with responsibility to care for it. When the world was finished it was ``very good,'' declaring the glory of God. (Gen. 1; 2; Ex. 20:8-11; Ps. 19:1-6; 33:6, 9; 104; Heb. 11:3.)

7. The Nature of Man:

Man and woman were made in the image of God with individuality, the power and freedom to think and to do. Though created free beings, each is an indivisible unity of body, mind, and spirit, dependent upon God for life and breath and all else. When our first parents disobeyed God, they denied their dependence upon Him and fell from their high position under God. The image of God in them was marred and they became subject to death. Their descendants share this fallen nature and its consequences. They are born with weaknesses and tendencies to evil. But God in Christ reconciled the world to Himself and by His Spirit restores in penitent mortals the image of their Maker. Created for the glory of God, they are called to love Him and one another, and to care for their environment. (Gen. 1:26-28; 2:7; Ps. 8:4-8; Acts 17:24-28; Gen. 3; Ps. 51:5; Rom. 5:12-17; 2 Cor. 5:19, 20; Ps. 51:10; 1 John 4:7, 8, 11, 20; Gen. 2:15.)

8. The Great Controversy:

All humanity is now involved in a great controversy between Christ and Satan regarding the character of God, His law, and His sovereignty over the universe. This conflict originated in heaven when a created being, endowed with freedom of choice, in self-exaltation became Satan, God's adversary, and led into rebellion a portion of the angels. He introduced the spirit of rebellion into this world when he led Adam and Eve into sin. This human sin resulted in the distortion of the image of God in humanity, the disordering of the created world, and its eventual devastation at the time of the worldwide flood. Observed by the whole creation, this world became the arena of the universal conflict, out of which the God of love will ultimately be vindicated. To assist His people in this controversy, Christ sends the Holy Spirit and the loyal angels to guide, protect, and sustain them in the way of salvation. (Rev. 12:4-9; Isa. 14:12-14; Eze. 28:12-18; Gen. 3; Rom. 1:19-32; 5:12-21; 8:19-22; Gen. 6-8; 2 Peter 3:6; 1 Cor. 4:9; Heb. 1:14.)

9. The Life, Death, and Resurrection of Christ:

In Christ's life of perfect obedience to God's will, His suffering, death, and resurrection, God provided the only means of atonement for human sin, so that those who by faith accept this atonement may have eternal life, and the whole creation may better understand the infinite and holy love of the Creator. This perfect atonement vindicates the righteousness of God's law and the graciousness of His character; for it both condemns our sin and provides for our forgiveness. The death of Christ is substitutionary and expiatory, reconciling and transforming. The resurrection of Christ proclaims God's triumph over the forces of evil, and for those who accept the atonement assures their final victory over sin and death. It declares the Lordship of Jesus Christ, before whom every knee in heaven and on earth will bow. (John 3:16; Isa. 53; 1 Peter 2:21, 22; 1 Cor. 15:3, 4, 20-22; 2 Cor. 5:14, 15, 19-21; Rom. 1:4; 3:25; 4:25; 8:3, 4; 1 John 2:2; 4:10; Col. 2:15; Phil. 2:6-11.)

10. The Experience of Salvation:

In infinite love and mercy God made

Christ, who knew no sin, to be sin for us, so that in Him we might be made the righteousness of God. Led by the Holy Spirit we sense our need, acknowledge our sinfulness, repent of our transgressions, and exercise faith in Jesus as Lord and Christ, as Substitute and Example. This faith which receives salvation comes through the divine power of the Word and is the gift of God's grace. Through Christ we are justified, adopted as God's sons and daughters, and delivered from the lordship of sin. Through the Spirit we are born again and sanctified; the Spirit renews our minds, writes God's law of love in our hearts, and we are given the power to live a holy life. Abiding in Him we become partakers of the divine nature and have the assurance of salvation now and in the judgment. (2 Cor. 5:17-21; John 3:16; Gal. 1:4; 4:4-7; Titus 3:3-7; John 16:8; Gal. 3:13, 14; 1 Peter 2:21, 22; Rom. 10:17; Luke 17:5; Mark 9:23, 24; Eph. 2:5-10; Rom. 3:21-26; Col. 1:13, 14; Rom. 8:14-17; Gal. 3:26; John 3:3-8; 1 Peter 1:23; Rom. 12:2; Heb. 8:7-12; Eze. 36:25-27; 2 Peter 1:3, 4; Rom. 8:1-4; 5:6-10.)

11. The Church:
The church is the community of believers who confess Jesus Christ as Lord and Saviour. In continuity with the people of God in Old Testament times, we are called out from the world; and we join together for worship, for fellowship, for instruction in the Word, for the celebration of the Lord's Supper, for service to all mankind, and for the worldwide proclamation of the gospel. The church derives its authority from Christ, who is the incarnate Word, and from the Scriptures, which are the written Word. The church is God's family; adopted by Him as children, its members live on the basis of the new covenant. The church is the body of Christ, a community of faith of which Christ Himself is the Head. The church is the bride for whom Christ died that He might sanctify and cleanse her. At His return in triumph, He will present her to

Himself a glorious church, the faithful of all the ages, the purchase of His blood, not having spot or wrinkle, but holy and without blemish. (Gen. 12:3; Acts 7:38; Eph. 4:11-15; 3:8-11; Matt. 28:19, 20; 16:13-20; 18:18; Eph. 2:19-22; 1:22, 23; 5:23-27; Col. 1:17, 18.)

12. The Remnant and Its Mission:
The universal church is composed of all who truly believe in Christ, but in the last days, a time of widespread apostasy, a remnant has been called out to keep the commandments of God and the faith of Jesus. This remnant announces the arrival of the judgment hour, proclaims salvation through Christ, and heralds the approach of His second advent. This proclamation is symbolized by the three angels of Revelation 14; it coincides with the work of judgment in heaven and results in a work of repentance and reform on earth. Every believer is called to have a personal part in this worldwide witness. (Rev. 12:17; 14:6-12; 18:1-4; 2 Cor. 5:10; Jude 3, 14; 1 Peter 1:16-19; 2 Peter 3:10-14; Rev. 21:1-14.)

13. Unity in the Body of Christ:
The church is one body with many members, called from every nation, kindred, tongue, and people. In Christ we are a new creation; distinctions of race, culture, learning, and nationality, and differences between high and low, rich and poor, male and female, must not be divisive among us. We are all equal in Christ, who by one Spirit has bonded us into one fellowship with Him and with one another; we are to serve and be served without partiality or reservation. Through the revelation of Jesus Christ in the Scriptures we share the same faith and hope, and reach out in one witness to all. This unity has its source in the oneness of the triune God, who has adopted us as His children. (Rom. 12:4, 5; 1 Cor. 12:12-14; Matt. 28:19, 20; Ps. 133:1; 2 Cor. 5:16, 17; Acts 17:26, 27; Gal. 3:27, 29; Col. 3:10-15; Eph. 4:14-16; 4:1-6; John 17:20-23.)

14. Baptism:
By baptism we confess our faith in the death and resurrection of Jesus Christ, and testify of our death to sin and of our purpose to walk in newness of life. Thus we acknowledge Christ as Lord and Savior, become His people, and are received as members by His church. Baptism is a symbol of our union with Christ, the forgiveness of our sins, and our reception of the Holy Spirit. It is by immersion in water and is contingent on an affirmation of faith in Jesus and evidence of repentance of sin. It follows instruction in the Holy Scriptures and acceptance of their teachings. (Rom. 6:1-6; Col. 2:12, 13; Acts 16:30-33; 22:16; 2:38; Matt. 28:19, 20.)

[The official Seventh-day Adventists baptismal vows
Seventh-day Adventists do not believe in baptizing infants. A person must be old enough to accept responsibility for his/her own actions. Baptism is by immersion. In order to be baptized, a person must agree to this set of thirteen baptismal vows:

1. I believe in God the Father, in His Son Jesus Christ, and in the Holy Spirit.
2. I accept the death of Jesus Christ on Calvary as the atoning sacrifice for my sins, and believe that through faith in His shed blood I am saved from sin and its penalty.
3. I renounce the world and its sinful ways, and have accepted Jesus Christ as my personal Savior, and believe that God, for Christ's sake, has forgiven my sins and given me a new heart.
4. I accept by faith the righteousness of Christ, recognizing Him as my Intercessor in the heavenly sanctuary, and claim His promise to strengthen me by His indwelling Sprit, so that I may receive power to do His will.
5. I believe that the Bible is God's inspired Word, and that it constitutes the only rule of faith and practice for the Christian.

6. I accept the Ten Commandments as still binding upon Christians; and it is my purpose by the power of the indwelling Christ, to keep this law, including the fourth commandment, which requires the observance of the seventh day of the week as the Sabbath of the Lord.
8. I look forward to the soon coming of Jesus as the blessed hope in my heart, and I am determined to be ready to meet the Lord, and to do all in my power to witness to His loving salvation, and by life and word to help others to be ready for His glorious appearing.
9. I accept the Biblical teaching of spiritual gifts, and believe that the gift of prophecy is one of the identifying marks of the remnant church.
10. I believe in church organization, and it is my purpose to support the church by my tithes and offerings, and by my personal effort and influence.
11. I believe that my body is the temple of the Holy Spirit, and I will honor God by caring for it, avoiding the use of that which is harmful, abstaining from all unclean foods, from the use, manufacture, or sale of alcoholic beverages, the use, manufacture, or sale of tobacco in any of its forms for human consumption, and from the misuse of or trafficking in, narcotics or other drugs.
12. I know and understand the fundamental Bible principles as taught by the Seventh-day Adventist Church. It is my purpose, by the grace of God, to order my life in harmony with these principles.
13. I accept the New Testament teaching of baptism by immersion, and desire to be so baptized as a public expression of faith in Christ and His forgiveness of my sins.
14. I accept that the Seventh-day Church is the remnant church of Bible prophecy, and that people of every nation, race, and language are invited

and accepted into its fellowship. I desire to be a member in this local congregation of the world church.]

15. The Lord's Supper:
The Lord's Supper is a participation in the emblems of the body and blood of Jesus as an expression of faith in Him, our Lord and Savior. In this experience of communion Christ is present to meet and strengthen His people. As we partake, we joyfully proclaim the Lord's death until He comes again. Preparation for the Supper includes self-examination, repentance, and confession. The Master ordained the service of foot washing to signify renewed cleansing, to express a willingness to serve one another in Christlike humility, and to unite our hearts in love. The communion service is open to all believing Christians. (1 Cor. 10:16, 17; 11:23-30; Matt. 26:17-30; Rev. 3:20; John 6:48-63; 13:1-17.)

16. Spiritual Gifts and Ministries:
God bestows upon all members of His church in every age spiritual gifts which each member is to employ in loving ministry for the common good of the church and of humanity. Given by the agency of the Holy Spirit, who apportions to each member as He wills, the gifts provide all abilities and ministries needed by the church to fulfill its divinely ordained functions. According to the Scriptures, these gifts include such ministries as faith, healing, prophecy, proclamation, teaching, administration, reconciliation, compassion, and self-sacrificing service and charity for the help and encouragement of people. Some members are called of God and endowed by the Spirit for functions recognized by the church in pastoral, evangelistic, apostolic, and teaching ministries particularly needed to equip the members for service, to build up the church to spiritual maturity, and to foster unity of the faith and knowledge of God. When members employ these spiritual gifts as faithful stewards of God's varied grace, the church is protected from the destructive influence of false doctrine, grows with a growth that is from God, and is built up in faith and love. (Rom. 12:4-8; 1 Cor. 12:9-11, 27, 28; Eph. 4:8, 11-16; Acts 6:1-7; 1 Tim. 3:1-13; 1 Peter 4:10, 11.)

17. The Gift of Prophecy:
One of the gifts of the Holy Spirit is prophecy. This gift is an identifying mark of the remnant church and was manifested in the ministry of Ellen G. White. As the Lord's messenger, her writings are a continuing and authoritative source of truth which provide for the church comfort, guidance, instruction, and correction. They also make clear that the Bible is the standard by which all teaching and experience must be tested. (Joel 2:28, 29; Acts 2:14-21; Heb. 1:1-3; Rev. 12:17; 19:10.)

18. The Law of God:
The great principles of God's law are embodied in the Ten Commandments and exemplified in the life of Christ. They express God's love, will, and purposes concerning human conduct and relationships and are binding upon all people in every age. These precepts are the basis of God's covenant with His people and the standard in God's judgment. Through the agency of the Holy Spirit they point out sin and awaken a sense of need for a Savior. Salvation is all of grace and not of works, but its fruitage is obedience to the Commandments. This obedience develops Christian character and results in a sense of well-being. It is an evidence of our love for the Lord and our concern for our fellow men. The obedience of faith demonstrates the power of Christ to transform lives, and therefore strengthens Christian witness. (Ex.

20:1-17; Ps. 40:7, 8; Matt. 22:36-40; Deut. 28:1-14; Matt. 5:17-20; Heb. 8:8-10; John 15:7-10; Eph. 2:8-10; 1 John 5:3; Rom. 8:3, 4; Ps. 19:7-14.)

19. The Sabbath:

The beneficent Creator, after the six days of Creation, rested on the seventh day and instituted the Sabbath for all people as a memorial of Creation. The fourth commandment of God's unchangeable law requires the observance of this seventh-day Sabbath as the day of rest, worship, and ministry in harmony with the teaching and practice of Jesus, the Lord of the Sabbath. The Sabbath is a day of delightful communion with God and one another. It is a symbol of our redemption in Christ, a sign of our sanctification, a token of our allegiance, and a foretaste of our eternal future in God's kingdom. The Sabbath is God's perpetual sign of His eternal covenant between Him and His people. Joyful observance of this holy time from evening to evening, sunset to sunset, is a celebration of God's creative and redemptive acts. (Gen. 2:1-3; Ex. 20:8-11; Luke 4:16; Isa. 56:5, 6; 58:13, 14; Matt. 12:1-12; Ex. 31:13-17; Eze. 20:12, 20; Deut. 5:12-15; Heb. 4:1-11; Lev. 23:32; Mark 1:32.)

20. Stewardship:

We are God's stewards, entrusted by Him with time and opportunities, abilities and possessions, and the blessings of the earth and its resources. We are responsible to Him for their proper use. We acknowledge God's ownership by faithful service to Him and our fellow men, and by returning tithes and giving offerings for the proclamation of His gospel and the support and growth of His church. Stewardship is a privilege given to us by God for nurture in love

and the victory over selfishness and covetousness. The steward rejoices in the blessings that come to others as a result of his faithfulness. (Gen. 1:26-28; 2:15; 1 Chron. 29:14; Haggai 1:3-11; Mal. 3:8-12; 1 Cor. 9:9-14; Matt. 23:23; 2 Cor. 8:1-15; Rom. 15:26, 27.)

21. Christian Behavior:

We are called to be a godly people who think, feel, and act in harmony with the principles of heaven. For the Spirit to recreate in us the character of our Lord we involve ourselves only in those things which will produce Christlike purity, health, and joy in our lives. This means that our amusement and entertainment should meet the highest standards of Christian taste and beauty. While recognizing cultural differences, our dress is to be simple, modest, and neat, befitting those whose true beauty does not consist of outward adornment but in the imperishable ornament of a gentle and quiet spirit. It also means that because our bodies are the temples of the Holy Spirit, we are to care for them intelligently. Along with adequate exercise and rest, we are to adopt the most healthful diet possible and abstain from the unclean foods identified in the Scriptures. Since alcoholic beverages, tobacco, and the irresponsible use of drugs and narcotics are harmful to our bodies, we are to abstain from them as well. Instead, we are to engage in whatever brings our thoughts and bodies into the discipline of Christ, who desires our wholesomeness, joy, and goodness. (Rom. 12:1, 2; 1 John 2:6; Eph. 5:1-21; Phil. 4:8; 2 Cor. 10:5; 6:14-7:1; 1 Peter 3:1-4; 1 Cor. 6:19, 20; 10:31; Lev. 11:1-47; 3 John 2.)

22. Marriage and the Family:

Marriage was divinely established in Eden and affirmed by Jesus to be a lifelong union between a man and a woman in loving companionship. For the Christian a marriage commitment is to God as well as to the spouse, and should be entered into only between partners who share a common faith. Mutual love, honor, respect, and responsibility are the fabric of this relationship, which is to reflect the love, sanctity, closeness, and permanence of the relationship between Christ and His church. Regarding divorce, Jesus taught that the person who divorces a spouse, except for fornication, and marries another, commits adultery. Although some family relationships may fall short of the ideal, marriage partners who fully commit themselves to each other in Christ may achieve loving unity through the guidance of the Spirit and the nurture of the church. God blesses the family and intends that its members shall assist each other toward complete maturity. Parents are to bring up their children to love and obey the Lord. By their example and their words they are to teach them that Christ is a loving disciplinarian, ever tender and caring, who wants them to become members of His body, the family of God. Increasing family closeness is one of the earmarks of the final gospel message. (Gen. 2:18-25; Matt. 19:3-9; John 2:1-11; 2 Cor. 6:14; Eph. 5:21-33; Matt. 5:31, 32; Mark 10:11, 12; Luke 16:18; 1 Cor. 7:10, 11; Ex. 20:12; Eph. 6:1-4; Deut. 6:5-9; Prov. 22:6; Mal. 4:5, 6.)

23. Christ's Ministry in the Heavenly Sanctuary:
There is a sanctuary in heaven, the true tabernacle which the Lord set up and not man. In it Christ ministers on our behalf, making available to believers the benefits of His atoning sacrifice offered once for all on the cross. He was inaugurated as our great High Priest and began His intercessory ministry at the time of His ascension. In 1844, at the end of the prophetic period of 2300 days, He entered the second and last phase of His atoning ministry. It is a work of investigative judgment which is part of the ultimate disposition of all sin, typified by the cleansing of the ancient Hebrew sanctuary on the Day of Atonement. In that typical service the sanctuary was cleansed with the blood of animal sacrifices, but the heavenly things are purified with the perfect sacrifice of the blood of Jesus. The investigative judgment reveals to heavenly intelligences who among the dead are asleep in Christ and therefore, in Him, are deemed worthy to have part in the first resurrection. It also makes manifest who among the living are abiding in Christ, keeping the commandments of God and the faith of Jesus, and in Him, therefore, are ready for translation into His everlasting kingdom. This judgment vindicates the justice of God in saving those who believe in Jesus. It declares that those who have remained loyal to God shall receive the kingdom. The completion of this ministry of Christ will mark the close of human probation before the Second Advent. (Heb. 8:1-5; 4:14-16; 9:11-28; 10:19-22; 1:3; 2:16, 17; Dan. 7:9-27; 8:13, 14; 9:24-27; Num. 14:34; Eze. 4:6; Lev. 16; Rev. 14:6, 7; 20:12; 14:12; 22:12.)

24. The Second Coming of Christ:
The second coming of Christ is the blessed hope of the church, the grand climax of the gospel. The Savior's coming will be literal, personal, visible, and worldwide. When He returns, the righteous dead will be resurrected, and together with the righteous living will be glorified and taken to heaven, but the unrighteous will die. The almost complete fulfillment of most lines of prophecy, together with the present condition of

the world, indicates that Christ's coming is imminent. The time of that event has not been revealed, and we are therefore exhorted to be ready at all times. (Titus 2:13; Heb. 9:28; John 14:1-3; Acts 1:9-11; Matt. 24:14; Rev. 1:7; Matt. 24:43, 44; 1 Thess. 4:13-18; 1 Cor. 15:51-54; 2 Thess. 1:7-10; 2:8; Rev. 14:14-20; 19:11-21; Matt. 24; Mark 13; Luke 21; 2 Tim. 3:1-5; 1 Thess. 5:1-6.)

25. Death and Resurrection:
The wages of sin is death. But God, who alone is immortal, will grant eternal life to His redeemed. Until that day death is an unconscious state for all people. When Christ, who is our life, appears, the resurrected righteous and the living righteous will be glorified and caught up to meet their Lord. The second resurrection, the resurrection of the unrighteous, will take place a thousand years later. (Rom. 6:23; 1 Tim. 6:15, 16; Eccl. 9:5, 6; Ps. 146:3, 4; John 11:11-14; Col. 3:4; 1 Cor. 15:51-54; 1 Thess. 4:13-17; John 5:28, 29; Rev. 20:1-10.)

26. The Millennium and the End of Sin:
The millennium is the thousand-year reign of Christ with His saints in heaven between the first and second resurrections. During this time the wicked dead will be judged; the earth will be utterly desolate, without living human inhabitants, but occupied by Satan and his angels. At its close Christ with His saints and the Holy City will descend from heaven to earth. The unrighteous dead will then be resurrected, and with Satan and his angels will surround the city; but fire from God will consume them and cleanse the earth. The universe will thus be freed of sin and sinners forever. (Rev. 20; 1 Cor. 6:2, 3; Jer. 4:23-26; Rev. 21:1-5; Mal. 4:1; Eze. 28:18, 19.)

27. The New Earth:
On the new earth, in which righteousness dwells, God will provide an eternal home for the redeemed and a perfect environment for everlasting life, love, joy, and learning in His presence. For here God Himself will dwell with His people, and suffering and death will have passed away. The great controversy will be ended, and sin will be no more. All things, animate and inanimate, will declare that God is love; and He shall reign forever. Amen. (2 Peter 3:13; Isa. 35; 65:17-25; Matt. 5:5; Rev. 21:1-7; 22:1-5; 11:15.)

B ARE SEVENTH-DAY ADVENTISTS HERETICAL?

(I) ORTHODOX?
Walter Martin, in his book *Kingdom of the Cults*, spoke of the Seventh-day Adventist Church as orthodox and refused to label it as a cult.

Seventh-day Adventists reject Joseph Smith and his *Book of Mormon*, they reject Mary Baker Eddy and her book *Science and Health with Keys to Scripture*. They reject the Jehovah's Witnesses, which have the *Watchtower* to guide them. Seventh-day Adventists reject all beliefs that cannot be supported by the Bible.

(II) TEACHING ABOUT MRS. ELLEN WHITE
Some Seventh-day Adventists, however, accept Ellen White's erroneous additions to the Bible.

The Seventh-day Adventist Church state that:

The writings of Mrs. White were never designed to be an addition to the canon of Scripture. They are, nevertheless, the messages of God to the remnant church and should be received as such as were the messages of the prophets of old. As Samuel was a prophet to Israel in his day, as Jeremiah was a prophet to Israel in the days of the captivity, as John the Baptist came as a special messenger of the Lord to prepare the way for Christ's appearing, so we believe that Mrs. White was a prophet to the Church of Christ today. And the same as the messages of the prophets were received in olden times, so her messages should be received at the present time.

Review and Herald, *October 4, 1928*

Ellen White was one of the founders of the Seventh-day Adventists and an acknowledged spiritual leader. Rather than calling herself a "prophet," she preferred the title, "messenger." She did, however, claim to have the "spirit of prophecy." She said that her messages were given to her by God himself and that they should guide and direct the Church.

Some of the official publications of the Seventh-day Adventist Church continue to defend Ellen White so that it even appears that some support the idea that there was no difference in the degree of inspiration she received from that received by Bible writers. In their June 2000 General Conference, the Seventh-day Adventists voted to more aggressively affirm and support the "Spirit of Prophecy through the ministry of Ellen White."

C DOCTRINAL DIFFERENCES

THE SABBATH
Seventh-day Adventists' teaching

> The divine institution of the Sabbath is to be restored. . . . The delivering of this message will precipitate a conflict that will involve the whole world. The central issue will be obedience to God's law and the observance of the Sabbath....Those who reject it will eventually receive the mark of the beast
>
> *Seventh-day Adventists Believe*

According to Ellen White in her book *The Great Controversy Between Christ and Satan,* Sabbath observance would be the "line of distinction" in the "final test" that

will separate God's end-time people who "receive the seal of God" and are saved, from those who "receive the mark of the beast."

In one of her (supposedly) direct visions from God, Ellen White wrote, "I saw that the Holy Sabbath is, and will be, the separating wall between the true Israel of God and unbelievers." (*Early Writings*)

The work of proclaiming the gospel, God has commanded to his church. They are to teach the perpetuity and binding force of the holy commandments delivered at Sinai.

Mrs. E. G. White,
The Watchman, *August 7, 1906*
The Perfect Standard, *par. 9*

The Bible's teaching
Adventists teach that the law is still binding on Christians today, and is the dividing line between the saved and the lost in the end time. But the Old Testament Sabbath is seen by most Christians today as the shadow of the substance. The teaching of the New Testament is that the rest prefigured by the Sabbath is the rest of God, which is Christ himself. (Hebrews 4:1–10).

INVESTIGATIVE JUDGMENT
Seventh-day Adventists teaching

> In 1844...[Christ] entered the second and last phase of His atoning ministry. It is a work of investigative judgment which is part of the ultimate disposition of all sin... It also makes manifest who among the living are abiding in Christ, keeping the commandments of God and the faith of Jesus, and in Him, therefore, are ready for translation into His everlasting kingdom. This judgment vindicates the justice of God in saving those who believe in Jesus. It declares that those who have remained loyal to God shall receive the kingdom
>
> *Seventh-day Adventists Believe*

7 SEVENTH-DAY ADVENTIST GROUPS

THE BRANCH DAVIDIANS
The Branch Davidians were a sectarian splinter from the Seventh-day Adventists. This split occurred in 1929 when Victor Houteff, who believed himself to be a messenger of God was, disfellowshiped because of his deviations from the main-line Church teachings.

A unique feature of the Davidians was their doctrine of proselytizing only among Seventh-day Adventists because they believed that only Adventists had the proper beliefs and understanding to receive the spiritual truths that Houteff taught.

TWO CAMPS
There are now two distinct camps in Adventism. The split became apparent in the late 1970s when pastors of many years' standing began to question some of the peculiar doctrines of their prophetess, Ellen G. White arguing that these could not be supported fully by the Scriptures.

8 QUOTATIONS

We realize that it's God's love and care for the world that we're trying to embody-that in the end it is Jesus who transforms the world, and that we are instruments of His grace. Jesus is the Messiah. He is God; we're not. Some of the more secular humanitarian agencies burn out because they think that they alone will save the world. Adventists don't save the world. God does.
Charles C. Sandefur

The Holy Scriptures, Old and New Testaments, are the written Word of God, given by divine inspiration through holy men of God who spoke and wrote as they were moved by the Holy Spirit. In this Word, God has committed to man the knowledge necessary for salvation. The Holy Scriptures are the infallible revelation of His will. They are the standard of character, the test of experience, the authoritative revealer of doctrines, and the trustworthy record of God's acts in history.
Fundamental Beliefs of Seventh-day Adventists, General Conference of Seventh-day Adventists

The primary mission of the Seventh-day Adventist Church is the vindication of God. It will be accomplished though the cleansing of the heavenly sanctuary. But before the

sanctuary in heaven can be cleansed from all the records of sin, the sanctuary of our hearts must be cleansed from the pollution which continues to dishonor God's name. Adventism is all about God's victory in the great controversy, as He finishes His six thousand year struggle against the lies of Satan.
Dennis Priebe

The matchless love of God for a world that did not love Him! The thought has a subduing power upon the soul and brings the mind into captivity to the will of God. The more we study the divine character in the light of the cross, the more we see mercy, tenderness, and forgiveness blended with equity and justice, and the more clearly we discern innumerable evidences of a love that is infinite and a tender pity surpassing a mother's yearning sympathy for her wayward child.
Ellen White

One of the things I admire most about Seventh Day Adventists, in addition to your faith, is your commitment to preach, teach and heal. Your emphasis on educating and nurturing your fellow man is a model for all people of faith to follow. And your network of schools and health care facilities put into action the tenets of those beliefs.
Senator Hillary Rodham Clinton

WORLDWIDE CHURCH OF GOD

CONTENTS

1 An overview   727

2 Founder   727

3 Worldwide Church of God's holy book   729

4 Facts and figures   730

5 Worldwide Church of God practices   730

6 Worldwide Church of God beliefs   732

7 Splits from the Worldwide Church of God   733

8 Quotations   734

1 AN OVERVIEW

SUMMARY

Under the leadership of its founder, Herbert W. Armstrong, this church rejected the essential doctrines of evangelical Christianity, denying the doctrine of the Trinity, the full deity of Jesus Christ, and the personality of the Holy Spirit. The church epitomized the somewhat eclectic set of beliefs and practices that became known as Armstrongism. Beginning in the early 1990s under the leadership Armstrong's successors, Joseph W. Tkach and his son Joe Tkach, this group has undergone remarkable doctrinal transformation. They now hold to a traditional evangelical position on the nature of God and the gospel, teaching the Trinity and salvation by grace alone, through faith alone. Large numbers of its membership have left to join splinter groups that still teach classic Armstrongism.

The Watchman Expositor

Factfile
- Date of origin: 1934
- Founder: Herbert W. Armstrong, 1892-1986
- Holy book: The Bible
- Number of adherents: 70,000

2 FOUNDER

A CRITICAL VIEW
[Exit & Support Network™ (ESN) began in 1993 as a resource and investigative service to aid those who were questioning or exiting the Worldwide Church of God and affiliated offshoots. The founder of ESN was former WCG member L. A. Stuhlman who had a background in business management, psychiatric nursing, and crisis intervention counseling.]

ESN'S VIEW OF THE WORLDWIDE CHURCH OF GOD
Herbert W. Armstrong founded the Worldwide Church of God in 1934 in Eugene, Oregon.

The Radio Church of God, as it was originally called [its name was changed to *Worldwide Church of God* on January 5, 1968], was a major proponent of British Israelism/the Lost Ten Tribes movement in the United States.

Herbert Armstrong moved to Pasadena, California in 1947 at which time he started the Ambassador College to train ministers for "the Work."

Membership peaked in 1973 with 52,000 recruits. By the time of Armstrong's death in 1986, the WCG had approximately 35,000 members; operated two campus locations (Big Sandy, Texas and Pasadena, California), and owned and operated considerable real estate, several airplanes and investment corporations.

The Worldwide Church of God reached annual revenues of two hundred and twenty-two million dollars annually by the late 1980s. The church demanded a three tier tithing system up to 30% of members' gross income.

L. A. Stuhlman, Founder of Exit and Support Network (ESN)

THE NEW WORLDWIDE CHURCH OF GOD

In the early 1930s, Herbert Armstrong began a radio ministry, a magazine and a church that eventually became *The World Tomorrow, The Plain Truth*, and the Worldwide Church of God. He had many unusual doctrines. These he taught so enthusiastically that eventually more than 100,000 people attended weekly services. After he died in 1986, church leaders began to realize that many of his doctrines were not biblical. These doctrines were rejected. Today the church and *The Plain Truth* are in full agreement with the statement of faith of the National Association of Evangelicals.

NEW LEADERSHIP AND DOCTRINE UNDER JOSEPH TKACH (1986-PRESENT)

Before Armstrong died in 1986, he appointed Joseph Tkach, who had supervised the church's ministers, to be his successor. Tkach came to believe that many of Armstrong's teachings could not be validated in scripture. This statement was made:

> We acknowledge that many of our doctrines were erroneous. We acknowledge that the WCG would not exist without those erroneous doctrines. But we do not conclude that Jesus Christ rescued us as a group merely to have us disband. He has bought and paid for this church. It belongs to him, and we have told him that he can have it! If it is of any value to him, he can use it as his instrument, and we are happy to let him lead us. We rejoice in the fellowship we have with him, and we believe that he is already leading us into usefulness.

> Our strengths as a denomination include a fresh awareness of the importance of grace, a high respect for Scripture, and a willingness to do what it says. We recognize that Jesus, as our Savior and as our Lord, gives us instructions for our thoughts, words and actions. We know that Christ makes a difference in the way we live. He transforms our lives in this age, as well as giving us eternal life. Of course, Jesus is not done with us yet. We are still being shaped and fashioned for his purpose. We praise him and worship him, and seek to know his will for our lives.

Worldwide Church of God

3 WORLDWIDE CHURCH OF GOD'S HOLY BOOK

We believe that the Bible constitutes the accurate, infallible and divinely inspired written word of God, the foundation of truth, the fully reliable record of God's revelation to humanity.
The Plain Truth Ministries Statement of Faith

The Worldwide Church of God always has, and continues to have the Bible as its sacred text. But, especially under Armstrong's leadership, unusual interpretations of the Bible have been taught.

BELIEFS ABOUT THE BIBLE UNDER ARMSTRONG'S LEADERSHIP
OLD TESTAMENT PRACTICES

Basing his beliefs on his strict interpretation of the covenant laws in the Old Testament, Armstrong gave the following teaching:

- traditional Christian celebrations and holidays such as Christmas and Easter are not to be observed
- the eating of certain meats is forbidden
- it is forbidden to engage in any type of politics or military service
- to observe Saturday as the Sabbath is an essential part of the faith. Armstrong saw this as the "test commandment" that set real Christians apart from all others.

THREE TITHES

Armstrong also encouraged the observance of certain major Jewish holidays, as well as participation in three tithes.

- the First Tithe, amounting to one tenth of one's earnings, was used in financing church administration, publishing, and education.
- the Second Tithe was spent on financing family and personal spiritual growth.
- the Third Tithe, collected twice every seven years, went to a specific charity.

BRITISH-ISRAELISM

Armstrong taught that it is essential for Christians to believe in British-Israelism, that is, that present-day Anglo-Saxons are the true descendents of the ancient Israelites. This doctrine states that as Jews were associated with the house of Judah, they are not entitled to the lands promised in Scripture to the Israelites. Instead, England and its people are seen to be the throne of David and should, by divine right, possess these lands.

4 FACTS AND FIGURES

The Worldwide Church of God claims to have nearly 70,000 members worshiping in 860 congregations in about 90 nations.

However, its active membership has been estimated at being nearer to 40,000.

A CRITICAL VIEW

The main recruiting strategy of the Worldwide Church of God consisted of *The World Tomorrow* telecast, the *Plain Truth* magazine, the Youth Magazine and massive amounts of printed booklets luring the readership into the church.

During the past eight years controllers of the WCG has strategically implemented a de-culting strategy and aggressive marketing appeal to Ecumenical Evangelicals. The WCG marketing strategy centers on doctrine issues and Herbert W. Armstrong. The multimillion-dollar empire has simultaneously downsized its lucrative holdings, creating factions within the membership. The current WCG has formed association with Promise Keepers, National Association of Evangelicals and other ecumenical entities.

L. A. Stuhlman, Founder of Exit and Support Network (ESN)

5 WORLDWIDE CHURCH OF GOD PRACTICES

MISSION

The motto of the Worldwide Church of God is "Living and Sharing the Gospel."

The church seeks to fulfill this mission by:

- Building healthy, Christ-centered congregations that are sanctuaries of worship, friendship, and nurturing pastoral care.
- Providing sound biblical teaching through congregations, media, and personal outreach in relevant, meaningful forms for people of diverse backgrounds and ages.
- Expressing the love of God to all through the work of the Holy Spirit in our lives.
- Equipping people for Christian service so that the gospel can be known, understood, and experienced.
- Sharing in the work of the gospel with the broader Christian community, acknowledging that we can learn from one another and that Christ's love goes beyond denominational boundaries.

Worldwide Church of God

A CRITICAL VIEW

Throughout its sixty years of existence the WCG has been responsible for considerable devastation to the lives of thousands. Families have been left destroyed and financially impoverished. Members have been victimized by emotional, spiritual, and physical abuse.

During the 1970's considerable documentation exposed the massive corruption, sexual improprieties, hypocrisy, duality of agenda and deception that prevailed under the guise of religion and God.

While some have disputed doctrinal issues in the Worldwide Church of God, other professionals deal with the psychological impact and mental distress associated with cult victimization.

Techniques consisting of coercion, manipulation, authoritarian rule, fear, threats, etc. have been employed in efforts to hold the membership under control.

L. A. Stuhlman, Founder of Exit and Support Network (ESN)

PLAIN TRUTH MINISTRIES (PTM)

The Bible says that you are not a cosmic mistake or a result of chance but that your life, far from being meaningless, is filled with eternal significance. This truth is behind everything we do at Plain Truth Ministries (PTM).

As a non-denominational media ministry, PTM uses modern technologies of radio, the internet and publishing to help change the lives of those we serve.

Our purpose is not to bring people to any specific church, but to lead people who are seeking answers to life's most important questions to Jesus Christ through magazines, books and booklets, on the internet, and with videos and radio programs.

Many of those whom we serve are burned out with religion and legalism and want to be given spiritual help and inspiration from a distance, rather than risk repeating some of the negative experiences they have had in the past.

PTM helps identify the pitfalls and roadblocks that cause many Christians to lose sight of Jesus Christ, the central focus and foundation of Christianity.

PTM offers spiritual insight and encouragement to Christians of all denominations as well as those who are not members of any church. PTM is honest and forthright about the problems and shortcomings of organized religion. PTM helps by serving as a resource for Christians everywhere, of all denominations and creeds. PTM believes that the gospel of Jesus Christ is the truth that everyone needs, and we believe that truth should be plain.

PTM makes the truth plain for those who are seeking it. With such a confusing array of philosophies and religions in today's world, we think Christianity should be understood as plain, clear and sensible.

PTM is a member of the Evangelical Press Association (EPA) and the National Religious Broadcasters (NRB).

Plain Truth Ministries

6 WORLDWIDE CHURCH OF GOD BELIEFS

PLAIN TRUTH MINISTRIES STATEMENT OF FAITH

God

We believe in one eternal, triune God in three co-essential, yet distinct Persons: Father, Son and Holy Spirit.

Jesus Christ

We believe in the Lord Jesus Christ, begotten of the Holy Spirit, born of the Virgin Mary, fully God and fully human, the Son of God and Lord of all, worthy of worship, honor and reverence, who died for our sins, was raised bodily from the dead, ascended to heaven and will come again as King of kings.

Salvation

We believe that human salvation is the gift of God, by grace through faith in Jesus Christ, not earned by personal merit or good works.

The Church

We believe in the spiritual unity of believers in our Lord Jesus Christ.

Plain Truth Ministries

A CRITICAL VIEW OF WORLDWIDE CHURCH OF GOD BELIEFS

Members were indoctrinated with the following:

- It is the one true Church.
- Herbert Armstrong was the one true apostle appointed by Christ in this age. He alone had the truth to the Bible.
- The church is God's one true government on earth which is government from the top down.
- Leaving the church means loss of salvation and annihilation in the Lake of Fire.
- The church demands obedience to authority.

L. A. Stuhlman, Founder of Exit and Support Network (ESN)

7 SPLITS FROM THE WORLDWIDE CHURCH OF GOD

INTRODUCTION

As a result of the doctrinal and practical changes brought in by the new leadership of the Worldwide Church of God since Armstrong's death, as many as 104 organizations have been listed as having splintered from the Worldwide Church of God to form separate entities. The list, compiled by Joseph Tkach Jr., includes the following breakaway churches:

- the Global Church of God
- the Philadelphia Church of God
- the United Church of God
- Triumph Prophetic Ministries (Church of God)
- Christian Churches of God.

All of these splinter groups continue to promote Armstrongism.

THE PHILADELPHIA CHURCH OF GOD

The Philadelphia Church of God was founded in 1989 and headquartered in Edmond, Oklahoma and is a strong promoter of Armstrongism.

It is led by Gerald Flurry, who was ejected from the Worldwide Church of God "for disagreement with the new direction" taken by Armstrong's appointed successor, Joseph W. Tkach, Sr.

The Philadelphia Church of God has now 6,000 members in 115 countries.

It publishes the monthly *The Philadelphia Trumpet* which has a circulation of some 80,000, replacing, and in many ways replicating, Armstrong's *The Plain Truth*, and *True Education*.

A booklet called: *WCG Doctrinal Changes and the Tragic Results* urges old Armstrongites to accept the "restored truths lost to the Church over the centuries . . . restored to the Church during Mr. Armstrong's ministry."

THE UNITED CHURCH OF GOD

In 1995, a group of the WCG's most senior pastors, along with 12,000 members, formed a new group called the United Church of God. It is led by David Hulmes of Pasadena.

The United Church of God has about 220 churches in the US, and about 150 in the rest of the world. It claims to have 21,000 members.

8 QUOTATIONS

If the leaders of the Worldwide Church of God want to obey the Word of God, let them disband their unscriptural organization and exhort their members to get saved by trusting the finished atonement of Jesus Christ and to join sound New Testament churches. By attempting to reform an unscriptural organization which has such a wretched and apostate history, the leaders of the WCG are creating tremendous confusion.

Bible Discernment Ministries

Sadly, Christians outside the WCG have been suspicious and slow to extend the right hand of fellowship.

David Neff, an editor of Christianity Today

PART FOUR

OCCULT

CONTENTS

Introduction

Divination

Magic, Magick

Spiritism and Spiritualism

CONTENTS IN DETAIL

INTRODUCTION   739

1 DIVINATION   743
  Introduction   743
  Astrology   744
    The Zodiac
      Twelve signs of the Zodiac
      Two Poems
    Fortune-tellers
    Horoscopes
  Tarot Cards   750
    Cartomancy
  Crystal ball, mirrors, psychometry   752
  Palm reading, phrenology.   752
  Rod and pendulum   753
  Tea leaf reading   753
  Dice and dominoes   754
  I Ching   754
  Snail shells and coconuts   754
  Tables of fate and the wheel of fortune   754
  Telepathy, clairvoyance   755
  Dreams   755
  Numerology   755
  Selenomancia   755

2 MAGIC, MAGICK   756
    Introduction   756
  White magic, black magic   756
    Introduction
    Biblical assessment
    Acupuncture
    Typical rite of magic
  Witchcraft   756
    Introduction
    Witchcraft assessed
    Types of witchcraft
    Witch doctors
    Membership and history
    What it is
    Covens
    Women

    Gods
    Esbat and Sabbat
    The rite
  Wicca   762
    Introduction
    History and background of Wicca
    Wicca beliefs and practices
    Mother Goddess, Horned God
    Maiden, Mother, and Crone
    Mother Goddess' names
    Horned God
    Horned God's names
    A Wicca view of god
    The Wiccan Rede
    The Law of the Three
    Relativism and moral relativity
    Wicca Practices
  The Church of Satan   768
    What it is
    Founder
    Revered texts
    The Satanic Bible
    Nine Satanic statements
    Satanic sins
    Black mass

3 SPIRITISM AND SPIRITUALISM   770
    Introduction   770
    History of spiritism   770
    Extent of spiritism and spiritualism   770
    Spiritism and Christianity   771
    The creed of Spiritualism   771
    Séances   771
      Critical view of séances
      Séances in churches
    The spirit world   772
      Poltergeists
      Ouija boards

Glossary   773

INTRODUCTION

WARNING TO READERS

This section is not for the faint-hearted. This encyclopedia pitches us into the world of heresy, false teaching, anti-Christian organizations, atheism, Satanism, doomsday cults, hidden and mysterious groups, naked evil, and the world of the occult. None of this is to be taken light-heartedly. Christians should only ever enter this world if they are fully armed with the Christian's spiritual weapons of warfare, as they are outlined in Ephesians 6:10-17.

While the greatest need in the world today is for the truth of the Christian gospel to be spread, a necessary part of that activity is to identify and expose evil in all its forms. That is one of the purposes of this part of *The Encyclopedia of World Religions, Cults, and the Occult.*

DEFINING THE OCCULT

The term, "occult" comes from the Latin *occultus* meaning "hidden."

The word "occult" may be defined as any practice to do with the supernatural that is forbidden in the Bible or is self-evidently evil.

> The term is applied to practices which are below the surface of normal life. They may be contacts with the evil spirit world, deliberately sought through (black) magic or Satanism. Or they may be the fostering of experiences that occasionally comes to Christians or non-Christians alike, such as second-sight, prevision and telepathy.
>
> *J. Stafford Wright*

The word "occult" is most often used to describe any attempt to gain supernatural power or knowledge apart from the God of the Bible. Generally it refers to witchcraft, Satanism, Neo-Paganism, or various forms of psychic discernment (astrology, séances, palm reading, etc.).

THE OCCULT AND THE OLD TESTAMENT

If you wanted to summarize the teaching about the occult in the Old Testament in a sentence, it might be: "Don't touch it with a barge-pole: give it a wide birth."

God's people were instructed in Deuteronomy 18:9: "When you enter the land the LORD your God is giving you, do not learn to imitate the detestable ways of the nations there." Verses 10 to 11 list these "detestable ways." Anyone who:

- sacrifices his son or daughter in the fire
- practices divination
- practices sorcery
- interprets omens
- engages in witchcraft
- casts spells
- is a medium
- is a spiritist
- consults the dead.

Verses 12 and 13 continue: "Anyone who does these things is detestable to the LORD, and because of these detestable practices the LORD your God will drive out those nations before you. You must be blameless before the LORD your God."

THE OCCULT AND "CLUELESS" CHRISTIANS

It may not be a good idea for all readers to be closely acquainted with all the material on the occult given in this book. But the problem is that occult practices are so widespread and invasive, and at the same time so deceitful and cloaked, ministries of darkness that are paraded as agencies of light, that Christians are deceived. All too often the only people in the world who have the spiritual armory to defeat these practices are the last people in the world to be aware of their insidious, malignant influence. Sadly, many Christians are blissfully ignorant of satanic activities going on under their noses. This results in weak and vulnerable people not being warned and steered away from the vice-like, demonic grip of the occult. The chapters in *Encyclopedia of World Religions, Cults, and the Occult* on the occult have been written to remedy this.

HEADING DEXPOSING THE OCCULT

One of the aims of *The Encyclopedia of World Religions, Cults, and the Occult* is to give a factual account of every sect, cult or group it mentions. But *The Encyclopedia of World Religions, Cults, and the Occult* also deliberately sets out to expose evil. In the light of the teaching of the Bible, the warped beliefs and sordid practices of the occult are shown up to be what they are. What matters is not what any book or person may think about the schemes of Satan – but what God's inspired teaching in the Bible has to say. This encyclopedia compares the teaching of the occult with the teaching of God's word. It also leaves the reader in no doubt about the biblical teaching on how God's followers should act when faced with devilish practices.

DISCERNMENT IN THE FACE OF DECEPTION

The greatest need amongst Christians and Christian leaders is for discernment which is so sadly lacking in the Church today.

David E. Garner

Deception of any kind is a terrible thing, but spiritual deception is a monstrous evil.

Gordon Sears

QUOTATIONS TO HEED

It is difficult to communicate the dangers of the occult to anyone who has not been personally involved in some kind of occultism or who has never tried to help a person who has been deeply immersed in the occult. The following quotations makes us all pause for thought as we consider the evil nature of the occult.

In contemporary Western society there has been a phenomenal increase in occult

activity. There are estimated to be over 2,000 occult sects in France, with over 70,000 fortune-tellers, clairvoyants and astrologers.

Paul Young

It is estimated that 10 million Americans are addicted to occultism of some kind. Canadians are going in for what is probably the biggest revival of astrology since the fall of Babylon.

MacLean's Magazine

Man's fiercest foe from the Garden of Eden right to the end of time is not cancer, communism, disease or death. It is the devil!

Billy Graham

Satanism is alive and well, and the sad thing is that it is growing among teen-agers.

Roger Burt

Satanism is a blatantly selfish, brutal religion. It is based on the belief that man is inherently a selfish, violent creature . . . that the earth will be ruled by those who fight to win.

(Satanist) Anton LaVey of the First Church of Satan, California

There are two equal and opposite errors into which our race can fall about the devils. One is to disbelieve in their existence. The other is to believe, and to feel an unhealthy interest in them. They themselves are equally pleased by both errors and hail a materialist or a magician with the same delight.

C. S. Lewis

POSSIBLE DEMONIC ENTRY POINTS

The following list of possible demonic entry points into our own lives and the lives of any Christian fellowship seems to be endless. To be aware of the possible danger is half the battle.

Abstract art (under hallucinogenic stimulus)
Acupuncture
Amulets (tiger's claw, shark's tooth, horseshoe

over door, mascots, talisman (magic picture)

Ankh (a cross with a ring top used in satanic rites)

Apparitions (occultic)

Astral travel

Astrology

Augury (interpreting omens)

Automatic writing

Birth signs

Black arts

Black magic (involving hidden powers for bad ends)

Black mass

Blood subscriptions (pacts)

Cartomancy (using playing cards)

Chain letters

Charming or enchanting (attempts to use spirit power)

Charms and charming for wart removal

Chinese astrology

Clairaudience (ability to hear voices and sounds supernormally – spirited voices alleging to be those of dead people giving advice or warnings)

Clairsentience (supernormal sense perception)

Clairvoyance (ability to see objects or events spontaneously or supernormally above their normal range of vision – second sight)

Color therapy

Concept therapy

Conjuration (summoning up a spirit by incantation)

Coven (a community of witches)

Crystal ball gazing

Crystals

Death magic (where the name of the sickness plus a written spell is cast into coffin or grave)

Demon worship

Disembodied spirits

Divining rod or twig or pendulum (see Hosea 4:12)

Dowsing or witching for water, minerals, underground cables, finding out the sex of unborn child using divining rod, pendulum, twig or planchette

Dream interpretation (as with Edgar Cayce books)

Dungeons and dragons

Eastern meditation/religion – gurus, mantras, yoga, temples, etc.

Ectoplasm (unknown substance from body of a medium)

Enchanting

ESP (extra sensory perception)

Findhorn Community

Floating trumpets

Fortune-telling

Gothic rock music

Gurus

Gypsy curses

Hallucinogenic drugs (cocaine, heroin, marijuana, sniffing glue, etc.)

Handwriting analysis (for fortune-telling)

Hard rock music

Heavy metal music

Hepatoscopy (examination of liver for interpretation)

Hex signs (hexagrams)

Horoscopes

Hydromancy (divination by viewing images in water)

Hypnosis

Idols

Incantations

Iridology (eye diagnosis)

Japanese flower arranging (sun worship)

Jonathan Livingstone Seagull (Reincarnation, Hinduism)

Kabbala (occult lore)

Karma

Levitation

Lucky charms or signs of the Zodiac or birthstones

Magic (not sleight of hand but use of supernatural power)

Mantras

Martial arts (aikido, judo, karate, kung fu, etc.)

Mediums

Mental suggestion

Mental telepathy

Mental therapy

Mesmerism

Metaphysics (study of spirit world)

Mind control

Mind dynamics

Mind mediumship

Mind reading

Moon-mancy

Motorskopua (mechanical pendulum for

diagnosing illness)
Mysticism
Necromancy (conjuring up spirits of the dead)
Numerical symbolism
Numerology
Occultic games
Occult letters of protection
Occult literature
The Greater World
The 6th & 7th Book of Moses
The other side
The book of Venus
Pseudo-Christian works of Jacob Lorber
Works by the following authors:
Edgar Cayce
Aleister Crowley
Jean Dixon
Levi Dowling
Arthur Ford (*The Overt Worship of Spirit Beings*)
Johann Greber
Andrew Jackson Davis
Anton Le Vay
Ruth Montgomery
John Newborough
Eric Von Daniken
Dennis Wheatley.
Omens
Ouija boards
Pagan fetishes
Pagan religious objects, artifacts and relics
Pagan rites (Voodoo, Sing sings, Corroborees, Fire walking, Umbahda, Macumba)
Palmistry
Pk (parakineses – control of objects by the power of the mind and will)
Parapsychology (PS) – especially study of demonic activity
Pendulum diagnosis
Phrenology (divining/analysis from the skull)
Planchette (divining)
Precognition (foreknowledge of the occurrence of events)
Psychic healing
Psychic sight
Psychography (use of heart-shaped board)
Psychometry (telling fortunes by lifting or holding object belonging to the enquirer)
Punk rock music
Pyramidology (mystic powers associated with models of pyramids)
Rebirthing
Reincarnation
Rhabdomancy (casting sticks into the air for interpreting omens)
Satanism
Séances
Self hypnosis
Significant pagan days
Silva Mind Control (SMC – psychorientology)
Sorcery
Spells
Spirit knockings or rappings
Star signs
Stichomancy (fortune-telling from random reference to books)
Stigmata (occultic types)
Superstitions (self or parents or grandparents)
Table tipping
Tarot cards (twenty-two picture cards for fortune-telling)
Tea-leaf reading
Thought transference
Tk (telekineses – objects move around room, instruments play, engines start, etc.)
TM (Transcendental Meditation
Trances
Transmigration
Travel of the soul
UFO fixation
Uri Geller
White magic (invoking hidden powers for "good ends")
Witchcraft
Yoga (which may involve Eastern demon worship)
Zodiac charms, birthdates
Zodiac signs

The following pages follow the three kinds of Occult in this order:
1 Divination
2 Magic
3 Spiritism

1 DIVINATION

Introduction
A Astrology
   (i) The Zodiac
      a. Two poems
      b. The twelve signs of the Zodiac
   (ii) Fortune-tellers
   (iii) Horoscopes
B Tarot cards
   (i) Cartomancy.
C Crystal ball, mirrors, psychometry
D Palm reading, phrenology

E Rod and pendulum
F Tea leaf reading
G Dice and dominoes
H *I Ching*
I Snail shells and coconuts
J Tables of fate and the wheel of fortune
K Telepathy, clairvoyance
L Dreams
M Numerology
N Selenomancia

INTRODUCTION

Divination is a generic term for attempting to foretell or explore the future, and to shape our lives according to what is coming. Someone who practices divination is called a fortune-teller.

A ASTROLOGY

WHAT IT IS

Divination based on the supposed influence of the stars upon human events. Astrology is "the art of judging the occult influence of the stars upon human affairs." *The Shorter Oxford English Dictionary*

> Astrology is an ancient fatalistic system of divination using the position of the planets, moon and sun in the twelve Zodiac positions at the moment of one's birth to gain occult or hidden knowledge of the future.

> The Watchman Expositor

Astrology claims that the arrangement of the stars, planets, and constellations at the time of one's birth sets a determined pattern in a person's life.

(I) THE ZODIAC

The word "Zodiac" comes from the Greek *zoe* (animal, life) and *diskos* (wheel), and so means "the wheel of life," or "the parade of animals."

The zodiac is a name given to the path of the Earth's orbit around the sun. This path is divided into thirty degree segments or sectors, each with its own sign: there are thus twelve signs. The signs of the zodiac, also known as "sun signs," indicate which sector the sun was in at the time of someone's birth. The signs follow a pattern that never changes: Aries, Taurus, Gemini, Cancer, Leo, Virgo, Libra, Scorpio, Sagittarius, Capricorn, Aquarius and Pisces. The sun is in one sign or another, it cannot be in two signs at the same time.

Each of these twelve signs is supposed to represent certain positive as well as negative characteristics in human behavior. These signs are also associated with four elements: fire, earth, air and water and three modalities: cardinal, fixed and mutable.

The Zodiac is one of Satan's big lies, but it is consulted regularly by 40 million Americans. Horoscopes run in 1,220 of the 1,750 dailies in the United States and are considered authoritative. There are three times as many astrologers and psychics as there are clergymen in America. More than $500 million is earned annually on telephone consulting lines giving enquirers their horoscopes.

A list of the dates, signs, symbols and elements of the signs of the Zodiac follows.

Dates (birth period)	Sign	Symbol	Element
Mar 21/Apr 20	Aries	the ram	F
Apr 21/May 20	Taurus	the bull	E
May21/June 20	Gemini	the twins	A
Jun 21/Jul 20	Cancer	the crab	W
Jul 23/Aug 22	Leo	the lion	F
Aug 23/Sep 22	Virgo	the virgin	E
Sep 23/Oct 22	Libra	the scales	A
Oct 23/Nov 22	Scorpio	the scorpion	W
Nov 23/Dec 22	Sagittarius	the archer	F
Dec 23/Jan 20	Capricorn	the goat	E
Jan 21/Feb 19	Aquarius	the water-bearer	A
Feb 20/Mar 20	Pisces	the fish	W

The right-hand symbols F, E, A,W denote the four elements fire, earth, air and water. Each zodiacal sign is associated with one of these elements in turn.

E. Cobham Brewer tells the order of the twelve constellations by describing their symbols rather than names.

A. TWO POEMS

Our vernal[1] signs the RAM begins,
Then comes the BULL, in May the
TWINS;
The CRAB in June, next LEO shines,
And VIRGO ends the northern signs.

The BALANCE brings autumnal fruits,
The SCORPION stings, the ARCHER
shoots;
December's GOAT brings wintry blast,
AQUARIUS rain, the FISH comes last.
(◊vernal: of/in the season of spring)
E. Cobham Brewer

The RAM, the BULL, the heavenly
TWINS,
And next the CRAB, the LION shines,
The VIRGO and the SCALES;

The SCORPION, ARCHER and SEA-
GOAT,
The MAN who pours the water out
And FISH with glittering tails.
*Isaac Watts (1674-1748), English hymn-
writer*

B. THE TWELVE SIGNS OF THE ZODIAC

Aries (March 21-April 21)
Aries, the ram, is the first sign of the zodiac and symbolizes a new beginning. It is endlessly creative, but never completes a task. It is not very sympathetic, and hates weakness. It is the sign of the eternal warrior. Aries rules the head.

Element: fire
Quality: cardinal
Ruling planet: Mars
Key phrase: "I am"

Taurus (April 21-May 21)
Taurus, the sign of the bull, is the sign of purposeful determination and productivity. Very resourceful, perceptive and alert for good business opportunities, it maximizes profit through reliance on its own talents. It can generate great wealth. Can be very materialistic, and can be quite cruel to those who stand in its way. Taurus rules the neck.

Element: earth
Quality: fixed
Ruling planet: Venus
Key phrase: "I have"

Gemini (May 21-June 21)
Gemini, the twins, represents curiosity and the urge to learn and communicate. It is quick-witted, restless and mentally brilliant, but lacks depth - it is the jack of all trades and master of none. It adjusts quickly to circumstances, and can juggle many things at once. Gemini rules the arms, hands, shoulders and lungs.

Element: air
Quality: mutable
Ruling planet: Mercury
Key phrase: "I think"

Cancer (21 June-July 21)
Cancer, the crab, introduces personal meanings and values. It represents the urge to build a home and is the nurturing sign. It is very intuitive, imaginative, and illogical. It always seeks to preserve life and protect the rights of individuals and property. It is talented at managing others. Cancer rules the stomach.

Element: water
Quality: cardinal
Ruling planet: Moon
Key phrase: "I feel"

Leo (July 21-August 21)
Leo, the lion, is the sign of confidence and power. Those with Leo traits radiate warmth to all and bask in adoration and affection. They love to give and receive love. They are dramatic, great organizers and leaders – others always feel great confidence in them. They are also stubborn, dogmatic and egotistic. Leo rules the heart and the spine.

Element: fire
Quality: fixed

Ruling planet: Sun
Key phrase: "I will"

Virgo (August 21-September 21)
Virgo, the virgin, is the sign of work and duty.
It takes care of all the details. Its desire for
perfection and order makes it prudish, and
obsessed with efficiency. Since it is
uncomfortable with the unknown, Virgo is
the sign of technology and scientific research.
It has a strong need to help the poor and the
sick. Virgo rules the intestines.

Element: earth
Quality: mutable
Ruling planet: Mercury
Key phrase: "I analyze"

Libra (September 21-October 21)
Libra, the scales, is the most cultured, refined,
artistic and musical of the signs. It has a strong
sense of justice and balance, and it brings
reconciliation through negotiation. Libras are
constantly evaluating and able to see both
sides of an issue, though they can be quite
indecisive. It is the sign of war as well as peace.
Libra rules the kidneys and loins.

Element: air
Quality: cardinal
Ruling Planet: Venus
Key phrase: "I balance"
Back to Zodiac Signs

Scorpio (October 21-November 21)
Scorpio, the scorpion, is the most passionate
and strong-willed sign. It seeks to penetrate
beneath the surface, probe the mysteries, and
uncover what is hidden. Aware of
vulnerability and death, it has iron
determination, and is steadfast in its struggles
with its enemies and for fulfillment of its
desires. It is the sign of spiritual rebirth.
Scorpio rules the sex organs.

Element: water
Quality: fixed
Ruling planet: Pluto
Key phrase: "I desire"

Sagittarius (November 21-December 21)
Sagittarius, the centaur, is the sign of

philosophy, the higher mind, higher
education, publishing, the press, organized
religion, diplomacy and flight. Well adjusted,
it insists on freedom for itself and others. It
thinks big, and speaks openly regardless of the
outcome. Sagittarians are daring and
adventurous, and tend to exaggerate
achievements. It rules the hips and thighs.

Element: fire
Quality: mutable
Ruling planet: Jupiter
Key phrase: "I see"

Capricorn (December 21 to January 21)
Capricorn, the goat, is ambitious and has the
aim to achieve status. Capricorns are very
good organizers, and can be persistent and
focused, never cutting corners since the aim is
right and truth rather than expedience. They
tend to be conscientious, realistic and possess
a high integrity which can be relied upon,
until they decide to use others for their own
needs. Capricorn rules the hips and thighs.

Element: earth
Quality: cardinal
Ruling planet: Saturn
Key phrase: "I rule"

Aquarius (January 21-February 21)
Aquarius, the water bearer, challenges
authority and seeks the new and unfamiliar. It
stands for knowledge and friendship toward
all. Aquarians are charismatic leaders, non-
conformists who try to understand the world
as it is and reinvent it. They are objective,
unemotional and can be detached. They are
original, unpredictable, intellectual and
independent. It rules the legs and ankles.

Element: air
Quality: fixed
Ruling planets: Uranus and Saturn
Key phrase: "I know"

Pisces (February 21-March 21)
Pisces, the fishes, the twelfth and last sign of
the zodiac, seeks to understand and identify
with the whole of creation and find ultimate
redemption. It wishes to be part of all, but not

to enclose itself. It seeks escape from the limits of form and this gives it the capacity to shirk responsibility and deceive itself and others. Pisces rules the feet.

Element: water
Quality: mutable
Ruling planets: Neptune and Jupiter
Key phrase: "I believe"

(II) FORTUNE TELLERS

A fortune-teller is anyone who tries to predict the future using any means, such as psychic divination, telepathy, astrology, the zodiac, cards, crystal balls, palm reading, pendulum, numerology, dreams, etc.

ENTICING CLAIMS
Four psychic providers advertise in the following ways:

Uncover your future – romance, passion, money, health, career, ask psychic advice, read your horoscopes, get a Tarot and palmistry reading, interpret your dreams, biorhythms and numerology readings."
Psychic Realm

This stunning new astrology service offers free horoscopes personalized just for you! They take your birth details and calculate the daily planetary alignments back to the alignment of the planets on the day you were born, to give you an accurate reading, day by day, different from everyone else's!"
Astrocall horoscopes

Natal astrology charts, forecast reports and compatibility astrology. Explore a large selection of reports designed to take your awareness of yourself and others to the next level of personal growth.
Sky View Zone Astrology

The story of your life told in 25 amazing pages you will never forget!
Your unique in-depth kozmik horoscope is sent to you within 24 hours when you pay by credit card.

What does your own unique horoscope tell you about your life?
Now you can find out, really fast, by simply sending me the place, time and date of your birth.
Your horoscope reading and birth chart will be emailed to you within 24 hours when you pay by credit card online in just one minute.
You'll receive a highly detailed and precise 25-page report telling the story of your life with a level of accuracy that will astonish you.
My world-exclusive super-powerful horoscope interpretation program has taken over five years to develop. And is designed to reveal the many hidden sides to your talents, your abilities and the baffling events of your life we call fate.
In fact, the highly detailed 25 pages of the report will astound you with the precision of their analysis and predictions.
Find out what the heavens had in store for you at the moment of your birth.
It will prove highly illuminating!
Kozmikhoroscopes

CHARLATANS
In 1990, 186 distinguished scientists issued a no-nonsense statement savagely attacking astrology:

The time has come to challenge directly and forcefully the pretentious claims of astrological charlatans. It's simply a mistake to imagine that the forces exerted by stars and planets at the moment of birth can in any way shape the future.

(III) HOROSCOPES

The word "horoscope" means "scope of the hour." From your geographical place of birth and the date and hour when you were born, it is supposedly possible to calculate your future, and whether or not conditions are favorable for anything your propose to do, from a business transaction, a career, an airplane trip, or a marriage.
In America, 30,000 people pay $20 to receive monthly computerized horoscopes.

CASTING A HOROSCOPE

Those who cast (give) a horoscope, have a circle (which represents the heavens) divided into twelve segments called "houses."

The Twelve Houses

1. Personality generally
2. Money and finance
3. Brothers and sisters, short journeys
4. One parent (usually father), the last period of life
5. Children, pleasure, theatres, gambling
6. Health and servants, Armed Forces
7. Marriage and open enemies
8. Death and other people's money
9. Religion, long journeys
10. Profession and standing in the world, one parent
11. Friends, children
12. Secret enemies, hospitals

Birth chart

A horoscope or a birth chart is a representation of the start of an event, and shows the positions of all the planets in our solar system. It claims to be a picture of your connection to the universe.

SEEKING CUSTOMERS

Here is one person seeking new customers by promising to reveal to your more details about yourself by telling you your horoscope.

Horoscopes and star signs as popularly published within magazines, newspapers and web sites are a very simple form of an Astrologers work. You may be typical of your Sun sign but the full flavor of your characteristics and forecast is dependent on much more, and this is very unique to each individual or event.

This subject enables greater self awareness so that we can learn to live life to the full and according to our innermost natures, enhancing our individuality and self expression.

A professional astrologer draws a birth chart or horoscope using tables of data or a computer to work out where all the planets are at the time of the event to be determined.

Most people are familiar with the idea that this event could be your birth, but in fact it could be the start of any event, country, venture, or business and of course it is excellent for determining character, timing of events and who will get on with who.

When full account is taken of all the planets in your birth chart and an accurate time and place of birth are known, a considerable degree of accuracy can be obtained in character and timings for life events leading to a more fulfilled life.

Annabel Burton

BIBLICAL RESPONSE

Astrology is a part of both divination and worship of the heavens, and both are condemned by the Bible.

• Astrology is prohibited

All the counsel you have received has only worn you out!
Let your astrologers come forward, those stargazers who make predictions month by month, let them save you from what is coming upon you.

Surely they are like stubble;
the fire will burn them up.
They cannot even save themselves from the power of the flame.
Here are no coals to warm anyone;
here is no fire to sit by.

Isaiah 47:13-14

And when you look up to the sky and see the sun, the moon and the stars – all the heavenly array – do not be enticed into bowing down to them and worshiping things the LORD your God has apportioned to all the nations under heaven.

Deuteronomy 4:19

- The Bible warns against the false predictions of astrology (Jeremiah 10:2; 27:9-10; Daniel 2:1-4; 4:7; 5:7-9)

- The Bible condemns the worship of the sun, moon and stars as well as the deities or demons associated with them. (Deuteronomy 17:2-5; 2 Kings 21:3, 5; Zephaniah 1:5; Job 31:26-28; Jeremiah 8:1-2)

- Seeking guidance from astrology is not only condemned, it is of no value:

Daniel replied, "No wise man, enchanter, magician or diviner can explain to the king the mystery he has asked about, but there is a God in heaven who reveals mysteries. He has shown King Nebuchadnezzar what will happen in days to come."

Daniel 2:27-28

DANGERS

As an ancient pagan system of divination, astrology easily traps people in occult practices and philosophy.

The consequences of false predictions in all areas of life, such as finance, relationships, and health, have resulted in spiritistic influence, spirit-possession, or even death.

QUOTATIONS

Astrology likes to pass itself off as a scientific and psychological tool, ignoring its roots in pagan worship of the stars and in occultism.

The Watchman Expositor

Though some advocates of astrology claim their practice is supported by the Bible, the Assemblies of God believes and teaches that God's Word strongly denounces astrology because of its association with the occult and demonic.

The General Council of the Assemblies of God

Astrology is not to be confused with astronomy, the science that studies the size, movement, and composition of celestial bodies. Astrology, a pseudo science, claims that stars and other heavenly bodies influence human personality and activity and that the position of celestial bodies at a given time can foretell future events in the lives of people.

The Encyclopedia of New Age Beliefs, *Harvest House, 1996*

There are dozens of ways to foretell the future! All of them, like astrology and the psychics, are schemes to obtain money from stupid people. But they are not "fun games," they are the work of Satan, says the Bible. So don't even try them, you are going to be burned in this life!

J. Dominguez, M.D.

The person who dabbles in fortunetelling expresses a lack of trust in the wisdom of God, who has revealed to us what we need to know.

John M. Parlow, author

B TAROT CARDS

"Tarot," means "tablets of destiny." A pack of Tarot cards has seventy-eight cards, twenty-two of them with "major mysteries," corresponding to the twenty-two letters of the Hebrew alphabet, inscribed with symbols that vary from pack to pack. All packs contain four major suits called wands, cups, pentacles, and swords. Court cards include the king, queen, knight, and page, symbolizing spirit, soul, vitality and body.

The Tarot is a deck of cards that originated over 500 years ago in northern Italy. Although the Tarot was first used in a game called Triumphs, it was quickly adopted as a tool for divination, and popularized by occult societies such as the Hermetic Order of the Golden Dawn. The early Tarot symbolism was deeply rooted in Medieval and Renaissance Europe, but over the centuries it has grown to incorporate everything from astrology and Kabbalah to runes (which predate the Tarot by 1,000) and the *I Ching* (which predates the Tarot by 2,500 years). Today, the Tarot is far and away the most popular tool for spiritual introspection in the West.

INTRODUCTION TO TAROT READINGS

Tarot readings are arrangements of cards drawn from a shuffled deck. The layout of the cards is known as a spread, and determines what each card refers to. For example, the Two Paths spread is used to understand an upcoming decision, and hence it uses cards to represent the different options and their outcomes.

DECKS

Tarot decks consist of seventy-eight cards. Twenty-two of the cards are major arcana (trumps), such as The Lovers, The Fool, The Pope, and The World. The remaining fifty-six cards are minor arcana divided into four suits of fourteen cards each. The suits are Swords, Cups, Wands (sometimes called Rods or Staves), and Pentacles (sometimes called Coins or Discs).

REVERSALS

About half of the cards in a reading are drawn reversed (upside down), which either negates or inverts their meaning. For example, Death upright means "change," but Death reversed means "stagnation."

MAJOR ARCANA CARDS

Here is a brief explanation of each card's meaning:

Fool	new beginnings, adventures, innocence
Magician	power, action, concentration, mastery
High Priestess	intuition, wisdom, education, mystery
Empress	mother, fertility, nature, life, teacher
Emperor	father, power, authority, wealth, success, courage
Hierophant	knowledge, education, conformity, dogma
Lovers	relationships (lovers and family), love
Chariot	journey, travel, success
Strength	strength, courage, conviction, resolve
Hermit	inner strength, loneliness, solitude, introspection, spiritual guidance
Wheel of Fortune	fortune, wealth, change, unexpected events, luck
Justice	balance, equality, harmony, legal dealings
Hanged Man	reversal, self-sacrifice, new beginnings, meditation
Death	unexpected change, transformation, loss, rebirth
Temperance	harmony, balance, self-control, moderation
Devil	violence, negative energy (and the need to release it), obsession

Tower	sudden change, loss (of friends or financial security)
Star	faith, hope, optimism, courage
Moon	illusion, confusion, deception, imagination, dreams, intuition
Sun	love, joy, happiness, success, material happiness, family happiness
Judgment	forgiveness, rebirth, positive career choice, awakening
World	fulfillment, completion, success

Each card is supposed to carry different meanings to different people, depending upon their life situation.

MINOR ARCANA CARDS

The fifty-six minor arcana cards represent the energy, emotions and activities of our daily lives and are divided into four suits: pentacles, cups, swords, and wands.

PENTACLES

Also known as Disks, Coins and Diamonds in the modern deck of cards, Pentacles represent business, money, material possession, practical skills and tangible accomplishment.

This suit corresponds to the astrological Earth signs of Capricorn, Taurus, and Virgo.

CUPS

Also known as Chalices and Hearts in the modern deck, these are cards of emotion and reflection and indicate spiritual authority, contemplation and inner feelings.

Cups corresponds to the astrological Water signs of Pisces, Cancer and Scorpio

SWORDS

Also known as Spades in a modern deck, the Swords indicate temporal authority, leadership, wisdom, ideas, creativity and decisiveness.

This suit corresponds to the astrological Air signs of Aquarius, Gemini and Libra

WANDS

Also known as Staves, Staffs or Clubs in the modern deck of cards, these cards indicate practical strength, productivity, confidence, physical power and self-reliance.

Wands corresponds to the astrological Fire signs of Aries, Leo and Sagittarius.

Each suit has fourteen cards.

COURT CARDS

Court cards are the influence of your personality on others:

Page	youth innocence
Knight	energy drive
Queen	understanding awareness
King	strength of will

ACE TO NUMBER 10

Ace	beginning
2	formation, coming together of opposites (initiative).
3	growth
4	practical attainment, material achievement (stability), work
5	new circle, change, stability upset (activity)
6	finding equilibrium, harmony in the face of constant change,(ambition)
7	facing complex choices, development of soul (versatility)
8	setting priorities, putting things where they belong, balancing (shrewd), reaping what you sow.
9	bring things to an end, completion, conclusion, (dependability)
10	over but not finished and about to begin again (persistent).

(I) CARTOMANCY

Cartomancy is like Tarot but uses the fifty-two regular playing cards, or only thirty-two, discarding the 2s, 3s, 4s, 5s, and 6s.

Cartomancy forecasts the future by means of using cards. The elaborately illustrated cards used in this technique are called Tarot Cards. Supposedly these cards hold the secrets to the future.

DANGERS

Stay away from Tarot cards as you stay away from a serpent.

J. Dominguez, M.D.

Since these readings invariably lead a person away from the God of the Bible, and attempt to invade an area of knowledge God has determined should remain secret, we must conclude that they are demonic.

Each of these fifty-two cards in a deck (pack) of cards has a secret meaning. Nicknames for a deck of cards include: "The Devil's Bible" and "The Devils Picture Book."

Some witches, psychics, and Satan worshipers use playing cards for divination and to cast spells and curses.

BIBLICAL RESPONSE

See Deuteronomy 7:26; 1 John 2:15-17; Romans 12:1,2; 2 Corinthians 6:17, 18; 1 Timothy 6:12.

C CRYSTAL BALL, MIRRORS, AND PSYCHOMETRY

CRYSTAL BALL

A crystal ball is used by fortune-tellers, clairvoyants, and diviners in the technique known as skrying. Gazing into the glass, the diviner enters into a trance-like state, claiming to see present and future events (crystalomancy).

MIRRORS

Mirrors are used in Rosicrucianism. The initiate has to stare in a mirror, and trace a five-inch cross on it while repeating "Hail, Rosi Cross," until his imagination or the devil gives him a hallucination.

PSYCHOMETRY

Psychometry can also be classed in the area of fortune-telling. In psychometry, someone holds a physical object and then claims to be able to make statements and identify characteristics of the owner of that object, perhaps also foretelling part of the future.

WARNING

Psychometry has no place in a Christian's life.
Michael (Manouchehr) Ghaemmaghami

D PALM READING, PHRENOLOGY

PALM READING

Palmistry, or chiromancy, is the practice of telling a person's future and character from the shape and markings of the hands and fingers. It is not to be confused with chirology, which is the scientific study of the development of the shape and lines of the hands, or with graphology, which is handwriting analysis. It has been said that: "Everything, yes, absolutely everything about you is in your hand!"

Traditional palmists are typically fortune-tellers, and may also read your personality.

Contrary to modern handanalysts, they directly link a single feature or symbol on the hand to something significant, such as luck in a certain area of your life. They may have you believe that the following can be read from your hand:

* evil signs
* signs that show you will be rich or will receive money
* your past – accurate to the year
* your future
* your life-span

- your state of health (although to show signs of some conditions, doctors may typically look at your nails)
- how many kids you'll have and
- when you'll marry
  Michael (Manouchehr) Ghaemmaghami

While you are free to believe in what you like, hearing such things can be harmful and outright dangerous, and people's lives have been wrecked by palmists claiming that they will die or other such bad omens, living in fear of something that would of course never happen (at least, not because such a thing is in your hands, which it is certainly not!). Do not believe such claims for a second! Try to avoid such palmists at all costs.

Larry Rodrigues

What palmists do know is that a strong fate line reveals a determination to succeed in finding a definite purpose and reason to exist as well as a determination to find stability and security.

Palmistry International
Palm Reading is based in apparent scientific data, the lines and mounts on the palm; but as divination, to read the future, it is also a fake or a lie of the devil, in spite of being probably the oldest and most sophisticated method of divination.
J. Dominguez, M.D.

PHRENOLOGY
Phrenology is the study of the bumps and shape of the head in order to tell someone's character.

E ROD AND PENDULUM

The rod and pendulum are objects used by a diviner for detecting so-called "earth rays."

- The "rod" is usually a forked twig taken from a willow tree. Fish bone and metals are also used.
- The pendulum, is a metal disk suspended by a thread.

- The "earth rays" have their basis in the earth's magnetic field.

The lack of understanding of this phenomenon has lent credence to the sorts of superstitions that are prominent in occult practices.

F TEA LEAF READING

Tasseography is the reading of the tea or coffee cup deposits in different imaginary shapes.

Tea leaf reading is also a form of divination. It interprets the shapes and relative positions left by tea leaves at the bottom of a cup. Fortunes are told using the same principles as are found in the oriental *I Ching* readings.
Michael (Manouchehr) Ghaemmaghami

G Dice and dominoes

Dice and dominoes are the simplest methods of fortune-telling. They are carried out by giving an arbitrary meaning to each number.

1   unity
2   marriage

3   trinity

or:

1   the sun
2   the moon, etc.

H *I Ching*

The *I Ching*, or *Book of Changes*, predates recorded history. The diviner throws fifty yarrow sticks. The hexagram formed from six lines in the sticks is read and interpreted from the *Book of Changes* to read the present and the future.

Practitioners believe that the spirits are communicating with them through the medium of chance, as expressed in the fall of the sticks, coins, or wands.

I Snail shells and coconuts

Snail shells and coconuts are used in "Santeria" (a syncretistic Caribbean religion) to read the present and the future.

The "Snail Shells" is the most important divination procedure in Santeria. The priests throw eighteen shells, some of which fall on their base and others on their side. The meaning of these positions is read in the "Table of Ifa."

The "coconuts" are thrown and they fall with the white down or the white up, and the results are read in the Table.

J Tables of fate and the wheel of fortune

The "Tables of Fate" and the "Wheel of Fortune" are based in the same idea as the *I Ching* only numbers or a wheel of fortune are used.

K TELEPATHY, CLAIRVOYANCE

MENTAL TELEPATHY

Mental telepathy is communication from one mind to another without verbal exchange or other physical and empirical modes of communication. It is a branch of parapsychology.

CLAIRVOYANCE

Clairvoyance refers to the ability to see and describe events without using the normal means of perception (sight, touch, hearing, taste, smell). Some Christians have had this gift, but so has Satan.

L DREAMS

Oneiromancy is divination by interpreting dreams.

Dreams are normal psychological states, in the Bible used by God as a means of communicating warnings or promises about future events, as in the cases of Joseph (Geneses 40-41), and Joseph, Jesus' foster-father (Matthew 1:20, 2:13).

But dreams can also be used by psychics as a way of obtaining money, and their interpretations of dreams may by be guided by the lies of the devil.

M NUMEROLOGY

Numerology assigns arbitrary specific values and meanings to numbers. Pythagoras influenced the Kabalistic Cornelius Agrippa (the kabala/cabbala/qabalah was a secret mystical tradition of Jewish rabbis, who read hidden meanings into the Old Testament and other writings; the word is also applied to other secret or occult or mystic teachings and groups).

Cornelius Agrippa drew up the following numbering system:

1 stands for origin;
2 stands for marriage;
3 stands for trinity, wisdom;
4 stands for permanence;
5 stands for justice;
6 stands for creation;
7 stands for life;
8 stands for fullness.

N SELENOMANCIA

Selenomancia is divination by use of the moon.

2 MAGIC, MAGICK

INTRODUCTION

Magic is the second kind of occultism. While divination attempts to foretell the future, magic tries to change the future, as well as the present. It tries to manipulate nature and even spirits by means of spells, rituals, charms, and prayers.

Magic is the attempt to control the present, our lives, the lives of others, or events of nature, by ceremonies, charms, or spells believed to have supernatural powers. Aleister Crowley added a "k" to the end of the word ("Magick") to distinguish it from the "magicians" who entertain an audience with tricks and illusions.

Magic was used in all the ancient cultures long before the advent of Christianity. It is not, however, to be confused with priests, shamans, and doctors of old cultures, who heal with herbs, or prayers to God.

ALEISTER CROWLEY (1875-1947)

Aleister Crowley was a self-proclaimed drug and sex "fiend," a mostly self-published author of books on the occult and magick, a poet and mountaineer, and a leader of a cult called Ordo Templi Orientis (OTO) whose tenets he detailed in one of his many writings, *The Book of the Law*. The latter contains his version of the Law of Thelema, which Crowley claims he channeled for a "praeterhuman intelligence" called Aiwass.

Do what thou wilt shall be the whole of the Law is his motto for OTO. In practice, for Crowley this meant rejecting traditional morality in favor of the life of a drug addict and womanizer.

Robert Todd Carroll,
The Skeptics Dictionary

A WHITE MAGIC, BLACK MAGIC

(I) INTRODUCTION

White magic is used for good purposes, such as healing the sick, or making it rain or stopping a thunderstorm.

Black magic is used for bad purposes, such as harming people, or creating a hurricane, or starting a fire. Some forms, called "sex magic," involve the ritual sexual abuse of adults and children. This has reached epidemic proportions in many countries.

(II) BIBLICAL ASSESSMENT

In Ezekiel 13:17-23 Black Magic is discussed. Verses 17-19: "Now, son of man, set your face against the daughters of your people who prophesy [Psychic people] out of their own imaginations.

Prophesy against them and say, 'This is what the Sovereign LORD says : Woe to the women who sew magic charms on all their wrists and make veils of various lengths for their heads in order to ensnare people. Will you ensnare the lives of my people but preserve your own? You have profaned me among my people for a few handfuls of barley and scarps of bread. By lying to my people, who listen to lies, you have killed those who should not have died and have spared those who should not live.'"

And in verses 20-23: "'Therefore this is what the Sovereign LORD says: I am against your magic charms with which you ensnare people like birds and I will tear them from your arms; I will set free the people that you ensnare like birds. I will tear off you veils and save my people from your hands, and they will no longer fall prey to your power. Then you will know that I am the LORD. Because you disheartened the righteous with your lies, when I had brought them no grief, and because you encouraged the wicked not to turn from their evil ways and so save their lives, therefore you will no longer see false visions or practice divination. I will save my people from your hands. And then you will know that I am the LORD.'"

The pillows (amulets) and kerchiefs mentioned were objects used in connection with magical practices. An amulet is an object of superstition. It can be defined as "a material object on which a charm is written or over which a charm was said, worn on person to protect the wearer against dangers, disease, to serve as a shield against demons, ghosts, evil magic, and to bring good luck and good fortune." In the ancient world, along with many present day primitive tribes, the carrying of an amulet is a common everyday occurrence. These objects also called fetishes, talismans and charms supposedly to ward off evil spirits or bring luck to the wearer.

Note the mention of hunting the souls of "my people." Most people mistakenly assume that witchcraft cannot affect a Christian. They foolishly believe that being born again automatically protects against any kind of curse, spell or hex, etc., sent by people practicing witchcraft. Ezekiel 13 indicates that we are a favorite target of witchcraft practices which is the hunting (catching or snaring) of our souls (mind, will, emotions). Through witchcraft God's people can be brought into bondage, thus becoming captives. Notice key words in this passage which show the effects of this type of magic or witchcraft. To slay! (Ezekiel 13:19). Not only to hunt and snare, but to slay the souls that should not die. There was no

reason why these people should die, but through witchcraft they could be slain prematurely. God states flatly that people should not live when they go to a witch to seek help to lengthen their life or be restored in health through magical arts.

In verse 22 of Ezekiel 13 the charge is, "with lies you have made the heart of the righteous sad." Depression comes to the heart of the righteous through magical practices. Other translations state that the heart of the righteous are discouraged or disheartened. The righteous are the targets and this shows the effects of witchcraft on God's people.

God says in Ezekiel 13:19 that witchcraft will, "Turn away my people from me." How many ministers and other Christians have backslidden because of heavy demonic influence induced by witchcraft? Such terrible things can happen to God's people through witchcraft.

- They can be saddened (depression)
- they can be ensnared (captivity)
- they can be slain (premature death)
- they can be turned away (backsliding).

Remember the things which can happen to God's people (to the righteous) if they are unaware of the perils of witchcraft. They can be brought into a state of oppression or depression; unexplainable sadness, anguish, and heart affliction when there is no reason for feeling downcast or disheartened. Everything can be going well for the believer. He can be healthy, prosperous and yet be covered with a strange pall of oppression, a dark cloud which settles in from nowhere. It can come from witchcraft!

Believers can become ensnared losing the power to make the right kind of decisions. Those who have experience in dealing with witchcraft have seen many killed by occult power. This power can also turn one away from the truth and cause backsliding.

Christians should put on the full armor of God for protection against witchcraft as Paul advised us in Ephesians 6:10-18. Both the Old and the New Testaments make repeated references to the practice of witchcraft and sorcery, and whenever these practices are referred to, they are always condemned by God. The Bible condemns all forms of witchcraft.

Michael (Manouchehr) Ghaemmaghami

(III) ACUPUNCTURE

In common with many other seemingly harmless practices, the medical practice of acupuncture may seem to have no connection with the occult. However, it is instructive to listen to Christians who think otherwise.

WHAT IT IS

Acupuncture is the practice of ancient Chinese needle stimulation based upon the occultic religion of Taoism. It involves the insertion of very fine needles along certain points in the body's Meridians, or channels of energy flow. In this way, it is claimed, the cosmic energy of the universe (*ch'i*) flows through the body and so keeps one in good health.

DANGERS

Taoist practice and philosophy, and other occult-linked practices, may be used in conjunction with acupuncture therapy.

Classical acupuncture involves the practice of an ancient pagan medicine inseparably tied to Taoism.

QUOTATIONS

Needle stimulation has occasionally produced physical complications and injuries, some serious;misdiagnosis of a serious illness; occult influence."

Biblical Discernment Ministries

Those who adhere to acupuncture's roots in traditional Chinese medicine and religion may try to convert patients to their Eastern world view, although this is not the case with every practitioner. Others may call upon spiritual powers to assist in treatments, thus exposing people to occult influences.

Donal O'Mathuna, Ph.D. and Walt Larimore, M.D
Alternative Medicine: The Christian Handbook, *Zondervan, 2001, p. 194.*

The main point to remember is that we should use discernment when investigating any medical treatment, because any treatment based on a false worldview can be harmful not only physically but spiritually as well.

Steve Goodwin

(IV) TYPICAL RITE OF MAGIC

The rites in white and black magic vary greatly from place to place, but a typical rite of magic is as follows:

a. The person seeking to engage in magic places himself in the presence of Satan.
b. The spell. The magician asks for a good or bad deed, using an established ritual or using his own words, with prayers to the devil.
c. The rite. The destruction of a wax image to harm a victim, or putting pins or needles into a doll. Water may be sprinkled to obtain rain.
d. The fetish. This is giving the client something to use, such as a potion, herbs, a charm, a prayer, an amulet to wear on the neck, a ring, or a crystal.
e. The client is given a blasphemous prayer addressed to the devil. This may have to be prayed five times a day for a month.

These rituals may include incenses, candles, drinks, herbs. Drinks may be include drugs such as belladonna, aconite, and hemlock.

B WITCHCRAFT

(I) INTRODUCTION

Witchcraft is the practice of sorcery, black or white magic, the operation of supernatural powers with the aid of the devil or a spirit.

Witchcraft is a form of polytheistic nature religion. It believes in reincarnation and *karma*, and practices such things as clairvoyance, divination, and astral projection.

Witches may be linked with any of the following:

- Pagans
- Druids
- earth or nature religion
- positive magick
- the craft
- the craft of the wise
- wisecraft
- Goddess worship
- wimmin religion
- shamanism.

(II) WITCHCRAFT ASSESSED

Witchcraft can be defined as the performance of magic forbidden by God for non-biblical ends. The word witchcraft is related to the old English word Wiccian, "practice of magical arts."

When a person became a witch, he or she entered into a pact with Satan to worship him. They deny the Creator of heaven and earth. They deny their baptism with Christ. They deny the worship paid to God. They adhere to the devil and believe only in him. They are re-baptized in the devil's name.

They promise to sacrifice children to the devil, a step which led to the stories of witches murdering children. Also, they request of the devil for their names to be written in the Book of Death. They tattoo themselves with the devil's mark in various parts of their body. The mark might vary in shape – magic circle or number 666, serpent, evil eye, spider, bat, a rabbit foot, a toad etc.

Witches were supposed to have had a variety of different powers which kept the people in fear of them. Witchcraft practitioners place spells by some spoken word(s) or form of words believed to have magic power, binding by spell or charm.

In witchcraft there is white magic which is supposedly curative and black magic, also voodoo (Africans name it joojoo) which are destructive. However, the most feared power thought to be held by witches was that of bewitchment, the ability to cause sickness and death. Practically speaking, a gray area of magic exists between black and white magic.

Most black magic advocates believe that through the use of charms, spells, fetish bags containing potions and animal bones, spiritual powers can be manipulated for one's own advantage. Thus, people selfishly practice all types of magic to obtain a means to their own ends, seldom distinguishing between black and white versions.

Some black magicians poke pins into voodoo dolls to inflict pain or misfortune upon those who have angered them. Still others cast black magic curses on career opponents to frighten or intimidate them into resigning their positions. Black magicians inflict disease, physical danger, and unfortunate circumstances on victims.

Many people are tempted to use black magic to get even with enemies or get ahead in life. Charms and spells can eliminate an enemy or protect against someone else's black magic. Fetishes supposedly make one person love another or cause him to follow someone else's wishes. They can also be used to persuade someone toward benevolence or to change a bad fate into a good destiny. With the help of hexes, black magicians hope to advance in the world of professional rivalry.

Witchcraft practitioners are also involved in water witching, levitation (the lifting of one's body in the air with no support), dowsing to use a divining rod (a forked stick alleged to dip downward when held over an underground supply of water), table tipping, psychometry (divination through objects), healing by witch doctors (a person who practices primitive medicine involving the use of magic, as among the tribes in Africa); this kind of temporary healing never cures a sick person but only transfers the sickness from one specific area of the body to another part of the body. This is totally different from the permanent healing which comes from God.

Is witchcraft an act of the Devil manipulating people's minds? Witches claim that witchcraft has nothing to do with the Devil but it is a form of goddess or demon worship; a form of nature or idol worship. Satan's followers believe their holy book is written on the earth. They study lay lines, mountain tops, rivers, trees, giving meaning to the way they lay, stand, or flow.

Witchcraft is an act of the devil which not only manipulates the minds of people, but it can wreak havoc physically, emotionally and spiritually too.

Those who engage in witchcraft, literally open themselves up to the attacks and manipulations of enemy, Satan. This then demonstrates the awesome power which can be wielded by those who practice the occult sciences.

Witch doctors, magicians and sorcerers all receive satanic power, not for edification, but for destruction.

The practice of spiritual prostitution both deprives and corrupts us. We must be very careful that we ourselves and those under our spiritual authority avoid engaging in any of the occult practices.

If a person dabbles with psychic phenomena (spiritism, séances, levitation, necromancy, astral projection, table lifting, handwriting analysis, automatic type writing, visionary dreams, telepathy, materialization, clairvoyance, ghosts, healing magnetism, mental suggestion, speaking in a trance, amateur hypnosis, self-hypnosis, fortune-telling of any kind, Tarot cards, palm reading, biorhythm, rod and pendulum (dowsing), horoscopes and astrology, ouija boards, witchcraft whether white, black, or gray, voodoo or joojoo, blood pacts, sorcery, love potions, fetishes, magic charming and talismans, eastern religions, Zoroastrian, Bahai Faith, Freemasonry, mysticism, transcendental meditation, Zen, Buddhism, karate, *I-Ching*, yoga, reincarnation, ESP, telepathy, hypnosis, scientology, the writings of mystics, and psychics such as Jean Dixon, Edgar Cayce and incubi , succubi [sexual spirits] and others . . .) which are so widely accepted today, they can expect to be invaded by these spirits. They have opened up the door.

As our defenses are dropped by our meddling curiosity, occult spirits can and will enter in and establish themselves. These are the spirits which travel to the third and fourth generations through the parents (inheritance) because consorting with them breaks the first commandment by contacting another god. A curse from God results (Deuteronomy 18:9-12 and Exodus 20:3-5).

In the beginning, the experimenter with psychic phenomena can control when and to what degree they can become involved with the occult spirits. However, as they continue on, lured deeper into the mysteries of the spirit world by clever adversaries, their God-given defenses are forced down again and again. Increasingly, the demons have free access and control. Before long they will exercise their capricious whims upon the unwitting victim and make a slave-victim, driving their victim ever deeper into the mire of sin and slavery. They will force their victim down every path which will open up ever increasing spiritual depravity.

They may be able systemically to destroy self-respect, family life, and afflict with many hurtful and destructive desires and hungers. In time, spirits of infirmity and sickness will also be brought under attack to further weaken the victim. Demons are not satisfied with mere compliance to their wishes, they work to reduce their victim to a helpless state, filled with mental and physical anguish almost beyond a person's ability to endure.

Michael (Manouchehr) Ghaemmaghami

BIBLICAL RESPONSE

The Bible condemns witchcraft in the strongest terms: "You shall not permit a sorceress to live" (Exodus 22:18).

(III) TYPES OF WITCHCRAFT

There are many different types of witchcraft. The following is a list of different religions and religious movements related to witchcraft. Some of them vary greatly from that of Wicca, but they are related in one form or another.

Witchcraft
Wicca
Witta
Pagan
Neo-Pagan
Ceremonial magick
Kemetic
Tameran
Discordian
Erisian
Chaos magician
Gardnerian
Alexandrian
Reclaiming
Dianic
Norse
Asatru
Odinism
Shamanism
Hindu
Huna
Mama Chi
"Native" or indigenous
Druid
Earth religion
The Craft
Old Religion
Voodoo
Vodun
Santeria
Yoruba
Golden Dawn
Circle
Yoruba
Bruja
Cunandero
Silva mind control
Recon
Reconstructionist

(IV) WITCH DOCTORS

The witch doctor of the ancient religions is different. He most often engages in the solo practice of white magic to heal the sick, but he may also practice black magic.

(V) MEMBERSHIP AND HISTORY

There are about 300,000 witches in the USA, 15,000 in England, 60,000 in France, and they are almost universal in non-literate societies.

In 1496, the *Malleus Maleficarum* (*The Witches' Hammer*) was published by two German Dominicans, with a definitive statement that witchcraft depends on a pact with the devil.

The principal period of persecution of witches was during the sixteenth and seventeenth centuries, when it is estimated that from 300,000 to 9 million witches were executed by hanging or burning. This persecution was led by the Inquisition, but both Catholics and Protestants participated.

In America, the most famous outbreak of witch persecutions occurred at the end of this period, in 1692, at Salem, Mass., where twenty-two witches were hanged.

The last trial for witchcraft in England took place in 1712, and in France in 1718.

(VI) WHAT IT IS

Witchcraft is a secret society of evildoers, who have a pact with the devil, whom they worship at night in obscene rites in the form of a black goat. Usually, on the initiation, the candidate has to worship Satan.

(VII) COVENS

While the magician practices on his own, with his client, witchcraft is a religion organized in groups, or covens, of thirteen people, one of whom is the High Priestess, and another the High Priest.

(VIII) WOMEN

Witchcraft focuses on nature worship and fertility rites, and so has been dominated by women, who are called witches or sorceresses. The male counterparts are called wizards, sorcerers, or warlocks.

(IX) GODS

The main god is the Great Mother Goddess, the Earth, identified in different cultures as Diane, Aphrodite, Artemis, Astarte, Kore, or Hecate.

The male consort Pan, the Horned God, is identified in different cultures as Apollo, Adonis, Dionysius, Lucifer, Osiris, Thor, or Baphonet.

The Mother Goddess is represented by the moon, and the Horned God by the sun. The ceremonies are called "Drawing down the Moon," and "Drawing down the Sun."

(X) ESBAT AND SABBAT

Regular meetings are called Esbat, while the special meetings, which are held eight times a year, are called Sabbats.

Sabbats pinpoint key phases in the seasonal progress of Mother Earth to harmonize with the rhythm of nature in the following way:

1 Spring Equinox: March 21
2 Summer Solstice: June 22
3 Autumn Equinox: September 21
4 Winter Solstice: December 22
5 Imbolg: February 2 (Christian Candelaria)
6 Beltane: April 30
7 Lugnasad: July 31
8 Samhain: October 31 (Halloween)

(XI) THE RITE

There is a wide variety of beliefs and practices, however, all meetings have the four features that are found in black magic:

• the presence of Satan
• the spell
• the rite
• the fetish.

C WICCA

(I) INTRODUCTION

Wicca, which means "wise one," is the name for a contemporary pagan revival of witchcraft.

Wicca, also called "the craft," or "the craft of the wise," is an ancient witchcraft religion which honors the gods of nature.

Wicca has been described as a marriage between witchcraft and Hinduism in modern dress.

Most Wiccans do not believe in Satan or use Satanic symbols, and they do not summon demons or try to hurt people or animals in any way. They do not always use magick, and they never use black magick.

(II) HISTORY AND BACKGROUND OF WICCA

Wicca is a common and much older name for witchcraft. The term witchcraft has been defined in different ways. In the past it has most often referred to the human harnessing of supernatural powers for the malevolent purpose of practicing black magic. For this reason, witchcraft, sorcery, and magic are nearly synonymous. Witchcraft is not, however, synonymous with Satanism. Not all witches worship Satan, and in fact most do not believe in Satan at all.

The definitive start of the modern

witchcraft era began with Gerald Gardner (1884-1964). As an archaeologist, Gardner had accumulated an extensive occult background. While in Southeast Asia, he learned the secrets of the Malaysian magical knife and became a Mason and a nudist. In 1939 when he returned to England an avid occultist, he became a member of the Corona Fellowship of Rosicrucians where he met Dorothy Clutterbuck. Clutterbuck initiated Gardner into witchcraft. Gardner took the magical resources he acquired in Asia and a selection of Western magical texts and created a new religion centered upon the worship of the Mother-Goddess. This was an important beginning in witchcraft, for it is the worship of the Mother-Goddess that has become the focus of modern witchcraft. From Gardner's writings, greatly influenced by Aleister Crowley, Theosophy, Freemasonry, ritual/sex magic, and numerous other occult sources, emerged modern day Wicca.

Contender Ministries

Modern witchcraft, commonly called Wicca, started in England with Gerald Gardener in 1949, with the publication of *High Magic's Aid*, and *Witchcraft Today*, where he blends the old Mother Goddess Religion with the teachings of Margaret Maori, and by borrowing practices from his friend, the British Satanist Aleister Crowley, and ideas from Hinduism, Theosophy, Freemasonry, Rosacrucians.

J. Dominguez, M.D.

(III) WICCA BELIEFS AND PRACTICES
There are a wide variety of beliefs and practices in modern-day Wicca. However, despite the pluralism and diversity, distinct principles derived from Gardnerian Wicca are common to most modern witches.

BELIEFS
Some of these beliefs are as follows:

* everyone has the divine (or goddess) within

* one should develop natural gifts for divination or occult magic (often spelled "magick" by occultists)
* divine forces or nature spirits are invoked in rituals
* the Goddess, as either a symbol or a real entity, is the focus of worship
* nature and the earth are sacred manifestations of the Goddess
* everyone has his or her own spiritual path to follow
* rituals and celebrations are linked to the seasons and moon phases
* meditation, visualization, invocation (calling on forces or gods/goddesses), chanting, burning candles and special rituals trigger a sense of the mystical, thus reinforcing the core belief system.

These beliefs will often be mixed with a combination of mystical traditions, Celtic or Norse paganism, Greek and Roman goddess worship, ancient Egyptian spirituality, Eastern Shamanism, or even Native American spiritual practices depending on the group. All of these groups revere nature, support peace, and believe society cannot be at peace if we are out of harmony with nature or are mistreating Mother Earth (also known as Gaia, the name of a pagan goddess given to Earth). This aspect of Wicca is very similar to the New Age Religion supported by the United Nations and many of its members, NGOs and leaders.

Contender Ministries

DIVINATION TECHNIQUES
Divination techniques such as Tarot cards, astrology, runes, the *I Ching* (from Chinese Taoism), clairvoyant or psychic readings, candle magick and other occult practices are not only common but encouraged by most groups.

THE SERPENT
As in Hinduism, the serpent is believed by Wiccans to be a symbol of eternal life and female spiritual awakening or power. In Hinduism, the practice of yoga and meditation result in enlightenment, the result of awakening the kundalini, or power, known as the serpent power, believed to be coiled at the base of the spine.

OTHER SYMBOLS
Other symbols used in witchcraft are:

- pentagram and pentacle – a 5-pointed star used for protection, spells, conjuring, etc.
- the Ankh – Egyptian cross-like symbol with a loop at the top associated with the worship of Isis
- the crescent moon – a symbol of the Goddess, also used in Islam
- crystals – believed to contain healing and spiritual properties; crystals are also used by many other new age cults.

WITNESSING TO WICCA MEMBERS

One hurdle that will have to be crossed in witnessing to a person involved in Wicca is their lack of belief in a need for forgiveness or salvation. To the witch, there is no sin therefore no need for forgiveness. There is no need for salvation, as there is nothing to be saved from.

Contender Ministries

BIBLICAL RESPONSE

It may be argued that sorcery is black magic used for evil, and that they practice white magic, magic for good. But the Bible makes no distinction between good or bad magic or sorcery. All sorcery comes from the same source and is abhorred by God. See Ex. 22:18; Lev. 19:26, 31; 20:6, 27; 1 Sam.15:23a; 2 Kings 23:24; I Chron. 10:13; Is. 2:6; 8:19-20; 47:13-14; Ez. 13:20-23; Dan. 2:27-28; 5:15-17; Acts 13:7-10a; 16:16-18; Gal. 5:19-20; Rev. 22:15.

Contender Ministries

(IV) MOTHER GODDESS, HORNED GOD

God, for the Wiccan (like the Hindu) is not a person, but is the Energy, the Force, the Power, the Universal Mind, the Absolute, the Unknown, the Divine Being.

God is not a "he" but an "it." It is not somebody but something, but something powerful, able to do wonderful things for you by using Magic, which involves you

worshiping it, that is, worshiping the Force or the Energy.

Wiccans worship any god, but most especially the great Mother Goddess (earth and moon) and her male consort, the Horned God (sun and stars). They worship any god, except the one God of the Jews, Christians, and Muslims.

Since god is not a person, there are no revelations from a non-person. In Wicca as in Hinduism, they do not speak of: "God said," or, "Yahweh calls".

The Goddess and God are the personification of the natural force, or power, that created, and is, the universe. The different deities representing the different aspects of this power. Far from being removed from us, humans are part of that power. We are affected by it, and can use and affect it, and that's what is called magick.

The Goddess in Wicca represents the feminine side of nature, is a mother, lover, the earth and moon.

The God represents the masculine side, a father, hunter, the sun and the stars.

Both are believed to be immanent deities accessible to humanity. This is what is called Magick! Immanent means in us. So the Energy, the Force, is inside us.

(V) MAIDEN, MOTHER, AND CRONE
Most Wiccan traditions recognize the tripartite nature of the Mother Goddess. It mirrors both a woman's life cycle and the cycles of the moon.

It is Maiden, Mother, and Crone.

The Maiden, the young woman, full of potential, unattached, is usually associated with the waxing new moon.

The Mother, pregnant both in body and in mind, the giver of life, the nurturer, the protectress, is usually associated with the full moon.

The Crone, old woman full of wisdom, done with the struggles of learning and bringing forth, offering guidance to her daughters, is usually associated with the waning moon.

(VI) MOTHER GODDESS' NAMES
The Mother Goddess, who is believed to be

eternal, is invoked in history by a variety of names:

Aphrodite, Artemis
Astaroth
Astarte
Athene
Brigit
Ceres
Cerridwen
Cybele
Diana
Demeter
Friga
Gaia
Hecate
Isis
Kali
Kore
Lilith
Luna
Persephone
Venus.

(VII) HORNED GOD
The Horned God is Mother Goddess's consort.

The male Horned God is associated with the sun. According to most witches, he dies and is reborn every year.

(VIII) HORNED GOD'S NAMES
Horned God is called and invoked in history by many names, including:
Adonis
Ammon-Ra
Apollo
Baphomet
Cernunnos
Dionysius
Eros
Faunus
Hades
Horus
Nuit
Lucifer
Odin
Osiris
Pan
Thor
Woden.

(IX) A WICCA VIEW OF GOD
ANIMISM
Animism is the basis of Wicca and of Hinduism. The "Life Force" is the soul or *anima* of everything, of a rock, a tree, a star, an animal, a human. So everything is sacred and everything and everyone is to be cared for and revered. Everything on earth or the sky is like a drop of water from the same ocean, which is the Life Force, the Absolute.

PANTHEISM
Pantheism is the consequence of animism. In pantheism all the world is divine. So a mountain is god, and you are god!

POLYTHEISM
Polytheism is the next obvious consequence. In polytheism there are thousands of gods.

BIBLICAL RESPONSE
The first verse of the Bible contradicts these views: "In the beginning God created the heavens and the earth." The Bible teaches that there is one Creator God, a person, and everything in the world has been made by him. God by his Holy Spirit is the soul and life and is within everything, but everything is not God.

(X) THE WICCAN REDE
The main tenet of Wicca is the *Wiccan Rede,* which states, "And it harm none, do as ye will." Wicca teaches that this has two aspects:

a. a witch means to seek harmony with the world, nature, and other human beings;
b. effects of magic will be returned threefold upon the person working it, limiting severely the pronouncing of "curses," that will return threefold upon the magician.

Unlike most mainstream religions, Witchcraft does not have a long list of laws governing our behavior. Witches generally adhere to what has become known as *The Wiccan Rede* and *The Three-fold Law.* These two principles contain the basics of what Witches define as ethical and moral behavior within the Craft and the society in which we live.
Wren Walker

FULL VERSION OF THE WICCAN REDE

Bide the Wiccan Rede ye must,
In Perfect Love and Perfect Trust;
Live ye must and let to live,
Fairly take and fairly give;
Form the Circle thrice about,
To keep unwelcome spirits out;
Bind fast the spell every time,
Let the words be spoke in rhyme.

Soft of eye and light of touch,
Speak ye little, listen much;
Deosil go by waxing moon,
Sing and dance the Witches' Rune;
Widdershins go by waning moon,
Chant ye then a baleful tune;
When the Lady's moon is new,
Kiss hand to her times two;
When the moon rides at peak,
Heart's desire then ye seek.

Heed the North wind's mighty gale,
Lock the door & trim the sail;
When the wind comes from the South,
Love will kiss them on the mouth;
When the wind blows from the West,
departed souls have no rest;
When the wind blows from the East,
Expect the new and set the feast.
Nine woods in the cauldron go,
Burn them quick, burn them slow;
Elder be the Lady's tree,
Burn it not or curs'd ye'll be;
When the wind begins to turn,
Soon Beltane fires will burn;
When the wheel has turned to Yule,
light the log, the Horned One rules.

Heed the flower, bush or tree
By the Lady blessed be
When the rippling waters flow
cast a stone – the truth you'll know;
When ye have & hold a need,
Hearken not to others' greed;
With a fool no seasons spend,
Or be counted as his friend.
Merry meet and merry part
Bright the cheeks, warm the heart;
Mind the threefold law ye should,

Three times bad and three times good;
When e'er misfortune is enow,
Wear the star upon your brow;
True in troth ever ye be
Lest thy love prove false to thee.

'Tis by the sun that life be won,
And by the moon that change be done;
If ye would clear the path to will,
Make certain the mind be still;
What good be tools without Inner Light?
What good be magick without wisdom-sight?
Eight words the Wiccan Rede fulfill
An it harm none, do what ye will.

It has been said that:

Love, life and peace are described in a few sentences in the Wiccan Rede. In the opening statement we read: "Bide the Wiccan Rede ye must, In Perfect Love and Perfect Trust; Live ye must and let to live, Fairly take and fairly give." The middle statement says, "Merry meet and merry part, Bright the cheeks, warm the heart; Mind the threefold law ye should, Three times bad and three times good."

(XI) THE LAW OF THE THREE

The other law of witchcraft is the "THREE-FOLD LAW OF RETURN," which is also known as "The Law of the Three." Basically, this is the natural law of cause and effect. The Goddess charges us to exercise great care in all that we, as witches, do and say and even think. The Threefold Law takes the notion that "what we reap, we will sow," a few steps further, in fact, three steps further. For what we do "for good or for ill, shall be returned to us threefold." In light of this fact, witches are loath to cause any harm, lest it be returned to them in spades!!"

Wren Walker

(XII) RELATIVISM AND MORAL RELATIVITY

From the doctrine of pantheism comes the

notion that ultimately there is no right or wrong.

Relativism in all areas of life is the rule, including ethics, metaphysics, religion.

Truth is what is true for you; right what is right for you; but neither are necessarily so for anyone else.

The only absolute is that there are no absolutes. But this statement is contradictory, it is an absolute itself!

Thus, all have the right to believe and practice "what they will."

(XIII) WICCA PRACTICES

Witches view themselves as fun-loving, life-celebrating and affirming folk who worship the Mother Goddess and her consort, the Horned God.

The practice of Wicca may be solitary or in circles of a coven, a group of about thirteen.

The "circle" has several uses. It is used protect a witch from harm and/or interference, and to contain the power raised during magical working (rituals or spells) until it is released.

Magic is a key component of the witches' world. The working of magic and diverse techniques of divination are part-and-parcel of their religion. Astrology, astral projection (out-of-body experiences), incantations, mediumship (channeling), necromancy, raising psychic power, sex magic, spell casting, trance states, are all tools of their craft.

ALTERED STATES OF CONSCIOUSNESS

Altered states of consciousness are another integral part of many witchcraft practices and rituals; these are induced to facilitate the working of magic and divination. Much of a witch's training is with a view to enabling him or her to enter these states at will. This is done by means of chanting, ecstatic dancing, hypnosis, meditation, and rituals. Even sex magic and drugs are used in many circles.

POSSESSION

For many witches, trance states are the high point of their religious practice. Of especial importance among these are the type termed "drawing down the moon," the Goddess, or "drawing down the sun," the Horned God.

These involve the Goddess or God entering or possessing a priestess or priest respectively during a ritual with mediumistic utterances given or magic worked.

EXPERIENCES

These experiences are essential in Wicca. It is not so much what you believe in, but what you personally experience that really matters.

Wicca has been called the "creed of experience." Experience is exalted dogmatically above, and often set in opposition to, creeds or doctrines. Experience is said to be superior to doctrine. Witchcraft is therefore a religion based first and foremost on the sense of being one and in harmony with all life.

NATURE AND SATAN

Wicca has given a new face-lift to witchcraft. It is part of nature. The occultic realm is now described as simply beyond-the-physical, but still a part of nature. It is not super-natural, but natural-super.

"I BELIEVE IN MAGICK"

This is how a Wiccan describes being a Wicca:

I believe in magick. Not the "I'll turn you in to a frog" misconception that some have, but the real thing. I believe in the magick that brought my wife, my son, and my daughters to me. I believe I can use this magick to influence the world around me, that I can make this existence better for my children. I guess it really doesn't matter how you perform magick, it all works. We perform a ritual, and some desired change occurs, along with all its consequences. You don't have to know how the filament in a light bulb is excited by an electron flow and releases photons to turn on the hall light, you just flick the switch.

Wicca, A Guide for the Solitary Practitioner

CHRISTIAN RESPONSE

While some witches may be skeptical about the existence of the Goddess and God, they all emphatically deny the existence of Satan and Hell. Therefore, they vigorously reject the charge that they worship the devil, which many Satanists would admit to.

But here is Satan's big trick. He is a liar, a thief, a murderer. His biggest lie is to make us believe he does not exist. In reality, Satan is the main reason, the source, of most of the ecstatic experiences a Wicca has, while he is emphatically denying the very existence of the devil.

Jesus said: "Worship the Lord your God, and serve him only" (Luke 4:8).

Jesus said: "I am the way and the truth and the life. No-one comes to the Father except through me" (John 14:6).

St. Paul wrote: "Satan himself masquerades as an angel of light" (2 Corinthians 11:14).

D The Church of Satan

(I) WHAT IT IS

The Church of Satan is a religion that mixes a hedonistic philosophy with the rituals of black magic. The Church of Satan does not promote the belief of Satan as a supernatural being. It does, however, use Satan as a symbol of defiance and rebellion against a conformist, God-fearing society.

The Church of Satan is pre-Christian, and derived from the pagan image of power, virility, sexuality and sensuality. Satan is viewed as a force of nature, not a living quasi-deity.

We are the first above-ground organization in history openly dedicated to the acceptance of Man's true nature – that of a carnal beast, living in a cosmos which is permeated and motivated by the Dark Force which we call Satan. Over the course of time, Man has called this Force by many names, and it has been reviled by those whose very nature causes them to be separate from this fountainhead of existence. They live in obsessive envy of we who exist by flowing naturally with the dread Prince of Darkness. It is for this reason that individuals who resonate with Satan have always been an alien elite, often outsiders in cultures whose masses pursue solace in an external deity. We

Satanists are our own Gods, and we are the explorers of the Left-Hand Path. We do not bow down before the myths and fictions of the desiccated spiritual followers of the Right-Hand Path.

Church of Satan

(II) FOUNDER

Anton Szandor LaVey (1930-1997) founded the Church of Satan (CoS) in 1966/1967. LaVey was a former carnival worker, whose personal interactions with Christians led him to conclude that Christianity was hypocritical and morally restrictive.

Today, we continue to uphold our legacy by building on the solid foundation created by Anton LaVey, and set forth in his writings, recordings, and videos. Since we were the first organization dedicated to Satan, we have had extensive media coverage and been referred to by several names over the course of the last thirty-seven years: The First Church of Satan, The Satanic Church, as well as The Satanic Church of America, yet we maintain the simplest and boldest moniker, embodied in the words Church of Satan.

Church of Satan

(III) REVERED TEXTS

The revered texts of the Church of Satan are:

- *The Satanic Bible* (1969)
- *The Satanic Witch* (1970)
- *The Satanic Rituals* (1972)

These three books were all written by LaVey.

(IV) THE SATANIC BIBLE BY ANTON SZANDOR LAVEY

The Satanic Bible, which can be found in most large secular bookstores, is perhaps the most common source of satanic ritual and understanding available to young people today. It has sold more than 600,000 copies since it was first published by Avon Books in 1969.

(V) NINE SATANIC STATEMENTS

LaVey summarized his philosophy in *The Satanic Bible* (1969) in what he described as The Nine Satanic Statements:

1. Satan represents indulgence instead of abstinence!
2. Satan represents vital existence instead of spiritual pipe dreams!
3. Satan represents undefiled wisdom instead of hypocritical self-deceit!
4. Satan represents kindness to those who deserve it instead of love wasted on ingrates!
5. Satan represents vengeance instead of turning the other cheek!
6. Satan represents responsibility to the responsible instead of concern for psychic vampires!
7. Satan represents man as just another animal, sometimes better, more often worse than those that walk on all-fours, who, because of his "divine spiritual and intellectual development," has become the most vicious animal of all!
8. Satan represents all of the so-called sins, as they all lead to physical, mental, or emotional gratification!
9. Satan has been the best friend the Church has ever had, as He has kept it in business all these years!

(VI) SATANIC SINS

The nine Satanic sins are:

- stupidity
- pretentiousness
- solipsism
- self-deceit
- herd conformity
- lack of perspective
- forgetfulness of past orthodoxies
- counterproductive pride and
- lack of aesthetics

QUOTATION

The worship of Satan has deep historical roots. Known as Satanism, it is found expressed in various ways. Black magic, Black mass, all types of drug culture, blood sacrifice and sexual perversion associated with the devil all have connections with Satanism. The worship of a personal and powerful devil is traditional Satanism and associated with witchcraft and ritualism. Evil spirits manifest in blasphemy, profanity and filthy conversation. Persistent and violent opposition to God manifests in the lives of the demonically tormented individuals.
Michael (Manouchehr) Ghaemmaghami

(VII) BLACK MASS

The Black mass is said in honor of the devil at the witches' sabbath. It is practiced by many satanic groups. The ritual reverses Roman Catholic mass, desecrating the objects used in worship.

The black mass prevents and desecrates the true worship of God and is a blasphemous affront to all believers in Christ. The black mass is today's perfect image of the occultism so clearly condemned by the LORD in the Old and New Testaments. It is not possible to serve Satan and Jesus Christ. Christians should have nothing to do with the black mass or any satanic or witchcraft practices.

Satan worshipers are perversions of the true Gospel. As perversions, they bring eternal death rather than the eternal life promised by Jesus Christ. A day will come when even Satan, his demons and those who are bound in the occult will no longer celebrate the black mass, but will be forced to bow to the Lord Jesus Christ.

According to Philippians 2:10, 11, "that at the name of Jesus every knee should bow, in heaven and on earth and under the earth, and every tongue confess that Jesus Christ is Lord, to the glory of God the Father."

Michael (Manouchehr) Ghaemmaghami

3 SPIRITISM AND SPIRITUALISM

INTRODUCTION

Spiritism is the third division of occultism. Divination attempts to foretell the future, magic to change it, spiritism tries to communicate with the dead to receive information and help from them.

Spiritualism is in many ways akin to spiritism but, additionally, it uses Christian prayers and holds services, which look like Christian services.

A HISTORY OF SPIRITISM

Most ancient civilizations practiced Spiritism.

KATE FOX

Although spiritualistic practices seem to be widespread, they were virtually unknown in modern civilized society until March 1848 when odd happenings were reported at the house of a farmer named Fox in the small town of Hydesville, in New York state, USA. Previous occupants of this house had been disturbed by unexplained raps at night. Kate Fox, the Fox family the youngest daughter, was said to have successfully challenged the supposed spirit to repeat the number of times she flipped her fingers. Once communication had apparently been established, a code was agreed upon by which questions could be answered: one rap meant "yes," two raps meant "no." The spirit identified himself as the spirit of a Mr. Splitfoot, who had been murdered in the house. Later a skeleton was dug up in the basement.

Two other sisters joined Kate: Margaret and Leah. In 1855, Kate and Margaret publicly admitted at the New York Academy of Music that they themselves had caused the rapping noises with their toes. Later they retracted this confession, claiming to have been bribed into making it originally. Kate and Margaret gave much of their lives to acting as mediums in the USA and England, and spiritism flourished through the world.

The tale of the Fox sisters spurred immediate interest, and helped to produce a revival of spiritualism. Many people were drawn to spiritualism through mere curiosity and the fascination of the supernatural along with the desire to convince themselves about survival after death. Many other people were primarily interested in communicating with their departed love ones. Other people wanted information about the future life.

B EXTENT OF SPIRITISM AND SPIRITUALISM

Spiritism may be humankind's oldest religion. Today there are an estimated 70 million Spiritists.

USA

In America, the "National Spiritualist Association of Churches," dating from 1893, was the first branch to be founded, and now has 300 churches and 10,000 members.

The "International General Assembly of Spiritualists" has 250 churches and 200,000 members.

The "Universal Church of the Master" (UCM), founded in 1908, now has over 300 congregations, 1,300 ministers, and 10,000 members.

The "National Spiritual Alliance of the USA" has 40 churches with 4,000 members.

C SPIRITISM AND CHRISTIANITY

The Bible condemns all kinds of spiritism and mediums in the strongest terms: see, for example, Acts 13:6-12

The greatest difference between Christianity and Spiritism is that in Christianity the supernatural manifestations and the prophecies are made by God or are inspired by God, while in Spiritualism they are ultimately derived from Satan. This occurs as living mediums contact the fake spirits of dead people.

Satan can simulate many supernatural manifestations of God, like the magicians did in the times of Moses, using living people. 2 Thessalonians 2:9 speaks of "the work of Satan, using all kinds of counterfeit miracles and signs and wonders, and every kind of wicked deception." See also Exodus 7; 2 Cor. 11:14; 1 Tim. 4.

Spiritism, also called Necromancy, involves the magic of calling spirits (séances), in which spiritists try to communicate with the dead. Spiritism, sometimes called spiritualism, is the oldest form of religious counterfeit known to man. The Bible speaks of spiritistic practices going back as far as ancient Egypt. The book of Exodus records to the Egyptians' many occultic activities, including magic, sorcery and speaking to the dead (Exodus 7 and 8).

Michael (Manouchehr) Ghaemmaghami

D THE CREED OF SPIRITUALISM

Spiritualistic churches have codified their beliefs in their Seven Principles:

1. The Fatherhood of God.
2. The Brotherhood of Man.
3. Continuous Existence.
4. Communion of Spirits and Ministry of Angels.
5. Personal Responsibility.
6. Compensation or Retribution Hereafter for Good or Evil Done on Earth.
7. A Path of Endless Progression.

E SÉANCES

A séance is a gathering of spiritualists who meet to receive messages from the spirits. They usually do this in small groups, but also in churches. Talking with or receiving information from the dead is the essence of spiritualism.

In a séance the participants sit quietly in a circle, in dimly lit surroundings. The medium is the center of a séance. He is a person on earth who is, supposedly, sensitive to vibrations from the spirit world and is able to convey messages between that world and this one and to produce other spiritualist phenomena.

The medium may be taken over by a "spirit control," that is, a spirit who, through the medium, answers all the inquiries of those present.

A spirit guide is usually a departed human being who speaks through the medium.

In New Age terminology, the word "medium" has been replaced by the word "channeler," a more contemporary, scientific term. The channeler is like a human telephone connecting the living to the spirit world.

(I) CRITICAL VIEW OF SÉANCES

Séances are meetings at which mediums try to communicate with the dead. During séances people who seek to communicate with loved ones are often startled to hear familiar voices supplying details about their lives which no one else present could know. In addition to impersonating the voice of the dead, these may well be the voices of the unclean spirits who actually lived within the person during their lifetime.

According to the Bible the dead cannot communicate with the living. Jesus made this very clear with the account of the rich man and Lazarus (see Luke 16:19-31).

Mediums or sorcerers absolutely have no access to the spirits of dead people. Any manifestation belongs to evil spirits whose job is to deceive the people and bring them under the curse of God to get control over them and their offspring.

Michael (Manouchehr) Ghaemmaghami

(II) SÉANCES IN CHURCHES

Séances in the churches may mimic Christian services, but are always satanic.

The service may resemble the church gatherings of small Christian denominations. The furniture may include a pulpit, pews, a crucifix, and an organ. But members receive "spirit greetings." The presiding minister's sermon may be delivered while in a trance. Psychic readings replace prayer, and familiar hymns such as "Just as I am" and "Holy, Holy, Holy" contain a few subtle changes to their words to avoid affirming Christian doctrine.

F THE SPIRIT WORLD

For Spiritualism, a "spirit" is the essential part of a man or woman. After the death of the body the spirit lives on. The "spirit world" is the world of spirits without bodies.

Belief in a spirit world is accompanied by belief in other phenomena, for example:

materialization:	the appearance of a spirit in matter
telepathy:	the communication of ideas through other than physical means
clairvoyance:	seeing by means other than the physical eye
clairaudience:	hearing by means other than the physical ears
psychometry:	foretelling a person's future by possessing an object belonging to that person

(I) POLTERGEISTS

The word is derived from the German *poltern* ("to make a racket") and *Geist* ("ghost"). Sometimes objects may appear to move or be thrown without a physical cause, or noises may be heard that have no apparent cause. The cause, some people say, is a particular type of ghost, called a "poltergeist." Poltergeists are also said to be responsible for the passing of objects or humans through walls (known as "apport").

(II) OUIJA BOARDS

An ouija board is an instrument for communicating with the spirits of the dead. Made in various shapes and designs, it has a flat surface marked with the letters of the alphabet, and with various signs and numbers and the words "yes" and "no." It is used with a planchette (a small board on two castors, with a pointer or pencil attached to it) or a similar device. When lightly touched this device spells out messages by successively pointing to the letters of the alphabet, to the numbers, and to the "yes" or "no" sections.

Ouija boards: "ouija" means "yes, yes" in a combination of French and German. It is widely marketed as a game and is commonly known as "spirit in the glass." Forms of it were used as long ago as six centuries before Christ. Fingers are placed on the glass and the spirit is asked a question and moves to "Yes" or "No." Words are spelt and messages given. This "harmless" fun game has caused many to have direct contact with the world of Satan.

Paul Young

GLOSSARY

Acupuncture
The practice of inserting needles into certain points on the body to influence the flow of *ch'i* (chee) - the energy or life force of the mind, body and universe. Believed to balance the yin and yang energies.

Aeromancy
This form of divination observes atmospheric conditions or ripples on the surface of an open body of water.

Age of Aquarius
It is believed that the Earth takes more than 25,000 years (called the "Great Year") to pass through the influence of each sign of the Zodiac and has now passed into the Age of Aquarius. The Age of Aquarius is an era of time that begins a new transformation of all living things into a period of love, light and life. It is a tremendous period of enlightenment as all inhabitants look to find the higher meaning of life, spiritual purpose and expression.

Age of Cosmic Consciousness
A period of time within an astrological cycle beginning in 1920 and lasting to 2020. A time when the planet Earth is affected by a shift within the Milky galaxy producing a struggle of purification. This struggle can be seen within the physical shifts of the planet, as well as within the human race, as mankind opens to an awareness of higher states of consciousness.

Ages (astrological)
A cycle of civilization, approximately 2,500 years in length, wherein the soul mind of humankind grows, progresses and attains some level of enlightenment.

Akasha
The fifth occult element, the omnipresent power that permeates the universe. It embraces the other elements (earth, air, fire, water), which are said to stem from it. Some

consider it the "other" of the two worlds that a witch walks between.

Air
The first element of the alchemical tradition. Air is the essence of intuition and learning, the element of the north and the nature of the mind.

Alexandrian
That tradition of Wicca descended from the teachings of Alex Sanders.

Altar
A flat surface used for religious and magickal rituals, preferably of natural materials such as wood or stone.

Amulet
A small ornament, commonly worn around the neck, to guard a person from misfortune, disease, witchcraft, evil magic, demons, etc. A common practice is to have a charm written on or spoken over the amulet.

Ankh
Egyptian "Cross of Life," which represents the union of male and female and was regarded as a universal life charm. The symbol is a cross with a looped, oval top. Also called the Key of the Nile.

Apparition
The conscious energy that was left from a living person after death.

Aradia
Daughter of the Goddess Diana and Lucifer, God of the Sun (sometimes said to be her brother), Aradia is called the Queen of Witches. Though used in many Wiccan traditions, she is central to the Italian witchcraft tradition, *Strega*.

Arcana
A deck of Tarot cards is divided into two halves or arcanas. The Major Arcana has

twenty-two cards representing dominant events and forces in life. The Minor Arcana (lesser Arcana) has fifty-six suit cards representing smaller and/or more mundane events in life.

Archetypes
Universal symbols that speak to us in the language of the subconscious. They are the ideal images of deities and other powers that embody concepts such as knowledge and beauty, and allow us to communicate such concepts to the subconscious in order to perform magick, divination and other rituals.

Arithmancy
Divination by numbers, especially by attaching mystical significance to the numbers associated with a person, especially those numbers associated with the letters of the person's name.

Astragalomancy
Divination by the use of small bones.

Astral body
The invisible spirit of a person (or, more likely, an animal).

Astral plane
The level of existence through which spirits of the dead first pass. The level in which an astrally projected spirit travels.

Astral projection
The separation of the astral body (or spirit) from the physical body. The astral body travels in the astral plane to places both near and far.

Astral/soul travel (commonly called "out-of body experience")
The separation of the soul from the physical body in order to travel to various parts of the universe. Used in ritual magic to carry out the task of delivering messages or of gaining information.

Astrology
The practice of gaining hidden knowledge about the future by observing the relationship of one's time of birth to the position of the planets and the twelve constellations of the Zodiac.

Athame
A double-edged knife used in rituals to cast and open circles, serving the same function as the magickal sword. It is the Witch's ceremonial knife, never to be used for mundane purposes (cutting anything on the material plane).

Augury
Divination by the flight of birds. The word is used for many kinds of divination, as well as for any omen or sign on which divination is or can be based. Augury is also known as Ornithomancy.

Aura
An energy field around a living object, such as a person, plant or animal. Depending on the energy level and vibrational frequency of the energy, it can be seen in varying colors that move or glow around a living object.

Automatic writing
Writing that is inspired by a controlling spirit while a person is in a trance state and is without conscious control of the body.

Bane
An archaic word meaning "bad," "evil," "destructive."

Banish
To magically send away or repel negative energies or entities from the person, home, or ritual area.

Besom
The witch's broomstick. Often used to sweep away negative energies from a space before casting a circle there.

Balefire
The traditional bonfire of the sabbats, still used in many Pagan celebrations.

Biofeedback/mind control
A means for gaining control of one's brain

waves and body processes such as heart rate and respiration to induce altered states of consciousness. This type of mind control is used to move and control the Qi or the energy and life force within the body in order to improve health, longevity, psychic powers and spiritual development.

Bind
To magically restrain something or someone.

Black magic
The practice of conjuring preternatural forces for a specific evil purpose.

Black mass
The mass said in honor of Satan by Satanists and also at the black witches' Sabbath.

Blood pacts
The sealing of a covenant agreement between one person and another person or group or demonic spirit by cutting themselves and co-mingling their blood and then drinking or signing a document. The blood seals the agreement.

Book of Shadows
A book of spells, rituals, recipes, and other guides and materials written by a witch or coven. It is often handwritten, though today many witches write their book on computers. Also, traditionally, the book was kept secret, either by the individual witch or the coven.

Burning times
Reference to the period during the Middle Ages when many people were executed by the Church or by public officials for practicing witchcraft. Some estimates suggest as many as nine million were killed while other estimates are far more conservative. Also, it is unlikely that they were all witches in that this became a favored means for officials to get rid of personal enemies or any unwanted person in the community. While burning was the method of execution in Scotland and some parts of Europe, in other areas the convicted "witches" were hanged.

Call
To invoke divine forces, as when one calls the Guardians of the Watchtowers before casting a circle.

Capnomancy
This form of divination uses the smoke of an altar or sacrificial incense as a means of foretelling the future.

Cardinal points
North, south, east, and west, often marked by candles of green, red, yellow, and blue.

Cartomancy
Divination by use of playing cards. Cartomancy is almost like Tarot Cards. The comes from the Italian *carta* ("card") and the Greek *manteia* ("divination").

Catoptromancy
Divination by use of mirrors. Mirrors are still used in fortune-telling by clairvoyants and for scrying.

Cauldron
A tool of witches, this three-legged cooking pot has many uses. It may be used to cook potions, for scrying (see below), and as a censer. On an altar, the cauldron symbolizes the Goddess.

Chakras
Seven major intersections of energy located on the vertical axis of the body. Each is associated with a color and an area of the body. They are also associated with life experiences such as love and may be used when meditating on those experiences. Starting from the tailbone, they are Root (Red), Sexual/Generative (Orange), Solar Plexus (Yellow), Heart (Green), Throat (Blue), Third Eye (Indigo), and Crown (Violet).

Chalice
A witch's tool that can be used to represent the element of water and may also be used to hold the juice or wine for the offering.

Channeling
A New Age word for mediumship, channeling

involves allowing a spirit entity to speak through the channeler. The authenticity of this process is virtually impossible to prove and therefore channeling does not enjoy a particularly good reputation.

Charms
A charm is an amulet or talisman worn for its magical power. It is also the chanting or recitation of a verse or formula to conjure spirits to activate magical powers. Religious verses are often used.

Chiromancy
See: palm reading.

Circle
The area in which magickal worship and spells takes place. Can also be used to designate a particular group of witches or Pagans such as "Silver Acorn Circle."

Clairvoyance
Clairvoyance is also called second sight. It is the ability to "see" mentally beyond time and space without the use of the five senses. Psychic information such as historical or future events and other phenomena are attained.

Color therapy
Color as energy is used to improve and balance one's health and emotional state. Different colors are said to govern different aspects of the soul, mind and body and have different effects. For example, violet energy is said to enhance spiritual power and creativity. The color and shape of one's aura (the forcefield surrounding the body) make diagnosis possible.

Cone of power
Energy or power raised within a circle by either an individual or group for a specific purpose. After the power is raised and visualized it is released to work the magick.

Conjuring
The process of calling preternatural forces into aid or action through the use of sorcery or ceremonial black magic.

Correspondences
Sets of ideas, concepts or objects that are regularly found together. Most magickal workings involve the use of correspondences. For example, the moon is associated with Monday, moonstones, the color white, and purity, among other things.

Coven
An organized group of witches, led by a High Priestess and/or a High Priest who meet regularly for worship and fellowship. The traditional membership is thirteen, but in reality most covens have fewer members.

Craft, The
A word used as a label for magickal rituals, ceremonies and beliefs as a whole. Often associated with witchcraft, this label could be applied to any form of magickal belief systems.

Crystal ball gazing
A form of divination or fortune-telling by gazing into a crystal ball or a crystal rock.

Crystallomancy
See: crystal ball gazing.

Curse
A curse is the invocation of an oath, formula or charm with the intention of causing evil misfortune to another person or property.

Dark moon
Another name for the new moon. Often refers to a time of rest when no magickal ceremonies or rituals should be conducted.

Death magic
The act of placing a death spell upon another. One procedure is considering the person as already dead thus forcing the soul to depart from the body as it is called by the spirits of death to enter into their domain.

Demonic tongues
The counterfeit gift of speaking in tongues that is under the control of demonic spirits.

Divination
The attempt to obtain information about the past, present, or future through occultic methods such as astrology, channeling, crystal balls, Tarot cards, etc.

Divination channel
A person who has developed the knowledge and awareness to tap into divine energies to interpret their patterns or meanings in order to gain spiritual understanding, or to forecast a coming event or issue.

Divining rods/dowsing
The divining rod is a V-shaped or forked rod, wire or branch used for dowsing. Dowsing is a form of divination (the attempt to gain hidden knowledge supernaturally) used to locate people, objects or underground substances (water).

Dowsing
See: divining rods.

Drawing
In Magick, practices such as "drawing a circle," and "drawing down the moon" are rituals or ceremonies by means of which you pull divine energies into yourself and your environment.

Drawing down the moon
Ritual invocation of the spirit of the Goddess into the body of the High Priestess by the High Priest.

Dungeons and Dragons
An occult fantasy role-playing game in which players seek to build up personal power using all kinds of satanic, evil, or witchcraft practices, including demonology, spells, murder, sexual perversion, and cannibalism.

Druid
Originally a Celtic order of Astronomers and Healers, the association has migrated to people who have a strong understanding of nature and hold an attachment to divine energies and the spiritual purpose to preserve it.

Earth magic
A form of magick in which the powers of the Earth are sought and used to conduct ritual and magickal workings.

Elements
Earth, air, fire, and water, plus spirit, or Akasha. Each is associated with a direction and a color (among other things): Earth (east, green), Air (north, yellow), Fire (south, red), and Water (west, blue), plus Spirit (center, white).

Energy
A force or inherent power that is part of all living things, seen and unseen.

Entity
The conscious energy that is left from living people after they have died.

Equinox
One of the two times in a year when the sun crosses the equator and the day and night are approximately the length. The spring equinox is March 21 or March 22; the fall equinox is September 21 or September 22.

Esbat
Meeting of witches on the full moon or the new moon, usually to perform rituals. Esbat rituals may also be performed by solitary witches.

Extra sensory perception
The knowledge of an experience, an influence, an event, or an object apart from the five senses. With this knowledge a person can predict the future, identify hidden things and perform supernatural feats of knowledge.

Familiar
An animal, either a pet or a spiritual entity, who serves the Witch as a magickal helper.

Fantasy role-playing games
Role-playing games in which players acquire the identity of mythical characters and engage in fantasy adventures. Most of these games are occult in nature.

Fates
The three goddesses of fate who determine the birth, life and death of human beings.

Fetishism
An amulet or talisman that is magically charmed with symbols, charm formulas or inscriptions. It is said to bring about occult transference of power.

Fire
The second element of the alchemical tradition. Fire is the essence of purification and change, the element of the east and the nature of the will.

Fire-walking
The ancient occult ritual of walking barefoot through fire or hot coals without experiencing pain or burns by entering a trance state. It is said to demonstrate one's psychic power over one's body.

Fivefold kiss
Also known as the fivefold salute. The witches' ritual salute, with kisses: on each foot; on each knee; above the pubic hair; on each breast; and on the lips – really eight kisses in all. It is only used within the Circle.

Full moon
Full moon nights are used for all magickal endeavors. These nights in particular are perfect for magickal works and for drawing favorable energy in ceremonies and rituals.

Geomancy
This system of divination employs a map with twelve divisions in which the symbols of geomancy are placed in conjunction with the planets.

Ghost
The conscious energy that was left from a living person after death.

Goblin
A mischievous gnome (small creature, dwarf, who lives underground).

Great rite
The rite which is the main feature of the third

degree initiation, and which is also laid down for certain festivals. It is sexual in nature, but may be "actual" (and private to the couples concerned) or symbolic, as the participants wish.

Great Spirit
Often associated with Native American terminology, this is a label assigned to the Divine force of all creation. Like the God/Goddess of the Pagan, the Great Spirit symbolizes all aspects of the universe. Can also be associated with Celtic beliefs as "the Great Spirits," making the word plural to recognize fully that all things are part of the Divine forces of all creation.

Guardians
The energies/entities of the four elements, four directions and four watchtowers of nature. Can also be associated with an individual's personal guide.

Guide
A spiritual being who assists an individual through certain aspects of their life. There are four types of spiritual guide in one's life: Spirit Guide, Relative Guide, Guardian Angel, Master Teacher. Always seen from head to torso, floating on air; never with legs and feet.

Halloween participation
All Hallow's Eve – October 31. A pagan/occult religious high or holy day that celebrates the transition from fall to winter. On this day the spirits of departed relatives return. Satan and his witches have the greatest power on this day, as all portals from Hades to the heavens are open. This day had its origin in ancient Druid rituals honoring their god Samhain, lord of the dead.

Handfasting
Wiccan equivalent of a wedding. It can be made legal if the Priestess and/or Priest are registered as clergy with the local authorities, or it may only be considered binding within the coven.

Haruspicy
Divination by reading the entrails of a sacrificed animal.

Healing channel
A person who has developed the knowledge and awareness to direct energy from the Divine forces to a person, animal, plant, place or thing for the purpose of healing.

Herbalism
Using various plants as creams, powders, deodorizers and other such productions to promote health. Scientists today have proven that many of the "old wives' remedies" handed down from the Middle Ages, do hold value.

High priest/ess
Technically speaking, a witch who has received the third degree initiation. More usually, the male and female leaders of a coven.

Hypnosis or mesmerism
Hypnosis is a technique to induce a trance or altered state of consciousness by verbal or non-verbal stimuli. In this state, a person is open to external suggestion.
Mesmerism was named after F. A. Mesmer. It is a hypnotic state termed "magnetic sleep" that is induced by "magnetic fluid" energy that comes from the practitioner's hands, voice or nervous system.

Hate magic
The act of placing a spell on a hated victim. One procedure is to write the hated enemy's name on a parchment paper with blood and then burn it over the flame of a black candle to bring great sorrow and even death to the hated person.

Healing magic
A holistic health technique used to restore a person's health by the balancing of healing energy through touch or hand movements over the person. Spirit guides are often used to aid the healing process.

Iridology or iris diagnosis
A holistic health technique used to diagnose physical ailments and emotional or mental problems by reading the color patterns of the eye's irises.

Iris diagnosis
See: iridology or iris diagnosis.

Invoke
To call energies into oneself from outside, as in calling the Goddess or drawing down the moon.

Jinx
To place bad energy or negative purpose on an individual, situation or spiritual tool.

Kaballah
Mystical teachings from the Jewish-Gnostic tradition that formed the basis of ceremonial magick and the Alexandrian tradition. An elaborately structured Tree of Life is central to the system of study.

Karma
In Hindu belief, where the term originated, it is the idea that the good and evil a person does will return either in this life or in a later one. Among some Pagans, the theory is that whatever negative or positive energies one sends out will come back to the sender in like kind. The "Three Fold Law" is a Wiccan version of this belief.

Levitation
The occult practice of raising or moving an object or person by supernatural or psychic means.

Lucifer
See: Satan.

Magic
The art of producing illusions
Magic card game
Fantasy role playing card games that involve Satanism, witchcraft and the occult. A popular magic card game is *The Gathering*.

Magic eight ball
A liquid filled black ball containing the printed words "yes," "no," and "maybe" on a die. Spirits provide guidance and insight to the person who asks questions directed at the eight ball.

Magick
The practice of performing acts with the aid of a spirit. The act of focusing will, emotion and energy to effect change within yourself and in the world. Whether it is good or bad depends on the intentions of the magician.

Magick circle
An area designated as a sacred space for spiritual practices. Outlined by items of nature, such as a rope of natural fibers, stones, wood or even people, the sacred circle is based on the principles of the "Wheel of Life."

Magick name
A name given to an individual for spiritual purpose. The name can be given by a Spiritual Guide, a Spiritual Teacher or a family relative. This name is used in magickal ceremonies, or as a means to identify the "spiritual" nature of a person.

Magickal herbalism
Combining the scientific with the spiritual, this is a means of mixing plants into herbal remedies while enhancing the known attributes and energies of the plants to aid its effectiveness through magickal rituals and/or consecrations (or spells).

Magickan
Someone who has studied several styles or sects of magick and has chosen bits and pieces from all for the basis of their own personal spiritual ideals. A person with very loose affiliations, if any at all, to any particular esoteric belief system.

Materialization
The ability to summon the dead into a visible form so that they can be seen. This is usually performed by a medium at a séance.

Mesmerism
See: hypnosis or mesmerism.

Metascopy
Divination by use of lines on the forehead.

Mirror mantic
Mirror mantic uses crystal balls, mirrors, rock crystals or still water as "mirrors of the future." This is an ancient method of divination.

Moon magick
A magick ritual, ceremony or practice conducted in association with a particular phase of the moon. Most often aligns one's energies and purpose to the feminine aspects of the Divine.

Namapathy
The practice of conducting healing through combining sound and music composed for the specific purpose of healing.

Necromancy
Necromancy is the practice of summoning the spirits of the dead to discover secrets from the past, to gain information about the future or to secure news of deceased loved ones.

Neo-Pagan
Neo-Pagan: literally, new-Pagan. A member, follower or sympathizer of one of the newly formed Pagan religions now spreading throughout the world.

New Age
A cultural movement combining beliefs in various eclectic, Pagan and Eastern religions or philosophies. Also connected with a period of time of intense spiritual growth from 1920 to 2000.

New moon
A phase of the moon when the lunar planet is between the earth and the sun and the dark side of the moon is facing the earth. A phase in magick that is used for personal growth, healing and blessing of new projects or ventures. It is also thought to be a good time to consecrate new tools and objects for use during rituals, ceremonies or an up-coming festival.

Numerology
The practice of attributing meaning or characteristics to numbers, such as birth dates.

Occult
The word "occult" means "hidden" and is

applied to a range of beliefs and activities that are outside of the mainstream philosophies and religions. It may also imply something that is secret, magickal, or supernatural.

Old path
Another name for Witchcraft.

Old religion
Another name for Witchcraft.

Old ways
Another name for Witchcraft.

Omens
A prophetic sign about some future event that has been received either through divination or spontaneously.

Oneiromancy
Divination by interpreting dreams.

Ornithomancy
See: augury.

Ouija board
The occult board with letters and numbers and a pointer that spells out messages from spirits during a séance. It is a form of necromancy.

Out of the body experiences
See: astral / soul travel.

Pagan
From the Latin *paganus*, country-dweller. Today used as a general term for followers of Wicca and other magical, shamanistic and polytheistic religions. It can be interchanged with Paganism. Historically, paganism has been used as a generic term to describe primitive non-Christian religions and superstitions, including religions centered on the occult. More recently Paganism is used as an umbrella term referring to Wicca/witchcraft, ceremonial magic, nature worship, polytheism (especially female deities), and ancient mythologies (Celtic, Norse, Egyptian, Greek and Roman).

Palm reading, chiromancy
The occult practice of divination by reading

the location, length and shape of the lines and markings on the palm of the hand.

Paranormal
Anything beyond the present accepted explanations of science. Often pertains to psychic events, gifts or beliefs.

Parapsychology
The scientific study of phenomena that natural laws cannot explain.

Pendulum
A tool made of string, thread or chain with a weighted object attached to one end. Used for communicating between the physical and spiritual worlds.

Pentacle (From the French: "to hang")
A pentagram surrounded by a circle. It may be a disc placed on an altar, a pendant to be worn, or any such representation.

Pentagram
The five-pointed star. With a single point uppermost, it represents the human being. Inverted, with two points uppermost, it can have Satanist associations; but not necessarily. Some traditions of Wicca use the inverted pentagram to signify an initiate of the second degree.

Phantom
An astral body or spiritual entity showing itself as a human being, but hazy or less dense than a physical body. Most often a soul that has transitioned to death, but does not want or does not know it has passed on. Seen always in full form from head to toe. Can also be called a ghost.

Phrenology
Phrenology is the study of the structure of the skull to determine a person's character and mental capacity.

Physiognomy
Divination by reading a person's character according to the shape of his features.

Precognition
To perceive mentally, or through a "gut feeling," the future of one's self, other people or society as a whole. Most often comes in the form of a precognitive dream, or a precognitive vision during a meditative state.

Psychic (Greek: *psychiokos* "psyche, soul or that which is mental" / Tibet: "vital or secret")
The sensitivity of the mind and body to subtle vibrations within the universe, often called the sixth sense. Everyone is psychic to some degree. As with the other five senses, each person has their own level of awareness or ability to use the sixth sense. Just as some people have better eyesight than others, so some people have a heightened awareness of the unseen energies and vibrations within the universe.

Psychometry
Divination by reading an object. The psychic ability to identify characteristics, events or future events of another person by holding a material possession, such as a ring, watch, or article of clothing, belonging to that person.

Pyromancy
Divination by use of fire configurations.

Quarters
The north, east, south, and west parts of a magickal circle or other ritual area.

Rede
Rule or law.

Reincarnation
The belief that each person possesses a soul that is independent of the body and can be reborn into another body.

Rhapsodmancy
This form of divination is based upon the line in a sacred book that strikes the eye when the book is opened after the diviner prays, meditates or invokes the help of spirits.

Rhobdomancy
See: divining rods.

Ritual Magick
(Europe, West Africa) Proven processes and ceremonies used to execute a particular form of magick such as summoning natural forces, conducting incantations, consecrating and dedicating magickal tools.

Rod and pendulum
The rod and pendulum are tools used for dowsing. The pendulum is becoming a popular means by which to diagnose disease, to determine the sex of an unborn child, and for physical and spiritual healing.

Runes
A set of symbols that are used both in divination and magickal workings. These symbols may be engraved in small pieces of wood for divination purposes. Runes that fit one's magickal goals are often carved into candles for candle magick.

Sabbat
One of the eight festivals or high holy days of Wicca that are observed in the Wicca calendar. They are: Samhain, Yule, Imbolc, Ostara, Beltane, Litha, Mabon, Lammas (Lughnasadh).

Santeria
Literally "worship of the saints," a syncretism of Roman Catholicism and traditional African polytheistic religions established when African slaves were introduced to the Caribbean. Elements include animal sacrifice and voodoo.

Satan, Lucifer
The leader of the rebellious angels. He was God's adversary, and was expelled from heaven for rebelling against God.

Scrying
Divination, usually using such methods as crystal gazing, incense smoke, or water, as opposed to Tarot or other manipulative means.

Séance
A séance is the session that is conducted by a

medium through which the spirit speaks to others in the room.

Selenomancia
Divination by use of the moon.

Self-mutilation
The act of destroying one's own body tissue by carving, scratching, cutting, burning, excessive tattooing or excessive body piercing. It is a way of dealing with overwhelming emotions, obsessive thought or dissociation. In SRA DID it is a way of cleansing the body of evil.

Sex magic
The use of sex (intercourse, actual or symbolic) within a ritual or spell-casting session to facilitate or augment the efficacy of a given magical rite. That is, sexual activities are used to accomplish the desired goal of the occultist.

Shamanism
Spiritual worldview of Native American and other early cultures that believe that "shamans," witch doctors or spiritual leaders, can provide healing, guidance (that is, divination), or wisdom through the occult, spiritism, or altered states of consciousness. The shaman's soul is sometimes believed to leave the body during a trance, at which time the shaman will speak with beings from the other worlds or assume animal forms.

Skyclad
The act of doing magickal workings or rituals in the nude. It is common in some traditions such as the Alexandrian, as well as among some solitary practitioners. Working skyclad does not imply anything sexual, but rather is an attempt to remove all barriers to the energies with which one is working.

Sorcery
The practice of black magic.

Sorcerer
A male who has made a pact with the devil in exchange for magical powers.

Sorceress
A female who has made a pact with the devil in exchange for magical powers.

Soul travel
See: astral/soul travel.

Speaking in trance/channeling
A person in an altered state of consciousness and under the control of a spirit speaks forth messages given from a spirit being. Also known as mediumistic trance.

Spell
A spell is a ritual performed with incantations, herbs, candles, knives and other witchcraft paraphernalia to affect the future of another person.

Spiritism
The worldview of those who believe that "spirits" reside in everything: people (including ancestors), rocks, wind, trees, rivers, etc.

Alleged contact with spirits through occult techniques. Specifically, the belief found in many primitive cultures that inanimate objects, plants and/or animals are possessed by spirits (good or evil) that must be appeased through occult practices... it is the French equivalent of the English "spiritualism." It is associated with Allan Kardec's doctrine of reincarnation, which does not figure in spiritualism.

Spiritualism
Communication, by means of mediumship, with those who live in the spirit world. It is similar to Spiritism, but uses Christian rituals and prayers.

Spiritualism "is the Science, Philosophy and Religion of continuous life, based upon the demonstrated fact of communication, by means of mediumship, with those who live in the Spirit World." (Definition adopted by the National Spiritualist Association of America)

Supernatural
Activity caused by God or his angels, or by Satan and his devils, commonly referred to as anything outside the bounds of natural laws.

Sympathetic magic
The control by magic of a person, animal, object or event based upon two basic principles:

1. "The Law of Similarity" states "like produces like" or that an effect may resemble a cause. In other words, things which resemble each other have a magical relationship (voodoo).

2. "The Law of Contact" states that things that have been in contact with each other will continue to act upon each other, even at a distance or with the passing of time. In other words, whatever happens to an object (hair, nails, clothing) that has been in contact with a person will happen to that person as well.

Table lifting

The lifting or movement of a seance table in response to communication with spirits of the dead. To elicit a response, participants usually place their hands palm down with fingers spread and connecting to form an unbroken circle.

Talisman

An object carried for protection or other goals that has been charged for that purpose. Examples are gemstones, shells, drawings and virtually any small object that one may carry.

Tarot cards

Fortune-telling or divination using Tarot cards, a deck of seventy-eight cards, twenty-two illustrated cards, or Minor Arcana cards, a deck of fifty-two cards, which hold the secrets to the future. The origin of the cards is unknown.

Tattoos

The practice of marking the skin with indelible patterns by making punctures in the skin and injecting pigment.

Tea leaf reading

The practice of divination by reading the patterns of tea leaves found in the bottom of a cup. Also called tasseography.

Telekinesis

A form of psychokinesis, the psychic ability to move objects without the use of known physical force.

Telepathy

Communication mind to mind without the natural senses.

Transference of sprits through laying on of hands

Demonic spirits are transferred from one person to another by "praying" over and placing one's hands upon another. Note: demonic tongues may be used.

Voodoo

Magical practice considered to be a form of black magic but also considered a religion by some.

Warlock

A male witch.

Witchcraft

The practice of performing acts with the aid of a spirit.

Wheel of the year

The Pagan calendar which symbolizes the eternal cycle of time. It usually begins with Samhain.

White-handled knife

The knife used by a witch for Craft tasks such as carving candles, making tools, chopping herbs, etc. Though it is not as sacred as the athame, it is reserved for Craft work exclusively.

White witch

A witch whose practice is solely for the purpose of good.

Wicca

An ancient witchcraft religion that honors the gods of nature. Wicca means "wise one."
An alternative name for modern witchcraft.
A Neo-Pagan nature religion with spiritual roots in Shamanism, having one main tenet: the Wiccan Rede.

Wiccan Rede

A simple and benevolent moral code of Wiccans.

Witch

Witches are Pagans and generally follow a nature religion, and usually (though not always) practice some form of magick.

Yang
(China) Energy that contains a positive or masculine charge of polarity. It is active and has the characteristics of sunlight, fire, strength and heaven. It is the white side of the yin/yang symbol.

Yin
(China) Energy that contains a negative or feminine charge polarity. It has the characteristics of darkness, the moon, weakness and water. It is the black side of the yin/yang symbol.

Yin/Yang
(China) The symbol of divine polarity. The balance of all things. It indicates that everything in and around the universe has an opposite.